CW00823573

The Complete Dramatic Works of Tang Xianzu

Edited by Wang Rongpei and Zhang Ling

BLOOMSBURY CHINA

LONDON · OXFORD · NEW YORK · NEW DELHI · SYDNEY

BLOOMSBURY CHINA
Bloomsbury Publishing Plc
50 Bedford Square, London, WC1B 3DP, UK

BLOOMSBURY, BLOOMSBURY CHINA and the Diana logo are trademarks of
Bloomsbury Publishing Plc

First published in China in 2014 as *The Complete Dramatic Works of Tang Xianzu*
by Shanghai Foreign Language Education Press, Shanghai
First published in Great Britain in 2018

Originally written in Chinese by Tang Xianzu.
Translated from Chinese into English by Wang Rongpei, Zhang Ling, Gu Wei,
Zhu Yuan and Huo Yuehong.
English translation edited by Wang Rongpei & Zhang Ling
English translation copyright © Wang Rongpei & Zhang Ling, 2014

This edition of *The Complete Dramatic Works of Tang Xianzu* is published
by arrangement with Shanghai Foreign Language Education Press, Shanghai, China.

Tang Xianzu has asserted his right under the Copyright, Designs and Patents Act, 1988,
to be identified as Author of this work.

Every reasonable effort has been made to trace copyright holders of material
reproduced in this book, but if any have been inadvertently overlooked
the publishers would be glad to hear from them.

This is a work of fiction. Names and characters are the product of the author's
imagination and any resemblance to actual persons, living or dead, is entirely coincidental.

All rights reserved. No part of this publication may be reproduced or transmitted in any
form or by any means, electronic or mechanical, including photocopying, recording, or
any information storage or retrieval system, without prior permission in writing from the publishers

No responsibility for loss caused to any individual or organization acting on or
refraining from action as a result of the material in this publication
can be accepted by Bloomsbury or the author.

A catalogue record for this book is available from the British Library

Library of Congress Cataloguing-in-Publication data has been applied for

ISBN: TPB: 978-1-9123-9201-8
ePub: 978-1-9123-9200-1

2 4 6 8 10 9 7 5 3 1

Printed and bound in Great Britain by CPI Group (UK) Ltd, Croydon CR0 4YY

MIX
Paper from
responsible sources
FSC® C013604

To find out more about our authors and books visit www.bloomsbury.com
and sign up for our newsletters

Foreword

Tang Xianzu (1550–1616), alias Yiren, was a dramatist, poet, essayist and a profound thinker. He lived a legendary life at the end of the Ming Dynasty, styling himself Ruoshi, Hairuo, Qingyuan Taoist and Hermit of the Jade Tea Studio. He was born into an intellectual family in Linchuan (in present-day Fuzhou of Jiangxi Province) on 24 September, 1550. At the age of twelve, he was a well-known poet; when he was fourteen, he passed the imperial examination at the county level; when he was twenty-one, he passed the imperial examination at the provincial level, but not until he was thirty-four did he pass the imperial examination at the national level. He served in Nanjing successively as adviser in the Court of Imperial Sacrifices, as secretary to the Office of Imperial Affairs and as administrative aide in the Sacrifice Bureau of the Ministry of Rites. In 1591, he wrote the famous "Memorial to Impeach the Ministers and Supervisors", criticizing the court for its misadministration since the ascendance of Emperor Shenzong and impeaching prime ministers Zhang Juzheng and Shen Shixing. As a result, he was demoted to the position of clerk in Xuwen County, Guangdong Province. A year later, he was transferred to be the magistrate of Suichang County, Zhejiang Province, where he took some enlightened measures for social development. After five years in office, he returned to his hometown, giving up all ideas of an official career and devoting himself to writing. On 29 July, 1616, he died in the Jade Tea Studio in Linchuan.

Tang Xianzu has left behind more than 2,000 poems, essays and rhymed essays, besides his chief achievement, dramatic works. His masterpieces "The Peony Pavilion" (also entitled "The Return of the Soul"), "The Handan Dream", "The Nanke Dream" and "The Purple Hairpins" are known as the "Four Dreams of Linchuan" or the "Four Dreams of the Jade Tea Studio". His plays, including the "Four Dreams" and "The Purple Flute", have passed down through numerous printings in the Ming and Qing dynasties, together with his *Leisurely Poems from the Red Spring Studio, Collected Poems by Tang Xianzu* and *The Complete Works of the Jade Tea Studio*. In contemporary China, *The Collected Works of Tang Xianzu* edited by Qian Nanyang and Xu Shuofang was published in 1962, and *The Complete Works of Tang Xianzu* annotated by Xu Shuofang was published in 1999.

Although Tang Xianzu was highly esteemed in the literary drama circles, "Tang Xianzu Studies" gradually came into being in the twentieth century. The studies on Tang Xianzu, especially on his dramatic works, can be roughly divided into two stages – the first half and the second half of the twentieth century. The studies in the first half of the twentieth century inherited the tradition of the Ming and Qing dynasties in tracing the origin of the stories, composing the music for them, singing the arias and appreciating the verse, but lacked new ideas and elucidation. The researchers were confined to certain experts in drama and literary circles, including Wang Guowei, Wu Mei, Wang Jilie and Lu Qian in the early period, and Yu Pingbo, Zheng Zhenduo, Zhao Jingshen, Zhang Youlan, Jiang Jiping and Wu Zhonghan in the later period. The studies in the second half of the twentieth century, in spite of the interference of vulgar sociology and ultra-left ideology, saw a small high tide around 1957 in commemorating the 340th anniversary of Tang Xianzu's death. Since the end of the 1970s, Tang Xianzu Studies has developed in depth. In commemorating the 366th anniversary of Tang Xianzu's death, China's academic circles held grand ceremonies in his native town and published a number of theses and other works, thus bringing Tang Xianzu Studies into a new era. The international symposium and the commemorative meeting held respectively in Dalian and Linchuan in 2000, with large numbers of participants and research papers, marked a new height in Tang Xianzu Studies. The conference of the China Association for Tang Xianzu Studies was held in Suichang, Zhejiang Province, for the first time in August 2001, and has been held several times in the following years, with its *Journal of Tang Xianzu Studies* published biannually since 2004.

To readers outside China, Tang Xianzu's name is inseparable from his magna opus "The Peony Pavilion", which reached Japan at the beginning of the seventeenth century. According to *The Catalogue of the Royal Library* in Japan, six copies of "The Peony Pavilion" (Zang Maoxun's adapted version) published in the Ming Dynasty were kept in the the Royal Library as early as 1636. "The Return of the Soul" or "The Peony Pavilion" translated into Japanese by Kishi Shunpulo was published by the Culture and Education Press in 1916. "The Return of the Soul" translated by Miyahara Minpei was published by the Tokyo National Library Publishing Association, and contained in Volume 10 of *Collection of Chinese Works Translated into Japanese* (1920-1924). Yiwashiro Shideo also translated "The Return of the Soul" into Japanese.

"The Peony Pavilion" also has various full-length and abridged English versions by Harold Acton, Cyril Birch, Zhang Guangqian, Wang Rongpei, Lindy Mark, Ben Wang, Xu Yuanchong and Xu Ming. The numerous translation and performances in the West have brought high acclaim to this play. According to *The Drama 100, A Ranking of the Greatest of All Times* (Daniel S. Burt, Facts on File, Inc. 2007), "In world drama there is no more extensive and beautiful exploration of love than Tang Xianzu's "Mudanting" ("The Peony Pavilion"). In fifty-five scenes and a performance time of eighteen hours, "The Peony Pavilion" merits the designation of epic. Its central character, the young woman Du Liniang, embarks on a journey of discovery to reach her heart's desire, facing down life-and-death obstacles in this world and the next. Along the way an entire culture's values and traditions are displayed. In a western context "The Peony Pavilion" combines elements of Homer's *Odyssey*, Virgil's *Aeneid*, Dante's *Divine Comedy*, and John Milton's *Paradise Lost*. Moreover, arguably it is the first great epic with a complex, believable woman protagonist. Despite its vast scope, "The Peony Pavilion" is anchored by a remarkable psychological depth and earthy realism. It turns lyrical, philosophical, satirical, fantastical, and bawdy, interweaving sentiment and humor. "The Peony Pavilion" provides one of the great entry points for an understanding of Chinese culture and Chinese classical dramatic traditions."

Tang Xianzu has been long acclaimed as China's Shakespeare but has not reached the Western readers in his entirety. With the 400th anniversary of the death of these two great dramatists in 2016, we offer *The Complete Dramatic Works of Tang Xianzu* to commemorate the historic occasion. We are relieved to have completed this endeavor after an effort of nearly two decades, and we hope that this English edition has presented the full grandeur of these plays. We shall be eagerly awaiting the comments from the international reading public.

紫箫记
The Purple Flute

汪榕培、张 玲、顾 薇 译

Translated by Wang Rongpei, Zhang Ling & Gu Wei

Table of Contents

Scene One
Prelude

(Enter the narrator)

NARRATOR (*To the tune of **Xiaochongshan***):

> When the auspicious sun bestows a new look on the earth,
>
> The young lady invites a man of worth
>
> To take a stroll to enjoy the grass and blooms.
>
> They glow with life when they pick the peaches and plums,
>
> Where the people go happy and gay
>
> And the mansion detains their returning way.
>
> When bright candles illuminate the lady's red dress,
>
> The moon and the flowers do impress
>
> The man at this hour and this place.
>
> Elegantly she would dance with grace
>
> And sweetly she would sing
>
> And play the music of "Warm Spring".

Dear audience, please keep quiet! Now please watch our performers playing *Li Yi's Story of the Purple Jade Flute,* but first of all I'd like to introduce the main plot to you.

> *(To the tune of **Fenghuangtaishangyichuixiao**)*
>
> The gifted scholar Li Yi
>
> And Princess Huo Xiaoyu
>
> Are brought together by a poem.
>
> The story concerns a purple jade flute
>
> That was picked up on the Lantern Festival.
>
> After a successful palace test,
>
> Li serves in the troops, separated with his wife.
>
> When he comes back,
>
> A peace-making marriage with Tubo is arranged,
>
> But successive wars bring him into trouble.
>
> Pretty as a blossom,
>
> Princess Xu from the palace
>
> Is married to Li as a concubine,
>
> Going through thick and thin.
>
> Trapped in the groundless slander,
>
> Princess Huo sells the jade flute.
>
> With the help of his bosom friend,
>
> Li escapes death and becomes a high official at court.
>
> Princess Huo resumes marriage with him
>
> When all the previous suspicions
>
> Are thrown into the wind.

When Li Yi wins reputation in the court,
Princess Huo picks up a jade flute by chance.
Shang Zipi saves Li out of the siege on the fort;
Princess Xu went to Tubo and returns in advance.

Scene Two
Friends' Get-Together

(*Enter Li Yi*)

LI YI (*To the tune of* **Zhenzhulian**):

When the Spring God in the east is auspicious at dawn,

I look eastward

To see the sun rising from behind the colorful clouds.

When the sun shines over the capital city,

People watch the weathercock by the Divine Terrace.

The juniors toast to the seniors in the family

To wish them a happy New Year

And a long life.

Paper flowers are cut by the palace maids

To rival with the blue robes and willow trees.

"To welcome the advent of New Year,

The palace gates are open at twilight.

From the treasure tripod coils the incense smoke,

Spreading its fragrance over the Divine Terrace.

Each family pastes paper-cuts on the windows

While ministers toast to the long life of the emperor.

The court abounds in literary talents,

Who are excellent in drafting documents."

I am Li Yi from Longxi, styled Junyu. My departed father Li Kui was Prime Minister for the late emperor. My departed mother, surnamed Xin, was entitled Lady Didao. We have marten coats, golden seals, ten carriages with horses, and a thousand imperial decrees. We boast valuable books like the calligrapher Wang Zijing, who held bestowed books of rarity, and paintings from Emperor Taizu of Liang, who collected famous paintings of great value. I have been keen on probing into metaphysics and the theory of being hard and white. My youthful talent shines like the rising sun, and radiates like the precious jade. Like the swords flying to the azure sky, I wish to soar to the dragon's height. I read widely when I was a kid like Huang Xiang from Jiangxia at the age of nine, and showed interest in astronomy like Guan Luo from Qinghe at the age of eight. As I am the youngest of ten brothers, I am also called Shilang, the tenth brother. It is just like what happens in a story,

"Among Jias' three brothers in the Han Dynasty,
Weijie is the best;
Among Xun Shu's eight sons in the Han Dynasty,
Ciming is to not to be equaled."

I am as assiduous as Zhu Mu, who studied so hard as to forget to have meals. I am also as profound as Qiao Zhou, who was so lost in reading as to smile to himself. I can write good essays in refined diction, and produce beautiful handwritings in elegant styles and with natural grace. On the spacious ground for ritual ceremonies, among the grass and trees, and in the grand courtyard with mansions, I give vent to my incomparable talent and emotion without restraint. I make two hundred annotations to *The Smaller Prajnaparamita Sutra*, and write a verse-essay entitled "The Famous Capital", briefly describing eighty scenic spots. I consider Guo Xiang's commentaries and annotations on "Wandering in Absolute Freedom" by Zhuangzi inferior to Xiang Xiu's. I am confirmed that He Pingshu's commentaries and annotations on *Book of Tao and Virtue* by Laozi not equal to Wang Bi's. When I chant the poem "Requiem" by Qu Yuan, I call to mind the mystical excursions of immortals by Li Bai. I sneer at the celebrities nowadays who attach more importance to daily trifles than to morals and ethics; I despise the Confucian scholars whose intelligence is lower than sunflowers. I grieve over Kuai Tong, whose repeated farsighted advice was rejected by Han Xin; I marvel at Mozi, who resisted nine offensives by Gongshu Ban and had six more tactics in reserve. I am very satisfied with the life in the garden and by the pond without any thought of an official career. However, my friends come to congratulate me while the county magistrates and city governors come to persuade me to assume an official post. Zhao Yi in the Eastern Han Dynasty visited an honest official Yang Zhi in Henan, while Zhang Changzong in the Tang Dynasty was elected as a distinguished scholar in Danyang. I feel myself unworthy of being recommended to be a high official, just like an ordinary branch among the cassia-bark trees in the imperial garden. As I was about to sit for the imperial examination in the palace, it was reported that the Tubos had captured several counties in the Longxi area and was pushing up to the city of Xianyang. The war fire spread to the Ganquan prefecture, and the imperial armies were stationed in Xiliu. So the imperial examination was postponed and everyone escaped for a safe place. The Longxi area falls into Tubo's hands to become part of their territory. There are but weak willows in Yang Zude's home while there are but withered pagoda trees in Yin Zhongwen's yard. The Sanchuan region serves as the fountain to drink horses while the Luhun area is disturbed by wars. The cities and towns there are frequented by the soldiers. No trees are seen beside the wells, but weapons are scattered everywhere. What a pity it is that the prosperous life is ruined! How regrettable it is that the cultural relics and classical works are destroyed! Tears are shed when people look at the ancestral graves and hometowns are forsaken for faraway places. I am detained in the imperial capital from the spring to the autumn, by staying in a hotel with my health damaged. However, it is fortunate that things are turning for the better and spring is at hand. Today is New Year's Day in the fourteenth year under the Yuanhe Reign, and it happens to be the day of Beginning of Spring. All the court officials and the imperial examination candidates enter the Cloud and Dragon Gate and come to the Taiji Palace for a greeting audience. As people peep at the sun through the morning glow, so the officials have an audience with the emperor on New Year's Day. The carriages and horses jingle with bells while the nine grand golden tripods stand in the courtyard. An audience is given to the ministers in the Yuzhang Palace while variety shows provide entertainment before the Flower and Calyx Building. When the Emperor ascends the throne, showering his grace over all the families and households, the people look up to him and cheer loudly, "Long live the Emperor!" After the audience is over, meals are granted in the Imperial Kitchen. Showered with the emperor's kindness, the ministers get intoxicated, in a harmonious atmosphere and in full vitality. Who would say that the country is in turmoil and upheaval? The music is always echoing in peace and tranquility. There is only one thing I am concerned about. I am nineteen years old but still single and have not carved out an official career by this festival. I am like the pepper flower that is worth lauding but has not yet met Mrs. Liu who wrote "Ode to the Pepper Flower"; I am also like the cypress leaf in the wine cup that is passed in vain but has not reached the seat of Dai Ping who expounded the classics. So I can only sigh deeply at that on New Year's Day. But it is a relief that many people of valor and gifts know about me, and many people of noble birth and superior positions come to visit me. An old friend of mine named Hua Qing, styled Jingding, used to be governor of the Xichuan area and has been promoted to the position of the Grand General. A candidate of the martial arts examinations named Shi Xiong, styled Ziying, is both intelligent and brave beyond comparison. Shang Zipi, son of the king of Tubo's Yangtong tribe in the Kunlun Mountains, is now studying in the Imperial Academy. The three of them are of different ages but are all valiant men. When we gathered at the palace gate for the New Year celebrations, we made the appointment to meet in my house. I have told my servant Qing'er to prepare the meal and wine, but I wonder whether everything is ready.

008

(*Enter Qing'er*)

QING'ER:

"*Before plum flowers bloom to the music,*
Orchid fragrance has permeated the wine."

Master, the cypress-leaf wine and the five-spice vegetable plate are ready.

LI YI:

Wait at the door! Inform me immediately when the three masters arrive!

QING'ER:

Yes, I see.

(*Enter Hua Qing, Shi Xiong and Shang Zipi*)

HUA QING, SHI XIONG, SHANG ZIPI (*To the tune of* **Heshengchao**):

The weather grows mild in the capital as seasons change,
With stars and candles illuminating the sky and the earth.
New Year is celebrated outside the Cloud and Dragon Gate;
In pleasant warmth the spring brings.

(*Greet and pay respect to each other*)

"*On New Year's Day,*
Auspice radiates from the sun.

All the deities bring us blessings

When spring is welcomed in all places."

(Chat)

HUA QING:

Mr. Li, you talented scholars compose poems on the first day of every year. Have you produced a new piece this year?

LI YI:

On my way back from the audience granted by the emperor in the palace, I looked and made several bows in the direction of my hometown to express my homesickness. As soon as I reached home, I have been busy preparing for food and drinks to serve you as my honorable guests and have not got time yet to write a poem.

HUA QING:

We can improvise some quatrains today, but not repeat the former poems on New Year's Day. Let's adopt a new style. The first line should mention our full name, style name or pen name. The next three lines should mention our aspirations in this coming year.

LI YI:

Will you start first, please?

HUA QING (*Chants a poem*):

> *"Hua Qing is a remarkable general,*
>
> *Once feasted at the Terrace of Heavenly Gods.*
>
> *In the celebration at the Cloud and Dragon Gate,*
>
> *Auspicious birds encircle the sky."*

LI YI:

This poem shows the aspiration of the Grand General. The next will be Shi Xiong's turn.

SHI XIONG (*Chants a poem*):

> *"I'm Shi Xiong from Huainan,*
>
> *I'll display my martial arts before the emperor.*
>
> *I wish that warfare will end this spring,*
>
> *But my name will be honored in the Qiling Pavilion."*

LI YI:

Good! This poem displays the aspiration of the Number-One Martial-Arts Candidate. The next will be Shang Zipi's turn.

SHANG ZIPI (*Chants a poem*):

> *"I am Shang Zipi from the Kunlun Mountains,*
>
> *Paying homage to the emperor as the son of the Tubo King.*
>
> *I make the wish to the Heavenly Queen Mother in the west,*
>
> *That the western tribes be blessed by spring wind."*

LI YI:

This poem displays the aspiration of a Tubo prince.

HUA QING, SHI XIONG, SHANG ZIPI:

The next will be Li Yi's turn.

LI YI (*Chants a poem in smiles*):

"I am Li Yi endowed with well-known talent,

With the Heavenly Gate opening for me in spring.

Like the pepper flower in the wine, I'll meet the noble lady today;

Like the cypress leaf in the wine, I'll serve the emperor this year."

HUA QING, SHI XIONG, SHANG ZIPI:

Li's aspiration to be listed at the top in the imperial examinations will surely come true.

(*Enter Qing'er holding wine*)

QING'ER (*Kneels*):

Please let me improvise a few lines too on New Year's Day!

HUA QING, SHI XIONG, SHANG ZIPI (*Laugh*):

Fine! You have also learned to chant poems.

QING'ER:

My master has a large number of precious books, among which many are rare ones. The books are classified into different types. My master can recite from memory what he reads at first sight. And I frequently jot down his comments on what he reads.

HUA QING:

You are really the one who stays near ink and gets stained black. Now you chant a poem!

QING'ER (*Chants a poem*):

"I am Qing'er, a page boy

Preparing a seasonal dish on New Year's Day.

When I am old and weak,

I'll tell my son to fetch paper for me to write a poem."

HUA QING (*Laughs*):

Wonderful! Du Fu is my old friend. His poems have been copied by page boys like you so often that you are familiar with them, too.

QING'ER:

I have only copied *Du Fu's Poems with Annotations by Yu Ji* in the Yuan Dynasty.

LI YI:

Stop your nonsense! Serve the wine!

(*Makes a toast*)

(*To the tune of **Yufurong***)

The pepper flowers in the wine usher in the spring

While the cypress leaves in the wine emit fragrance.

I wish that the Floral God would take actions

To hasten the blooming of flowers.

Now that valiant scholars go outing in a group,

Shang Zipi will return home when the weather warms up.

ALL:

The advent of spring

Is marked by the gentle caress of the east wind

And the budding of flowers in the New Year,

With each spring fairer than the last.

HUA QING (*To the previous tune*):

> With auspicious clouds in the sky,
>
> The brilliant sun shines over Chang'an.
>
> We celebrate the New Year together
>
> In one toast after another.
>
> Seasons are reckoned according to three calendars
>
> While dishes are loaded with five vegetables.

ALL:

> Gently fondling the temples,
>
> The vernal breeze greens the willows
>
> Before it greens the woods
>
> While youngsters drink the Tusu wine to their hearts' content.
>
> (*Enter a messenger from the Imperial Academy*)

MESSENGER (*Reports*):

> *"The scenic spots suitable for young people*
>
> *Take on a new look in the spring season."*

By His Majesty's decree, "All the students of letters and martial arts in the capital city as well as all the sons of ethnic-group kings studying in the Imperial Academy and waiting upon the emperor are to study music in the academy." So Master Shi and Master Shang have to take leave now.

SHI XIONG, SHANG ZIPI (*Take leave*):

Respectable general Hua, please drink a few more cups before you leave.

> *"We admire plum flowers in leisure*
>
> *And appreciate willows together.*
>
> *We now leave but will come back,*
>
> *To commit our emotions to the wine cups."*
>
> (*Exeunt Shi Xiong and Shang Zipi*)
>
> (*Songs within, accompanied by flutes and drums*)
>
> *"It is a delight to see spring*
>
> *Come back at the year's beginning."*

LI YI (*Asks*):

Who is singing outside?

HUA QING:

I suppose that the performers from the palace troupe are returning from the New Year celebrations.

LI YI:

Qing'er, tell the singers outside to come in and propose a toast to General Hua.

> (*Enter the chief of the palace troupe*)

CHIEF OF THE PALACE TROUPE (*Kowtows*):

We have heard of Master Li for a long time. We are passing by your house on our way back from the New Year celebrations. Let's present a song for you with all our respect!

> (*Sings*)

(*To the tune of* **Yanlaihong**)

Delighted to see spring

Come back at the year's beginning,

We indulge ourselves in the spring times

Under the azure sky far beyond reach

When auspice descends upon the palace.

With the change of seasons,

A stretch of willows heralds the warm spring in the fields.

PERFORMERS:

When auspicious clouds appear

And people touch the holy spring,

Water in the immortal dew-plate is drunk

In the banquet held in the Palace of Constant Joy.

LI YI:

Thank you!

CHIEF OF THE PALACE TROUPE:

We'll also present a dance.

(*Sings*)

(*To the previous tune*)

The goddesses chant a song

To the accompaniment of the zither

And dance in swirling movements

With paper flowers as their headwear,

To wish you enjoy women, wealth and position.

Paper-cuts of swallows are pasted on the windows

To greet another year of willow twigs and peach blossoms.

PERFORMERS:

Presenting precious books with respect,

With dragon-shaped pendants

And silk-tinsel flags on their heads,

Scholars smile from the bottom of their hearts.

LI YI:

Thank you! Qing'er, fetch some satin handkerchiefs and money as tips to the performers!

CHIEF OF THE PALACE TROUPE:

There is no need for that. When we perform for the emperor, we do not sing old songs. So we long to get the new poems and songs written by famous gifted men of letters. Emperor Taizong was fond of the music "The Flowers in the Leafy Backyard" from the Chen Dynasty and "The Tune of Companions" from the Qi Dynasty; in Emperor Xuanzong's time, "The Clear and Peaceful Tune" was played to the north of the Fragrance Pavilion late at night. When Li Qiao was alive, we chanted his "The Fenshui River"; after Wang Wei died, we no longer sing his poem "The Yangguan Pass". Now Master Li, with your name well-known in the capital city, your poems "The Spring" and "The Midnight" are repeatedly set to music. As we are going to compose new tunes for famous poems, what we seek from you is an exquisite poem rather than satins to wrap our heads.

LI YI (*Laughs*):

So you are ambitious to have been singing new songs. But as a traveler I have composed only a few poems, which have already been spread by people who show great interest. You can come when you need to perform for the emperor later on.

CHIEF OF THE PALACE TROUPE:

We present our songs for the emperor on certain occasions. Now we need some new poems for urgent use, because Prince Huo pays much attention to climbing the mountain on the seventh day of the first month, that is, the Man's Day. And the emperor will hold a banquet on the fifteenth day of the first month, that is, the Lantern Festival. Could you please wield your pen and compose two poems for us?

HUA QING:

Why not grant her the favor!

LI YI:

All right!

> (*Chants and writes*)
>
> (*Hands the poems to the entertainer*)

"The Amiable Spring" is fit to be set to music for the Man's Day, while "Searching for Spring Lantern" is fit to be set to music for the Lantern Festival.

CHIEF OF THE PALACE TROUPE (*Aside, reads the new poems and smiles with approval*):

Wonderful! Wonderful indeed! He is worthy of an extraordinary talent in Luoyang.

> (*Turns back*)

Please allow me to express my thanks with your wine!

> (*Sings*)
>
> (*To the tune of **Cuyulin***)
>
> Around the Copper-Camel Gate,
>
> A lot of talented youngsters gather;
>
> At the Golden-Horse Gate,
>
> Numerous prominent persons can be found.
>
> With your lines of poems like strings of pearls,
>
> You'll surely be summoned by the emperor for your brilliance.

PERFORMERS:

> In the New Year,
>
> The palace garden
>
> Will take on a new look.

HUA QING:

To tell you the truth, these poems are easy to compose for a great talent.

> (*To the previous tune*)
>
> A heaven-sent talent
>
> Produces poems on the white snow.
>
> If he is extolled,

He should be sent to the sky.

His broad mind is to be admired,

For his wonderful poems reveal his mind.

PERFORMERS:

In the New Year,

The palace garden

Will take on a new look.

(*Take leave*)

LI YI:

Thank you for your performance in my shabby house!

CHIEF OF THE PALACE TROUPE:

"*When beauties raise toast after toast,*

The talent writes poems to boast."

(*Exit*)

LI YI (*To the tune of* **Coda**):

When flowers are about to bloom in the magnificent garden,

Spring songs bring warmth to the sky.

HUA QING:

Shilang, please come to my house for a drink tomorrow or the day after tomorrow! I will ask a
charming female singer, Bao Siniang, to toast for you. Come and see

Peach and plum blossoms outgrow my living quarters.

When spring permeates Chang'an from heaven divine

The friends meet and drink with lofty airs.

We watch the flowers and drink the mellow wine,

With "The Warm Spring" played without compares.

Scene Three
Spring Outing

(*Enter Zheng Liuniang with maidservant Huansha*)

ZHENG LIUNIANG (*To the tune of* **Mangonghua**):

When the field paths are covered with vernal green,

And the mansions are beautiful as pictures,

I live in luxury with a slender waist.

HUANSHA (*Rolls up the curtain*):

The gilded birdcage, gold lock, and sleeping mandarin-ducks,

The tall scroll, painted curtain, and headwear of pearl and jade.

ZHENG LIUNIANG (*In the pattern of* **Suzhongqing**):

"*With plum blossoms climbing the terrace,*

Flowers bloom in the warm breeze.

> *I wake up*
> *To see that spring has returned,*
> *Resting my rouge cheeks on the sandalwood pillows.*
> *With my sleeves smelling of musk,*
> *I walk on the steps.*
> *The butterflies are flirting amid the flowers,*
> *But how many times can they come?"*

I am Zheng Liuniang. Du Qiuniang and I used to be leading musicians in the palace troupe. When the emperor invited the princes to appreciate singing and dancing performances on one occasion, we were both conferred to Prince Huo's residence. Though we were not as pretty as the beauty Biyu, we participated in performances on important occasions. I was envied to the extreme, but I never even peeped at men. When talented friends gathered at the House of the Prince and I entertained them in the west garden, they would be attracted by me as if the three stars in the sky would not gaze at the moon when the concubine of the First Emperor of Qin, Mi Bazi waited on the banquet. I have given birth to a daughter named Xiaoyu, sixteen years old. She is extraordinary in both talent and appearance. She is like the fairy in the paintings and the goddess in the moon. The black dye from the south beautifies her eyebrows as fine as a couple of willow leaves. The red rouge from the north colors her cheeks as pretty as the lotus flowers. She is taught to act strictly according to the moral standards, and learns to despise the female showing love to the male. She is innately good at elegant singing and dancing, unlike the ancient beauty Xishi, who learned to do so. She is attractively dressed in fanciful embroidery, but she has neither been engaged nor found her sweetheart. She lives in the Red Mansion, surrounded by beautiful flowers and luxuriant trees. The inside of the mansion has red walls painted in green copper-coin patterns. The young beauty, longing for the outside world, often looks out of the window like an immortal in the Lingguan Hall and watches the paths crowded with people on spring outings to the mountains in rain. Today is sunny, with plum blossoms about to fall and willows leaves newly sprouting. There are men and women on spring outings from the noble residences. I may as well call Xiaoyu out to enjoy the spring sights. Indeed,

> *"The ice is thawing and the pond is turning green,*
> *While the clouds are dispersing and the sky is clearing up.*
> *I should not be so excited about the spring outing,*
> *But I must go for my daughter's sake."*

Huansha, tell Yingtao to invite the princess out.

> (*Yingtao invites Miss Huo*)
> (*Enter Huo Xiaoyu, followed by Yingtao*)

HUO XIAOYU (*To the tune of* **Mangonghuahou**):

> A tender-skinned beauty is standing by the bamboo window,
> When a sudden rain startled a pair of golden orioles.

YINGTAO:

Princess,

Ladies go outing for the spring fragrance;

Look,

The flowers are blooming but willows are just sprouting.

(*Huo Xiaoyu greets Zheng Liuniang; Huansha and Yingtao kowtow*)

HUO XIAOYU:

"I while away my time doing embroidery."

Why do you call me out, mom?

ZHENG LIUNIANG:

Let's go on a spring outing, enjoying the beautiful sights by the pond and in the pavilion this early spring morning!

(*Walks*)

ZHENG LIUNIANG:

"When spring displays its beauty at its advent,

HUO XIAOYU:

People pass by in the spring sun and breeze.

HUANSHA:

While the breeze brushes past on spring days;

YINGTAO:

Tender affection is stirred up on spring nights."

Mistress, here we are at the green pavilion and the silver pond.

ZHENG LIUNIANG (*To the tune of* **Miandaxu**):

In the quiet and solitary chamber,

Gorgeous satin enhances the beauty of the lady.

The mica screen splendidly painted

Faces the duck-shaped smoking-oven in solitude.

HUANSHA:

Please feel relaxed, mistress!

ZHENG LIUNIANG:

When flowers are no longer in bloom,

People can still contemplate over them,

Disregarding their elapsing beauty

And the boredom of fond dreams.

ALL:

With sleeves stained by the rouge,

I am not in a mood to adjust the silver-decorated flute.

HUO XIAOYU (*To the previous tune*):

While the chamber is bathed in the spring sunshine,

The golden headwear sways in my thick and raven hair.

YINGTAO:

Princess, please listen to the sound of chess playing in the side yard!

The jingling jade chess-pieces

Rouse the sleeper in the Red Mansion.

(With the twittering of birds within, Yingtao walks by the side of Huo Xiaoyu)

While the orioles sing amid the leaves,

The weeping willow twigs are sprouting.

At the time when plum blossoms are about to drop,

The spring breeze keeps brushing the sleeves.

ALL:

We stroll in the serene places,

Along the narrow paths and painted bridges.

HUANSHA (*To the previous tune*):

The petals fall when the birds peck

And skim past our silk skirts.

(Slightly lifts her hands and dances)

I try on the spring dress,

Walking with fragrance floating around.

In tender and graceful manners

I sway my slender waist.

(Unloosens her dress and shouts, "How warm it is!")

I love to see waters rippled by the warm spring breeze

And the halcyons dancing on the orchid stems.

ZHENG LIUNIANG:

Huansha, why do you unloosen your dress?

ALL:

She secretly tightens her embroidered corsage

So as to conceal her tender emotions.

YINGTAO (*To the previous tune*):

As smiling faces are like seasonal flowers,

How many times can we treasure the spring nights?

Dressed in satin coats and silver-lined skirts,

The twelve courtesans whisk their sleeves.

At the apricot branch tips,

We feel the approach of spring warmth.

HUANSHA:

Look, Yingtao, how handsome are those young gentlemen jogging on the narrow paths!

YINGTAO (*Sighs*):

We are eager to gaze at the youngsters on horseback

With alluring eyes.

ZHENG LIUNIANG:

Yingtao, how do you comment on those youngsters?

ALL:

With lockers of jade and gold jewelry by our side,

We paint our raven eyebrows by ourselves.

*(To the tune of **Yuwen**)*

While spring grass beside the steps is to be adored,

Exquisite bowers are enveloped in smoke in the dusk.

ZHENG LIUNIANG:

When you go back to your chamber,

You'd better do the embroidery.

As willows and spring breeze work wonders,

The sun has warmed the copper grooves by then.

When you pick the flowers at the railings,

The man will come as grass turns green again.

Scene Four
Exchanging the Concubine for a Horse

(*Enter Hua Qing*)

HUA QING (*To the tune of* **Yeyouchao**):

The halberds, the spears, and rare steeds;

The mink tails, the ribbons, and jade quivers.

I rejoice to see my armors covered with dust

And my spears lying idle with moss gathering around,

As *The Military Stratagem* is useless at peaceful times.

"Flags flutter after I return from the border area,

But my grey head is still wearing the helmet.

I adjust zither strings and sing 'The Moon at the Fortified Pass',

As if I were singing before the mirror-like mountain rocks."

I am Hua Qing, the Grand General of the Tang Dynasty. I used to be the governor of West Sichuan, but have returned to the capital and lived at leisure, receiving a salary of two thousand hectoliters of grain a year and wearing a jade belt and a dragon-design robe. I have a concubine named Bao Siniang, who is pretty, affectionate and sociable. She is the best singer among all the performers in the military camp, and the best *pipa* player among all the musicians in the palace. As there are honorable guests to visit me now and then, I have kept her in my house to sing over the wine. Where is Bao Siniang?

(*Enter Bao Siniang*)

BAO SINIANG (*To the tune of* **Shanggonghua**):

While plum blossoms display their beauty in the painted hall,

Soothing music is played on the jade flute,

Enshrouded in the fragrant smoke amid willow twigs.

Awakened from my dream in the chilly morning of early spring,

I am so delicate as to fear the east wind.

Blessings on you, General!

HUA QING:

I've summoned you because I have something to say. I met my friend the talent Li Yi the other day on the spring festival and invited him to my camp for a drink. I've told the cooks to prepare a dinner. I suppose he'll be coming soon. And I I'd like you to sing and dance at the dinner.

BAO SINIANG:

Yes, I see.

HUA QING:

By the way, I remember a couplet in one of Li Yi's poems,

> "*Beyond the screen, winds sway the bamboo trees;*
> *I wonder whether it's my friend who comes at ease.*"

You may set it to music and sing with the new words. Li Yi will soon be promoted to be a standing member of the Imperial Academy.

BAO SINIANG:

I see.

> (*Enter Li Yi*)

LI YI (*To the tune of* **Buchangong**):

> Duckweeds float in the defrosted palace stream,
> Flowers and trees are lush in the beautiful garden.
> East of the fragrant house and painted bridge,
> A bosom friend of mine stays with me.
> (*Greets Bao Siniang and says "I've heard of you for a long time."*)

HUA QING:

Bao Siniang, fill his cup for me and sing a new song!

BAO SINIANG (*Serves wine*):

> (*To the tune of* **Wugongyang**)
> When the shade is rolled up, the wind blows
> To stir the curtain in the evening glows
> And the coils of smoke above the tripod.
> The fan dance starts with the music of "Riding the Cloud",
> When the mica folding-screen shields the mountain view
> With its painted green outshining the glaring flowers.
> In the verdant spring come the romantic young men
> Dressed in elegant robes,
> Of whom one is a burly general
> And the other is a renowned scholar.

HUA QING:

Mr. Li, it's so wonderful that you wrote the lines "Beyond the screen, winds sway the bamboo trees" and Bao Siniang composed a song bearing the same theme. The literary piece and the musical piece present themselves at the same time; therefore, we should each drain a goblet of wine.

BAO SINIANG (*To the previous tune*):

> Steaming dishes are served,

Mellow wine is drunk,

And melodious music is enjoyed.

My pleated dress is painted with colorful flowers,

While my fragrant and dense hair is curled like clouds.

The guest writes essays circulating in the capital

And rides along the paths stirring up dusts.

With flowers on my satin headband swirling,

I dance in such graceful steps

That even bamboo leaves and peach blossoms

Enjoy themselves to the full.

LI YI:

I'm drunk!

HUA QING:

Now, remove the wine and the dishes!

> *"When I get drunk with mellow wine,*
>
> *I look at the mountain village in spring.*

Alas!

> *I see so many gallant men*
>
> *Riding with the flowers and grass."*

Mr. Li, look at the roads in spring!

> (*To the tune of* ***Jiang'ershui***)
>
> On the smooth roads with green grass,
>
> Well-equipped horses gallop like winds.
>
> (*A horse neighs and bells ring within*)

HUA QING:

Attendants, go and ask whose noble horse it is!

> Galloping noble horses can follow the sun like floating clouds.
>
> (*Enter an attendant, reporting*)

ATTENDANT:

Guo Xiaohou is shooting on horseback with his men.

HUA QING:

Mr. Li, do you know this man? He is the grandson of the Duke of Fenyang.

> Followed by numerous attendants, he is beamish,
>
> Son of the noble lineage
>
> Fully enjoying the romping pleasure in youth.

Alas! How well he does in horse archery!

> His arrow sends the plate to flight
>
> And hit the two golden pellets in a row.

LI YI:

Why do you admire him so much? He has just bought an excellent horse with a thousand ounces of gold and tries his bow with ten thousand pellets. But if you have such a horse, you can quell the barbarians and be conferred the title of a marquis.

(*To the previous tune*)

The white horse can gallop in the south like a belt

And fly in the north like a yellow crane.

If you get this horse,

You can move like the swift wind,

Winning praise by your military exploits.

By that time, you'll always be busy in the position of a general until you are very old.

Going to the court with a gold bow-sack and a jade horse-bridle,

You will be unanimously considered the most remarkable man.

In his old age, General Ma Yuan with the honorary title of General Quelling-the-Waves in the Han Dynasty conquered the savage tribes in Wuling and cast a copper statue of a stalwart steed to be presented to the emperor.

If you love his statue of a Golden Horse,

You'd better do merits in the savage Emerald-Rooster Cave.

HUA QING:

What you say sounds reasonable, Shilang. Attendants, go and chase after Guo Xiaohou! Invite him in and ask him whether he is willing to sell his horse!

(*Hustles of people and horses as well as voice of invitation within*)

(*Enter Guo Xiaohou, whipping his horse*)

GUO XIAOHOU (*To the tune of **Cuidijindang***):

Except for his contact with the courtesans,

Hua Qing is a peerless gallant man.

Fastening his horse in the forest,

Where is the hero in the song-and-dance house?

HUA QING (*Smiles and greets Guo Xiaohou*):

I am waiting at the gate to welcome you.

(*Invites Guo Xiaohou in and introduces him to Li Yi*)

GUO XIAOHOU:

Who is this scholar?

HUA QING:

This is Mr. Li Yi from Longxi for the imperial examinations.

GUO XIAOHOU:

Then, is this beauty your beloved concubine Bao Siniang?

HUA QING:

Yes.

(*Guo Xiaohou greets Bao Siniang*)

GUO XIAOHOU:

As I was riding to shoot at the birds with pellets just now, I am wondering what you want me for.

HUA QING:

I admire both you and your horse. So I invite you for a drink and want to ask where you got this stalwart horse.

GUO XIAOHOU:

I am not as valuable as jade, but the horse is indeed as valuable as gold. Since you admire the horse, let's go to the gate and have a look at it before we drink!

(*Looks at the horse*)

(*To the tune of* **Yujiaozhi**)

As to this steed,

> It is of noble birth as if coming from heaven,
>
> Puffing out an immortal breath.
>
> Both its appearance and equipment
>
> Show it to be an incomparable horse.
>
> It looks like a tiger or a dragon of the arhats,
>
> Or like a rainbow of whirling satin when it gallops.

LI YI:

Will you sell it?

GUO XIAOHOU (*Laughs*):

> As we are gallant men on horseback encountering on the way,
>
> Why does a wealthy marquis need more money?

HUA QING:

I see. It's impossible for me to get it from you. Now let's drink!

GUO XIAOHOU:

Was Bao Siniang with you when you watched me shooting at the birds with pellets?

HUA QING:

She witnessed your valiant and heroic manner together with me.

GUO XIAOHOU:

May I trouble her to play a piece of music for me?

HUA QING:

Bao Siniang, fill in our cups and play the music!

BAO SINIANG (*To the previous tune*):

> Dressed in green and red,
>
> I move my steps in the shadows of the window lattice.
>
> Leaning on the railings, I cast rounds of amorous glances
>
> With my face blushing like a half-drunken lotus.
>
> A tender, languid butterfly faintly powdered,
>
> I sing in an oriole voice as smooth as the silk handkerchief.
>
> I roll up my sleeves to hold the golden cups in smile,
>
> And pour the silver kettle in a drunken mode.

GUO XIAOHOU:

I have long heard of Bao Siniang's stunning beauty and charming voice. In face of a beauty worth a million ounces of gold, a horse worth a thousand is incomparable!

LI YI:

General Hua Qing loves the good horse, while Guo Xiaohou appreciates the heavenly voice of the beauty. If you make an exchange, both of you will be satisfied.

GUO XIAOHOU:

> *"If you really wish for the stalwart steed,*
>
> *I am willing to ask for your beloved beauty.*

HUA QING:

> *If at a heavy cost I can get the noble horse,*
>
> *I might as well give away my graceful beauty."*

Bao Siniang, serve the wine and I will send you to Guo Xiaohou's residence!

HUA QING, LI YI, GUO XIAOHOU (*To the tune of* **Qiyanhui**):

> With the beauty in exchange for a noble horse,
>
> The smoking-oven is a petal less for its fragrance.
>
> A scented beauty of scarlet jade
>
> Is aligned with a precious steed of flowing speed.
>
> The famous steed and the gifted beauty
>
> Will take flight abreast in the evening glow,
>
> Disturbing the white clouds.
>
> The rabbit will weep for the fairy in the moon
>
> While even the copper peacock will soar to the sky.

BAO SINIANG (*Weeps*):

General, how can you be so heartless!

023

> (*To the previous tune*)
>
> You put me in such embarrassment!
>
> For a good horse a pretty woman is exchanged.
>
> As beautiful as the peach blossom,
>
> I am just expected to dance in the spring breeze.
>
> When I lean against the window
>
> Or saunter in the garden,
>
> I will lament over my lot.
>
> When I hear the neighing of the foaming steed,
>
> I will deplore my unsettled fate as the dandelion.

HUA QING:

You need not cry! As a truly ambitious man cherishes aspiration for honor and success, I will guard the frontier for the most of my life in the future.

> (*To the tune of* **Shantaohong**)
>
> I sigh over the lost beauty and the cold bed-curtain,
>
> For I shall sleep alone.
>
> After you play the tunes of "The Lingering Phoenix",
>
> You are to leave as a lonely swan.
>
> You are a lovely green-feathered phoenix,

But when I see this bloody-sweat steed,

> All my thoughts go with the roaming dragon.

Siniang, don't call the wrong name in your dream!

> When you wake up,

Don't mistake the new master

For the pair has separated in your Pear-Blossom Dream.

As Guo Xiaohou is a young childe, Bao Siniang, wait on him with heart and soul!

You should be loyal and obedient

As the tender moon and the mild spring breeze.

As for you, Guo Xiaohou,

She is frowning

For her grievance on us.

You should be kind and soft to her

And not hurt her heart.

GUO XIAOHOU:

No need to say any more! Siniang will feel at home.

BAO SINIANG (*To the tune of* **Xiashanhu**):

My eyebrows would be reflected in another mirror,

As the beloved bird has left its cage.

My desire is like the cloud,

Which will float with the wind.

The master suddenly longs for a noble horse,

So that the female swallow has to part in woe with the male one.

Master, would you look for another concubine to wait on you day and night when I leave you?

HUA QING:

I only have the frontier on my mind and will not consider to have a woman any more.

BAO SINIANG:

You are an elderly man now. Do take care of yourself! Take care!

With my sentiments of departure filling the sky,

You should take care of your precious health

And not say that the steed will secure you a high rank.

Master, I have been waiting on you for a long time. After I leave here, who can do that well since the servants are either male or maids who sleep soundly at night?

As no one will take care of your bedding,

I am afraid that in the spring cold and heavy drunkenness,

You will feel sad and lonely at night.

LI YI:

Master Guo has been waiting for a long time. You'll have to say goodbye after all.

(*To the tune of* **Manpailing**)

When the horse is ready to set on its way,

The beauty weeps with tears all over her face.

BAO SINIANG (*Blames Li Yi*):

Damn you! Your visit has caused all my trouble! The general might visit Xiaohou by riding to his house some day, but I can never come to the general's residence!

The leaving horse longs to go back to its former bridle,

But the falling petal will never return to its stem.

How I wish to kill that horse!

　　The purple steed has ruined my life!

Master, I hope you will drop by Xiaohou's house. He's hospitable and will surely treat you well.

　　Separated by numerous high mountains,

　　We can only keep contact

　　Through messages brought by the swan or the wild goose.

Master, you said Guo Xiaohou loves my voice and looks, but I am afraid

　　Dancing and singing will stop

　　When my beauty fades as a burnt candle.

　　(*Collapses in tears*)

HUA QING:

Now I'll have Bao Siniang escorted to your house in a sedan. Master Guo, you can ride on that steed back with her.

GUO XIAOHOU:

I have got another horse.

BAO SINIANG (*Takes leave*):

　　(*To the tune of* **Zhegutian**)

　　The clouds are bleak at the time of departure,

　　As the Tartar horse still loves the north wind.

HUA QING:

　　When can I welcome the peach blossom again?

BAO SINIANG:

　　When will the deserted woman meet her former husband?

　　(*Exit Bao Siniang, followed by attendants*)

　　(*Guo Xiaohou takes leave*)

HUA QING (*Laughs*):

Mr. Li, the lady's chamber is deserted tonight, so I will feel lonely tonight and you may drink with me overnight.

LI YI:

I will come again tomorrow.

HUA QING:

Attendants, see off Mr. Li on the new horse!

　　One is my pretty concubine

　　And the other is a stalwart steed.

　　A noble horse will see off a noble guest,

From tomorrow on,

　　The northern horse will follow me to the north.

　　As a beauty has been hard to find,

　　The steed has cost me much more than it'd need.

　　I'll cast all memory of her behind,

　　With my attention on the noble steed.

Scene Five
Indulging His Mistress

(*Enter Guo Xiaohou*)

GUO XIAOHOU (*To the tune of* **Tianxiale**):

>Spring hunting follows the youngster's bent,
>But to avoid startling the beauty I keep my steps soft.
>When I appreciate the sword, I fill the cup again;
>When I sit in face of a beauty, I fiddle the zither again.
>*"The pretty concubine departs from her lover in resentment,*
>*As the early bird recalls its former nest.*
>*Where is the affection inscribed?*
>*Tears soak her spring garment."*

I am Guo Feng, by the style name of Xiaohou. Guo Ziyi, Prince of Fenyang, is my grandfather. My elder sister is the current first-rank imperial concubine in charge of the empress's jade seal and her daughter is Princess Taihe. Because of my sister, I was made a marquis in my childhood. When I was going on a hunting ride yesterday, I passed by the gate of Grand General Hua, who took a fancy on my horse, invited me to his singing-and-dancing hall and exchanged his beloved concubine Bao Siniang for my horse. Bao Siniang was in deep woe when she left her former master Hua Qing. She has been crying all day without eating anything since she came to my house. Well, how can a true gentleman bear to hurt other's feelings? Attendant, I have told you to escort Bao Siniang to my alternate mansion, where she can do whatever she pleases. But she is supposed to come to my house to perform singing and dancing on festivals.

ATTENDANT:

Bao Siniang has already been sent to your alternate mansion, but shortly upon arrival she was invited to Prince Huo's residence to teach singing, by a person who calls herself Zheng Liuniang.

GUO XIAOHOU:

I see. There is a Du Qiuniang in Prince Huo's residence, who used to be Bao Siniang's disciple. Therefore, Zheng Liuniang invites Bao Siniang to her place. I came to know at Hua Qing's banquet that Li Yi had just succeeded in the imperial examinations after reading numerous books, while Hua Qing made the exchange in order to perform meritorious service in the border areas at his old age. Who can be as happy as I am, for I have been made a marquis since my childhood!

ATTENDANT:

It is true indeed,

>*"There are Taoist priests in the immortal realm,*
>*As there are marquises in the human world."*

GUO XIAOHOU:

Just look at me,

(*To the tune of* **Wugongyang**)

With a fungi-cicadae tattoo on my arm,

I only wear a streamer-adorned hat,

Holding the ribbon under my arm and hiding my official garment.

I lead the horse out of the stable

And change clothes for the polo game several times.

I drink mellow wine from the silver or jade cup,

With my servants wearing satin boots and red coats.

Song and music accompany me all the time,

With candles waiting for me to return.

While flowers and birds flourish for three spring months,

The nobleman enjoys the longevity of a hundred years.

ATTENDANT:

The Xinfeng lads enjoy expensive wine,

GUO XIAOHOU:

To stay with steeds and beauties day and night.

ATTENDANT:

They do not know that lonesome Yang Xiong stayed

GUO XIAOHOU:

In temples for the night, without delight.

Scene Six
Discriminating the Tunes

(*Enter Zheng Liuniang, Huo Xiaoyu and Huansha*)

ZHENG LIUNIANG, HUO XIAOYU, HUANSHA (*To the tune of* **Raochiyou**):

The mansion is colorfully decorated

When spring arrives

With mists enshrouding the foliage in the empty yard.

ZHENG LIUNIANG (*In the pattern of* **Yuegongchun**):

"Spring arrives at our house when days grow longer,

With sandal scent risings from the smoking-oven.

HUO XIAOYU:

In shoes embroidered with mandarin ducks,

I move my steps in the magnificent hall.

HUANSHA:

Beautiful flowers allure us to the courtyard,

Which is showered with golden sunlight.

ZHENG LIUNIANG:

Having trained the parrot across the screen,

I'll teach my daughter a fresh tune."

HUO XIAOYU:

What do you mean by teaching me a fresh tune? You know, I cherish peace and quietude rather than the music.

ZHENG LIUNIANG:

Buddhist chants and hymns will not disturb your peace and quietude. I've told Yingtao to invite Bao Siniang. I guess she has arrived.

(Enter Bao Siniang)

BAO SINIANG (To the previous tune):

> The luxuriant pistacias and thin angelicas
>
> Echo the swift clapping of sandal clappers,
>
> But who is behind the latticed windows?

I am Bao Siniang. I had just arrived at Guo Xiaohou's alternate residence when Zheng Liuniang from Prince Huo's residence invited me to teach her daughter to sing. Here I am. I may as well go in.

(Bao Siniang and Zheng Liuniang exchange greetings)

ZHENG LIUNIANG:

> "As she waits and waits but you do not come,
>
> She has to draw on the spring water by the pond.

BAO SINIANG:

> Since I have not met her even once,
>
> How can she have so much affection?"

(Asks Huo Xiaoyu)

Is this the young princess?

(Huo Xiaoyu bows to Bao Siniang)

BAO SINIANG:

What a cute girl!

> "Only when the young bird learns to comb its bun,
>
> Can it use pearls and beads as its earrings.
>
> When you learn newly-composed love songs,
>
> You will tacitly stir your lover's heart."

(Huo Xiaoyu blushes)

ZHENG LIUNIANG:

She is young and shy. You see, while ladies walk in sunny spring days, from the mansions along the roads come the newly composed pleasant songs, with the accompaniment of sandal-clappers. The songs sound like the "Lush Trees" by the goddess on the Xiangshui River while the tunes sound like "Plain Orchids" by the honored scholar Sima Xiangru. The songs from *The Flower Basket* are written with words as bright and smooth as pearls and with tunes as beautiful as kingfisher's feather. *The Cloud Ballads* from the northwest will allure the cranes to dance in pairs while the line "The Sun Rises in the Southeast" in *The Yuefu Poetry* echoes "The Fish" in *The Book of Poetry*. A noble young lady should be instructed by a good teacher.

BAO SINIANG:

Liuniang, I used to dance the elegant dances but despise those who dance like desmodium gyrans, the dancing grass; I can sing "The Beauty at Night" by Xue Daoheng in the Sui Dynasty but deplore the chics who indulge in the singing-and-dancing hall. I have followed Guo Changsheng in playing the flute and taught Shi Chong and his disciples in playing the zither. My music can stop the floating clouds to do justice to my name as a famous musician; my songs can linger for a long time as Han E in the Warring States Period; and my tunes of Huainan are so popular that I can count my money like Cha Nu in Hejian. It is up to you to decide what to teach, Liuniang.

(*Enter Yingtao*)

YINGTAO:

"*Cold weather is hardly felt by drinking from jade cups*
While abandoned love abounds in beauty's chamber.
Pendants chink with the dancing steps
While sleeves are rolled up in a wait for the new song."

Mistress, when I was playing in the palace troupe, I copied a new poem by Li Yi from Longxi. Would you read it with the young princess?

(*Huo Xiaoyu, Zheng Liuniang and Bao Siniang read the poem together*)

HUO XIAOYU, ZHENG LIUNIANG, BAO SINIANG:

Alas! It is the *ci*-poem "Mountain Climbing on Man's Day" set to the tune of *Yichunling*. Well-done! Well-done!

BAO SINIANG:

Li Yi is a young man. I know him.

ZHENG LIUNIANG (*Laughs*):

Siniang, you know a lot of people! I'll have this poem sent to Du Qiuniang's alternate mansion to have it practiced. When Prince Huo climbs the mountain tomorrow, we'll serve the wine with this tune. Xiaoyu, learn the song by heart from Siniang!

BAO SINIANG:

Liuniang, I'd like to ask you for a favor. Du Qiuniang used to learn singing from me, but she still owes me the tuition fee. Now that she has taught her own disciple Shancai, it's time for her to requite me.

ZHENG LIUNIANG (*Smiles*):

You have such a good memory!

(*Exits*)

BAO SINIANG (*Smiles to Huo Xiaoyu*):

Xiaoyu, now you should call me the tutor. Please concentrate your mind when I teach you!

HUANSHA:

Siniang, we won't be able to sing what you teach us.

BAO SINIANG:

Nonsense! You can do it well as long as you become familiar with the tune. Xiaoyu, please sit upright and listen to me! There are three keys to singing. The first, remember the tunes; the second, keep to the rhythm of the clapper; and the third, display your voice to the full.

HUO XIAOYU:

How many tunes are there altogether?

BAO SINIANG:

It's hard to tell all the tunes at one go. I'll give you a general idea. There are twenty-four chapters of the *Huangzhong* tune, twenty-five chapters of the *Zhenggong* tune, twenty-one chapters of the *Dashi* tune, five chapters of the *Xiaoshi* tune, forty-two chapters of the *Xianlü* tune, thirty-two chapters of the *Zhonglü* tune, twenty-one of the *Nanlü* tune, a hundred chapters of the *Shuangdiao* tune, twenty-five chapters of the *Yue* tune, sixteen chapters of the *Shang* tune, six chapters of the *Shangjiao* tune, and eight chapters of the *Banshediao* tune, altogether three hundred and thirty-five chapters. From the time when Emperor Xuanyuan created seventeen tunes, only twelve of them are passed down to the present day. There are different designations for the same tunes. For example, *Yizhihua* and *Zhanchunkui* are the same tune. So are *Yangchunqu* and *Xichunlai*, *Paoqiule* and *Cailouchun*, *Douhama* and *Caochichun*, *Liuyaobian* and *Liushaoqing*, *Shengpingle* and *Maihuasheng*, *Gumeijiu* and *Qionglinyan*, *Hanjiangqiu* and *Jingxiangyuan*, *Caichage* and *Chujiangqiu*, *Ganheye* and *Cuipanqiu*, *Zhiqiuling* and *Wuye'er*, *Jingshanyu* and *Cezhuan'er*, *Xiaoshamen* and *Tusi'er*, *Hanguolang* and *Mengtong'er*, *Cunlixiucai* and *Bandushu*, *Dianqianhuan* and *Fengjiangchu*, *Guayugou* and *Guadagu*, *Zuiniangzi* and *Zuiyemosuo*, *Qiaomuzha* and *Yinhancha*, *Tiaoxiaoling* and *Hanxiaohua*, *Shuahai'er* and *Moheluo*, *Yebuluo* and *Yeluosuo*, *Leiguti* and *Cuihuale*, *Lingshouzhang* and *Daiguduo*, *Yingwuqu* and *Heiqinu*, *Didijin* and *Tianshuiling*, *Zhenzhenying* and *Deshengling*, *Liuyingqu* and *Zhai'erling*, *Jiquzi* and *Jizhuoling*, *Guisaibei* and *Wangjiangnan*, *Xuanheming* and *Kuhuangtian*, *Chuwenzhan* and *Bujinqian*, *Bobuduan* and *Xuduanxian*, *Lian'erhong* and *Mapozi*, *Lingboxian* and *Shuixianzi*, *Panfeiqu* and *Bubujiao*, *Xianggong'ai* and *Fumahuanchao*, *Hongna'ao* and *Hongjinpao*, *Nüguanzi* and *Shuangfengqiao*, *Zhulüqu* and *Hongxiuxie*, *Santaiyin* and *Guisantai*, *Xiaobaimen* and *Bubaimen*, *Chaotianzi* and *Yejinmen*, *Shouyangqu* and *Luomeifeng*, *Zheguiling* and *Buchangong*. At the same time, my young princess, there are the same designations for different tunes. For example, both the *Huangzhong* and the *Shuangdiao* tunes have the designation of *Shuixianzi*; both the *Xiangong* and the *Zhenggong* tunes have the designation of *Duanzhenghao*; both the *Zhonglü* and the *Yue* tunes have the designation of *Dou'anchun*; both the *Zhonglü* and the *Nanlü* tunes have the designation of *Hongshaoyao*; both the *Zhonglü* and the *Shuangdiao* tunes have the designation of *Zuidongfeng*. They are not to be confused in singing. Words may be added or subtracted for some tunes, for example, *Duanzhenghao*, *Huolang'er*, *Hunjianglong*, *Houtinghua*, *Qinge'er*, *Meihuajiu*, *Xinshuiling* and *Zheguiling*. Besides, see to it that you do not confuse the tones in *Daogong Gaoping Xiezhi* and *Zimu Yichuanlizhu*! As you will soon be married to someone who has passed the imperial examinations, I'll sing for you in advance the tune of *Zheguiling*, which means "The Tune of Passing the Imperial Examinations",

> (*To the tune of* **Northern Zheguiling**)
> Relaxing your delicate eyebrows
> And wearing casual spring dress,
> You do up your beautiful hair randomly.
> You round up your night dream at the windows
> When the moon wanes.

Your eye-shadow has been erased by lover's caress,

And the sandal trace on your arm has been wiped off.

When you sleep behind the screen

And beside the smoking-oven,

You turn a deaf ear to the parrot's parody.

HUO XIAOYU:

You are a good singer, but this song fits the dandies and wenches rather than gentlemen and recluses. Can you show me some poems by the talented scholars?

BAO SINIANG:

Who else is a better talent? The poem "Mountain Climbing on Man's Day" circulated by the palace troupe is composed by a talent. As he is an acquaintance of Hua Qing, I've been familiar with his poems.

HUO XIAOYU:

Please tell me some lines!

BAO SINIANG:

I remember his couplet

"Beyond the screen, winds sway the bamboo trees;

I wonder whether it's my friend who comes at ease."

HUO XIAOYU (*Chants the poem and sighs*):

He is no less elegant and refined than the ancient poets Shen Yue and Jiang Yan. Siniang, let's have a walk along the carved railings by the green pond!

(*To the tune of **Huangying'er***)

On the beautiful screen is a colorful painting,

With the silk flower-clusters embroidered with thin threads

And the crystal-clear pond water glittering like a spring sea.

With her purple jade hairpins florid and translucent,

On the exquisite dressing table,

The sweet and charming beauty leaves her delicate trace.

Siniang, what wonderful lines!

HUO XIAOYU, BAO SINIANG:

The talent is admirable in writing

"Beyond the screen, winds sway the bamboo trees;

I wonder whether it's my friend who comes at ease."

BAO SINIANG (*To the previous tune*):

Her charming cheeks wearing the smile in her night dream,

Her white skirt draping on the ground to chase the butterfly,

She stands by the twisting railings for a moment.

The mossy ground bearing her footprints,

Plum blossoms falling on her skirt,

She betrays her lovesickness between her eyebrows.

HUO XIAOYU, BAO SINIANG:

The talent is admirable in writing

The Purple Flute

"Beyond the screen, winds sway the bamboo trees;

I wonder whether it's my friend who comes at ease."

BAO SINIANG:

I can see that you admire his poems very much although you have not met him yet.

(To the tune of **Cuyuling**)

He is impressive

With handsome looks,

Like an immortal

Coming out of his residence.

His appearance and bearing are extraordinary;

His personality is noble and lofty.

HUO XIAOYU, BAO SINIANG:

The talent is admirable in writing

"Beyond the screen, winds sway the bamboo trees;

I wonder whether it's my friend who comes at ease."

HUO XIAOYU:

What a lovely man!

BAO SINIANG (To the previous tune):

He is virtuous

With graceful manners.

You are not alone in adoring him,

Numerous pretty ladies

Have been chasing after him,

As he is a lady-killer.

Once you see him,

You'll peep behind the screen and expect his return.

HUO XIAOYU, BAO SINIANG:

The talent is admirable in writing

"Beyond the screen, winds sway the bamboo trees;

I wonder whether it's my friend who comes at ease."

HUO XIAOYU:

Where is he from?

BAO SINIANG (To the tune of **Coda**):

The talent comes to the capital from Longxi.

HUO XIAOYU:

What is his name?

BAO SINIANG:

His name is Li Shilang, as far as I know.

HUO XIAOYU:

Has he written any other new poems?

BAO SINIANG:

Why do you want more of his poems?

HUO XIAOYU:

To be used for songs I'll sing.

(*Bao Siniang takes leave and exits*)

What excellent poems he writes! What a pity that I cannot remember all his lines! What I remember is but bits and pieces of his gems. Indeed,

Beyond the curtain, bamboos sway in breeze;

I brush away the dust upon the lute.

The boudoir ladies love the amorous songs,

For "Orchid" tunes are from the sheer grass-root.

Scene Seven
Conversion to Taoism

(*Enter two attendants of Prince Huo*)

ATTENDANTS (*To the tune of **Shenzhang'er***):

From the azure sky on Man's Day

The sun sheds its warm light.

The orioles are passing on the message

That spring comes earlier this year.

As today is Man's Day,

Prince Huo will climb the mountains

And he's calling us in the West Garden.

"The guests enjoy much amusement

In the large palace garden.

Prince Huo will hold festival celebrations

While spring breeze brushes away the dusts."

We are attendants of Prince Huo. As today is the Man's Day, Prince Huo will climb the mountains and entertain the guests. His concubines Zheng Liuniang and Du Qiuniang are to play some music and they are waiting at the Spring Terrace. Here comes Prince Huo.

(*Enter Prince Huo*)

PRINCE HUO:

(*To the tune of **Wangwuxiang***)

I am entertained by the emperor as a prince,

With auspicious clouds floating over the palace,

Where the Chaoyuan Hall is bright and clear in the spring

And the Liangyuan Garden is full of birdsongs after snow.

With carriages followed by the guards of honor

And red robes permeated with smoking scent,

The Man's Day is full of vigor and vitality.

"The green grass decorates the prince's residence

While auspicious clouds loom over the palace.

The jade terrace is empty most of the time,

Except for drinking in front of the spring flowers."

I am Prince Huo, brother of Emperor Shunzong and uncle of the present emperor. The blue blood, descended from the dragon and the phoenix, is extraordinary. The emperor allots land to the lords, so that they are willing to leave the palace and go to the fiefs assigned to them. When three princes are conferred the title on the same day, why should they rival with each other in the north? Why should they rival with each other in comparing themselves to the lotus flowers in Yexia, instead of rivaling with each other in comparing themselves to the peach and plum blossoms in Yichun? I am below Kong Rong in literary talent and lack the wisdom of Mi Heng. I have not taken up any official position, but have been granted by the emperor numerous wagons decorated with flags; I have a large collection of books and attend the ritual and musical ceremonies in the Three Palaces of Harmony. Although I ride in magnificent carriages, I prefer to concoct pills of immortality. In picturesque surroundings, I am carefree to watch the flowers and willows. I have two concubines, Zheng Liuniang and Du Qiuniang, both bestowed on me by the emperor, who have lived with me for over twenty years. However, only Zheng Liuniang gave birth to a daughter. The two concubines are possessed with sweet voices like Bao Mingyue who rises with the singing birds at dawn and with delicate figures like Shi Xuanfeng who sleeps on the scented bedding. They give improvised performances at the banquets and never feel sad on hearing the music. Today is the Man's Day on which people climb mountains. The weather is sunny and pleasant. I shall wine and dine with my attendants. Indeed,

"On his visit to Nanpi, Wang Shuzi

Was impressed by Xie Zhuang's 'Verse Essay on the Moon';

The Prime Minister in Beidi

Was impressed by Song Yu's 'Verse Essay on the Wind'."

Kitchen chief, as I think the wine and dinner is ready, tell Zheng Liuniang and Du Qiuniang to come to the terrace!

(Enter Zheng Liuniang and Du Qiuniang)

ZHENG LIUNIANG (*To the tune of* **Guazhen'er**):

With the dressing mirror not in use for long,

My graying hair is combed at random.

DU QIUNIANG:

I copy scores at leisure

And learn them by heart in the rounds of wines,

With the flowers and leaves witnessing my joys.

(They come into the hall and greet Prince Huo)

ZHENG LIUNIANG:

Zheng Liuniang kowtows to wish Your Lordship longevity!

DU QIUNIANG:

Du Qiuniang kowtows to wish Your Lordship longevity!

PRINCE HUO:

034

Sing some new songs for the Man's Day!

ZHENG LIUNIANG, DU QIUNIANG:

Yes, Your Lordship!

(*Get up and stand at Prince Huo's sides*)

(*The attendants offer the wine*)

ZHENG LIUNIANG, DU QIUNIANG (*To the tune of* **Huangying'er**):

In the magnificent mansion in early spring,

A dinner is set in the evening glow,

With the flowers and leaves bathed in the moonlight.

The spring rape sprouts

And the spring willow twigs

Add fragrance to the road in the mist.

ALL:

In peaceful times,

On time-honored Man's Day,

Wine is drunk at the banquet.

PRINCE HUO:

Fill in the cups of my attendants!

(*To the previous tune*)

With "The Clean and Clear Music" to entertain the guests,

When we walk along the riverbank dotted with orchids,

The pond floating with water grass seems not big enough.

The spring rouses joyous emotions,

Presents pretty looks

And smiles with the flowers and wild geese.

ALL:

In peaceful times,

On time-honored Man's Day,

Wine is drunk at the banquet.

(*Zheng Liuniang and Du Qiuniang present the wine*)

ZHENG LIUNIANG (*To the tune of* **Yichunling**):

To celebrate the Man's Day,

Men read "Ode to the Pepper Flowers"

While young ladies decorate screens with paper-cuts.

With gold and silver headwear,

Pretty women decorate the windows in happiness.

Their fragrant belts wave like the floating cloud,

And their ribbons sway like the rising smoke.

ALL:

We wish Your Lordship

Many happy returns of Man's Day

And rejuvenation from your age!

PRINCE HUO:

Good wording! Good wording! Have you got any other songs?

DU QIUNIANG:

There is one more song.

(*To the previous tune*)

As days become longer

And the year grows shorter,

I fill in the passage of time with wine.

Even the Queen Mother of the West

Laments in face of the messenger bird.

People are busy all day long,

Sad for the growing of age.

ALL:

We wish Your Lordship

Many happy returns of Man's Day

And rejuvenation from your age!

PRINCE HUO:

Who has composed this song? It obviously reminds me to drink the wine of longevity and to live in the realm of longevity. How talented and kind-hearted the composer is! What is his name?

ZHENG LIUNIANG:

It's said that the composer is scholar Li Yi from Longxi.

PRINCE HUO:

I hear that there is a Li Yi in the court, who is full of jealousy. How can he write such a poem?

ATTENDANTS (*On their knees*):

There are two men by the name of Li Yi. Old Li Yi is serving in the court, while young Li Yi is well-read and well-versed in poetry. The jealous one is the old Li Yi.

PRINCE HUO:

Oh, I see. There are two Li Yi's. This song makes me oblivious of all the worldly affairs. Now I am old. If I do not cultivate myself to be an immortal, I will not be able to enjoy rejuvenated youth. So, attendants, I'll go into the Huashan Mountain and live as a recluse. Zheng Liuniang and Du Qiuniang, fill in my cup and listen to me!

(*To the tune of* **Xinujiao**)

Both pretty women

And the beautiful moon

Are present today.

By the Jade Terrace,

We make merry in laughters.

You are graceful and charming.

You are pretty

For your fair skin

And expressive bright eyes.

Your gauze skirts

Sway when you walk.

Your fragile figures

Keep the beauty of your earlier years.

ZHENG LIUNIANG, DU QIUNIANG:

We wish Your Lordship immense pleasure in the palace!

PRINCE HUO (*Laughs*):

But I am old.

ZHENG LIUNIANG, DU QIUNIANG:

We wish Your Lordship longevity!

PRINCE HUO:

I'm afraid I won't escape from fate.

(*To the previous tune*)

I won't escape from fate.

You don't know, snow-white hair is inevitable after all. Look at me,

Even the spring breeze is not able

To brush away my grey hairs.

I remember my former days.

In my youth,

I led an amorous life,

Flirting around.

I had liaison with women

In the dewy night

Until dawn in the spring.

I am too old to enjoy the bed pleasure with you.

I'll sneer at

My impotent sex play

As if in the erotic color paintings.

ZHENG LIUNIANG, DU QIUNIANG:

Your Lordship must be fed up with our fading beauty. Why don't you select other beauties
to rouse you up in your old age?

PRINCE HUO (*Laughs*):

Zheng Liuniang and Du Qiuniang,

(*To the tune of* **Doubaochan**)

For all their

High buns

And slim waists

In their prime of life,

They are nothing to me.

Now,

I only stare blankly at the old mansion

And the ancient road leading to Suiyang.

I glance in leisure at

The towers and mansions

In the mundane world.

In the bleak shadows,

I loathe the flutes and zithers

Beside the ape woods and swan pond.

ZHENG LIUNIANG, DU QIUNIANG:

Where is your retreat if you are tired of such a life?

PRINCE HUO:

I'd like to look for a friend.

(*To the previous tune*)

The fabulous immortal Wang Qiao

Is inviting me

From the remote region.

ZHENG LIUNIANG, DU QIUNIANG:

How can you find the immortal in the remote region?

PRINCE HUO:

Zheng Liuniang and Du Qiuniang, even if I fail to find him, it is much better than to live a worldly life.

Knocking the bells at dawn

And chanting the scriptures at night

Is better than dreaming of the fairy in Song Yu's mind

And the goddess at the Luo River in Cao Zhi's poem.

ZHENG LIUNINAG:

You'd better wait until our daughter is married before you pursue your immortal's life. By that time, Du Qiuniang and I will follow you in pursuit of Tao.

PRINCE HUO (*Laughs*):

When I think of the ins and outs, I won't be able to care for my daughter.

You must recognize

That all deep affections

Will vanish with floating life.

ZHENG LIUNIANG:

You can practice Taoism in your secluded residence. What's the need of going far away?

PRINCE HUO:

I cannot be clear-minded enough in the mundane world. When I am gone,

I'll wander freely,

Searching in the rolling Guiling Mountains

For the immortals' residences.

ZHENG LIUNIANG, DU QIUNIANG:

Before you leave, you'd better send in a memorial to the emperor and appoint your inheritor.

PRINCE HUO:

If I send in a memorial, I am afraid that the emperor will not let me go. I may as well go to the

Huashan Mountain first before I send in a memorial to him. You may take leave now and look for a dwelling place.

ZHENG LIUNIANG, DU QIUNIANG:

In spite of your wealth and honor, you will search for the immortals. We are willing to follow you in pursuit of Tao, like followers of Liu An, Prince of Huainan, and like Cainü, Peng Zu's faithful female disciple.

ZHENG LIUNIANG (*To the tune of* **Heimaxu**):

> As you are like the cloud in the sky,
>
> With the aura of an immortal,
>
> Why should we change our master to serve King Zhao of Yan,
>
> Who indulged himself in song and dance,
>
> Leaving his concubines to sleep by themselves?

Your Lordship, the concubine of King of Zhao was remarried to a kitchen soldier, while Princess Gaoyang in the Tang Dynasty was married to a general. I despise them although I am of humble origin.

> It is ridiculous
>
> That those pretty concubines
>
> And dancing girls from the palace
>
> Lost their dignity and grace.

ZHENG LIUNIANG, DU QIUNIANG:

> We'd rather be the Golden Rooster in the clouds
>
> And the Blue Bird messenger
>
> Than assume charms for other men.

DU QIUNIANG (*To the previous tune*):

> It is grievous
>
> That the unicorn flags,
>
> The pearl-stringed wrapper
>
> And all the fond dreams of a luxurious life have come to an end.
>
> The disrupted love between us
>
> Has made me dull and depressed.

I admire the hairy Maid Maonü who flies to the sun and the goddess Chang'e who occupies the moon although I am of humble origin.

> It is fantastic
>
> That Maonü soars to the sky
>
> While Chang'e pounds the immortal medicine
>
> With her ribbons swaying in the wind.

Your Lordship, we have been following you for over twenty years since we served you in Jinling city. Now that you will be away to pursue an immortal life, where shall we stay?

> How can we bear cold spring night,
>
> When Chang'e stops pounding the medicine
>
> And Queen Mother of the West stops roaring?

PRINCE HUO:

I see that both of you have strength of character. However, as Zheng Liuniang has a daughter Xiaoyu who has not been married yet, how can you go into seclusion? Now I bestow on you the temporary Taoist name of Jingchi and on your daughter a mansion plus ten caskets of jewelry. She can take the entitled surname of mine, Huo. As for Du Qiuniang, since you are determined to go into seclusion, you can go to the Nunnery of the Queen Mother of the West near the Jinbiao Gate and be converted to a Taoist nun, to be waited on by your disciple Shancai. I bestow on you a gilded chime stone and a purple Taoist garment. Zheng Liuniang and Du Qiuniang, refrain from grief after I leave! You will sing Blue Bird songs again when I come back as an immortal riding a crane. Attendants, fetch the Taoist hat and robe for me to change clothes!

> (*Changes clothes*)
>
> (*To the tune of* **Coda**)
>
> Removing my gold crown and red robe,
>
> I need no guide to go to the Peach-Blossom Spring.

Zheng Liuniang and Du Qiuniang,

> I hope that you will not be waiting in solitude.
>
> (*Zheng Liuniang and Du Qiuniang see off Prince Huo on their knees. Re-enter Zheng Liuniang and Du Qiuniang, taking leave of each other*)

ZHENG LIUNIANG:

Qiuniang, when are you leaving for the Taoist nunnery?

DU QIUNIANG:

I will leave soon with my disciple Shancai.

> (*Zheng Liuniang and Du Qiuniang embrace each other and weep*)

How despondent it is for us to be separated all of a sudden after being together for twenty years!

ZHENG LIUNIANG (*To the tune of* **Zuitaiping**):

> It is deplorable
>
> That concubines good at singing
>
> Are disbanded and go different ways
>
> Like the slender Zhao Feiyan and the plump Yang Yuhuan.
>
> In blooming times we'll beat the drums
>
> And play the game of women warriors on the purple terrace.
>
> It is no easy matter for us,
>
> For the departure of our master leaves us in tears
>
> And we have to call him in a different world.
>
> We shall be expecting him in tearful eyes,
>
> For the immortal mansions and trees
>
> Are hard for us to claim.

DU QIUNIANG (*To the previous tune*):

> With dizzy eyes,
>
> We knit our brows and expect his return,
>
> Throwing the jade hairpins and gold combs

Toward the deep mountains.

We will grudge that gone is the Prince,

Who will play the flute in the immortal land.

We shed woeful tears,

For we are left in the human world of spring flowers,

When the banquet is over and the lamps removed.

(*Sobs*)

After I wash my charming face by myself,

I shall play the flute in rains of tears,

With my disheveled hair getting moistened.

ZHENG LIUNIANG (*To the tune of* **Coda**):

A world of difference occurs to us within a day,

With Taoist nuns wearing the laurels,

DU QIUNIANG:

But we shall meet on the immortal mount in the sea someday.

The Prince of Huainan follows immortals,

Leaving for at least a thousand years.

To follow him to the Peach-Blossom Spring,

The weary beauties will live without cheers.

Scene Eight
A Visit to an Old Acquaintance

(*Enter Li Yi*)

LI YI (*To the tune of* **Siniang'er**):

With my home beside the mountains and rivers

Seized by invaders from the north,

How roamers as I grieve for it in the spring wind!

Wearing a wretched hat

And a shabby coat,

I am looking for the singing house.

"Poplar trees grow luxuriant by the riverbank,

Where fairies may be seen among the flowers.

On the Jade Terrace I see the worry-free grass,

Which is not at all free from worries."

Everyone says that I am a wanton talent, but actually I am honest and decent. On a recent visit to Hua Qing, I heard the singing of Bao Siniang, whose beauty disgraces the moon and whose voice halts the floating cloud. As long as you are a man, who can be devoid of emotions? Hua Qing is really ridiculous to exchange such a charming beauty for a horse

without rhyme or reason. How sentimental Bao Siniang was when she left Hua Qing! When she wept, all the people present felt sad for her; when she looked back, all the people present were tormented by her departing woe. Luckily, Guo Xiaohou is generous indeed. When he sees that she is in low spirits, he shows much sympathy for her by settling her in his alternate residence without locking the door. She can teach others singing and dancing as she likes. I have never committed any misconduct with women although I am a young man. "As the stones are visible in clear waters, man should not covet the neighbor's wife; as the orchids are pure and white, man should not violate the master's daughter." However, with my heart stirred this spring, I feel that it is time now for me to aspire for love. I have indited love-pledging poems and now I'd like to seek love. As it is bright and sunny today, I may as well wander alone and go to Guo's alternate residence to pay Bao Siniang a visit, but I wonder whether I will meet her or not. Qing'er, I'm going out for a stroll in the street. You will stay at home and look after the house. Do not let the sparrows spoil my inkstones or the wind blow off my books!

QING'ER:

Yes, I see.

LI YI (*Walks*):

Alas! The willow trees along the palace ditches have turned green in the couple of days I stayed indoors!

(*To the tune of **Jinchandao***)

In the Copper Pond,

Green water ripples in the bright and clear spring days

While willow-twigs waver in the mist.

I still remember the beauty

In the general's mansion,

Who filled my wine cup

And sang songs in a crispy voice

Which was affectionate and melodious.

Her shy look behind the gilded screen in the breeze

Tickled the sentiment in my heart.

When I ride to the alternate residence,

I hear melodious singing amid the flowers.

Alas! At the crossroads, there are two pathways. One is the Huayang Street and the other is the Shangguan Lane. Let me ask the way? Where is Guo Xiaohou's residence, brother?

VOICE WITHIN:

It is the tall mansion in the Shangguan Lane.

LI YI:

Thank you! Now I'll go ahead and make more inquiries. Indeed,

From behind the charming flower beds,

The beauties raise their voices and sing aloud.

I ask and get the answer from the guards,

Hou's scarlet mansion towers in the cloud.

Scene Nine
Inviting the Matchmaker

(*Enter Bao Siniang, followed by the maidservant*)

BAO SINIANG (*To the tune of* **Boxing**):

> While clouds float and cast shadows through the trees,
>
> The foliage fragrance permeates the cool mist.
>
> In face of the distant mountains,
>
> I am not in a mood to make up.
>
> Like a butterfly dangling from the spider web,
>
> I have not made up my mind where to fix my affection.
>
> For an unfortunate woman like me,
>
> The song and dance before the flowers
>
> Have become a memory in my mind.

(*In the pattern of* **Nangezi**)

> "*The joss-stick burns outside the bed-curtain;*
>
> *The sandal smoke brushes at my make-up.*
>
> *Riding on a saddled steed,*
>
> *A childe came to drink by the bridgehead,*
>
> *And I had to entertain him with a forced smile.*
>
> *A fickle man was not to be relied on,*
>
> *While a fragile woman was ill at ease.*
>
> *When I woke in cold tears at cockcrow,*
>
> *I found myself a frightened butterfly*
>
> *Returning from the nightly flight.*"

I am Bao Siniang. The wretched Hua Qing exchanged me for a horse, while the kind-hearted childe settled me in his alternate residence. Since I taught the young Princess Xiaoyu to sing in the mansion of Prince Huo the other day, I've been feeling bored and have never gone beyond the railings carved with flowers. Have you heard of any news in the street, my maid?

MAIDSERVANT:

When I went to master's main mansion this morning, I heard that Prince Huo was so depressed after the dinner-party that he went to the Huashan Mountain to pursue an immortal's life. He presented Zheng Liuniang and Xiaoyu a red mansion for the young princess to look for a satisfactory son-in-law and bestowed the surname of Huo on Xiaoyu. Another concubine Du Qiuniang who said that she had no heirs was inclined to practice Taoism in the Nunnery of the Queen Mother of the West. All those in our master's main residence sighed over this. That's all I have heard.

BAO SINIANG (*Startled*):

Alas! The young princess is delicate and intelligent. Why doesn't Prince Huo leave after she comes of age? How can he have the heart to do so? Du Qiuniang is my disciple. She is determined to live a secluded life, while I am still entangled in the worldly affairs. It is true that the master is below par with the disciple, who is like a lotus with its root in the mud and its flowers immaculately white.

MAIDSERVANT:

You live in the alternate residence by yourself, sitting in the fragrance of smoking scents, without being disturbed by our master. And you are free to teach singing. You are living a fairy's life.

BAO SINIANG:

Oops! It is inappropriate for you to say so. Seclusion for Taoist cultivation is far better than the worldly life!

(*To the tune of* **Bubujiao**)

How can the worldly life be as peaceful as the secluded one?

A debauched dream-like life is hard to get rid of.

The noisy flute and zither music is loathsome to the ears

While health is damaged by excessive drinking at banquets.

Nothing is comparable to chanting scriptures in tranquility,

Which clears away the frivolous nature.

(*Enter Li Yi*)

LI YI (*To the tune of* **Bushilu**):

Having done her make-up in the bower,

The mistress is known for her outstanding charm.

My visit is like tapping at the pedicel,

Which startles the butterfly from its dream in the mist.

BAO SINIANG (*Surprised*):

Who is it at the door?

It must be a childe for a sudden whim.

LI YI:

I am Hua Qing's old friend.

BAO SINIANG (*Pleasantly surprised*):

It sounds like Li Yi from Longxi. I'll open the door at once.

As I had not heard your voice clearly,

I did not answer the door at once.

Excuse me for the delay!

Excuse me for the delay!

LI YI:

It may be inconvenient if Guo Xiaohou comes at this time. I'll just stand at the door and have a word with you before I take leave.

BAO SINIANG (*Choking with sobs*):

Please come in and sit for a while!

(*To the previous tune*):

In the alternate residence,

LI YI:

I'll just sit in the hall for a while.

    Let's have a chat in the main hall.

BAO SINIANG:

There's a lot for us to chat about.

    Please listen to me with patience

    Because your presence reminds me of Hua Qing.

LI YI:

Siniang,

    It is a blessing for you

    To wait on the young nobleman

    Instead of staying in the military camp.

BAO SINIANG:

    Don't taunt me like this

    For you witnessed the whole business!

    What a virtuous deed!

    What a virtuous deed!

    (*Sits down*)

Shilang, have you visited Hua Qing recently?

LI YI:

I have been staying in the hostel in a depressed mood without visiting anyone since I saw you last time. As your sweet songs have been lingering in my ears, I've come on purpose for some relaxation.

BAO SINIANG:

I am not in the mood to sing. Even if I sing, my song will not be pleasant, as I have been bearing constant resentment for Hua Qing. Now listen to me!

    (*To the tune of **Haojiejie***)

    In my bower with orchids and screens,

    I paste my decorations in front of the mirror.

The merry-going dandies would pay for the pleasure with me.

    I would wag my sweet tongue

    To produce melodious songs.

    In high spirits,

    Prompted by oxhide gelatin mixed with wine,

    I would bring joy with slight perspiration.

But since I came to Hua Qing' residence, I have lost interest in the merry-making.

    (*To the previous tune*)

    I would be inwardly startled when the lamps are to go out.

Shilang, you are late in seeking pleasure from me. How can I sing well in such a mood?

    As to playing the zither at the end of spring,

    I don't feel like plucking the strings

    Because of my deep remorse.

As I am about to fall ill,

How can I bear to entertain the guests

With my fragile figure?

LI YI:

I am sorry that you are not in the mood to sing. Would you please tell me some other female singers?

BAO SINIANG:

Shilang, it is improper for a noble person like you go to the sporting house for entertainment. Why not marry a famous beautiful singing girl to keep you company?

LI YI (*Laughs*):

How difficult it is to find such a girl! I have three requirements on her: noble birth, extraordinary beauty, and deep compassion.

BAO SINIANG:

Alas! Speaking of compassion, there is a girl to whom I told your couplet of "*Beyond the screen, winds sway the bamboo trees; / I wonder whether it's my friend who comes at ease,*" which I heard in Hua Qing's residence. That girl adores your lines. Does she really have compassion for you?

LI YI (*Surprised*):

Such a girl must have a good countenance.

BAO SINIANG:

She is an absolute beauty.

LI YI:

Is she born in a noble family?

BAO SINIANG:

Yes.

LI YI:

Who is she?

BAO SINIANG:

She is the daughter of Prince Huo.

LI YI:

May I manage to seek her love?

BAO SINIANG:

It is possible in some ways.

LI YI:

Why do you think so?

BAO SINIANG:

Please listen to what I have to say!

(*To the previous tune*)

Beautiful red flowers and green leaves

Are set against the delicacy of the noble beauty.

Shilang, she pondered over your lines for quite a while.

Inertia caused by her spring sentiments

Accompanied a pensive mood.

Chanting your lines,

She sensed your affectionate tenderness

As well as romantic sentiments.

LI YI:

Would you act as my matchmaker?

BAO SINIANG:

Yes.

(*To the previous tune*)

Making a good match

Also needs predestination.

LI YI:

I'm afraid she has not come of age yet.

BAO SINIANG:

Romantic affairs should be enjoyed

With such a young talent.

Shilang, this girl is sixteen of age. Please offer betrothal gifts as soon as she agrees on the marriage!

LI YI:

I see.

BAO SINIANG:

For the beautiful girl,

An auspicious day will be chosen to offer betrothal gifts.

I'm sure the girl

Will shelter her face with her sleeves to conceal her affection.

LI YI:

Please see to the matter as soon as possible! I am leaving now.

BAO SINIANG:

As you are an old friend of Hua Qing's, I must help you fulfil your wish. I'm only afraid that I haven't treated you well enough today.

(*Sobs with her eyes covered*)

LI YI:

Do you have anything else to say?

BAO SINIANG (*To the tune of* **Coda**):

Please tell Hua Qing about my tears

And my negligence of making up since we parted.

Shilang, I have to put up with my unsettled life since I came from the pleasure quarters. When you marry Princess Huo, you should not be as heartless as Hua Qing.

How can I get rid of my fickle name?

LI YI:

I long for youthful love of pretty maids,

BAO SINIANG:

While I won't like to sing in joyous tone.

LI YI, BAO SINIANG:

> *Keep away from the pleasure-seeking grounds,*
> *Lest your spouse is left at home alone.*

Scene Ten
Tactful Inquiry

(*Enter Zheng Liuniang*)

ZHENG LIUNIANG (*To the tune of* **Yichichi**):

> With shreds of clouds flying over the mansion,
> I have long forsaken my dream for the immortal land.
> When dewdrops hang on the jade hooks,
> The curtain wavers in the spring breeze.
> I pluck the strings and meditate
> That even the immortal king has his concubines.

(*In the pattern of* **Huanxisha**)

> *"When spring brings a different scene*
> *With withering plum blossoms and daffodils,*
> *I languish by the smoking-oven.*
> *Instead of going on spring outings like the fairy concubines*
> *Or wearing the pendant in the immortal mountains,*
> *I return to my youthful times in my dreams."*

I, Zheng Liuniang, used to serve Prince Huo heart and soul like a humble and diligent ant, wishing that he would cherish longevity. Before I could requite his kindness with my efforts as meager as the the light of the fireflies, he has gone to pursue an immortal's life, leaving me alone without anyone to rely on and his daughter Xiaoyu living with her deserted mother. As Xiaoyu does not feel well these days, I have to stroll alone in the yard. How melancholy I am to recall the days when Du Qiuniang and I served Prince Huo together!

(*To the tune of* **Xiaotaohong**)

> With the painted flowers fading on the screen
> And the copper mirror blurring in the air,
> I think of the pretty concubines of the ancient king Gaoyang.

In the song and dance at that time,

> Flowers were merrily passed
> And reddened the silk ribbon.

It was known that the life in Huo's residence was luxurious.

> The emerald-decorated reed-pipe was played,
> With the phoenix ring attached to the jade,
> While the fans in the dance turn toward the clouds

And the dragon flags wave in the wind.

It seems that extreme luxury and amusement would rouse gloomy sentiments. In his old age, Prince Huo has to take immortal cultivation in seclusion as his last resort.

> He would live in a dream in his old age,
>
> With all his merriment lost.

Prince Huo, you have left in pursuit of an immortal's life in seclusion, disregarding me and my daughter. You have not even said good-bye to her!

> Wife and daughter are thus discarded,
>
> Sad and lonely in the ostentatious world.
>
> (*Enter Bao Siniang*)

BAO SINIANG (*To the tune of **Lülüjin***):

> Flowers in solitude
>
> And willows in the hazy shade
>
> Accompany the pretty ladies in their sleep
>
> Amid birdsongs.
>
> Knitted eyebrows reflect
>
> Their deep meditation.
>
> They paint the Wushan Mountains on Sichuan paper,
>
> With their beautiful hair done at random.

I used to be Hua Qing's concubine, and today I'll make the match for Mr. Li. When I come to make the match, I'll talk to the fair lady as beautiful as the moon-goddess. The Red Mansion is not far away. I suppose Princess Xiaoyu has finished with her make-up.

> (*Chants "They paint the Wushan Mountains on Sichuan paper, with their beautiful hair done at random" and calls Yingtao to open the door*)

YINGTAO (*Opens the door*):

Oh! It's Bao Siniang.

> (*Bao Siniang and Yingtao greet each other*)

BAO SINIANG:

> "*For what was the prince intent on departure?*

ZHENG LIUNIANG:

> *For he is attached to an immortal's fate.*

BAO SINIANG:

> *Why did he not wait until his daughter is married?*

ZHENG LIUNIANG:

> *Because he thought that it would be too late.*"

BAO SINIANG:

Has the young princess dressed and made up?

ZHENG LIUNIANG:

I don't know why she seems to be dizzy all day these days. Since her father left, she has always been in tears, with no spirited look in her eyes, no mood for doing her hair and no appetite for meals. I was sitting here in a depressed mood when you came.

BAO SINIANG:

Is she being sentimental in sight of the swift passage of spring?

ZHENG LIUNIANG:

Nonsense! How can a young girl be sentimental over spring?

BAO SINIANG:

Alas! How can a young girl be not sentimental over spring?

ZHENG LIUNIANG:

As no one is sentimental over spring nowadays, how can my daughter be sentimental like this?

BAO SINIANG:

Unlike crude people, all intelligent people have such sentiments. What an intelligent girl your daughter is! Please listen to me.

(*To the tune of* **Jiang'ershui**)

Her slim waist can only bear the weight of dewdrops.

ZHENG LIUNIANG:

Where is she to beg for the dewdrops of tender love?

BAO SINIANG:

She has started to expect that.

Her light figure tends to lean against the wind.

ZHENG LIUNIANG:

Xiaoyu is a decent girl. She does not want to lean against any man.

BAO SINIANG:

You are not accurate in your judgment.

Judgment should be made according to her behavior.

Listen to her playing the music tunes!

She plays the tender note on her lute in her bower.

Liuniang, do you think the princess is lovesick?

ZHENG LIUNIANG:

She has been acting like this in these two days.

BAO SINIANG:

You know,

Stains of her menses in her crotch show her adolescence.

Liuniang, I'm afraid that the princess has learned to dream.

She may laugh out in her fond dreams.

Liuniang, you know, the youngest daughter of King Fuchai of Wu by the name of Ziyu in ancient times hated her mother for spoiling her fond wishes. Liuniang, consider her health,

I am afraid that her unnamed desire

Would cost her life just as Ziyu died for her lover Han Zhong.

ZHENG LIUNIANG:

You are right in saying so. But where can we find the man to whom we can entrust Xiaoyu?

BAO SINIANG:

You are predestined to have an excellent son-in-law. I don't know whether you will agree to accept him.

ZHENG LIUNIANG:

How is he compared with Xiaoyu in terms of talent and appearance?

BAO SINIANG:

They are a natural couple like a pair of screens! Now listen to me!

(*To the previous tune*)

His writings

Are like the shining ink on the white silk;

His books

Are as numerous as pollens for the bees.

ZHENG LIUNIANG:

I'm afraid he is such a bookworm that he lacks romantic traits.

BAO SINIANG:

He is gifted

In revealing his affections through music tunes.

ZHENG LIUNIANG:

How about his family?

BAO SINIANG:

He comes from a family

Of good education and high official status.

ZHENG LIUNIANG:

How many betrothal gifts can he offer?

BAO SINIANG:

If you'd like to accept him,

You will get wagons of Tartar jars and embroidered satin.

ZHENG LIUNIANG (*Laughs*):

I just asked casually. If he is really so excellent, we need no money except two white jade pendants.

BAO SINIANG:

A pair of jade pendants will soon bring a son.

ZHENG LIUNIANG:

What is his name?

BAO SINIANG:

He is Li Yi, the gentleman who wrote a poem on climbing the mountains on the Man's Day.

ZHENG LIUNIANG:

Oh, it's him! He is really the best choice as Prince Huo loves his poems very much. There is just one thing to consider now. My daughter was bestowed his father's surname *Huo*, but actually the true surname of the Huos is *Li*, which is the same as that of the young man. It's not good that a couple share the same surname.

BAO SINIANG:

Huo is to be used since it is bestowed by Prince Huo. In the past, a couple in the court bearing the same surname brought good prosperity to the posterity.

ZHENG LIUNIANG:

Let me apply to divination first!

BAO SINIANG:

The result is sure to be "marrying your daughter to this man".

> The affable mother's divination
>
> Predicts a pair of noble phoenixes after marriage.

ZHENG LIUNIANG:

As marriage is a lifelong matter, I must ponder it over.

BAO SINIANG:

As he is a young talent of noble birth, he will find other choices if you don't agree. You'd better make up your mind in a day or two.

ZHENG LIUNIANG:

When a girl is in her childhood, her mother will make the nuptial decision for her. As she has grown up by now, I must discuss it with her. When we have made the decision, I'll tell Yingtao to give you a reply.

BAO SINIANG:

The princess will surely agree if you ask her, because she knows Li Yi's poems and appreciates them very much. When you meet her, just tell her that I've brought more of Li Yi's new poems to her. As she is still asleep, I must be going now.

ZHENG LIUNIANG (*Smiles*):

As you please!

BAO SINIANG:

I'm leaving now and I'll be waiting for your reply. You know, the matchmaker has recommended the most graceful man.

> (*Exit*)

ZHENG LIUNIANG:

Yingtao, go and tell the young princess to come here!

> (*Enter Huo Xiaoyu*)

HUO XIAOYU (*To the tune of* **Santailing**):

> Raindrops fall onto the flowers from the eaves
>
> When evening glows are reflected on the red wall.
>
> After a sweet dream,
>
> I'm awakened by the wind when the setting sun shines on the windows.

Blessings on you, mother! Why do you call me here?

ZHENG LIUNIANG:

Bao Siniang came here just now.

HUO XIAOYU:

Did she come for a casual visit?

ZHENG LIUNIANG:

She came here to set a poem to music.

HUO XIAOYU:

Now that my father is away for immortal seclusion, how can you be in a mood to listen to her?

ZHENG LIUNIANG:

She said that she had Li Yi's new poems.

HUO XIAOYU:

It's Li Shilang instead of Li Yi.

ZHENG LIUNIANG:

It's the same person. How do you get to know him?

HUO XIAOYU:

Bao Siniang came with his poems the other day, and mentioned that he was a remarkable talent. Father is not at home; otherwise I'll ask him to come. I suppose that he has the bright talent of the ancient scholar Sima Xiangru and a better appearance than the ancient poet Wang Can.

ZHENG LIUNIANG:

You want to see him and he also wants to see you.

HUO XIAOYU:

How can he want to see me?

ZHENG LIUNIANG:

As he wants to marry you, he asks Bao Siniang to be the matchmaker.

HUO XIAOYU:

Don't let Bao Siniang hoax you! She knows that I like Mr Li's poems, so she takes the chance to tease you. Besides, as Father has become an immortal, I should become a fairy maid. In ancient times, there were filial maids who refused to marry after their fathers died, so that they could look after their mothers. This is also my set wish!

(To the tune of **Xiudai'er**)

I sat on the bed, trying to conceal my affection

And feeling shy to be called a wife.

ZHENG LIUNIANG:

My daughter, only fairies are absent from desires for love. Once they come to the human world, they also seek love.

HUO XIAOYU:

I am not the fairy Du Lanxiang who visited the man Zhang Shuo,

And I sneer at the fisherman who seeks the peach blossom.

I am not boasting

That I am determined to retain my chastity.

Why should I dismiss my wish to stay single?

(Sobs)

As mother and daughter keep to each other,

How can I leave you alone?

ZHENG LIUNIANG (*To the previous tune*):

With the passage of time,

Why should a widow, like the frosty cloud and the solitary moon,

Keep her pretty daughter at her side?

Xiaoyu, even the immortal fairy Magu has human affections.

The Purple Flute

Luofu, Queen Mother's young daughter, was married to Xuandu

While the magnolia was reluctant to bear lotus flowers.

As to the immortal fairies,

The Weaver Girl in the sky would arrange her own marriage,

And meet her lover across the Milky Way on the magpie bridge.

So today,

Your braceleted arm should be twined with red gauze

When you are married to a talent of noble origin.

HUO XIAOYU:

How am I to look after you once I get married? I am determined not to be married!

YINGTAO (*To the previous tune*):

Don't be in the wrong!

The most adorable miss

Would be eager to be married to an ideal man.

Madam, as the old saying goes, "How can you have a grandson if you do not get your daughter married?"

HUO XIAOYU (*Displeased*):

You naughty maid! I won't get married because I love my mother. It's none of your business!

YINGTAO:

Young princess, are you caring for your mother?

If you hesitate between the two,

Neither of them will be happy in the end.

HUO XIAOYU:

Nonsense! What on earth do you know?

YINGTAO (*Aside*):

I won't be hoaxed!

She has reached the age of sixteen,

An age to break away from her cloistered life.

As she has come of age,

She is firm in speech but vexed at heart.

(*Turns round and kneels*)

Madam, the young princess is not willing to be married as she cannot tear herself away from you. But it is possible that Li Yi, who is a kind young man, will agree to live with you and look after you together with the princess. Why don't we ask Bao Siniang to inquire about this?

ZHENG LIUNIANG:

My daughter, what she says sounds reasonable. Yingtao, go and invite Siniang here!

HUO XIAOYU:

Mother, Bao Siniang is sure to speak for Li because they are old acquaintances. I think it impossible for such a talent to remain single till now. So this time he must be looking for a concubine to be taken back to Longxi. As Longxi is ten thousand miles away from here, how can I go to that place? I have an idea. Let's have Yingtao disguised as an adopted daughter of Bao Siniang and go to Li's hostel to discuss the marriage! He will surely let out the truth. What do you think of it?

ZHENG LIUNIANG (*Smiles*):

You are really sophisticated, Xiaoyu! Yingtao, do as the princess tells you and don't let the cat out of the bag! It is true indeed,

> *"We shall depend on the Blue Bird messenger*
> *Who is like the nimble-tongued go-between."*

> (*Exit*)

YINGTAO:

Young princess, tell me what I am to do for you, for I am at your service!

HUO XIAOYU:

I'm wondering about two things. Listen to me!

> (*To the previous tune*)

> I am afraid

> That I shall be a concubine to be despised

> And that the man will not stay in the capital.

There is no doubt that he is a young talent, but

> Why should the talented scholar

> Do without a perfect mate?

> Try to make it clear

> That he marries for the first time

> And will settle down in the capital!

> In that case, I will give my consent

> To form the wedlock with him as soon as possible.

YINGTAO:

Princess, you said that you wanted to remain single like an immortal fairy, but now you'll seek a pleasant life!

HUO XIAOYU:

You fool! If I become an immortal, I'll keep you as my disciple; if I live a pleasant life, I'll bring you pleasures as well.

> (*To the tune of* **Coda**)

> Try to be flexible when you speak!

Yingtao, you are cleverer than Huansha. I will be expecting you in the bower.

> I will be waiting until all the ravens return to their nests.

When you make clear of everything, tell him that I'll entrust myself to him after he offers the betrothal gifts!

YINGTAO:

Princess, just now you said that you would bring me pleasures as well. May I ask what rewards you would grant me after the matter is settled?

HUO XIAOYU (*Laughs*):

I would ask Shilang for a cute boy to be your match.

YINGTAO:

Thank you, princess!

People cherish reunion everywhere under the full moon.
In beautiful garment without restraint,
Princess Fufei met her lover in her prime.
Who knows that Nongyu fell in love with Xiao Shi
And played incessant flute tunes at nighttime?

Scene Eleven
Presentation of the Betrothal Gifts

(*Enter Li Yi*)

LI YI (*To the tune of* **Qingjiangyin**):

On the bed-curtain are embroidered red plum-blossoms,

With delicate leaves clustering around a golden halcyon.

In distress and puzzlement I travel alone,

With dreams of spring in the far distance.

After the intoxicating wine,

The ideal princess

Is weighing on my mind.

(*In the pattern of* **Chouyilan**)

"With the petals dropping

And the scent permeating in the rain,

Spring appears all the more lovely.

The wincing willows dangle in the wind,

In their full verdancy.

When the moon goes dim at dawn,

Where is the one in my heart?

I tell the oriole not to call out at dawn,

For fear of adding sorrow to my depression."

Yesterday I went to visit Bao Siniang, who promised to make a proposal for me to Huo Xiaoyu, the daughter of Prince Huo. When I returned, I tossed and turned on the pillows for the spring night. As I did not sleep well or wake up in the right mood, I'll read *Zhaoming's Literary Selection* for a lift up.

(*Turns a page*)

Alas! How auspicious it is that I happen to come across the character of *love* in Volume Nineteen, followed by verse-essays of "A Verse-Essay on Gaotang", "A Verse-Essay on the Goddess", "A Verse-Essay on Dengtuzi's Lubricity" and "A Verse-Essay on the Goddess of the Luo River". Oh! It turns out that talents through the generations are all full of affections!

(*To the tune of* **Zhaoluopao**)

In "A Verse-Essay on Gaotang",

Recalling the bed pleasure in Gaotang with the goddess,

The king had the banners prepared on a propitious day

To pay tribute to all the gods.

The Gaotang area was pathetic and quiet as if the ghosts and the spirits were about to come.

The plaintive music of nature increased the woe

When the rustling of the pine needles faded in the deep valley.

King Huai of the Chu State was looking around when suddenly he saw a goddess on the cloud wait on him in his day nap. It was a pity that this episode was over in the twinkle of an eye. If they could stay together longer, the king would certainly obtain longevity.

Followed by colorful banners and green shades,

The king ascended the mountain at that time;

In the morning rain and in the evening dew,

He met a pretty goddess.

Perusal of the verse-essay soothes my body and soul.

In "A Verse-Essay on the Goddess",

(*To the previous tune*)

The poet Song Yu dreamed of a remarkable lady

Like the morning sun above the rafts

That shone over the room.

With the swift passage of time in the human world,

His mind and thought went with the goddess.

Oh, King Xiang of Chu! It was fortunate enough to dream of such a goddess! Why should you call her to your mind after you woke up?

She was still gazing at him,

But her fragrance had vanished;

He still kept in his mind

The sweet words she had mouthed.

A reading of the verse-essay brings tears to my eyes.

In "A Verse-Essay on Dengtuzi's Lubricity",

(*To the previous tune*)

The girl next door

Smiled with a charm

That distracted any man's mind around Xiacai.

Why should Song Yu speak ill of her?

She was a true beauty at any rate.

Oh Song Yu! With such a pretty neighbor, you were sure to produce writings much more eloquently than anyone else! What's the use of talking about the beauties in the states of Zheng and Wei on your way to Handan!

For three years she remained single

And peered at Song Yu over the east wall.

The pretty flower is inclined on him,

But when will the spring breeze brush on her?

A reading of the verse-essay arouses my willow-breaking desire.

In "A Verse-Essay on the Goddess of the Luo River",

> On his sailing along the Luo River,
>
> Cao Zijian presented the goddess with the jade,
>
> While she raised herself and passed on the message.
>
> Her garments looked like the drifting snow in the winds;
>
> Her hair looked like the light clouds sheltering the moon.

Oh, Cao Zijian! What could you do with this affectionate goddess whom you had not proposed earlier but felt the regret at a later date!

> As he had not proposed at an earlier date,
>
> He was too late to present the precious pearl;
>
> Now that man and goddess went different ways,
>
> How could he tear himself from the goddess?
>
> A reading of the verse-essay fills me with tears.

In the four verse-essays, the appearance of the goddess on the Luo River has left a thousand years of remorse while the affection on the Yangtze River has passed down for ten thousand years. Although I am not an amorous man, I have some fancies for the goddesses on the river. I may as well quit reading and go to bed as Song Yu did at Gaotang during the daytime and imagine the coming of clouds at the Wu Gorge. Oh, Sister Xiaoyu, are you the goddess at the Jade Terrace in heaven, or the neighbor girl of Song Yu, or the mulberry-picking beauty near the Zhanghua Terrace, or the goddess on the Luo River? Why hasn't Bao Siniang brought any message and given me the reply?

(Falls asleep)

(Enter Yingtao)

YIGNTAO (*To the tune of* **Tianxiale**):

> My embroidered shoes step in the fragrant breeze,
>
> While the garnet skirt offsets my slim waist.
>
> Under disguise I'll make inquiry about the marriage proposal,
>
> To see how deep his love is.

I am Yingtao from the residence of Prince Huo, serving the young Princess Xiaoyu. At Madam's behest, I come under the disguise of Bao Siniang's daughter to visit Li Yi. I am supposed to inquire whether he has married before and whether he is willing to stay in the capital. I will also try to find out his intelligence and appearance. Here I am at his hostel. Let me make a cough!

LI YI (*Wakes up with a startle*):

Alas! The moment I fell asleep, I saw a beauty with remarkable looks. She smiled and knitted her brows, appearing and disappearing before me. I looked up and down at her and approached her to make inquiries. We were about to exchange words when wind and rain woke me up from my fond dream as experienced by the King of the Chu State. Indeed,

> *"As I am not aware that I am a guest in my dream,*
>
> *I cannot distinguish the rain from the cloud when I wake up."*

It turns out to be neither the rain nor the wind, but someone knocking at the door. It must be some diligent scholar to discuss learning with me or some old friend to ask me for an inscription. Oh! In a lady's voice, it must be Bao Siniang.

(*Opens the door and greets Yingtao*)

May I ask where you are from and why you are here?

YINGTAO:

I am Bao Siniang's daughter on an errand to report good news.

LI YI:

Hasn't Huo Xiaoyu agreed to the marriage?

YINGTAO:

His fond dream will soon come true, but I'll keep him in the dark for a while.

LI YI:

Isn't she fond of me?

YINGTAO:

She is fond of you for several things, as my mother has words of praise for you.

(*To the tune of **Lanhuamei***)

She says that

 You have a round face like the lotus on the waters,

LI YI:

I have inherited this appearance from my parents.

YINGTAO:

She says that

 You wear a black hat on your raven hair and a satin robe,

LI YI:

Love of beauty is my nature.

YINGTAO:

She also says that

 You are from a noble family of high officials.

LI YI:

It's not necessary to talk about my family. She only needs to say that I am fit for the marriage.

YINGTAO:

She also mentioned this.

 She says that you have talent and prestige,

And therefore,

 You're entitled to invite a go-between to make the proposal.

LI YI:

Now that everything goes well, I only need to rent a big house for the wedding.

YINGTAO:

Wait! I shall hoax him a bit. She still has doubts about two things.

(*To the previous tune*)

She says that

 A noble family like yours has many relations.

It is impossible that

> There are no suitable girls to marry.

LI YI:

Are you asking me why I have not got a wife and am making a proposal in the capital? Does she suspect that she will be a concubine?

YINGTAO:

That's true. She doubts

> Why you arrange a marriage far away from home.

There is another thing. As Prince Huo went in pursuit of an immortal's life, the mother and daughter are staying by themselves. She is afraid that you will only make a short stay here and discard her some day. She is afraid that

> You are but a passing traveler.

Mr. Li, my mother suggests that you make the proposal and promise to settle down in the capital. When the wedlock is tied, you can take her back home sometime in the future. It's up to you whether Huo Xiaoyu is the legitimate wife or the concubine, as long as

> You obtain a high official rank and scholarly honor.

LI YI (*Laughs*):

It turns out that she makes such remarks!

> (*Aside*)

I'll take this chance to put on a show and scout out some details about Huo Xiaoyu's appearance and family background.

> (*Turns round and asks*)

Alas! According to what you said, the young princess is picky and choosey. What gifts and looks does she boast to match such a talent as me and to be my legitimate wife?

YINGTAO:

Mr. Li, it is no exaggeration that there are many excellent men in Longxi, but few girls of Huo Xiaoyu's gifts and looks in the capital. Now listen to me,

> (*To the tune of* **Zuiluoge**)
>
> She is as delicate as the weeping willows
>
> And as beautiful as the spring flowers.

This morning I saw her when she had just finished her make-up.

> She removed the extra rouge with her tender fingers,
>
> And fondled her drooping spring gown.
>
> She wetted her lips with saliva
>
> And spat on the velvet.
>
> Even the lotus smiled at her stealthily,
>
> And the azure clouds stole a look
>
> At her petite and dainty feet.
>
> As she is so charming
>
> And so fragile,
>
> Do you have the luck to marry her?

LI YI (*Laughs*):

I would approach her even if she is Chang'e in the moon, let alone a young princess in the human world. But I have another misgiving. I am used to a luxurious way of life. How can I quit homesickness if I am not satisfied with their plain life as Prince Huo is gone?

YINGTAO:

Speaking of Huo's residence,

> The tranquil courtyard is good for leisure,
>
> With the bamboo curtains dyed dark green.
>
> The musk incense coils in the warm bower,
>
> With the smoking-oven sitting in the center.
>
> Delicate food is bestowed by the heaven,
>
> While dews drop from lichen onto the earth.
>
> The lovely pet dog plays with the fireflies
>
> While the idle cat sleep in the flower shrubs,
>
> Enjoying her tasty food, bean-powder bath and golden ring,
>
> Along the soft flower path
>
> Permeated with the sweet scent
>
> Of willows relaxing at dusk and lotuses blossoming at night.

LI YI:

If there is such a good residence, young miss, I must thank you for this match-making. I wish that someday you will be married to a man as excellent as I am. Now I have made up my mind to settle down all my life in the residence of Prince Huo.

YINGTAO:

How heartless you are to leave your wife behind at home!

LI YI:

I have talents and handsome looks, but I do not have a wife or a home. My parents deceased long ago, and my hometown suffered from wars. The flowers here are so beautiful that travelers forget to return home. As the Lantian jade is precious, the true beauty is hard to seek. She is my legitimate wife and we will respect each other all our lives. Now that I am determined about the marriage, what does she have to hesitate and doubt about? Listen to me!

> (*To the previous tune*)
>
> I am solitary and miserable,
>
> Escaping from the flames of war.

Dozens of cities in the Longxi area have been seized by the Tubos, not to mention the terraces and ponds at my home.

> After areas west of the Yellow River were cut off,
>
> People fled helter-skelter in fright.
>
> Where is my hometown at present?
>
> Floods of tears are shed in the west wind.
>
> The capital city is in peace and serenity,
>
> A harmonious picture in early spring.
>
> I try hard to cheer up by the flowers.

As a homeward journey is impossible,

I can only long for it in the music.

YINGTAO:

Mr. Li, it will be a happy marriage since you've never married and will settle down in the capital city.

(*To the previous tune*)

Surely, surely, all the matters are settled;

Happily, happily, you'll become a couple.

Mr. Li, the young princess is famous for her gifts and looks in the capital city. Numerous young men from noble families seek her hand. Whatever treasure you have, just give me and my mother will bring it to Huo's residence. By so doing, the marriage is settled.

Trade a fortune as you may for the spring night,

Which you will enjoy to your heart's content.

The zither stand and the writing-brush rack

Will be left unattended.

Sharing the same pillow with your love,

You will enjoy the warm spring night,

Holding her legs up close and tight.

Three days after the wedding,

In the early morning,

You'll thank your matchmaker with ten rolls of red silk gauze.

LI YI:

As a traveler, I cannot get the betrothal gifts fully prepared. But I do have two treasures which are passed down from my parents. They have always been with me through weal and woe in my life. The princess is undoubtedly worthy of the priceless beauty of the treasures. Qing'er, fetch from my gold carved trunk the copper mirror with nine golden dragons and the jade swallow-shaped hairpins inlaid with three pearls.

(*Enter Qing'er with the two treasures*)

LI YI:

Thank you for bringing them to Huo's residence for the young princess's adornment! I cannot present them in person without taking a scented bath. And I will call on you someday to requite your kindness. The mirror was forged in the middle of the Yangtze River, while the pair of jade swallow-shaped hairpins were patterned after the Terrace of Song'e. Madam and the young princess will surely set high value on them when they see them.

(*To the tune of* **Dong'ouling**)

The jade swallows

Inlaid with pearls

Will reflect in the mirror with the flowers and the curled dragons.

It is difficult for me to offer more than these as I am traveling away from my home. Otherwise, for the worth of the princess,

A million ounces of gold is needed to buy her eyebrows,

But can her love be bought at this price?

I wonder whether the young princess has me in her heart. As long as we are of one heart, what is the use of money?

> If she has me in her heart,
> She will have a safe lock to secure her love.

YINGTAO:

The marriage is settled. Speaking of her heart,

> (*To the previous tune*)
> It is dear
> And kind,
> Not cold, or deep, or broad.

LI YI:

Hurry, hurry! I will soon go to her residence!

YINGTAO:

The scholars are too much in a haste, but people in Huo's residence are like tempering pills of immortality: it must be slow and steady.

> It is like dragon and tiger gnawing at each other,
> By bits and bites.

LI YI:

I do not mean in that haste. I say that I will visit her in her residence tomorrow or the day after tomorrow.

YINGTAO:

I see. I will wait on you when you visit her because Bao Siniang does not always stay there.

LI YI:

Please allow me to express my thanks to you in advance!

YINGTAO:

Mr. Li, I dare not ask for your thanks. I only hope that you will not scold me for my blunders in serving you. At that time, please do not

> Keep all the pleasures to yourself
> Without anyone else in your mind.
> (*To the tune of* **Coda**)
> As the couple is a perfect match,
> Why should you turn to the spring wind for help?

Mr. Li,

> You'll need some silk fabric when you make love.

LI YI:

Please send my regards to her!

> *The maid goes on an errand with a scheme,*
> *At the behest of the mistress to test the man.*
> *Where is he to roam in tonight's dream?*
> *He'll fly and flirt as freely as he can.*

Scene Twelve
Carrying the Locket

(*Enter Yingtao, carrying a locket*)

YINGTAO (*To the tune of* **Liuyaoling**):

> Amidst the fragrant flowers,
>
> The beauty is ill at ease
>
> With her knitted eyebrows ridden with sorrow.
>
> In the tree of red plums,
>
> Purple orioles are singing
>
> In a voice so heart-breaking,
>
> In a voice so heart-breaking.

There are always admiring glances at me wherever I go. As I wait upon the young princess all day, I have no chance for frolics. Now I am walking on the imperial road lined with delicate plum flowers and orioles. I'd like to grasp this moment of leisure to play for a while. What about putting the locket in the grass and climbing onto the tree to pick some flowers and tease the birds?

(*Climbs the tree and teases the birds*)

(*Enter Bao Siniang*)

BAO SINIANG (*To the previous tune*):

> In this prosperous city,
>
> Many talents are fit for the Red Mansion,
>
> Where the beauty has come of age in the flowery garden.
>
> Walking on the verdant road
>
> In the fragrant breeze,
>
> I see something glittering in the grass,
>
> I see something glittering in the grass.

Oh! What is it that glows in the grass? Who has left the dressing-case here?

(*Opens the locket and looks*)

There is a copper mirror and a pair of jade hairpins in it. Where are they from? There are characters inscribed on the back of the mirror saying, "Prime Minister Li of Longxi, the fifth day of the fifth month in the fifth year of the Tianbao reign. Forged in the middle of the Yangtze River." There are four characters on the hairpins, "Lady of the Didao County." Well! Who is that Prime Minister Li? I will ask Li Yi as I am about to pass on a word to him about his marriage. I think he must know about them.

(*Walks*)

> "With the Lantian spirit embodied in the jade,
>
> Golden lights are emitted from grass.
>
> Without asking anyone else,
>
> I know that they must be betrothal gifts."

YINGTAO (*Sees Bao Siniang and shouts from the tree*):

Why are you stealing my locket, Bao Siniang?

BAO SINIANG:

Oh, you are Zheng Yingtao from Huo's residence. Why are you sitting on the plum tree?

YINGTAO:

I'm waiting to make a match.

BAO SINIANG:

Quit your nonsense! Come down and I have something to ask you!

(*Yingtao walks around the plum tree*)

BAO SINIANG:

What are you doing here?

YINGTAO:

This is called match-making around the plum tree.

BAO SINIANG:

Nonsense! Tell me why Zheng Liuniang lets you out?

YINGTAO (*To the tune of* **Bubujiao**):

The old mistress

    Hears that Mr. Li is of remarkable looks and talents,

    And tells me to pay him a visit.

She has two misgivings. One is that

    He has a wife in Longxi;

The other is that

    He will return home with Xiaoyu after marriage.

Therefore,

    I am disguised as your daughter

    To inquire about the details.

BAO SINIANG:

Zheng Liuniang is really sophisticated. I have not visited him for that. Then what is his reply?

YINGTAO (*To the previous tune*):

He said that

    He has never been engaged with anyone,

    Though he is eager for a spouse.

BAO SINIANG:

So he is not married yet.

YINGTAO:

    Like lovebirds sleeping on entwined branches,

    He will live with the mother and the daughter.

BAO SINIANG:

So he will settle down in the capital city. What did he ask you?

YINGTAO:

He asked me how the young princess thinks.

BAO SINIANG:

What did you say?

YINGTAO:

I said I was not the one to ask about her thoughts.

> My thin underwear
>
> Gets a little wet when I come.

BAO SINIANG:

Nonsense! Are the jade hairpins and the copper mirror in the locket from Li Yi?

YINGTAO:

Yes.

> (*To the previous tune*)
>
> Inherited from his parents,
>
> These are genuine treasures.

BAO SINIANG:

Why did he give them to you?

YINGTAO:

He said that since I was your daughter, I could bring them to you so that you can forward them to the Huos as the betrothal gifts.

> Open the golden locket to take out the betrothal gifts.

With such a young man, Madam and the young princess

> Must be satisfied from the bottom of their hearts.

But the young princess tends to put on airs, so it's not suitable for me to tease her as a maidservant. You'd better go back with me, open the locket and then persuade her to put on the hairpins and look into the mirror. You can make fun of her for a while.

> After she puts on the hairpins and looks into the mirror,
>
> You can ask her whether she likes them or not.

BAO SINIANG:

Then why were you sitting on the tree?

YINGTAO (*To the previous tune*):

> I was driving away the oriole
>
> Because it was eating the plums.

Siniang, you've made the match for the princess. As I have grown up too, you'll also find a man like Shilang to match me.

BAO SINIANG:

Pooh! Where can I find such a man?

YINGTAO:

Well, forget about it! Today when I was in Shilang's studio, I saw his boy-servant Qing'er, who is lovable with comely looks. When Shilang comes tomorrow, please do me a favor by having him grant Qing'er to me!

> The young Qing'er is a lovable lad.

BAO SINIANG:

Qing'er is only about fourteen. What can he do for you? Do you really take a fancy on him?

YINGTAO:

If he cannot do much for me now, he will grow up sooner or later.

> He is a man in spite of his young age.

Siniang, please make the match for me as soon as possible! If I do not find a man, my good looks will make the young princess jealous when Shilang comes to live with us. If I am married to Qing'er,

> I do not have to sneak around at midnight
> Like an egret looking for fish.

BAO SINIANG:

If you ask for your man, Huansha will also ask for one.

YINGTAO:

She can be matched to Wu'er, Shilang's kitchen boy.

BAO SINIANG:

You just leave the ugly one to others! Now stop wagging your tongue and go home with me!

BAO SINIANG, YINGTAO (*To the tune of* **Lülüjin**):

> When flowers are in full bloom
> And little orioles sing,
> Red flower-petals scatter
> Into the spring pond.
> When a woman worries about the loss of beauty,
> She will have to look back into the past at leisure.
> When she is in lovesickness,
> She will look at her boudoir with knitted eyebrows.

YINGTAO:

Siniang, our residence is in sight. The young princess is sitting alone in the Red Mansion, waiting for my reply. When you arrive at the residence, sit in the pavilion holding the locket! I will go and report to the princess, and then she will let you in.

> *Old treasures shining with youthful brilliance,*
> *The pearls and mirror serve as betrothal gifts.*
> *For the princess to be happily married,*
> *A maid is sent on an errand as makeshifts.*

Scene Thirteen
Accepting the Betrothal Gifts

(*Enter Huo Xiaoyu*)

HUO XIAOYU (*To the tune of* **Fanbusuan**):

> Leaning against the incense burner outside the screen,
> I find the rouge on my lips faded after a night's sleep.

With the floral fragrance return the bees

Flapping their wings to wilt the flowers.

(*In the pattern of* **Manjianghongqian**)

"When the sun shines through the mist,

I sleep soundly behind the bed curtains.

I may have disturbed the birdlings in pairs

On the warm embroidered quilts.

I mess up the rouge in my sleep,

Leaving a red trail on my pillows.

Leaning against the painted railings,

I watch the aquatic fowls."

I am Huo Xiaoyu, fully aware of the worldly affairs although I am still young. But my old mother does not know that many things are now different from those when she was young. This morning I sent Yingtao to coax Li Yi into telling the truth about himself and report to me first when she comes back. The sun is setting, but she has not come back yet. How bored I am!

(*To the tune of* **Sanhuantou**)

After a sound sleep,

I can hardly remember the dream when I wake up.

When blooming flowers bend the tree branch

And dust falls on my sleeve,

I feel weak all over in the spring.

The young lass,

Without rhyme or reason,

Turns lovesickness

Into love affairs.

In the late spring afternoon,

I rub the tassels on my dress

In a trance and in indolence,

Wondering why the reply has not come yet.

(*Enter Yingtao and Bao Siniang*)

BAO SINIANG (*To the tune of* **Chuanyanyunü**):

With a chill in my sleeves,

I walk on the spring roads.

YINGTAO:

The dress shows my emaciation in the spring,

When dusk clouds enshrouds the sky.

YINGTAO, BAO SINIANG:

In the fading sunlight,

Curtains are raised at sunset.

YINGTAO:

Here we are at our residence, Siniang. Please sit in the east hall and wait to offer the betrothal gifts! When I come back with words from the princess, the old mistress will come to accept the betrothal gifts.

BAO SINIANG:

Yes, I see.

> (*Exit Bao Siniang*)
>
> (*Yingtao greets Huo Xiaoyu*)

HUO XIAOYU (*Asks in a haste*):

So you've returned at last! What did you find out about that man?

YINGTAO:

Congratulations! Congratulations! How elegant and amorous the man is! He is perfect for he has not married and has settled down in the capital.

HUO XIAOYU:

How can he be willing to discard his hometown?

YINGTAO:

He is a native of Longxi. As it has been occupied by the Tubos, he has no hometown to turn to now.

HUO XIAOYU:

I see! It's just the thing I want.

YINGTAO:

My princess, he is to sleep with you tomorrow.

> (*Huo Xiaoyu is shy*)

YINGTAO (*To the tune of **Sanhuantou***):

069

> He is young and good-looking;
>
> His words are affectionate and loving.
>
> He will be a good husband,
>
> Like a butterfly enchanted by the flower,
>
> Panting while twisting his waist.

My princess, how happy you will be on the day when you are called "wife"!

> Here comes
>
> Your beloved one.
>
> When he calls you "wife",
>
> How would you react at that time?
>
> You would answer in a trembling voice,
>
> With your mind in a trance.
>
> Please remember your maidservant,
>
> Who has contributed to this blessed marriage!

HUO XIAOYU:

You want to be remembered before the matter is settled. Did he say when he will present his betrothal gifts?

YINGTAO:

Bao Siniang has been waiting outside with his betrothal gifts.

HUO XIAOYU:

Make haste and invite my mother here!

> (*Enter Zheng Liuniang*)

The Purple Flute

ZHENG LIUNIANG (*To the tune of* **Shenghulu**):

> A bright and beautiful make-up is done
>
> For the marriage over which we still hesitate.
>
> The future son-in-law
>
> Is extraordinary in looks and talents.
>
> I'm afraid he is already married
>
> And will one day leave for good.

(*Enter Bao Siniang with Yingtao*)

ZHENG LIUNIANG:

Oh! Yingtao is back. What did you find out?

YINGTAO:

It's really good that he is unmarried and has settled down in the capital city. He has offered the betrothal gifts and Bao Siniang is waiting outside.

ZHENG LIUNIANG:

Invite her in!

BAO SINIANG (*Greets Zheng Liuniang*):

The curtains embrace the spring breeze while the lintel of the door is decorated with blessings. The young princess is as beautiful as jade, while Li Yi is as firm as a rock. The marriage across a thousand miles will last as long as a hundred years. You can prepare the red candles for me to display the mirror and the pearl-decorated hairpins.

ZHENG LIUNIANG:

Siniang, please hold them for a while! Yingtao, where did you meet Siniang?

YINGTAO:

On my visit to find out the details about him, Mr. Li mistook me for Siniang's daughter, so he told me to forward the two treasures to you as his betrothal gifts. On my way back, I met Siniang under the plum tree around the corner of the Five-Phoenix Gate. So she came back together with me to give you the reply.

ZHENG LIUNIANG:

Oh, I see.

BAO SINIANG:

You are really prudent!

ZHENG LIUNIANG (*Smiles*):

Yingtao will get half of the wedding gifts tomorrow.

(*To Huo Xiaoyu*)

From now on you are the wife of Mr. Li. Have a look at the betrothal gifts!

HUO XIAOYU (*In shyness*):

Your inspection is enough.

ZHENG LIUNIANG:

You can get ready for the wedding ceremony.

(*To the tune of* **Yueshanghaitang**)

> In full brilliance,
>
> The lamps and candles send up a scented smoke.

The fragrance of the spring breeze

Permeates in the princess's boudoir.

The pair of jade hairpins in the locket shine with luster,

While the beloved daughter wears interlocked jade pendents.

ALL:

A marvelous match it is,

With the precious mirror and hairpins

Lasting forever as love tokens.

BAO SINIANG (*Congratulates*):

(*To the previous tune*)

I am an enthusiastic matchmaker,

Who ties the true love-knot with silk threads.

The moon rises from behind the laurel-tree,

When the phoenix hovers above the locust-tree.

The wife is like the courtesan Biyu playing the flute;

The man is like the prefect in the court of the Han Dynasty.

ALL:

A marvelous match it is,

With the precious mirror and hairpins

Lasting forever as love tokens.

ZHANG LIUNIANG (*Looks at the mirror and hairpins*):

He comes from the family of a prime minister. When I was in the palace, I heard of a mirror forged in the middle of the Yangtze River during the reign of Emperor Xuanzong. But I did not know then that it belonged to the Li family. Xiaoyu, I heard that there were two dragons guarding the boat where the mirror was being forged, so the back of the mirror bears the design of two coiling dragons, which was created by nature rather than by man. The pair of swallows carved on the jade hairpins are so lifelike, rarely seen in the world. The day after tomorrow is an auspicious day. As Mr. Li stays in the hostel in solitude, we might as well have the wedding settled on that day. Siniang, you just stay here with Xiaoyu and I will arrange with Huansha a dinner for you.

BAO SINIANG:

All right!

(*Exit Zheng Liuniang*)

BAO SINIANG:

Today is a good date. Yingtao, hold the mirror and hairpins! I will adorn her hair with the hairpins in her room.

HUO XIAOYU:

It is brighter here in the hall.

BAO SINIANG:

But it is more convenient in your room.

(*Walks*)

YINGTAO:

This is where the princess washes and dresses.

BAO SINIANG:

I see. Let's put up the mirror beside the gauze window! Please look into the mirror, princess!

HUO XIAOYU (*In shyness*):

(*To the tune of* **Erlangshen**)

Behind the gauze window,

The coral headwear in the mirror

Turns the moon-lit sky into a vast expanse of sea.

The moon-goddess in the mirror

Sees the dawning clouds approach her terrace.

The pair of green and red swallows in the mirror

Reflect the two tranquil and pure hearts.

BAO SINIANG:

Don't mention

The wandering shadows any more,

For you'll see a pair of smiling faces!

Let me plant the hairpins into your hair!

HUO XIAOYU:

Just leave that till tomorrow!

BAO SINIANG:

They should be planted in your hair today.

(*Puts on the hairpins*)

HUO XIAOYU:

Be careful! It hurts.

BAO SINIANG:

It surely hurts to have something stuck in.

HUO XIAOYU:

Pooh!

(*To the previous tune*)

It is resplendent

That green buds are set in the jade flowers

And carved swallows hold scented grass in their mouths.

The decorative silk button-loops are exquisite;

The jade swallows seem to flutter with feathers spread.

The swaying pendants of the hairpins hang on the temples

And the thin rods are stuck into the smooth thick hair.

BAO SINIANG:

I'm afraid that the rod thrusts into your hair too loosely. You'll thrust it more tightly tomorrow.

HUO XIAOYU:

Pooh!

BAO SINIANG:

Don't make haste to contradict,

As you'll soon lie on the same pillow with your man.

HUO XIAOYU:

Siniang, what you say sounds scaring because it is vulgar!

BAO SINIANG:

You'll be scared by your man, not me!

HUO XIAOYU:

Why should I be scared by him?

BAO SINIANG:

Because he will ask you to cook for him.

HUO XIAOYU:

That is not difficult for me.

(*To the tune of* **Fengrusong**)

I would cook for him with pleasure.

BAO SINIANG:

He will ask you to prepare wine for him.

HUO XIAOYU:

With good grace,

I would fill the jade cup with the silver pot,

Warm the mellow wine as Zhuo Wenjun did

And present it to him with due respect.

BAO SINIANG:

He will ask you to sing for him.

HUO XIAOYU:

It's no problem.

I would sing songs of devoted couples.

BAO SINIANG:

He will also ask for several night meals to trouble you.

HUO XIAOYU:

He can eat to his fill as long as he has the appetite.

A talent like him can have a feast of the eye at will.

BAO SINIANG:

You are really not afraid of these troubles. He will also ask you to put on his cap.

HUO XIAOYU:

It's no problem either.

(*To the previous tune*)

I'll brush his official hat and put it on for him.

BAO SINIANG:

He will ask you to make clothes for him.

HUO XIAOYU:

It is easy.

With sharp scissors,

I'll cut and sew at quick speed

To display my needlecraft.

BAO SINIANG:

How can you know his height? And how can you be familiar with his waist-size?

HUO XIAOYU:

I can figure that out.

    I'll figure that out by stealthily wrapping a band around his waist.

BAO SINIANG:

His waistband must be very long.

HUO XIAOYU:

You have a discerning eye in match-making. How come you are so familiar with him?

    You have sharp eyes but evil sentiments.

BAO SINIANG:

As my disciple, you should not scold your matchmaker. I used to teach you music, so I am your teacher. Now I'll teach you something, which your mother is not fit to do.

HUO XIAOYU:

What is it that you'll teach me? There are no early learners or late learners because those who have mastered come first.

BAO SINIANG:

Don't be pretentious! The newly-weds will feel very shy in facing the red candles on silver stands.

    (*To the tune of* **Yujiaozhi**)

    Sitting alone listless in the candlelight,

    You'll fondle your jade hairpins,

    Expecting your love to embrace you.

You should put on some airs by

    Knitting your brows, sheltering with your sleeves and shyly evading him.

Don't respond immediately when he speaks to you!

    You should pretend to be reluctant in response.

When he flirts with you with trifles,

    You should respond with tactics.

When he asks you to go to bed, you just wait by the bedside until he carries you onto it.

    The embroidered bed-curtains will be opened with trembling hands.

You should not undress by yourself. Rather, you should refuse him at first, preferably wait for him to snap open your band,

    And unloosen the knots from the loops on your short red coat.

HUO XIAOYU:

I see. You are babbling too much.

BAO SINIANG:

I'll tell you some sex techniques. When you go to bed, you should go to the west side if he lies in the east side and go to the east side if he lies in the west side.

    (*To the previous tune*)

You should pretend

    To be startled by the blissful delight;

You should pretend to pinch him with your finger-nails

    And push him away with your slim fingers.

He will definitely not give up,

But try to reach the lilac bud of your virginity.

You just give him the chance,

Not caring about getting pregnant at your age;

And you should prepare a white silk handkerchief because

You'll see red stains when he breaks the path.

Oh! That really hurts. Listen!

The juice will be drawn out to spray inside you.

The climax will come in a full blast

When your waist and limbs quiver.

HUO XIAOYU:

Master, how can you know the ropes so well?

BAO SINIANG:

I have my life experience. On my wedding night,

(*To the tune of* **Jiangshuiling**)

I was pretty and young

When I first experienced the ecstasy

Of flirtations in the arms of my man.

I took off my socks beside the smoking-oven,

And laid my embroidered shoes on the bedside.

My slim body lay on the bed,

And my eyebrows were frowned,

When I tasted the joy and endured the hurt.

I cleaned the stained silk,

I cleaned the stained silk,

And cast a side-glance by the candlelight.

I moved the pillow,

I moved the pillow,

Pulled the quilt tight and feigned to reject.

HUO XIAOYU:

You do have much to say!

BAO SINIANG (*To the previous tune*):

I got off the bed with my make-up messed up,

And sat at the dressing mirror facing the Jade Terrace,

Giggling and sighing at my recent experience.

I stole a glance at the blood-stains

And wiped the scratched spot in sorrow.

In front of the clothes-stand

And outside the curtains,

I made deep bows to the bridegroom in the bridal room.

Congratulations on the newly-weds,

Congratulations on the newly-weds,

Who glowed with happiness!

My bridegroom,

My bridegroom

Had such tenderness and affections!

HUO XIAOYU:

No wonder you are so shrewd!

BAO SINIANG:

Tomorrow you will be shrewd too.

(*Enter Zheng Liuniang*)

ZHENG LIUNIANG:

The evening dinner is ready in the hall. Bao Siniang, what have you got to say to keep you in the room for such a long time?

BAO SINIANG:

Just an idle chat.

ZHENG LIUNIANG:

We haven't prepared many dishes today.

(*To the tune of* **Coda**)

On the green jade plate

And in the purple glaze cup,

There are delicious food and mellow wine.

When Shilang moves in here,

The matchmaker will be entertained with a candle-lit banquet.

(*Exit*)

Scene Fourteen
Borrowing a Stalwart Steed

(*Enter Li Yi*)

LI YI (*To the tune of* **Yueyungao**):

With the thick scented smoke,

My heart goes out of the bamboo curtains.

The smoke coils like the swallow tails

Or the floating ribbons.

The tender willows sway in the sun

While plums come into full blossom in the breeze.

The butterflies stop at the flower petals

In the warm courtyard.

The albizzia flowers that are about to bloom

Come into my dream hand in hand with my love.

(*In the pattern of* **Baizilingqian**)

"The windows of the hostel

Shut out the spring and shut in the woe.

A cluster of flowers sway

In the sweet-smelling rain.

The zigzag railings stretch like a ribbon,

Encircling the the joyous flowers.

Gathering into crowds and floating slowly,

What do the morning clouds have in mind?"

Bao Siniang's daughter took my betrothal gifts to Huo's residence yesterday. Now that the sun is shining over the flower-beds, I suppose the reply must be coming. For the moment, I'd like to imagine what to do as a bridegroom. It is true indeed,

"As I am longing to cherish the love of a beauty,

There is no need for her to long for me."

(*Enter Bao Siniang*)

BAO SINIANG (*To the tune of **Jinlongcong***):

The young phoenix twitters on the tree branch,

Dripping tears of woe on the smooth grass.

Dressed in silk coats of bright designs,

The beauty leans against the curtains to steal a peep.

I am Bao Siniang. I have rejected playing the lute or flute with my companions, but am still good at going around the houses. Last night Lady Zheng gave me the wedding card to invite her future son-in-law. I got drunk last night and woke up late this morning. So I did not come out until noontime.

(*Calls*)

LI YI:

Oh, it's Bao Siniang! What brings you here in person? I gave your daughter the precious mirror and the pearl-decorated hairpins for her to bring to Huo's residence. How is the matter going on?

BAO SINIANG:

It's settled. Here is the wedding card from the old mistress.

LI YI (*Reads the card*):

(*To the tune of **Yifengshu***)

This is from Zheng, yours respectfully,

To Mr. Li Junyu.

Huo Xiaoyu, daughter of Prince Huo,

Is not outstanding in wit or beauty.

You are misled into believing that she makes a good wife

And offer the betrothal gifts of the mirror and the hairpins.

As the auspicious date has been fixed,

We shall wait for your arrival

To attend the wedding ceremony.

LI YI (*Laughs*):

The blissful event is just around the corner! Tomorrow is an auspicious day. Siniang, I'm too happy now, but I don't know how the princess thinks about it. And I'd like you to tell me more about her.

BAO SINIANG (*Laughs*):

She is no less preoccupied with the blissful event.

> (*To the tune of* **Xiaoshunge**)
>
> She got up languidly
>
> With a drowsy countenance,
>
> Negligent of the birdsongs and floral fragrance after rain.

She is not concerned about anything else.

> She has neither interest in playing the dice game
>
> Nor in the mood of cleaning with the bristle duster.

LI YI:

Is she shamming?

BAO SINIANG:

No, it is her natural disposition.

> During her daily smile and chat
>
> In the casual manner,
>
> She often appears like this.

Shilang, with such a nice girl as your partner,

> She will be a good companion
>
> With special attraction.

Shilang, please arrive early tomorrow, as she is expecting you eagerly!

> With her smooth skin in the new bedding,
>
> She is ready for you to enter.

LI YI:

What should I wear tomorrow?

BAO SINIANG:

Your scholar's robe will do.

LI YI:

How many servants should I bring along with me?

BAO SINIANG:

Of course you will not walk there. You must borrow from Hua Qing a horse as well as some young attendants.

LI YI:

I see.

> (*To the previous tune*)
>
> With the wedding date fixed
>
> And the wedding card granted,
>
> I'll borrow a noble steed with an embroidered saddle.
>
> From numerous men I am chosen
>
> To match this delicate beauty.

Siniang, please tell them to start meals after one or two cups of wine tomorrow evening as I'm not good at drinking!

> After drinking the mellow wine
>
> And eating the savory rice,
>
> I'll enter the bridal chamber.
>
> Against the comfortable bed,
>
> I shall enjoy the jade of a beauty to the full.

Tonight I'll stay in the hostel, but tomorrow night,

> Like a butterfly enticed by the flowers and a bird hidden in the willows,
>
> I shall experience all the warmth and fragrance.

BAO SINIANG:

After I leave, you shall visit Hua Qing and ask him whether he still remembers me.

> (*Sighs*)

LI YI:

I'm sorry that I won't dine and wine with you today. But I won't forget to express my thanks tomorrow in Huo's residence.

> (*To the tune of* **Coda**)
>
> Tomorrow I'll ride a magnificent wagon like Sima Xiangru,
>
> But my wife will not serve the wine like Zhuo Wenjun.

BAO SINIANG:

When you see Hua Qing, don't tell him that I've come to visit you in the hostel! Just tell him that

> I am chanting "Picking the Sweet Herbs" alone up the hill.
>
> (*Exit Bao Siniang*)

LI YI:

Qing'er, follow me to borrow a horse from Master Hua Qing for my wedding!

QING'ER:

As you'll be a donkey after marriage, you might as well borrow a donkey.

LI YI:

Shut up and make haste!

> (*Walks*)
>
> (*To the tune of* **Yueyungao**)
>
> The poets chant of the spring,
>
> About the "eastern neighbor" and the "southern road".
>
> The green poplar trees bend with luxuriant leaves
>
> While the plum flowers turn from pink to white.
>
> When the willows become glossy in the warm spring,
>
> The rippled pond water displays double colors.
>
> This explains why the amorous beauty
>
> Tosses and turns in the arms of her man.
>
> When the embroidered curtain is pushed aside
>
> She points to the floating silver clouds in smiles.

Qing'er, Master Hua Qing's residence is around the corner. You go and tell the gatekeeper that Mr. Li Yi has come for a visit!

(Qing'er calls)

(Enter the gatekeeper)

GATEKEEPER:

At present I am a new soldier in the Xiliu Camp;

In the past I was a drunkard in the city of Xianyang.

Who is making such a noise at the gate?

QING'ER:

Mr. Li from Longxi area is waiting at the gate.

GATEKEEPER:

Wait for me to report!

(Enter Hua Qing)

HUA QING (To the tune of **Jinlongcong**):

Wearing satin robes at home,

I am in command of the army at the frontier.

When the yellow-robe dandy rides a spotted horse,

Where does the flute music come from?

Oh, it's Li Yi.

(Bows)

LI YI:

"Leaves has just begun to sprout in the Xiliu Camp,

HUA QING:

When the horse is trained by the flowers in the sun.

LI YI:

I'll spare no money to borrow a good steed.

HUA QING:

And I know what you have on your mind."

(Li Yi and Hua Qing sit down)

LI YI:

Why did you say that you know what is on my mind?

HUA QING (Laughs):

I told my maidservant to visit Bao Siniang, who said that she had been away for a visit to Shilang in the hostel. So there is no distance between our hearts.

LI YI:

You know, she has done a lot for me recently.

HUA QING:

What is it?

LI YI:

I've asked Siniang to make a match between Prince Huo's daughter and me.

HUA QING:

When I was attending the court the other day, I read Prince Huo's memorial to the emperor about his pursuit for an immortal's life and the abandonment of his fief. It says that a poem by a talent inspires him for immortal cultivation, and that he leaves home for a life in the mountains before his daughter is married. I suppose that the talent refers to you, but I did not expect that his daughter would become your wife. Since the father is on immortal cultivation, both the daughter and you are fairies too. That is really a big event. I've been on the night patrol with the court guards until General Shesheng takes my turn today. I am about to visit you with some wine when you come for a vist. I am sorry for being late to greet you. Attendants, serve the wine!

(*Enter the attendants with wine*)

ATTENDANTS:

"*Good steeds enjoy a good fame far and wide*
While metal kettles are filled with mellow wine."

Master, here is the wine!

HUA QING (*Makes a toast*):

(*To the tune of* **Yifengshu**)

When spring permeates the camp,

I take kinostemon ornatum flowers to ease drunkenness.

The birdsongs are sweet and weak,

Just as the courtesan Niannu sings to the lute accompaniment.

Sweet wine in the jade cup stains the satin garment.

Oh, as to Bao Siniang,

Is her hair as thick and beautiful as before?

LI YI:

She is also lovesick for you.

HUA QING:

If she were here today, I would be coaxed into drinking more.

An expert of the jade flute

And the bamboo pipe,

She can drink a hundred kettles if necessary.

LI YI:

Please quit drinking for the moment! I want to ask you for a favor. Please listen to me!

(*To the tune of* **Xiaoshunge**)

I would marry the Frost Star of a beauty

Like the legendary Cowboy Star,

Coming into her embrace in the morning glow.

They've asked me to be the bridegroom tomorrow.

With her red shoes lit up by the candles,

I will stay in the bridal room.

HUA QING:

Is everything ready for the wedding?

LI YI:

They are a rich and powerful prince family, while I have few horses and attendants in the hostel.

I'd like to borrow a noble steed from you.

HUA QING:

So you need a horse?

LI YI:

Yes.

    I also need some attendants

    To follow me to the wedding house.

HUA QING:

I have a lot of handsome servants. I'm afraid you also need some money. I'll offer as much as you need.

LI YI:

There's no need for that.

    To be carefree,

    I try to take it easy.

I'm leaving now.

    I am taking leave rather than staying for dinner,

    But I respect the general for his generosity and thoughtfulness.

HUA QING:

Attendants, choose a good steed and some capable servants to escort Mr. Li to Huo's residence tomorrow!

    (*Two attendants respond*)

HUA QING:

I've long been thinking of finding a nice girl to be your spouse, but now,

    (*To the previous tune*)

    You excel in the imperial exam

    And chance on a remarkable wife.

For such a blessing we should drink some wine

    By the oilcloth wine sack and the flower-covered oven.

Shilang, what a coincidence it is that your matchmaker is my concubine and your wedding escort is my noble steed! This horse,

    With its bristles resembling the purple velvet

    And its saddle lined with gold,

    The horse gallops like a piece of flying red jade!

When such a horse bears a young talent to the noble house,

    Your extraordinary elegance

    Perfectly fits the remarkable family.

Shilang, you can keep the clever servants from my house at your disposal.

LI YI:

They have enough servants.

HUA QING:

Why not have some more?

    Even my vegetable gardener

Needs some heralds when he goes out.

Shilang, I won't urge you to stay.

    The colt equipped with the gilded saddle and the satin canopy

    Will carry you to your fairy beauty in the blooming spring.

    (*To the tune of* **Coda**)

    Tonight the fireflies will shed silver sparkles

    Illuminating the fructus corni seed pillows.

The day after tomorrow, I will come to Huo's residence to offer congratulations together with Shi Xiong and Shang Zipi. At that time,

    Your face will blush like the spring flower or the brimming wine.

    Her willow-leaf brows and her peach-blossom face

    Will belong to the man after the wedding feast.

    Tonight the beauty shines alone as the moon,

    But tomorrow guests will swarm in from the east.

Scene Fifteen
The Wedding

(*Enter Huo Xiaoyu, followed by Yingtao*)

HUO XIAOYU (*To the tune of* **Queqiaoxian**):

    The quilts are embroidered with lovebirds,

    The screens are painted with phoenixes,

    And the dressing locket is opened at dawn.

    Smoke coils from the candle on silver stands,

    Illuminating my shy face.

    (*In the pattern of* **Haoshijin**)

    "When the gauze curtain is rolled up at dawn,

    I get up with my skirt drooping.

YINGTAO:

    You are quite different in the usual days

    When you sleep until the sun shines high above.

HUO XIAOYU:

    Flowers are hastened by the spring breeze,

    Which prevents me from sleeping deep.

YINGTAO:

    You have a man in your mind

    As well as in your heart."

HUO XIAOYU:

How can I sleep well with such an important event for me in my mind?

YINGTAO:

I wonder when Mr. Li will come.

HUO XIAOYU:

He has no one to wait on him in the hostel.

YINGTAO:

I'm afraid he will take it ill as I sat poking fun with him face to face.

HUO XIAOYU:

He won't be particular about that as he is a man of honor. Bao Siniang said she would come early, but she has not arrived yet. You go to the hall and wait for her over there!

YINGTAO:

You have too many things to consider!

    (*Enter Bao Siniang*)

BAO SINIANG (*To the tune of* **Lameihua**):

    In the flourishing spring with flowers and trees,

    The curtain is rolled up in fragrance and verdancy.

    With a wed-lock across a thousand miles,

    The beauty in her natural raven hair

    Will be married in the magnificent mansion today.

YINGTAO:

So you've arrived, Siniang. My young princess got up very early this morning to dress up and have breakfast so that no congratulatory poem is needed to hasten the bride. Make haste and go upstairs! Has the bridegroom come with you?

BAO SINIANG:

It's still early.

    (*Goes upstairs and greets Huo Xiaoyu*)

You should have a good sleep, my young princess, as you will have no sleep tonight. I've never come upstairs, so let's have a look into the distance from here as Li Yi has not arrived yet!

    (*Looks*)

My young princess, look to the east at the row of government offices around the palace. There are military camps along the city wall, among which the residence of the Cavalry General Hua is located. There is a tall building called the residence of the military governor near the Shangguan Lane in the west, where my Guo Xiaohou lives.

HUO XIAOYU:

Siniang, you know quite a lot.

BAO SINIANG:

I can't conceal that from you. I also know another place in the north, which is neither big nor small. The wall is white and the gate opens wide, facing the Zhangtai Street. Behind the red curtain there is a remarkable man whom I know.

HUO XIAOYU:

Your eyes can wander.

BAO SINIANG:

But your eyes should not wander astray. Wait to see the man come out from there!

HUO XIAOYU (*Looks*):

Alas! Siniang, there is really an official on horseback coming out from there.

BAO SINIANG:

Where is he going?

HUO XIAOYU:

Oh! He is coming southward.

> (*Li Yi rides on a horse, followed by three attendants*)

LI YI (*To the tune of* **Sudijindang**):

> Intoxicated by the spring flowers, I hold a whip in my sleeve,
>
> Riding along the lush foliage by the river.
>
> Wearing a jade pendant from Lantian,
>
> I look from afar at my bride's house in the mist.
>
> (*Exit*)

HUO XIAOYU (*Pleasantly surprised*):

Siniang, look at the man riding along the river! He is as alluring as the willows, like the scholar Zhang Xu in his youth! How freely he is whirling his whip backwards, with the horsemanship of Wang Zhan in the past! How lovely he is!

> (*To the tune of* **Zhaojiao'er**)
>
> Who is that handsome man by the river?
>
> He is riding a horse like dancing peach blossoms.
>
> He seems to sit on the clouds, soaring to the sky,
>
> With glamour and grandeur along the way.

BAO SINIANG:

My young princess, when you look at the man on horseback, you are brimming with joy, but when I look at him, I am sighing with remorse.

HUO XIAOYU:

Why?

BAO SINIANG:

That is the very horse which General Hua took a fancy to when Guo Xiaohou rode on it to visit him.

HUO XIAOYU:

Siniang, a good horse can be compared to a noble man. Is it the horse that was exchanged for you?

BAO SINIANG:

I won't conceal it from you.

> Against the dancing shadows and the ringing music,
>
> I long for my former master at the sight of the bridegroom
>
> In deep melancholy,
>
> While still missing the former lover
>
> And feeling sad before the flower.

My young princess, I'm predestined to contribute to a happy marriage. Do you know who the handsome young man is on horseback? It is Li Yi!

HUO XIAOYU (*Delighted*):

Thank you for what you've done for us!

> Dressed in blue and vitalized on the face,
>
> The young man
>
> Is adorable indeed.
>
> At the jade dressing-table, two knots are interlinked
>
> By a red thread.

BAO SINIANG:

Let's make haste to go downstairs and ask the madam to sit in the hall to greet the bridegroom!

> (*Goes downstairs*)
>
> "*I'd rather listen to the Queen Mother in the emerald palace*
>
> *Than hear the lovebirds chirping on the magpie bridge.*"
>
> (*Enter Zheng Liuniang*)

ZHENG LIUNIANG (*To the tune of* **Xiaopenglai**):

> From the exquisite mansion comes the floral fragrance,
>
> Mixed with sweet scents from the smoking-ovens and red candles.
>
> Having reached the marriage age,
>
> The flower of a girl is in full bloom
>
> In prospect of leaves thick and dense.

Bao Siniang, thank you for what you've done for us! As Li Yi is arriving soon, the young princess will change clothes to greet him.

> (*Enter Li Yi*)

LI YI (*To the tune of* **Shanglinchun**):

> Drizzling rain and dense mist
>
> Disappear when the sky clears up,
>
> With phoenixes barely visible in the floating clouds.
>
> In the fragrant candleslight
>
> I come with the tinkling of jade rings and pendants.
>
> (*Bao Siniang goes out to greet*)

MASTER OF CEREMONY (*Chants a poem when Li Yi and Huo Xiaoyu bow to Heaven and Earth*):

> "*The Heavenly Emperor comes down to the earth*
>
> *While the Weaving Girl goes up to the sky.*
>
> *With the sun and the moon chasing after each other,*
>
> *The stars of fortune, prosperity and longevity shine o'er high.*"
>
> (*Chants a poem when Li Yi and Huo Xiaoyu bow to Zheng Liuniang*)
>
> "*The Queen Mother of the West*
>
> *Is wished a long life by her daughter Taizhen.*
>
> *The snowball viburnum flowers will bear seeds*
>
> *While the peach leaves look their best.*"
>
> (*Chants a poem when Li Yi and Huo Xiaoyu bow to each other*)
>
> "*You'll be a couple for a hundred years,*
>
> *Like phoenixes flying wing to wing.*

Your son will be a general or a prime minister
While your daughter will be married to the blue blood."
(*Proposes a toast*)
(*To the tune of* ***Jintangyue***)
In the serene sky,
The sun brings warmth
And bathes the courtyard in springtime.
Behind the painted curtains
Hides a hibiscus of a pretty face.
A butterfly lifts its wings on the flower stem
While silkworms swarm on the tree to spit threads.

ALL:

We make toasts
To wish the happy marriage to last for a hundred years.

MASTER OF CEREMONY (*To the previous tune*):

A banquet is held
For the fairy-like beauty
And the handsome talent
In the flowery courtyard.
Mellow and pure wine
Is tasted in silver cups.
With gilded chopsticks we eat minced leeks;
In painted caskets we fetch delicious food.

ALL:

We make toasts
To wish the happy marriage to last for a hundred years.

MASTER OF CEREMONY (*To the previous tune*):

With ups and downs,
With embroidered shoes placed in the corner
And satin quilts piled on the bed,
The music of the jade lute echoes in the room.
Hairpins of a new design
Adorn the hair to add charm to the beauty.
Noises can be heard outside the bamboo curtain
To hasten the beauty to make up.

ALL:

We make toasts
To wish the happy marriage to last for a hundred years.

MASTER OF CEREMONY (*To the previous tune*):

With expecting emotion,
The Weaving Girl Star passes message
When the beauty casts a glance

At her coat embroidered with a golden-thread phoenix.

She is dressed in red silk to fit her slim figure,

In the bridal chamber lit by the candles.

The talent and the beauty wish for the birth of many children,

While the double pillow blesses its realization.

ALL:

We make toasts

To wish the happy marriage to last for a hundred years.

ZHENG LIUNIANG (*To the tune of* **Zuiwengzi**):

Enviably,

The talent will surely rank among eminent people.

Your excellent essays increase the paper demand for copy use;

The resulting rising price devalues Luoyang's peonies.

LI YI (*On his knees*):

I'm fortunate enough

To be granted your kindness and grace.

Where can I find the pearls and jewelry to requite?

ALL:

The couple

Would be like the full moon

And be united all the seasons.

HUO XIAOYU (*To the previous tune*):

Stop the chat,

You'll surely come atop in the imperial test.

At home you will read my essays and poems

And watch me cutting white silk into dancing fans.

LI YI, HUO XIAOYU (*On their knees*):

Willingly,

We will face the fiery plum-blossoms

And hold the joss-sticks to make the pledge of eternal love.

ALL (*To the tune of* **Jiaojiaoling**):

The red candlelight flickers

On the lotus-shaped stand.

In the stillness of the night,

She holds fragrant breath,

And wears sparkling jewelry,

Expecting her young man.

(*To the previous tune*)

With their faces flushing as if in intoxication,

They can hardly fall asleep on the enchanting night.

Yet the stars move and time flies fast;

With her beautiful hair messed up, they wait for the daybreak.

(*To the tune of* **Coda**)

While the tassels on the bed curtain will witness

The constant love between man and wife,

We wish you a family of dozens of children and grandchildren.

(*Exeunt Li Yi, Huo Xiaoyu and Huansha*)

(*Bao Siniang takes leave*)

ZHENG LIUNIANG:

Siniang, you may as well take some marriage-blessing money home.

BAO SINIANG:

There is no need for that. I'll come tomorrow to greet the blissful bridegroom.

(*Exit*)

The trees bear flowers in the palace woods,

With usnea vines entangled like love-knots.

As flute tunes are played in the bridal room,

There's no need for the mother's lute.

Scene Sixteen
Congratulations

(*Enter Yingtao*)

YINGTAO:

"The purple ribbon with silver flowers

Is tied to the affectionate bride.

With the window gauze brushing my eyebrows,

I bow in a tilting manner to my elegant master."

My name is Yingtao. I've been with the young princess ever since my childhood when I accompanied her doing embroidery. Last night my young princess was married to Mr. Li. As her maid, I slept at the back of the bed, so how could I fall asleep? How would Mr. Li feel about it? What would be my mistress's grace and dignity? Anyway, I don't have to care about all these. Now that the sun has risen high and it is almost noon, the madam still bids me not to disturb her sleep. However, the young princess woke up early and has already got up to do her make-up.

(*Enter Huo Xiaoyu*)

HUO XIAOYU (*To the tune of* **Tanchunling**):

The bridal room was warm all through the night,

With the spring breeze behind the the bed-curtain.

(*Yingtao goes up to support Huo Xiaoyu*)

HUO XIAOYU:

With Yingtao supporting my frail figure,

I smile and feign to be angry when she asks me.

The Purple Flute

What can I do with such an affectionate man?

(*In the pattern of* **Heyebei**)

"*I remember the night encounter with him,*

With a trembling heart.

In messed hair and weakened limbs,

I kept silent and did not raise my head.

How embarrassing! How embarrassing!"

Yingtao, how distressed I am for my neck gets stiff from last night's sleep!

YINGTAO (*Laughs*):

That is what you enjoyed and what you suffered!

(*Pretends to rub where it hurts*)

HUO XIAOYU:

As soon as you got into bed, you fell asleep and slept till dawn. What can be hurting you?

YINGTAO (*Laughs*):

My young princess, you are hoaxing me. But I really heard something.

HUO XIAOYU:

What did you hear?

YINGTAO:

I heard you moan as soon as you got into the bed.

(*To the tune of* **Yingtixu**)

When the two of you became one behind the bed curtain,

The man wanted to get into the flower cave.

In the moonlight you moaned like an oriole

And promised him to continue the next night.

But how could he easily give up?

He thrust and throbbed to his heart's content.

When the bed shook hard,

How could you stop him with your fragile waist?

HUO XIAOYU:

Nonsense! Go and help him wash and dress as I don't need you here!

YINGTAO:

I'm afraid Mr. Li is still asleep.

(*Aside*)

As my young princess tells me to go, I'll hide behind the curtain and see what she is doing here.

(*Pretends to go away*)

(*Enter again, peeking stealthily*)

HUO XIAOYU (*Murmurs to herself*):

How embarrassing! How embarrassing! A girl should always avoid being seen by strangers. But now all of a sudden a strange man came to sleep with me side by side and did many movements. It hurts badly as if I were to die. When I got up and approached my dressing-table at dawn, he looked out of the bed-curtain again. So I had to sit here alone. I touched where it hurt most but was afraid of being sneered at by the maidservants. Now that Yingtao is away, I'll have a look at the silk handkerchief.

(*Looks*)

Alas! Where did these red stains come from? No wonder it hurt so much! But he seemed to have red stains too. How come I didn't hear him say "It hurts"?

(*When Yingtao tries to snatch the handkerchief, Huo Xiaoyu puts it into her sleeve*)

YINGTAO:

The stains are left by you rather than by Mr. Li. My young princess, let me have a look as it is something precious from you!

HUO XIAOYU:

It is nothing precious but a handkerchief. What is worth seeing?

YINGTAO:

It was a white brocade kerchief with bird patterns on it last night, but now it has turned red. Isn't it precious?

HUO XIAOYU:

It was originally reddish.

(*To the previous tune*)

On the pink brocade kerchief is woven

The evening glow and the wailing phoenix.

YINGTAO (*Laughs*):

This is in fact the peach-blossom spring

To be imprinted with the virgin stains.

HUO XIAOYU (*Sings to scold Yingtao*):

When you look askew and peep for no good reason,

What's the use of babbling about this?

When you joke with me,

Where is your respect for your mistress?

(*Pushes and Yingtao falls on her knees*)

YINGTAO:

I am intent on having a look at it for me to model after you.

HUO XIAOYU:

In that case, I'll tell the madam about it.

YINGTAO:

Then I would rather kneel here to be punished by you in whatever way.

(*Huo Xiaoyu walks*)

(*Enter Li Yi, running into Huo Xiaoyu and holding her in his arms*)

LI YI (*To the tune of **Ruanlanggui***):

When spring warms the water and greens the lotus,

I enjoy myself under the embroidered quilt

Oh, my dear wife,

Where are the morning clouds drifting?

It's disgusting that the sun casts shadows on the curtains.

(*Li Yi and Huo Xiaoyu greet each other*)

LI YI:

"When flowers bloom in the sunny spring,

HUO XIAOYU:

I meet you by chance and offer my virginity.

LI YI, HUO XIAOYU:

We hope that we shall never part

But melt into one person."

(Sit down)

LI YI:

Oh! As Bao Siniang's daughter, you need not make obeisance to me.

HUO XIAOYU (*Smiles*):

She's my maidservant. I ordered her to kneel for some reason.

LI YI:

Why did she act as the go-between who passed on the betrothal gifts?

HUO XIAOYU:

I told her to go and inquire about you.

LI YI:

You are scheming! No wonder this young lady said that you were prudent!

HUO XIAOYU:

Young lady! Just call her Yingtao!

LI YI:

Please allow her to rise to her feet for my sake!

YINGTAO:

I dare not get up before I receive the reward.

LI YI:

What reward do you want?

YINGTAO:

My young princess has made a promise.

LI YI (*Asks Huo Xiaoyu*):

What did you say?

HUO XIAOYU (*Smiles*):

I promised to grant her a young attendant.

LI YI:

Then I'll match Wu'er with her.

YINGTAO:

He is more than I can enjoy.

LI YI:

You can choose whomever you like from my attendants.

HUO XIAOYU:

You may as well match her with Qing'er.

LI YI:

I'm afraid Qing'er is too clever for her.

YINGTAO:

Yingtao is also very clever.

LI YI:

It would be a good match between the clever and unclever.

YINGTAO:

My mistress is clever, and she is matched with a clever husband. What do you say about that?

LI YI (*Laughs*):

Then Qing'er is settled on. Go and tell him to come!

(*Report within, "Report to the master that the guests have arrived."*)

(*Enter Huansha*)

HUANSHA:

> *"The horses are heralded by guards of honor*
> *While the men are smoked with exotic scent."*

Master, Master Hua, Master Shi and Master Shang have come to extend their congratulations.

LI YI:

Since we have guests, Yingtao can get up and serve the wine. My wife, they are my sworn brothers, so you may as well go to the hall and serve wine in your formal dress.

HUO XIAOYU:

I see.

(*Exit Huo Xiaoyu*)

LI YI:

Invite the three masters into the hall!

(*Enter the three guests Hua Qing, Shi Xiong and Shang Zipi*)

HUA QING, SHI XIONG, SHANG ZIPI (*To the tune of **Queqiaoxian***):

> When the spring breeze swirls the flowers
> And sways the willow twigs,
> We see an expanse of brilliant flowers and verdant trees.
> With towers and mansions against the green mountains,
> The palms of the immortals have painted the spring beauty.
> (*Li Yi and the guests greet one another*)

It's a shame that we did not contribute to your wedding expenses.

LI YI:

As I stayed in the hostel, I did not ask you for your suggestions. You give me the honor to visit me instead, but I am not considerate enough to wait at the gate.

HUA QING, SHI XIONG, SHANG ZIPI:

Please allow us to offer our congratulations to your wife!

LI YI:

She is obliged to come here and greet you.

(*Enter Huo Xiaoyu, greeting the guests*)

LI YI:

The new bride will serve the wine.

The Purple Flute

(Enter Yingtao with wine)

YINGTAO:

> *"Wine is offered to friends as worthy as gold*
> *By the lady who is as pure and pretty as jade."*

Here is the wine!

HUO XIAOYU (*Makes a toast*):

> (*To the tune of* **Yushantui**)
>
> When guests arrive at the splendid hall,
>
> I go downstairs putting on pretty headwear.
>
> With stirring dust under my tiny feet,
>
> I push aside the bead-decorated curtain.
>
> Like the rippled water in the breeze,
>
> My eyebrows are half knit in shyness.
>
> I wrap up my hands to pick up the kettle,
>
> With my hairpins at my temples slanting down
>
> And my cheeks flushing for the wine.

HUA QING, SHI XIONG, SHANG ZIPI (*To the previous tune*):

> The beauty sends her fragrance all over,
>
> Standing by the noble guests.
>
> Her eyebrows are like the verdant mountains,
>
> Or like a stretch of green amid the morning flowers.
>
> The painted beams in the morning sun
>
> Are not as gaudy as the silk garments.
>
> The light willow catkins
>
> Take wings in the spring
>
> And lean against the painted screen with the lady's ringing words.

LI YI (*To the previous tune*):

> After years of picking and choosing,
>
> I settled my marriage through a couplet of a poem.
>
> As Cao Zhi followed the goddess on the Luo River,
>
> I pursue the song and music as if I were in Yangzhou.
>
> Settling down in the capital city,
>
> I am destined to marry the charming beauty.
>
> When I halt my horse
>
> But float with the cloud,
>
> I will drink the beauty's toasts till I am intoxicated.

HUA QING, SHI XIONG, SHANG ZIPI (*To the previous tune*):

> What adorable grace!
>
> Time slows down in the coiling smoke.
>
> On the bed draped with fragrant curtains,
>
> The beauty enjoys her first wedding night.
>
> As your wild and undisciplined friends,

We've come to ask about your love affairs last night.

We're happy to see that the bride is half drunk

With enchanting smiles on her face

And keeps filling the wine cups.

HUA QING:

So much for the wine! I have a word with you. Shilang carves a career together with us in Chang'an far away from home. His official career is close at hand. The young princess should advise Shilang to make efforts for the bright future rather than waste time indulging himself in pleasure-seeking.

(*To the tune of* **Zhunu'er**)

A successful man is excellent in looks and manners,

As well as in writing remarkable essays sold at a high price.

May the wife encourage her man to strive for a grand career,

Instead of indulging himself in the domestic affairs.

HUA QING, SHI XIONG, SHANG ZIPI:

We wish that you would receive a lady's title

And ride in carriages decorated with gold and pearls,

Flying wing to wing with your man.

HUO XIAOYU:

Now you three gentlemen are present today. I'm afraid that Shilang may forsake me when he attains honor and wealth.

(*To the previous tune*)

When I have the official seal of a lady's title,

He may find a new silk weaver at home.

HUA QING:

Shilang is a faithful man.

Look how he treasures the perfume pouch behind his elbow!

He will not be a fickle man who forsakes his wife.

HUA QING, SHI XIONG, SHANG ZIPI:

We wish that you would receive a lady's title

And ride in carriages decorated with gold and pearls,

Flying wing to wing with your man.

LI YI (*To the tune of* **Coda**):

As dusk has descended on the woods and the palace,

Wagons will start on your way back before complete darkness.

HUA QING, SHI XIONG, SHANG ZIPI:

Shilang, it is the Lantern Festival tomorrow. As His Majesty grants the people the opportunity to light lanterns, the lantern fair will be the most prosperous. You may have a good time tomorrow night with the young princess. It is not convenient for us friends to follow you.

It is frightening how time flies.

(*Exeunt the three guests Hua Qing, Shi Xiong and Shang Zipi*)

HUO XIAOYU:

My man, judging from their appearances, the three of them will be high officials.

LI YI (*Laughs*):

What does a girl like you know about that?

HUO XIAOYU:

The wife of Minister Xi Fuji in the State of Cao recognized the talents of Zhao Shuai and Hu Yan while the wife of Minister Shan Tao in the Jin Dynasty peeped at Ji Kang and Ruan Ji. From these stories it can be seen that women can surpass men and the contemporary people can surpass the ancient people.

LI YI (*Laughs*):

I understand. Let's go to the hall and greet the madam!

> *In the bridal room invigorated by the spring,*
> *The peach blossom of a beauty sees off the guests.*
> *With the intoxicated wife in a fragrant scent*
> *Behind the heavy curtains now he rests.*

Scene Seventeen
Picking Up a Flute

(*Enter courtier Yan Zunmei*)

YAN ZUNMEI (*To the tune of* **Dianjiangchun**):

> Myriads of stars hang in the sky,
> When the sunset sheds evening glows
> Over the palace garden.
> The lantern trees on the Lantern Festival
> Light up the yellow silk fans of the court maids.
> Under the crimson clouds in the sky,
> Officials attend the emperor's banquet.
> The blazing candles and lanterns
> Illuminate the slow-moving chariots with dangling fringes.
> *"When the moon shines over the sacrificial altar,*
> *People enjoy the peaceful gathering in palace.*
> *The dragon lanterns make up the fiery trees;*
> *The phoenix lanterns give display to the lotus flowers."*

I am Yan Zunmei, vice director of the military ministry. I am a student of Ma Cunliang, the courtier supervisor, and I used to be in charge of the harem affairs together with Ximen Jixuan. In my opinion, courtiers should only attend to the daily affairs of the palace rather than the military affairs. Taking care of the documents is not the business of the courtiers. Having long been thinking about reclusion in the Qingcheng Mountains, I've just quit the official post of head of the secretariat. My mission now is to be His Majesty's bodyguard, managing his carriages. On this Lantern Festival, people are allowed to light lanterns. I'm now waiting for His Majesty to finish the banquet with the officials and tour around the palaces. What fabulous lanterns there are in the Huaqing Palace! The gauze-and-bamboo lanterns are ball-shaped with many light-emitting holes. The lotus-shaped lanterns are like the stars over the Huashan Mountain. And the lanterns with bamboo holders are like the torches. The light of the lanterns is as bright as the shining mica pieces that decorate the bed-curtains. It is also as bright as thousands of glowing glaze beads. The lantern light reflected on the bead curtains is as dazzling as the chinking pearl-and-jade strings. The glowing bright light comes from the lanterns that are shaped in the deer, the beast and the dog. The fish swim around in the glaze fish-tank, stirring shiny ripples on the satin-like water as in the Dongxiao Cave of the immortals. The horse-shaped lanterns are really like the fabulous galloping steeds, sending out flames before the mountains on the agate screen. The ball-like lanterns are like stars from the sky, with red balls rolling on the earth. On reaching the households, the moon seems to drop silver candles from the sky. The giant boat-shaped lantern sails off and on upon the Morning-Glow Terrace to the vast sea with coiling red smoke. The grand fire-mirror lantern hangs in front of the Sun-Viewing Temple. When the gate of the lantern is opened, numerous bright candles are seen to cluster round on the Heavenly Terrace. The palace outline is visible in the lantern light, dotted by the tulip-shaped lanterns. The canopies above the wagon-shaped lanterns turn round and round while the vines of the purple grape-shaped lanterns are swaying to and fro. The attached green jade pieces are made of white crepe from the immortal Fanghu Mountain; the silk bands with chessboard designs wrapped around the bamboo frames are woven from the silk threads in the immortal Yuanqiao Mountain. Unlike the roaring of dragons, tigers, or various breeds of steeds, the beating of night-curfew drums and the neighing of the startled horses in the six streets of the capital sound like rumbling thunders as if Goddess Axiang were pushing the thunder cart. Various dancing troupes such as the Halting-Cloud Troupe, the Flying-Casket Troupe, the Feigned Kinsmen Troupe, the Feigned Greeting-Wine Troupe, and the Feigned Music-God Troupe play in the roadside sheds and in the parades while the pretty ladies throw arrows into a pot before the windows. The shapes and styles of the lanterns are ingenious and exquisite. The lanterns with the pattern of verdant trees and hanging ears of grains, accompanied by the flute music echoing to the skies, are fixed on the frames like the dew-holders. The lanterns with the pattern of embroidered clouds lined in circles look like icicles about to melt in the jade bottle. The crystal candle-stands are like the white phoenixes in the clear and transparent Guanghan Palace on the moon. The dragon-shaped candles on coral stands illuminate the tiny state of Ronggao on the lantern. Various snacks are sold on the lantern fair, such as slimming paste and amber malt sugar in scraps and crumbs, lotus roots filled with petals, moths and insects on the red plates. There are also ornaments like the plain tassels and fragrant papal leaves, while silk dress pinned with dried plums and cocoons are the popular fashion. Special lantern devices are made to create exotic movements. High towers are set up in imitation of the three immortals' mountains. Lively performances of stories are given. On the railings are the flower-clustered words "Long Live the Emperor". It is true indeed,

> *"People in satin and brocade swarm in the street,*
> *Where the melodious music of 'Rainbow Skirts' is played.*
> *Wherever the wagon of the emperor goes,*
> *He is escorted by myriads of lanterns."*

His Majesty has arrived before I can finish my remarks.

(*Enter Emperor Yuanhe, escorted by followers*)

EMPEROR YUANHE (*To the tune of **Wangwuxiang***):

> All the households in early spring are bathed
>
> In peace and prosperity.
>
> The buildings along the way are lit
>
> By the candles as if morning glows had spread.
>
> Along the roads painted with mashed pepper
>
> And the corridors decorated with silk ribbons,
>
> My carriage proceeds amid jade flute music.
>
> *"With the city gates open all night,*
>
> *Songs come late in the spring.*
>
> *Dragon lanterns on archways are quiet in the moonlight;*
>
> *Candles in the mansions are tranquil in the breeze."*

I am the thirteenth-generation descendant of the founder of the Tang Dynasty. Since I ascended the throne, my country has been in peace and prosperity, thanks to the harmony between Heaven and Earth as well as the blessings from the ancestors. The sun and the moon always shine brightly while the cloud and the wind always correspond to the forecast at the beginning of the year. There are bumper harvests of crops in the fields and there is enough silk for weaving the satins. The branches in the wind will predict the seasons for a thousand years and the birds in the snow will sing for ten thousand years. It is pleasing that on this Lantern Festival night, the lanterns and the moon set off each other. At the prediction of a fruitful year, I'd like to have a good time with the people. Let me wander around for a while in the Huaqing Palace here. Tell the courtiers that the palace musicians are requested to stop other music and perform the hand-joining and ground-kicking singing and dancing.

(*Song and music within*)

SONG AND MUSIC WITHIN (*To the tune of **Huanglongtanchundeng***):

> The magpie songs in the refreshing wind
>
> And the lotus flowers at night
>
> Are signs of peace and prosperity.
>
> The evening glow,
>
> The evening glow
>
> Are succeeded by the candlelight
>
> And the moonshine.
>
> The country is in peace and prosperity
>
> Thanks to the favorable weather.
>
> The song and dance in the moonlight
>
> Wish the emperor eternal youth,

Wish the emperor eternal youth.

EMPEROR YUANHE:

Sing another song!

SONG AND MUSIC WITHIN (*To the previous tune*):

> The misty scarlet clouds
>
> And the arrayed blue-birds
>
> Are above the graceful plum blossoms.
>
> The half-hidden gauze lanterns,
>
> The half-hidden gauze lanterns
>
> Overhear the giggling chats
>
> And detect the fragrant dresses.
>
> Gently approach the beauties
>
> And cast glances of affection.
>
> The song and dance in the moonlight
>
> Wish the emperor eternal youth,
>
> Wish the emperor eternal youth.

EMPEROR YUANHE:

Who wrote the lines of the songs?

VOICE WITHIN:

Li Yi, a scholar from Longxi who passed the imperial tests.

EMPEROR YUANHE:

He is the talent of talents! Yan Zunmei, paste his name on the imperial screen!

> (*Yan Zunmei: "Long live the emperor!"*)

EMPEROR YUANHE:

I'll idle away some more time here.

> (*To the tune of **Wangwuxiang**)*
>
> Across the candles and incense burners
>
> I walk around on patterned mats.
>
> The evening glow lingers over the imperial banquet
>
> While the clouds float in the heavenly breeze.
>
> When the turtle lanterns rejoice over the cheers
>
> And the quail lanterns light up the galas,
>
> I ascend the heights.

Yan Zunmei, my banquet with the ministers finished too early for this Lantern Festival. I can see that they have not enjoyed to the full. Pass on my decree that all the men and women of whatever social status in the capital are allowed to view the lanterns in the Huaqing Palace till midnight! The city patrols should not prevent them as I intend to share the pleasure with the people.

> (*Yan Zunmei: "Long live the emperor!"*)
>
> (*Exit Emperor Yuanhe*)

YAN ZUNMEI:

Tell the gate captain to inform the patrol general of the imperial decree: "All the men and

women of whatever social status in the capital are allowed to view the lanterns in the Huaqing Palace till midnight. The city patrols should not prevent them as I intend to share the pleasure with the people."

(*Shouts of "Long live the emperor!" within*)

(*Exit Yan Zunmei*)

(*Enter Guo Xiaohou with Bao Siniang, viewing lanterns*)

GUO XIAOHOU:

"Spring warmth can be felt even at midnight

When the moon becomes full at the year's outset."

I am Guo Xiaohou. After I attended the banquet granted by His Majesty to the royal relatives, I hear that all the people are allowed to view the lanterns in the Huaqing Palace. Bao Siniang accompanies me to the palace to have a good time.

(*To the tune of* **Chuduizi**)

The lanterns hanging on the trees,

The lanterns hanging on the trees

Have holes on the painted gauze to leak out the light.

The golden knockers glitter on the illuminated gates

When clouds float in the bright light of the candles.

Siniang, let's go back to keep some joyful mood!

GUO XIAOHOU, BAO SINIANG:

We are going back to Guo's residence,

In the fragrant wind of the broad streets.

(*Exeunt*)

(*Enter Du Qiuniang and Shancai dressed as Taoist nuns*)

DU QIUNIANG:

"The buildings are like the Ever-Bright Palace,

With candles burning in a sleepless city."

I am Du Qiuniang. I used to wait on the late emperor before I was bestowed to Prince Huo. Now I am a Taoist nun in the Queen Mother Nunnery. Tonight's festival activities rekindle my worldly desires. On hearing the imperial decree to allow the people to view the lanterns, I come to the Huaqing Palace. Shancai, this is where we used to stay. The lanterns and music are the same, but the people are different.

(*To the previous tune*)

The lotus-shaped lanterns shed light,

The lotus-shaped lanterns shed light

On the palace at night under the moonlit sky.

Over the Penglai immortal mountain the Taiyi Star shines

With the pearl-like distant stars moving in the Milky Way.

Shancai, let's go back! To stay here for long induces sadness.

We'll go back to the nunnery

To saunter in rainbow skirts.

(*Exeunt Du Qiuniang and Shancai*)

(*Enter Zheng Liuniang, Li Yi and Huo Xiaoyu*)

ZHENG LIUNIANG:

    "The palace is open till midnight

    With the star-lit moat winding under the bridge."

I am Zheng Liuniang. I used to wait on the late emperor before I was bestowed to Prince Huo. I used to stroll in the Huaqing Palace, but Shilang and Xiaoyu have not been here before, so we'll take this chance to have a good time.

    (*To the previous tune*)

    The capital city celebrates the Lantern Festival,

    The capital city celebrates the Lantern Festival

    With willows and flowers lining the jade steps.

    When wagons pass and raise dusts in the bright lanes,

    Lost flutes and hairpins are seen scattered on the road.

Shilang and Xiaoyu,

    In viewing the lanterns,

    Shilang should slightly support the tender Xiaoyu.

LI YI, HUO XIAOYU (*To the previous tune*):

    On the mica lamp-stands,

    On the mica lamp-stands

    The candles on the red shacks move on the shafts.

    Around lanterns in the shape of moths, phoenixes and dragons,

    Well-dressed people happily sing and dance.

Mother,

    Viewing the candles and the smoke,

    We are not to fear the patrols tonight.

    (*Enter the patrol general, shouting*)

PATROL GENERAL:

It is midnight, yet you are saying that you do not fear the patrols. Leave here quickly! The site-clearing courtier is coming!

    (*To the tune of* **Langtaosha**)

    I am the patrol general

    To lead the imperial guards

    In dispersing the merry-going people.

    In the depth of the night,

    Water is dripping from the hourglass,

    Water is dripping from the hourglass.

Leave here quickly! Leave here quickly! Arrest him!

    (*Exit*)

    (*Enter Zheng Liuniang and Li Yi, shouting*)

ZHENG LIUNIANG, LI YI:

Xiaoyu, hurry up!

ZHENG LIUNIANG (*To the pervious tune*):

Hurrying on the moonlit ground,

We are chased by the harsh officer.

Alas! Where is Xiaoyu?

(*Alarmed*)

All of a sudden mother and daughter are separated.

The laughing voice over there sounds like hers.

LI YI (*Looks around, shouting and crying*):

As the smiling beauty is missing before the lanterns,

I shed tears like the weeping candles,

I shed tears like the weeping candles.

(*Shouts of "Arrest him!" within*)

(*Exeunt Zheng Liuniang and Li Yi*)

HUO XIAOYU:

Oh, dear me! Where are my mother and my man?

(*Alarmed at the shouts within*)

(*Walks*)

(*To the previous tune*)

Loud shouts to clear the way echo above the patrolled road,

When the moon begins to set beyond the horizon.

Oh, dear me! Where can I find my way out from the zigzagging palace paths?

Which gate should I choose to get out of the palace?

(*Stumbles and picks up a flute*)

Oh! Here lies a purple jade flute! An idea hits upon me. Even if I get out of here, a tender girl as I am might fall victim to bad guys on the crowded lantern fair outside. I might as well hold this purple jade flute in my hand. I would have a chance to explain about this if I am arrested and taken to the palace hall by the site-clearing courtier. If His Majesty asks me, I would tell him about Shilang's talent and fame. In that case, I might be pitied and sent out of palace.

I picked up a purple flute and played it,

Hoping to be led out of the palace,

Hoping to be led out of the palace.

(*Enter Yan Zunmei, shouting*)

(*Huo Xiaoyu bends over on the ground in alarm*)

YAN ZUNMEI (*To the previous tune*):

With lanterns still hanging on the trees,

Orders are relayed to lock the palace gate.

Search everywhere carefully, my men, in case there should be a spy!

Is there anyone hiding in the corners?

CITY GUARDS (*Shout*):

We've arrested a young woman who stole Lady Taizhen's purple jade flute and hid at the west end of the palace hall.

YAN ZUNMEI:

Well! She has broken the law!

    Why did she steal the jade flute?

    Ask her who she is!

    Ask her who she is!

    (*Exeunt all*)

    (*Enter Lady Guo*)

LADY GUO (*To the tune of* **Yijiangfeng**):

    With the kingfisher feather crowning my bun,

    In the palace in early spring,

    I feel chilly although my forehead is covered with a kerchief.

    On the Lantern Festival night,

    Trees and buildings are brightly lit

    By lanterns and stars.

    With smoke rising from the lion-shaped incense burner,

    The courtiers are patrolling around the palace

    While peace-eulogizing music is played in the spring wind.

    (*In the pattern of* **Genglouzi**)

    "In the palace,

    By the lantern,

    Bright light shines over noble men and women.

    On the grand banquet

    Where gorgeous candles are lit,

    The spring breeze bathes the painted hall.

    Under the pearl-like stars

    And the silver moon,

    The flute is played on the phoenix bridge.

    I put on my headwear,

    Select my silk skirt

    And smoke myself with fragrant scents."

I am Lady Guo. My ancestor is Guo Ziyi, Prince of Fenyang. My father is Guo Ai, a supreme official in charge of military affairs. My mother is Princess Taichang of the State of Qi. I became Prince Guangling's concubine when I was very young, and I was promoted in rank after the prince succeeded to the throne. I am in charge of the jade seal of the Changqiu Palace. My daughter is Princess Taihe. I have only one nephew, Guo Xiaohou. As I was born in a noble family, I had a pleasant time with my mother in my childhood and my father was promoted to an official in Gaomi. Lady Ban Jieyu in the Han Dynasty refused to ride with the emperor on pleasure trips, but the pretty girls in the Ganquan Palace who bribed the painter so as to enter the palace did not enjoy life at all. Empress Ma Mingde confined herself in the back hall, instructing the Crown Prince and reading classics, but the nice royal instructors have never been commended in the court. Therefore, whenever I read the poems, I would recite the famous lines of "The Cooing"

from *The Book of Poetry*, which is about the virtue of the king's lady. It is pleasing to see in the candlelight the imperial concubines wait upon His Majesty in good order. After the banquet with His Majesty for the Lantern Festival today, I return to the palace and stay here on His Majesty's decree to interrogate whichever maidservant who has committed mistakes or crimes. Here comes a courtier before I finish my words.

(*Enter Yan Zunmei with the detained Huo Xiaoyu*)

YAN ZUNMEI (*To the previous tune*):

> With auspicious clouds floating in the sky,
>
> And the palace curtains sheltering the spring dawn,
>
> The dragon and phoenix candles burn with coiling smoke.
>
> On the Lantern Festival night,
>
> The halo of the moon
>
> Shines over the lotus-shaped lanterns.

The court-maid

> Is causing trouble
>
> By offending the law
>
> In stealing a jade flute.

His Majesty decrees, "On this grand festival, I attended the lantern fare and listened to the wonderful poems by the talents. I had a good time with the people until midnight. On their patrol duty, the courtiers caught a girl who stole Lady Taizhen's purple jade flute. Is she a court-maid who went out of the palace because she got tired of the palace life? Or is she a palace musician who passed the flute out for her to play the music? Now she is sent to be interrogated in the Changqiu Palace. If she is from the capital city, ask her the reason why she was lagging behind!"

LADY GUO:

Long live the emperor!

(*To the tune of* **Guizhixiang**)

(*Interrogates*)

Are you a court-maid?

> The light of the moon and candles shines
>
> Over the beautifully dressed ladies amidst crowds.
>
> Are you a maid in the palace
>
> Who feels lonely behind locked doors,
>
> Who feels lonely behind locked doors?
>
> After the night candles are put out,
>
> The chamber is lonely and desolated,
>
> While the mirror reflects your pretty face in vain.
>
> You were taking the chance to stroll about
>
> And to look for someone who knows your heart.

Therefore,

> You tried to steal the flute from the palace.

HUO XIAOYU:

How can I be disguised as a court-maid since I do not wear the right dress?

(*To the previous tune*)

As the fish in the palace pond

And the crane at the palace steps

Are both securely confined,

How can they find an escape?

The old courtiers,

The old courtiers

Will summon them according to the portraits

Or call their names according to the list.

When their duty is done,

They appear pale and languid,

Feeling ashamed when they walk across the yard.

LADY GUO:

If you are not a court-maid, you must be a palace musician who has the chance to use the purple jade flute.

(*To the previous tune*)

Look,

Your jade hairpins

And skillful make-up

Show that you must be a good singer like Han E in the State of Qi

Or a popular courtesan like Su Xiaoxiao.

In pleasing His Majesty,

In pleasing His Majesty,

You act as the plum-blossom to win a smile

And sing of the orchids to the tunes.

As your songs are accompanied by the flute,

You stole it

By taking the chance of a performance.

HUO XIAOYU:

I am no longer a court-musician.

(*To the previous tune*)

My career in the palace is gone like a dream

That fades away into the distance.

Your Ladyship,

If I am a palace singer,

Why don't I wear a singer's hat

And a dancing skirt,

And a dancing skirt?

I no longer clean the performing stage

Or dance on the red carpet

With the charming dancers.

Speaking of the flute,

It was once played by the slim-fingered fair lady Nongyu.

LADY GUO:

How can you be compared with Nongyu in the State of Qin? She was the king's daughter. Now that you are not a palace musician, why did you come to the palace? Have you come to steal the flute? Who on earth are you?

HUO XIAOYU:

My name is Huo Xiaoyu, the daughter of Prince Huo.

LADY GUO:

Prince Huo's fief is in the Huo area, while you are surnamed Huo. So how can you be his daughter?

HUO XIAOYU:

My mother is Zheng Liuniang, a former court musician. She was bestowed by the emperor upon Prince Huo and lived with him for twenty years. I am sixteen now. Prince Huo thought that I was born of a humble mother, so he changed my surname to Huo. He granted me a red mansion and ten caskets of jewelry and bid me to marry whom my mother may choose for me. All that I have said is the truth, Your Ladyship.

LADY GUO (*Helps Xiaoyu up*):

Prince Huo is the brother of Emperor Shunzong, bestowed the title of Supreme Duke. Since you are the daughter of Prince Huo, please get up and explain the matter!

HUO XIAOYU (*To the tune of **Jixianbin***):

My mother

Used to enjoy pleasures with the emperor,

And she was bestowed upon a man of blue blood.

LADY GUO:

Why did he leave his home?

HUO XIAOYU:

He went to live in the mountains for Taoist ideals,

For he was bored with the life of a grey head and a young beauty.

LADY GUO:

Was he sad about it?

HUO XIAOYU:

Yes, he was.

His pretty wife

Is set free at her own disposal.

LADY GUO:

Has he succeeded in the Taoist practice?

HUO XIAOYU:

As he began to practice a long time ago,

He's sure to be an immortal as Prince Liu An in the Han Dynasty.

LADY GUO:

Are you married, young princess?

HUO XIAOYU:

Yes, I am.

> (*To the previous tune*)

> A young scholar from a noble family in Longxi,

> He is full of soaring aspirations.

> He has refined and graceful bearings

> And writes wonderful poetic works.

LADY GUO:

Did his ancestors serve in the court?

HUO XIAOYU:

> Each dynasty has his ancestors in high ranks.

LADY GUO:

Who is he?

HUO XIAOYU:

His name is Li Yi.

LADY GUO:

It is often heard in the palace that there is a talent called Li Yi from the province. Is he the man you refer to?

HUO XIAOYU:

Yes.

> He is famous for his grace and talent.

LADY GUO:

Has he achieved success as a scholar?

HUO XIAOYU:

He has entered the imperial examination and will soon be on the spring list of those who have passed.

> As a successful imperial test candidate,

> He will have a bright future within the sight.

LADY GUO:

How long have you been married, young princess? I suppose you two were viewing the lanterns in the Huaqing Palace?

HUO XIAOYU (*To the previous tune*):

> As we have just formed the wedding-tie,

LADY GUO:

What a well-matched couple of a talent and a beauty!

HUO XIAOYU:

> I feel ashamed that my humble body is not as precious as jade.

> With the moon and the lanterns illuminating the streets,

> I am excited at the bustling sight.

LADY GUO:

Why didn't Shilang look after you as he was with you?

HUO XIAOYU:

As the watchtowers are magnificent late at night,

LADY GUO:

Were you two separated when the patrol general and the site-clearing courtiers locked the palace gate?

HUO XIAOYU:

Yes.

> The wild goose has lost its way when it leaves the flock.
>
> (*Sad*)
>
> (*Aside*)

Shilang, my husband!

> On pins and needles,
>
> I shed tears at the extinguishing candles.

LADY GUO:

How did you steal Lady Taizhen's purple jade flute?

HUO XIAOYU (*To the previous tune*):

> Walking in the darkness with my small feet,
>
> I picked up a jade flute at the west end of the hall.

At that time, I wondered how I could get back alone. On the lantern fair,

> With light-minded youngsters sauntering in the streets,
>
> I feared to be bullied if I walked alone at night.

If I fell victim to them, where would my grace be even if I were let go and returned home? I bring this flute along,

> As I would rather be punished by the law.
>
> If I am brought to the emperor and the empress,
>
> I can explain to them what has happened.

I won't regret even if I am executed in the palace, because

> I shall be proved innocent in my deeds at night.

LADY GUO:

What a strong will you have! And how clever you are!

> (*To the tune of* **Hupomao'erzhui**)
>
> The young lady is bright
>
> With incomparable wit.
>
> She defends herself when suspected
>
> And displays a noble mind.
>
> At daybreak,
>
> She is to be sent back
>
> To where she lives.

HUO XIAOYU (*Bows and begs*):

> (*To the previous tune*)
>
> The sleeping birds get startled and wail
>
> When the moon falls behind the dew-container column.

Your Ladyship,

I beg to thank His Majesty for being pardoned.

LADY GUO:

I am afraid that no report can be made now since His Majesty has gone to bed.

HUO XIAOYU:

Your Ladyship, amid merry laughter from the other palace

    I hear His Majesty's voice soaring to the sky.

LADY GUO:

But I am afraid that the day will soon break.

HUO XIAOYU:

    The dawn has not arrived yet,

    But I wish that the rooster will crow

    So that I can soon return to my man.

LADY GUO:

If you are in a hurry to go back, you may as well come with me to the other palace and tell His Majesty about Prince Huo.

HUO XIAOYU (*To the tune of* **Coda**):

    I beg you to report to His Majesty

    That I might be pardoned for my taking the flute.

LADY GUO:

You are welcome!

    You are to be escorted out of the palace with respect.

LADY GUO:

    When sandglass tells the midnight,

HUO XIAOYU:

    In the palace yard alone I roam.

LADY GUO, HUO XIAOYU:

    His Majesty will have the candles rekindled

    And the gate unlocked for you/me to go home.

Scene Eighteen
Bestowing the Flute

(*Enter the female courtier with court-maids*)

FEMALE COURTIER (*To the tune of* **Tianxiale**):

    The incense burner is tended by the court-maids,

    Whose headwear glitters in the light of the lanterns.

    As people disperse at late night,

    Songs and music fade in the distance.

Good evening, everyone!

"The night is bright as broad daylight

With the lanterns on the city gates shining as stars.

In the shadows of flowers and candles,

We escort the beauty to her home."

Lady Huo got lost from her husband when they viewed the palace lanterns. As she was afraid to be bullied by the dandies outside the palace, she would rather be caught in the palace when she found Lady Taizhen's purple jade flute. She was brought to Lady Guo in the Changqiu Palace for an interrogation and finally had her integrity verified before His Majesty. We female courtier and court-maids are ordered to escort her home with four gilded lanterns. The purple jade flute she found and a palace decree were bestowed on her. She is now in the Changqiu Palace to express her gratitude to Her Ladyship. As she will be here soon, we are waiting for her at the gate of the Huaqing Palace.

(*Enter Huo Xiaoyu, holding the flute*)

HUO XIAOYU (*To the tune of* **Wanxiandeng**):

With the moon shining over my homeward path,

The palace is bathed in brilliant lights.

Thank you for taking all the troubles to implement His Majesty's decree!

FEMALE COURTIER:

It is already past midnight. Please get on your way!

HUO XIAOYU (*To the tune of* **Sibianjing**):

The spring is in full swing in the palace,

Permeating the zigzagging corridors.

I make my way in the starlight

Passing by the tall copper dew-container.

ALL:

With hanging hairpins swaying with each step,

We walk lightly in soft socks.

FEMALE COURTIER (*Supports Huo Xiaoyu*):

We escort the beauty on her way back,

A file of ladies dressed in deep red.

HUO XIAOYU:

Don't bother to support me!

(*To the previous tune*)

Now that the night is deep in the palace,

It is high time to remove the make-up.

One will feel the cold when she sits by the candle

And weeps over her fond dreams.

ALL:

We escort the beauty on her way back,

A file of ladies dressed in deep red.

HUO XIAOYU (*To the previous tune*):

The glazed brick road looks like a silk band,

On which I walk slowly and step on the moss.

Who will sleep soundly in the bright moonlight,

Facing the cloudless sky?

ALL:

We escort the beauty on her way back,

A file of ladies dressed in deep red.

HUO XIAOYU (*To the previous tune*):

Escorted by the court guards, the palace wagon rumbles

On this lantern-illuminated night.

One can hardly fall asleep

When the day is about to break.

ALL:

We escort the beauty on her way back,

A file of ladies dressed in deep red.

HUO XIAOYU:

Here we are! My Red Mansion is in sight.

While lights are dimly visible in the cold moon,

The tune of "Rainbow Skirts" swiftly fleets.

With the dance still lingering in my mind,

I turn my eyes toward the busy streets.

Scene Nineteen
Returning with the Imperial Decree

(*Enter Zheng Liuniang and Li Yi*)

ZHENG LIUNIANG, LI YI (*To the tune of **Fendie'er***):

On holders in the shapes of camels and ducks

Are stuck the weeping red candles.

ZHENG LIUNIANG:

"The lonely lamp is easy to go out

While the scattered moon is difficult to wax to the full."

Shilang, you got married for only three days and should be enjoying the pleasant views on the Lantern Festival in the palace tonight. Who would have expected that you got severed from Xiaoyu? Now that she is nowhere to be found, I wonder whether she is left behind in the palace or somewhere else. How agonizing it is!

LI YI:

How painful my wife Xiaoyu must be now! If you are detained in the palace, I am afraid that your delicate body cannot withstand the inquisition by tortures. But if you are detained somewhere else, you would suffer more!

(Sobs)

*(To the tune of **Shizixu**)*

If she is detained in the palace,

She must be scared as a delicate girl.

The roads are dark as lights go out,

But there are still young wanderers.

ZHENG LIUNIANG:

If she is harassed by the ruffians, she will surely stab herself with a thin-toothed comb, or jump headlong into a well.

She would surely struggle with the ruffians,

Cursing them in a rage

Or wailing under a plum tree.

She would be sad and distressed

In the light of the setting moon.

Shilang, sit in the chamber waiting till cockcrow to find out her whereabouts at dawn!

(Wails and sits down in sorrow)

(Enter the female courtier with court-maids holding lanterns and Huo Xiaoyu with the flute)

HUO XIAOYU *(To the tune of **Fendie'er**)*:

I return in the company of the lanterns

At the time of daybreak.

(Knocks at the door)

ZHENG LIUNIANG, LI YI *(Open the door in surprise)*:

Oh! It is Xiaoyu in the bright candlelight!

FEMALE COURTIER:

Fall on your knees and listen to His Majesty's decree: "As I am fond of poetry, I search widely for well-written lines. I have heard that Li Yi from Longxi is well-versed in poetry and that his wife Huo Xiaoyu is the daughter of my uncle Prince Huo. She lost contact with her husband on the Lantern Festival and was afraid to walk alone at night. I greatly appreciate her wits in preserving her chastity when she happened to find a jade flute. Now she is escorted back to Li Yi's house with bestowed candles from the palace as well as the jade flute she found. The memorial of her thanks to the court does not need to be submitted. The decree is to be sent to Prince Huo's residence." Kowtow and thank His Majesty's grace!

(All cup their hands in obeisance)

LI YI:

Please stay for a cup of tea!

FEMALE COURTIER:

As His Majesty will have an audience early in the morning, we dare not stay here for long. We must be leaving now. Good-bye!

(Exeunt the female courtier and court-maids)

(Zheng Liuniang and Huo Xiaoyu embrace each other)

ZHENG LIUNIANG:

You must have been scared, my daughter!

LI YI:

You must have been scared, my dear wife!

HUO XIAOYU:

Thanks to His Majesty's favor, I have not been scared. How could I get out of the palace in the hastening order of the courtiers after I lost contact with you? I was walking in haste when I stumbled on a purple jade flute. I considered that there were lots of pleasure-seeking dandies wandering outside the palace. Even if I got out of the palace, I might lose my chastity. So I hid myself at the western end of the hall and allowed myself to be arrested and taken to Lady Guo's palace in the Yongxiang Lane for interrogation. I told her my fathers' name and Li Yi's talent as well as his family. Lady Guo showed due respect to me and brought me in the presence of His Majesty, who bestowed on me the jade flute and the palace candles. I can hardly requite the favor from His Majesty.

ZHENG LIUNIANG, LI YI, HUO XIAOYU (*To the tune of* **Yifengshu**):

> It is a blessing that the stainless jade
> And the palace candles are bestowed.
> His Majesty has granted me the favor
> To leave the palace in great honor.
> When the court-maids snuff out the candles,
> I return from the palace in the cold night.
> It will be a tale on everybody's lips
> That I walk in the flowery palace
> Until I return with the flute at dawn.

ZHENG LIUNIANG:

Shilang, you'd better accompany Xiaoyu to take a nap.

> *Startled from the festivities in the palace,*
> *The phoenix was separated from her mate.*
> *She met the emperor in escaping the city guards*
> *And daybreak saw her return to her own gate.*

Scene Twenty
A Happy Stroll

(*Enter Yingtao*)

YINGTAO:

> *"To paint a person's mien is difficult*
> *But the flowers are beautiful in a round shape.*
> *Over the new tunes of 'Cold Armors',*
> *We taste the mellow and fragrant rice wine."*

I am Yingtao. After my princess was married to Li Yi, they matched Qing'er with me and Wu'er with sister Huansha. It is true indeed,

"*The white is fit for the white,*
While the black is fit for the black."

But there is one thing that I feel worried about. As Qing'er is witty and smart, he is always bossed around by Shilang so that I cannot stay with him except at night. In contrast, Wu'er and his wife enjoy themselves together all the time in the kitchen. As the saying goes,

"*The quick-witted runs here and there*
For everybody to see day and night,
While the slow-witted stays indoors
For his wife to see at night."

Mr. Li and my princess stay together all the time deeply attached to each other because he has not taken up a position yet and has enough leisure time. Today he told Qing'er to have the servants open the garden of Prince Huo and have the mattress, cushions and couches ready for them to take a nap when they stroll in the garden. The madam told me to prepare the white jade pot to be filled with new wine and ten lotus-shaped bowls to be placed on the lacquer tea-table with delicious snacks in the bowls. Here comes the couple to the garden now!

(*Enter Huo Xiaoyu*)

HUO XIAOYU (*To the tune of* **Yumeiren**):

I have a slim waist, a white neck and tender skin,

My thick black hair spreading at my temples.

With raven eyebrows of deep attachment

At my youthful age,

I display my affection in attractive manners.

(*In the pattern of* **Chunguanghao**)

"*By the warm gauze window*

And behind the painted mica screen,

I stand with my hair drooping casually.

I feel all the drowsiness after sleep

In this season of high spring."

YINGTAO:

"*By beautiful fingers I cut silk flowers*

As topping on the crunchy refreshments.

Princess,

Your worries on your mind

Are shown on your knitted eyebrows."

HUO XIAOYU:

What worries do you think are on my mind?

YINGTAO:

Before you were married to Mr. Li, you had fun on the swings with me, played the games of casting the gold coins, fighting the quails, betting on the litchi, throwing the red beans, and hide-and-seek with me, and you were always in a happy mood. Since you met Mr. Li and got married a month ago, you have been staying with him in your chamber without playing games with me anymore. Now I see you frown all the time. There must be something disturbing with you.

HUO XIAOYU:

Yingtao, how can you understand me? Before marriage, I could do whatever I liked. But I am not allowed to act like this now, as I am a wife and I should please my man day and night, which makes me a bit bored. Today he wants me to stroll around the garden with him. How can I walk ten miles a day? But I have to keep him company.

YINGTAO:

Princess, you used to sleep the whole night until daybreak, but now you chat with Mr. Li till well after midnight, and then you toss and turn and can hardly get enough sleep. It is true that to be a good wife is not easy.

HUO XIAOYU:

Quit your nonsense! You are supposed to get all the tableware ready by now. Shilang is coming soon for a stroll in the garden.

> (*Enter Li Yi*)

LI YI (*To the tune of **Shanglinchun***):

> I read in my leisure time,
>
> With the books piled on the desk
>
> And the ink-slab dotted with petals drifting through the window.
>
> A rooster is fluttering its wings with vigor over the wall,
>
> While people feel drowsy in the lengthy daytime.
>
> (*Turns around and snuggles up to Huo Xiaoyu*)
>
> "*Your frivolity is worthy to be painted,*
>
> *Which stirs the amorous desire in my heart.*"

I have been reading some poetic essays and practicing calligraphy, which makes me feel tired. Let's go for a stroll in the garden and walk around the ponds and hills!

HUO XIAOYU:

It is about ten miles to walk along those hills and ponds in the garden. If we are not in a hurry, it will be dark when we return. I have told Huansha and Wu'er to wait on my mother at home and prepare some snacks and wine so that we can set out at an early time. But I am afraid that my small shoes would slip on the moss, so will you please keep a steady pace?

LI YI:

That is my duty as the husband. Yingtao, go ahead and wait for us at the Pavilion of a Hundred Flowers! We shall walk slowly.

> (*Walks*)
>
> "*Spring comes at the end of the second month*
>
> *When the day begins to grow longer.*
>
> *The overhanging willows herald the warming rooms*
>
> *While the blooming flowers bring a fragrant house.*"

Alas! What a winding and quiet view the garden entrance presents! Let's walk in slowly!

> (*To the tune of **Huameixu***)
>
> The willows sway along the petal-dotted path,
>
> Leading to a natural retreat in the garden.

It is time for the tender flowers to grow in warmth

And for the young people to enjoy their youth.

(*Lowers his head and enters the garden*)

Tilt your head for your protruding hairpin!

(*When a hairpin falls, Li Yi picks it up and sticks it in Huo Xiaoyu's hair*)

The golden goose and insect hairpin drops from your head,

On the mossy ground slightly imprinted with footsteps.

Let's enjoy love in private behind the flowers!

HUO XIAOYU:

Shilang, why did you say in private?

LI YI:

There is an Ever-Spring Pavilion ahead amid the flowers, where no one ever goes and the lawn looks like a green blanket. We should not miss our love there.

HUO XIAOYU;

It is a lovely place. Let's walk around the flowers near the Ever-Spring Pavilion!

(*To the tune of **Huangying'er***)

I steal a glance at the sunny spring

In morning splendor, moistening mist,

Steaming glow and gentle wind.

When the filaments shiver in the breeze

And the stamens and pistils enfold,

The bird's nest weighs down the willows.

The flower-shaped gold pin

Is stuck into the hair sideways

By my slim fingers.

LI YI:

Here we are! In the pavilion is a couch equipped with a gold-threaded cushion.

HUO XIAOYU:

As I thought that you would come alone, I asked Qing'er to put them here so that you can take a nap. Now that I've come with you, you'll have no time for a nap. After you drink a cup of wine, we'll go for a stroll.

LI YI:

We may sleep here for a while as well.

HUO XIAOYU:

How embarrassing it is!

(*Makes a toast to Li Yi*)

Let's pray to the Flower God! Flower God, do bless us with a happy life together!

(*Feeds Li Yi with the wine*)

(*Li Yi holds the wine cup and feeds Huo Xiaoyu with the wine*)

(*Huo Xiaoyu gets intoxicated*)

LI YI (*Supports Huo Xiaoyu to sit down*):

(*To the tune of **Sishihua***)

The beauty is intoxicated by the nectar,

With her skin fair and delicate

And her voice in a tremor.

When she smells the flowers,

How charming she is!

The golden threads hang from her hairpin,

Her light yellow trousers blow up in the wind,

And her embroidered skirt is creased when she is seated.

Her sandal-powdered face

Is rosy and tender,

Blushing after a few drinks

Beside the weeping willows.

It is not her tiredness from viewing the flowers

But the after-effects of her drunkenness

That enliven her flower of a face.

HUO XIAOYU (*Struggles to get away from the clasp of Li Yi's arms*):

Release your embrace! I can sit by myself.

LI YI:

You were at my disposal since you were drunk just now.

HUO XIAOYU:

I was not drunk.

YINGTAO:

The Huashan Mountain and the Kunming Lake are dimly visible ahead, while the eight streams flowing through Chang'an can be seen from the tower. Was this tower built by Prince Huo, Princess?

HUO XIAOYU:

Yes, it was. And it is called the Halting-Spring Tower. Look, Shilang, how delicate the inside of the tower is! A pity that Prince Huo is gone!

(*To the tune of* **Zhaoluopaodai**)

By the twelve screens with phoenix designs,

We gaze at the verdant mountains

Fading away into the distance.

The world is filled with transient foams,

Like the infinite stars and mists in the sky.

In the cave surrounded by flowers,

Prince Huo cultivated for years in pursuit of immortality.

The Huaqing Palace on Mount Xiulin

Used to be his abode.

The beauties play the zither music

Of woe over the flowing Zhanghe River that never returns.

Shilang, you have never met my father.

He solicited talents

For the imperial court,

And pursued the Taoist canons.

He frowned all day long

And counted the moss by himself,

But who knows that he aspired for immortality?

LI YI:

Don't be so melancholy, Xiaoyu! Let's go for a walk to the rockery!

(*Li Yi and Huo Xiaoyu step downstairs*)

LI YI (*To the tune of **Jiesancheng***):

The uneven path zigzags along

Under the lingering purple-colored clouds

And across the luxuriant flowers and plants.

With the waterfall pouring from the top,

The rockery looks like a lotus flower cutting from the clouds

Or like the Xiangjiang River rushing through the Wuxia Gorge.

This place is worth a visit,

But it is discarded by the Yan Jidao-like genius,

Who aims at attaining immortality.

HUO XIAOYU:

Why did you mention the Wuxia Gorge and the Xiangjiang River?

LI YI:

The Wuxia Gorge is where the king of the Chu State met with a goddess, while the Xiangjiang River is associated with the two concubines of King Shun who were not allowed to follow their husband after he became an immortal in the Jiuyi Mountains. It is the same case as your mother who cannot follow your father when he goes to live in the Huashan Mountain for Taoist practice.

HUO XIAOYU (*Sighs*):

It is true indeed. In speaking of the Xiangjiang River,

"Please look at the riverside bamboos,

Whose flecks are not the tear-stains of men."

(*Walks*)

(*To the tune of **Huanxisha***)

With the wind seemingly blowing at the Xiangjiang cliffs,

This garden is a miniature of the natural wonders,

Where the river water splatters the silver pearls.

I shall play the zither and the flute

To express my lovesickness when I look into the mirror.

The music will tinkle and permeate into the water

When I strike the bamboo with my golden hairpin

To win a betting of gold coins.

LI YI:

Why should we bet by gold coins between man and wife?

HUO XIAOYU:

We shall bet by the gold-coin flower.

LI YI:

Then let's take the nuptial flower as the gold-coin flower!

HUO XIAOYU:

You will begin with the Bamboo Tune, and I will follow you.

LI YI:

That's a good idea.

    (*Starts the tune*)

    (*Sings*)

    The matchmaker's red thread is tied

HUO XIAOYU:

    Into a tight knot,

LI YI:

    While the silk produced in the Yue area extends

HUO XIAOYU:

    To express my profound love.

LI YI:

    The willows dangle on me

HUO XIAOYU:

    With care and affection,

LI YI:

    And the lotus flower withers

HUO XIAOYU:

    To reveal its seed of a pure heart.

LI YI:

It is a real case of man singing and wife following!

YINGTAO:

The Kunming Lake is ahead. It is drizzling now, Master and Princess, so let's hurry to the Pearl Pavilion built by Prince Huo at the lakeshore and drink a few more cups before we go back!

    (*Li Yi and Huo Xiaoyu walk fast*)

    (*To the tune of* **Qiaohesheng**)

    We'll shelter from the drizzling rain,

    We'll shelter from the drizzling rain,

    To keep warm against cold.

    The looming clouds drape low like the beauty's hair,

    While the mist and fragrance drift in the breeze.

    With the round fan covering our heads,

    We step on the soft lawn,

    A green carpet to hold our weight.

    The cushion is embroidered with gold threads

In designs of tiny ripples

And dashing swallows through the flowers.

When mandarin ducks play in the lake,

We exchange charming glances of flirtation.

We'll walk shoulder to shoulder

Until we reach our chamber

To take off our underwear.

HUO XIAOYU:

Here we are in the Pearl Pavilion! Shilang, you should behave yourself and speak properly.

(*To the tune of* **Zhuomu'er**)

The frivolous man and the amorous wife

Add vitality to the painting of spring cardamoms.

Shilang, you are embracing so tightly that my headwear gets messed up.

But your joy and love have brightened up my headwear.

I did some embroidery on my collar at home before I came out for a walk.

Several stitches were done to embroider the grapes,

But I did not expect that we would walk such a distance.

Shilang, I do this for your pleasure. Look!

Our happy faces are mirrored in the wine.

LI YI:

You just ask me to drink rather than listen to me.

HUO XIAOYU:

None of your idle talk! There seems to be a voice beyond the bamboo grove.

It seems to be Bao Siniang from the sporting house.

LI YI:

Call Bao Siniang at once!

(*Twittering of birds within*)

Oh! I can see nobody over there.

(*To the tune of* **Yujiaozhi**)

In the depth of the garden,

The birdsong is mistaken for someone's voice.

Xiaoyu, look at the startled birds taking flight!

A couple of startled green birds

Are hovering above the lilac flowers.

As your toasts have intoxicated me, I will make you drunken too.

(*Huo Xiaoyu refuses and chews at the flower petals with a smile*)

LI YI:

Xiaoyu,

Don't feign your reluctance to drink

And ask for exemption in coyness.

You bite at the flower buds

And steal a peep at me while looking at the oriole.

HUO XIAOYU:

Shilang, you may have placed your love on the wrong person, as I shall be pining away. What worries me is that your newly-wed wife will become old sooner or later while men are always longing for a change. Lyrics of deserted wives have been chanted in sighs since ancient times. I have heard of the tales of women who were firm in love and willing to be buried in the same grave with their lovers. I am predestined to serve you and my heart is as firm as the grinding stone in my love for you. I can make my vow to the heaven, but you have great ambitions as you come from a distinguished family in Longxi. When the disturbances there are quelled, you will surely go back and look for a spouse of your equal status. As a withered flower will naturally be cast away, how can I complain about your frivolity! I'd like to tell you my long-cherished desire.

LI YI:

Please speak it out!

HUO XIAOYU:

Now I am eighteen and you are twenty. When you are thirty, I will be twenty-eight. At that time, if you'd like to marry a woman from Maoling and discard a woman like Su Hui, I will have nothing to complain even if I die.

LI YI:

What nonsense you are talking! You are not the ancient Zhuo Wenjun, married to the frivolous Sima Xiangru who was once intent on a woman from Maoling, while I am the faithful Dou Tao, whose wife was Su Hui. We will be man and wife forever who live in the same room and be buried in the same grave.

HUO XIAOYU:

It is hard to predict the future. I am just joking.

> (*To the tune of* **Yubaodu**)
>
> I will serve you for ten years,
>
> Pleasing you with my beauty and youth.
>
> With tender affection I will keep your company
>
> By day and by night.

When we are nearing thirty,

> I will be losing my beauty,
>
> And everything then will be changed,
>
> Leaving behind a fond dream or a sweet memory.

LI YI:

You should not make wild guesses. My heart will always be loyal to you.

> (*To the tune of* **Yushantui**)
>
> You are young and beautiful as a peach-blossom,
>
> With your petticoat soft and fragrant,
>
> Your delicate voice inducing lovesickness,
>
> And your slim body enticing endearment.
>
> Now that I have a rare beauty like you,
>
> What other distinguished flowers shall I admire?

A heartless man will be condemned by the heaven.

If I should betray you,

I would be sick every spring.

HUO XIAOYU:

Shilang, in my jewelry locket, there are pieces of columned writing-paper, a bamboo-tube writing-brush and a conch-shaped ink-stick. You can write a few lines as a keepsake for the rest of my life. When you leave for an official position one day, I will read it as if I saw my man!

LI YI:

That will do!

(*Yingtao fetches the writing-paper and the writing-brush*)

LI YI:

Xiaoyu, look at the Kunming Lake, where the statues of the Cowboy and the Weaving Girl are erected! I shall make my vow in front of it and write a few lines.

(*Chants the poem*)

"*Our overlapped shadows have linked hearts*

In a chamber by the Kunming Lake.

I vow by the Weaving Girl by the water

And the Cowboy on the opposite bank.

My love will last till final destruction of Heaven and Earth,

When the seas have gone dry and the rocks melted with the sun.

We shall be of the same ashes through all the kalpas,

And I shall never forget my vow for a day."

HUO XIAOYU:

Thank you!

(*Bows to express her thanks*)

(*To the tune of* **Chuanbozhao**)

I am grateful for your love,

My dear man,

As your vow shows your boundless love.

I am afraid that you merely write in black and white,

I am afraid that you merely write in black and white

To love me till the seas have gone dry.

You might be mouthing fine words,

But do not remember to keep your own vow.

Shilang, now that you have made your vow, this tour is worthwhile for me. As it is getting late now, please be on our way back as early as possible!

YINGTAO:

By a path near the rockery and the lake, we are not far away from home.

(*Returns*)

HUO XIAOYU (*To the tune of* **Yiduojiao**):

The spring sights are becoming dim

When we walk on the fragrant path at dusk,

Hearing the birds sing in the distant mountains.

Over the mountain summit,

The sun is still hanging high,

And the night clouds are floating in the sky.

The flowers and leaves will fall asleep,

The flowers and leaves will fall asleep,

While the returning crows no longer croak.

(*Huo Xiaoyu stumbles*)

LI YI (*Helps her up*):

I enjoy walking in the moonlight since I am by your side. Why do you walk in such a hurry that you stumble and get your shoe-seams split? Now walk slowly! The moon is rising.

(*To the tune of* **Yueshanghaitang**)

On her delicate feet,

The red embroidered shoe-seams split.

I am reluctant to open the gate

And block the garden flowers.

This happy spring tour

Gives my eyes a charming view.

We return home

In the moonlight,

And Yingtao will knock the copper gate-bell.

(*Knocks at the door*)

(*Huansha opens the gate, holding a candle and letting them in*)

HUO XIAOYU:

Has my mother gone to bed?

HUANSHA:

She is waiting for you in the living-room with wine ready. Please come in!

LI YI (*To the tune of* **Coda**):

With profound love

And in high spirits,

I see the shadow of flowers casting on the railings.

HUO XIAOYU:

Shilang, I'd like to appreciate the moon after drinking the wine with you.

We'll watch the silk-tree flowers in the spring courtyard.

The breeze brushes at the sleeves and tilts the hair,

When we have dinner in the bright red room.

I will soon have a cozy sleep tonight,

To best enjoy the music in the bloom.

Scene Twenty-One
Winning the Laurel

(*Enter officials and officers*)

OFFICIALS, OFFICERS (*To the tune of* **Tianxiale**):

> The Imperial Academy leads to the court,
>
> Where the palace hall is glorified by the lotus flowers.
>
> The sun shines beyond the capital city,
>
> Where the meritorious deeds are inscribed on the steles.

Good morning, everyone! The results of the imperial examinations are announced today. His Majesty nominates in person that Li Yi is the Number-One Scholar, who is allowed to present himself at the court. All the scholars are supposed to be waiting outside the palace gate now.

(*Enter Li Yi*)

LI YI (*To the tune of* **Busuanzi**):

> The lucky bird is flying around me
>
> While auspicious clouds are hovering above my head.
>
> The best scholar is nominated by His Majesty,
>
> Who rejoices over the gathering of talents.

(*Enter a courtier*)

COURTIER:

Here is His Majesty's decree, which says, "All the wise ancient emperors tried to solicit the gifted and the talented. This righteous practice has been widely followed to carry on the old tradition. Distinguished people are selected and promoted to their respective posts while their descendants likewise are bestowed high honor and positions. All the emperors, whether wise or mediocre, follow this practice. Since I ascended the throne, talents of all kinds have swarmed in to serve the country. If I lay too much emphasis on men of literary talents, there will be no guarantee to the peace of the territories. Therefore, I have nominated various talents to consult on the literary and military strategies. I am relieved to see that each of them will give full play to his special talents. I have nominated five hundred candidates who have passed the imperial examinations. At the top of the list is Li Yi, whose essays and poems I have been reading for long and whose high reputation I have been appreciating. He is allowed to express his gratitude in the Taiji Hall and to take office as an Imperial Academician as soon as possible. He is to go to serve as the military consultant in the army under Prime Minister Du Huangshang in the Shuofang area. His appointment document is to be drafted by the Secretariat."

LI YI (*Expresses his gratitude to the emperor and goes out of the palace gate*):

> (*To the tune of* **Diliuzi**)
>
> The sage emperor,
>
> The sage emperor
>
> Gives an audience to his ministers.
>
> The ministry of rites,

The ministry of rites

Has eight important sections.

From among the people,

Excellent officials are selected

And recommended to the court,

Where they are given due honor and positions

And are granted a grand banquet beside the Qujiang Pool.

(*To the previous tune*)

In the past,

In the past

I wrote essays in vain.

In the palace yard,

In the palace yard

I got drunk when I was not nominated.

In the brothel house,

With all the curtains rolled up,

I will pick from those I know.

To pick the name written on the fragrant paper,

Which one should I sleep with tonight?

(*To the tune of* **Coda**)

As flowers bloom all over the yard when the bells ring,

So there is no limit to wealth and rank when you are nominated.

There are always stories for people to pass down.

For one more talent in the court

He has a brilliant future of high rank.

The Apricot Garden is in the late spring,

But he is the topmost candidate who drank.

Scene Twenty-Two
Parting with Reluctance

(*Enter Li Yi*)

LI YI (*To the tune of* **Fanbusuan**):

The spring is in its last phase

When ministers retreat from the court.

With urgent tidings from the border area,

The sword will have to leave the sheath.

(*In the pattern of* **Huanxisha**)

"*As the court abounds in capable people,*

The Purple Flute

I am sent from the palace

To the remote frontier regions.

When frontier wars draws me away from home,

I shall serve in the army that is stationed there

But my heart is linked with a faithful heart."

I am Li Yi. I am ranked at the top among the talented scholars, so I am appointed an Imperial Academician. As the war in Shuofang is still under way, Prime Minister Du Huangshang is dispatched to the frontier and I am decreed to be his military consultant. I am happy to learn that Shi Xiong came at the top in the imperial test of martial arts, Hua Qin wrote a report to His Majesty yesterday and asked to be dispatched to the frontier to make contributions, and Shang Zipi has asked His Majesty for permission to return to the west. I have sent Qing'er to go to the Secretariat and inquire about His Majesty's response.

(Enter Qing'er)

QING'ER:

"While time passes slowly in the palace,

Flowers bloom over the Ministry of Justice."

Master, here is the court gazette!

LI YI (*Reads the gazette*):

Oh! The Personnel Ministry handed in the memorial on the sixteenth day of the second month that to handle the affairs in the Songpan area, Grand General Hua Qin is to be transferred to Xichuan because there is no military governor there. On the seventeenth day, the Military Ministry handed in the memorial that Shi Xiong, the champion in the imperial test of martial arts, is to be transferred to Longxi to handle the affairs related the Tubos. On the eighteenth day, the Ministry of Rites handed in the memorial concerning the rites for the return of Shang Zipi, son of the Tubo King, that a banquet is to be held in the Guanglu Temple, and that the Imperial Academy is to draft a document of response to the Tubos. Alas! The three friends of mine will be separated when I go to Shuofang as the military consultant. How sad I am since I do not know when we can meet again! Qing'er, go and inquire when they are going to set out!

QING'ER:

It is decreed that all of you are to set out early tomorrow morning. I have just met their gateman, who told me that the three masters would come here to say farewell.

LI YI:

In that case, prepare a banquet as soon as possible!

(Enter Hua Qing, Shi Xiong and Shang Zipi)

HUA QING, SHI XIONG, SHANG ZIPI (*To the tune of **Yeyouchao***):

Eminent people leave for the northwest one after another,

Feeling the deep sorrow of parting in times of war.

Riding on jade bridled steeds,

And holding the sharp-edged swords,

We have loyal hearts for our country.

(Greet each other)

"Having just enjoyed a happy spring outing,

> *We now have to part from each other.*
> *There's no need to talk about the distance between us,*
> *Since we are separated by rivers and mountains."*

LI YI:

The Songpan area where Hua Qing will go to serve as the military governor is inland. But the Longxi area where Shi Xiong will go is the place ravaged by the Tubos, and I wonder when Shang Zipi will come back again after he returns home in the Tubos' territory. How sorrowful we are for us sworn brothers to leave for different remote places!

HUA QING:

Shang Zipi will come back sooner or later after he returns home this time. Shi Xiong will have a bright future since he is making contributions at his young age. As I am old, I'm afraid that I will stay at the frontier for the rest of my life and I will not have the chance to see you again.

LI YI:

You will return to the court in victory like the ancient generals Jiang Ziya and Ma Yuan. It is just the separation at this very moment that makes you feel sentimental and upset. When Shi Xiong recovers the Longxi area by depending on His Majesty's power and prestige, please visit my father's grave for me! When Shang Zipi sends messengers, please drop me a line! I will set out for Shuofang tomorrow or the day after tomorrow. It is hard to predict the future as I shall go through tortuous and dangerous passes and mountains. A true man must cherish great ambitions and aim at achieving success and reputation. Let's drink and sing to our hearts' content at today's parting!

HUA QING, SHI XIONG, SHANG ZIPI:

We don't feel like drinking now because we'll soon be on our way.

LI YI:

Please do drink a cup since we won't be able to drink together any more. Qing'er, fill in the wine cups!

QING'ER:

> *"The horse neighs at the road of departure*
> *While the wine fills the cup of separation."*

Here is the wine, Master!

(Fills in the wine cups)

LI YI (*To the tune of **Zaoluopao***):

> The wine adds woe to the sorrow at our farewell,
>
> When the generals will leave for the frontier
>
> And Shang Zipi will go a long way back home.
>
> Feather-decorated army flags flutter past the parting pavilion,
>
> With their bright colors mirrored in the river water.

LI YI, HUA QING, SHI XIONG, SHANG ZIPI:

> The mountain paths wind forward
>
> When the black steeds start off late in the day.
>
> The companions are decreed to set out,

With parting sorrow at the moment.

We have to tear ourselves away from our friends.

HUA QING (*To the previous tune*):

Departure is made in overwhelming sorrow,

Which can even make the monkeys wail

And the cranes linger above.

It is hard to imagine the reunion date for the long distance

And for the various detentions we might encounter.

The four of us

LI YI, HUA QING, SHI XIONG, SHANG ZIPI:

Bear well-made bows

And sharp-edged swords.

Full of energy and aspiration,

For what are we to show valiance at the frontier?

In Seleukia we shall meet the envoy from the west again.

SHANG ZIPI:

Shilang, when you say that you will meet the envoy from the west again in Seleukia, you are expecting me to return to the middle kingdom. But you know, although I am reluctant to leave Mount Tai and Mount Hua in China, I have to go back home as I am an envoy. And I am afraid that it will be hard for me to keep in touch with you as I will live in seclusion in the Kunlun Mountains after I go back. I will remain single and will not serve as a bureaucrat.

LI YI:

Zipi, although you are indulged in the mountains such as Mount Tai, Mount Hua and the Kunlun Mountains, the Tubo King might not allow you to do so. If he insists on your service, how can you live up to his expectations? Jurong after his mission to the State of Jin and Youyu after his mission to the State of Jin did meritorious deeds in consolidating the friendly contact between the central plain and the western regions. Zipi, you should persuade the Tubo King to pacify the frontier and secure the stability in the border regions. In that case, how can you confine yourself in the mountains and look on with folded arms?

SHANG ZIPI:

I see. So much for the wine today!

LI YI:

I will escort you till we get out of the Yanqiu Gate.

(*Bids farewell to Shang Zipi*)

(*To the tune of* **Xiangliuniang**)

I see off the traveler with tears in my eyes,

I see off the traveler with tears in my eyes

When the horses gallop neck to neck,

With flags fluttering in the evening glow.

I can hardly contain myself,

I can hardly contain myself

In pressing for the reunion date

So eagerly that I might knock the spittoon to pieces.

LI YI, HUA QING, SHI XIONG, SHANG ZIPI:

> The flute will be played in the frontier,
>
> The flute will be played in the frontier
>
> To express our depression
>
> In letters to our friends.

HUA QING (*To the previous tune*):

> I am reluctant to say farewell,
>
> I am reluctant to say farewell
>
> As we shall live under different skies,
>
> Leaving me waving to you under the sun.
>
> The wild geese flying south in the spring,
>
> The wild geese flying south in the spring
>
> Are wailing on their way of departure
>
> But hailing on their way of return,
>
> Which upsets those who pass by.

LI YI, HUA QING, SHI XIONG, SHANG ZIPI:

> The flute will be played in the frontier,
>
> The flute will be played in the frontier
>
> To express our depression
>
> In letters to our friends.

Let's say good-bye now!

> (*Bow to each other*)
>
> (*To the tune of* **Coda**)
>
> The roadside willows intoxicated in the spring warmth
>
> Cannot detain the neighing horses of departure,
>
> But remind us of the palace bells at dawn.
>
> (*Exeunt Hua Qing, Shi Xiong and Shang Zipi*)

LI YI (*To Qing'er*):

Qing'er, let's go back! You see, when the three of them took departure, I saw them off. But there is no one to see me off when I leave tomorrow. In pursuit of scholarly honor and official rank, we all suffer the woe of hardship and separation.

> (*To the tune of* **Xiangliuniang**)
>
> The spring breeze blowing at my hair,
>
> The spring breeze blowing at my hair
>
> Sweeps here and there
>
> In absolute freedom.
>
> Life running on like a galloping horse,
>
> Life running on like a galloping horse
>
> Brings sadness to the passenger
>
> For the long and tortuous way ahead.
>
> So why seek for a high official rank?

So why seek for a high official rank?

By selling the medicine and repairing the zither,

You can likewise spend your floating life as if in a dream.

As war dusts rise amid the whistling sands,

I shall go northwest bearing bow and sword.

Although I shall serve in the frontier regions,

I see off friends in tears of my own accord.

Scene Twenty-Three
Bidding Farewell

(*Enter Zheng Liuniang*)

ZHENG LIUNIANG (*To the tune of* **Bubujiao**):

The beauty weeps when she goes to bed,

With her palms stained by the silver on her skirt

And her hair tied to her dreams.

By the window

With a view of peach blossoms in full bloom,

Xiaoyu leans against her husband in tenderness

Like an oriole afraid of being disturbed by the wind.

(*In the pattern of* **Yejinmen**)

"*I cannot ask him to stay,*

Because this is only my vain hope.

In view of the flowery garden with whistling spring breeze,

The beauty weeps with her sleeves covering her face.

Why does he discard her soon after they are conjugated?

Tomorrow they'll snap willows as keepsake at Baling Bridge.

I cannot bear to see mandarin ducks in couples

When she will be a lonely pheonix."

I am Zheng Liuniang. My daughter Xiaoyu is married to Li Yi, who came at the top in the imperial test and is appointed an Imperial Academician. They are indeed an unparalleled couple of talent and beauty. But he is assigned to be the military consultant for Prime Minister Du in Shuofang as soon as he took office in the Imperial Academy. I hear that Tubo is to the west of Shuofang, while Huihu is to the northwest. And these two nations often fight with each other in the areas of Shuofang. I am worried that Shilang will have a hard time in dealing with the military affairs there. But I dare not tell Xiaoyu about this as she might be startled, so the only thing for me to do is have a dinner prepared for tomorrow's farewell. Where is Yingtao?

(*Enter Yingtao*)

YINGTAO:

"*I whisk the sheath to see the sword*

And open the casket to fold the army uniform."

What do you want me to do, Madam?

ZHENG LIUNIANG:

As Mr. Li will leave tomorrow, we should prepare a dinner for I shall bid farewell to him tonight, while the Princess will see him off tomorrow.

YINGTAO:

I see.

ZHENG LIUNIANG:

Where are Mr. Li and the Princess?

YINGTAO:

They are upstairs making a most tearful farewell.

ZHENG LIUNIANG (*Sadly*):

Oh my daughter,

> (*To the tune of* **Zuifugui**)
>
> Wrapped by the double quilt
>
> And resting on the double pillow,
>
> The couple keep at each other's side.
>
> Like butterflies disturbed by drafts of wind,
>
> Mr. Li will follow the steps of General Li Guang
>
> To serve at the frontier and leave his wife alone.

YINGTAO:

Mistress, my husband Qing'er will go with Mr. Li.

> (*Wails*)
>
> (*To the previous tune*)
>
> The pair of bamboo shoots fit into each other
>
> While the pair of horse statues stand together.

Wu'er

> Becomes the housekeeper to stay at home,

But my Qing'er

> Will soon leave me behind.

From now on,

> I will sigh behind closed doors,
>
> With my heart burning like the candlewick.

ZHENG LIUNIANG (*To the tune of* **Coda**):

> Man with high ambition
>
> Pays no regard to the delicate beauty,
>
> Who will be left to paint her eyebrows alone.

YINGTAO:

The dinner is ready. Please drink to your heart's content tonight with Mr. Li and the Princess, Madam!

ZHENG LIUNIANG:

Yingtao, how can I drink to my heart's content? It is true indeed,

For an ideal nuptial tie that is newly knotted,

The man will leave his wife to go to war.

The drops of bloody wine she drinks tonight

Will turn into her tears in the boudoir.

Scene Twenty-Four
The Seeing-Off

(*Enter Huo Xiaoyu, followed by Yingtao*)

HUO XIAOYU (*To the tune of* **Busuanzi**):

Tall and dense tree branches shelter the house

While light and soft catkins flow everywhere.

When swallows spread their wings in their flight,

I feel sad at the separation with my man.

(*In the pattern of* **Hechuan**)

"*The company of spring*

And the warmth of flowers

Pay no attention to my sorrow at departure.

My dress is wet through

With rain and sweat.

When we say good-bye by the palace stream,

My tears will flow into my side hair.

I hold the full cup with tears in my eyes,

Pestering him like a spoiled child,

With my soul following him for thousands of miles.

When his wagon embarks on the road,

I will recall our happy old days,

And harbor a grudge for being unable to go with him."

Yingtao, I have been feeling grieved to death before I see off Shilang today.

(*Enter Li Yi, followed by attendants*)

LI YI (*To the previous tune*):

Mixed with the hubble-bubble is her tender moan,

Which is faint like the fog outside the window gauze.

With her tears moistening the rouge like dewdrops on the petals,

Where will the beloved one be when her tears run dry?

"*After the grand banquet in the palace,*

I cherish affections at home.

Who knows that the Number-One Scholar

Is to serve in the troops in the northwest?"

Attendants, halt the wagon outside the post station of the Baling Bridge and wait until I finish the farewell drinks with my wife!

(*Greets Huo Xiaoyu*)

Thank you for your trouble to see me off! Isn't the madam with you?

HUO XIAOYU:

She will be here soon. Shilang, I can't help feeling sad when I see you off. I'll have a word to say about my reluctance to part with you. Fetch the wine!

(*To the tune of* **Northern Jishengcao**)

The parting tune of "The Yangguan Pass"

Enters the jade wine kettle.

Standing on the green grass by the rippling river,

I am overwhelmed with sorrow at dusk

At the view of the weeping willows by the Baling Bridge.

I hope that my slim waist will turn into a ribbon to detain him,

But he is like a floating catkin that cannot rein himself.

LI YI:

"How can I be so heartless?

I have to pursue fame and honor.

I am in extreme sorrow

When the parting music comes to its close."

HUO XIAOYU:

You are certainly heartless, because you should feel sad as soon as the music begins. Fill in your cup again!

(*To the previous tune*)

Dressed in the golden-threaded skirt,

I nestle against my man on the red blanket.

After I experience the transient joy time and again

With my heart stirred by love and desire,

Where can I find the intimate pleasure once more?

When we are about to part with each other,

I'd like to ask you who has cut short my joy and hope.

(*Li Yi utters a long sigh and lowers his head*)

HUO XIAOYU (*To the previous tune*):

When the black hair is no longer glossy, the flowers are sad;

When the eyebrows knit, the willows will not unfold.

My slim fingers wipe off the tears from my rosy cheeks,

With watery and bright eyes below my knitted brows,

When I drag my long skirt along the way.

Why do I feel sad when I see off my man?

I'll have a lovesick dream with no pleasure tonight.

LI YI:

Play one more tune, and we'll have to say good-bye!

The Purple Flute

HUO XIAOYU (*To the previous tune*):

> I am reluctant to pluck the strings,
>
> Wearing a coat of lovebirds in vain.
>
> I shall doze the spring off
>
> With my waist-belt turning loose,
>
> And the candle and incense burning to the end.
>
> Looking at the clouds and mountains on the screen,
>
> I expect to meet you again but you may have new love then.

LI YI:

Do you have anything to give me as a souvenir?

HUO XIAOYU:

I have floods of tears for you to keep in your sleeves.

LI YI (*To the previous tune*):

> Oh my tears!
>
> How they roll down my cheeks
>
> In rouge strings of jade-beads!
>
> My tears ooze like rose-dews from the jade pot,
>
> Or like raindrops from the petals of pear-flowers,
>
> Or like the drizzle-mist from the mermaid.
>
> My tears will drop till the sea clouds dry up,
>
> With my sleeves stained with blood of the Xiaoxiang bamboos!

HUO XIAOYU:

You can shed your tears on my sleeves as well, Shilang!

LI YI:

> "*A true man will never shed tears*
>
> *On the dress of a woman.*"

HUO XIAOYU (*Annoyed*):

What a heartless man you are!

LI YI:

Xiaoyu, I will have to swallow my tears by myself.

> (*To the previous tune*)
>
> I will have words that touch my heart
>
> And move me all the time.

After I leave, take care not to catch a cold as you'll sleep alone!

> Tie the silk belly-slip,
>
> Fasten the soft waistband,
>
> And make your bed warm and cozy.
>
> As you may have dreams haunting your mind,
>
> Make sure to ease your sorrow when you wake up!

HUO XIAOYU:

On hearing these remarks, I feel that you are not a frivolous man. But at this moment,

> (*To the tune of **Jiesancheng***)

The embroidered oriole perches alone on the screen

While the butterfly rests by itself on a branch.

I shall play the music in loneliness

And present it to the flowers.

Even if I fail to rival the beauty in the northwest,

I will send you a wife's letter of deep yearning.

For the sake of a new beauty,

You might leave me behind

To look at the mirror in solitude.

LI YI (*To the previous tune*):

When the zither music comes to an end at separation,

The army flags will flutter along the mountain path.

When the beauty frowns and lowers her head at the last note,

The river water seems to stop flowing for the moment.

The sorrow of separation for three years

Will be witnessed from the mirror with sighs.

The pursuit of fame and honor

Will leave the beauty in solitude,

Only sending letters in words of woe.

HUO XIAOYU:

When will you return? I'll be longing for you all the time!

(*To the previous tune*)

With your term of service not numbered,

You'll embark on the road to the frontier.

I'll be expecting in the east to receive your letters,

Delivered by the horse or the camel well-equipped.

The wild flower which butterflies visit has no spouse,

But I have my man far away at the frontier.

Reluctant to waste my youth,

I hope to live like wild geese in pairs

Or mandarin ducks swimming side by side.

LI YI:

Let's say good-bye now!

(*To the previous tune*)

After seeing me off in the setting sun,

My lovesick wife will go home in the nightly moon,

To see the satin seat, the red ceiling, and the broad window

With silver latches and purple fringes.

When clouds hover over the lovesick tree,

Her tears will flow like strings of beads.

As I have missed the honeymoon,

I will be on the watch for the phoenix in the parasol tree

And the wailing crow amid the laurel leaves.

(*Enter Zheng Liuniang*)

ZHENG LIUNIANG:

"*He makes farewell with the jade sword in hand*

And empties the golden cup from the horseback.

With his strong will and ambition,

He goes for fame and honor today."

Shilang, you are whiling away your time, but they are urging you to start early with the chariots.

Fetch the wine and I'll see Shilang mount the horse!

(*To the previous tune*)

Shilang, please take leave on your horse,

With your pretty wife waving good-bye on the roadside.

You should face hardships with a light heart

And refrain from looking back or hesitating.

While winning honor is the duty of a man,

Taking care of the household is the duty of a wife.

With the army flags flapping in the wind,

You will soon allot the ivory tallies

In the embroidered military tent.

LI YI (*To the previous tune*):

The drums are beaten when the parting song is sung

And the coral on the whip is broken when the horse is spurred on.

When clouds and sands enshroud the old sentry post,

I set out to defeat the enemy as an eagle snatches the rabbit.

I shall set out for the northwest frontier,

With my wife dancing her dance of departure.

I'll travel at double speed,

In full confidence to win victories

And make my name go down on historical records.

ALL (*Bow and bid farewell*):

(*To the tune of **Zhegutian***)

He bids farewell with much hesitation

Before embarking on the long and intriguing journey.

As long as wealth and rank can be achieved,

The loneliness of his wife at home is worthwhile.

(*Li Yi leaves, followed by attendants*)

LI YI:

Good-bye! Please go back!

(*Exit*)

(*The attendants follow Li Yi*)

(*Zheng Liuniang and Huo Xiaoyu stay behind*)

HUO XIAOYU:

Mother,

> He is escorted
>
> By multitudes of horses and men.

ZHENG LIUNIANG:

He is a prospective hero and a desirable husband.

> (*Enter the neighborhood head, kneeling down*)

NEIGHBORHOOD HEAD:

When Mr. Li bid farewell to the ministers of the six court departments, he told me to ask Madam Zheng and Mrs. Li to return early.

ZHENG LIUNIANG:

Thank you! Please take good care of Mr. Li on the way!

HUO XIAOYU:

Please tell him to

> Have the sword in his hand along the way
>
> And send home letters whenever there is a post station.
>
> *The parting tune is played*
>
> *Until farewell has been made.*
>
> *He is to leave for years,*
>
> *His wife at home in tears.*

Scene Twenty-Five
Journey to the Frontier

> (*Enter a soldier*)

SOLDIER (*To the tune of* **Jinqianhua**):

> When the rain washes away the dust from Weicheng,
>
> When the rain washes away the dust from Weicheng,
>
> The moon casts its yellow light over Luntai,
>
> The moon casts its yellow light over Luntai.
>
> On our journey to the west frontier,
>
> We wear battle armour and ride on saddled horses,
>
> Leaving with battle flags and returning with victory songs.

The Military Department orders me to escort Military Consultant Li to Shuofang. I suppose he has arrived.

> (*Enter Li Yi*)

LI YI (*To the tune of* **Mantingfang**):

> Before I left the Xiliu Camp
>
> And the Changyang Palace behind,

I bid farewell by the painted bridge in the tree shade.

As a scholar in the Imperial Academy,

For what am I to make the expedition to the frontier?

When I asked why my wife was in distress,

She shed tears which wet her sleeves.

As I had to depart,

I stood on the Baling Bridge,

Looking back alone at Chang'an, the imperial capital.

"When the carriage arrives with sunshine over the walls

Of the garrison with blooming flowers and open stables,

The music of reed pipes and long horns

Will resound in the ancient town of Luntai.

I hate the green willows along the field paths,

For they entangle my dress but cannot detain me.

My longing wife weeps in vain to the south of the Weishui River,

But I have to leave for the north of the Jiaohe River."

The departure with sister Xiaoyu at the Baling Bridge by the weeping willows has been haunting my mind. However, military orders must be obeyed without any delay, so I have to restrain my sentiments for her. Attendant, is our team ready to go?

138

(*The soldier responds*)

LI YI:

Let's be on our way!

(*To the tune of* **Chaoyuange**)

When the horses stir up the dusts in the breeze,

The carriage and three is bathed in the morning sun.

The rolling wheels on the riverbank

Follow the green waters of the river.

The black troop pushes its way forward

With banners patterned with falcons,

At the lightning speed of shooting stars.

To the beat of drums and gongs,

I march from the court in the south to Shuofang,

On my mission traversing the grass

In full imperial splendor.

ALL:

Tighten the reins

And we'll win honors and titles by making great feats.

SOLDIER (*To the previous tune*):

The Great Wall is dimly visible from the mountain peak,

With military spears pointing to the clouds

And white feathers decorating the flowery gates.

With flags twisting and turning in the ravine

And trees at the beacon towers guiding the way,

We turn to Shangjun by the Jiaohe River.

The horsemen gallop to and fro in both directions,

Delivering letters of emergency.

We water the horses at the creeks,

With flags fluttering in the frontier dust.

ALL:

Tighten the reins

And we'll win honors and titles by making great feats.

LI YI (*To the previous tune*):

When I look back at Chang'an, the sun is rising,

As if seeing me off from the east,

With my wife standing in the southern fields in deep woe.

The rouge from Yunling

And the white powder from Yuntai

Can hardly conceal her solitude and sorrow.

I have the dagger to defend myself,

But dusts will wither my face and winds will ruffle my hair.

When a roaming young man joins the army,

Wealth and fame will turn to hardship and bitterness.

ALL:

Tighten the reins

And we'll win honors and titles by making great feats!

SOLDIER (*To the previous tune*):

When he searches for spring flowers in the frontier,

He neglects himself in requiting the imperial grace,

But keeps his dear wife in mind.

For all the reed pipes at the ancient fortress

And the bamboo flutes in the mountains,

The music of "Falling Plum Blossoms" can be heard no more.

In observing the source of the Yellow River,

We see that the war star has not set yet.

We laugh and get ready for the heroic exploits,

Expecting the mellow wine for our frontier victory.

ALL:

I used to wait at palace gates at dawn,

Without a thought that camps are my sojourn.

I have the war-challenge letter in hand;

The court will wait for my triumphant return.

Scene Twenty-Six
Arrival at the Frontier

(*Enter Du Huangshang*)

DU HUANGSHANG (*To the tune of* **Qitianle**):

> In the magnificent palace hall,
> I am ranked at the top as the Prime Minister.
> In the Zhique Temple
> And the Qilin Tower,
> I am honored as a distinguished minister.
> When the weapons are laid up in peaceful times,
> You can see the brave soldiers patrol in the fortress
> And the prime minister serve in the frontier
> With absolute authority
> In the Yumen Pass.
> *"Under His Majesty's decree I command the army*
> *As the prime minister in the reigns of three emperors.*
> *With great power and influence,*
> *I do not covet to have my portrait enshrined in the Qilin Tower."*

I am Du Huangshang, styled Zunsu, a native of the Wannian prefecture in Chang'an. I passed the imperial examinations when I was young, then assisted in managing the affairs in Shuofang under the leadership of Guo Ziyi, Prince of Fenyang. I have served the three emperors — the Daizong Emperor, the Dezong Emperor and the Shunzong Emperor — before I serve the current emperor. I take up a high-ranking post and have great authority in handling the court affairs. As the prime minister, I have made great contributions in the military affairs, quelling Qing and Qi in the east, Huai and Cai in the south, Yinxia in the north, and Jin and Jiang in the west. I am entitled the Duke of Fen with a fief of ten thousand households. Now I am appointed to manage the frontier affairs following the ancient practice. His Majesty allows me to set up another military office as I used to be in charge of the Shuofang area. Recently I hear that Li Yi, the Number-One Scholar in the latest imperial examination, will be here to be my military consultant, and that he has settled down outside the Shouxiang city. He is about to meet me this morning. Although he has not become a court official, he comes with His Majesty's decree. As he will be relied on later, a grand ceremony would be appropriate to greet him. Attendant, has Mr. Li arrived?

ATTENDANT:

He is waiting to be received at the gate.

DU HUANGSHANG:

Invite him in!

(*Enter Li Yi*)

LI YI (*To the tune of* **Shengzhazi**):

> My red robe is burning bright,

While my horse is exhausted from the hard journey.

You have the countenance of a prime minister,

Who commands the army in the military camp.

(*Du Huangshang and Li Yi greet each other*)

LI YI:

"You made great contributions in the former times,

DU HUANGSHANG:

But your talent as a military consultant will be eminent.

LI YI:

You serve His Majesty with shining glory,

DU HUANGSHANG:

But I'll respect you as an emissary.

LI YI:

You are a prime minister with august gravity,

DU HUANGSHANG:

But your writings are appreciated by His Majesty.

LI YI:

You are the pillar of the country,

DU HUANGSHANG:

But you will have your name passed down."

I have long heard that you were appointed as the Imperial Academician, but how come you are dispatched to the frontier as a military consultant?

LI YI:

Even a prime minister has come to the frontier by the order of the court, so I am honored to be dispatched here and work under you as a military consultant. I have always admired your prestige,

(*To the tune of* **Suochuanglang**)

Always by the side of His Majesty,

You have succeeded in the government of the state.

Surrounded by the noble pagoda-trees,

The frontier military camp is your present abode.

You are the prime minister

As well as a competent scholar-general.

ALL:

High posts are held by literary and military talents,

Who contribute to the ending of wars

And the building of a peaceful society.

DU HUANGSHANG:

I am requiting His Majesty's grace by my military service, and I shall soon go back home with honor. You are highly regarded by His Majesty as a young scholar and esteemed by the people for your talent. So I shall entrust my duty to you when I am too old.

(*To the previous tune*)

It is admirable that you come to the frontier

With a high official rank in the prime of youth.

With your splendid writings presented to His Majesty,

You will be remembered from generation to generation.

More precious is your voluntary frontier service

In composing the military documents.

ALL:

High posts are held by literary and military talents,

Who contribute to the ending of wars

And the building of a peaceful society.

(*Military officers come to pay respect to Li*)

MILITARY OFFICERS (*To the previous tune*):

The remote frontier region is garrisoned,

With our flags waving at all the forts.

Among all the military camps, which one is like ours, with the prime minister as the commander and the Number-One Scholar as the military consultant?

We are commanded by the prime minister

And the renowned court official.

Their presence by His Majesty's decree

Brings a breath of spring to the Yumen Pass.

ALL:

High posts are held by literary and military talents,

Who contribute to the ending of wars

And the building of a peaceful society.

DU HUANGSHANG:

Mr. Li, I'll show you around the frontiers tomorrow.

DU HUANGSHANG, LI YI (*To the previous tune*):

The chief commander makes his presence at the front,

Burning the enemy camps and chasing the barbarian chief.

With yellow dust of sand comes

The war fire and the gun smoke.

When the frontier region is under our control,

The enemy will give allegiance to our government.

ALL:

High posts are held by literary and military talents,

Who contribute to the ending of wars

And the building of a peaceful society.

DU HUANGSHANG:

Attendant, escort Mr. Li to settle down in the hostel for the envoy of our tributary states and have an official banquet prepared!

(*To the tune of* **Coda**)

The literary talent is smart as a military consultant,

Who brings the strong army so much credit
That there will be no more wars in our region.
Stay here before the war comes to an end
And let's enjoy the tunes of pipes and flutes.
When the moon sheds light over frontier camps,
I'll dream of hearth and home in backward routes.

Scene Twenty-Seven
Profound Longings

(*Enter Huo Xiaoyu and Yingtao*)
HUO XIAOYU (*To the tune of* **Yumeiren**):
  Amidst the oriole's heart-breaking cry in the late spring wind,
  I fall asleep with the golden phoenix hairpin on my head.
  I knit my light eyebrows and rouge my lips,
  With the dressing locket in front of me
  And the fond dreams in my mind.
  (*In the pattern of* **Pusaman**)
  "*With my jade hairpin swaying in the wind,*
  My dewy begonia of a face is stained with tears.
  I cannot see the lotus flowers from my bower,
  Shielded by the rolling-mountain screen.
  I look at my face from before and behind in the mirror,
  Which reflects both my face and the flowers.
  I admire the ancient Zhang Chang
  Who painted his wife's eyebrows."

Yingtao, it has been a month since Shilang left for the army and there is not a line from
him. As it is late spring of azalea flowers now, how dreary the weather is!
  (*To the tune of* **Haoshijin**)
  When the warm breeze gently blows,
  My hair is tossed and spreads over my shoulders.
  The incense has reduced its fragrance,
  Leaving only the faint curly smoke.
  How miserable I am,
  Twisting the golden thread in loneliness,
  As the prime time of spring has gone!
  With my beloved going far away,
  I gaze at the flowers in full bloom
  In silence all day.

YINGTAO:

The young couple would never forget each other for their mutual love and pleasure. You two are separated when you have just started your sweet nuptial life, but you are clever enough to relax and enjoy yourself.

> (*To the tune of **Jinchandao***)
> A young girl as you
> Should always be cheerful
> By blowing the bamboo flute
> Or playing on the swings
> To idle away your time.
> How can you be in a sad mood
> Just for the falling petals?
> (*Aside*)
> Your delicate body is lovely indeed.
> (*Turns back*)
> Your attachment to him
> Makes it hard for you to fall asleep.

HUO XIAOYU:

You are right. When I was a girl, I went to bed early and covered myself with an embroidered quilt without feeling lonely. I used to sneer at those lovesick companions, but it is my turn now.

YINGTAO:

You have been attached to him for some time, and you will soon get over it.

HUO XIAOYU:

I'm afraid I'll be lovesick too.

> (*To the tune of **Jintingle***)
> In the past I was neither sad nor grieved,
> And did not feel sentimental in the spring.
> I wondered why some people would feel lovesick,
> But it is my turn to feel lovesick now.
> It is my fond wish
> To lean against the zigzag railings
> As if I were leaning against the endless frontier walls.

HUO XIAOYU, YINGTAO (*To the tune of **Guluntai***):

> Two young people
> Make a happy couple
> And enjoy the newly-wed pleasure.
> The bridegroom used to steal a glace
> At the blushing face of the bride,
> But it is a pity that the man has gone to the frontier.
> He is ready to leave
> For a future bright and prospective,
> Rather than stay in company with his wife.

From this night on,

The man will be in the remote West,

While the wife will stay alone waiting for the dawn.

As the beloved is not by her side

And there is no need to be shy,

The bride would cry by herself like a cuckoo.

When can they meet again?

The bride would be too distressed to put on her headwear.

(*To the tune of* **Coda**)

Does the beauty have to wait for years

Before she gets a line saying that he is safe and sound?

HUO XIAOYU:

Yingtao, where can I find a temple to burn the joss-sticks to wish for Shilang's safety?

YINGTAO:

Du Qiuniang is now living in the Nunnery of Queen Mother of the West. As the fifteenth of the fourth month is Queen Mother's birthday, we can go there and burn joss-sticks to while away some time.

HUO XIAOYU:

I'll ask my mother to go with me on that day.

YINGTAO:

I see.

The heart-shaped incense will be burnt to make a wish.

Spring birds are dimly visible in the clouds,

While I do my embroidery in the bower.

When spring breeze brushes in a teasing way,

I'm pining for my husband like a flower.

Scene Twenty-Eight
Tubo's Harassment

(*Enter the Tubo King*)

TUBO KING (*To the tune of* **Yizhihua**):

The fragrant rice grows along the roads in Bailan,

While tamarisk willows cover the Lhasa ferry.

Shiny weapons and large flags are displayed

At the gates of the military camps.

Wearing tiger-skin belts and eagle-shaped hats,

Our soldiers are accompanied by the sorcerers,

Carrying protective shields and beating platform drums.

I wear a hat with feathers
And a dark brown robe,
With my sword glittering against the gold threads.
"*With domes of tents crawling on the Altai Mountains,*
There are our warriors buried in the sands every year.
Spring never touches upon the white grass in the city
While wild geese wail above the yellow flowers in the garrison."

I am King Yitai of the Tubos. Our country borders with Junmao and Liangsong in the east, Qiuci and Shule in the west, Borneo in the south and Turkey in the north, occupying a territory of ten thousand miles with a population of several hundred thousands. Our country abounds in gold and treasures and each household has its books of poetry. Areas to the west of the upper reach of the Yellow River are all under our control after the Huihe nation was annexed by us. I am now spending the summer by the Zanghe River to escape from the heat. Dissatisfied as my ambition has not been fully realized, I am considering an invasion to the south. The chief of my secretariat, Shang Qixin, is a resourceful man, so I shall seek advice from him.

(*Enter Shang Qixin*)

SHANG QIXIN (*To the tune of* **Fendie'er**):
We eat by hands from the felt plate
And drink over the camel hoof and the crispy cheese.
"*With our horses wearing saddles studded with green jade,*
The battle has ended at moonrise.
The drumbeat is still loud on the city wall,
While the broad sword in the box is still wet with blood."

I am Shang Qixin, Tubo's chief of the secretariat. As the king is summoning me to have an audience, I'll go and meet him.

(*Greets the Tubo King*)

TUBO KING:

Chief of the Secretariat, we have failed to snatch any land from the Central Plains this summer. The detestable Huihus have not surrendered to us for their blood relation with the Tang court. Now I intend to invade the south and attack the north at the same time. I'd like to seek your advice.

SHANG QIXIN:

My uncle Shang Zipi used to wait upon the Tang emperor and study in their imperial academy. When he returned from the Central Plains, he said that the people there lived a harmonious and prosperous life, and that the emperor is sagacious while the people are loyal. The military chief in Shuofang is the aged Prime Minister Du Huangshang, who promotes strengthening the country and is very resourceful. His military consultant is the new Number-One Scholar Li Yi, who is good at military strategies and brilliant in literary talents. Their fortresses are firmly connected and can withstand attacks from all directions, so I'm afraid we will not succeed if we attack them. The Longxi area has been annexed by us, but I hear recently that the Tang court has dispatched a man called Shi Xiong, styled Ziying, to lead an army into that area. That man is bold and valiant as well as expert in military tactics. The Tang's tribes in Longxi are mostly weak in their defense except in the Songzhou area, where the land is fertile with abundant produces. The commanding general there is Hua Qin, who is at an old age now, so we can consider seeking that place. Most of the Huihe's areas have been occupied by us. Therefore, we may as well pretend to be weak and go westward to that area. When the Tang court asks, we can just say that we do not intend to attack the southern area so that they will surely replace the commanders in Shuofang. Then we can wait to launch an attack by the mid-autumn.

TUBO KING:

Is it true that we should not attack the Central Plains, as your uncle has suggested? I suppose Shang Zipi knows much about the Central Plains since he stayed there for half a year. I will appoint him the chief commander and attack the empire of Tang. What would you say about that?

SHANG QIXIN:

My uncle Shang Zipi has a wide scope of knowledge in astronomy and is not interested in the worldly affairs. As soon as he returned from his mission to Tang, he went back to Yangtong and had a house built at the foot of the Kunlun Mountains without any intention to get married or be an official. Neither is he concerned about what is happening currently. If you want to appoint him to a position, you must wait until late autumn and visit him in person. Only then might he be willing to take the post.

TUBO KING:

There is something reasonable in what you say. I shall dispatch General Lunkongre to attack Songzhou for the moment, and go to Yangtong in person in late autumn to invite Shang Zipi.

(*To the tune of* **Hongxiuxie**)

Qiang's ancient chief Yuanjian showed his valiancy in Qin,

Qiang's ancient chief Yuanjian showed his valiancy in Qin,

And Liang's ancient chief Wugu annexed Qiang's Ruo tribe,

And Liang's ancient chief Wugu annexed Qiang's Ruo tribe.

The war will be started in Fuhan

And be fought in Yunya.

We shall fight our way to Babu

By way of Guazhou and Shazhou.

Zanxinya

Will be appointed the commander.

Chief of the Secretariat, select thirty thousand soldiers and horses and order Lunkongre to close on Songzhou!

SHANG QIXIN:

Yes, I see.

TUBO KING (*To the previous tune*):

I am imbued with all-conquering spirits,

I am imbued with all-conquering spirits,

And you are resourceful in military tactics,

And you are resourceful in military tactics.
Shoot an arrow to convey urgent message
Across the river;
Beat the drum at one tempo
And sound the conch trumpets;
Drive away the Hans
And sing our Qiang songs.
When stars throw lights upon our glorious state,
Tonight our army flags will flutter in Xizhou.
The Hans are playing tunes of "Frontier Life",
With songs of birds inducing grief and woe.

Scene Twenty-Nine
A Sincere Wish

(*Enter Du Qiuniang and Shancai dressed as Taoist nuns*)

DU QIUNIANG (*To the tune of* **Linjiangxian**):

The pale purple dress of a Taoist nun
Outlines my weary and slender figure.

SHANCAI:

Featuring like an immortal with a jade pendant,
She presents herself as a quiet portrait
Amid the curling incense smoke.

DU QIUNIANG (*In the pattern of* **Nüguanzi**):

"I wear a Taoist hat and dress,
Residing in a nunnery.

SHANCAI:

Her delicate figure dims the ornaments
While her slim fingers put up a light make-up.

DU QIUNIANG:

With fallen petals dotted on my shoes,
I burn the incense like a thin and long bamboo.

SHANCAI:

The fairy messenger bird will carry tidings
To her dear sweetheart."

DU QIUNIANG:

I am Du Qiuniang, a native of Jiankang. I used to wait on the late emperor but was later bestowed upon the old Prince Huo to perform song and dance for him. I stayed in his residence for twenty years before he felt melancholy over the music he heard on the seventh day of the first month and dismissed all his singing girls to live a reclusive life in the deep mountains. I was instructed to become a nun in the Nunnery of the Queen Mother of the West. As I came from the prince's residence, the disciple Shancai was assigned to look after me. My palace companion Zheng Liuniang, who was good at palace music and was called a master in the Palace Troupe, was also bestowed upon Prince Huo. With her daughter Xiaoyu not yet married, she was granted to live in the Red Mansion for the time being. I have never heard from her since we parted. As today is the fifteenth of the fourth month, birthday of the Queen Mother of the West, we have just finished all the worshipping rituals. Shancai, I see that you've been pining away since you came to the nunnery. Now that you have come to this, why don't you quit your secular thoughts and cultivate yourself through Taoism? Won't you pacify your mind and diminish your desires?

SHANCAI:

Qiuniang, how can I pacify my mind and diminish my desires? I still remember the days in the past when

> (*To the tune of* **Miandaxu**)
>
> Flowers came into blossom in the early summer
>
> And mandarin ducks swam in pairs in the warm water,
>
> While the rain accompanied my dreams in the pleasure boat.
>
> The verdant scenes
>
> Aroused my tender affection,
>
> As well as the memory of playing on the swing
>
> In the happy bygone days.

Since I was languid and sickly in days of song and dance, what am I to cultivate as a nun?

> With sweet memories of the past in my mind,
>
> How can I bear the burning desire in my heart?

DU QIUNIANG:

As bygones are bygones, you have to be contented with your life as a nun.

SHANCAI:

Even an immortal in the fairyland are badly in need of a companion! The fairy Yuqing had a rendezvous with Taibai; the star of the Weaver Girl was grim all the time; the fairy Chenggong Zhiqiong was married to the man Xian Chao; and the fairy Du Lanxiang had illicit relations with Zhang Shuo. How can I bear the loneliness and boredom when I still cherish human desires?

DU QIUNIANG:

You have to restrain yourself, Shancai.

SHANCAI:

You are already forty, but I'm not yet thirty. How can I bear it all?

DU QIUNIANG:

It's most difficult for a woman of forty to restrain her desires, but I'm no longer in the mood to talk about the past.

> (*To the previous tune*)

My hometown is by the beautiful Wujiang River.

When I served as a singing girl in Jiankang,

    I often sang the song of "Cherish while Ye May"

    Till I was separated from my beloved one.

    After my youthful life was ruined,

    I seemed to be half-tinted with autumn bleakness.

    Later I served the young Crown Prince with all my heart,

    But was given the cold shoulder in the house of Prince Huo.

Now that I am practicing Taoism,

    What's the use of talking about make-up?

    I am nothing but a lonely azalea.

Shancai, go and see whether there are ladies burning joss-sticks in the Queen Mother Hall!

SHANCAI:

Who will come after noontime?

DU QIUNIANG:

Have a look outside for all that!

    (*Enter Zheng Liuniang and Huo Xiaoyu*)

ZHENG LIUNIANG (*To the tune of* **Yijiangfeng**):

    This is a clean and serene place,

    With tall green trees around

    And drifting white clouds above.

Look, my daughter!

    Rising into the sky,

    The magnificent mansion

    Stands against the setting sun.

    When the beaded curtain is raised,

    Fragrant incense smoke permeates the place.

Here comes Sister Shancai!

SHANCAI (*Comes out and greets in a pleased surprise*):

It turns out to be Liuniang and Princess Xiaoyu! Judging from your headwear, are you married, Princess?

ZHENG LIUNIANG:

She is married to Li Yi from Longxi. He is the latest Number-One Scholar and has been appointed an Imperial Academician, serving as the military consultant in Shuofang. Today we come on purpose to burn some joss-sticks to pray for his safety and to bring regards to Qiuniang.

SHANCAI:

I see!

    Tears of joy are shed at our meeting again.

Please wait a minute and I'll report to Qiuniang!

    (*Reports*)

Qiuniang, here come Zheng Liuniang and Princess Xiaoyu!

DU QIUNIANG (*In a pleased surprise*):

As they never go outdoors, how can they be here?

> (*Comes out and greets in sorrow*)
>
> (*To the tune of* **Kuxiangsi**)
>
> The swallows seldom fly together,
>
> But we are fortunate to meet each other.
>
> *"We stayed together like sisters for twenty years,*
>
> *But have lost contact once we went our own ways.*
>
> *With our happiness gone with the prince,*
>
> *Who will lament over our unfortunate days?"*

Now that you are here, won't you burn some joss-sticks in the Hall of the Queen Mother?

ZHENG LIUNIANG:

Qiuniang, my daughter has been married to the latest Number-One Scholar Li Yi. He has been appointed an Imperial Academician and now serves as the military consultant in Shuofang. I am accompanying Xiaoyu here to burn some joss-sticks to pray for his safety and to pay you a visit.

DU QIUNIANG:

What a pleasure for you to be married to a talent! Now I'll do the prayer for you.

> (*They walk*)

Please offer the joss-sticks, Liuniang and Xiaoyu! I'll make the prayer.

> (*Zheng Liuniang and Huo Xiaoyu offer the joss-sticks*)

DU QIUNIANG (*Prays*):

Zheng Liuniang, concubine of Prince Huo, and her daughter Xiaoyu now pray to the Queen Mother of the West. Xiaoyu offers her incense for her husband Li Yi, the latest Number-One Scholar and the military consultant in Shuofang. She prays for the immortal power to ensure Li Yi's safety in the remote place, to help him make great achievements and rise smoothly to a higher rank. Liuniang and Xiaoyu, say something on your own behalf!

> (*Zheng Liuniang and Huo Xiaoyu kowtow*)

ZHENG LIUNIANG (*To the tune of* **Tingqianliu**):

> My son-in-law is a scholar,
>
> But now serves in the army,
>
> Ready for the battle and slaughter,
>
> By writing declaration of war to the enemy.

ZHENG LIUNIANG, HUO XIAOYU, DU QIUNIANG:

> We wish for Queen Mother's immortal power
>
> To help him achieve grand feats
>
> And return to the capital with honor.

SHANCAI:

Princess Xiaoyu and I will make the second prayer.

> (*To the previous tune*)
>
> The princess is young and pretty,

But her man has left for the battlefields.

I wish that she would appear in his dream

And accompany him in whatever yields.

ZHENG LIUNIANG, HUO XIAOYU, DU QIUNIANG:

We wish for Queen Mother's immortal power

To bless the love between man and wife

As well as their proliferate progeny.

DU QIUNIANG:

So much for the prayer! Let's have a chat in the tea hall!

(*They walk*)

Liuniang, where is your son-in-law Li Yi from?

ZHENG LIUNIANG:

From Longxi. He is the one who composed the poem *Yichunling* on the theme of ascending the heights on the Man's Day.

DU QIUNIANG:

He really lives up to his reputation. Who is their matchmaker?

ZHENG LIUNIANG:

It's Bao Siniang.

DU QIUNIANG:

Oh, it turns out to be Siniang! How is she doing these days?

ZHENG LIUNIANG:

She is looking quite languid now.

DU QIUNIANG:

The three of us are of the same age and are all growing languid! It's time for the young people like Xiaoyu to enjoy their time. Liuniang, not only is my appearance not as good as before, but my fingers are also not so nimble either.

ZHENG LIUNIANG:

Why do you say so?

DU QIUNIANG:

I haven't played the music for a long time, so I felt very awkward when I played a piece of palace music in leisure the other day, with my fingertips, silver nails and strings all in disorder.

ZHENG LIUNIANG:

Qiuniang, your music talents used to excel the elders while your beauty was above par with the others. I still keep it in my memory after twenty years.

DU QIUNIANG:

Liuniang, I did not know much in my young age when I was proud and jealous, but I did not expect that one day I would shed tears of woe when I departed with my man. When I recall the past, those days have turned into a dream! At that time,

(*To the tune of **Shanpoyang***)

Wearing green dress and forming lissome lines,

We dancers gathered and scattered by turns.

Our singing was like orangutan's cry in the twilight

And oriole's chirp in the forest.

We danced around the lamps,

Which lit up our figures and our voice.

But now,

With no audience, I have quit song and music,

But still remember His Majesty asking my name.

I would wake up with a start,

Singing sweet tunes in my old age.

With tears in my eyes,

A mixture of feelings would well up in my mind.

ZHENG LIUNIANG:

Speaking of the past, I still faintly remember the song and dance of "Rainbow Skirts".

(*To the previous tune*)

By railings mirrored in the waters,

Jade pendants chinked with the prelude.

The dancers swirled with skirts wavering in wind

When the music proceeded to its middle.

The dancing dress swept graceful and light

As the music ended with a prolonged echo.

Now,

I cannot remember the song and dance clearly,

Though I used to be an excellent performer.

In making idle comments,

I lie on the silver bed in my aging days;

In resting at leisure,

I expect the youngsters to be experts in music.

SHANCAI:

Speaking of the youngsters, I am still young. Your performance was surely excellent at that time, and I was an outstanding singer when I drank with the wealthy dandies in the capital.

(*To the previous tune*)

My headwear would tilt when I felt dizzy;

I would play the fool when I was in the wrong mood.

I would gamble in drunkenness

And play the wager games in a brisk manner.

I would make up in the early morning

And play the music in a silk dress.

I would feel sickly for no reason at all,

And learn from Zhenniang, the famous courtesan.

But now,

Homeless,

I stay in the Temple of the Queen Mother of the West.

Coy,

I have the fragrant wind brushing my sleeves.

HUO XIAOYU:

Sister Shancai, how come that you are emaciated when you practice Taoism? In my eyes, a nun's life is simple and much better than the mundane life!

(*To the previous tune*)

You wear a soft silk dress

And pink headwear.

You play the melodious music on the lute

And strike the resounding chime-stone.

You study the sacred Taoist scriptures

In an undisturbed state of mind.

The pretty looks of Zhang Juan and Li Tai

Do not enable them to be immortals;

In a tranquil mood,

The love affairs of Linglong and Yuqing are not to be admired.

For no good reason,

Their lives are wasted in romantic affairs.

DU QIUNIANG:

Young as you are, you have made remarks with Taoist connotations! Liuniang, after I have learned the Taoist scriptures by heart, I will go to the Huashan Mountain to follow the footsteps of Prince Huo.

ZHENG LIUNIANG:

I'll go with you.

DU QIUNIANG:

I live here in the nunnery in solitude, but I suppose there are messages from Prince Huo brought to the Red Mansion where you stay.

ZHENG LIUNIANG:

We often dispatch someone to send him regards, but there is no reply from him at all. He is really uninterested in the worldly life!

DU QIUNIANG:

I have quit thinking of the worldly life, let alone the old prince!

(*To the tune of **Haojiejie***)

I burn the incense

To pay homage to the immortals.

Standing by the silver lined screen,

I look far beyond

At the verdant spring.

I have not the slightest interest

In the swallows fluttering past the flowers

Or the orioles hidden in the willow branches.

ZHENG LIUNIANG:

Darkness is descending and the moon will soon come up.

ZHENG LIUNIANG, HUO XIAOYU (*To the previous tune*):

> In front of the eaves,
>
> Willows and flowers fall asleep.
>
> Birds perch and sing in the tree
>
> On the moonlit and dewy night,
>
> When the wind whistles through the trees like flute music.
>
> Behind the curtain,
>
> The poet Lu Jin is no longer so romantic
>
> While the cute Biyu has left words of cheers.

ZHENG LIUNIANG:

We must be leaving now.

DU QIUNIANG:

I am sorry that I have nothing to entertain you but bland tea and random chat. Please excuse me, Xiaoyu!

ZHENG LIUNIANG, HUO XIAOYU (*To the tune of* **Liupomao**):

> A refreshing heart-to-heart talk is conducted
>
> Over the fine green tea which brings warmth
>
> And excels the mellowest wine.
>
> The water in the jade teapot
>
> Cleanses the earthly mind.

ZHENG LIUNIANG:

We shall invite you to our Red Mansion.

SHANCAI:

How can I go to the earthly places in such attire? You may come whenever you have time.

DU QIUNIANG, SHANCAI (*To the previous tune*):

> Uninterested in visiting the earthly places,
>
> We ask whether you would come at leisure times.
>
> It is hard to tell when we shall separate and meet again,
>
> Even when we live close to each other
>
> In the same city.
>
> (*To the tune of* **Coda**)
>
> When the two guests are gone, I can only see
>
> The cold moonlight and the shadowy paths.

ZHENG LIUNIANG:

Qiuniang, how can you bear a separation like this without paying us a visit?

DU QIUNIANG:

Liuniang, I would only feel all the more sorrowful if I went and saw the old house and the old friends. Let me show you to the gate,

> As we have been good sisters for twenty years.
>
> *With fragrant breeze into the fairyland,*
>
> *Two ladies visit former Taoist friend.*

When they talk about the worldly affairs,

They nearly forget when time will end.

Scene Thirty
Stationed in the Frontier

(Enter Military Commander Du Huangshang, followed by the subordinates)

DU HUANGSHANG *(To the tune of* **Baoding'er***):*

    Our camp hall looks imposing,

    With the Emperor Star shining above

    And the War Stars setting in the west.

    When the frontier warfare is over,

    The swords and chariots will be left aloft.

    A military commander will stay behind

    And enjoy the mellow wine in the hot weather.

ALL:

    It is time to enjoy the grapes

    And the delicious food

    Over the cool drinks.

DU HUANGSHANG:

    "The wine is cool, bubbling with foams,

    When mountains are still covered with snow in this season.

    With music heard all over the town,

    There is nothing like the frontier."

I am Du Huangshang, in a high position appointed by His Majesty for my literary and military talent. Now stationed in Shuofang, I am glad that our barbarian enemies have fled for fear of His Majesty's imposing authority and power. I went a long way beyond the border with my military consultant Li Yi yesterday and returned without seeing the barbarians. As summer has begun in this area, ice and snow has vanished. We would like to taste the cool drinks to kill the heat. I have told my men to prepare some fruits to have a good time with Mr. Li over the drinks. I think he has arrived by now. Attendant, go to the gate and get ready to welcome Mr. Li!

    (Enter Li Yi)

LI YI *(To the tune of* **Hudaolian***):*

    I drop the pen and take up the sword in the frontier,

    Where the Yellow River flows from its source to the capital.

    When the sun sets in Chang'an,

    The flowers by the window mirrors the beauty's face.

ATTENDANT *(Reports):*

Here comes Mr. Li!

(*Du Huangshang gets up and greets Li*)

LI YI:

"*You hold a high official post;*

DU HUANGSHANG:

You boast incomparable talent.

LI YI:

The warfare has come to an end,

DU HUANGSHANG:

To give place to music day and night."

LI YI:

The weapons are laid off for display when war is over. Why are you summoning me today?

DU HUANGSHANG:

By relying on His Majesty's authority and power as well as the collective wisdom and efforts, I have recovered a thousand miles of territory and taken command for years. I have suffered from the hardship of night marches, but have not enjoyed the pleasure of daytime entertainments. As I have been in this remote region of Duqu and Heyuan for years, I am expecting His Majesty's decree to summon me back but in vain. I have spent some pleasant time with you, and today we shall listen to the ancient music and drink the cool wine.

LI YI:

You have quelled the barbarians in the western frontier, grasped the fortress in the northern area, controlled the passage to the south, and are now facing the east to host a grand dinner party. I feel sorry that I have not put forward many valuable proposals. In the frontier regions, there is the music of "Bronze Hooves". I have the honor of attending the banquet and listening to the songs of victory with respect. On this occasion, let me propose a toast first!

DU HUANGSHANG:

You are my guest here. Fill in the cups, attendant!

(*Holds the wine cup*)

(*To the tune of* **Zhumating**)

In the peaceful military camp,

The tent is magnificently decorated.

It is the season when chinaberry flowers fall,

The bamboos grow up

And the daylilies are the most luxuriant.

Fish play among the water lotuses,

While orioles peep at the red berries in the trees.

Mellow wine is drunk,

While songs are chanted loud and clear.

We are living an idle life like Prince Cao Zhi,

With green moss gathering around our camp.

LI YI (*To the previous tune*):

When the weapons are laid aside,

We view flowers and grass in the daytime.

The breeze arises,

The sunflowers sprout

And the rainy spell is over.

The mists and clouds are merged in the sky,

Enshrouding the verdant peaks.

The snow-mountains are high and steep;

The snow-mountains are high and steep.

The luxuriant woods on the peaks

Are dimly discernable in the distance.

DU HUANGSHANG:

Mr. Li, I am growing old now, but am still contributing my share to the country. Sooner or later I shall make retirement and return to the south, while you ought to remain in the northern frontier. Let's drink a few cups at this gathering!

(*Drinks the wine*)

(*To the previous tune*)

In intoxication,

I am proud that my feats have excelled the ancient generals.

The red flowers are in full bloom,

The green grass overgrows

And the bright foliage shines in the sun.

Experiencing the coolness on the bamboo mat,

I appreciate the picturesque landscape.

Holding the wine cup, I talk in a lofty strain;

Holding the wine cup, I talk in a lofty strain.

It would be amusing to ask where the war hero is,

For he is reading books at leisure by the window!

LI YI:

You have brought peace to the northern frontier and invited us to the music, but after the grand banquet, you say that you will return to the capital. I am not as talented as you, but I am willing to inherit your ambition and strive to make new achievements. Today,

(*To the previous tune*)

When horses are grazed by the Golden River,

Their neighs are heard in the deep summer mansion.

Fortunately, with round feather fans

Spreading heat-relieving fragrance,

Echoes the music of "Clear Waters" and "Auspicious Clouds".

When singing and dancing are over, the mansion will be deserted,

For the swallows to make nests on the beams.

Time is wasted in the song and dance;

Time is wasted in the song and dance.

But with dancing girls serving in the camp,

I feel happy and contented.

(*Enter the post station chief*)

POST STATION CHIEF:

"*The moonlight links the Great Wall with the frontier,*
Where barbarian waters flow into the Hans' area."

Sir, here comes the imperial envoy!

DU HUANGSHANG:

Get the incense-burner table ready to greet the imperial decree!

VOICE WITHIN:

Here is His Majesty's decree. Fall on your knees and listen the decree: "When I compose this decree, I have long missed my worthy subjects, both valiant officers and intelligent officials. Prime Minister Du Huangshang, Duke of Fen, bears the appearance of an immortal and masters the military tactics and strategies. I have been converted to follow the Taoist teaching of Huang Shi and have subdued the tribes of Wuzhu. When I look west, I think of Du Huangshang who has served at the frontiers for a long time. So I give consent for him to be fetched in a special wagon. The military consultant, Li Yi, is to return to the court at the same time and take charge of decree-writing. The military affairs in the frontier are committed to Left General Hao Pin, and Right General Yan Chao is to be his assistant. Once you receive this decree, you should start the journey to come back as soon as possible to fill the vacancy of the official postition." Now look towards the palace and express your gratitude to His Majesty!

(*All shout "Long live the Emperor!"*)

DU HUANGSHANG:

Invite the court courier to have a rest in the Huanghua courier house. I will start soon after I give some instructions to my men. Mr. Li, Shuofang is of military importance and used to be harassed by Tubo and Huihu tribes. The late emperor appointed me as Prime Minister to be stationed in the frontier, and appointed Your Honor as Grand Academician to serve as the military consultant in Shuofang. On hearing the news, the tribes realized the seriousness of the situation and dared not to make harassment at the borders anymore. I am afraid that when both of us leave our positions, they will consider harassing this area again. The two generals, Hao Pin and Yan Chao, are audacious, but not strategic enough, so I suggest that you stay for half a month more after I leave tonight. You will give advice to the two generals about the management of the frontier affairs. I shall dispatch my men to pick you up when I reach the Great Wall. What do you think?

LI YI:

I will surely obey your order!

DU HUANGSHANG:

Attendant, invite generals Hao and Yan here!

(*Enter generals Hao Pin and Yan Chao*)

HAO PIN, YAN CHAO:

"*Weathered by wind and dust in the frontier land,*
We are full of heroic spirits that go with rewards.

With jade-decorated swords in hand,

What is the use of broad swords?"

We greet you with respect!

DU HUANGSHANG:

Please rise to your feet! General Hao built a fortress in Linjing so that the enemy from the west dare not come near. The Tubo King made a golden figure the same size of General Hao as a reward to whoever kills the general. Your name is also used to stop the babies from crying. General Yan kept guard of the Shazhou fortress. When you were besieged by the enemy and our rescue forces could not reach you, not a single soldier gave up during these ten years. Now you are required by the court to stay, so you are the real defenders. I will return to the south to-night and Military Consultant Li will stay here for half a month before he leaves. I will send for him when I reach the Great Wall. The Shuofang area is committed to you!

HAO PIN, YAN CHAO:

Please don't worry! We guarantee that the enemy will not be able to cross the border and drive south!

DU HUANGSHANG:

You are heroic and audacious enough to wipe out the enemy.

(*To the tune of* **Douheima**)

(*To General Hao*)

You suppress the enemy in the Linjing county

And breed steeds to be used in battles.

Your name is awesome enough to stop babies' cry

And you are worth the gold of your size.

(*To General Yan*)

You guarded the Shazhou area,

Slaughtering the enemy

With no reinforcements available

In the ten years' fierce battle under siege.

DU HUANGSHANG, HAO PIN, YAN CHAO:

When the sharp-edged swords are drawn out,

The imposing momentum soars to the star.

Great ambitions are realized in the frontier

To make contributions to the country in the long run.

LI YI (*To the previous tune*):

Skilled in the military strategies,

We boast an awe-inspiring army.

We are bold and wise

In various defenses and attacks.

I will leave

While you will stay

When the singing and dancing

Come to an end.

DU HUANGSHANG, HAO PIN, YAN CHAO:

> When the sharp-edged swords are drawn out,
>
> The imposing momentum soars to the star.
>
> Great ambitions are realized in the frontier
>
> To make contributions to the country in the long run.

DU HUANGSHANG:

I am leaving. When I reach the Great Wall, I'll dispatch my men to pick up Military Consultant Li, and inform your family of your return. You two generals are not to go far away from here to see me off.

REPORT WITHIN:

The tribe chiefs in Shouxiang city are here to see you off.

DU HUANGSHANG:

Tell them that there is no need to see me off, and that their loyalty should be manifested in the devotion to the court with no act of offence or betrayal!

> (*Takes leave*)
>
> (*To the tune of* **Huichaohuan**)
>
> I'll return to the court,
>
> I'll return to the court
>
> From this wide-stretching desert.
>
> The Central Plains are prosperous
>
> With rich natural beauties.
>
> "The Frontier's Moonlight",
>
> "The Frontier's Moonlight",
>
> The farewell music is coming to my ears.
>
> You are seeing me off from the battlefield,
>
> While my hair has turned gray on my forehead,
>
> But there is no need for you to feel sad.
>
> Dressed in a silk robe that sets against my graying hair,
>
> I will return to the capital in the east.
>
> *Through the Yumen Pass under the bright moon,*
>
> *The Prime Minister is to go home soon.*
>
> *With a valiant army under his command,*
>
> *No barbarians will dare to invade our homeland.*

161

Scene Thirty-One
Conversion to Buddhism

(*Enter an old Buddhist master*)

OLD MASTER (*To the tune of* **Northen Dianjiangchun**):

> For the saintliness of Buddhism,

All creatures fall under the influence

Of the All-Powerful Tathagata Buddha.

In the shadow of the temple pillars

Appear all the Buddhas and Bodhisattvas.

The All-Powerful Buddha sheds brilliant light

Over the whole universe

And submits all the creatures.

The fallen petals in the Buddhist yard

Regain life in the warm breeze.

(*In the pattern of* **Changduanju**)

"*Anxiedaerma,*

Why do people become so wretched?

Doubuluobawo,

Why do people incite disharmony?

Xiduntageduo,

People should chant the Buddhist scripture.

Zayueeluda,

People should pay homage to Buddha earlier."

I am Sikong, a Buddhist monk from the Zhangjing Temple. I am now one hundred and eight years old. I did not fully understand the Buddhist scriptures until I became older. I practice Buddhism all day, so I am greatly illuminated. The immaterial tree in your mind may grow in the sky as you can see the reflection of the tree in the pond; the immaterial lotus in your heart may bloom in the fire as you can smell the fragrance of the lotus on the sea. You may talk about the ashes after the destruction at the end of a kalpa, but the Weaver Star is still hanging in the Milky Way; you may try to ascertain the fall of the stars at night, but the moon is always shedding its light over the dews. I have an old acquaintance by the name of Du Huangshang, who used to study and talk about Buddhism with me in this temple when he was a young scholar. Now he is stationed in the Shuofang area as Military Commander and Prime Minister in the rank of dukedom. His Majesty decrees him to return to the court and he will soon be here in the capital city. It is very likely that he will come here to pay homage to Buddha when he drops by this temple. This man not only holds the topmost official position with meritorious deeds as the ancient prime ministers Xiao He and Guan Zhong, but also cherishes high aspirations. When he comes here, I will illuminate him with a few Buddhist chants so that he will soon reap the fruits of Buddhist attainment and cut himself off from the material world. For a better afterlife, he should be converted to Buddhism. I'll call my disciples Faxiang and Fayun to wait at the gate.

(*Enter Faxiang and Fayun*)

FAXIANG, FAYUN:

"*While vulgar people are rejected at the Buddhist door,*

When are we disciples permitted to present flowers?"

We make reverence to you, Master!

OLD MASTER:

Where did you come back, Faxiang and Fayun?

FAXIANG, FAYUN:

We are not called Faxiang and Fayun, but called Sikong.

OLD MASTER:

I am your master Sikong, meaning "Four Sunyata, Four Vanities, Four Voids, or Four Emptiness." How come you have the same name?

FAXIANG:

I am afraid that our Sikong is different from yours.

OLD MASTER:

In what way are they different?

FAXIANG:

When I went out for amusement after I finished sitting in meditation today, I saw monks from the Shaolin Temple practicing martial arts. As I was hot and thirsty, I asked an alchemist for some silver to have some drinks at an inn. When the waiter brought the wine, I drained a kettle at one gulp. He laughed to see that I could drink so much wine. He asked whether I could chant the Buddhist hymns. When he asked me to compose a hymn rhyming with "*vain*", I managed to compose half of a hymn with the four words of wine, woman, money and pride.

OLD MASTER:

What is your hymn?

FAXIANG:

> "*The wine is vain,*
> *For the waiter only serves the wine cups from day to day;*
> *The woman is vain,*
> *For the whorehouse runner only buys powder from day to day;*
> *The money is vain,*
> *For the alchemist only tempers copper from day to day;*
> *The pride is vain,*
> *For the boxer only makes a show from day to day.*"

Thus, men in the street call me Sikong, Four Vanities.

OLD MASTER:

How come Fayun is also called Sikong?

FAYUN:

Faxiang returned and told me about the first Four Vanities, but I think that none of the four types of people in his lines enjoys wine, woman, money or pride. What's the use of talking about them? He's left out that those who enjoys the four things are also vain. Therefore, I say that his lines are but the first half of the hymn.

OLD MASTER:

What is your half?

FAYUN:

> "*The wine is vain,*
> *For the drunkard only dwells in dreams from day to day;*
> *The woman is vain,*

For the palace courtesan only lives in tears from day to day;

The money is vain,

For Dong Zhuo's wealth could not be hoarded from day to day;

The pride is vain,

For the ambitious Sima Xiangru was laid in bed from day to day.

Thus, the disciples in the temple also call me Sikong, Four Vanities.

OLD MASTER:

In my opinion, wine, women, money and pride are not vain.

"The wine is not vain,

For the Buddha's teaching is the mellowest nectar;

The woman is not vain,

For the Buddha has the round face of a pretty woman;

The money is not vain,

For the Buddha lives in the Pearl Palace;

The pride is not vain,

For the Buddha is the great hero who conquers the demons."

FAYUN:

Then, why are you called Sikong, Four Vanities?

OLD MASTER:

I am not referring to wine, woman, money and pride, but referring to earth, fire, water and wind. They come from nowhere and go nowhere.

FAXIANG:

In that case, you are the Old Sikong, Fayun is the Big Sikong and I am the Small Sikong.

OLD MASTER:

Fayun, go and boil the tea! Faxiang, wait at the gate! Prime Minister Du Huangshang is likely to drop by on his way back to the capital.

(*Exit Fayun*)

(*Faxiang waits at the gate*)

(*Enter Du Huangshang, followed by attendants*)

DU HUANGSHANG (*To the tune of* **Lülüjin**):

Over the road where the sands whistle,

The flying fire-wheel of the sun

Scorches the way of my journey.

Where are the cool clouds arising,

Amid winds blowing across the earth?

I remember having taken a rest in the temple,

And wonder when I can enjoy a life of ease.

Attendants, I'll visit Master Sikong in this temple.

FAXIANG (*Reports*):

Prime Minister Du is at the gate!

DU HUANGSHANG (*Greets Old Master*):

"I still remember the day of my departure from you

And your seeing me off all the way.

For what have I been kept busy till my hair turns grey?

I ask myself when I return in triumph."

OLD MASTER:

What's the use of asking yourself, Your Excellency? I have a similar question to ask myself.

DU HUANGSHANG:

At over a hundred years of age, you have reached the highest stage of Buddhist practice. So what do you have to ask? As I am only sixty, how shall I practice Buddhism to reach the age of a hundred?

OLD MASTER:

I have been ignorant in these hundred years.

DU HUANGSHANG:

Please tell me in detail!

OLD MASTER:

When I intended to devote my body to Buddhism, my parents did not agree. They gave my body love and care by providing me with dwellings, clothes, food, bedding, medicine, horses, wagons and servants, kept me healthy and contented all the time. Instead of being grateful, my body bore grudges against them and deteriorated according to the laws of impermanence of life. Moreover, my body could not remain permanently strong, and would not benefit my eternal self either. The insatiable desires were hateful as thieves and ugly as poisoned sores. Except for excretory functions which are normal, my body was fragile as the foams in water and filthy for the parasites. It was but a terrible nuance, kept together by veins, blood, skin and bones. If it was observed in this way, it was abhorrence indeed. Constrained by the worldly rituals, sexual intercourse was dirty and sanguinary but was considered love. With the passage of time, I was like fish living in decreasing waters — what pleasure was there? I strove hard as if in imminent danger. As I studied the sutras and abided by the disciplines, I have lived more than a hundred years. I have resisted multitudes of nameless worries, and am now devoid of all the nameless worries. What's more, there is a change in every ten years of human life. Let me describe the life process from the age of ten to the age of one hundred!

(*To the tune of* **Shuahai'er**)

At the age of ten,

Children have pretty countenance

And play games all day long.

At the age of twenty,

People ride splendid wagons driven by stalwart steeds

And make lofty and refined speeches.

At the age of thirty,

People cherish noble ambitions

And devote themselves to fame and name.

At the age of forty,

People hold high official posts

165

The Purple Flute

And serve at the court in all splendour.

(*To the tune of* **Wusha**)

At the age of fifty,

People enjoy prestige

And live a life full of singing and dancing.

At the age of sixty,

People enjoy a life of affluence and comfort.

At the age of seventy,

People have no more pleasure

And seldom look into the mirror.

At the age of eighty,

People lose their wits and memory

And store their wagons in the garage.

(*To the tune of* **Sisha**)

At the age of ninety,

People do not have many days in store.

What is left of the body and mind?

They speak wrong words

And harbor their fear in heart.

They shed tears for the bygone days

But do not recognize their grandchildren.

At the age of one hundred,

People lose interest in anything,

With their eyes smeared and blurred

And their mouths dripping saliva.

DU HUANGSHANG:

When life comes to this stage, it is useless to talk about the rewards and punishments by Heaven! If the saints cannot escape life and death, how can I hope to live longer? What happened in the past is but a transient dream!

(*To the tune of* **Sansha**)

When will their vitality be lost?

The old tree will grow decayed,

Ready to leave the earthly world.

Why do birds singing in the trees move from place to place?

Autumn cicadas chirping in the temple will increase my sadness.

Overwhelmed with the sad sentiments,

The blooming cycas flowers will wither

And the arjaka leaves will fall.

OLD MASTER:

Why do you worry about the arjaka trees?

DU HUANGSHANG:

In my opinion, there are multiple sufferings brought about by the transmigration of life. Today

I will take off a jade belt and make confessions to Buddha with a bunch of precious incense. Tomorrow I will write an application of resignation and go to practice Buddhism in the mountains. I am afraid that it is already too late to solve this matter of life and death.

OLD MASTER:

Everyone has the Buddhist nature, so why do you say "too late"? You may walk to the Buddhist hall as well.

(*Walks*)

Now make your confessions, please!

DU HUANGSHANG:

Please ask one of your disciples to take the trouble to invite the Bodhisattvas to listen to my confession!

(*Tells Faxiang to invite the Bodhisattvas*)

On the fifth day of the sixth month in the first year of the Taihe reign in the Tang Dynasty, Duke of Fen and Prime Minister Du Huangshang piously offers a jade belt and precious incense and wishes to be converted to Buddhism, honoring all the Bodhisattvas, arhats, four grades of saintship and sanctity, Shakyamuni, and eight divisions of gods and dragons. I have been the prime minister, patrolling in the frontier, but I consider that there are multiple sufferings brought about by the transmigration of life and death. Therefore, I would like to extend my wish to the Bodhisattvas that I am willing to abandon all the worries and begin to practice Buddhism. As a newly-converted Buddhist still tormented by various disturbances, I prey to the Bodhisattvas in the east and in the west, in the north and in the south, to guard and protect me so that I will grasp the essence of Buddhism. I hope that when the end of my days comes, I will be in a happy state and leave in auspiciousness for the pure land in the west. Now I pay my utmost homage to Buddha and make my sincerest prayer!

(*Finishes the rite*)

FAXIANG:

Please take a vegetable meal in the Bamboo Hall!

DU HUANGSHANG:

There is no need for that. I will come and stay here after I make my resignation. And I am grateful to you for salvaging the rest of my life, Master!

(*To the tune of **Ersha***)

Time passes but I have not realized the sufferings

Of sleeping late and getting up early to fulfill the official duty,

But I'll get rid of human bondage and devote myself to Buddha.

As fragile as grass in the vain shape of a prime minister,

I will finally enter the Buddhist realm after death.

The precious incense is fragrant in the hot sunshine;

What people do is just like having a short dream,

Seeking Buddha's shelter like frightened doves.

I must take leave now, Master. I beg you to enlighten me from now on!

FAXIANG:

Please don't cheat the Bodhisattvas, Your Excellency!

DU HUANGSHANG (*To the tune of **Shawei***):

> I feel sad to live to an advanced age in vain,
>
> So why should I be afraid of falling sick from strange diseases?
>
> I've made the oath to the Bodhisattvas over the incense.

Master,

> My wish to convert myself to Buddhism comes too late.
>
> *I return to the south in gray hairs,*
>
> *For I keep the Lotus Pond of the temple in mind.*
>
> *I used to be occupied with court affairs,*
>
> *But from now on I'll never leave the master behind.*

Scene Thirty-Two
Border Thoughts

(*Enter Li Yi*)

LI YI:

> *"The Grand Academician at the court*
>
> *Makes military exploit in the front.*
>
> *Leaving wife and capital city behind,*
>
> *I live a rough life in the frontier fort.*
>
> *Keeping my separated wife in mind,*
>
> *I go on expedition in the west.*
>
> *While warriors look in the direction of the homeland,*
>
> *Their wives shed tears that wet the dresses."*

When Prime Minister Du left, he said that he would send for me as soon as he reached the Great Wall. But it has been half a month with no one to pick me up. I wonder whether my wife Xiaoyu is going on well at home. Tonight the crescent moon shines over the tent when the clouds are dispersed. Wind from the snow-topped mountains cools the heat. I gaze at the Milky Way, imagining the bridge that brings the Cowboy and the Weaver Girl together. It is true indeed,

> *"The fleabanes that drift all the time*
>
> *Do not return when the melons ripe.*
>
> *While I am weathering cold and heat,*
>
> *My wife is declining in her beauty.*
>
> *In longing for my dear wife,*
>
> *I look far beyond the Yumen Pass.*
>
> *After I parted with my dear wife,*
>
> *I suffer increasing lovesickness."*

My wife, I know that you are also longing for me.

(*To the tune of **Luojiangyuan***)

When the stars move in their orbits,

The night watch breaks the silence

In the clear sky.

The Milky Way looks like the white silk,

While the moon shines over the general's camp

And illuminates the fairyland.

With the Red Mansion in my mind,

In face of the rolling mountains barely visible in the distance,

I watch the wild geese in their southward flight.

My wife, it is the hottest season in the Central Plains, and yet it is still cool here in early summer. In this season,

(*To the tune of **Xiangbianman***)

You sleep in a pretty posture on the fragrant bed,

Waving a fan after bath

And wearing a transparent dress over your fair skin.

Your beautiful hair is loosely woven in a bun,

On which a hairpin is stuck askew.

Peeping at the moon,

You show signs of bitterness.

Gazing in the direction of the borders,

You lean against the railings.

Xiaoyu, when you saw me off at the Baling Bridge, you shed tears on my war robes, leaving stains still visible now. Caressing the tear stains, I recollect the parting scene at the red pavilion.

(*To the tune of **Jinguyuan***)

Grasping my sleeves, you sang a song of separation;

Holding my horsewhip, you blamed me for heartlessness.

In the ancient fortress dotted with flowers by the green peaks,

I recall your parting tears when you plucked a flower

And snapped a farewell willow-twig.

How difficult it was to say good-bye at that time!

(*To the tune of **Jiaqingzi***)

You saw off your man in tears

With catkins floating about and disturbing the mind,

Not to be pacified by tying golden threads to the flowers.

The separation was really painful,

But departure had to be made

And the journey had to be hastened.

Though I thought of quitting the post,

(*To the tune of **Yaobian***)

169

The Purple Flute

I was decreed to obey this military order,

Which is harsh and permits no delay.

I was sad that her hairpin fell off

And reminded her to watch her steps on the petal-covered path

When I saw that she felt bitter and hated to be left alone.

Xiaoyu, since we parted at the red pavilion, the pleasures between us have been lost!

(*To the tune of* **Pinling**)

I recall her rubbing the skirt ribbon

And walking round the stairs,

With her eyebrows contracted in woe

And her eyes gazing after the flapping flags.

Her eyes full of tears

That dropped in strings

On tear-stained dress,

She adjusted the zither, but was afraid to listen.

As to the wind and the moon afar,

The full moon might bring about high wind.

I can remember how we enjoyed ourselves strolling in Prince Huo's Ever-Spring Garden.

(*To the tune of* **Biyefa**)

We were pleased to appreciate the flowers

And stopped occasionally on the lawn.

The lute was played in the warm spring breeze,

The lute was played in the warm spring breeze,

In tunes about the cold clouds mirrored on the autumn pond.

When lotus flowers were in full bloom

And bamboos were green and clear,

Distant green mountains were enshrouded in the mist,

Distant green mountains were enshrouded in the mist.

Why were the orioles separated in the spring?

They were chirping the song of separation.

(*To the tune of* **Yujiaozhi**)

With fading powder and fragrance,

The beauty was left at the pavilion of departure.

We nestled together with sleeves wavering in the wind,

When the blooming season was leaving with the spring.

We hugged like the twining hoisting-tackle of the well,

And kept close as the toad biting at the lock of the burner.

We were full of tender affection to each other,

Yet I had to part with her for rank and honor,

Yet I had to part with her for rank and honor.

I am so lovesick now!

(*To the tune of* **Sanfanliuyaoling**)

She may keep awake longing for her man in the frontier,

While I am like Sima Xiangru dreaming of Zhuo Wenjun.

In her chamber by the Yuniang Lake,

She may shed tears by the silver screen;

In the frontier near the Guanglu fortress,

I wear the warrior's robe holding the sword,

Seeing glowworms fly around the eaves

And the beacons' fires announcing safety.

I did not cry at departure, but shed tears in loneliness on the borders. It is true indeed,

"I used to think that it was pleasant to join the army

But not until today do I know the hardship for a traveler."

(*To the tune of* **Jiang'ershui**)

My tears are drained in meditation in the remote land,

While my eyebrows are knit in sadness in the green grassland.

My dress still bears the fragrance at home

And I act in the manners of a counselor like Xun Yu.

I recall the past in the moon shadow,

Fearing that the insects' chirp will stop at moonset.

As the long distance is difficult to transcend,

I feel bored all day afraid of hearing the flute music,

For boudoir poems cannot be composed in the frontier.

I suppose that I can soon hand over military duties and take leave.

(*To the tune of* **Yicuozhao**)

Having made contributions and won honors,

I am eager to return from the frontier.

Sima Xiangru was good at wielding the sword and the pen,

Feigning to be ill to shun his official post.

After I return from the hard journey,

I will sip the wine in the night rain till dawn.

Xiaoyu, at that time,

We will face the stars and unfasten the waistband,

Indulged in our love with double affection.

(*Enter the messenger*)

MESSENGER (*To the tune of* **Liuyaoling**):

Peace reigns in the frontier,

Peace reigns in the frontier,

Where veteran soldiers drink to intoxication.

The distinguished Prime Minister has crossed the Great Wall

And dispatched us to pick up the military consultant

To return to the court by day and night.

Your Excellency, we have escorted Prime Minister Du to the Great Wall and come back to pick you up.

LI YI:

Oh, you've come to pick me up at last! I have handed the documents to General Hao and General Yan. Now I will bid farewell to them and start on my journey tonight.

(*Enter generals Hao Pin and Yan Chao*)

HAO PIN, YAN CHAO:

"The sad clouds carry the frontier thoughts for home;

The homesick heart takes wings with the moon.

It has always been the case,

Let alone when the consultant is to go back soon."

We bow to you with respect! When we heard shouts from the beacon tower, we knew that Prime Minster Du had dispatched his men to escort you back to the south. We have come to inquire about the date of your departure, and hope that you can stay for several days more.

LI YI:

Both of you are very brave generals. You have awe-inspiring valiance and hardship-weathering royalty. You will be able to assist each other and support each other. The military affairs in the area of Shuofang, a spot of strategic importance, are entrusted to you. As it is very hot now, I'll take leave and set out by night. I have two precious swords for you as souvenirs.

(*Enter Qing'er with the swords*)

QING'ER:

"The swords shimmer with blue gleams

In the military camp at the frontier."

(*Li Yi presents the swords*)

LI YI (*To the tune of **Shanhuazi***):

The swords are etched with lotus patterns,

Decorated with seven stars.

Their cutting edge induces a chilly feeling,

With glossy silk tassels hanging on their handles.

LI YI, QING'ER:

With golden gleams outshining the bright moon,

The swords are gifts from an old friend with goodwill.

When you command the army and quell the riots,

Your names will be passed down the generations.

HAO PIN, YAN CHAO (*To the previous tune*):

You are an Academician well-versed in essays,

Always in company of the heroes and the elite.

As we are in the low military rank,

How can we make the precious swords shine?

LI YI, QING'ER:

With golden gleams outshining the bright moon,

The swords are gifts from an old friend with goodwill.

When you command the army and quell the riots,

Your names will be passed down the generations.

LI YI:

Now I'll be on my way.

HAO PIN, YAN CHAO:

Let's escort you out of the pass!

 (*Walk*)

 (*To the tune of* **Hongxiuxie**)

 The travelers and wagons are like meteors;

 The travelers and wagons are like meteors.

 The journey back home is made in the moonlight;

 The journey back home is made in the moonlight.

 The galloping horses

 Will startle the sleeping crows,

 Which peep at the black shadows

 And listen to the sound of the wheels.

 You serve as a military consultant

 As well as a civil official at court.

 (*Bow and bid farewell*)

 (*To the tune of* **Coda**)

 I present the swords to my bosom friends,

 Not knowing whether I shall meet them again.

When you meet Prime Minister Du, please tell him that

 We will guard the frontier and subdue the enemy.

 The royal envoy leaves for south in grace,

 Riding past the mountains topped with snow.

 He commits to the moon his departing woe,

 And gives his friends the precious swords in case.

Scene Thirty-Three
Coming Out of Seclusion

 (*Enter Shang Zipi*)

SHANG ZIPI (*To the tune of* **Juhuaxin**):

 Auspicious haze from Kunlun Mountains permeates the land,

 Where twelve magnificent palaces mirror the capital town.

 Long and sharp swords are produced in the western area,

 Where letters are carried by wild geese to the Central Plains.

 "*When trees and leaves wilt in the west wind,*

 The immortal palace manifests its full splendor.

 At the windows I gaze at the stars setting to the sea

 And the rain showering over the river source."

I'm Shang Zipi. My family name was Molu, and my first name was Zanxinya. I was a native of the Yangtong Kingdom, and my ancestors were prime ministers of the Tubo tribes. During the reign of late king, I was granted an audience together with my father Shang Jiezan at the Tang court by Emperor Xianzong, who appreciated my talents and enrolled me into the Imperial Academy to read the classical books and learn the ceremonial dances. At that time, I got to know Li Yi from Longxi and styled Junyu, Shi Xiong from Xuzhou and styled Ziying, as well as Hua Qing from Duling and styled Jingding. The three of them are full of soaring ambitions and substantial literary talents. We became bosom friends although we were together only for a short period of time. We first met in the hostel in spring and bid farewell at the city gate. We could not help weeping and could not refrain ourselves when Junyu asked me when we would meet again. I told him I would not intend to pursue the official career any more, but rather reside in the Kunlun Mountains reading Taoist canons, playing the music, worshipping the Sun God in the east, and begging for the elixir of life from Queen Mother in the west. If I should get entangled in worldly affairs from which I can't extricate myself, or get into a serious strife, I would resign myself. If decrees should arrive from the Central Plains for me to go to the court in your country, I would take this opportunity to have a chat with you again. If I should fail to meet you again, I would have someone look for your whereabouts, from Mount Zhongnan to the Weihe River. It is said that disorders often arise in the Central Plains and traffic was cut off in the Hetao and Longyou area. Lunkongre of our kingdom controls a powerful army, while the king is incompetent and tyrannical in these years. Now I am past forty. Although I am not engaged in learning for an official career, I cannot help making some lamentations! Looking at my graying hair, I wonder how Mr. Li is going on. It is true indeed:

> *"We parted as green grass*
> *And lament as withered flowers.*
> *When I ask my brothers in the Central Plains,*
> *How many of them are alive and kicking?"*

I cannot refrain from sighing to myself.

> (*To the tune of* **Jinluosuo**)
> I open the Buddhist scriptures and the River Diagram
> In the stone house near the Mysterious Garden.
> I recall the spring outings in the fields near Chang'an,
> Drinking wine with my friends
> Till we were drunk.
> In the warm chamber with embroidered curtains and red stove,
> We were so excited that we crushed the silver drum
> And broke the jade spittoon in indignation.

I was enjoying the happy get-together with Li Yi, Hua Qing and Shi Xiong, when the Tang emperor hastened me to visit the Imperial Academy. At that time, the old scholar Han Yu was the instructor. All the scholars were supposed to recite his writings, but I consider his works dull and boring after I read a few of his essays.

> I lived a leisurely life,
> Studying like a bookworm in firefly gleams

And reading a bed of books each year.

Since we four parted at the Yanqiu Gate, we have had no contact for ten years because the traffic was cut off in the Hetao and Longyou area and the city of Songpan was besieged. Although I came from the Tubo tribes, my heart runs along the Han road.

> With correspondence among friends cut off,
>
> I have vague dreams as a Taoist master,
>
> But still remember the way to the capital city.

(*Enter the attendant boy reporting*)

ATTENDANT BOY:

> *"In the splendid Queen Mother Temple,*
>
> *We ride the bamboo-stick to become immortals.*
>
> *Dongfang Shuo stained his dress in the Purple Mud Sea,*
>
> *And so the one who stole the peach must have been a child."*

Master, I don't know where the Tubo King has been hunting. There is much noise and it is said that he comes here to visit you.

SHANG ZIPI (*Laughs*):

I suppose he is led here by Shang Qixin, the head of the secretariat from my family, to coerce me back to assume an official post.

> *"How can I be driven by hunger and cold?*
>
> *It's only funny for him to force me with power and wealth."*

But I have to open the gate and welcome them.

(*Enter the Tubo King, followed by Shang Qixin*)

SHANG QIXIN (*To the tune of* **Shuangtianxiaojiao**):

> When the clouds are golden and the dewdrops are blue,
>
> The leopard hides in the den to keep away from the fog.
>
> The immortal Queen Mother wears hair ornaments;
>
> The reclusive scholar is greeted by noble attendants.

(*The Tubo King and Shang Zipi greet each other, making long bows*)

TUBO KING (*Asks in anger*):

You were born and grew up in the state of Yangtong bordering Tubo, and studied in the Central Plains, yet now you do not pay homage to your king. Where do you find your reason in the scripture?

SHANG ZIPI (*Smiles*):

> *"In the Guye Mountains resided a pure and noble immortal;*
>
> *The Milky Way was visited by a man from the earth.*
>
> *India's Sakyamuni became Buddha in his old age;*
>
> *Prince Moonlight followed Buddha from his childhood."*

Why have you come to visit me? I call this your philosophy of life for the moment. You've come to visit a reclusive scholar who does not wish to be an official and would like to close the door and never go out of the wall, but does not mind provoking the king. If you require courtly formalities, what is the necessity of seeking them from a reclusive scholar?

TUBO KING (*Laughs and apologizes*):

Just now I was trying to sound out your true intention, and you really deserve your reputation. Today I've come as your guest and implore you to tell me how to stabilize our state.

(*Bows*)

"*You've long enjoyed a high reputation,*

SHANG ZIPI:

But I keep to the mountains for convalescence.

TUBO KING:

Health and young appearance should be well preserved.

SHANG ZIPI:

What if I'm idle and indolent in nature?"

What do you have to ask about in my humble house on your hunting chase?

TUBO KING:

Please sit down and listen to me! My ancestors,

(*To the tune of* **Dashengle**)

King Nongzan, who was heroic and generous,

And King Lisuo, who was stout from childhood,

Presented gold and jade to marry the Tang princesses.

Today's Tubo King

Is their descendent.

Now the Tang court looks down upon us and is more intimate with the Huihe nation. So I intend to lunch an attack on the Tang territory.

I am the leader of a big and powerful nation,

Above par with the smaller ones of Wuhe and Jitian.

What I'm concerned about now is that the important forts of Tang to be attacked are no more than the areas of Shuofang, Longxi and Songzhou. I've ordered Lunkongre's army to attack and make a breakthrough into Songzhou and I suppose there won't be any problem with that. As to Longxi, I hear that there is an audacious general Shi, who is hard to conquer. As to Shuofang, the prime minister and the consultant who used to be stationed there have been summoned back. I hear that there is left on the assistant generals Hao Pin and Yan Chao, who used to build the defense in the Linjing area and keep the guard of the Shazhou city respectively. I fought battles with them in the past. So it's difficult to attack Shuofang with these two men guarding there. I want to march toward Longxi and wonder what the will of Heaven is.

As I will go on a southward raid,

I'd like to make a divination through the cloudscape

To know about the prospect.

SHANG ZIPI:

Let me make the divination outside!

(*Aside*)

Dear me! I'm glad that Li Junyu has returned and Shuofang is still kept in the guard. But I'm not sure whether Hua Qing in Songzhou is able to withstand Lunkongre's attack. Shi Xiong will have a hard job if the Tubo King marches to Longxi.

(*Sings in a low voice*)

(*To the previous tune*)

His attack against Longxi is reckless

Because the army is not strong enough,

But to the Tubo King I must offer indirect and tactful advice.

(*Turns round and sings*)

According to the cloud and wind,

There will be loss and gain.

Your Highness, to the south of the Mao star and the Bi star, in the areas between Qing and Long, purple and auspicious clouds float in the sky; while to the north of the Mao star and the Bi star, west to the areas of He and Huang, there are dark masses of clouds. Besides, the sun's aureole is in the east in recent days, which signifies the victory of the eastern army; the star flags fall in the north, which signifies the defeat of the western army. The momentum in the east is powerful and overwhelming, while the momentum in the west is like the swirling leaves, the hanging clothes or a carriage cover. Our mounted troops are deployed, but the moon aureole does not signify victory. Our noble steeds neigh, but the North Star signifies they will be harmed. So I advise you to forge a marriage with Tang because it's hard to win if you attack Longxi.

You'd better welcome the Tang Princess in Fengchi and Bohai,

Instead of dressing the peaceful messenger general in war array.

TUBO KING:

If I fail to make a marriage with Tang, I will launch an attack.

SHANG ZIPI:

It's not necessary.

You may as well take military actions against the Huihe nation

So as to avoid the momentum of the Central Plains

And handle the frontier affairs.

TUBO KING:

I accept your advice. What about your coming along with me?

SHANG ZIPI:

I haven't got married or taken up an official position, and am turning fifty. I reside in the Kunlun Mountains and when I look far into the distance, I see hustle and bustle everywhere in the earthly world. Indolent and unrestrained by nature, I go against the worldly ways of life. Besides, I lived in the Central Plains of the Tang Dynasty when I was very young, so I admire the people's way of life there. I should evade anything that would bring aspersion by not being entangled in the important and confidential affairs. So I dare not obey your order.

TUBO KING:

How can there be aspersion between gentlemen? When the war is over and achievement is made, you can do whatever you want.

SHANG ZIPI:

Shall I make a divination outside by judging from the wind?

(*Aside*)

I have nothing to seek after in this world, but I'm concerned that the fate of the Tubo nation is declining as his top-rank general Lunkongre harbors evil intentions. I may as well take this opportunity to get away. Besides, it's likely that I can get back to the Tang court and meet Li Yi, Shi Xiong and Hua Qing.

(*Turns around*)

According to prophecy by the wind, we use the word "date" instead of day. The date is the guest star while the hour is the host star. Today the wind comes from the southeast while I stay in the west. The date today is *geng-xu* and the hour now is from five to seven in the afternoon, nearing dusk. Both the date and the hour are positive. As "*geng*" indicates "righteousness" and "*xu*" indicates "impartiality", I am able to go with you but won't accept your conferment of the title. When the job is done, please allow me to go wherever I want!

TUBO KING:

That's fine! That's fine! Your nephew, Shang Qixin, head of the secretariat, is to stay and keep you company. You can take your time and join me, while I go back hunting at night.

(*Bids farewell*)

"The Shaowei star joins the invasion of the Beiluo star

When the Taibai star launches the western army.

If you had recognized the auspicious air moving to the east,

You would be a cloud leaving the mountains in vain."

(*Exit*)

(*Shang Qixin and Shang Zipi stay on the stage*)

SHANG QIXIN:

It's Tubo King's goodwill to assign you the position of grand prime minister or military governor. Why should you reject his offer now that you agree to follow him? Besides, all our family members are Tubo officials, and the Tubo nation is strong and powerful now, so we should make contributions to its prosperity.

(*To the tune of **Yicuozhao***)

The Tubo ancestors Tang and Kun

Built the ancient tribe called the Powerful Hu.

There are prime minister and vice prime minister,

Plus grand prime minister.

Wearing gold and gems,

The high officials smear silver over their arms.

The high and mighty are painted with tiger designs,

While the cowards have fox-tails attached at their back.

Military viceroys are needed for the camps

And governors are needed for the forts of importance

So that the Tang's territory

Can be seized with ease.

SHANG ZIPI:

It's not easy at all! If we forge a marriage alliance with Tang, we can suppress other nations. I may as well get on my way now since I've agreed to follow the King.

SHANG QIXIN:

The King has left carriage and horses here.

SHANG ZIPI:

I have nothing but several Taoist books and a zither in my thatched cottage. Just put them in my luggage, attendant boy. It's a pity that I can no longer look back to the Kunlun Mountains with its five cities and twelve bowers. I will bring with me the gilded earthen statuette of Queen Mother of the West. The Kunlun Mountains can only be visited in my dreams, but the Zhongnan Mountains is likely to be reached in person.

SHANG QIXIN:

You are mistaken, my uncle! You can still come to the Kunlun Mountains after you make achievements and retreat in seclusion. But how can you reach the Zhongnan Mountains in the capital city of Tang?

SHANG ZIPI:

My nephew, it's likely that I will have a chance to go to the Central Plains if a marriage tie is formed with Tang. Once a man enters the official career, he will be like a leaf blown about by the wind independent of his own will. Therefore, is there any certainty for me to become a recluse? After I leave the Kunlun Mountains, I'll live in woe and sorrow. When things are packed, I'll get on the horse and start on my way.

> (*Rides*)
>
> (*To the tune of* **Xiangliuniang**)
>
> I am fully aware,
>
> I am fully aware
>
> That engagement in military affairs for the king's prosperity
>
> Is not the intention of my inner mind.

SHANG QIXIN:

> Who is there in the west,
>
> Who is there in the west
>
> That keeps to the Kunlun Mountains
>
> And looks at the Menlu River.

SHANG ZIPI, SHANG QIXIN:

> The affair is handled with expedience,
>
> The affair is handled with expedience.
>
> The involvement in the worldly affairs
>
> Will finally be discarded.
>
> *The swords were shelved to get rusty,*
>
> *As the Hans sought peace with the Huns for a truce.*
>
> *Since he enjoys living in the mountains,*
>
> *Why should one try to persuade the recluse?*

179

The Purple Flute

Scene Thirty-Four
Reunion on the Double-Seventh Day

(*Enter Huo Xiaoyu*)

HUO XIAOYU (*To the tune of* **Queqiaoxian**):

> With Han tunes resounding amid the heavenly elms
>
> And moon laurels beside the Milky Way,
>
> The Gedao Star is amazed at the flute music.
>
> With her earrings swaying, the Weaver Girl drops spinning,
>
> Unable to sleep all the night.

(*In the pattern of* **Wuyangufeng**)

> "The man failed to return to Heyang in autumn
>
> And brought no news to Hanyin.
>
> In the moonlight silk cloth is woven
>
> On which there is the ripple pattern.
>
> When the fairy carriage is gone,
>
> The eyebrows of the wife contract in lovesickness.
>
> The clear dew falls on the silk garment
>
> And the autumn wind blows at the zither strings.
>
> As the better part of the night has passed,
>
> On whom will the remaining light shine?"

It has been several years since I bid farewell to Li Yi when he left for Shuofang as the military consultant. I used to long for him on the Double-Seventh Festival every year, and it is the festival again today. Several days ago Prime Minister Du returned to the court and sent a message that Li Yi will soon be home. How anxious I am when I wait for him!

(*To the tune of* **Putianle**)

> I expect the day of reunion in the crescent moonlight,
>
> Shaded by the flimsy clouds in the autumn.

The lovesickness grows every day,

> Tears are shed in lovesickness.

And tonight,

> With tears soaking my dress,
>
> I fail to sleep in the autumn wind and dew.
>
> After years of separation,
>
> The short reunion on the Double-Seventh
>
> Will be over when the day breaks in deep remorse.
>
> I'll send him words to hurry him back
>
> And do not want the magpies to fly away
>
> Which build the bridge with mud carried in mouths.

My man, if you don't come back tomorrow,

Tears will again soak the silk handkerchief,

While I sit by the empty weaving loom.

(*Enter Zheng Liuniang*)

ZHENG LIUNIANG:

"By the clear Milky Way

Laments the Weaver Girl Star to herself.

Without the painstaking Jingwei bird,

How could the Silver River be filled?"

Since my daughter Xiaoyu parted with Li Yi, she always feels sad on festivals. The Cowboy Star will reunite with the Weaver Girl Star tonight. She will surely stop weaving and sit silently in lovesickness. I have asked Yingtao and Wu'er to invite Bao Siniang and Du Qiuniang to the Red Mansion to thread the needles so as to while away the time with my daughter. I suppose they have arrived.

(*Greets Huo Xiaoyu*)

Xiaoyu, today is the Double-Seventh Festival. Prime Minister Du informed us that Li Yi will soon be home. I have invited Bao Siniang and Du Qiuniang to keep you company.

(*Enter Bao Siniang and Du Qiuniang*)

BAO SINIANG, DU QIUNIANG (*To the tune of* **Raochiyou**):

In early autumn,

The beloved is expected to come back.

Why are you lamenting all the year round?

(*Greet Zheng Liuniang and Huo Xiaoyu*)

"The Weaver Girl flies across the tent carrying a round fan,

To reach the star bridge formed by the magpies.

How can we turn endless departure in the human world

Into a heavenly reunion once a year?"

It has been a long time since we last visited you, and it is the Double-Seventh Festival again today.

ZHENG LIUNIANG:

Indeed. We invite you here to wait for the stars to meet.

BAO SINIANG:

When the Weaver Girl Star crosses the magpie bridge over the Milky Way, we can make wishes, but we can make no more than one wish, which should be kept in heart and not be spoken out within three years. Let's lay the incense table here in the courtyard! Liuniang shall be the first to make the wish.

ZHENG LIUNIANG (*To the tune of* **Zhuyunfei**):

The Weaver Girl in the remote Milky Way

Weaves the bright white silk away from the Central Plains.

She stops in anticipation for a letter

And puts away her make-up locket.

Well,

She caresses the golden hairpin in joy

And does the evening make-up in elegant manners.

With dimples on her rosy cheeks,

She is all charming smiles,

Unable to fall asleep tonight.

BAO SINIANG (*To the previous tune*):

When the fairy magpies began to sing,

The goddess Chang'e presented evening beauty.

When drum beat and wagon rumble came in the distance,

The Weaver Girl unfastened her belt and softened her heart.

Well,

Before she met the Cowboy in a languid manner,

She wore the pendant on her skirt with fragrance.

After their transient reunion,

They parted at the flowing Silver River

And had to wait another year before they meet again.

HUO XIAOYU (*Aside*):

The Cowboy Star and the Weaver Girl Star are just like Li Yi and me!

(*To the previous tune*)

Since the marriage and reunion were so happy,

Why did they stay awake over the night?

Her eyes looked back in tears,

When the Cowboy returned in a carriage.

Well,

With lingering thought in her mind,

The Weaver Girl Star falls low.

As she goes down the magpie bridge

And I am filled with increasing bitterness,

Where shall I rest my tender emotion?

DU QIUNIANG:

I remember that when I entered the palace at a young age, there was a Needle Threading Tower where I made my wish and was praised by my companions. Now that the prince has gone for seclusion, I am left behind in the Nunnery of the Queen Mother of the West.

(*To the previous tune*)

The Blue Bird messenger did not bring any message,

But we enjoyed a luxurious night.

We did not wash our faces

Or do any make-up.

Well,

When the emperor went into seclusion,

The court ladies out of favor bore grudges.

By the palace pond,

When we recalled the Palace of Eternal Youth by the lake,

We seemed to see fairy boys and girls singing at the banquet.

Now that we have made our wishes, let's go upstairs to thread the needle!

 (*Goes upstairs*)

 "With wishes to walk on the moon,

 We can hardly refrain from our emotion.

 Each draws a thread from the hank

 And put it through the needle."

BAO SINIANG:

Liuniang, the young princess should be blessed with all the good luck, so she should be the first to thread the needle and Liuniang is the next.

HUO XIAOYU:

Thank you!

 (*Threads the needle*)

 (*To the tune of* **Chanqiao'er**)

 There is needle-threading in every household tonight,

 With hearts tied to the beloved ones away from home.

 The round fans are sewn for conjugal happiness,

 With the tassels hanging like our longing thoughts.

ALL:

 In the flowery courtyard,

 The wish will come true

 And good luck is acquired

 Because parted couples are reunited!

ZHENG LIUNIANG:

Thank you for letting me thread the needle after Xiaoyu!

 (*Threads the needle*)

 (*To the previous tune*)

 When the Cowboy Star chases after the swallows flying west,

 The needle is hard to thread for the blowing wind and dim light.

My daughter, you do it for me.

HUO XIAOYU (*Threads the needle for Zheng Liuniang*):

 With shyness I reach out my fingers,

 Which are slim and lovely.

ALL:

 In the flowery courtyard,

 The wish will come true

 And good luck is acquired

 Because parted couples are reunited!

DU QIUNIANG:

Now it's Bao Siniang's turn.

BAO SINIANG:

 Thank you!

183

(To the previous tune)

In pale yellow silk in the autumn,

I go up the stairs in tenderness.

Young princess, please do it for me!

(Huo Xiaoyu threads the needle for Bao Siniang)

BAO SINIANG:

How nimble your fingers are!

You can compare with the ancient Dowager Empress Hu,

Who shot at the needle-eye with an arrow,

In terms of your nimble fingers.

ALL:

In the flowery courtyard,

The wish will come true

And good luck is acquired

Because parted couples are reunited!

BAO SINIANG:

Now it's Du Qiuniang's turn.

DU QIUNIANG:

From a palace maid then to a Taoist nun now, what good luck do I have to wish?

(To the previous tune)

I have sewn numerous dancing dresses with gold thread,

But I have no good luck to enjoy constant love.

Young princess, please do it for me!

(Huo Xiaoyu threads the needle for Du Qiuniang)

DU QIUNIANG:

How nimble your fingers are!

Like Xue Yingyun who could sew in the darkness,

Your nimbleness is a blessing to your husband.

ALL:

In the flowery courtyard,

The wish will come true

And good luck is acquired

Because parted couples are reunited!

(Enter a messenger)

MESSENGER:

"Today is the Double-Seventh Day,

When man and wife shall be reunited.

I am glad to be like the Blue Bird messenger

That brings the news to the lady."

Old madam, Master Li has arrived!

ZHENG LIUNIANG:

What a coincidence!

DU QIUNIANG:

I'm so glad to see today's reunion!

(Enter Li Yi)

LI YI (To the tune of **Lingboxianzi**):

When the Cowboy Star sheds its first light on Chang'an,

The starlight shines amid the splendid lanterns.

I am like the imperial envoy Zhang Qian

Returning after his term of service.

(They exchange greetings)

ZHENG LIUNIANG:

"The Departure Song is sung along the way,

LI YI:

The autumn moon shines over the bed curtain.

ZHENG LIUNIANG:

The sadness and bitterness of a traveler can be imagined,

LI YI:

Fortunately the appearance has not changed.

HUO XIAOYU:

With tears shed for the separation worlds apart,

LI YI:

The beauty in the boudoir is longed for in the frontier.

HUO XIAOYU:

The conjugal stars are reunited in the sky tonight,

LI YI:

Lest they face the Milky Way in unkempt appearance."

ZHENG LIUNIANG:

Du Qiuniang has never met Li Yi, and Bao Siniang is also here to greet you.

BAO SINIANG:

"The respectable court official returns to the capital.

DU QIUNIANG:

I have long heard of your reputation.

LI YI:

With songs and laughter Heaven and Earth hail,

BAO SINIANG, DU QIUNIANG, LI YI:

For the encounter of a fairy maid and a worldly man."

HUO XIAOYU:

Shilang, since you left, I've been suffering from lovesickness which grows all the more bitter on the festivals. I put your clothes and books in the sun on the Double-Seventh Day each year, and our reunion happens to fall on this very date this year. I remember that we made an oath toward the Cowboy and Weaver Girl stars by the Kunming Pond. Is it with the stars' help that we get together tonight?

(*To the tune of* **Zhuanlinying**)

When the trees brush the sky and stir the autumn breath,

My lovesickness is infinite when I look at the sky.

I weep by the gauzed window in the mist,

Tears moistening my dress when I sort out your robes.

I keep in mind our oath by the Kunming Pond

And look at the Weaver Girl Star against the railings.

In the glaring golden plate,

The spider weaves a web as an auspicious sign

Of the return of the long separated one.

LI YI:

My wife, I was in the north while you were in the south. Although we could not meet every day, we often saw each other in our dreams.

(*To the previous tune*)

I watch the Cowboy and Weaver Girl stars

And come back to you on their immortal canoe,

Lamenting over the sudden separation years ago

And seeing that everything goes unchanged.

In the bright candlelight,

The house is full of weeping beauties.

On this happy date,

Holding the needle and thread,

The long-separated people reunite like new friends.

ZHENG LIUNIANG (*To the tune of* **Changpai**):

By the silver screen,

By the silver screen,

In the magnificent courtyard and at the precious table,

We see the wagon dust and smell the fragrance in the distance.

You look like the fairy Cowboy in the west of the Milky Way!

The fairy man gets happily reunited,

With music resounding amid the bamboos.

BAO SINIANG, DU QIUNIANG:

From where has the sun returned,

Shining over the exquisite carved railings,

While the clouds are brightly colored?

Numerous wisps of silk are prepared

To embroider the mandarin ducks.

The round flower patterns are now woven at last,

Much better than when hastily done.

ALL (*To the tune of* **Duanpai**):

With their hearts fastened in a loop,

With their hearts fastened in a loop,

They are linked together as sealed swallow-tails,
Though the happy night is but transient.
She is nimble in her fingers,
But not nimble enough to tie her man's heart.
What is the intimate love between man and wife?
They get undressed against the silver lamp in smile,
Pushing aside the embroidered pillows
And lowering the silk bed-curtain.
(*To the tune of* **Coda**)
Holding the incense and the truelove knot,
They make love oath toward the sky.
From now on they will tie the five-colored threads
So as to be blessed every year.
For Double-Seventh every year they wait,
But they'll no longer be kept worlds apart.
Don't envy fairy lovers for their fate,
As there is more bliss for the human heart.

紫钗记
The Purple Hairpins

汪榕培、朱　源、张　玲 译

Translated by Wang Rongpei, Zhu Yuan & Zhang Ling

Table of Contents

192

Scene One
Prelude

(*Enter Narrator*)

NARRATOR (*To the tune of* **Xijiangyue**):

Swallows fly to and fro in the hall

While belles pencil their eyebrows by the sill.

With wonderful songs and dances that enchant us all,

I adapt a courtesan's tale for a moving opera.

I revise my old work at Hongquan

And add new lyrics at Yuming.

Where on earth can I express my feelings for love?

Only people like us are devoted to passions as such.

(*To the tune of* **Qinyuanchun**)

A scholar named Li Yi

And a lady named Huo Xiaoyu

Make a perfect match by talent and charm.

They chance to meet on Lantern Festival Eve

When she drops a hairpin and he keeps it as a token.

With Bao Siniang as the matchmaker in between,

They make an oath for their love.

The scholar wins the laurel in the imperial exam

But never succumbs to the power,

And is thus dispatched far away,

Leaving the bride alone with woe.

General Lu schemes to beckon for a son-in-law,

And has Li Yi dispatched to Mengmen in the west.

Back in the capital but confined in General Lu's estate,

Li Yi is tormented by the letters' delay.

With anxieties in her heart,

Xiaoyu looks for her man at all cost

And sells her hairpins to General Lu for her man,

Thus rousing suspicion on her man's mind.

Old friends Cui Yunming and Wei Xiaqing invite Li Yi to a flower show,

Intending to satirize him for his betrayal,

Only to find all but a rumour and a mistake.

The Gallant Knight revitalizes their love

And makes the hairpins shine again.

When the Gallant Knight helps by doing what he can,

Huo Xiaoyu sells her swallow hairpins for her man.

General Lu beckons for a son-in-law in vain,
And Officer Li Yi meets his wife once again.

Scene Two
A Scholar's Ambition in Spring

(*Enter Li Yi*)

LI YI (*To the tune of* **Zhenzhulian**):

> I've been studying hard for a good career,
>
> With an ambition as vast as the ocean waves,
>
> Yet now I'm still stuck in poverty and solitude.
>
> I write rhyme prose, discuss essays,
>
> And present my views on state affairs.
>
> A lonely traveller, often cold and tired,
>
> I hear the spring bird whisper in my ear:
>
> "How much talent have you gained?"
>
> It echoes so deep in my heart
>
> That this spring seems my lucky time.

(*In the pattern of* **Qingyu'an**)

> *"A scholar in prosperous times travels and reads widely;*
>
> *He enjoys peach blossoms with contentment in leisure.*
>
> *His dreams may come true through his magic words.*
>
> *When spring days become longer and longer,*
>
> *He expects a call from the imperial court,*
>
> *But who's to invite him to the court?*
>
> *He waits and waits in his robe tidy and clean.*
>
> *Oh, how many youthful years have passed away!"*

I am Li Yi, styled Junyu, from Longxi. My father was a former minister and my mother was conferred the title of Grand County Lady. Wealth and fame are elusive, but talent has its roots. I make myself known in the literary circle, and comment on the celebrities at will. Calligrapher Wang Zijing held bestowed books of rarity; Emperor Liang collected famous paintings of great value. They appreciated paintings all the year round, and enjoyed songs and dances in all the seasons. My youthful talent shines like the rising sun, and radiates like the precious jade. Like the dragon swords flying to the azure sky, I wish to break free and soar with the wind. Yet one thing upsets me: Well over 20 years old, I'm still single. Without a belle as my mate, how can I call myself a talented scholar? I've come to Chang'an recently, and am now staying at Xinchang Lane. Today is the first day of spring, the 14th year of the Yuanhe Reign. This morning I paid a visit to Mr. Liu Gongji, my old friend who is the Governor of Guanxi. On my way home, I came across my cousin Cui Yunming and my bosom friend Wei Xiaqing. So we are going to have a feast at this hour. Qiuhong, fetch the wine.

(*Enter Qiuhong*)

QIUHONG:

"*Let's drink the wine on this early spring day*

And enjoy the plum blossoms fresh and fair."

Now the wine is ready.

(*Enter Wei Xiaqing and Cui Yunming*)

WEI XIAQING, CUI YUNMING (*To the tune of* **Heshengchao**):

Spring has turned around in a heavenly cycle,

Yet the lonely dweller stays cold in the setting sun.

Decorations have been made to celebrate the spring,

But homesickness grows in the season of blossoms.

(*Greet one another*)

WEI XIAQING:

"*Happiness has traveled a thousand miles;*

CUI YUNMING:

Spring has brought us under the same roof.

LI YI:

Only the wine from Yichun

Can prolong the prime of our youth."

(*Raises the wine cup*)

(*To the tune of* **Yufurong**)

Pepper flowers charm the early spring;

Cypress leaves enhance the fragrant wine.

May the flower goddess help

The flowers bloom early in spring.

When the pond thaws, fish come up in shoals;

When the imperial garden warms up, wild swans move north in flocks.

LI YI, WEI XIAQING, CUI YUNMING:

The arrival of spring

Is marked by the gentle caress of the east wind,

And house decorations attract swallows at every door,

With each spring fairer than before.

WEI XIAQING, CUI YUNMING (*To the previous tune*):

As the yellow cloud brings luck to the new year,

The scholars stay in Chang'an on a sunny day.

We climb up to the Chaoyuan Temple on Mount Lishan

To celebrate the coming of the new year.

Spring wine cannot drive away the cold,

Though the warmth of spring is coming near.

LI YI, WEI XIAQING, CUI YUNMING:

Gently fondling the temples,

The spring breeze greens the willows

Before it does the woods.

Young men drink the Tusu wine to their hearts' content.

LI YI:

When I hear you talk about young men, I seem to be getting old.

(*To the tune of* **Cuyulin**)

My friends in need

Are only the two of you,

But spring melancholy depresses me all alone.

Grass and trees turn green in the garden,

And the east wind is tearing my patterned gown.

LI YI, WEI XIAQING, CUI YUNMING:

Thanks to the spring god,

Every branch and leaf

Heralds early spring in the imperial garden.

WEI XIAQING:

By saying that "the east wind is tearing my patterned gown", you mean that you haven't established yourself in career and fame, so you want to change for a purple gown with the gold badge of a high rank. That's nothing too difficult. I hear that your old friend Mr. Liu Gongji is the Governor of Guanxi. As His Majesty is going on an inspection tour to the east this year, the imperial civil examination dates have not been decided yet. You may follow Mr. Liu to the west. That'll offer an opportunity for your career and fame.

LI YI:

A true scholar must depend on himself to pass the imperial examination for a career.

CUI YUNMING (*Laughs*):

Xiaqing, you've made a terrible mistake. "The east wind is tearing my patterned gown" means that he has nobody to mend his torn gown. For this, there is someone who can offer a hand.

LI YI:

Who is it?

CUI YUNMING:

Bao Siniang in the deep alley. She's an old hand at matchmaking. Why not ask her for help?

LI YI:

To tell you the truth, I've visited Bao Siniang. But I haven't revealed much of my intention.

WEI XIAQING, CUI YUNMING:

A talented scholar matches a fair lady. That's the most natural thing in the world.

WEI XIAQING (*To the previous tune*):

You've been much travel-stained

On your way to the imperial exam,

When spring comes and water rises.

LI YI:

Well, it depends on one's luck!

CUI YUNMING:

Your appearance is attractive enough for a lady's favour.

LI YI:

Well, it depends on one's money!

CUI YUNMING:

Your inner talent is worth a fortune.

LI YI, WEI XIAQING, CUI YUNMING:

Thanks to the spring god,

Every branch and leaf

Heralds early spring in the imperial garden.

WEI XIAQING, CUI YUNMING:

(*To the tune of* **Coda**)

Good luck falls upon your brow;

Why not cater to a lady pretty and fair?

Oh, my friend,

How can we see you cold and dreary all alone!

As spring comes to the capital town,

So grace and wealth are born with you.

Without a matchmaker, your hair will turn grey;

With a matchmaker, your bride is on the way.

Scene Three
Appreciating the New Hairpins

(*Enter Lady Zheng*)

LADY ZHENG (*To the tune of* **Mangonghua**):

Spring is showing its fullest charm,

Yet sadly I seem to be getting old

And losing interest in making up my face.

The east wind pulls the green gauzes in the mist,

And coldness lingers on in the early morn.

(*In the pattern of* **Dielianhua**)

"Who'll cut paper flowers and wear them in the hair

To display her youthful life

And welcome the caress of spring breeze?

It's sad for me to recall the past,

For flowers bring regrets in spring.

I long for spring before it comes,

And hate to see the delay of the blooming,

With plum blossoms left in solitude.

Spring is drawing near this year,

But it's uncertain when it will arrive in the end."

I'm Lady Zheng from the House of Prince Huo. In an ordinary family I would be praised for my stellar beauty, and in a noble house I would be recommended for my services on gilded cushions. Afraid of the jealousy from my woman peers, I had never been indiscreet enough to have an affair. Talented friends gathered at the House of the Prince and I was often called upon to entertain them in the west garden. However, in my old age I start to worship Buddha and is renamed Jingchi. I have a daughter named Xiaoyu. She's sixteen with a most good-looking face. She used to study poems and essays by my side, and now she is learning how to play musical instruments and sing songs from Bao Siniang. The black dye from the south beautifies her eyebrows as fine as a couple of willow leaves. The red rouge from the north colours her cheeks as pretty as the lotus flowers. She's most attractively dressed with fanciful embroidery, but she has neither been engaged nor found her beloved man. She loves to wear swallow hairpins of purple jade. I have commissioned Jade-smith Hou Jingxian to carve and trim a pair of hairpins for her. We have to wait till they are sent here. Now that it's early spring, I'll call her out to enjoy the spring scene near the Wei Bridge. Huansha, where is your young mistress?

(*Enter Huo Xiaoyu with Huansha*)

HUO XIAOYU (*To the tune of **Mangonghuahou***):

Staying alone in my chamber all day long,

I pencil eyebrows as pretty as the natural beauty of spring.

HUANSHA:

Preparing embroidered shoes for an outing in spring,

We expect the flowers to bloom soon.

HUO XIAOYU:

May bliss be forever yours, Mom!

LADY ZHENG:

Don't stand on ceremony, my dear daughter.

HUO XIAOYU:

Why are you calling me, Mom?

LADY ZHENG:

As the sunlight is so bright in early spring, let's take an outing near the Wei Bridge.

(*Starts to move*)

"*The ice is thawing and the pond is turning green;*

The cloud is dispersing and the sky is clearing up.

I should not be so excited,

But I must go for my daughter's sake."

Old as I am, I'll take an outing in the fresh spring.

(*To the tune of **Miandaxu***)

A lady's chamber is quiet and solitary;

Her pretty forehead mirrors her light fur-coat.

The painted silvery screens

Faces the duck incense burner in solitude.

For my dear daughter,

I'll go on a spring outing

Despite my old age

And lonely dreams!

Time has passed and will never return;

I fear to hear the oriole's song soaring to the sky.

HUO XIAOYU (*To the previous tune*):

Smiling to the dressing mirror,

I see a blush upon my face.

The east wind last night

Blew at the spring decorations in my chamber.

Greeting the spring morning,

I amble with my slender waist.

Now the rain and cloud

Begin to disperse and disappear.

In the shade of the window gauze

I stitch more threads

To while away my days doing embroidery.

HUANSHA (*To the previous tune*):

Young as she is,

She must have youthful vigor in spring.

Spring has come all of a sudden,

But she shows no joy behind closed doors.

All along the streams and bridges,

Beautiful ladies greet one another.

They are ready for poems and songs

To express their passions on the spring day.

Oh, my young mistress,

Let's saunter along and enjoy the fresh spring day,

Instead of penciling your dainty brows all by yourself.

(*Enter Hou Jingxian*)

HOU JINGXIAN:

"The new swallow hairpins are imbedded with gold;

They have been carved with the old toad knife for jade."

Your Ladyship, I, Hou Jingxian, the jade-smith, have completed the jade hairpins. Please allow me to present them to you.

LADY ZHENG (*Tells Huansha to accept them and takes a look*):

What deft hands! I'll award you with ten thousand coins.

HOU JINGXIAN (*Expresses gratitude*):

"How can I express my gratitude for the award of ten thousand coins,

As I've finished the carving of the swallow jade hairpins?"

(*Exit*)

LADY ZHENG:

Huansha, today is the best time to cut the decorations out of the Xizhou brocade and

attach them to the hairpins for your young mistress.

(*Exit Huansha, who reenters with a mirror*)

HUANSHA:

Here are the brocade flowers.

(*Lady Zheng shows Huo Xiaoyu the hairpins with the decorations*)

HUO XIAOYU (*Takes a look at the hairpins*):

(*To the previous tune*)

The jade-smith is so deft

That he carved the jade red and clear.

Swallows and patterned flowers

Decorate the pins for a lady's hair.

(*Tries on the hairpins while Huansha holds the mirror*)

HUO XIAOYU:

In light brocade,

Dainty decorations are pinned in the bun.

The swallows signify the coming of early spring,

While bees and butterflies dance in the clear sky.

ALL:

When will a pair of swallows be matched

And clean the mirror for the best luck?

(*To the tune of* **Coda**)

Behind the curtains stays the pretty maid;

Behind the screens hides the youthful heart,

But her beautiful eyes must fix on the needlework.

The graceful mother is dwelling in her rooms

When fresh spring scenes call for an outing there.

The daughter is as fair as jade and blooms

When she puts the pretty hairpins on her hair.

Scene Four
Paying a Visit for the Fair Lady

(*Enter Bao Siniang*)

BAO SINIANG (*To the tune of* **Zhuyingtaijin**):

The green screens stand idle;

The exquisite mirror stays cold.

I often count the passing years

And recall the time when I lived with my man.

Wine perplexes me and spring depresses me;

I add more incense to prolong the night,

Comforting myself in warm seclusion.

(*In the pattern of* **Shaonianyou**)

"With curtains drawn and the courtyard cold and bleak,

Spring scenes are far from me.

In the dark corner full of dust,

My stringed musical instruments lie,

Tears dropping on my handkerchief.

Nobody visits the old house any more.

My quilt is patterned with mandarin ducks

And the incense is half burnt.

What beautiful time has passed away!

But who can cherish a thought

As dull as mine?"

I'm Bao Siniang. I used to be a singing girl in the royal son-in-law Xue's house. But I was exempt from the bond and have been free for over ten years. I am lively and glib in nature. The wealthy and the distinguished are all associated with me. I offer advice and seek for fashion. Thus, I'm considered as the flower queen. Whenever Mr. Li Yi from Longxi comes for a visit, he will give me lots of money and silk fabrics. In my eyes, he is good-mannered, smart and exceedingly handsome. By ample gifts and sweet talk, he is bound to have ulterior motives. It's certain that he wants me to find a bride from a house of distinction. I find Lady Zheng's daughter an ideal choice. She's pretty, literate and bright, adoring Mr. Li's elegant manners. I just need to wait for Mr. Li to express his intention, and then I can pass the message. Don't worry, he'll come sooner or later.

201

(*Enter Li Yi*)

LI YI (*To the tune of* **Tangduoling**):

A traveler's longing is far and deep;

I enjoy myself deep in the alley.

Whose house is it in the back street?

Its pink curtains are half drawn.

To seek girls and belles

Is my pastime.

(*Greets Bao Siniang*)

"You are as young as ever before,

And I shall paint your pretty brows again.

BAO SINIANG:

Nobody here ever tries pigment in early spring;

Only the spring wind greens the willows."

LI YI:

Siniang, I've been visiting you for years, but for this early spring visit, why is it so desolate in your house?

BAO SINIANG:

Let me tell you,

(*To the tune of* **Zhuyingtai**)

    In my youth I certainly had my share of charm,

    But now I've become a withered flower left in the rain.

    I used to have the smile that's worth gold,

    And have the voice that's worth a fortune,

    For families of great esteem.

    Alas, my look has faded when I look at the mirror,

    And carriages have stopped coming by.

LI YI:

Why don't you find a spouse?

BAO SINIANG:

    Well, times have changed!

    Who would care to stop by?

Mr. Li, you've given me gifts from time to time, and I haven't repaid your kindness. So what can I do for you today?

LI YI (*To the previous tune*):

    I roam with spring passion

    That turns into melancholy.

    In an excursion to the outskirts,

    I walk to your tranquil courtyard

    To have a pleasant chat with you.

BAO SINIANG:

My charm is half gone. How could you have such inclinations?

LI YI:

    Still charming!

    You are talented in your profession,

    All the more skillful in making matches.

    As a mature lady,

    You are no less attractive.

BAO SINIANG (*To the previous tune*):

    Don't be silly!

    Among those I like and those who like me,

    I know quite a few people.

    Your talent and demeanor,

    Your courteous and chivalrous deeds,

    Are not meant for a withering flower.

Mr. Li, you must have sent me gifts for something on your mind. Please tell me your real intention so that I can do my best to help you.

LI YI:

    Good heavens!

    I'm talented but still a bachelor,

    So I need a belle to take care of me.

Who can offer me the picture of such a belle?

BAO SINIANG (*To the previous tune*):

> Don't you know?
>
> For your genuine passions,
>
> I've been seeking for such a belle everywhere.

LI YI:

Have you found one?

BAO SINIANG:

Mr. Li, your fond dream will soon come true. A fairy of a lady has descended into the human world. She doesn't seek wealth but adores elegant manners and handsome figure. You're her perfect image in talent and appearance.

> Her age is twice eight,
>
> Or thrice five,
>
> From a family more distinguished than the others.

LI YI (*Surprised and delighted*):

Really?

> You must have made up a story of a fairyland,
>
> And I'm afraid I'll wait for the love in vain.
>
> (*Kneels down*)
>
> This marital match
>
> Must be arranged by you, my lady.

BAO SINIANG:

Please rise to your feet and let me tell you the details. The former Prince Huo had a daughter named Xiaoyu whom he loved dearly. Her mother is called Jingchi, who was the prince's favorite concubine. When the prince died, his brothers refused to let her stay due to her humble origin. Therefore, she was allotted some money and property and moved to live elsewhere. She changed her family name to Zheng. Nobody knows she has a daughter with the prince.

> "*Her daughter has stunning looks,*
>
> *Never seen elsewhere in my life.*
>
> *She has strong passions and graceful manners,*
>
> *Surpassing others in every way.*
>
> *As for music and poetry,*
>
> *She's most at home in her way.*"

It was yesterday that she asked me to find her a good man to match her taste. She was delighted when I mentioned your name to her, for she had heard about you. She's now living in the eastern spare chamber at Sanqufu in Shengyefang Lane.

LI YI:

Can I pay her a visit?

BAO SINIANG:

This young lady usually stays in her chamber, but in the Lantern Festival celebration this year, she might be ambling out to the main street. If you are interested, you can try to find

her near the creek.

LI YI:

I see.

BAO SINIANG:

After you meet the angel under the palace lanterns, I'll go to your study and arrange the marriage.

LI YI (*To the tune of* **Coda**):

I'll express my sincere love to her,

BAO SINIANG:

But the final say is still in her hands.

LI YI:

This is no joke but you've prepared my future.

Amid the crowd to watch the lanterns here,

I'm excited to find my adorable love.

If this is not the best scene far and near,

There is no spring bestowed from above.

Scene Five
Enjoying the Palace Lanterns

(*Enter Prefect of the Capital*)

PREFECT (*To the tune of* **Dianjiangchun**):

His Majesty makes the edict:

As wind and rain turns out propitious at our will,

To celebrate the bumper harvest,

A lantern festival is arranged.

"*When all the gates are left open in the capital,*

Spring is approaching amid songs.

The streets are lit by moonlight bright and lanterns dim

While breeze is gentle and lanterns dim within the palace walls."

I'm Prefect of the Capital. On the Lantern Festival Eve, the moonlight is tender and the breeze is mild. His Majesty has issued the edict that all residents are allowed to enjoy the lanterns throughout the night. All city gates are left open tonight. As the poem goes,

"*As there is no curfew tonight,*

Time, please take no flight."

(*Exit*)

(*Enter Lady Zheng*)

LADY ZHENG (*To the tune of* **Wanxiandeng**):

Lanterns are in display on this Festival Eve;

Horn music and plum blossoms fill the night.

Gentle breeze sends over warmth and laughter;

Ladies and maids dress themselves in their best.

(*Enter Huo Xiaoyu*)

HUO XIAOYU (*To the previous tune*):

The beautiful springtime is locked deep in the court,

And tonight spring shows its fullest splendour.

(*Enter Huansha*)

HUANSHA:

People spend the sleepless night at this wonderful time,

With countless joyful couples passing by.

LADY ZHENG (*In the pattern of* **Yiqin'e**):

"On the wonderful Festival Eve,

Beaded curtains are drawn up at every door.

HUO XIAOYU:

At every door,

Flowers come out late at dawn

Though spring comes early in every street.

HUANSHA:

Pretty faces are reflected in the candlelight;

Flute music and songs make maidens smile.

ALL:

Maidens smile

To the halo of the moon

And the twinkling of the stars."

HUO XIAOYU:

On the Lantern Festival Eve, please allow me to offer you a cup of wine.

LADY ZHENG:

That's very considerate of you, my dear. As the saying goes,

"When the daughter presents wine in spring,

The Mother-Goddess lights the lamps in the sky."

(*To the tune of* **Teteling**)

Every year when we celebrate the Lantern Festival Eve,

The main street looks like a fairyland of eternal spring,

And the fairy courts are lit up on the Milky Way.

It is high time for belles in red to gather,

Imperial banners to wave,

Joyous laughter to fill the air,

And peace to return to the world.

HUO XIAOYU (*To the previous tune*):

It's never cold but warm on the Lantern Festival Eve;

Spring has climbed up to the railings of upper stories;

All the ladies appear in red from every place.

This is when incense smoke floats,

Fragrant breeze softens,

Human voices muffle,

And flute music fades away.

HUANSHA (*To the previous tune*):

The moon is round in its perfection on the Lantern Festival Eve;

Beaded curtains are drawn up all along the streets;

Starry lights dot every door.

This is the time when flutes are played

And laughter roars,

And we'll have the most fun

In the joyful crowd.

Your Ladyship and young mistress, please walk along the main street and enjoy the sight.

LADY ZHENG:

Go ahead.

(*To the tune of* **Coda**)

Spring night is as bright as the day,

The evening is as joyous as the Spring Festival,

And the incense smell floats over the streets.

Who cares for sleep on this Lantern Festival Eve?

Fair ladies can't bear staying at home;

They join the festival crowd at night.

All gates are left open for the eve;

The Milky Way seems to merge with the lantern light.

Scene Six
A Hairpin Dropped on the Festival Eve

(*Enter Li Yi*)

LI YI (*To the tune of* **Fenghuanggeyin**):

On the spring night in the capital,

The white moon hangs low as if falling.

When the streets are filled with the crowd,

The moonlit Forbidden City is as bright as day.

(*Enter Wei Xiaqing and Cui Yunming*)

WEI XIAQING, CUI YUNMING:

When a gentleman meets a lady,

There must be attendants and horses.

LI YI:

> "*Songs and music fill the taverns,*
>
> *And fanciful lanterns light up every tree.*
>
> *Who can sit still at home under the beautiful moon?*
>
> *And who would not come to enjoy the lanterns so dainty?*"

My brothers, Bao Siniang instructed me last night to steal a glance at the lady who'd come out on the Lantern Festival Eve. Let's watch for her giggling voice and fragrant dress in the light of numerous candles and shades of countless flowers. In this way we'll make this year's lantern tour worthwhile. Before I can finish my words, there come the noble families to enjoy the lanterns.

> (*Exeunt all*)
>
> (*Enter the noble families, laughing and smiling*)

NOBLE FAMILIES (*To the tune of* **Yuanlinhao**):

> Thank His Majesty for the bright lanterns and the bright moon;
>
> Thank Heaven for a prosperous spring and a prosperous year.
>
> Peace and prosperity spread all over the empire,
>
> With songs and dances along the streets.
>
> (*Exeunt*)
>
> (*Enter Lady Zheng, followed by Huo Xiaoyu and Huansha*)

LADY ZHENG:

What splendid lanterns!

> (*To the previous tune*)
>
> The lanterns are the best at Nantianmen;
>
> Grand carriages crowd with red lantern hung.
>
> Shouts stop our carriages and make us turn;
>
> Who is coming with the swirling dust?

Ah! There comes a stout man dressed in yellow riding a white steed.

> (*Exeunt all*)
>
> (*Enter the Gallant Knight, followed by a couple of Tartar servants, all on horseback*)

GALLANT KNIGHT (*To the previous tune*):

> I come from Shandong for a pleasure tour in Chang'an,
>
> And roam around with fun on this Festival Eve.
>
> There sounds the beating of street drums for the time.
>
> (*Laughing voices inside*)

VOICES INSIDE:

Who's that stout man over there? You are so tall and your steed is so big that you've blocked our way to watch the lanterns.

GALLANT KNIGHT (*Laughs*):

As for my name, I'm the Gallant Knight. Since we are in your way, let's go, my Tartar boys.

> So I whip my horse and depart in the lantern light.
>
> (*Exit*)

(Enter Li Yi, Wei Xiaqing and Cui Yunming)

LI YI, WEI XIAQING, CUI YUNMING *(To the previous tune)*:

> There's such a huge crowd for the sight;
>
> Laughter and songs come from ladies and maids.
>
> The main street is glazed green and yellow by the lantern lights;
>
> There'll be a more spectacular scene as if in a fairyland.
>
> *(They look around and then exit)*
>
> *(Enter Lady Zheng, Huo Xiaoyu and Huansha)*

LADY ZHENG:

Enough fun, let's have a rest!

> *(To the previous tune)*
>
> The crimson buildings are tall with flowing rosy clouds,
>
> And light gleams over beaded curtains and glazed tiles.
>
> Let's take a break in the corridor in the moonlight
>
> And smell the fragrance of plum blossoms at leisure.
>
> *(Enter Li Yi, Wei Xiaqing and Cui Yunming)*
>
> *(Exit Huo Xiaoyu with Lady Zheng and Huansha, much startled, dropping a hairpin)*

LI YI:

Wait! My brothers, is that maid the one from Shengyefang Lane? How stunningly beautiful she is! Is this a hairpin that touches the plum twigs and falls to the ground?

> *(To the tune of **Jiang'ershui**)*
>
> Moonlight slants from the plum branches;
>
> A swallow hairpin hangs on the plum twigs.
>
> A belle was just taking a break a moment ago;
>
> She was half hidden behind the silk lanterns;
>
> Dressed in red, she was shy in front of men.

LI YI, WEI XIAQING, CUI YUNMING:

> Fondling the hairpin and murmuring,
>
> We're lucky to have the chance encounter
>
> On the Lantern Festival Eve.
>
> *(Enter Huansha with a lantern, leading the way for Huo Xiaoyu)*

HUANSHA:

Well, Her Ladyship has returned home. Let's go and find the hairpin.

WEI XIAQING:

There comes someone for the hairpin. Yunming and I are going to the front gate to watch the lanterns, so you may stay and talk with her for a while to see if she's the right person.

LI YI:

Fine, please go ahead.

> *(Exeunt Wei Xiaqing and Cui Yunming)*

HUO XIAOYU *(Looks for the hairpin)*:

I can't find the hairpin anywhere. Oh, the plum twigs, what a nuisance!

> *(To the previous tune)*

Crowded with lady folk in red and green,

The path drags me to a halt by the plum twigs.

(*Acts as if to shun Li Yi*)

I'd like to tarry in the corridor in the shade of moonlight,

But I'd hate to stay in the corridor lit up in candlelight.

(*Li Yi bows to Huo Xiaoyu*)

Why does the handsome man cast a look at me?

LI YI (*Smiles to her*):

You must have dropped a hairpin.

HUO XIAOYU:

Have you found one, gentleman?

LI YI, HUO XIAOYU:

Fondling the hairpin and murmuring,

We're lucky to have the chance encounter

On the Lantern Festival Eve.

Li Yi (*To the tune of **Yujiaozhi***):

Which affluent family are you from?

Why are you going in such a hurry, my fair lady?

HUANSHA:

My young mistress is the daughter of Prince Huo.

LI YI:

What a coincidence! What a coincidence! So it's Sister Xiaoyu?

HUANSHA:

Yes, it's her.

LI YI:

I've been adoring your mistress for a long time! Why is she coming alone?

HUANSHA:

She's looking for her hairpin.

LI YI:

The walk on the crowded street tires her delicate feet,

So it's all for the dropping of the hairpin.

HUANSHA:

Hey, scholar, have you seen the hairpin?

LI YI:

Yes, I have. But please allow me to greet Sister Xiaoyu.

HUO XIAOYU (*In a whisper*):

Huansha, that won't do! But ask the scholar where he's from.

LI YI:

I'm Li Yi from Longxi, and my secondary name is Junyu, the 10th son of the family. I've come here to take the imperial examination.

HUO XIAOYU (*Takes a look at Li Yi, lowers her head and smiles*):

I've heard of Mr. Li's talent for poetry from Bao Siniang, and I've been thinking of him

all day long. Now I see you in person, but you don't look as good as I've imagined. A talented scholar must be handsome as well, right?

LI YI (*Listens and goes forward for a greeting*):

Well! You adore talent, Miss, and I admire good looks. We two are a perfect match. What a lucky coincidence for tonight!

HUO XIAOYU (*Shuns him shyly*):

Luckily, the hairpin's fallen into the scholar's hands!

    What a pretty hairpin in my bun viewed from the mirror!

    But now it's in the scholar's sleeve due to the plum twigs.

Huansha, ask the scholar to return my hairpin.

HUO XIAOYU, HUANSHA:

    It'd be a pity if this one remains single before the lanterns;

    It'd be a pity if that one remains single before the lanterns.

LI YI:

Please allow me to tell you, maid. I've remained single for over twenty years, not even engaged. I thought I could never see such lady's jewelry. Luckily, I've met a fairy from the moon, and picked up the hairpin before the plum blossoms. The plum blossoms are a token of matchmaking, and the swallows carved on the hairpin symbolize the happiness of a married couple. So I'll treasure this hairpin as a token for the marital tie. What would you think?

HUANSHA (*Gets annoyed*):

How rude you scholar are! You take advantage of the opportunity to express your passions. I must scold you for that!

HUO XIAOYU:

You lousy maid, how could you do that?

    (*To the previous tune*)

    The lanterns get us in trouble,

    By which the scholar expresses his intention.

Scholar, my hairpin is worth a fortune!

LI YI:

I have the fortune to meet you.

HUO XIAOYU (*Smiles aside*):

    The meeting is worth a fortune tonight;

    It seems as joyful as that of the Lanqiao tale.

Return my hairpin!

LI YI:

I'll choose a good matchmaker and present it to you by then.

    Oh, hairpin,

    How she sighs and sighs!

    But I've got the chance to talk with her by the plum twigs.

LI YI, HUO XIAOYU:

    It'd be a pity if this one remains single before the lanterns;

    It'd be a pity if that one remains single before the lanterns.

HUANSHA:

Her Ladyship would be waiting for long, so let's go home.

> (*To the tune of* **Chuanbazhao**)
>
> The flute tune is low
>
> And time urges us to return.

HUO XIAOYU:

> I tarry for the scholar's talent and grace,
>
> I tarry for the scholar's talent and grace,
>
> Without knowing the moon has glided down.

Huansha, ask the scholar to return my hairpin!

> (*Bows to Li Yi sidewise*)

HUO XIAOYU, HUANSHA:

> We've got to return though we've just met,
>
> We've got to return though we've just met.

LI YI (*Bows*):

> (*To the previous tune*)
>
> On the Lantern Festival Eve,
>
> I've the luck to meet the fairy from the moon.

HUANSHA:

Scholar,

> It's enough to gaze at the fair miss for so long;
>
> It's enough to gaze at the fair miss for so long.
>
> Why are you still keeping the hairpin in your hands!

HUO XIAOYU, HUANSHA:

> We've got to return though we've just met;
>
> We've got to return though we've just met.

LI YI (*To the tune of* **Coda**):

> Such a fairy shines brighter than the moon;
>
> Spring love is revealed on the Festival Eve.

HUO XIAOYU (*Whispers to Huansha*):

Remember not to leak a word to anybody tomorrow.

> (*Exeunt Huo Xiaoyu and Huansha*)

LI YI (*Left alone on the stage*):

How miraculous! How miraculous! I've met a fairy tonight.

> (*To the tune of* **Yulouchun**)
>
> It's a wonder to meet such a fairy from the moon;
>
> Though sleepy I'll think of my love all night through.
>
> She departs in the red candlelight far away;
>
> I'll wait to gallop my horse on this moonlit night.

Oh! The carriage is returning in a hurry, and the swallow hairpin is still in my hand, but how could I go home alone?

> (*Enter Cui Yunming*)

CUI YUNMING (*To the tune of* **Yulouchunhou**):

> The flute tune has been low all through the night,
>
> And the dropping of the hairpin matches the love.
>
> (*Enter Wei Xiaqing*)

WEI XIAQING:

> The couple's been under the lanterns for quite long;
>
> They've whispered softly like fragrant snow falling on plum blossoms.

Hey, Brother Li, is that your miss?

LI YI:

She is truly extraordinary!

> (*To the tune of* **Liufanqingyin**)
>
> She is a nymph of a lady,
>
> Like the fairies led by the goddess,
>
> Shimmering in the corridor in the moonlight.
>
> On that most precious moment,
>
> Heaven made the hairpin hang on the twigs.
>
> As I picked up the hairpin, she met me with a blush,
>
> Speaking to me affectionately with a smile.
>
> From her tender look and her lowering brows,
>
> I can see that she accepts my love
>
> And we know each other by heart.

WEI XIAQING, CUI YUNMING:

> With songs under the lanterns and the moon,
>
> Plum blossoms of love fall into her sleeves.

LI YI:

> It's a pity that the lanterns are distracting
>
> And the crowd is everywhere.
>
> How I wish that the streets would turn narrower
>
> And time would pass slower!
>
> I'll keep the hairpin as a token of love.

LI YI, WEI XIAQING, CUI YUNMING:

> A dream has just faded away,
>
> And in the flute songs and moonlight,
>
> The people are returning home.

CUI YUNMING:

Since the miss has such affection for you, you should never betray her!

> (*To the tune of* **Coda**)
>
> The fairy's departure takes away the spring.

Look at the pair of eyes,

> But how would these eyes endure so many glimpses?

LI YI:

> All my fortune in my later life depends on this occasion.

The fragrance of the hairpin lingers in the sleeve
As I return from the chance encounter on the Eve.
As I haven't fully expressed my feelings to my love,
I can't help searching for her, reluctant to leave.

Scene Seven
Marriage Proposal Broached

(*Enter Li Yi*)

LI YI (*To the tune of* **Daolianzi**):

The blossoms were serene and the moon was full.

The hairpin dropped near the corridor in the lanterns' light;

Sparkles of affection were transmitted from the starry sky.

(*In the pattern of* **Rumengling**)

"Ladies are passing by outside the door

When stars throw light into the windows at dawn.

Quiet and alone at the inn,

I dream of the return path in the moonlight.

Forlorn,

Oh, forlorn,

I murmur to myself in the candlelight."

I enjoyed the lanterns with Sister Xiaoyu last night. By our eyes and brows, how we exchanged our affections!

(*To the tune of* **Putianle**)

Leaning on the railing,

I recall the numerous lanterns and the colourful clouds.

Keeping the red lanterns bright and warm in spring,

She looked back with so much charm upon our first encounter,

As if she were riding on a phoenix toward the moon.

The flute tune faded, the crowd moved, and the hairpin dropped;

She held the plum blossoms in silence.

Now I take off my pendants in the clear moonlight,

And my dream suddenly ends after my return at dawn.

Yet the east wind still intoxicates me,

And the fragrance still lingers with me.

(*Enter Bao Siniang*)

BAO SINIANG (*To the tune of* **Bushilu**):

In the courtyard deep and quiet,

He is reputed for his elegant manners.

He holds the flower stalk in hand,

To seek his flower after awakening from the butterfly dream.

LI YI (*Greets Bao Siniang with a smile*):

Oh, it's you!

Your hair is loose though you are well dressed.

You are kind enough to come to this isolated studio.

BAO SINIANG:

Thanks for your compliment!

To see the gentleman greet me with such a smile,

I feel much flattered,

I feel much flattered.

"With a wonder in the world as your true love,

Did you see her clearly before the lanterns?

Don't frown and don't worry;

Please tell me your intention in every detail."

So tell me what you saw before the lanterns last night.

LI YI:

It was such a noisy crowd, so I didn't see much of anything. But I did pick up a dropped purple swallow jade hairpin. Please take a close look.

BAO SINIANG (*Looks at the hairpin*):

What a purple jade hairpin!

(*To the tune of* **Zhuomugongzi**)

The waves are clear, the knots are bright,

And the jade is neatly embedded.

The frames and leaves are so well carved

That they seem to shine in the sun.

Oh, swallow,

Why are you flying in such a disconcerted manner?

You'll sit still on the dressing case or the fragrant kerchiefs,

Or perch on the lady's bun in the mirror.

Who's conveyed so much affection into this adorable pin?

LI YI (*To the previous tune*):

Amid laughter from behind the lanterns,

The flood of moonlight ensured true love.

I waited where the hairpin lay,

To greet the one who'd come for the pin.

Thanks to the swallow hairpin,

We talked gently though nothing seemed to settle down,

And linked our hearts in the fragrance of plum blossoms.

I hid the hairpin in my sleeve,

A windfall bestowed by Heaven.

BAO SINIANG (*To the tune of* **Haojiejie**):

When Heaven makes such a match,

This swallow hairpin is the token.

The fair miss made the promise in person,

And you met each other before the token.

BAO SINIANG, LI YI:

With the lanterns lit,

The meeting is a fairy tale on its own,

So none would go for another fairyland!

LI YI (*To the previous tune*):

Is this some arrangement like the Lanqiao tale?

This is some wonder descending from the moon.

Though it's still chilly for the dew and flowers in early spring,

She comes down from the fairyland for true love.

BAO SINIANG, LI YI:

With the lanterns lit,

The meeting is a fairy tale on its own,

So none would go for another fairyland!

LI YI:

Please take this hairpin as the token for the marriage. Then I'll present her a pair of precious white jade pendants.

BAO SINIANG (*To the tune of* **Coda**):

A single swallow longs to match a mate.

LI YI:

The hairpin loser leans on the dressing-table in pensive mood.

BAO SINIANG:

The sparkling light last night presages the marriage of the couple.

To meet a fairy before the lanterns under the moon

Is like meeting Yunying in the wonderful Lanqiao tale.

The hairpin in the sleeve is like the fabled jade pestle,

So there's no more need for a match by Heaven.

Scene Eight
Marriage Proposal Granted

(*Enter Huo Xiaoyu and Huansha*)

HUO XIAOYU (*To the tune of* **Boxing**):

I sit still in my chamber with light makeup,

Feeling the warmth and chill in early spring.

The lamplight is dim and the moonlight is pale;

How I gaze and gaze, feeling desolate and lonely!

Although the hairpin swallow circles in the sky,

The curtains are too thick for the reunion.

HUANSHA:

She seems intoxicated in her heart,

And yet feels shy in her mind.

Who is she longing for?

She wakes up only to find

The moon is still above the plum branch.

HUO XIAOYU (*In the pattern of* **Yingtianchang**):

"While the lantern wheels were turning round

And the moonlight was flooding,

I tried to recognize him from the laughter.

He half hid himself behind the lanterns

And inquired leisurely, the hairpin in his hand.

Who could truly understand his inquiry?

Then our hearts touched each other,

Yet my intention might be mistaken in the encounter.

When the crowd dispersed,

I returned alone,

Leaning on the railing in a pensive mood."

Huansha, where goes the scholar who picked up the hairpin?

(*To the tune of* **Zizijin**)

Spring crawled into the boudoir;

The moonlight shone on the plum blossoms.

Time urged us to enjoy the blossoms,

And I wore the most exquisite hairpins for the Festival.

On my way back from watching the lanterns,

Due to the plum blossoms in the moonlight,

I got my hairpin caught on the plum twigs.

Hairpin, hairpin,

Although I found out at once,

Why should it fall into the scholar's hands?

What a scholar!

He took it in his hands!

HUO XIAOYU, HUANSHA:

One of the hairpins flew away,

So it's missing from the pair.

What could I do when I met the scholar?

He held the missing hairpin in his hand,

And held it so elegantly and leisurely,

So happily and merrily.

It made me so annoyed,

So eager.

It's all for the meeting on the spring night.

HUANSHA (*To the previous tune*):

Two swallows were torn apart by accident,

But the true lover won the trophy.

He put the hairpin into his sleeve,

Imagining how the hairpin stuck on the lady's hair.

He walked along the street at leisure,

And the moonbeam was dim on the plum trees at dusk.

Hairpin, hairpin,

The scholar held it in his hand.

He met a fair miss,

Such a fair miss,

Who bowed to him in a trance.

HUO XIAOYU, HUANSHA:

One single hairpin flew away alone,

So it's missing from the pair.

What could I do when I met the scholar?

He held the missing hairpin in his hand,

And held it so elegantly and leisurely,

So happily and merrily.

It made me so annoyed,

So eager.

It's all for the meeting on the spring night.

(*Enter Bao Siniang*)

BAO SINIANG (*To the tune of **Ruzhuan***):

As the chill of spring is thawing,

It's time for an outing to collect the herbs.

I move my delicate feet

And arrive at the vermilion gate.

I wonder who is inside the door.

(*The parrot mimics inside: "Guest's coming! Guest's coming!"*)

HUO XIAOYU (*Startled*):

When curtains stir up the shadows,

The parrot reports the coming of a guest.

HUANSHA:

It's a fine day today.

Who's at the door?

(*Greets Bao Siniang*)

HUO XIAOYU:

Ah! It's Bao Siniang.

How come that you are here?

BAO SINIANG:

I know you must be in your boudoir.

Miss Huo, you love to wear the purple swallow jade hairpins. Where are they now?

HUO XIAOYU:

I don't feel like wearing them today.

BAO SINIANG:

You must have lost one, I dare say?

HUO XIAOYU (*Smiles*):

How could I have lost it?

BAO SINIANG:

If I say you lost one, you have surely lost one; but if I say you'll make the pair, you'll surely make the pair. It all depends on your will.

HUO XIAOYU (*Smiles*):

Then you say I'll make the pair.

BAO SINIANG:

So that's it! But let me ask you how your hairpin fell into the scholar's hands?

HUO XIAOYU (*To the tune of* **Xueshizi**):

    In the Lantern Festival on the moonlit street,

    The moon shone through the plum trees.

    I tarried outside the corridor smelling the fragrance of the plums.

    Then the plum branch shivered,

    The plum branch shivered and caught the hairpin.

    It's Heaven that bestowed it on the scholar.

HUO XIAOYU, BAO SINIANG:

    A single swallow hairpin now, and a pair of swallow hairpins then;

    One is missing from the pair, and is now returning to make the pair.

    Can it fly back to my dressing-table

    Like spring entering the curtains?

BAO SINIANG (*To the previous tune*):

    Lanterns bright as day and crowds huge as the sea,

    It's a wonder that he should have picked up the hairpin!

    Nobody else saw it on the Lantern Festival Eve.

    Plum blossoms were falling,

    Plum blossoms were falling,

    But they could only be picked up by those who keep an eye.

    The scholar is the one who keeps an eye on them.

HUO XIAOYU, BAO SINIANG:

    The hairpins are mentioned directly, and then indirectly;

    One is missing directly, and is now returning indirectly,

    Can it fly back to my dressing-table

    Like spring entering the curtains?

BAO SINIANG:

As you mention the dressing-table, I'd like to tell you that Mr. Li is taking the hairpin as a token for the marital tie.

HUO XIAOYU:

But what family is he from? How talented is he? How come that he is still single at the age over twenty?

BAO SINIANG:

As to the scholar, he is from a distinguished family and is exceptionally talented. He has no rivals in poetry and prose. The sages strongly recommend him for his talent. He prides himself for elegant manners. He has been looking for an ideal mate from prestigious families, but hasn't found one yet.

HUO XIAOYU:

I see. As for this matter, you need to consult my mother.

> (*To the tune of* **Gewei**)
>
> As you talk about the dressing-table,
>
> How could the poor scholar put the hairpin on my hair?

I'm afraid

> My dear mom might not recognize his talent!
>
> (*Exit*)

BAO SINIANG (*Remains on the stage*):

May I talk with Your Ladyship?

> (*Enter Lady Zheng*)

LADY ZHENG (*To the tune of* **Yijianmei**):

> Outside the red gauze appear the greens in fog and mist;
>
> Flowers wave to the window gauze,
>
> And the sun shines through the window gauze.
>
> Who has brought luck to my door?
>
> Spring makes me old
>
> And makes my daughter thin.
>
> (*Greets Bao Siniang*)

So it's Bao Siniang.

> "*With one third of spring gone,*
>
> *The day is getting longer.*

BAO SINIANG:

> *To make a match,*
>
> *I've come to talk in details.*"

Your Ladyship, guess why I've come here today! It's for your daughter's marriage.

LADY ZHENG:

My daughter is too young to marry. Now let me tell you,

> (*To the tune of* **Yichunling**)
>
> To be born a fairy,
>
> My daughter always stays by my side.

Behind the layers of curtains,

How could she bare her heart?

Incense smoke curls upward from the burner;

Flowers exhibit charm in the jade vase.

Like other maidens she has hidden her heart.

BAO SINIANG (*To the previous tune*):

She's growing up,

And you're getting old.

She'll not take your words seriously.

She's been so touched in her heart

That she is growing too slender for her spring dress.

Nobody from the marriage list would remain single;

Belles are eager to express their affections.

You'd like to stay with her,

But she burns the incense sticks so as to find her ideal groom.

LADY ZHENG (*To the previous tune*):

Time and tide await no one;

It's true that a lady must marry a man.

Yet how could I let her marry outside my house;

I might invite the groom to marry inside my house.

So I may prepare the west room as their hall,

And the east room as their chamber.

Who is so concerned like me for the daughter's happiness?

Then how's the man?

BAO SINIANG (*To the previous tune*):

Young, handsome and talented,

Mr. Li is from a distinguished family in Longxi.

By relying on him,

You'll be surely secure and stable.

The Jiangchu Tune will lead to their union;

The Qiufeng Tune will bring him here.

(*Takes out the hairpin*)

So you must accept the swallow jade hairpin.

LADY ZHENG (*Looks at the hairpin*):

Well! This hairpin looks like the one Xiaoyu wears. How can the scholar have it? Marriage must be based on my daughter's will. Huansha, please call your young mistress.

(*Huansha calls*)

(*Enter Huo Xiaoyu*)

HUO XIAOYU (*To the tune of* **Yijianmei**):

I wake up to find the spring breeze fondling the flowers;

I pity my youth

And I pity the spring flowers.

Showers of rain brought the flowers to blossom;

I saw lanterns last night,

And I see plum blossoms today.

(*Greets Lady Zheng and Bao Siniang*)

LADY ZHENG:

My dear daughter, Bao Siniang has come to arrange Mr. Li's marriage with you. What's your opinion?

HUO XIAOYU:

Why should you mention his name?

(*To the tune of* ***Xioudai'er***)

Content to sit on my chair and bed,

I feel shy to be called a man's wife.

I'm not the fairy Lanxiang eager for a man;

And this isn't the Peach Blossom Valley for a fisherman to visit.

Without exaggeration, I'm determined to remain chaste

And to stay in my own boudoir.

(*Sobs*)

I've been living with you for so many years,

Staying together all the time.

How could I ever leave you?

LADY ZHENG (*To the previous tune*):

Oh, with the passage of time,

Like the frosty clouds and the solitary moon,

How can I keep my pretty daughter all to myself?

My dear daughter, even the fairy Minggu has human feelings.

I wish you a happy marriage,

So that you won't live alone all the time.

Even the fairy weaver would arrange her marriage,

And meet her lover on the magpie bridge across the Milky Way.

So today,

When you have your spouse

With the help of a matchmaker,

I won't be worrying for you any more.

HUANSHA (*To the previous tune*):

Please don't sigh.

As a most adorable miss,

You will soon be married to your ideal man.

You are caring too much for your mom.

If you hesitate between the two,

None of them will be happy in the end.

(*Aside*)

I won't be coaxed.

She has reached the age of sixteen,

An age with undisciplined impulses of a youthful heart.

It's high time for her to get married;

A flawless jade as she is,

She will soon pass her prime.

BAO SINIANG (*To the previous tune*):

With your glib tongue,

You are slashing me the matchmaker.

Eager to win your hand,

Why should the talented scholar

Do without a perfect mate?

The miss longs for love but gives no reply

While the mother chatters all in vain.

To tell whether their love is true or not,

You may look at the swallow jade hairpin,

And recall what happened before the plum blossoms.

LADY ZHENG:

That's right. It's the hairpin on my daughter's dressing-table. How did it fall into the hands of a

young man?

(*Huo Xiaoyu blushes*)

(*Asks Huansha*)

What happened last night?

HUANSHA (*To the tune of* **Taishiyin**):

On our leave for the lanterns on the Festival Eve,

We turned to the winding corridor in front of the moonlit plums.

We were about to leave when her hairpin got caught on the twigs;

As we were searching for it, he put it into his sleeve.

LADY ZHENG:

Was he Mr. Li the scholar?

HUANSHA:

While the scholar was bold enough,

My young mistress appeared a bit shy and timid.

LADY ZHENG:

What did the scholar say?

HUANSHA:

He said that as he was still single at his age,

He kept the hairpin so as to have access to the miss.

LADY ZHENG:

What did your young mistress say?

HUANSHA (*To the previous tune*):

She has heard of his talent and grace,

But chanced to meet him on the Festival Eve.

I stood by the lanterns in the moonlight,

Overhearing the dialogue between the scholar and belle.

How happy he was when he held the hairpin!

How shy she was behind the plum blossoms!

LADY ZHENG:

Then what?

HUANSHA:

She looked with a charming smile,

For she was much enticed.

LADY ZHENG:

Why?

HUANSHA:

As we know, a smile often predestines a happy marriage.

LADY ZHENG (*Asks with a smile*):

Is that true, Xiaoyu?

HUO XIAOYU (*In a low voice*):

(*To the tune of* **Sanxueshi**)

As I tarried by the plum blossoms at spring dusk,

I saw him sigh and sigh.

He was watching my face behind the lantern

When I asked him to return the exquisite hairpin.

Suddenly we seemed to make a vow for marriage

And smiled to each other at the encounter.

LADY ZHENG (*To the previous tune*):

Marriage is no joking for you,

But he might be too rash about it.

Is he ready to settle down in Chang'an?

I'm afraid that he might discard you in the future.

So lightly you made your vow under the moonlit plums

That I fear your encounter might be a mistake.

BAO SINIANG (*To the previous tune*):

Xiaoyu,

You are in the prime of your life,

And the scholar is from a prestigious family.

When he took your swallow hairpin,

Does it mean that the swallow flew into an ordinary family?

As I also made my vow under the moonlit plums,

I can assure you of a happy marriage.

HUANSHA:

Your Ladyship, please give your consent!

(*To the previous tune*)

Spring night in a fairyland

Foretells the best luck for a joyful life.

Oh, talented scholar,

    Do you have a fine steed

    To match the swallows on the belle's hairpins?

    Your vow under the moonlit plums

    Will bring about the happiest marriage.

LADY ZHENG:

They talked heart to heart and took the hairpin as the token of engagement. It's all arranged by Heaven! It's all arranged by Heaven!

    (*To the tune of* **Coda**)

    Please ask the would-be son-in-law to fix the date;

    I'll prepare the ceremony for the wedding day.

BAO SINIANG:

    He has a pair of white jade pendants to highlight the best day.

    A chance encounter ends with a smile,

    With the hairpin as a token of engagement.

    With the swallow on the hairpin in his sleeves,

    The scholar will meet the belle in her boudoir.

224

Scene Nine
Receiving Good News

    (*Enter Li Yi*)

LI YI (*In the pattern of* **Siyueren**):

    "Ambling through the capital to view the lanterns,

    I saw a jade swallow as if in a dream.

    Tarrying in the street and listening to the flute music,

    I seemed to hear her voice ringing around.

    The spring is early and the jade is real;

    When can I fly with her as a floating cloud?

    I try my luck of love for the belle,

    And eagerly expect news from the matchmaker."

I've asked Bao Siniang to make the match, but I fear that my love's mother might not agree.

    (*To the tune of* **Yingjilinchun**)

    We met and chatted before the lanterns for a while,

    And walked quietly along the corridor in the moonlight.

    I felt it a pity that time passed so quickly,

    For she seemed to regret dropping the hairpin under the trees.

    Walking back and forth among the flowers,

I thought of her slim and slender charm.

As spring chill still pervaded the air,

I sank into a melancholy mood.

I could only reveal my gloom

To the clear and bright moon.

(*To the previous tune*)

I'm still uncertain about the depth of her feeling;

How she smiled when I met her by chance!

Faintly I heard the oriole leaving in the moonlight;

The morning breeze blew here and there at daybreak.

I reckon that as she is so rarely smart,

It'd take some time to truly understand her.

So close by, yet so far away,

There's still some distance to get near her,

But much easier than to enter the Peach Blossom Valley.

(*To the tune of* **Sifanying'er**)

What I love is her sweet and charming manners;

What I fear is her mother's stubborn attitude,

As scholars are not esteemed in society these days.

I have no chance to explain to her again,

And this is a most unfortunate matter,

As we just met and then had to part.

I neither have lust for her beauty,

Nor have greed for her wealth.

From the bottom of my heart,

I must feel sure and secure.

(*To the previous tune*)

For all my talent and knowledge,

So many maidens crave for me.

She loves me fine though without words.

The hairpin on the plum twigs

Is to be used as a token by the matchmaker,

Who is as glib as the oriole warbling in spring.

I wear out my eyes waiting for the outcome

In a melancholy and longing mood,

But the matchmaker is yet to come.

(*Enter Bao Siniang*)

BAO SINIANG (*To the tune of* **Lanhuamei**):

The day is getting fine with bluish clouds and azure sky;

After the Lantern Festival, the spring scene quiets down

When I slipped out of bed with my hair dishevelled.

(*Greets Li Yi*)

LI YI:

Sorry to have troubled you! But did she give consent?

BAO SINIANG:

> She agreed not by words, but by heart.
>
> As the saying goes, "Spring breeze brings good luck."

LI YI:

So what did she say?

BAO SINIANG (*To the previous tune*):

> She said that as you were a talented scholar
>
> With fine manners and a grand style,
>
> As you were from a distinguished family,
>
> Your marriage was predestined by Heaven,
>
> For you to pencil her eyebrows at the dressing-table.

LI YI:

What was the young mistress doing then?

BAO SINIANG:

When I arrived there, she had just got out of bed.

> (*To the tune of* **Zuiluoge**)
>
> She was charming after a night's sleep,
>
> And she was fresh after careful make-up.
>
> She removed the extra powder with delicate fingers,
>
> And fondled her drooping spring gown.
>
> She rinsed her mouth with fragrant water,
>
> And wiped her dainty lips clean.
>
> Even the lotus smiled to her stealthily,
>
> And the azure clouds stole a look at her,
>
> Only to find her spring affection by her eyebrows.
>
> But don't be hasty.
>
> As she's so supple and charming,
>
> Do you have the luck to marry her?

LI YI (*To the previous tune*):

> Surely, surely, it's been settled down;
>
> Happily, happily, we've become one.
>
> It'll take a fortune to trade for the spring night,
>
> Which I enjoyed so much.
>
> To drink alone in melancholy spring,
>
> A single man may feel a bit cold;
>
> To share the same pillow with your love,
>
> You may feel warm in spring night.
>
> She can wait with patience but I can't wait any more.
>
> After three days,
>
> In the early morning,

I'll thank my matchmaker with precious gifts.

BAO SINIANG:

Mr. Li, we'll hold the wedding ceremony on the birthday of flowers, but you look so humble. A man from such a family as yours must ride a fine horse with a gilded saddle and be followed by some servants.

LI YI:

I see.

BAO SINIANG (*To the tune of* **Coda**):

>As you are truly a first-rank scholar,

>You must make your wife all the more charming.

Oh, yes, Mr. Li,

>You also need some silk fabric for lovemaking.

>(*Exit*)

>(*Li Yi remains on the stage*)

LI YI:

Bao Siniang says that I look humble, so I'll ask my brothers Wei Xiaqing and Cui Yunming to borrow some servants and horses for a grand show.

>*The jade hairpin is on the moon fairy's head,*

>*While the matchmaker arranges for the marriage.*

>*The magpies spreading good news for the couple*

>*Signify the harmony between phoenixes.*

Scene Ten
Asking for Servants and Horses

>(*Enter Qiuhong*)

QIUHONG:

>*"The public goes after a grand fashion,*

>*But what matters most is one's actual achievement.*

>*When the man and the horse are both respectable,*

>*The two families will shine brightly."*

My master, Mr. Li, is exceptionally talented, and so Heaven arranges for his marriage. All are ready except for some servants and horses. He went to consult Mr. Cui and Mr. Wei. How seriously he takes it!

>(*Enter Li Yi*)

LI YI (*To the tune of* **Wanxiandeng**):

>I'm talented as Sima Xiangru,

>And yet I need a hall and a carriage.

Qiuhong, I've invited Mr. Cui and Mr. Wei to come for some consultation. They'll be coming any moment.

(*Enter Wei Xiaqing and Cui Yunming*)

WEI XIAQING, CUI YUNMING (*To the tune of* **Xiaopenglai**):

> When spring breath blows to the deserts,
>
> Extravagant gentlemen have gathered in the capital.
>
> One of us from the esteemed Wei family from Zhongnan,
>
> And the other from the distinguished Cui family from Boling,
>
> We are both free and elegant.

(*Greet Li Yi*)

CUI YUNMING:

How's your love affair out of the hairpin?

LI YI:

The date of marriage has already been fixed. As not much time is left, I shall ask you for help.

CUI YUNMING:

I'll be glad to hear it.

LI YI:

> "*The noble and distinguished families*
>
> *Must present expensive and respectable gifts.*
>
> *In these traveler's humble clothes,*
>
> *I feel truly hard to pose myself in a grand fashion.*"

Now let me tell you,

> (*To the tune of* **Zhumating**)
>
> I travel only on donkeys,
>
> Without showy silvery saddles.
>
> When I become the bridegroom,
>
> I certainly need a grand carriage and four.
>
> Walking by the flowers, I quite hesitate,
>
> For where could I get the proper sets for a grand style?

WEI XIAQING, CUI YUNMING:

> With escorts at the front and the back,
>
> We must make a glorious scene for your family.

CUI YUNMING:

Brother Li, you aren't going to marry a lady with the same family name as yours. So what has caused you "Wu Maqi", to have no horse to ride, as the story goes in the *Analects*? I have horses for you in my Cui family.

WEI XIAQING:

As the *Analects* goes, Mr. Cui killed the king of the State of Qi, and Chen Wenzi gave up his horses. So it's Mr. Chen that has forty horses. How could the Cui family have any horses? I have horses in my Wei family.

CUI YUNMING:

How would you explain it?

WEI XIAQING:

As the line of the *Book of Family Names* goes, Lu Wei Chang Ma, so the Wei family has lots of horses.

CUI YUNMING:

Let's stop kidding! There's a rich family in Chang'an. They have a dozen fine horses with gilded saddles and jade bridle bits. I'll borrow the horses for you.

(*To the previous tune*)

Let's forget about the inferior nags.

I have a fabulous knightly friend,

Who can lend you a horse and a saddle,

So you can be a bridegroom on a horse.

A fine horse to ride is a must,

To bring a belle into a grand house,

With silvery saddles and embroidered kerchiefs.

WEI XIAQING, CUI YUNMING:

With escorts at the front and the back,

We must make a glorious scene for your family.

LI YI:

Besides the horses, I've one more thing to ask for!

(*To the previous tune*)

In a declining family,

One servant or two would be enough.

But since I'm going to marry now,

I need some servants to tend the horse,

So they can carry my clothing

And shoulder my zither and books.

With this luck, I won't feel lonely any more,

But I do need some servants.

WEI XIAQING, CUI YUNMING:

With escorts at the front and the back,

We must make a glorious scene for your family.

CUI YUNMING:

Before you marry, you even want to change your servants as the *Book of Poetry* goes. That won't do. A man's wife is called "Madame", and she calls herself a "servant" before her man as the *Book of Rites* goes. If you bring several pretty "servants", your bride will be jealous. If you want pretty servants, you can carve some from the plum trees.

WEI XIAQING:

What do you mean?

CUI YUNMING:

Well, it's all explained in the *Book of Family Names*, "Jiang Tong Yan Guo, Mei Sheng Lin Diao," that is, if you want pretty servants, you can carve some from the plum trees, you see.

LI YI:

You're kidding!

WEI XIAQING:

That knight has servants too. They are all professionally dressed with very special green sleeves and patterned head-coverings.

> (*To the previous tune*)
> We'll have fabulous servants
> To compare with the ancient famous servants.
> Instead of appointing servants to play the flutes
> Or to make decorations,
> We'll have short-haired Tartar servants.
> So you can hold the whip and ride the horse led by a handsome boy,
> And your suitcase will be carried by other male servants.

WEI XIAQING, CUI YUNMING:

> With escorts at the front and the back,
> We must make a glorious scene for your family.
> (*To the tune of* **Coda**)
> Just go ahead and be a bridegroom with ease,
> And we'll take care of the rest.

We'll celebrate your marriage with enthusiasm.

> We wish you to enter the bridal chamber safe and sound.
> *What is one's natural state?*
> *It takes efforts for a grand style.*
> *Mr. Li must ride a fine horse,*
> *But who will order the servants?*

Scene Eleven
Advice for the Wedding Night

(*Enter Huo Xiaoyu*)

HUO XIAOYU (*To the tune of* **Fanbusuan**):

> Leaning against the incense burner outside the screen,
> I find the rouge on my lips gone after a night's sleep.
> With flushing dainty brows I accept the wedding date
> And treasure the intention vowed before the blossoms.
> (*In the pattern of* **Pusaman**)
> *"One festival passes after another for Heaven and Earth;*
> *In the flickering red candle lights I shed my sorrow on the pillow.*
> *When spring enters my chamber,*
> *I blush like a blooming cardamom.*
> *With a spider caught on my skirt as a sign of happiness,*
> *I feel delighted in my heart.*
> *The nearer the day draws, the more anxious I feel*

For the uncertainty of the wedding night."

Mr. Li's proposal was accepted yesterday, but how soon or late is the wedding day? This truly bothers me!

(*To the tune of* **Wugongyang**)

We did meet once,

But with whom can I spend the springtime now?

He feels sorry for the spring

Especially when the feast is over at night.

As he has just left,

Who understands my tender feelings?

We parted on the Lantern Festival Eve,

And expect to meet again on flowers' day.

Even the affectionate Spring Goddess

Would blame human indifference and alienation.

(*To the previous tune*)

Lingering obscurely in my dream,

Our encounter sticks firmly to my mind.

Wavering in the wind at night,

For whom was the jade hairpin fondling the plum twigs?

It's said that one does not have to roll the heavy curtains

For the swallows to bring good news.

They delay the wedding at will

Without considering my anxious heart.

Why not marry him sooner

To receive his true and loving care?

(*Enter Bao Siniang*)

BAO SINIANG (*To the tune of* **Jinlongcong**):

The phoenix flaps on the green branches;

The flower fragrance seeps into the emerald moss.

The young lady drowses in the painted hall in spring;

Who's behind the beaded curtains over there?

(*Greets Huo Xiaoyu*)

HUO XIAOYU:

"*Butterflies flutter wings for their mates among flowers;*

BAO SINIANG:

Willow branches whip the bees to report the news.

HUO XIAOYU:

When spring makes you drowsy behind the tree-shaded door,

BAO SINIANG:

I'll teach you, young lady, how to spend the happy time."

HUO XIAOYU:

What happy time do you mean?

BAO SINIANG:

I mean to teach you what "happy time" means. Of course, I mean the wedding night.

(*To the tune of* **Yujiaozhi**)

Idling alone in the candle light,

You fiddle with the jade hairpins.

You expect your groom's loving embrace,

Yet you hesitate, frowning and evading shyly.

When the happy hour comes at midnight, you turn and smile;

This is the time worth a fortune.

With trembling hands you lift the embroidered bed-curtains,

And unbutton the chained knots on your red short coat.

(*To the previous tune*)

Startled with blissful delight,

You have no time to hold your rosy cheeks with your fine fingers.

You try to protect the lilac bud of your virginity,

Yet he gains the cardamom of your girlhood.

He ventures to violate your body of jade and fragrance,

And you willingly accept the lovemaking of cloud and rain.

Then the climax comes in full bloom

When your waist and limbs quiver.

That's what you are to do in the bridal chamber.

(*To the tune of* **Chenzuidongfeng**)

You need to tailor a vest with a pair of mandarin ducks

Embroidered by your own fingertips.

For your luscious pussy,

You need to prepare an undershirt of light gauze

To do the cleanup in the course.

Coyly you half open your eyes,

And light up the lamp,

Revealing your figure of a newly-wed bride.

HUO XIAOYU:

That's enough!

BAO SINIANG:

All right, enough.

(*To the previous tune*)

Out of the loving bed with the rising sun,

He steals a look when you dress yourself up before the mirror.

You frown and contemplate by yourself,

Secretly looking and wondering at the red stain,

Calling the maid to take it away without being seen.

Bliss on the bride!

Bliss on the bridegroom!

This is the happiness between man and wife.

HUO XIAOYU:

I appreciate your advice! My mother is calling for you.

BAO SINIANG (*To the tune of* **Coda**):

> I'll go and explain most clearly,
>
> So as to fix the luckiest wedding day.
>
> You'll have to endure the muddle these days.
>
> *From a slim lady of virginal innocence,*
>
> *You'll become the respectful wife of a man.*
>
> *This is the first sign of happiness in life,*
>
> *Like the yearly spring for flowers and grass.*

Scene Twelve
Servant and Horse at the Door

(*Enter Qiuhong*)

QIUHONG:

> *"My master is fond of me by nature,*
>
> *So we live in the same chamber.*
>
> *But he neglects me in recent days,*
>
> *For he found his love not long ago."*

My name is Qiuhong. For my rough knowledge of etiquette, I get the chance to serve at Mr. Li's house. I've been at his service for a couple of years, feeling most at home. Now that my master is to marry the young mistress of the Huo family, he has no time to notice me. So I call it the master's neglect of the servant. Despite the neglect, the Huo family is certainly not lacking in maids. For old time's sake, my master may also find me a mate. So he has a lady for his wife and I have a maid for my spouse. That's no problem. Yesterday my master asked Mr. Wei and Mr. Cui to borrow some horses and servants, so that he can have a grand show for the wedding. I was told to take care of them when they arrive. But you know how difficult it is: Servants want rice to eat and horses need to be fed with grass, and yet I have neither. How I am to manage all these things! Oh, how annoying! Let me see what's going on outside.

(*Enter the Gallant Knight's short-haired Tartar servant with a horse*)

TARTAR SERVANT:

> *"A young gentleman is well matched with a fine horse,*
>
> *And yet such a talent has to borrow a bearded servant."*

Yesterday Mr. Wei and Mr. Cui borrowed a servant and a horse for Mr. Li from Longxi. Here is his residence. Let me call out. Who's at the door?

QIUHONG:

Good gracious. Here arrives the servant and the horse. Yet we need one more horse.

TARTAR SERVANT:

Why?

QIUHONG:

As my master is to marry the young mistress, I will take the lucky day to match with a plain-looking chambermaid of the house. That's why we need one more horse.

TARTAR SERVANT:

How fortunate! You've just rid yourself of being ridden, and now you want to ride a horse. It's too early yet!

QIUHONG:

All right, forget about it. Let me look at your horse. Fine. Then let me look at the servant. (*Laughing*) So you were a horse in your previous life.

TARTAR SERVANT:

How come?

QIUHONG:

A horse needs to have its mane cut, and you need to have your beard cut; a daddy horse is dark-skinned, and your face is dark-skinned all over, too. So you must be a horse in your previous life.

TARTAR SERVANT (*Angrily*):

What! You borrow our man and horse without giving any rice and fodder. Instead, you try to insult me. You deserve a beating, you bastard!

> (*Beats Qiuhong*)
>
> (*Enter Li Yi*)

LI YI (*To the tune of Wanxiandeng*):

> I choose the lucky day to send my wedding invitation.
>
> Tonight is the last night for me to sleep alone.

Oh, no! The borrowed servant and horse are our guests. Qiuhong, you rogue, how could you be so rude! My guests, please forgive us.

> (*The Tartar servant kowtows*)

TARTAR SERVANT:

At your service. Please check the horse, Mr. Li!

LI YI:

A fine horse! An excellent man!

TARTAR SERVANT:

Please forgive me for asking: Where are you going?

LI YI (*To the tune of Xiaoshunge*):

To Huo's residence.

> A gentleman matches a lady like a pair of phoenixes.
>
> He borrows a fine horse to shine for the family.

Look at the horse!

> Its hair is dark red like the purple velvet,
>
> And its saddle decorations are plated with gold.
>
> What a fabulous young gentleman,

With all the ease and grace,

Proceeding to a promising career!

With the servant going ahead,

The young master is crowded all around.

When you arrive, answer with courtesy.

You must be decent and smart,

As theirs is a family of manners and etiquette.

TARTAR SERVANT:

Yes, I see.

(To the previous tune)

You are a top scholar from a distinguished family.

The horse

Matches the handsome gentleman perfectly well.

Our Knight has an extraordinary habit,

Of fondly helping the gifted scholars.

Mr. Li,

You'll ride on a fine horse with a gilded saddle,

With servants accompanying you,

Going to the bridal chamber.

By that time, I'm afraid after drinking,

You won't have time to care for us

But lie in the chamber for your bride.

So we just have one request: The horse will have good fodder, the servants will have good wine, and you our master will eat well, so that we'll all be high-spirited.

You draw the reins tight and call the servants at will,

Showing your best extravagance.

LI YI:

Thanks a lot! All retire for tonight now.

The man eats cooked rice,

While the horse feeds on chopped grass.

When I ride on the miraculous horse,

I'll advance with fancy decorations.

Scene Thirteen
The Wedding in Spring

(Enter Huo Xiaoyu and Huansha)

HUO XIAOYU (*To the tune of* **Queqiaoxian**):

With the beaded curtains rolled up high,

And the painted screens spreading low like fans,

I open my dressing case in the morning sun.

Blue smoke curls up from the silvery candle on the crimson stand,

And the dim candlelight makes me blush.

(*In the pattern of* **Haoshijin**)

"*As the window gauze is rolled up in the morning light,*

I get up half dressed in my silk gown.

HUANSHA:

Why do you get up so early,

As the sun is just rising?

HUO XIAOYU:

When the spring wind blows into our storeyed house,

I cannot stay asleep in bed in the chamber.

HUANSHA:

Well, there's a special person

To be kept in your heart."

HUO XIAOYU:

The time for the wedding is drawing near, but Bao Siniang has not arrived yet.

(*Enter Bao Siniang*)

BAO SINIANG (*To the tune of* **Lameihua**):

The candles, the incense burners and the feast are all set;

The screens are decorated with foggy hills and phoenixes.

With the red thread to link the couple for marriage,

The handsome bridegroom will soon come

To meet his fairy bride in hundreds of flowers.

(*Greets Huo Xiaoyu*)

Your darling will be arriving soon. My young mistress, let's climb to the Phoenix & Flute Mansion to take a look. (*Looks*) The Shengyefang Lane is over there, that is the end of the street, and this is your residence hall.

HUO XIAOYU:

Ah, look, Siniang! A man is riding this way.

BAO SINIANG:

Right! He's coming to the south.

(*Enter Li Yi riding a horse, followed by the Tartar servant, Qiuhong and a few other servants*)

LI YI (*To the tune of* **Sudijindang**):

Intoxicated by spring flowers, I hold a whip in my sleeve,

Riding a horse along the lush foliage by the river.

I'm a fabulous man more attractive than the Lantian jade,

Looking from afar at my bride's house in the mist.

(*Exit*)

HUO XIAOYU (*Delightfully surprised*):

Siniang, look at him riding along the river! He's as elegant as the willow, like Zhang Xu in his young days! How freely he's whirling his whip backwards, with the horsemanship of Wang

Zhan in the past! He's indeed the man of men!

(*To the tune of* **Diaojiao'er**)

Who's that handsome man by the river?

He's riding a horse like dancing peach blossoms.

He seems to sit on the clouds, soaring to the sky,

With glamour and grandeur along the way.

With my image in his heart,

He gazes, casts the spring wind of his eyes,

Greets the morning sun, and sways before the blossoms.

Clothed in blue and glowing on the face,

There comes such an adorable young man,

Far surpassing Song Yu,

And Sima Xiangru as well.

BAO SINIANG:

This mansion has become the platform to look forward to her man. Let's go downstairs and ask Her Ladyship to greet the bridegroom.

(*Goes downstairs*)

"*The bridegroom must listen to the mother-in-law,*

And the pair of mandarin ducks must meet on the magpie bridge."

(*Enter Lady Zheng*)

LADY ZHENG (*To the tune of* **Ruihexian**):

My daughter in the prime of her youth

Is committed in marriage by a red thread.

In deep spring with a radiant scene

Where flowers blossom with time,

Good luck brings happy marriage.

Swallows send the good news

That the pair of swallow hairpins have been matched.

My sole concern goes with my daughter

For her to get happily married,

And for the couple to love and respect each other forever.

Mr. Li has arrived. Huansha, where's the Wedding Master of Ceremony?

(*Enter the Wedding Master of Ceremony*)

MASTER:

Here I am. Here I am.

"*Appearance and rite, which is more important?*

So come on, bridegroom, dress yourself up.

Rite and food, which is more important?

So come on, waiters, prepare the best food.

The rites intoned at the hall are to be watched;

Yet the rites intoned on the bed are only to be listened to."

BAO SINIANG:

How can the rites be intoned on the bed?

MASTER:

> *"They just prostrate themselves, bow and kowtow to each other;*
> *In fact, they don't intone anything, but act."*

BAO SINIANG:

Why don't they intone the rites on the bed?

MASTER:

> *"The bridegroom nods to perform the rites on the bed.*
> *If he intones out of the tune, it will surely ruin the pleasure."*
>
> (*Enter Li Yi*)

LI YI (*To the tune of* **Baodinger**):

> When I ride on my horse holding my whip,
> I see the decorated house before my eyes,
> And hear the flute music from the court.
> Candle smoke slowly curls up from the crimson stand,
> While the embroidered gauze is stirred by the wind.
>
> (*Enter Huo Xiaoyu*)

HUO XIAOYU:

> The swallows on the pair of jade hairpins are delightfully matched,
> Remaining affectionate as they first met before the plum blossoms.

LI YI, HUO XIAOYU:

> Facing the dense incense smoke from the tripod,
> We pray from the bottom of our hearts
> That our marital ties will last forever.

MASTER (*Gives the blessing*):

> *"First bow to Heaven and Earth.*
> *When Heaven and Earth meet, they bring happiness to man and wife,*
> *Because everything goes well now that the water goes above the fire.*
> *You are to have a son this year*
> *And a daughter next year.*
> *Next bow to your mother.*
> *When you bow to the Mother Goddess,*
> *You receive the blessing of the Mother Goddess.*
> *The Mother Goddess marries her daughter this year*
> *And will see her grandson next year.*
> *Then bow to each other between man and wife.*
> *When you are married today,*
> *You'll share whatever wealth and prosperity.*
> *One aims at high position and fame,*
> *While the other gives birth to offspring."*

BAO SINIANG (*Cuts in jokingly*):

What a wife from a grand family!

MASTER:

Now the rites are over. The bride and bridegroom, please be seated. Now it's time for the servants to kowtow.

(*Qiuhong and the Tartar servant come to the fore*)

QIUHONG:

Your closest servant little Qiuhong kowtows to you.

LADY ZHENG:

Are those servants all from the Li family?

QIUHONG:

Not the Li family of plums, but the Tao family of peaches.

LADY ZHENG:

Which Tao family?

TARTAR SERVANT:

The grand Hao family.

LADY ZHENG:

Which Hao family?

TARTAR SERVANT:

Now the Li family has become rich, so it's called the Hao family of grand status.

LADY ZHENG:

I see. So Mr. Li comes from a rich and grand family. Is the horse also from the Li family?

QIUHONG:

Not from the Li family of plums, but the Tao family of peaches.

LADY ZHENG:

How come it's from the Tao family again?

LI YI:

It's not the horse from the Tao family of peaches, but it's the peach-flowered horse, you know.

LADY ZHENG:

Mr. Li, so your horse is as fine as the peach flower or your horse is simply gone? Huansha, show our guests to the banquet at the other hall.

TARTAR SERVANT:

Great! Let's go and have a drink.

"*The horse bathes in the spring pond outside the door,*

And the red candles greet guests before the house."

(*Exit*)

LADY ZHENG:

Fetch the wine.

LI YI:

Please wait a moment. I have a pair of Lantian white jade pendants and ten bolts of patterned brocade to present to you with my humble respect.

LADY ZHENG:

Please accept them, my daughter. Mr. Li, I've often heard about your talent and manners.

Now that I see your elegant bearing in person, you are truly remarkable. Though my daughter needs more cultivation, she is above the plain looks. So she is lucky to match you perfectly.

LI YI (*Gratefully*):

I'm far from satisfactory, and I don't aspire too highly. I feel most lucky to be chosen as your son-in-law. It's my great honour in this life or after.

> (*To the tune of **Jintangyue***)
>
> (*Raises the wine cup*)
>
> With embroidered curtains linked by red drapes,
>
> With doors and gates surrounded by verdant trees,
>
> The spring scene spreads over the courtyard of tradition.
>
> Fragrance lingers and mist floats;
>
> The couple hold fans and laugh as if in a fairyland.
>
> The new beauty shuns the morning sun with her dress,
>
> And saunters along the Luo River to exhibit her charm.

LI YI, HUO XIAOYU:

> What a fairylike couple!
>
> Coming together from afar for the marriage,
>
> We are sure to enjoy the happiness for a hundred years.

HUO XIAOYU (*To the previous tune*):

> Luckily, by the fairy pond
>
> And at the Lantern Festival Eve,
>
> The phoenixes appeared in the dreamland.
>
> Once we drink the nectar,
>
> We'll be married as if in the Lanqiao legend.
>
> We'll soar to the clouds
>
> And dance around like the fairies.

LI YI, HUO XIAOYU:

> What a fairylike couple!
>
> Coming together from afar for the marriage,
>
> We are sure to enjoy the happiness for a hundred years.

LADY ZHENG (*To the previous tune*):

> Pitifully, my daughter's been pretty
>
> And shy since she was small,
>
> And she has never met a young man before.
>
> Now that she's married,
>
> There'll be harmony in the family.
>
> She dresses herself up before the fancy mirror
>
> And she is lucky to find her ideal man.

LI YI, HUO XIAOYU:

> What a fairylike couple!
>
> Coming together from afar for the marriage,
>
> We are sure to enjoy the happiness for a hundred years.

ALL (*To the previous tune*):

    Warmly, mist comes up from the green,

    The red dress shines in the sun,

    And people sing together all the time.

    Congratulations to the talent and beauty,

    Who are married in the prime of their youth.

    The starlight mingling with the candlelight

    Seems to enter the spring scene of the fairyland.

LI Yi, HUO XIAOYU:

    What a fairylike couple!

    Coming together from afar for the marriage,

    We are sure to enjoy the happiness for a hundred years.

LADY ZHENG (*To the tune of* **Zuiwengzi**):

    Enviably, the happy marriage dwells in the prime of youth,

    Yet laurels of success hang up cold on the moon,

    And the peonies in Luoyang may be devalued.

LI YI:

    I'm fortunate enough

    To have such kindness and mercy.

    Where could I find the riches to repay?

LI YI, HUO XIAOYU:

    So treasure the happiness together,

    And remember the vows under the moon

    And the swallows on the pair of jade hairpins.

HUO XIAOYU (*To the previous tune*):

    Stop the chat, time for my man to paint my eyebrows,

    When the three stars still twinkle,

    And the lucky clouds hang over our bridal house.

LI YI:

    To our will, I'm sure to win His Majesty's conferment,

    And then return home for reunion with wealth and fame.

LI YI, HUO XIAOYU:

    So treasure the happiness together,

    And remember the vows under the moon

    And the swallows on the pair of jade hairpins.

LI YI (*To the tune of* **Xingxingling**):

    On the high lotus-shaped stand,

    The red candlelight flickers.

    In the stillness of the night,

    She holds fragrant breath,

    And wears sparkling jewelry,

    Expecting her young man.

HUO XIAOYU (*To the previous tune*):

> Flushed with intoxication
>
> I can't fall asleep at the enchanting night.
>
> Yet the stars move,
>
> And time passes by.
>
> Dressed in my best
>
> I wait for the daybreak.

LI YI, HUO XIAOYU (*To the tune of* **Coda**):

> With the brocade curtains fragrant for a hundred years,
>
> Man and wife will live together forever,
>
> As the talent matches the beauty perfectly well.
>
> *When the spring moonlight reflects the spring flowers,*
>
> *The marital ties are linked across a thousand miles.*
>
> *Blissful is the time when candles are lit in the bridal chamber;*
>
> *Fortunate is the time when one succeeds in the imperial exam.*

Scene Fourteen
The Chivalrous Friends' Congratulations

(*Enter Huansha*)

HUANSHA:

> "*Spring lingers in the bed-curtain with tassels in the morn;*
>
> *Flowers toss their buds and spread fragrance after fresh rain.*
>
> *The window gauzes wave and the dainty eyebrows come in sight*
>
> *As I bow in a tilting manner to my elegant master.*"

Funny, really funny. As my young mistress is married to Mr. Li, I, as a maid, sleep at the back of the bed. So how would Mr. Li feel about it, and what would be my mistress's grace and dignity? Anyway, I don't have to care about these. Now that the sun rises up high and it's almost noon, my young mistress is starting to dress up.

(*Enter Huo Xiaoyu*)

HUO XIAOYU (*To the tune of* **Tanchunling**):

> We tasted our bliss in the couple's quilt for the first time
>
> With the spring breeze behind the curtain of our bed.
>
> (*Huansha supports Huo Xiaoyu*)
>
> Supported and frail as I am,
>
> I smile, afraid that someone might ask:
>
> What can I do with such an affectionate man?
>
> (*In the pattern of* **Heyebei**)
>
> "*I offered my first love to my man last night,*

My heart trembling, my hair messed up and my limbs most weakened.

With my adorable softness, how could I silently raise my head?

How embarrassing!

How embarrassing!"

HUANSHA (*Laughs*):

Ah, this is what you enjoy and what you suffer! The white and clean kerchief must have been stained.

> (*To the tune of **Yingtixu***)
>
> The scarlet stain on the brocade kerchief has just faded;
>
> Sweat was mixed with the powder on your tender face.
>
> He could hardly wait to experience such passion of love,
>
> And had already penetrated your delicate parts.

Oh, how you suffered!

> Suddenly you gave out an oriole-like cry,
>
> Folded up your soaked parts and became his wife.
>
> Oh, what a dream-like spring!
>
> How the rain matched the cloud with fragrance strong!
>
> (*Enter Li Yi*)

LI YI (*To the tune of **Ruanlanggui***):

> When the morning light shines through the green window gauze,
>
> My darling comes into sight like a goddess from a fairyland.
>
> I gaze at her sitting and smiling by the screens,
>
> So fresh and quiet in her new make-up.
>
> (*Greets Huo Xiaoyu*)
>
> *"You pencil your eyebrows with proper dark and light shades,*
>
> *As if the beauty of spring mountains were brought indoors.*
>
> *Soon the sun will shed light on your rouged cheeks,*
>
> *As if the red cream were starting to melt."*

Xiaoyu, when I took the first look at you in the chamber, you looked like a tree of jasper and jade, glimmering all over. When I took a second look at you, you were radiating with charm and grace. Your voice was soft and your expression was subtle. When you were undressing yourself, you showed the best glamour. As we turned intimate on our pillows in the curtain, how lovingly you attracted me! I thought to myself: Even the goddess of beauty could not compare with you!

HUO XIAOYU (*Smiling*):

You're flattering me! You're flattering me!

LI YI:

My friends Wei Xiaqing and Cui Yunming are coming to extend their congratulations. We must get wine and food ready.

HUO XIAOYU:

Certainly, we will.

> (*Enter Wei Xiaqing and Cui Yunming*)

WEI XIAQING, CUI YUNMING (*To the tune of* **Queqiaoxian**):

> Zhang Sheng peering through the red wall for Yingying,
>
> Lady Yang bathing in the Huangqing Pond,
>
> Both of them rouse youthful passions in spring.
>
> Like Xiao Shi and Nongyu flying to the fairyland,
>
> What colourful clouds we have today!
>
> (*They enter to greet the new couple*)

Right on time, right on time. Congratulations on the bride and bridegroom! A talent matches a beauty, what a heavenly couple!

> "*The bridegroom shows new talent for loving his bride,*
>
> *And the bride keeps the same tune with her bridegroom.*

LI YI, HUO XIAOYU:

> *Stars match each other in pairs in heaven;*
>
> *Guests offer congratulates on earth.*"

LI YI:

Fetch the wine.

HUANSHA (*Presents the wine*):

> "*Old wine smells more aromatic;*
>
> *Familiar guests greet the new couple.*"

Here is the wine.

> (*Li Yi and Huo Xiaoyu hold up the wine cups*)

LI YI (*To the tune of* **Yushan'er**):

> On arriving at the painted hall,
>
> The guests straighten up their silken robes with phoenixes and cranes.
>
> The crimson candles on the silvery lotus-shaped stands flicker brightly,
>
> While the fine incense smoke curls up slowly from the tripod burner.

HUO XIAOYU:

> Before the old friends who come for the congratulations,
>
> I can't help blushing with my eyebrows half knit,
>
> Holding up my sleeves to make toasts to our friends.

LI YI, HUO XIAOYU:

> With the hairpins slanting down,
>
> She slightly bows by the bridegroom,
>
> Feeling most delicate and charming.

CUI YUNMING (*To the previous tune*):

> Born in a noble family,
>
> She's a daughter that shines like jade and gold.
>
> Her eyebrows are like the spring mountains,
>
> Or like a thin and green line brightly lit.

WEI XIAQING:

> When the morning sun shines brightly on the painted house,
>
> The beauty sends her fragrance all over —

A true belle in the world!

WEI XIAQING, CUI YUNMING:

> With the luckiest fate,
>
> You wander under most usual circumstances
>
> Yet to meet such a fairy!

LI YI (*To the previous tune*):

> For years and years,
>
> I've been searching for a plum flower under the moon.
>
> Then I saw the belle loiter alone,
>
> And won the chance to talk with her face to face.

HUO XIAOYU:

> It must be the predestined fate
>
> That blessed me with such charm
>
> To be appreciated by such a talent.

LI YI, HUO XIAOYU:

> In favour of our will,
>
> Both in the prime of our youth,
>
> We make a perfect couple.

WEI XIAQING (*To the previous tune*):

> What adorable grace!
>
> Time slows down in the study and at the court.
>
> The fragrant breeze attracts the fairy beauty,
>
> And the spring peony adds more to her allurement.

CUI YUNMING:

> As your cavalier and extravagant friends,
>
> We've come to ask the green cardamom
>
> About your love affair at the wedding night.

WEI XIAQING, CUI YUNMING:

> May the daylilies
>
> Bloom early,
>
> So that you waste no time for such a beauty.

WEI XIAQING:

Enough of wine. Please allow me to offer some advice: Now that you have become the son-in-law in a noble family to enjoy the beauty and luxury, our mistress must learn from Yue Yangzi's wife to encourage her man to succeed in distinguishing himself in his career. Indulgence in pleasure may hinder great accomplishment.

> (*To the tune of **Zhunu'er***)
>
> A fabulous man is famed for his look and manners,
>
> In accompanying his belle at the moon palace.

CUI YUNMING:

> May the wife encourage her man for a grand career,
>
> And not just care for her domestic affairs.

WEI XIAQING, CUI YUNMING:

    May you respect and love each other at home,

    And you are sure to win the conferment by His Majesty.

HUO XIAOYU:

Now you two gentlemen are present today. Mr. Li is sure to have a grand career, but I'm afraid when he does succeed, he may forsake me.

    (*To the previous tune*)

    Now the marriage certificate registers me as his wife,

    But when he wins the laurel, he may have other's name registered.

CUI YUNMING:

Mr. Li is not that kind of person.

    Look how he treasures the perfume pouch in his sleeve!

    He can't be a heartless man who'll forsake his wife.

WEI XIAQING, CUI YUNMING:

    May you respect and love each other at home,

    And you are sure to win the conferment by His Majesty.

CUI YUNMING:

Mr. Li, now you've got a phoenix nestle of a family among us three while we two are still poor birds without a nestle and a family, nor do we have enough food or clothing. So how are we going to make a living?

LI YI:

As long as you have me as your brother, I'll take care of everything.

CUI YUNMING (*To the tune of* **Coda**):

    The man and wife make the perfect couple,

WEI XIAQING:

    And no other couple can compare with this pair.

WEI XIAQING, CUI YUNMING:

    This pair of phoenixes are about to fly from the flute tower.

    The guests send their congratulations to the new couple,

    Advising the bride to aim high and waste no time.

    With bosom friends, one can never drink too much;

    With talks in accord, one never feels like stopping.

Scene Fifteen
Boasting Power and Selecting Talents

    (*Enter General Lu with his retinue*)

GENERAL LU (*To the tune of* **Manpailing**):

    I command the controlling power at the court,

Taking a carriage almost the same as His Majesty's.

His Majesty releases the edict in the springtime

To line up guards before the palace in Luoyang,

When he takes a tour to the east.

For fear of delaying the imperial examinations,

His Majesty has chosen this very spot as the examination place.

So how can I block the entrance to selecting talents?

"Of a noble family much favoured by His Majesty,

I follow His Majesty and stay in Luoyang.

When talented scholars come to vie for the spring laurel,

His Majesty is concerned about the winners in the capital."

I am General Lu. Prime Minister Lu Qi is my brother. The court eunuch Lu Zhonggui is my younger brother. We are all from a noble and distinguished family, taking full charge of the state affairs. This year I escort His Majesty to Luoyang in the east. For fear of delaying the spring imperial examinations, we decide on Luoyang as the examination site to select the talents. Now I think of my daughter who is about to be fifteen. This would be a good opportunity to choose a true talent as my son-in-law. Where are my attendants?

(The attendants kowtow)

Here is my instruction: Inform the Minister of Education that whoever passes the imperial entrance examination must pay a visit to General Lu's residence. Only after the visit can he get registered in the official list of the candidates. This is exactly what is versed:

The pavilion near the waterfront gets the moonlight first;

The flowers and trees facing the south greet spring early.

(Exit)

Scene Sixteen
The Vow of Love in the Garden

(Enter Huansha)

HUANSHA:

"The mood and spirit are hard to paint;

Flowers grow full all over the twigs.

New tunes are played by the silvery fingertips;

Fragrant rice wine is filled with cold foams."

I am Huansha. As my young mistress is married to Mr. Li, I am awarded with Qiuhong. Qiuhong is smart and sensible, but he is dispatched by Mr. Li to run errands back and forth all the time. In contrast, when Wu'er is married to Yingtao in our house, they work around the stove all day long, never far apart from each other. Just as the saying goes, "The quick-minded are busy like the grain stone-rollers only to gain temporary excitement,

while the slow-minded remain indoors yet to enjoy amorous pleasures every night." I can see Mr. Li and my mistress are in deep love. This morning I was told to prepare for a garden tour. I have taken the carved white-jade wine-cups, fetched the fresh green-peach wine, and set a dozen of lotus-leave-shaped bowls on the red low table. My mistress is fond of writing poems and doing calligraphy during the break after playing music, so I have also brought the brush stands and ink stones in the case, most of which belong to the family heritage. There they come along.

(*Enter Huo Xiaoyu*)

HUO XIAOYU (*To the tune of* **Yiqin'e**):

Deep at the courtyard,

On a clear day the east wind blows mildly.

The east wind blows mildly,

The day is long,

And the early orioles warble on a warm day.

HUANSHA:

My mistress tells me to add incense after she has a dream;

Her penciled eyebrows are like the green mountains far away.

HUANSHA, HUO XIAOYU:

The green mountains far away,

The flower fragrance comes in as the curtain is rolled up

And the night has changed their shade of colour.

HUO XIAOYU (*In the pattern of* **Chunguanghao**):

"The window gauze is light,

The painted screen is dark,

And the mood is deep;

Spring touches my dress,

Makes my waist weak, and I know why it is so.

HUANSHA:

The hair flowers are well cut by the swallowtail-shaped scissors;

The green silk and velvet decorate the flowery hairpins.

Ah, my young mistress,

How you frown for myriad worries,

Worries that knit your eyebrows!"

HUO XIAOYU:

Huansha, what's wrong with my eyebrows?

HUANSHA:

My mistress, before you met Mr. Li, you went playing on the swing, throwing copper coins, betting for litchi stones, and feeding birds with red beans. How relaxed your eyebrows were at that time! Ever since Mr. Li came to our house, you've been frowning behind the window gauze all day long, lamenting over the passing youth by yourself.

HUO XIAOYU:

Oh, Huansha, how can I behave to my heart's content as before my marriage?

HUANSHA:

As the saying goes, "A grown-up person has to restrain himself."

(*Enter Li Yi*)

LI YI (*To the tune of **Yeyougong***):

> The morning sun shines again in the house after rain,
>
> With mist hanging over the flowers and trees.
>
> Why not meet my love
>
> And embrace her tenderly every day!
>
> The night never gets chilly,
>
> When I hold her in my arms.
>
> (*In the pattern of **Huanxisha***)
>
> *"When the zither is played, even mud is heard dropping from the swallow's nest;*
>
> *The gossamer hangs high on the painted west house.*

HUO XIAOYU:

> *The red-crowned rooster crows on the wall at the corner.*

LI YI:

> *The dainty brows catch the eye on the grass-covered path;*
>
> *The flowery dimples slightly bloom by the green-peach stream.*

HUO XIAOYU:

> *Why does one have to stay alone in the chamber?"*

LI YI:

As you ask why one has to stay alone in the chamber, now I'd like to take a spring tour with you for half a day.

HUO XIAOYU:

The wine box and the suitcase are both ready. Now let's go.

> (*All start to go*)

LI YI:

> *"In a famous garden with an attractive spring scene,*

HUO XIAOYU:

> *The man walks ahead and the young wife follows behind.*

LI YI:

> *Nobody is around when we climb up in the bamboo grove;*

HUO XIAOYU:

> *The birds are startled when we find our path in the flowers."*

HUANSHA:

This is the front gate of the Garden of a Hundred Flowers.

LI YI (*To the tune of **Huameixu***):

> I call the fairies in the flower grove,
>
> As we saunter on the zigzagging path in the garden.

HUO XIAOYU:

> In the spring scene that fills our eyes and hearts,
>
> The peach and plum flowers call us to tarry.

The path is lined up with green trees and the meadow covered with tender grass;

The weeping willow twigs softly fondle the painted eaves and the golden banks.

(*All arrive at the gate*)

LI YI, HUO XIAOYU:

Spring fills the garden,

But few come to enjoy the beauty.

Only orioles and swallows fly around freely.

Let's walk around the flowers.

LI YI (*To the tune of **Huangying'er***):

I steal a look at the sunny day,

Fresh with the morning clouds and the dusk rain.

HUO XIAOYU (*Picks up a flower*):

A branch bends low in the garden,

With buds in half bloom

That have a few red petals on them,

While an oriole flies amid the branches and whistles in the splendour.

Petals fall on my fine shoulders,

And I pin a flower in my hair with my delicate fingers from my sleeve.

LI YI (*Offers the wine*):

(*To the tune of **Zaoluopao***)

Gently I make a toast to my darling,

Who stands with her back to the spring breeze,

Smiling before the flowers.

With hairpins tilting on her hair,

She suddenly starts to move along the path.

(*Huo Xiaoyu gets a little drunk*)

LI YI:

Her silk dress wrinkles and falls;

Gossamer waves in the mist and clouds.

In the colourful and fragrant garden,

She acts like a spoiled child,

With beads of sweat rolling down her red cheeks.

HUO XIAOYU (*To the tune of **Zhuomu'er***):

To our hearts' content we enjoy

The spring scene that dots the garden.

We leisurely tend the withering flowers;

Grapes grow on the vines like works of embroidery.

How come I've dragged my long dress on the grassy path thus far?

With you I look at my pretty face on the silvery pond,

Yet take care not to let the hairpins slant down from my bun.

HUANSHA:

Oh, it's raining!

(*They take shelter from the rain*)

LI YI (*To the tune of **Yujiaozhi***):

> The shower of rain makes petals fall,
>
> And spreads grass fragrance to the pavilion by the pond.
>
> Flying swallows startle the dragonflies away,
>
> And hover over the pond for its fresh mud.
>
> We walk shoulder to shoulder
>
> With the fan unfolded before our faces.
>
> We stop to watch the scenic drawings on the rails,
>
> And sit awhile on cushions embroidered with golden threads.
>
> (*Sits down*)
>
> (*Enter Qiuhong*)

QIUHONG:

> "*Scholars in Luoyang are eager to win the laurel;*
>
> *Fair ladies in Qinzhong are fond of watching flowers.*"

Please allow me to report to you, Master. As His Majesty takes a tour to Luoyang, the examination will be held right there. The prefecture announcement has been made and will be sent without delay.

LI YI:

In that case, get the baggage ready at once. I'll go aboard at the Wei River.

QIUHONG:

> "*The prefecture officials are to meet the scholars for the exam tomorrow;*
>
> *The scholars will gallop to the Luoyang Bridge in the spring wind.*"
>
> (*Exit*)

HUO XIAOYU:

We've been married for just a few days, but we will part tomorrow. What am I to do? My man,

> "*Why do you think I wear fashionable dress and make-up?*
>
> *Because I want to vent my feelings like orioles warbling on the willows.*
>
> *There's so much concern in a wife's heart,*
>
> *That even an affectionate man may not know.*"

I know I'm an insignificant person, not to be matched with you. Today you love me for my beauty and take it as my virtue. But once my beauty wanes, you may change your love and affection, and I may end up rootless and forsaken. So I can't help feeling sad in the time of our best joy.

> (*Sobs and sighs*)

LI YI:

My lifetime desire has been fulfilled today. I will never leave you whether I live or die. How could you say that, Xiaoyu? Please give me a piece of white fine silk fabric, so I can write a vow of my love for you.

HUO XIAOYU:

Huansha, fetch three feet of fine silk fabric from the case, together with the ink, the

The Purple Hairpins

writing brush and the ink stone.

HUANSHA:

Here's the silk fabric.

LI YI (*Writes*):

I've done it. Please take a look.

HUO XIAOYU (*Reads*):

> "Duck and drake on the water,
> Or jasper and jade in the clouds,
> Stick to each other day and night,
> Without regret alive or dead.
> With mountains and rivers as our witnesses,
> With the sun and the moon as our observers,
> We shall share the quilt when we live,
> And share the grave when we die."

Mr. Li, this vow will be kept in the jewelry box as the proof in the future.

> (*To the tune of* **Yubaodu**)
> We make a vow before the heart-shaped incense
> To remain devoted in our hearts.
> We'll cling to each other heart to heart,
> And spend sleepless nights enjoying ourselves.
> In an incense pouch,
> I'll keep the silk fabric with the vow
> And wear the pouch on my waist.

LI YI:

Please trust my heart.

> (*To the tune of* **Yushantui**)
> You have tranquil and spiritual attraction,
> Born to be mild and tender.
> Your sweet voice induces my endless thoughts of love;
> Your slim waist against the rail arouses my fond affection.
> Now that we are still in our honeymoon,
> Why do you refrain from smile and laughter?
> You must obey the will of the spring god.
> Yet you keep silent
> And let the cuckoos warble out
> Your thoughts of love.

HUO XIAOYU (*Bows*):

I, your humble wife, thank you for your consideration!

> (*To the tune of* **Chuanbozhao**)
> With boundless feelings,
> You love me
> In spite of my low status.

I'm afraid the matchmaker will come to you to make proposals,

I'm afraid the matchmaker will come to you to make proposals,

Though you've vowed to love me till the sea goes dry.

You'd better not go in such a hurry

But stay and lean on the rails to enjoy the pretty flowers.

My man, it's getting late.

(*All start to return*)

LI YI, HUO XIAOYU (*To the tune of* **Yiduojiao**):

The spring scene is dimming,

When dusk falls on the fragrant path

And ravens crow lonely and timidly to the capital.

We trace the faint scene in the dim light,

When rosy clouds tint our garments.

Now that our mood for the spring scene is fading,

Now that our mood for the spring scene is fading,

We hurry back on the stone steps covered with green moss.

(*Huo Xiaoyu slips*)

(*To the tune of* **Yueshanghaitang**)

Tiny feet in embroidered shoes

Move on step by step.

Instead of the front gate,

We walk through the garden gate.

Spring mountains on the tour

Provide many a beautiful sight.

We come back from the swings and flower grove,

And knock the copper ring on the door.

(*Enter Huansha, holding a candle*)

HUANSHA (*Opens the door*):

(*To the tune of* **Coda**)

When the spring scene fades like the clouds,

I light the candle and let it burn till daybreak.

The couple seem to have toured the imperial garden in the spring breeze.

The candle in the silvery bowl reddens the evening gown,

And stirs up tender feelings for departure tonight.

The harmony between man and wife will last;

Youth like the bright moon never shines in vain.

Scene Seventeen
Going to Luoyang for the Spring Exam

(*Enter Qiuhong*)

QIUHONG:

> *"The orioles warble beautifully on a warm day;*
>
> *The horses gallop briskly in the light breeze.*
>
> *If the master can pass the imperial exam,*
>
> *His servants may also rise in their status."*

My master instructed me yesterday to prepare for today's departure for the exam. But he hasn't got up yet at this time of the morning. I'll call Huansha.

> (*Enter Huansha*)

Please call the master for departure. The prefecture officials are waiting. As the saying goes,

> *"It's easy for the talent to achieve fame,*
>
> *But hard for the beauty to endure the parting."*
>
> (*Exit*)
>
> (*Enter Huo Xiaoyu*)

HUO XIAOYU (*To the tune of **Shi'ershi***):

> Why does spring pass in such a hurry?
>
> How I meditate in a melancholy mood!
>
> Our honeymoon comes late,
>
> But your departure arrives early.
>
> My sweet dreams break with my soul lost;
>
> I can hardly rise with my eyebrows knit.
>
> *"Water dribbles from the silver hourglass to urge morning dressing;*
>
> *Tears drip from the red candle in the morning light.*
>
> *The jewelry all over makes me cold,*
>
> *For nobody will embrace me warmly in my sweet dream."*

I've been married to my man for only a few days, but unexpectedly when His Majesty takes a tour in Luoyang, he calls for the imperial exam. My man is going to the prefecture hall for the exam. Though the trip takes only half a month, I still feel sad about our parting. He's already bid farewell to Mother.

> (*Enter Li Yi*)

LI YI (*To the tune of **Raodiyou***):

> Once the path is paved for promotion,
>
> I'm bound to write a grand piece for His Majesty.
>
> Yet looking at the morning clouds, I hesitate and hesitate.

HUO XIAOYU:

My dear man, it's high time for departure.

> (*To the tune of **Huangying'er***)

I wipe tears from my face with the red sleeves,

For I'm suddenly awakened from my loving dream

When peach blossoms are struck by the early spring thunder.

After you leave,

The clouds will float above the branches,

The grass will turn fresh after the rain,

And you will ride along the capital street.

Looking at the road leading far away,

I can't bear giving you the whip,

For who'll share the pride as you ride on the fine horse?

LI YI (*To the previous tune*):

Don't shed tears on your handkerchief like this!

For a grand future I have to be away for a while

And take the opportunity to pass the imperial exam.

To be listed in the successful candidates' roll,

And pay homage to His Majesty at the palace,

I'll compete with the best among the talents.

Looking at the road leading far away,

I'll return to hold your hands

When fragrance from the palace wafts from my sleeves.

(*Enter Qiuhong*)

QIUHONG:

I'm going to tell my master that the boat is waiting on the Wei River.

HUO XIAOYU (*To the tune of* **Hupozhui**):

Young and talented,

My man accepts the edict for the exam.

But don't get drunk by His Majesty's wine,

And don't forget that I'm waiting for your good news by the red door.

Handsome and proud man!

I hope you'll get on well with your spring exam.

LI YI (*To the previous tune*):

For my elegant style,

I'll surely win the first place with my poems,

Composing my poems as Li Bai did at the Chenxiang Pavilion.

But I'm afraid that your longing for me may make you thin.

Lovely and charming woman!

You deserve the title of the County Lady,

And the most extravagant carriage.

(*Enter Qiuhong*)

QIUHONG:

Master, the prefecture officials want you for the farewell reception.

HUO XIAOYU (*To the tune of* **Coda**):

After your departure,

    The orioles' warbling will soon vanish,

    But I'll still stand on the meadow at dusk.

Mr. Li, when you go for your grand career,

    Learn how to care for your loving wife.

    When a roamer has a belle as his wife,

    She longs for the setting sun.

    Knowing it's only half a month's separation,

    They still feel sad when they part.

Scene Eighteen
A Parting Dinner at the Prefecture Hall

(*Enter the Prefect*)

PREFECT (*To the tune of* **Fanbusuan**):

    When His Majesty takes a tour to the east,

    The imperial edict comes from the capital in the west.

    Scholars gather to vie for promotion in spring,

    Just as the carps vie to leap over the dragon's gate.

    "The imperial exam is to be held in Luoyang to select talents;

    By His Majesty's favour I've been appointed Prefect.

    According to His Majesty's edict from the secretary's office,

    We'll offer flowers and wine to the scholars for their departure."

I am Prefect of the capital. As His Majesty takes a tour to Luoyang, the imperial exam is to be held there. We have chosen Scholar Li Yi as the only candidate from Chang'an County of the prefecture, and today we'll host a farewell dinner for him. He is coming soon.

    (*Enter Li Yi*)

LI YI (*To the tune of* **Haoshijin**):

    The prefecture officials have chosen me as the talented scholar,

    And will bid me farewell at the Baling Bridge in Chang'an.

    I'll try to write the finest poetical piece with the grandest style

    To win the laurel in the imperial garden.

    (*The reception is announced by the reporter*)

REPORTER:

Mr. Li Yi is to kowtow to the Prefect.

LI YI (*Kowtows*):

    "The clouds have dispersed for me to see the sun;

PREFECT:

    Your excellent work has long been reputed.

256

LI YI:

You offer your generosity for the scholars;

PREFECT:

I expect you to soar high like the phoenix."

Attendants, get the wine ready.

(*To the tune of **Changpai***)

His Majesty has issued an edict

For the young talents

To try their best in their writings.

Scholar Li, when you go this time,

Your writing will be the most flowery and vivid,

Like the dragons flying around the palace and soaring in the blue.

Today,

On this auspicious day,

You may get drunk with the wine and show a flushing face.

May you win the official hat and the palace flowers,

As well as the robe with green patterns and soft belts.

Drink three cups of the bestowed wine before getting on your horse,

So that you'll parade around the central district of the capital,

For your manners to be admired by the passers-by.

LI YI:

I'm not much of a drinker, so please let me be on my way.

PREFECT:

Not yet. When you win the laurel as a young man, there are more advantages.

(*To the tune of **Duanpai***)

You'll have an easy position in the Imperial Academy,

In the Penglai Palace close to the Son of Heaven,

With imperial incense floating in the air.

The scholars draft the edicts in the Imperial Academy,

And shine with decorations of golden fish and purple pouches.

Eventually you'll take charge of the seal of the State Council,

Where you work hard and get yourself established,

In high spirits when you have more fame and wealth.

(*Sees Li Yi off*)

(*To the tune of **Coda***)

Now I see the virtuous talent off,

I wish you high spirits among the myriad talents at the palace,

And have your image painted on the Lingyan Tower for your achievement.

When a scholar makes early progress through hardships,

Even recommenders may feel surprised at his success.

The scholar cultivates his wisdom in peaceful time,

And dedicates it to the state in times of need.

Scene Nineteen
The Frontier Governor Ascends the Altar

(*Enter the officers*)

OFFICERS (*To the tune of* **Dianjiangchun**):

> The cold mist hangs over the desolate frontier grass,
>
> When the sun shines on the bannered camp gate
>
> Through the crack of red clouds.
>
> In the beating of drums and waving of flags,
>
> All are watching the general's grand manners.
>
> *"When spring refreshes everything in the frontier,*
>
> *The new general has come to protect the western border.*
>
> *On the day when the mighty general ascends the alter,*
>
> *The resounding martial music scares away the clouds."*

Your attention, please! As the officers at the Yumen Garrison, today we welcome the new frontier governor Lord Liu to take the position. Attendants, serve our new governor.

(*Enter Liu Gongji with the attendants*)

LIU GONGJI (*To the tune of* **Xidijin**):

> With my spirits soaring into the blue sky like the phoenix,
>
> I defend the great frontier like the tiger and the leopard.
>
> Taking charge of three hundred thousand brave warriors,
>
> I wear my silken robes and jewelry belt with vitality.

(*In the pattern of* **Zhegutian**)

> *"When the cold morning wind stirs the banners on the posts,*
>
> *An air of valiancy rises from the general's halberds and flags.*
>
> *The western nomadic tribes all follow the Han Governor,*
>
> *While numerous bordering states obey the rule of the Empire.*
>
> *Travelling far to the western frontier through wind and cloud,*
>
> *I have my tent pitched at the strategic position.*
>
> *For what are the horns blown from camp to camp?*
>
> *The new general is to ascend the alter as of old."*

My name is Liu Gongji. To be born a general, I'm most familiar with the military strategies. I defeated the Tartars in the northern frontier, and now I've been entitled Governor of the western frontier. I've chosen today as the auspicious day to take my position. Call the officers to meet me.

OFFICERS (*Come forward to pay respect to Liu Gongji*):

Congratulations, my lord! Wish you be conferred titles of high position!

LIU GONGJI:

Rise to your feet. How are things going on along the western frontier in recent days?

OFFICERS:

Under the brilliance of His Majesty's sun, there's no warfare and peace reigns. The Han Dynasty opened up the western territories, diminishing the Tartars' power in the west. The Tang Dynasty divided the western Qiang territories into two states of Dahexi and Xiaohexi. Incited by the Tubo State recently, the two states might pose a threat to the border areas in the future.

LIU GONGJI:

So we must do more military training to crack down on the rebels.

OFFICERS:

We will obey your order!

    (*The military training starts*)

LIU GONGJI (*To the tune of* **Shanhuazi**):

    The Great Tang Dynasty was worshipped as the Heavenly Khan,

    But the Hexi states now follow the Hun Regime.

    Then how are we to tackle with the Tubo State?

    In great rage I'm determined to defeat the western barbarians.

ALL:

    When the news of dispatching the army spreads to the Yumen Pass,

    We point our gigantic swords beyond the Tianshan Mountains,

    Toward the origin of the Yellow River, toward the galaxy.

    We are bound to be conferred titles of high positions,

    With our images painted on the Lingyan Tower.

LIU GONGJI:

Officers, I need a military consultant at the Guanxi Fortress. Now that the Tubo troops have waged wars against us, the drafting of military messages is very urgent. I've already written a request to send for a new scholar from the Imperial Academy to be a military consultant and secretary. Then our troops in Hexi will be much better equipped.

OFFICERS:

We will obey your order!

LIU GONGJI (*To the previous tune*):

    We not only need weapons but writing brushes in our army;

    Military consultants and secretaries have their own advantages.

    Messages will be drafted and sent efficiently

    In smooth and fluent diction and style.

ALL:

    When the news of dispatching the army spreads to the Yumen Pass,

    We point our gigantic swords beyond the Tianshan Mountains,

    Toward the origin of the Yellow River, toward the galaxy.

    We are bound to be conferred titles of high positions,

    With our images painted on the Lingyan Tower.

LIU GONGJI (*To the tune of* **Coda**):

Officers!

    Raise our banners, get our weapons ready,

Beat the drums and blow the horns outside the camp!

A scholar may also make his contributions in the troops.

A grand general descends from the floating clouds,

To issue orders and lead the army to the west.

The military consultant will soon send the message

Of capturing the western tribal chief alive.

Scene Twenty
Expecting Success in Spring Melancholy

(*Enter Huo Xiaoyu and Huansha*)

HUO XIAOYU (*To the tune of* **Jinlongcong**):

When the wind blows and tosses my hair,

And green shades move quietly on the walls of the well,

A sudden chill pierces my thin dress.

When tender swallows carry fresh mud in their bills,

And green water sparkles as crow-feathers wrinkle the pond,

The rain on flowers soaks through my spring melancholy.

(*In the pattern of* **Xifenfei**)

"*The spring melancholy drags on like the golden threads,*

And the fragrance of dreams lingers on, reluctant to depart.

HUANSHA:

Awakened from sleep from time to time,

I shoot at the magpies to enliven my heart.

HUO XIAOYU:

A grand prose poem elegantly presented,

It should be my man's masterpiece.

HUO XIAOYU, HUANSHA:

We gaze beyond and eagerly expect

That the horse arrives with good news."

HUO XIAOYU:

Huansha, Mr. Li has gone for the exam, but who knows what would be the result? Oh, what vexation!

(*To the tune of* **Bangzhuangtai**)

By the dressing table,

I feel reluctant to have my hair combed,

Though the sun rises high over the garden pavilion.

Hardly have I enjoyed love to my heart's content

When I am overwhelmed by spring melancholy.

Dizzily I feel hot on my face;

Yawningly I have my brows knit.

Turtledoves whistle and young swallows fly around;

Spring and youth are in the prime of their time.

Gossamer floats and willow catkins fall

Under the sway of the east breeze.

In such a season, how I regret letting my man go for the exam!

HUANSHA (*To the previous tune*):

I gaze longingly

To see if he is counting the days till the boat returns home.

What you hope is the joy between man and wife;

What he shares is the concerns of His Majesty.

So how could you act as an ordinary couple,

Like the insects male and female living together all their lives?

As a talent in the capital,

How could he give up his ambition?

Now that spring is passing away in Luoyang,

He is still staying there and trying his best.

I hope that he'll succeed in winning the laurel,

And gaining the first place among the candidates.

HUO XIAOYU (*To the previous tune*):

When he tours around the capital streets in silken robes,

Some matchmaker might stop his fine horse.

She might spread a belle's picture,

And beg him to accept the engagement.

Casually he might receive the keepsake,

And find it hard to return home.

Flute music and songs might lure him in the daytime

And brothels might attract him with seductive smiles.

If he is to embrace the harlots at night,

How could I argue with them then?

To be allured at that time,

How could he refrain from feeling extravagant and fashionable?

HUANSHA (*To the previous tune*):

You knit your brows like the new moon or the curtain hooks,

For you are separated from your man after a brief honeymoon.

The aroma of your lovemaking still exists,

And the marriage vow is hard to break.

You murmur longingly by the flowers at night,

For him to return in silken robes under the moonlight.

As you're bound to win the phoenix crown of a lady,

What makes you so worried?

As you're bound to take the grand carriage,

What makes you so sad?

You'll surely love each other intimately

And dwell in the luxurious house in glory.

(*To the tune of* **Coda**)

When the good news

Is brought back to the deep painted hall,

The notice with the imperial seal will shine in your hands;

Only now, you'll fondle the hairpins in the candlelight.

The exam is not far away from here,

With auspicious clouds looming clear.

My man is vigorous in the prime of his youth,

Yet where is he drunk and asleep tonight?

Scene Twenty-One
Celebrating Success at the Apricot Garden

(*Enter officials and officers*)

OFFICIALS, OFFICERS (*To the tune of* **Tianxiale**):

The Imperial Academy and the Imperial Palace are closely linked,

Leading scholars from here on earth to there on Heaven.

The sun sheds light from Heaven over the capital and beyond;

Rivers and mountains are bathed in brilliance all over the country.

Attention, please! Today we announce the results of the imperial examination. His Majesty confirms Li Yi from Longxi as having extraordinary talents for his replies and judgments in the examination, and therefore confers the title of Number One Scholar on him. Please go to the Wufeng Gate to wait for his arrival.

(*Enter Li Yi*)

LI YI (*To the tune of* **Busuanzi**):

Phoenixes fly around me,

Surrounded by auspicious clouds.

With my name reputed all over the capital,

I will soon see His Majesty.

ALL:

Number One Scholar, please express your gratitude for His Majesty's favour.

LI YI (*Expresses his gratitude*):

(*To the tune of* **Diliuzi**)

The Saintly Emperor,

The Saintly Emperor will reign over the world eternally.

The Virtuous Ministers,

The Virtuous Ministers are firm pillars of the Empire.

The selected most talented scholar

Will be sent to the Penglai Palace.

My gratitude goes to His Majesty

For his palace robes and grand feast,

All scented with the imperial incense.

ALL:

Now please show Number One Scholar to the feast!

(*Move*)

(*To the previous tune*)

We smile at the past,

We smile at the articles written in the past;

We rejoice at the present,

We rejoice at the imperial music and songs at present.

With curtains all rolled up along the capital streets,

People see what it's like to be flushed with success in the spring wind.

With auspicious clouds floating over the blooming flowers,

The scholar gets intoxicated at the feast by the Qujiang River.

(*To the tune of* **Coda**)

Flowers with ringing bells bloom all over the garden

To show boundless elegance and wealth,

Leaving stories to pass from generation to generation.

Thousands of people are making merry in the capital,

While trees are bearing peaches by the Qujiang River.

This is where you express your gratitude for a grand career

And drink to your heart's content in silken robes.

Scene Twenty-Two
General Lu's Rage and His Scheme

(*Enter General Lu*)

GENERAL LU (*To the tune of* **Yiluosuo**):

Stepping out of the palace bearing my sword now,

I have got steady promotion in my official career.

With students and attendants all around me,

I'm sure no one dares to disobey my orders and wills!

"I hold up the sky with the mightiest power,

With silken robes and jewel belts showing my youthful vigour.

The rich and powerful in Luoyang are eager to accompany me,

While most scholars are my enthusiastic students and attendants."

I, General Lu, have served His Majesty for a long time, assisting Him in the state affairs. As the imperial examination is held in Luoyang, I've ordered all the scholars who passed the examinations to pay visits at my residence. When the results were released yesterday, I noticed that a scholar by the name of Li Yi from Longxi was conferred the title of Number One Scholar. But when I checked the register book of my residence, I did not find his name. How arrogant and outrageous he is! How infuriating he is! How infuriating! Now I have a scheme. Yesterday Liu Gongji, Governor of the Yumen Pass, sent a report asking for a military consultant. I will appoint Li Yi to take the position and never allow him to return to the capital. He will fall into my trap. Secretary!

(*Enter Secretary*)

SECRETARY:

"Attendants line up in the Prime Minister's hall

When spring flowers blossom in the city of Luoyang."

Here I am, my lord. What can I do for you?

GENERAL LU:

All the scholars have paid respects to me at the hall, except for the new Number One Scholar Li Yi. Now I have recommended him to be the military consultant at the Yumen Pass. Go to the office and have the recommendation report drafted.

(*To the tune of* **Fengtie'er**)

The report says that his writing style is mighty for a general;

Yet there are no records about him in the Imperial Academy.

Governor Liu,

Asks for a military consultant with high reputation.

GENERAL LU, SECRETARY:

It must be executed with care,

For secret military reports are most urgent.

SECRETARY:

I see.

GENERAL LU:

And more to add,

(*To the previous tune*)

As war is imminent at the Yumen Pass,

You draft the edict ordering him to set off without delay.

The official appointment is urgent,

So order him not to take any rest at home.

GENERAL LU, SECRETARY:

It must be executed with care,

For secret military reports are most urgent.

An idiot of a scholar as he is,

He'll go to the border for his stubbornness.

Gentlemen must have a sense of justice,
While politicians must have a sense of malice.

Scene Twenty-Three
Joy over His Glorious Return

(*Enter Huo Xiaoyu and Huansha*)

HUO XIAOYU (*To the tune of* **Xiqianying**):

Now that the sky is clearing up and magpies are tweeting,

We have to part soon after our wedding,

And he might be listening to the orioles in the imperial garden.

With clouds in the sky

And mists over the river,

It's time to enjoy the tenderness of spring.

Why does my sorrow seem to return like silk threads?

Why does my dream seem to stop around the incense smoke?

In spring drowsiness

When the setting sun throws light on my dress,

I wish that my man would soon return to renew our love.

"For his wonderful writing he is called to the palace gate,

Distinguishing himself as the most talented scholar in Luoyang.

The east wind does not visit the beauty behind the curtain,

But favours the contented scholar by the flowers."

Last night, I dreamed that my man had passed the examination and I was dressed up to accompany him to his new post. How happy I was!

(*To the tune of* **Erlangshen**)

Leaning against the rail in the spring breeze,

I see my man standing in the flower shade by the Luoyang Bridge.

A belle tries to unbutton the neck of her spring dress,

And adds incense to the burner with her fine fingers,

With fragrance as enchanting as that from Xun Yu of old.

He urges his belle

To wear her best to tour the office.

I awaken from my dream

To dress up before the mirror with my back to the gauze window.

(*To the previous tune*)

I still remember

The wine and powder stains on my sleeves upon departure.

HUANSHA:

Mr. Li must have had a lot of fun parading the streets.

HUO XIAOYU:

> I think he may also feel lovesick for me.

> I'm reluctant to rise though the sun is high,

> And find excuse for my drowsiness in spring intoxication.

HUANSHA:

Look at the gossamer signifying the best luck in the early morning!

HUO XIAOYU:

> After the drizzle and mist,

> It clears up and the lucky spider comes out.

> But spring in full display makes the dainty brows knit.

> Gazing in deep thought,

> I hear the orioles warble in touching tunes.

> (*Enter Lady Zheng*)

LADY ZHENG (*To the tune of* **Wanxiandeng**):

> Amid warm greetings for the carriages,

> The new Number One Scholar will come along the street.

Xiaoyu, the Prefect is arriving to greet Number One Scholar. It's said to be Mr. Li. Get the flutes and drums ready at once for the celebration.

> (*Enter Li Yi with his attendants*)

LI YI (*To the tune of* **Qitianle**):

> In the long spring day along the busy capital streets,

> The scholar returns to his residential hall in full splendour.

> With carriages blocking the view of flowers,

> And the horses stopping by the meadow,

> The distinction today is fabulous.

> (*Greets all*)

> "*After I presented my writing and entered the dragon gate,*

> *The phoenix sent me the edict for my success.*

> *With warm sunshine and colourful flowers all along the way,*

> *I saw the painted bridal house in front of my eyes.*"

LADY ZHENG:

Our Number One Scholar has received the most honorable title from His Majesty. Congratulations! Congratulations!

LI YI:

Soon after my arrival in Chang'an, I received the imperial edict for my conferment. Thanks for your compliment! Thanks for your compliment!

LADY ZHENG:

Fetch the wine, Huansha.

> (*Enter Huansha*)

HUANSHA:

> "*In green silken robes bestowed by His Majesty,*

> *He drinks the best wine for Number One Scholar.*"

266

Here's the wine.

LADY ZHENG (*To the tune of* **Huameixu**):

Flowers warm the city of Luoyang,

As if the Heyang peach blossoms had returned.

What a joy to extol the scholar

And send him to soar to the sky.

He has returned with the spring laurel,

And brought back the auspicious clouds.

ALL:

As the title of Number One Scholar matches the family status,

We celebrate the success with flutes and drums in our painted hall.

HUO XIAOYU (*To the previous tune*):

You shot the peacock screen and became the bridegroom;

You showed your talent and became the Number One Scholar.

Take me with you as the County Lady

While you are still young.

You have Sima Xiangru's ambition and style,

And Prefect Zhang Chang's loving care to pencil his wife's brows.

ALL:

As the title of Number One Scholar matches the family status,

We celebrate the success with flutes and drums in our painted hall.

LI YI (*To the previous tune*):

I still remember the day under the plum tree,

A spring scene in the south that warmed my heart.

I'm happy that the Moon Goddess gave consent,

And the plum blossoms linked us together.

My hat touched the plum blossoms under the moon,

And her hairpins got caught on the plum tree in the moonlight.

ALL:

As the title of Number One Scholar matches the family status,

We celebrate the success with flutes and drums in our painted hall.

HUANSHA, QIUHONG (*To the previous tune*):

Spring fills up the fairy mountain;

Candles are lit in the lanterns and incense smoke curls up from the burner.

How he catches her eye in his silken robes,

As she wears her black hair colourfully dressed!

Merciful rain and dew ripen the celestial peaches;

Spring breeze blows, swallows fly and apricot flowers bloom.

ALL:

As the title of Number One Scholar matches the family status,

We celebrate the success with flutes and drums in our painted hall.

(*Enter the envoy*)

ENVOY:

> *"Travellers come and go every day on the road;*
>
> *Orioles' warbling can be heard everywhere.*
>
> *I've come to inform the scholar of the Imperial Academy*
>
> *To take his position at the Yumen Pass."*

I serve as General Lu's subordinate officer. I've come all the way to inform Number One Scholar Li Yi to take the position of military consultant at Governor Liu's Guanxi Prefecture, and urge him to depart for the border post without delay. Here I am.

> (*Notifies and meets Li Yi*)

LI YI:

I've already accepted the imperial appointment. Please allow me a few days before I set out.

ENVOY:

That'll do. I'll be waiting to the west of the Bating Pavilion.

> (*Exit*)

HUO XIAOYU (*Asks in surprise*):

That officer outside, where did he inform you to go?

LI YI (*In a subdued voice*):

The imperial edict urged me to go to the Yumen Pass to be Governor Liu's military consultant. But I'll be returning soon.

LADY ZHENG (*To the tune of* **Diliuzi**):

> Forget about the long and rough journey for the moment,
>
> But go into the west chamber to spend the night.
>
> Seize the time to enjoy your youth,
>
> As we expect good news
>
> And expect our bridegroom to return home soon.
>
> Oh, why can't my son-in-law stay long with my daughter?

LI YI:

I'm drunk.

HUO XIAOYU (*Supports Li Yi*):

> (*To the tune of* **Baolaocui**)
>
> With blessing from Heaven,
>
> I respect my man for his talent
>
> And support him in his drunkenness.
>
> Instead of getting drunk as such,
>
> You must show your grand style and manners
>
> To chant and sing.
>
> I'll accompany you till the end of spring
>
> When you parade the capital streets in fragrant breeze
>
> And we'll start our happy life anew.

ALL (*To the tune of* **Shuangshengzi**):

> The family thrives, the family thrives;
>
> The scholar returns in silken robes in charming spring.

268

This is no fluke, this is no fluke;

It's the man's happy lot and the wife's good fortune.

What a perfect match! What a perfect match!

What imperial grace! What imperial grace!

In admiration for the man's honour and the wife's distinction,

We wish them everlasting happiness.

(*To the tune of* **Coda**)

From now on the perfect couple ride in a grand carriage in the capital,

Thanks to the grace of His Majesty.

LI YI:

But I'm afraid I'll have to leave the capital in dismay.

With guards of honour leading the horses in spring,

The scholar returns home in silken robes with grace.

He shows his best like the golden peacock in full display,

But remembers not to have the mirror broken into two.

Scene Twenty-Four
A Farewell Chat

(*Enter Lady Zheng*)

LADY ZHENG (*To the tune of* **Bubujiao**):

When colourful clouds disperse and the Qin flute music ends,

They'll say farewell near the flowing imperial river,

With soft choking weeps from time to time.

The departing horses startle the fragrant flowers,

While the rolling wheels seem to spin around the moon.

Dust in gusty wind covers the sky over the frontier;

My son-in-law has to depart soon with a farewell song.

(*In the pattern of* **Yejinmen**)

"We can't ask him to stay,

And it's no good asking him to stay.

Xiaoyu sheds tears on her red sleeves by the window;

She stays in solitude in her chamber.

Why does he have to tear away from her once again?

The willows are weeping today at the Baling Bridge.

Mandarin ducks all stay in pairs;

How can I bear seeing my daughter staying alone?"

I'm Lady Zheng. My daughter Xiaoyu is married to Li Yi who passed the spring
examination and became the Number One Scholar. However, soon after he entered the

Imperial Academy, he was assigned to be the military consultant on the western frontier. I hear that the military actions against the Tubo forces are urgent on the western border.

(*Sorrowfully*)

Oh, my daughter!

(*To the tune of* **Zuifugui**)

The couple's quilt has just been made ready for the bed;

The pair of pillows have just been made fit for sleep.

The couple can't be away from each other even for a while,

Yet wind blows and shakes all the decorations of saucers and plates.

As the lady's carriage can't go along with the gentleman's horse,

The appointment to the frontier breaks the union in the chamber.

HUANSHA (*To the previous tune*):

When the couple enjoyed their marital life in the capital,

How could he be assigned to write military reports in the army!

Oh, Mistress,

Last night you were packing for the master, tears running down your cheeks;

This morning his departing wheels are grinding the tenderness of your heart.

Now that the cuckoos' cry makes people sigh,

When are you going to meet again?

(*Enter Bao Siniang*)

BAO SINIANG:

"When spring grows old in changeable weather,

People in sadness feel the slow passage of time.

They listen to orioles' whistling as time passes by

And seem to complain the departure of willow catkins."

I hear that Mr. Li has returned home as Number One Scholar, but he is going far away for the military mission. I'm taking the fine spring day to see the scholar off for his long march to the front.

(*Greets Lady Zheng*)

Your Ladyship, for your son-in-law's long expedition, how bitterly you weep as I can see from the corners of your eyes!

LADY ZHENG:

How unfortunate we are!

(*Enter Li Yi*)

LI YI (*To the tune of* **Nüguanzi**):

With my eyes filled with departing sorrow,

I steal a look at the coupling swords.

In my wandering mind,

I dream of banners waving,

War horses neighing,

And phoenixes soaring.

(*Enter Huo Xiaoyu*)

HUO XIAOYU:

> My tears pour on the dressing table,
>
> As I'll send you off to the frontier,
>
> The talented scholar of Luoyang.

ALL:

> On the old paths around the screen,
>
> There's been so much joy,
>
> Yet the young scholar is going to stay away from home.

LADY ZHENG (*Weeps*):

Oh, Mr. Li, how we suffer from your departure! Oh, it's killing your mother-in-law!

LI YI:

So you are here too, Siniang.

LADY ZHENG (*To the tune of* **Gu'nüguanzi**):

> Looking at my son-in-law, the new Number One Scholar,
>
> We're celebrating our happy gathering.
>
> I propose a spring toast to the scholar's journey,
>
> But how could I let him go when I haven't seen enough of him?

LI YI:

I'll be returning soon. Please take good care of everything at home.

LADY ZHENG:

> Ladies stay deep in the chamber,
>
> So what are you worrying about?
>
> We'll wait till you are entitled the hero on the frontier,
>
> And I'll shoulder the responsibility of our home.

ALL:

> No matter how long he is away from home,
>
> He will not forget his love and his home.

LI YI (*To the previous tune*):

My dear wife,

> You need not roll up the curtain, just stay deep in the house
>
> And follow the steps of your mother.

Your Ladyship,

> I feel sorry for not staying with you
>
> Neglecting my care for both of you.

LADY ZHENG:

Mr. Li, please return home soon. I'm already in my old age.

LI YI:

> You are like the Queen Mother of the West,
>
> Taking good care of Xiaoyu as the celestial crimson peach.
>
> I'd pray to Heaven for your longevity,
>
> And call my dear from the frontier far away.

ALL:

No matter how long he is away from home,

He will not forget his love and his home.

HUO XIAOYU (*To the previous tune*):

He must hate the separation too as he departs,

While I'll shed tears in the chamber for our transient joys.

Man and wife look at each other without a word;

My old mother also suffers great sorrows.

She sees her daughter married,

And soon to be separated.

As man and wife have to part,

Mother and daughter can only weep to the moon in vain.

ALL:

No matter how long he is away from home,

He will not forget his love and his home.

BAO SINIANG (*To the previous tune*):

The couple complain about the lack of care for the flowers,

For they'll be parted like a pair of swallows.

Nothing can stop him from his grand career,

And we can't delay him for the bright future.

Then what will happen when he departs?

How can we ask him to stay?

The traveller will be heart-broken at the apes' cries on his way,

But must strive for his career, even if it's trivial as ants.

ALL:

No matter how long he is away from home,

He will not forget his love and his home.

(*Enter the military officer*)

OFFICER:

"*As time is urgent,*

We can't stay long at Baling."

So please hurry up, military consultant.

LI YI (*Kowtows for departure*):

Ah, Your Ladyship,

(*To the tune of **Yicuozhao***)

Though it's cold in your own chamber,

You must show warm care for your solitary daughter.

LADY ZHENG:

Mr. Li,

As life is hard on the frontier,

You must cherish your own health.

LI YI:

Siniang,

Please take care

Of the mother and daughter when I'm away.

BAO SINIANG:

I'll surely do,

But you must return soon.

HUO XIAOYU:

As I see my man leaving,

How much more I'd express for his departure!

LADY ZHENG, HUO XIAOYU, BAO SINIANG:

As you are departing,

We expect to receive your letters soon.

LADY ZHENG:

Mr. Li, when are you to return?

LI YI:

No more than a year.

(*To the tune of* **Kuxiangsi**)

How a bamboo-shoot of a son-in-law suffers upon departure,

And how the mother and daughter have to endure the sorrow!

(*Lady Zheng faints*)

(*Exeunt Li Yi and Huo Xiaoyu*)

BAO SINIANG:

Your Ladyship, stop worrying. He goes to the frontier for a grand career, and will return in glory.

When the man is to leave for the western frontier,

The adorable wife behind hides her knit brows.

With tears rolling down her cheeks,

The broken-hearted wife is to break weeping willows.

Scene Twenty-Five
Breaking Willow Twigs upon Departure

(*Enter Huo Xiaoyu and Huansha*)

HUO XIAOYU (*To the tune of* **Jinlongcong**):

With thin and tender fingers

I embroider coats for my man to the frontier.

When my carriage stops beside the Baling Bridge,

I see the fine horses marching on the road.

The guards of honour play reed pipes in the woods,

But none of them is in a joyful tune.

*(In the pattern of **Haoshijin**)*

"I rest my head on my wrist for fear of dreaming of my man,

For we parted when rain and clouds stop.

HUANSHA:

Hearing the dripping of time from the imperial river,

We can't help giving out a choked cry.

HUO XIAOYU:

I dare not look westward in my carriage,

Finding it hard to describe how we'll part.

HUO XIAOYU, HUANSHA:

When do cuckoos cry in the flowers?

Just look at the old blood stains!"

HUO XIAOYU:

Huansha, this Baling Bridge is truly a heart-breaking bridge!

(Enter Li Yi with his attendants)

LI YI *(To the tune of **Northern Dianjiangchun**)*:

In the solemn military style I depart for the frontier in glory;

I stop at the solid Baling Bridge to bid farewell to my kinsfolk,

And then I tread on the road to the Yangguan Pass.

Escorted at the front and back,

I hold the rein amid hustle and bustle.

"When fluttering banners and warm sun disperse the spring cold,

Wine drops on the western desert with tears that never dry.

After I watch my love in the flowers for a while,

She'll stay in my memory on the journey tomorrow.

Attendants, stop the guards of honour beside the Baling Bridge, so that I'll bid farewell to my wife.

(Meets Huo Xiaoyu)

Why should I have to head for the frontier?

HUO XIAOYU:

My man,

Tarry no more on your horse today.

LI YI:

When will my journey come to an end?

HUO XIAOYU:

All my heart-breaking music is meant for you."

My dear man, although you're setting off in a grand style, I can't help feeling dreary and sad. The Baling Bridge is right ahead. I'll go and break the willow twigs, in imitation of a tune for your departure. Fetch the wine, please!

*(To the tune of **Northern Jishengcao**)*

The Tune of the Yangguan Pass terrifies me,

And it even chills the Weishui River.

The ancient Peach Blossom Ferry still stands where lovers bid farewell;

The islets are green with grass where clouds and water meet;

The willows whisper gently to the breeze at the Baling Bridge.

(*Breaks the willow twigs*)

Ah, willows,

I wish you would bind my man with your threads,

Yet knowing they can't stop their own catkins from floating away.

LI YI:

Think of the bliss we had last night!

(*To the previous tune*)

Nothing can block our hearts for love;

Our joy goes beyond description.

Spring love fills our quilt;

Intoxication satisfies our souls.

Where do we find our momentary ecstasy?

But when we wake up, it's time to depart.

Let me ask you, my dear, for whom spring ends so soon.

HUO XIAOYU:

How myriad tears drop upon your sleeves!

(*To the previous tune*)

Oh, the tears,

How they roll down my cheeks like red threads!

How my tender weep brings jade-beads of tears!

My tears splash like pure rose-dew from the jade pot,

Breaking into depressive pieces like falling pear-petals,

Soaking the red-gauze kerchiefs like pearls dropping on plates.

How the tears drop till the sea clouds dry!

Ah, the sleeves,

How they are stained like the spotted Xiaoxiang bamboos!

LI YI:

Oh, how bitterly you weep!

(*To the previous tune*)

You keep silent and dreary,

Knitting your eyebrows with a lonely heart.

Casually you make up your face with fine fingers,

Your bright eyes roll with restraint,

And your long wrinkled dress drags along as you walk.

A precious moment is worth a fortune — so what

For we can't consummate our dream and love tonight.

HUO XIAOYU:

My man, in which direction is the Yumen Pass?

(*To the previous tune*)

My eyes will follow you till the road bends,

And my teardrops will float with the dust.

After you go,

My bed-curtain will be cold and desolate,

My belt will turn loose,

And the candlelight and incense smoke will fade.

Looking at the clouds and mountains on the screen,

I think of our meeting again but you may have new love then.

My man, is there anything you'd like to advise me?

LI YI (*To the previous tune*):

I'll spend my leisure in boredom,

Keeping you in my mind to console my soul.

Please tie up the drooping button loops,

Fasten the soft and colourful bellybands,

And make your bed warm and comfortable.

You may have some dreams lingering in your mind,

So please try to ease your sorrow when you wake up.

HUO XIAOYU:

Hearing these remarks, I feel you are not a frivolous man. But at the moment,

(*To the tune of* **Jiesancheng**)

My pain fills the court flowers in the rain;

My sorrow covers the wild grass in the mist.

Forget about the separation of paired mandarin ducks

And their yearning for reunion.

I'll knock the hairpins to call the parrot to talk

Or drowsily glance at the amorous picture-books after making the bed.

My bridegroom is gone,

Disappearing from my sight in no time,

Leaving the phoenix alone in the mirror.

LI YI:

How can I leave abruptly! Fetch more wine!

(*To the previous tune*)

For a scholar who's just made some success,

I feel overwhelmed by your passionate love.

Swallows feed their young with sweet milk around the Cold Food Day,

While pelicans cry, "Don't go darling!"

I tether my steed to a lovesick tree,

With homesick tears that can link the crooked beads.

When I'm lost in my soul,

It's the time when I return drunk

And chant poems lamenting the passing spring.

HUO XIAOYU:

When you are gone, how am I to spend my time?

 (*To the previous tune*)

 How can I have the mood listening to orioles sing?

 I don't even care to do make-up any more.

 From now on I'll be in a melancholy mood all day long,

 Expecting your horse clacking or your letters arriving.

 With the master of the house gone from the bridal chamber,

 The setting sun will find my man on the western frontier.

 Along the road to the Baling Bridge,

 What I see is only the callous painted boats,

 With my carriage laden with sorrow.

LI YI:

My love, I'm afraid the wind and sand on the frontier will make me old!

 (*To the previous tune*)

 I'm like Wang Can in the service in the north,

 While you're like Xiao Qiao married to the State of Wu.

 The talent and belle should enjoy their time together,

 So how can I waste my time on the long journey?

 This departing sorrow can only be relieved by string music;

 The void of time can only be filled by sighs before the mirror.

 When time betrays your intentions for love,

 Can you still recognize me when I return home?

 What would happen on my journey to the frontier?

HUO XIAOYU:

My man, people admire you for your looks and fame. There must be many ladies who'd like to be married to you. As you are departing, it's not certain when you'll return. When you get official promotion, there may be other better proposals of marriage for you. By then our vows might be annulled. However, as your humble wife, I have a modest desire to discuss with you. If you will excuse me, please listen to me.

LI YI (*Startled*):

What's wrong with me that makes you utter such a remark? Please tell me exactly, and I'll certainly respond with all seriousness.

HUO XIAOYU:

I'm now eighteen, and you're twenty-two. There are still eight years to go before you enter the prime of your life. Yet the cream of my life might have ended by then. At that time, you might have better choices for your marriage. That won't be too late for you yet. By then I'll leave the secular world, have my hair cut, wear the black robe and be a nun. All my past desire will be satisfied by then.

 (*To the previous tune*)

 The incense stick might be broken in my previous life;

 Can the candle sparks bring any happiness?

 Just remember that lovers will stick to each other till they're thirty;

277

Don't take the vows and oaths too seriously.

My man,

> Belles are many who'd like to offer you silk whips for keepsake;
>
> I'm just one lonely songster who cares for you.
>
> I must take care
>
> Neither to saturate my green handkerchief with tears
>
> Nor to write palindrome poems to express my longings.

LI YI (*Weeps*):

> *"With my vow as clear as the sun,*
>
> *I will stick to it alive or dead."*

To live and grow old with you is what I long for. How could I think of other choices? So please trust me, and we'll love and respect each other all the time.

> (*To the previous tune*)
>
> Who can compare to you in the town of ladies?
>
> Even the Queen's Kingdom has no match with you.
>
> So trust your man who pencils your eyebrows,
>
> As no other beauty or wine has any charm for me.
>
> Even if another belle can dance and sing on the palm,
>
> I'll never forget you, my dear wife, who sighs by the window.
>
> What grief it is
>
> To look at your raven eyebrows,
>
> And cold dainty crimson lips!
>
> (*Enter Wei Xiaqing and Cui Yunming*)

WEI XIAQING, CUI YUNMING (*To the tune of* **Shengchazi**):

> The talent rides on his horse to the west,
>
> While the wife laments on her beauty.
>
> Orioles warble on the grass fragrant and green;
>
> Fallen petals urge the horse on its way.

We heard quite some time ago that Li Junyu would depart soon. Now it's already noon but he's still tarrying in a gloomy mood at the red pavilion.

> (*Greet Li Yi*)

CUI YUNMING:

Li Junyu, with flutes and drums in the camp on this auspicious day, it's high time to hit the road! It's time for the departure!

LI YI:

To tell the truth, Xiaoyu has a lot to say, so it's hard for me to say good-bye to her.

WEI XIAQING:

As Lu Guimeng's poem goes,

> *"I carry my sword to fill the cup;*
>
> *It's a shame to make a fuss about departure."*

Li Junyu, you are a real man, yet how could you linger like this? Mistress, we will accompany Junyu for a few miles. When we return, we'll bring back the news that all is well. The military mission is urgent, so he can't be delayed. As the saying goes,

"The flapping banner shades away the setting sun,

And the dagger cuts off the sentiments upon departure."

(*Exeunt*)

(*Flutes and drums from within*)

LI YI:

My love, listen to the reed pipes and drums. They're urging me to hurry up. Our intimate love is beyond words. Now I really have to depart.

(*To the tune of **Zhegutian***)

Hiding my tears I send you to your carriage,

Clinging to the dream where we may enjoy the reunion.

HUO XIAOYU:

My man, you don't have to see me back.

I wish you would return in silken robes;

That wouldn't bother my life of solitude.

(*Exit Li Yi with his attendants*)

Escorted by hundreds of horses

And supported by thousands of people,

He's a wealthy, valiant and handsome man.

Huansha, send my words to my man,

Wherever he goes, be sure to bring the sword with him;

Whomever he meets at the post, ask them to bring letters home.

Once we part, we seem to live in two worlds;

Broken-hearted, I look back with weeping eyes.

As the Yumen Pass is three thousand miles away,

It is no easy matter to hear from him.

Scene Twenty-Six
Composing Poems on Mount Longshan

(*Enter the attendants*)

ATTENDANTS (*To the tune of **Jinqianhua***):

The rain washes away the dust,

The dust over Weicheng;

The moon casts the yellow light,

The yellow light over Luntai.

The drumbeats urge us to join the army,

For us to bid farewell to our wives

And to achieve feats with our swords.

Hi, everyone! How heart-breaking it is when we saw the military consultant parting with his wife! There appears the red streamer, and there comes the military consultant.

(*Enter Li Yi*)

LI YI (*To the tune of* **Mantingfang**):

 With catkins dotting the road,

 I broke willow twigs overwhelmed with sorrow,

 In the shades of trees beside the Baling Bridge.

 As a scholar in the Imperial Academy,

 For what did I venture to the frontier?

 When I fondly asked my wife why she wept by the window,

 The wine turned cold and the fragrance on her sleeves dispersed.

 But still I had to leave

 The Baling Bridge,

 Which was bathed in the spring of the imperial capital.

 "The sun shines over the city gate and the envoy's carriages come along;

 The frontier is warm with spring flowers and horse courts are open.

 Suddenly I hear the reed pipes and long horns resounding;

 The sound spreads all the way to the ancient town of Luntai.

 How fresh and green the willows are along the paths in the fields;

 They drag my blue gown but I can't stay behind.

 The longing wife weeps in vain to the south of the Weishui River;

 The man has already gone to the north of the Jiaohe River."

I left my wife's chamber the other day and bid farewell to her at the Baling Bridge by the weeping willows. The scene has been haunting my mind. However, military orders must be obeyed on all accounts, so I have to restrain my tears, bid farewell to my wife and lead my men on the road. Attendants, let's be on our way!

ATTENDANTS (*To the tune of* **Chaoyuange**):

 The breeze blows and the horses stir up the dust;

 The morning sun shines on the carriage and three.

 It's bright and colourful on the banks of the river;

 The carriage moves on along the green water.

 The black troop snakes its way forward,

 And the banners patterned with falcons move onward,

 All taking place swiftly like lightning or shooting stars.

 When we march on with the beating of drums and bells,

 How far is the Southern Hun capital in the north?

 The green grass accompanies the entrusted mission,

 And His Majesty will award the envoys.

ALL:

 Hold the reins tight,

 And we'll win imperial bestowals by making great feats.

LI YI (*To the previous tune*):

When we look back, Chang'an is far and the sun is near.

The officials in the east send us off with enthusiasm,

While my wife in the south suffers from the sorrow of love.

Looking at the rouge, black dye and white powder,

She finds it hard to express her solitude and sorrow.

I have the dagger to protect me,

Yet the frontier sands wither my face and the rough wind ruffles my hair.

The extravagant young man joins the army,

Yet all the wealth and fame turn to be hardship and bitterness.

ALL:

Hold the reins tight,

And we'll win imperial bestowals by making great feats.

ATTENDANTS:

My lord, the Longtou River lies ahead. One distributary enters the Han territory and the other the Hun territory.

LI YI:

This divided river forks into heart-breaking creeks! I'll compose a poem on Mount Longshan, but there's nobody to bring it home. So let me do it orally,

"Green willows touch the water and grass is in the mist;

This is where the Tartars used to water their horses.

The sounds of reed pipes come up at the moonlit night;

Who's pointing the gigantic sword high up to the sky?

The frozen river used to be a mountain path,

Yet today it forks before the Han envoys.

Don't ask the travelers to mirror their faces and hair,

For they fear it might bring weariness into the new year!"

ATTENDANTS (*To the previous tune*):

He's been looking for the spring scene over Mount Longshan,

And neglecting his health to repay the imperial grace,

Still keeping his dear wife in mind.

At the ancient fortress the reed pipes are blown;

In the mountains the flutes are played;

Yet the music of *Falling Plum Blossoms* can be heard no more.

When he prowls on his horse,

He hears the endless sound of flowing waters.

As he waters his horse at the heart-breaking creeks,

Tears of homesickness wet his handkerchief.

ALL:

Hold the reins tight,

And we'll win imperial bestowals by making great feats.

(*Enter the officers from the western town, amid flute and drum music*)

OFFICERS:

Officers from the western town are here to greet the military consultant.

ATTENDANTS (*To the previous tune*):

> When the Great Wall turns dim after sunset,
>
> Stars start to wink from behind the clouds,
>
> And the moon shines over the Huamen tribes.
>
> The general's standard blows on the frontier,
>
> While military banners turn around in the valley.
>
> Past trees lining up along the beacon towers,
>
> We make our way toward the Upper Yellow River.
>
> Observing the atmosphere over the origin,
>
> We see that the war stars have not fallen yet.
>
> We laugh and get ready for the heroic exploits,
>
> Expecting the intoxicating wine for our frontier victory.

ALL:

> Hold the reins tight,
>
> And we'll win imperial bestowals by making great feats.
>
> *We expect the reclusive haven in the moonlit mountains,*
>
> *When we break through the clouds over the gigantic peak.*
>
> *We'll stick to our books and swords till we grow old,*
>
> *And follow armoured General Li Guang in the Han Dynasty.*

Scene Twenty-Seven
The Chivalrous Mistress Offers Rewards

(*Enter Huo Xiaoyu*)

HUO XIAOYU (*To the tune of* **Yue'ergao**):

> As I hate to be single but love to be coupled,
>
> My waist grows thin for my loneliness.
>
> Departing sorrow breaks my heart,
>
> Leaving me in a most melancholy mood.
>
> The early summer seems to me the desolate autumn;
>
> Who could bear such solitude and negligence?
>
> Don't you know it?
>
> In the green waves that ripple the pond,
>
> Mandarin ducks swim head by head in pairs.
>
> (*In the pattern of* **Shengchazi**)
>
> *"The flowers and the moon like to arrange for new happiness;*
>
> *One feels most delighted after the fresh rain.*
>
> *My man is not a man of frivolity;*

He falls in love with me and cares for me with devotion.

Once he's gone, how could he turn back?

The road bends as if the screens blocked the view.

Knitting my brows in sorrow,

I feel reluctant to do any make-up."

Huansha, How many days has your master been away?

HUANSHA:

Quite a few days.

HUO XIAOYU:

The two scholars, Cui Yunming and Wei Xiaqing, promised to bring the news after they saw your master off across the river, but they haven't come yet. Oh, I think of the time when we first met.

(*To the tune of* **Xiaojinzhang**)

When we chanced to meet on the Lantern Festival,

We fell in love at first sight.

When my short jade and golden hairpin slipped down my hair,

Our happy marriage was consummated

Like the perfect match between the spokes and the axis,

With our two hearts beating together.

We're born an ideal couple with the heart-to-heart communion.

Holding my hands fondly among the red flowers and green leaves,

He intimately,

Intimately embraced me with passionate love.

HUANSHA (*Aside*):

(*To the previous tune*)

She's soft and tender in love,

Indulged in the blissful dream of the Goddess on Mount Wushan.

She sang *The Yangguan Pass* for the passage of spring,

Looking so alluring,

So sad and dreary.

She exhibited her slim waist in the rain at dusk,

In the rain at dusk breaking the willow twigs by the bridge.

They were linked heart to heart,

Tears wetting her sleeves.

At last they had to say farewell,

A farewell that was so reluctant.

HUO XIAOYU:

Huansha, last night I had a dream:

(*To the previous tune*)

My feelings and mood remained the same,

Clinging to my heart and mind all the time.

I whispered to ask if he would still have to go,

The Purple Hairpins

But he would not answer,

Nor would he move.

(*In a subdued voice*)

By the window,

I pushed the pillow aside and expected his embrace.

Oh, when I looked back at the empty bed,

I only saw the slanting moonlight and heard the ringing bell.

I suddenly jumped up, only to find my love gone,

And all I could do was to beat the pillow.

HUANSHA:

Mistress, let's go to the master's study to relax for a while.

(*They move*)

HUO XIAOYU (*To the previous tune*):

The green windows are covered with dust;

The ink slab seems glazed in the centre.

HUANSHA:

How come Qiuhong left the four stationary articles?

HUO XIAOYU:

They certainly have them in the trunk.

The windows are covered with new moss.

The moss is wrinkled here

And drawn there like embroidery.

Don't take the green moss lightly,

For it has more profound feelings.

Huansha, there seems somebody coming.

(*In a subdued voice*)

Behind the bright windows and on the shadowed bed,

I used to be with him in the study.

HUANSHA:

Somebody's coming.

HUO XIAOYU (*Startled*):

I raise my head all of a sudden to listen,

And hear the orioles warble on a sunny day.

Huansha, there're some green plums on a half of the branch outside the window. Pick them for me!

(*Steps aside*)

(*Enter Wei Xiaqing and Cui Yunming*)

WEI XIAQING, CUI YUNMING (*To the previous tune*):

At the farthest end of Chang'an,

We bid farewell to the fine scholar.

The heart-broken wife dwelt in the chamber,

Then happy,

And now sad.

It's for all that,

For all that tenderness and intimacy.

Ah, is that Xiaoyu walking away indoors?

Seeing the guests coming,

She walks away in her socks,

With her golden hairpins slipping down.

Bashfully she walks away,

She walks away, holding and smelling the green plums.

HUO XIAOYU:

Huansha, there come Mr. Wei and Mr. Cui. Ask them to what place they accompanied your master, and ask them if they've brought back any message.

(*To the previous tune*)

I wonder after his departure

Whether he still misses me.

Seeing each other all the time may be boring,

So I try to restrain myself from sorrow

And put it aside for some time.

Even if I could see him off some pavilions away,

Out of the Qin territory, I would have to stop weeping.

Once he writes lyrics of sentiments,

He'll send them to my dressing table.

These solitary days make me thin.

WEI XIAQING, CUI YUNMING (*To the tune of* **Fengrusong**):

Huansha, now listen to us:

We sent him off all the way to the riverside,

And stayed with him for a few days.

We saw him look back from time to time

And shed tears on his blue gown.

Please tell your mistress,

His letter home has yet to wait as he has just left;

She should take good care of herself and not worry too much.

HUANSHA:

Then what else?

CUI YUNMING:

Qiuhong wants me to tell you not to wander about.

HUANSHA:

Nonsense! Why can't I roam about with my own feet?

HUO XIAOYU (*Sighs*):

So Li Yi sent back the message for me to take a good rest. The Huo residence is big. Does Li Yi have any relatives in Chang'an after his departure? It would be better if we can find one to keep our gate. Please ask Mr. Wei and Mr. Cui to be seated outside, and I'll inquire

285

here inside.

(*Huansha asks Wei Xiaqing and Cui Yunming to sit outside*)

WEI XIAQING, CUI YUNMING:

What would you like to know, Mistress?

HUO XIAOYU:

Li Yi left in a hurry before I had time to ask about his family in detail. As his old friends, do you know what relatives he has?

CUI YUNMING:

Mistress, are you worried about whether he has other wives?

(*To the previous tune*)

He's remained single,

And like a flatfish never wont to ogle.

HUO XIAOYU:

Not that. I'm asking what attendants he has with him.

CUI YUNMING:

He only has Qiuhong as his attendant.

Are you asking where to find his former spouse?

HUO XIAOYU:

Not that. I'm asking who his relatives are.

WEI XIAQING:

He's destined to have no relatives,

But rove all over the country by himself.

HUO XIAOYU:

Pity on him. Such a young talent, but so poor and all lonely!

CUI YUNMING:

But what a blissful chance for him.

At Lanqiao he met a fairy,

And that revealed his elegance and luck.

HUO XIAOYU (*Talks to herself*):

So it is! But wait, we don't have other relatives in the house either. We don't even have one who can follow the news about my man. The other day my man told me that the two scholars were his bosom friends. Besides, they are two poor visiting scholars, and our family is well-to-do. So why not help them and they can help us in return? Huansha, please ask the two scholars to listen to me,

(*To the previous tune*)

The male phoenix has left the female phoenix,

Leaving the mate alone in the nest.

Since my man has no relatives, I'll treat you two scholars as his close kin.

One way or the other we need your help as his brothers.

CUI YUNMING:

We're busy making a poor living, so we're afraid we don't have much time to help.

HUO XIAOYU:

Don't worry about that. For clothes, food or firewood, please come to my house and get your share.

> For the daily allowance of gold coins you need,
>
> Feel free to obtain it from our rich wealth.

As *The Book of Poetry* goes,

> *"To my man's friends,*
>
> *I'll present jade pendants."*
>
> Why do I present jade pedants?
>
> I hope they'll offer help in return.

WEI XIAQING:

Since we are so entrusted, whatever we hear about Mr. Li, Mr. Cui will come and report it.

CUI YUNMING:

That'll do.

WEI XIAQING (*To the previous tune*):

> Please stay well in the best mood in your chamber.

If there's anything for our help, simply send Huansha to tell us.

CUI YUNMING:

> She's as deft as the blue bird in passing the message.

It's not convenient for us to frequent your house.

> We fear it's not proper for others to see us here too often,
>
> So we'll focus on the news from the frontier.

WEI XIAQING:

> Though we are brothers and friends,
>
> You need to take charge of the affairs in the house.

Huansha, please pass our respect to your mistress. We're leaving now.

> (*To the tune of* **Coda**)
>
> We stay poor and desolate in Chang'an,
>
> Yet we offer help and consolation to the wealthy.

This is an extraordinarily virtuous lady!

> Among the chivalrous heroines she's one of the best.
>
> (*Exeunt Wei Xiaqing and Cui Yunming*)

HUANSHA:

Two poor bookworms! Why do we have to subsidize them?

> *As the man serves as military consultant on the frontier,*
>
> *There must be assistance and help in times of need.*
>
> *Courtesy comes from a sense of humanity,*
>
> *So why not act with generosity and chivalry?*

Scene Twenty-Eight
The Tubo General Seeks Hegemony

(*Enter the Tubo General*)

TUBO GENERAL (*To the tune of* **Dianjiangchun**):

Bold and powerful are we Tubos,

Who dominate the western areas

Covering a large expanse.

Born in a family of senior officials,

I have a thousand stalwart steeds.

"Grass rolls with the chilly wind along the western frontier;

Rustling in the wind are imposing armors of the warriors;

Our boundless territory stretches to the horizon,

With soldiers prepared for fierce invasion."

I'm a Tubo general. We Tubos have a wide-spreading territory and numerous brave soldiers. Braving the snow and holding the sharpest swords, we have extended our sphere of influence to as far as the west of the Kunlun Mountains and the north of the Chibin River. All the states in the east of the upper reaches of the Yellow River are subjugated to us, but now the Tang emperor wants to conquer them and take them from us. The state of Dahexi produces wine and the state of Xiaohexi produces watermelons. It is time to plunder them. I'll gather my brave soldiers and give them orders.

(*Enter the soldiers*)

SOLDIERS (*To the tune of* **Shuidiyu**):

With wild geese in the sky and chrysanthemums on the ground,

The western area is enshrouded with dusts.

In our teens,

We Tubos can blow horns and ride horses.

We wear leather hats,

Adorned with feathers of the sacred crows.

Any enemy that comes into our hand

Is bound to lose his head.

(*Greet the Tubo General*)

TUBO GENERAL:

We take wine from Dahexi and watermelons from Xiaohexi every summer. It's time to go again. Now listen to my orders!

(*Soldiers answer in chorus*)

TUBO GENERAL (*To the tune of* **Qingjiangyin**):

With wine pots and yurts we wander everywhere

In the endless expanse of the western area.

Why do Hans guard against us in autumn?

All the products are the richest in summer here.

Let's all mount the horses, warriors!

(*The soldiers smell the wine*)

TUBO GENERAL (*To the previous tune*):

As the wine is fragrant and sweet,

We'll enjoy ourselves to our hearts' content.

We'll bite watermelons when intoxicated,

While galloping and tramping on the flowers.

We'll beat the drums while hurrying on our way to loot.

When grass is luxuriant in early summer,

Our horses are in the best condition.

The soldiers are busy with archery training,

In preparation for successful military action.

Scene Twenty-Nine
Writing a War Proclamation

(*Enter Liu Gongji*)

LIU GONGJI (*To the tune of* **Yizhihua**):

With feather-decorated army flags fluttering in the breeze,

Our soldiers are patrolling to guard against invaders.

When all military activities have ceased,

We'll enjoy leisure fully relaxed.

Listening to the twitters of cicadas,

I suddenly find a few gray hairs on my head.

Under the shadows of green trees,

I, like the famous ancient general Feng Yi, gradually turn old,

But still have a bearing both scholarly and refined.

(*In the pattern of* **Linjiangxian**)

"Life is prosperous in the middle empire,

While there's an endless desert in the northwest.

With the beloved native land in mind,

Stationed near the windy west frontiers,

I'll render a service meritorious and splendid.

Blowing horns can be heard near the Great Wall all night;

Stars can be seen in the western area at dawn.

Around me are civil officials of literary talent,

As well as consultants of far-reaching insight

And generals of military aptitude."

I'm Liu Gongji. His Majesty appoints me as Governor to guard the western frontier. I have recently moved our camps outside the Yumen Pass. Approved by His Majesty, I assign the Number One Scholar Li Yi, an old friend of mine, to be my military consultant. As he will report to duty today, I have ordered my troops to drill in battle array as a welcome for him. Attendant, get the wine ready.

(*Drum and horns within*)

(*Enter Li Yi, followed by subordinates*)

LI YI (*To the tune of* **Manjianghong**):

> While horse-neighs resound to the sky,
> I tighten my silk rein and hold up the whip.
> I can hear horns and drums by the riverside
> Echoing in the mountains.
> When songs from the campsite come to my ears,
> Red flags on watchtowers flutter before my eyes.

SUBORDINATES:

> The grass is green at the waterfront,
> To welcome a man of superior talent.

(*Liu Gongji and Li Yi greet each other*)

LIU GONGJI:

> "You are the best poet today,

LI YI:

> But I must obey you in military affairs.

LIU GONGJI:

> You are my most honoured guest,

LI YI:

> But I depend on you to do meritorious deeds."

LIU GONGJI (*Smiles*):

Li Junyu, I'm so glad today. Attendant, serve the wine!

ATTENEANT:

> "A sunny day is the best for painting;
> A breezy day is the best for drinking."

Here's the wine.

LIU GONGJI (*To the tune of* **Liangzhouxu**):

> Officials at court praise in one accord
> Your elegant appearance
> And your literary talent.
> As it's our fate to co-operate at the frontier,
> I'm now welcoming you with great respect.
> With your rich literary knowledge
> And resourceful military skills,
> The frontier will be an impregnable fortress.
> Since I come here as the chief commander,

I've been dreaming of an outstanding figure

To act as a competent helper.

ALL:

In a weather so clear and mild,

A military report reaches the headquarters

That it is peaceful on the frontiers.

People are jubilant

At the grand banquet.

LI YI (*To the previous tune*):

With extraordinary appearance and graceful manners,

As well as ruddy complexion and black hair,

You are indeed a dashing commander.

By the Great Wall of thousands of miles,

You'll station here in the military camp.

Looking at our army in gallant spirits,

You'll take authoritative command

And become the most brilliant hero in the world.

The frontier will be impregnable

Under your command,

And you will be highly awarded by the court.

ALL:

In a weather so clear and mild,

A military report reaches the headquarters

That it is peaceful on the frontiers.

People are jubilant

At the grand banquet.

LIU GONGJI:

I have something important to consult with you. Beyond the Great Wall, there are two states, Dahexi and Xiaohexi, which has blocked the Hans since Emperor Wu of the Han Dynasty set up the four counties in the western area. The two states have been paying tributes to us. Dahexi presents wine to our Jiuquan County, while Xiaohexi presents watermelons to our Beiguazhou County. But recently, threatened by the Tubo state, they dare not pay tributes to us any longer. So we intend to declare a war on them. I want you to write a report to His Majesty.

LI YI:

Let me think it over.

LIU GONGJI (*To the previous tune*):

The green tents are patterned with birds flying in the wind;

The army flags are adorned with coiling dragons and snakes in the clouds.

With the tunes *Dachanyu* and *Xiaochanyu* played all night,

No presence of enemy has been reported.

His Majesty attaches great importance to the western frontier;

The Purple Hairpins

His order to guard it is determinate and clear,

And your report can well settle the military affairs.

With your report written in quick wit,

We will soon dispatch troops westward.

ALL:

In a weather so clear and mild,

A military report reaches the headquarters

That it is peaceful on the frontiers.

People are jubilant

At the grand banquet.

LI YI:

It is not a bad idea to start a war on Dahexi and Xiaohexi since they no longer pay tributes to us. But the weather is not desirable with irregular sunny days and rainy days in the fourth month and the fifth month. Let me write a false war proclamation just to scare Dahexi and Xiaohexi. And we can also consider dispatching troops to cut off Tubo's route of retreat so that they dare not send all their troops to invade Dahexi and Xiaohexi. In this way, tributes to us will be continued.

LIU GONGJI:

That's a good idea. You have both literary talent and military strategy. Attendants, serve wine in a goblet!

LI YI (*To the previous tune*):

Your worth will be appreciated and win you a promotion;

Your post of chief commander doesn't interfere with your relaxation.

You discard an exquisite life filled with formalities

And numerous attendants crowding around.

You prefer a life unrestrained,

A gallant and martial life

Those high officials would hardly believe

You can enjoy in the west.

Working under such an outstanding commander as you,

Even a man of letters will never feel hard and strenuous.

ALL:

In a weather so clear and mild,

A military report reaches the headquarters

That it is peaceful on the frontiers.

People are jubilant

At the grand banquet.

(*Enter female singers and dancers*)

FEMALE SINGERS AND DANCERS:

"*Bringing along our dancing costumes to the frontier,*

We sing and dance with the bright moon in the sky."

(*Play music*)

(*To the tune of **Jiejiegao***)

When the decorated drum

Is beaten,

Various musical instruments begin to play.

The melodies from the Qiuci state

And the songs from the Yutian state

Are full of joy.

The tunes from Yizhou and Liangzhou

And the music from Ganzhou soar to the sky.

ALL:

Wearing military robes we drink wine to the wind

And sing of our happiness in the front.

FEMALE SINGERS AND DANCERS (*Dance*):

(*To the previous tune*)

As soon as the flute music stops,

Dance performance begins,

With ribbons flying around.

The dancing girls can dance on plates held in hand,

With lithe and graceful movements

Like whirlwind.

Young are the dancing girls,

Who perform under bright lamps.

ALL:

Wearing military robe we drink wine to the wind

And sing of our happiness in the front.

LIU GONGJI (*To the tune of **Coda***):

As every piece of tune is pleasant to the ear,

People whistle in satisfaction after the festival.

I'm really like Ban Chao, the famous ancient general.

As the grand banquet in the camp is held at night,

Our patrolman hurries with war information to report.

When the proclamation is quickly written by candlelight,

All the people agree that Li Yi is an outstanding talent.

(*Left alone on the stage*)

Tell the adjutant to fetch two proclamations from Li Yi tomorrow morning. We will, in the name of His Majesty, order Dahexi and Xiaohexi to continue their tributes. If they still disobey, we'll start a war. Li Yi can really solve the problem well. It is true indeed,

"*While battle steeds should not be left idle,*

The report will bring us into high spirits."

(*Exit*)

Scene Thirty
Subjection of Dahexi and Xiaohexi

(*Enter the Dahexi king with a blue face, a big nose and a thick beard*)

DAHEXI KING (*To the tune of* **Fendie'er**):

> The Dahexi state prospers in radiant splendour,
>
> Having a vast territory
>
> And taking absolute possession of this land.
>
> Nourished by horse-milk wine and delicious meals,
>
> We are stalwart and strong.
>
> Our chest is wrapped in expensive colourful cloth;
>
> From our eyes never drop tears.

I am king of the Dahexi state. It is time for grapes to ripe. We will make grape wine to present to the Tubo state when the east wind blows. I heard that the Tang emperor stations troops at the Yumen Pass and wants us to be subjugated to them. I don't care whether it is the Tubo state or the Tang Empire that we'll be subjugated to. "First come, first served." Now that we are brewing wine, let's look and see who comes first.

(*Enter a Dahexi soldier*)

DAHEXI SOLDIER:

Report! Report! Ambassador from the Tang Empire has arrived.

VOICE WITHIN:

Here comes the ambassador! The Tang Emperor's edict orders the Dahexi king to kneel and listen, "It has been a convention that grapes must be presented to us, the Hans. We have sent the chief military commander Liu Gongji and the military consultant Li Yi to govern you. War will be proclaimed on you if you do not obey." Now you kowtow and give thanks to the imperial decree.

DAHEXI KING (*Rises to his feet*):

Invite the Tang ambassador to a banquet with horse milk.

VOICE WIHTHIN:

As I'm now going to the Xiaohexi state, I can't stay any longer. Goodbye.

DAHEXI KING:

Now we are subjugated to the Tang Empire.

> "*We have been a powerful country,*
>
> *But are now subject to the Hans.*"

(*Exit*)

(*Enter the Xiaohexi king with a blue face, a big nose and a thick beard*)

XIAOHEXI KING (*To the tune of* **Xinshuiling**):

> Once a state like a powerful and invincible lion,
>
> We are now conquered and no longer awe-inspiring.
>
> Having just enjoyed a sweet watermelon

And bathed a comfortable bath in the river,

I now play a sharp iron sabre skillfully,

To boil stinky fat mutton.

I am king of the Xiaohexi state. We used to be subjugated to the Tang Empire, but were later forced by the Tubo state to pay tributes to them. Whenever the grapes are ripe, they would come to loot. If they come to loot again, I'd rather submit to the authority of the Tang Empire again.

VOICE WITHIN:

Ambassador from Tang has arrived. The Tang Emperor's edict orders the Xiaohexi king to kneel and listen: "Considering that Xiaohexi is located in a remote region, we have sent the chief military commander Liu Gongji and the military consultant Li Yi to govern you. War will be proclaimed on you if you do not obey." Now you kowtow and give thanks to the imperial decree.

XIAOHEXI KING (*Rises to his feet*):

Invite the ambassador to a banquet of mutton.

VOICE WITHIN:

As I'm going to have Tubo's retreat route cut off, I can't stay any longer. Goodbye.

XIAOHEXI KING:

Let us subjugate ourselves to the Tang Empire.

"*When the imperial edict comes,*

We are awfully scared."

(*Exit*)

(*Enter the black-faced Tubo General, followed by soldiers*)

TUBO GENERAL (*To the tune of **Yizhihua***):

Chilly winds blow hard on the road to the Bailan Mountains;

Places with water are the best resort of escape from summer heat.

Shining weapons are displayed at military camp gate.

In the sweeping sandstorm,

We are in battle array under flapping flags

And in battle roar.

Wearing a coloured cloth hat

And a felt garment,

I proudly flick my sword to the music.

"*A state situated against the mountains,*

We've subjugated all the states in the west.

Dahexi and Xiaohexi are exceptions,

Who're subjugated to the Hans."

I'm a Tubo general. Now I am gathering my soldiers to loot Dahexi and Xiaohexi. What beautiful scenery along the way!

(*Hunting while traveling on*)

(*To the tune of **Duanzhenghao***)

With military flags fluttering in the sun,

Our horses march on under clouds.

With grass growing luxuriantly along our way,

I lead my soldiers to hunt all the day

And camp near the Yellow Flower Valley now.

(*To the tune of* **Gunxiuqiu**)

While strong winds sweep over the grass,

When can we see the scenery of swaying willows?

We can hear the cooing wild geese and foxes,

The rushing river deer,

The racing rabbits,

The shivering porcupines,

And the frightened tigers.

With the hard-blowing wind

Come spasms of drumbeats.

The flying arrows redden the grass,

And the vulture blood stain my sleeves.

Oh! Here we are in the Dahexi state. Ask them whether grape wine is ready for us.

VOICE WITHIN:

The Tang Empire has sent an ambassador to our state and we have surrendered.

TUBO GENERAL (*Angry*):

Alas! Dahexi has been conquered by the Tang Empire!

(*To the tune of* **Tangxiucai**)

The Tang Empire conquers the silly Dahexi state

That abounds in luscious grapes,

Of which mellow wine is made.

You used to submit to us with wine as tribute,

But now do the same with Tang.

You are a shameless blackguard!

Warriors, let's loot them!

(*Killing while walking*)

Oh! The Xiaohexi state is ahead. Ask them whether watermelons are ready for us.

VOICE WITHIN:

The Tang Empire has sent an ambassador to our state and we have surrendered.

TUBO GENEARL (*Angry*):

The Xiaohexi state has also been conquered by the Tang Empire.

(*To the tune of* **Yaopian**)

Stubborn and strange are the little Xiaohexi men.

Luscious are their watermelons with black seeds and red pulp,

Whose coolness penetrates to the heart.

If you present watermelons, you'll erase my annoyance in the heat.

Otherwise I will carve up your land

And see what you are to do!

VOICE WITHIN:

The Tang Empire has sent troops to cut off your retreat. Are you afraid of them?

TUBO GENERAL:

Is that true?

> (*To the tune of* **Coda**)
>
> We allow you to obey the Tang Empire for the moment,
>
> Which may not be dependable for long.
>
> We have just known your betrayal to us,
>
> But someday will vanquish you in battle drums.
>
> *We are hunters with great vigor and high spirits,*
>
> *But Dahexi and Xiaohexi make us distressed.*
>
> *Subjugation to Tang retains your king's leadership,*
>
> *But don't you know we pose to you a great threat?*

Scene Thirty-One
Escaping the Summer Heat on the Tower

> (*Enter Liu Gongji*)

LIU GONGJI (*To the tune of* **Xidijin**):

> No heat is felt here in the northwest
>
> Because there are high buildings to prevent sunstroke.
>
> As our military victory is worth boasting,
>
> I'm indulged in drinking wine.
>
> (*In the pattern of* **Yiluosuo**)
>
> *"With a view of shining weapons, swaying willows*
>
> *And singing birds under the eaves,*
>
> *A summer tower is newly built.*
>
> *With beaded curtains lowered at twilight,*
>
> *We lustily sing an ancient melody.*
>
> *All the consultants gathered here are prominent,*
>
> *With no one jealous of others' talent.*
>
> *While rain is pouring down outside,*
>
> *There is singing and dancing at the banquet."*

I, Liu Gongji, am now stationed in the west of the Yumen Pass. Li Junyu, my consultant, is really a talented and graceful man. Since there are no longer any wars, we are holding a banquet to escape the summer heat. Recently, Dahexi and Xiaohexi have begun to pay us tributes. What good news it is!

> (*Music within*)
>
> (*Enter Li Yi*)

LI YI (*To the tune of **Fanbusuan***):

>   In June when warfare ends,
>   Breeze gently sways the curtain.
>   Governor Liu is very considerate
>   To hold a grand banquet in my honour.

>   (*Liu Gongji and Li Yi greet each other*)

LIU GONGJI:

>   *"A high tower is built for cool enjoyment;*

LI YI:

>   *A magnificent banquet is held at the military camp.*

LIU GONGJI:

>   *You're a man of marvelous literary talent;*

LI YI:

>   *A great commander like you shows a useful man due respect."*

LIU GONGJI:

We're sworn brothers and co-operate well in the military affairs. I've been too busy these days to hold a celebration banquet in your honour. Let's have a drink of wine on this summer tower on such a hot day. Attendant, serve wine.

>   (*Enter the attendant*)

ATTENDANT:

>   *"So high and cool is the tower as if it has snowed;*
>   *So long is the daytime that much incense is burnt."*

Here's the wine.

LIU GONGJI (*To the tune of **Xinujiao***):

>   On our expedition a long way from home,
>   We hold a victory banquet
>   In jubilant atmosphere.
>   Now that warfare has come to an end,
>   We can now be fully relaxed.
>   At noontime,
>   Under the tree shade which looks like a chariot awning,
>   On the mossy steps where spears are laid unused,
>   Drumbeats are heard from behind the flowers.
>   At long last,
>   When this hard military expedition is over,
>   How can we not enjoy full relaxation?

LI YI (*To the previous tune*):

>   When you give orders
>   In your commander's office,
>   The wind has stopped on the embroidered flags,
>   And the clouds have dispersed on the travel pass
>   All the way to Liangzhou.

The scorching heat is unbearable,

Yet with silk kerchief on head,

And feather fan in hand,

You play the flute in high spirits

For the good news from the front.

At the serene dusk,

Swallows return to the nest

And incense smoke curls up above the windows.

(*Enter the attendant with a wine jug*)

ATTENDANT:

"We have pure and mellow wine

That gives off an aroma so fine."

My lord, here's the wine Dahexi has presented to our Jiuquan County.

LIU GONGJI:

This should be attributed to our consultant, Mr. Li Yi. Attendant, serve the wine.

(*To the tune of* **Heimaxu**)

The wine

Smells better than ghee.

Made from ripe grapes,

It's fresh, green and crystal clear.

For this alone I'd rather move to Jiuquan County,

Than to be stationed here in Liangzhou.

LI YI:

The wine,

Stored in the basement for one year,

Is mellow and pure.

With the grapes squeezed

And the impure contents removed,

Crystal-clear wine is produced.

(*Enter the attendant with watermelons*)

ATTENDANT:

"As the Northern Dipper is as high as the Southern Dipper,

So the watermelons are as big as the white gourds."

My lord, our Ganzhou County brings you watermelons, the tribute from Xiaohexi.

LIU GONGJI:

This should be attributed to our consultant, Mr. Li Yi. Attendant, serve the watermelons.

(*To the previous tune*)

The watermelon

Is taken out of an icy well.

We cut open the green, clear and smooth shell,

Wrap it in gauze and store it in a shady place.

So fresh is the red pulp,

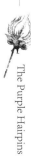

With luscious juice flowing out!

LI YI:

> The icy juice in the shell,
> Sweet as the nectar,
> Drops onto the plate like pearls.
> Iced in the well water,
> The pulp is bright red and crisp,
> Which other fruits lack.

LIU GONGJI:

Let's enjoy the view on the Tower of Watching the Capital.

LI YI:

What's the point of watching the capital?

LIU GONGJI (*To the tune of Jinyixiang*):

> Trees beyond the Yumen Pass are luxuriant,
> With a thick leafy shade.
> Duckweeds are rising and falling in river,
> Stirred by the gentle breeze.
> When you look out of the tower, where is the capital?

LI YI:

> I'm afraid that one day
> This tower will be deserted,
> Leaving behind the frontier music
> And the floating clouds.
> In the dense leafy shade,
> I strike up a tune
> And sing aloud by the pillars.
> I listen to the reed pipe playing,
> Which seems to lament on the elapse of time.
> Chattering birds fly around for branches to alight,
> While the startled cicada falls on the dewy ground.

LIU GONGJI, LI YI (*To the tune of Jiangshuiling*):

> I wonder where my settled home is,
> With these mountains, rivers and passes in my dream,
> And my drunken shadow in the moonlit cup.
> In my drunkenness I might spoil the jade kettle
> Or break the coral.
> My hair has turned grey
> Before my ambition is realized
> And I still have a long way to go in my service for the court.
> At the banquet,
> At the banquet,
> Brilliant talents gather;

Outside the camp gate,

Outside the camp gate,

The moon shines and stars glitter.

LIU GONGJI:

Mr. Li Yi,

(*To the tune of* **coda**)

We now enjoy watermelons in high spirits;

Sooner or later you'll win merits in the battles.

At that time you may leave here for the court

And write articles to sing praise of His Majesty.

LI YI:

As I'm grateful for your appreciation of my talents, I'll improvise a poem for you.

LIU GONGJI (*Laughs*):

I'll be glad to hear.

LI YI (*Chants the poem*):

Day by day we drink to our hearts' content,

Indulged in music and songs of every kind.

As I'm grateful for your kindness,

I'll keep my promotion out of mind.

Scene Thirty-Two
Scheming to Take in the Talent

(*Enter General Lu*)

GENERAL LU (*To the tune of* **Yexingchuan**):

As the highest-ranking official at court,

I intermarry with the emperor's in-laws

And socialize with the most influential eunuchs.

Not knowing the way of the world

Or the importance of connections,

That young scholar is really an idiot.

"Holding the key military power and post,

I'm sent by His Majesty to guard a strategic fort.

Li Yi is too arrogant for his talent,

Which definitely does him no good."

I'm General Lu. Three years ago, I managed to dispatch Li Yi to the outlying west frontier as a military consultant, because he was too arrogant and did not obey me. I heard that he expressed his dissatisfaction with the court in his poem for Governor Liu, "*As I'm grateful for your kindness, / I'll keep my promotion out of mind*", which I should have reported

to His Majesty. But the situation now is that I've just been decreed to guard a strategic fort, and that Governor Liu is summoned back to act as chief commander of the imperial armies. I'd better act accordingly and ask for the permission from His Majesty to transfer Li Yi to my army as a consultant without being allowed to go back home first. I'll try to take him in as my son-in-law when he is under my command in the army. If he is still disobedient, I'll report his dissatisfaction with the court to His Majesty. I've sent for his friend Wei Xiaqing for a discussion on this matter. Now here he comes.

(*Enter Wei Xiaqing*)

WEI XIAQING (*To the tune of* **Boxing**):

> When the hot summer has just passed,
>
> Autumn displays different sights.
>
> On prosperous roads in Chang'an,
>
> Senior officials bustle about in the autumn wind.
>
> When can I meet
>
> My friend in a remote place?
>
> Now I am at the gate of General Lu's house,
>
> Which is magnificently decorated,
>
> And I shall soon meet him in person.

GENERAL LU (*Greets Wei Xiaqing*):

> *"I'll treat a friend from afar with hospitality;*

WEI XIAQING:

> *A powerful person like you will guard the western frontier.*

GENERAL LU:

> *I want you to recommend a talent as my consultant;*

WEI XIAQING:

> *I pay homage to you amidst the military flags."*

GENEARL LU:

Mr. Wei, you are Li Junyu's best friend. What would you say if I were to transfer Mr. Li to my army as a military consultant?

WEI XIAQING:

Li Junyu has been in the army at the west frontier for as long as three years, so I think he should be transferred to work at the imperial court. Moreover, I'm afraid that the position of a military consultant is beyond his ability.

GENERAL LU:

What is the point of transferring Mr. Li to the imperial court since he expresses dissatisfaction with His Majesty in his poem for Governor Liu? To work under me is just as good.

(*To the tune of* **Luoguling**)

> As Li has much literary talent,
>
> I'd like to befriend him and promote him,
>
> But how eccentric his temperament is!

WEI XIAQING:

> Mr. Li naively takes it for granted

That his articles would be appreciated and bought.

Even though he is a man of great genius,

Who would admire him with loud cheers?

GENERAL LU:

I won't mind if he doesn't come,

But no one else would appreciate him.

GENERAL LU, WEI XIAQING:

Days and years have elapsed

In a place far from the court.

By order from His Majesty,

Li will soon come back.

We'll meet here in such a happy mood

That even the bleak scenery will look good.

GENERAL LU (*To the previous tune*):

The idea has always been in my mind

To have Li Yi under my command

As a resourceful military consultant.

WEI XIAQING:

Li's promotion and appointment by the court is doubtless;

But what is the duration of his military service?

GENERAL LU:

Fortunately, the strategic fort we guard is not at the frontier.

WEI XIAQING:

No matter where the fort lies,

Working at the imperial court is the best choice.

GENERAL LU:

How impressive and vigorous we officers look!

How do you know military consultants won't be officials at court?

GENERAL LU, WEI XIAQING:

Days and years have elapsed

In a place far from the court.

By order from His Majesty,

Li will soon come back.

We'll meet here in such a happy mood

That even the bleak scenery will look good.

WEI XIAQING:

Since you attach so much importance to Li Junyu, he will surely contribute his brilliant talent. I'm afraid I must be off now.

(*To the tune of **Coda***)

For friendship

I've come at your invitation;

GENERAL LU:

Because of Li's talent I have a transference intention.

Mr. Wei,

> Who dare say I'm a rash and thoughtless general
>
> That doesn't know how to recruit talented people?

(*Exit Wei Xiaqing*)

GENERAL LU (*Left alone on the stage*):

How funny! Mr. Wei surely doesn't know my scheme. How is it that my attendant has not come yet?

(*Enter the attendant*)

ATTENDANT:

> "*Hearing the bell ringing from the imperial palace,*
>
> *I bring back the decree that concerns Mr. Li.*"

My lord, His Majesty decrees that Li Yi is to be transferred to your garrison as a military consultant and to set off at once without going back home first.

GENERAL LU (*Laughs*):

He's now under my control. Give my orders that the troops are to set off at once.

> *With brave soldiers at my command,*
>
> *A clever scheme comes up in my mind.*
>
> *When he is under my control,*
>
> *There is no way out for him to find.*

Scene Thirty-Three
Woes on an Autumn Night

(*Enter Huo Xiaoyu followed by Huansha*)

HUO XIAOYU (*To the tune of **Niannujiaoxu***):

> No sooner has the rain stopped
>
> Than the sky clears up
>
> And everything is enveloped in the mist at dusk.
>
> By the flapping curtain with jade hooks,
>
> I stand still looking far into distance.

HUANSHA:

> Other houses are filled with music,
>
> But you have no desire for elaborate dressing,
>
> While stars are glittering and the sky is clear.

HUO XIAOYU, HUANSHA:

> The tryst with my lover is long in waiting,
>
> Yet I hear nothing but the tingling of my pendants.

HUO XIAOYU (*In the pattern of **Linjiangxian***):

> "*As spring passes and autumn comes with the rain,*

My longing for the distant lover is transferred by the shooting stars.

HUANSHA:

Now that your hair ornaments sway in the autumn wind,

Please stop weeping for the moment

And expect your lovers' reunion on the celestial bridge.

HUO XIAOYU:

For celestial lovers this is a happy night,

And so all anxieties in one year are erased

HUANSHA:

When decorated houses are full of whispers and fragrance.

HUO XIAOYU, HUANSHA:

Who will have the best luck?

Who will let slip the precious night?"

HUO XIAOYU:

Huansha, today is the seventh day of the seventh month when the celestial lovers will meet on the celestial bridge. Now that candles and fruits to celebrate this festival have been prepared and displayed, you can send for my mother and Bao Siniang. They may have come already.

(*Enter Lady Zheng*)

LADY ZHENG (*To the tune of* **Siniang'er**):

As staying indoors all day I don't feel autumn's advent,

This good night makes me all the more distressed

At the thought of the celestial lovers in long separation.

Looking at the sky,

Hearing crows fly on this autumn night,

I find that my hair has turned grey.

Why do you want me here, my daughter?

HUO XIAOYU:

Bliss on you, Mom! Today is the Double-Seventh Festival. I want to spend the night with you and Bao Siniang.

LADY ZHENG:

Is Bao Siniang coming?

(*Enter Bao Siniang*)

BAO SINIANG (*To the tune of* **Raochiyou**):

Your decorated house is quiet,

With candlelight flickering on the beautiful garment.

Who can have the most wishes realized on this night every year?

(*Greets Lady Zheng and Huo Xiaoyu*)

Bliss on you, Your Ladyship and Miss Huo. I see you have fruits and candles ready tonight. Do you also follow the custom of praying for good luck?

LADY ZHENG:

What's the point of my praying for good luck? I'm here just because my daughter invites

me. I suppose you are also invited here.

BAO SINIANG:

We can only keep our wishes at heart without speaking them out. And the wishes can be realized if a spider weaves webs in this house. Your Ladyship, let's do obeisance to the sky for our wish.

> (*Does obeisance to the sky*)
> "*A celestial bridge is formed tonight*
> *For separated lovers to meet again.*
> *Fruits and candles are displayed for unsaid wish;*
> *We expect spiders to weave webs that bring good luck.*"

LADY ZHENG:

What a good sight tonight!

> (*To the tune of* **Niannujiaoxu**)
> For both Heaven and the human world,
> This is the most enjoyable night,
> Under a clear and pure sky.
> The courtyard is enclosed in the twilight,
> With stars glittering overhead,
> While celestial lovers clearly see the lonely sight
> In the moonlight.
> The mica screen is unfolded,
> The crystal curtain is rolled up,
> And the faint moon in a light breeze
> Makes a hazy scene.

ALL:

> Let's look and see
> How many separated lovers can meet
> Like those in the celestial world.

HUO XIAOYU (*To the previous tune*):

> The sky
> Looks different tonight.
> Lest the texture be moistened by the mist,
> The Weaving Girl stares in expectation,
> While her separated lover
> Is looking at her in the far distance.
> Who can bear witness to their love and tenderness?
> The Weaving Girl,
> Too glad to dress up
> And too excited to weave on,
> Walks with her eyes on the Cowboy across the river.

ALL:

> Let's look and see

How many separated lovers can meet,

Like those in the celestial world.

BAO SINIANG (*To the previous tune*):

The birds,

Let's beg the dimly discernable silver birds,

And the numerous black crows,

To form a bridge across the celestial river.

The crispy sound of pendants can be vaguely heard,

Like the raindrops.

Tonight we are in the mood

To look at the sky by the window,

To walk about in lithe steps,

And to enjoy the most unforgettable sights.

ALL:

Let's look and see

How many separated lovers can meet,

Like those in the celestial world.

HUANSHA (*To the previous tune*):

In a manner so sedate and dignified,

I put up a windscreen with patterns of cloud,

To bathe my face in moonlight

And to pour out my long lovesickness.

It is a quiet place here,

Overflowing with sweet air.

The celestial lovers clearly hear

Through the breeze

The happy whispers

(*Laughter within*)

Of the emperor and his mistress.

ALL:

Let's look and see

How many separated lovers can meet,

Like those in the celestial world.

LADY ZHENG (*To the tune of* **Guluntai**):

Through the soft and tender night cloud,

The bright moon and candlelight illuminate the painted screen,

While fragrant smoke curls up from the incense burner.

BAO SINIANG:

When the bright moon shines o'er the decorated houses.

Who is walking quietly at night

And celebrating the love so precious?

Celestial lovers are enjoying an untroubled tryst,

Which embodies the wish of all human lovers.

HUO XIAOYU:

There are endless words to tell her lover

In a gentle breeze that flaps the silk ribbons on her dress.

The love is as gentle as water;

The date is as happy as a dream.

The sky is clean and bright,

But this precious night will soon be over.

HUANSHA:

On this beautiful and bright night

Who is lamenting over her fate in the moonlight?

BAO SINIANG (*To the precious tune*):

For love,

Temporary reunion and joy

Can be abandoned,

As long as the love is loyal and permanent.

HUO XIAOYU (*In sorrow*):

While time slips away without a sound,

The woeful west wind moans on and on.

Having to part with the remote lover

And suffer from long separation,

The Weaving Girl returns to her loom

And continues to weave her web of love.

ALL:

With the Cowboy lover in her mind's eye,

She sheds pearls of tears

That soak her bolt of silk.

A hairpin is given

As a keepsake in private.

The celestial river would surge and roar,

Let alone the waters in the human world.

(*To the tune of* **Yibujin**)

A celestial bird will come to the human world

And ask the frivolous husband

Whether he sees the love between the Cowboy and the Weaving Girl.

Mother and daughter are both filled with woe,

And have to face the dim and flickering lamp.

As the way to true love is hard to trail,

It's better to keep a lovesick lady company.

Scene Thirty-Four
Distress in the Frontier

(*Enter the generals and soldiers*)

GENERALS (*To the tune of* **Northern Dianjiangchun**):

> When frost falls on the Great Wall
>
> And the bright moon shines over the smooth sand,
>
> Our military flags are fluttering in wind.
>
> Against the wall is the array of weapons
>
> That shines towards the tent of the generals.
>
> *"Our consultant leaves for Lanzhou at commander's order;*
>
> *His green wagon runs fast under red clouds.*
>
> *The patrol flags in the frontier may have been changed,*
>
> *And the fortress in the mountains needs to be renovated."*

We are subordinates of Governor Liu Gongji. His consultant Mr. Li Yi has dispatched troops to the Huile Peak and the city of Shouxiang to cut off Tubo troop's retreat. As Mr. Li Yi will inspect the frontier tonight, all the watchmen, heighten your vigilance!

(*The soldiers respond in chorus*)

(*Enter Li Yi, followed by attendants beating drums and holding lanterns*)

LI YI (*To the tune of* **Jinlongcong**):

> Numerous and fully armoured are our warriors
>
> Who fight bravely in the deserted western areas.
>
> The gongs are ringing high and low
>
> While the horns are resounding solemn and stirring.
>
> I feel chilly in the wind wearing a gorgeous embroidered robe,
>
> But our troops are assembled for training at dawn.
>
> *"Frost fell in the frontier last night*
>
> *When the moon was shining and horns were blowing loudly.*
>
> *The wild geese can never fly over the Great Wall;*
>
> *The music of Xiaochanyu is blown here by autumn wind."*

I'm a man of letters, but am now acting as a military consultant in the frontier. The military affairs make me very tired. Now pass my order for all the generals and soldiers to sharpen their vigilance!

(*The generals and soldiers respond in chorus*)

LI YI:

Roll up the tent curtain so that I can watch the view of the frontier!

> (*To the tune of* **Yijiangfeng**)
>
> After I get off the wagon,
>
> We roll up the tent curtain
>
> And ascend the city wall.

Our flags flutter

Against the light of lanterns —

What a sight of beauty!

Are the flames in the distance from the night hunting by the Huns?

GENERALS:

It's not the night hunting,

It's not the night hunting,

It's the beacon signaling peace and safety.

The generals guarding the Yumen Pass are to be promoted.

It's the Huile Peak ahead.

LI YI (*To the previous tune*):

Have a look over there,

Where the endless wildness

Arouses bleak and sad feelings.

Is that snow?

GENERALS:

It's the sand.

LI YI:

The dense and thick sands over there

Look like swirling snow.

I should drink wine beside the desert,

I should drink wine beside the desert.

GENERALS:

You can also write poems on the ancient battlefield,

But you have to build barriers before the enemy arrives.

Here we are in the city of Shouxiang.

LI YI (*To the previous tune*):

Cold and desolate,

Everything is shrouded in the slight mist

And shimmering in the shadow.

Is it frost?

GENERALS:

It's the moonlight.

LI YI:

The moon palace is visible

When the moon is crystal-clear and bright.

My robe bears the trace of frost,

My robe bears the trace of frost.

GENERALS:

The moon goddess above the city wall

Brings grief to the warriors here.

LI YI:

Now I'll sit here for a while.

(*To the previous tune*)

Sitting on the chair,

I watch the bright moon over the desert,

(*Flute music within*)

With loud music coming into my ear.

GENERALS:

Where does the flute music come from? Is it *Guanshanyue* or *Siguiyin*?

(*Look back in the direction of their hometowns*)

(*Point at the clouds*)

Isn't that my hometown Luoyang? Isn't that my hometown Chang'an? Isn't that his hometown Longtou?

(*Li Yi also looks in the direction of his hometown and weeps*)

GENERALS:

Startled by the flute music,

We miss our hometowns all the night.

Where are our hometowns?

Where are our hometowns?

We feel sad for parting with families,

And weep with heart-broken tears.

(*Enter Scout Wang*)

SCOUT WANG:

"Weeping at the sound of the flute,

We tie our letters home to the geese's feet."

Your Excellency, I'm Scout Wang from General Lu's official residence in the capital. I'm sent here to inquire Governor Liu Gongji about the situation in the frontier. Do you want me to take a letter home for you?

LI YI:

I really have to trouble you for this. I'm afraid that a single letter isn't enough to convey my love and longing for my wife. So let me paint the night scene here on foldable paper screen to tell her my loneliness. Qiuhong, bring me the painting brush and colourings.

(*Enter Qiuhong*)

QIUHONG:

"Painting paper is unfolded,

On which homesickness is conveyed."

Here is the painting brush and ink.

LI YI (*Paints*):

(*To the tune of **Sanxianqiao***)

There's withering grass all round

In the frontier at sunset.

Along the riverside,

I vaguely see wild geese in flight.

On the city wall in the painting,

I add several small points

That represent our fluttering flags,

While the Huns are far away from this place.

Alas!

I take out the silk handkerchief

To wipe off my tears of lovesickness.

Following the regular way of painting,

With my brush dipped in ink,

I draw the sight of wind and sand.

On the screen,

I paint sections and sections of the Great Wall,

But cannot paint my fond dream of family reunion.

Let me add the snow-like sand and the frosty moonlight.

(*To the previous tune*)

Why is the remote snow-like desert

Providing little joy for the Huile Peak?

With frost over the Shouxiang City,

My picture represents warriors

Accompanying sand and moonlight.

When shadows are swaying,

And everything is shrouded

In misty light greenness,

Our tents are quiet in the chilly night.

Looking around, I'm overwhelmed with sorrow,

In unbearable coldness and loneliness.

My brush falls softly on paper,

Depicting the evening glow

And the dim twilight.

On the paper screen,

I paint with ingenuity

In the hopes of depicting this place for my lonely wife.

Let me add a warrior looking in the direction of his hometown and listening to the flute music.

(*To the previous tune*)

The wind blows on a moonlit night,

Carrying the refined flute music

Of warriors' homesickness

Throughout the night.

Together we look into the distance

With homesick tears,

Snuggling up on the Great Wall

And staring blankly in trance.

The willows in the hometown

Might be shivering and falling in the west wind.

When I stay in the frontier at dawn,

I play some music in the open air,

But *The Liangzhou Tunes* can hardly express my feelings.

On the paper screen,

How can I send the music I play

To the pining wife at home?

Now the painting is finished. Let me inscribe a poem on it.

"The sand before the Huile Peak is like snow;

The moonlight in the Shouxian City is like frost.

Where is the flute music coming from

That makes us homesick all night?"

Now you can bring this to my wife, Scout Wang.

SCOUT WANG:

You'll surely have a letter in reply.

LI YI (*To the tune of* **Coda**):

No match to General Li Guang in old times,

I depict the snow, moon, frost and sand here,

For the south-flying geese to bring home.

(*Exit Scout Wang*)

(*Enter the messenger*)

MESSENGER:

"It's good anyway that the birds fly south,

But for whom has the messenger come?"

I'm a messenger from the capital to inform Mr. Li Yi that he'll be transferred to another place. Let me go straight inside.

(*Greets Li Yi*)

Congratulations! By His Majesty's decree, you're appointed to work in the Secretariat as the military consultant to General Lu. And you're required to leave immediately.

LI YI:

How come this happens? Let me tip the messenger first and then write a farewell letter to Governor Liu.

MESSENGER:

Governor Liu is also ordered back to the court to take charge of the imperial military affairs.

LI YI:

Oh, I see.

Before I come from frontiers to the court,

With weeping eyes I paint a paper screen.

Now that my wife is waiting there for nought,

She'll have more woe for what she's seen.

Scene Thirty-Five
The Frontier Governor Returns

(*Enter Liu Gongji, followed by the subordinates*)

LIU GONGJI (*To the tune of* **Baoding'er**):

> Our military camp looks imposing,
>
> With beautiful clouds floating in the sky
>
> And the stars of war setting in the west.
>
> When the frontier's warfare is over,
>
> The swords and chariots will be left unused.
>
> A frontier governor will stay behind,
>
> To patrol the peaceful borders.

ALL:

> When autumn hears the sound of drums
>
> And sees the fluttering military flags,
>
> Brave warriors gather in the camp.

LIU GONGJI:

> *"With all the military affairs under my command,*
>
> *I serve in the army in the autumn frost.*
>
> *General Ban Chao was promoted in his old age*
>
> *While General Li Guang was never given a title."*

I'm Liu Gongji, now stationed beyond the Yumen Pass. Since I came here, I've put quiet a few talents in important positions and have expanded our territory.

> *"When the nomads' tents are swept away at last,*
>
> *The entire Yellow River flows into the Han territory."*

His Majesty's decree came yesterday that I should go back to the court to take charge of the imperial military affairs. Mr. Li was appointed to work in the Secretariat as General Lu's military consultant. I suppose Li's letter to me will soon arrive.

(*Enter a soldier with Li Yi's letter*)

SOLDIER:

> *"The geese bring the letter at dawn,*
>
> *While the scouts return at dusk."*

(*Kowtows*)

Here's a letter from Mr. Li Yi.

LIU GONGJI (*Smiles and reads the letter*):

"Dear respected Governor Liu,

During the three years I work here under you, I've received great care and favour from you. But I am still suffering from great homesickness. As we are far away from each other, I cannot say goodbye to you personally. Fortunately, I shall benefit from your return and promotion at the court. I am sending you this letter to shorten the distance between us. Your grand feats will surely bring you a bright future. So much for this letter. Respectfully yours, Li Yi."

Alas! Mr. Li Yi has already left for General Lu's garrison. Now that I've received His Majesty's decree, I should not stay here any longer. Attendants, fetch the golden seal of the Frontier Governor and hand it over to the vice commander. I'll be on my way today.

(*Enter the vice commander, followed by the subordinates*)

VICE COMMANDER:

> "*We work under your command*
>
> *And pay you great respect.*
>
> *We all envy your return with grand feats*
>
> *That excel the ancient heroes.*"

Congratulations on your return to the court!

LIU GONGJI:

What contributions have I made to get such favour from His Majesty?

> (*To the tune of **Zhuomu'er***)
>
> I am old but still have a heart of devotion,
>
> Remaining energetic and high-spirited.
>
> How many ancient generals enjoyed their retired life?
>
> To my relief I can now enjoy a leisurely life.
>
> (*Raises his hand*)
>
> I've served my duties with your assistance;
>
> Now that I have to part with you by His Majesty's decree,
>
> (*Weeps*)
>
> I cannot help dropping tears on my robe.

GENERALS:

Ah, Your Excellency!

> (*To the previous tune*)
>
> You can deploy the army and handle the warfare
>
> By studying intensively the arts of war.
>
> By reversing the desperate situation and settling the military affairs,
>
> You are more meritorious than the most famous ancient generals.
>
> (*Kowtow*)
>
> In chorus we congratulate you on your promotion!
>
> (*Weep*)
>
> With tearful cheers echoing in the gloomy music,
>
> We'll no longer enjoy wine and songs at the banquet.

LIU GONGJI:

It's time to say goodbye.

GENERALS:

Please stay a couple of nights longer so that the people here can express their thanks to you for your heroic deeds.

LIU GONGJI:

The imperial military affairs are busy and urgent, so I must be off at once. The Frontier

Governor's golden seal is now handed over to the vice commander. Please take good care of it!

(*Hands over the seal*)

(*To the tune of **Sanduanzi***)

Tie the big golden seal with ribbons

And hang it on your elbow.

When you do not hang it on your elbow,

Keep it safely in front of your bed.

If the seal should be stolen,

Military affairs might be mismanaged.

The seal should never be misused,

For military affairs are no joking matters.

GENERALS:

Which is the most important among military affairs?

LIU GONGJI:

In the Han Dynasty, four counties were set up to cut off the Huns' entry into the Qiang state. So now we should prevent the Qiangs from forming an alliance with the Tubos. In this way, we can keep peace in this area.

(*To the previous tune*)

The frontier and the capital are far apart

Like two ends of the world.

Why are military camps set up and fields reclaimed?

It is to prevent invasion from Tubo and Qiang.

GENERALS:

Please give us your suggestions on the military strategies.

LIU GONGJI:

Please listen to my suggestion.

Beware of Qiang's tricks;

Never relax in times of peace.

The two catch phrases are:

"Share weal and woe;

Implement fair reward and punishment."

Now I'll be on my way. You are not to go beyond the base to see me off.

(*Reports within*)

The minority group leaders want to bid you farewell.

LIU GONGJI:

It's not necessary. Just tell them to keep in accord with the empire.

(*Starts to leave*)

(*To the tune of **Guichaohuan***)

I'll return to the court,

I'll return to the court

From this wide-stretching desert.

The central plain is prosperous

With rich natural views.

On my way home,

On my way home,

I hear the farewell music.

A general returns from the battlefield,

With his hair turning gray on his head.

In autumn when the frontier is picturesque,

His Majesty orders me back to court,

Where I can enjoy warm spring wind.

Through the Yumen Pass under the bright moon,

The general is to go home soon.

With a valiant army under his command,

No Huns will dare to invade our homeland.

Scene Thirty-Six
Reading the Paper Screen in Tears

(*Enter Huo Xiaoyu and Huansha*)

HUO XIAOYU, HUANSHA (*To the tune of* **Juhuaxin**):

I suddenly see a single file of wild geese

When I look at the autumn sky and lean against the railings.

The cold rain patters on the flowers

And spoils the beautiful scene.

(*In the pattern of* **Hemanzi**)

"Lotus flowers wither in the cold dew,

Leaving lingering fragrance in the courtyard.

I stay behind the half-rolled curtain,

Longing for my man more eagerly in the autumn.

I often stand there motionless and silent,

Looking at the wild geese flying past.

I haven't received a line from my man since he left three years ago. It's true indeed,

Chrysanthemums have bloomed and withered twice,

But my man hasn't returned home,

And the heartless geese won't bring me a line from him."

HUANSHA:

He'll come back sooner or later, so don't worry.

HUO XIAOYU (*To the tune of* **Guizhixiang**):

On a clear day without a cloud,

I make up and get dressed.

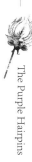

In the sun I'm leaning against the screen,

Filled with sorrowful feelings.

Every day I'm getting thinner

And thinner,

Sighing lonely in my bridal chamber.

With no one to admire,

The moon will soon disappear;

Why is the autumn scenery so hard to endure?

HUANSHA:

Let's climb the Fengxiao Tower to look into the distance!

HUO XIAOYU (*To the previous tune*):

I roll up the curtain

And see the picturesque water and mountains.

The sunset glow is shining over the clear river,

Where the leaves fall in the frost.

There is a place in the far distance,

There is a place in the far distance,

Where there are abundant sands and geese.

Leaning against the high railings,

I can imagine my man's tearful face,

But where exactly can I find his trace?

(*Enter Scout Wang with a paper screen*)

SCOUT WANG (*To the tune of* **Zhuan**):

I gallop all the way from the frontier,

With a cheerful message for the lady in chamber.

HUO XIAOYU:

I stay alone behind closed doors,

With no mind for make-up.

Why do I feel so depressed

And have the beaded curtain rolled up?

(*Scout Wang shouts*)

HUANSHA:

At the calling of some visitor

To the lonely and quiet house,

I peep out from the corridor.

Who is it?

SCOUT WANG:

A scout bringing message from the frontier.

HUO XIAOYU (*Pleasantly surprised*):

You may be working under my man,

To whom I haven't sent the winter coats yet.

SCOUT WANG (*Takes out the paper screen*):

> In case a letter may not express his feelings well,
>
> He paints on a paper screen instead.

HUO XIAOYU:

> It takes several nights to bring the screen here,
>
> Even by a wild goose.
>
> To reward my messenger, chrysanthemum wine is the best.
>
> (*Huansha takes out some wine for Scout Wang*)

SCOUT WANG:

> By my master's order I can't stay for long.

HUANSHA:

> Our young lady entertains you with sincerity.

HUO XIAOYU:

Who's his new superior?

SCOUT WANG:

It's General Lu.

HUO XIAOYU:

Who is General Lu?

SCOUT WANG:

He's the younger brother of the prime minister Lu Qi and the elder brother of the favoured eunuch Lu Zhonggui. So he is very powerful and wealthy.

HUO XIAOYU:

Can you tell me when my man will return home?

SCOUT WANG:

When I was in the frontier, I heard that Mr. Li said to Governor Liu Gongji, "I'll keep my promotion out of mind."

> (*Huo Xiaoyu is annoyed*)

SCOUT WANG:

Don't worry.

> I've heard about His Majesty's decree
>
> That another post will soon be assigned to Mr. Li,
>
> Who is bound to return in honour for his grand feats.
>
> I'll drink the wine and take leave at once.
>
> (*Exit*)

HUO XIAOYU:

> At last the message comes from a remote place,
>
> Which is very precious,
>
> Which is very precious.
>
> (*To the tune of **Jinsuoguawutong***)
>
> The crows fly in the glorious sunset glow,
>
> And the magpies bring enjoyable weather.
>
> I gaze at the river far away,

Which flows with green ripples.

(*Unfolds the paper screen*)

Oh my man,

In three years not a letter comes from you;

Is it because you don't miss me at all?

The screen,

Why is it delivered to me in so many folds?

My man, you're grateful for the kindness and appreciation from Governor Liu Gongji, so you'll keep your promotion out of mind.

Indulged in the sumptuous banquet with beauties,

You don't care how I live in sorrows.

In fierce sandstorms,

Fallen tree-leaves settle on the flower roots.

HUO XIAOYU, HUANSHA:

We don't know his date of return yet,

But we're happy for his message for the moment.

HUO XIAOYU:

Now I know he'll soon come back. Let me unfold the paper screen and see what he says in the poem. Oh! It's a painting by himself.

(*Reads the poem aloud*)

"*The sand before the Huile Peak is like snow;*

The moonlight in the Shouxian City is like frost.

Where is the flute music coming from

That makes us homesick all night?"

In this paper screen, the poem and the scenery enhance each other. What a gloomy frontier!

(*To the previous tune*)

The sands are like snow;

The moonlight is like frost.

The dim moonlight and hazy desert

Best represent the frontier sight.

I've never been to the Great Wall,

But it seems that someone is absent

From the painted landscape.

My man,

I'm pointing at the painted desert,

And you're playing the flute in moonlight.

Please remember

That in the dream we'll meet each other.

HUO XIAOYU, HUANSHA:

We don't know his date of return yet,

But we are happy for his message for the moment.

HUANSHA:

Our family has declined since Mr. Li left home three years ago.

(*To the tune of* ***Wutonghua***)

We used to enjoy to our hearts' content

The untold wealth and high honour,

As well as the beautiful flowers and moonlight.

But who cares about all this for the present?

Seeing the lonely daughter and the declined house,

The old lady is tormented by great sorrows.

HUO XIAOYU, HUANSHA:

Only Li's return is the best solution.

HUO XIAOYU:

It's no use talking about wealth. What a pity that our best time is wasted!

(*To the previous tune*)

For what reason

Are tears dropping down?

By the lotus pond in autumn,

I mix the painting rouge.

Who knows my great sorrows and distresses?

I'll send my man a painting of autumn sights.

HUO XIAOYU, HUANSHA:

Only Li's return is the best solution.

HUO XIAOYU (*To the tune of* ***Yibujin***):

Wives are busy making winter clothes for husbands;

HUANSHA:

Mr. Li will be back before we send the clothes.

HUO XIAOYU, HUANSHA:

How happy we'll be when he returns!

The lonesome lady weeps for her man,

And moistens the painted screen.

If her man fails to come back next year,

She'll turn into a cloud and fly to the west.

Scene Thirty-Seven
Transference to Another Garrison

(*Enter General Lu*)

GENERAL LU (*To the tune of* ***Fanbusuan***):

The frontier in autumn is dreary and hazy with grass and mist;

The fierce west wind has stopped.

A talented young man will come to work under my command,

So I hold in his honour a reception banquet with music.

"Our family boasts countless wealth

And wields great power and influence.

So far we've achieved great military victories,

Now I welcome the meritorious young man of genius."

I'm General Lu, now guarding the Mengmen Pass. I've asked for His Majesty's permission to have Li Yi as my military consultant. He'll report to the post today, so I'll welcome him. Attendants, wait at the camp gate.

(*Enter Li Yi, followed by attendants*)

LI YI (*To the tune of* **Shenzhang'er**):

Leaving the northwestern frontier,

Leaving the northwestern frontier,

I go to work under General Lu.

SCOUT WANG (*Kowtows*):

Your Excellency, I've sent the paper screen to your wife.

LI YI:

Thank you. Is she well?

SCOUT WANG:

Yes, she's expecting you home.

LI YI:

Now give him some silvers. Scout Wang, you're my native, so I'll tip you well if you can bring me letters from my wife when you are on an errand to Chang'an.

SCOUT WANG:

Yes, no problem!

LI YI:

Now I'm told my wife is well,

But even so,

How can I not miss her?

Confined in the military camp,

I can't see my house.

(*Greets General Lu*)

GENERAL LU:

"You did well through your literary talent;

LI YI:

You have great prestige and influence.

GENERAL LU:

To realize your ambition this is the best place;

LI YI:

A free and carefree life is my wish."

GENERAL LU:

I've had high esteem for you since I saw you last, Mr. Li. How lucky I am to have you as my military consultant! Now serve the wine!

(*Enter the attendant*)

ATTENDANT:

"*A talented man is sought after*

To work under my master."

Here's the wine.

GENERAL LU (*To the tune of* **Suohanchuang**):

On the boundless central plain with its sandy storms,

I am the general that gives command.

Beyond the Mengmen Pass,

Before the Shaohua Peak,

Numerous military flags are fluttering

Along the riverside.

Our victory also depends on your literary talent.

GENERAL LU, LI YI:

As it's hard to predict

Whether we'll meet or not,

We must treasure the banquet today.

LI YI (*To the previous tune*):

Wars can be suppressed through my proclamations,

The power of which needs no flatteries.

Transferred from the Yumen Pass to this garrison,

I've never left the battlefields.

Even the most talented literary consultants

And the greatest generals

Are not always on the move like me.

GENERAL LU, LI YI:

As it's hard to predict

Whether we'll meet or not,

We must treasure the banquet today.

GENERAL LU:

I've heard of your poem that says you'll keep promotion out of your mind. Is that true?

LI YI:

It's casual talk after drinking. Don't take the trouble thinking about it!

GENERAL LU (*Laughs*):

(*To the previous tune*)

You write the poem out of gratitude

To express your indifference to coming back.

Please don't look down on your post, Mr. Li.

You have an outstanding talent,

And produce prominent essays.

No matter how profusely you write,

Or how brilliantly you compose,

You have to serve in the court.

GENERAL LU, LI YI:

As it's hard to predict

Whether we'll meet or not,

We must treasure the banquet today.

GENERAL LU:

Do you have a wife?

LI YI:

I've been married and lived with my wife Huo Xiaoyu's family.

GENERAL LU:

I see. In ancient times, it often happened that a man would desert his first wife when he became wealthy and powerful. With your talent and achievement, why don't you enter the wedlock with an influential family? It's helpful to your promotion.

LI YI:

I won't go back on the vow I made to her.

(*To the previous tune*)

The tears my wife dropped on my sleeves give off a sweet smell;

Several years have passed but she is still young and pretty.

GENERAL LU:

Have you sent a letter to your wife?

LI YI:

One of your men sent a letter for me, the first within three years.

GENERAL LU:

You've been serving His Majesty, so how can you be over-concerned about love affairs?

LI YI:

When the wife prepares her man's clothes at night,

He will return in the moonlight.

Swallows and wild geese are flying to and fro,

To bring messages between man and wife.

How can they be ever severed?

GENERAL LU, LI YI:

As it's hard to predict

Whether we'll meet or not,

We must treasure the banquet today.

LI YI:

I can't drink any more.

GENERAL LU:

We've military banquets every day here.

(*To the tune of* **Coda**)

I cherish your talent and reputation;

LI YI:

This is because you're broad-minded.

GENERAL LU, LI YI:

We'll soon win the war and return to the capital.

(*Exit Li Yi*)

GENERAL LU (*Left alone on the stage*):

Who's the one that brought a letter home for Li Yi?

SCOUT WANG:

It's me.

GENERAL LU:

Now I'll have you bound and imprisoned.

(*Scout Wang begs for mercy*)

GENERAL LU:

I'll give you a chance to make amends for your fault. Now you go to Governor Liu Gongji's office to congratulate him on his return to the court. Then you go to Li Yi's house and tell his wife that Li Yi has married my daughter and lived with us. Let her be driven crazy. This is a chance for you to render a service.

SCOUT WANG:

Yes, I see.

> *With great power and influence in his hand,*
> *He has the scholar under his command.*
> *He will not hurt the scholar in the dark,*
> *But have him hooked through his scheme.*

Scene Thirty-Eight
Taking a False Message

(*Enter Bao Siniang*)

BAO SINIANG (*To the tune of* **Boxing**):

> The clouds are drifting in the sky,
> When the rain has just wetted the balcony.
> The setting sun sheds placid light
> On the infinite autumn sight.
> I'm looking into the mirror,
> Wondering if you can make a guess
> Of how old I am exactly.
> The phoenix tree by the well often appears in my dream;
> Now the rain dripping on it increases my solitude and gloom.

(*In the pattern of* **Xijiangyue**)

"*Long skirts and broad sleeves were popular in the past,*

But are now replaced by tight socks and bowed shoes.

Evening flowers bloom when morning flowers wither,

Which no one would buy without the vendor's cries.

I frequently do embroidery with the maids

And write poems with the lasses.

All the year round I wind silk threads,

Which are like the traces of my tears."

I'm Bao Siniang. I've been keeping company with Miss Huo Xiaoyu recently. She's heard that her man Li Yi has been ordered back by the court, but there has been no message from him yet, which makes her wan and shallow. Thinking of the old days when I enjoyed the company of dandies from rich families, I also feel sad now.

(*To the tune of* **Luojiangyuan**)

When beautiful autumn sights fade,

I become increasingly thin and pallid.

I'm kept awake by the crickets' chirp,

Counting the fireflies and waving a round fan in hand,

So lonely with no one to talk to.

There's no companion by my side

Except for the candlelight and my own shadow.

How lonely and sad I am!

(*Enter Scout Wang*)

SCOUT WANG:

"I was entertained with wine last time,

But now I come again with bad news."

I'm Scout Wang, now sent by General Lu on an errand to Huo's house to tell them that Military Consultant Li Yi has married and lived with the general's daughter, which the general thinks will surely drive Li's former wife crazy. General Lu is selfish but I have to obey him and do as he tells. I was kindly entertained by Mrs. Li last time when I brought her Mr. Li's letter. This time I must take care how to tell her the bad news. I hear there's a well-informed Bao Siniang around here. Let me ask for her advice.

(*Greets Bao Siniang*)

Will you please give me some water to drink?

BAO SINIANG:

Where are you from?

SCOUT WANG:

I'm a scout from Military Consultant Li Yi's camp.

BAO SINIANG (*Surprised*):

Where's Mr. Li now?

SCOUT WANG:

He's ordered back by the court but has been appointed by General Lu to be the Military Consultant for the Mengmen Garrison.

BAO SINIANG:

Will he come back soon?

SCOUT WANG:

No. I'm afraid he has to yield to Miss Lu.

BAO SINIANG:

What do you mean?

SCOUT WANG:

He may be married to and living with Miss Lu.

BAO SINIANG:

How heartless he is!

(*To the tune of* ***Xiangbianman***)

That guy is so shameless

That he must have a bad end.

He's most refined and talented,

But also hard to be known inside out.

Now what a sin he has committed!

The pretty young lady is unfortunate

And always in a daze.

Even an outsider like me

Will strike the railings in great wrath.

Now you come with me to Miss Huo and tell her in detail what has happened. You'll surely be tipped for your information.

SCOUT WANG:

Yes, I see.

BAO SINIANG (*To the previous tune*):

We get some information

That will soon be leaked out.

It brings a lot of complicated feelings,

Other than mere sadness.

Tonight,

Let's curse that relentless man

To bring the poor wife some comfort.

When he comes back,

We'll give him a sound beating.

(*To the tune of* ***Coda***)

Is your information true or false?

SCOUT WANG:

It's true and doubtless.

Please pass it to the lady alone in her house.

SCOUT WANG, BAO SINIANG:

The poor lady surely can't bear the sad news.

Autumn brings a message from a remote place,

While spring witnesses orioles and swallows.

The egrets can't be seen until they fly up from the snows;
The parrots' voice betrays their hiding place in willows.

Scene Thirty-Nine
Writing a Poem in Tears by Candlelight

(*Enter Huo Xiaoyu*)

HUO XIAOYU (*To the tune of* **Wangyuanxing**):

With jade hairpins dangling on head,

I stand by the window admiring autumn flowers outside.

The incense has burnt out when I sober up from wine last night,

With tears soaking the rouge on my face,

Feeling all the more lonely and miserable in the west wind.

(*In the pattern of* **Haoshijin**)

"*When it's drizzling outside,*

Bitterness and sadness increase at my heart.

Emaciated by the west wind,

I even lack the strength to miss my man.

The sound of autumn insects and working looms comes into my ears,

While the hazy and dismal autumn scenery spreads before my eyes.

The red lotus petals have fallen in the pond,

Leaving bitter seeds alone at the flower's heart."

Autumn has deepened since I received my man's letter. I wanted to drop him a line, but there's no messenger to carry it for me. How melancholy I am! Huansha, I haven't seen Bao Siniang these days. What's happened? Indeed,

"*When the house is desolate in the cold autumn wind,*

Staying alone at dusk is the hardest for me to stand."

(*Enter Bao Siniang*)

BAO SINIANG (*To the tune of* **Yan'ermei**):

With important information I hurry to Huo's house,

Unable to walk faster in my small embroidered shoes.

The young lady must be feeling lonely at dusk,

And playing the flute in a depressed mood,

Looking all the more pallid and languid.

(*Greets Huo Xiaoyu*)

HUO XIAOYU:

Why didn't you come recently?

BAO SINIANG:

I didn't pay you a visit as I've been busy these days. May I ask how long Mr. Li has been away?

HUO XIAOYU:

He's been away for nearly three years.

BAO SINIANG:

He's struck some good luck!

HUO XIAOYU (*Surprised*):

What good luck?

BAO SINIANG:

Have a guess.

HUO XIAOYU (*To the tune of* **Hongna'ao**):

> Has he fended off the enemy with his literary talent?
>
> Has he been promoted to a high official position?
>
> Is he now on the way back to the court,
>
> Proudly riding a horse followed by fluttering flags?
>
> He's accomplished so many military merits
>
> That I can also win an honour from His Majesty.
>
> Good news comes before his arrival,
>
> No wonder there's propitious snuff in the candle.

BAO SINIANG (*To the previous tune*):

> We thought he'd won great prestige;
>
> We thought the notes of his triumphant bugle reached the capital;
>
> We worried about whether his official appointment encountered obstacle;
>
> We worried about whether his homeward journey ran into trouble.
>
> Who'd expect he did not return home after his promotion?
>
> You have been waiting patiently at home for his return these years,
>
> So it's hard to tell you the truth
>
> That may throw you into great sadness.

HUO XIAOYU:

Then why did you say he's struck some good luck?

> (*To the previous tune*)
>
> Is he detained in the frontier by military affairs?
>
> Has he fallen ill because of awful homesickness?
>
> Has he suffered failure in battles,
>
> Or has he been struck by bad luck?

My man,

> If you died from bad luck,
>
> My tears would flood the Great Wall.
>
> And there'll be only my lonely reflection in the mirror
>
> That you gave me as a betrothal gift.

BAO SINIANG (*To the previous tune*):

> You worry about his hard life in the frontier;
>
> You worry about his safety on the battlefield.
>
> But he might have been attracted by another girl,

Casting your love and tenderness out of mind.

If he should be indulged in his fancy for the new sweetheart,

You can write a letter to change his mind.

If you are in doubt,

There's a messenger here

To tell you more.

(*Enter Scout Wang*)

SCOUT WANG:

"*All the trouble comes from the frivolous man,*

And will bring the lady much annoyance."

I kowtow to madam.

HUO XIAOYU:

Are you Scout Wang who brought my man's painted screen last time?

SCOUT WANG:

You have watery eyes.

BAO SINIANG:

Nonsense!

SCOUT WANG:

Oh, pardon me. I mean you have expressive eyes.

HUO XIAOYU:

How many daughters has General Lu got? Is it true that Mr. Li has become his son-in-law?

SCOUT WANG:

He's got only one daughter. She is talented and pretty. When Mr. Li worked under General Lu in the Mengmen Garrison, the two fell in love with each other. So now the wedding is being arranged.

HUO XIAOYU:

Is it settled?

SCOUT WANG:

Yes, it's being settled.

HUO XIAOYU (*Weeps*):

How heartless you are, my man!

(*To the tune of* **Qiyanhui**)

I can't help weeping upon hearing the news,

And recalling our first encounter by the moonlit plum blossoms.

We are unfortunately destined

To enjoy transient happiness.

Hoaxing me with honeyed words,

He won my heart with ease.

Fooled and deserted by the heartless man,

I would die in vain even if I commit suicide.

(*Enter Lady Zheng*)

LADY ZHENG:

>In leisure I lean by the window,
>
>Admiring flowers in full bloom.
>
>There's fragrance of incense in the room
>
>While crows are cawing above the willows.

So Bao Siniang is here. Where is this scout from? Why is the young lady crying so hard?

BAO SINIANG:

This is Scout Wang who brought Mr. Li's painted screen last year. He comes to inform us that Mr. Li is going to marry General Lu's daughter.

LADY ZHENG:

Which General Lu? How relentlessly Li treats us!

>(*To the previous tune*)
>
>Beautiful flower
>
>Are cultivated through years of care.
>
>The spring
>
>Embodies all their beauty
>
>That is full of energy.
>
>They enhance the magnificence of our house
>
>And raise the decent family status.
>
>I expected to depend on that young man,
>
>But he's relentlessly deserted us!

SCOUT WANG:

It's late. I must be off now.

HUO XIAOYU:

Huansha, light the candle. I will write a poem to my man.

>(*Enter Huansha with a candle*)

HUO XIAOYU (*Writes*):

>(*To the tune of **Liuhuaqi***)
>
>Immersed in shock and resentment,
>
>I recall the vow of love between us
>
>On a cold day by the dim candlelight.
>
>I can't see my man
>
>Except in constant dreams.
>
>He doesn't care how I feel,
>
>But only sees the new sweetheart in her beauty,
>
>Forgetting all about my deep love for him.

LADY ZHENG:

Have you finished your poem?

>(*Reads the poem*)
>
>"*The orchids flourish with leaves luxuriant and green,*
>
>*To match the pomegranate blossoms delicate and bright.*

We used to enjoy a happy life together,

Indulged in deep love for each other.

Our love was as valuable as flames in the winter stove,

Yet you should desert it like an unused fan in autumn.

There are so many high mountains

That ruthlessly separate and estrange us.

Even grass will sprout in the warmth of spring,

How can you be indifferent to my tender feelings?

Whoever you please and pay attention to,

Don't forget that I am still waiting for you.

Looking in the direction of your garrison,

I eagerly send my best regards.

Please learn from migrating geese that return every year,

Rather than flowing water that never comes back."

(*To the previous tune*)

The letter is written with eyebrow pencil,

Dipped in waves of tears

And sealed with meticulous care.

BAO SINIANG:

You have great faith and sincerity in him,

And weigh with deliberation the words in your poem.

LADY ZHENG:

Why not tell him directly your feelings?

Your love has suffered too much disturbance.

HUO XIAOYU (*To the tune of* **Yujiafan**):

Why am I so wan and indolent?

Why do I contract my eyebrows so tight?

Because there's family discipline to restrain my faraway man,

But no law to deal with the willful minister.

You will remarry the daughter of an influential family,

Like all other officials who have their first wives and concubines.

Of course we shall wait and see

Who enjoys the higher status

To make everyone happy at home.

LADY ZHENG (*To the previous tune*):

You write such a long poem that the incense has burnt down,

And seal the letter with such sad tears that the candle has gone out,

Because Li has cast a heavy shadow on our house.

(*Points at Bao Siniang*)

Your wrong matchmaking brings us pains.

BAO SINIANG:

We should blame the pair of purple jade hairpins

That led to this marriage.

Who could have expected

He would cast off the old love

And bring in the new.

HUO XIAOYU (*To the tune of* **Pudeng'e**):

He's a scoundrel and lecher

That hunts beautiful women one after another.

I hate what he's done to me,

But won't hold a grudge against him.

As he's graceful and talented,

But a little unrestrained,

Let's give him a lenient rebuke.

Just tell him I'm afraid

That anyone would snatch away my man.

LADY ZHENG (*To the previous tune*):

As you two are destined to meet again,

You will have a lot to say by then.

BAO SINIANG:

The first time he heard about the young lady,

He was immediately happy and satisfied.

It did not take him long and much money

To succeed in his offer of marriage.

Since the young lady is from a decent family,

How can she be treated so casually

Like wild flowers with no one to care.

(*Scout Wang kowtows and is about to leave with the letter*)

HUO XIAOYU:

Scout!

(*To the tune of* **Yibujin**)

Tell my man to read the poem seriously

And to remember my increasing gloom

For his heartlessness and mischief.

(*Exit Scout Wang*)

Though you have become a senior officer,

I suffer so much when we stay apart.

Leaning by the window in cold candlelight,

I write to you with a broken heart.

Scene Forty
Crying over Wife's Letter

(*Enter Li Yi*)

LI YI:

> "*Luxuriant and fragrant with no one to admire,*
> *Flowers and grass will wither at night.*
> *As I always have my mind set on home,*
> *My wife appears everyday in dream.*"

Since I was transferred to General Lu's army as a consultant, I have heard that General Lu intends to take me in as his son-in-law, but I'll just pretend not to know anything about it. How can I forget my wife?

> (*To the tune of* **Guaguling**)
> In my idleness, I miss my wife,
> So pretty, so graceful and so elegant.
> She used to get up late,
> With her pretty face tilted on her slim fingers in bed,
> Enjoying the orioles' sweet songs,
> And then dressing herself before the mirror.
> With a contented heart,
> She'd gaze at her beautiful hair.
> It's hard to paint her infinite charm
> Like the splendour of the moon in spring.
> (*To the previous tune*)
> She was much spoiled in my presence;
> How is she now when I'm not beside her?
> The inscribed screen for her embodies my great attachment,
> But will it be left covered with dust?
> Dark night comes too soon for my lonely wife,
> Who yearns day and night for my sweet love.
> Anxiously she'll think about me from dawn to dusk,
> With delicate eyebrows tightly contracted.
> (*Enter Scout Wang*)

SCOUT WANG:

> "*My clothes still bear the fragrance in Lady Li's house;*
> *My horse is still sweaty after traveling long ways.*"

I am Scout Wang. By General Lu's order, I went to visit Consultant Li's wife and passed on the fake information that Mr. Li would be taken in as General Lu's son-in-law. And I came back with a letter from Mr. Li's wife. Here I am at his residence. Let me enter the house and greet him.

LI YI:

Oh, it's you, Scout Wang. Where have you been?

SCOUT WANG:

I've just come back from your home. You know, I was scolded by General Lu for taking your letter to your wife last time. Recently, General Lu sent me to your hometown on an errand, so I went to visit your wife. Here is her letter for you.

(*Kowtows and presents the letter*)

LI YI:

Oh, it's a poem by my wife.

(*Reads the poem*)

"*The orchids flourish with leaves luxuriant and green,*
To match the pomegranate blossoms delicate and bright.
We used to enjoy a happy life together,
Indulged in deep love for each other.
Our love was as valuable as flames in the winter stove,
Yet you should desert it like an unused fan in autumn.
There are so many high mountains
That ruthlessly separate and estrange us.
Even grass will sprout in the warmth of spring,
How can you be indifferent to my tender feelings?
Whoever you please and pay attention to,
Don't forget that I am still waiting for you.
Looking in the direction of your garrison,
I eagerly send my best regards.
Please learn from migrating geese that return every year,
Rather than flowing water that never comes back."

(*To the tune of **Sanhuantou***)

Between the lines of your verse,

I read your suspicion and doubts;

From the trace on the writing paper,

I see your weeping eyes.

While the wild geese come back in files,

They cannot bring enough messages

To clear the misunderstanding between us.

How much of your sad feeling

Has been expressed through words?

LI YI, SCOUT WANG:

Instead of bringing good news,

The letter arouses worries.

LI YI:

Scout Wang, did you talk nonsense to my wife?

SCOUT WANG:

No.

LI YI:

The poem sounds strange.

SCOUT WANG:

Indeed. General Lu threatened to torture me because I sent the letter for you. He warned me not to do it again, because he intended to take you in as his son-in-law. So I had to tell your wife about it.

LI YI:

What nonsense!

(*To the previous tune*)

General Lu,

    How can you be serious with jokes in a banquet,

    With casual remarks by the flowers,

    Or with totally unfounded rumours?

    You spread the rumours

    And try to separate us.

My dear wife,

    You should try to find the ins and outs

    When you hear the rumours.

    What you write in your poem

    Makes me all the more upset.

LI YI, SCOUT WANG:

    Instead of bringing good news,

    The letter arouses worries.

    Although I am a thousand miles away,

    I dream of my dear wife every day.

    She must have written the poem at night,

    With tears glittering in the candlelight.

Scene Forty-One
Arranging a Marriage

(*Enter Attendant*)

ATTENDANT (*To the tune of* **Zizishuang**):

    I'm an attendant

    Of no important official status.

    I smell bad

    With a running nose.

    I'm most obedient

    To my master's instructions.

    I try my best

    To snatch money by all means.

I'm General Lu's attendant. Though I have no official rank, I have enough money to spend. My master General Lu commands seventy-two squads of guards in the capital and sixty-four military camps outside the capital. I ask for some reward from them for my daily service and pocket a small portion of money from the businesses in my charge. Thus, I can always collect a little money each day.

VOICE WITHIN:

Aren't you an upstart?

ATTENDANT:

Of course not. My purse is always leaking. Now I hear the signals that General Lu will soon begin office.

(*Enter General Lu*)

GENERAL LU (*To the tune of* **Yipibu**):

>Favoured by His Majesty,
>
>I'm a minister
>
>That exerts the mightiest power.
>
>With all the seals in my hands,
>
>Who dares to show disobedience?
>
>*"I'm the most influential official,*
>
>*And I have a daughter called Mo Chou.*
>
>*She is pretty yet single,*
>
>*Waiting for a proper man as her spouse."*

I'm General Lu, summoned back to the court to take charge of military affairs. I'm granted the delegated power to take action before reporting to His Majesty. As I've got a single daughter not yet married, I have much interest in a young man, but he acts strangely and always talks nonsense to evade the issue. So far he hasn't yielded to my intention to marry my daughter to him. Yesterday he returned to the capital. Afraid that he would go home, I've put him in the guesthouse without allowing him out. When he sees how powerful I am, he will have to yield. In spite of all the measures, I've invited his friend Wei Xiaqing to persuade him. Here he comes.

(*Enter Wei Xiaqing*)

WEI XIAQING (*To the tune of* **Baoding'er**):

>What can I do to help the general
>
>Who has great influence and power?

(*Greets General Lu*)

It's been a long time since I came here last. Now I'm here again to pay you great respect.

GENERAL LU:

Please don't stand on formalities. I have something to consult you.

WEI XIAQING:

What can I do for you?

GENERAL LU (*To the tune of* **Suochuanglang**):

>Mr. Li is an outstanding literary talent;
>
>My daughter is young and beautiful.

Mr. Wei,

> Please persuade your good friend
>
> To yield and be my son-in-law.

Don't you know I have great power and influence?

> However he persists,
>
> He can't escape
>
> From my command and trap.

WEI XIAQING (*Aside*):

It turns out that General Lu wants Mr. Li to marry his daughter. If that happens, Huo Xiaoyu is betrayed and deserted. I'll tell him the real situation with Mr. Li.

> (*To the previous tune*)
>
> No one can compare with you in wealth and position,
>
> But please take this into consideration.
>
> With a solemn vow of love to his wife,
>
> He would not do anything unfaithful.

GENERAL LU (*Laughs*):

I can destroy anything and anyone if I want, let alone Huo Xiaoyu.

WEI XIAQING (*Aside*):

Mr. Li,

> As the general is powerful and sinister,
>
> I'm really afraid
>
> To be such a matchmaker.

ATTENDANT (*Whispers*):

Mr. Wei, my master asks you to be a matchmaker for his daughter. How dare you disobey?

> (*To the previous tune*)
>
> He commands all the officials in the court,
>
> And must find a talent for his daughter.
>
> He must have his wish fulfilled,
>
> So take the pledge of marriage and make Li change his mind.

WEI XIAQING (*Whispers back*):

It's not necessary for me to take the pledge of marriage to him as a matchmaker. I'll try to persuade him as a friend.

> (*Turns around*)

WEI XIAQING, ATTENDANT:

> Marriage is predestined.
>
> I just try my best to persuade him
>
> And let him decide.
>
> *For the daughter of the powerful general,*
>
> *A young talent is willfully chosen as son-in-law.*
>
> *He shouldn't make any vain attempt*
>
> *To escape from this marriage any more.*

Scene Forty-Two
Refusing a Forced Marriage

(*Enter Li Yi*)

LI YI (*To the tune **Xiaopenglai***):

> I become wan and sallow
> To be confined in the guesthouse.
> I have no one to share the flowers,
> I have no one to drink with,
> And I get drunk in loneliness.

(*In the pattern of **Nanxiangzi***)

> "*For how many years have I been away from my wife?*
> *I have no choice but to weep by myself.*
> *I dream of returning home,*
> *But detained here,*
> *I have no freedom.*
> *I'd like to ascend a high tower*
> *Until I see my house.*
> *If my wife knows we're so close,*
> *Her sadness*
> *Will be profound and endless.*"

I'm Li Yi, now summoned back to the court from the Mengmen Garrison. I intended to return home immediately and reunite with my wife, but the domineering General Lu puts me in house arrest here. As I wonder why he does this, I'll ask his attendant, who will come here soon.

(*Enter Wei Xiaqing, followed by Attendant*)

WEI XIAQING (*To the tune of **Xixiangfeng***):

> Who can restrain a talented scholar?
> The general's flower of a daughter.
> But the general's marriage arrangement
> Might cause much resentment.

(*Greets Li Yi*)

LI YI:

> "*I didn't expect to see you here*;

WEI XIAQING:

> *You know our friendship is profound.*

LI YI:

> *I've been eager to return home,*

WEI XIAQING:

Junyu,

> *But you'll be the most unfaithful man.*"

LI YI:

Why do you say I'll be the most unfaithful man?

WEI XIAQING:

Let's stop talking like this. General Lu's attendant is here.

(*Attendant greets Li Yi*)

LI YI:

Xiaqing, why do you say I'll be the most unfaithful man?

WEI XIAQING:

Junyu, have you forgotten our conversation about your faithfulness to your wife on your wedding day?

LI YI:

How can I forget it?

> (*To the tune of* **Yanyujin**)
> I miss my wife's dainty figure
> Against the blooming lotus in autumn.
> Our happy life was so transient
> And I had to start on the journey,
> Leaving my wife behind.

WEI XIAQING:

Did you send a letter home?

LI YI:

> I sent her a painted screen to erase her worries,
> And she returned with a poem dotted with tear stains.

WEI XIAQING:

The wild geese have long been back.

LI YI:

> I have got used to loneliness;
> Like a wild goose,
> I wonder when I can meet my love again.

WEI XIAQING:

Now I introduce you to a new love.

LI YI (*Startled*):

To whom?

WEI XIAQING (*To the tune of* **Erduan**):

> A beauty,
> Not yet married,
> Is to share your love.

LI YI:

Where is she from?

WEI XIAQING:

General Lu has a daughter. He asks me to act as the matchmaker.

> You can marry again,

To enjoy a privileged and luxurious life.

LI YI (*Sighs*):

Don't say so!

> Not predestined to marry Miss Lu,
>
> How can I agree to the marital tie?
>
> I have to pretend ignorance.

WEI XIAQING (*In a low voice*):

Won't you enjoy such a marriage?

LI YI (*In a low voice*):

Xiaqing, why won't I enjoy something else? But I know General Lu and his brothers are influential persons in the court. So I can't offend him too much.

> I'll be grateful
>
> If you can tell General Lu I'm hesitant and dismal.

Attendant,

> How hoary and sick now I look!

Miss Lu,

> Born in such a noble family,
>
> How will you love a frustrated man?

ATTENDANT (*To the tune of **Sanduan***):

> Like a high mountain,
>
> General Lu dominates all the officials;
>
> He selects you for your unique excellence.
>
> How can you decline his offer?
>
> Your refusal to the arrangement
>
> May bring about an unhappy result.
>
> (*In a low voice*)

Your Excellency, don't you know General Lu is the most powerful official?

> Please don't be so obstinate,
>
> And give consent for the present;
>
> You can still find other ways out.

WEI XIAQING:

What he says sounds reasonable and convincing.

> You can disregard your official career,
>
> But General Lu's punishment is really hard to bear.

LI YI (*To the tune of **Siduan***):

> Without my knowing it,
>
> I've got stuck in my office.
>
> Without rhyme or reason,
>
> I fall into the trap.
>
> (*In sadness*)
>
> With my wife staying alone for so many years,
>
> I long to see her again,

Now that I have left the remote frontiers.

Attendant, please pay tribute and respect to General Lu for me.

> I'm suffering boundless agitation
>
> Which depends on your favour
>
> For a satisfactory solution.

ATTENDANT:

I know what to say before General Lu. But you shouldn't be too obstinate.

LI YI:

> How can I forget the pledge of jade hairpins
>
> And the vow I made for my faith?

ATTENDANT (*To the tune of* **Wuduan**):

> You are anxious
>
> To defer the wedding,
>
> Which needs my intervention.

WEI XIAQING:

The attendant will report this to General Lu, so it's not necessary for me to go again.

> (*Whispers to Attendant*)
>
> This marriage is heaven blessed,
>
> In which Mr. Li has an interest
>
> But won't speak it out.

LI YI:

> Already tangled in this marriage,
>
> I just need more time to consider.
>
> (*Attendant takes leave*)

Wait a moment.

> Please attend to the matter for me.

Xiaqing,

> Detained here with no freedom at all,
>
> I don't want the information to get around.

WEI XIAQING:

I know what you mean. See you later.

LI YI:

> "*We're old friends but can't talk for long*;

WEI XIAQING:

> *You've found a new wife to bring you wealth and fame.*

ATTENDANT:

> *A bond brings you together over great distances*;

LI YI:

> *Without a bond you won't meet though face to face.*"
>
> (*Exit*)

WEI XIAQING (*Left alone on the stage*):

> "*When his wife is out of his sight,*
>
> *Leisurely thoughts fill his mind.*

As we can paint a tiger's skin, but not its bones;

So we can know a man's face, but not his heart."

Why do I say so? I still remember the first time Li Yi met Huo Xiaoyu in the lantern light. He picked up Xiaoyu's missing hairpin and gave it back to her as a pledge of love, and he made the vow by incense that they would stay together in life or in death. But he did not send a single letter home during his three years in the army. Now staying in General Lu's house, he still denies that it's his intention. He's not at all resolved in refusing this marriage arrangement. All he says is ambiguous and shows his reluctance to refuse. It seems that all women are infatuated but it's not the same case with men. I'll make a comment on Li Yi,

> (*To the tune of* **Jinwutong**)
>
> Overflowing with talent,
>
> The man is well liked.
>
> He keeps the old jade hairpin,
>
> And wears a new marital belt.

Look at him,

> He's eager to get the new and better,
>
> But mouthing fine words all the time.

He could just tell me his idea directly, but why did he say that he didn't "want the information to get around"?

> What he does and says
>
> Will surely breed suspicion and bitterness.

I'll talk with Cui Yunming. As to Xiaoyu,

> She'll be deeply hurt by Li's love and betrayal.
>
> *His speech in hesitation and panic*
>
> *Shows how inconstant he is in love.*
>
> *For a talent to be married into a wealthy house,*
>
> *People have different comments below and above.*

Scene Forty-Three
Jewels to Be Bought for the Wedding

(*Enter General Lu*)

GENERAL LU (*To the tune of* **Wangjiangnan**):

> Endowed with imperial favour,
>
> I have a luxurious house
>
> And a pretty daughter with no flaw.
>
> I'll choose the most excellent
>
> From the young talents to be my son-in-law.
>
> *"Warriors with swords guard my residence in autumn wind;*

Lotuses are blossoming in the exquisitely carved pond.

My daughter would be as noble as a phoenix,

Once married to a man of genius."

I'm rich and powerful enough, but I have yet to select an excellent young man to match my daughter. By my order, Wei Xiaqing and my attendant went on an errand to Li Junyu's residence as matchmakers. His residence is not far from here. Why are they not back yet?

(*Enter Attendant*)

ATTENDANT:

"*Music and songs provide great pleasures;*

I act as a messenger bird to make the match."

My lord, I've just been to Li Junyu's residence with Mr. Wei. That young man dare not refuse our proposal of marriage, and just said that he wanted to think it over. Mr. Wei asked me to tell you about it.

(*To the tune of* **Chanqiao'er**)

Mr. Li says that he must do justice to his wife,

As they have taken a solemn vow of love by the flowers.

GENERAL LU (*Laughs*):

Does he know I like him?

ATTENDANT:

He is thankful for your appreciation,

And will depend on you for promotion.

GENERAL LU, ATTENDANT:

An auspicious date is to be set;

A happy wedding is to be arranged.

When the wedding day finally arrives,

Jewels are to be worn on the bride's head.

GENERAL LU (*To the previous tune*):

Though sons of prime ministers have literary grace,

Dare that young man say a general's daughter is rude?

ATTENDANT:

How dare he!

GENERAL LU:

Then why didn't he accept the offer at once?

Does he think it will bring him disgrace?

GENERAL LU, ATTENDANT:

An auspicious date is to be set;

A cheerful wedding is to be arranged.

When the wedding day finally arrives,

Jewels are to be worn on the bride's head.

ATTENDANT (*To the previous tune*):

The bird startled by strong winds quickly flees the woods;

The fish hiding in slow waters finally take the bait.

To reach our goal, we need time and patience,

For he has not learned to appreciate favours.

GENERAL LU, ATTENDANT:

An auspicious date is to be set;

A happy wedding is to be arranged.

When the wedding day finally arrives,

Jewels are to be worn on the bride's head.

GENERAL LU:

As I have settled on him, he'll have to obey me sooner or later. My daughter will soon be fifteen years old. We must get all kinds of first-rate jade hairpins ready for her.

(*To the previous tune*)

My daughter

Will soon get married,

With pairs of phoenix-shaped hairpins on her hair.

We'll buy superb jade,

Regardless of prices.

GENERAL LU, ATTENDANT:

An auspicious date is to be set;

A happy wedding is to be arranged.

When the wedding day finally arrives,

Jewels are to be worn on the bride's head.

ATTENDANT:

My lord, there's a pawnshop run by an old jade-smith, Hou Jingxian. Pearls and jade often find their way there.

GENERAL LU:

Tell him to show me some exquisite ones.

Wearing superb hairpins dotted with superb jewels,

My daughter is destined to marry that young man.

As a phoenix can be held in a charming net,

So a mandarin duck can be confined in a jade cage.

Scene Forty-Four
Selling the Hairpins

(*Enter Huo Xiaoyu*)

HUO XIAOYU (*To the tune of* **Boxing**):

My lonely bower is shrouded in hazy mist,

With a hint of the moonlight through the curtains.

Leaning against the fragrant incense burner,

I admire the jade-like plum flowers.

On the paper screen is painted

Yellow sands and wild geese.

Looking at it with fixed attention,

I feel cold with gooseflesh,

At the thought of frontier's low-flying dark clouds.

(*In the pattern of* **Suzhongqing**)

"*Rolling up the curtain I feel the misty frost,*

Timid to see my remaining rouge after illness.

The affection under the plum flowers

Has weathered the snowstorm.

My slimmed shadow

And thought of the withered flowers

Have ridden me to bed.

In cold winter the scared crows

And moaning wild geese,

Arouse my tender sentiments."

Since my man left home, there has been no one to take charge of the family affairs. I've been looking forward to his return so that everything will come to the normal. But I heard that he was going to marry Miss Lu and abandon this home forever. How unexpected it is! Still, I wouldn't believe this is true. I've been looking for sorcerers far and near to foretell whether my man has returned to the capital or is still in the Mengmen Garrison. And I would be very generous giving out rewards if they can give me useful information. I've been paying friends so that they can help inquire about Li's whereabouts. I'm so eager to know where he is. I've spent almost all my money. So I told Huansha to put some valuable things on sale in Bao Siniang's place, but she has not come back yet. Gracious heavens! I'm painful and distressed, but there's no information about Li at all.

(*Enter a Buddhist nun with a lot-stick holder*)

BUDDHIST NUN (*To the tune of* **Shuidiyu**):

I'm an ordinary person

Now practicing Buddhism.

Those stupid lovesick people hope in vain

For help from Heaven.

I'm a Buddhist nun from the Water and Moon Bodhisattva Nunnery. I hear that Huo Xiaoyu gives alms for her man. I'll use my lot-sticks to hoax some money out of her. Here comes a Taoist nun.

(*Enter a Taoist nun with a scroll of painting and a small tortoise*)

TAOIST NUN (*To the previous tune*):

I wear my cap awry,

To fake an immortal's ability.

I have a lovely and clever tortoise,

With which I defraud people of some money.

BUDDHIST NUN (*Annoyed*):

You're snatching away all the money that can be deceived out of people!

TAOIST NUN:

I don't mean that. I'm from the Western Mother Goddess Taoist Nunnery. Hearing that Miss Huo Xiaoyu is paying for the information about her man's whereabouts, I've come here to hoax some money from her.

BUDDHIST NUN:

What's the use of a tortoise and a scroll of painting?

TAOIST NUN:

On the painting, there are stories of joys and sorrows, and of departures and reunions. I tell the people what will happen to them according to where the tortoise goes on the painting.

BUDDHIST NUN:

I see. Let's go together.

HUO XIAOYU (*Greets the two nuns*):

Where are you from, sisters?

BUDDHIST NUN:

I'm a Buddhist nun from the Water and Moon Bodhisattva Nunnery.

TAOIST NUN:

I'm a Taoist nun from the Western Mother Goddess Nunnery. We've heard that you are inquiring by all means about the whereabouts of your man, who has been away for a long time and has not come back yet. So we've come to help you with our Buddhist and Taoist wisdom.

HUO XIAOYU:

In that case, I'll burn joss-sticks to show my sincerity to Buddhism and Taoism.

BUDDHIST NUN:

Please show obedience to Avalokitesvara, the Goddess of Mercy first.

TAOIST NUN (*Annoyed*):

Our Taoist Western Mother Goddess has a husband, so your obedience to Taoism first will surely help you find your man. Avalokitesvara is a widow. She can't help you at all!

BUDDHIST NUN (*Annoyed*):

Pooh! Your Western Queen Mother is an unfaithful woman. She's not qualified to be a goddess. What is the use of showing obedience to her?

HUO XIAOYU:

They are both genuine goddesses, but let me do obedience to Avalokitesvara first.

(*Shows obedience with burning joss-sticks in hand*)

(*To the tune of **Jiang'ershui***)

I show obedience to the merciful Avalokitesvara,

Who comes in a pure white lotus.

To relieve my resentment of parting

And the endless lovesickness and waiting,

Avalokitesvara be with us.

BUDDHIST NUN (*Invites Huo Xiaoyu to draw a lot*):

Good, good! The lot you draw says that you'll be reunited with your man. Please write the amount of your offering on this book.

HUO XIAOYU (*Writes*):

Huo Xiaoyu, the female Buddhist devotee, offers 300,000 strings of coins for the Buddhist rites held by the Water and Moon Bodhisattva Nunnery.

HUO XIAOYU, BUDDHIST NUN:

> Don't begrudge your layman's money;
>
> It's used to show obedience to the gods.

TAOIST NUN:

Now it's the Taoist Western Mother Goddess's turn to predict your fate.

HUO XIAOYU (*Shows obedience with burning joss-sticks in hand*):

> (*To the previous tune*)
>
> A letter to my man
>
> Does not bring him back.
>
> Are we to live together happily till our dying day,
>
> Or am I to die early
>
> Without fully enjoying my precious youth?

TAOIST NUN:

I don't use lot-sticks. But my painting and tortoise can well predict your fate.

> (*Holds the tortoise and clumsily forces its crawling route on the painting*)

Good, good! The tortoise comes to the story of a couple's reunion. So you'll soon have your man back. Now please write the sum of your offering on this book.

HUO XIAOYU (*Writes*):

Huo Xiaoyu, the female Taoist devotee, offers 300,000 strings of coins for the Taoist rites of the Jade Pond Assembly.

HUO XIAOYU, TAOIST NUN:

> Don't begrudge your layman's money;
>
> It's used to show obedience to the gods.

BUDDHIST NUN, TAOIST NUN:

Thank you.

HUO XIAOYU:

Sorry to have bothered you. I'll offer you more if I can be reunited with my man. It's true indeed,

> "The record books witness the man's heartlessness;
>
> The incense of religious faith shows a vow of love."
>
> (*Exeunt the Buddhist nun and the Taoist nun*)

HUO XIAOYU (*Left alone on the stage*):

Good! Both the Buddhist and the Taoist goddesses will bless our reunion. I'll wait for Huansha to bring back the money from the sale.

> (*Enter Huansha*)

HUANSHA:

> "The talented young man has been away for long;

You may ask where this young lady has come from."

We've got more than 700,000 strings of coins from the sale, mistress.

HUO XIAOYU:

Good! Take out 600,000 strings as offerings to the goddesses. The rest is for the daily expense in this winter. When spring comes, my man will have returned.

> *"I show my gratitude to Heaven*
>
> *That blesses me with my man's return."*
>
> *(Enter Cui Yunming)*

CUI YUNMING (*To the tune of* **Tingqianliu**):

> The Huo's house is half-dilapidated,
>
> With the painted screen unfolded in the wind.
>
> Masses of clouds won't disperse;
>
> Moss grows on the steps.
>
> I'll pass the message with great care,
>
> And tell it to his wife in detail.
>
> *(Knocks at the door and greets Huansha)*

HUANSHA:

Mr. Cui, have you heard of anything about Mr. Li?

CUI YUNMING:

Yes indeed, I've come here with some information for your mistress.

> *(To the tune of* **Yifengshu**)
>
> I've got the information
>
> That Li has left the Mengmen Garrison for some time.

HUANSHA:

Is he going straight home?

CUI YUNMING:

> How can he go straight home?
>
> He's staying in General Lu's guesthouse.

HUANSHA (*Surprised*):

So he's staying with the Lu's? Why doesn't he come back now that he is in this city? Who has seen him?

CUI YUNMING:

Wei Xiaqing has seen him.

> A young lady urges Li to stay,
>
> Which easily arouses suspicion.

HUANSHA:

So it really happened.

HUANSHA, CUI YUNMING:

> It's deplorable
>
> That he is so mischievous
>
> And so perverse.
>
> *(Huansha tells Huo Xiaoyu the information)*

HUO XIAOYU (*Astonished*):

We didn't believe Scout Wang's words, but according to what Mr. Cui says it seems to be true that Li has found a new spouse.

CUI YUNMING:

Please don't worry. Though General Lu is a most influential official and Mr. Li now stays in his house, I'm afraid that what Wei Xiaqing says isn't credible. I'm telling you the truth for your kindness.

HUO XIAOYU:

Can you do me a favour by going to General Lu's house to find out the truth?

CUI YUNMING:

But how can I enter their house as I'm so poor and shabby?

HUO XIAOYU:

Huansha has just come back from the pawnshop. Here're 300 strings of coins for your drinks. I'll give you more after I sell my jade hairpins.

CUI YUNMING:

"*Pitiable is the young lady*
Who has so little money left!"

(*Exit*)

HUO XIAOYU:

Huansha, it's easy to inquire about the heartless man since he's so close to us in General Lu's house. But I've no money to reward those who help me. Take out my jade hairpins from the dressing table. It can sell for a million strings, which I'll use to pay for the information.

HUANSHA:

That pair of hairpins is your marriage pledge. How can we sell it?

HUO XIAOYU:

What's the use of it now that he's thrown me out of his mind!

(*To the tune of* **Luojiangyuan**)

At the mention of the jade hairpins,

I'm too embarrassed to go to the dressing table.

A work of art by a master jade-smith,

I began to wear them at the age of fifteen.

One hairpin was lost in the street,

But where is the man who picked it up?

Holding the hairpins in my hand,

I wonder whether my man will come back.

Now for money I have to sell them.

(*To the previous tune*)

The hairpins are destined

To come into my possession.

They're dear and precious on my head

But devalued in other hands.

Who'll get them now

And put them on?

I'll sell them for money

For someone else to wear.

How do I know they won't be sold again?

HUANSHA:

I'm going to sell them.

HUO XIAOYU (*Weeps*):

(*To the tune of* **Xiangliuniang**)

The jade swallows on the pins,

The jade swallows on the pins

Have beaks and wings as if alive

And pearly eyes so lovely.

They used to stay on my dressing table,

They used to stay on my dressing table

And bring us together,

Yet now I have to bid them adieu.

HUO XIAOYU, HUANSHA:

What extraordinary pins they are!

What extraordinary pins they are!

Let's wrap them up with red silk

And close the jewelry case.

HUANSHA:

Now I'm going to sell them.

HUO XIAOYU:

Wait a minute. The jade hairpins,

(*To the previous tune*)

You're now flying away,

You're now flying away.

I sincerely cherish you

And still want you back.

If my man returns one day,

If my man returns one day,

I must reclaim you

With a million strings of coins.

HUANSHA, HUO XIAOYU:

What extraordinary pins they are!

What extraordinary pins they are!

Let's wrap them up with red silk

And close the jewelry case.

(*To the tune of* **Coda**)

For love I use up all the money

And have to part with the jade pins.

351

Doomed to wear bramble hairpins,

I'm afraid the unlucky jades won't sell.

After I part with the hairpins,

Spider web will soon fall on my dressing table.

Why do I have to suffer such fate?

I still want my hairpins back.

Scene Forty-Five
Jade-smith's Sentiments

(Enter Huansha with the jade hairpins in a jewelry case)

HUANSHA (*To the tune of* **Lülüjin**):

I wear spiral-shaped hair

And paint my eyebrows.

My clothes smell fragrantly

Of rouge and powder

But also of tea, salt and vinegar.

The jade hairpins are carefully put

In a case lined with velvet.

To whom will the jade hairpins be sold?

I'm reluctant to act like a broker.

"What I'm accustomed to do

Is such light housework as cooking.

But now I am told

To sell the jade hairpins."

There's someone coming this way. It seems to be Hou Jingxian the jade-smith. I'll just wait a while and ask for his help. How can a girl sell things in the street?

(Enter Hou Jingxian)

HOU JINGXIAN (*To the tune of* **Fanbusuan**):

With a sharp knife,

I've carved all kinds of precious jade.

Now I stop working in my old age,

Tired of a busy and bustling life.

"I'm aging with dim eyes

And deaf ears.

But I used to make gold chains

And jade pendants."

HUANSHA:

Where are you from?

HOU JINGXIAN:

I might have seen you somewhere. I can't remember exactly. Who are you?

HUANSHA:

I have something as a reminder.

    (*Takes out the hairpins*)

HOU JINGXIAN:

This is a pair of purple jade hairpins. I've seen them somewhere.

    (*Looks at the hairpins closely*)

    (*To the tune of* **Taishiyin**)

    I scrutinize the crystal pure hairpins

    With delicately inlaid jadeite and pearls.

Ah! They were carved by me!

    I remember selecting a cockscomb-shaped jade

    And carving them with elaborate effort.

HUANSHA:

How did you acquire such fine craftsmanship?

HOU JINGXIAN:

    Experience of perfect craftsmanship comes from years' accumulation;

    The carved flowers and birds on them surely withstand scrutinization.

HUANSHA:

Do you remember for whom you carved the hairpins?

HOU JINGXIAN:

No. I can't remember. But where are you from?

HUANSHA:

I'm from the Huos.

HOU JINGXIAN:

Oh I remember. I was asked to carve this pair of hairpins for Miss Huo Xiaoyu when she reached the age of fifteen. I was paid a million strings of coins for doing it. How can I forget that?

    When the beautiful hairpins were put on with fair fingers,

    Miss Huo's face lit up with bliss.

HUANSHA:

So you remember right. Miss Huo is the daughter of Prince Huo.

HOU JINGXIAN:

The hairpins are very precious. Why do you take them to the streets?

HUANSHA:

For sale.

HOU JINGXIAN:

Miss Huo is the heir to a rich and senior official's family, and she is so young and pretty. Why does she have to sell the hairpins?

HUANSHA:

The Huos have come down in the world. They're not as wealthy as before.

HOU JINGXIAN:

Is Miss Huo married?

HUANSHA (*To the previous tune*):

> She's married happily to a talented scholar.

HOU JINGXIAN:

A scholar. That's great.

HUANSHA:

> But he left home and never comes back.

HOU JINGXIAN:

Alas! He's deserted Miss Huo.

HUANSHA:

> So she is pitiably left alone.

HOU JINGXIAN:

Fortunately, she has a rich family.

HUANSHA:

> All valuable things have been sold.

HOU JINGXIAN:

Is she still waiting for her man?

HUANSHA:

> She remains loyal to him.

HOU JINGXIAN:

Is she living a luxurious life?

HUANSHA:

> How can she when she's so short of money?

HOU JINGXIAN:

Then what does she depend on for a living?

HUANSHA:

She keeps selling valuable clothing and jewelry to pay for the information about her man.

> Now the jade hairpins are the most valuable things left.

HOU JINGXIAN:

It's good if Miss Huo can get information about her man. Otherwise,

> The pretty lady will suffer illness and ill fate.

> (*Weeps*)

Even those who have enjoyed privileged status and wealth would be reduced to such a pitiful state when they come down in the world! Seeing such ups and downs in my old age, I feel very sentimental.

> (*To the tune of* **Huaqiao'er**)
> Yours is a wealthy and influential family
> Living a luxurious and leisurely life.
> You have richly-decorated mansions
> And delicately-set ornaments.
> Why do you act so decisively

Instead of leaving yourself some leeway?

I've witnessed the life of many influential families. Now this Miss Huo is so down on her luck.

HOU JINGXIAN, HUANSHA:

>Short of money for basic needs,
>
>How can she deal with illness?
>
>It's saddening and heartbreaking
>
>To sell her jade hairpins.

HOU JINGXIAN:

I must continue my way now.

HUANSHA (*Sighs*):

I'm a young girl, but I have to peddle such luxuries in the street.

>(*To the previous tune*)
>
>Closing the jewelry case,
>
>I hold it in distress.
>
>How come I walk to such a bustling street?
>
>There's nothing here of interest.
>
>Holding the jade hairpins cautiously for sale,
>
>I have to try many unfamiliar places.
>
>(*Stops*)

Mr. Hou, I'd like to ask you for a favour.

>(*Bows*)
>
>I'm not bowing to ingratiate you,
>
>But really need your help,
>
>As I feel like crying to sell the hairpins.
>
>Please look at my small and tight shoes.

HOU JINGXIAN:

What's the point of looking at your small and tight shoes?

HUANSHA:

It's painful for me to walk too much.

HOU JINGXIAN (*To the previous tune*):

>Speaking sweet words with a kind look,
>
>You are lively and eloquent.

HUANSHA:

I'm not lively and eloquent. I'm afraid that the Huo family will lose dignity if people know about the sale of Miss Huo's hairpins.

HOU JINGXIAN:

>At the mention of the Huo's dignity,
>
>I am deeply absorbed in thought.
>
>(*Aside*)

What a smart girl!

>With a sense of honour,

She comes straight to the point.

All right, I'll take it.

> I'll examine the jewelry case
> And pluck the thread ends.
> It's heartbreaking to sell the hairpins;
> But I'll do what I can to help.

HUANSHA:

Mr. Hou, please sell it at a fair price.

> (*To the previous tune*)
> On the hairpins inlaid with pearls,
> The pair of swallows are resting in the case.
> They will fly to another lady's chamber
> And peep around on her hair.

Mr. Hou, please make sure the money is paid immediately when the hairpins are sold.

> Please be smart
> With the price paid.

Mr. Hou, let go of the hairpins when the money is paid.

> You have to go out of your small store
> To peddle them in rich men's magnificent houses.
> I feel like crying to sell the hairpins,
> And look at them sadly with tightly knitted eyebrows.

Now I'll go back home. We'll reward you for your help.

HOU JINGXIAN:

Just a moment. Tell me who is that heartless man? It will be convenient for me to inquire about him while selling the hairpins.

HUANSHA:

I have an idea. You just put placards in the street saying: Miss Huo's husband Li Yi left home and never comes back. Born in Longxi, he is the tenth child of his family. Now he is in his twenties and is appointed Military Consultant. He wears a black-gauze official cap, a purple-coloured robe, a gold-decorated belt and cloud-patterned official boots. He is of middle height, with a round, pale face and a small moustache. Anyone who sees him will be rewarded one ounce of silver. Anyone who provides information about him will be rewarded two ounces.

HOU JINGXIAN:

The reward sounds too small.

HUANSHA:

I once got lost and was found by putting up such a placard. The reward for people who offered help was one or two ounces.

HOU JINGXIAN:

But your bones are of different weights.

HUANSHA:

Then give the reward with the money from the hairpins.

> "*We depend on you in this business,*

And want the money back."

(Exit)

HOU JINGXIAN (*Left alone on the stage*):

"Precious jade will be recognized by a jade expert;

Gold must be sold to those who need it."

Miss Huo is not married to the right man. Now she has to sell the precious hairpins for the information about her man to get the family reunion. But the pair of purple jade hairpins is too expensive, so it's hard to find a buyer immediately. Let me see — who is the most likely buyer? Oh yes, several days ago the attendant of General Lu came to ask for a pair of purple jade hairpins for Miss Lu, who is going to get married. Here is their residence with a red gate and weapons displayed outside. Is the attendant at the gate?

(Enter Attendant)

ATTENDANT:

"Who is knocking at the door

Without fear for the cudgel?"

It turns out to be Mr. Hou. Have you brought purple jade hairpins with you?

HOU JINGXIAN:

Yes, I happen to have a pair. So your Miss Lu is fortunate enough.

ATTENDANT:

Where did you get them?

HOU JINGXIAN:

It's hard to tell.

ATTENDANT:

We won't accept them without knowing where they are from. Take them to other places.

HOU JINGXIAN:

To tell you the truth, it's from the Huos.

ATTENDANT:

Is it sold by Miss Huo?

HOU JINGXIAN:

How strange that you know about it! Who tells you?

ATTENDANT:

You don't know that Miss Huo has been married to our Military Consultant Mr. Li. Now Mr. Li is staying here and is going to marry the daughter of General Lu. The purple jade hairpins are prepared for the bride, Miss Lu. So you come at the right time.

HOU JINGXIAN:

Maybe this Mr. Li is not Miss Huo's husband.

ATTENDANT:

He is called Li Yi, and is a native of Longxi.

HOU JINGXIAN:

So it's really the same man. His wife has been searching for him up and down the world. But it turns out that he becomes the son-in-law of General Lu. Can you take me to see him?

ATTENDANT:

How can you see him so casually in such a big and awe-inspiring house? Besides, he has vowed not to go back home.

HOU JINGXIAN:

I hear he made a vow of love with his former wife as well.

ATTENDANT:

It's none of your business. Wait here, I'll fetch the money for the hairpins.

HOU JINGXIAN:

The pair of hairpins is worth a million coins.

ATTENDANT:

I'll charge thirteen thousand coins for commission.

HOU JINGXIAN (*Sighs*):

What a heartless man Li is! I'll sing a tune to curse him.

> (*To the tune of* **Qingjiangyin**)
>
> Li's unfaithfulness is now disclosed;
>
> Everyone knows he is iron-hearted.
>
> If a lot-stick is drawn in each temple,
>
> All the lots indicate that he's a wicked man.

Li Yi, Li Yi,

> A single betrayal will multiply into many more.
>
> (*Enter Attendant with money*)

ATTENDANT:

Here are a million coins for the hairpins and a hundred thousand coins as your commission. Now go away quickly. General Lu will begin to handle official business.

HOU JINGXIAN:

I'd like to know what Military Consultant Li is going to do with his former wife.

ATTENDANT:

What to do with her? He won't ask her to be a lifetime widow!

> The home is near but far apart;
>
> Who'll get the pair of hairpins at last?
>
> Tell the ill-fated beauties in the world
>
> Not to do nothing but lament the past.

Scene Forty-Six
Weeping Over the Jade Hairpins

(*Enter General Lu*)

GENERAL LU (*To the tune of* **Fengma'er**):

> With my delegated power and talented subordinates,

I wear a brilliantly embroidered official robe.

With all senior and junior officials under my command,

I come from the most influential family at court.

"I exercise omnipotent power

To do whatever I like.

Everything goes on as I wish,

Except for this stubborn young man."

I'm General Lu. There are enough young men for me to pick and choose as my son-in-law. But I have singled out Military Consultant Li Yi and have decided on him as my son-in-law. As he's so arrogant and disobedient, I must have him yield to me. Now I order my men to collect jade hairpins for my daughter, but so far, there aren't enough satisfying ones. How worthless is the attendant!

(*Enter Attendant*)

ATTENDANT:

"On the screen are painted colourful golden-tailed birds;

Reflected in the mirror are jade hairpins of red swallows."

My lord, I get a pair of purple jade hairpins from Hou Jingxian.

GENERAL LU:

How delicately carved it is! Where did he get it?

ATTENDANT:

It's pitiable that the former wife of Military Consultant Li has to sell her purple jade hairpins for a living.

GENERAL LU (*Keeps silent and ponders*):

I'm thinking of a good idea to vanquish Li. Do you know whether there are any women in frequent contact with the Huos?

ATTENDANT:

I hear that Scout Wang mentioned a Bao Siniang who often goes to the Huos'.

GENERAL LU:

You go to invite Military Consultant Li here, then ask your wife to pretend to be Bao Siniang's sister Bao Sanniang. Tell your wife to say that the hairpins are sold by Li's former wife because she has another man in her heart. Li will surely be angry at this and agree to marry my daughter. Now you can go for Military Consultant Li. It's true indeed,

"I secretly play tricks with the hairpins

To make the young man suspicious."

(*Exit Attendant*)

(*Enter Li Yi*)

LI YI (*To the tune of **Shuangtianxiaojiao***):

General Lu's residence is picturesque

With a painted gate and neatly displayed weapons.

Tree branches and leaves brush my hat,

As I get down from the steed.

(*Attendant reports the arrival of Li Yi*)

GENERAL LU:

"You enjoy spring sights in the guesthouse;

LI YI:

I'm willing to bow to your superiority.

GENERAL LU:

You're honoured as a meritorious hero;

LI YI:

But I'll be incapacitated by kindness."

GENERAL LU (*Laughs*):

How tactful it is of you to say you'll be incapacitated by kindness! Now please take a seat. We have something to discuss. You know I have a daughter who is fifteen years old. I want to marry her to you. I have invited Mr. Wei to be the matchmaker for us. But he says you cannot forget your former wife. I wonder how you were taken into the Huos as a son-in-law.

LI YI:

Please allow me to tell you in detail.

(*To the tune of* **Dongouling**)

The first time I saw her,

She was charming amidst colourful lanterns,

Having had her hairpin hooked on tree branches.

I took up the pin as a good excuse

To ask her for her hand.

We have taken serious vows of love,

And I'll never forget my promise to her.

GENERAL LU:

It's not good to get married so rashly.

(*To the previous tune*)

It's easy to fall in love

At first sight,

But it's dishonourable to talk love in the street light

And take fallen hairpins as a betrothal gift.

I am afraid

Her love is not constant and profound

And she will easily desert her man.

(*Enter Bao Sanniang with a jewelry box containing the jade hairpins*)

BAO SANNIANG:

"My mouth projects with blood-red lips;

My face is lean with pale hollow cheeks.

I look like Bao Siniang in appearance,

But my big feet are uncomfortable in small embroidered shoes."

(*Greets General Lu*)

I kowtow to you, my lord.

GENERAL LU:

Who are you?

BAO SANNIANG:

I am from the Baos.

GENERAL LU:

Why do you come here?

BAO SANNIANG:

I hear that your daughter needs a pair of purple jade hairpins. I happen to have a pair to present to you.

GENERAL LU:

That's good. Let me have a look.

> (*Attendant takes the hairpins out of the jewelry box and hands them to General Lu*)
>
> (*General Lu and Li Yi have a close look at them*)

GENERAL LU:

How nice! The swallows and flowers are delicately carved. Where have you got them? Look, they are tied with red silk threads and put in a box inlaid with golden threads.

LI YI (*Aside, surprised*):

I've seen the hairpins somewhere. She says that she is from the Baos. Maybe she knows Bao Siniang. If so, I can inquire about my wife.

> (*Turns around*)

Do you have sisters?

BAO SANNIANG:

We are seven sisters. I am the third.

LI YI:

Is there a Bao Siniang?

BAO SANNIANG:

She's my younger sister. She's eloquent and good at matchmaking. I can only do some petty business because I'm too straightforward.

LI YI:

Where are the hairpins from?

BAO SANNIANG:

They are mine.

LI YI:

They don't seem to be yours judging from your clothes.

BAO SANNIANG:

To tell you the truth, my younger sister Bao Siniang asks me to sell them.

LI YI:

When did she get them?

BAO SANNIANG:

She picked them up in the street in the Lantern Festival.

LI YI (*To the tune of **Shizixu***):

> Whose hairpins are they?
>
> I suddenly think of the Lantern Night.

Though the owner is not present,

I can still remember all that happened.

What's stirring my feelings now?

It is the happy bygone days

When my wife casually combed her beautiful hair

At the dressing table

In the moonlight.

BAO SANNIANG:

What a good memory you have!

LI YI (*Surprised*):

Are they really from the Huos?

(*Looks at the hairpins*)

They are the swallows

And flowers.

(*Feels sad*)

How come they are brought here?

(*To the tune of* **Taipingge**)

I've been away from my wife for three years,

During which I often shed tears.

The sight of the marriage pledge makes me sad at her death.

BAO SANNIANG:

She's still alive.

LI YI:

Does she sell the hairpins

For lack of money?

BAO SANNIANG:

How can she go begging from house to house?

LI YI:

Is she remarried?

Would she go so far

As to remarry a vulgar man?

BAO SANNIANG:

You look worried and sad. Do you know her? I feel distressed to speak of her story. I hear the Huos took in a man as the son-in-law. But that man left home and never returned. There's a scholar, a Mr. Cui, who told her that her man had been remarried. She wouldn't believe it at first, but when she got the exact information of his remarriage, she cursed him for a whole month. This time, my younger sister acted as the matchmaker again and found for her a new husband. So she has the hairpins sold now.

LI YI (*Weeps*):

Oh, my wife!

BAO SANNIANG (*Surprised*):

Now I see that she's your wife. I'm sorry for what I said. I'm sorry for what I said.

LI YI (*Faints, falls to the ground and is helped up*):

Oh my wife! It's me that have brought you all the misfortunes.

> (*To the tune of* **Shanggonghua**)
>
> Is it true or false?
>
> Your slim fingers come into mind again.
>
> Though the hairpins are priceless,
>
> The jade may not be flawless.

BAO SANNIANG:

Mr. Li, your wife has deserted you.

LI YI:

Oh my wife!

> Who will accompany me from now on?
>
> I am still infatuated with you
>
> Although I am deserted.

BAO SANNIANG:

What an infatuated man Mr. Li is!

LI YI (*Looks at the hairpins again*):

> (*To the tune of* **Xianghuanglong**)
>
> There is no doubt now
>
> That they are the same hairpins.
>
> What has happened
>
> Makes me panicky and alarmed.

Oh my wife! The old saying goes that the first spouse is the best. Now you are persuaded by your second husband to sell the hairpins. You will regret doing this when you think of me one day. Oh my wife,

> How is your present husband?
>
> I still remember how you loved me at that time.

GENERAL LU:

Mr. Li, this woman is of easy virtue. But you needn't worry about finding another good girl. I asked Wei Xiaqing to persuade you yesterday. Now that we know your former wife has remarried, it's your destined fate to marry my daughter.

LI YI:

> Good heavens!
>
> The hairpins remind me of my wife.
>
> Is she really so casual in marriage?

Oh, Xiaoyu, you're killing me!

> With a lump in my throat,
>
> I wish I could swallow the hairpins right now!

GENERAL LU:

You needn't be so sad! If you're choked to death, you won't be able to regain your life. You'd better keep the hairpins. I'll pay for you.

LI YI (*Thanks General Lu and takes the hairpins*):

(*To the tune of* **Dashengyue**)

    I put the pins in my sleeves with great care,

    As I once did by the plum flowers.

    I still remember how she pinned them on her hair,

    Which cascaded over her shoulders.

GENERAL LU:

How about having Bao Sanniang as the matchmaker and taking the hairpins as the marriage pledge?

LI YI:

    Won't the hairpins be separated in this way?

    I must try to unite the pins and see her again.

GENERAL LU:

Let me break the hairpins.

LI YI:

    If you break the hairpins,

    I will weep in sad tears.

GENERAL LU:

Attendant, escort Mr. Li to his residence.

    (*Attendant escorts Li Yi back*)

LI YI (*To the tune of* **Kuxiangsi**):

    The jade-hairpin marriage is thus broken!

    (*Exit*)

GENERAL LU (*Left on the stage*):

Ask the attendant's wife to come here. Now you are forbidden to leak any information. When the marriage is settled, I'll reward your husband a secretarial post.

    (*Bao Sanniang kowtows*)

    Maple leaves drift forlornly in the autumn wind;

    The swallows in spring's courtyard knows this sight.

    True love should be entrusted to the moon,

    Which rises over the flower branches at night.

Scene Forty-Seven
Scattering Money in Sorrow

    (*Enter Huo Xiaoyu looking sick, followed by Huansha*)

HUO XIAOYU (*To the tune of* **Xingxiangzi**):

    Gone will be the spring

    With its beautiful moon and flowers,

    While I'm emaciated with lovesickness.

To inquire about my man's whereabouts,

I've been racking my brains.

HUANSHA:

He'd better come back,

Otherwise, what's the use

Of your waiting in vain without end!

HUO XIAOYU (*In the pattern of* **Collected Poems**):

"With the incense going out,

I'm doomed to part with the hairpins.

I don't feel like looking in the dusty mirror;

Sicknesses and sadness do harm to my body and mind."

Huansha, that pair of hairpins are my favorite. When will we find a buyer? How distressed

I am!

(*To the tune of* **Yushanying**)

When I began to wear hairpins at fifteen,

I was carefree and healthy.

When my hair remains while my man is gone,

I'm always absent-minded the whole day.

Every day when I get up,

I look at the empty dressing table,

Doubting whether the hairpins are left on the pillow

Or put away in the jewelry box.

But suddenly I remember in sorrow

That they have been sold —

The thought left me alone in tears.

(*To the previous tune*)

They have been sold!

I've sold the hairpins;

What buyer is enjoying their beauty now?

She might be bargaining patiently about the price, and maybe

She's scoffing at my raising the price

In my poverty and distress.

I fell in love with Li Yi at first sight, but now I have to sell the marriage pledge.

People are rumouring

About the story of the hairpins

And how I have reduced myself to such misfortune.

For whom

I sell the pins on my hair

With my face pallid in the mirror?

(*Enter Hou Jingxian*)

HOU JINGXIAN:

"Plum flowers wither when azaleas are in bloom;

Of the two young ladies one is in gloom,

Because one is becoming poor and penniless,

But the other is graced by pretty hairpins."

I'm Hou Jingxian. I sold Huo Xiaoyu's jade hairpins for a million coins, but they haven't come to take the money yet. So I have to bring them the money myself. Is anyone at the door?

HUANSHA:

Here comes Mr. Hou. Let me report to my young lady.

HUO XIAOYU (*Greets Hou Jingxian*):

Are the hairpins sold at a good price?

HOU JINGXIAN (*To the tune of* **Guihuasuonanzhi**):

I sold the hairpins

At once

And at a good price.

Here's the money for you to count.

HUANSHA (*Counts the money*):

It's a millon coins indeed. Did they give you the commission?

HUO XIAOYU:

Who is the buyer?

HOU JINGXIAN:

It's the influential General Lu,

For his daughter to wear when she reaches the age of fifteen.

HUO XIAOYU (*Surprised*):

Huansha, did Mr. Hou get any information when he went to sell the hairpins in Lu's house?

HOU JINGXIAN:

Right! Right! There's indeed a Military Consultant Mr. Li.

You're looking for your lost man,

While he's to become the bridegroom.

HUO XIAOYU:

So the rumour is true.

HOU JINGXIAN:

At the gate of Lu's house,

I stayed for a long while.

It was Lu's attendant

That told me the truth.

HUO XIAOYU (*Weeps*):

How can such a thing happen in our world today? My hairpins are on the head of Lu's daughter!

(*Faints*)

HOU JINGXIAN:

"The jade-smith helps to find her missing man;

The sale of the hairpins breaks the lady's heart."

(*Exit*)

HUO XIAOYU (*To the tune of **Xiaotaohong***):

    I no longer care about my appearance and beauty,

    While Miss Lu must be eager to look more pretty.

    I expected to spend the whole life with my man,

    But have given up our marriage pledge with a sigh.

    When my man is gone,

    My figure is emaciated

    And my eyebrows unpainted.

    I intend to keep company with the pins,

    But the pledge is now gone with the wind.

    When the jade hairpins are gone,

    I won't have the pair of swallows on my head.

HUANSHA:

How I love the money!

HUO XIAOYU:

What's money for, anyway?

    (*To the tune of **Xiashanhu***)

    A red string

    Of copper coins

    Does not bring wealth

    Or family reunion.

    General Lu takes in a son-in-law

    By cruelly breaking up a happy couple.

    Listen to me, you deaf God of Wealth,

    That blind and unsympathetic thing called money

    Brings me floods of tears

    That dim my eyes.

    (*Throws away the money*)

    I scatter the money in the wind

    Like the worthless coin-like elm seeds drifting about.

HUANSHA:

How can you throw away money like this? How extravagant you are!

HUO XIAOYU (*To the tune of **Zuiguichi***):

    A happy couple

    We once were.

    I married him not for money, but for permanent love;

    Who knows the hairpins will change hands!

    Separated from each other,

    I wonder whether he'll weep over my letter.

    He is good at cheating and hoaxing,

    But is Miss Lu to bear misfortunes as I did

    And admire my jade hairpins?

(*To the tune of* **Wubanyi**)

I remember my first encounter

With the young man,

Who took me as a celestial beauty

Smiling by the flowers,

And picked up the hairpins in full joy.

That encounter brought about transient joy of marital life,

But now another young lady takes over the hairpins

While I have to lead a wretched existence.

Does she have extraordinary attraction?

There might be predestination behind our separation!

(*Enter Cui Yunming*)

CUI YUNMING:

"*A poor scholar takes time enjoying the spring sight,*

While a lovesick wife fears to see the beautiful flowers."

These days I haven't been to the Huos to inquire about Li Yi and get some money. What's the sad noise inside? I'll walk in and have a look.

(*Surprised to see money scattered on the ground*)

Huansha, I'm busy all day eking out a living, while you're throwing money on the ground. Why?

HUANSHA:

You know, we've spent all our money inquiring about Mr. Li's whereabouts. So we have to ask the jade-smith to sell the jade hairpins for us. It turns out that the hairpins were bought by General Lu as dowry for his daughter's marriage with Mr. Li.

CUI YUNMING:

So the rumour turns out to be true! Li Junyu, I'll surely rebuke you if I meet you. I'll make you change your mind!

HUO XIAOYU:

For your efforts to make him change his mind, here is the money as the reward. I'm sincerely thankful to you for your help.

(*Bows to Cui Yunming*)

(*To the tune of* **Yiduojiao**)

With your help,

A broken marriage might be renewed;

However, man proposes, heaven disposes.

CUI YUNMING:

With fallen petals beneath trees in late spring,

For your marital reunion,

For your marital reunion,

We need another accidental encounter.

HUO XIAOYU (*To the tune of* **Kuxiangsi**):

As I love him who does not love me,

Please tell him to keep his word.

He's enjoying a wealthy and merry life,

But I'm lamenting over my hairpins and lost youth.

(*Cui Yunming takes leave*)

HUO XIAOYU:

Try to persuade him

With gentle words

Not to desert me like this.

If you make him change his mind,

Your words are worth a thousand ounces of gold.

"When I think over my unlucky fate,

I often doubt the dreams that my heart knows to be true.

I've experienced so many unhappy things,

But still expect money to buy a reunion."

(*Exit*)

CUI YUNMING (*Left alone on the stage*):

"While beautiful flowers wait for viewers in vain,

Sick and moaning birds evoke popular sympathy."

Huo Xiaoyu has spent all her money inquiring about Li Yi. I've received much from
her during these three years, but haven't offered any help. I'd like to visit Li Yi but he's
detained in Lu's house. And he's not allowed to receive guests after coming back from the
court every day. What can I do then?

(*Thinks*)

I've got an idea. The peony flowers in the Chongjing Temple are in full bloom this spring.
I'll discuss with Wei Xiaqing at an inn, to see how we can invite Li Yi to admire flowers
with us. We'll take the opportunity to persuade him, and might make him change his
mind. It's true indeed,

"The stable relationship between man and wife

Relies on the advice from friends."

Scene Forty-Eight
The Gallant Knight's Drunken Comments

(*Enter the old waiter*)

WAITER:

"When sightseers come to enjoy flowers in leisure,

We take the chance to sell wine of rice.

Our wine is sold at a cheap price,

But it can bring great pleasure."

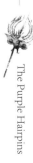

I'm a waiter from a famous public house in the street before the Chongjing Temple. The peony flowers have been in full blossom for about half a month this year. A lot of viewers come to enjoy the beauty of flowers, and I'm waiting here for customers. Whatever requests they make about the wine, I will satisfy them. It's true indeed,

> "*Wine is served at people's request,*
>
> *After flowers are viewed to their hearts' content.*"

Here comes a living immortal!

(*Enter the Gallant Knight wearing a gauze kerchief and a yellow robe, holding an arrow and riding a horse, followed by several servants*)

GALLANT KNIGHT (*To the tune of* **Suonanzhi**):

> In beautiful scenes that unfold before my eyes
>
> With clouds drifting across the sky,
>
> I wear gorgeous yet light clothes.
>
> Galloping on a noble horse among flowers,
>
> I'm born unyielding and chivalrous.

As an obscure gallant knight, I come out and shoot birds for pleasure in the delightful spring scenery of flourishing flowers and verdant grass. Well, there's a big public house ahead. I have my servant ask the waiter whether he's got enough delicious wine, as I'll come to drink here when I finish shooting the pellets with my arrow.

WAITER:

Yes, sir.

GALLANT KNIGHT:

> Mellow wine is to be prepared
>
> In several barrels.
>
> When I come back from hunting,
>
> I'll enjoy drinking amidst flowers and birdsongs.

So I'm on my way now.

(*Exit*)

(*Enter Cui Yunming*)

CUI YUNMING (*To the previous tune*):

> In the vast spring sight
>
> Of beautiful red blossoms,
>
> I feel sorry when I watch the flowers.
>
> Walking along the bridge in leisurely steps,
>
> I conceive a sentimental poem on vanishing spring.

Hey, where's the waiter?

(*Enter the waiter*)

CUI YUNMING:

> Bring me sorghum wine
>
> Without heating or warming,
>
> Plus scallion stalk
>
> That is mildly salted.

I'll have a talk with my friend Wei Xiaqing here. Prepare several dishes to go with the drink.

WAITER:

Please come in and take a seat.

> (*Cui Yunming drinks by himself*)
>
> (*Enter Wei Xiaqing*)

WEI XIAQING (*To the previous tune*):

> Seeing a fluttering black flag
>
> With the big character of "wine",
>
> I walk in the spring breeze to meet an old friend of mine.

Cui Yunming has arrived ahead of me.

> (*Greets Cui Yunming*)

CUI YUNMING (*Laughs*):

How can we not be intoxicated with such beautiful scenery!

WEI XIAQING:

> You are poor but not wretched;
>
> You wear shabby clothes but look smart!

CUI YUNMING:

Waiter, wine please.

> We'll enjoy the birdsongs
>
> And admire the spring sights,
>
> Lest you get an old scholar
>
> Deadly drunk.

WEI XIAQING:

Yunming, are you here to talk about Li Junyu with me?

CUI YUNMING:

Yes. I hear the peony flowers are in full blossom in the Chongjing Temple. I'd like to use the money given by Huo Xiaoyu to invite Li Junyu to a dinner, so that we can take the opportunity to persuade him to change his mind.

WEI XIAQING:

Maybe you don't know that General Lu is the most influential official at court, to be escorted by soldiers and guards. He has ordered that anyone who talks about this matter be cudgeled. And it's tricky of him to deploy a lot of lackeys around the city of Chang'an.

CUI YUNMING:

As we've got Miss Huo's money, let's do something for her.

> (*To the previous tune*)
>
> As we've got her money
>
> And promised to help her,
>
> We should not look on with folded arms.

For us,

> As we've helped them to come together,
>
> We'll have to hope for the better.

WEI XIAQING:

>I'm afraid he's cold-hearted
>
>And pretends not to understand.
>
>In that case all our cares and worries
>
>Would be wasted.

CUI YUNMING:

Waiter, get a dinner for three ready here and invite Military Consultant Li to enjoy the peony flowers the day after tomorrow.

WAITER:

It's not easy to be admitted into Lu's residence. I'm afraid they might grow suspicious.

WEI XIAQING:

I've got an idea. You just say the Buddhist Master Wuxiang invites him.

WAITER:

All right. Let me pour another pot of wine for you.

>(*Enter the Gallant Knight*)

GALLANT KNIGHT (*To the previous tune*):

>Where the flying orioles are brisk
>
>And the green trees are delicate,
>
>I shoot pellets to the sky.
>
>Now I gallop by on the horse
>
>And see the silver bottle hanging outside the inn.

Well, there're two scholars here. Tell them to stay out of my sight.

>The two silly scholars
>
>Are not afraid to be ridiculed.
>
>They won't realize their ambition
>
>In this public house.
>
>(*Raises his hand*)

Excuse me!

WEI XIAQING, CUI YUNMING (*Leave for another place*):

>"*We are driven away by the late comer;*
>
>*The virtuous wife is displaced by another girl.*"
>
>(*Exeunt*)

GALLANT KNIGHT (*Smiles, following them with his eyes*):

Where are these two silly scholars from?

SERVANT:

They look so familiar. One of them seems to be the Mr. Wei who borrowed our horse three years ago. The other seems to be the Mr. Cui who borrowed our Tartar servant.

GALLANT KNIGHT:

Why did they borrow our horse and servant?

SERVANT:

Mr. Li Yi was taken into the Huo family as a son-in-law. He borrowed the horse and the tartar servant to add grace to his wedding.

GALLANT KNIGHT:

How long have the two sour scholars been here?

WAITER:

They've been here for a long time.

GALLANT KNIGHT (*Looks at the leftover in the dishes and laughs*):

What did they eat from this dish just now?

WAITER:

Fermented soybeans.

GALLANT KNIGHT:

What about that dish?

WAITER:

Assorted bean-curds.

GALLANT KNIGHT (*Laughs*):

How wily it is of you to serve the poor scholars with such things! How many bottles of wine did they drink?

WAITER:

Each of them drank a bottle.

GALLANT KNIGHT (*Looks at the pot*):

Oh! It's a poor-quality wine. Others won't drink more than five cups of such wine. What's so important to discuss that they stay here for long?

WAITER:

Li Yi has deserted his wife and married General Lu's daughter. Now his former wife is very sick. The two scholars have decided to ask us to prepare a banquet. And they ask me to invite Mr. Li to the Chongjing Temple to enjoy peony flowers, which is a chance for them to persuade Mr. Li to change his mind. But they are afraid of the influential General Lu, so they dare not talk about the details. It's really sorrowful to mention Li's former wife.

(*Weeps*)

GALLANT KNIGHT:

What a miserable story it is! Waiter, serve the wine.

(*Wine is served*)

GALLANT KNIGHT:

Is there any talented female entertainer around here?

WAITER:

There's a Wang Dajie opposite this inn. And there's a Liu Ba'er next door. Both are good.

GALLANT KNIGHT:

How can I enjoy such cheap and inferior prostitutes?

(*To the previous tune*)

Rolling up my sleeves

And stroking my whiskers,

I see sightseers flocking the road.

It's nothing but the plum and peach flowers

The Purple Hairpins

That bring the beautiful ladies so much pleasure.

Enjoying the mellow wine

Amidst beautiful flowers,

I'm a gallant man

Whistling with grace.

WAITER:

May I ask what a gallant man is?

GALLANT KNIGHT:

You are not in a position to speak of gallantry.

WAITER:

I know a gallant woman around here.

GALLANT KNIGHT:

What do you mean by gallant woman?

WAITER:

There's a Bao Siniang around here, who spares no money making friends and entertaining guests. She has all the desirable qualities a woman can have, and she is very careful with her reputation. Ordinary men, even those of wealth, cannot win her favour. Only refined and romantic men can win a look from her beautiful eyes. Isn't she a gallant woman?

GALLANT KNIGHT:

I've heard of her for years. Will you go and invite her here?

WAITER:

Isn't that Bao Siniang coming?

    (*Enter Bao Siniang*)

BAO SINIANG (*To the previous tune*):

    Wearing a red coat

    And emerald headwear,

    I stand by the window enjoying cuckoo songs.

    I've seen the pretty yet sick young lady,

    Who weeps for being deserted by her promising husband.

WAITER (*Goes out and greets Bao Siniang*):

Bao Siniang, a guest here wants to see you.

BAO SINIANG (*Peeps*):

    The man is graceful

    In tasteful clothes.

    He must be full of affection and tenderness

    Rather than do evil deeds.

WAITER:

You've made a correct judgment.

GALLANT KNIGHT (*Greets Bao Siniang*):

So this is Siniang. Really striking, as people say.

    (*To the previous tune*)

    She is the most gallant

Among all the women

And still looks young at her age.

A glance from her beautiful eyes

Fills me with jubilance.

A woman looking so nice

Must have refined taste.

(*Turns around*)

Look at the bottles of wine;

Let's get drunk together today.

(*Bows to Bao Siniang*)

I've heard of your gallantry for a long time, so I'm eager to see you.

(*In the pattern of* **Pusaman**)

"*The red-banister bridge reaches the downtown street;*

Willows sway in the wind by the peony flowers.

BAO SINIANG:

My gorgeous clothes are worn out

And my youth is spent when I meet you.

GALLANT KNIGHT:

Wearing a yellow robe and riding a noble horse,

I seek pleasure every day in hilarious places.

BAO SINIANG:

Let your pellets spare the orioles,

For they sing beautiful songs."

GALLANT KNIGHT (*Laughs*):

My shots are not accurate. Right on with your songs, bird!

BAO SINIANG (*Fills the wine cup*):

(*To the tune of* **Xiudai'er**)

With a small golden cup,

You drink away your leisure time,

For affection is better than humdrum.

With subtle fragrance from the distance,

Music of song wafts from the brothel

By a versatile courtesan.

Her tunes reveal her smile

And delicate figure,

Echoing in the sky

For a long time.

GALLANT KNIGHT (*To the tune of* **Bailianxu**):

It is so pleasant

To see the beauty.

Well-known flowers are particularly pretty,

Whose sight I'd like to see every day.

Wandering everywhere with graying hair,

I enjoy the subtlest fragrance this year.

I have no mind

To play with women

Or get married.

BAO SINIANG (*To the tune of* **Zuitaiping**):

Don't pretend;

You are so refined and graceful.

For mellow wine,

You can give up anything valuable.

You drink and talk

About your grand ambition.

Looking far into the distance,

I see luxuriant willows, beautiful pheasants

And roads with hunting-fire traces.

With green grass like my skirt waist

And red flowers like my sleeves,

The late spring is nice and pleasant.

GALLANT KNIGHT (*To the tune of* **Bailianxu**):

For vanity

In my youth,

I spent many a wonderful night with women.

It's like a dream

That never recurs.

After my hangover wears off, I'll take care

Not to be too melancholy,

But just neglect

The comment

People make about the spring sorrow.

Where have you been just now, Siniang?

BAO SINIANG:

I'm from a visit to the sick young lady Miss Huo.

GALLANT KNIGHT:

How did she fall ill?

BAO SINIANG:

She fell in love with Li Yi and married him. But Li is a heartless man and remarries the daughter of General Lu. So Huo Xiaoyu is now lying sick in bed.

GALLANT KNIGHT:

Is she remarried too?

BAO SINIANG:

She'll stick to the vow of love with Li till her dying day.

GALLANT KNIGHT:

How unfair it is! What about her family condition now?

BAO SINIANG (*To the tune of* **Zuitaiping**):

> She is pretty
>
> And lovesick.
>
> To inquire about her missing man,
>
> She has spent all the money.
>
> Her jade hairpins are sold
>
> To pay for any information of her man.
>
> She lies sick in bed
>
> In a gloomy mood,
>
> Wetting her pillows with tears.

GALLANT KNIGHT:

Is she well now?

BAO SINIANG:

> She cannot get up or walk about.

GALLANT KNIGHT:

Has her man returned?

BAO SINIANG:

> Don't mention the cruel-hearted man
>
> To bring me further distress.

GALLANT KNIGHT (*Annoyed*):

> (*To the tune of* **Xianghuanglong**)
>
> I can hardly keep at ease
>
> To hear of her miserable story.
>
> Leaning against the banister,
>
> I'm irritated by the blowing wind.

Siniang, what about drinking a large cup of wine?

> Refill my cup,
>
> Refill my cup
>
> And wipe my tears
>
> With your sleeves.
>
> (*Gets drunk, and is supported by Bao Siniang*)

GALLANT KNIGHT:

> Please take the trouble
>
> To support me.
>
> There're few women as amorous as you.

Boy, give Siniang ten bolts of red silk as reward for her company.

> Where will my heart linger under the dusk clouds?
>
> I'm just intoxicated in beautiful songs.
>
> (*To the tune of* **Coda**)
>
> You don't have the mood for enjoying the cup,
>
> And I have no way to rescue the broken marriage.

(Raises his hand)

Siniang,

> We understand each other at the first smile.

(Exit Bao Siniang)

GALLANT KNIGHT (*Left on the stage alone*):

> *"It's inhumane to look on with pocketed hands;*
> *I'm warm-hearted and cry out against injustice.*
> *I see beauties smile amidst flowers*
> *And my anger appeases when I get drunk."*

I think that Li Yi is detained by General Lu in his residence, thus reducing his former wife Huo Xiaoyu into such poverty. This is the worst injustice in the world! If I don't do something to help, how can I be called a gallant man? Boy, send five thousand ounces of silver to Huo's residence and tell them to hold a lush banquet the day after tomorrow. If they ask why, you just say that they'll see the point by then.

SERVANT:

But my lord, why on earth are we to do that?

GALLANT KNIGHT:

Don't ask. Tell all my men to get the horses ready the day after tomorrow. We'll admire flowers in the Chongjing Temple. It's true indeed,

> *"I'll offer immediate help as a gallant man,*
> *And bring relief to the young lady at the banquet."*

(Exeunt the Gallant Knight and his servant)

Scene Forty-Nine
Interpreting a Dream

(Enter Huo Xiaoyu in sickness, supported by Huansha)

HUO XIAOYU (*To the tune of **Yijiangfeng***):

> I sleep all day,
> Dreaming many dreams,
> With killing lovesickness.
> For love I'm frantic and absent-minded,
> Too weak to withstand a gust of wind.

VOICE OF PARROT WITHIN:

How pitiable you are!

HUANSHA:

What a clever parrot! It says you are pitiful.

HUO XIAOYU:

> The parrot knows how to show mercy,
> The parrot knows how to show mercy,

But the man has no sympathy.

Sad and distressed, I am forgetting about the past.

(*In the pattern of* **Collected Poems**)

"The flowers and willows are jealous of my beauty,

But I'm now like the withering peonies.

I cannot sleep well in such loneliness,

But other people won't understand my feelings."

Huansha, I've been living in sorrow and resentment for over a year since I heard of Li's remarriage with Miss Lu. Lying in bed sick and lonely, what am I to do?

HUANSHA:

You weep all day without eating and sleeping well. Now that your hope to see him again is shattered, your accumulated grievance has led to illness. But I don't think Master Li is really so heartless, judging from his sincere vow to you. You just set your mind at ease and wait for the reunion with him.

HUO XIAOYU (*To the tune of* **Jixianbin**):

With your words of ambition still in my ears,

I'll be satisfied if that's realized.

As the absence of letters from you after parting makes me suspicious,

I've become sick

And penniless,

With nothing left but people's sympathy.

Thin and pallid,

I lament over the past.

(*Vomits*)

HUANSHA (*To the previous tune*):

Your vomitting from stomachache,

With blood in your spit,

Reduces your weight.

Although you suffer from straitened circumstances

And grave sorrows,

You keep on waiting for your man.

What's the point of all these?

Please get well-dressed and forget your sadness.

Please get some relaxation by playing music.

HUO XIAOYU:

Take the musical instrument away!

(*To the previous tune*)

I've no mind to play music

And leave the musical instrument covered with dust.

Why is my man snatched away from me?

Left desperate in loneliness,

Without my man by my side,

I'll live a meaningless life in my remaining days.

It's useless to regret

Over our first encounter in the Lantern Festival.

HUANSHA (*To the previous tune*):

Please take care of your health,

Though it's hard to live in loneliness.

For the final reunion you should preserve your youthful looks

By having enough food

And taking good sleep

In soft and fragrant quilts.

It is likely

That you'll dream of your man.

HUO XIAOYU:

Maybe you are right. I'll sleep for a while.

HUANSHA:

I'll fetch some food for you.

(*Exit*)

(*Enter Bao Siniang*)

BAO SINIANG:

"The talented young man is heartless,

Leaving the pretty lonely wife in sickness."

I'm Bao Siniang. Busy eking out a living, I've not seen Xiaoyu for many days. I wonder how she is now. Well, she's sleeping in bed. Where is Huansha?

HUO XIAOYU (*Wakes in surprise*):

How long have you been here, Siniang?

(*To the tune of **Huangying'er***)

I'm startled awake

From the dream I had.

BAO SINIANG:

Did you have a nice dream?

HUO XIAOYU:

There is only grief, with a rain outside the balcony in the dusk.

BAO SINIANG:

Did you see Li Yi in your dream?

HUO XIAOYU:

I long to see him in my dream,

But who would he care about in his mind?

Siniang, in the dream,

I saw a gallant knight,

In a yellow robe

Handing me

A pair of shoes.

BAO SINIANG:

The shoes symbolize harmony. You'll surely reunite with Li Yi in harmony.

>(*To the previous tune*)
>
>There'll be no doubt about your dream
>
>That the man in yellow
>
>Will bring you the shoes of harmony.
>
>Much money is spent and lot-sticks drawn,
>
>As you try looking for your man
>
>And praying for your man.
>
>Now you're requited with a dream of reunion like shoes in pairs.
>
>Congratulations on your man's return,
>
>To live with you in harmony,
>
>Like mandarin ducks in pairs.
>
>(*Enter the Gallant Knight's servant, holding money in his hands*)

SERVANT:

>"*Our gallant master conceals his name,*
>
>*But he cares about unjust things.*
>
>*He spares no money and effort*
>
>*For benevolence and righteousness.*"

My master is a gallant knight who conceals his name. He asks me to offer a hundred thousand ounces of silver to the Huos for a grand banquet. I don't know why he does so. Here is the Huo residence. Anyone at the door?

>(*Enter Huansha*)

HUANSHA:

Who is it?

SERVANT:

Our master wants to hold a banquet in your house, so he asks me to give you a hundred thousand ounces of silver to cover the expense.

HUO XIAOYU:

You must be mistaken. This is not a public house. Why do you want to hold a banquet here?

SERVANT:

We'd like to hold the banquet in the pavilion by the flowers and bamboos.

HUO XIAOYU:

Bao Siniang, you see, our house is so different from the past.

>"*Luxuriant bamboos used to grow here;*
>
>*They are standing lonely in the deserted garden.*
>
>*The dancing terrace is about to collapse;*
>
>*The singing stage is covered with moss.*
>
>*The walls are dust-covered,*
>
>*For wild birds to build their nests.*
>
>*All the curtains are gone from the windows,*

Leaving a saddening bleak sight."

This is really not a good place for a banquet.

SERVANT:

"As you'll know everything by then,

There's no need for you to refuse now."

(Exit)

HUANSHA:

What on earth are they up to?

HUO XIAOYU (*To the tune of* **Cuyulin**):

We are not relatives.

What is their purpose?

A windfall comes to my hands.

HUANSHA:

The money comes easily like falling petals of a flower;

The man must be someone of great power.

HUO XIAOYU, HUANSHA:

I doubt

For what reason

We are so blessed.

BAO SINIANG (*To the previous tune*):

I can interpret your dream,

But I can't understand

What the money is meant for.

HUO XIAOYU:

Is Li's current wife playing another trick?

Or is a man coming to woo for my love?

HUO XIAOYU, BAO SINIANG:

It's hard to predict

Whether an unexpected guest

Brings good luck.

BAO SINIANG:

Huansha, help your young mistress to bed for a sleep. I'm leaving now.

HUO XIAOYU (*To the tune of* **Coda**):

Siniang,

I can't see you out as I'm so sick.

As to the heartless man,

He remarries in a place so close to me;

I hate him to the marrow of my bones.

As the right medicine will cure the disease,

So the dreamland shoes will cure lovesickness.

Who'll hold the strange banquet?

Whether it's bane or boon is hard to predict.

Scene Fifty
Sighs of Doubt at the Hairpins

(*Enter Li Yi*)

LI YI (*To the tune of **Jinlongcong***):

> I see singing orioles
>
> And flying wild geese,
>
> But not my wife any more.
>
> By luck I get her hairpins,
>
> The sight of which
>
> Strikes a cord in my heart.
>
> (*In the pattern of **Zhegutian***)
>
> *"My wife suffers a tragic and bitter fate,*
>
> *But I still wouldn't believe what I heard.*
>
> *So delicate and devoted,*
>
> *How can she remarry and sell the hairpins?*
>
> *Lamenting over the present and recalling the past*
>
> *I seem to see her putting them on her hair at fifteen.*
>
> *Do I wake or sleep?*
>
> *I put away the hairpins in tears."*

I'm Li Yi. General Lu tries to force me to yield to him through power and influence. I had been out of contact with my wife for a long time, so I didn't know how she was until I heard of her remarriage and got the hairpins sold by her. I'm shocked and nearly grieved to death. I've nothing to do today and feel much bored, so I tell Qiuhong to take out the hairpins. I'd like to look at them more closely.

(*Enter Qiuhong with the hairpins*)

QIUHONG:

> *"The jade hairpins*
>
> *Are taken out of the golden case."*

Master, here're the hairpins.

LI YI (*To the tune of **Jiangtoujingui***):

> Holding the hairpins in hand,
>
> I shed a flood of cold tears.
>
> They're winded with red silk threads
>
> By my wife's slim fingers
>
> For fear the pair of swallows might separate.
>
> As we are destined to be a couple,
>
> Why are we separated like this?
>
> Through sophisticated handcraftsmanship,
>
> Lifelike swallows are carved
>
> Out of the superb jade.

The swallows accompanied her,

The swallows accompanied her

Day and night.

Having the eyebrows gently painted,

She would stand still before the mirror,

With the hairpins quivering on her head.

QIUHONG:

What is the value of the hairpins as you cherish them so much?

LI YI (*To the previous tune*):

Ornamenting the beautiful hair,

The hairpins added much grace.

With paper flowers adorning the jade pendants

And silk threads stringing the jade pearls,

The hairpins were neatly set.

We played the flute on warm days,

And looked at our happy reflections in the mirror.

We admired beautiful flowers

And walked on the green grass,

With a love beyond description.

When it got dark,

Her beauty was set off by dusk clouds.

By the candlelight,

She took down the hairpins

And spoke in a gentle and soft voice.

QIUHONG:

It's unexpected that she should have sold the hairpins.

LI YI (*To the previous tune*):

People say beautiful ladies suffer a bad fate,

But you're living a happy life.

Where are you at present?

Are you enjoying yourself with your new man?

You take our marriage too lightly

By deserting me

And remarrying another man.

Who is fortunate

To be your new sweetheart?

You forget all about our love.

It must have brought you grief

To have the hairpins sold.

You rush with haste

Into the life with another man,

Leaving the happy time with me behind.

QIUHONG:

Why are you looking at the hairpins? Just agree to General Lu's marriage arrangement.

LI YI (*To the previous tune*):

> I'm talented but not cruel-hearted;
>
> I make complaint but have attachment.
>
> She didn't give much thought
>
> To her second marriage.
>
> Recalling the past and thinking it over,
>
> I believe she's far-sighted and clever
>
> And will cherish our love vow forever.
>
> She wouldn't bring blame on herself
>
> By reducing me to a lonely and homeless life.
>
> Maybe she is misguided by the dreams she had!
>
> It's our fate
>
> To have met through the hairpins.
>
> We were such a happy couple
>
> That I doubt the rumour I heard
>
> About her easy virtue.

QIUHONG:

It's good that these are just rumours. If these were true, I might have lost my Huansha as well!

385

LI YI (*To the tune of **Dayagu***):

> She demeans herself
>
> By deserting me
>
> For the rest of her life.
>
> She should have endured her loneliness
>
> To wait for my success.

LI YI, QIUHONG:

> Holding the hairpins,
>
> I make the love vow.

LI YI:

Qiuhong, the Huos must have come down in the world!

> (*To the previous tune*)
>
> Though many things may happen,
>
> She should have thought well before she acts
>
> And been able to endure loneliness.

My wife, do you believe I'm really taken into the Lus as the son-in-law?

> I live a lonely life in detention,
>
> In fear of being forced into a marriage.

LI YI, QIUHONG:

> Holding the hairpins,
>
> I make the love vow.

The Purple Hairpins

(Enter the old waiter with an invitation card)

WAITER:

> "I come to invite the brilliant young man
>
> To admire our temple's peonies."

I'm the waiter of the public house. Tomorrow the two scholars Wei and Cui will have a dinner in the Chongjing Temple, and they ask me to invite Military Consultant Li to admire peonies together with them. We just say it's the Buddhist Master that invites him for fear that General Lu may prevent him from going to the banquet.

(Enter the gateman)

GATEMAN:

Hey! Who's at the gate?

WAITER:

The Buddhist Master Wuxiang of the Chongjing Temple invites Military Consultant Li to a banquet.

GATEMAN:

Where's the banquet to be held?

WAITER:

Where do you think it can be? It's the Buddhist Master who invites Li.

(Gateman reports to Li Yi)

LI YI *(Reads the invitation card)*:

I see. I'll go tomorrow as the Master is an old acquaintance of mine.

GATEMAN:

General Lu has ordered that wherever you go, there should be ten armed military men with cudgels to escort you.

LI YI:

All right.

> Detained in the powerful general's residence,
>
> I hope to relieve boredom by chatting with friends.
>
> Forever separated from my wife,
>
> I begin a lonely and woeful life.

Scene Fifty-One
Meeting the Gallant Knight

(Enter the Buddhist Master)

BUDDHIST MASTER *(To the tune of **Sudijindang**)*:

> Fragrant peonies in the Buddhist temple
>
> Come into full bloom in late spring.
>
> The flowers and grass in the yard add much grace;

How many people can enjoy such beautiful sights?

I'm the Buddhist Master Wuxiang in the Chongjing Temple. When I finish my meditation session, I see flocks of people coming to admire blossoming peonies. So I'll ask my disciples to greet the sightseers. Where are my disciples?

(*Enter two disciples*)

DISCIPLES A and B (*To the previous tune*):

> Monks are stirred by spring sights as well;
>
> Even in meditation they smell of the fragrance.
>
> The shimmering mirror of clear pond water
>
> Reflects the flowers and branches to perfection.

Here we are, Master. Why don't we pluck a twig of peonies and present it in a bottle before the statue of Buddha?

BUDDHIST MASTER:

Which one is the most beautiful?

DISCIPLE B:

There are more than a hundred colours of peonies including red, rosy, pink and purple. The first choice for you is the breed of the Intoxicated Princess Yang or the Plump Beauty Xishi — either is the most beautiful.

BUDDHIST MASTER:

Nonsense!

DISCIPLE A:

How about the fair and plain-coloured breeds like the Avalokitesvara Face or the Buddha Head?

BUDDHIST MASTER:

All right. People flock here to admire the blooming flowers. You two stay here to receive the guests. I'll go back to my meditation. It's true indeed,

> *"Among the fragrant flowers in multiple colours*
>
> *Stands out the moonlit datura in heavenly rain.*
>
> *At the sight of the pure yellow peony in breeze,*
>
> *You don't need to watch the red or purple ones."*
>
> (*Exit*)

DISCIPLE B:

Brother, greeting and entertaining those sightseers will give us great troubles. The two scholars Cui and Wei went to invite Military Consultant Li to a banquet, so we may as well lock the meditation hall and enjoy ourselves elsewhere. It's true indeed,

> *"Wine makes sightseers intoxicated;*
>
> *Beautiful sights make monks unsettled."*
>
> (*Exeunt*)
>
> (*Enter Wei Xiaqing and Cui Yunming*)

CUI YUNMING (*To the tune of **Xidijinyin***):

> Green leaves enhance the beauty of charming flowers,
>
> Fully nourished by spring flavours.

WEI XIAQING:

>The flowers are delicate
>
>With layers of petals
>
>Like red clouds.

CUI YUNMING:

Xiaqing, the banquet is ready, and Mr. Li will be here soon. What flourishing peonies!

(*Enter Li Yi, followed by guards with cudgels*)

LI YI (*To the tune of **Gaoyangtaiyin***):

>In a sunny day of blooming flowers,
>
>With incense smoke curling up from the palace,
>
>The temple is permeated with Buddhist splendour.
>
>With thick clouds floating in the sky,
>
>I'm not afraid of getting drunk and catching cold.
>
>Hearing singing orioles everywhere,
>
>I'm to meet old friends here.
>
>I watch the palace in the distance,
>
>Where there are diaphanous long curtains
>
>In richly ornamented mansions.

(*Greet Wei Xiaqing and Cui Yunming*)

WEI XIAQING, CUI YUNMING (*Laugh*):

Junyu, we've not seen each other for a long time!

>How much leisure do we have in spring?
>
>Now we admire the numerous fragrant flowers
>
>With flying bees and butterflies,
>
>While richly-dressed people are enjoying music
>
>In the beautiful and charming springtime.

LI YI:

>As time flies when I work at court,
>
>I long to enjoy spring breeze and flowers all year round.

WEI XIAQING, CUI YUNMING:

>By the Chenxiang Pavilion,
>
>The Tang emperor and his empress used to enjoy flowers
>
>And order a famous talented poet to compose poems.

(*Greet each other*)

CUI YUNMING:

>"*A swallow returning to nest is out of flock*;

WEI XIAQING:

>*We're afraid that the spring will soon be past*;

LI YI:

>*I'm lonely and melancholy, confined in the official residence*;

WEI XIAQING, CUI YUNMING, LI YI:

>*We meet here again amidst peonies.*"

CUI YUNMING:

Mr. Li, we've not seen each other for several years since we parted in Qinchuan. You've forgotten all about us!

WEI XIAQING:

We invite you to admire flowers today. Let's forget about it and just drink.

GUARD:

Why does scholar Wei hold the banquet in the name of the Buddhist Master?

WEI XIAQING:

You don't know that the Master is nicknamed "man shy of flowers".

(*Enter the waiter*)

WAITER:

"*In the flower world of a Buddhist temple,*

Enjoyment of spring sights must go with wine."

Here is the wine.

(*Wei Xiaqing and Cui Yunming fill the cup*)

WEI XIAQING (*To the tune of* **Gaoyangtaixu**):

Verdant leaves

And delicate flowers

Enhance the beauty of spring sights.

Extravagant wagons are rumbling

Through the capital's downtown streets.

Amidst roaring laughter,

Beautiful ladies are sure to hope

That spring won't so soon be past.

There are various peony flowers

That display their beauty all at once.

LI YI (*To the previous tune*):

Who plants

The intoxicated crane-head peonies

And the fainting sandalwood peonies

With their overlapping petals and charming pistils?

The purple peonies turn crimson,

Surrounded by other peony flowers.

On sunny days,

The red-gauze peonies are not in full bloom,

As if still in a dream.

A fringed gauze tent is needed,

To shade the sun-facing peonies in the shape of rainbows.

CUI YUNMING (*To the previous tune*):

Please cherish

The misty camel-brown peonies

And the bright-orange peonies,

Which do not have green tight buds.
The dusk rain and the morning clouds
Provide them with rich nourishment.
In leisure,
The Flower Goddess will doubt that the flowers are dyed,
As if they are taken from the fairyland.
Who's injected such vitality into the peonies
That they are entitled flower queens in the world?

LI YI (*To the previous tune*):
We admire flowers,
Some of which tilt like jade plates
While others cluster like velvet balls,
All enclosed in beautifully carved railings.
In their bright colours,
They are like floating clouds.
In addition,
Some are touched by people,
To bear finger prints on the petals;
Others are clipped off gently,
To be presented to lovers.

WEI XIAQING (*To the previous tune*):
Admiring flowers and chanting poems,
You wait for your beloved beauty
Amidst the sightseeing ladies,
Singers and dancers.
When they approach the flowers,
Their clothes become fragrant.
We're afraid
That the flowers will be snipped off as gifts,
But we're happy that they rank the first.
How can we get the beauties
To share with us the enjoyable moments?

CUI YUNMING:
Junyu, how can we not admire such beautiful flowers? But a fragrant plain white peony in the corner is neglected by people!
(*To the previous tune*)
A lovable flower it is
With a unique flavour
Of plain colour
And beautiful shape.
It comes from a fairyland,
With no one to share with it the spring breeze.

WEI XIAQING:

    Ironically,

    No one appreciates

    Its beauty and tenderness.

WEI XIAQING, CUI YUNMING:

Mr. Li,

    Although it suffers endless bitterness,

    It gives off faint fragrance.

WEI XIAQING:

Junyu, we've come to admire flowers today. What about collecting ready-made lines for a quatrain on the peonies?

LI YI:

Excellent!

CUI YUNMING:

Will you start first, Junyu?

LI YI:

    "To cherish the late spring sights,

CUI YUNMING:

    We rush here to appreciate the peonies.

WEI XIAQING:

Let me finish the quatrain,

    But there is a lonely flower

    Attracting no one to admire."

    (Li Yi sighs)

CUI YUNMING:

Why are you sighing? Let's enjoy ourselves over the corridor.

    (They walk)

    (Enter the Gallant Knight, with a short-haired Tartar servant holding a sword)

GALLANT KNIGHT (*Laughs broadly*):

What flourishing peony flowers!

    "The fingerprint peony in full bloom

    Radiates the most charm among all the flowers.

    Its red petals are spring's hair-bun;

    Its green leaves are spring's sleeves."

I'm a gallant knight with my name concealed. I hear the heartless Military Consultant Li is admiring flowers here. Where are they drinking now?

    *(To the tune of **Northern Xinshuiling**)*

    For their gathering in the spring breeze,

    I thought that they would hold a grand banquet.

    But the sour scholars are here

    Neither to inscribe names,

    Nor to compose poems,

But to have idle chats about this or that.

It's very easy for me to kill the heartless man. However,

> *"One should not take up the axe if he likes the trees;*
> *One should build shelters for delicate flowers."*

I'll first listen to the scholars' talk.

CUI YUNMING (*To the tune of* **Bubujiao**):

Miss Huo is really wretched.

LI YI (*In a low voice*):

How is she doing now?

WEI XIAQING:

She sheds tears of blood all day long.

As time goes by,

She becomes lonely and destitute,

Without getting any help from you.

LI YI (*In a low voice*):

I hear she's remarried.

CUI YUNMING:

She's determined to stick to you,

But how can you desert her like this?

(*Enter the guard*)

GUARD:

Why did you say "stick to you", Scholar Cui? It's none of your business. Here comes a man in a yellow robe.

GALLANT KNIGHT (*To the tune of* **Northern Zheguiling**):

He's so graceful and elegant;

No wonder he deserts his wife

And finds another sweetheart.

Frivolous as he is,

How can he grudge about his wife?

Hearing his injustice done to his devoted love,

I'm more sympathetic for his wife.

Hearing how he's remonstrated by his friends,

I myself cannot wait

To take immediate actions.

I'd better listen a little while longer.

LI YI (*To the tune of* **Jiang'ershui**):

The touch of leaves induces my sadness;

The sight of flowers evokes my tears.

WEI XIAQING:

> *"The spring sight is enticing*
> *With its luxuriant trees and flowers.*
> *But Miss Huo is immersed in grave sorrow*

As well as resentment and loneliness."

It's lamentable that the pretty young lady will die of lovesickness.

LI YI (*Weeps*):

You don't know the truth. I've tried to put General Lu off by giving equivocal answers. I haven't agreed to his marriage arrangement.

How can the love vow be discarded?

I won't betray my conscience to fawn on the power.

CUI YUNMING:

Junyu, how about paying a visit to Xiaoyu right now?

LI YI (*Sighs*):

How can I go there in haste?

WEI XIAQING:

She's waiting to bid you farewell. How can you be so cruel as to lay her aside?

WEI XIAQING, CUI YUNMING:

Please take a second thought,

For a true man should not act like you.

(*Enter the guard*)

GUARD:

It's none of your business, Scholar Cui. The man in a yellow robe comes again.

(*Enter the Gallant Knight*)

GALLANT KNIGHT:

Hi, everyone! I've been listening to you for a long time. Aren't you Mr. Li Yi? I'm a native of Shandong and I'm an in-law relative of His Majesty. Though I don't have any literary talent, I appreciate those who have. I've been eager to see you for your fame. Today I'm lucky to see your grace. My residence isn't far away from here. There are music, pretty women entertainers and noble horses for you to enjoy. Please come with me.

WEI XIAQING, CUI YUNMING:

Let's go with him to enjoy mellow wine and wonderful music to our hearts' content.

GALLANT KNIGHT:

I have several horses here. Let Mr. Li mount a noble horse and you two please follow us.

WEI XIAQING, CUI YUNMING:

All right.

"Here comes a noble horse,

Carrying him to his happiness."

(*Exeunt*)

GALLANT KNIGHT:

Boys, fetch me two noble horses.

(*Enter two servants, riding on neighing horses*)

GALLANT KNIGHT (*To the tune of **Northern Yan'erluo** with **Deshengling***):

I have noble horses

And handsome servant boys.

Horses,

The Purple Hairpins

I'll whip you on;

Boys,   .

I'll boss you around.

Horses,

Your hairs will be neatly combed;

Boys,

Your faces will be handsome.

As for me,

Why do I offer a noble horse

And handsome servants

As well as my belongings?

At my home,

I have considerable wealth;

If you refuse to accept it,

I'll wield my whip in wrath,

I'll wield my whip in wrath.

GUARD (*Annoyed*):

Another interfering man! Don't you know General Lu's powerful and influential? Military Consultant Li is going to be the general's son-in-law. Where are you taking him? I'll let you taste my cudgel!

(*To the tune of* **Jiaojiaoling**)

I brandish the cudgel,

On which there's the character of Lu,

To strike the wretched man.

GALLANT KNIGHT (*Laughs*):

What then?

GUARD:

Pretending to be blind to the character,

You'll meet your death if you're obstinate!

As for the Military Consultant,

He'll be the son-in-law of a powerful family.

How contented he'll be!

Your wealth is to be left for your own consumption!

GALLANT KNIGHT (*To the tune of* **Northern Shoujiangnan**):

Wow!

You guard the scholar against anyone.

So General Lu must be a sissy!

I'd rather court with his daughter

Than invite him to be my guest.

(*Draws out the sword*)

Let's see whose sword prevails at last;

You may come on if you don't fear death.

GUARD (*Puts down the cudgel in fear*):

I'm just kidding with you! Why are you drawing your sword? Aren't we responsible for killing? We'll go with you to your residence and drink to the fill!

GALLANT KNIGHT:

Help Mr. Li onto the horse, boys.

    (*Rides side by side with Li Yi*)

LI YI:

It seems to be the Shengyefang Lane.

    (*Rides on*)

    (*Asks*)

Is it the Creek Head ahead?

    (*Rides on*)

Is it Huo's residence further on?

GALLANT KNIGHT:

Why do you ask such questions?

LI YI (*To himself*):

How is it that I know this place?

    (*To the tune of **Yuanlinhao***)

    The horse and the servant look so familiar.

SERVANT:

You have a good memory.

LI YI:

    I used to live in the neighborhood.

May I ask if there's another way leading to your residence?

GALLANT KNIGHT:

We must go this way.

LI YI:

    He takes a winding course to this place;

    What's his intention to pass her residence?

    What's his intention to pass her residence?

GALLANT KNIGHT:

It doesn't matter. There are many places that look similar.

    (*To the tune of **Northern Gumeijiu** with **Taipingling***)

    You sit tight on the horse amidst flowers,

    On the horse amidst flowers,

    And bring with you a servant as a messenger of love.

    At this time who won't enjoy himself with his sweetheart?

    But who is this lonely pretty lady?

    Whose residence is so similar?

    I know the whole story

    Though we meet by chance.

    How can we not be moved by your love affair?

Alas!

> You may as well be indulged in tender affection
>
> Rather than pretend not to care about all this.

LI YI:

As it's late, I must be off now. I'll keep your company another day.

> (*Intends to turn round the horse*)

GALLANT KNIGHT (*Pulls Li Yi by the sleeve*):

My residence is close at hand. How can you leave like this?

> (*To the tune of* **Coda**)
>
> What's so embarrassing to you?
>
> Let's just go forward,
>
> For I'm aware of your feelings now.
>
> (*Exeunt*)

Scene Fifty-Two
Family Reunion

> (*Enter Huansha*)

HUANSHA (*To the tune of* **Yuandongfeng**):

> Now that the spring will soon be past,
>
> Our young lady is still seriously sick.
>
> The maidservant has exerted great efforts
>
> And feels much distressed.
>
> Divination is groundless,
>
> Special prescriptions are effectless,
>
> And prayers to God go useless.

I'm Huansha. I've been waiting on our young lady, who has been ill for several years. Now spring will soon be past. All the ladies are coming out to enjoy spring sights; only we stay at home in distress. I'm afraid she'll not hold out for long. Let me help her outdoors for some relaxation.

> (*Calls Huo Xiaoyu*)
>
> (*Enter Huo Xiaoyu in sickness*)

HUO XIAOYU (*To the previous tune*):

> I'm dejected and apathetic from lovesickness,
>
> With the flower petals falling in strong winds.
>
> It's difficult to see my man again,
>
> Which brings me great pains.
>
> I can't enjoy a sweet dream for long;
>
> My sense and soul seem to be gone;

Even when supported, I walk in faltering steps.

Huansha, my illness can't be cured! Why do you help me out of bed?

HUANSHA:

"The spring sight wasn't bright in recent years,

But this year the peony flowers come into full bloom."

Young mistress, please have some relaxation by enjoying the beautiful scenery.

HUO XIAOYU:

Huansha,

"One bird is lonely while many others are singing in happiness;

One tree is sick while many others are growing in lushness."

How on earth am I to relax myself?

(*To the tune of **Shanpoyang***)

My ill luck brings me infinite loneliness

And throws me into disturbance and agitation.

I'm now ill and weak

With no grace or elegance.

Oh! Huansha,

Dazed from illness,

I wonder how soon the spring will pass.

I can hardly sleep well,

At the sight of the withering flowers

And the extinguishing incense.

With my mind distressed

By my missing man,

I am overwhelmed,

Feeling weak and dizzy as a cloud.

HUANSHA (*To the previous tune*):

She is thin and languid,

Her eyes no longer bright.

She has only faint breath,

Unable to vent her distress.

She's entirely changed,

Changed beyond reorganization

Even to the man who painted her portrait.

Sometimes she is clear-minded;

Sometimes she is muddle-headed.

God of Flowers,

You've sent withering flowers to the late spring;

God of Spring,

You'll redeem the lady's health and youth.

(*Huo Xiaoyu faints*)

(*Enter Bao Siniang*)

BAO SINIANG (*To the tune of* **Wanxiandeng**):

> The young lady's lingering illness
>
> Discolours the courtyard scattered with fallen flowers.

I'm Bao Siniang. I wonder how the sick lady is now. Alas, she's again sleeping here. Where's Her Ladyship?

(*Enter Lady Zheng*)

LADY ZHENG:

> "*A young lady cannot always keep her youth and beauty;*
>
> *The Lady in the Moon fears that the moon is not her permanent residence.*"

Siniang, what do you think of my daughter's illness?

HUO XIAOYU (*Awakes*):

How terrible it is, Mom! When did Siniang come here?

> (*To the tune of* **Shantaohong**)
>
> Clouds are slowly drifting apart;
>
> Man and wife can hardly get together.
>
> I had a happy marriage in the previous incarnation,
>
> So I pay for it with my life in the present existence.
>
> When my thoughts wander like the rosy clouds in the wind,
>
> You cremate me with the smoke melting into the evening mist.
>
> I am dying,
>
> But my heart and soul remain
>
> To speak to him in his dream.

LADY ZHENG, BAO SINIANG, HUANSHA (*Weep*):

> You shed tears before flowers,
>
> As a virtuous yet pitiful lady
>
> Who will miss the last farewell with her man.

LADY ZHENG:

What else do you want to say, my daughter?

HUO XIAOYU:

What do I want to say? Please pass my word to my man.

> (*To the previous tune*)
>
> He should come to see my mother,
>
> Which he should do as the son-in-law.

Huansha, if Qiuhong comes back, you two should take care of my mother. Now I bow to pay you respect.

> (*Stumbles*)
>
> You'll be her direct descendant
>
> And look after her from now on.

Bao Siniang, please come to see my mother once in a while. You were the matchmaker for Li and me. If one day you see him,

> Tell him to treat kindly his new wife
>
> And not to let their happiness be overshadowed by me.

If he comes to my grave for past love's sake,

Just ask him to pour a bowl of cold water as a memorial mark.

Even if I die,

I'll die in loneliness without my lover by my side.

LADY ZHENG, BAO SINIANG, HUANSHA:

You shed tears before flowers,

As a virtuous yet pitiful lady

Who will miss the last farewell with her man.

(*They turn aside*)

LADY ZHENG:

What shall we do without Li's presence?

BAO SINIANG:

Look, she's now a mere sack of bones, and her face is deathly yellow. Is it an omen?

HUANSHA:

She faints.

(*Massages Huo Xiaoyu*)

LADY ZHENG:

How heartless Li is!

BAO SINIANG:

How unfortunate Xiaoyu is!

HUO XIAOYU (*Awakes*):

Oh, Mom! Now I feel better. Li is coming.

LADY ZHENG:

Why do you say so, my daughter?

HUO XIAOYU:

Let me get up. Mom, please wash and dress me.

LADY ZHENG:

My daughter, you're in confusion from chronic illness. Now take a rest!

HUO XIAOYU:

You don't believe me, Mom. Please help me up, Siniang.

(*To the tune of* **Coda**)

I may as well make up and dress up,

Because I hear the sounds of hooves.

Huansha,

They are approaching our house.

(*Exeunt all*)

(*The Gallant Knight rides side by side with Li Yi, who is abashed and reluctant to ride on*)

(*Enter Li Yi on horse, pushed by the Gallant Knight's servants*)

GALLANT KNIGHT (*To the tune of* **Bushilu**):

The road winds past the bridge

And reaches the Shengyefang Lane.

The flowers are like icy graupels,

Or withered and neglected peach blossoms by the Wuling River.

The dusk falls;

How can you return in such high spirits?

I won't allow your horse to turn back like this.

LI YI (*Covers his face*):

I'm ashamed!

Feeling ashamed, my eyes

Have been eager to see my home,

But I'm afraid it's no longer mine now,

But I'm afraid it's no longer mine now.

GALLANT KNIGHT (*To the previous tune*):

For the destruction of your happy life,

I hold my sword in wrath.

Now you finally come out

From Lu's gorgeous residence.

Scholar Li, I'm not inviting you to my house but rather to your own house.

How dilapidated it is!

Have a good look on my horse

At a declining scene of wild grass and flowers!

LI YI:

I'm afraid General Lu will take cruel actions to harm us.

GALLANT KNIGHT:

Why do you fear him so much?

Li Yi:

You don't know that when I was a Military Consultant in the Yumen Garrison, I wrote a poem to thank Governor Liu for his kindness, which contained the line "*I'll keep my promotion out of mind.*" General Lu often threatens that he would report it to His Majesty that I hated to look in the direction of the court. This is the first thing I fear. Besides, General Lu says that if I return to the Huos, he will get rid of Xiaoyu first. This is the second thing I fear. What's more, he has armed military men to follow me all day and they may hurt my friends. This is the third thing I fear. Therefore, I've been hesitating all the time. Otherwise, how can I be a heartless man? And I have no face to see my wife today!

GALLANT KNIGHT:

You become man and wife by your first marriage. An apology to her is enough. As to General Lu, I know how to deal with him. You needn't worry about that.

You have nothing to worry about;

Just stop your horse and bid your servant

To knock at the door hard,

To knock at the door hard.

(*The servant knocks at the door*)

(*Enter Lady Zheng and Huansha*)

LADY ZHENG, HUANSHA (*To the previous tune*):

Swallows have flown away;

Only a few of them stay.

Who's come for a visit

And pounds on the door so hard?

SERVANT:

The dilapidated house

Might become gorgeous again

With a bliss that is coming.

LADY ZHENG, HUANSHA:

It's noisy outside;

The guests might have arrived for the banquet.

Let's have a peep,

Let's have a peep.

(*Enter Li Yi on horse, pushed by the Gallant Knight and his servants*)

GALLANT KNIGHT (*Points at Li Yi*):

Do you know him?

LADY ZHENG (*Astonished, weeps*):

Where are you from, heartless man?

GALLANT KNIGHT:

When he gets down the horse, leave him to Xiaoyu!

LADY ZHENG:

My daughter has been ridden in bed for a long time. She needs help all the time.

HUO XIAOYU (*From within*):

I get up now, Mom.

(*Enter Huo Xiaoyu, supported by Bao Siniang*)

HUO XIAOYU (To the *tune of* **Kuxiangsi**):

My heart flies out

To the voice outside.

(*Greets the guests*)

GALLANT KNIGHT:

So Bao Siniang is here. Xiaoyu, do you know this scholar?

LI YI (*Weeps*):

My wife, you are so sick!

(*Huo Xiaoyu looks at him sideways, covers her face with her hands and utters a long sigh*)

GALLANT KNIGHT:

How pitiable she is!

(*To the tune of* **Bushilu**)

She leans sick against the railings

Like falling flowers in the strong, cold wind.

She looks sideways

With eyes half shut.

Xiaoyu, now I hand the heartless man over to you. You're so sick.

You've suffered misfortunes and pains.

Mr. Li, Mr. Dongfang Shuo says that wine erases worries. I've paid for a banquet to be held here. As for the wine,

> It cures worries and cares;
>
> It brings a prescription
>
> (*Points at Li Yi*)
>
> Of getting back.

Now I'm leaving.

LI YI:

I'll propose a toast to you in thanks for all your help. Why are you leaving in such a hurry?

GALLANT KNIGHT:

But I'm not here to drink with you.

LI YI:

Please tell us your name. I'll write down your name to remember you.

GALLANT KNIGHT (*Laughs*):

It's not necessary!

> I chanced
>
> To hear about your trouble in marriage.
>
> Who's got entangled?
>
> Who's got entangled?
>
> (*Raises his hand*)

Bye-bye!

GALLANT KNIGHT, SERVANTS:

> *"We'll ride back amidst flowers,*
>
> *Leaving the couple to themselves in tears."*
>
> (*Exeunt*)

LI YI:

What the Gallant Knight said is reasonable. Now let me propose a toast to my wife.

> (*Hands the wine cup to Huo Xiaoyu*)

HUO XIAOYU (*Sighs*):

> *"I'm a woman*
>
> *Suffering an unfortunate fate.*
>
> *You are my man*
>
> *With a cruel heart.*
>
> *I'll die in bitterness*
>
> *With my youth and beauty wasted.*
>
> *I'll leave my loving mother*
>
> *Without my filial piety.*
>
> *I'll leave behind the enjoyment*
>
> *Of beautiful clothes and music.*
>
> *I'll die in great grievance,*
>
> *All caused by your heartlessness."*

Mr. Li, we'll part forever today!

(*Holds Li Yi's arm with her left hand, drops the wine cup onto the ground, utters several sighs and faints out*)

LADY ZHENG (*Tries to help up Huo Xiaoyu, who falls into Li Yi's arms*):

(*Weeps*)

Wake her up, Li Yi!

LI YI (*To the tune of* **Erlangshen**):

> In all these years,
>
> I've disappointed my wife.
>
> What have I got from my official career?
>
> My lack of concerns for you is like shears
>
> That cut short your tender life.

My wife,

> No one in the world is your peer.
>
> (*Tries to help Huo Xiaoyu up but fails*)
>
> How can I lift a rock of deep lovesickness!

LI YI, LADY ZHENG, BAO SINIANG, HUANSHA:

> We wonder
>
> How you can be willing to leave us like this?

HUO XIAOYU (*Awakes*):

> (*To the previous tune*)
>
> I've lost consciousness;
>
> Where am I now?
>
> Am I drunk or dreaming,
>
> To have my man by my side?

Mom,

> I feel like the flying willow catkins in wind.
>
> Who has lifted me up into the air?

LI YI:

I am supporting you.

HUO XIAOYU:

Why are you supporting me?

> Let's be separated till my death,
>
> And I'll complain about you in the netherworld.

LI YI, LADY ZHENG, BAO SINIANG, HUANSHA:

> We wonder
>
> How you can be willing to leave us like this?

HUO XIAOYU:

I don't want to recall your words when you left for the frontier!

LI YI (*To the tune of* **Zhuanlinying**):

> It's hard to explain my experience in a few words,
>
> But the paper screen well represents my lovesickness.

And I'm grateful for your poem written by candlelight

When I was transferred to the Mengmen Garrison.

HUO XIAOYU:

So you received the poem?

LI YI:

Yes.

You hinted at my remarriage with Lu's daughter,

But it is mere rumour.

HUO XIAOYU:

Didn't Wei Xiaqing act as the matchmaker and then Cui Yunming tell me the truth? Is this the case, or is it mere rumour?

HUO XIAOYU, LI YI:

For a false and pretended love,

Tears have been soaking the dress.

HUO XIAOYU (*To the previous tune*):

Miss Lu is pretty;

How long will you keep her waiting?

She can still enjoy happiness,

But I have few days left.

I would rather die

Than put you in a plight.

LI YI:

We'll share the same grave when we die.

HUO XIAOYU:

Who'll believe you?

HUO XIAOYU, LI YI:

For a false and pretended love,

Tears have been soaking the dress.

HUO XIAOYU:

Now you know I sold the hairpins out of poverty. Aren't the hairpins worthy of her attention?

LI YI:

Nonsense!

(*To the tune of* **Zhuomuli**)

The sight of the hairpins off your hair

Shoots daggers to my heart.

HUO XIAOYU:

How do they look on the new wife's hair?

LI YI:

How can I give her your hairpins

To enhance her prettiness?

HUO XIAOYU:

She must have been annoyed and so given the hairpins to her maidservant.

LI YI:

Nonsense! The person who sold your hairpins spoke "good" about you.

> She said you deserted our love and sold the hairpins,
>
> But I didn't believe it and hid the hairpins in my sleeves.

HUO XIAOYU:

Why did you put them in your sleeves?

HUO XIAOYU, LI YI:

> I will cherish
>
> The sight of your beautiful hair
>
> Adorned by the hairpins.

LI YI:

When you get better, I want to see a person.

> (*Looks around*)

HUO XIAOYU:

Who are you looking for?

LI YI:

When Bao Sanniang came to sell your hairpins, she said you had a new lover.

HUO XIAOYU (*Annoyed*):

How shameful it is to say so! Where is the so-called Bao Sanniang? It is Hou Jingxian who sold the hairpins for me. What nonsense it is to speak of a new lover! It's you who want to shift the blame on me!

> (*To the previous tune*)
>
> You don't have respect for your wife
>
> And try to play dirty tricks on her.
>
> Now what outcome have you seen?

LI YI:

You're annoyed again!

HUO XIAOYU:

> I'd rather die now than be wronged.

You said I deserted our love. Now give me back the hairpins.

LI YI:

That's easy.

HUO XIAOYU:

Give me back the hairpins and let's clear up the matter.

> She must have grown bored of the hairpins,
>
> So she throws them away for a new hairstyle.

Now give me back the hairpins!

HUO XIAOYU, LI YI:

> I will cherish
>
> The sight of your beautiful hair
>
> Adorned by the hairpins.

LADY ZHENG:

Let's ask Qiuhong what on earth had happened.

(*Enter Qiuhong*)

QIUHONG:

It's true that he did not agree to marry Miss Lu.

(*To the tune of* **Tiying'er**)

For that General Lu,

It's funny of him to put my master in house detainment,

But my master,

My master would not agree to his marriage arrangement.

HUANSHA:

Then why didn't he come back?

QIUHONG:

My master,

He resents the forced marriage arrangement,

But has to fear General Lu's threat.

He is afraid that Lu will find faults with you.

For the final reunion with you,

He had to live under house arrest.

QIUHONG, HUANSHA:

Hearing why you sold the hairpins,

He put them away

In his sleeves.

BAO SINIANG:

Military Consultant Li, you've forgotten all about how I made the match for you.

QIUHONG:

Your family members do matchmaking as well as business. The person who sold the hairpins is your elder sister.

BAO SINIANG:

I have many sisters.

QIUHONG:

So it was General Lu's trick!

LADY ZHENG (*To the previous tune*):

He tried to break your love tree with strong wind;

Fortunately you are reunited as man and wife.

BAO SINIANG:

The Gallant Knight in the yellow robe comes to my mind.

We womenfolk could do nothing but look on,

While the Gallant Knight offered immediate help.

Miss Huo,

How accurate your dream was about the man in yellow,

Who indicated that the matter would be well solved.

QIUHONG, HUANSHA:

Hearing why you sold the hairpins,

He put them away

In his sleeves.

HUO XIAOYU:

All right then, but have you brought the hairpins with you?

(*Li Yi takes out the hairpins from his sleeves*)

HUO XIAOYU:

So they are really in your sleeves.

(*Holds the hairpins in joy*)

(*To the tune of* **Yuying'er**)

The smooth jade hairpins

Are still tied with silk threads.

Inlaid in them are several pearls,

Shining with vernal green.

They are about to take flight from the hair,

Or to sleep on the dressing table.

But how can I put them on in my sickness?

HUO XIAOYU, LI YI:

How strange it is

That the hairpins we see

Look the same as we did at the Lantern Festival!

LADY ZHENG:

Huansha, bring the jewelry box, mirror and rouge, and put the hairpins on Xiaoyu's hair.

LI YI (*Supports Huo Xiaoyu and laughs*):

You look more beautiful and delicate in frailty.

(*Huo Xiaoyu puts on the hairpins with trembling hands*)

LI YI:

It's indeed,

(*In the pattern of* **Huanxisha**)

"*She makes up and dresses up;*

LADY ZHENG:

She combs her beautiful hair;

BAO SINIANG:

She holds the hairpins beside her man.

HUO XIAOYU:

Mr. Li,

Although I've recovered from illness,

I'm still too weak in health.

HUO XIAOYU, LI YI:

Our reunion gives us a second life."

LI YI (*To the previous tune*):

We are blessed with happiness

From the reunion through the hairpins.

The pair of swallows on them seem to fly

Yet reluctant to leave the flowers.

With the hairpins stuck in your hair

That sways slightly in breeze,

The chirping swallows can't tell our whole story.

LI YI, HUO XIAOYU:

How strange it is

That the hairpins we see

Look the same as we did at the Lantern Festival!

LADY ZHENG:

All of us should be grateful to the Gallant Knight.

HUO XIAOYU:

I seem to have seen him on the Lantern Festival.

(*To the tune of* **Coda**)

My man,

The same Gallant Knight appeared in my dream,

But it's your turn to take care of your sick wife.

My man, don't leave again!

Burn another joss stick to make a vow of love.

I've gained a second life and met my man,

With a mixed feeling of gratitude and resentment.

Let's light the candle all through the night,

As I'm still afraid that we're meeting in a dream.

Scene Fifty-Three
His Majesty's Decree Is Declared

(*Enter Cui Yunming and Wei Xiaqing*)

CUI YUNMING, WEI XIAQING (*To the tune of* **Yiduojiao**):

After a few toasts,

We rush to admire flowers,

Indulged in beautiful music and sights.

For propitious signs from candlewicks last night,

We come to congratulate,

We come to congratulate,

On the conferment of honorable titles by His Majesty.

"There is too much injustice in this world,

But too few people who stand out to offer help."

We've received a lot of money from Huo Xiaoyu for helping to find her man. Not until the Gallant Knight in the yellow robe comes to redeem their broken marriage does their trouble come to an end. Now all the people celebrate the happy ending brought about by the Gallant Knight, which is not at all accidental.

WEI XIAQING:

But I'm afraid that General Lu won't give up so easily. We'll all come to trouble if he wishes. What can we do to deal with him?

CUI YUNMING:

The Gallant Knight has secret connections with the imperial family, although he conceals his name. Recently His Majesty is not satisfied with General Lu for his monopoly of power. And someone reported Lu's evil deeds to His Majesty, which makes His Majesty angrier. Now General Lu has no mind to plan his daughter's marriage. Besides, one of the Gallant Knight's subordinates had the story of Xiaoyu's virtue and the forced marriage arrangement by General Lu reported to His Majesty, who dispatched Governor Liu to confer Xiaoyu a title of honour. So you can just set your mind at ease.

WEI XIAQING:

I see. What a satisfactory result! Let's go to report the news and offer our congratulations!

(*Enter Li Yi, Huo Xiaoyu and Lady Zheng*)

LI YI, HUO XIAOYU, LADY ZHENG (*To the tune of **Changmingnü***):

> In the spring breeze,
>
> We have a reunion after a long separation.
>
> (*Greet Cui Yunming and Wei Xiaqing*)

Here are Mr. Cui and Mr. Wei. Welcome to our house, old friends!

CUI YUNMING (*Laughs*):

Xiaoyu, your money is not all squandered. Now please get prepared to welcome Governor Liu, who will come with His Majesty's decree.

(*Enter Liu Gongji with His Majesty's decree*)

LIU GONGJI:

> "*His Majesty gives entitlement and promotion,*
>
> *And blesses the reunion between man and wife.*"

Now you kowtow and accept His Majesty's decree. The affection between man and wife is not to be neglected; the sense of justice and chivalry are to be commended. This has always been emphasized throughout the history. With both military and literary talents, Military Consultant Li Yi does not yield to a forced remarriage arrangement in pursuit of power. He is a faithful husband. Now he is entitled Jixiandian Scholar and Luantai Assistant Minister of the Six Boards. With extraordinary wisdom, Huo Xiaoyu vows to be faithful to love until the dying day, and got destitute and ill for love. Now she is entitled Lady of Taiyuan Prefecture. Lady Zheng helped her husband to achieve meritorious deeds and brought up an excellent daughter. She is benevolent and good at disciplining child; she is old yet virtuous. Now she is entitled Lady of Xingyang Prefecture. General Lu takes advantage of his power to force Li to yield to his marriage arrangement. He almost caused people involved to die and broke a happy family. Now he is deprived of General's post to

make up for Huo Xiaoyu's grievances. The Gallant Knight in yellow offers help to the young lady and upholds the moral standard and virtues. Now he is entitled The Nameless Prefect. Whoever supports the imperial creeds will be highly commended. That's all for the decree. Now you kowtow and give thanks to His Majesty.

(*Li Yi, Huo Xiaoyu and Lady Zheng kowtow and extend their thanks*)

LIU GONGJI:

Junyu, we haven't seen each other for a long time. Will you tell me in detail the story of the purple jade hairpins?

LI YI (*To the tune of* **Cuipai**):

> In the street on the Lantern Festival night,
> We met for the first time,
> And immediately fell in love.
> And immediately fell in love.
> Fortunately I picked up her lost hairpins
> In the pale moonlight by the plum flowers,
> And took it as a pledge
> That contributed to our marriage.

LI YI, LIU GONGJI:

> By His Majesty's decree
> Man and wife are happily reunited.

HUO XIAOYU (*To the previous tune*):

> Well dressed on the sunny spring day,
> I visited the imperial garden in splendour.
> My man returned with honour and wealth,
> My man returned with honour and wealth,
> But he used to stay in another lady's residence
> And forget all about me.
> He nearly married another woman,
> But fortunately he has now returned.

LI YI, LIU GONGJI:

> By His Majesty's decree
> Man and wife are happily reunited.

LADY ZHENG (*To the previous tune*):

> We thought you had found new love,
> As you did not return for several years.
> See how declined we are,
> See how declined we are.
> And to know your whereabouts,
> We used up all our resources.
> Words failed our resentment and pains
> When we had to sell the hairpins.

LI YI, LIU GONGJI:

> By His Majesty's decree
>
> Man and wife are happily reunited.

BAO SINIANG (*To the previous tune*):

> It's your predestined fate
>
> To get the hairpins back.
>
> Now put them onto your hair,
>
> Now put them onto your hair,
>
> As if you were the new wife
>
> And his new love.
>
> I'll burn the incense
>
> To bless your new life.

LI YI, LIU GONGJI:

> By His Majesty's decree
>
> Man and wife are happily reunited.

WEI XIAQING:

This should be attributed to the Gallant Knight.

CUI YUNMING (*To the previous tune*):

> He offered help at once
>
> When he heard of the injustice.

WEI XIAQING:

> Now the couple stay together,
>
> Now the couple stay together.
>
> You renew your happy life
>
> Under the candlelight
>
> And stick to the love vow
>
> Made before the flowers.

LI YI, LIU GONGJI:

> By His Majesty's decree
>
> Man and wife are happily reunited.

ALL (*To the tune of* **Yicuozhao**):

> Parting and reunion
>
> Are predestined fate.
>
> He has talent
>
> But not a cruel heart.
>
> We should always bear in mind
>
> The scenes by the flowers and lanterns,
>
> The pair of swallows on the hairpins,
>
> The shoes in dream and the banquet.
>
> A love-filled world and predestined marriages
>
> Are to be yearned for.
>
> All lovers in the world
>
> Are to be happy couples.

*(To the tune of **Coda**)*
Any scholar is able to compose poems,
But difficult to find an appreciative wife.
The story is spread because of the anonymous Gallant Knight.
If the hairpin love cannot withstand setbacks,
The Gallant Knight in yellow will be out of the way.
As resentments appear every year,
So love sentiments arise every day.
The millets are cooked in the Handan dream,
While ants are personified in the Nanke dream.
The poetic justice at the end of the play
Makes the audience happy and gay.

牡丹亭
The Peony Pavilion

汪榕培 译

Translated by Wang Rongpei

Table of Contents

414

Scene One
Prelude

(*Enter Announcer*)

ANNOUNCER (*To the tune of **Dielianhua***):

> All the men prefer remaining free;
> Yet howe'er they try,
> They are as worried as can be.
> Among the sentimental tales I write,
> Love is as mysterious as the sea.
> I write the tale from morning till night.
> With candles burning bright,
> Enlightening me in the brightest ray.
> When a beauty falls in love with a man,
> The Peony Pavilion sees her ardent way.
> "*Du Bao, the magistrate,*
> *Has a daughter by the name of Liniang,*
> *Who strolls on a sunny springtime date.*
> *When she dreams of a scholar breaking willows,*
> *She's thrown into a grievous state.*
> *She draws a self-portrait*
> *And pines away lamenting o'er her fate.*
> *When three years have passed by,*
> *Liu Mengmei comes along*
> *To meet her in the garden once again.*
> *Du Liniang gains her second life.*
> *When Liu is about to seek office in Lin'an,*
> *There arrives a mob of rebellious men.*
> *As Du Bao is besieged inside the town,*
> *His daughter is in a panic then.*
> *Liu Mengmei goes to seek information,*
> *But his good will is beyond Du's ken.*
> *When his love affair is in great trouble,*
> *News comes that Liu is allotted office*
> *And Liu at last fulfills his yen.*"
> *Du Liniang draws a portrait true to life;*
> *Chen Zuiliang brings about the peace once more;*
> *Liu Mengmei meets his resurrected wife;*
> *Du Bao gives tortures to his son-in-law.*

Scene Two
A Scholar's Ambition

(*Enter Liu Mengmei*)

LIU MENGMEI (*To the tune of **Zhenzhulian***):

> Among the houses of distinction in Hedong,
>
> The most renowned has been the house of Liu.
>
> In astrologic terms,
>
> The fortune star is due.
>
> As their descendants are poor scholars,
>
> They do not have a brilliant sight in view.
>
> The saying goes that studies bring the wealth,
>
> But where is pretty lady
>
> And where is gold?
>
> Although wretched poverty may discourage me,
>
> I am as honest as of old.
>
> *"I've studied hard but have made no success,*
>
> *A southern scholar in the deepest stress.*
>
> *Howe'er, endowed with favours from above,*
>
> *Profoundest learning is what I possess.*
>
> *Because I study hard till late at night,*
>
> *I can write essays with far-reaching sight.*
>
> *When I win the laurel in the future days,*
>
> *I'll prove that I am really smart and bright."*

My name is Liu Mengmei, also called Chunqing. A descendant of Liu Zongyuan, poet and Prefect of Liuzhou in the Tang Dynasty, I have lived with my family in Lingnan. My father was a minister without portmanteau and my mother was conferred the title of County Lady.

(*With a sigh*)

As an orphan since my early childhood, I have scraped a bare living. Now that I have grown up to be over twenty, I am intelligent enough to pass the county examination. Unfortunately, as I haven't got the right opportunity to hold an office, I'm still living in cold and hunger. My ancestor Prefect Liu had a servant Hunchback Guo, a gardener for his official residence in Liuzhou. This man has a hunchback descendant who works as a gardener here in Guangzhou and helps me with my daily life. However, this is not the right way for a worthy man to live through his life. Day by day I am in a melancholy mood. It happens that I had a strange dream half a month ago. I dreamed of a belle standing under a plum tree in a garden. She was of medium height and looked at me in a coy manner. She said, "Sir, sir, you are destined to meet me as your love and then start your career." That is why I change my name to Mengmei which literally means "dreaming of the plums" and also call myself Chunqing which literally means "spring lord". Truly,

"Long dream or short, it is anyway a dream;
Year in year out, time and tide moves like a stream."
(*To the tune of **Jiuhuichang***)
　　Although I've changed my name offhand,
　　Does the beauty know in her dreamland?
　　Although I long to wed and get a post,
　　I Liu Mengmei will never make a boast.
　　For fear that beauty fades away too soon,
　　I seem to sit on pins and needles
　　And cry for the moon.
　　I use no fireflies when I read and learn;
　　Beyond the east wall stays the girl I yearn.
　　The lucky star will shine on me someday
　　And I'll no longer fidget in dismay.
　　By then I'll ride across the streets,
　　Accept the hearty greetings
　　And pick from beauties on their seats.

Let me forget about it. I have a friend by the name of Han Zicai. As a descendant of Han Yu, he stops over at the Terrace of Prince Zhao Tuo. He is tending to his ancestral shrines, but he is an eloquent speaker. I'd like to pay a visit to his place.

When plums and willows grow before the gate,
I see the king but doubts arise when dreams abate.
My heart contains a hundred blooms in buds,
But as to find a branch, I have to wait.

Scene Three
Admonishing His Daughter

(*Enter Du Bao*)

DU BAO (*To the tune of **Mantingfang***):
　　A well-known scholar from Sichuan
　　And now the prefect of Nan'an,
　　In and out of office, I've done what I can.
　　In robes and golden belt I'm dressed,
　　Which shows my ranking higher than the rest.
　　As my hair is turning grey degree by degree,
　　I'd like to retire and have time free,
　　But I'm afraid the emperor will not agree
　　And I still have to wait and see.

"All my life an honoured official in Nan'an,

I do much better than the ordinary man.

I serve my term of office with clean hands;

When I retire, I'll stay in my native lands."

I am Du Bao, Prefect of Nan'an, also called Zichong and descended from Du Fu of the Tang Dynasty. I have lived with my family in Sichuan and now I am past fifty. I passed the imperial examination when I was twenty and became a prefect three years afterwards. I have been renowned for my clean government. My wife is Lady Zhen, a descendent of Empress Zhen of the Wei Dynasty. Her family has been living near Mount Emei and has enjoyed a good reputation for generations. My wife has given birth to a daughter only, a gifted and pretty girl by the name of Liniang. I have not made any arrangements for her marriage yet. It is universally acknowledged that a virtuous girl should be well educated. As I have some time free from my office, I'll call my wife and discuss it with her. As the saying goes,

"Well learned, Cai Yong had a daughter of good fame;

A poor official, Deng You lost his son but earned his name."

(*Enter Lady Zhen*)

LADY ZHEN (*To the tune of* **Raochiyou**):

A descendent from Princess Zhen

And a resident in Sichuan,

I've been conferred the title Lady of Nan'an.

(*Greets her husband*)

DU BAO:

"Without much worth, I serve the court although I'm aged;

LADY ZHEN:

Without much work, I've got a title from the king.

DU BAO:

How does Liniang pass her time in spring?

LADY ZHEN:

In needlework alone is she engaged."

DU BAO:

Our daughter is good at needlework. In the past and at present, virtuous girls should be well educated. When she marries a scholar, she can share a talk with him. What do you think about it?

LADY ZHEN:

I agree with you.

(*Enter Du Liniang, followed by her servant maid Chunxiang carrying a tray of wine vessels*)

DU LINIANG (*To the previous tune*):

The oriole is fond to sing

At such a lovely time of spring.

How can I e'er requite

My parents for their caressing light?

(*Greets her parents*)

Bliss on you, Dad and Mom.

DU BAO:

Why do you tell your maid to bring the wine here, child?

DU LINIANG (*Kneels*):

In such a fine spring day, you are taking a rest in the rear hall. I'd like to offer you three cups of wine with my best wishes to you in the spring.

DU BAO (*With a smile*):

Thank you very much.

DU LINIANG (*To the tune of* **Yushantui**):

> With bliss on you, my dad and mom,
>
> That is where all my joy comes from.
>
> With everlasting spring air in the hall,
>
> You drink the wine and bring joy to all.
>
> Oh father dear, oh mother dear!
>
> I wish you'd have a son this year
>
> To stay with you and bring you cheer.

DU BAO, LADY ZHEN:

> Fill high the cups with vernal wine
>
> For our dear son and daughter fine!

DU BAO:

Fill in a cup for your mistress, Chunxiang.

> (*To the previous tune*)
>
> My ancestor Du Fu wandered all his life
>
> And felt ashamed to face his son and wife.
>
> (*Weeps*)
>
> My lady, I am more pitiable than my ancestor Du Fu.
>
> He could yet write about his lovely son
>
> While I have my daughter as my only fun.

LADY ZHEN:

Don't get worried, my lord! If we find a good son-in-law, he will be as good as a son.

DU BAO (*Smiles*):

Yes, indeed!

LADY ZHEN:

> A daughter brings the same bliss as a son.
>
> There is no need to make the grudge
>
> When only half of your life-course is run.

DU BAO, LADY ZHEN:

> Fill high the cups with vernal wine
>
> For our dear son and daughter fine!

DU BAO:

Take the wine vessels away, my child!

> (*Exit Du Liniang*)

DU BAO:

Chunxiang, tell me what your young mistress does by the day in her bower.

CHUNXIANG:

She does embroidery in her bower.

DU BAO:

How much embroidery does she do?

CHUNXIANG:

She does her embroidery with a nap.

DU BAO:

What do you mean by "nap"?

CHUNXIANG:

A brief sleep.

DU BAO:

So, so! Madam, you just said that she was engaged in needlework alone, and you went as far as to allow her to take naps! How are you teaching your daughter! Call the girl back!

(Enter Du Liniang)

DU LINIANG:

What can I do for you, Dad?

DU BAO:

Just now I asked Chunxiang about you. How can you be taking naps during the day? After you've finished your embroidery, you have plenty of books to read on the shelves. When some day you are married, you will be learned and know the rites. In this way, your dad and mom will feel honoured. Your mom has not done her duty to teach you.

(To the tune of **Yubaodu**)

Although I always live a meagre life,

I've ne'er neglected learning in my strife.

In my home as my daughter you have grown,

But very soon you'll stand upon your own.

As I'm too busy to teach you every day,

You should follow your mom in every way.

LADY ZHEN (To the previous tune):

Liniang, although you're not a boy,

You've brought me all the joy.

I look upon you as the pearl of pearls

And you are really now the girl of girls.

My dear, please keep your father's words in mind,

You must be of the intelligent kind.

DU LINIANG:

I've grown up in a prefect's home,

Indulging myself in the paint and comb.

Now I draw a picture of the swing,

Then I weave the lovebirds on the wing.

From now on I'll make full use of my time,

Reading all the books sublime.

LADY ZHEN:

That's good indeed, but you'd better have a lady tutor to teach you.

DU BAO:

That won't do.

(*To the previous tune*)

In my official residence,

Her tutor ought to be a scholar with common sense.

LADY ZHEN:

My daughter does not have to read all the books,

But she should know something about the rites.

DU BAO, LADY ZHEN:

In this way she will not only know how to spin,

But also be an intelligent virgin.

DU BAO:

It's not difficult to find her a tutor, but he must be well treated.

(*To the tune of* **Coda**)

Madam, as you love your daughter, grudge no expense

And give the tutor tasty food from hence.

When I do anything with creed,

The books are all I need.

Why is a tutor summoned to the house?

He is to teach my daughter under age.

As I have not a son born by my spouse,

Can my daughter be a genuine sage?

Scene Four
A Pedagogue's Complaints

(*Enter Chen Zuiliang*)

CHEN ZUILIANG (*To the tune of* **Shuangquanjiu**):

Perusing books by night and day,

I'm poor but always wait and wait.

As lucky star ne'er shines my way,

I am reduced to this sad state.

To add pain to my deep distress,

The asthma gets me in a mess.

"*I drink less for my bad disease;*

I cook less for my scanty fees.

> *While no one lives high in the sky,*
>
> *A grey-haired sage on earth would sigh."*

I am Chen Zuiliang, also called Bocui, student of the Confucian Academy in the Prefecture of Nan'an. I came from a doctor's family but have pursued the Confucian learning since early childhood. I entered the academy at the age of twelve and received stipend from the government. In these forty-five years I sat for examinations fifteen times without success. Unfortunately, I turned out to be the last in the previous examination and was deprived of my stipend by the supervisor. To make things worse, out of work as a tutor for two years, I only scraped a meagre existence. Therefore, those young fellow students mockingly changed my name from Chen Zuiliang to Chen Jueliang, which literally means "Devoid of Food". Besides, as I am well-versed in medicine, prophecy and geomancy, they have changed my other name from Bocui to Baizasui, which literally means "Jack of All Trades". Now that I shall arrive at the age of sixty by next year, I do not cherish any more hope. I am now running the pharmacy handed down from my grandfather. As the saying goes, "A Confucian scholar becomes a doctor, just as the vegetable becomes the pickles." — Forget about it. Yesterday I heard that our Prefect Du was looking for a tutor for his daughter. A lot of people vie with each other for the post. But why? First, to have something to show off to their kith and kin; second, to make some connections in the government office; third, to earn some money; fourth, to alter the archives through the help of the servants and butlers; fifth, to prepare for posts somewhere else; sixth, to scare the inferior officials; seventh, to cheat their family members. These seven considerations drive them to vie with each other for the post. However, they have not realised that official residence is a hazardous place. Besides, a girl student is even more difficult to deal with. Neither soft words nor hard words will do with her. If I get into some trouble with her, I'll really be in a dilemma. As an old man, I'd better follow the saying,

> *"Nowhere am I to fix my look*
>
> *But bury my head in the book."*
>
> *(Enter the janitor)*

JANITOR:

> *"The scholars in the world are poor*
>
> *While janitors are smart for sure."*
>
> *(Greets Chen Zuiliang)*

Congratulations, Sir.

CHEN ZUILIANG:

For what?

JANITOR:

Prefect Du would like to find a tutor for his daughter, but is not satisfied with anyone recommended by the director of the Prefectural Academy because he wants an experienced tutor. I spoke to the director and recommended you. Here is the letter of invitation from Prefect Du.

CHEN ZUILIANG:

Mencius teaches us, "Man's anxieties begin when he would like to teach others."

JANITOR:

But man's hunger is more tormenting than man's anxieties. You don't have to worry about your stomach at least.

CHEN ZUILIANG:

In this case, let's go now.

> (*They begin to leave*)
>
> (*To the tune of* **Dongxiange**)
>
> I sew my scarf when it is torn
>
> And mend my shoes when they are worn.

JANITOR:

> When you take the tutor's post,
>
> You'll share the honour of the host.

CHEN ZUILIANG, JANITOR:

> Rinse with water from the writing tray
>
> Before the tasty dinners every day
>
> And use toothpicks to keep the stink away.

JANITOR (*To the previous tune*):

> I have found such a precious job for you;
>
> Don't you forget to give me a gift or two!

CHEN ZUILIANG:

> I know you want me to repay,
>
> But I don't know if I can stay.

CHEN ZUILIANG, JANITOR:

> On festivals when days are fair,
>
> Be sure to go out in the air
>
> And bring something for us to share.

JANITOR:

The prefect's gate is in sight now.

> *The worldly honour comes and goes,*

CHEN ZUILIANG:

> *But who cares for old men in their woes?*

JANITOR:

> *When Prefects sit at home in ease,*

CHEN ZUILIANG, JANITOR:

> *The favour-curriers come in rows.*

Scene Five
Employing the Tutor

> (*Enter Du Bao with his butler and attendant*)

DU BAO (*To the tune of* **Huanshaxi**):

> The mountains look their best;

The court now takes a rest.

The birds come and go above the hall;

The petals cover my seal stand and curtains fall.

"Although Du Shi exceeds me in esteem,

I've earned a good reputation in Nan'an.

For all my contributions so supreme,

I have begot no male heir to my clan."

As Prefect of Nan'an, I only have my wife and my daughter on my side. I intend to find a tutor for my daughter. Yesterday, the Confucian Academy of the prefecture recommended to me a scholar by the name of Chen Zuiliang, a learned man about sixty years old. He can teach my daughter and also chat with me. Today I have laid off official duties so that I can entertain him with a dinner. Butler, get ready for the guest.

(*The butler and the attendant answer the order*)

(*Enter Chen Zuiliang in a blue robe and a scholar's cap*)

CHEN ZUILIANG (*To the previous tune*):

I'll do away with fear

And put on my best cheer.

In shabby coats for my old age,

I'll face my master like a sage.

ATTENDANT (*Announces*):

Mr Chen is at the gate.

DU BAO:

Invite him to come in.

ATTENDANT (*Announces*):

Here comes the scholar from the prefectural academy.

(*Exit*)

CHEN ZUILIANG (*Kneels, rises to his feet, bows and kneels again*):

Chen Zuiliang from the prefectural academy kowtows to Your Excellency.

(*Kowtows*)

"After schools are set up in the town,

DU BAO:

A scholar is deemed of high renown.

CHEN ZUILIANG:

Toasts after toasts are now exchanged,

DU BAO:

When host and guest are properly arranged."

Now all the attendants may go home since I shall have a chat with Mr Chen. Tell the servants to attend on us.

(*The attendants answer the order and withdraw*)

(*Enter the servant boy*)

I've long heard that you are well learned. May I ask how old you are and whether you come from a Confucian family?

CHEN ZUILIANG:

Yes, of course.

> (*To the tune of* **Suonanzhi**)
>
> I'm over sixty years of age,
>
> On my way toward three score and ten,
>
> A scholar whose youth will ne'er come again.

DU BAO:

And now?

CHEN ZUILIANG:

> I practise medicine to earn some pay,
>
> A practice passed down from the ancient day.

DU BAO:

So medicine is your family heritage. What else do you know?

CHEN ZUILIANG:

> I can do prophecy for men;
>
> And geomancy is within my ken.

BU BAO:

These skills are all the more useful.

> (*To the previous tune*)
>
> I've heard of your name for many years,
>
> But it's the first time for me to meet
>
> A scholar of enormous feat.

CHEN ZUILIANG:

You're over-praising me.

BU BAO:

> My daughter knows how to read and write
>
> And will surely learn from you with delight.

CHEN ZUILIANG:

I'll do my best, but I'm not sure whether I can teach her well enough.

BU BAO:

> Lucky is my daughter
>
> To have you as her tutor.
>
> As this is a day of bliss
>
> For my daughter to meet her tutor.

Butler, strike the summoning plate to call the young mistress.

> (*Enter Du Liniang with Chunxiang*)

DU LINIANG (*To the previous tune*):

> With eyebrows craven-black
>
> And pendants emerald-green,
>
> A beauty steps from behind the screen.
>
> In buoyant footsteps to the hall,
>
> I act properly in front of all.

CHUNXIANG:

Now that the tutor has arrived, what shall we do?

DU LINIANG:

I have to meet him anyway, Chunxiang.

>   The names of virtuous ladies never fade;
>
>   A little learning makes you a better maid.

BUTLER:

Here comes the young mistress.

>   (*Du Liniang bows to her father*)

DU BAO:

Come forward, my child. As *The Book of Rites* says,

>   "*Uncarved jade is unfit for use;*
>
>   *Uneducated men are unaware of Tao.*"

As today is a day of bliss, come and meet your tutor.

>   (*Sounds of drums and music within*)

DU LINIANG (*Makes obeisance*):

I'm an unworthy student for an experienced teacher.

CHEN ZUILIANG:

It's an honour for an old man like me to teach a talented student.

DU BAO:

Chunxiang, come and kowtow to Mr Chen. This servant maid will accompany my daughter in her studies.

>   (*Chunxiang kowtows*)

CHEN ZUILIANG:

May I ask what books the mistress has studied?

DU BAO:

She's able to memorise the *Four Books* both for men and for women, and now she'd better read something from the *Five Classics. The Book of Changes* deals with the duality of *yin* and *yang*; that's too profound for her. *The Book of History* deals with political affairs; that's of no concern for women. *The Spring and Autumn Annals* and *The Book of Rites* are too fragmented. *The Book of Poetry*, however, starts with the eulogy of the virtue of queens and consorts and is easy to remember with its four-syllabic verse. Moreover, poetry conforms with my family tradition. It's better for her to study *The Book of Poetry*. I have all kinds of books and histories, but the pity is that she is a girl.

>   (*To the previous tune*)
>
>   At fifty years of age,
>
>   I'm fond of books myself,
>
>   With thirty thousand on the shelf.
>
>   (*Sighs*)
>
>   What's the use of my great name,
>
>   If I have not a son to carry on the fame?

Mr Chen, my daughter has all the books at her disposal. If she's done anything wrong, just punish the maid.

CHUNXIANG:

Alas!

DU BAO:

> I hope that you will make my daughter
>
> A worthy scholar of the topmost grade.
>
> Meanwhile, just watch out
>
> For the naughty maid.

CHEN ZUILIANG:

Yes, I'll do my best.

DU BAO:

Chunxiang, see your young mistress to her room while I have a drink with Mr Chen.

DU LINIANG (*Makes obeisance*):

> *"The tutor has his wine to drink;*
>
> *The daughter has her books to think."*
>
> (*Exit Du Liniang with Chunxiang*)

DU BAO:

Mr Chen, let's have a drink in the back garden.

> *A tutor teaches pupils in the day,*

CHEN ZUILIANG:

> *Poor scholars have but rice upon the tray.*

DU BAO:

> *A loving daughter as my single heir,*

CHEN ZUILIANG, DU BAO:

> *She has a tutor now to guide her way.*

Scene Six
An Outing

> (*Enter Han Zicai*)

HAN ZICAI (*To the tune of **Fanbusuan***):

> With family name tracing back to Tang,
>
> I now dwell in the town Chaoyang.
>
> Now that I watch the boundless roaring sea,
>
> Will my career be promising for me?
>
> *"On the Ancient Terrace under banyan trees,*
>
> *I watch the Jiazi Bay below in breeze.*
>
> *Without a trace of former song and dance,*
>
> *I see a partridge come and go at ease."*

I am Han Zicai. My ancestor Han Yu was banished to Chaozhou in the south because he wrote the essay *On the Bones of Buddha*. As soon as he arrived at the Languan Pass, his horse was unable to go on because of heavy snow. He thought that this was an ill omen. In distress, he saw his nephew Han Xiangzi, one of the eight immortals, approach him in rags. All the more distressed, he thawed his frozen brush and wrote a poem in the hostel. The last two lines read:

> "*I know that you have come to me*
> *To take my relics to the sea.*"

Han Xiangzi thrust the poem in his sleeves and soared into the sky with a prolonged laugh. It so happened that my ancestor Han Yu died of malaria in Chaozhou with no relatives beside his deathbed. Han Xiangzi witnessed all this up in the clouds. As he recalled the poem, he lowered his clouds and collected the remains. When he came to the official residence, he saw no one but his former wife. As they looked at each other, his mortal instinct was aroused. A son was born in Shuichao to carry on the family line and I am descended from this line. In times of turmoil, I moved here to Guangzhou and was assigned as an assistant to the Temple of Han Yu because I was his descendant. And so I'm now living near the Terrace of Prince Zhao Tuo. As the poem goes,

> "*A scholar of the poorest kind*
> *May have the loftiest mind.*"

Here comes a friend of mine. Who can it be?

(*Enter Liu Mengmei*)

LIU MENGMEI (*To the previous tune*):

> With learning and experience
> Behind an inconspicuous appearance,
> I'd like to mount the hills to watch the cloud
> Above the flat sea like a shroud.

(*Exchanges greetings with Han Zicai*)

HAN ZICAI:

Hi, Liu Mengmei! What wind has brought you here?

LIU MENGMEI:

I'm wandering alone and happen to climb onto this terrace.

HAN ZICAI:

This terrace commands an excellent view.

LIU MENGMEI:

But it's not easy to climb such a height.

HAN ZICAI:

I'm having a good time here.

LIU MENGMEI:

It suddenly occurs to me that the illiterate have the best time.

HAN ZICAI:

Whom do you mean?

LIU MENGMEI:

Prince Zhao.

(*To the tune of* **Suohanchuang**)

When Qin's First Emperor was dead,

Across the land the turmoil spread.

Prince Zhao usurped a stretch of land

And thus became a sovereign head.

A hero without any dread,

With people under his command,

He built a palace tall and grand.

But for scholars like you and me, do we have a single bit of land?

Confucian books bring no land to our hand.

LIU MENGMEI, HAN ZICAI:

Oh, Gracious Heaven,

It's no use dwelling on the past;

The terrace alone will stand and last.

HAN ZICAI:

You look as if you were upset. My ancestor Han Yu wrote,

"Never mind whether the official is bright,

But mind whether your essay is right;

Never mind whether the official is fair,

But mind whether your knowledge is there."

Brother, I'm afraid we still have something to learn.

LIU MENGMEI:

Let's forget about it. Both my ancestor Liu Zongyuan and your ancestor Han Yu were men of great learning, but they were born under the wrong star. Your ancestor was banished to Chaozhou — he should not have written *On the Bones of Buddha*; my ancestor was banished to Liuzhou — he should not have played chess with Prime Minister Wang Shuwen in the Chaoyang Hall of the palace and thus disturbed the Emperor. Both Chaozhou and Liuzhou were located in the foggy coastal areas. While they travelled together to the south, they chatted under the lamp in the hostel. "Zongyuan, Zongyuan," said Han Yu, "your essays are as good as mine. I wrote *A Biography of Wang Chengfu, the Bricklayer* and you wrote *A Biography of a Carpenter;* I wrote *A Biography of Minister Mao Yin* and you wrote *A Biography of Hunchback Guo, the Gardener*; I wrote *A Funeral Oration to the Crocodile* and you wrote *Reminiscences of a Snake-Catcher*. So far so good. When I submitted *An Epigraph on the Pacification of Huaixi* to curry favour with the throne, you wrote in your turn *Ode to the Pacification of Huaixi*. You competed with me essay by essay. Now that we are banished to the remote regions, we are in the same boat. What has brought us together, the time, the chance or the fate?" Brother, let's forget about things in the distant past but comment on you and me. Should we deserve such destitution? Why hasn't my ancestor's essay *Pursuit for Fortune* brought any fortune to the twenty-eight generations of my family? Why hasn't your ancestor's essay *Farewell to Poverty* bid farewell to poverty all through the twenty-odd generations of your family? The time and the chance seem to be the only answer.

HAN ZICAI:

Exactly. Chunqing,

> (*To the previous tune*)
>
> You buy the books to enrich your mind,
>
> But oft-times knowledge may be left behind.

However, Lu Jia, a scholar in Prince Zhao's time, came here on an imperial errand and was entitled a high-ranking official. How well he was received by Prince Zhao!

> In honour he returned to court,
>
> With treasures of various sorts.

Emperor Gaozu in the Han Dynasty detested scholars. Whenever he saw a Confucian cap, he would piss on it. One day Lu Jia went for an audience in his square cap and dark robe. On seeing Lu Jia, Emperor Gaozu said to himself, "Another piss pot for me!" and shouted at Lu Jia, "I have won my empire on horseback; what's the use of poems and books?" Lu Jia was witty enough to retort: "Your Majesty has won the empire on horseback, but can you rule over the empire on horseback?" The emperor smiled at these words and said, "True as you are, let me hear a passage." Lu Jia took his time and drew from his sleeves a scroll of *Latest Remarks*, thirteen essays written at home. The emperor was delighted when he heard the first essay, and praised each essay when they were read out. Lu Jia was immediately entitled Interior Marquis. What a glory for him! Not only the emperor but also the ministers and generals gave high credit to him.

> A word of wisdom from the learned man
>
> Roused applause from whole clan.

LIU MENGMEI (*Heaves a sigh*):

> As for my essays, no one would like to scan.

LIU MENGMEI, HAN ZICAI:

> Oh, Gracious Heaven,
>
> It's no use dwelling on the past;
>
> The terrace alone will stand and last.

HAN ZICAI:

Chunqing, may I ask how you manage to make a living?

LIU MENGMEI:

I'm living with my gardener.

HAN ZICAI:

In my opinion, you'd better find a patron to help you out.

LIU MENGMEI:

You know, nowadays very few people care for men of learning.

HAN ZICAI:

Haven't you heard that Miao Shunbin, Imperial Envoy for treasure appraisal, cares for men of learning? Before his term of office ends this autumn, he will go as usual to assess treasures in the Treasure Temple near Xiangshan Bay in Macao. Shall we go and try to see him at that time?

LIU MENGMEI:

I'll be glad to.

A man of sorrow fears to live alone,
Who never hopes to make himself well-known.
The prince takes pride in his own terrace
While men who never read ascend the throne.

Scene Seven
Studying at Home

(*Enter Chen Zuiliang*)

CHEN ZUILIANG:

"I read and copy poems I wrote last spring;
After meals I guess what tea to bring.
An ant is creeping to the ink-slab pool;
A bee is sucking at blooms with its sting."

I, Chen Zuiliang, am a tutor in the prefect's residence, to teach Miss Du *The Book of Poetry*, following her family tradition. Madam Du has treated me very well. Now that breakfast is over, I'm going to review the notes on *The Book of Poetry*.

(*Reads*)

"The waterfowl would coo
Upon an islet in the brooks.
A lad would like to woo
A lass with pretty looks."

"Like" means "love" while "woo" means "seek after".

(*Looks around*)

At this late hour, there's yet no sign of my pupil. She must have been pampered badly. I have to strike the summoning plate.

(*Strikes the summoning plate*)

Chunxiang, ask Miss Du to come to class!

(*Enter Du Liniang, followed by Chunxiang with books in her hands*)

DU LINIANG (*To the tune of **Raochiyou***):

I've made up for the day

And come into my study,

A room so bright and full of ray.

CHUNXIANG:

Wise Sayings from the Ancient Times

Really bothers me;

It's only fit to make the parrots cry for tea.

(*Du Liniang and Chunxiang greet Chen Zuiliang*)

DU LINIANG:

I wish you happiness, respected tutor.

CHUNXIANG:

I wish you kindness, respected tutor.

CHEN ZUILIANG:

According to *The Book of Rites*, it is proper for a young mistress to get up at the first cockcrow, wash her hands, rinse her mouth, brush and comb her hair, and then pay respects to her parents. After sunrise, each will attend to her own work. And now your work is to study. You must get up early.

DU LINIANG:

I won't be late from now on.

CHUNXIANG:

I see. I won't go to bed tonight and I shall ask you to give us lessons at midnight.

CHEN ZUILIANG:

Have you gone over the poem I taught yesterday?

DU LINIANG:

Yes, I have. I'm expecting your interpretation today.

CHEN ZUILIANG:

Please read the poem.

DU LINIANG (*Reads*):

> "The waterfowl would coo
> Upon an islet in the brooks.
> A lad would like to woo
> A lass with pretty looks."

CHEN ZUILIANG:

Now listen to me. "The waterfowl would coo." "Waterfowl" is a bird and "coo" describes the birdcall.

CHUNXIANG:

What kind of call is it?

> (*Chen Zuiliang imitates the birdcall*)
> (*Chunxiang imitates Chen's birdcall*)

CHEN ZUILIANG:

This kind of bird is fond of the quietness "upon an islet in the brooks".

CHUNXIANG:

That's it. It happened yesterday or the day before yesterday, this year or last year. When my young mistress set free the waterfowl in the cage, it flew to the house of Mr Brooks.

CHEN ZUILIANG:

Nonsense! This is an analogy.

CHUNXIANG:

What does it analogise?

CHEN ZUILIANG:

An analogy is the beginning of a poem. It leads to the pretty lass, a quiet girl wooed by a lad.

CHUNXIANG:

Why should he give her wood?

CHEN ZUILIANG:

Shut up!

DU LINIANG:

Mr Chen, I can follow the notes by myself, but will you tell me the general idea of the book?

CHEN ZUILIANG (*To the tune of* **Diaojuese**):

  Among the Six Classics,

  The Book of Poetry is the best

  To tell about ladies who are blessed:

  About the life in the wild,

  There's Jiang Yuan who conceived a child;

  Against jealousy,

  There're consorts who were e'er carefree.

In other poems,

  The roosters crow at break of day;

  The swallows sadden travellers on the way;

  The river rouses great dismay;

  The streams are where the lovers stay.

  The poems in plain and simple style

  Teach the people all the while

  To build their homes in smile.

DU LINIANG:

How can it contain so many things?

CHEN ZUILIANG:

In a word, of the three hundred poems in *The Book of Poetry*,

  For you, the mere short phrase

  "Without evil thought"

  Is of great import.

So much for the poems. Chunxiang, fetch the stationery set for calligraphy.

CHUNXIANG:

Here's the paper, the ink, the brush and the ink-slab.

CHEN ZUILIANG:

What kind of ink is this?

DU LINIANG:

She's fetched the wrong kind of ink. It's the paint for the brows.

CHEN ZUILIANG:

What kind of brush is this?

DU LINIANG (*Smiles*):

It's a kind of brush to paint the brows with.

CHEN ZUILIANG:

I've never seen these things. Take them away! Take them away! And what kind of paper is this?

435

DU LINIANG:

It's ladies' writing paper.

CHEN ZUILIANG:

Take it away! Take it away! Fetch the writing paper for the gentleman. And what kind of ink-slab is this? Is it single or double?

DU LINIANG:

It's a mandarin-duck ink-slab.

CHEN ZUILIANG:

Why are there so many eyes on the slab?

DU LINIANG:

They are called "weeping eyes".

CHEN ZUILIANG:

What are they weeping for? Go and change the whole set.

CHUNXIANG (*Aside*):

What a boorish old man! I'll go and change them.

    (*Exit and re-enter with a new set*)

Will these things do?

CHEN ZUILIANG (*Examines the writing-set*):

Yes.

DU LINIANG:

I know how to copy the characters, but Chunxiang needs your help.

CHEN ZUILIANG:

I'll watch how you copy the characters.

    (*Du Liniang copies*)

    (*Chen Zuiliang is surprised*)

I've never seen such fine writing. What style is it?

DU LINIANG:

It's the beauty-bloom style, invented by Lady Wei.

CHUNXIANG:

I'll imitate my young mistress.

DU LINIANG:

It's too early for you to do that.

CHUNXIANG:

May I ask permission to wash my hands?

    (*Exit*)

DU LINIANG:

May I venture to ask the age of your wife?

CHEN ZUILIANG:

She's just reached sixty.

DU LINIANG:

I'll embroider a pair of shoes for her if you tell me the pattern she likes.

CHEN ZUILIANG:

Thanks. As for the pattern, you can follow the teaching of *Mencius*: "Make shoes without knowing the feet."

DU LINIANG:

What's the matter with Chunxiang?

CHEN ZUILIANG:

Shall I call her back?

> (*Calls Chunxiang three times*)
>
> (*Re-enter Chunxiang*)

CHUNXIANG:

Old rascal!

DU LINIANG (*Angrily*):

Where have you been, nasty maid?

CHUNXIANG (*Smiles*):

I've been to the toilet. I went by a big garden overgrown with flowers and willows. It's fun over there.

CHEN ZUILIANG:

Alas! Instead of studying, you played in the garden! I'll get a cane.

CHUNXIANG:

What do you need a cane for?

> (*To the previous tune*)
>
> How can a maid
>
> Become a scholar of the topmost grade?
>
> It's but a literary game she played.

CHEN ZUILIANG (*Stands up*):

There were students in ancient times, who read by the light of the fireflies and the moon.

CHUNXIANG:

> The moonlight glares the eye
>
> While fireflies burn and die.

CHEN ZUILIANG:

How about the student who tied his hair to the beam to keep awake and the student who stabbed his thighs?

CHUNXIANG:

> You hang on the beam and hurt your hair;
>
> You stab in the thigh and leave a scar there.
>
> What's the use even if you dare!
>
> (*A flower-peddler's cry within*)

Listen, mistress,

> A flower-peddler's cries
>
> Distract my reading eyes.

CHEN ZUILIANG:

You're again diverting the attention of your mistress. I'll give you a sound beating.

> (*Raises the cane*)

CHUNXIANG (*Dodges*):

> Oh, dear me,
>
> A tutor beats a maid
>
> In spite of her plea.
>
> (*Grabs the cane and throws it to the ground*)

DU LINIANG:

You naughty maid! As you have offended the tutor, down on your knees!

> (*Chunxiang kneels*)

Mr Chen, as this is her first offense, it'll be enough to give her a scolding.

> (*To the previous tune*)
>
> Keep your hands off the garden swing
>
> And keep your feet off the garden ring.

CHUNXIANG:

It all depends.

DU LINIANG:

You're talking back!

> I'll scorch your wicked mouth with incense-stick
>
> And give your wicked eyes a needle-prick.

CHUNXIANG:

What can I do for you if I'm blind?

DU LINIANG:

> You'll hold the slab beside the desk,
>
> Recite the poems and read the lines
>
> And never do anything grotesque.

CHUNXIANG:

Please pardon me for doing something grotesque.

DU LINIANG (*Seizes Chunxiang's hair*):

> How many hairs will you lack?
>
> How many welts will be on your back?
>
> My mother keeps whips on the stack!

CHUNXIANG:

I'll never do it again.

DU LINIANG:

Now you understand?

CHEN ZUILIANG:

Well, I'll spare you this time. Stand up!

> (*Chunxiang rises to her feet*)

CHEN ZUILIANG (*To the tune of* **Coda**):

> A girl just learns for joy;
>
> Otherwise, she's like a boy.

You may go back when your homework is done. I'll have a chat with your father.

CHEN ZUILIANG, DU LINIANG, CHUNXIANG:

> It is indeed a shame
>
> To waste the time as in a game.

(*Exit Chen Zuiliang*)

CHUNXIANG (*Points scornfully at Chen's back*):

A bull! A silly old dog! He's an out-and-out boor!

DU LINIANG (*Pulls at Chunxiang*):

You naughty maid! "Your teacher for a day is your father for a lifetime." Hasn't he got the right to beat you? By the way, where's the garden?

CHUNXIANG (*Feigns to ignore, but points when Du Liniang asks a second time with a smile*):

Over there!

DU LINIANG:

What are the sights?

CHUNXIANG:

As for the sights, there are half a dozen of pavilions and a couple of swings. There's a meandering stream and an artificial hill, plus beautiful flowers and grass.

DU LINIANG:

I didn't know there's such a wonderful place. But let's go back to my room for the moment.

> *I can sing poems just as a lark;*

CHUNXIANG:

> *A pity that we miss the park.*

DU LINIANG:

> *With boundless sorrows in my heart,*

DU LINIANG, CHUNXIANG:

> *We'll walk on lawns before it's dark.*

Scene Eight
Inspecting the Farms

(*Enter Du Bao, followed by his attendants and butler*)

DU BAO (*To the tune of **Yeyouchao***):

> Where shall I go inspecting the farm?
>
> I'll gather poems of springtime charm.
>
> The turtledove's song I hear;
>
> Behind my carriage runs the deer.
>
> Under trees I'll take a rest in good cheer.
>
> "*The season, the season*
>
> *Is now in the middle of the spring.*

After timely rain the fog is thick

When I go around to check everything.

As farm-work takes the foremost place,

Peace and order I shall bring."

Spring comes early to the Nan'an Prefecture, which is located between the Yangtze River and the Guangdong Province. As a prefect, I spend most of the time in my mansion and know little about what is happening in the remote villages and who is neglecting his farm-work. Yesterday I ordered that sweet wine be prepared to reward the farmers. I believe everything is ready by now.

(*Enter the county official*)

COUNTY OFFICIAL:

"I carry out the order from above

And have it done by villagers I love."

Your Excellency, the sweet wine for your inspection is ready.

DU BAO:

Get ready to set out. See to it that when we approach the village, people should be kept in order.

(*The attendants answer the order and the party sets off*)

DU BAO:

As the poem goes,

"I'm on a tour to ensure the yields,

Not to see the sights in the fields."

(*Exeunt all*)

(*Enter village elders*)

VILLAGE ELDERS (*To the previous tune*):

Grey-hairs care less for daily strife;

The children's games enrich our life.

Here comes the prefect on his tour,

With his horse trotting slow and sure.

Will he meet the farmers, rich and poor?

We are village elders from Qingle Township of the Nan'an Prefecture. We are glad to have Prefect Du in office for three years. Kind and honest, he gets rid of evil practice and promotes virtue. In all the villages, rules and regulations are established, local organisations are set up, and public granaries and village schools are in operation. It's indeed our blessing. Now he's on a tour to inspect the farms, and so we'll go and greet him in the official pavilion. Here come the bailiffs carrying sweet wine.

(*Enter the bailiffs carrying sweet wine*)

BAILIFFS (*To the tune of **Puxiange***):

We outrun thieves in chasing race;

Today we leave the office without a trace,

Bearing sweet wine at quick pace.

(*Stumble*)

We nearly spilt the wine,

But the fault is not mine.

VILLAGE ELDERS:

Welcome to our village.

BAILIFFS:

As the jar is cracked and some wine is leaking, please find some excuse for us.

VILLAGE ELDERS:

No problem. Put the jars aside and then have a drink in the village tavern.

    (*Step aside*)

    (*Exeunt the bailiffs*)

Community chiefs, put the chair in the proper place. Prefect Du is coming.

    (*Enter Du Bao with his attendants*)

DU BAO (*To the tune of* **Paige**):

    The apricot flowers turn red

    And green sweet sedges spread —

    It's getting warmer day by day.

    Above the fence the tavern flags float high;

    While chimney smoke spirals to the sky.

    (*Village elders come forward to welcome Du Bao*)

ALL:

    The pelicans sing;

    The cuckoo songs ring;

    The office closes for the spring.

    Bring no guards;

    Make no clamour;

    Don't disturb farmers in the yards.

ATTENDANT:

Your Excellency, here we are at the official pavilion.

    (*Village elders greet Du Bao*)

DU BAO:

Respected elders, what's the name of this village and township?

VILLAGE ELDERS:

This is the Number One Township Qingle.

DU BAO:

Let me have a good look.

    (*Looks around*)

A pretty place with a pretty name Qingle — tranquil and happy. Just look,

    "The hills are clear;

    The rills are clear.

    When you walk in the wilds,

    Spring clouds appear."

VILLAGE ELDERS:

Indeed,

> "The officials are clear;
>
> Their followers are clear.
>
> When lawsuits decrease,
>
> The pastorals appear."

DU BAO:

Respected elders, do you know the purpose of my spring inspection?

> (*To the tune of* **Bashengganzhou**)
>
> When wheat grows lush in the fields,
>
> Green waves rise and fall,
>
> Predicting bumper yields.
>
> Gentle is the rain
>
> That moistens the plain.
>
> As the fields are richly spaced,
>
> I hate to have them lie in waste.
>
> I also fear that a pointless feud
>
> Delays the work you've pursued.

VILLAGE ELDERS:

442

In the old days, we were harassed by the officials during the day and by the burglars during the night, but since Your Excellency took office,

> (*To the previous tune*)
>
> Our life is turning better day by day.
>
> That's why we elders greet you on the way
>
> And children hail you while they play.
>
> Like spring sunshine from above,
>
> You shower us with endless love.
>
> When dogs no longer bark at night
>
> And farmers plough the fields with might,
>
> The country life presents a thriving sight.
>
> (*The song "The Slippery Track" is heard from within*)

DU BAO:

Listen, there rings a village song.

> (*Enter a farmer*)

FARMER (*To the tune of* **Xiaobaige**):

> Along the slippery track
>
> I glide my way,
>
> With a rake and a plough upon my back.
>
> I sow the seedlings after a nightly rain
>
> And spread manure in sunny weather,
>
> With stinky smell across the plain.

DU BAO:

It's indeed a good song.

> "I sow the seedlings after a nightly rain
>
> And spread manure in sunny weather,
>
> With stinky smell across the plain."

He's referring to the stink of the manure, but respected elders, he fails to realise that the manure can be fragrant. As is said in a poem,

> "While sumptuous dinners scarcely bring
>
> Delicious savour to a king,
>
> The smell of rice in hungry times
>
> Is better than a fragrant thing."

Give him flowers to wear and some wine to drink.

FARMER (*Smiles as he puts on the flowers and drinks the wine*):

Thank you, my good lord, the wine tastes good.

ALL:

> The tasty wine from the gracious lord
>
> And the flowers on my head
>
> Are farmers' best reward.
>
> (*Exit the farmer*)

BUTLER (*Reports*):

Here comes a cowboy singing.

> (*Enter a cowboy with a flute in his hand*)

COWBOY (*To the previous tune*):

> A whip in hand,
>
> A flute on lips,
>
> I ride an ox upon its hips.
>
> (*Points his flute at the butler*)
>
> He's of my size
>
> And wears my hair,
>
> But rides a mighty mare!

DU BAO:

He sings a good song, but why should he point at the butler and sing,

> "He's of my size
>
> And wears my hair,
>
> But rides a mighty mare?"

Respected elders, he fails to know that an ox provides a steadier ride. As is said in a poem,

> "I used to envy wealthy men,
>
> Who ride the horses now and then.
>
> Yet when I ride a horse in hills,
>
> I'd rather ride an ox again."

Give him flowers to wear and some wine to drink.

> (*The cowboy puts on the flowers and drinks the wine*)

ALL:

    The tasty wine from the gracious lord

    And the flowers on my head

    Are cowboys' best reward.

    (*Exit the cowboy*)

BUTLER (*Reports*):

Here come two women singing.

    (*Enter a young woman and an old woman, picking mulberry leaves*)

TWO WOMEN (*To the previous tune*):

    Under mulberry trees,

    With baskets on our backs

    We pick the leaves at ease.

Oh, who is the official over there?

    Like Luo Fu who had her man,

    We'll not be tempted as of old

    By silver or expensive gold.

DU BAO:

They sing a good song. Tell them that I'm not a man who flirts with women in the old days. I am the prefect inspecting the farms. I respect them for they work hard picking mulberry leaves. As is said in a poem,

    "*The peach and plum inspire the song,*

    But mulberry trees here are ten acres strong.

    Unlike the useless plants that grow around,

    They turn out silk that will prolong."

Give them flowers to wear and some wine to drink.

    (*The two women put on the flowers and drink the wine*)

ALL:

    The tasty wine from the gracious lord

    And the flowers on our heads

    Are mulberry pickers' best reward.

    (*Exeunt the two women*)

BUTLER (*Reports*):

Here come two more women singing.

    (*Enter two women, carrying baskets and plucking tea-leaves*)

TWO WOMEN (*To the previous tune*):

    In late spring days

    We pluck the fresh tea-leaves,

    Leaves of topmost tea on trays.

Oh, who is the official over there?

    A scholar brews the tea with snow;

    A weary student longs for tea —

    They both make tea with fire aglow.

444

DU BAO:

They sing a good song. Tell them that I'm not the famous scholar or the weary student in the old days. I am the prefect inspecting the farms. I admire them for they work hard plucking tea-leaves. As is said in a poem,

"*As there's no tea-star in the sky,*

The young tea-nymph on earth is sly.

When girls engage in bets for tea,

In grander games the men would vie."

Give them flowers to wear and some wine to drink.

(*The two women put on the flowers and drink the wine*)

ALL:

The tasty wine from the gracious lord

And the flowers on our heads

Are tea-leaf pluckers' best reward.

(*Exeunt the two women*)

VILLAGE ELDERS (*Kneel*):

Your Excellency, the villagers have set the table for dinner in your honour.

DU BAO:

There's no need for the trouble. Just take the rest of flowers and wine to share with people in smaller villages as a token of the government's concern for farming. Tell the attendants to get ready to start.

VILLAGE ELDERS (*Rise to their feet and call out loudly when they fail to ask Du Bao to stay*):

Those who have received the flowers and the wine, come forward to see His Excellency off.

(*Enter the farmer, the cowboy and the four women, wearing flowers*)

FARMER, COWBOY, FOUR WOMEN (*To the tune of* **Qingjiangyin**):

On his grand inspection tour,

The prefect rides a horse that looks so fine.

He brings to us his deep concern

With his flowers and wine.

Come along, villagers,

We'll sing of the deeds that'll always shine.

(*Exeunt*)

DU BAO:

The houses wind their way uphill,

With verdant fields along the rill.

When I halt my horse at dusk,

I see peach blossoms glowing still.

Scene Nine
Cleaning the Garden

(*Enter Chunxiang*)

CHUNXIANG (*To the tune of* **Yijiangfeng**):

> I am Chunxiang, a little maid;
>
> Long favoured by my miss,
>
> Within her rooms I've stayed.
>
> I wait on her,
>
> Make up for her,
>
> Dress up for her.
>
> And stand by her.
>
> I do silk-work with care
>
> And listen to her prayer,
>
> But Madam gives me punishment unfair.
>
> *"A pretty lass in early teens*
>
> *Has sensed the female ways and means.*
>
> *A young man of the proper kind*
>
> *Will wholly occupy her mind."*

I've been attending on my young mistress day and night. Beautiful as she is, she places her family honour in the first place. Gentle and shy as she is, she is in fact sombre and elegant. Her father has engaged a tutor for her. When she read the first poem in *The Book of Poetry* and came across the lines

> *"A lad would like to woo*
>
> *A lass with pretty looks",*

She quietly laid down the book and sighed, "In these lines are revealed the passions of the sage to the fullest extent. Isn't it true that people in ancient times and in modem times share the same passions?" On hearing her words, I suggested, "If you're tired of reading the books, why don't you try to have some fun?" After a few moments of hesitation, she rose to her feet and asked, "Chunxiang, what fun would you suggest that I have?" I replied, "Well, my mistress, as far as I can see, why don't we take a stroll in the back garden?" She said, "Nonsense, what if my father should find it out?" I answered, "Lord Du has been to the countryside for several days." She walked up and down the room without a word for quite a few moments before she began to consult a calendar. "Tomorrow's no good," she said, "The day after tomorrow is little better, and only the next day will be auspicious because it is the day of the god of minor trips." She told me to order the gardener to clean the garden paths. I said yes but I'm afraid that Madam will find it out. I have to wait and see. For the moment I'll go and tell the gardener. Alas, here comes Tutor Chen along the corridor. As the poem goes,

> *"The springtime here is full of glee;*
>
> *Old fools alone will fail to see."*

(Enter Chen Zuiliang)

CHEN ZUILIANG (*To the previous tune*):

> The scholar in old age
>
> Is teaching here to earn some wage,
>
> With classroom curtains flapping in the sun.

Now,

> On the corridor
>
> Stands a young girl with coiled hair,
>
> Who seems to murmur something.
>
> I'll go and see who's staying there.

Oh, it's Chunxiang. Tell me,

> Where is the gracious master?
>
> Where is the madam?
>
> What keeps my pupil from attending class?

CHUNXIANG:

Hello, Mr Chen. My young mistress has no time to attend class these days.

CHEN ZUILIANG:

What's she doing now?

CHUNXIANG:

Let me tell you.

> *(To the previous tune)*
>
> In this time of the year,
>
> You should be smart enough to know
>
> That there is something severe.

CHEN ZUILIANG:

What is it?

CHUNXIANG:

Don't you know, Mr Chen, that the master is angry with you?

CHEN ZUILIANG:

What is he angry for?

CHUNXIANG:

He says that your exposition of *The Rook of Poetry* goes way too far. For the young mistress,

> These poems of ancient art
>
> Have touched her to the heart.

CHEN ZUILIANG:

I've just started with the very first line "The waterfowl would coo".

CHUNXIANG:

That's it. The young mistress said, "Now that a caged waterfowl would like to coo upon an islet in the brooks, how could a human being be less passionate!"

> Delve deep in books by all means,
>
> And raise your head to view the scenes.

She's told me to get ready for a stroll to the back garden in a day or two.

CHEN ZUILIANG:

What's her intent for the visit?

CHUNXIANG:

> With spirits low when spring is on the way,
>
> She fears that spring would leave too soon,

And in the back garden,

> She'll try to cast her woe away.

CHEN ZUILIANG:

How can she do that!

> (*To the previous tune*)
>
> When a girl proceeds from place to place,
>
> She has to wear a veil
>
> Lest man should see her face.

I'm over sixty, but I've never worried about the hasty passage of spring nor been sightseeing in a garden.

CHUNXIANG:

Why?

CHEN ZUILIANG:

Haven't you heard that the sage Mencius' sayings can be boiled down to this: men should "restrain his strayed heart"?

> If you stick to the normal state of mind,
>
> Why do you feel depressed in spring?
>
> Why do you need spring tour of any kind?

Upon your return from the sightseeing,

> Nothing but disquiet you'll bring.

Since the young mistress is not going to class, I'll leave for home for a few days. Chunxiang,

> Please often go to the classroom
>
> And check the windows with looped hooks,
>
> Lest the swallows soil the books.

I'm leaving now.

> "*Young ladies play grass games to waste their prime;*
>
> *Old scholars read the classics all the time.*"
>
> (*Exit*)

CHUNXIANG (*To herself*):

Mr Chen is gone at last. Where on earth is the gardener?

> (*Calls out*)

Gardener!

> (*Enter the young gardener, in a tipsy state*)

YOUNG GARDENER (*To the tune of* **Puxiange**):

> Tending flowers is what I do,
>
> But sometimes I sell a few.
>
> The sheriffs may catch me,

The sergeants may grab me,

And now strong liquor nearly kills me.

(*Greets Chunxiang*)

Hi, Sister Chunxiang.

CHUNXIANG:

You deserve a sound beating, sneaking out to the streets and wining around. And you haven't delivered vegetables for days.

YOUNG GARDENER:

That's the greengrocer's business.

CHUNXIANG:

And you haven't carried the water yet.

YOUNG GARDENER:

That's the water carrier's business.

CHUNXIANG:

And you haven't delivered the flowers yet.

YOUNG GARDENER:

I deliver the flowers every morning, one bunch for the madam and another bunch for the young mistress.

CHUNXIANG:

And yet another bunch for me?

YOUNG GARDENER:

Oh, I'm to blame.

CHUNXIANG:

What's your name?

YOUNG GARDENER:

They just call me Gardener.

CHUNXIANG:

Well, just make up a song to explain your name. If I like the song, I'll spare the rod.

YOUNG GARDENER:

Please listen,

(*To the tune of* **Lihuaer**)

I've seen so many flowers surge and surge,

But from the flowers you emerge.

Let's go and seek for pleasure in the day;

Ah,

At dusk a morning bud may sing its dirge!

CHUNXIANG:

Now it's my turn,

(*To the previous tune*)

You've seen too many flowers surge and surge,

But can you have me now that I emerge?

YOUNG GARDENER:

Oops!

CHUNXIANG:

> When I report to Master of your words,
>
> (*Grasps the young gardener by the hair*)
>
> I'm sure you'll have a pleasant scourge.

YOUNG GARDENER (*Topples*):

Now I give up. Well, what has brought you here to the garden?

CHUNXIANG:

The young mistress is coming to visit the garden in two days. So be sure to clean the garden paths.

YOUNG GARDENER:

Yes, I see.

> *In eastern suburbs flowers are at their best;*
>
> *By Lady Star is the hometown fully blessed.*
>
> *Once lads and lasses are aware of love,*
>
> *Their youthful hearts can hardly be suppressed.*

Scene Ten
An Amazing Dream

(*Enter Du Liniang with Chunxiang*)

DU LINIANG (*To the tune of **Raochiyou***):

> When I'm awakened by the orioles' songs
>
> And find the springtime beauty all around,
>
> I stand in deep thought on the courtyard ground.

CHUNXIANG:

> With burnt incense
>
> And silk yarns scattered here and there,
>
> This spring no longer holds back maidens fair.

DU LINIANG:

> *"With the distant pass in view at dawn,*
>
> *In my night-gown I stand forlorn.*

CHUNXIANG:

> *In spring-style braid,*
>
> *You lean against the balustrade.*

DU LINIANG:

> *That which scissors cannot sever,*
>
> *And, sorted out, is tangled again,*
>
> *Makes me bored than ever.*

CHUNXIANG:

>   *I've told the early birds*
>
>   *To meet the spring and send your words."*

DU LINIANG:

Have you ordered the garden paths to be cleaned, Chunxiang?

CHUNXIANG:

Yes, I have.

DU LINIANG:

Bring my mirror and gowns.

>   (*Exit and re-enter Chunxiang with the mirror and gowns*)

CHUNXIANG:

>   *"Face the mirror when she's done her hairs;*
>
>   *Perfume the gowns once more before she wears."*

Here are your mirror and gowns.

DU LINIANG (*To the tune of* **Bubujiao**):

>   In the courtyard drifts the willow-threads
>
>   Turn by spring breeze into flimsy shreds.
>
>   I pause awhile
>
>   To do my hairstyle.
>
>   When all at once
>
>   The mirror glances at my face,
>
>   I tremble and my hair slips out of lace.
>
>   (*Walks in the room*)
>
>   As I pace the room,
>
>   How can anyone see me in full bloom!

CHUNXIANG:

You're so pretty today.

DU LINIANG (*To the tune of* **Zuifugui**):

>   You say my dress is fine
>
>   And hairpins shine,
>
>   But love of beauty is my natural design.
>
>   My beauty is concealed in the hall,
>
>   But it'll make fish delve and birds fall
>
>   And outshine blooms, the moon and all.

CHUNXIANG:

It's time for breakfast. Let's go.

>   (*Begins to move*)

Look,

>   *"How the painted corridor shines!*
>
>   *How green the moss appears in endless lines!*
>
>   *To walk on grass I fear to soil my socks;*
>
>   *To love the blooms I want to keep them under locks."*

DU LINIANG:

If I had not come to the garden, how could I have tasted the beauty of spring!

(*To the tune of* **Zaoluopao**)

The flowers glitter brightly in the air,

Around the wells and walls deserted here and there.

Where is the "pleasant day and pretty sight"?

Who can enjoy "contentment and delight"?

Mom and Dad have never mentioned such pretty sights.

DU LINIANG, CHUNXIANG:

The clouds at dawn and the rain at dusk,

The bowers in the evening rays,

The threads of shower in gales of wind,

The painted boat in hazy sprays:

All are foreign to secluded maids.

CHUNXIANG:

All the seasonal flowers are in full blossom, but it's still too early for the peony.

DU LINIANG (*To the tune of* **Haojiejie**):

Amid the red azaleas cuckoos sing;

Upon roseleaf raspberries willow-threads cling.

Oh, Chunxiang,

The peony is fair indeed,

But comes the latest on the mead.

CHUNXIANG:

Look at the orioles and swallows in pairs!

DU LINIANG, CHUNXIANG:

When we cast a casual eye,

The swallows chatter and swiftly fly

While orioles sing their way across the sky.

DU LINIANG:

It's time to leave.

CHUNXIANG:

There's more than enough to be seen in the garden.

DU LINIANG:

No more about it.

(*Du Liniang and Chunxiang begin to leave*)

(*To the tune of* **Quasi-coda**)

It's true that there's more than enough to be seen,

But what though we visit all the scenic spots?

We'd better find more fun behind the screen.

(*They arrive at the chamber*)

CHUNXIANG:

"I open doors of chambers east and west

And sit on my own bed to take a rest.

I put azalea in the earthen vase

And add incense unto the proper place."

Mistress, please take a rest now and I'll go and see the madam.

(*Exit*)

DU LINIANG (*Sighs*):

"Back from a brief spring tour,

I know my beauty now for sure."

Oh spring, now that I love you so much, what shall I do when you are gone? How dizzy I feel in such weather! Where's Chunxiang?

(*Looks around and lowers her head again, murmuring*)

Oh heavens! Now I do believe that spring is annoying. There is some truth about what is written in various kinds of poems about maidens in ancient times, who felt passionate in spring and grieved in autumn. I've turned sixteen now, but no one has come to ask for my hand. Stirred by the spring passion, where can I come across one who will go after me? In the past, Lady Han met a scholar named Yu, and Scholar Zhang came across Miss Cui. Their love stories have been recorded in the books *The Story of the Maple Leaves* and *The Life of Cui Hui*. These lovely ladies and talented scholars started with furtive dating but ended in happy reunion.

(*Heaves a long sigh*)

Born and brought up in a renowned family of high officialdom, I've come of age but haven't found a fiancé yet. I'm wasting my youth that will soon pass.

(*Weeps*)

What a pity that my face is as pretty as a flower but my fate is as dreary as a leaf!

(*To the tune of **Shanpoyang***)

Indulged in springtime passion of all sorts,

I'm all of a sudden roused to plaintive thoughts.

I have a pretty face

And so my spouse must be as good,

With a noble place.

What is there to meet my fate

That I must waste my youth to wait!

When I go to bed, who'll peep

At my shyness in my sleep?

With whom shall I lie in my secret dream,

Drifting down the springtime stream?

Tormented day by day,

To whom can I say

About my woe,

About my wretched fate?

Only the heavens know!

I feel dizzy. I'll lean on the table and take a short nap.

(Falls asleep and begins to dream)

(Enter Liu Mengmei with a willow-twig in his hand)

LIU MENGMEI:

"In warm days orioles' songs ring apace

While man in deep affection has a smiling face.

I chase the fragrant petals in the stream,

To find the fair lady in my dream."

I follow the footsteps of Miss Du along the path, but how is it that I lose sight of her now?

(Looks back)

Hi, Miss Du! Hi, Miss Du!

(Du Liniang rises in astonishment and greets Liu Mengmei)

I've been looking for you here and there. Now I find you at last.

(Du Liniang looks aside without a word)

I just snapped a willow-twig in the garden. Miss Du, as you are well-versed in classics, why don't you write a poem to honour the twig?

(In happy astonishment, Du Liniang is about to speak but holds back her tongue)

DU LINIANG *(Aside)*:

I've never seen this young man before. Why does he come here?

LIU MENGMEI *(With a smile)*:

I'm up to the neck in love with you. Miss Du!

*(To the tune of **Shantaohong**)*

For you, a maiden fair,

With beauty that will soon fade,

I've been searching here and there,

But alone in chamber you have stayed.

Come with me and let's have a chat over there, Miss Du.

(Du Liniang smiles but does not move)

(Liu Mengmei pulls her by the sleeve)

DU LINIANG *(In a subdued voice)*:

Where to?

LIU MENGMEI:

Beyond the rose grove,

Beside the mount we'll rove.

DU LINIANG *(In a subdued voice)*:

What to do, sir?

LIU MENGMEI *(Also in a subdued voice)*:

I shall unbutton your gown

And strip it down.

You'll bite your sleeve-top with your teeth,

Then make a hug and lie beneath.

(Du Liniang is shy, but Liu Mengmei comes forward to embrace her. She feigns to push him away)

LIU MENGMEI, DU LINIANG:

> Is it absurd
>
> That we seem to meet somewhere before
>
> But stand here face to face without a word?
>
> *(Exit Liu Mengmei, holding Du Liniang in his arms)*
>
> *(Enter Flower God with bundled hair, dressed in red and strewn with flowers)*

FLOWER GOD:

> *"The flower god looks after flowers here*
>
> *And keeps the springtime busy year by year.*
>
> *When petals fall from flowers in a rain,*
>
> *The flower gazer starts to dream in vain."*

I am the flower god in charge of the prefect's back garden in Nan'an. As the prefect's daughter Du Liniang and the scholar Liu Mengmei are predestined to get married, Miss Du is so affected by her spring tour that she has enticed Liu Mengmei into her dream. I am a flower god to take care of all the beauties in this area, and so I've come here to protect her in order that she will enjoy herself to the full.

> *(To the tune of **Baolaocui**)*
>
> In the surge of earth and sky,
>
> He swirls like a busy bee
>
> And looks into the flowery maiden's eye.
>
> That is a meeting in the dream,
>
> A wedding in the mind,
>
> An outcome of the fate
>
> That brings defilement of the foulest kind.

I'll drop a flower petal to wake her up.

> *(Scatters some petals to the entrance of the stage)*
>
> How can they tear themselves away from a dream?
>
> They'll wake up when the petals gleam.

The scholar is still indulged in his dream, but when he wakes up, he'll see Miss Du to her chamber. I've got to go now.

> *(Exit)*
>
> *(Enter Liu Mengmei and Du Liniang, hand in hand)*

LIU MENGMEI *(To the tune of **Shantaohong**):*

> With heaven and earth as our bridal room,
>
> We sleep on grass and bloom.

Are you all right, my dear?

> *(Du Liniang lowers her head)*
>
> Look at her pretty hair,
>
> Loosened here and there.

Please never forget the day when we

> Lie together side by side,
>
> Make love for hours and hours,

And hug as man and bride,

With your face red as flowers.

DU LINIANG:

Are you leaving now, my love?

LIU MENGMEI, DU LINIANG:

Is it absurd

That we seem to meet somewhere before

But stand here face to face without a word?

LIU MENGMEI:

You must be tired, my dear. Sleep awhile, sleep awhile!

(*Sees Du Liniang to her sleeping position, and pats her on the back*)

I'm going, my dear.

(*Looks back*)

Please sleep awhile, my dear, and I'll come and see you again.

"She comes like a gentle rain in spring

And wets me like clouds on the wing."

(*Exit*)

DU LINIANG (*Wakes up with a start and murmurs*):

Are you leaving, my love?

(*Dozes off again*)

(*Enter Lady Zhen*)

LADY ZHEN:

"My husband holds high office here;

My daughter stays without much cheer.

Her worry comes from the skirts she wears,

Adorned with blooms and birds in pairs."

How can you doze off like this, my child?

DU LINIANG (*Wakes and calls the scholar*):

Oh! Oh!

LADY ZHEN:

What's wrong with you, my child?

DU LINIANG (*Stands up with a start*):

Oh, it's you, Mom!

LADY ZHEN:

Why don't you, my child, enjoy yourself by doing some needlework or reading some books?

Why are you dozing off like this?

DU LINIANG:

Just now I took a stroll in the back garden, but I was annoyed by the noise of the birds and so

I came back to my chamber. As I could not find a way to while away the time, l dozed off for a

moment. Please forgive me for having not greeted you at the door.

LADY ZHEN:

As the back garden is a desolate place, my child, don't go there again.

DU LINIANG:

I'll follow your advice, Mom.

LADY ZHEN:

Go and study in the classroom, my child.

DU LINIANG:

As the tutor is on leave, I have a few days off.

LADY ZHEN (*Sighs*):

A girl has her own emotions when she has come of age. I'd better leave her alone. As the saying goes,

> "*Busy for the children all her life,*
> *A mother always has her strife.*"
>
> (*Exit*)

DU LINIANG (*Sighs deeply and watches Lady Zhen leave*):

Alas, heavens! I'm lucky enough today. A whimsical stroll to the back garden made me pathetic in spite of the beautiful scenery. After I came back in low spirits, I took a nap in my chamber. In my dream I saw a handsome scholar by the age of twenty. He broke a willow-twig in the garden and said to me with a smile, "Miss Du, as you are well-versed in classics, why don't you write a poem to honour the twig?" I was about to reply when it occurred to me that I should not speak to him because he was a total stranger and I did not know his name yet. When I was hesitating, he came forward, spoke a few melancholy words and carried me to the Peony Pavilion. We made love there beside the peonies. With mutual passion, we stuck to each other in tenderness. When it was all over, he brought me back and said time and again, "Sleep awhile." I was about to see the scholar to the door when my mother came and startled me out of my dream. I was wet in cold sweat from my daydream. I made haste to greet my mother and then had to listen to her talk. I kept silent but was still troubled in my heart. I seemed to be sitting on pins and needles, utterly at a loss. Oh, Mother, you told me to go back to my classroom, but what kind of books can bring me relief?

457

> (*Covers her eyes with her sleeve and weeps*)
>
> (*To the tune of **Miandaxu***)
>
> The youthful joy in love regime
> Had reached the verge of dream
> When Mother came into the room
> And woke me back to my deep gloom.
> With cold sweat that soaked my dress,
> I was simply rooted to the ground,
> My mind and hair in utter mess.
> In a sunken mood,
> Not knowing how to sit or stand,
> I'd go and sleep in solitude.
>
> (*Enter Chunxiang*)

CHUNXIANG:

> "My make-up is undone at night.
>
> With only incense burning bright."

Your quilts have been scented, Mistress. It's time to go to bed.

DU LINIANG (*To the tune of* **Coda**):

> As the springtime tour has tired me out,
>
> There is no need to scent my quilts.

Good heavens,

> I wish that pleasant dreams would soon sprout.
>
> *A springtime tour from painted halls*
>
> *Brings near the scent of bloom that falls.*
>
> *If you should ask where lovers meet,*
>
> *I say that hearts break where they greet.*

Scene Eleven
Madam's Admonishment

(*Enter Lady Zhen*)

LADY ZHEN:

> "Each day becomes worse than the last;
>
> Each year grows older than the past.
>
> My daughter is deprived of weal,
>
> Who stands before the window seal."

I had not been to my daughter's chamber for several days. When I went to see her at noontime, I found her listless and dozing alone in her room. She told me that she felt tired because she had just returned from the back garden. She's too young to realise that girls should never visit a deserted place in full make-up. That must be all Chunxiang's fault to give her the temptation. Where's Chunxiang?

(*Enter Chunxiang*)

CHUNXIANG:

> "A maid who wants a moment's sleep
>
> Will soon be called to clean and sweep."

How is it that you haven't gone to bed at such late hours, Madam?

LADY ZHEN:

Where's your young mistress?

CHUNXIANG:

After you left her chamber, Madam, she kept murmuring to herself and gradually fell asleep. She must be dreaming now.

LADY ZHEN:

You good-for-nothing! You tempted the young mistress to the back garden. What if something should happen to her?

CHUNXIANG:

I won't any more.

LADY ZHEN:

Now mark my words.

（*To the tune of* **Zhenghubing**）

A girl should stay in her own room,

To work with hands or at the loom.

As far as sewing is concerned,

A stitch more is a moment earned.

In summer when daytime is slow,

There're lutes to play and books to read;

The garden isn't the place to go.

CHUNXIANG:

There're pretty things to see in the garden.

LADY ZHEN:

Let me tell you, ignorant maid,

（*To the previous tune*）

The garden is a lonely place by day,

With terraces and pavilions in decay.

Even when a mature lady like me has to go there,

I have to hesitate.

What are you girls to do o'er there?

Her luck depends upon her fate.

CHUNXIANG:

What if she's ill-fated?

LADY ZHEN:

If it comes true

That something should go wrong,

What can her mother do?

As she didn't have supper today, get her an early breakfast tomorrow. Tell her what I said to you.

In stormy woods the ghosts and demons groan,

CHUNXIANG:

But flower pickers seldom stay alone.

LADY ZHEN:

As pretty maidens have their way of life,

CHUNXIANG:

There are admonishments from Prefect's wife.

Scene Twelve
Seeking the Dream

(*Enter Chunxiang*)

CHUNXIANG (*To the tune of* **Yeyougong**):

> I wash my face at early dawn
>
> And put on hairpins in the morn.
>
> I serve the miss from morn till night
>
> With drowsy eyes in candlelight:
>
> Before the wardrobe,
>
> Beside the dressing-table,
>
> Between the painted screens.

I'm Chunxiang, maid to serve Miss Du. Miss Du has a tutor, who is like a cat watching over the mice. It happens that she was affected by *The Book of Poetry* and thus chose an auspicious day to have a walk in the back garden to while away the time. Miss Du was just dozing off when the madam dropped in. She scolded Miss Du and laid the blame on me. I kept silent and then promised never to do that again, but the madam would not let me off and I had to vow and swear.

VOICE WITHIN:

What did you vow and swear, Sister Chunxiang?

CHUNXIANG:

"If I should make trouble again," I said, "I would never be able to get married." Although I answered like that, how can a crow control a phoenix? Miss Du tossed and turned all night. She got up early this morning and urged me to fetch water for her to make up. She has been talking to herself all the time till now the sun is shining over the flowers and windows.

VOICE WITHIN:

Hurry up! It's time for Miss Du to have breakfast.

CHUNXIANG:

> "The cook has word for me
>
> To fetch the soup and tea."
>
> (*Exit*)
>
> (*Enter Du Liniang*)

DU LINIANG (*To the tune of* **Yueergao**):

> Like arching hills on painted screens,
>
> My brows are drawn by various means.
>
> Why couldn't quilts conceal my care?
>
> The moon doesn't call for my weary stare.
>
> Isn't it the fallen bloom
>
> That draws me from my room?
>
> *"Among the flowers rose a dream*

> *That drove my thoughts to riotous stream.*
>
> *I stayed awake with candlelight,*
>
> *To watch my maid sleep well all night."*

A random spring stroll yesterday brought me face to face with someone in the dream. I fixed my eyes on him as if he had been my true love. When I sit alone thinking over the dream, I feel depressed. How piteous I am!

(*In a depressed mood*)

(*Enter Chunxiang with tea and food*)

CHUNXIANG:

> *"The tray contains pearl-like rice*
>
> *And fragrant tea of good price."*

Breakfast is ready, Mistress.

DU LINIANG:

I'm not in a mood for breakfast.

> (*To the previous tune*)
>
> I have just washed and done my face
>
> And left the glass not yet in place.
>
> I see life as a total waste;
>
> How can I have a pleasant taste?

CHUNXIANG:

The order from Madam is that you have an early breakfast.

DU LINIANG:

> For you to use my mother's word
>
> To push a hungry soul appears absurd.

Do you know how people eat to keep alive?

CHUNXIANG:

Three meals a day.

DU LINIANG:

Alas,

> Not strong enough to hold the bowl,
>
> I've had enough as a hungry soul.

Take the breakfast away and have it by yourself.

CHUNXIANG:

> *"I would prefer the leftover food*
>
> *To paints and rouge that are no good."*
>
> (*Exit*)

DU LINIANG:

Chunxiang is gone at last. Oh heavens, the lake and the pavilion in yesterday's dream were real enough. I tried to relive the old dream but new disappointment ensued. I tossed and turned all night without a moment's sleep. Now that Chunxiang is gone, I'll take this opportunity to sneak into the garden and have a look.

(*In a sad mood*)

Oops, I feel as if

> *"The dream displays no phoenix on the wing,*
>
> *But links the yearning hearts with one tough string."*

(Walks)

Here's the garden. As luck has it, the gate is left open and the gardener is not here. How the ground is scattered with fallen petals!

*(To the tune of **Lanhuamei**)*

This spring has strongly stirred my heart.

High above the garden walls,

The blooms and branches stretch and dart.

(Stumbles)

Oh, the raspberries are pulling at my skirt,

As if they tried to grasp my heart and flirt.

How the streamlet flows!

(To the previous tune)

Why should lovers try to find the same old place?

The blooms and streams must have left a trace.

For flowers, the heavens need not pay a cent

But people cried o'er fallen petals

As lovely spring thus came and went.

(Enter Chunxiang)

CHUNXIANG:

When I came back from breakfast, I lost sight of Miss Du. I have to look for her here and there. Oh, here you are, Mistress!

*(To the tune of **Bushilu**)*

How come my pretty mistress stands

By plum trees with a twig in her hands?

What brings you to this zone

So early in the morn alone?

DU LINIANG:

On the corridor,

I saw the swallows build a nest

And followed them without a rest.

CHUNXIANG:

If Madam comes to you

And finds you out of view,

She'll say, "Where's she fooling around?

Where's she fooling around?"

DU LINIANG *(Feigns to be annoyed)*:

(To the previous tune)

I came here all by chance,

But you suggest I seek after leisure.

CHUNXIANG:

Well, you're not seeking after leisure, but after pleasure.

DU LINIANG:

> Don't treat me as a child
>
> And say the garden's wild.

CHUNXIANG:

> I dare not be so bold,
>
> But Madam gave the order that
>
> You do more needlework in spring
>
> And scent the paper twofold.

DU LINIANG:

What else did she say?

CHUNXIANG:

> This garden is a haunted place.
>
> With ghosts and demons all apace.
>
> Back to your secluded chambers!
>
> Back to your secluded chambers!

DU LINIANG:

Yes, I see. You go first and make promise for me to my mother and I'll be back in no time.

CHUNXIANG:

> *"Wild flowers lie unstirred*
>
> *While caged birds utter many a foul word."*
>
> (*Exit*)

DU LINIANG:

Now that Chunxiang is gone, it's time for me to seek my dream.

> (*To the tune of* **Teteling**)
>
> Here the lakeside rocks are piled,
>
> With the Peony Pavilion lying wild.
>
> There the peonies dot the way,
>
> And the twigs of willows sway;
>
> The elm fruits dangling from the trees
>
> Are mourning in the springtime breeze!

Oh, this is the place where the scholar asked me to write a poem in the name of willow twigs and forced me to make love with him. It's a long, long story!

> (*To the tune of* **Jiaqingzi**)
>
> Who was the handsome man
>
> That lured me through the garden tour?
>
> I felt ashamed for sure.
>
> He stroked me, my eyes blurred;
>
> I tried to speak, but without a word.
>
> (*To the tune of* **Yinling**)

How enticing the scholar is!

In my previous life I had not been his wife

And never saw him in this life.

In my afterlife I shall be his wife

And dream appears first in this life.

Overcome by his enticing charms,

I left myself in his strong arms.

What a splendid moment!

(*To the tune of* **Pinling**)

He leaned against the rocks and stones;

I stood beside him with faint groans.

He pulled me softly to the ground,

Permeated with springtime warmth around.

Above the fence,

Across the swing,

My skirt spread out from hence.

We lay on grass and faced the sky,

But what if heavens should spy?

It was eternal time

When we enjoyed life's prime.

At the best time of the dream, some petals dropped from the flowers!

(*To the tune of* **Douyehuang**)

He grew much bolder

And kissed my shoulder.

I played with him in little haste,

But soon became less graced,

Soft and tender

With a sensual taste.

But floral rains that gleam

Bewildered me in my sweet dream.

Alas, here and there I seek my dream, but I've found nothing. The Peony Pavilion, the rose grove, how can they be so desolate! How can they be so lifeless! How the sight breaks my heart!

(*Weeps*)

(*To the tune of* **Yujiaozhi**)

In a place forlorn,

Without pavilions far and near,

How is it that I can neither see nor hear?

In the broad daylight,

I fail to find the dreamland sight.

The visions flash before my eye

And would not linger though I try.

Well, it's here that we meet and sigh.

Oh that I see my man again!

(*To the tune of* **Yueshanghaitang**)

How can I explain

Why he appears again?

Here he comes at leisured pace;

There he leaves without a trace.

He is not far away —

Before the rain and cloud disperse,

Behind the blooms I see him stay.

At this time yesterday,

On this very spot,

I was transformed and went astray.

I'll stay here for another moment.

(*Looks around*)

Why! In this lonely place where no one comes, a huge plum tree stands before me, hanging with lovely fruits.

(*To the tune of* **Erfanyaoling**)

How can its fragrance spread

And its leaves crown like a shed?

When plums are ripe and rain is clean,

The vernal leaves are thriving green.

How can the plum contain a bitter heart?

I love the shade provided by the tree,

For in my dream I'll play another part.

Well, the plum tree is lovely indeed. After my death, I would be lucky enough if I could be buried underneath.

(*To the tune of* **Jiangershui**)

All of a sudden my heart is drawn

Toward this plum tree by the lawn.

If I were free to pick my bloom or grass,

If I were free to choose to live or die,

I would resign to fate without a sigh.

I'll risk my life

And weather raging storms

To be your faithful wife.

(*Sits down on the ground wearily*)

(*Enter Chunxiang*)

CHUNXIANG:

"She tours the garden in spring days;

Her maid burns incense in court maze."

Well, Miss Du is dossing off under the plum tree as she is tired from the garden tour.

(*To the tune of* **Chuanbozhao**)

465

How does the plum tree allure

You to end the garden tour?

DU LINIANG:

When I gaze,

When I gaze at the endless skies,

Woe and sorrow moist my eyes.

(*In tears*)

DU LINIANG, CHUNXIANG:

Who knows from where the woe arises?

Who knows from where the tear arises?

CHUNXIANG:

What's weighing on your mind, Mistress?

DU LINIANG (*To the previous tune*):

How absurd

That we gazed without a word!

I should have held,

I should have held the twig and yelled.

Now I regret,

Now I regret that not a word he did get.

CHUNXIANG:

What is the riddle you have set?

DU LINIANG, CHUNXIANG:

Who knows from where the woe arises?

Who knows from where the tear arises?

CHUNXIANG:

We'd better go back now.

DU LINIANG (*Starts to move but stops again*):

(*To the previous tune*)

Spring, stay a while

And linger in exile.

(*Birds sing within*)

Listen,

Listen to the cuckoo's song.

Is it true that I can only come —

Come here to see the plum —

In dream or death that will prolong?

DU LINIANG, CHUNXIANG:

Who knows from where the woe arises?

Who knows from where the tear arises?

CHUNXIANG:

Here we are. Let's go and see Madam, Mistress.

DU LINIANG:

Not now.

> (*To the tune of **Yibujin***)
>
> I dragged my weary steps to my own room,
>
> About to greet my mom,
>
> But I alone sleep with bedside bloom.
>
> *Where on earth can fairy love be found?*

CHUNXIANG:

> *The tourist's zeal can hardly be profound.*

DU LINIANG:

> *In dreams my man will show up off and on;*

CHUNXIANG:

> *Eternal woe will ne'er be dead and gone.*

Scene Thirteen
Leaving Home

> (*Enter Liu Mengmei*)

LIU MENGMEI (*To the tune of **Xinghuatian***):

> Although my learning is beyond compare,
>
> My stomach is empty most of the time,
>
> Filled with dismal air.
>
> In dreams I stalk in the splendid court,
>
> But when I wake up in the hut,
>
> My vision quickly thaws.
>
> *"When dragons leave, ink-slabs are dry;*
>
> *When hares are gone, pen-brushes are bare.*
>
> *I've tried in vain to find a way,*
>
> *Like a bird that hovers here and there."*

I'm Liu Mengmei, an outstanding scholar in the Guangzhou academy. I have studied hard there for several winters and summers, but now I still have to live in a desolate garden and depend on my gardener for a living. The more I think about it, the more ashamed I feel. I'd better follow Han Zicai's advice to move to some other county to seek a better living. As the saying goes,

> *"An empty house provides no food;*
>
> *The scanty trees don't brood a good mood."*

Where are you, gardener?

> (*Enter Hunchback Guo*)

HUNCHBACK GUO (*To the tune of **Zizishuang***):

> With a curved front and a humped back,
>
> I'm a hunchback.

Like fully stretched bows,

I pose.

To walk with bumble, tumble, stumble,

I'm humble.

To roll down the street like a ball,

I fall.

I am Hunchback Guo, the gardener. My ancestor who followed Prefect Liu to Liuzhou in the Tang Dynasty was also a hunchback. It's been quite a few years since I followed his twenty-eighth generation descendant, Liu Mengmei's father, to escape the war and settle down in Guangzhou. Now that I have sold the fruit, I'll go and greet my master.

(*Greets Liu Mengmei*)

Hello, Master, how hard you've been working on your books!

LIU MENGMEI:

Well, gardener, I've something to discuss with you. After twenty years of studies, I still have no hope of getting into office. I think I'm still young, and how can I idle away my time here like this! Thank you for all you've done for me: carrying firewood and water for me. Now, all the fruit trees in the garden are yours. Listen to what I have to say:

(*To the tune of* **Guihuasuonanzhi**)

All these years I have relied on you:

Such faithful men like you are very few.

Life is hard and food is plain,

But I should owe all this to you.

What am I like in your eyes?

I sit and daydream like a fool all day,

And never give you help in any way.

My very daydream is a shame;

Who else am I to blame?

I'll leave the garden trees to you;

That is all I can do.

HUNCHBACK GUO (*To the previous tune*):

For years with you I've stayed

And gardening is my family trade.

(*Makes a bow*)

As a hunchback I'm not of much use,

But I shall do my best without excuse.

By the way, may I ask where you're going now that you've given me the garden?

LIU MENGMEI:

I'd rather go begging with a stick than sit idle and wait to eat at home.

HUNCHBACK GUO:

What do you mean by "go begging with a stick"?

LIU MENGMEI:

That's another term for "going with the autumn wind", that is, seeking favour from the rich.

HUNCHBACK GUO:

Good Gracious,

> Rather than go begging from town to town,
> You'd better study hard to win renown.

LIU MENGMEI:

Do you mean that "going with the autumn wind" is no good? Have you ever heard of the poem "Emperor Wu Goes with the Autumn Wind"? Life is short indeed, but he became the emperor in the end.

HUNCHBACK GUO:

No more of your allusions, Master. Which wind are you going with?

> When luck is with you,
> The wind will go with you.
> When luck is against you,
> The wind will go against you.

LIU MENGMEI:

As I've made up my mind, don't try to stop me.

HUNCHBACK GUO:

I'll pack some clothes for you.

> (*To the tune of* **Coda**)
> I'll wash and pack your shabby dress;

LIU MENGMEI:

> A scholar is a beggar in distress.

HUNCHBACK GUO:

Good-bye, master,

> I hope to see you come back with success.

LIU MENGMEI:

> *I have to wander east and west,*

HUNCHBACK GUO:

> *When blooms on trees are at their best.*

LIU MENGMEI:

> *Where am I to seek the "autumn wind"?*

HUNCHBACK GUO:

> *In spring you'd better pass the imperial test.*

Scene Fourteen
Drawing Her Own Image

> (*Enter Du Liniang*)

DU LINIANG (*To the tune of* **Poqizhen**):

> The man fades with the garden dream;

The gems in chambers hear my soul scream.

Like blooms seen through the mist,

Like moonlight piercing through the cloud,

My precocious emotions will persist.

(Enter Chunxiang)

CHUNXIANG:

My mistress seems to get a troubled heart

And lends her ear to songs of shrikes;

With spring it's hard for her to part.

DU LINIANG:

"Entangled in affairs I see and hear,

I linger in the dreamland now and here.

CHUNXIANG:

With sorrow painted on her brow,

She knows not where it comes and how.

DU LINIANG:

With endless grief,

In flimsy dress,

I shed teardrops in distress.

DU LINIANG, CHUNXIANG:

The fairy on Mount Wu is hard to depict,

Her fate still harder to predict."

CHUNXIANG:

Mistress, since your stroll to the back garden, you have never had enough food or sleep. Is it your spring thoughts that make you pine away? Although I am not in a position to give you any advice, I'd venture to suggest that you never go to the back garden again.

DU LINIANG:

How can you get to know my mind! As the poem goes,

"A dream in spring contains the season's flight;

The morning chill destroys the vernal sight."

(To the tune of **Shuazixufan**)

(In a low voice)

When spring departs with chilly pace,

For days I keep a weary face

And sit alone with thoughts in a race.

I'd not have peace of mind

Unless the troubled thoughts declined

And the way of life gets realigned!

For him I smiled with hearty cheers;

In dreams I shed large drops of tears.

CHUNXIANG *(To the tune of* **Zhunu'erfan**):

Mistress,

Why has your passion not yet died?

Why have your cold tears not been dried?

It's clear that the recent garden-tour

Has worn you out with songs of birds for sure.

Just think,

How you will make Madam's heart sink!

If you go on with this downcast attitude,

Your beauty will be nothing but platitude.

DU LINIANG (*In surprise*):

Oh, do you mean that I'm utterly worn out? I'll have a look in the mirror to see what has happened to me.

(*Looks in the mirror and feels sad*)

Where's my former beauty! How can I look so haggard! If I don't paint a picture of myself now to be preserved in the world, who will ever know of my beauty once I pass away? Chunxiang, fetch me some silk, ink and pen, and then watch how I paint.

CHUNXIANG (*Goes off and re-enters with silk, ink and pen*):

"It's easy to paint a scene in springs,

But hard to paint how her heart stings."

Here's the silk, ink and pen.

DU LINIANG (*In tears*):

I'm painting a picture of myself at the age of sixteen. Why should things come to this!

(*To the tune of **Putianle***)

My beauty in its fullest prime

Is spent within a few days' time.

It's true that youth can hardly last,

But why does it dissolve so fast?

There have been beauties in the world

Who pined away at early age, I've heard.

I'll calm my burning soul

And wield the drawing pen

To paint my beauty on a scroll.

(*Looks in the mirror and sighs*)

(*To the tune of **Yanguosheng***)

With silken cloth,

I wipe the mirror clean

And move my pen to paint the scene.

Oh, my image,

This is how you look like:

Two dimpled cheeks,

A cherry mouth,

Two thin brow-streaks,

The hair-locks floating north and south.

My eyebrows stretch to the hair

Above my eyes that talk

And shine with ornaments I wear.

CHUNXIANG (*To the tune of* **Qingbeixu**):

With a pleasant smile,

The slender mistress stands against the eastern breeze,

But feels depressed when springtime flees.

DU LINIANG:

Against the background of hills,

With huts beside the rills,

I paint a picture of a maid,

A maid who wanders in the shade,

Fumbles plums and feels dismayed.

She leans against a rocky seat,

Beside the willow-tree retreat.

With palm-tree leaves the picture is complete.

Chunxiang, hold up the picture. Does the maid in the picture look like me?

CHUNXIANG (*To the tune of* **Yufurong**):

It's easy to paint a picture of a maid,

But hard to show her inner trait.

You see in the picture the reflections

Of flowers in the mirror or the moon in the lake.

DU LINIANG (*Cheers up*):

What a lovely picture! Oh,

I know full well how I look like;

Additional strokes will spoil my psyche.

CHUNXIANG:

It's a pity that you do not have a husband by your side.

If you become a bride

At an early date,

The pair will feel elated side by side!

DU LINIANG:

To tell you the truth, Chunxiang, I met a man during my garden stroll.

CHUNXIANG (*In surprise*):

How was it possible, Mistress?

DU LINIANG:

It was a dream!

(*To the tune of* **Shantaofan**)

I had a merry time with the man;

I'll search my mind and do what I can

To add him in the picture here,

But that'll reveal my secret love, I fear.

My delicate figure in the picture

 Is like the lonely autumn moon;

 Which handsome man will join me soon?

It occurs to me, Chunxiang, that the scholar in my dream snapped off a willow-twig as a gift for me. Is it an omen that my would-be husband is a Mr Liu, which means "willow"? I've composed an occasional poem that alludes to my yearning. What about inscribing it at the top of the picture?

CHUNXIANG:

A good idea!

DU LINIANG (*Recites the poem when she inscribes it*):

 "A close inspection shows her as her self;

 A distant look displays her as an elf.

 Her future spouse who shares the pillow

 Will be found by the plum or willow."

 (*Puts down the pen and sighs*)

Chunxiang, in the past and at present, beauties either have pictures drawn by their husbands or draw their own pictures as gifts to their lovers. But to whom shall I present this picture?

 (*To the tune of **Weifanxu***)

 My heart is filled with weal and woe:

 A joy to see her dress shine bright

 And her pendants glow;

 A grief to see her pine away

 As time and tide relentlessly flow.

 Love's labour's lost!

 Who will shed his tears for her?

 Who will ever call for her?

 (*In tears*)

 What ill fate

 That she must wait to see her mate!

Chunxiang, bring the gardener quietly.

 (*Chunxiang calls for the gardener. Enter the young gardener*)

YOUNG GARDENER:

 "I live among the flowers all my days;

 The mistress loses her brilliant rays."

What can I do for you, Mistress?

DU LINIANG:

Have this picture mounted by the scroll-maker. Make sure that the job is well done.

 (*To the tune of **Baolaocui***)

 Who will mount this picture here

 To make a better souvenir?

 The silk material must be white

While margins must not be wide.

To keep secret, you must keep your mouth shut tight.

In sunny days, the scroll must be well dried

Lest it decay in the broad daylight

And my painting be vilified.

YOUNG GARDENER:

When the picture is mounted, where shall I hang it, Mistress?

DU LINIANG (*To the tune of* **Coda**):

In my chamber it shall be displayed;

CHUNXIANG:

It fits much better in the fairy temple.

DU LINIANG, CHUNXIANG:

But with the rain and wind it'll fade.

CHUNXIANG:

As pearls and jewels go against her bent;

DU LINIANG:

She weeps for flowers to her heart's content.

CHUNXIANG:

When it reveals its genuine worth,

DU LINIANG:

It pales the prettiest maid on earth.

Scene Fifteen
Brooding on an Invasion

(*Enter the Jin Emperor, followed by his attendants*)

JIN EMPEROR (*To the tune of* **Yizhihua**):

At heaven's will we overthrew the Liao

And share the world with House of Zhao;

The ceremonies at court have altered now.

With beat of drums and sound of bells,

The ministers arrive with northern smells.

Our countenances make the southerners laugh:

Our beaked noses,

Our freckled faces,

Our curls of hair.

"Upon our vast terrain of land and dust,

New ministers enjoy the new king's trust.

Why should we northerners put up with the sands?

Why should they southerners live on fertile lands?"

I'm Dignai, emperor of the great Jin Dynasty. Although I am a barbarian, I love to read poems. It's over thirty years since my grandfather Ogda grabbed the northern part of the Song Dynasty while Emperor Zhao Gou fled and made Hangzhou the new capital. It's said that Zhao Gou has built Hangzhou into a city more beautiful than Bianliang, the former capital. He and his followers make merry day and night on the West Lake. As a *ci* poem has it,

> *"Osmanthus blossoms during autumn days*
> *And lotus flowers bloom along the bays."*

So I can easily raise a million troops and occupy that part of the land. According to military strategy, I'd better employ a southerner as my guide. It happens that Li Quan, a bandit chief in Huaiyang, is brave enough to fight ten thousand men. As he is loyal to me, I have bestowed upon him the title of Gilded Prince. I've told him to raise his own troops in three years and to cause trouble in his area. At the same time, he should look for the opportunity for me to start my military excursion. How I wish I could find some fun on the West Lake!

(*To the tune of* **Northern Erfanjiang'ershui**)

Share and share alike,

Share and share alike,

But I have made a lucky strike.

The arrow on my map is pointed to the south,

To the best dominion in the south.

JIN ATTENDANTS:

What's good over there?

JIN EMPEROR (*With a laugh*):

Have you heard of

> The charming maiden on the shore,
> Who smiles and leans against the oar?

JIN ATTENDANTS:

Is the West Lake as large as our Nanhai and Beihai Lakes in Beijing?

JIN EMPEROR:

> The lake is over a hundred miles in circumference.
> Upon the waves the flowers dance in crowds
> And send their scent beyond the clouds.
> All through the endless nights,
> The songs and music ring around.

JIN ATTENDANTS:

Your Majesty, let's borrow it and have some fun.

JIN EMPEROR:

I've sent some painters in disguise and made a sketch of the whole scene. I am painted as riding a horse on the highest peak of Mount Wu by the lake. How mighty and powerful I am!

Mount Wu is unique,

But I ride atop the peak.

The southern land is low

And I have seen it lie below.

(*Dances for joy*)

Look, how I make the show!

JIN ATTENDANTS:

Your Majesty, as we can't reach the West Lake at once, where will you stay over the night?

JIN EMPEROR (*To the tune of* **Northern Coda**):

Before I ride my horse around the West Lake,

I'll march toward Luoyang and take a break.

The rest of Zhao's realm will soon be at stake.

Narrow is the river, small the sky;

How our military flags float high!

Can we drink up all the southern wine

When all the southern land is mine?

Scene Sixteen

Inquiring about the Disease

(*Enter Lady Zhen*)

LADY ZHEN (*To the tune of* **Sandengle**):

What does this life mean to me?

My daughter has not many days to see

And I'll be childless, like a lonely tree.

(*In tears*)

Like a pearl held on my palm,

Like flesh torn from my heart,

For my daughter I weep and lose my calm.

Oh heavens!

Why should health stay with others

While illness strikes my daughter who has no brothers?

"Delicate as a bloom,

She should be blessed, I presume.

Yet cruel wind and rain

Torment her with grave pain.

She should have stayed in her room,

Instead of going out to watch the moon.

Filled with sorrow in my growing years,

I feel so dizzy with large drops of tears."

Now that I am approaching fifty years of age, I've got my only daughter Liniang. What disease is it that has laid her down for half a year? Judging from her appearance and behaviour, her disease does not seem to have come from cold or heat. I'll question Chunxiang as she must know something about the reason. Where's the mischievous Chunxiang?

(*Enter Chunxiang*)

CHUNXIANG:

I'm coming.

> *"Without a clever boy to help me out,*
> *I serve a miss who can't be up and about.*
> *When I hear the madam call my name,*
> *I know I have to bear the scold and blame."*

LADY ZHEN:

Your young mistress used to be in perfect health, but she has been ill since you became her maid half a year ago. I'm really distressed, distressed! Now tell me about her appetite these days.

CHUNXIANG (*To the tune of **Zhumating***):

> Little does she eat,
>
> Nothing does she do,
>
> And nobody does she meet.
>
> She weeps by herself,
>
> She laughs by herself
>
> And thinks by herself.

LADY ZHEN:

She's seen the doctor.

CHUNXIANG:

> No doctor can put her at ease;
>
> No pills can cure her disease.

LADY ZHEN:

What is she suffering from?

CHUNXIANG:

I don't know.

> She lies in bed in autumn days,
>
> But caught the illness in spring days.

LADY ZHEN (*Sobs*):

What's the matter with her?

> (*To the previous tune*)
>
> Her slender form
>
> Grows thinner than the norm.

It must be your fault!

> She was tempted by spring flowers,
>
> Enticed by flighty birds

And lured by frivolous words!

On your knees, you devil! Hand me the rod!

CHUNXIANG (*Kneels on the ground*):

I really don't know.

LADY ZHEN:

> How do you make her pine away?
>
> How do you lead her astray?

CHUNXIANG:

My young mistress went to the garden, picking flowers and playing with willows, but I don't know how she got ill.

LADY ZHEN (*Gets irritated and beats Chunxiang*):

> I beat you for your artful tongue
>
> And honeyed tunes you've sung!

CHUNXIANG:

Please pardon me, Madam, and I'll tell you the whole story. It happened on the day when we visited the back garden and you came across us on our way back. She told me about a young scholar who snapped off a willow-twig and asked her to write a poem. She said she did not write anything because he was a stranger.

LADY ZHEN:

Well, so far so good. And what happened then?

CHUNXIANG:

Then, then the scholar came forward and carried my young mistress straight to the Peony Pavilion.

LADY ZHEN:

What for?

CHUNXIANG:

How can I know? It's just her dream.

LADY ZHEN:

Her dream?

CHUNXIANG:

Yes, her dream.

LADY ZHEN:

She must be haunted. Ask the master to come here and I'll talk it over with him.

CHUNXIANG:

Master, please come here.

> (*Enter Du Bao*)

DU BAO:

> *"An aged man cares not for the title of earl,*
>
> *But for his daughter precious as a pearl."*

Madam, how's our daughter like this?

LADY ZHEN (*In tears*):

Listen to what I have to say, my lord,

(To the previous tune)

It gives me pain to speak

About what ails her and makes her weak.

Confined in bed most of the time,

Now she smiles, now she weeps;

Her illness comes without reason or rhyme.

It so happened that when Liniang visited the back garden, she dreamt of a man holding a willow-twig and carrying her away.

(With a sigh)

She smeared the willow sprite with sod

Or maybe upset the flower god.

My lord,

Invite a Taoist priest to use his charm

Lest ill fate should do her harm.

DU BAO:

No more of your nonsense! I've engaged Mr Chen as her tutor to teach her proper manners, but you as her mother allows her to take spring strolls.

(With a smile)

She's been exposed to the sun and wind and has caught a cold. There's no need for Taoist charms. If you like, you can ask Sister Stone from the Purple Sunlight Nunnery to chant a few scriptures. As the ancient saying goes, "To prefer the witch to the doctor is one way to avoid cure." I've told Mr Chen to feel her pulse.

LADY ZHEN:

What's the use of feeling her pulse! If she had been engaged, she would not have caught the disease.

DU BAO:

Well, in ancient times, man married at thirty and woman married at twenty. Liniang is too young to know anything about it.

(To the previous tune)

Innocent as a dove,

How can she know such things as love?

It's just a fever,

Or a cold,

Or a disease untold.

As her mother, you

Neglect your pearl upon your palm

And for her illness you cannot keep calm.

(In tears)

DU BAO, LADY ZHEN:

For man and wife,

Oh heavens above,

The daughter means our life,

(*Enter Steward*)

STEWARD:

> *"The visitor comes from the hills;*
>
> *The vessel sails down the rills."*

DU BAO (*To the tune of* **Coda**):

> With official work to do,
>
> I'll leave the daughter unto you:
>
> In autumn chills her illness cannot subdue.
>
> (*Exit Du Bao with the steward, leaving Lady Zhen and Chunxiang on the stage*)

LADY ZHEN:

> *"Man is free when official work is done;*
>
> *Man is snug when he has a son."*

My man ignores his daughter when a messenger comes. How sad it is!

> (*Weeps*)

Now I'll ask Sister Stone to chant the scriptures and ask Mr Chen to prescribe some medicine, but I don't know what will come out of all this. Indeed,

> *"A mother is the dearest to her daughter,*
>
> *But all the same requires the witch and doctor!"*

480

Scene Seventeen
A Taoist Nun

(*Enter Sister Stone*)

SISTER STONE (*To the tune of* **Fengrusong**):

> The world is busy getting wed
>
> With *yin* and *yang* as linking thread.
>
> Resigned to my destined fate,
>
> I wore a Taoist robe from early date.
>
> For over forty years,
>
> I've lived a tasteless life,
>
> A dream without the slightest cheers.
>
> *"The Taoist temple stands upon the earth,*
>
> *Near where the rocks and bamboos idly lie.*
>
> *I grieve that human heart is even worse*
>
> *And runs wild when temptation chances by."*

I am Sister Stone in the Purple Sunlight Nunnery. Stone was not my surname, but I've got the title Sister Stone because I was born sterile and was thus deserted by my husband. Come to think of it: if I want to return to secular life, "Stone" is contained in *Hundred Surnames* and my personal life is described in *The Thousand Character Text*. Oh heavens, I do not want to

"Find proof from ancient texts",
But, on the contrary, I just want to be
　　"As straightforward as the historian Shi Yu".
Why have I been living in this
　　"Magnificent nunnery"
And striving to be
　　"Diligent and strict with myself"?
It is because the Taoist practice is like
　　"Virtue which leads to bliss"
While retribution means that
　　"Vices add up to misfortune".
What is the
　　"Prestigious foundation of my family"?
For generations my ancestors have
　　"Lived in retirement".
When I was born, I had
　　"A good shape and good manners",
With an aptitude for
　　"Peace and tranquility".
My feces was like
　　"Twigs of the chaste tree",
And my urine was like
　　"Drips from the lotus leaves".
At the delta where there should have been
　　"A vast lake or swamp",
There was only a stretch of land, which is
　　"A dried pond with an arid rock".
Although the pebbled path could
　　"Clutch the scholar-trees",
How could the barren land
　　"Grow corns and millets"?
Who would marry me for
　　"Unproductive echoes in the empty valley"?
I had to stay by mother's side and
　　"Do my filial duties".
However, there were those
　　"Aunts and uncles",
Who babbled about
　　"Getting married and bearing children".
My mother said that although I would
　　"Remain chaste all my life",
I looked like

"*The fairest of the fairest*".

Since all the other women could live

"*A harmonious family life*",

Why shouldn't I have

"*A husband to accompany me*"?

So she hired a matchmaker with a glib tongue to

"*Pass on words of honour*"

And had me engaged to a licentious man with a big nose, whose

"*Lust was insatiable*".

All was fixed very soon. The bridegroom picked a day of good omen with

"*The sun and the moon in the best phase*"

And checked the horoscope to see to it that

"*The stars were aligned in good order*".

He sent me betrothal money of

"*Pure gold from River Li*"

And I stepped on the bridal sedan chair as

"*Genuine jade from Mount Kungang*".

I covered my face with

"*A round silk fan*"

And went in a procession with

"*Candles burning bright*".

The bridegroom in his holiday best

"*Sat on my right in a high hat*"

And I the bride was also well dressed

"*With an elegant air*".

We invited some

"*Kith and kin*"

To greet us on the way

"*With goblets and wine*".

I was led

"*Up the stairs and into the hall*",

With bridesmaids

"*Waiting on me in the nuptial chamber*".

We drank our wedding drink amidst

"*Songs and music in the feast*"

And scattered coins and candies to the children from the nuptial bed amidst

"*Chants and hymns in praise of the lamb*".

Inch by inch the guests

"*Examined my figure and countenance*";

Item by item the guests

"*Assessed my precious dowry*".

In the deep of night, the bridegroom came forward and sat close to me, saying that we were like

"Phoenixes echoing in the bamboo grooves"

And that we would soon

"Graze like snow-white colts".

With a quilt

"Covering our body and hair",

We removed

"Our last shreds of clothing".

Oh heavens, on seeing his

"Beastly male organ",

I went through a moment of

"Fright and fear".

When he saw how nervous I was, he said that I had

"Grown in years"

And that he would take his time to

"Tune in with me".

I made no reply but smiled to myself, thinking that however hard he was

"Busy with his hands and feet",

He'd better

"Refrain from overconfidence in his strength".

When night grew deeper, he was still

"Pushing and thrusting",

But how could he break through

"The frozen land"?

For a moment he was confused and wondered what the matter was. He asked for a lamp
and leaned his head, trying to

"Find his way to the right spot",

And fixed his eyes on

"The ivory bed".

I said nothing but grinned to myself, thinking that my private parts were for him to

"Look and see",

But not for him to

"Taste and satiate his desire".

After he tried in vain several more times, he was so annoyed that he mumbled about

"Practice makes perfect",

And he was tired out before he made a hole in

"The chaos of heaven and earth".

All through the night, he

"Grabbed every minute";

And, to speak of what he did, it would put to shame

"The walls that had ears".

On several occasions I would like to hang myself or drown myself so as to

"Escape from his blame",

And if I were to drill a hole or burn a hole, how could I violate the commandment
"Thou shalt not hurt yourself"?
I would even rather run away and
"Live a solitary life",
But how could I make him
"Feel satisfied"?
Yes, there was a way out. In the end he had to take
"The back position"
While I had to comply with him by
"Storing what he offered".
Alas, when we were face to face, I acted as if I
"Had striven to keep chaste",
But when I turned round, I acted as a
"Male partner".
Although for the moment I
"Satisfied his desire",
I knew the meaning of
"Nuptial love".
If he kept me as his wife, he would
"Have no sons and heirs"
And if he divorced me, he would be denounced as
"Betraying his former wife".
So I tried to persuade him to wed a concubine to
"Weave and spin"
Lest he should feel annoyed to be
"A husband in name only".
I would like to
"Resign from my post as a genuine wife"
If only he did not
"Forget his first lady".
Later he did get a concubine. Not long afterwards his concubine
"Won greater favour and challenged my authority",
And deprived me of my position as
"The rooster of the house".
Bearing no grudge against her, I
"Engaged myself in introspection"
And decided to leave the family and become a nun,
"Living in seclusion".
My nunnery had never been
"A magnificent edifice",
And it was me that
"Turned chaos into order".

I had a picture painted of the Taoist immortal king
    "Swinging his mighty sword"
And started to make pills of immortality
    "Under the starry sky".
I offered to the immortals
    "Fruits and cakes",
And ate vegetables
    "With mustard and ginger seasonings".
I no longer cared about the worldly affairs
    "With its ups and downs",
Having escaped from the human bondage,
    "Scot-free".
Since I converted to Taoism several years ago, the fluid from my husband
    "Has been washed away"
And my lust as a wife has dropped
    "From the boiling point to the freezing point".
It is a pity that as the head of the nunnery I,
    "Living all alone",
Have to
    "Take pains to give consultations".
Those who come for the service must be
    "Provided with meals"
And those travelling nuns must be
    "Provided with grains".
How is it that there are no other nuns in the nunnery? I live
    "A secluded life"
And have no one to
    "Write to for alms".
When I grow old
    "With passing years",
My beauty fades
    "Like the waning moon".
Although I am not as beautiful as those ladies
    "Who will forever live in the portraits",
I hope to live among the immortals
    "Who are pious and chaste".
Too lazy to
    "Wander around the world",
I spend all the time
    "Sitting in deep contemplation".
Few nuns
    "Share my views"

While few monks are worthy of my
> "Coy smiles".

For fear of their
> "Underhand means",

I'm like a fish in cold waters that
> "Does not bite the bait".

My only attendant is my
> "Nephew who is treated as my son",

who is called Scabby Turtle,
> "Ridiculed as an ignorant man".

VOICE WITHIN:

Why are you calling names, Auntie? I'm a lovely boy.

SISTER STONE:

Shame on you! Don't you know
> "Loss of sense of shame is a disgrace"?

Do you really think that you are
> "Lovely and attractive"?

VOICE WITHIN:

A bailiff from Prefect Du is coming to arrest you.

SISTER STONE:

Why?

VOICE WITHIN:

He says that you are a witch of a Taoist nun.

SISTER STONE:

Oh, those bailiffs are
> "Runners from the office",

Taking me as a witch
> "On the wanted list".

I may well
> "Stay at ease"

And care nothing for their
> "Bluffs and intimidations".
>
> (Enter Bailiff)

BAILIFF:
> "A bailiff from the office hall,
> On the Taoist nun I call."

SISTER STONE (Greets the bailiff):

What can I do for you, Mr Bailiff?

BAILIFF (To the tune of **Dayagu**):
> The prefect stays in office;
> His wife has sent her word
> To cure some pain absurd.

Her dainty daughter

Has caught a strange disease,

And half a year now flees.

SISTER STONE:

I'm not a gynaecologist.

BAILIFF:

You'll hold a service for her,

Then pray for her and see what will occur.

SISTER STONE (*To the previous tune*):

We Taoists have our secret way:

Use tiny talismans to pray

Beside her bed

And illness will flee from her head.

BAILIFF:

As you have such magic talismans, let's hurry!

(*They start to move*)

SISTER STONE:

Boy!

(*Response from within*)

Take good care

And stay o'er there.

As no one is in the hall,

Watch the lights and all.

VOICE WITHIN:

Yes, I see.

SISTER STONE:

While fairy ladies burn incense at night,

BAILIFF:

The mountain nunnery hides itself from sight.

SISTER STONE:

Since Goddess carries remedies of life,

BAILIFF:

Make no excuse but rush in for the strife!

Scene Eighteen
Making Diagnoses

(*Enter Du Liniang in illness, supported by Chunxiang*)

DU LINIANG (*To the tune of **Yijiangfeng***):

I feel so dizzy in disease.

Why am I not feeling well?
The reason is hard to tell.
When I woke up from my dream,
I saw the swallows in the sky
And bamboo blinds nearby.
I watch the spring depart,
I watch the spring depart.
While flowers fall apart,
The rustling tree-leaves break my heart.

Well, Chunxiang,

"How can a dreary lass,
Like a leaf in breeze,
Endure the long disease?

CHUNXIANG:

In every act
And every deed,
You show your charm,
Your noble breed
And lofty creed.

488 DU LINIANG:

My longing for plum bloom
And the man with willow-twigs
Vanish with the spring in gloom.

CHUNXIANG:

When incense burns at noon
And tranquil air is known,
Who makes you groan?
Who makes you pine?
Who makes you feel alone?"

DU LINIANG:

Chunxiang, I've been laid in bed since my dream during the spring stroll. Although I'm not afflicted by pain or itches, I feel dizzy all the time. What's the matter with me?

CHUNXIANG:

Mistress, a dream is a dream. Forget about it!

DU LINIANG:

How can I forget about it!

(*To the tune of **Jinluosuo***)

For a moment's joy,
I'm entangled with the boy.
I'd like to stop recalling him,
But how can I stop recalling him?
I pine away

And live in fear from day to day,

Coughing all the way.

Alas!

Who will feel for me?

Who will share my woe with me?

How I regret,

How I regret for dreamland fret!

CHUNXIANG:

Madam has arranged a Taoist service to rid you of the evil spell.

DU LINIANG:

What's the point to rid me of the spell?

Was it in the garden

That I met the evil spirit from the hell?

CHUNXIANG (*To the previous tune*):

When spring has left, does she think so?

When bedtime comes, does she think so?

Can she retain her breath as seasons flow?

She frowns in stress,

Like a beauty in distress.

My dear mistress,

Is the dreamland man your genuine wealth

That damages your fragile health?

You pine away before you wed your man.

What's the use

Of unrequited love in your life span?

There is no sultry heat,

But you seem to be drunk by chance,

Always in a trance.

(*Enter Chen Zuiliang*)

CHEN ZUILIANG:

"*To air the books, I fear the birds on roads;*

To make the medicine, I need the fluid of toads."

I am instructed by the prefect to make a diagnosis for the young mistress. Here I am in the inner court. I'll call for someone to show me the way. Where's my pupil Chunxiang?

CHUNXIANG (*Greets Chen Zuiliang*):

Mr Chen, Miss Du is now sleeping.

CHEN ZUILIANG:

Don't disturb her. I'll enter the room by myself.

(*Greets Du Liniang*)

Mistress!

DU LINIANG (*Startled*):

Who is it?

489

CHUNXIANG:

It's Mr Chen.

DU LINIANG (*Sits up on bed*):

Mr Chen, as I'm confined to bed, I haven't paid respects to you for some time.

CHEN ZUILIANG:

Mistress, as the saying goes in the classics, "Studies start from diligence and end in negligence." Since you were exposed to the sun and the wind in the back garden the other day, you have been taken ill and have neglected your studies. I've been worried about your health although I did not come to see you. And so I'm delighted to see you and make a diagnosis for you when orders come from the prefect. But I have not expected to see that you are so frail. In this case, when will you be able to get up and go on with your studies? I'm afraid the Dragon-Boat Festival is the earliest.

CHUNXIANG:

You'll have your share for the festival, Mr Chen.

CHEN ZUILIANG:

When I speak of the Dragon-Boat Festival, I don't mean to ask for my share of the gift. As a part of the diagnosis, may I ask how you got ill?

CHUNXIANG:

There's no need to ask. It must have come from *The Book of Poetry*, especially from the line "*A lad would like to woo*".

CHEN ZUILIANG:

Which lad do you mean?

CHUNXIANG:

Who knows!

CHEN ZUILIANG:

If that is the case, I'll use *The Book of Poetry* to cure a disease contracted from it. There is a magic prescription for women's diseases in the first volume.

CHUNXIANG:

Do you remember the prescription in *The Book of Poetry,* Mr Chen?

CHEN ZUILIANG:

According to the prescription, the young mistress should take a lad as she is sick for the lad. As *The Book of Poetry* has it,

> "*As I have seen my dear,*
> *Why shouldn't I rejoice?*"

If the lad gives her a few thrusts, the disease will be thrust out of her at once.

DU LINIANG (*Embarrassed*):

Oh!

CHUNXIANG:

What else would you prescribe?

CHEN ZUILIANG:

Ten sour plums. As *The Book of Poetry* has it,

> "*You see seven plums drop*

From the tree, lying on the way."

There is also the line

"You see three plums drop from the tree."

Three and seven makes ten. That is a good cure for sour memory of lovesickness between men and women.

(*Du Liniang sighs*)

CHUNXIANG:

What else?

CHEN ZUILIANG:

Three southern stars.

CHUNXIANG:

Will three be enough?

CHEN ZUILIANG:

Add a few more if you like. It's said in *The Book of Poetry*,

"I see three stars of Orion rise."

This is a good cure for acute lovesickness between men and women.

CHUNXIANG:

What else?

CHEN ZUILIANG:

I can see that the young mistress has much internal heat. You go and get a closet-stool ready and I'll feed her with some purgatives. This is part of the prescription:

"If you are married to me,

I'll feed your horse for thee."

CHUNXIANG:

Feeding the mistress is quite different from feeding the horse.

CHEN ZUILIANG:

In both cases, you are feeding somebody with something.

DU LINIANG:

Mr Chen proves to be a quack doctor.

CHUNXIANG:

Experienced like an elderly lady in her monthly periods.

DU LINIANG:

Don't stick to your prescriptions, Mr Chen. You'd better start by feeling my pulse.

(*Chen Zuiliang tries to feel her pulse on the back of her hand*)

CHUNXIANG:

Please turn over her hand, Mr Chen.

CHEN ZUILIANG:

According to the *Pulse Know-how* by the famous doctor Wang Shuhe, you must feel the female pulse upside down. Well, for the time being, I'll turn her hand over.

(*Feels her pulse*)

Good Gracious, her pulse is so weak!

(*To the tune of **Jinsuoguawutong**)*

491

Her mind is meek;

Her pulse is weak.

In the prime of her day,

What makes her pine away?

(Rises to his feet)

Listen to me, Chunxiang,

Sick in spring and summer days,

Your mistress needs more care

When autumn brings despair.

I'll go and prepare your medicine, Mistress.

DU LINIANG (*With a sigh*):

Well, Mr Chen,

Deep-rooted out of amour,

My lovesickness is beyond cure.

(Weeps)

You try to cure me but in vain;

When will you come to see me again?

CHEN ZUILIANG, CHUNXIANG:

As patients cannot bear alarm,

You'd better take a rest

And keep away from harm.

DU LINIANG:

Take your time, Mr Chen, I'm afraid I can't see you off. By the way, have you made a divination for me?

CHEN ZUILIANG:

Yes, you'll turn for the better after the Mid-Autumn Festival.

"From fate no one has ever fled;

No doctor can revive the dead."

(Exit)

CHUNXIANG:

Here comes a Taoist nun.

(Enter Sister Stone)

SISTER STONE:

"While no fairy is heard to give salute,

Another lady tastes forbidden fruit."

I'm Sister Stone from the Purple Sunlight Nunnery. I've received orders from the Madam to pray for Miss Du. What is she suffering from?

CHUNXIANG:

She's suffering from lovesickness.

SISTER STONE:

Who is her lover?

CHUNXIANG:

Someone in the back garden.

> (*Sister Stone raises three fingers and Chunxiang shakes her head, then Sister Stone raises five*
> *fingers and Chunxiang shakes her head again*)

SISTER STONE:

Well, tell me whether it is three or five and I'll pray for her.

CHUNXIANG:

Go and ask her by yourself.

SISTER STONE (*Greets Du Liniang*):

Good morning, Miss Du. I'm a Taoist nun!

DU LINIANG (*Taken aback*):

Where are you from?

SISTER STONE:

I'm Sister Stone from the Purple Sunlight Nunnery. I've received orders from the Madam
to pray for you. It's said that you were haunted in the back garden, but I don't believe it.

> (*To the previous tune*)
>
> For a maiden as smart as you,
>
> Can your distracted state be true?

DU LINIANG (*In a trance*):

Oh my dear!

SISTER STONE, CHUNXIANG (*Aside*):

> In a trance she said,
>
> As if she'd lost her head.

SISTER STONE (*Takes a hairpin from Du Liniang, hangs a talisman on it, and makes an incantation*):

> "Beaming bright, beaming bright,
>
> The sun is shedding light.
>
> This talisman dispels the spell
>
> And drives the evils to the hell.
>
> Going, going, gone!"
>
> (*Puts the hairpin back onto Du Liniang's head*)
>
> Keep this talisman
>
> When you sit and sleep
>
> To keep the wild thoughts under ban.

DU LINIANG (*Comes to her senses*):

Well, is this talisman effective? Isn't my lover

> A sprite among the trees
>
> That puts me ill at ease!

SISTER STONE:

If she loses her senses again, I'll strike her with a thunderbolt from my palm.

DU LINIANG:

> It makes just little sense
>
> That while I weather the wind and rain,

You add a thunder to my pain.
SISTER STONE, CHUNXIANG:

In a trance she said,

As if she'd lost her head.
SISTER STONE:
If she goes on like this, I'll hoist a magic flag ten feet high.
DU LINIANG:
What can I say to a nun like this!

(*To the tune of* **Coda**)

With the handsome man dim in my mind,
Oh, Sister Stone,

You have no need for flags of any kind.
When I'm in a pensive mood,

I will be in my dreams confined.
CHUNXIANG (*Supports Du Liniang and goes off stage*):

My mistress is too weak to lift an eye;
SISTER STONE:

As a Taoist nun I pray and lie.
DU LINIANG:

I stay away from crimson bloom
ALL:

To stop the east wind in its gloom.

Scene Nineteen
The Female Chieftain

(*Enter Li Quan with his men*)
LI QUAN (*To the tune of* **Northern Dianjiangchun**):

A smell of mutton struck the land

While aliens dashed and hurled.

Against the winds of war,

We bandit heroes

Outshine the burglars who break the door.

"The army of a thousand hoofs

Raises dust and ashes o'er the roofs.

When Hans acquire an alien tongue,

They curse their natives old and young."

I'm Li Quan, a native of Chuzhou. As a warrior brave enough to fight ten thousand men, I was neglected by the southern dynasty and so I became a bandit chieftain of five hundred men, roaming in the Huaiyang area. At a time when I did not know where to turn to, the emperor of the great Jin Dynasty bestowed upon me the title of Gilded Prince, told me to cause trouble in this area and try to find the opportunity to start a military excursion. To tell the truth, I have more courage than wisdom, but my wife Lady Yang helps a lot. With a pear-blossom spear in hand, she has no match among ten thousand men. What a valiant couple we are on the battlefield! The only pity is that my wife is a bit jealous — all the women captives must be handed over to her at once. All my men are more afraid of her than me. It's true that

> "A snake of a wife swallows the elephant;
>
> A prince of a bandit is the dragon."
>
> (*Enter Lady Yang, carrying a spear*)

LADY YANG (*To the tune of* **Fanbusuan**):

> A bandit's wife with spear and shield
>
> Adds blood to rouge on battlefield.
>
> (*Wields her spear*)
>
> With swirls of wind I wield my spear
>
> And sparkles of pear-blooms appear.
>
> (*Raises her hand as a sign of salutation*)

Your Highness, as I'm fully armoured, I won't do the formal greeting.

LI QUAN:

Do you know, Madam, that the emperor of the great Jin Dynasty has bestowed upon me the title of Gilded Prince?

LADY YANG:

What's Gilded Prince?

LI QUAN:

"Gilded" means "brilliant".

LADY YANG:

Why did he bestow upon you the title?

LI QUAN:

He asked me to cause trouble in Huaiyang for three years. Then, when we have amassed a large troop with ample provisions, we'll cross the river and overthrow the Song Dynasty. If we succeed, I'll be crowned the king.

LADY YANG:

What a wonder! Congratulations! We'll take this opportunity to buy horses and enrol soldiers.

> (*To the tune of* **Liuyaoling**)
>
> Like thunders in the sky,
>
> In the camps the battle drums will roar
>
> While spies are sent across the eastern shore.

ALL:

> A valiant pair
>
> Sit within the camp

And threaten people everywhere.

LADY YANG (*To the previous tune*):

    Amass the grain, enrol the men,

    And buy the battle steeds.

    My hairpins glitter now and then.

ALL:

    A valiant pair

    Sit within the camp

    And threaten people everywhere.

LI QUAN:

    Rebellions start all o'er the land,

LADY YANG:

    With broken swords stuck in the sand.

    No cattle graze on fertile grass

    When wildfire spreads afield, alas!

Scene Twenty
Premature Death

(*Enter Chunxiang*)

CHUNXIANG (*To the tune of* **Jinlongcong**):

    In nightly storm

    Endless woes reduce her form.

    No Taoist magic will prevail;

    No medicine is of avail.

    "You frown when you should frown;

    You smile when you should smile.

    If you can't smile or frown,

    You will die in a while."

I've done my best to wait on Miss Du, for she has been ill from early spring till late autumn. Today is the Mid-Autumn Festival, but it is blowing and raining hard outside. Miss Du is growing from bad to worse, and still I'll bring her here to idle away the time. Yes,

    "A heavy rain enshrouds the autumn moon

    While prayer lamps will die out soon."

    (*Exit*)

    (*Enter the sickly Du Liniang supported by Chunxiang*)

CHUNXIANG (*To the tune of* **Queqiaoxian**):

    There is no moonlight in the hall,

    When floating clouds conceal the sky.

Her chilly dream is bitter as gall.

Earth has not anything to show more smart

Than her affection in her broken heart.

DU LINIANG:

"The water clock drips weaker than my breath

While I still linger on the verge of death.

Amid the fragrance in the nightly rain,

With autumn chill my strength is on the wane."

In my serious illness, Chunxiang, I don't know what day today is.

CHUNXIANG:

It's the fifteenth of the eighth month.

DU LINIANG:

Oh, it's the Mid-Autumn Festival! Are my parents too distressed to enjoy the moon?

CHUNXIANG:

Never mind about that.

DU LINIANG:

Mr Chen made the prophecy that I'd get better after the Mid-Autumn Festival. However, my health is going from bad to worse and I don't feel too well this evening. Open the window and I'll have a look at the moon.

(*Chunxiang opens the window and Du Liniang looks at the moon*)

DU LINIANG (*To the tune of **Jixianbin***):

In the boundless skies,

From where does the moon arise?

In the autumn skies,

Who helps the fairy arise!

Does the west wind make the dream vaporize?

When he has left, he is hard to see again;

I blame gods and ghosts for this in vain.

On my brows and in my heart,

Waves of sorrow start.

(*Falls into a depressed mood*)

CHUNXIANG (*To the previous tune*):

Spring fancy drove her into a trance;

Spring fog and smoke aroused romance.

As human life is not a joke,

It starts and ceases in due time;

Who knows her life recedes like smoke!

For whom, for whom

Has she pined away in gloom?

I'll try to give her a little cheer. Mistress, the moon is hanging in the sky.

The silvery moon o'er there

Will send your gloomy dreams into the air.

DU LINIANG (*Looks up to the sky and sighs*):

> "I've yearned for this Mid-Autumn Day,
>
> *But festivities have filled me with dismay.*
>
> *Just like the solitary moon,*
>
> *I'll vanish in the rain too soon."*
>
> (*To the previous tune*)
>
> Whom does the autumn moonlight please?
>
> The rain and the west wind hurt the trees.
>
> I'm growing thinner on sickbed,
>
> Like a wild goose hurrying to its shed.
>
> I hear the crickets chirrup on the plains
>
> And fierce wind whistle through the window-panes.
>
> (*Shivers, about to faint*)
>
> I feel so chilly in a fit;
>
> My limbs can hardly move a bit.

CHUNXIANG (*Alarmed*):

Miss Du has fainted. Come please, Madam!

> (*Enter Lady Zhen*)

LADY ZHEN:

> "My husband is so rich in wealth;
>
> *My daughter is so poor in health."*

How are you feeling now, my dear daughter?

CHUNXIANG:

She's not feeling well, Madam, she's not feeling well.

LADY ZHEN:

What's to be done!

> (*To the previous tune*)
>
> The dream in your last garden tour
>
> Has put you in a trance;
>
> There is no way of any cure.
>
> (*Weeps*)
>
> How I wish she find a spouse!
>
> If she's alone like this,
>
> She'll soon die in the house.
>
> Everything is null and void;
>
> Our lives will be destroyed.

DU LINIANG (*Comes to senses again*):

> (*To the tune of* **Zhuanlinying**)
>
> What has brought my soul out of the hell?
>
> I am awakened by the tinkling bell.
>
> (*Weeps*)

Thank you for coming, Mom.

(*Falls on her knees in a shaky way*)

> You've treasured me since early days,
> But I can't serve you in my filial ways.

Oh Mom, it's fate!

> I bloom and pine before my prime,
> And so I'll serve you in my next lifetime.

DU LINIANG, LADY ZHEN, CHUNXIANG (*Weep*):

> O wild West Wind, why should you
> Strike me like a bolt out of the blue!

LADY ZHEN (*To the previous tune*):

> With no sons by my side,
> I only have a dainty daughter,
> Who plays with joy and pride.
> We hoped we'd have her all the time.
> But now she's dying before her prime.

My child,

> As evil omens do suggest,
> Your weary heart will go to rest.

DU LINIANG, LADY ZHEN, CHUNXIANG:

> O wild West Wind, why should you
> Strike me like a bolt out of the blue!

DU LINIANG:

If the worst comes to the worst, Mom, what are you going to do with my remains?

LADY ZHEN:

We'll send you back to our ancestral burial ground.

DU LINIANG (*Weeps*):

> (*To the tune of* **Yuyinger**)
> In the coffin I shall stay,
> For fear of hills on homeward way.

LADY ZHEN:

We'll send you home although it's a long way.

DU LINIANG:

However, I have but one request to make. In the back garden there's a plum tree, which I love very much. Will you bury me under that tree?

LADY ZHEN:

How do you come across this idea?

DU LINIANG:

> As I can't become a fairy queen,
> I'll lie beneath a tree that's fresh and green.

LADY ZHEN (*Weeps*):

> She bends her head and sheds large drops of tear,
> Soaked with sweat that chills her heart;

At sight of this, I'd give my life for my dear.

DU LINIANG, LADY ZHEN, CHUNXIANG:

> Oh, relentless heaven,
>
> Why should flowers suffer from the blight
>
> While the moon is full and bright?

LADY ZHEN:

I'll have to go now and prepare with your father for a Taoist service, my child.

> *"When medicine becomes of little use,*
>
> *A Taoist service we shall introduce."*
>
> (*Exit*)

DU LINIANG:

Do you think, Chunxiang, that I may revive someday?

> (*Sighs*)
>
> (*To the previous tune*)
>
> You've always been servile to me;
>
> All the time our thoughts agree.

From now on, Chunxiang, be sure to take good care of my parents.

CHUNXIANG:

Of course I will.

DU LINIANG:

Chunxiang, one thing comes to my mind. My portrait, with a poem inscribed on it, should not be exposed to others. When I'm buried, put it in a red sandalwood case and conceal it under a Taihu rock.

CHUNXIANG:

What for?

DU LINIANG:

> My portrait, by a maiden fair and smart,
>
> May find an echo in another heart.

CHUNXIANG:

Please rest at ease, Mistress. If you should pass away, you would stay in the grave all by yourself. But if you take a good rest and get recovered, I'll beg your father to find a scholar by the name of Plum Mei or Willow Liu as your life companion. Wouldn't that be wonderful?

DU LINIANG:

I'm afraid there's no time for me to wait. Oops, oops!

CHUNXIANG:

> How can we lessen her disease?
>
> How can we make her heart at ease?

DU LINIANG:

After my death, Chunxiang, come and stand before my memorial tablet from time to time, calling aloud to me.

CHUNXIANG:

> Her murmur makes my feeling freeze.

DU LINIANG, CHUNXIANG:

> Oh, relentless heaven,
>
> Why should flowers suffer from the blight
>
> While the moon is full and bright?
>
> (*Du Liniang faints away*)

CHUNXIANG:

Help, help! Hurry up, Master, Madam!

> (*Enter Du Bao and Lady Zhen*)

DU BAO, LADY ZHEN (*To the tune of* **Yiyinger**):

> The night is deep;
>
> The woe is deep.
>
> The gloomy window is wet with rain;
>
> Our daughter fills our hearts with pain.

CHUNXIANG (*Weeps*):

Mistress! My dear mistress!

DU BAO, LADY ZHEN (*Weep*):

Oh, our dear daughter!

> When you pass away
>
> And leave us far behind,
>
> Which heir can we then find?

DU BAO, LADY ZHEN, CHUNXIANG:

> Alas, alas! The human life is brief,
>
> As a floating dandelion or a fading wave,
>
> Or a lonely wind-borne lotus leaf.
>
> (*Du Liniang regains consciousness*)

DU BAO:

Come on, my child! Your dad is here.

DU LINIANG (*Looks at Du Bao*):

Oh, Dad, help me to the middle hall.

DU BAO:

Lean on me, my child.

> (*Supports Du Liniang*)

DU LINIANG (*To the tune of* **Coda**):

> When I lose life as a dropping bloom,
>
> Please erect a stone before my tomb.

Dad, is it the Mid-Autumn Festival tonight?

DU BAO:

Yes, it is, my child.

DU LINIANG:

> It has been raining all through the night.
>
> When the moon is set, I'll meet my doom!
>
> (*Exeunt all*)

(Re-enter Chunxiang in tears)

CHUNXIANG:

Mistress, my dear mistress!

> *"In nature there are unexpected storms;*
>
> *In life there are ill lucks of various forms."*

Miss Du died of sorrow for the brevity of spring. My master and madam are deep in grief over her death. Dear audience, what can I do but have a good cry? Mistress, no more will you ask me

*(To the tune of **Hongna'ao**)*

> To burn the incense slicks,
>
> Remove the candle drips,
>
> Entice the whistling birds,
>
> Or paint your tender lips.

I still remember the sight when you

> Laid down your scissors late at night
>
> And drew your portrait till daylight.

Well, speaking of the portrait, my master saw it and told me to bury it with the coffin lest it should make the madam sad. However, I'll follow my mistress' last wish to

> Conceal it under Taihu rock, but fear
>
> That colours fade before her man comes here.

Oh, here comes Sister Stone.

(Enter Sister Stone)

SISTER STONE:

You're having a good cry and I'll join you. Chunxiang, no more will your mistress

(To the previous tune)

> Teach you how to play the flute,

CHUNXIANG:

True.

SISTER STONE:

> Or stamp on grass and pick the fruit.

CHUNXIANG:

Naturally.

SISTER STONE:

Now that your mistress is dead and gone, life is easier for you.

CHUNXIANG:

What do you mean?

SISTER STONE:

You don't have to

> Chat with your young mistress,
>
> Stay up late at night
>
> Or get up before the day is bright.

CHUNXIANG:

I've got used to it.

SISTER STONE:

There's less trouble for you, too. You don't have to

    Pout your lips when you pick her corn,

    Or clean the night-stool in the morn.

    (*Chunxiang spits with scorn*)

What's more, when your mistress has come of age, she might

    Have a rendezvous off the track,

    And then her mom will break your back.

CHUNXIANG:

None of your nonsense! Here comes the madam.

    (*Enter Lady Zhen*)

LADY ZHEN (*In tears*):

My dear child!

    (*To the previous tune*)

    You stayed around me from day to day

    And never smiled to men nor went astray.

    You learned the maiden classics from the start

    And I had not a worry in my heart.

    Indeed I had been worried about your health

    But never thought that death would strike by stealth.

    (*Sobs*)

    I'll have no daughter in my future days;

    This thought inflicts me in a thousand ways.

    (*Falls in a swoon*)

CHUNXIANG (*In alarm*):

Madam has fainted, Master! Hurry, hurry!

    (*Enter Du Bao, in tears*)

DU BAO:

My poor child! Alas, here lies my lady in a faint. My lady,

    (*To the previous tune*)

    Had you not been fated to be without an heir,

    I must have made mistakes without compare.

    It's best to have more daughters by our side,

    When we haven't well-known doctors as our guide.

Oh, heavens, heavens! At my age when my hair turns grey,

    What's the use of having massive wealth,

    When our daughter dies of broken health?

Take care of yourself, my lady. Even if you

    Are filled with woe and pain,

Your daughter won't

    Come back to life again.

    (*Enter the butler*)

BUTLER:

> "The scared crow flies away with worldly woes;
>
> The magpie brings in bliss the king bestows."

My lord, here's the government bulletin on your promotion.

DU BAO (*Reads the government bulletin*):

The Ministry of Personnel issues the following imperial decree: "In view of the intended southward invasion by the bandits from the Jin Dynasty, Du Bao, Prefect of Nan'an, is promoted to the Envoy of Appeasement in charge of the defense of Huaiyang. Du Bao is to go to his new office without delay. So much for the imperial command."

> (*With sighs*)

As the imperial decree impels me to go north, my lady, I won't be able to send Liniang's remains to the west. Butler, send for Tutor Chen at once.

BUTLER:

His Excellency wants to see you, Mr Chen.

> (*Enter Chen Zuiliang*)

CHEN ZUILIANG:

> "Long life, short life, a grave contains them all;
>
> For weal, for woe, the guests meet in the selfsame hall."
>
> (*Greets Du Bao*)

DU BAO:

Mr Chen, my daughter has left you for good.

CHEN ZUILIANG (*Weeps*):

I know. I'm deeply grieved at the passing away of Miss Du, which has left me out of a job. I'm glad that you have been promoted, but I have nowhere to dwell in.

> (*All weep*)

DU BAO:

I've something to talk over with you, Mr Chen. I've received the imperial decree to go to my new office immediately. My daughter will be buried under a plum tree in the back garden according to her last wish. As I'm afraid that there might be inconvenience for my successor, I've ordered that the back garden be exclusively separated and be named the Plum Blossom Taoist Nunnery, where my daughter's memorial tablet will be placed. I'd like to ask Sister Stone to tend to the shrine. Sister Stone, do you agree?

SISTER STONE (*Kneels*):

I'll burn incense and add fresh water to the shrine, but I need someone else to take charge of other duties.

LADY ZHEN:

Will you be so kind as to do this, Mr Chen?

CHEN ZUILIANG:

I'll be glad at your service.

LADY ZHEN:

My lord, we'd better assign some land to cover the expenses for the maintenance.

DU BAO:

There are two hectors of uncultivated land in the public cemetery. The yield from the land can be used to cover the expenses for the nunnery.

CHEN ZUILIANG:

I'll take care of the land.

SISTER STONE:

As I'm the nun of the nunnery, naturally I'll take care of it. As you're nicknamed Chen Jueliang, which means "Devoid of Food", how can you take care of it?

CHEN ZUILIANG:

A scholar can find food everywhere, including the nunnery. You are the nun of the nunnery, but I am an elderly scholar. Why shouldn't I take care of the land and reap the harvest?

DU BAO:

You don't have to argue. Mr Chen will take care of the land. Mr Chen, in my term of office here, I've always favoured the schools.

CHEN ZUILIANG:

That is known to all. According to the time-honoured practice, at the time of your promotion, I'll have the local scholars write a eulogy on the love you've left behind for the people and erect an inscribed monument in the memorial hall. Copies of the eulogy and the inscriptions go well with the gifts to your superiors when you arrive in the capital.

SISTER STONE:

Mr "Devoid of Food", is the eulogy on the love of your mistress?

CHEN ZUILIANG:

It's a eulogy on the prefect's love for the people. It has nothing to do with the mistress.

SISTER STONE:

And what is a memorial hall?

CHEN ZUILIANG:

It's a large worshipping hall with a statue of the prefect in it. Above the door there is a horizontal board with the inscription "Memorial Hall for Lord Du".

SISTER STONE:

In this case, why not have a statue of the young mistress too and we'll take care of them both?

DU BAO (*Annoyed*):

None of your nonsense! Although this is a time-honoured practice, I'll do away with it. Mr Chen, Sister Stone,

> (*To the tune of* **Yibujin**)
> Our daughter's grave mounts three feet high;
> My wife and I entrust it to you hereby.

We do not expect you to watch over it all the time, but we hope that on festivals

> A bowl of rice for her you will supply.

DU BAO:

> *Her soul and spirit have gained eternal life,*

LADY ZHEN:

After eighteen years of earthly strife.
CHEN ZUILIANG:
As sorrow for her will forever last,
DU BAO, LADY ZHEN, CHEN ZUILIANG, SISTER STONE:
We feel deep grief when we retrace her past.

Scene Twenty-One
An Audience with the Envoy

(Enter the head monk)
HEAD MONK (*To the tune of* **Guangguangzha**):
In a ragged sakaya here and now,
I am a Buddhist monk in Macao.
With bodhisattvas of abundant wealth
Live many monks of soundest health.
I'm the head monk of the Treasure Temple near the Xiangshan Bay, Guangzhou Prefecture.
This temple was built by the foreign merchants to receive the officials of treasure appraisal.
The Imperial Envoy Lord Miao, whose term of office has just ended, will display his treasures
before the Treasure Bodhisattva. Here I am to welcome him.
(Enter the imperial envoy Miao Shunbin, followed by the interpreter, two attendants and a foreign merchant)
MIAO SHUNBIN (*To the tune of* **Guazhen'er**):
As Southern Song begins its foreign trade,
My men approach the Pearl House in a parade.
(The monk welcomes Miao Shunbin)
ALL:
The God of Southern Sea,
Treasure Boy and Virgin Maid
Listen to Bodhisattva's decree.
MIAO SHUNBIN:
"Although the traffic to the cliff was hard,
The marshal marched to the sea in disregard.
As the Vietnamese sent corals of their free will,
The envoy need not go through hills and rills."
I am Miao Shunbin, Imperial Envoy for treasure appraisal. Now that my three years' term of
office is over, I'm going to pay my last tribute to the Treasure Bodhisattva. Interpreter!
(The interpreter greets Miao Shunbin)
FOREIGN MERCHANT (*Greets Miao Shunbin*):
Galala ...

(The head monk greets Miao Shunbin)

MIAO SHUNBIN:

Interpreter, tell the foreign merchant to present his treasures.

INTERPRETER:

All the treasures are ready for your inspection.

MIAO SHUNBIN *(Rises to his feet and inspects the treasures)*:

What rare treasures! They are as crystal as mountain torrents and as brilliant as the sun and the moon. This Treasure Temple indeed deserves its name! Offer incense to the Bodhisattva.

(With ringing of bells within, Miao Shunbin kowtows)

MIAO SHUNBIN *(To the tune of **Tingqianliu**)*:

> While the monks chant of three virtuous deeds,
>
> I watch the seven treasures none exceeds.
>
> They make the earthly world sedate and bright
>
> And bathe the universe with brilliant light.
>
> By displaying this,
>
> The Bodhisattva showers his bliss.

ALL:

> Oh, Bodhisattva,
>
> Give us a great store,
>
> And much makes more.

MIAO SHUNBIN:

Monk, chant a blessing for the foreign merchant.

HEAD MONK *(To the previous tune)*:

> The sea abounds in treasures of all kinds,
>
> But waves may toss the ships and minds.
>
> The merchants with their treasure hoard
>
> Fear to brave the wind and waves aboard.
>
> Bodhisattva Guanyin,
>
> Your name brings bliss through thick and thin.

ALL:

> Oh, Bodhisattva,
>
> Give us a great store,
>
> And much makes more.

(Enter Liu Mengmei)

LIU MENGMEI *(To the tune of **Guazhen'er**)*:

> The capital lies in the westernmost,
>
> But I was born beside the southern coast.
>
> The treasure-loving lamas
>
> And bead-reckoning monks
>
> Are worthless as the junks.

I often sneer at myself, a penniless loafer without home. As chance would have it, the

imperial envoy is inspecting the treasures in the temple and I'll try to obtain an audience with him. I don't know whether I can persuade him into giving me some help.

(*Greets the attendant*)

Sir, will you be kind to announce that Liu Mengmei, student of the Confucian Academy in the Prefecture of Guangzhou, would like to ask permission to have a look at the treasures?

(*The attendant announces*)

MIAO SHUNBIN:

These treasures are gifts to the emperor, not for public display. However, as he's a Confucian scholar, let him come in and have a look.

LIU MENGMEI (*Greets Miao Shunbin*):

"As pearls in southern palace are the best,

MIAO SHUNBIN:

There is no need to have jade from the west.

LIU MENGMEI:

Here I am to bare my thoughts to you,

MIAO SHUNBIN:

And I am glad to meet a brilliant guest."

May I ask why you come to this temple?

LIU MENGMEI:

I am a poor scholar. Hearing of your inspection of the treasures, I've come here to ask your permission to let me have a look at the treasures so that I can be enlightened.

MIAO SHUNBIN (*With a smile*):

As you are a pearl of a man from the south, I don't have to conceal the western jade from you. Feel free to have a look round.

(*Shows Liu Mengmei around to inspect the treasures*)

LIU MENGMEI:

I thought I knew the names of precious jewels and jades, but I cannot recognise some specimens here. Your Excellency, will you be kind to enlighten me?

MIAO SHUNBIN:

Here you see

(*To the tune of **Zhuyunfei**)*

The Divine Pebbles of the Milky Way,

The Pills of Gold, the Iron Tree Bloom,

The Cat's-eyes that emit the brilliant ray,

And Emeralds that dispel the gloom.

Look, there you see

The Rubies from the foreign land,

The Magic goblet from the west,

The Toad of Jade that sucks moon-sand,

The Sun-flint Pearls and Ice-plate blest.

LIU MENGMEI:

In southern Guangdong, we have moonlight pearls and coral trees.

MIAO SHUNBIN:

> The inch-wide pearls will have no place to stay;
>
> The three-feet corals will all be thrown away.

LIU MENGMEI:

If I had not come to this sacred place, how could I have witnessed such miracles!

> (*To the previous tune*)
>
> The rarest treasures come from foreign lands
>
> And in the end will reach imperial hands.

Your Excellency, may I ask how far away these treasures came from?

MIAO SHUNBIN:

Some came from thirty thousand *li* away and the others at least ten thousand *li* away.

LIU MENGMEI:

Is that possible? Did they fly here or did they walk here?

MIAO SHUNBIN (*Laughs*):

How could they fly or walk! The foreign merchants have brought them here as the court has offered a high price.

LIU MENGMEI (*With a sigh*):

Your Excellency, these insensible and footless treasures can reach the emperor from thirty thousand *li* away, while a competent scholar like me cannot reach the emperor from three thousand *li* away. I have feet but I cannot fly!

> Attracted by alluring prices,
>
> The crafty merchants came by ship;

Alas!

> The waves have lent wings to the trip.

MIAO SHUNBIN:

Do you suspect that these treasures are all shams?

LIU MENGMEI:

Your Excellency, even if they are genuine, you can't eat them when you are hungry and you can't wear them when you are cold. They are but

> Useless small devices!

MIAO SHUNBIN:

Then, what is your idea of genuine treasures?

LIU MENGMEI:

To be frank, I am a piece of genuine treasure.

> At court I'll prove my worth,
>
> The rarest treasure here on earth.

MIAO SHUNBIN (*Laughs*):

I'm afraid that there are too many rare birds at court now.

LIU MENGMEI:

> I'm better than the treasures in the sea
>
> Or all the treasures people ever see.

MIAO SHUNBIN:

509

In that case, you should be presented to His Majesty.

LIU MENGMEI:

As a poor scholar, I'm unable to serve the officials; how am I in a position to see His Majesty?

MIAO SHUNBIN:

You see, it's easier to see the emperor than the officials.

LIU MENGMEI:

But the travel expenses for three thousand *li* are more than I can afford.

MIAO SHUNBIN:

That won't be a problem at all. As the ancients gave pieces of gold to valiant men, I will give you pieces of silver from the official revenue to cover your travel expenses.

LIU MENGMEI:

With your help I'll set off at once because I have no family burden.

MIAO SHUNBIN:

Attendants, get some silver for the scholar and prepare some wine.

> (*Enter the attendant*)

ATTENDANT:

> "The Guangzhou folk prefer the litchi wine;
>
> The north-bound scholar meets a patron benign."

The wine is ready and here's the silver.

MIAO SHUNBIN:

Sir, please accept the silver for your travel expenses.

LIU MENGMEI:

Thank you very much.

MIAO SHUNBIN (*Offers the wine*):

> (*To the tune of Sanxueshi*)
>
> When you leave here with wine on your lips,
>
> You'll make fair progress on your trips.

LIU MENGMEI:

> When emperor offers lofty price,
>
> I'll serve him with my sound advice.

MIAO SHUNBIN, LIU MENGMEI:

> Make haste to shed the scholar's gown;
>
> Become a high official with renown.

LIU MENGMEI:

I'm really afraid that

> (*To the previous tune*)
>
> Although the emperor has discerning eyes,
>
> The heaven may be blind.
>
> Oh that I be a gem the Persians find!

MIAO SHUNBIN:

> As the gold is always there,
>
> The panner is aware of what to spare.

MIAO SHUNBIN, LIU MENGMEI:

> Make haste to shed the scholar's gown;
>
> Become a high official with renown.

LIU MENGMEI:

I'm leaving now.

> (*To the tune of* **Coda**)
>
> It's kind of you to give me gold.

MIAO SHUNBIN:

> A cup of wine has made you bold.

I wish you

> A brilliant future ahead of you!

LIU MENGMEI:

> *Above my black silk hat is lucid air;*

MIAO SHUNBIN:

> *You are a man with noble grace and wit.*

LIU MENGMEI:

> *I hear that the imperial court is just and fair;*

MIAO SHUNBIN:

> *I've helped you make your journey there.*

Scene Twenty-Two
A Hard Journey

(*Enter Liu Mengmei, with an umbrella and a bundle, looking sick*)

LIU MENGMEI (*To the tune of* **Daolianzi**):

> A man en route without a rest
>
> Is like a bird out of its nest.
>
> (*Howling wind within*)
>
> I brave the dreadful wind and snow,
>
> Feeling cold and thus depressed.
>
> *"I packed my bundle in the south*
>
> *And took a boat toward the north.*
>
> *With homesick thoughts in chilly days,*
>
> *I see plum blossoms bursting forth."*

The autumn wind was blowing when I left Envoy Miao Shunbin and had farewell dinner with my kith and kin. Winter has now been well under way when I get off the boat and climb over the Plum Ridge. As the wind north of the ridge is unexpectedly bitter, I've caught a cold but do not want to turn back. After one day's trudge in the wind and snow, now I see Nan'an in the distance. What a wretched journey!

(*To the tune of* **Shanpoyang**)

With hungry vultures howling in the trees,

Alone the sick man leaves the ridge behind.

The hailstones hit my head and make me freeze;

The whistling umbrella stirs my mind.

A shortcut I take,

But no inns can I find.

Alas, snow,

Why do you play tricks on me flake by flake?

Look, there's a broken bridge across the stream!

My footsteps shake.

Well, here's a willow tree. I'll hold onto it and walk across the bridge.

It is a hunchback friend, I deem.

(*Holds onto the willow tree and walks across the bridge*)

Snap,

It is a withered tree I've found.

Thump,

I slip and fall flat on the ground.

(*Falls to the ground*)

(*Enter Chen Zuiliang*)

CHEN ZUILIANG (*To the tune of* **Bubujiao**):

Free from care, free from woe,

On a donkey I ride,

Toward a bridge I go.

To find a tutor's job I've tried.

(*Liu Mengmei groans*)

Why is there such a groan?

(*Looks around*)

Well, from which broken kiln

Comes such a man of skin and bone?

LIU MENGMEI:

Help! Help!

CHEN ZUILIANG:

I, Chen Zuiliang, have come out in the cold weather to look for a tutor's job. As my luck would have it, the first thing I meet is someone who falls in the stream. It's none of my business.

LIU MENGMEI (*Cries again*):

Help!

CHEN ZUILIANG:

Help? A good deed is always a double blessing. I'll ask him what's happened.

(*Asks Liu Mengmei*)

Who are you and how did you have a fall here?

LIU MENGMEI:

I'm a scholar.

CHEN ZUILIANG:

As you are a scholar, let me help you to your feet.

(*Slips when he tries to help Liu Mengmei to his feet, and make fun at each other*)

May I ask where you come from?

LIU MENGMEI (*To the tune of* **Fenrusong**):

> From Guangzhou I've come by boat
>
> To offer treasures I can boast.

CHEN ZUILIANG:

What are your treasures?

LIU MENGMEI:

> On my way to take imperial tests,
>
> I've caught a cold in flimsy coat.
>
> When I tried to cross the bridge,
>
> I nearly broke my back and throat.

CHEN ZUILIANG:

It seems to me that you are fully confident of your success, otherwise you won't be going through all the hardships.

LIU MENGMEI:

As a matter of fact, I'm a jade pillar that holds up the sky and a gold bridge that runs across the sea.

CHEN ZUILIANG (*Laughs*):

How comes that the pillar cracks with the cold weather and that the bridge collapses in the middle? Well, so much so. I'm quite well-versed in medicine. There is a Plum Blossom Nunnery nearby, where you can stop over till spring comes.

> (*To the previous tune*)
>
> A scholar came across the bridge,
>
> A blissful sign to have a fall.
>
> I'll get you medicine on the ridge,
>
> For you to take in nunnery best of all.

LIU MENGMEI:

How far is the nunnery away from here?

CHEN ZUILIANG (*Points the way*):

> Over there where snow-white blossoms smile
>
> And silken banners wave above the wall.

LIU MENGMEI:

Will you please lead the way?

> *At thirty still without a home,*

CHEN ZUILIANG:

> *I saw you at first sight a friend.*

LIU MENGMEI:

> *In holy places where the fairies roam,*

LIU MENGMEI, CHEN ZUILIANG:

The east wind escorts them to a good end.

Scene Twenty-Three
The Judgement in Hell

(*Enter the Infernal Judge, followed by a ghost carrying a writing-brush and a register-book*)

INFERNAL JUDGE (*To the tune of* **Northern Dianjiangchun**):

> I did my service well
>
> For Prince of the Tenth Hell.
>
> The human beings,
>
> When they are no more,
>
> Will be led into our door.

I am Judge Hu under Prince of the Tenth Hell. There had been ten princes in the hell, but when the population dwindled due to the wars between the house of Zhao and the house of Jin, the Jade Emperor in the heaven decreed to cut the staff. One prince was to take charge of one of the nine territories, and only the tenth prince was dismissed from his office. As there was no one to take care of the official seal, the Jade Emperor placed it in my charge as a reward to my honesty and intelligence. Today is my first day to be in office. At the sight of the lines of ghosts and yakshas with knives and swords in their hands, I can sense that this is no small occasion.

GHOST (*Presents the writing-brush*):

Every new official on his inauguration day will use this brush to allot the punishment and sign his name. Will Your Lordship sing praise of the brush?

INFERNAL JUDGE (*Examines the brush*):

You see, ghost, this writing-brush is of great significance.

> (*To the tune of* **Hunjianglong**)
>
> This brush is resting on the rack,
>
> Made of human flesh.
>
> The clerks and copyists at the back
>
> Are always smart and fresh.

GHOST:

What's the brush-shaft made of?

INFERNAL JUDGE:

It's made of an arm-bone or a shin-bone,

> As round as a bamboo pole.

GHOST:

What about the brush-hairs?

INFERNAL JUDGE:

They are hairs from the heads of the ox-head ghosts and the yakshas,

Or scarlet beard encircled by a wire.

GHOST:

Who selected the hairs?

INFERNAL JUDGE:

The hairs were picked

According to the special desire.

GHOST:

What is the name of this writing-brush?

INFERNAL JUDGE:

This tube of a pen

Is honoured by the sire.

GHOST:

What would you do if you are in high spirits?

INFERNAL JUDGE (*Laughs and then dances*):

I'll make a whistle

To scare away the evil force,

Or start a dance

To track the heavenly course.

GHOST:

What if you are merry?

INFERNAL JUDGE:

When I'm merry,

I'll bring my brush toward the bridge to hell.

GHOST:

What if you are bored?

INFERNAL JUDGE:

When I'm bored,

I'll throw my brush toward the door to hell.

GHOST:

Did you succeed in the celestial examination?

INFERNAL JUDGE:

When I took the test for gods,

My name was listed on the top.

GHOST:

Are you good at writing poems?

INFERNAL JUDGE:

With the help of literary stars,

My flow of poems will never stop.

GHOST:

You are a highly gifted scholar.

INFERNAL JUDGE:

Although I'm no match with Li He

Whose songs resounded to a height,

I'm on a par with Shi Manqing

Who wrote his poems at night.

Although I can't depict the whole wild world,

I can well stir up trouble with all might.

GHOST:

What position are you holding now?

INFERNAL JUDGE:

You ask about my position?

In Polaris' hall, in Yama's palace,

I stand erect with pride.

You say I've no office?

In temples of mountain gods and city gods,

My statue stands on the left-hand side.

GHOST:

Is there anyone whom you respect?

INFERNAL JUDGE:

With upraised hands I stand there in my place,

And let the Buddha sit in solemn grace.

GHOST:

Is there anyone who annoys you?

INFERNAL JUDGE:

Well, a statue of mine less than three feet tall is by no means majestic. I have to face

Inferior ghosts of various kinds

With grotesque shapes and minds.

GHOST:

Your official hat is somewhat outworn.

INFERNAL JUDGE:

As I stand all day,

With a writing-brush and a register-book in hand,

My hat is stained with dust and clay.

GHOST:

There's no ink on your writing-brush.

INFERNAL JUDGE:

To moisten the brush,

If you give me gold, silver or money,

I will not blush.

GHOST:

Here's the register-book of the dead.

INFERNAL JUDGE:

To find the names I take a casual look

And fetch the dead men at the proper date.

I'll make a tick and sign my name
Behind one man or another
According to his destined fate.
In the register-book
Is recorded every name,
Be it small or great.

GHOST:

I'll prepare the ink for you.

INFERNAL JUDGE:

On the slab he prepares the ink;
Scritch-scratch, scritch-scratch,
The shiny black ink is filled to the brink.

GHOST:

The rooster is crowing.

INFERNAL JUDGE:

The death-knell tolls,
Ding-dong,ding-dong.
While roosters invoke the wandering souls.

GHOST:

Will you please tick the names now?

INFERNAL JUDGE:

When I tick some names.
These souls will enter samsara,
A multitude of weal and woe.
When I tick the other names,
Those souls will enter bottomless hell,
To suffer endless torments down below.

GHOST:

Your signature, please.

INFERNAL JUDGE:

Alas, with my signature,
They will go through severe ordeal.

GHOST:

What about "invitations"?

INFERNAL JUDGE:

As for invitations,
They're for the sick that cannot heal.

GHOST:

Hang up the scales!

(Petty ghosts respond in chorus)

INFERNAL JUDGE:

With a pair of scales hanging on hair,

We find their bodies lighter than their crime,

And so we'll finish with them in no time.

(*Cries of pain and begging for mercy are heard from within*)

GHOST:

The Ninth Prince is torturing the dead souls next door.

INFERNAL JUDGE:

The torture is music of the flesh.

The wails and howls of those dead souls

Are masterpieces of pain.

At this time,

The slightest smile is thought to be insane.

(*Wails are heard from within*)

In this place,

The faintest moan is held in rein.

GHOST:

So you are afraid!

INFERNAL JUDGE (*Annoyed*):

Oops!

By infernal law

I mete out different awards.

In the dreadful hell,

I wield my judicial swords.

My bearded face is fierce and stern;

My uplift eyes are burning bright.

I've got recorders on my left

And secretaries on my right.

Like the gold county judge,

Like the silver prefectural judge,

Like the copper provincial judge,

Like the iron ministerial judge —

Like all the judges in the earthly courts,

I make my judgements according to laws.

With a humidity samsara,

With a universe samsara,

With a womb samsara,

With a shell samsara —

With different samsara forms,

I've been promoted because I have norms.

In dignity I rule the fate of men;

In majesty I fulfil the godly yen.

Send for the secretary. As is recorded in the register-book, how many cases are to be dispatched today?

(*Enter the secretary*)

SECRETARY:

> "*A secretary in the human world*
>
> *Becomes a secretary in the netherworld.*"

Your Lordship, since the Tenth Prince was dismissed, his office has been vacant for three years. In the City of Innocent Deaths, there are four males of minor offenses Zhao Da, Qian Shiwu, Sun Xin and Li Houer, in addition to a female Du Liniang. They haven't been sentenced yet.

INFERNAL JUDGE:

Bring in the four male offenders first.

> (*The ghost leads in the four male offenders: Zhao Da, Qian Shiwu, Sun Xin and Li Houer*)

GHOST:

Here are the male offenders.

INFERNAL JUDGE (*Calls the roll*):

For what offense, Zhao Da, are you detained in the City of Innocent Deaths?

ZHAO DA:

I'm not guilty. When I was alive, I would like to sing some songs.

INFERNAL JUDGE:

Step aside. What about you, Qian Shiwu?

QIAN SHIWU:

I'm not guilty. When I built a small hut, I mixed some allalloch eaglewood in the mud.

INFERNAL JUDGE:

Step aside. And you, Sun Xin?

SUN XIN:

When I was young, I used to spend some money in the brothel.

INFERNAL JUDGE:

And you, Li Houer?

LI HOUER:

I committed a minor offense. I'm homosexual.

GHOST:

That's true. Even here in the hell he seduced a little monkey of a man.

INFERNAL JUDGE (*Annoyed*):

Shut up! Stand back and mind your own business!

> (*Writes on the register-book*)

Now listen carefully to the verdicts.

> (*The four male offenders kneel on the ground*)

As I have just come into office, I'm not going to put you to tortures. You are remitted and allowed to have a shell samsara.

LI HOUER:

Would Your Lordship tell us what shells you mean? If they are of Arabian eggs, we'll be reborn in the remote border-area.

INFERNAL JUDGE:

Pooh, do you want to be reborn a man? You'll enter the eggshells.

ZHAO DA, QIAN SHIWU, SUN XIN, LI HOUER (*Wail loudly*):

Oh, we'll be devoured by men!

INFERNAL JUDGE:

All right. I won't have men devour you. Zhao Da, as you were fond of singing, you shall be reborn as an oriole.

ZHAO DA:

It's nice of you. I shall be Miss Oriole in my next life!

INFERNAL JUDGE:

Qian Shiwu, as you used to live in a spiced mud hut, you shall be reborn as a swallow to enjoy your next life in a swallow's nest.

QIAN SHIWU:

I'll be glad to be Empress Swallow in my next life!

INFERNAL JUDGE:

Sun Xin, as you used to spend money in the brothel, you shall be reborn as a butterfly.

LI HOUER:

I'd like to go with Sun Xin and be a butterfly too.

INFERNAL JUDGE:

Li Houer, as you used to be a homosexual, you shall be reborn as a bee with a needle in your asshole.

LI HOUER:

Why, whom am I to sting?

INFERNAL JUDGE:

Now you four insects, listen to me.

(*To the tune of* **Youhulu**)

Oh Butterfly,

How pretty is your powdered coat!

Oh Bee,

How bitter is your biting sting!

Oh Swallow,

How fragrant is your mudded nest!

Oh Oriole,

How pleasant is the song you sing!

You friends will fly among the blooms abreast.

In the earthly world, the lads and lasses may

Pelt you oriole all around,

Or strike you butterfly with a perfumed fan.

At the same time,

In paintings you swallow is found;

In spring you bee will buzz as hard as you can.

LI HOUER:

When I come here again as a bee, I'll sting your head.

INFERNAL JUDGE:

You're asking for a sound beating.

LI HOUER:

Oh, pity on me!

INFERNAL JUDGE:

All right, be gone with the wind! Get out at once!

> (*The Infernal Judge puffs at the four males. Exeunt the four, each flying in his own manner. The Infernal Judge whistles towards the exit. Enter the ghost, ushering in Du Liniang*)

GHOST:

> *"You won't meet me on Heaven's path;*
>
> *I'm not to blame for Hell's fierce wrath."*

Here's the female offender.

INFERNAL JUDGE (*Raises his head. Aside*):

What a fair lady-ghost!

> (*To the tune of* **Tianxiale**)
>
> A fairy of a ghost is standing here,
>
> Heigh-ho, heigh-ho,
>
> Come near, please come near.
>
> (*Du Liniang complains*)

INFERNAL JUDGE:

> Bodhisattva Guanyin's cry in hell, I hear.

GHOST (*Whispers in the Infernal Judge's ear*):

Why don't you take her as your concubine?

INFERNAL JUDGE:

Pooh, according to the celestial law, those who flirt with women prisoners will be beheaded.

> *"You may go on with your wild talk,*
>
> *But without my head, how can I walk?"*
>
> (*Du Liniang moans*)

INFERNAL JUDGE (*Turns back*):

> Doesn't she seem to flirt with me?

Bring her forward!

> (*To the tune of* **Nuozhaling**)
>
> With rosy cheeks,
>
> Are you going to a garden or a pub?
>
> With pretty hairpins,
>
> Are you going to a concert or a club?
>
> With honeyed smiles,
>
> Are you going to a date?
>
> Of what illness did you die?
>
> Where is your family estate?
>
> Your colour is alien to hell at any rate.

DU LINIANG:

I've neither married nor drunk any wine. My skin has looked like this since I was born. Under a plum tree in the back garden of Nan'an Prefect's residence, I dreamed of a scholar who snapped off a willow-twig and asked me to write a poem about it. He was gentle and affectionate. When I woke up, I wrote a poem,

> "Her future spouse who shares the pillow
> Will be found by the plum or willow."

As a matter of fact, I died of lovesickness.

INFERNAL JUDGE:

You liar! How can anyone die as a result of a dream?

> (*To the tune of* **Quetazhi**)
> Young and tiny as you look,
> You cling so strongly to your dream.
> Who can read your dream?
> Who can guess the theme?
> Heigh-ho, heigh-ho,
> Where is this young scholar?
> Who else did you see in your dream?

DU LINIANG:

I didn't see anyone else. When a flower dropped off, I was frightened.

INFERNAL JUDGE:

Send for the flower god in charge of the prefect's back garden in Nan'an.

> (*The ghost repeats the order*)
> (*Enter Flower God*)

FLOWER GOD:

> "The flowers drop with springtime rain;
> A moment's joy is mixed with pain."

How do you do, Your Excellency!

> (*Salutes the Infernal Judge*)

INFERNAL JUDGE:

Flower God, she says that she had a dream in the back garden and died of a startle caused by a fallen flower. Is that true?

FLOWER GOD:

Yes. She was dreaming of a rendezvous with a young scholar when she was wakened by a fallen flower. She died of lovesickness.

INFERNAL JUDGE:

Were you dressed as a young scholar to allure her?

FLOWER GOD:

Do you mean that I allured her?

INFERNAL JUDGE:

Do you think that we are all fools in the netherworld?

> (*To the tune of* **Houtinghuagun**)

> Spring is a carefree time for all,
> But you disturb the peace of mind.
> With flowers you decorate the hall;
> You should have left your lust behind.
> With blossoms at your beck and call,
> An overabundance glares mankind.
> Now, enumerate the flowers you find.

FLOWER GOD:

I'll enumerate for you. The peach blossom —

INFERNAL JUDGE:

> Leads to a lover's tryst;

FLOWER GOD:

The pear blossom —

INFERNAL JUDGE:

> Gives love a twist.

FLOWER GOD:

The gold-coin blossom —

INFERNAL JUDGE:

> Is a wedding gift;

FLOWER GOD:

The seven-barks blossom —

INFERNAL JUDGE:

> Serves as a wooing shift.

FLOWER GOD:

The peony blossom —

INFERNAL JUDGE:

> Links the hearts;

FLOWER GOD:

The brush-pen blossom —

INFERNAL JUDGE:

> Practices the writing arts.

FLOWER GOD:

The water chestnut blossom —

INFERNAL JUDGE:

> Stands on the dressing-table there;

FLOWER GOD:

The plantain lily blossom —

INFERNAL JUDGE:

> Adorns the hair.

FLOWER GOD:

The rose blossom —

INFERNAL JUDGE:

Applies to the face;

FLOWER GOD:

The winter-sweet blossom —

INFERNAL JUDGE:

    Paints the forehead with grace.

FLOWER GOD:

The mullein blossom —

INFERNAL JUDGE:

    Decorates the skirt;

FLOWER GOD:

The narcissus blossom —

INFERNAL JUDGE:

    Looks like a fairy shirt.

FLOWER GOD:

The lantern blossom —

INFERNAL JUDGE:

    Is shining bright;

FLOWER GOD:

The roseleaf raspberry blossom —

524 INFERNAL JUDGE:

    Causes a drunken sight.

FLOWER GOD:

The pot marigold blossom —

INFERNAL JUDGE:

    Serves for a wedding cup;

FLOWER GOD:

The ribbon blossom —

INFERNAL JUDGE:

    Ties the skirt up.

FLOWER GOD:

The mulga blossom —

INFERNAL JUDGE:

    Hangs her head in taste;

FLOWER GOD:

The willow blossom —

INFERNAL JUDGE:

    Sways like slender waist.

FLOWER GOD:

The trumpet-vine blossom —

INFERNAL JUDGE:

    Blows like a cock;

FLOWER GOD:

The hot-pepper blossom —
INFERNAL JUDGE:
　　Removes her block.
FLOWER GOD:
The Michelia figo blossom —
INFERNAL JUDGE:
　　Expects her love;
FLOWER GOD:
The red sunflower blossom —
INFERNAL JUDGE:
　　Turns to her face above.
FLOWER GOD:
The liana blossom —
INFERNAL JUDGE:
　　Twines like a bitch;
FLOWER GOD:
The crape myrtle blossom —
INFERNAL JUDGE:
　　Fears the itch.
FLOWER GOD:
The day lily blossom —
INFERNAL JUDGE:
　　Prophesies a son;
FLOWER GOD:
The lilac blossom —
INFERNAL JUDGE:
　　Blooms in the sun.
FLOWER GOD:
The cardamum blossom —
INFERNAL JUDGE:
　　Is pregnant with seeds;
FLOWER GOD:
The milk blossom —
INFERNAL JUDGE:
　　Is sufficient for needs.
FLOWER GOD:
The gardenia blossom —
INFERNAL JUDGE:
　　Is discrete beyond compare;
FLOWER GOD:
The wild-apple blossom —
INFERNAL JUDGE:

> Is free from any care.

FLOWER GOD:

The citrus blossom —

INFERNAL JUDGE:

> Leans against the fence;

FLOWER GOD:

The crabapple blossom —

INFERNAL JUDGE:

> Has a drowsy sense.

FLOWER GOD:

The boy blossom —

INFERNAL JUDGE:

> Is a smiling lad;

FLOWER GOD:

The sister blossom —

INFERNAL JUDGE:

> Is a jealous lass.

FLOWER GOD:

The knotweed blossom —

INFERNAL JUDGE:

> Is reluctant to bud;

FLOWER GOD:

The winter daphne blossom —

INFERNAL JUDGE:

> Sleeps in the mud.

FLOWER GOD:

The dryland lotus blossom —

INFERNAL JUDGE:

> Attracts her spouse to come again;

FLOWER GOD:

The pomegranate blossom —

INFERNAL JUDGE:

> Is kept in vain.
> There are more riddles for you to guess,
> Riddles that put the heaven in stress.
> What made her take bated breath?
> Why did she die an early death?

FLOWER GOD:

It is the heaven that predestines the colours and shapes of flowers. I do nothing but carry out the heaven's decrees. How dare I tempt anyone? I've never heard of any beautiful lady dying of love for flowers.

INFERNAL JUDGE:

You say that no beautiful ladies died of love for flowers? I'll name a few for you.

(*To the tune of **Jishengcao***)

The flowers make the maidens in a mess;

The flowers make the maidens in distress.

There was a lotus that bloomed at night,

And Empress Feiyan died on the site.

There was a crabapple that never quit,

And Lady Yang was buried with it.

There was a winter daphne that caught man's breath,

And Concubine Feiyan was flogged to death.

How can you say that flowers bring no harm?

You Flower God roused all the alarm!

FLOWER GOD:

I know I'm guilty. From now on I'll allow no blooming.

INFERNAL JUDGE:

I've just given verdicts to the four friends among the flowers. You are now to watch over them. Since this female offender died of lovesickness, she'll go with them as a swallow or an oriole.

FLOWER GOD:

Your Excellency, this female offender committed a crime in her dream, which is as invisible as the morning breeze. Besides, as her father is an upright official and she is his only child, I think she should be remitted.

INFERNAL JUDGE:

Who is your father?

DU LINIANG:

My father was the Prefect of Nan'an, and is now promoted to be Envoy of Appeasement in charge of the defense of Huaiyang.

INFERNAL JUDGE:

So you're a maiden with blue blood. Well, on account of Prefect Du, I'll report your case to the celestial emperor before I pass a sentence on you.

DU LINIANG:

Will you be so kind as to check why I was reduced to such misery?

INFERNAL JUDGE:

It must have been recorded in the Book of Heartbreaks.

DU LINIANG:

Will you do me another favour by checking the name of my husband? Is he Liu or Mei? Has he anything to do with Willow or Plum?

INFERNAL JUDGE:

Get me the Marriage Book.

(*Turns aside and looks up the Marriage Book*)

Yes, here is Liu Mengmei, the new Number One Scholar. Wife, Du Liniang. A secret love at first, official wedding in the end. Destined to meet in the Red Plum Blossom Nunnery.

Top secret.

(*Turns round*)

You are destined to marry this man. I'll release you from the City of Innocent Deaths so that you can float with the wind and look for this man.

FLOWER GOD:

Miss Du, kowtow to the Judge!

DU LINIANG (*Kowtows*):

Thank you for giving me a second life. However, as my parents are in Yangzhou, may I see them again?

INFERNAL JUDGE:

Yes.

> (*To the tune of* **Yaopian**)
> With many years of human life ahead,
> You should not have come here yet.
> While wanton love shall be what you dread,
> The plum and willow shall be what you get.
> To stare at parents now that the sky is clear,
> You mount the Home-gazing Terrace to see
> Night scenes of mourning in Yangzhou from here.

Flower God, show her around the Home-gazing Terrace.

DU LINIANG (*Mounts the terrace with Flower God and wails in the direction of Yangzhou*):

Yangzhou is over there! Dear Dad, dear Mom! How I wish to fly to you at once!

FLOWER GOD (*Stops her*):

It's not the time for you to go yet.

INFERNAL JUDGE:

Come back and listen to me. Attendant, prepare a passport for her. Flower God, take care to protect her body of flesh.

DU LINIANG:

Thank you very much, Your Excellency.

INFERNAL JUDGE (*To the tune of* **Semi-coda**):

> Remember to keep your passion in control,
> As where there're hills there's wood.
> Keep away from rain and sunshine when you stroll.
> You'll be allowed to wed your lover,
> And free to come and go will be your soul.
> Now that you are released,
> You will resume your human role.
> Four friends among the flowers are at your command:
> The butterfly and bee, the swallow and oriole.
> You'll wait for the man who digs the grave,
> To fulfil your dream and console your soul.

> (*Exit*)

FLOWER GOD:

Come, Miss, let's return to the back garden.

> *I wear my hat awry in drunken state;*

DU LINIANG:

> *By day the flags keep still in breathless air.*

INFERNAL JUDGE:

> *Year by year I check the human fate;*

FLOWER GOD, DU LINIANG, INFERNAL JUDGE:

> *We all await a judge who's just and fair.*

Scene Twenty-Four
Picking up the Portrait

(Enter Liu Mengmei)

LIU MENGMEI (*To the tune of **Jinlongcong***):

> Who cares more for spring days than I?
>
> To stormy weather I am on alert.
>
> The wind has pierced my shabby gown;
>
> The rain has soaked my yellow shirt.
>
> When I woke to a day without rains,
>
> I found my bed-sheets wet with dreamland stains.
>
> *"The yard in spring is fragrant with pear bloom,*
>
> *But still my bygone worries can be traced.*
>
> *How come that spring is casting endless gloom?*
>
> *I am appalled to see my slimming waist."*

My illness has confined me to the Plum Blossom Nunnery. I'm lucky to get acquainted with a Mr Chen who is good at medicine, and I'm feeling much better now. However, the spring weather makes me bored and depressed these days. I don't know where I can go to kill some time. Well, here comes Sister Stone.

(Enter Sister Stone)

SISTER STONE (*To the tune of **Yiluosuo***):

> A nun may have discerning eyes
>
> To read a scholar's deep dismay.
>
> From where does endless daydream rise
>
> That he keeps yawning all the day?

How are you feeling now, young scholar?

LIU MENGMEI:

I'm feeling much better these days, but I feel a little bored sitting idly all the time. In such a big nunnery, there must be a garden or some pavilions where I can walk around.

SISTER STONE:

There is a garden in the back. Although it has been deserted, you can find some flowers here and there. You can while away some time there, but don't get sentimental.

LIU MENGMEI:

Why should I get sentimental!

SISTER STONE (*With a sigh*):

Forget about it. Go ahead and enjoy yourself. Follow the west corridor and turn around the painted wall. In a hundred yards you will find a wicket gate. There are ponds and pavilions for three *li* around. You can enjoy yourself as much as you please and as long as you like. There's no need for me to go with you.

> *"The tourists come and go,*
> *But who will know such woe!"*

> (*Exit*)

LIU MENGMEI:

As there's such a back garden, I'll take a leisurely stroll there.

> (*Walks*)

Here is the west corridor.

> (*Walks on*)

What a green wicket gate! A pity that half of it is collapsed.

> (*With a sigh*)

> *"While marble balustrades as yet stand there,*
> *The painted garden walls have lacked repair.*
> *Where pleasant scenery used to meet the eyes,*
> *The withered willows dangle in the air."*

> (*Arrives at the garden*)

Oh, what a spacious garden!

> (*To the tune of **Haoshijin***)

> With years of constant wear and tear,
> The painted walls remain in bad repair.

> (*Slips*)

> Now that the slippery moss
> Intrudes the broken wall,
> Why should the door be closed to all?

This garden must have been haunted by many visitors, judging from the numerous names inscribed on the bamboo stems.

> This is a place where tourists used to come,
> And as years went by,
> Only names on bamboo stems defy the sky.

Alas, what I see now is nothing but

> Wild flowers overgrowing the path,
> With weeds and bushes as an aftermath.

Isn't it curious that a Taoist nun in the Plum Blossom Nunnery could have built such a magnificent garden? It's puzzling indeed. Just look at the meandering stream:

(*To the tune of **Jinchandao***)

Behind bolted gates

There lies a fairyland;

Why is it in such decay?

Beside the lake are misty estates

And painted boats stuck in the sand,

While swings would never sway.

But for a fire or war,

Why is it in such a wretched state?

Does it contain a mournful lore

Or people with a doleful fate?

Although I try to think of it no more,

The lakeside rocks have made me hesitate.

What a hill of mounted rocks!

(*Looks around the hill*)

Oh, there's a little box in the crevice. I'll lean against the left side in order to see what it is.

(*A rock slides down*)

Why, it's a red sandalwood case.

(*Opens the case to find a portrait*)

Well, it's a portrait of Bodhisattva Guanyin. Bliss on me! I'll take it to my study and pay my homage to her, rather than have it buried here.

(*Walks back, holding the case in his hand*)

(*To the tune of **Qianqiusui***)

Under cragged rocks

Is a case of sandalwood,

Where Bodhisattva Guanyin is enshrined.

The peak of rocks,

The peak of rocks

Seems to fly across from foreign lands —

A wonder of the fate destined.

I shall perfume the portrait with incense

And kowtow on the ground;

I'll add oil to the lamp from hence

To be endowed with bliss profound.

I'll pay my homage here,

But will she ever hear?

(*Arrives at the nunnery*)

Now that I'm back in the nunnery, I'll shelve the portrait till an auspicious day to do the service.

(*Enter Sister Stone*)

SISTER STONE:

So you are back already, Mr Liu!

LIU MENGMEI (*To the tune of* **Coda**):

Sister Stone,

> A stroller can hardly find relief,
>
> And daytime in the garden seems so brief.

You told me not to be sentimental, but you'd better show me

> A place without regret or grief.
>
> *Although I love to live near hills and rills,*

SISTER STONE:

> *I can't escape from dreamy thrills.*

LIU MENGMEI:

> *Where shall I hang the portrait in the hall?*

LIU MENGMEI, SISTER STONE:

> *The flowery maid is smiling on the wall.*

Scene Twenty-Five
Recalling Her Daughter

(*Enter Chunxiang*)

CHUNXIANG (*To the tune of* **Wanxiandeng**):

> At sight of things their owner comes to my mind;
>
> Once the owner dies, things lose their charm.
>
> It's true that "fairy fruits are hard to find
>
> While precious blooms are prone to serious harm".

(*With a sigh*)

> Dear Miss Du, I couldn't die with you;
>
> To clear the incense ash is what I do.

I, Chunxiang, am maid to the Du family, with whom I came to Yangzhou. It's been about three years since my young mistress died. Every day Madam wept at the thought of her daughter. My old master tries hard to console her, but can hardly reduce her sorrow. Even I, the maid, feel sad when I recall the kindness of Miss Du and her words on her deathbed. As today is Miss Du's birthday, Madam orders me to prepare incense sticks and candles for a memorial service in the direction of Nan'an. Now everything is ready. Madam, will you come for the service?

(*Enter Lady Zhen*)

LADY ZHEN (*To the previous tune*):

> Between Heaven and Earth,
>
> There is no place to rest my bones.
>
> I can't see my daughter on the day of her birth;
>
> Her soul is now in unknown zones.

(*Weeps*)

Oh Liniang, my dear daughter!

> My life on earth has but limited lease,
>
> As my heart is torn apart piece by piece.
>
> *"The clouds loom o'er the ridge,*
>
> *The dense trees veil the distant pass.*

CHUNXIANG:

> *The dreams in spring are groundless,*
>
> *Yet they deprived the life of a lass.*

LADY ZHEN:

> *Close to her mother's heart,*
>
> *My daughter is dead and gone,*
>
> *But her scents won't depart.*

CHUNXIANG:

> *Incense smoke rises to the sky*
>
> *While silver candles burn bright.*

LADY ZHEN:

> *I pray to Buddha on her birthday,*
>
> *And shed my tears of blood upon the rite.*
>
> (*Wails*)

LADY ZHEN, CHUNXIANG:

> *Can her soul return?*
>
> *Her second birth is what we yearn."*

LADY ZHEN:

Chunxiang, since Liniang died, I've been like a living corpse tormented by sorrow all the time. The books she read, the flowers she embroidered, the powder and perfume she used, the hairpins and shoes she wore — the sight of all these things would bring tears to my eyes and break my heart. It's been three years now since she passed away, and today is her birthday again. The incense seems to burn from my heart, and the candles seem to shed tears from my eyes. I've told you to prepare for a service. I suppose everything is ready by now.

CHUNXIANG:

Yes, Madam, everything's ready. Will you start the service?

LADY ZHEN (*Kowtows*):

> *"Incense smoke swirls and candles weep;*
>
> *I sprinkle wine and burn incense as last year.*
>
> *Where lies her lonely tomb of cloddy heap?*
>
> *Her soul flies south toward eternal sphere."*

I, wife of Envoy Du, pray to great Buddha that my daughter Du Liniang be blessed by his mighty power and ascend to Heaven in no time.

> (*Rises to her feet*)

Chunxiang, now that I've prayed to the Buddha, it's time to offer some tea and rice to Liniang.

(*To the tune of* **Xiangluodai**)

Where is Liniang's grave?

The heaven will not answer me.

Her shape in dreams I cannot clearly see;

Her voice alone rings wave on wave.

I raise myself on bed

And turn my head

To find flickering lamps instead.

(*Weeps*)

Oh Liniang my dear,

How can you bear to leave me here!

CHUNXIANG (*Kowtows*):

(*To the previous tune*)

With a fragrant stick I kowtow to you

To show my gratitude for you,

Wearing coats I got from you.

(*Rises to her feet*)

On your deathbed, you told me to call out for you from time to time. Now I'm calling you, "Mistress! Mistress!"

Can I get a response from you?

LADY ZHEN, CHUNXIANG (*Wail*):

With all her tender love

And boundless woe,

Why should she be doomed by Heaven above?

CHUNXIANG (*Turns to the memorial tablet again*):

Oh my mistress dear,

Will you go back to your old house from here?

(*Kneels*)

At your age, Madam, you can't sustain too much grief. As Miss Du can't come to life again, it's worthless to hurt yourself by grieving over the dead. Take good care of yourself so that you can enjoy lasting wealth and honour with the master.

LADY ZHEN (*Weeps*):

Did you know, Chunxiang, that my lord had been considering to have a concubine as he did not have a son? His love for Liniang alone made him drop the idea. Now that Liniang is dead, we are left without an heir. What can I say to console him when we sit facing each other? Oh, good gracious!

CHUNXIANG:

Madam, I'm not in a position to give any advice, but from what you have said, I get to know that the master would like to have a concubine. In that case, you'd better let him have one so that he'll beget a son.

LADY ZHEN:

Chunxiang, do you suppose that a concubine's son will be as good as my own son?

CHUNXIANG:

Madam, I'm lucky to be brought up by you and I treat you as my own parent although we have no blood ties at all. If you treat the concubine's son as your own, he'll treat you as his own mother, I'm sure.

LADY ZHEN:

Well said! Well said!

My daughter perished like the waning moon;

CHUNXIANG:

My moans resound like wailing poplar trees.

LADY ZHEN:

Our sorrows cannot fade and vanish soon;

LADY ZHEN, CHUNXIANG:

Tears fall into the wintry pond and freeze.

Scene Twenty-Six
Cherishing the Portrait

(Enter Liu Mengmei)

LIU MENGMEI:

"The palm leaves seldom hold the drops of rain;

The tips of peony stop the wind in vain.

Although the portrait itself throws no light,

The vernal sight illuminates the brain."

When I felt bored for my sojourn at the nunnery, I took a leisurely walk in the back garden. Under the Taihu rocks, I picked up a scroll of a painting. It seems to be a portrait of Bodhisattva Guanyin, concealed in a precious case. As it has been raining for the past ten days, I didn't think it fit to open the case. It happens that today is bright and clear. I'll open the case and pay my homage to the portrait.

(Opens the case and unscrolls the portrait)

*(To the tune of **Huangying'er**)*

Like the autumn moon upon the Milky Way,

She stretches herself as a virgin.

Oh, Bodhisattva Guanyin

With her magnificence in full display!

An image of the goddess in Putuo

Reveals herself before me in full glow.

(Thinks)

But why doesn't she sit on the lotus seat?

Wait, there's something wrong:

Why does the skirt reveal a pair of tiny feet?

How can Bodhisattva Guanyin have a pair of tiny feet? Let me look more closely.

> (*To the tune of* **Erlangshenman**)
> Once more,
> Let me have a closer look soon.

Well, I've got it.

> This must be the portrait of Chang E,
> A fairy lady dwelling in the moon.

If it's Chang E, I'll pay more homage to her.

> I'd like to ask Chang E
> Whether I will take the laurel with festoon.

But if it is Chang E,

> Why is there no cloud to uphold her?
> Why is there no laurel surrounding her?

If it's neither Bodhisattva Guanyin nor Chang E, who on earth could look like this?

> To my surprise,
> I seem to know this maid.
> Who is this maid of such fair size?

Let me have another look. Is this portrait done by a painter or by the fair maid herself?

> (*To the tune of* **Yingtixu**)
> Tell me, fair maid, where you were born,
> And who has drawn your pretty form.
> A maid with such a pretty form
> Makes all the flowers feel forlorn.
> A piece of nature as its norm,
> Who could have got so close to her?

It's impossible for a painter to get so close to her.

> She must have painted her own form!

Wait, here at the top of the scroll, a few lines are inscribed in fine characters.

> (*Looks*)
> Why, it's a quatrain!
> (*Reads*)
> *"A close inspection shows her as her self;*
> *A distant look displays her as an elf.*
> *Her future spouse who shares the pillow*
> *Will be found by the plum or willow."*

Oh, it's the self-portrait of a fair lady. But why did she say "Will be found by the plum or willow"? It's really fantastic!

> (*To the tune of* **Jixianbin**)
> Across the hill and rill, across the sky,
> How could she know that I'll come by?
> Does it mean that I'll gain fame?

I'll wait, wait all the same
And have a closer look.
How could she know my name?
Let me think anew!
Has my dream come true?
How I long to see her!
(*To the tune of* **Huangying'er**)
As Chang E the fairy lady from the sky,
She moves her dainty shape
And trails her gown of crape.
Her virgin love is locked between her brows,
Which curve like verdant hills
With mists of hair from rills.
I gaze at her and she at me:
Up and down, right and left,
Our four eyes yearn to see.
How is it that she carries a twig of green plums in her hand as if she were holding me in
her arms?
(*To the tune of* **Tiyingxu**)
Green plums in hand, she sings her verse,
Disturbing my quiet universe.
I seem to draw a cake to ease my greed;
She seems to look at plums to quench her need.
Oh my dear, my dear,
Her lotus bud of a tiny mouth
And rosy lips that smile
Display a graceful style.
She has a saddening tale to tell,
But lacks the breath to yell.
This fair lady is good at painting, poetry and calligraphy. Learned as I am, I'm no match to
her. At this chance encounter, I'll write a poem in the corresponding rhyme.
(*Writes on the scroll*)
"A precious painting shows her genuine self,
A wondrous fair lady if not an elf.
Here comes your spouse who'll share the pillow,
Just as spring dwells in the plum and willow."
(*To the tune of* **Cuyulin**)
She can paint,
She can write,
Her portrait has the hills and rills in sight.
Let me call out: "Fair lady, fair lady! My dear, my dear!"
Have you heard me calling you?

537

I'll call out till you call back.

You seem to move your feet anew

And walk out of the scroll,

But you are still out of view.

Well, in my solitude, I'll cherish, revere, call and praise her portrait from morning till night.

(*To the tune of* **Coda**)

It is my luck to find this portrait of a maid.

Is she someone I can't evade?

Mistress, mistress!

Your intangible form will kill me, I'm afraid.

The painting art is by no means to blame;

I'll always hang the portrait on the wall.

I'm puzzled by the verse that hides my name;

To wake from vernal dream is hard for all.

Scene Twenty-Seven
The Roaming Soul

(*Enter Sister Stone*)

SISTER STONE (*To the tune of* **Guazhen'er**):

Now that spring arrives at every hall,

The pillars find reflections on the pond.

When smoke of incense coils around the wall

And sounds of death-knells echo in a drawl,

I read the scripture for the World Beyond.

"When flowers fall onto the yellow earth,

The moon will gaze upon the mountain flanks.

I pick a solitary rose in mirth

As the east wind blows o'er riverbanks."

I've been looking after Miss Du's memorial shrine for over three years now. I've chosen this auspicious day to hold Taoist rites for guiding her soul to Heaven. The ritual banners have been hoisted outside the gate. I'll wait and see who will attend the rites.

(*Enter Young Nun and Novice*)

YOUNG NUN (*To the tune of* **Taipingling**):

Above the hills and rills,

The moon ascends the rainbow.

A nun and a novice come and go.

NOVICE:

As it's getting late, let's stop over at the Plum Blossom Nunnery.

YOUNG NUN:

The incense smoke leaks from the windowsills.

I am head of the White Cloud Nunnery in Shaoyang County. We have just travelled to this place. As the ritual banners announce the Taoist rites, we're just in time to mount the altar and join in the rites.

(*Greets Sister Stone*)

"*The curling incense floats in the sky;*

SISTER STONE:

You bring your wand and banner to the shrine.

YOUNG NUN:

I'd like to find a place where I can lie;

SISTER STONE:

Well, in your case,

A worldly nun recites a Taoist line."

Where are you from, young sister?

YOUNG NUN:

I come from Shaoyang County and would like to stop over for the night here.

SISTER STONE:

You have to put up with the side room because the guestroom has been occupied by a Mr Liu from Lingnan, who is recuperating from his illness.

YOUNG NUN:

Thank you very much. By the way, may I ask the purpose of the evening rites?

SISTER STONE (*Sighs*):

Alas,

"*Three years ago Miss Du died here;*

We'll send her soul to top celestial sphere."

YOUNG NUN:

I see.

"*It's best to hold the Taoist rites tonight;*

The incense I burn adds wings to the sprite."

SISTER STONE:

That's nice of you.

(*Sound of bells and drums within*)

YOUNG NUN, NOVICE:

It's time for you to offer the incense.

SISTER STONE:

Lady Star of Life and Death, Lady Star of Rebirth,

(*Offers the incense and kowtows*)

(*To the tune of **Xiaonange***)

I kindle a new fire

To light a pious stick

And offer it for Du Liniang.

YOUNG NUN, NOVICE (*Kowtow*):

> Around the banners is the incense dense and thick;
>
> In the breeze the gentle music rings.

Ladies of Stars,

> With your mighty power,
>
> Please send this flower
>
> To the top celestial sphere.
>
> As she still has her time on earth,
>
> Please render her a rebirth.
>
> Let her be reborn as a boy,
>
> Let her be reborn as a maid,
>
> Be married with eternal joy
>
> And live long with your aid.

SISTER STONE:

I remember that Miss Du died of love for flowers. I've picked a sprig of plum blossoms today and placed it in a purified vase.

> (*Kowtows to Du Liniang's memorial tablet*)
>
> (*To the previous tune*)
>
> The purified vase in the room
>
> In early spring sunshine
>
> Holds a sprig of rosy bloom.

Miss Du,

> Who is walking with you in your dream?
>
> What a lonely soul with high esteem!

YOUNG NUN, NOVICE:

Sister, what would you say the purified vase represents? And what does the sprig of plum blossoms represent?

SISTER STONE:

> The vase with its void
>
> Holds the world minute.
>
> It's like the bloom of plums,
>
> Which carries water and has no root
>
> But still gives off fragrance acute.

YOUNG NUN, NOVICE:

Miss Du, the offer you receive here will add

> Coolness to your bone
>
> And fragrance to your soul.
>
> If you resume the human role,
>
> Will you return to this selfsame zone?
>
> (*Sound of wind within*)

SISTER STONE:

How strange! There arises a blast of chilly whirlwind.

(Sound of bells and drums within)

YOUNG NUN, NOVICE:

It's time for evening meal. Let's go and have meal first, then we'll come back and finish the rites. As the saying goes,

> *"The morning dispels darkness all along;*
> *The evening bell suspends the holy song."*

(Exeunt all)

(Enter Du Liniang, wailing as a ghost and hiding her face with her sleeves)

DU LINIANG *(To the tune of **Shuihonghua**)*:

> With the Home-gazing Terrace out of sight,
> My soul walks in the shimmering night;
> Outside the grave-gate is a quiet site.

(Startled at the sound of barking dogs within)

> With flower-shadows out of sight,
> A dog barks in the chilly night;
> Pear blossoms foretell a flowery site.

Well, here is the Peony Pavilion, and there is the rose grove. They are both in ruins. It's three years since my parents left this place.

(Weeps)

> Deserted paths and broken walls are sad.
> But what is this place in sight
> With a ghostly light?

(Listens)

> What? Human voices nearly make me mad!
> *"An elegant maiden in the former days,*
> *I'm like a faded flower now.*
> *For such a dainty bloom beyond praise,*
> *Why should I wither on the bough!*
> *Destined to lead a lonely life,*
> *I gaze at stars in vain tonight.*
> *In life or death I yearn to be his wife,*
> *As love gets hold of me too light."*

I'm Du Liniang in the ghost form. I died of a dream that made me lovesick. As the Prince of the Tenth Hell was dismissed from office, I was left in the cell for three years with no one to dispatch my case. I'm lucky to meet with a sympathetic old judge and to be allowed to take leave so that I can roam at will in this moonlit night. Why, how is it that the back garden to the study has become the Plum Blossom Nunnery? How distressing!

*(To the tune of **Xiaotaohong**)*

> A broken heart awakened from dream,
> I wonder who'll bring me to life again.
> Although ghosts ne'er travel in a team,
> I still put right my garment now and then.

In the shadowy night

When dews settle in the breeze,

The clouds obscure the moonlight,

And stars lie hidden ill at ease,

I wander as I please;

The first drumbeat finds me in a flowery site.

(*Startled at the sound of tinkling bells within*)

What gives me sudden fear

Is the bells that tinkle here.

What a fragrant smell of incense!

(*To the tune of **Xiashanhu***)

The smoke of incense curls;

The light of lanterns glows.

When I see the holy portraits,

My fear suddenly grows.

Who are those goddesses? Oh, one is Lady Star of Life and Death, and the other is Lady Star of Rebirth.

(*Kowtows*)

Du Liniang in the ghost form kowtows to you Ladies of Stars.

542

I've quietly come back to the earth

To pray for my rebirth.

Let me see what are the words of the prayers. Sister Stone is presiding over the rites for my rebirth in Heaven. Sister Stone, I'm deeply indebted to you. In the purified vase is a sprig of plum blossoms from my grave. Oh, plum blossoms, both you and I are nipped in the bud! How sad it is!

The sound of bells and drums and chants

Has roused me from a dream of mine.

I'll step into the plants

To leave some sign.

(*Weeps*)

If I do not leave some sign, how can the pious nuns know that I appreciate their efforts? Let me scatter some petals of plum blossoms on the shrine.

(*Scatters the petals*)

My love stays with the petals on the shrine.

Where are my parents and where is Chunxiang? Well, there comes the sound of moaning and calling. Let me listen carefully!

VOICE WITHIN:

My dear! My fair lady!

DU LINIANG (*Startled*):

Who is calling? Whom is he calling? Let me listen again.

(*The voice calls again from within*)

DU LINIANG (*Sighs*):

(*To the tune of* **Zuiguichi**)

Alive and dead,

I'm destined to roam alone.

There's no reply to what you've said;

Why do you just moan?

Lonely tears I shed;

Where is the man of my own?

A voice unknown

Continues to groan.

I'll try to find the tone.

(*The voice calls again from within*)

Who is the scholar there,

Whose cries in his sleep fill the air?

(*To the tune of* **Heimaling**)

His moans have touched my heart;

Repeated moans and screams

Make my chilly teardrops start.

Is he the man I met in dreams?

I remember the blooms and streams;

I remember the breeze and moonbeams.

Now that I am a roaming soul,

Can I ever play the bridal role?

I'd like to find out more about it, but as the day is soon to break, I can't linger here any longer.

(*To the tune of* **Coda**)

Why do the lanterns shimmer in the hall?

VOICE WITHIN:

There are noises in the hall.

(*Enter Novice, standing aside and looking around*)

(*Sound of another whirlwind within*)

DU LINIANG:

Why do the banners flutter?

This wind is what I leave behind them all.

(*Exit Du Liniang wailing as a ghost, coming face to face with the novice*)

NOVICE (*Cries out in horror*):

Holy sisters, come, come!

(*Enter Sister Stone and Young Nun in a hurry*)

SISTER STONE, YOUNG NUN:

What's the matter?

NOVICE:

When I hid behind the lantern shadows, I saw a goddess flapping the banners with her sleeves and vanishing in a flurry. How terrible! Terrible!

SISTER STONE:

What does she look like?

NOVICE (*Gestures*):

About this height, this size, a pretty face with golden headwear, dressed in a red skirt and green coat, clinking with jade ornaments. Isn't she a goddess from Heaven?

SISTER STONE:

That's exactly what Miss Du looked like in her lifetime. Hasn't her spirit come to earth?

YOUNG NUN:

Look! The shrine is scattered with petals of plum blossoms. Fantastic! It's really fantastic! Let's chant another hymn for her.

SISTER STONE, YOUNG NUN, NOVICE (*To the tune of* **Yiduojiao**):

> When the incense has burned up
>
> And corridors are flooded in moonlight,
>
> Appearance of a lonely soul
>
> With scattered petals is a saddening sight.
>
> May you have peace in celestial sphere,
>
> In celestial sphere,
>
> And linger no more in homeland here.

YOUNG NUN:

May I ask how Miss Du died? Why does her spirit come to earth again?

SISTER STONE (*To the tune of* **Coda**):

> Don't be in a fright;
>
> Don't ask whys!
>
> Let's put away instruments for the rites;
>
> Now, listen.
>
> The tinkling sounds again arise.

SISTER STONE:

> *It's hard to show her genuine stuff,*

YOUNG NUN:

> *Because to tell the truth will make her wail.*

NOVICE:

> *If the vernal breeze is wise enough,*

SISTER STONE, YOUNG NUN, NOVICE:

> *It should have known the fairy tale.*

Scene Twenty-Eight
Union with the Ghost

(*Enter Liu Mengmei*)

LIU MENGMEI (*To the tune of* **Yexingchuan**):

Where is the fairy maid I saw?

She's empty as the moon in mist.

My woe can hardly thaw,

While endless thoughts persist.

The sun has long set in the west.

"A rosy cloud descended from the sky,

Like a flower in broadest smile.

Whose hand has drawn a face so shy,

With loving glances all the while?"

Since I saw the portrait of a loving lady, I've kept thinking of her day and night. In the small hours tonight, I'm spending some time reading her poem and cherishing her portrait. Even if I could meet her in my dream, I would enjoy every minute of it.

(*Unrolls the scroll and cherishes it*)

Oh, what a beauty! She seems to have something to say, and her eyes are eloquent too. As a quotation goes,

"With evening glows the lonely swan would fly;

The autumn waters share the same hue with the sky."

(*To the tune of* **Xiangbianman**)

The evening breeze has brought about

A glow of sunlight from the fairyland —

A fairy maid without doubt.

Pure and simple is her claim,

Like the crimson gauze of window-frame.

This portrait of a dainty maid

Has set my heart aflame.

Oh, my dear, how I yearn to see you!

(*To the tune of* **Lanhuamei**)

The maid is delicate and shy,

A daughter from a noble house.

She sits before the mirror with a yearning heart

And draws her portrait with a sigh.

But does she know that

The one who's picked it yearns to be her spouse?

(*To the tune of* **Erfanwulongshu**)

Her moon-shaped visage full of glow

Has brought about a sky of woe.

In the past I could fall asleep facing the moon, but in recent nights

Her radiance is so bright

That I can hardly bear the light.

Disturbed by the thought of her,

I have her on my mind day and night.

But for the fear of spoiling it,

I'll sleep with it at night.

It must be fate that has brought her to me. Let me read the poem again.

> (*Reads the poem*)
>
> (*To the tune of* **Huanshaxi**)
>
> These lines she wrote
>
> For her future mate —
>
> For willow and plum remote.
>
> From the lakeside hills comes the fairy soul,
>
> Who lands on the scroll.

Whoever she is, I'll pay homage to her.

> (*Lights the incense and kowtows*)
>
> It gives me pain
>
> To have your image deep in my brain.
>
> Your lover is here, expecting in vain.

During my stopover here, how can I have a brief rendezvous with you?

> (*To the tune of* **Liupomao**)
>
> One scroll does not contain a loving pair;
>
> I wish I were a reed by your side.

My dear,

> As your ears are covered by your hair,
>
> Can you hear the sorrow I confide?
>
> (*To the tune of* **Qiuyeyue**)
>
> I am a fool indeed
>
> To daydream like a child.
>
> You are the moon above the clouds;
>
> You are the mist above the wild.
>
> You may amuse the crowds,
>
> But not to be beguiled.
>
> (*To the tune of* **Dong'ouling**)
>
> It is a magic spell I read;
>
> It is a prayer I said.
>
> A stone would nod its head;
>
> A rain of blooms would spread.
>
> But why won't you descend?
>
> It is too hard for you to come ahead.
>
> (*Sound of wind within. Liu Mengmei places his hand on the portrait*)
>
> For fear the portrait be blown away,
>
> I'll hold it under sway.

In case the portrait is torn apart by the wind, I'll find a skilled painter to make a copy of it.

> (*To the tune of* **Jinlianzi**)
>
> Just imagine
>
> How I can bring you to my bed!

If I could meet you face to face,

I'd hold you in embrace,

To prove what you have said.

I'll trim the wick to have a better look at you.

(*Holds the lamp to the portrait*)

(*To the tune of* **Quasi-coda**)

A human fairy oft involves a scheme.

(*Sound of wind within, nearly blowing out the lamp*)

What a chilly blast!

The portrait nearly caught on fire.

Well, think no more about the portrait.

I'll shut the window and meet her in my dream.

(*Dozes off*)

(*Enter Du Liniang in the ghost form*)

DU LINIANG:

"My dream left unfulfilled in my eternal sleep,

I cherish human love profound and deep.

When the portrait guides me in the moon,

I hear a man sigh in a woeful tune."

I'm Du Liniang in the ghost form. I pined away for a dream in the garden. Before I died, I drew a self-portrait and buried it under a Taihu rock. On the portrait is the inscription

"Her future spouse who shares the pillow

Will be found by the plum or willow."

When my soul roamed the nunnery these nights, I heard him calling in the guestroom: "Oh my dear, my fair lady!" The sad voice touched my heart. When I glided into his room, I saw a tiny scroll hanging on the wall. When I looked more closely, I recognised that it was the portrait I left behind. Below my inscriptions, he wrote a poem in the corresponding rhyme. The signature is Liu Mengmei from Lingnan. While *liu* means willow and *mei* means plum, isn't it predestined that he is the man to be found "by the plum or willow"? Therefore, I asked for leave from the Infernal Judge to fulfil the dream at this pretty night. Alas, how I have suffered!

(*To the tune of* **Chaotianlan**)

A faded beauty in ghost form,

I fear it's second dreamland love affair.

As I'm abashed and got my curls dishevelled,

Let me arrange my hair.

Well, here I am at his room.

Lest I make the wrong tour,

I'll wait and make sure.

LIU MENGMEI (*Recites the poem in his sleep*):

"Her future spouse who shares the pillow

Will be found by the plum or willow."

Oh my dear!

DU LINIANG (*Listens and weeps*):

> (*To the previous tune*)
>
> I shed a flood of tears to hear his call,
>
> While my verse lines echo in the hall.

Is he still lying awake?

> (*Looks into the room while Liu Mengmei talks again in his sleep*)
>
> He talks to himself in his sleep.

Wait!

> I'll tap at window-frames and peep.

LIU MENGMEI (*Wakes up with a start*):

My dear!

DU LINIANG (*Sadly*):

> I shall go forth and meet my mate.

LIU MENGMEI:

I seem to hear a tapping at the bamboo frames. Is it the wind or someone there?

DU LINIANG:

Here I am.

LIU MENGMEI:

Someone's at the door. Are you Sister Stone bringing tea? It's so kind of you, but I don't want any tea now.

DU LINIANG:

I'm not Sister Stone.

LIU MENGMEI:

Are you the travelling Young Sister?

DU LINIANG:

No, I'm not.

LIU MENGMEI:

Strange, it's strange. She's not the young nun, either. Who else can it be? Let me open the door and have a look.

> (*Opens the door to have a look*)
>
> (*To the tune of* **Wanxiandeng**)

Oh,

> A beauty stands before me,
>
> A beauty rare to see.
>
> (*Du Liniang smiles and slips into the room. Liu Mengmei closes the door in haste*)

DU LINIANG (*Adjusts her hair and dress, and then greets Liu Mengmei*):

Blessing to you, sir.

LIU MENGMEI:

May I ask, young lady, where you are from and why you come at this late hour?

DU LINIANG:

Will you have a guess, sir?

LIU MENGMEI (*To the tune of* **Hongnaao**):

> Are you the Weaving Star in the sky?
>
> Are you the Fairy Waitress coming by?

DU LINIANG:

How can the heavenly immortals come here?

LIU MENGMEI:

> Are you a phoenix following the crow?
>
> (*Du Liniang shakes her head*)
>
> Are you an old acquaintance to see me now?

DU LINIANG:

We've never seen each other before.

LIU MENGMEI:

> Have you mistaken me for someone else?
>
> Have you lost your way to the hotels?

DU LINIANG:

No, I haven't lost my way.

LIU MENGMEI:

Are you here to borrow a lamp?

> Is it because you walk at night
>
> That you come here for the candlelight?

DU LINIANG (*To the previous tune*):

> I have not come to send you bloom,
>
> Nor read books in your room.
>
> I'm not Zhao Feiyan who had a sad fate
>
> Nor Zhuo Wenjun who lost her mate.

Dear sir,

> Have you had a dream of love and hate?

LIU MENGMEI (*Tries to recall*):

Yes, I have.

DU LINIANG:

> That's why I come here all the way.

If you ask me where I live, I'd say

> In the neighbourhood where beauties stay.

LIU MENGMEI:

Yes, I see. When I was turning west in the back garden at dusk, I saw a fair lady walking in the distance.

DU LINIANG:

That's me.

LIU MENGMEI:

Who lives with you in your family?

DU LINIANG (*To the tune of* **Yichunling**):

> In the west

549

The Peony Pavilion

Where grows the grass,

With lonely parents lives the lass.

At sixteen years of age,

I'm like a flower in the vase.

When I took a stroll in ebbing spring,

I stole a glimpse of your handsome face.

Here I am

To sit by the candlelight

And chat with you all night.

LIU MENGMEI (*Aside*):

Fantastic! Fantastic! What a rare beauty in the world! Now that I've chanced upon a pearl of a young lady, what am I to do?

(*To the previous tune*)

Amazing beauty,

Rare beauty bright,

Her smile outshines the candlelight.

By looking at the brilliant moon,

I wonder what day is today.

A graceful maid should have come to me!

A fairy maid should have come to stay!

(*Aside*)

Yet,

Yet who is this naughty maid

That comes to me to play?

I'll ask her a few more questions.

(*To Du Liniang*)

Am I dreaming now that I see you in the deep of night?

DU LINIANG (*Smiles*):

No, you're not dreaming. I'm my true self, but I'm afraid you won't accept me.

LIU MENGMEI:

I'm still afraid it's not real. If you are really fond of me, I shall be too glad to accept your love. How can I say no?

DU LINIANG:

In this case, my dream has come true.

(*To the tune of* **Shuabaolao**)

In the peaceful vale of love,

You brought my heart to bloom at night.

Since then no other men have come to sight;

And you're the one who knows the reason why:

I am a daughter graceful and polite.

At the Peony Pavilion,

We were tender toward each other.

By the lakeside hills,

   We felt bashful with each other.

   Near the window-frames,

   We sat silent facing each other.

   We shared the night at ease

   And knew the price of moon and breeze.

LIU MENGMEI (*To the tune of* **Didijin**):

   When I wake up with a start,

   I see the cool moon gleam.

   But is this sudden bliss

   A love affair in dream?

Oh, my dear, it is inconceivable that

   You dread not when you cross the shade,

   You slip not when you tread on the moss,

   You fear not when you shun your parents,

   You err not when you come to my aid.

Look,

   The Dipper is aslant;

   The petals fold;

   The flowers slumber in the cold.

   We shall laugh

   And sing

   In the moon and breeze of spring.

   You are tender; you are coy.

   How can I let you down?

   For every minute, we shall enjoy.

DU LINIANG:

I have one request to make. Will you please listen to me?

LIU MENGMEI:

Go ahead, please.

DU LINIANG:

Once you have me, body and flesh, heart and soul, please never give me up. My lifelong
desire is fulfilled if only we share the pillow night after night.

LIU MENGMEI:

Now that you devote yourself to me, how can I ever forget you?

DU LINIANG:

I have one more word to tell you: please let me go before cockcrow. You don't have to see
me off because the morning breeze is chilly.

LIU MENGMEI:

I'll do what you tell me, but may I ask your name?

DU LINIANG (*With a sigh*):

   (*To the tune of* **Yibujin**)

Though each thing has its root and form,

My name may stir up a roaring storm.

LIU MENGMEI:

I hope that you'll come every night.

DU LINIANG:

My dear sir,

Let's make this first night sweet and warm.

LIU MENGMEI:

I spend the night with a beauty ne'er seen;

DU LINIANG:

The moon goes west before the nighttime ends.

Morning clouds come from an unknown ravine;

LIU MENGMEI:

Who knows from where the fairy maid descends?

Scene Twenty-Nine
The Nun's Suspicion

(*Enter Sister Stone*)

SISTER STONE (*To the tune of* **Bubujiao**):

I have been born to be a nun,

Without a spouse,

Without a son.

I tend the shrine of gods in Heaven and Hell,

Adding water and joss-sticks to the shrine,

Beating drums and striking the bell.

But now I must watch this roaming nun,

Who has lewd looks and a wagging tongue.

"There is not any genuine trust on earth;

Suspicion proves to be a thing of worth."

Since Prefect Du established this Plum Blossom Nunnery, I have been looking after it for three years. Everything has been in good order and above suspicion, except for the young scholar Liu Mengmei from Lingnan. He was brought here by the old scamp Mr Chen and was put up in the eastern guestroom for recovery from illness. When he came back from the back garden a few days ago, he seemed to be in a trance, as if he were haunted by ghosts. I began to have suspicions at once. It happens that a young nun from Shaoyang travelled to this place and has stayed here for a few days. Twenty-eight years of age, she has an attractive face. At night I hear people chatter in Mr Liu's room and it seems that there is a female voice. I guess that the young nun is visiting him behind my back and Mr Liu has accepted her offer. I'll try to find out the truth when she comes back.

(*Enter Young Nun*)

YOUNG NUN (*To the previous tune*):

    A nun as pretty as a fairy maid,

    I'm well behaved,

    Although my sweetness would not fade.

    I've worshipped gods and prayed

    And hoped to turn into a fairy maid.

    (*Sighs*)

    A fairy maid will have her mate,

    But why should I be in this wretched state?

    (*Greets Sister Stone*)

    "Remain dispassionate to watch the soul;

SISTER STONE:

    Remain passionate to watch the body hole."

Young sister, did you roam to the young scholar's room last night to watch his soul or his hole?

YOUNG NUN:

What are you driving at, old sister? Who saw me going there?

SISTER STONE:

I did.

    (*To the tune of* **Tiyindeng**)

    As a nun, you paint your face

    And wear a simple Taoist cloak.

    With adorned hair you smile from place to place,

    So appealing to the folk.

    I can imagine

    How you went to the scholar's room

    And shared the bed with him in the gloom.

YOUNG NUN:

Which scholar do you mean? You're simply talking nonsense.

    (*To the previous tune*)

    Although I am still young,

    I have a crystal heart.

    You accuse me with a vicious tongue

    But I have played a better part!

SISTER STONE:

You are turning the slander on me!

YOUNG NUN:

    Just consider

    How there can be a scholar's face

    In this sacred Taoist place.

SISTER STONE:

Alas, are you alluding that I have an affair with the young scholar? In this Plum Blossom Nunnery, you stop over as a travelling nun and he stops over as a travelling scholar. Why can I put you up but not him? He used to sleep well all through the night; however, since you came here, he has opened his door at night and whispered all night. Who is he whispering to but you? I'll bring the case against you in the Taoist court.

(*Grabs at Young Nun*)

YOUNG NUN:

Off we go! You put up a wandering vagabond in the nunnery established by the former prefect. Do you think they'll easily let you go?

(*Grabs at Sister Stone*)

(*Enter Chen Zuiliang*)

CHEN ZUILIANG (*To the tune of* **Yifengshu**):

> I go to the nunnery alone
> To meet the young scholar Liu
> And visit Sister Stone.

(*Sees the two nuns grabbing at each other*)

Oh,

> How can two nuns fight for a single man?
> Both disciples of Tao,
> Why don't you quietly spend your life span?
> You are older and she is younger now,
> Who are you seeking after in your clan?

SISTER STONE:

Let me tell you, Mr Chen. I heard the scholar open his door at night and whisper all the time. When I asked the young nun politely, "Have you chatted with him", it was all right that she answered, "Who has chatted with him?" It was too much for her to say that I kept a scholar under my roof. Tell us, Mr Chen, who brought him into my nunnery! Take her to the Taoist court to get the truth out of her. I'm Sister Stone, with a heart of stone.

YOUNG NUN:

Do you mean to say that I am as frivolous as water?

CHEN ZUILIANG:

Shut up, both of you! You are ruining the reputation of Mr Liu. Now, listen to me.

(*To the previous tune*)

> Do not draw conclusions in haste.
> Are you sure you know the truth?
> A man of lofty taste,
> Mr Liu is an honest youth.
> If the court should know you are not chaste,
> You'll be dispelled and sneered for sooth.

YOUNG NUN:

Indeed we'll make a show.

CHEN ZUILIANG:

> Arrange your hairpins and comb your hair;
>
> Your cloak has gone through wear and tear.

SISTER STONE:

All right, let's forget about it. Mr Chen, let's go and have a vegetarian dinner.

CHEN ZUILIANG:

No, thanks. I'll come again when Mr Liu is in.

> (*To the tune of* **Coda**)
>
> In this holy place,
>
> I lag my pace.
>
> (*Weeps*)

Alas,

> Against the wind I shed large drops of tear.

Sister Stone, shall we go to Miss Du's grave?

SISTER STONE:

It's raining.

CHEN ZUILIANG (*With a sigh*):

> How I hate the rainfall here!
>
> (*Exit Chen Zuiliang, leaving Sister Stone and Young Nun behind*)

SISTER STONE:

Mr Chen is gone and you don't have to worry now.

YOUNG NUN:

Let's try to find out who's been chatting with the young scholar.

SISTER STONE:

> *The Taoist nuns have never shunned the world!*

YOUNG NUN:

> *Seldom do they behave like a sage.*

SISTER STONE:

> *When parrots learn to say the human word,*

YOUNG NUN:

> *They start to quarrel with the golden cage.*

Scene Thirty
Disrupting the Love Affair

(*Enter Liu Mengmei*)

LIU MENGMEI (*To the tune of* **Daolianzi**):

> When it is in the deep of night,
>
> The moon moves to the zenith.

Is the joss-stick burning bright?
"Her finger-nails are painted scarlet-red,
On fingers slender as the bamboo-shoots.
With a pretty maiden on my bed,
I am completely stricken deaf and mute."

As a diligent student, I've been devoted to studies. When I reached Nan'an on my way north to the capital, I met a fair lady from the neighbourhood. Her sweet smile has brought about a series of rendezvous. She is gone with the wind before the day breaks. We'll have a date tonight, but I'm not sure when she will come. As the poem goes,

"Before her tiny feet would move with grace,
The candle has been thus burned down apace."

The point is, I must be fresh and energetic to meet her, and so why not take a nap now!

(*Takes a nap*)

(*Enter Du Liniang in the ghost form*)

DU LINIANG (*To the tune of* **Chengrenxin**):

I suffer in the netherworld,

But would not die a second death.

I have the scholar in my mind,

Who waits for me with bated breath.

(*Moves into Liu Mengmei's room*)

Oh,

He slumbers on a low settee,

Without a quilt to shun spring cold.

There he lies and waits for me.

Let me wake him up. Scholar, scholar!

LIU MENGMEI (*Wakes up*):

Oh. It's you, my young lady! I'm sorry.

(*Rises to his feet and bows*)

I should have been well-dressed

And gone to meet you.

But haven't the wind and dew

Put nocturnal flowers to rest?

DU LINIANG:

In my place the night is long and deep,

But thoughts of you deprived me of my sleep.

LIU MENGMEI:

My young lady, how is it that your steps are so quiet?

DU LINIANG:

"Of course I leave no trace and stir no dust;

LIU MENGMEI:

I long for you by day and dream by night.

DU LINIANG:

> *Through the windows I find you sit awake;*

LIU MENGMEI:

> *I'm waiting for you to come in sight."*

Tonight you're later than usual, my young lady.

DU LINIANG (*To the tune of* **Xiudaier**):

> Don't be annoyed, please.
>
> I do not want to come so late;
>
> I've always kept you in my heart.
>
> Only when the evening incense was lit,
>
> From my parents could I depart.
>
> I leant against my bed
>
> And laid my needlework down.
>
> At once I came here in the breeze,
>
> Without making up or changing my gown.

LIU MENGMEI:

Thank you for your kindness. But how are we to spend this wonderful night without wine?

DU LINIANG:

I nearly forget that I've brought a kettle of wine and some fruit and flower. They are left on the corridor. I'll get them for you.

> (*Fetches the wine, fruit and flower*)

LIU MENGMEI:

Thank you very much. What's the fruit you've brought?

DU LINIANG:

Some green plums.

LIU MENGMEI:

And what's the flower?

DU LINIANG:

It's canna.

LIU MENGMEI:

The green plum is as sour as I, and the canna is as red as you. Let's share a cup of wine.

> (*Liu Mengmei and Du Liniang drink from the same cup*)

DU LINIANG (*To the tune of* **Bailianxu**):

> Fill in the golden cup
>
> With fragrant wine.

LIU MENGMEI:

> The wine you brewed
>
> Brings a flush to your cheeks
>
> As the east wind makes the blooms ashine.

DU LINIANG:

> No other flower or fruit

Is better than canna or plum,

For, you know,

The kernel of fruit is fine,

The flower has its root.

LIU MENGMEI (*To the tune of* **Zuitaiping**):

What's more,

The canna flower

Is like a fragile maid,

While the plum kernel like a learned man.

When canna's pistil is displayed,

The plum petal is lured into her span.

What comes next?

With a smile and flush upon your face,

You will be showered with my kiss.

Very soon,

You'll shut your eyes with grace,

And, in your scarlet spot,

Accept the green-plum juice.

DU LINIANG (*To the tune of* **Bailianxu**):

I pant,

And heave

In this paradise of love on earth.

Behind the window screen,

We'll make love in the eve;

Why do we speak so many words?

LIU MENGMEI:

It's time to go to bed.

DU LINIANG:

Let's gaze at the moon.

Sit here for a while

And share the pretty scene

With the moon-land fairy queen.

LIU MENGMEI (*To the tune of* **Zuitaiping**):

Leave the fairy queen alone.

In the flower shade,

Let's go to bed,

My pretty maid.

The charming vernal night

Will fly away, I am afraid.

My dear,

You were too shy last night;

Tonight you'll be all right.

When we're in bed,

I'll feel your creamy breast,

Embrace your sweaty chest

And hold your waist tight.

    (*Enter Sister Stone and Young Nun stealthily*)

YOUNG NUN:

    "Tao can be defined as Tao,

    But are you aware of Tao?

    Names can be used for its name,

    But are you aware of its name?"

    (*Liu Mengmei and Du Liniang laugh heartily*)

YOUNG NUN:

Listen, Sister Stone, someone's talking in the scholar's room. Now you know it's not me.

SISTER STONE (*Listens attentively*):

There's a woman's voice. Let me knock at the door.

    (*Knocks at the door*)

LIU MENGMEI:

Who's at the door?

SISTER STONE:

It's me, Sister Stone, to bring you some tea.

LIU MENGMEI:

It's too late for tea now.

SISTER STONE:

You seem to have a guest with you.

LIU MENGMEI:

No, I haven't.

SISTER STONE:

Yes, you have a lady guest.

LIU MENGMEI, DU LINIANG (*In a panic*):

What's to be done?

SISTER STONE (*Bangs on the door*):

Be quick, sir. Open the door. The patrolmen are coming. I don't want any trouble.

LIU MENGMEI (*At a loss*):

What shall I do! What shall I do!

DU LINIANG (*Smiles*):

Never mind. I'm from the neighbourhood. If they won't let you go, you can accuse them of seduction.

    (*To the tune of* **Quasi-coda**)

    If they want you to open the door, they have to be polite;

    Beside the windows, can they stand the whole night?

Dear Mr Liu, just unbolt the door.

    I'll hide behind the beauty scroll to stand out of sight.

SISTER STONE, YOUNG NUN (*Rush in, giggling, as Liu Mengmei opens the door and shields Du Liniang, who hides behind him*):

Congratulations!

LIU MENGMEI:

What for?

(*Sister Stone tries to look over Liu Mengmei's shoulder, but Liu Mengmei blocks her way*)

SISTER STONE, YOUNG NUN (*To the tune of* **Gunbian**):

> Hour by hour the night will pass;
> The nunnery's gate is closed tight.
> From where comes the pretty lass,
> Who stirs the man at night?

LIU MENGMEI:

> Just look ahead!
> Do you indeed believe
> That you'll find something on the bed?
> Or in the trunk?
> Or up my sleeve?

(*Sister Stone and Young Nun push forward. Liu Mengmei fails to keep them back. Sound of wind within. Du Liniang slips offstage*)

LIU MENGMEI:

You nearly blew out the lamp.

SISTER STONE:

I saw someone's shadow a moment ago, but now there is only the beauty scroll on the wall. Was the painting enchanted?

> (*To the previous tune*)
> The beauty on the scroll would dance and sing
> To form a pair with you.
> If it were not demon or something,
> Why should it flee while the wind blew?

What painting is this, sir?

LIU MENGMEI:

> It is a work of art
> To bless me all along the way.
> I worship it from the bottom of my heart,
> But you disturb me when I pray.

SISTER STONE:

Oh, that's it. I never thought of it. When I heard someone murmuring in your room, I suspected that it was this young nun. Now I see. Excuse me, sir, for I'll have a word with her.

LIU MENGMEI:

Please.

YOUNG NUN (*To the tune of* **Coda**):

> You want to drag me to the Taoist court!

LIU MENGMEI:

   And give an honest man a bad report!

Sister Stone, by what you did,

   My sweet dream tonight is cut short.

   (*Exeunt Sister Stone and Young Nun*)

LIU MENGMEI (*Laughs*):

My sweet rendezvous is ruined by these two nasty nuns! What a distress! How they have startled my beauty!

   I should escort you in the night,

   But spring breeze brings woes hand in hand.

   When rolling mountains come in sight,

   My dream has borne me to the fairyland.

Scene Thirty-One
Preparing for War

   (*Enter an official and an officer*)

OFFICIAL, OFFICER (*To the tune of* **Fanbusuan**):

   The Yangtze flows, the sea roars,

   Yet rebel armies are malign.

   Yangzhou has reinforced its walls;

   We toast the river with our wine.

How do you do! We are the official and officer of the Yangzhou Prefecture. As Li Quan is making harassment in this area, Envoy Du has ordered us to build an outer city wall. Today we're going to hold a banquet to celebrate the completion of the outer wall. Here comes Envoy Du.

   (*Enter Du Bao, followed by subordinates*)

SUBORDINATES (*To the previous tune*):

   Three thousand followers line the hall;

   Our strength is doubled by the wall.

   (*The official and the officer welcome Du Bao*)

DU BAO:

   Yangzhou commands sights ever seen;

   Let's climb the tower for a better scene.

SUBORDINATES (*Greet Du Bao*):

   "*To guard the gate we need a warrior old and bold;*

DU BAO:

   I wish I were a warrior crowning all.

SUBORDINATES:

   The heaven sets a hill as our stronghold;

DU BAO:

> *I'll guard the city as an iron wall."*

The swift completion of the Yangzhou outer wall is the result of the joint efforts of the officials, officers and civilians.

SUBORDINATES:

You have made all the plans while we have just followed your instructions. Will you accept our toast as a time-honoured tradition?

DU BAO:

Excellent! Now let's have a look around the gate tower.

> *(Looks around)*

What a magnificent wall! It is truly

> *"The strongest city in the north;*
> *The topmost tower in Huainan."*

SUBORDINATES:

A toast to you!

> *(To the tune of **Shanhuazi**)*
> Cheers to the towering wall,
> With a bird's-eye view of the stream.
> A safeguard to us all,
> It is indeed supreme.

ALL:

> On watchtowers above the wall,
> We sprinkle wine beside the banners.
> When we think of past glories,
> Our mournful teardrops fall,
> For the world has changed its manners.

DU BAO:

What are those forty or fifty snowy mounds that rise in the distance?

SUBORDINATES:

They are salt piles stored in the yards to be paid to the merchants.

DU BAO:

Where are the merchants?

> *(Enter two merchants)*

TWO MERCHANTS:

> *"The jades from brines are piled and sold;*
> *The salt has thus become pure gold."*

We merchants pay our respect to you.

DU BAO:

Merchants, as I'm afraid that provisions will be needed here, please bring them in as soon as possible.

> *(To the previous tune)*
> The salt piles stand as snowy mounds,

In exchange for fodder and grain.

The salt stored on the spacious grounds

Will soon become the merchants' gains.

ALL:

On watchtowers above the wall,

We sprinkle wine beside the banners.

When we think of past glories,

Our mournful teardrops fall,

For the world has changed its manners.

DU BAO:

Now, so much for the sprinkling of wine. I'm glad that we have abundant provisions in store, but I still hope that you must be on the alert to guard the frontiers.

SUBORDINATES (*To the tune of* **Wunishang**):

We are the frontier guards,

The frontier guards,

Protecting farms and fields,

Protecting people in the yards.

ALL:

Should the Jins dare to invade the land,

We'll greet them with our bows and guns.

When war cries roll along the border,

At your command,

All the soldiers are brave ones.

SUBORDINATES (*To the tune of* **Hongxiuxie**):

We offer sacrifice to the city god,

The city god,

We thank the heaven for our peace,

For our peace.

Let us salute the army flags

And get our weapons piece by piece.

When battles start,

Who will fight with pride?

Behind the battlements,

Our archers hide.

DU BAO (*To the tune of* **Coda**):

When I deploy the troops,

All of you must take good care

To wait for battle summons there.

With battle flags flying on the wall,

We'll crash the enemy's daydream.

The outer walls are strong and tall,

Guarded by a valiant team.

Scene Thirty-Two
Vowing between Man and Ghost

(*Enter Liu Mengmei*)

LIU MENGMEI (*To the tune of* **Yueyungao**):

> When gilded roofs are shadowed by the cloud,
>
> The prayer banners flutter in the breeze.
>
> The evening bells no longer ring aloud,
>
> And I begin to feel so ill at ease.
>
> A scholar as poor as can be,
>
> I have a pretty maid who loves me.

The time is early yet.

> When flowers tremble in a gale,
>
> The moonlight dots the garden trail.
>
> (*Shields the lantern*)
>
> When I roam along the garden trail,
>
> I shield the lantern from the gale.
>
> (*Smiles*)
>
> "It's easier to finish learned books
>
> Than wait for maid with pretty looks."

As I did not take any precautions when my fair lady came last night, our rendezvous was disrupted by the nuns. Before she comes tonight, I'll go and chat for a while with the nuns, lest suspicion should arise again.

> (*Leaves the door ajar and walks along*)
>
> I leave the door ajar for my beloved one.

Oh heavens,

> What mood do I have to chat with the nun?
>
> (*Exit*)
>
> (*Enter Du Liniang in the ghost form*)

DU LINIANG (*To the previous tune*):

> In lonely fear I ran
>
> When my pendants rang in a tinkling tune.
>
> (*Taken aback*)
>
> I thought it was the shadow of a man,
>
> But it was a cloud drifting past the moon.
>
> (*Reaches the door*)

Here I am at Mr Liu's study, but where is he now?

> The lantern quivers in the gloom,
>
> Adding dimness to the room
>
> As the oil
>
> Ignites the lantern flame,

So the wick

Ignites my loving claim.

(*Sighs*)

My rendezvous with Mr Liu is kept unknown to the mortals but not the ghosts.

(*Weeps*)

As grapevine always stretches fast,

Who knows how long our rendezvous can last?

"From my mouth comes hardly a word;

On my brows comes hardly a beam.

I'd like to taste the pleasure in this world,

But fear that it happens only in a dream."

Although I've entered the netherworld, I still keep my body intact. I'll soon leave the netherworld and return to the human world. I died for Mr Liu and shall return to life for Mr Liu. It is our fate to be man and wife; therefore, if I don't tell him about it tonight, what good will come of a rendezvous between man and ghost? I'm afraid that my story will give him a shock, but that's my only choice. It is true to say that

"A ghostly story that he hears

Will fix the marriage of a hundred years."

(*Enter Liu Mengmei*)

LIU MENGMEI (*To the tune of* **Lanhuamei**):

The bamboo wavers in the breeze;

(*Sound of startled birds within*)

The crows are startled in the trees.

Oh, my door is now opened.

A fairy has arrived at ease.

(*Du Liniang comes out of the door to greet him*)

DU LINIANG:

So you're back.

LIU MENGMEI (*Makes a bow to Du Liniang*):

So you've come.

DU LINIANG:

I trimmed the wick while I waited here;

LIU MENGMEI:

You are indeed true to me, my dear.

DU LINIANG:

While I was waiting for you, sir, I made up a quatrain by collecting lines from the Tang poets.

LIU MENGMEI:

I'll be pleased to hear it.

DU LINIANG:

"I need someone to tell my love

While the cold moon shines above.

565

The Peony Pavilion

When from somewhere the dirges ring,

I yearn for the man of bygone spring."

LIU MENGMEI:

You're indeed a gifted poet.

DU LINIANG:

Sir, where have you been in the small hours?

LIU MENGMEI:

As we were disturbed last night by the nuns, I visited them before your arrival to make sure that they would not suspect us. I didn't expect that you come so early.

DU LINIANG:

I can hardly wait till the moon rises.

LIU MENGMEI (*To the tune of* **Taishiyin**):

> What a bliss that I have this maid,
>
> So kind and faithful to a man like me.
>
> Her tender eyes that I can't evade
>
> Enchant me degree by degree.

What a pity that the nuns last night

> Disturbed us while we were in glee.

My dear,

> The nuns distressed your mind
>
> And brought you such a fright.
>
> If you leave the woes behind,
>
> We'll start the game again tonight.

DU LINIANG (*To the tune of* **Suohanchuang**):

> Their visit caught me unawares
>
> And scared me out of my wits.
>
> When the moon is hidden in the air,
>
> I stood behind the scroll and quit.
>
> I nearly stumbled on the trail,
>
> As I had never been so scared.
>
> If Dad should hear about the tale,
>
> I won't easily be spared.

LIU MENGMEI:

I'm sorry for the trouble I've brought you, but am I indeed worthy of your love?

DU LINIANG:

I love you because you are the man of men.

LIU MENGMEI:

May I ask whether you have been engaged, my dear?

DU LINIANG (*To the tune of* **Taishiyin**):

> No one has offered me his hand.

LIU MENGMEI:

What kind of husband would you like to have?

566

DU LINIANG:

>A loving scholar is what I demand.

LIU MENGMEI:

I do have a loving heart.

DU LINIANG:

>A scholar with a love so deep,
>
>You distract me in my sleep.

LIU MENGMEI:

Be my wife, my dear.

DU LINIANG:

>While from Lingnan you roam,
>
>I don't know whether you have a wife at home.

LIU MENGMEI:

I'm not married yet.

DU LINIANG (*Smiles*):

>You have deep roots in the native land,
>
>Why should you offer me your hand?

Will you tell me something about your parents?

LIU MENGMEI:

My late father served as a minister in the court and my late mother was entitled Lady of
the County.

DU LINIANG:

In that case, you are from an official's family. How is it that you are not married yet?

LIU MENGMEI (*To the tune of* **Suohanchuang**):

>Although I live a roaming life,
>
>I will not take a homely wife.
>
>But where's the maid who'd marry
>
>A man like Xiangru who had to roam?
>
>Where's the maid who'd marry
>
>A man like Xiao Shi who had no home?
>
>Your smiles on me are the highest praise,
>
>And as I'm blessed with smiles from you,
>
>Although I'm not up to men of ancient days,
>
>My love will not be like the morning dew.

DU LINIANG:

Since you have a strong love for me, why don't you get a matchmaker for our engagement,
so that I don't have to worry about our rendezvous?

LIU MENGMEI:

I'll visit your parents tomorrow morning and ask for your hand.

DU LINIANG:

When you come to my home, you'll only meet me. It's not the time yet for you to meet
my parents.

LIU MENGMEI:

Do you mean to say that you are from a distinguished house?

> (*Du Liniang giggles*)

LIU MENGMEI:

What's up your sleeves?

> (*To the tune of* **Hongshan'er**)
>
> Your beauty of tremendous worth
>
> Does not belong to mortal earth.

DU LINIANG:

If it does not belong to the mortal earth, does it belong to the heaven?

LIU MENGMEI:

> How can you walk alone in the nightly shade
>
> Without a servant-maid?

Will you tell me your name?

> (*Du Liniang sighs*)

LIU MENGMEI (*Aside*):

> Why does she conceal her name?
>
> Does she enjoy immortal fame?
>
> (*To Du Liniang*)

Since you won't disclose your name, you must be a fairy. As I am not worthy of your trust, I dare not have any rendezvous with you.

> For all the love you have for me,
>
> The lord of heaven will not agree.

DU LINIANG (*To the previous tune*):

> You take me as an immortal friend,
>
> But my previous life has come to an end.

LIU MENGMEI:

If you are not an immortal, are you a human being?

DU LINIANG:

> If I can elope with you,
>
> My name should not have been taboo.

LIU MENGMEI:

If you are not a human being, are you an elf amid the flowers?

DU LINIANG:

> I'd like you to dig my root,
>
> But fear to spoil our pursuit.

LIU MENGMEI:

What do you mean?

DU LINIANG (*Hesitates*):

> I should have made it clear,
>
> But hesitate with fear.

LIU MENGMEI:

My dear,

"Tell me now;

Tell me how.

If you say no,

Who else should know?"

DU LINIANG:

I'll tell you now;

I'll tell you how.

Dear sir,

An elopement is not fair.

I'll tell you if you swear."

LIU MENGMEI:

If you want me to swear to marry you, I'll make a vow by burning a joss-stick with you.

(Kowtows with Du Liniang)

(To the tune of **Diliuzi**)

Heavens above,

Heavens above,

The incense proves the man.

Liu Mengmei,

Liu Mengmei

Now stays in Nan'an.

I'll have this beauty in life

As my dearest wife.

We'll live to share the room

And die to share the tomb.

If I break my word,

I'll perish from this world.

(Du Liniang weeps)

LIU MENGMEI:

How is it that you're weeping now?

DU LINIANG:

I'm moved to tears by your strong love.

(To the tune of **Naofanlou**)

A scholar with a loving heart

Will never tear his words apart,

Alas,

But my account can hardly start.

Now listen, my dear,

And do not fear.

But I'm afraid when you hear

What I have to say,

You'll stumble and fade away.

LIU MENGMEI:

What is it that you have to say?

DU LINIANG:

Dear sir, where did you find the portrait on the wall?

LIU MENGMEI:

I found it in a crevice of lakeside rocks.

DU LINIANG:

How would you say if you compare me with it?

LIU MENGMEI (*Compares her with the portrait and gets surprised*):

Why, you look as like as two peas!

DU LINIANG:

You know, it's a portrait of me.

LIU MENGMEI (*Bows to the portrait with folded palms*):

I haven't burnt my incense in vain. My dear, would you tell me more about yourself?

DU LINIANG (*To the tune of* **Zhuomufan**):

> Now listen, my dear man,
>
> My father was the Prefect of Nan'an.

LIU MENGMEI:

Well, the former Prefect of Nan'an has been promoted to Yangzhou, but why are you left behind?

DU LINIANG:

Trim the wick, please.

> (*Liu Mengmei trims the wick*)

DU LINIANG:

> Now that the lamp is bright,
>
> I'll bring the truth to light.

LIU MENGMEI:

May I ask your name and your age?

DU LINIANG:

> Du Liniang stands by your side,
>
> Sixteen years of age,
>
> The right time to be a bride.

LIU MENGMEI:

Oh, Liniang, my dear sweetheart!

DU LINIANG:

Wait, dear sir, I'm not a mortal being yet.

LIU MENGMEI:

If you are not a mortal being, are you a ghost?

DU LINIANG:

Yes, I am a ghost.

LIU MENGMEI (*Frightened*):

Oh, terrible! Terrible!

DU LINIANG:

> Stand back, Mr Liu,
>
> And hear my words.
>
> As I told you,
>
> I live between two worlds.

LIU MENGMEI:

My dear, how did you manage to return to this world to meet me?

DU LINIANG (*To the previous tune*):

> When I was in the world of hell,
>
> The judge knew that I was from an official's house
>
> And treated me well.
>
> He promised me a second life
>
> And sent me to this world,
>
> As I am fated to be your wife.

Dear sir,

> As you yearn to take me as your wife,
>
> My chilly bones are again warm with life.

LIU MENGMEI:

As you are my wife, I have no reason to be afraid, but how can I make sure that you are revived? Would I be just like fishing the moon in the lake or picking the flower in a dream?

571

DU LINIANG (*To the tune of* **Sanduanzi**):

> As my senses still survive,
>
> Although a ghost, I can walk like you.
>
> With my spirit still alive,
>
> I shall soon start a life anew.

My dear, are you well-versed in classics?

> Alive or dead, my heart remains the same;
>
> You hardly know if now you sleep or wake.
>
> You may pick the flower in a dream,
>
> But not fish the moon in the lake.

LIU MENGMEI:

Since you are experiencing a living death, where is your burial place?

DU LINIANG:

Under a plum tree beside a Taihu rock.

> (*To the previous tune*)
>
> In the garden I have stayed
>
> And dreamt alone
>
> Beneath the plum-tree's shade.
>
> When the plums are ripe,
>
> For the man I love,
>
> Large drops of tear I wipe.

LIU MENGMEI:

Haven't you found a way out?

DU LINIANG (*Sighs*):

> Even when I've met my doom,
>
> I'm still a fragrant bloom.

LIU MENGMEI:

You must have felt very cold.

DU LINIANG:

> Although my soul is cold,
>
> My faith is as of old.

LIU MENGMEI:

Wouldn't I disturb your soul?

DU LINIANG (*To the tune of* **Doushuangji**):

> The flower roots are in a place
>
> Which leads to the human world,
>
> Where I'm warmed up by your embrace.
>
> If you fear to "disturb my soul",
>
> > My soul already flies to you.
>
> Since I saw you for the first time,
>
> > Revival has always been in view.

LIU MENGMEI:

In that case, it's a long story.

DU LINIANG:

> To be a couple for a night
>
> Brings about three generation's delight.

LIU MENGMEI:

I appreciate your devotion, but I'm afraid I can't do it all by myself.

DU LINIANG:

Why don't you talk it over with Sister Stone?

LIU MENGMEI:

As I don't know how deep you lie, I'm not sure how long it will take to get through to you.

DU LINIANG (*To the tune of* **Dengxiaolou**):

> A man who sticks to his aim
>
> Is a man worthy of his name.
>
> If you dig three feet deep,
>
> You'll reach where I lie asleep.
>
> You'll feel the chilly breeze down there,
>
> Some distance from the open air.
>
> (*Sound of cockcrow within*)
>
> (*To the tune of* **Baolaocui**)

Alas,

> For eternal sleep in eternal night,

The cockcrow does not bring daylight.

But tonight,

> When cockcrow breaks my dream,
>
> I know the human world is supreme.
>
> Now that the morning breeze dies out in the south
>
> And the moon sets amid cuckoo-songs,
>
> Less than half of my words pass my mouth.
>
> (*To the tune of* **Shuabaolao**)
>
> Bit by bit,
>
> I've bared my heart.
>
> Since you know my inner part,
>
> You must save my outer part.
>
> Lose no time;
>
> Make haste;
>
> I've told you my story from the start.
>
> (*Sound of a gale within*)
>
> With the gale I have to depart.
>
> (*Exit in a hurry*)

LIU MENGMEI (*Astonished*):

Absurd! Absurd! I've become the son-in-law of Prefect Du. Am I in a dream? I'll recall what's happened. Her name is Du Liniang, aged sixteen, buried beneath a plum tree in the back garden. Pooh, she's alive and kicking, with flesh and blood. Why on earth did she say that she was a ghost?

> (*Re-enter Du Liniang*)

DU LINIANG:

You're still here, dear sir?

LIU MENGMEI:

Why are you back again?

DU LINIANG:

I have another word with you. If you take me as your wife, please be quick to act. Otherwise, this is our last rendezvous, for I've revealed my secret to you. See to it that you do not lose the opportunity. If I cannot come to life again, I'll bear you hatred in the netherworld.

> (*Kneels on the ground*)
>
> (*To the tune of* **Coda**)
>
> You can give me a second life.
>
> (*Liu Mengmei kneels to help her to her feet*)
>
> Have pity on your wife.

If you do not want me to hate you in the netherworld,

> Make an oath and you're out of the strife.
>
> (*Exit with a ghostly wail, casting a final glance*)

LIU MENGMEI (*Whispers softly to himself*):

573

I'm haunted. However, her words ring loud and sincere in my ears. Be it real or not, I must follow her instructions. I'll go and talk it over with Sister Stone.

> *What's better than the dreamland in the room?*
> *The fairy lady makes me moan alone.*
> *Who on earth will guide me to the tomb?*
> *Someone says that it is Sister Stone.*

Scene Thirty-Three
Clandestine Schemes

(*Enter Sister Stone*)

SISTER STONE (*To the tune of* **Raochiyou**):

> In a lotus cloak,
> I wear my hair so short.
> Amid the smoke and bells, I invoke.
> *"The empty hall is humming in the breeze*
> *While I sit alone under verdant trees.*
> *With the lotus pond at sight,*
> *I smell the scent at night.*
> *The man will soon grow old;*
> *The scheme is uncontrolled;*
> *The dream can hardly hold.*
> *The love, howe'er profound,*
> *Is buried underground,*
> *With sunshine on the mound."*

This Plum Blossom Nunnery was built in memory of Miss Du. Prefect Du entrusted it to the care of Tutor Chen, who has collected the land rent for the past three years but seldom minded the business. After Prefect Du's departure, Tutor Chen raised donations to build a memorial hall for him. But when I passed by the memorial hall yesterday, I saw shit and dung littering the ground. Chen Zuiliang, Chen Zuiliang, why don't you get someone cleaning the hall? As a contrast, I've kept Miss Du's shrine clean and tidy, offering incense and changing sacrificial water every day. It's true to say,

> *"Don't trust Confucian scholars now;*
> *Better trust disciples of Tao."*

(*Enter Liu Mengmei*)

LIU MENGMEI (*To the previous tune*):

> With a ghost I date,
> A spiritual mate.
> I'd like to talk, but hesitate.

(*Greets Sister Stone*)

"The fallen petals are fragrant in the hall;

SISTER STONE:

Have the petals disturbed your heart?

LIU MENGMEI:

The fairy maiden makes a distant call;

SISTER STONE:

The human world has made another start."

LIU MENGMEI:

Sister Stone, I've lived in your nunnery for quite some time, but I've never visited the main hall yet. Will you show me around today?

SISTER STONE:

No problem. Go after me, please.

(*They reach the main hall*)

SISTER STONE:

High above stands the Jade Emperor, and on either side stand Lady of Mount Tai and Lady of the Southern Dipper.

(*Bell rings within*)

LIU MENGMEI (*Kowtows*):

"High above in the sky,

The emperor's strength and power pervade.

When River God is beating drums,

We get to know the fairy maid."

What a magnificent hall! On the memorial tablet on the left is the inscription "The Spiri of Miss Du". What's the meaning of "spiri"?

SISTER STONE:

To complete the service, we need someone to add the final letter. It's "The Spirit of Miss Du".

LIU MENGMEI:

And who is this Miss Du?

SISTER STONE (*To the tune of **Wugengzhuan***):

I'll tell you

For whom this nunnery is built.

It has been built by Prefect Du.

Liniang, his daughter fair and dear,

Who died young,

Is buried here.

On his departure for his latest post,

He left the inscription incomplete

And left alone the ghost.

LIU MENGMEI:

Who's taking care of the graveyard and the shrine?

SISTER STONE:

She has land attached to her grave,

With inscriptions to make her name last.

As her kith and kin are far away,

For years she has to go on a fast.

LIU MENGMEI (*Weeps*):

Judging from what you've said, Miss Du must be my dear wife.

SISTER STONE (*Astonished*):

Are you telling the truth, Mr Liu?

LIU MENGMEI:

The truth, nothing but the truth.

SISTER STONE:

Then you know the date of her birth and the date of her death?

LIU MENGMEI (*To the previous tune*):

As I don't know the date of her birth,

How can I know the date of her death?

I only know she has been dead for years

And will soon have a rebirth.

SISTER STONE:

When did you hear of her death?

LIU MENGMEI:

I heard of her in the morning

And she died in the evening.

SISTER STONE:

If she's your wife, it's your duty to make offerings to her.

LIU MENGMEI:

As I haven't looked after her alive,

How can I look after her after death?

SISTER STONE:

Since you've married her, have you ever met her?

LIU MENGMEI:

The plum blossom here

Is our nuptial chamber,

Behind your eye and ear.

SISTER STONE:

When was that?

LIU MENGMEI:

The night before when you spoilt our cheer.

SISTER STONE (*Astonished*):

You are haunted. Incredible! Incredible!

LIU MENGMEI:

If you don't believe me, fetch a brush-pen. When I complete the word "spirit", the memorial tablet will stir.

SISTER STONE:

Is that possible? Here is a brush-pen.

LIU MENGMEI (*Completes the word*):

> I'll give you life,
>
> My dear, dear wife.

Look, look!

SISTER STONE:

Fantastic! Fantastic! The tablet is stirring! Oh, my young mistress!

> (*To the previous tune*)
>
> I thought that the plum before the tomb
>
> Served to protect you,
>
> But Mr Liu has been the bloom.
>
> Mr Liu, since she's your wife, you'd better
>
> Build a hut beside her tomb
>
> And live there as your room.

LIU MENGMEI:

I'm going to bring her to life.

SISTER STONE:

> Do you have the spell
>
> Endowed by the Prince of Hell?

LIU MENGMEI:

I need some labourers to help me.

SISTER STONE:

> You need a wife,
>
> She needs a life
>
> And ghosts help with your strife.

LIU MENGMEI:

I need your help too.

SISTER STONE:

According to the present law, grave-robbers are to be beheaded, be he the instigator or the accomplice.

> A scholar from the dynasty of Song
>
> Is unaware of the present law:
>
> To rob a grave is wrong.

LIU MENGMEI:

It doesn't matter to realise Miss Du's own wishes.

> (*To the previous tune*)
>
> It's she down in the hell,
>
> Who asks you to give aid.
>
> Who knows so well
>
> As the pretty maid?

SISTER STONE:

As I'm carrying out Miss Du's order, I'll try to find an auspicious date.

(Consults the almanac)

It happens that tomorrow is an auspicious day to dig the grave.

LIU MENGMEI:

Tomorrow is an auspicious day,

But I still need a robust man

To dig the clay.

SISTER STONE:

My nephew by the name of Scabby Turtle will be at your service, but what if people should know about it?

LIU MENGMEI:

Once we bring her to life,

We'll keep our mouth shut tight

About my dearest wife.

Who needs a corpse in the broad daylight?

One more thing: when Miss Du comes to life again, she must need some herbs to relieve her mind.

SISTER STONE:

Tutor Chen keeps a pharmacy. We'll just say that the wandering young nun has run against an evil spirit and that she needs some herbs to calm down.

LIU MENGMEI:

Will yon please go and get the medicine at once?

To save a life today

Is no child's play!

SISTER STONE:

Amid the mist and raindrops from the skies,

LIU MENGMEI:

I'll go to visit that magician's cave.

SISTER STONE:

Not far from where the pretty maiden lies,

LIU MENGMEI:

I tread the withered grass to watch her grave.

Scene Thirty-Four
Asking for Medicine

(Enter Chen Zuiliang)

CHEN ZUILIANG:

"Confucian learning shows its effect:

I'm now a doctor all admire.

> *The servants greet me with respect*
> *While neighbours call a doctor squire."*

Since I lost my tutor's position, I've kept a pharmacy for a living. I wonder which customer is coming today.

(*Enter Sister Stone*)

SISTER STONE (*To the tune of* **Nüguanzi**):

> Be it in Heaven or on Earth,
>
> Good sense is difficult to find.
>
> From dreams a fancy comes in birth;
>
> From Hell a lover comes to mind.

Good luck to your business, Mr Chen.

CHEN ZUILIANG:

How do you do, Sister Stone.

SISTER STONE:

What a fine store you've kept! The inscription "Confucian Doctor" must have been written by Prefect Du. The inscription on the signboard "Choicest Herbs" is well said, but what's the use of these two clods of earth?

CHEN ZUILIANG:

It comes from beneath the widow's bed. If a man is haunted, just resolve some earth in water and have him drink it. It's very effective.

SISTER STONE:

Then what's the use of this rag?

CHEN ZUILIANG:

It comes from the crotch of a strong man's pants. If a woman is haunted, just burn them to ashes and have her eat it. It's also very effective.

SISTER STONE:

In that case, what about exchanging the earth from beneath my bed for the crotch from your pants?

CHEN ZUILIANG:

I'm afraid you're not much of a widow.

SISTER STONE:

Phew! I'm afraid you're not strong enough.

CHEN ZUILIANG:

Well, forget about it. What can I do for you?

SISTER STONE:

To tell you the truth, I've come for the young nun who the day before yesterday

> (*To the tune of* **Huangying'er**)
>
> Did not take sufficient care
>
> And late at night
>
> Came back from the fair.

CHEN ZUILIANG:

Was she in trouble?

579

SISTER STONE:

> Who knows in which wild wasteland
>
> She was caught by some evil turn.
>
> At the ghostly command,
>
> Her soul departed, never to return.

CHEN ZUILIANG:

How careless she was!

SISTER STONE:

> You can do your job well
>
> To save her from the living hell.

CHEN ZUILIANG:

Is she dead or alive?

SISTER STONE:

She's been dead for a couple of days.

CHEN ZUILIANG:

Can the dead nun take medicine? At any rate, burn this rag of pants and have her take it with warm wine.

> (*To the previous tune*)
>
> A magic medicine I grant:
>
> The crotch of strong man's pant.

SISTER STONE:

If that's the medicine, I have some in my place.

CHEN ZUILIANG:

> Perhaps you don't know which is fine.
>
> Just cut a little piece,
>
> Burn and mix it with sweet wine,
>
> Then force it down between her teeth.
>
> The medicine retrieves her soul
>
> In a unique way
>
> And plays a magic role.

SISTER STONE:

Thanks a lot.

CHEN ZUILIANG:

> *She went to markets with her friends,*

SISTER STONE:

> *But fell ill for her dearest love.*

CHEN ZUILIANG:

> *As caves are closed when her life ends,*

SISTER STONE:

> *She needs a helping hand above.*

Scene Thirty-Five
Returning to Life

(*Enter Scabby Turtle*)

SCABBY TURTLE (*To the tune of* **Zizishuang**):

> I have a swine's bladder like a gourd —
>
> A scabby head.
>
> My spade will dig into something soft —
>
> The soil bed.
>
> The scholar wants a ghost of a wife —
>
> How can they wed?
>
> A grave-digger will be buried alive —
>
> What a dread!

(*With a laugh*)

I'm Scabby Turtle, nephew of the head of the Plum Blossom Nunnery. She has agreed to help Mr Liu to open up Miss Du's grave. What a funny thing that he says Miss Du would like to be his wife again. Well, that's none of my business. I've brought some yellow paper to burn. I'll put it on the Taihu rocks and then light some incense.

(*Enter Sister Stone, carrying some wine, and Liu Mengmei*)

SISTER STONE (*To the tune of* **Chuduizi**):

> Where is the pretty lass?
>
> Where is the pretty lass?
>
> Beside her tomb grows luxuriant grass.
>
> Now that love-songs ring around,
>
> Has cuckoo's song reached her native town?
>
> With woe in her grave,
>
> In her dreams she would still frown.

LIU MENGMEI:

Here we are at the back garden, Sister Stone. Alas, the pavilion has nearly tumbled down, with thorns and brambles all around. Miss Du's sash-trails have been covered with vines and flowers while her skirt-traces have been overgrown with verdant grass. I only remember the Taihu rocks, where I picked up the portrait, but everything is vague and obscure as if in a dream. What can I do about it?

SISTER STONE:

Take it easy, Mr Liu. Here it is, the mound beneath the plum tree.

LIU MENGMEI:

Oh, dear Miss Du! What a great sorrow you've brought me!

(*Weeps*)

SCABBY TURTLE:

It's no use weeping at this time. Let's get to work.

(*Burns the yellow paper*)

LIU MENGMEI (*Kowtows*):

God of Hills and God of Earth, please show your divine power!

> (*To the tune of* **Zhuomuli**)
>
> The yellow paper burns beside the grove
>
> And lights a fire just like a stove.

SCABBY TURTLE:

> How dare you dig the earth upon this seat
>
> And build a tunnel to her feet?

LIU MENGMEI:

God of Earth, I dig the grave today in order to bring Du Liniang to life again. I don't want her dead, but I want her alive.

> You are a god upright and fair,
>
> And so we do our job without care.
>
> If it should become widely known,
>
> I'll say I've wed the daughter of your own.
>
> Oh, how the plum blossoms in the spring air!

It's time to dig the earth!

SISTER STONE, SCABBY TURTLE (*Dig the earth*):

> (*To the previous tune*)
>
> Let's dig the earth, dig the earth.
>
> Are you here, Miss Du, to have a rebirth?

LIU MENGMEI:

Handle with care!

> (*Watches the digging*)

Here's the coffin!

SCABBY TURTLE (*Throws away the spade in alarm*):

The cop? We're finished.

LIU MENGMEI (*Waves his hands*):

Shut up!

> (*Du Liniang moans within, which frightens all*)

SISTER STONE, SCABBY TURTLE:

The living ghost is making a noise!

LIU MENGMEI:

Don't frighten Miss Du!

> (*The three of them squat, facing the entrance, and open the coffin*)

SISTER STONE:

Oh, the nails have rusted away and the joints are loose. Miss Du must be making love somewhere.

> (*Moaning sounds within*)

LIU MENGMEI (*Sees Du Liniang and goes to support her*):

Hurrah, Miss Du is here, with heavenly fragrance and former beauty! Oh, my heaven, look!

> There's dirt on the coffin lid,

But not a single ant is in the grave.

The fragrant planks have sheltered her

On her way to the netherworld,

For her to lie at ease in the cave.

(*Supports Du Liniang, who leans limply on him*)

I'll hold her sleeping head with care,

Lest I hurt the funeral stone there.

(*Du Liniang vomits quicksilver from her mouth*)

SCABBY TURTLE:

A piece of silver! Well, it's heavy enough. Will you give me as a gift?

LIU MENGMEI:

This is her crystallisation of the dragon and the phoenix for me to keep as an heirloom. You'll get some other reward.

(*Du Liniang opens her eyes and sighs*)

SISTER STONE:

Miss Du has opened her eyes.

LIU MENGMEI:

The heaven has opened its eyes! My dear!

DU LINIANG (*To the tune of* **Jinjiaoye**):

Is it real or illusory

That I awake from a nightmare?

(*Covers her eyes*)

I fear the light might vanish with the wind

As that is too much for me to bear.

LIU MENGMEI:

She fears the wind. What's to be done?

SISTER STONE (*Supports Du Liniang*):

Why not take the magic medicine in the Peony Pavilion. Mr Liu, please cut this piece of a man's pants-crotch.

(*Liu Mengmei cuts the pants*)

SCABBY TURTLE:

Let me add some stronger smell to it.

LIU MENGMEI:

Away with your smell! Warm some wine for me, please. Be quick.

(*Mixes the medicine with the wine and feeds it into Du Liniang's mouth*)

(*To the tune of* **Yingtixu**)

Drink the medicine and you are blessed.

(*Du Liniang vomits*)

Why do you vomit it on your chest?

Take some more, Miss Du.

You've only taken three tiny sips.

(*Keeps a close look at her face*)

Wonderful! Wonderful!

> Now she's looking her best.

DU LINIANG (*Looks around*):

Who are these people around?

> Look how you scoundrels behave!

> Are you robbing me of my grave?

LIU MENGMEI:

I'm Liu Mengmei.

DU LINIANG:

> As for the moment I'm blind and numb,

> I'm not sure if you are the man beside the plum.

LIU MENGMEI:

Sister Stone will be the witness.

SISTER STONE:

Can you recognise me, Miss Du?

> (*Du Liniang looks but does not speak*)

SISTER STONE (*To the previous tune*):

> How is it that you can't recall me?

LIU MENGMEI:

Do you remember the back garden?

> (*Du Liniang does not speak*)

SISTER STONE:

I've got it.

> She's still in a dream and cannot see.

DU LINIANG:

Are you Mr Liu?

> (*Shows signs of recognition when Liu Mengmei replies yes*)

You've kept your word, Mr Liu.

> I thank you for your pains

> And now you have your gains.

Take the jewellery from the coffin and throw the rest into the lake.

LIU MENGMEI, SISTER STONE, SCABBY TURTLE:

Phew!

> (*Throw away the coffin*)

DU LINIANG:

> I'll start my human life anew

> When the evil coffin flows out of view.

LIU MENGMEI, SISTER STONE, SCABBY TURTLE:

What hard time for you to sleep for three years!

DU LINIANG:

> The flowing time

> In the grave

Has wasted my prime.

LIU MENGMEI:

My dear, it's windy and wet here. Let's find a better place for you to have a good rest.

(*To the tune of* **Coda**)

My efforts have saved you from hell;

A bath and dinner will make you well.

DU LINIANG:

Where are you leading me?

SISTER STONE:

To the Plum Blossom Nunnery.

DU LINIANG:

You know, acts of love

Will drive away the spell.

LIU MENGMEI:

Heaven has bestowed on you pretty cheeks;

DU LINIANG:

With your help I've left the nether creeks.

SISTER STONE:

We haven't dug the pit as vain attempt;

LIU MENGMEI:

Don't refuse my hand with contempt.

Scene Thirty-Six
Wedding and Departure

(*Enter Du Liniang, supported by Sister Stone*)

DU LINIANG (*To the tune of* **Yinanwang**):

I smile, I stare;

In the web of love,

The dreamland is always there.

SISTER STONE:

Far, far away from hell and curse,

You left the netherworld in your hearse.

DU LINIANG:

Sister Stone,

I'm trying hard to raise

My feeble legs,

But to recover needs a lot of days.

DU LINIANG, SISTER STONE:

There is still doubt

Whether this will end up in smoke
Or shadow that dies out.

DU LINIANG:

"For three years in the deepest gloom,
My dream still lingers in the lonely tomb.
With fallen petals on my skirt,
My rosy cheeks are covered with dirt.

SISTER STONE:

Although the wind might start anew
And incense fragrance might ensue,
She puzzles deities down and above
With her ardent love."

DU LINIANG:

Sister Stone, I was away from this world for three years, but ardent love has brought me back to this world again. I owe my second life to you and Mr Liu. Your delicious food and meticulous care have given me fresh energy within a few days.

SISTER STONE:

That's nice. Mr Liu has asked me time and again to prepare for your wedding.

DU LINIANG:

Sister Stone, it's not the right time yet. I have to go to Yangzhou and ask Dad and Mom to find a matchmaker.

SISTER STONE:

What a trite idea! But it's up to you to decide. By the way, do you still remember what happened before you died?

DU LINIANG (*To the tune of* **Shengruhua**):

What happened then
I've always kept in mind.
I took a stroll when I felt bored
And for my vernal dream I pined.
When the scholar picked up my portrait,
He was so earnest
And tried hard to find.
He was so eager to meet me
That he looked as if dumb and blind.

SISTER STONE:

I've heard something about it, but how do you get to know?

DU LINIANG:

Although I was buried in earth,
I was moved by his words.
For his devoting heart,
I left the netherworld
And came back brisk and smart.

SISTER STONE:

Here comes the young scholar.

> (*Enter Liu Mengmei*)

LIU MENGMEI (*To the tune of* **Shengchazi**):

> Buried for years in earth,
>
> She gained a second birth.
>
> See how she smiles with pins on her head
>
> And how her sash trails when she walks ahead.
>
> (*Greets Du Liniang*)

Oh, my dear wife!

> (*Du Liniang is abashed*)

LIU MENGMEI:

My dear, it's me who helped you out of the grave.

DU LINIANG:

I owe more to you than to my parents.

LIU MENGMEI:

Let's get married this very night.

DU LINIANG:

I still feel dizzy and weak.

SISTER STONE:

You just said that you were full of fresh energy. She's not telling the truth, Mr Liu.

DU LINIANG:

Mr Liu, you must know the quotation from *Mencius*: "Await the injunctions from the parents and the discussions of the go-betweens."

LIU MENGMEI:

The other day I did not "make holes and crevices in order to catch sight of you", to quote the same book, but I did dig the grave. And now you are quoting from the classics!

DU LINIANG:

There's a world of difference. I was a ghost then, and I am a maiden now. A ghost can ignore the ethic codes, but a maiden can't. Listen to me:

> (*To the tune of* **Shengruhua**)
>
> Gone is the night;
>
> The day is bright.
>
> (*Kowtows to Liu Mengmei*)

Mr Liu,

> With deep respect I kowtow to you,
>
> But a matchmaker is needed too.
>
> (*Weeps*)
>
> My parents must be on the site.

LIU MENGMEI:

When we visit your parents after we get married, they will be overjoyed. Sister Stone will be the matchmaker.

DU LINIANG:

What's the hurry, Mr Liu?

    I've waited upon you night by night.

LIU MENGMEI:

But what special night is this?

DU LINIANG:

    You're lustful, right?

LIU MENGMEI:

You are being naughty!

DU LINIANG (*Smiles*):

You are being naughty!

    Not that I make a pretentious show,

LIU MENGMEI:

But what?

DU LINIANG (*Abashed*):

    But that I'm just back to life,

    Not fit to make love, you know.

    Here I stand before you,

    Give me time to rest;

    (*Aside*)

    Of course I love you best.

    (*Enter Chen Zuiliang*)

CHEN ZUILIANG (*To the tune of* **Bushilu**):

    In the vacant yard,

    The flower and moss are wet with dew.

    (*Knocks at the door*)

    Is anyone in?

    I've come to visit Mr Liu.

    (*Liu Mengmei, Du Liniang and Sister Stone are startled*)

LIU MENGMEI:

Tutor Chen is at the door. What shall we do?

DU LINIANG:

Sister Stone, I'd better withdraw.

    (*Exit with Sister Stone*)

CHEN ZUILIANG:

    It's strange to me

    That I hear a girl's voice

    While the door is closed fast.

    (*Knocks at the door again*)

LIU MENGMEI:

Who is it?

CHEN ZUILIANG:

It's me, Chen Zuiliang.

LIU MENGMEI (*Opens the door and greets Chen Zuiliang*):

> Your visit honours me all the more;
>
> I'm sorry to be late to open the door.

CHEN ZUILIANG:

> There's something unusual here.

LIU MENGMEI:

> What is unusual here?

CHEN ZUILIANG (*To the previous tune*):

> But for the fairyland,
>
> Where comes the gentle voice offhand?
>
> (*Enter Sister Stone*)

SISTER STONE:

Oh, it's you, Tutor Chen.

LIU MENGMEI:

The gentle voice inside is from Sister Stone.

SISTER STONE:

Oh I see what you mean.

> What you hear
>
> Comes from a young nun who comes here.

CHEN ZUILIANG:

Is she the young nun who came the other day?

SISTER STONE:

It's another nun.

CHEN ZUILIANG:

Well, the Plum Blossom Nunnery is thriving, thanks to the blessing from Miss Du. I've come to invite Mr Liu to make offerings to Miss Du's tomb tomorrow at noontime. See you tomorrow.

> That's why I've come to your room.
>
> So that's settled for tomorrow —
>
> We'll sprinkle the wine on her tomb.

LIU MENGMEI:

> Thank you for inviting me;
>
> Sorry we haven't prepared tea.
>
> I'll pay a return visit soon.

CHEN ZUILIANG:

> See you soon.
>
> (*Exit*)

LIU MENGMEI:

Well, Mr Chen's gone at last. Please ask Miss Du to come for a chat.

> (*Enter Du Liniang*)

SISTER STONE:

What's to be done? What's to be done? Mr Chen will go to Miss Du's tomb tomorrow. If our act is known to the public, firstly, Miss Du will be accused of witchcraft; secondly, Prefect Du will be blamed for a lack of family discipline; thirdly, Mr Liu will be ridiculed for his bewilderment; fourthly, I'll be accused of grave-robbing. What can we do about it?

DU LINIANG:

What is the way out then, Sister Stone?

SISTER STONE:

Miss Du, as Mr Liu is going to Lin'an for the imperial examination, why don't you just get married, have Scabby Turtle find a boat and sail off this very night so that no one will know anything about it? What's your opinion?

DU LINIANG:

That's the only choice.

SISTER STONE:

The wine is ready and you two just kowtow to Heaven and Earth.

> (*Liu Mengmei and Du Liniang kowtow, each holding a cup of wine in hand*)

LIU MENGMEI (*To the tune of **Liuhuaqi***):

> It's really something rare
>
> For us to be a pair.
>
> In the golden cup,
>
> The wine is for us to share.
>
> Freshly brewed with spring flair,
>
> It makes your cheeks rosy and fair.

DU LINIANG (*In sorrow*):

> I died of vernal sorrow
>
> And slept for three long years.
>
> One thing still worries me now:
>
> How can I be your match,
>
> Back from the nether spheres?

LIU MENGMEI:

Don't talk like that!

> (*To the previous tune*)
>
> I'm fortunate to meet you on the way;
>
> How can I have doubt on our wedding day?
>
> To share the bed with you
>
> Is worth all that I pursue.
>
> You are a lady of good name,
>
> But I am not a man of far-reaching fame.

DU LINIANG (*Sighs*):

> In the intercourse,
>
> I was tempted by his manly force.

Mr Liu, I'm still a virgin.

LIU MENGMEI:

We've made love several times. How can you remain a virgin?

DU LINIANG:

You met my spirit at that time. Now I'm standing before you in my real self.

> You touched my spirit for sure
>
> While my real self is a virgin pure.

> (*Enter a boatman*)

BOATMAN (*Singing a ditty*):

> The maid is fond of tavern house,
>
> And never comes back late with care.
>
> She says the master's spouse
>
> Needs her help to comb the hair.

> (*Singing another ditty*)

> For maids by this name or that name,
>
> Each can drink a pot of tea.
>
> They steal from the storehouse without shame,
>
> Taking everything for free.

> (*Enter Scabby Turtle*)

SCABBY TURTLE:

Boatman! Boatman! Boatman! There're passengers to Lin'an!

BOATMAN:

Coming, coming, I'm coming.

> (*Rows his boat toward the bank*)

SCABBY TURTLE:

The boat has arrived. Mr Liu, please help Miss Du on board.

SISTER STONE (*Says farewell to Liu Mengmei and Du Liniang*):

Take care, Mr Liu and Miss Du.

LIU MENGMEI:

There's no one to wait on my wife. Would you come with us, Sister Stone? I'll requite your kindness when I obtain an official position.

SISTER STONE:

I haven't got my belongings yet.

> (*Aside*)

If the story is known to the public, I'll be punished. Flight is the best policy.

> (*Turns to Liu Mengmei*)

All right. Mr Liu, please give my nephew something as a reward and ask him to take care of the nunnery. I'll go with you.

SCABBY TURTLE:

Agreed.

LIU MENGMEI:

I'll give him this robe.

> (*Takes off hig robe and gives it to Scabby Turtle*)

SCABBY TURTLE:

Thanks. Who will take the blame if the story leaks out?

LIU MENGMEI:

Just say you don't know.

SCABBY TURTLE:

Bye-bye, then.

> "A scabby boy gives the nun some aid
>
> While Taoist nun becomes the servant maid."
>
> (*Exit*)

LIU MENGMEI, DU LINIANG, SISTER STONE (*Board the boat*):

> (*To the tune of* **Jibanling**)
>
> By night we sail off Nan'an,
>
> On our way toward Lin'an.
>
> (*Du Liniang weeps*)

LIU MENGMEI:

Why are you weeping now?

DU LINIANG:

> We'll start to roam;
>
> We'll start to roam.
>
> I lived here for three years;
>
> I lay dead here for three years.
>
> When I was dead, I was away from home;
>
> Now that I've revived, I'm going home.

LIU MENGMEI, DU LINIANG, SISTER STONE:

> What special night is this?
>
> From this very night,
>
> The bliss is
>
> That a couple unite.

LIU MENGMEI (*To the previous tune*):

> A beauty has regained her soul,
>
> As well as her female role.
>
> (*Du Liniang sighs*)

Why are you weeping again?

DU LINIANG:

> I was so helpless, so alone.
>
> I was so helpless, so alone.
>
> My perfume sachet was lost in grass;
>
> On my golden pin, dust has grown.
>
> I feared that between two worlds,
>
> Our hearts could hardly be known.

LIU MENGMEI, DU LINIANG, SISTER STONE:

> What special night is this?

From this very night,

The bliss is

That a couple unite.

SISTER STONE:

As the night is deep, I'll tell the boatman to moor the boat and you two can have some sleep.

LIU MENGMEI:

The breeze, the moon, the boat — all have added joy to our wedding night.

(*To the tune of* **Yicuozhao**)

With a fairy maid as my wife,

I've now brought love to life.

DU LINIANG:

My dear, only now do I understand the joy of the human world!

The love between the ghost and man

Was where the wedding began.

Tonight,

We have attained our goal;

I'll serve you body and soul.

SISTER STONE:

You've fastened your belt in the breeze;

It's time to make yourself at ease.

LIU MENGMEI:

With your heavy woe,

Can the boat bear the weight?

To bed we shall go

And your terror will abate.

(*To the tune of* **Coda**)

Our love is bound with mortal life;

DU LINIANG:

With persistent love I become your wife.

Mr Liu,

We've gone through a life-and-death strife.

LIU MENGMEI:

We take flight under the shining moon,

SISTER STONE:

With gentle breeze to whisper soon.

DU LINIANG:

Who knows what happens on the boat?

SISTER STONE:

On the water true love sails afloat.

Scene Thirty-Seven
The Pedagogue's Alarm

(*Enter Chen Zuiliang*)

CHEN ZUILIANG:

"My hair is unstirred in the gentle breeze;

I take a stroll out in late spring at ease.

As hundred years elapse in endless dreams,

The nightly storm has sent the blooms to streams."

I, Chen Zuiliang, am looking after Miss Du's tomb out of my gratitude for Prefect Du. Yesterday I invited Mr Liu to visit Miss Du's tomb with me. It's time to go now.

(*Walks on*)

"The gate is open and enwrapped in clouds;

The yard is overgrown with grass in crowds."

Let me call at the gate.

(*Calls aloud*)

Oh, the gate used to be closely shut, but today it's left open. I'll pay respects to the Bodhisattva.

(*Looks around the statue*)

Why, there's neither lamp nor incense today. And where's Miss Du's memorial tablet? I'll ask Sister Stone about it.

(*Calls three times*)

She's out. Let me ask Mr Liu.

(*Calls aloud*)

Mr Liu, my friend!

(*Calls again*)

Mr Liu! Still no response.

(*Looks around*)

Oh, Mr Liu is gone. I cured him of his disease, but he has never said a word of gratitude, not even saying good-bye when he left. It's a shame! It's a shame! Let me look at the living room in the west wing. Ah, Sister Stone is gone, too. The bells, the pots and the mattress are all gone. How strange!

(*Thinks*)

I've got it. There have been some rumours about a young nun, and I heard voices of a young nun again yesterday. There must be something fishy between Mr Liu and the young nun and they must have eloped last night. It's a shame! It's a shame! Forget about it! Forget about it! Let me go to the back garden and have a look at Miss Du's tomb.

(*Walks on*)

(*To the tune of **Lanhuamei***)

The moss is thick along the garden trail

While the pavilions are lying waste.

Here we bury the beauty and here we wail.

(*Stares around*)

Oh, the high mound has been levelled.

What's happened to the grave?

Has it collapsed into the cave?

The Taihu rocks have been moved to the left and the plum trees are still there.

(*Alarmed*)

Alas! Miss Du's tomb has been robbed!

(*Cries out*)

Oh, heavens! Miss Du!

(*To the tune of **Chaotianzi***)

What heartless scoundrel has robbed the grave?

How much gold has he found in the cave?

Miss Du, if you had been married, your body would have been buried in your husband's ancestral cemetery.

Without a spouse of her own,

She died and lay alone.

I feared that snakes and roots

Might disturb her bone,

But did not expect a man with heart of stone.

That's it. Liu Mengmei is from Lingnan, and grave-robbing must be something common there. He must have hidden the coffin in a nearby place and cut off a corner as a demand for ransom money. He must have expected Prefect Du to pay the money after learning about it. The coffin must have been buried somewhere near. Let me search for it.

(*Discovers the coffin*)

Oh, isn't it the coffin-head in the grass? Isn't it the rusted coffin-nails? The coffin has been broken open. Oh, heavens! Where are Miss Du's remains?

(*Looks around*)

A coffin plank is floating on the pond. Yes, Miss Du's remains must have been thrown into the pond. What a brutal robber!

(*To the tune of **Putianle***)

Oh heavens! How can you bear

To see her remains be thrown away?

She does not owe anyone a debt;

Why should her remains in water decay?

The lotus would have shed tears,

For her remains to be thrown into evil spheres.

When the pond is drained and her remains recovered,

Her scattered bones will look the worst.

How I wish that she were buried in water at first!

The robber is a brute of a man;

How can he care for the fair maiden

595

When he wants to grab whatever he can!

Confucius said, "When a tiger or a rhinoceros gets out of a cage, or tortoise-shell or jade is damaged in a box, the keeper cannot escape the blame." I'll first report it to the Nan'an prefectural office for them to apprehend the grave-robber, and then leave for Huaiyang this very night to report to Envoy Du.

(*To the tune of* **Coda**)

Sister Stone knew the jewels in the cave;

Mr Liu ventured to dig the grave.

Miss Du, can you see why

Like a housebreaker they behave?

When he dug the grave to gain his aim,

The mound was levelled with shame.

Although it's not my fault to bring the harm,

The robber drunkard is to blame.

Scene Thirty-Eight
The Invasion

(*Enter Li Quan with his men*)

LI QUAN (*To the tune of* **Shuangtianxiaojiao**):

A hero rises above all;

The drums and banners are the battle-call.

For three years in a coat of mail,

I've joined in battles big and small.

"Here I stand, the bravest chieftain Li Quan,

For the alien emperor I'll do whatever I can.

My troops will sweep across the Yangtze River,

To stun the cowards of the southern clan."

At the behest of the great Jin Dynasty, I, Gilded Prince, have been making trouble in the area between the Yangtze River and the Huaihe River for three years. Reports have it that the great Jin Dynasty has amassed sufficient troops and supplies for a southward expedition and that I am ordered to make advances on the Huaiyang area. I'd better discuss with my wife. Attendants, call for my spouse.

ATTENDANTS (*Call out*):

His Highness calls for his louse.

(*Enter a soldier with arrows*)

SOLDIER:

I've got arrows to shoot the louse.

LI QUAN (*Scolds with amusement*):

What did you say, son of a bitch?

SOLDIER:

Your Highness just said that you want to shoot the louse.

LI QUAN:

Nonsense! I called for my spouse Lady Yang, not to shoot a louse.

SOLDIER:

Your Highness will discuss with your spouse and I'll shoot my louse.

> (*Exit, amid shouts from Li Quan*)
>
> (*Enter Lady Yang*)

LADY YANG (*To the previous tune*):

> In the inner tent,
>
> The chieftain's wife is a brilliant portent.
>
> (*Salutes Li Quan*)

Prosperity to Your Highness!

> How fierce your assault was last night,
>
> Which wore me out with great delight.

My chieftain husband, I had been so exhausted that I was nearly torn out of bed. What is it that you'd like to discuss with me?

LI QUAN:

Reports have it that the Jin emperor will be on a southward expedition and that I am ordered to invade Huaiyang so as to clear his way of advance. I'm afraid that Yangzhou is guarded by Envoy Du and is not an easy prey for us. What's the best policy?

LADY YANG:

As far as I can see, you'd better besiege Huai'an first so that Envoy Du will come to its rescue. Then I'll lead some of our troops to attack Yangzhou so as to cut his provisions. At that time the ball is in our hands.

LI QUAN:

Marvellous idea! Marvellous idea! On hearing this scheme, I am stricken with awe myself.

LADY YANG:

And when were you not stricken with awe?

LI QUAN:

Quite right. Before I was made a prince, I had been a henpecked robber; since I was made a prince, I have been a henpecked prince.

LADY YANG:

Stop your nonsense. Now order the troops to set off to Huai'an at once.

LI QUAN (*To the tune of **Jinshanghua***):

> When I move my troops,
>
> I've sent the vanguard groups.
>
> Onward march, men of valiant deeds!
>
> Onward gallop, my brave steeds!
>
> Beat the drum!
>
> Beat the drum!
>
> Huaiyang will be deaf and numb!

ALL (*To the previous tune*):

> We have a tigress that would roar,
>
> Whom we regard with awe.
>
> She makes her plan;
>
> She controls her man.
>
> Laugh with cheer!
>
> Laugh with cheer!
>
> Huaiyang will tremble with fear!

LADY YANG:

Gilded Prince, now take my orders! Wherever your troops go, leave women alone! If you violate my order, you'll be punished in a court-martial.

LI QUAN:

I won't violate your order.

LADY YANG:

> *On the stormy field of ancient warfare,*

LI QUAN:

> *The warriors imitate a woman's wear.*

ALL:

> *Beneath the scarlet battle-flag,*
>
> *We honour golden brooches on her hair.*

Scene Thirty-Nine
Sojourn in Lin'an

(*Enter Liu Mengmei*)

LIU MENGMEI (*To the tune of **Tangduoling***):

> The mirror is clean and clear,

(*Enter Du Liniang*)

DU LINIANG:

> In my new dress I appear.

LIU MENGMEI:

> I see the Qiantang sights from my room.

DU LINIANG:

My dear husband,

> A fragrance came from the sky last night —
>
> The laurel on the moon in bloom.

LIU MENGMEI:

> "Long trips are boring for the man and wife;

DU LINIANG:

> *A cup of wine will add pleasure to your life.*

LIU MENGMEI:

> *The Qiantang bore is surging like the snow;*

DU LINIANG:

> *They foretell good tidings heavens bestow."*

LIU MENGMEI:

We have travelled together to the capital of Lin'an. Now that we've rented an empty house, I should be able to study the classics and histories. However, as the date for the imperial examination is still far off, I'm growing more and more homesick. How can I cheer up?

DU LINIANG:

This morning I asked Sister Stone to buy a kettle of wine to relieve your melancholy. She's not back yet.

LIU MENGMEI:

Thank you for your kindness, my dear. There's still one thing we haven't talked about. When we first met each other, you said that you were from the neighbourhood. Who knows that the netherworld prince was moved and we were married in haste! Throughout the journey I've never asked this question. Did you first see me in the west wing of the nunnery? How could you allude to my name in the poem "Will be found by the plum or willow"? How did you come across this magical idea?

DU LINIANG (*Smiles*):

Mr Liu, it is sheer fabrication to say that I first saw you in the west wing of the nunnery. In my previous life,

> (*To the tune of **Jiang'ershui***)
>
> I chanced to meet you in my garden dream
>
> And wrote poems on the willow theme.

I was just beginning to write the poem when you took me to the Peony Pavilion.

LIU MENGMEI (*Laughs*):

How did you like it?

DU LINIANG (*Smiles*):

Alas, while we were enjoying ourselves, petals fell and woke me up. From that time on I was simply sitting on pins and needles and fell seriously ill.

> Cleverness may hurt a clever man;
>
> Sincerity does not requite a sincere man;
>
> Predestined love is destined to befall the man.
>
> With profound love for you,
>
> I'm brought back to life again.
>
> That's my story from a different point of view.

LIU MENGMEI (*To the previous tune*):

> Although I am amazed at your strange tale,
>
> My faith tells me to believe in you.
>
> I feared the nether prince would blame our love,
>
> And for grave-digging I would rue.

599

As I'm destined to have a nether wife,

You have kept your body intact, too.

You'll see the splendour of the capital

When you start your life anew.

(*Enter Sister Stone with a kettle of wine*)

SISTER STONE:

"*I walked by the Phoenix Palace and beyond,*

Then bought my wine in Goldfish Pond."

Oh, Mr Liu and Miss Du, I've something to tell you. When I was buying the wine by the river, I saw scholars from all over the country going to the examination halls. Don't you miss your chance, Mr Liu!

(*Liu Mengmei and Du Liniang get into a flurry*)

DU LINIANG:

You must make haste, my dear.

SISTER STONE:

Please let me toast to your success in the examination.

DU LINIANG (*Holds up a cup of wine*):

(*To the tune of* **Xiaocuoda**)

The pleasure of one night's love

Is cut short by the two words: fame and name.

Please drink three cups of wine;

I wish that quadruple bliss be to our claim.

You'll stand at palace gate at five o'clock

And hear the bustle in the six streets.

With your talent to write a poem in seven steps,

You'll ascend the eight-treasure terrace for your feats.

With a drink from the royal "nine palaces",

You'll watch flowers along ten miles of streets.

LIU MENGMEI (*To the previous tune*):

After ten years of studies,

The plums will bloom in the coldest nine days.

Our fates are fixed by eight points of time —

You'll ride in a carriage of seven fragrant trees,

Have an audience with the queen in her six halls,

And receive your title on the five-coloured silk.

A model of four virtues

And three laws of obedience, you'll live well.

When you see my name on golden lists two inches long,

I'll be meeting you on a magnificent carriage.

DU LINIANG:

My dear, I still remember the poem I wrote on my portrait.

(*To the tune of* **Coda**)

I shall see you in your best

When you do well in the imperial test.

When you succeed in your examination, we'll go and meet your parents-in-law. They will say that

From Hell to Heaven I am blessed.

DU LINIANG:

My dearest husband is indeed sublime;

SISTER STONE:

Yon must hurry lest you miss your time.

LIU MENGMEI:

Forget not to count the days in your bedroom,

LIU MENGMEI, DU LINIANG, SISTER STONE:

From high above there comes joyous chime.

Scene Forty
Looking for His Master

(*Enter Hunchback Guo, carrying his luggage on a shoulder-pole*)

HUNCHBACK GUO (*To the tune of* **Gufeiyan**):

The human life is long and tedious;

I keep decades of life in mind.

My master, Mr Liu, is a learned man,

With no other means of life

Than relying on the orchard trees,

Which nature makes them ripe.

As years go by,

The orchard lies in waste.

Master, where are you?

I have no idea as to what to do.

I do not know

Where to find my revenue.

"The servants do their work well

When their master's there.

When Master says farewell,

The orchard trees are bare."

For all my life I have grown trees for the Lius. Strange to say, when Mr Liu was at home, each tree could bear over a hundred fruits; but since Mr Liu was gone, each tree has born over a hundred worms. For the few fruits on the trees, they are all stolen by the boys. With no master to help me, I have been bullied all the time. At last I decided to look for my master. I heard that he had crossed the Five Ridges and was put up in the Plum

Blossom Nunnery for illness. I followed him all the way to this place only to find that the city-gate had been sealed by the Nan'an Prefecture. I learned that the nun had fled for some crime and that she had a nephew, Scabby Turtle, who lived near the west city-gate. I'll go and try to find out the whereabouts of my master.

(*Walks on*)

"Follow the eastern road,

And reach the western gate."

(*Exit*)

(*Enter Scabby Turtle in Liu Mengmei's robe, laughing*)

SCABBY TURTLE (*To the tune of **Jinqianhua***):

I have a scabby head since my boyhood,

Since my boyhood.

I was put in jail for my aunt's sake,

For my aunt's sake.

I was tied

And was tried.

I was released,

But my house was leased.

I run errands in the open air,

From lane to street, from here to there.

"Nobody will know it,

Unless you haven't done it."

I am Scabby Turtle. As there's nobody around, I'll tell you my story. Indeed, my aunt and Mr Liu did a good job and escaped at the right time. After Tutor Chen the rascal reported it to the Nan'an Prefecture, I was put in custody and questioned: "Where's your aunt? Who's robbed the grave?" I was not clever, but I was cunning enough. I hung my head and kept my mouth shut. The damned judge said, "Truss up a horse and it grows; squeeze a man and he talks. Put the head-hoop on that scoundrel's head!" Oops, oops, what a pain! The torturers had got a golden bell and a jade chime out of me, so they did me a favour by reporting to the judge that they had squeezed my brains out of me. The damned judge said, "Take some and show it to me." He looked and said with a wave of his nose, "It's true you've squeezed his brain out of him." As he didn't know that it was the pus from my scabby head, he let me off. And so I was released on bail. Now that my life is preserved, I put on the robe Mr Liu gave me and swagger in the street.

(*Sings*)

Sway and strut,

Strut and sway.

In the empty street,

I swagger on the way.

(*Enter Hunchback Guo*)

HUNCHBACK GUO (*Bows to Scabby Turtle*):

How do you do, sir.

SCABBY TURTLE (*Does not return the bow, but sings with a laugh*):

> I've got a pain in my back
>
> And cannot bow.
>
> For a hunchback,
>
> You are stretching yourself now.

HUNCHBACK GUO:

You thief, you're mouthing dirty words. Have you never bowed?

SCABBY TURTLE:

I'll slap on your face. What have I stolen from you? Me, a thief?

HUNCHBACK GUO (*Inspects Scabby Turtle's robe*):

I don't care about anything else, but how is it that you're wearing a robe that belongs to Mr Liu from Lingnan?

SCABBY TURTLE:

Well, why can't I have a decent coat or two by myself? When you say that it belongs to the Lius of Lingnan, who has seen me stealing it from across the ridge?

HUNCHBACK GUO:

His name is woven into the ribbon. If you don't tell the truth, I'll call the cop.

> (*Tries to grab at Scabby Turtle*)

SCABBY TURTLE (*Frightened, stumbles on the ground*):

All right, I'll give back the robe to you.

HUNCHBACK GUO:

No more kidding! I just want to ask you about someone.

SCABBY TURTLE:

Who is it?

HUNCHBACK GUO:

Where is Mr Liu, the scholar?

SCABBY TURTLE:

I don't know.

> (*Hunchback asks the question three times and Scabby Turtle says he doesn't know all the time*)

HUNCHBACK GUO:

If you won't tell, I'll call the cop.

SCABBY TURTLE:

Well, I'll tell you, but it's not convenient to talk in the street. Let's go to the army's training ground.

> (*Scabby Turtle and Hunchback Guo walk on*)

HUNCHBACK GUO:

What a quiet place!

SCABBY TURTLE:

So there was a Mr Liu, but I don't know whether he's the man you're looking for. If you tell me that he's the right person, I'll tell you; if you can't, I won't tell you even if you call the cop or the judge.

HUNCHBACK GUO:

How cunning you are! Now listen to me:

> (*To the tune of* **Weifanxu**)
>
> This Mr Liu
>
> Has a fair face
>
> Full of grace.

SCABBY TURTLE:

Yes, and what is his age?

HUNCHBACK GUO:

> From his appearance,
>
> He looks less than thirty.

SCABBY TURTLE:

Yes, and what's your relationship?

HUNCHBACK GUO:

> For years and years in his home,
>
> I've tended flowers and grown the rice.
>
> From his childhood,
>
> I was in his place.

SCABBY TURTLE:

So you're his steward. When did you part with him and do you know what he has done?

HUNCHBACK GUO:

> We parted in the spring
>
> And I have traced him all the way here.
>
> As to what he has done,
>
> I am not clear.

SCABBY TURTLE:

What this old man says makes sense. Old man, I'll tell you what he has done.

> (*Whispers to Hunchback Guo, who cannot hear clearly*)

Phew! As no one is around here, I'll make some fun of him. Old man, now listen.

> (*To the previous tune*)
>
> He was ill when he arrived here.

He happened to meet Mr Chen, tutor to the prefect's daughter Miss Du, and

> Was tempted to live in the nunnery
>
> And was shown around the back garden.

HUNCHBACK GUO:

What happened next?

SCABBY TURTLE:

When he came across Miss Du's tomb, he picked up a portrait of a young lady. As he was haunted by the portrait day and night, he made some trouble.

HUNCHBACK GUO:

What's the trouble?

SCABBY TURTLE:

He took it for a genuine maid

And dug the grave.

HUNCHBACK GUO (*Surprised*):

What happened next?

SCABBY TURTLE:

I'll tell you. When Tutor Chen reported it to the prefecture, the cops came and surrounded the nunnery. They arrested and bound up Mr Liu and my aunt, Sister Stone, and clamped their fingers. They were forced to confess their crimes and sign their confessions. When they were brought to the provincial prison, the magistrate checked the civil codes as to how they were going to be punished and found out that all the grave-robbers should be silenced.

HUNCHBACK GUO:

What does "silenced" mean?

SCABBY TURTLE (*Presses Hunchback Guo's head as if ready to chop his head*):

It means this!

HUNCHBACK GUO (*Astonished and in tears*):

Oh my master, I have nowhere to go.

SCABBY TURTLE (*Laughs*):

Don't worry, please.

Later they were acquitted, and Miss Du came back to life.

605

HUNCHBACK GUO:

How could that happen!

SCABBY TURTLE:

The revived ghost became his wife;

My aunt became their servant maid.

HUNCHBACK GUO:

Where are they now?

SCABBY TURTLE:

They went to Lin'an.

When I saw them off,

He gave me this old robe.

HUNCHBACK GUO:

I was really scared to death, but it turned out to be good news.

(*To the tune of **Coda***)

He went to Lin'an for imperial exams;

SCABBY TURTLE:

I see.

HUNCHBACK GUO:

I must be on my way to the capital town.

SCABBY TURTLE:

Look out on the way, old man, for at this moment

The portraits are posted to hunt them down.

HUNCHBACK GUO:

To search for hermits in the fairy spring,

SCABBY TURTLE:

Just follow main roads on the western wing.

HUNCHBACK GUO:

Amid the bustling crowd we cannot talk

SCABBY TURTLE:

About a scholar who will see the king.

Scene Forty-One
Late for the Examination

(*Enter Miao Shunbin with his attendants*)

MIAO SHUNBIN (*To the tune of **Fenghuangge***):

When border areas are aflame with battle-fire,

How can the scholars fulfil their desire?

When flowers blossom on the bough,

Who will obtain the laurel now?

MIAO SHUNBIN, ATTENDANTS:

Tightly close the door

When we mark the score.

MIAO SHUNBIN:

"Examiners await the gifted man,

Ready for him to appear.

He can requite the love of spring,

If he writes good essays here."

I am Miao Shunbin. As I did a good job in examining the treasures presented by the foreign merchants, I have been appointed chief examiner in the imperial examinations. In face of the Jin invasion, His Majesty decreed the topic for this year's examination: "Among appeasement, offence and defence, which is the best policy?" Now that top-rank papers have been picked out from examinees in different sections, I am instructed to make the final selection. To my mind, it is easier to judge treasures than to judge essays. The reason is that my eyes are like cat's eyes, no different from green crystals. They will glow when they meet genuine treasures, while they won't glow when they meet words. However, I have to carry out the imperial decree. Attendants, open the cases and hand me the papers.

(*Reads the papers when the attendants have fetched the papers*)

Well, there are not many papers. I'll first have a look at three essays from the first section. The first essay reads, "His Majesty's topic is: Among appeasement, offence and defence, which is the best policy?" "In my opinion, The nation's appeasement with the invaders can be compared to the village elder's settlement of a quarrel." Oh, if the village elder fails to settle a quarrel, nothing serious will happen, but, if the nation fails to appease the invaders, who knows what will happen! There's no reason for me to rank it as the first. The second essay is in favour of defence.

(*Reads*)

"In my opinion, the emperor's defence of his nation can be compared to the virgin's defence of her body." This is an improper comparison. The third essay is in favour of offence.

(*Reads*)

"In my opinion, the southern dynasty's combat with the north can be compared to *yang's* offence on *yin*." It's a fantastic comparison, but there is indeed the saying "*yin* and *yang* in conflict" in *The Book of Changes*. Years ago, Qin Hui's appeasement policy impaired the nation. Now I'll put offence in the first place, defence in the second place, and appeasement in the third place. The other papers will be ranked in the same order.

(*To the tune of* **Yifengshu**)

The essays are of various kinds,

But the scholars make their essays trite.

They try to rack their minds,

But few of them are bright.

The chances are still there,

But slim for those in plight.

I can hardly do anything about it —

The annual test is fair and square,

But not a genius comes in sight.

(*Seals the papers*)

(*Enter Liu Mengmei*)

LIU MENGMEI (*To the tune of* **Shenzhang'er**):

This is a battleground,

A battleground

For gifted men from all around.

ATTENDANT:

You come at the right time when the examination is over.

LIU MENGMEI:

Alas, the examination is over, but may I present my essay?

ATTENDANT:

No, you can't. Do you suppose that we are waiting for you? It is said that

When scholars gather round,

We close the testing ground.

LIU MENGMEI:

But I'm afraid the Number One Scholar has not been decided yet.

ATTENDANT:

Not many, but there are three already.

LIU MENGMEI:

> In a race of ten thousand steeds,
>
> The topmost one is yet to prove in deeds.

Will you go in at once and announce that a scholar for the make-up examination is at the door?

ATTENDANT:

There's no make-up examination in the imperial court. You can have it in your county or prefecture.

LIU MENGMEI:

Are you not going indeed, brother?

> (*Weeps*)

Oh, heavens! Mr Miao offered the fare for me to present treasures, but

> As I fail to present treasures here,
>
> How can I stop my tear?

MIAO SHUNBIN (*Overhears the talk*):

Doorman, who's making a fuss in a solemn place like this? Bring him in.

> (*The attendant drags Liu Mengmei in*)

LIU MENGMEI:

I've come for the make-up examination. I beg you to give me a try.

MIAO SHUNBIN:

Now that His Majesty has decreed the topic and the examination hall has been locked, who dares to accept you?

LIU MENGMEI (*Weeps*):

I've come all the way from Lingnan with my family. As I have no way out, I'll bump my head at the steps and die in front of you at once.

> (*Tries to bump his head but is stopped by the attendant*)

MIAO SHUNBIN (*Aside*):

This scholar looks like the Mr Liu I met before. He's a pearl of a man from the South Sea.

> (*Turns to Liu Mengmei*)

Come forward, young scholar. Do you have the paper to write your answers?

LIU MENGMEI:

Yes, I have.

MIAO SHUNBIN:

Well, you are admitted to enter the examination and will be judged on the same footing as the other scholars.

LIU MENGMEI (*Kneels*):

Once in a blue moon am I bestowed such a favour.

MIAO SHUNBIN (*Reads the topic*):

"His Majesty decrees the topic: In face of the Jin invasion, which is the best policy, among appeasement, offence and defence?"

LIU MENGMEI (*Kowtows*):

I've got the imperial topic.

> (*Rises to his feet*)

ATTENDANT:

Go to the eastern section.

>   (*Liu Mengmei writes*)

MIAO SHUNBIN (*Reads the three papers again*):

The first essay is in favour of appeasement, the second essay is in favour of defence, and the third is in favour of offence. I'm afraid that His Majesty won't like the idea of appeasement.

>   (*Liu Mengmei hands in his paper*)

MIAO SHUNBIN (*Reads the paper*):

He's written a thousand words in the twinkling of an eye. Marvellous, marvellous! As I can't finish your paper in a glance, just tell me briefly what policy you are in favour of: appeasement, offence, or defence.

LIU MENGMEI:

I'm not in favour of any particular policy. Either offence or defence will do, and then appeasement will also do. It's like a doctor prescribing the medicine. Offence can be used to cure outward symptoms, defence can be used to cure inward symptoms, and appeasement can be used to harmonise the two.

MIAO SHUNBIN:

A wonderful idea! Simply wonderful! What do you think of the present situation?

LIU MENGMEI (*To the tune of **Matihua***):

His Majesty

>   Remains here
>
>   By the scenic West Lake,
>
>   Where autumn cassias bloom
>
>   And lotus flowers perfume,
>
>   Mixed with worries for border war's sake.

I hope that

>   The alien king should cease to expand,
>
>   So that we can recover the lost land.

If we adhere to appeasement,

>   The court will bear the shame henceforth;
>
>   If we adhere to offence or defence,
>
>   The court should move to the north.

MIAO SHUNBIN:

Your comments are reasonable.

>   (*To the previous tune*)
>
>   His Majesty on the throne
>
>   Would like to retrieve the lost zone.

Over a thousand candidates have come to attend the imperial examination, but

>   Few understand the times
>
>   Or know the imperial care;
>
>   How can they be worthy scholars there?

It is you alone that

> Have come to the point
>
> And exhausted the urgent affair.

LIU MENGMEI:

I'm from Lingnan.

MIAO SHUNBIN (*In a low voice*):

I know.

> From a scholar you have hoped to rise
>
> And will be awarded the first prize.

Scholar, wait outside the palace gate for the imperial decree.

LIU MENGMEI (*Responds and withdraws, aside*):

This examiner is Envoy Miao, but to avoid suspicion I have to keep my mouth shut.

> *"Outside the gate I'll wait for the decree;*
>
> *I only hope the envoy will choose me."*
>
> (*Exit*)

MIAO SHUNBIN:

I've finished marking all the papers. Attendants, make way to the court and I'll make a report to His Majesty.

> (*Walks on, followed by the attendants*)
>
> *"It's quiet when I send in the report*
>
> *While time draws on inside the court."*

Well, where comes the beating of drums?

> (*Rapid drum-beating within*)

ATTENDANT:

The drum-beating comes from the War Ministry to announce the border conflict.

> (*Neighing of horses within*)

MIAO SHUNBIN:

There are urgent reports from the border-area. What's happened? What's happened?

> (*Enter the elderly War Minister*)

WAR MINISTER:

> *"A walled alley leads to the court;*
>
> *From War Ministry comes the war report."*
>
> (*Miao Shunbin and War Minister greet each other*)

MIAO SHUNBIN:

Are you going to report the border conflict, sir?

WAR MINISTER:

Yes. Are you here to report the examination results?

MIAO SHUNBIN:

Yes.

WAR MINISTER:

As my business is more urgent today, I have to report first. Excuse me.

> (*Kowtows and reports*)

The War Minister is now reporting to Your Majesty.

VOICE WITHIN:

What do you want to report?

WAR MINISTER (*To the tune of* **Diliuzi**):

> The Jin invaders,
>
> The Jin invaders are launching an attack.

VOICE WITHIN:

Who is the vanguard?

WAR MINISTER:

> Li Quan,
>
> Li Quan is taking the lead.

VOICE WITHIN:

Where are they now?

WAR MINISTER:

> It's said they've reached Huaiyang.

VOICE WITHIN:

Whom shall we dispatch for the defence?

WAR MINISTER:

Du Bao is now the Envoy of Huaiyang, but

> As they cannot hold on for a long time,
>
> We must send more troops at once.

MIAO SHUNBIN (*Kowtows and reports*):

The imperial examiner Miao Shunbin is now reporting to Your Majesty.

> (*To the previous tune*)
>
> The papers,
>
> The papers have been scored.
>
> Your Majesty,
>
> Your Majesty shall select the best.
>
> It's an auspicious day
>
> To proclaim the results.
>
> Officials are waiting at the palace gate
>
> For the celebration feast.

VOICE WITHIN:

Both of you, wait at the palace gate.

> (*War Minister and Miao Shunbin rise to their feet*)

MIAO SHUNBIN:

Do you know why the Jins launch the invasion, sir?

WAR MINISTER:

I dared not mention it just now. The Jin emperor has come to grab the scenic area near the West Lake.

MIAO SHUNBIN:

Those crazy aliens! The West Lake is for us to enjoy. If they should occupy the West Lake,

The Peony Pavilion

the capital Hangzhou would be useless for us.

VOICE WITHIN:

Now listen to my decree: In my reign over the world, there are things urgent and less urgent and I should consider the military affairs as well as the civil affairs. Now that the Huaiyang areas are in danger, I order Envoy Du Bao to lose no time in fighting against the enemy. As to the proclamation of the examination results, it will be postponed to a time when the military actions are over and then we shall consider these civil affairs. My decree is to be made known to the public. Kowtow!

(*War Minister and Miao Shunbin kowtow, shout "Long live the emperor" and then rise to their feet*)

WAR MINISTER:

When national war affairs now prolong,

MIAO SHUNBIN:

The scholars stick to reading all day long.

WAR MINISTER:

The gifted man expects brilliant success,

MIAO SHUNBIN:

But border conflicts need scholars less.

Scene Forty-Two
Military Transfer

(*Enter Du Bao, followed by attendants*)

DU BAO (*To the tune of* **Yeyouchao**):

When west winds shake the river trees,

The flowing waters make me ill at ease.

In shielding the south

Against the north,

Is there any better place?

"The sound to pound the winter coat

Dies with river waters that flow remote.

Where does the native country lie?

A wild goose flies past the tower of Huai.

The state affairs

That fill me with woe

Eastward flow.

I envy my ancestor poet Du,

Who dreamt with Yangzhou in view."

I'm Du Bao, Envoy of the Huaiyang area. Since I came here three years ago, Li Quan has been making disturbances but I've had the overall situation under control. When I learned yesterday that the invading troops were coming from the frontiers, I was deeply worried. However, my wife knew nothing about this and kept weeping for our departed daughter.

(*Enter Lady Zhen, followed by Chunxiang*)

LADY ZHEN (*To the tune of **Siniang'er***):

> My lord commands the army here,
>
> And brings me closer to the frontier.
>
> (*Sighs*)
>
> I see the Qinhuai trees beyond the screen,
>
> With Jin Hill and Jiao Isle in sight.
>
> I knit my brow
>
> At the sight that looms bright.

Blessings on you, my lord.

DU BAO:

Sit down, please, my lady.

LADY ZHEN:

My lord,

> "Ever since we left Nan'an,
>
> Several years have gone by.

DU BAO:

> We vainly long for the native land
>
> While in Yangzhou pleasure is a far cry.

LADY ZHEN:

> If you strike your sword and search,
>
> Is there an idle hero that meets your eye?
>
> (*Weeps*)

DU BAO, LADY ZHEN:

> With no son to relieve our woe,
>
> Away from home we weep and sigh."

LADY ZHEN:

You always keep silent whenever I mention our departed daughter. But can you imagine how sad I am? On the one hand, I'm sad for our departed daughter; on the other hand, I'm sad for the lack of an heir. I'll look for a concubine to bear a son for you. What do you think about it?

DU BAO:

No, that won't do. I can't take a concubine from my jurisdiction.

LADY ZHEN:

Then, how about having one from Jinling across the Yangtze River?

DU BAO:

As I'm busy with my official business, how can I find the time for such things?

LADY ZHEN:

Oh, Liniang, my poor daughter!

> (*Weeps*)

(*Enter Messenger A*)

MESSENGER A:

> "*The imperial decree sheds its brilliant light*
> *To heighten spirits of warriors in their fight.*"

Your Excellency, here are instructions from the imperial court.

DU BAO (*Stands up and reads the instructions*):

Instructions from the War Ministry, concerning the invasions on the Huaiyang area. His Majesty decrees: "Envoy Du Bao of the Huaiyang areas is to be transferred to Huai'an without delay." With urgent military affairs comes this stern decree. My lady, we must set off for Huai'an at once.

> (*Enter the stationmaster*)

STATIONMASTER:

> "*The plumed letters are sent pile by pile;*
> *The time is counted mile by mile.*"

Your Excellency, the ship is ready.

> (*Sound of drums and pipes within. Du Bao, Lady Zhen and their attendants board the ship*)

VOICE WITHIN:

All the local officials are here to see you off.

DU BAO:

Thank you, good-bye.

> (*To Lady Zhen*)

My lady, the river is again in its autumn best.

> (*To the tune of* **Changpai**)
> Autumn's just arrived,
> Autumn's just arrived.
> Here comes a gentle breeze
> Over the painted bridge and misty trees.
> The summer heat no longer hurts
> And coolness starts to leave its trace
> As a drizzle moistens our skirts.
> Our ship is sailing in the scene of fairyland,
> With rising tides, a chilling wind,
> The spraying waves
> And white gulls near at hand.

The wind has lulled, and at sunset

> The ship's reflection quivers on the water
> While sounds of drums and pipes rise to the clouds.
> From where comes the country song
> That draws me away from the madding crowds?

Look, who's galloping on the bank toward us?

> (*Enter Messenger B on horseback*)

MESSENGER B (*To the tune of* **Bushilu**):

I call out on horseback

To anchor ships for plumed letters.

DU BAO:

What does the letter say?

MESSENGER B:

The Prefecture of Huai'an

Is invaded by Li Quan.

DU BAO:

Shall I send reinforcements?

MESSENGER B:

How can they withstand the foe?

You must deploy the troops tonight.

As it's too slow to go by water,

You'd better go by land to join the fight.

DU BAO:

Do not fear.

My lady,

I'll go by land.

You just turn back,

Turn back.

LADY ZHEN:

Well, another messenger's coming.

(*Enter Messenger C*)

MESSENGER C (*To the previous tune*):

Ten thousand rebels on horseback

Threaten to grab our native lands.

Please make haste, Your Excellency,

Do not delay.

I must take leave at once,

For fear that Huai'an will fall into rebels' hands.

(*Exit*)

LADY ZHEN (*Weeps*):

What will you do?

You'll fight the foes when your hair is grey,

When battle cries arise all along the way.

DU BAO:

What worries me

Is that the way to Yangzhou is cut off.

In that case, where shall we meet again,

Where shall we meet again?

I'm leaving now, my lady. If Yangzhou is in danger, you can go to Lin'an directly.

(*To the tune of **Duanpai***)

The ageing man and wife depart,

The ageing man and wife depart,

Just as the poet Du Fu

Separated with his wife with a weeping heart.

LADY ZHEN (*Weeps*):

When my child is no more,

I must now send my lord to war!

DU BAO, LADY ZHEN:

Man and wife with rank and title

Are without child or spouse.

Life and death

Come in dreams and word of mouth.

LADY ZHEN (*To the tune of* **Coda**):

I have to take my fate in my own hand;

DU BAO:

In this area I take command.

LADY ZHEN:

Take care, my lord,

Of your men and your own life.

(*Exit Du Bao*)

LADY ZHEN (*Sighs*):

Oh heavens! As Yangzhou seems to be aflame with battle fire, Chunxiang, let's go to Lin'an directly.

Bleak are the sights upon the canal dike;

The riversides are battlefields alike.

Ignorant of sounds of spear and gun,

We flee along the route of setting sun.

Scene Forty-Three
Military Defence

(*Enter Du Bao, followed by attendants in battle array*)

DU BAO, ATTENDANTS (*To the tune of* **Liuyaoling**):

With the wild west wind

Spreads the clamour of the battle cry,

While tides are surging to the sky.

The army is deployed

And tactics are employed

To have the foes destroyed.

DU BAO:

I'm exhausted by the march. Attendants, where are we now?

ATTENDANTS:

The city of Huai'an comes in sight.

DU BAO (*Looks ahead*):

Oh heavens!

> *"The remaining native lands*
> *Will fall into alien hands.*

ATTENDANTS:

> *The ancient battlefield*
> *Smells of sanguine sword and shield.*

DU BAO:

> *I hear the soldiers moan and groan,*
> *With tears soaked to the bone.*

ATTENDANTS:

Your Excellency,

> *It's not the time for tears;*
> *We'll march and do away with fears."*

DU BAO:

My men, my sons! Look, Huai'an is near in sight and in imminent danger. Let's set death aside and break into the city. At the same time, I'll ask for reinforcement from the court. Now follow my command: beat the drums and advance!

ATTENDANTS (*In tears*):

Yes, advance!

DU BAO (*Walks on*):

> (*To the tune of **Sibianjing***)
> I sit on the saddle and give command,
> With banners on every hand.
> Our banners flutter left and right
> And dim the sunlight.

DU BAO, ATTENDANTS:

> The alien troops are full of pride;
> The southern troops have had a tiring ride.
> Besieged and bathed in blood,
> What will happen to this town on our side?

DU BAO:

The alien bandits have blocked the way. Break our way through the enemy troops!

> (*Exeunt all*)
> (*Enter Li Quan, followed by his men and Lady Yang, yelling*)

LI QUAN (*To the previous tune*):

> I can shoot at the heart of flying geese;
> I can mount a galloping steed.

617

When I prick with my stirrup,

My pennants flutter in the breeze.

LI QUAN, LADY YANG, SOLDIERS:

The alien troops are full of pride;

The southern troops have had a tiring ride.

Besieged and bathed in blood.

What will happen to this town on our side?

LI QUAN (*Laughs*):

With my ten thousand soldiers, I've besieged the city with seven rings of troops. I think it's tight enough!

(*Drums and shouts within*)

Well, there are troops ahead. It must be Envoy Du and his men. I'll bring a thousand men to fight against him.

(*Li Quan, Lady Yang and soldiers go to the rear of the stage*)

(*Re-enter Du Bao and his attendants*)

DU BAO, ATTENDANTS:

The alien troops are full of pride;

The southern troops have had a tiring ride.

Surrounded and bathed in blood,

What will happen to this town on our side?

(*Li Quan, Lady Yang and soldiers turn back to fight with Du Bao and his attendants. Li Quan and Du Bao fight. Li Quan and his men form a line to block the way. Du Bao calls on his men to break through and fight their way into the city*)

LI QUAN:

Alas, Du Bao and his men have fought their way into the city. Let them go. When their provisions come to an end, they will surrender in due time.

LI QUAN, LADY YANG, SOLDIERS:

The alien troops are full of pride;

The southern troops have had a tiring ride.

Besieged and bathed in blood,

What will happen to this town on our side?

(*Exeunt*)

(*Enter two officials*)

OFFICIAL A, OFFICIAL B (*To the tune of **Fanbusuan***):

The battle storm that swirls all day

Almost blows our official hats away.

(*Enter two officers*)

OFFICER A:

I guard the bridge with spear and sword;

OFFICER B:

The drums and horns sound like the dragon's roar.

(*The officials and the officers exchange greetings*)

OFFICIAL A:

> *"Beside the river of Huai,*
> *Not far from the sea,*

OFFICIAL B:

> *The battle cries resound in the sky.*

OFFICER B:

> *The drums and guns*
> *Terrify me.*
> *I wish I could put on wings and flee.*

OFFICER A:

> *With our swords,*
> *With our arrows,*
> *We'll fight to the last.*

OFFICIALS, OFFICERS:

> *We fear the tunnels;*
> *We fear the armoured carts.*
> *When shall we see Envoy Du?"*

OFFICIAL A:

We are officials in the Huai'an Prefecture. Besieged by the enemy troops, we've been waiting for Envoy Du for a long time, but he has not arrived yet . May I ask you generals for some advice?

OFFICER B:

In my opinion, we'd better surrender.

OFFICIAL A:

How can you talk like this?

OFFICER B:

If we don't surrender, we'd better escape.

OFFICIAL A:

One out of ten can escape at the best.

OFFICER B:

In that case, what shall I do with my wife?

OFFICIAL A:

Lock her in the wardrobe.

OFFICER B:

Where shall I put the key?

OFFICIAL A:

Leave it to me. If Li Quan does not come, I'll take care of your wife and your son.

OFFICER B:

What if Li Quan comes?

OFFICIAL A:

I'll present them to him for you.

OFFICER B:

You're a friend in need! A friend indeed!

(*Drums and shouts within*)

(*Enter Messenger*)

MESSENGER:

Report, report, report! An army from the south has broken through the enemy lines. Envoy Du is coming!

OFFICIALS, OFFICERS:

Let's open the city gate at once and meet His Excellency.

"Blood is shedding day and night;

Who's come to join the fight?"

(*Exeunt*)

(*Enter Du Bao, followed by attendants*)

DU BAO (*To the tune of **Jinqianhua***):

The battle cries soar to the sky,

To the sky.

The town is tightly besieged,

Tightly besieged.

The wind whistles;

The banners flutter.

Open the city gate

And let down the drawbridge!

(*Enter the officials and the officers*)

OFFICIALS, OFFICERS (*Kowtow*):

The local officials and officers are here to welcome Your Excellency.

DU BAO:

Stand up, please. I'll meet you in the city tower.

(*The officials and the officers respond, rise and exeunt*)

DU BAO (*To the previous tune*):

The dust has soiled my battle-robe,

My battle-robe.

The blood has stained my treasured sword,

My treasured sword.

(*Drums within*)

Amid Huai'an drums

And Yangzhou flutes,

I hoist the flag

And mount the city tower.

DU BAO, ATTENDANTS:

Meet in the hall

And talk to all.

(*Reach the city tower*)

(*Enter Clerk*)

CLERK:

Please take the chair, Your Excellency.

DU BAO (*To the tune of **Fendieeryin***):

> Miles and miles the troops go,
>
> But how can I expel the foe?

CLERK (*Announces*):

Officials and officers, come in please.

> (*Enter the officials and the officers*)

OFFICIALS, OFFICERS (*Kneel to greet Du Bao*):

Our besieged city is in imminent danger. Your Excellency, an excellent warrior, has come to our rescue. The local officials and officers are most grateful to you.

DU BAO:

As I am slow in coming, you have suffered from all the trouble in the battles. Therefore, please accept my deep bow.

> (*The officials and the officers respond, rise and return a bow*)

DU BAO:

It seems to me that this Li Quan is good at strategy. He must be playing a trick by letting me break into the city.

OFFICIALS, OFFICERS:

He will rely on no more than digging the tunnels or raising the ladders. We know something as to take precautions.

DU BAO:

I'm afraid he's trying to block the city.

OFFICER B:

May I ask what it means? Is he going to block from the inside or from the outside? To block from the outside, they'll block Gilded Prince out; to block from the inside, they block me in too.

DU BAO:

Forget about it for the moment. How many troops are there in the city?

OFFICER A:

Thirteen thousand troops.

DU BAO:

What are the provisions in the city?

OFFICIAL B:

The provisions will last us half a year.

DU BAO:

As long as all the officials and officers share one mind, we can hold out and wait for the reinforcement.

> (*Drums and shouts within*)
>
> (*Enter Messenger*)

MESSENGER:

Report, report! Li Quan's troops are closer to the city.

DU BAO (*With a long sigh*):

What a rascal!

> (*To the tune of* **Chanqiaoer**)
>
> With ample men and grain we can hold out,
>
> But all of you must fight in one mind.

OFFICIALS, OFFICERS:

> We'll keep watch day and night,
>
> With all our efforts combined.
>
> (*Yells within*)

ALL (*Weep*):

> Amid the alien yells,
>
> Our silent hatred swells.

DU BAO (*Kowtows to the sky while the officials and the officers join him*):

> With our tears rolling down the wall,
>
> We pray that Heaven bless us all.

OFFICIALS, OFFICERS (*To the previous tune*):

> A good commander can expel the foes;
>
> To guard the frontier depends on the heroes.

DU BAO:

> The Yangtze and Huai rivers are strategic parts,
>
> So we have to take arms with all our hearts.

ALL:

> Amid the alien yells,
>
> Our silent hatred swells.

DU BAO:

From now on, the officials shall defend the city walls while the officers shall go out to fight. You must support each other as the situation demands.

OFFICER B:

But I'm afraid the main forces of the Jins will come soon.

DU BAO:

As to the Jins,

> (*To the tune of* **Coda**)
>
> It's hard to say whether the Jins will come by now,
>
> But you should not smear the banners of Zhao.

Even if they should come,

> To fight to the end is our solemn vow.

OFFICER A:

> *The aliens run riot day by day,*

OFFICER B:

> *With three thousand troops on the way.*

DU BAO:

> *I have my scheme to quell the foe,*

OFFICIALS, OFFICERS:

A feat that will always stay.

Scene Forty-Four
Concern for Her Parents

(*Enter Du Liniang*)

DU LINIANG (*To the tune of* **Juhuaxin**):

When magpies greet me for my happy dream,

I tap my golden hairpins with a smile.

The incense smoke coils in autumn breeze

And makes me anxious for news all the while.

"A ghost expects to gain a second life;

A wretched scholar hopes to gain fame.

An honoured husband makes a glorious wife;

I do hope he indeed achieves his name."

I've come with my husband Mr Liu to attend the imperial examination. It happens to be
the right time for His Majesty to select talented scholars, but the announcement has not
been made yet. It is true to say,

"The court is a distant place to seek fame;

Will my husband gain his name?"

(*Enter Liu Mengmei*)

LIU MENGMEI (*To the tune of* **Chuduizi**):

I was lucky in the imperial exam,

But news of war destroyed my dream.

Awaiting news of my success at home,

My wife expects the rise of my esteem.

Like a homeless soul,

She is adrift with the stream.

(*Greets Du Liniang*)

DU LINIANG:

I'm glad you're back at last, Mr Liu. I expected you to come back in a grand carriage, but
how is it that you come back on foot?

LIU MENGMEI:

Now, listen to my explanation.

(*To the tune of* **Wapen'er**)

As I was late for the exam,

The gate was locked and scholars gone.

DU LINIANG:

Oh, so you were late.

LIU MENGMEI:

    I happened to meet someone I knew.

DU LINIANG:

Did he allow you to make up for the exam?

LIU MENGMEI:

    He picked me as another pearl that shone.

DU LINIANG (*Delighted*):

Wonderful! Have you learned of the results?

LIU MENGMEI:

    When we waited outside the palace gate

    For the announcement,

    It happened ...

DU LINIANG:

What happened?

LIU MENGMEI:

Don't you know that the Jins are sending their armies to the Huaiyang area?

    As the troops are busy with the war affair,

    The scholars' business is put aside

    And thus you are delayed to get your share.

624 DU LINIANG:

It doesn't matter to be delayed for some time. By the way, you just mentioned Huaiyang. Is it the area where my father takes command?

LIU MENGMEI:

Yes, it is.

DU LINIANG (*In tears*):

Oh heavens, what's happened to my parents?

    (*Weeps*)

LIU MENGMEI:

    You are nearly mad,

    So sad

    And depressed.

    In the hell were you so distressed?

DU LINIANG:

Forget about it. But there's something I hesitate to say.

LIU MENGMEI:

Go on.

DU LINIANG:

Mr Liu, as we have to wait a long time for the announcement, will you be kind enough to go to Huaiyang and try to find out about my parents?

LIU MENGMEI:

I'll be willing to, but I'm reluctant to leave you here.

DU LINIANG:

Don't worry. I'll take care of myself.

LIU MENGMEI:

Then, I'll be leaving in an instant.

DU LINIANG (*To the tune of **Liuhuaqi***):

    My parents lived below the distant clouds

    While I was buried under the plum tree.

    Away from the crowds,

    My soul was bent on thee.

    Between Huaiyang and here,

    My soul wandered to and fro.

    I'm afraid they will be filled with fear.

Oh, Dad and Mom,

    As resurrection is something they hardly know,

    How can they expect a son-in-law,

    Who marries their deceased daughter

    And comes to their door!

LIU MENGMEI (*To the previous tune*):

    To go or not to go,

    I'm in two minds.

    My desires to stay with my dear wife grow.

DU LINIANG:

I have Sister Stone to keep me company.

LIU MENGMEI:

    A nun won't help you spend the long cold night;

    I'm afraid you'll change your mind

    And wander again like a sprite.

DU LINIANG:

I won't.

LIU MENGMEI:

    In the exam I wrote the best essay;

    I'm afraid I'll miss the announcement day.

DU LINIANG (*Weeps*):

Oh, Dad and Mom!

LIU MENGMEI:

    In view of your deep love for your parents,

    I'm ready to meet them as a son-in-law.

My dear, as soon as I meet your parents, the first thing they'll mention is how you came back to life again.

DU LINIANG (*Sighs*):

    (*To the tune of **Yujiadeng***)

    As it seems to be a fantastic tale,

    My dad might not believe what you say.

(Ponders for a moment)

Well, I have an idea. Bring my portrait with you.

> When they see my portrait,
>
> They'll ask about you and me right away.

LIU MENGMEI:

> What shall I say then?

DU LINIANG:

> You just say that it's our fate
>
> To be man and wife
>
> And you opened the grave for me.

LIU MENGMEI:

I should say you came to my study first.

DU LINIANG:

> I don't agree.
>
> You'll make them laugh at me,
>
> But you can hint at it to Chunxiang.

LIU MENGMEI *(To the previous tune)*:

> I hoped to go with you in carriage and four
>
> And see them as a man of renown;
>
> But now I'll go in times of war
>
> And wear a shabby gown.

DU LINIANG:

It doesn't matter for a son-in-law to be plainly dressed. I'm only worrying about your lonely trip.

LIU MENGMEI:

> At autumn dusk,
>
> The wild geese are on a returning flight.
>
> On Qinhuai River I'll spend the lonely night.

DU LINIANG:

My lord, this might be a lonely trip, but when you come back ranking first in the imperial examination ...

LIU MENGMEI:

> What a splendour then!
>
> It'll make a grand show
>
> When I meet them again.

(Enter Sister Stone)

SISTER STONE:

> *"As the umbrella shelters sun and rain,*
>
> *So the portrait endures autumn and spring."*

Here's the parcel and umbrella for you.

(Liu Mengmei and Du Liniang take leave of each other)

DU LINIANG *(To the tune of **Coda**)*:

> You're going to the family of Du;

626

LIU MENGMEI:

At the news of your revival, great joy will ensue.

DU LINIANG:

Mr Liu, come back as soon as things are settled there.

Don't let the Yangzhou music detain you.

LIU MENGMEI:

To Du's family a scholar will go,

DU LINIANG:

Without a precious gift to show.

LIU MENGMEI:

On the lonely trip to Yangzhou,

DU LINIANG:

Both man and wife are filled with woe.

Scene Forty-Five
The Bandits' Wily Scheme

(*Enter two bandit sentries, patrolling here and there*)

SENTRY A (*To the tune of* **Baoziling**):

Our prince came from the rank and file,

The rank and file.

His wife was once a female courier,

A female courier.

Not content with their rule on the mount,

They start to grab more land on no account.

SENTRY A, SENTRY B:

Up and down the hill we're on patrol;

We strike the gongs to play our role.

SENTRY A:

Brother, our prince is besieging the city of Huai'an and he wants to find someone to bring a message to Envoy Du. As there's not a single shadow on the highway, let's turn to the byways.

SENTRY A, SENTRY B:

Up and down the hill we're on patrol,

We strike the gongs to play our role.

(*Exeunt*)

(*Enter Chen Zuiliang, bearing an umbrella and a parcel*)

CHEN ZUILIANG (*To the tune of* **Zhumating**):

I used to teach in Nan'an,

But I've lost my position there.

If I want to be a millionaire,

I have to teach a thousand years

To get my share.

I, Chen Zuiliang, am on my way to Yangzhou to report to Envoy Du on Miss Du's affairs. But who knows that he's besieged in Huai'an with the result that I have nowhere to turn to. As it's too dangerous on the highway, I'll go along the byways.

Like Confucius who wandered here and there,

I am a scholar who lives in worry and care.

When tree shadows meet my eye,

The wails of apes and tigers make me sigh.

(*Enter the two bandit sentries*)

SENTRY A:

"Aware of tigers in the hill,

He goes to the den with a stubborn will."

Where are you going, old man?

(*The sentries catch hold of Chen Zuiliang*)

CHEN ZUILIANG:

Mercy on me, rebel king!

SENTRY B:

There's another king here!

CHEN ZUILIANG:

On, heavens! As the saying goes,

"With crows and magpies in the sky,

Who knows if I'll live or die!"

(*Exit Chen Zuiliang with the sentries*)

(*Enter Li Quan, followed by his men and Lady Yang*)

LI QUAN (*To the tune of **Puxiange***):

When I become a bandit head,

Who says that I'm full of dread?

Although I'm alien to the south

And foreign to the north,

The heaven has reserved my bed.

My lady, we've besieged Huai'an for quite some time, but haven't conquered it yet. We'd better find someone to bring a message there and find out what Envoy Du is up to. But I have no idea as to whom to send.

LADY YANG:

The man must know old Envoy Du well and can cope with the situation.

(*Enter Chen Zuiliang, tied up and led by Sentry B*)

CHEN ZUILIANG (*To the tune of **Fendieer***):

I got caught on the byway;

Oh, heavens!

In the butcher's house what could I say?

SENTRY B (*Greets Li Quan*):

My lord, we've captured a man from the south.

LI QUAN:

Well, it's an old chap. Where are you from? What is your trade?

CHEN ZUILIANG:

Now, listen,

> (*To the tune of **Dayagu***)
>
> I, Chen Zuiliang,
>
> A scholar from Nan'an,
>
> Am going to visit a friend in Huaiyang.

LI QUAN:

Who is it?

CHEN ZUILIANG:

It's Envoy Du.

> I used to teach in his home.

LADY YANG:

So you were a tutor in his home. How many pupils did you teach?

CHEN ZUILIANG:

His wife Lady Zhen gave birth to a single daughter.

> Dead and gone was his daughter Du Liniang.

LADY YANG:

Who else is there in his family?

CHEN ZUILIANG:

> His adopted daughter,
>
> A former maid by the name of Chunxiang.

LADY YANG (*Sniggers aside*):

I've never heard about old Du's family affairs. Now that I get to know of it, I've a scheme ready.

> (*To the attendants*)

Take this pedant outside the camp.

> (*The attendants respond and take Chen Zuiliang off stage*)

My lord, I've conceived a scheme. As we killed some women yesterday, we can pick out two heads and say that they are the heads of Du's womenfolk, caught by my men and killed on their way back to Yangzhou. Then we'll let the pedant go and pass the word to old Du. Overcome by grief, he will lose his heart in defending the city.

LI QUAN:

A good idea! A good idea!

> (*Rises to his feet and speaks in a low voice*)

Call my adjutant.

> (*Enter the adjutant*)

LI QUAN (*To the adjutant*):

When I speak with the pedant, you just come in to present two heads of the women killed yesterday and say that they are the heads of Lady Zhen and her maid Chunxiang. Do as I tell you.

(*Exit the adjutant after a response*)

LI QUAN:

Now bring the pedant in.

(*Enter Chen Zuiliang, escorted by the attendants*)

CHEN ZUILIANG:

Mercy on me, my lord!

LI QUAN:

I won't spare a spy of your sort.

LADY YANG:

Won't you unbind him and let him speak something on the art of war, my lord?

LI QUAN:

In that case, do as you say and let him loose.

(*The attendants let loose of Chen Zuiliang*)

CHEN ZUILIANG (*Kowtows*):

Thank you, my lord and my lady, for sparing me my life.

LI QUAN:

Stand up and say something about the art of war.

CHEN ZUILIANG:

When Duke Ling of Wei asked Confucius about the deployment of troops, Confucius refused to answer the question but said, "I've never met anyone whose desire for virtue is as strong as his desire for sex."

LI QUAN:

What does he mean?

CHEN ZUILIANG:

As Duke Ling's wife Nanzi was present, Confucius would not like to speak.

LI QUAN:

His wife's name Nanzi sounds like a man's, but my wife is a woman.

(*Drums within*)

(*Enter the messenger*)

MESSENGER:

Report, report! Our troops to Yangzhou killed the womenfolk of Envoy Du. They've come to present the heads for a reward.

LI QUAN (*Looks carefully at the heads*):

I'm afraid they are not the heads of Envoy Du's womenfolk.

MESSENGER:

They are as true as can be. His wife is Lady Zhen, and his maid is Chunxiang.

CHEN ZUILIANG (*Looks at the heads and wails in astonishment*):

Oh heavens! This is Lady Zhen's head and that is Chunxiang's head!

LI QUAN:

Tush, none of your wailing, old pedant! We'll soon break through the city of Huai'an to kill old Du as well.

CHEN ZUILIANG:

Please have mercy on him, my lord!

LI QUAN:

I won't spare him unless he gives up the city of Huai'an.

CHEN ZUILIANG:

Will you please let me bring your words to him and report to you in no time?

LADY YANG:

If you want to save your neck, old pedant, get out of here at once!

> (*Drums and shouts within. The gate is opened*)

CHEN ZUILIANG (*In terror*):

> (*To the tune of* **Coda**)
>
> The mighty Gilded Prince
>
> Will always linger on my mind.

LI QUAN, LADY YANG:

Go and tell Envoy Du

> To surrender and leave his airs behind.
>
> We're bound to grab more land,
>
> With manoeuvres well designed.
>
> (*Exeunt*)

CHEN ZUILIANG (*Bows to see them off*):

Sheer robbers and bandits! They've killed Lady Zhen and Chunxiang. I'll bring the news to Huai'an.

> *The sea god blows an ill wind to the east*
> *And swirls dusts when the sun sets in the west.*
> *The present envoy is my former host,*
> *Who'll honour me as his distinguished guest.*

Scene Forty-Six
Outwitting the Bandits

> (*Enter Du Bao, fully armoured and bearing a sword, followed by his attendants*)

DU BAO (*To the tune of* **Pozhenzi**):

> In various formations I deploy the troop;
>
> To guard the frontiers I shall never stoop.
>
> (*Drums and shouts within*)

DU BAO (*With a sigh*):

> Like thunder the cannons roared;
>
> Like whirling snow flashes the sword.
>
> Li Quan, Li Quan,
>
> To grab the land,

You have to grab it from my hand.

"Who can break through the siege in tease?

In the northern sky not a single bird flees.

Since rebels started skirmish in despair,

The worries for the war have greyed my hair."

Since I, Du Bao, arrived in Huai'an, I have been involved in warfare. The city has been completely isolated and heavily besieged. As I can do nothing but manage the provisions and keep up the morale, I cherish no hope of returning alive and entrust the survival of the city to the heavens. Now that I sit upon the city tower, I cannot but think of the fall of the former capital and grieve at the sight of the lost territory.

(*To the tune of* **Yuguizhi**)

Oh heavens, what do you mean

By showing favour to the alien tribe?

The stink of mutton is hard to describe;

The desert sands are here to be seen.

(*Annoyed*)

How my anger rises!

How my anger rises!

Who is to blame

To bring our land to shame?

(*Sighs*)

Our central plains are in alien hands at last!

Entrapped in siege

And devoid of hope,

I'll still defend Yangzhou

And Huai River in my scope.

With tens of thousands of troops, I don't think it difficult for Li Quan to break our defence. There must be some reason for him to be hesitating.

To break the siege I have a plan,

But I fail to find a suitable man.

(*Drums within*)

(*Enter a messenger*)

MESSENGER:

"On the battlefield no wild geese dwell,

But a man has come from Hell."

Funny indeed that a scholar has penetrated the siege and come to pay tribute to his patron. I'll make a report all the same. Your Excellency, a former acquaintance of yours is at the gate.

DU BAO:

Would he be a spy?

MESSENGER:

He says that he's Mr Chen, a scholar from Nan'an Prefecture in the south.

DU BAO:

How can a pedant like him break through the siege? Show him in at once.

> (*Enter Chen Zuiliang*)

CHEN ZUILIANG (*To the tune of* **Huanxisha**):

> The battle-flags provide a good display.
>
> It's not the Lantern Festival now,
>
> But firecrackers crackle away.

Where is Lord Du?

DU BAO (*Comes out to welcome Chen Zuiliang with a smile*):

> Which distant friend appears?
>
> (*Sighs*)

Oh, it's you, Mr Chen.

> Your arrival startles me into tears.

CHEN ZUILIANG:

Your hair has turned completely grey, Lord Du.

DU BAO, CHEN ZUILIANG:

> Two worried grey-heads
>
> Meet again after three years.
>
> (*They greet each other*)

CHEN ZUILIANG:

> *"A donkey ride is hard for a grey-head;*

DU BAO:

> *This meeting makes me think of olden days.*

CHEN ZUILIANG:

> *With a thousand li and more to tread,*

DU BAO:

> *I now take Nan'an for my native place."*

CHEN ZUILIANG:

Lord Du, you always linger on my mind, but I do feel sorry that Lady Zhen on her way
back to Yangzhou was captured and killed by the bandits.

DU BAO (*Startled*):

How did you get to know it?

CHEN ZUILIANG:

I saw with my own eyes her head in the bandit camp; Chunxiang was killed as well.

DU BAO (*Wails*):

Oh heavens! How my heart pains!

> (*To the tune of* **Yuguizhi**)
>
> You have shared my name and fame,
>
> My lady, my dearest wife!
>
> You deserve the highest claim,
>
> A worthy mate all through your life.
>
> When I recall our marital years,

Our marital years,

You seem to stand before me

And my eyes are filled with tears.

(*Faints as he wails and is helped to his feet by the attendants*)

CHEN ZUILIANG:

Oh respectable lady, respectable lady! How can you come to this! Join me in weeping, officers and officials!

ALL (*Weep*):

Oh, respectable lady!

DU BAO (*Wipes off his tears in irritation*):

Well, I shouldn't have acted like this! My wife is a lady of an honoured title. It befits her to die cursing the enemy. How can I lose control of my temper and cause disturbance among my men?

As the commander,

I'll do away with my private woe.

Come what may,

I'll sustain the blow.

What did the Gilded Prince say, Mr Chen?

CHEN ZUILIANG:

His words are beyond mentioning. He said that he'd kill you.

DU BAO:

Oops!

Why does he want to take my life?

I'll kill him for the national strife.

CHEN ZUILIANG:

In my opinion, there's no sense in all the killings.

(*Whispers in Du Bao's ears*)

The Gilded Prince intends to occupy the city of Huai'an.

DU BAO:

Shut up! Tell me whether there's one seat or two seats in his camp?

CHEN ZUILIANG:

He sits side by side with his wife.

DU BAO (*Laughs*):

In that case, I'm sure that I can lift this siege. But may I ask why you came all the way here?

CHEN ZUILIANG:

If you hadn't reminded me, I nearly forgot about it. I've come all way to report to you that your daughter's grave was robbed.

DU BAO (*Taken aback*):

Oh, heavens! Her dried bones in the grave couldn't have offended the robbers. They must have come for the buried treasures. Who were the robbers?

CHEN ZUILIANG:

After you had left, the nun took in a vagabond from Lingnan, Liu Mengmei, as her companion.

With greed for the treasures, they robbed the grave and escaped by the night, casting her remains in the pond. That's why I went all the way to report to you.

DU BAO (*With a sigh*):

My daughter's grave was robbed and my wife was killed. As the saying goes,

> *"It's hard to live a safe life*
> *Before you are buried.*
> *It's harder still to keep a safe grave*
> *After you are buried."*

There's nothing we can do about it. But I must thank you all the same for your kindness.

CHEN ZUILIANG:

Since you left me, my life has gone from bad to worse.

DU BAO:

As I'm now in the camp, I've got no gift for you. However, I'll give you a chance to do some service.

CHEN ZUILIANG:

I'm ready at your service.

DU BAO:

I've written a short letter to demand Li Quan to dismiss his army, but I haven't found a suitable messenger yet. Will you go on the errand? Attendants, fetch the letter. If you can persuade Li Quan into surrender, I'll report your meritorious deeds to the court and you will be offered a position.

635

ATTENDANT (*Brings in the letter and some money*):

> *"The scholar wags his tongue;*
> *The general writes his letter."*

Here's the letter and the travel fare.

CHEN ZUILIANG:

Thank you for the money, but this errand is risky indeed.

DU BAO:

Set your heart at ease.

> (*To the tune of **Liuhuaqi***)
> Through the tightest blockade
> The scholar will go.
> With a letter from me,
> He will appease the foe.

Mr Chen,

> I'm sure you'll convince the foe,
> For, wicked as they are,
> They'll change with the ebb and flow.

CHEN ZUILIANG:

Scholars are not good at appeasement.

DU BAO:

You know, as he let you through the blockade, he had his ulterior motives.

To bring the message, you are the suitable man.

CHEN ZUILIANG:

With your letter to defeat the foe,

I'll be as dignified as I can.

(*Drums and bugles within*)

DU BAO (*To the tune of* **Coda**):

On the watchtower our meeting is brief.

When you succeed,

You'll be an honoured man.

This letter will bring

Safety to the city of Huai'an.

DU BAO:

Few soldiers come back from the battlefield

CHEN ZUILIANG:

When the prefect comes to meet his men.

DU BAO:

Your mission will foretell a bumper yield;

CHEN ZUILIANG:

I hope I'll be lucky in the bandit den.

636

Scene Forty-Seven
Lifting the Siege

(*Enter the interpreter*)

INTERPRETER (*To the tune of* **Chuduizi**):

Under the selfsame sky,

A war begins between north and south.

A bandit gang lies in between,

Helping the aliens fight the Hans.

As an interpreter,

I meddle in disputes with my mouth.

Where there is a dispute, there is a root. I am an interpreter under the Gilded Prince. It's ridiculous that our chieftain should assist the Jins to besiege the Hans and attack the city of Huai'an while the Jins sent secret envoys to negotiate with the southerners. The saying is true indeed,

"*Even if you speak the words of the beast,*

You don't understand them in the least."

(*Exit*)

(*Enter Li Quan followed by his men*)

LI QUAN (*To the tune of* **Shuangquanjiu**):

> Across the river camps lie
>
> While towering racks rise to the sky.
>
> Amid sounding drums and waving flags,
>
> Our armoured steeds and vehicles ally.
>
> We have besieged the town,
>
> Ready to bring it down.
>
> Envoy Du,
>
> Even if you have wings, we'll catch you.

I am the Gilded Prince. For days we've been attacking the city of Huai'an, but without success. I put up a fierce appearance, but I'm filled with doubts within my heart. On the one hand, I'm afraid that there will be reinforcements from the south; on the other hand, I'm afraid that there will be reprimands from the north. Caught in a dilemma, I'm waiting for my lady for consultation.

> (*Enter Lady Yang*)

LADY YANG:

> *"I'm a demon through thick and thin,*
>
> *A leopard in woman's skin."*

My lord, have you heard that the Jin messenger to the south is back at the gate of our camps?

LI QUAN:

Is that possible?

> (*Enter the Jin General on horseback, sword in hand*),

JIN GENERAL (*To the tune of* **Northern Yexingchuan**):

> I'm the envoy from the north,
>
> With a passport shedding the light forth.
>
> (*Enter the groom, chasing after him*)

GROOM:

Slippery! The ground is slippery!

JIN GENERAL:

> Whose camp is this,
>
> With soldiers running here and there?

Why is it

> That no one comes to give me any care?

GROOM (*Shouts*):

Your Highness Gilded Prince, the envoy from the north is at the gate.

> (*Exit*)

LI QUAN, LADY YANG (*In a panic*):

Send for the interpreter at once.

> (*Enter the interpreter*)

INTERPRETER (*Kneels to welcome the Jin General*):

The Gilded Prince is too ill to meet you at the gate. Come in please, General!

JIN GENERAL:

Kubla kubla ...

(*Dismounts and takes the main seat*)

Durr durr ...

LI QUAN (*To the interpreter*):

What did he say?

INTERPRETER:

He's angry.

(*Li Quan and Lady Yang raise their hands in salutation, but the Jin General ignores them in anger*)

JIN GENERAL (*Points at Li Quan*):

Tieli wendo dala ...

LI QUAN (*To the interpreter*):

What did he say?

INTERPRETER:

I'm afraid to repeat — he wants to kill you.

LI QUAN:

For what?

JIN GENERAL (*Stares at Lady Yang and grins*):

Hulin hulin ...

(*Lady Yang asks the interpreter*)

INTERPRETER:

He admires your good looks.

JIN GENERAL:

Kulo kulo ...

INTERPRETER:

He says he's thirsty after the long journey.

JIN GENERAL (*Waves his hands and feet*):

Ergai dala ...

INTERPRETER:

He wants horse-milk wine.

JIN GENERAL:

Yorr erchi ...

INTERPRETER:

He wants baked mutton.

LI QUAN (*Aloud*):

Get him some mutton and milk wine. Be quick!

(*Enter the attendant with mutton and wine*)

JIN GENERAL (*Drinks by himself, slices the mutton and eats it, laughs, and wipes his greasy hands on his chest*):

Yelu erlada ...

INTERPRETER:

He's not angry now. He says you've done the right thing.

JIN GENERAL (*Drunk*):

Sodoba sodoba ...

INTERPRETER:

He says he's drunk.

JIN GENERAL (*Stares at Lady Yang*):

Dola dola ...

LADY YANG (*Smiles*):

What did he say?

INTERPRETER:

He wants you to sing a song.

LADY YANG:

No problem.

    (*To the tune of* **Northern Qingjiangyin**)

Ha,

    The dumb Bodhisattva Guanyin meets a foreign guy,

    And smiles with her face awry.

    General from the north,

    You're welcome to come by.

    We greet you with a loud cry.

Interpreter, I'll pour a cup of wine and you'll hand it over to him.

INTERPRETER (*Hands over the wine*):

Arar galie ...

LADY YANG:

What did you say?

INTERPRETER:

I said that you poured the wine for him.

LADY YANG:

Right.

JIN GENERAL (*Stares at Lady Yang in a drunken state*):

Bach bach ...

INTERPRETER:

He asks you to dance for him.

LADY YANG:

No problem. Get my pear-blossom spear.

    (*To the previous tune*)

    As I twist my pretty waist

    And wield the spear like a whirl,

    There flies a shower of cold pear blooms.

    I show the foreign guy

    A shower of pear blooms.

JIN GENERAL (*Turns aside, flaps his sleeves and collapses with laughter*):

Hulin hulin ...

(*Lady Yang helps the Jin General to his feet*)

JIN GENERAL (*Waves his hands and collapses on the ground*):

Ala bulai …

INTERPRETER:

He's encoring. He wants you to sing another song.

JIN GENERAL (*Laughs and nods to Lady Yang for her to come nearer*):

Hasa hasa …

INTERPRETER:

He wants to ask you a question.

LADY YANG:

What did he want to ask?

JIN GENERAL (*Pulls Lady Yang by the sleeve and whispers*):

Hasa erge hairkela, hairkela …

LADY YANG (*To the interpreter with a smile*):

What did he say?

INTERPRETER (*Shakes his head*):

He begged something from you.

LADY YANG (*Smiles*):

What is it?

INTERPRETER:

I dare not repeat his words.

JIN GENERAL (*Collapses with laughter*):

Gulu gulu …

LI QUAN (*Aside, to the interpreter*):

What did he want from Lady Yang, by *gulu-gulu* all the time?

INTERPRETER:

As for this, he should not have wanted. Even if he wants it, Her Ladyship would not give him. Even if she will give him, Your Highness would not allow her. Even if you will allow her, I would not hand it over to him.

LI QUAN:

What is so precious?

INTERPRETER:

His words are clear enough: *hasa erge hairkela …* He wants Her Ladyship's hairy private parts.

LI QUAN (*Annoyed*):

What a shame! What a shame! That son of a barbarian bitch! Get me the spear!

(*Dashes at the Jin General with a spear in his hand*)

JIN GENERAL (*Fends off the spear with his wine jar*):

Gulu gulu …

LI QUAN (*To the tune of **Northern Coda***):

How can you fend off my spear with a jar?

You son of a barbarian bitch,

What do you aliens think we are!

(*Pushes the Jin General to the ground*)

I'll pull your scarlet beard;

I'll choke you and have you speared.

(*Lady Yang grasps Li Quan and lets the Jin General go*)

JIN GENERAL:

Yela yelaha ...

(*Points at Li Quan*)

Lilo chiding chiding mulash, lilo chiding mulash ...

(*Exit with a flap of his sleeves*)

LI QUAN:

What a shame! What did he mean by *yelaha*?

INTERPRETER:

He's calling for the groom.

LI QUAN:

Why does he point at me, shouting *lilo chiding mulash*?

INTERPRETER:

He's going to report this to his emperor and ask him to send troops to kill you,

(*Li Quan is enraged*)

LADY YANG:

My lord, it's not the time for you to fly into a rage.

LI QUAN:

Oops, he wants your *hairkela*!

LADY YANG:

What if he gets it? You're too jealous.

LI QUAN (*After a pause*):

I was being outrageous. When the Jin emperor learns about it, my position as Gilded Prince is shaky enough.

LADY YANG:

As this alien envoy has just returned from the south, there must be some bargain between the south and the north.

LI QUAN:

What's your suggestion?

LADY YANG:

Let me think it over.

(*Drums within*)

(*Enter the messenger*)

MESSENGER:

Report, report, report! The scholar we released the other day has galloped back alone on horseback from Huai'an. He says that he's got an urgent message for Your Highness.

LADY YANG:

He's here at the right time. Show him in.

(*Enter Chen Zuiliang*)

CHEN ZUILIANG (*To the tune of* **Lülüjin**):

> On an errand beyond my power,
>
> I have to wait and see.
>
> A military mission fits the soldier
>
> Better than a scholar like me.
>
> (*Stumbles when he hears the yells within*)
>
> At the sound of cannon roar,
>
> I stumble on the ground.

Dear me, dear me,

> I try to find my way,
>
> With swords and spears around.

MESSENGER (*Announces*):

Here comes the scholar.

CHEN ZUILIANG (*Greets Li Quan and Lady Yang*):

The scholar Chen Zuiliang, after a narrow escape, bows a hundred times to Your Highness and Your Ladyship.

LI QUAN:

Has Envoy Du surrendered his city?

CHEN ZUILIANG:

A city is nothing, compared with the kingship he has to offer you.

LI QUAN:

I have been a king since long ago.

CHEN ZUILIANG:

He's offering you more titles and honours. Here's his letter to you.

LI QUAN (*Reads the letter*):

"Family friend Du Bao shows his respect to His Highness, Prince Li." Scholar, what family connections do I have with Envoy Du?

CHEN ZUILIANG:

In the Han Dynasty, there were two bosom friends named Li Gu and Du Qiao; in the Tang Dynasty, there were also two bosom friends named Li Bai and Du Fu. Therefore, Envoy Du ventures to say that you and he were family friends.

LI QUAN:

The old chap's clever enough. Let me see what he's got to say.

> (*Reads the letter*)
>
> (*To the tune of* **Yifengshu**)
>
> "I hear that you serve the alien king,
>
> Who is as fierce as wolf and tiger;
>
> Such friendship can hardly last.
>
> If you turn to serve the court of Song,
>
> You'll have abundant wealth
>
> And be promoted fast.
>
> Keep your crown

And turn over a new leaf.

As I try to persuade you

To stop the strife,

Please take my words in full belief."

(*Laughs*)

This letter is trying to persuade me to turn to the court of Song, but I can hardly follow his advice. "Enclosed is a private letter to Her Ladyship."

(*Laughs*)

Envoy Du has learned to show his respect to you, my lady.

LADY YANG:

Read it for me.

LI QUAN:

"Family friend Du Bao pays homage to Her Ladyship, Lady Yang." Well, Envoy Du is building family connections with Lady Yang, too.

CHEN ZUILIANG:

As he's a family friend of yours, so he's a family friend of hers.

LI QUAN:

There's some sense in it, but he should not say "pay homage" to a lady.

CHEN ZUILIANG:

If Her Ladyship is willing to pay homage to the court, why shouldn't the envoy pay homage to her?

LADY YANG:

Well said. Now read on!

LI QUAN (*Reads the letter*):

"Family friend Du Bao pays homage to Her Ladyship, Lady Yang. It is said that your husband has been entitled Gilded Prince by the dynasty of Jin, but that you have not been entitled. I have reported to our emperor to entitle you as Anti-Jin Princess. I hope Your Ladyship will accept the offer with pleasure. With best regards." He's so considerate as to gain some imperial favour for you!

LADY YANG:

Mr Chen, does he want me to fight the Jins by conferring on me the title Anti-Jin Princess?

CHEN ZUILIANG:

When you accept the offer, you can get gold from the dynasty of Song whenever you need it. That's why you're entitled Anti-Jin Princess.

LADY YANG:

I must thank the kindness from your emperor.

CHEN ZUILIANG:

Everybody is singing praise of Song.

LADY YANG:

I take your words for granted. I need a helmet of purest gold. As I am a woman general, I only wear a helmet without jewellery. I'd like to have a helmet in the southern style.

CHEN ZUILIANG:

I'll get it for you.

LI QUAN:

You only care about gold, gold. What about me, Gilded Prince?

LADY YANG:

Then, you'll be Anti-Jin Prince.

LI QUAN:

I accept the title with pleasure.

CHEN ZUILIANG (*Kowtows*):

I'm afraid that Your Highness and Your Ladyship will change your minds.

LADY YANG:

I've fixed my mind. We'll write a petition for surrender and ask you to bring it to the southern court.

LI QUAN (*To the previous tune*):

> When we turn to the court of Song,
>
> Our relations with Jin will go wrong.

LADY YANG:

Mr Chen,

> It's your task indeed
>
> For me to get all the gold.

CHEN ZUILIANG:

Your Highness,

> Conversion gives you peace of mind,

Your Ladyship,

> And brings you bliss of every kind.

CHEN ZUILIANG, LI QUAN, LADY YANG:

> Withdraw the troops
>
> And obey the royal call
>
> Lest our names be cursed by all.

LI QUAN:

Mr Chen, have dinner in the guesthouse. We'll draft a petition of surrender by night and see you off tomorrow morning.

> (*Raises his right hand as a gesture of farewell. Chen Zuiliang also bows his farewell*)

LI QUAN (*To the tune of* **Coda**):

> While I am but a skeleton,
>
> My wife carries the day.

CHEN ZUILIANG:

> With your petition of surrender,
>
> Our emperor will be happy and gay.

> (*Exit Chen Zuiliang, leaving Li Quan and Lady Yang on the stage*)

LI QUAN:

My lady, by deserting Jin, we've got two princely titles. For most people, one princely title is unattainable, but we've got two. Aren't we lucky!

LADY YANG:

Wait, we'll have a third title.

LI QUAN:

What's the third title?

LADY YANG:

Headless Prince.

LI QUAN:

What do you mean?

LADY YANG:

We'll be beheaded.

LI QUAN:

Now that we've surrendered, why should they kill us?

LADY YANG:

We became chieftains because we had Jins at our back. Now that we have no one to turn to, the southern court can easily capture us.

LI QUAN (*Annoyed*):

Alas! I'm strong enough to fight ten thousand men; why should I be afraid of the southern court?

LADY YANG:

You are but another Xiang Yu, who would not admit defeat until he reached the Wujiang River.

LI QUAN:

Nonsense! Even if I were Xiang Yu and you were Beauty Yu, I would not submit you to the southern court.

LADY YANG:

Well, you are not Xiang Yu and I'm not Beauty Yu. Let's find another way out.

LI QUAN:

What way out?

LADY YANG:

We'll be like Fan Li sailing with Beauty Xishi.

LI QUAN:

Where are the Five Lakes for them to sail? — You mean we'll go out to sea and be pirates?

LADY YANG (*Gives commands*):

Men in the camps, we've surrendered to the southern court. We'll lift the siege on Huai'an and then go out to sea!

ATTENDANTS (*In response*):

The siege is lifted.

(*Drums within*)

The ships are ready. Your Highness, it's time to set off.

(*All embark the imaginary ships and walk around the stage*)

LI QUAN (*To the tune of **Jiangtousongbie***):

Beyond Huaiyang,

Beyond Huaiyang,

The sea surges wave on wave.

With the east wind,

With the east wind,

The sails go to the sea.

We'll build our camps near the Penglai cave,

And raise our flags on ancient debris.

LADY YANG (*To the previous tune*):

Follow heavenly ways,

Follow heavenly ways,

And we'll live an easy life.

When we submit,

When we submit,

We'll do away with war.

We nearly hurt the Song court in the strife

But now we'll brave the sea with awe.

ATTENDANTS:

Your Highness, Your Ladyship, we are out at sea.

LI QUAN:

Lay anchor for the night. We'll set sail at dawn,

Each fights the war for his own lord

LADY YANG:

Until one side has gained the field.

LI QUAN:

I lead the troops to sea on board,

ALL:

No longer wielding sword or shield.

Scene Forty-Eight
Reunion with Her Mother

(*Enter Du Liniang*)

DU LINIANG (*To the tune of **Shi'ershi***):

My unconquerable love

Restored me to life.

Freed from the smell of earth,

New flesh grows in the world above.

I stay at an inn as a lonely wife.

(*Enter Sister Stone*)

SISTER STONE:

    You've pushed your man into the worldly strife.

DU LINIANG:

    "When bamboo mattress is left in the cold

SISTER STONE:

    And dust remains upon the pillowcase,

DU LINIANG:

    My man comes in my dreamland as of old.

SISTER STONE:

    Since the scholar met you in new bloom,

DU LINIANG:

    The yearning maid has come to life again,

DU LINIANG, SISTER STONE:

    But has to stay by herself in her room."

DU LINIANG:

Sister Stone, I was lucky to regain my life and get married to Mr Liu. I hoped that he would pass the imperial examination and that we could visit my parents at home. It happened that the announcement of results was postponed because of the disturbances in Huainan. As my parents are in the besieged city, I've sent Mr Liu to find out what has happened to them and I'm thus left alone at an inn by the Qiantang River. How melancholy the moon looks and the river moans!

SISTER STONE:

This sight is much more lovely than what you saw in the netherworld.

DU LINIANG:

Of course it is.

    (*To the tune of* **Zhenxianxiang**)

    Although I dwell in a lonely village inn,

    Compared with years of burial in the tomb,

    The broken door and ragged blinds

    Are heavens to me in my room.

Sister Stone,

    How about life with my parents far away?

    How about life with my man day by day?

    In a trance, I seem

    To live between life and death —

    I have only one man in my dream.

SISTER STONE:

Few have had your experience.

    (*To the previous tune*)

    I kept your memorial tablet in the house

    And waited for you to see your spouse.

DU LINIANG:

Sister Stone, do you know where I hid myself when you called on the scholar the other night?

SISTER STONE:

> To hide behind the painting shade
>
> Is a baffling trick by a maid.

DU LINIANG:

It's getting dark.

SISTER STONE:

> The moon and stars are obscure in the skies;
>
> The fireflies glitter like the devil eyes.

DU LINIANG:

It's time to light the lamp.

SISTER STONE:

We've run out of oil.

> Let's sit in the dark
>
> And save the last drop of oil
>
> For you to doff your dress in sparks.

DU LINIANG:

I cannot go to sleep in the long night. You'd better go and borrow some oil from the landlord.

SISTER STONE:

You just sit in the courtyard while I'll go and borrow some oil.

> *"When I go for the oil,*
>
> *My tiny feet will toil."*
>
> (*Exit*)
>
> (*Du Liniang gazes at the moon and sighs*)
>
> (*Enter Lady Zhen and Chunxiang, travelling on the way*)

LADY ZHEN (*To the tune of* **Yueergao**):

> When war starts in the north,
>
> We have to wander in the south.
>
> As I have to go on foot,
>
> I wear out my shoes away from my house.
>
> My lord commands the army,
>
> With his life oft in ordeals.
>
> I have no one to go with me
>
> But Chunxiang at my heels.
>
> I have no time to do my hair,
>
> Not even in the common Yangzhou style.
>
> Now that we've arrived in Lin'an,
>
> In the gloomy forest near the hills,
>
> Where can I put up for the while?

CHUNXIANG:

Thank heavens! We've arrived in Lin'an at last.

LADY ZHEN:

Alas,

> "It is a narrow escape
>
> That we have reached Lin'an.
>
> Where can we take refuge?
>
> On the road we haven't met a man."

CHUNXIANG:

The gate ahead seems to be ajar. Let's get in.

LADY ZHEN (*Steps into the house*):

It seems to be all empty house. Is there anybody in here?

DU LINIANG:

Who is it?

CHUNXIANG:

It's a woman's voice. I'll ask her to open the inner door.

DU LINIANG (*Taken aback*):

> (*To the tune of* **Bushilu**)
>
> When I lean on the porch,
>
> Who's calling at the door in a voice so soft and light?

LADY ZHEN:

> As we have travelled late,
>
> We ask you to put us up for the night.

DU LINIANG:

> Judging from the voice,
>
> They are not men;
>
> I'll open the door and have a look in the moonlight.
>
> (*Du Liniang and Lady Zhen greet each other*)

DU LINIANG:

Oh, it's a lady. Come in and sit down please.

LADY ZHEN:

> A helping hand is of great worth,
>
> Both in the heaven and on earth.

DU LINIANG:

> Sorry to have kept you waiting;
>
> Sorry to have kept you waiting.
>
> (*Du Liniang and Lady Zhen look at each other*)

LADY ZHEN (*In surprise*):

> (*To the previous tune*)
>
> In this dilapidated site,

Young lady,

> Why do you sit alone without a light?

DU LINIANG:

> In this empty court,

I watch the moon as a sport.

LADY ZHEN (*Aside, to Chunxiang*):

Chunxiang, whom do you think this lady looks like?

CHUNXIANG (*Alarmed*):

I dare not say it. She looks like Miss Du.

LADY ZHEN:

Take a quick look inside the room to see if anyone else is there. If no one else is inside the room, she must be a ghost!

(*Exit Chunxiang*)

DU LINIANG (*Aside*):

This lady looks like my mother and her maid looks like Chunxiang.

(*To Lady Zhen*)

May I ask where you are from?

LADY ZHEN (*Sighs*):

 I'm from Huai'an;

 My husband is the Envoy of Huai'an.

 To escape from the war,

 I've travelled a long way and come to your door.

DU LINIANG (*Aside*):

650

She must be my mother, but how shall I present myself?

(*Enter Chunxiang in a panic*)

CHUNXIANG (*Aside, to Lady Zhen*):

It's an empty house with no one around. She must be a ghost, a ghost!

(*Lady Zhen trembles with fear*)

DU LINIANG:

From what she's said, she must be my mother.

(*Throws herself in Lady Zhen's bosom and cries*)

Mom, Mom!

LADY ZHEN (*Tries to move away*):

Are you my daughter? I must have neglected your offerings and you appear before me in the human form! Chunxiang, get some sacrificial money and scatter it! Scatter the money!

(*Chunxiang scatters the sacrificial money*)

DU LINIANG:

I'm not a ghost.

LADY ZHEN:

If you are not a ghost, answer my three calls with increasing voice!

(*Calls three times and Du Liniang answers three times, but each time in a weaker voice*)

You must be a ghost!

DU LINIANG:

Mom, please listen to me.

LADY ZHEN:

 Please keep away,

For a chilly wind does blow

From where you stay.

DU LINIANG:

What comes from where I stay?

(*Pulls at Lady Zhen*)

LADY ZHEN (*In fear*):

Your hands are cold, my child.

CHUNXIANG (*Kowtows*):

Please don't hurt me, Mistress.

LADY ZHEN:

We should have held a ceremony to transcend your soul but for the objection from your

father.

DU LINIANG (*Wails*):

Why should you be in such fear, Mom? I won't let you go at any event.

(*Enter Sister Stone*)

SISTER STONE (*To the previous tune*):

Before I left, I closed the door,

But how come from the yard all the roar?

(*Lowers the lamp to light the ground*)

How is it that I've found

Sacrificial money on the ground?

CHUNXIANG:

Isn't it Sister Stone coming, Madam?

LADY ZHEN:

Yes, it is.

SISTER STONE (*Surprised*):

Where are you from, Madam and Chunxiang? Why are you making such a fuss? Look,

How they move about in fear —

The old mistress

Would like to leave a ghost from the grave;

The young mistress

Would like to get the light and draw near.

DU LINIANG:

Come over quickly, Sister Stone! My mom is greatly terrified.

CHUNXIANG:

Isn't the nun also a ghost?

SISTER STONE (*Grasps Lady Zhen by the sleeve and holds up the lamp to Du Liniang*):

Too much of your ado!

Have a close look in the light.

Isn't this the face you knew?

LADY ZHEN, CHUNXIANG:

This is the face we knew.

LADY ZHEN (*Embraces Du Liniang and weeps*):

I won't tear myself away from you, my child, even if you are a ghost.

>(*To the previous tune*)

>My heart has been broken for three years,

>But how did you leave the netherworld spheres?

DU LINIANG:

>Out of respect for Dad and Mom,

>The nether judge released me from the hell.

CHUNXIANG:

How did you manage to get out of your grave, young mistress?

DU LINIANG:

>It's a story hard to tell.

LADY ZHEN:

How did you manage it?

DU LINIANG:

>Thanks to the Goddess of Mount Tai,

>A scholar got the inspiration from a dream to dig my grave.

LADY ZHEN:

Where is the scholar's native place?

DU LINIANG:

The scholar Liu Mengmei is from Lingnan.

CHUNXIANG:

What a coincidence! His name indeed carries "willow" *liu* and "plum" *mei*!

LADY ZHEN:

Why did he bring you here?

DU LINIANG:

He's here to take the imperial examination.

LADY ZHEN:

Then he must be a nice scholar. Ask him to meet us.

DU LINIANG:

>I asked him to meet you in Huaiyang.

Therefore,

>Here I stay alone;

>Here I stay alone.

LADY ZHEN (*Aside, to Chunxiang*):

How is it possible!

CHUNXIANG:

I think so, for how can there be such a pretty ghost?

LADY ZHEN (*Turns back to Du Liniang and weeps*):

>(*To the tune of* **Fanshanhu**)

>I thought that you had soared to the sky,

>Seated on the lotus in the western spheres,

But I didn't expect to meet you again in three years.

I cried till my limbs were numb

And my eyes were dry.

My dreams would be haunted;

My thoughts would fly.

I was afraid that

You would lack food and drink;

In your graveyard cattle would saunter by.

ALL:

What night indeed is this?

What night indeed is this?

Oh,

We fear that this reunion is a lie.

DU LINIANG (*Weeps*):

(*To the previous tune*)

You put me in a grave that was shallow,

Where bones lay cold and sleep came slow.

I got your food and drink,

Offered on Festival for the Ghost.

I had no hope for the future;

The past terrified me the most.

This is a confounding puzzle,

Only heavens will ever know.

I'm no longer a ghost;

I've come back from down below.

If I had not cut off the nether tie,

How can I have you close by?

ALL:

What night indeed is this?

What night indeed is this?

Oh,

We fear that this reunion is a lie.

LADY ZHEN:

Sister Stone, thank you for watching over my child.

SISTER STONE (*To the previous tune*):

Never mention the past three years,

For they make me shudder all the time.

I observed all the rites for her;

Who knows she had a love affair sublime!

(*Whispers to Lady Zhen*)

I tried to find out about the love affair,

But she played tricks on me all the time.

ALL:

> Miraculous love!
>
> Miraculous love!
>
> Her soul made love on earth above!

CHUNXIANG (*To the previous tune*):

> I've heard about souls that stroll,
>
> Who cannot keep their bodies whole.
>
> A pity that they had no tomb-mates
>
> To love them heart and soul.
>
> My mistress alone has attained her goal.

Young mistress,

> Your love is obstinate,
>
> And now you've had your mate.
>
> I offered food and drink for you every day;
>
> Your mom never forgot the memorial date.
>
> Who knows that you have changed your fate
>
> And is sailing with your mate!

ALL:

> Miraculous love!
>
> Miraculous love!
>
> Her soul made love on earth above!

LADY ZHEN (*To the tune of* **Coda**):

> Thank heavens that you've come back to life,
>
> But your dad is still entangled in the military strife.

DU LINIANG:

Don't worry, Mom. My faithful man will

> Probe high and low
>
> To find the news for his wife.
>
> *Imaginary sprites are hard to meet;*
>
> *Where in the heaven flies the blossom sweet?*
>
> *Don't say that only mortals have some warmth;*
>
> *The morning mirror is like a chilly sheet.*

Scene Forty-Nine
Sojourn near the Huai River

(*Enter Liu Mengmei with a bundle and an umbrella*)

LIU MENGMEI (*To the tune of* **Sandengle**):

> There is no easy road
>
> In times of war.

At the sight of fallen leaves,

The traveller senses the coming fall.

As my wife worries about her father,

I'm on my way to Yangzhou.

When I know he's besieged in Huai'an,

To his rescue I must go.

"How can I go and see my kin?

I have to go through thick and thin.

For a scholar in times of distress,

Poverty will throw him in a mess."

As I, Liu Mengmei in the human world, was loved by Du Liniang in the netherworld, we became man and wife. We went together to Lin'an to enter the imperial examination. I was lucky enough to have my belated paper accepted, but the border conflict delayed the announcement of the results. As soon as my wife heard that her father was besieged in Huaiyang, she asked me to seek information on the way. Therefore, I set off with her self-portrait to report the news of her resurrection. My only means to cover the travel expenses is the jewellery unearthed from her tomb. Some little articles are not easy to sell or pawn on the spot, and some vessels of precious metal are of little weight. What's more, I'm a scholar who does not know much about the scales. The little cash I have is spent on my daily expenses on the way. Now that I have reached Yangzhou, I hear that my father-in-law has been transferred to defend the city of Huai'an. As the bandit troops have blocked the way, I dare not move on. However, the bandit troops seem to be dispersing and so I'm moving forward again.

(*To the tune of **Jinchandao***)

I cherished the hope that in Yangzhou

I would drink as much as I can

And relish in the song and dance,

But who knows that Envoy Du has gone to Huai'an.

I have no fortune

To take a pleasure ride on a crane.

I have to live with the rustic folk,

With sight of decayed lotus and willow

Scattered on the autumn plain.

What melancholy thoughts when I roam!

I have to wait for my fame and name,

And leave my dear wife at home.

Well, forget about it!

Woeful thoughts are a shame!

After a long journey, the towering city wall of Huai'an comes in sight at last! Around the city wall flows the clear Huai River; above the wall-tower floats the sixteen-feet military streamer. Amid drums and bugles, the city gate is closed. I'll try to find an inn to put up for the night.

(Enter the innkeeper)

INNKEEPER:

> "Add a lot of water to the wine;
>
> Don't earn money in indecent line."

Do you need a room for the night, sir?

(Liu Mengmei enters the inn)

Will you have wine with nuts and fruits or with dishes?

LIU MENGMEI:

I never drink wine.

INNKEEPER:

Will you have some food?

LIU MENGMEI:

I'll pay after I eat.

INNKEEPER:

No, you'll pay before you eat.

LIU MENGMEI:

Here are some scraps of silver.

INNKEEPER:

What scraps! I'd better weigh them.

> *(Weighs and calls out in surprise)*

The silver's gone.

LIU MENGMEI:

Why all the fuss?

INNKEEPER:

Sir, your silver has disappeared in the floor cracks. Look at the tiny drops!

LIU MENGMEI:

I've some more for you.

INNKEEPER *(Takes the silver and it vanishes again. The same happens a third time)*:

Oh, you're giving me quicksilver!

LIU MENGMEI:

Why do you call it quicksilver?

> *(Aside)*

I've got it. It must be the quicksilver my love held in her mouth at the burial. "The dragon soars to the sky when the earth in its mouth turns into pearls; the ghost resurrects to the human world when the quicksilver in its mouth turns into pellets." It conforms to the natural course of events that these things are gone with the wind. When my love died, the quicksilver was dead; when my love comes to life again, the quicksilver becomes alive. It's a pity that the common people do not understand these miraculous things.

> *(Turns to the innkeeper)*

Well, sir, you've squandered all my silver and I have no more left. Here is a book I read every day. It's worth a flask of wine.

INNKEEPER:

The book is too worn and torn.

LIU MENGMEI:

Here is a brush-pen to go with it.

INNKEEPER:

The pen is battered.

LIU MENGMEI:

From your numerous customers, haven't you ever heard of Du Fu's line "Wear out ten thousand books"?

INNKEEPER:

No, I haven't.

LIU MENGMEI:

Haven't you ever heard of Li Bai's line "Dream of a pen that bears a thousand blooms"?

INNKEEPER:

No, I haven't.

LIU MENGMEI (*With a giggle*):

(*To the tune of **Zaoluopao***)

It would be fun that he assumes

He'll "*wear out ten thousand books*"

And "*dream of a pen that bears a thousand blooms*".

I'm wrong to swap these things for wine.

INNKEEPER (*Smiles*):

"*An immortal leaves his jade pendant;*

A minister gives his golden plate."

LIU MENGMEI:

Where do you think these jade pendants and golden plates come from?

When a scholar serves the royal court,

His intelligence will be considered great.

You probably don't know that

A maid of noble birth

Will marry him;

A minister of lofty worth

Will visit him.

INNKEEPER:

What do they want of him?

LIU MENGMEI:

With his pen, a scholar quells the earth.

If you don't want my book or brush-pen, how about the umbrella?

INNKEEPER:

You're asking for rain!

LIU MENGMEI:

I won't leave tomorrow.

INNKEEPER:

Do you want to starve yourself to death here?

LIU MENGMEI (*Smiles*):

Do you know Envoy Du in this Huaiyang area?

INNKEEPER:

Oh, who doesn't know him? A Banquet of Peace will be held tomorrow.

LIU MENGMEI:

I'm his son-in-law to pay a visit to him.

INNKEEPER (*Startled*):

I'm lucky that you mention this early. Envoy Du has sent you a letter of invitation.

LIU MENGMEI:

Where's the letter?

INNKEEPER:

We'll go and read it.

> (*Shows the way for Liu Mengmei*)

I'll carry the bundle and umbrella for you.

> (*Goes with Liu Mengmei*)

LIU MENGMEI:

Where's the letter?

INNKEEPER:

There it is!

LIU MENGMEI:

This is an official notice.

INNKEEPER:

So it is. Just look!

> (*To the previous tune*)
>
> "Prohibition on Vagabonds and Impostors".

Envoy Du is from Sichuan:

> "I came here from Sichuan,
>
> Ten thousand *li* away from my hometown.
>
> I have neither kin by my side
>
> Nor son-in-law around."

This sentence is meant for you, sir:

> "Put him to jail
>
> If any swindler should be found."

The next sentence is for me:

> "The host will also be published
>
> If he takes in the swindler within his door.
>
> Let this notice be known to all."

"That's all for the notice. The fifth day of the fifth month, the thirty-second year of Jianyan, Song Dynasty." Look at the signature of Envoy Du at the end, with the glaring seal of "Imperial Envoy and Commander-in-Chief to the Huaiyang Region". Take your time, sir, and I'll be off now.

> *"Each one sweeps the snow from his own doorstep*
> *And heeds not the frost on his neighbour's roof."*
>
> (*Exit*)

LIU MENGMEI (*Weeps*):

My dear wife, do you know that I'm in such a wretched state here?

> (*Looks around*)

Well, there's a house ahead with big golden characters. I'll try to find shelter there.

> (*Looks*)

The characters read: "Memorial Hall to Mother Washer". Why is this called "Memorial Hall to Mother Washer"?

> (*Looks*)

There is an inscription on the wall:

> *"The ancient sage keeps a meal in heart;*
> *For a thousand years it lives in works of art."*

Yes, I see. This memorial hall was built in honour of Marquis of Huaiyin Han Xin's benefactress, Mother Washer. Just think that Han Xin was a sham-king of Qi and could still be fed by a woman; I am a genuine scholar but no one will provide me with a cup of cold wine. I'll bow a thousand times to Mother Washer.

> (*Bows*)
>
> (*To the tune of* **Yingzaopao**)
>
> When he fished in the land of Chu,
>
> Han Xin, the hungry gentleman, met Mother Washer.
>
> Compared with her,
>
> Xiang Yu the Conqueror was blind to virtue.
>
> She was praised by the great historian Sima Qian
>
> And honoured in the Prefecture of Huai'an.
>
> Therefore, a meal is of immense value.

It seems that women always have better vision.

> When Duke Wen of Jin went begging,
>
> Lady Xi gave him food.
>
> When Wu Zixu went begging,
>
> A washing woman did all she could.
>
> I'll give three thousand kowtows to those who did good.

Now goes the first night watch-beat. I'll put up for the night in the corridor and get up early tomorrow morning to enter the city gate. But there's no water to wash my face …

> (*Looks around*)

Wonderful, it's raining now.

> *None in the past could be compared*
> *To Mother Washer with discerning eyes.*
> *When I bow before official gates,*
> *I will control myself when tears arise.*

Scene Fifty
Spoiling the Banquet

(Enter Du Bao, followed by the gatekeeper and attendants)

DU BAO *(To the tune of **Liangzhouling**):*

A thousand steeds gallop along the Huai,

While wild geese flock across the cloudy sky.

Thoughts of homeland make me weep and sigh.

ALL:

With good cheer,

We've won the day,

But now we still stay here.

DU BAO:

"The road to peerage is tough and rough;

Of the hardship I've never had enough.

Amid sounds of drums and bugles bold,

I'm growing old.

When peace arrived amid cheers,

I dreamed of home and woke in tears.

The war has kept me from home,

Bringing endless thoughts on the roam."

As Envoy for Appeasement, I have been caught in the warfare. I broke through the blockade line to save the city and lifted the siege by a letter. Li Quan's bandits are gone and the Jin troops are not coming yet. During this interval, I have to deal with a lot of aftermath. Attendants, wait for my orders outside the gate.

(Exeunt attendants)

(The gatekeeper stands on guard at the gate)

DU BAO:

I'm glad that the city has been preserved, but I'm in deep woe that my wife died.

(In tears)

My dear wife, I sent a memorial to the court yesterday, asking for an honoured funeral for you and asking for leave to send your remains to Sichuan. For the moment, I don't know yet what the imperial decree will be. It is true to say,

"Fame and wealth is but the dew

While family union is extra hue."

(Reads the documents)

(Enter Liu Mengmei in ragged clothes, carrying Du Liniang's self-portrait in his sleeves)

LIU MENGMEI *(To the tune of **Jinjiaoye**):*

Poverty and weariness fill me with dismay,

In addition to the autumn decay.

(Straightens his clothes)

I straighten my cap and gown,

Not sure whether I'll be accepted today.

GATEKEEPER (*In a harsh voice*):

Who's coming outside?

LIU MENGMEI:

Envoy Du's son-in-law asks for admittance.

GATEKEEPER:

Are you serious?

LIU MENGMEI:

A scholar never tells falsehoods.

(*The gatekeeper comes in to report*)

DU BAO:

I've made it clear in the official notice.

(*To the gatekeeper*)

How does he look like?

GATEKEEPER:

Just so so. He carries a scroll of painting in his sleeves.

DU BAO (*Smiles*):

So he's a painter. Tell him that I'm occupied with military affairs.

GATEKEEPER (*To Liu Mengmei*):

His Excellency is occupied with military affairs. You are free to go anywhere else.

LIU MENGMEI:

If I'm free to go anywhere else, I'll be nobody.

GATEKEEPER:

If you are somebody, you'll not be free to go anywhere.

LIU MENGMEI:

Is His Excellency going out for a visit?

GATEKEEPER:

All the officials and officers will be attending the Banquet of Peace. No appointments will be made today.

LIU MENGMEI:

What is the Banquet of Peace?

GATEKEEPER:

It's an annual banquet in the border area. As we've dispelled the bandits this year, the banquet is more sumptuous. On the banquet there are gold-flower trees, silver plates, bolts of silk, silver ingots, and gifts of all sorts. If you are Envoy Du's son-in-law, you may bring some home.

LIU MENGMEI:

Yes, I see. I'm afraid when I meet him, what if he should ask me to improvise such poems as *"On the Banquet of Peace"*, *"Song of Triumph"* or *"Ode to the Pacific Huai"*. I'd better prepare a poem or two while I wait in the gatekeeper's room. As the proverb goes, "Better prepared, less embarrassed."

GATEKEEPER:

Will you step aside, sir? The officials and officers are coming.

> (*Exit Liu Mengmei*)
>
> (*Enter Official*)

OFFICIAL (*To the tune of **Liangzhouling***):

> When autumn arrives at the river Huai,
>
> We're glad that arms are laid by.
>
> It's time for us to sing praise
>
> Of peace with the best phrase.
>
> (*Enter Officer*)

OFFICER:

> Officials and officers,
>
> Generals and ministers,
>
> Enjoy the dishes on the trays.

How do you do!

OFFICIAL:

At the Banquet of Peace for the officials and officers, we've seen to it that aquatic food and land produce are sumptuous and that song and dance are splendid.

OFFICIAL, OFFICER (*Greet Du Bao*):

Under the rule of His Majesty who is beloved by all his subjects, Your Excellency has inspired awe from all sides. As the bandits have been dispersed with a mere letter from you, we've prepared a Banquet of Peace in the army tradition. Now that everything is ready, would you please join the banquet?

> (*Drums and pipes within*)

GATEKEEPER:

> "*The book on arts of war enhances eloquence;*
>
> *The limpid water sweetens cortex wine.*"

The wine, please.

DU BAO (*Sprays the wine*):

> (*To the tune of **Liangzhouxu***)
>
> To the north of the Yangtze,
>
> To the south of the Huai,
>
> The beats of night watch ring in the sky.

OFFICIAL, OFFICER (*Offer a toast*):

> What an honour for the frontier area
>
> To welcome Your Excellency here!

To our great joy,

> Without fighting a single battle,
>
> The war clouds are dispersed
>
> With a mere letter of persuasion.
>
> The alien horns are cursed
>
> On the first tower against invasion.

ALL:

> When autumn winds
>
> Sweep the border weeds,
>
> We drink to our hearts' content.
>
> For your meritorious deeds,
>
> Let's drink to your health in the tent.

DU BAO (*To the previous tune*):

> As His Majesty is amply blessed,
>
> With our unanimous efforts,
>
> The besieged city is no longer distressed.

OFFICIAL, OFFICER:

> Your commands are strict and stern;
>
> Your tactics are hard to learn.

DU BAO:

With my letter to Li Quan and his wife,

> I used the old trick of bribing the wife
>
> And playing mournful alien tunes —
>
> A word is as sharp as a knife.
>
> Without outside help, we would have no way;
>
> It is Heaven that blesses us today.

ALL:

> When autumn winds
>
> Sweep the border weeds,
>
> We drink to our hearts' content.
>
> For your meritorious deeds,
>
> Let's drink to your health in the tent.
>
> (*Drums within*)
>
> (*Enter Messenger*)

MESSENGER:

> *"The gifts and titles from the imperial court,*
>
> *Are given to him who valiantly fought."*

Your Excellency, the imperial decree has it that you are not allowed to retire. You are to return to the capital and be promoted to the position of Grand Chancellor. Her Ladyship has been conferred the posthumous title of first-rank Virtuous Lady.

OFFICIAL, OFFICER:

Grand Chancellor is equal in rank to the prime minister. As your subordinates, we're overjoyed to hear that Your Excellency has been a minister of the highest rank.

> (*Offer wine to Du Bao*)
>
> (*To the previous tune*)
>
> For years and years you will have high renown,
>
> When you serve His Majesty in the capital town.

After your departure,

We'll lay aside arms of any sort,

When you serve in the court.

The fragrance of osmanthus bloom

Will accompany your steed;

Amid flutes and drums, by night you'll speed.

When you serve in the palace,

Will you remember the place where you succeed?

ALL:

When autumn winds

Sweep the border weeds,

We drink to our hearts' content.

For your meritorious deeds,

Let's drink to your health in the tent.

DU BAO:

Talented and in the prime of your life, you are destined to attain peerage. As for me, I return to the capital in grey hair. It's nothing worth mentioning.

(*To the previous tune*)

When I look at the mirror every day,

I weep because old times won't stay.

The landscapes change;

The times change.

I caress my sword;

I tap the rails in melancholy tune,

Only to raise my head to see the moon.

When I leave this time,

My feat will go with the eastward stream,

(*Raises his hands in salutation*)

But with whom will you sing under the moon?

ALL:

When autumn winds

Sweep the border weeds,

We drink to our hearts' content.

For your meritorious deeds,

Let's drink to your health in the tent.

(*Enter Liu Mengmei*)

LIU MENGMEI:

"With a poem ready at the gate,

To see the envoy, I have yet to wait."

(*Greets the gatekeeper*)

Will you announce for me again, Sir?

GATEKEEPER:

His Excellency is still at the Banquet of Peace.

LIU MENGMEI:

I've composed a poem on the Banquet of Peace, but the banquet itself is not over yet.

GATEKEEPER:

Who told you to compose the poem?

LIU MENGMEI:

As I'm his son-in-law, sir, will you announce for me?

GATEKEEPER (*To Du Bao*):

Your Excellency, your son-in-law is at the door.

DU BAO:

You're asking for a spanking!

LIU MENGMEI (*As the gatekeeper angrily pushes him*):

> "The envoy is still at the fete;
>
> His son-in-law has to wait."
>
> (*Exit*)
>
> (*Enter two singing girls*)

SINGING GIRLS:

> "On the battlefield the warriors die when they advance;
>
> In the camp, the beauties sing and dance."

We camp-girls are kowtowing to you.

> (*To the tune of **Jiejiegao***)
>
> The flutes and drums resound in the camp
>
> When battle clouds disappear.
>
> Can His Excellency remain here?
>
> With a marten hat on your head,
>
> A belt of jade on your waist
>
> And a gold seal in your hand,
>
> You'll gallop in the autumn breeze
>
> And walk on a road covered with sand.

ALL:

> As you have defended the motherland,
>
> You'll be welcomed by the musical band.
>
> (*Enter Liu Mengmei*)

LIU MENGMEI:

> "You can enjoy a grander sight
>
> By climbing to a greater height."

Well, I suppose the songs have ended and the banquet is over by now. As I'm too hungry and tired, I have to force my way in.

GATEKEEPER (*Tries to stop Liu Mengmei*):

Don't you feel the shame, you hungry devil?

LIU MENGMEI (*Annoyed*):

How dare you a humble groom insult the son-in-law of an honoured lord? I'll give you a beating.

(*Beats the gatekeeper*)

DU BAO (*Calls out*):

Who's making such a noise outside the camp?

GATEKEEPER:

It's that son-in-law who came this morning, with a tattered gown, a battered hat, a ragged bundle, a broken umbrella and a torn portrait. He says that he's so hungry and tired that he has to force his way in. He beats whoever wants to stop him. He's beaten nine and a half men — only half of my face is spared.

DU BAO (*Angry*):

What a shame! I've issued an official notice of prohibition. Where comes the wretched guy, making all the disturbances?

OFFICIAL, OFFICER:

If he's really your son-in-law, we'll be honoured to meet him.

DU BAO:

You've been tricked! Tell the adjutant to arrest the scoundrel, send him by the postal route to Lin'an and put him to jail.

(*Enter Adjutant, shouting assent and tying Liu Mengmei up*)

LIU MENGMEI:

Injustice! Oh, my dear wife!

"Coming to Huai'an for my dear wife,

I, a Confucian scholar, is put up in jail."

(*Exit*)

DU BAO:

You know, my heart breaks as my family breaks in the war. I'm all the more grieved when this vagabond makes all the trouble.

OFFICIAL, OFFICER:

Her Ladyship has been conferred a posthumous title; her name has been recorded in the honourable list. You will have an heir in the future. So don't be grieved. Tell the singing girls to pour the wine.

(*To the previous tune*)

In the south you'll have a better career.

Now that the urgency is over,

Please have a drink with good cheer.

You'll enjoy a long and prosperous life,

And have numerous heirs

When you marry a second wife.

DU BAO:

I've got drunk.

(*Supported by singing girls*)

(*Weeps*)

I shed a hero's tears on beauties' sleeves,

But never for autumns a hero grieves.

ALL:

> As you have defended the motherland,
>
> You'll be welcomed by the musical band.

DU BAO:

I must say farewell to you now. As I'm eager to go to the capital, I must set off at once.

> (*Drums within*)
>
> (*To the tune of* **Coda**)
>
> Tomorrow we'll drink a cup of parting wine.

OFFICIAL, OFFICER:

> We hope to see your portrait in the Hall of Fame.

DU BAO (*Laughs*):

> But only portraits of grey heads are in line.
>
> *When bandits have been conquered in the west,*

OFFICIAL:

> *You go back to the court with flags abreast.*

OFFICER:

> *When wild geese fly across the sunset glow,*

ALL:

> *Quietly flows the Huai with your name impressed.*

Scene Fifty-One
Announcing the Results

> (*Enter two generals of palace guards, carrying the Imperial Squash and Mallet respectively*)

GENERALS:

> *"The dragon and phoenix symbolise the crown,*
>
> *With palace guards patrolling up and down.*
>
> *When results for imperial test are announced,*
>
> *News of triumph spreads in the capital town."*

How do you do! His Majesty is going to give an audience. Let's wait in attendance.

> (*Enter the aged War Minister*)

WAR MINISTER (*To the tune of* **Northern Dianjiangchun**):

> I manage state affairs firm and fast
>
> And raise funds for the border provisions.
>
> Our country will forever last.
>
> (*Enter Miao Shunbin*)

MIAO SHUNBIN:

> The scholars' essays
>
> Sing praise of prosperity unsurpassed.

How do you do! Congratulations on the surrender of Li Quan and his gang. It all owes to your excellent maneuver.

WAR MINISTER:

I'm here to report this to His Majesty. When you fixed the number-one candidate for the imperial examination the other day, His Majesty decreed that the results would be announced when the war ended. It's high time for the announcement.

MIAO SHUNBIN:

I'm here to submit my memorial to His Majesty. Well, here comes an old scholar. Strange, what has he to do here?

> (Enter Chen Zuiliang in shabby clothes, holding a memorial in his hand)

CHEN ZUILIANG:

> "Confucius, far and wide his name rang,
>
> Never met the emperor of his day,
>
> But the emperor of today
>
> Will meet me, Chen Zuiliang."

That's something unusual.

> (Greets Miao Shunbin and War Minister)

Your student Chen Zuiliang pays respect to you.

MIAO SHUNBIN (*Surprised*):

Are you another student who missed the imperial examination?

CHEN ZUILIANG:

No, I'm not. I'm brought here by the War Minister for an audience.

WAR MINISTER:

Oh, he is the student whom Envoy Du sent to appease Li Quan. He's carried Li Quan's petition for surrender with him. That's why I brought him for the audience.

> (Drums within)

VOICE WITHIN (*Solemnly*):

Those who have memorials to His Majesty, come to the royal court!

> (War Minister kneels at the front, with Chen Zuiliang at his heels, and kowtows)

WAR MINISTER:

Your Majesty's War Minister in charge of all forces begs to report with congratulations that Your Majesty's heavenly virtue and earthly power have brought the Huai bandits to submission and halted the Jin troops. Du Bao, Envoy to Huaiyang, has dispatched Chen Zuiliang, student in the official school of Nan'an Prefecture, to report on this and submit Li Quan's petition for surrender. That's all I have to report.

VOICE WITHIN:

Let Chen Zuiliang make a detailed report on Du Bao's appeasement of Li Quan.

WAR MINISTER:

Long live the emperor!

> (Rises to his feet)

CHEN ZUILIANG:

The letter carrier, student Chen Zuiliang, begs to report.

(*To the tune of **Zhuyunfei***)

In the area from Yangtze to Huai,

Plains and mountains lie.

Envoy Du devised

A royal pardon and made him surprised.

Ha,

The bandit Li Quan surrendered at once

And wrote a petition at this good chance.

When the Jin emperor heard about it,

He dared not advance.

He could only reach Luoyang,

And we shall soon defeat him in Bianliang.

VOICE WITHIN:

Wait for the imperial decree outside the palace gate.

CHEN ZUILIANG:

Long live the emperor!

(*Rises to his feet*)

MIAO SHUNBIN (*On his knees*):

Miao Shunbin, Your Majesty's Chief Examiner to the last imperial examination, begs to report.

(*To the previous tune*)

The scholars who took the imperial test

Are waiting for Your Majesty's behest.

Now that war has come to an end,

It's time for scholars to contend.

Ha,

Now that papers have been carefully marked,

It's time to announce the results.

We shall not keep the talented men

Waiting like dragons in the den.

The laurels are waiting for their owners;

The chrysanthemum wine is waiting for the winners.

VOICE WITHIN:

Wait for the imperial decree outside the palace gate.

MIAO SHUNBIN:

Long live the emperor!

(*Rises to his feet and moves aside*)

The results for the imperial examination will be announced today. These poor scholars have waited long enough.

WAR MINISTER (*Sneers*):

By smuggling a pirate's letter, this Mr Chen does not have to wait long.

VOICE WITHIN:

On your knees to listen to the imperial decree: "I am very, very pleased to learn of the appeasement of bandit Li Quan and the withdrawal of the Jin troops. These are the meritorious deeds of Du Bao, whose return to the capital has been made clear in my previous decree. For his eloquence, Chen Zuiliang is appointed Palace Announcer at the palace gate, with due attire of hat and belt. Among all the candidates for this imperial examination, Liu Mengmei has been selected as the Number One Scholar. He will attend the royal banquet, escorted by Imperial Squash and other guards of honour." Give thanks to the imperial decree.

(*All shout "Long live the emperor" and rise to their feet*)

(*Enter attendants with hat and belt*)

ATTENDANTS:

"When a student wins renown,

A purple robe replaces his blue gown."

CHEN ZUILIANG (*Changes clothes*):

Thank you very much, Your Excellencies.

WAR MINISTER, MIAO SHUNBIN:

Congratulations, congratulations to you. Tomorrow we'll have a new announcer at the palace gate to make announcements.

CHEN ZUILIANG:

Where is Liu Mengmei, the Number One Scholar proclaimed in the imperial decree, from?

MIAO SHUNBIN:

He's from Lingnan. His experience is quite unusual.

WAR MINISTER:

How is it unusual?

MIAO SHUNBIN:

When I finished marking the papers the other day and was about to submit the results to His Majesty, this scholar wailed loudly outside the palace gate and begged for a make-up examination. It happened that he missed the examination because he had moved his family to the capital. I included his paper in an appendix to my list and he, out of everybody's expectation, was selected as the Number One Scholar.

WAR MINISTER:

How remarkable!

CHEN ZUILIANG (*Aside, to himself*):

It sounds like that Liu Mengmei I knew! Does he have a "family"? He must have married that old nun!

(*To War Minister and Miao Shunbin*)

To tell you the truth, I knew this Liu Mengmei.

WAR MINISTER, MIAO SHUNBIN:

Another congratulation to you!

MIAO SHUNBIN:

The gilded names of candidates shine bright;

WAR MINISTER:

The border conflict makes a long report.

CHEN ZUILIANG:

> *Don't blame the official for displaying might;*

ALL:

> *He has a high position at the court.*

Scene Fifty-Two
Searching for Liu Mengmei

(*Enter Hunchback Guo, carrying a bundle and an umbrella*)

HUNCHBACK GUO (*To the tune of* **Wuxiaosi**):

> Ninety thousand *li* by air
>
> Or three thousand *li* by land is by no means near.
>
> A month's journey
>
> Takes me half a year.
>
> The bundle of lousy clothes weighs on me
>
> And makes my body awry;
>
> I crawl like a turtle to the sky.

Thank heavens, I've reached Lin'an at last. The capital is full of hustle and bustle. As I don't know where Mr Liu is, I'll try to look for him in the main street. Well, here comes a troop of dirty soldiers. I'd better step out of their way. As the saying goes,

> *"But for the fisherman to lead the way,*
>
> *How can I see the billows in the bay?"*

(*Exit*)

(*Enter two sergeants, with flags and gongs*)

SERGEANTS (*To the tune of* **Liuyaoling**):

> We've put posters on every gate,
>
> But where's the Number One Scholar Liu Mengmei?
>
> He can't be a rebel sneaking away.
>
> We go from door to door
>
> Without delay,
>
> Lest he miss the honourable day.

SERGEANT A:

How funny it is! How funny it is! Something strange has happened in our country. Isn't it unbelievable that the Number One Scholar makes light of his career! Isn't it incredible that the Number One Scholar brings so much trouble! Isn't it unthinkable that the Number One Scholar walks away without notice! Isn't it inconceivable that the Number One Scholar disappears like a coil of smoke! Men from Lingnan are the oddity of oddities. Just look at the placard. It reads, "Wanted: Liu Mengmei, the Number One Scholar by imperial decree, born in Lingnan, aged twenty-seven, of middle height, with a pale face."

The descriptions are clear, but the man is nowhere to be found! Has he gone home, or passed away, or gone to sleep? He'll miss the palace banquet for him.

SERGEANT B:

Brother, how can we pick him out in an ocean of people? Why don't we grab a Confucian scholar and bring him to the banquet? If the real person shows up, we'll pay him for the banquet he missed.

SERGEANT A:

That won't do. It will do to find a substitute for a banquet of our Palace Guards, but it won't do to find a substitute for a banquet of scholars. The Number One Scholar will have to compose a poem in the palace.

SERGEANT B:

Brother, how many Number One Scholars are heard of composing impromptu poems? Well, I'll do as you like and continue to call out.

> (*Walks and calls out*)

Where're you, Number One Scholar Liu Mengmei?

> (*Calls out three times*)

SERGEANT A:

No one answers at the twelve city gates and through all the main streets. Let's call out in the side lanes.

SERGEANT B:

There's a Hainan Regional Guild in Sumu Lane. Let's ask the community chief.

> (*Calls out*)

COMMUNITY CHIEF'S VOICE WITHIN:

What can I do for you, sirs?

SERGEANTS:

An earth-shaking event has happened and you are still sleeping! Now listen,

> (*To the tune of **Xiangliuniang***)
>
> We ask you about the new Number One Scholar;
>
> We ask you about the new Number One Scholar.

COMMUNITY CHIEF'S VOICE WITHIN:

Where's he from?

SERGEANTS:

> He's from Guangnan.

COMMUNITY CHIEF'S VOICE WITHIN:

What's his name?

SERGEANTS:

> Liu Mengmei with a pale face without spots.

COMMUNITY CHIEF'S VOICE WITHIN:

Who's searching for him?

SERGEANTS:

> The present emperor;
>
> The present emperor.

When the man is found,

The palace banquet will be held.

COMMUNITY CHIEF'S VOICE WITHIN:

The man of your description is nowhere to be found around here, but there's a southerner staying in Sister Wang's place in the marketplace.

SERGEANTS:

Well, let's go, let's go.

Ah Liu Mengmei,

Ah Liu Mengmei!

We've searched several rounds,

But he's nowhere to be found.

(*Exeunt*)

(*Enter Sister Wang, a harlot*)

SISTER WANG:

"Why doesn't a harlot know of her age?

She only grieves o'er flowing rivers in her cage.

While gorge by gorge the river flows down,

She mistakes Hangzhou for the capital town."

I'm Sister Wang, opening a little brothel here. Oh heavens, there's not a visitor today, but here come two sergeants.

(*Enter the two sergeants*)

SERGEANTS:

Congratulations, Sister Wang. The Number One Scholar Liu is in your house.

SISTER WANG:

What Number One Scholar Liu?

SERGEANTS:

A southerner.

SISTER WANG:

I don't know him.

SERGEANTS:

The community chief gives the information.

(*To the previous tune*)

A scholar sleeps with a flower of a girl;

A scholar sleeps with a flower of a girl.

SISTER WANG:

A visitor came yesterday and he went off before he got his pants on.

SERGEANTS:

Well said, well said,

The man slipped off from your bed!

Is the Number One Scholar in?

SISTER WANG:

I've only got a scalar.

SERGEANT B:

Let's go and get the scalar.

> (*The sergeants go into the house and search, molesting*)
>
> (*Exit Sister Wang, running away when she is molested by the sergeants*)

SERGEANTS:

> We seek for the amorous Number One Scholar;
>
> We seek for the amorous Number One Scholar.
>
> He's on which pillow
>
> To idle away his sorrow?

Let's go.

> Ah Liu Mengmei,
>
> Ah Liu Mengmei!
>
> We've searched several rounds,
>
> But he's nowhere to be found.
>
> (*Exeunt*)
>
> (*Enter Hunchback Guo, leaning on a stick*)

HUNCHBACK GUO (*To the previous tune*):

> Here I am in the capital;
>
> Here I am in the capital.
>
> It's a city for the elite,
>
> With marketplaces and crowded streets.

Oh, Mr Liu,

> You've left no trace;
>
> You've left no trace.
>
> With a pretty wife on your side,
>
> Where on earth will you hide?

I've no way out than walking on the streets.

> Ah Liu Mengmei!
>
> (*Enter the two sergeants*)

SERGEANTS:

> Ah Liu Mengmei!
>
> We've searched several rounds,
>
> But he's nowhere to be found.

HUNCHBACK GUO (*Yells when Sergeant B bumps into him*):

You're killing me! You're killing me!

SERGEANT B (*Catches hold of Hunchback Guo*):

We're calling Liu Mengmei and you're also calling Liu Mengmei. We'll put you in jail!

HUNCHBACK GUO (*Kowtows*):

Oh, I see. It must be for the Plum Blossom Nunnery affairs. I know nothing about it.

SERGEANTS (*Laugh*):

You must know something! What's your relationship with him?

HUNCHBACK GUO:

I'll tell you everything.

>(*To the previous tune*)
>
>> I tended the garden for him;
>>
>> I tended the garden for him.
>>
>> I've walked all the way to see him.

SERGEANTS (*Anxious to know*):

Have you found him?

HUNCHBACK GUO:

> There's nowhere to find him.

SERGEANTS:

You must know his whereabouts.

HUNCHBACK GUO:

Pity on me. I only know that he's been to Nan'an.

SERGEANTS:

Funny, funny indeed! He's been here in Lin'an to enter the imperial examination and has become the Number One Scholar.

HUNCHBACK GUO (*Surprised and overjoyed*):

> He's become the Number One Scholar;
>
> He's become the Number One Scholar.
>
> He came from the vegetable garden
>
> To make his way to the royal garden.

Now that he's the Number One Scholar, he can't get lost!

SERGEANTS:

We agree.

HUNCHBACK GUO, SERGEANTS:

> Ah Liu Mengmei,
>
> Ah Liu Mengmei!
>
> We've searched several rounds,
>
> But he's nowhere to be found.

SERGEANTS:

Well, we'll spare you this time but you'll search for him with us.

SERGEANT A:

> *After he won the imperial test,*

SERGEANT B:

> *He lets the honour slip out of his hand.*

HUNCHBACK GUO:

> *Along the road of dust and sand,*

SERGEANTS, HUNCHBACK GUO:

> *Where can he be in this strange land?*

Scene Fifty-Three
Interrogating Liu Mengmei

(*Enter Liu Mengmei*)

LIU MENGMEI (*To the tune of* **Fengrusongman**):

> I'm jailed for not a single reason at all;
>
> Is this due treatment for a son-in-law?
>
> All I've got is a bowl of porridge
>
> And a mattress of straw.

Oh heavens!

> All the way I've come
>
> To see my father-in-law,
>
> But who knows that he should put to jail
>
> His very son-in-law!
>
> *"To be detained here in a foreign place,*
>
> *A gentleman must learn to bear disgrace.*
>
> *If my father-in-law acts like this,*
>
> *Who else would understand the case?"*

I, Liu Mengmei, followed Miss Du's words to go to Huaiyang and meet Envoy Du. I was sent to jail in Lin'an, because he was not willing to accept me as his son-in-law before his subordinates. I think that he will have to accept me when he comes to question me and sees the self-portrait of his daughter. For the time being, however, I'm in a wretched situation.

(*Enter the warden, followed by a jailer holding a rod in his hand*)

WARDEN:

> *"When you have the prison god in sight,*
>
> *You'll know the warden's might."*

Well, where's the prisoner from Huai'an?

(*On hearing these words, Liu Mengmei raises his hands*)

What do you have for a gift for our first meeting?

LIU MENGMEI:

I've got nothing to give you.

JAILER:

What about your entrance fee?

LIU MENGMEI:

I've got nothing to give you, either.

WARDEN (*Annoyed*):

Then, how do you dare to raise your hands when you've got nothing for us!

(*Beats Liu Mengmei*)

LIU MENGMEI:

Oh, please don't! You can take whatever you find in my bundle!

JAILER (*Searches Liu Mengmei's bundle*):

What a wretched devil! He's only got a torn bed-sheet and a small scroll of painting.

(*Looks at the portrait*)

It's a portrait of Bodhisattva Guanyin. I'll give it to my grandma.

LIU MENGMEI:

Take everything except the scroll.

(*The jailer tries to grab the scroll from Liu Mengmei's hands*)

(*Enter the bailiff*)

BAILIFF:

"The son-in-law is put in jail,

Where he suffers from blackmail."

Where's the warden?

JAILER (*Bows his salutation*):

So you're from the Grand Chancellor's office.

BAILIFF (*Shows the warrant*):

Orders from the Grand Chancellor to fetch a prisoner for interrogation. He'll bring all his belongings with him.

JAILER:

The prisoner's here, but he's got no belongings.

LIU MENGMEI:

He's taken away everything.

BAILIFF:

What did he take? I'll bring the jailers to the Grand Chancellor's office.

WARDEN, JAILER (*Kowtow in panic*):

All he's got is a scroll of painting and a bed-sheet.

BAILIFF:

Give them back to the scholar, you dirty dogs, and bring him to the Grand Chancellor's office.

WARDEN, JAILER (*Respond and escort Liu Mengmei*):

Will you start moving, sir?

"If you learn the Confucian rites with awe,

You will not violate the law."

(*Exeunt all*)

(*Enter Du Bao, followed by attendants*)

DU BAO (*To the tune of **Tangduoling***):

In a crimson robe girdled by a belt of jade,

I'm promoted to serve in the court.

Standing with a sword of shining blade,

Now I take the Grand Chancellor's post,

But my hair has greyed.

"Now that I've quelled the autumn strife,

I'm thus promoted to the highest post.

When I look back at my eventful life,

I've suffered more than I can boast."

I'm Du Bao, the Grand Chancellor. As I've quelled the bandits in Huaiyang, I've been promoted by His Majesty to the position of Grand Chancellor. But a vagabond came the other day and pretended to be my son-in-law, and so I had him put in jail in Lin'an. Today I'm going to interrogate him.

(*Enter Liu Mengmei, escorted by the warden and the jailer*)

DOORMAN (*Announces*):

Here comes the prisoner from the Lin'an Prefecture!

LIU MENGMEI (*Bows*):

My respect to you, father-in-law.

(*Du Bao remains seated and laughs*)

Man should put courtesy and music in the first place.

(*Sighs when attendants shout at him*)

(*To the tune of **Xinshuiling***)

A scholar has to learn more

When he enters a noble house

And faces the deafening roar.

However I bowed,

However I showed courtesy,

He sat motionless and proud.

DU BAO:

Wretched pedant, what do you think you are? As an offender of the law, why aren't you on your knees before me?

LIU MENGMEI:

I'm Liu Mengmei, a scholar from Lingnan. I'm your son-in-law!

DU BAO:

My daughter has been dead for three years. She had neither accepted betrothal gifts, nor been engaged before her birth or in her childhood. How can I have a son-in-law? How ridiculous! How disgraceful! Attendants, have him tightly bound!

LIU MENGMEI:

Who dares to bind me!

DU BAO (*To the tune of **Bubujiao***):

I have no son, but have a daughter,

Who died young.

How can I believe your wagging tongue?

You cannot even wed my distant niece —

As you come from Lingnan

While I come from Sichuan,

We are so far away

That you cannot meet anyone from my clan.

You go begging here and there;

By claiming to be my relative,

    You're trying to stir up some smoke in the air.

LIU MENGMEI:

As your son-in-law, I study hard day and night, summer and winter, so that I can rank high in the imperial examination. As I'm talented enough to sustain myself, why should I beg from you?

DU BAO:

How dare you talk back! Now search his bundle to see whether he has some forged letters or seals. These evidences will be enough to put him in jail.

JAILER (*Unwraps the bundle*):

He's got a torn bed-sheet and a portrait of Bodhisattva Guanyin.

DU BAO (*Astonished to see the portrait*):

Now I've got you at last! This is my daughter's self-portrait. Did you go to Nan'an and meet Sister Stone?

LIU MENGMEI:

Yes, I did.

DU BAO:

Did you meet Tutor Chen?

LIU MENGMEI:

Yes, I did.

DU BAO:

Oh, the heaven is like an enormous net and its meshes allow no escape. So it's you who robbed the grave! Attendants, take him away and give him a sound flogging!

LIU MENGMEI:

Who dares to beat me!

DU BAO:

Then make confessions, you wretched thief!

LIU MENGMEI:

Whom are you calling a thief? You should catch the thief red-handed and catch the lovers in bed.

    (*To the tune of* **Zheguiling**)

    You take the portrait as the evidence.

DU BAO:

The portrait was buried in my daughter's grave.

LIU MENGMEI:

    Don't you know that rocks might crack

    And reveal the portrait at the back?

DU BAO:

Make confessions at once!

LIU MENGMEI:

    This is all I have to say —

    I opened the grave to save your daughter,

But I myself have fallen prey.

DU BAO:

There was also a jade fish and a gold bowl buried in the grave.

LIU MENGMEI:

The gold bowl is

    For man and wife to share;

The jade fish is

    To swim with me as a pair.

DU BAO:

Did you get anything else?

LIU MENGMEI:

    A roller made of jade

    And a lock made of gold.

DU BAO:

Sister Stone is to blame.

LIU MENGMEI:

    Sister Stone let the lovers go without grief

    While Your Excellency makes much ado about a thief.

DU BAO:

As he's made his confession, secretary, take a piece of official paper and write on it his confession and the verdict: "The criminal Liu Mengmei is sentenced to death because he opened the coffin and robbed its contents." When the document is completed, let the criminal sign his name under the word "death" and then keep the document in the files.

    (*Enter the secretary with a piece of official paper*)

SECRETARY:

Would Your Excellency indict the sentence here?

    (*Du Bao writes. The secretary forces Liu Mengmei to sign. Liu Mengmei refuses*)

DU BAO:

The thief is asking for a sound beating.

    (*To the tune of **Jiang'ershui***)

    You're born with eyes of a thief,

    Doing evils without grief.

Do you still refuse to sign?

LIU MENGMEI:

I've never done anything wrong.

DU BAO:

    With ink and paper you should confess.

LIU MENGMEI:

I've committed neither theft nor adultery.

DU BAO:

    You've committed theft and adultery to excess.

LIU MENGMEI:

What I did was for your daughter's sake.

DU BAO:

> Deceit and trickery are in your veins.

LIU MENGMEI:

Your daughter is now ...

DU BAO:

> You scattered my daughter's remains.

LIU MENGMEI:

Where did I scatter her remains?

DU BAO:

> In the garden lake,
>
> Where the chilly waves shiver for her sake.

LIU MENGMEI:

Who's the witness?

DU BAO:

Tutor Chen has told me everything.

LIU MENGMEI:

Only Heaven and Earth know my efforts for Miss Du. How can Tutor Chen know?

> (*To the tune of* **Yan'erluo**)

For Miss Du,

> I worshipped her portrait
>
> And called her name aloud.

For Miss Du,

> I had rendezvous with her
>
> And lived in fear but still avowed.

For Miss Du,

> I burned the sacred incense
>
> And opened up her grave.

For Miss Du,

> I took the quicksilver from her mouth
>
> And revived her from the cave.

For Miss Du,

> I warmed her with my flesh
>
> And made her come back to life.

For Miss Du,

> I gave her a sense of love
>
> And made her my dear wife.

For Miss Du,

> I raised her arms
>
> And stretched them up and down.

For Miss Du,

> I thawed her heart

And made her alive and well.

For Miss Du,

> I saved her life
>
> From the darkest hell.
>
> As a wonder of love,
>
> I have relieved her pain.
>
> Wonder or not,
>
> I've saved her life, but loved in vain.

DU BAO:

What nonsense is he talking about? He must have been haunted by the ghosts. Attendants, fetch the peach canes to flog him and fetch the water to spurt over him.

JAILER (*Goes off stage and enters again with peach canes*):

> "*To drive away the ghost,*
>
> *Grow peach trees for the host.*"

Here are the peach canes.

DU BAO:

Hang him up and flog him!

> (*The attendants hang Liu Mengmei up and flog him. As Liu Mengmei cries and twists in pain, the attendants mimic a show of dispelling the ghost and spurting the water*)
>
> (*Enter Hunchback Guo, with Sergeants A and B carrying Imperial Squashes*)

SERGEANTS A AND B:

> "*Heaven and Earth are in chaos all around;*
>
> *The Number One Scholar is nowhere to be found.*"

We've been looking for Liu Mengmei all these days. If we can't find him today, we'll give this hunchback a sound beating.

HUNCHBACK GUO:

Am I to blame? I'll buy some wine for you, but let's go on with our search now.

> (*Shouts*)

Where are you, Number One Scholar Liu Mengmei?

> (*Du Bao listens. Hunchback Guo and the sergeants go on with their shouting when they exit. Du Bao asks the jailer*)

JAILER:

As the Number One Scholar is missing, His Majesty decrees that they search for him by shouting along the streets.

LIU MENGMEI:

Have the results for the imperial examination been announced, sir? Who's the Number One Scholar?

DU BAO (*Annoyed*):

It's none of your business. Attendants, slap his face! Slap his face!

> (*Liu Mengmei protests when the jailer slaps him on the face*)
>
> (*Re-enter Hunchback Guo with Sergeants A and B carrying Imperial Squashes*)

SERGEANTS A AND B:

> *"From the chancellor's house comes a noisy sound,*
>
> *But the Number One Scholar is still nowhere to be found."*

Well, what's the row from the Grand Chancellor's house?

> (*Listen to the row*)

HUNCHBACK GUO:

My master's voice seems to come from within.

> (*Hunchback Guo and the sergeants enter Du Bao's house*)

HUNCHBACK GUO (*Bursts into tears when he sees Liu Mengmei*):

Why do you hang up my master?

LIU MENGMEI:

Help! Help!

HUNCHBACK GUO:

Who has ordered to beat you?

LIU MENGMEI:

The Grand Chancellor.

HUNCHBACK GUO (*Waves his stick to strike at Du Bao*):

I'll risk my life to strike at the Grand Chancellor.

DU BAO (*Irritated*):

Dare you!

SERGEANTS A AND B:

By the imperial decree, we're searching for the Number One Scholar Liu Mengmei.

LIU MENGMEI:

I'm Liu Mengmei, Sir!

> (*When Hunchback Guo goes forward to release Liu Mengmei, Du Bao tries to pull him but*
>
> *stumbles*)

LIU MENGMEI:

Oh, you're Hunchback Guo! How come that you are here?

HUNCHBACK GUO:

I've been looking for you all the way here. I'm overjoyed that you have become the Number One Scholar.

LIU MENGMEI:

Really! Go quickly outside the Qiantang Gate and tell Miss Du about it.

SERGEANTS A AND B:

Since we've found the Number One Scholar, we'll report the news to the Palace Announcer.

> *"Before the imperial audience,*
>
> *He has trouble with the chancellor."*
>
> (*Exeunt Sergeants A and B, and Hunchback Guo*)

DU BAO:

Now that these vagabonds are gone, I'll go on with my interrogation. Attendants, hang up this fellow again.

LIU MENGMEI:

Please listen to me. How can I feign to be the Number One Scholar?

DU BAO:

The Number One Scholar must have his name registered in the list. Can you show me the list?
Attendants, just hang him up and give him a sound flogging!

(*Liu Mengmei protests*)

(*Enter Miao Shunbin, followed by two officers carrying the official head-dress, robe and belt*)

MIAO SHUNBIN:

> "*You may wear out straw shoes and search in vain,*
>
> *But find the man by chance with little pain.*"

Your Excellency, please stop! Here's the list.

(*To the tune of **Jiaojiaofan***)

> As the most successful candidate,
>
> Liu Mengmei is a pillar of the state.

DU BAO:

I'm afraid he's not the right person.

MIAO SHUNBIN:

I'm his examiner myself.

LIU MENGMEI:

Oh, honourable Master Miao! Help me!

MIAO SHUNBIN (*Smiles*):

> You're hanging up a man of high seating
>
> And giving him a sound beating.

That's the whole story, Your Excellency. Officers, release the Number One Scholar at once.

(*Officer B releases Liu Mengmei, who groans with pain*)

MIAO SHUNBIN:

Poor fellow! Poor fellow!

> A scholar suffers from pains
>
> Inflicted with ruthless canes.

LIU MENGMEI:

He's my father-in-law.

MIAO SHUNBIN:

> The father-in-law has put you to ordains.

OFFICER A:

The Number One Scholar has to suffer somehow.

MIAO SHUNBIN:

Forget about it. Now give him the official garments.

DU BAO:

Give him the official garments? Tear up the garments!

(*Tries to tear up the official garments*)

LIU MENGMEI (*To the tune of **Shoujiangnan***):

> You defy royal orders to the excess

If you tear up the official dress.

The first visit by a son-in-law

Should be honoured all the more.

But you won't listen to what I explain

And put me to the cane.

(*Officer A helps Liu Mengmei into his official garments and puts a flower on his robe*)

LIU MENGMEI:

Your Excellency,

Just see what great honour I obtain.

DU BAO:

I'm afraid that he's not the right Liu Mengmei. If he were, he should have waited for the announcement after he took the imperial examination. How is it that he roamed to Huaiyang instead of waiting for the announcement in the capital?

LIU MENGMEI:

You don't know the whole story, Your Excellency. The announcement was postponed because Li Quan started an insurrection. On hearing that you were engaged in the battle against the bandits, your daughter told me to present myself to you, to inform you of her revival and to offer my service to you. My good intentions have been ill returned. Now, will you accept me as your son-in-law?

DU BAO:

I won't!

MIAO SHUNBIN, OFFICERS (*To the tune of* **Yuanlinhao**):

You are to blame

For your contempt for a scholar poorly dressed.

Like elderly men,

You put on airs to a guest.

(*Laugh*)

You have an honourable son-in-law at your behest.

DU BAO:

I regret that I didn't keep him in jail until death sentence for this grave-robber is confirmed.

LIU MENGMEI (*Laughs*):

(*To the tune of* **Gumeijiu**)

You put me in jail

Because I dug your daughter's grave.

As Grand Chancellor,

You can't answer for how you behave.

I thought I would be welcomed in the hall

And would ride through the street,

But instead of good reception,

A rude father-in-law I meet.

When I become a man of esteem,

685

You will bow and scrape

And treat me as an honoured guest —

Only then shall I realise my long-cherished dream.

I must take my leave now, Your Excellency. I'm going to the palace banquet.

(*To the tune of* **Beiwei**)

You nearly murdered the Number One Scholar

By inflicting upon him all the pains.

When I think of the glory I receive today,

I do admire my wife's gifts

And my father-in-law's canes.

(*Exeunt Liu Mengmei, Miao Shunbin and officers*)

DU BAO:

How queer! Queer indeed! Is he a thief or a ghost? Attendant, go and ask the Palace Announcer to come over for consultations.

ATTENDANT:

Yes, I see.

"The Palace Announcer looks like a ghost

While the Number One Scholar looks like a man."

(*Exit*)

(*Enter Chen Zuiliang, as the Palace Announcer*)

CHEN ZUILIANG:

"Now that I serve in the royal court,

I start my service with great joy.

As the emperor gives me food of every sort,

I no longer teach any rustic boy."

I am Chen Zuiliang. I've been appointed Palace Announcer because His Majesty was pleased with the news of victory I brought. I must owe everything to the patronage of Envoy Du, and therefore I'm going to his place to express my gratitude.

(*Re-enter the attendant*)

ATTENDANT (*Greets Chen Zuiliang*):

I'm on my way to invite you. Please wait and I'll report your arrival.

(*Comes in to report. Du Bao and Chen Zuiliang greet each other*)

DU BAO (*Smiles*):

Congratulations! Congratulations to you!

"The former wretched teacher

Has become the Palace Announcer."

CHEN ZUILIANG:

"New favours can hardly be repaid,

But old grief can easily fade."

I've just heard that you are blessed by triple happiness: your promotion to the position of Grand Chancellor, your daughter's revival, and your son-in-law becoming the Number One Scholar.

DU BAO:

You've tutored such a good pupil that she's become a sprite!

CHEN ZUILIANG:

Why don't you accept what she is?

DU BAO:

You are wrong. For witchcraft like this, a minister must report it to His Majesty and have it exterminated.

CHEN ZUILIANG:

If that's your intention, shall I report to His Majesty at once and ask for his decree?

DU BAO:

That suits me very well.

A monster listens when I read at night;

CHEN ZUILIANG:

It is ill clouds that blur the starry sight.

DU BAO:

Who is able to judge the human affairs?

CHEN ZUILIANG:

The sacred mirror overhead shines bright.

Scene Fifty-Four
Learning the Good News

(Enter Chunxiang)

CHUNXIANG (*To the tune of* **Raochiyou**):

> When autumn dew glitters cold,
>
> The parasol leaves fall into the well.
>
> Love's karma rotates Heaven and Hell.

Well, Miss Du died of lovesickness three years ago for a scholar who appeared in her dream. My master and my lady have been grieved over her solitary spirit. Who knows that she's revived and stayed with a poor scholar by the Qiantang River? Now she has been reunited with her mother. It's true indeed that nothing is impossible in the world. Today Miss Du told me to prepare for the embroidery table for her to do some needlework again. And here she comes.

(Enter Du Liniang)

DU LINIANG (*To the tune of* **Raohonglou**):

> At early sunset when autumn was half way through,
>
> The swallows chirped and my sorrow grew.
>
> Since my man sailed away,
>
> In a hotel I've stayed.
>
> I've waited, but seen no carriage in view.

> *"When chilly autumn winds pierce the window,*
> *My husband is still in Yangzhou.*
> *While tears drop on the northern grass,*
> *From my needles southern flowers grow."*

Chunxiang, as soon as I came here with Mr Liu, he entered the imperial examination. Before the announcement was made, an insurrection broke out in Yangzhou. I asked Mr Liu to set off by night and to find out what happened to my parents. To my great joy, I happened to meet my mother here, but I haven't got any news of my father yet. Mr Liu is expected to arrive at any time and I'm sure that his name will be on the top list. I'll make him a new garment for this grand occasion.

CHUNXIANG:

The embroidery table is ready at your disposal.

DU LINIANG (*Cuts out the garment*):

Now that the cutting is done, I'll start sewing.

> (*Sews the garment*)

CHUNXIANG:

Mistress, may I venture to ask what it was like in your dream and in the netherworld?

DU LINIANG (*To the tune of* **Luojiangyuan**):

> A sweet dream in the spring
>
> Became real love in the netherworld.
>
> While two shadows parted in the dream,
>
> We stuck together in the netherworld.

CHUNXIANG:

How did you feel like when you were revived?

DU LINIANG:

> As from a dream I came around,
>
> I looked back and fell to the ground.

CHUNXIANG:

Were there any places of interest in the netherworld?

DU LINIANG:

> There were samsara roads
>
> For perfumed carts,
>
> Amorous rivers for love odes
>
> And nether gates for broken hearts.

CHUNXIANG (*To the previous tune*):

> Your beauty allures the man;
>
> Your passion torments the man.

Mistress,

> While your soul wandered in a dream,
>
> Your mother shed tears like a stream.
>
> Now that your tomb lies in waste,
>
> You build your nest in graceful taste.

I'd like to ask

> How you managed to hide behind the light
>
> And how you bought the wine at night.

I'm afraid when you made love for the first time,

> Your virgin blood must have come in sight.

DU LINIANG:

You silly girl! I seemed to be in a dream when we made love. There is no sense for you to ask such questions. Look, my mother is coming in a hurry.

(Enter Lady Zhen in a hurry)

LADY ZHEN (*To the tune of **Wanxiandeng***):

> There is noise from the street;
>
> It's my daughter they seem to greet.

My child, from what I've heard from the street, I can gather that the latest Number One Scholar is Liu Mengmei from Lingnan.

DU LINIANG:

Is that so?

(Enter Sister Stone in quick steps)

SISTER STONE (*To the previous tune*):

> Holding flags amid the roar;
>
> Who are the messengers
>
> That approach our door?

(Greets Lady Zhen and Du Liniang)

Madam and Mistress, the imperial messengers are coming. I'll go and wait at the door.

(Exit)

(Enter two sergeants, with imperial flags)

SERGEANTS (*To the tune of **Ruzhuan***):

> Among the shabby houses in the narrow lane,
>
> We look for the scholar's home in vain.

This might be the one.

(Knock at the door)

LADY ZHEN:

> Terrified by the deafening roar,
>
> I'll peep through the door.

(Opens the door. The sergeants burst in)

Which office are you from?

SERGEANTS:

> We come here as quick as can be.
>
> Look at the flags,
>
> Look at the supreme flags.
>
> The Palace Announcer sends us to pass the decree.

LADY ZHEN (*Calls aloud*):

My child, they've come to pass the imperial decree.

DU LINIANG (*Steps forward*):

> May I venture to ask
>
> When the results will be announced?
>
> Is Liu Mengmei on top of the list?

SERGEANTS:

He's the Number One Scholar.

DU LINIANG:

Is that so?

SERGEANTS:

> Although he's on top of the list,
>
> His misdemeanor can hardly be dismissed.

DU LINIANG (*Taken aback*):

What happened to him?

SERGEANTS:

> In Huaiyang he offended Lord Du
>
> As grave-robbing was a taboo.

LADY ZHEN:

Thank heavens, my child! Your father has arrived in the capital safe and sound. Of course he won't believe that you're revived.

DU LINIANG:

What happened to him next?

SERGEANTS:

> When the flogging was not yet complete,
>
> He was rescued and paraded through the street.

DU LINIANG:

So he was rescued at the right time.

SERGEANTS:

But the Grand Chancellor was in a position to submit a memorial to His Majesty, saying that a grave-robber was not entitled to be the Number One Scholar.

DU LINIANG:

Did the Number One Scholar submit a memorial to defend himself?

SERGEANTS:

Yes, he did.

> The Grand Chancellor accused him of robbing the grave;
>
> The Number One Scholar argued that he was brave.
>
> His Majesty did not know how to behave.

DU LINIANG:

And then?

SERGEANTS:

It happened that the Palace Announcer, Mr Chen, was an old friend of the Grand Chancellor. He suggested that the Grand Chancellor, the Number One Scholar and you, Miss Du, appear before the throne at the same time so that His Majesty might make his judgement.

LADY ZHEN:

Well, who is that Palace Announcer Chen?

SERGEANTS:

>His name is Chen Zuiliang,
>
>Who said that he once taught in Nan'an.

Therefore,

>The Grand Chancellor recommended him
>
>To be the Palace Announcer.

LADY ZHEN:

Amazing indeed!

SERGEANTS:

It's him who sent us to bring you the imperial decree. Miss Du is to make up at the first watch-beat, have breakfast at the second watch-beat, get dressed at the third watch-beat and set out at the fourth watch-beat.

>Till the fifth watch-beat you'll wait
>
>And in tinkling ornaments,
>
>You'll enter the palace gate.

DU LINIANG:

I'm afraid to go alone.

SERGEANTS:

What is there to be afraid of?

>You're the daughter of the Grand Chancellor
>
>And wife of the Number One Scholar.

We'll be leaving now.

DU LINIANG:

Tell me something more before you leave.

SERGEANTS:

>Tomorrow at the court,
>
>Please give us tips of some sort.
>
>(*Exeunt*)

DU LINIANG:

Mom, Dad has been promoted and Mr Liu has become the Number One Scholar.

>The sergeants have brought the good news
>
>Of their safety and success.
>
>Let's thank heavens!
>
>Let's thank heavens!
>
>(*They kowtow*)

DU LINIANG (*To the tune of* **Diliuzi**):

>Years ago,
>
>Years ago we got acquainted at the plum and willow;
>
>Outside the nether gate,
>
>Outside the nether gate my soul met my mate.

My dream came true

At the garden behind our house.

In this way finally comes the day

For the success of my spouse.

The match in the netherworld

Awaits the judge of human world.

LADY ZHEN (*To the previous tune*):

Although we say,

Although we say things have gone astray,

Is there any need,

Is there any need for imperial decrees indeed?

You are thought

To be disturbed in your cave

While Liu Mengmei is thought

To have robbed a grave.

But your father

Has no magic powers

To summon the god of flowers.

(*To the tune of* **Coda**)

My child,

Get prepared to present yourself at court.

DU LINIANG:

What shall I say to His Majesty?

LADY ZHEN:

Your presence alone will clarify the day;

DU LINIANG:

His Majesty will listen to what I have to say.

(*Enter Hunchback Guo*)

HUNCHBACK GUO:

"*To find the turtle's cave,*

You have to cross the magpies' bridge."

I've looked for the Qiantang Gate for two days, but in vain. I was lucky enough to meet an old sergeant, who told me Miss Du's address. Now I'll venture to enter her house.

(*Greets Lady Zhen and Du Liniang*)

LADY ZHEN:

Who are you?

HUNCHBACK GUO:

I'm Hunchback Guo, serving in the Number One Scholar's house. I've come to offer my congratulations.

DU LINIANG:

Thank you for your congratulations. Have you seen the Number One Scholar?

HUNCHBACK GUO:

It was I who rescued him in the Grand Chancellor's office. He sent me to bring you to the palace.

LADY ZHEN:

The bygone dreams will come to light;

DU LINIANG:

Today the sky appears to be so bright.

HUNCHBACK GUO:

To gratify the deep love of the sprite,

DU LINIANG:

I'll see His Majesty in all his might.

Scene Fifty-Five
Happy Reunion at Court

(*Enter two generals of palace guards, carrying the Imperial Squashes*)

GENERALS:

"The sun and moon set forth Heaven's feat;

The hills and rills consolidate the royal seat."

When His Majesty gives an audience, we stand on duty here.

(*Enter Chen Zuiliang*)

CHEN ZUILIANG (*To the tune of* **Northern Dianjiangchun**):

The palace towers above the clouds

And incense coils to the skies.

Eternal peace blesses the crowds.

(*Turns to the throne and kowtows*)

When the sun shines over the stairs,

I kowtow and then rise.

"When phoenix banners flap in the morning breeze,

His Majesty issues his decrees.

In order to sweep away the monstrous airs,

He relies on gods and ghosts to appease."

I'm old Chen Zuiliang, newly-appointed Palace Announcer in the Great Song Dynasty. I was a learned scholar in the Nan'an Prefecture. As Liu Mengmei robbed Miss Du's grave, I brought the news to Yangzhou. For old times' sake, the Grand Chancellor sent me to appease the bandit Li Quan. When I completed my task, I was assigned the position of Palace Announcer. It happened that on his way to the capital, the Grand Chancellor received a visit by Liu Mengmei, who was arrested at once and sent to prison in Lin'an. The story was that Mr Liu had entered the imperial examination and was selected as

The Peony Pavilion

693

the Number One Scholar. When people were looking for him, he was being flogged and interrogated in Lord Du's office. The sergeants broke into the office to rescue him and carried him away on horseback. That was part of the story. It was said that my pupil Miss Du was revived and took up residence in the capital. To his greater annoyance, the Grand Chancellor heard that his daughter had become a wanton sprite. He told me to write a memorial to His Majesty for the extermination of evil spirits. Liu Mengmei was accused of grave-robbing and releasing an evil sprite which took on the name of his daughter; therefore, Liu Mengmei must be executed at once. Lord Du's memorial was justified, but Mr Liu also sent in a memorial in his own defence. There came the imperial decree, saying, "Due to the unusual mysticism as narrated in your memorials, the revived girl must appear in an audience so that I can make the final judgement." As I was afraid that Miss Du had indeed revived, I privately sent two sergeants to tell her of the imperial decree for her to appear before the throne at the fifth watch-beat tomorrow morning. As the saying goes,

> *"The past and present are shown on the Eternal Rock;*
> *Truth and falsehood are judged at the imperial court."*

Before I can finish my monologue, here come the Grand Chancellor and the Number One Scholar.

(*Enter Du Bao and Liu Mengmei, dressed in official hats and robes, each holding a memorial tablet*)

DU BAO (*To the previous tune*):

I hate to face confrontation at court

For no apparent reason at all.

It's a case of peculiar sort.

LIU MENGMEI:

To solve the riddle,

I wait for His Majesty's call.

My respect to you, father-in-law!

DU BAO:

None of your father-in-laws here!

LIU MENGMEI:

My respect to you, Grand Chancellor!

DU BAO:

None of your Grand Chancellors here!

LIU MENGMEI (*Laughs*):

As an old poem goes,

> *"When snow and plum blossom vie to win spring grace,*
> *The poet lays down his pen to settle the case."*

When I defend myself today, you'll have to lay down your pen.

DU BAO:

You are a criminal, but you are still playing with words now.

LIU MENGMEI:

What am I guilty of? In fact you are a criminal.

DU BAO:

I've done meritorious deeds for the country by quelling the bandit Li Quan. What am I guilty of?

LIU MENGMEI:

The court is unaware of the fact that you haven't quelled Li Quan, but quelled his better half.

DU BAO:

What do you mean by saying that?

LIU MENGMEI (*Sneers*):

You have tricked his wife into withdrawing the troops. This is not a complete victory.

DU BAO (*Grasps at Liu Mengmei in annoyance*):

Who told you that? Let's argue before the throne.

CHEN ZUILIANG (*Rushes toward Du Bao and Liu Mengmei*):

Who's making such a roar outside the royal palace?

(*Greets Du Bao and Liu Mengmei*)

Oh, it's Lord Du. This is the new Number One Scholar. Please let him off! Please let him off!

(*Du Bao lets off Liu Mengmei*)

How is it that he has offended you?

DU BAO:

He calls me a criminal. What am I guilty of?

LIU MENGMEI:

How can you say that you are not guilty? You have at least committed three errors concerning your daughter.

DU BAO:

What are the errors?

LIU MENGMEI:

First, as a prefect, you allowed your daughter to go on a spring stroll.

DU BAO:

That's true.

LIU MENGMEI:

Second, after your daughter died, you didn't send her remains to her native town to be buried in your ancestral cemetery, but set up a private nunnery instead.

DU BAO:

There's something in what you said.

LIU MENGMEI:

Third, in addition to dispelling your son-in-law because he is poor, you put a Number One Scholar to tortures.

CHEN ZUILIANG (*Laughs*):

Mr Liu, you have your errors to blame too. Just listen to me and make peace between you.

LIU MENGMEI:

What have I to do with you?

CHEN ZUILIANG (*Laughs*):

Probably you don't know that I used to be your wife's tutor.

LIU MENGMEI:

Are you a tutor for the ghosts?

CHEN ZUILIANG:

Have you forgotten your old friend, Mr Liu?

LIU MENGMEI (*Recognises Chen Zuiliang*):

Are you Tutor Chen from Nan'an?

CHEN ZUILIANG:

That's me! That's me!

LIU MENGMEI:

Oh, Mr Chen, we were on good terms, but why did you say that I was a robber? You didn't tell the truth when you were a tutor, and I'm afraid you will not tell the truth now that you become the Palace Announcer.

CHEN ZUILIANG (*Laughs*):

I'm telling the truth today. I see Miss Du approaching in the distance. Both of you, kowtow to His Majesty first.

VOICE WITHIN (*Solemnly*):

Those who want to make reports, stand in your places.

696

    (*Du Bao and Liu Mengmei kowtow*)

DU BAO:

Your Majesty's humble servant Du Bao kowtows.

LIU MENGMEI:

Your Majesty's humble servant Liu Mengmei kowtows.

CHEN ZUILIANG:

Rise to your feet.

    (*Du Bao and Liu Mengmei stand on separate sides*)

    (*Enter Du Liniang*)

DU LINIANG:

    "*Du Liniang, once a ghost,*

    Will have His Majesty as her host."

    (*To the tune of* **Huangzhong** *with* **Northern Zuihuayin**)

    Inside the palace with glazed tiles,

    The ceremonial whip calls for silence.

GENERALS (*Shout*):

Who is that woman stepping on the palace stairs? Have her arrested!

DU LINIANG (*Frightened*):

    The ugly guards

    Are shouting at me.

In the netherworld,

    The fierce demons

    Are not so frightening to see.

CHEN ZUILIANG:

Is my pupil Miss Du coming?

DU LINIANG:

The Palace Announcer coming to me seems to be Tutor Chen. Let me call out to him —
Tutor Chen! Tutor Chen!

CHEN ZUILIANG (*Responds*):

Here I am.

DU LINIANG:

Congratulations to you, Tutor Chen!

CHEN ZUILIANG:

Miss Du, since you are a ghost, I'm afraid you'll give a shock to His Majesty.

DU LINIANG:

None of your nonsense!

> Don't say that I've just come back to life;
>
> Here I am as Number One Scholar's wife.
>
> (*Exeunt the two generals*)

VOICE WITHIN:

Kowtow to His Majesty!

DU LINIANG (*Kowtows*):

Long live the emperor! Long live the emperor!

VOICE WITHIN:

Rise to your feet.

> (*Du Liniang rises to her feet*)

Now listen to the imperial decree: Du Bao and Liu Mengmei, step forward to see whether
this is the genuine Du Liniang.

LIU MENGMEI (*Gazes at Du Liniang and shows signs of woe*):

Oh Liniang, my dear wife!

DU BAO (*Gazes at Du Liniang and shows signs of annoyance*):

The ghost looks exactly like my late daughter. Sheer witchcraft! Sheer witchcraft!

> (*Turns back to face the throne and makes his report*)

Your humble servant Du Bao begs to report. My daughter died three years ago, but this
woman looks exactly like her. It must be a flower sprite or a fox sprite assuming the
human form. This is what I have to say:

> (*To the tune of **Southern Huameixu***)
>
> As my daughter has been dead for years,
>
> How can she come back to life again?
>
> If you strike her with a cane,
>
> Her demonic form soon appears.

LIU MENGMEI (*Weeps*):

What a stone-hearted father!

> (*Kowtows to the emperor and makes his report*)
>
> As her father, he pretends to be stern;

The Peony Pavilion

It's a good fame he wants to earn.

(*Rises to his feet*)

DU BAO, LIU MENGMEI:

Neither nether nor human judge can settle the case;

Only Your Majesty will decide with grace.

VOICE WITHIN:

Now listen to the imperial decree: "I've heard that men cast shadows while ghosts dread the mirrors. On the Timekeeping Platform there is a Penetrating Mirror from the Qin Dynasty. Palace Announcer, bring Du Liniang to the mirror and then take her along the flower tracks to see whether she leaves a shadow. When you've followed my instructions, report the results to me."

CHEN ZUILIANG (*Assents and then leads Du Liniang to the mirror*):

Are you a human being or a ghost, Miss Du?

DU LINIANG (*To the tune of **Northern Xiqianying***):

How can I say whether I am a ghost?

The mirror will soon tell the truth.

CHEN ZUILIANG:

As you have your exact image in the mirror, you prove to be a human being. Now let's go along the flower tracks and see if you cast a shadow. Then I'll report the results to His Majesty.

698

(*Walks and inspects her shadow*)

DU LINIANG:

Oh, dear me!

Along the flower tracks,

I leave my footprints to see.

CHEN ZUILIANG (*Reports to the emperor*):

Du Liniang has an image and a shadow, therefore she is a human being.

VOICE WITHIN:

Now listen to the imperial decree: "Du Liniang, as you are human, tell me your experience of death and revival."

DU LINIANG:

Your Majesty, I drew a self-portrait when I was sixteen years old. I once saw in my dream a scholar beside a plum tree beyond the willow trees. After I died of lovesickness for him, I was buried under a plum tree in the back garden. It happened that a scholar by the name of Liu Mengmei found my self-portrait and kept yearning for me day and night. That's why I came back to this world and married him.

(*Sadly*)

Oh how sad!

My revival after death

Implied all the mishaps I had.

VOICE WITHIN:

Now listen to the imperial decree: "Liu Mengmei, come forward and testify whether Du Liniang has told the truth. Why are you named Mengmei, which literally means 'dreaming of plums'?"

LIU MENGMEI (*Bows*):

Long live the emperor!

> (*To the tune of **Southern Huameixu***)
>
> When I sought marriage across the southern sea,
>
> I met a girl by the plum tree when the dream began.
>
> On my way to take the imperial exam,
>
> I fell ill and was detained in Nan'an.

As a result, I stayed at the Plum Blossom Nunnery in the Nan'an Prefecture. When I took a stroll in the back garden, I found the self-portrait of Du Liniang. Miss Du was so moved by my affection for her that she resumed her human form.

Du Bao (*Kneels*):

He is cheating Your Majesty and slandering my daughter as well. As for my daughter,

> She'd rather sink in the river and lie there
>
> Than have an illicit affair!

DU BAO, LIU MENGMEI:

> Neither nether nor human judge can settle the case;
>
> Only Your Majesty will decide with grace.

VOICE WITHIN:

Now listen to the imperial decree: "As the saying goes, 'Illicit love without the consent of parents and the introduction of matchmakers is despised by the parents and the people all over the country.' Du Liniang, how can you justify yourself?"

DU LINIANG (*Weeps*):

Your Majesty, I owe my second life to Liu Mengmei.

> (*To the tune of **Northern Chuduizi***)
>
> I won't use the word "illicit affair".

DU BAO:

Who was your matchmaker?

DU LINIANG:

> Our matchmaker was the Funeral Star above.

DU BAO:

Who were your wedding attendants?

DU LINIANG:

> They were the netherworld sprites.

DU BAO:

Sheer nonsense!

LIU MENGMEI:

It's a perfect match of Heaven and Hell.

DU BAO:

Perfect! Perfect lies from your scarlet lips!

LIU MENGMEI:

Sir, you are mocking at southerners chewing betel nuts, but I was born with scarlet lips

and white teeth.

DU LINIANG:

No arguments! A daughter alive and kicking is ignored by her father while a ghost for three years was married by Liu Mengmei.

> You cannot revive your daughter;
>
> Why are you reviling at my man?

Dad, if you refuse to accept me, Mom has accepted me.

> (*Points at the entrance*)
>
> The one to persuade you is my mother.
>
> (*Enter Lady Zhen*)

LADY ZHEN:

Why is my daughter kept so long in the palace? I'll enter the palace gate to plead for her.

> (*Steps into the palace and kneels on the ground*)

Your Majesty, the first-rank Lady Zhen, wife of Grand Chancellor Du Bao, presents herself before the throne.

> (*Du Bao and Chen Zuiliang are surprised*)

DU BAO:

Where are you from? You're my wife, aren't you?

> (*Kneels to the emperor*)

I beg to report that my wife died at the hands of the bandits in Yangzhou. I have applied for posthumous honours for her from Your Majesty. The mother and daughter must have been some devilish incarnation to fraud Your Majesty in the broad daylight.

> (*Rises to his feet*)

LIU MENGMEI:

I've never seen this lady before.

VOICE WITHIN:

Now listen to the imperial decree: "Since Lady Zhen has been killed by the bandits, how can she live with her daughter in Lin'an?"

LADY ZHEN:

Your Majesty,

> (*To the tune of **Southern Diliuzi***)
>
> On my way to Yangzhou,
>
> On my way to Yangzhou I encountered the bandits.
>
> I had to,
>
> I had to seek shelter in Lin'an.
>
> One night beside the river Qiantang,
>
> As blood is thicker than water,
>
> I happened to meet the likeness of Liniang.
>
> We have lived together as mother and daughter.

VOICE WITHIN:

According to what you said, your daughter must have been revived. As she lived in the netherworld for three years, she must have learned much about karma. What were the punishments for kings and ministers who neglected their duties? Tell me exactly what you know.

CHEN ZUILIANG:

DU LINIANG:

Better forget about it, but there are indeed many people under punishment.

CHEN ZUILIANG:

My pupil, "Confucius never talked about things grotesque." In the human world the archives of the prefectures and counties are checked from time to time, but how can similar things be done in the netherworld?

DU LINIANG:

Well,

> (*To the tune of* **Northern Guadifeng**)
>
> All the cases are clearly recorded in the netherworld,
>
> With no room for a denying word.
>
> The kings are honoured as of old
>
> While ministers are fettered with jade and gold.

CHEN ZUILIANG:

My pupil, there is no evidence for what you said. If that were the case, would Premier Qin Hui have suffered in the netherworld?

DU LINIANG:

I know something about him. To speak about his sufferings, as soon as he entered the netherworld,

> A hammer crushed his black heart
>
> And a knife cut his liver into three parts.

ALL (*Terrified*):

Why was his liver cut into three parts?

DU LINIANG:

Because he served one part for the Great Song Dynasty, another part for the Jin Dynasty, and a third part for his wife with a wagging tongue.

CHEN ZUILIANG:

What were his wife's sufferings?

DU LINIANG:

To speak about her sufferings, as soon as she entered the netherworld, she was stripped of her coronets and robes until she was naked. An ox-headed sprite jumped forward to clutch at her throat with nails seven or eight inches long.

> Her wagging tongue was torn out by the sprite.

CHEN ZUILIANG:

Why should she suffer so much?

DU LINIANG:

> Because her tricks had come to light.

DU BAO:

Sheer nonsense! Little devil, I'll ask you one question: In the human world there are punishments for elopement. Are there similar punishments in the netherworld?

DU LINIANG:

Yes, there are plenty. Liu Mengmei was flogged seventy strokes, which you administered by yourself, while I was detained in the netherworld for three years.

> Mr Liu was flogged,
>
> Blamed,
>
> And put under arrest
>
> For our love affair.
>
> Why don't you let us go now that we have confessed?

VOICE WITHIN:

Now listen to the imperial decree: "According to what Du Liniang said, she must have been revived. Palace Announcer, take her outside the palace gate so that the parents and daughter, the man and wife can be reunited. When they return home, a formal wedding ceremony should be held."

ALL:

Long live the emperor!

> (*Walk around the stage*)

LADY ZHEN:

My lord, congratulations on your promotions!

DU BAO:

My lady, I didn't expect that you had a narrow escape.

DU LINIANG (*Weeps*):

Dad!

DU BAO (*Ignores Du Liniang*):

You little devil had better stay away from broad daylight. Mr Chen, now I am beginning to suspect that Liu Mengmei is a devil too.

CHEN ZUILIANG (*Laughs*):

He's a devil of a literary star.

LADY ZHEN (*Elated*):

It's a double happiness to meet my Number One Scholar son-in-law and see my revived daughter. Come on, Number One Scholar, greet your mother-in-law first.

LIU MENGMEI (*Makes a bow*):

I'm sorry that I didn't greet you earlier.

DU LINIANG:

Congratulations on your success, Mr Liu.

LIU MENGMEI:

Who told you about it?

DU LINIANG:

Tutor Chen brought me the imperial decree.

LIU MENGMEI:

I was ill-treated by your father.

CHEN ZUILIANG:

Mr Liu, greet your father-in-law.

LIU MENGMEI:

I'd rather have the netherworld king as my father-in-law!

CHEN ZUILIANG:

Listen to me, Mr Liu,

> (*To the tune of* ***Southern Didijin***)
>
> As man and wife you have suffered your share
>
> But the emperor is almighty and fair.
>
> The Grand Chancellor has to marry his daughter.
>
> It's better for mother and daughter,
>
> Father-in-law and son-in-law,
>
> To make a deal then and there.

LIU MENGMEI:

Mr Chen, I'm a convicted robber.

CHEN ZUILIANG (*Laughs*):

You are lucky enough,

> But you still want to take advantage.
>
> When you were expected to win the imperial test,
>
> You stole a flower of a girl lying at rest.

DU LINIANG (*Sighs*):

If you had not allowed me to take a stroll in the back garden, how could I have met this scholar?

DU BAO:

Little devil, since Liu Mengmei is from a family inferior to ours, what is it that makes you love him so much?

DU LINIANG (*Smiles*):

> (*To the tune of* ***Northern Simenzi***)
>
> I love his hat and robe in official style,
>
> And so I smile and smile and smile.

Dad and Mom, in the human world people fail to pick a son-in-law in high position even if they build high platforms to attract wooers; in the netherworld, in my dream, I picked a Number One Scholar. How can you say that his family background is inferior to ours?

> You are from the honoured family of Du
>
> While he is from the honoured family of Liu.

Dad, please accept me as your daughter!

DU BAO:

I'll accept you as my daughter back at home if you do away with Liu Mengmei.

DU LINIANG:

> If you want me to go back to the family of Du
>
> And leave the family of Liu,
>
> All my life I'll weep and hate you.
>
> (*Weeps*)

Alas,

In front of my previous-world father

And present-world mother,

My soul will wander farther.

(*Faints*)

DU BAO (*Taken aback*):

Oh Liniang, my child!

CHEN ZUILIANG (*Looks ahead*):

How does it happen that Sister Stone is coming and Chunxiang is still alive? Ridiculous, ridiculous! What did I see in the bandit camp?

(*Enter Sister Stone with Chunxiang*)

SISTER STONE (*To the tune of* **Southern Baolaocui**):

The case is settled before the throne;

The case is settled before the throne.

(*Looks around*)

How is it that Mr Liu and Miss Du are standing there with pursed lips?

Lord Du makes a judgement of the worst sort;

Tutor Chen makes a speech of the worst sort.

CHEN ZUILIANG:

Here comes Chunxiang! This nun is a robber!

SISTER STONE:

Oops! Beggar Chen, who do you say is a robber? You made the false report that the lady was dead and Chunxiang was dead.

You put them in a paper coffin

And buried them with your tongue.

(*To Liu Mengmei*)

Congratulations, Mr Liu!

LIU MENGMEI:

Congratulations, Sister Stone! But where is it that I once saw this servant maid?

CHUNXIANG:

I was in the dream you and Miss Du experienced.

LIU MENGMEI:

So you're a living witness.

SISTER STONE, CHUNXIANG:

Who knows that ghostly union may turn true!

Who knows that ghostly love may renew!

Lord Du,

Even if you rule over the netherworld,

You will find the case absurd.

(*Exeunt Sister Stone and Chunxiang*)

CHEN ZUILIANG:

In front of the palace gate, both men and ghosts will have to show submission. Miss Du, it's up to you to persuade Mr Liu into greeting his father-in-law for everybody's benefit.

DU LINIANG (*Smiles and tries to persuade Liu Mengmei*):

My dear, just greet your father-in-law with a bow!

> (*Liu Mengmei is reluctant to do so*)

DU LINIANG (*To the tune of* **Northern Shuixianzi**):

> Oh, oh, oh,
>
> You are making a show.
>
> (*Pulls at Liu Mengmei's hand and presses his shoulder*)
>
> Now, now, now,
>
> By pressing your shoulder, I'll force you to bow.

LIU MENGMEI:

I won't forget the flogging!

DU LINIANG:

> Bow, bow, bow,
>
> Ancient kings were flogged anyhow.
>
> (*Pulls at Du Bao*)
>
> Pull, pull, pull,
>
> The father-in-law has to be cool.
>
> (*Points at Liu Mengmei*)
>
> He, he, he,
>
> He burnt paper money to marry me.
>
> I, I, I,
>
> I accepted the offer from this guy.
>
> (*Points at Chen Zuiliang*)
>
> You, you, you,
>
> You have indeed made much ado.
>
> (*Points at Liu Mengmei*)
>
> True, true, true,
>
> You opened my coffin to bring my corpse to view.
>
> (*Points at Du Bao*)
>
> Dad, dad, dad,
>
> Your swearing is indeed bad.
>
> (*Enter Han Zicai in official robe, holding the imperial decree in his hands*)

HAN ZICAI:

Here comes the imperial decree. Kneel and listen: "In regards to the extraordinary story, I hereby decree that the family be reunited. Grand Chancellor Du Bao is promoted to the topmost rank. His wife Lady Zhen is granted the title Lady of Huaiyin Prefecture. The Number One Scholar Liu Mengmei is appointed member of the Imperial Academy. His wife Du Liniang is granted the title Lady of Yanghe County. Master of Ceremony Han Zicai is to accompany them to their residence." Kowtow and thank the imperial grace.

> (*Greets Liu Mengmei*)

Congratulations to you, Number One Scholar.

LIU MENGMEI:

Oh, it's you, Mr Han Zicai! How did you become Master of Ceremony?

HAN ZICAI:

After I saw you off, the prefect showed special favour to me as the descendant of a renowned family by offering financial aid for me to enter the imperial examination in the capital. I passed the examination and was appointed Master of Ceremony. That's why we have the chance to meet here.

LIU MENGMEI:

It's all too fantastic!

CHEN ZUILIANG:

So Mr Han is also an old friend of ours.

> (*Walks around the stage*)

ALL (*To the tune of **Southern Shuangshengzi***):

> How absurd!
>
> How absurd!
>
> The match began with a dream in the netherworld.
>
> How fortunate!
>
> How fortunate!
>
> The wedding takes place in front of the palace gate.
>
> What the emperor has to say,
>
> What the emperor has to say
>
> Makes everybody happy and gay,
>
> Makes everybody happy and gay.
>
> By imperial decree,
>
> From the netherworld Miss Du is set free.

LIU MENGMEI (*To the tune of **Northern Coda***):

From now on,

> We shall enjoy the Peony Pavilion dream.

DU LINIANG:

> Thanks to your tender care,
>
> My ghostly love becomes supreme!
>
> *When verdant grass grows on the vernal sand,*
>
> *The Jin drums resound across the land.*
>
> *The yearning soul regrets to miss her mate;*
>
> *The Peony Pavilion sees her woeful trait.*
>
> *While ladies weep and sigh as blooms decline,*
>
> *Men come and go to drink a cup of wine.*
>
> *All raptures vanish when the curtain falls;*
>
> *From blooming twigs a charming birdsong drawls.*

南柯记
The Nanke Dream

汪榕培、张　玲、霍跃红 译

Translated by Wang Rongpei, Zhang Ling & Huo Yuehong

Table of Contents

Scene One
Reminding the World

(Enter the Narrator)

NARRATOR (*To the tune of **Nankezi***):

> The rain falls on the lake outside the Jade Tea House
>
> And the sun shines over the small Metal Brake Hall.
>
> Don't stop your song nor lower your cup
>
> When you see the heedless ants
>
> Show signs of passion to all.
>
> The country founded in July
>
> Was nothing but a castle in the sky.
>
> Master Qixuan is still preaching.
>
> May I ask the east wind
>
> When I'll wake up from my dream?
>
> *He ranks high in the State of Peaceful Locust,*
>
> *With the princess in his arms.*
>
> *In recording the feats of Nanke Magistrate,*
>
> *The venerable monk will speak the truth.*

Scene Two
Chivalrous Passions

(Enter Chunyu Fen, bearing a sword on his back)

CHUNYU FEN (*To the tune of **Poqizhen***):

> With soaring aspiration,
>
> I stay in Yangzhou although I often dream of home.
>
> I wander here and there,
>
> Sniffing the world,
>
> For the world is blind.
>
> Since childhood, I have been fond of wine,
>
> Never feeling sad for spring sights.
>
> And now in late autumn, I see a locust-tree behind me.
>
> *(In the pattern of **Dielianhua**)*
>
> *"A locust-tree stands in the empty yard,*
>
> *With its leaves ruffling in the autumn wind,*
>
> *Wailing o'er the passage of time.*
>
> *I never wield my precious sword,*

Wandering in Wu and Chu in my prime.
I do not want to live here for long,
For I will stay
Where there is wine and song.
Before my bosom friends arrive,
My sorrow has gone away."

I am Chunyu Fen, a native of Dongping. I am a descendant of Chungyu Kun, a man renowned for drinking deep and making people roar with laughter. A later ancestor the good doctor Chunyu Yi was made the Magistrate of Taichang. He had no sons but his daughter saved him from death. My father is a general in the border areas. He has been there for many years and I don't know whether he's alive or dead. I am skilled in the martial arts and am a man with a generous heart, having spent a thousand ounces of gold at a time. When carousing with good fellows of the rivers and lakes, I have led a nomad's life in the regions of Wu and Chu. Once I served as an assistant general in the Huainan troops and hoped to be promoted in Hebei. Alas, I had the misfortune of getting drunk and thus lost favour with the marshal. Hard times came again and I had to give up my official position. In the yard of my home, ten miles from the Guangling City, is an ancient locust-tree with a stout trunk and luxuriant branches, under which I drink with my fellow drinkers, but they do not turn up very often these days. I only have two bosom friends in Luhe County: one is Zhou Bian, a military candidate and a fellow drinker of mine; the other is Tian Zihua, a recluse and a pen friend of mine. Today is an autumn day in the seventh year of Emperor Dezong of the Tang Dynasty. I shall tell my boy-servant Partridge to get wine ready in the locust-tree yard so as to entertain these two friends. Where is Partridge?

(*Enter Partridge*)

PARTRIDGE:

"I have the legs of a buffalo
And the face of a partridge."

Master, the wine is ready under the locust-tree. The two guests have arrived.

(*Enter Zhou Bian and Tian Zihua*)

ZHOU BIAN, TIAN ZIHUA (*To the tune of* **Daolianzi**):

The flowers are nearing their end

When mountains are bathed in autumn air.

Men should get drunk in Yangzhou, where

We have a drinking friend.

ZHOU BIAN:

I am Zhou Bian from Yingchuan.

TIAN ZIHUA:

I am Tian Zihua from Pingyi.

ZHOU BIAN, TIAN ZIHUA:

As we shall soon return home to Luhe, we must bid farewell to Brother Chunyu.

PARTRIDGE:

My master is waiting for you in the locust-tree yard.

(*Greets Zhou Bian and Tian Zihua*)

(*In the pattern of* **Collected Tang Poems**)

"*The locust-tree bears its root in an ancient city*

In an autumn day when the west wind blows.

Before the gold is all spent,

All day long the wine flows."

CHUNYU FEN:

I feel depressed when guests do not come for days.

ZHOU BIAN, TIAN ZIHUA:

We've come to say good-bye as we shall take a boat home tonight.

CHUNYU FEN:

I feel so depressed now that the two of you are returning home too. Wine is ready. Let us raise a glass or two in the locust-tree yard!

(*The three of them drink*)

CHUNYU FEN (*To the tune of* **Yujiaozhi**):

    As I have wandered over the earth,

    I gladly squander money with such friends as you.

    I am skilled in martial arts,

    Well known through Chu and Wu.

    I care nothing for a low position,

    Neither do I enjoy a brief chat.

    I ease my sorrow with tasty brew

    And bare my heart in front of you.

ZHOU BIAN, TIAN ZIHUA:

Brother, you may enjoy yourself under the locust-tree.

CHUNYU FEN (*To the previous tune*):

    With its root branching out,

    The luxuriant locust-tree stands alone in the yard.

    Why should the heaven shower so much from above

    That the tree is ripped of its leaves?

    In this season of the imperial exam,

    The horses gallop the candidates to the capital.

    Face to face the heroes talk of woe;

    Heart to heart the heroes disperse their frowns.

ZHOU BIAN, TIAN ZIHUA:

We must be off now.

CHUNYU FEN:

I'll walk with you for part of the way.

(*To the tune of* **Jibanling**)

    From Yingluan you depart for the west;

    By the Rose Channel you take a boat west.

    I see you off in late autumn;

I see you off in late autumn.

I look into the distant sky

And see a boat at the Peach Ferry lie.

I hope you'll soon return;

For your good company I shall yearn.

ALL:

The river will disperse our woe

After we separate in the evening glow.

ZHOU BIAN, TIAN ZIHUA (*With a sigh*):

We are leaving now, but we might come back again.

CHUNYU FEN:

Why do you talk like this?

ZHOU BIAN, TIAN ZIHUA (*To the previous tune*):

When we part with our bosom friend,

We might not see you very soon.

Tears flow from our eyes;

Tears flow from our eyes.

Why do we gaze into each other's eyes,

Hand in hand as dear brothers?

With broken hearts we shall go

And always dream of Yangzhou.

ALL:

The river will disperse our woe

After we separate in the evening glow.

CHUNYU FEN (*To the tune of* **Coda**):

I long to go and drink with mates,

Whose friendship never dissipates.

When you are gone,

I shall have to drown myself in wine.

(*Exeunt Zhou Bian and Tian Zihua*)

CHUNYU FEN:

Now that they are gone, I feel so bored in the empty yard. Partridge, with whom can I while away some time in Yangzhou?

PARTRIDGE:

Let me see … As far as I know, Liu'er and Sha San beyond the Wazipu Pleasure Ground can help you while away some time.

CHUNYU FEN:

Go and bring them here.

Wandering in the south all my life,

I speak of swords in my prime.

When people leave after the wine,

The yard seems drearier in autumn time.

Scene Three
The Tree State

(*Enter the Ant King, followed by attendants*)

ANT KING (*To the tune of* **Haitangchun**):

> Countries may be founded anywhere,
> Among which is a miniature state.
> While households cluster in the north,
> One road leads to the locust-tree gate.

ATTENDANTS:

> Crimson costumes, majestic palaces,
> Propitious air and imperial terraces:
> These form an entirely different state.

ALL:

> We spray the wine before the steps of jade,
> To laud the king with attendants in parade.

ATTENDANTS (*Kowtow to the Ant King*):

Long live the king!

ANT KING (*In the pattern of* **Qingpingyue**):

> *"Under the locust-tree,*
> *The sun casts its shadows willy-nilly.*
> *Everything in the state is piled with soil,*
> *A treasury valuable beyond compare.*
> *The ants in a thousand years*
> *Are spiritualised with their king.*
> *There is a state within a state,*
> *With subjects like human beings."*

I am King of the Great State of Peaceful Locust, originally an ant, an insect that conforms to the movement of the universe. We live on the earth, which is also the dwelling place of dragons and snakes. One becomes two, and two becomes three — wealth is amassed by taxing ten thousand out of a hundred thousand and taxing a hundred out of a thousand — I thus become a king out of amassment of wealth. A miracle may be worked out of decadence — as the ancient saying goes, "Honesty may move the people, who may be transformed and turned from bad to good." A state may be founded on a tiny bit of land — as the ancient saying goes, "Equality removes poverty; harmony removes solitude; peace removes peril." People were gathered in the first year, a town was founded in the second year and a capital was established in the third year. All was achieved due to my virtue. For a memorial tablet to the god of the earth, pine was used in the Xia Dynasty, cypress in the Shang Dynasty, and chestnut in the Zhou Dynasty — while my country is founded in a locust-tree, immune from the fire and the axe. Virtue is the source of a powerful state; a tree is the pillar of a magnificent palace. I set up arsenals, built city walls and opened city gates; then I built houses, raised pavilions and erected mansions. Administration is divided among the six ministries; the Prime Minister exercises authority over all the offices. Heavy traffic flows on the thoroughfares in the capital; leafy trees shelter the inner palaces. In the northern palace are enshrined the memorial tablets of the Three Dukes to commemorate these great personages; in the southern palace are allotted official positions to reinforce the fortifications. On the right is the Justice Bureau where judicial cases are handled; on the left is the Military Headquarters where the general reviews military manoeuvres. The Prime Minister sits in front of the Inner Gate for the morning audience; the scholars gather in the fairs on the first and fifteenth days of every month. It is said that the locust-tree, like the auspicious star in the sky, is the sacrificial tree of the state. Following the practice of King Wu in the Zhou Dynasty, the tree is planted inside the Forbidden City to keep away the detrimental and to admit the beneficial; following the practice of Duke Jing in the Qi State, it is known among the neighbouring states that those who offend the locust-tree will be punished and those who damage the locust-tree will be beheaded. This is the law decreed by the king and is the foundation of the state. I am fortunate that I have a virtuous Queen and an efficient Right Prime Minister at my service. As I have some leisure time after the state affairs, I shall have an excursion with the ministers. The banquet is ready now and the Prime Minister has arrived.

    (*Enter Duan Gong*)

DUAN GONG (*To the tune of* **Haitangchun**):

    I left the court when the sun went west,

    But am coming again at the king's behest.

    (*Kowtows to the Ant King*)

Duan Gong, Right Prime Minister and Marquis of Martial Feats, kowtows to Your Majesty and wishes you a long life.

ANT KING:

Rise to your feet. Do you know why I have called for you today?

DUAN GONG:

No, I don't.

ANT KING:

The chief worry of a state is the discordance among Heaven, Earth and Man. We are fortunate that our state is neither threatened by storms from Heaven, nor threatened by floods on Earth, nor threatened by leniency in government or law. Free from any damage or disaster, our state has immigrant ants across the border. The peace we enjoy proves the efficiency of our judicial system. I'd like to invite you to accompany me on an excursion within our territory. What do you think?

DUAN GONG:

It is an excellent idea in times of peace for the king and the ministers to tour the state and see the lay of the land. However, there are eighteen dukes and four royal families in our country. They must attend on you as well.

ANT KING:

I shall have another banquet with them. I shall go to the locust-tree with none else but you.

(*Walks on*)

"*The palace stands in gloomy charm*
While the yard lies open, broad and wide.
When wind shakes twigs from side to side,
The sun shines o'er the cactus palm."

ATTENDANTS:

The wine is ready.

DUAN GONG (*Presents the wine to the Ant King*):

Here is longevity wine for Your Majesty.

ANT KING (*To the tune of **Xinujiao***):

    Nature is selfless,

    Making clear distinctions

    Between each tiny sect.

    Although the king is a tiger and man is a dragon,

    Still they must follow courtly etiquette.

    A miniature king like me

    Can share

    The royal air.

ALL:

    What a strange parade!

    In such a mild day as this,

    An excursion we have made.

DUAN GONG (*To the previous tune*):

    In the court,

    I am the newly-appointed Prime Minister.

    The high-ranking officials

    Are dressed in scarlet and yellow.

    All the households

    Are dotted with stars.

    In our tiny world,

    The king is crowned

    And inspects all his land.

ALL:

    What a strange parade!

    In such a mild day as this,

    An excursion we have made.

ANT KING (*To the previous tune*):

    Bear in mind

    That a grain of millet may fly in the air.

    Among all tiny creatures,

    Who lacks his valiant share?

    On a tiny territory,

I have become the king.

I have ambition

To follow the orbit of stars

And listen to the ocean roar.

ALL:

Linger a while

And see how the wind blows

Before you move a mile.

DUAN GONG:

Do you think that your territory is too small, Your Majesty?

(*To the previous tune*)

Think before you act

Although my words are of little consequence.

To found a state

Is a tough job in every sense.

I sigh with regret

That the ants busy themselves for grains.

Why should we

Look for trouble in a quiet life

And complicate the issue with more?

ALL:

Linger a while

And see how the wind blows

Before you move a mile.

ANT KING:

I haven't been on an excursion to the locust-tree for a long time. Let's enjoy ourselves to the full today.

(*To the tune of* **Jinyixiang**)

With verdant foliage,

Its leaves form a heavy screen;

In the spring time,

Its trunk looks green.

Intertwined

And crisscrossed,

The tree towers into the sky.

Like the village mulberries

And the temple willows,

Its branches constitute a shelter

That reaches palace windows.

I was predestined to found a state,

Small though others may consider it.

As a king who leads the ants,

I assume manners strict and regal.

(*To the tune of* **Jiangshuiling**)

Thanks to heavenly grace

And earthly power,

Within the walls stands the splendid palace.

With twists and turns,

The corridors extend afar

Into lanes

And street fairs.

They either bow

Or kowtow —

The ministers show their respect to the king;

They either walk

Or stand —

The common folk are ignorant.

(*To the tune of* **Coda**)

I have founded a state and ascended the throne;

Prime Minister,

You have become Prime Minister at court.

I wish that the State of Peaceful Locust

Shall last forever and put down the deepest of roots.

Everything is a being of its own,

Which constitutes a little world.

I dare to see through the absurd

And build the state in another zone.

Scene Four
Inviting a Monk to Preach Zen

(*Enter Master Qixuan*)

MONK QIXUAN (*In the pattern of* **Collected Tang Poems**):

"An old monk lives upon the Western Peak,

In a glazed temple lit by the hanging moon.

Although he sticks to jade and does not speak,

It's hard for him not to leave the forest soon."

I, Master Qixuan, a Pravrajana master since early childhood, am ninety-one years old now. Devoted to Buddha, I have always been following the Buddhist instructions, from what World-Honoured One preached in the west to what Bodhidharma moralised in the east. Under a shadowless tree, I play with the moon and sneer the wind; in the seamless

pagoda, I'll rest myself and live an eternal life. But for a sin I committed five hundred years ago, I should have recovered to my original nature just as the bubbles become water again or as the bright moon returns to the sky. In the first years of the Liang Dynasty, I was a Buddhist monk in my previous life and followed Bodhidharma to cross the river. There was in Yangzhou a pagoda in honour of Vipasyin, one of the seven bodhisattvas. One evening I was carrying a lotus lamp on the seventh floor of the pagoda when my lamp tilted, spilling the hot oil into an ant-hole. At first I did not notice that a young acolyte guarding the pagoda looked unhappy. When I asked him whether he was unhappy because he would have to clean the pagoda, the acolyte replied that he was unhappy for no other reason than that a sacred monk had enlightened on him that there were eighty-four thousand ant families in the hole. When the acolyte lit the lamp and prayed to Buddha, the ants would come out of the holes to listen to the chant. At such moments, the acolyte would scatter some rice and play with them. Now the spilt hot oil must have hurt many ants. When I heard about this story, I repented and reported it to Bodhidharma, who said, "Never mind! Never mind! These ants will soon be relieved from their karma as insects. A miracle will be worked out in five hundred years and they will ascend to the sky." These words have been kept in my mind, ringing at my ears for three lives. Five hundred years have passed since that time. I'll go to Yangzhou to settle this case at my senile age. Look, the city of Runzhou faces Mount Jin and Mount Jiao, thus providing magnificent scenery. Now that the meditation room is peaceful and secluded, I shall sit quietly and meditate for a while to see what state of mind I shall be in.

720

(*Enter a monk, followed by three laymen, with a letter of petition in his hands*)

MONK:

"*The cranes may leave the woe behind*

While dragons come to hear the preaching."

I am abbot to the Xiaogan Temple and the Chanzhi Temple in Yangzhou across the river. To meet the demands of the lay Buddhists, I have come to ask Master Qixuan to preach to them. Here we are at the meditation room of the Sweet Dew Temple. Let's enter the room to present the letter of petition. Well, as Master Qixuan is sitting in meditation, I'll strike the iron plate three times.

(*Strikes the iron plate*)

MASTER QIXUAN (*Wakes up*):

What have you all come here for?

MONK, LAYMEN (*On their knees*):

The monks and laymen in Yangzhou are respectfully inviting you to preach on the fifteenth day of the seventh month, the Ullambana Day. Here is the letter of petition from all the Buddhist disciples.

(*Present the letter of petition*)

MASTER QIXUAN:

Please rise to your feet and read the letter.

MONK (*Unfolds and reads the letter*):

"As we live in the decadent area of Yangzhou, how can we escape from our evil fate? At the same time, as we border on the area of ancient Runzhou with its Mount Jin and Mount

Jiao, we can cherish good fate as well. Those who come to the temple in Runzhou are all Buddhist disciples. Master Qixuan of the Sweet Dew Temple is magnanimous and benevolent, embodying the three pearls of inward virtue and the five phases of outward transformation. Since the bell and the drum do not mix their sounds, the sangha is enlightened on its way of life; since no wind or flag but the heart stirs, the sangha is to rid itself of human bondage. You are not only able to witness the true faces of Shakyamuni, Maitraya and Kassapa, but also to perceive the samadhi of all living creatures. In the basin of Ullambana, there is the purity of heart; in the lamp of bright moon, there is no web of complications. Like the smiling Kassapa, you will convert the sangha. We pray that you will convert us with your maitri and karuna."

MASTER QIXUAN:

I can hardly cross the river at my senile age of sickness.

(*Aside*)

Is the karma of the ants to appear in this trip of mine?

(*To the tune of* ***Zhenggong Duanzhenghao***)

I am the second Manjusri,

Descending from the three Indian Temples,

To convert the ants to the south of Yangtze.

With bells and drums near Mount Jin and Mount Jiao,

The temple is known as Sweet Dew.

(*Turns to reply*)

I'd better stay. The monks seem to be good at interpreting the sutra. However, what they preach in a glaring and yelling manner has nothing to do with the essence of the sutra.

(*To the tune of* ***Gunxiuqiu***)

I only hear of wild geese carrying the letters,

But never see them come back.

Why does a stone lady dance?

Why does a new bride ride a donkey?

Where is the man who picks a flower in smile

Or eats litchi in good taste?

If you come to the point,

How can you miss the target?

I can harmonise the world

And clear the path,

Because everyone is in the dark.

(*The monk and laymen implore him to go*)

MASTER QIXUAN:

Since you implore me to go, I'll pay a visit across the river.

(*To the tune of* ***Tangxiucai***)

As Buddha's wisdom enlightens the universe,

There is no need to print his verse.

The practitioners of Dhyana strike the plate

While worldly people read and contemplate.

What is the present state of mind

That you will find?

For me, the Buddha stands behind.

You go first and follow my instructions!

(*To the tune of* **Quasi-coda**)

Prepare an attendance-book in the Chanzhi Temple

And a painting of Sudhana attending the preaching.

On hearing my preaching, the stones may nod

And sparkling stars may dot the sky.

Get ready the canopy and banners

To wait for me to cross the river by a vessel.

By the time when I work the miracles,

All the ants will have to surrender.

Scene Five
Admonishing the Princess

(*Enter the Ant Queen, followed by maids of honour*)

ANT QUEEN (*To the tune of* **Yeyougong**):

With my palace under a locust-tree,

Female virtue is what the earth has endowed me.

MAIDS OF HONOUR:

We hold painted fans and go behind,

While in the palace,

The sound of clock

Vanishes beyond the garden flowers.

(*Kowtow*)

We kowtow to Your Majesty the Queen. We wish you a long life.

ANT QUEEN (*In the pattern of* **Qingpingyue**):

"*The State of Peaceful Locust in autumn*

Is away from the worldly din.

The sweet songs behind palace walls

Will not subvert the state.

In two lines with peacock fans in their hands,

The maids of honour wear short-sleeved dress.

Behind closed palace doors,

Their amazing dance entices the king."

I am Queen of the Great State of Peaceful Locust. When I was a young ant, I was married to a handsome mayfly. My waist is as slim as a louse, but my figure is as large as a gadfly. When my spouse was enthroned, I naturally became the Queen. I only have a daughter by the name of Yaofang, entitled Princess Golden Branch. With utmost beauty, she has reached the age of marriage. She studies classics and histories under the instruction of Sister Shangzhen and learns embroidery under the guidance of my sister-in-law Lady Lingzhi. I received the decree of His Majesty the King yesterday to find a spouse for my daughter in the human world. Only people with deep insight can pick out a passionate son-in-law. It comes to my mind that my niece Princess Qiongying has a penetrating eye for men. I shall first talk it over with my daughter and then tell my niece to follow my instructions.

MAIDS OF HONOUR:

Her Highness the Princess is at the door.

> (*Enter Princess Golden Branch*)

PRINCESS GOLDEN BRANCH (*To the previous tune*):

> Whether clever or foolish by nature,
>
> Any girl can apply the rouge and powder.
>
> Charming and tender,
>
> I have a heart
>
> That has been stirred
>
> In my chamber.
>
> (*Greets the Ant Queen*)

Your daughter Yaofang kowtows to you. I wish you a long, long life.

ANT QUEEN:

As you have reached the age of fifteen, Yaofang, you are a qualified princess to be well-matched. You are now staying with me, but sooner or later you'll get married. Do you know about the "four virtues and three obediences"?

PRINCESS GOLDEN BRANCH:

As I am still young, please tell me about them.

ANT QUEEN:

The three obediences are obedience to your father before marriage, obedience to your husband during married life and obedience to your sons in widowhood. The four virtues are propriety in speech, fidelity, physical charm and efficiency in needlework. With these three obediences and four virtues, you will be a virtuous lady. Now listen to me:

> (*To the tune of* **Bangzhuangtai**)
>
> By the spiritualised root of the locust-tree,
>
> I live in the magnificent chambers.
>
> In spite of my miniature size,
>
> I have assumed a human figure.
>
> First wife to your father the King,
>
> I am First Lady in the eyes of other states.
>
> In charge of ladies' education in the state,
>
> I live well with your father in dignity,
>
> As a woman of chastity and fidelity.

PRINCESS GOLDEN BRANCH (*To the previous tune*):

> A tiny beauty in the world,
>
> I am born in a royal family.
>
> Although it is not the human world,
>
> I am treasured as a pearl in your palm.
>
> In cold weather I stay in my chamber;
>
> In warm weather I feel the warms of parental care.
>
> With lectures from my father
>
> And instructions from my mother,
>
> How can I lack three obediences and four virtues?

(*Enter Princess Qiongying*)

PRINCESS QIONGYING (*To the tune of* **Wanxiandeng**):

> With hurried steps,
>
> I walk to the palace door.

I am Qiongying, niece of the Ant King. Summoned by Her Majesty, I shall wait for an audience with her.

(*Kowtows to the Ant Queen*)

Princess Qiongying kowtows to Your Majesty the Queen. I wish you a long life.

(*Greets Princess Golden Branch*)

How do you do, Princess Golden Branch.

PRINCESS GOLDEN BRANCH:

How do you do, Princess Qiongying.

ANT QUEEN:

Listen to my edict, Princess Qiongying. As Princess Golden Branch has come of age, she is to find a spouse. His Majesty the King has decreed that he is to find a son-in-law in the human world because she may not find a wise and valiant spouse in our clan to be the pillar to the state. I hear that the Xiaogan Temple in Yangzhou has invited Master Qixuan to expound the sutra on the fifteenth day of the seventh month. By the time when a multitude of monks and laymen gather in the Indian Yard of the Chanzhi Temple, you can go with Lady Lingzhi and Sister Shangzhen to listen to the preaching. See to it that you find a handsome and energetic young man.

PRINCESS QIONGYING:

Yes, I'll follow your edict to the letter.

ANT QUEEN (*To the tune of* **Bangzhuangtai**):

> When a girl has come of age for marriage,
>
> She will be matched disregarding social standings.
>
> The dragon's daughter may find a human spouse
>
> And a wedding may be held in the dream.

PRINCESS QIONGYING:

> Who is anticipated to be her spouse
>
> And requite the parental favours?
>
> I shall appear in public

But hide my smile

To find a proper spouse for her.

PRINCESS GOLDEN BRANCH:

May I go with you to the preaching, Qiongying?

PRINCESS QIONGYING:

As a royal princess, you'd better not go out with me.

PRINCESS GOLDEN BRANCH:

In that case, I'll present a pair of gold phoenix hairpins and a striped rhino-horn case to Master Qixuan as a token of my good will.

(*To the previous tune*)

In such a pleasant season,

I'd like to go but I am a girl.

I'll present him the gold phoenix hairpins

And a striped rhino-horn offering case.

PRINCESS QIONGYING:

All your good will

Will be heard by the Avalokitesvara.

I'll bring your token

And make it known to the congregation

So that you will find a spouse to your heart.

ANT QUEEN:

It's no small matter, Princess Qiongying.

(*To the tune of* **Coda**)

For brilliant young men in the congregation,

I hope you will fix your eye on one.

In this trip,

You must keep secret and make my heart at ease.

You shall select a man in the sacred place

And find him near the meditation bed.

In your trip, you must conceal your race

But bring me pleasant news instead.

Scene Six
A Random Pastime

(*Enter Liu'er*)

LIU'ER (*To the tune of* **Zizishuang**):

I live in ancient Yangzhou —

Beyond Wazipu.

I have inherited loose behaviours —

Since childhood.

I'm dressed in rags and a slanted hat —

With underarm odour.

I often scrape a meal or get some wine —

Smart enough.

I am the notorious Liu'er in Yangzhou. I've been dissolute and dissipated all my life. Those who are in bad luck need me to make quips and jokes; those who are dandies with or without taste want me to flatter and toady. I do not have many skills but have a ready tongue. When I meet a dupe, I just make him pay through the nose — this is a sharp practice of beating the grass to startle the snake; when I try to swindle someone, I let him take some advantages first — this is the simple trick of angling a carp with the bait of a shrimp. No matter in the south farm or in the north field, whoever provides for me is my parent of food and clothing; no matter whether I am invited by the neighbour in the east or in the west, Sha San is my brother for wining and dining. Those who understand me say that I am a wonderful man, a good man and an honest man; those who do not understand me say that I am a spendthrift, a ruffian, a rascal. I do not care who is sneering at me or scolding me; I care nothing but having a good time. As I haven't seen Sha San for several days, I'll look for him and idle away some time with him.

(*Enter Sha San*)

SHA SAN (*To the previous tune*):

I am Sha the thirteenth child —

Named Lan.

I'm like the water moon on the thirteenth day —

Floating round.

Six and seven is thirteen —

Sheer rubbish.

Thirteen strokes of flogging at court —

It's nonsense.

LIU'ER:

You've violated the curfew, Sha San.

SHA SAN:

If I do not violate the curfew, I won't be called a whore-master or an amateur performer, brother.

LIU'ER:

We haven't wined or dined for days, brother.

SHA SAN:

Let's saunter around the highway.

(*Enter Partridge*)

PARTRIDGE:

"*Where does the white cloud flow?*

Where does the bright moon go?"

SHA SAN:

The moon goes here, brother.

PARTRIDGE:

My master Chunyu wants to while away some time with Liu'er and Sha San. Where are they living?

LIU'ER, SHA SAN:

We are the men you're looking for. What business is your master doing?

PARTRIDGE:

He is serving as an assistant general.

SHA SAN:

Oh, he's an assistant cobbler. Does he want us to help with the drilling?

PARTRIDGE:

He's an assistant general in the military camp.

LIU'ER:

Is he the heavy drinker Master Chunyu?

PARTRIDGE:

Yes, he is.

LIU'ER, SHA SAN:

Let's go at once. Let's go at once.

> "*If you have wine, we are bosom friends;*
>
> *If you do not have money, we are total strangers.*"
>
> (*Exeunt all*)
>
> (*Enter Chunyu Fen*)

CHUNYU FEN (*In the pattern of **Collected Tang Poems***):

> "*Abandoned and having nothing to say,*
>
> *I wander lonely in Wu and Chu.*
>
> *Separated with my friends by a long way,*
>
> *I only hear the wind blow in autumn's view.*"

I, Chunyu Fen, have been in a dire strait since I gave up my position and have to relieve myself by drinking. As my friends have left me, I have to drink all by myself. What a tedious life I am leading!

> (*To the tune of **Jinchandao***)
>
> My youthful ambition
>
> Was to do meritorious deeds
>
> In full vigour.
>
> Who knows
>
> That the world may alter its needs?
>
> For all the aspirations you have,
>
> Your expectation soon flees.
>
> I'd learn from the hard drinker Liu Ling,
>
> Who achieved nothing all his life,
>
> And I am still addicted to drinking.
>
> I would that I be a bottle cork
>
> And sink upside down in the wine.

Is the poet Qu Yuan the only man awake?

(*Enter Partridge, followed by Liu'er and Sha San*)

PARTRIDGE:

"Here come three drunkards;

LIU'ER, SHA SAN:

Two of them are libertines."

PARTRIDGE:

The two gentlemen, Liu'er and Sha San, are at the door.

(*Chunyu Fen greets Liu'er and Sha San*)

LIU'ER:

"I am Liu'er;

SHA SAN:

I am Sha San.

CHUNYU FEN:

It's the first time we meet;

LIU'ER, SHA SAN:

Ten is more salty and sour to eat."

CHUNYU FEN:

What do you mean?

LIU'ER:

An old man said that he paid nine coins to have a bowl of noodles without salt and vinegar; therefore, I added one more coin.

CHUNYU FEN (*Smiles*):

May I ask whether you two live in town or in the countryside?

LIU'ER, SHA SAN (*To the tune of **Haojiejie***):

In Guangling,

A town in the county,

Liu'er and Sha San are well-known.

We are clever and smart,

Up to the mark in the zone.

To your liking,

We'll sing a pleasant tune

Or play tricks of our own.

(*Liu'er kneels on one knee, kowtows twice and chants "Uncle"*)

SHA SAN (*Hums a beggar's tune*):

Let's go to the Home for the Aged.

CHUNYU FEN:

How can we go to a place for the wretched?

SHA SAN:

No, I mean to say Home for the Adults, a whorehouse.

CHUNYU FEN:

I nearly know all the prostitutes in Yangzhou. Where else can I while away some time?

SHA SAN:

Yes, of course. As there will be an Ullambana service in the Xiaogan Temple, the monks and laymen have invited Master Qixuan from the Sweet Dew Temple in Runzhou to give the preaching.

CHUNYU FEN:

What about going to the preaching?

SHA SAN:

Meat and fish is abstained in the temple. I know you are fond of drinking.

CHUNYU FEN (*To the previous tune*):

> The world
>
> Is drunk all over,
>
> But there is a saint among the drunkards.
>
> A vegetarian in front of Buddha's portrait
>
> Will attain purity in the human world.

Get my horse ready, Partridge.

> In a joyful mood,
>
> I'll follow the Buddhist monk
>
> And find out to what he will allude.
>
> *In a deep frustrated mood,*
>
> *I try to while away my time.*
>
> *In the temple I shall brood*
>
> *Amid the autumn preaching chime.*

Scene Seven
A Chance Encounter

(*Enter an Un-tonsured Monk*)

UN-TONSURED MONK (*To the tune of* **Puxiange**):

> Men pray before Tathagata from morn till night
>
> Before a flesh-like lotus terrace.
>
> Encumbered by evils like wine and woman,
>
> Plus avarice and pride,
>
> By Buddhist disciplines they hardly abide.

I am an un-tonsured monk in the Chanzhi Temple in Yangzhou Prefecture. An un-tonsured monk is neither a monk nor a layman. As there is an Ullambana service in the Xiaogan Temple, the monks and laymen have invited Master Qixuan from Runzhou to give the preaching. Master Qixuan has made a strict directive that those who want to listen to the preaching will have to enter their names here before they go to the service. A Brahmin from the west by the name of Shi Yan is stopping over at our Indian Yard. Good

at the Indian swirl-dancing, he will make a performance whenever people come here to enter their names. Therefore, our temple is bustling with activity. Now that joss-sticks and candles are burning before the statue of Avalokitesvara, I'll wait and see who will come to enter their names. I'll stay away for the moment. It is true to say,

> "*While half of the Buddhist Hymn is left here,*
>
> *Three ways to perfection are laid elsewhere.*"

(*Exit*)

(*Enter Princess Qiongying, Lady Lingzhi and Sister Shangzhen*)

PRINCESS QIONGYING (*To the previous tune*):

> A tiny creature by nature
>
> Likewise pursues the incense to the temple.
>
> I wear a pair of red embroidered shoes,
>
> A pair of jade phoenix hairpins,
>
> A towel with jade pendants and long sleeves.

Together with Lady Lingzhi and Sister Shangzhen, I, Princess Qiongying, have come to enter our names in the Chanzhi Temple and listen to the preaching in the Xiaogan Temple. At the same time, I'll present Princess Yaofang's jade hairpins and rhino-horn case in front of the master's terrace. I'll see whether Princess Yaofang can find a satisfactory spouse. Here we are at the Indian Yard of the Chanzhi Temple, with a black-bamboo statue of Avalokitesvara beside the lake. There is an attendance-book on the altar. Let's burn the incense, make a kowtow and sign our names.

(*Princess Qiongying, Lady Lingzhi and Sister Shangzhen kowtow before the altar*)

PRINCESS QIONGYING (*To the tune of **Huangying'er***):

> We offer incense
>
> To Avalokitesvara.
>
> As descendents of humble origin,
>
> We venture to visit the temple.
>
> With your blessing,
>
> This life will be better than well.

ALL:

> We make a kowtow
>
> To wish for a harmonious marriage
>
> With ants' heart and soul.

PRINCESS QIONGYING:

Let's secretly pray for the success of Yaofang's marriage.

(*Princess Qiongying, Lady Lingzhi and Sister Shangzhen kowtow before the altar*)

PRINCESS QIONGYING (*To the previous tune*):

> To proliferate the State of Peaceful Locust,
>
> The royal princess is to get married
>
> To a spouse after her heart.
>
> We'll pick and choose,
>
> Wish and hope

That passion of love will melt her heart.

ALL:

We make a kowtow

To wish for a harmonious marriage

With ants' heart and soul.

SISTER SHANGZHEN:

Let's saunter beside the lake for a while. Look, a Brahmin is dancing toward us.

(*Enter a Brahmin*)

BRAHMIN (*To the tune of **Northern Dianjiangchun***):

Born in the west,

I am a Buddhist disciple

Practising in China.

I practise Dhyana

With overpowering faith.

I am Shi Yan, a Brahmin. As an itinerant monk, I stop over at the Indian Yard. Now I shall go dancing to drive away my boredom. Well, where are you three sisters coming from? Will you please watch my Brahmin swirl-dancing?

PRINCESS QIONGYING, LADY LINGZHI, SISTER SHANGZHEN (*In smiles*):

Yes, please.

(*Drumbeats within*)

BRAHMIN (*Dances*):

(*To the tune of **Duiyuhuan** with **Qingjiangyin***)

I clap my hands in front of the altar

While the embroidered flags wave in the wind.

Soft and flexible,

I bend and twist my waist.

I am dressed in a bright mantle,

Made of pretty satin in the west.

With my mantle flapping,

I pose as the seated Avalokitesvara.

I put my palms together as lotus petals

And smile back in Buddhist grace.

(*Bravo within*)

BRAHMIN:

As an official is riding towards us, I have to leave.

(*Exit*)

PRINCESS QIONGYING, LADY LINGZHI, SISTER SHANGZHEN:

Someone is coming. Let's wash our hands beside the lake.

(*Wash their hands*)

(*Enter Chunyu Fen on horseback, followed by Partridge*)

CHUNYU FEN (*To the tune of **Lülüjin***):

Time hangs heavy on my hands,

But I show no pity on myself.

I come to the Chanzhi Temple

To while away my time.

On mossy ground dotted with petals,

Who is dancing an Indian dance?

When I tie my horse and hold my whip,

I see someone over there.

(*Comes into the temple*)

"The bamboo-lined path leads afar,

Into the meditation room amid flowers."

The attendance-book is in front of the altar of Avalokitesvara. I shall offer some incense and enter my name here.

(*Kowtows with a joss-stick in his hand*)

(*To the tune of **Jiangshui'er***)

Your disciple Chunyu,

In deep sorrow,

Will listen to the preaching to relieve his woe.

Let me sign my name here.

(*Writes*)

I'll sign my name

To pray for relief from Avalokitesvara.

(*Notices Princess Qiongying*)

Beside the lake and bamboos,

Who is staying there?

PRINCESS QIONGYING (*Turns back in a smile*):

Where shall I hang the wet towel, Lady Lingzhi?

CHUNYU FEN (*Aside*):

What a fairy of a lady, with such tender skin and enchanting smile?

(*Turns back to reply*)

I'll hang the towel on the bamboo for you.

(*Princess Qiongying hands over the towel with a smile*)

CHUNYU FEN (*Accepts the towel and hangs it on a bamboo*):

What a sweet towel! I would that I become a towel to be held in her sleeves and to dry her sweet sweat!

(*Princess Qiongying, Lady Lingzhi and Sister Shangzhen smile but make no response*)

CHUNYU FEN:

What a beautiful sight of the lake and the flowers!

(*Sighs*)

Have I met a fairy? She whispers to herself and gives an enticing glimpse, but I cannot approach her for the moment. I'd better go to the Xiaogan Temple to listen to the preaching. Partridge, bring me the horse.

(*Gets on horseback*)

"*The horse neighs its way into falling petals;*

I hesitate but have to leave in grief."

(*Exit*)

PRINCESS QIONGYING:

This is a young man with a passionate heart. Since he is going to the preaching, let's go after him and have a closer look at him.

LADY LINGZHI:

Well, I'm not going. I have become such a genuine Buddhist disciple that I have become a Avalokitesvara with monthly flow.

SISTER SHANGZHEN:

What do you mean?

LADY LINGZHI:

My menses have arrived.

PRINCESS QIONGYING:

What a shame! In that case, I'll go with Sister Shangzhen.

(*To the tune of* **Coda**)

To listen to preaching in the temple,

I'll go with Sister Shangzhen

Now that Lady Lingzhi is gone.

When we reach the lecture hall,

I'll scrutinize the young man again.

In watching the Indian dancer,

We meet a young man on horseback.

We get the lotus-root for its buds' sake

While its flowers diffuse fragrance on the lake.

Scene Eight
Passion of Love

(*Enter the First-Rank Monk, holding a fishing-rod in his hand*)

FIRST-RANK MONK:

"*Buddha has passed down a lamp,*

Which remains alight all the time.

The lamp illuminates from year to year

While everywhere shine Buddhist wits sublime."

I am the first-rank disciple of Master Qixuan of the Sweet Dew Temple in Runzhou. A practitioner of Pravrajana since early childhood, I have served my master for years. I always mend my worn mantle in the morning and recite the Buddhist canons in the evening. As my master is invited by the Xiaogan Temple in Yangzhou to expound the sutra, I have led

all the monks to prepare the incense, lamps, flowers and fruits and to clean the meditation bed and table so that my master may ascend the rostrum. Play the ritual instruments, all the monks!

(Drums and music within)

(Enter Master Qixuan with a sceptre and a whisk)

MASTER QIXUAN *(Ascends the rostrum)*:

"*I ascend the rostrum to preach Buddhist laws*

And cite examples of man and beast.

All the stars centre around the north star

While all the waters flow toward the east."

(Holds up the sceptre)

"*Like an old liana on Mount Sumeru,*

I follow the flying sceptre in the sky.

When the sceptre blazes a way to Heaven,

All the antagonists stop their battle cry."

(Waves the whisk)

"*When gentle breeze scatters the cloud,*

Immense dusts have no room to hide.

The warrior has nothing to wield

When I wave the whisk before the crowd."

(Offers the incense)

Look at the incense!

"*What you cannot get from Bodhisattvas,*

You can hardly beg from the king.

The empty sky is so vast

That the earth cannot hold a thing."

I hold the incense toward the sky so that it will penetrate the Dharmadhatu and fume the continents; I'll burn the incense in the incense-burner to wish the Emperor and the crown prince a long, long life.

(Angles with the fishing-rod)

"*With a fishing-rod to angle the moon,*

A man sails to the mouth of the Milky Way.

The boat floats forever day by day,

But neither fish nor dragon touches the hook."

FIRST-RANK MONK:

Why is a phantom the reality?

MASTER QIXUAN:

"*The rising sun seems to be spit out in the east;*

The morning green seems to float to the south hill."

FIRST-RANK MONK:

Why is the reality a phantom?

MASTER QIXUAN:

"*You can neither see how the drizzle wets the dress*

Nor hear how the petals fall onto the ground."

FIRST-RANK MONK:

Why is non-reality a non-phantom?

MASTER QIXUAN:

"*Unconsciously, you face the moon in your return*

And see the cloud in your dream."

FIRST-RANK MONK:

Thank you very much, Master. I shall withdraw today and ask for your advice tomorrow.

(*Exit*)

MASTER QIXUAN:

If any of you monks or laymen has any uncertainties in your meditation or any doubts in your contemplation, I am ready to expound a few questions from you today. Any questions?

(*Enter an elderly monk*)

ELDERLY MONK:

Yes, I have some questions. May I ask what is the Buddha or the Enlightened One?

MASTER QIXUAN:

"*It's like the moon above worldly peaks*

Or like the daily breeze in the Milky Way."

ELDERLY MONK:

Then, what is the Dharma or the True Teaching?

MASTER QIXUAN:

"*It's like poem books under a straw rain-cape*

Or like wine-containers in a bamboo house."

ELDERLY MONK:

Then, what is the Sangha or the Buddhist Brotherhood?

MASTER QIXUAN:

"*It's like a man with grey hair that sits in the world*

Or like a lonely lamp that accompanies old friends."

ELDERLY MONK:

Thank you very much, Master. I shall withdraw today and ask for your advice tomorrow.

(*Exit*)

MASTER QIXUAN (*Angles with the fishing-rod*):

"*I often hold the fishing-rod in my hand,*

Which in the dusk stirs the fish breeds.

I can hardly keep the moon in the sky,

For I wake up to find myself in the reeds."

If any of you monks or laymen has any unawareness in your meditation, I am ready to answer some more questions from you today. Any questions?

(*Enter Chunyu Fen*)

CHUNYU FEN (*To the tune of **Yejinmen, Part One***):

I live a leisurely life,

Accompanied by wine and flower.

I sit near the incense-burner beside the rostrum,

To feel the sermon in its full power.

I, Chunyu Fen, have come here to listen to the preaching. As I have nothing to do and feel vexed all day long, for what advice can I ask the master? I shall inquire the master about the hetu-pratyaya or cause and effect.

(*Greets Master Qixuan*)

I, Chunyu Fen, bow to you and ask you for advice. What are the six principal moral afflictions?

MASTER QIXUAN:

"*They're like bare locust-trees in the empty palace*

Or like ethereal music played beside a luxuriant lake."

CHUNYU FEN:

Then, what are the twenty subsidiary moral afflictions?

MASTER QIXUAN:

"*They're like two wings stretching ten thousand miles,*

But halting to find a dwelling in the forest."

CHUNYU FEN:

Then, how can I break away from these moral afflictions?

MASTER QIXUAN:

"*When the dream has vanished,*

The homeward road is barely visible."

(*Chunyu Fen meditates*)

MASTER QIXUAN:

With my insight into the past and the future, I can perceive that this young man looks foolish but may become a bodhisattva in no time.

(*Enter Princess Qiongying with Sister Shangzhen*)

PRINCESS QIONGYING (*To the tune of* **Yejinmen**, **Part Two**):

I amble to the temple,

In the slow pace of an ant.

Sister Shangzhen,

As the man in the bamboo yard is full of passion,

Let's try to have a closer look at him.

MASTER QIXUAN (*Smiles*):

You have brought your kith and kin with you, Mr. Chunyu.

CHUNYU FEN (*Looks back*):

Oh, what a pair of pretty ladies!

(*Sighs aside*)

How do you know that I am not married, Master?

PRINCESS QIONGYING (*Makes a bow to Master Qixuan*):

I bow to you, Master.

MASTER QIXUAN:

What are you here for, Ant?

PRINCESS QIONGYING:

I've come for the hetu-pratyaya of five hundred years.

MASTER QIXUAN (*Smiles aside*):

Yes, I see. Lay the sheets on the ground, attendant!

ATTENDANT (*Gets the seats ready*):

> (*Aloud*)

The fifty-three sheets of Buddhist sutras are ready.

MASTER QIXUAN:

Name one of the sutras!

PRINCESS QIONGYING (*Aloud*):

Saddharma Pundarika Sutra, Avalokitesvara.

MASTER QIXUAN:

> *"Sixty thousand words in seven scrolls*
> *Contain impenetrable implications.*
> *From his white teeth flow sarira relics;*
> *From his tongue shed bright lights.*
> *In his throat drip sweet dews;*
> *In his mouth utter the enlightening truths.*
> *Even for the towering sins,*
> *A few lines of sutra will soothe."*
>
> (*To the tune of **Liangzhouxu***)
>
> In the temples on earth,
> The dharma provides enlightenment
> And attracts Buddhist disciples.
> From what hetu-pratyaya
> Comes the name Avalokitesvara?
> According to Buddha, when men call this name
> In times of difficulty,
> Avalokitesvara will appear in no time.

All the desire of greed, anger and delusion

> Will vanish at once.
> The converted men and women are blessed.

ALL:

> He who has such magnificence
> And compassion
> Is named Avalokitesvara.
> We prostrate ourselves before you
> In front of the terrace of lotus flowers.

MONKS, LAYMEN:

Why are you touring the world, Avalokitesvara? Why are you expounding the sutras for all the people? Why are you enlightening the world?

MASTER QIXUAN (*To the previous tune*):

By the name of the land,

All the people are to be converted

By various personifications.

To preach according to different causations

Is to witness the tormented world.

Various kinds of beings

In times of difficulty

Are to be rescued.

When he shows his generosity everywhere,

Numerous as the river sands,

Miracles are worked out in a moment.

ALL:

He who has such magnificence

And compassion

Is named Avalokitesvara.

We prostrate ourselves before you

In front of the terrace of lotus flowers.

CHUNYU FEN:

What about the Aksayamati Bodhisattva?

MASTER QIXUAN:

Aksayamati said to Buddha, "World-Honoured One, I now offer sacrifice to Avalokitesvara." Upon these words, he untied the pearl necklace which was worth hundreds of ounces of gold and offered it to Avalokitesvara, saying, "I hope that you will accept this offer." When Avalokitesvara refused to accept the offer, Buddha said to him, "Just accept the pearl necklace to show mercy on Aksayamati and the congregation." Avalokitesvara accepted the necklace in accordance with Buddha's decree, but divided it into two parts: one part for Shakyamuni Buddha and the other part for Opakut Buddha's pagoda. When you listen to my preaching, please remember that Avalokitesvara is all-powerful and to be worshipped by everyone from the bottom of their hearts.

MONKS AND LAYMEN:

We shall prostrate ourselves before him.

CHUNYU FEN:

Master, as I was a general, I have killed and wined. Am I not to be released from the purgatory?

MASTER QIXUAN:

As is stated in the sutra, in the case of valiant generals, Buddha is to appear at once to release him from the purgatory. What is the difference between the valiant generals and you?

PRINCESS QIONGYING (*Asks*):

What about women, Master?

MASTER QIXUAN (*Smiles*):

As is stated in the sutra, in the case of humans and non-humans, Buddha is to appear at once to release them from the purgatory.

PRINCESS QIONGYING (*Taken aback, aside to Sister Shangzhen*):

This master has great magic power. Instead of saying men and women, he says humans and non-humans. You ask him another question.

SISTER SHANGZHEN (*Asks Master Qixuan*):

Master, can I become a Buddhist disciple now that I am a Taoist nun?

MASTER QIXUAN:

It is said in the Taoist Classic that Tao exists in the ants.

> *"A few grains of rice are piled*
> *Into a Mini-Mount Sumeru."*

Why are you excluded?

PRINCESS QIONGYING, SISTER SHANGZHEN (*On their knees*):

You have a penetrating insight. We have a younger sister by the name of Yaofang. As she is too young to attend the service, she offers a pair of gold phoenix hairpins and a rhino-horn box. Will you kindly accept them?

> (*Rise to their feet*)
> (*To the previous tune*)

The Buddhist master

> Has a deep insight,
> But has he ever worn a necklace?
> When we make an ordinary offer,
> We can still hardly escape the samsara.
> Now that we offer the pearls,
> Can we become men as the Dragon Princess did?
> Tiny creatures as we are,
> We can make tiny offers.
> As we make but a small offer,
> Can it be divided into two parts?

ALL:

> He who has such magnificence
> And compassion
> Is named Avalokitesvara.
> We prostrate ourselves before you
> In front of the terrace of lotus flowers.

CHUNYU FEN (*Aside*):

What exotic ladies!

> (*Turns back*)

May I have a look at the gold hairpins and the rhino-horn case, Master?

> (*Looks at the gold hairpins and the rhino-horn case*)
> (*Turns to look at Princess Qiongying and Sister Shangzhen*)

Both the ladies and the offers come beyond the human world.

> (*To the previous tune*)
> The gold hairpins
> Are a pair of phoenixes in flight;
> The case is made of rhino-horn better than gold.

(*Aside*)

Their smiles are sweet;

Their eyes are coy.

They have brought rhino-horn

And phoenixes

To this sacred place.

(*Master Qixuan sneers*)

CHUNYU FEN (*Turns back*):

Worth hundred of ounces of gold,

These tiny objects

Are offered to Shakyamuni.

ALL:

He who has such magnificence

And compassion

Is named Avalokitesvara.

We prostrate ourselves before you

In front of the terrace of lotus flowers.

CHUNYU FEN:

Where are the ladies from, Master?

MASTER QIXUAN (*Aside*):

As he is stirred by a passion of love, I'll let the parrot wake him up before the terrace of Avalokitesvara.

SOUND OF PARROT WITHIN:

Turn around, ants! Turn around, ants!

MASTER QIXUAN:

Have you heard something, Mr. Chunyu?

CHUNYU FEN:

"Turn around, lasses! Turn around, lasses!"

MASTER QIXUAN (*Smiles*):

It's midday. The preaching is over and I'll go for meditations.

"*Inspect the universe of a billion universes*

And nod in the unspeakable path of truth."

(*Exit*)

CHUNYU FEN:

Now that the master is gone, I'll have a chat with the ladies. Can you tell me your names?

(*Princes Qiongying and Sister Shangzhen make no reply*)

CHUNYU FEN:

Where are you from?

(*Princess Qiongying and Sister Shangzhen make no reply*)

CHUNYU FEN:

Are you the ladies who watched the dances in the Chanzhi Temple?

PRINCESS QIONGYING, SISTER SHANGZHEN (*Smile*):

Yes, we are.

CHUNYU FEN:

Alas!

> (*To the tune of* ***Jiejiegao***)
>
> The two pretty ladies
>
> Are amazing,
>
> Fit to sit on the terrace of lotus flowers.

PRINCESS QIONGYING (*Smiles*):

I have a younger sister who is more amazing.

CHUNYU FEN (*Smiles*):

Are the phoenix hairpins and the rhino-horn case offered by your sister?

> Her simple words
>
> Are difficult to understand.
>
> It's hard to imagine
>
> That such treasures exist in the human world.

Sister, sister, you offer the phoenix hairpins and the rhino-horn case to the temple.

> Why don't you appear in person
>
> And enter wedlock with me before Avalokitesvara?

SISTER SHANGZHEN:

Oops! How can you call her "sister"!

CHUNYU FEN:

Well, I am asking for a rebuff! Good-bye, ladies!

> "*While a silent fallen petal smiles,*
>
> *Who can appreciate my passionate tunes?*"
>
> (*Exit*)

SISTER SHANGZHEN:

It seems that he is the most suitable person to be the royal son-in-law.

> (*To the previous tune*)
>
> ˙ He smiled when he met us,
>
> Full of passion of love,
>
> And will be in sorrow when he is home.
>
> With a glib tongue,
>
> A moving shadow
>
> And an assured heart,
>
> He is a perfect match for the princess.

PRINCESS QIONGYING:

I have often seen this gentleman.

SISTER SHANGZHEN:

You see, he lives close to our state. His name is Chunyu Fen.

PRINCESS QIONGYING, SISTER SHANGZHEN:

> A neighbour to the giant locust-tree
>
> Sleeps amid the plum-blossom in dreams.

Let's go back.

(*To the tune of* **Coda**)

In the magnificent lecture hall,

We can hardly find a suitable man.

Yaofang, Yaofang,

We've found one for you at last.

Rare in the multitude of men,

One man comes into our ken.

Look for men and they flee;

Flee the men and one follows thee.

Scene Nine
The Royal Son-in-Law

(*Enter the Ant Queen, followed by maids of honour*)

ANT QUEEN (*To the tune of* **Xijiangyin**, **Part One**):

While ants respond when spring is on the way,

The locust-leaves fold by night and unfold by day.

I have a tender daughter by my side,

But I don't know when she'll be the bride.

I am Queen to the Ant King. I have asked my niece Princess Qiongying to look for a royal son-in-law when she attends the preaching. She is about to come back. Maids of Honour, stand in wait.

(*The maids of honour respond*)

(*Enter Princess Qiongying*)

PRINCESS QIONGYING (*To the tune of* **Xijiangyin**, **Part Two**):

While men ride in black robes,

Women wear tiny shoes and narrow sleeves.

I don't know what will happen in the next life,

But now I have to obey royal decrees.

(*Kowtows to the Ant Queen*)

I've fulfilled your task and am ready to report to you, Your Majesty.

ANT QUEEN:

Have you found a man in the congregation?

PRINCESS QIONGYING:

I've found a handsome young man by the name of Chunyu Fen, a native of Guangling. When Sister Shangzhen and I presented the rhino-horn case and the gold hairpins in the temple, he looked at the offerings with great care and interest. As he showed his passion of love to us, we paid attention to him. If he becomes the royal son-in-law, he will be able to handle the state affairs.

(*To the tune of* **Huangying'er**)

    I saw him in the Indian yard

    And followed him to the temple,

    Where he showed signs of passion.

    From his outward appearance

    And inward talent,

    He revealed his innate distinction.

Do you know where he lives, Your Majesty?

ALL:

    What coincidence!

    Not far from the locust-tree

    Lives this young man.

ANT QUEEN (*To the previous tune*):

    As if predestined,

    He looked at the hairpins with passion

    And stood with prominence in the congregation.

    For his talent,

    I shall marry my daughter to him

    To pay the debt in my previous life.

ALL:

    What coincidence!

    Not far from the locust-tree

    Lives this young man.

ANT QUEEN (*To the tune of* **Coda**):

    If the King is satisfied,

    I will send the Royal Envoys to meet him.

    When he falls into a dream,

    He will become my son-in-law.

    My son-in-law must be a man of passion;

    Who can surpass Chunyu in the least?

    When I look for my son-in-law,

    I find him a neighbour in the east.

743

Scene Ten
Accepting the Invitation

(*Enter Chunyu Fen in a languid manner*)

CHUNYU FEN (*To the tune of* **Zhuyunfei**):

    Clever or foolish,

    It all depends on the word "cute".

The Nanke Dream

Some people are grown up in age,

But lack the mood.

Alas!

I stand alone under the locust-tree,

Which shades off the sun.

The chirping of the cicadas

Bores me to the death.

In a drunken stupor in Yangzhou,

How can I keep the gold phoenix hairpins in mind?

I, Chunyu Fen, do not lag behind the others in talents and capabilities. However, at the age of thirty, I have neither won a name nor married a wife. With nothing but the bare walls in my house, I stand beside this locust-tree, lonely and bored. If it were what human life means, I would rather give up my life. Since I came back from the Dhyana preaching in the Xiaogan Temple, I have felt all the more bored. I can do nothing to cheer me up but get myself drunk all the time. The ancient saying is correct enough that drunkenness gets rid of everything. Well, enough of my mumbling. Now I shall leave Partridge to himself and go rambling in the streets. I'll try to find a good inn and have a hearty drink. It is true to say,

"As it is useless to weep on the way,

I would drink to death on this very day."

(Exit)

(Enter Partridge)

PARTRIDGE:

It is funny indeed that my master looks for trouble when trouble does not look for him. Well-versed in martial arts, my master became an assistant general in Huaiyang, but lost his position because he was addicted to drinking. He has been in low spirits ever since. As his wine friends Zhou Bian and Tian Zihua have returned home to Luhe, my master was so lonely that he invited Liu'er and Sha San to chat with him. It so happened that Liu'er and Sha San induced my master to listen to the preaching in the Xiaogan Temple. Since his return from the preaching, my master has been in a delusion all the time, drinking and sleeping by turns in a depressed mood. When I come back from a nap under a sandal tree beside the stream, I can no longer find him. I am afraid that he will fall asleep intoxicated in the street as if haunted by a ghost. That would be a nuisance for him. I'd like to go out and look for him, but there is no one to keep the door. What shall I do then?

(Looks around)

Well, Liu'er and Sha San are coming.

(Enter Liu'er and Sha San)

LIU'ER, SHA SAN:

"To give wine when I want wine,

You are a friend of mine.

To give tea when I want wine,

You are a foe of mine."

Is your master in, Partridge?

PARTRIDGE:

I'd ask you to keep the door for me while I look for my master.

LIU'ER, SHA SAN:

No problem. You just go and look for your master.

(*Exeunt all*)

(*Enter Partridge carrying a wine-kettle in one hand and supporting the drunken Chunyu Fen*)

PARTRIDGE (*To the previous tune*):

> In whiling away your time,
>
> What's the use of getting dead drunk?
>
> You drank so much that you've lost your voice
>
> And you are so heavy that my shoulders ache.

VOICE WITHIN (*In laughter*):

What a drunkard!

PARTRIDGE:

Men,

> With sober eyes,
>
> You look down upon my master.
>
> He brings half a kettle of wine
>
> For a sip at home.
>
> Nothing is better than getting drunk;
>
> Sleeping is better than getting drunk.
>
> (*Enter Liu'er and Sha San*)

LIU'ER, SHA SAN:

Alas, what's happened to him?

PARTRIDGE:

Funny, funny indeed! I looked around and found him falling asleep, intoxicated at an inn by the side of Chanzhi Bridge. When I helped him downstairs, he could hardly tear himself away from this half-kettle of wine. What is he up to? We are home, Master, wake up a bit!

CHUNYU FEN (*To the previous tune*):

> In a delusion all these days,
>
> (*Tumbles on the ground*)
>
> I feel dizzy and can hardly move a step.
>
> I have Green Maid to support me
>
> But lack Red Lady to sleep with me.

SHA SAN (*To Chunyu Fen*):

Where are you from, Mr. Chunyu? You are very drunk.

CHUNYU FEN (*Fails to recognize Sha San*):

> Who is it
>
> That asks my whereabouts?
>
> I am often under the influence.
>
> Drunk at the faggot gate,

I stagger in small steps in the breeze,

With my face crimsoning like leaves on trees.

(*Vomits*)

LIU'ER, SHA SAN:

Alas, you've vomited on our trousers. What tasty wine! What tasty wine! Fetch some tea at once, Partridge.

(*To the previous tune*)

You've spat your wine all over

On your dishevelled coat.

We'll arrange your dress

For you to steady your steps.

(*Hand over the tea to Chunyu Fen*)

Brother,

Lean against the small screen

And have a cup of tea.

In the western breeze,

You'll feel better after you are sober,

And we'll enjoy the fireflies under the moon.

CHUNYU FEN (*Feels tired*):

Help me to the eastern room and I'll sleep a while. Keep that kettle of wine for me.

PARTRIDGE:

You are so drunk but you still keep that kettle of wine in mind.

(*To the previous tune*)

He is clear-headed,

But I am like a donkey

To carry his heavy weight,

A man without a spouse.

CHUNYU FEN:

In the emptiness,

The lotus-flowers float cold in the stream,

In the autumn sky and water.

With few visitors to my home,

I can hardly dream a prosperous dream,

(*Falls asleep, supported by Partridge*)

But like a cold cicada chirping alone.

PARTRIDGE:

I'm going to boil some more tea for him.

LIU'ER, SHA SAN:

We'll wash our feet and leave him sleeping by himself. As the saying goes,

"*While others drink wine in the hall,*

I'll have a sound sleep in the room."

(*Exeunt all except Chunyu Fen*)

(*Enter two Royal Envoys dressed in black, followed by attendants leading an ox-cart*)

TWO ROYAL ENVOYS:

> "*To invite the royal son-in-law,*
>
> *The Royal Envoys bring a cart for him.*"

We are Royal Envoys from the Great State of Peaceful Locust. At the decree of the King, we come here to bring Mr. Chunyu as the royal son-in-law. As he is now sleeping in the east room, we'll enter the room without announcement.

> (*To Chunyu Fen*)

Mr. Chunyu!

CHUNYU FEN (*Startled from his sleep*):

Who is it?

TWO ROYAL ENVOYS (*Kneel on the ground*):

> (*To the previous tune*)
>
> The State of Peaceful Locust
>
> Is ruled by the Ant King,
>
> Who sent us to deliver a message.

CHUNYU FEN:

Why are you here?

TWO ROYAL ENVOYS:

> As to the King's decree,
>
> How can we to reveal it at will?

CHUNYU FEN:

I was having a sound sleep.

TWO ROYAL ENVOYS (*Help Chunyu Fen to his feet*):

> Please rise from your bed!
>
> We'll help you to your feet.

In our state,

> A bed for the royal son-in-law
>
> Has been prepared for you.

CHUNYU FEN (*To the previous tune*):

> What is it
>
> That descends from the sky?
>
> The autumn wind is sweeping the locust leaves.
>
> When I wake from my sweet dream,
>
> Two messengers are at the door.
>
> As I still feel blurry from the sleep,
>
> I stretch myself in my room.
>
> I tidy my dress
>
> And move my languid steps.
>
> (*An ox-cart moves onto the stage*)

TWO ROYAL ENVOYS:

> With a canopy of black satin,

The small carriage

Is pulled by white oxen.

(*Invite Chunyu Fen to get on the cart*)

With attendants on both sides,

We'll support you out of your door.

CHUNYU FEN:

Where are we going?

TWO ROYAL ENVOYS:

Enter the cave of this ancient locust-tree.

CHUNYU FEN:

How can we enter it?

TWO ROYAL ENVOYS:

The cave of this ancient locust-tree

Is the site of our State.

If you hesitate,

Please drive onward and you will see.

(*Exit one Royal Envoy*)

CHUNYU FEN (*Asks the other Royal Envoy*):

How can a state capital be in such a small cave of a locust-tree?

ROYAL ENVOY:

Mr. Chunyu, don't you remember that there was a state in the Han Dynasty called the State of Expansive Cave? Although it had expansive territory, it was situated in a cave. There was another state called the State of Peaceful Hole. Although it was peaceful, it was situated in a hole. How do you know that there is not a state in the cave of a locust-tree?

The cave of this ancient locust-tree

Is the site of our State.

Do not hesitate!

Just drive onward and you will see.

(*Exeunt all*)

(*Enter Duan Gong*)

DUAN GONG:

"*The autumn sheds its light on locust leaves;*

The spring awaits the peach-trees to blossom."

I am Duan Gong, Right Prime Minister and Marquis of Martial Feats of the State of Peaceful Locust. The royal decree comes that Chunyu Fen from Dongping County has been selected as the royal son-in-law. When he arrives, he will stay in the Donghua Guesthouse for a while and meet me first before he has an audience with His Majesty. As he has just arrived, he seems to be in a trance. In order to relieve him from his uneasiness, I've reported to His Majesty that he used to have a wine friend by the name of Zhou Bian and a pen friend by the name of Tian Zihua. I have brought both of them here, with Zhou Bian as the Royal Captain to command a few hundred soldiers and patrol the palace, and Tian Zihua as the Ritual Announcer in the guesthouse. Let's drop this subject. Another decree comes from Her Majesty the Queen that

Sister Shangzhen, Lady Lingzhi and Princess Qiongying are to visit His Highness the royal son-in-law and ease his mind before he is invited to the Xiuyi Palace and attend the wedding ceremony with Princess Golden Branch. I shall visit His Highness when he arrives at the Donghua Guesthouse. It is true to say,

"*When the royal son-in-law comes,*

The Prime Minister visits him in a small cart."

(*Exit*)

(*Enter the two Royal Envoys, with Chunyu Fen in the cart*)

CHUNYU FEN (*To the previous tune*):

In a small cart,

I enter the ancient cave

And see spectacular sight before me.

(*Murmurs to himself*)

How can there be such a place?

The city walls rise high,

With carts and people passing by.

It's strange indeed. Whoever meets me on the way will stand erect in full respect. What's the matter?

Those who follow my cart

Are ushering the way.

How is it that

Those who pass by

Are shunning from my sight?

TWO ROYAL ENVOYS:

Here we are at the State Gate.

CHUNYU FEN:

What a splendid city with towers on the city walls and a golden plate inscribed with the words "Great State of Peaceful Locust"!

(*Enter a messenger*)

MESSENGER:

By the royal decree, His Majesty invites his honoured guest to stop at the Donghua Guesthouse.

(*Kowtows, and rises to his feet to follow the procession*)

CHUNYU FEN:

There is a placard "Dismount from the Horse" to the east of the city gate. How is it that the scarlet gate on the left is wide open?

TWO ROYAL ENVOYS:

Here we are at the Donghua Guesthouse. Please get off the cart!

CHUNYU FEN (*Gets off the cart and enters the gate*):

(*Smiles aside*)

There are colourful pillars and columns in the Donghua Guesthouse, with trees and fruits in the yard. Arrayed in the hall are tables and chairs, curtains and delicacies. How pleased

I am!

(*Sound of hailing the way within*)

TWO ROYAL ENVOYS:

The Right Prime Minister is at the door.

DUAN GONG (*Greets Chunyu Fen*):

His Majesty orders me to meet you here with respect and to announce your marriage with the royal princess.

CHUNYU FEN:

As a man of low social status, how can I expect such a favour?

DUAN GONG:

The Royal Envoys are here to practise the rituals for the ceremonies. You will have an audience with His Majesty at dawn.

> *In the Donghua Guesthouse*
> *You are to practise the rituals.*
> *When roosters crow at five,*
> *The royal son-in-law is to arrive.*

Scene Eleven
Going for the Audience

(*Enter Zhou Bian, followed by palace guards and the Palace Announcer*)

ZHOU BIAN (*To the tune of **Dianjiangchun***):

> The present dynasty in an ancient cave
> Remains the same —
> A small state.
> The ritual bells resound
> In the palace in the locust-tree.

Hello, everyone.

> "*In my service in the locust root,*
> *I wear costumes and carry a sword.*
> *As Royal Captain with immense repute,*
> *My life here is no match to the human world.*"

I, Zhou Bian, used to be addicted to drinking and assuming an air of arrogance. Now, I serve as the Royal Captain with hundreds of soldiers under my command and am in charge of guarding the palace. My old friend Chunyu Fen has been selected as the royal son-in-law and will have his first audience with His Majesty. The Palace Announcer and I are waiting at the palace gate.

(*Enter the Ant King wearing flowers on his crown, followed by attendants*)

ANT KING (*To the previous tune*):

> In a white satin robe,

I wear a red crown and jade hairpins

At dawn under rosy clouds.

My daughter in the locust cave,

Will have her distinguished spouse.

"In a red crown fit for an ant,

I stay in the palace within the cave.

With the gates open I look north,

To find the world less than what I crave."

I am King of the Great State of Peaceful Locust. To find a spouse for my daughter Princess Golden Branch, I have decided on Chunyu Fen, who must have arrived. It's time for me to grant an audience with him.

PALACE ANNOUNCER (*Kowtows*):

Here I am to report to Your Majesty that the royal son-in-law has arrived.

ANT KING:

Tell the Right Prime Minister to bring him to the royal court!

PALACE ANNOUNCER:

Yes, Your Majesty.

(*Enter Chunyu Fen, following Duan Gong, the Right Prime Minister*)

CHUNYU FEN (*To the tune of **Jiangduchunxu***):

In this tiny cave of a locust-tree,

How can there be so many households

With all the fairs and streets?

Now that I have arrived at the scarlet gate,

Prime Minister Duan,

How is it that smoke coils in the palace-hall?

DUAN GONG:

It comes from the dignity of His Majesty.

At both ends of the palace-hall,

The royal maces and poleaxes

Are shining bright.

CHUNYU FEN (*Frightened*):

With a thumping heart,

I enter the palace

In disheveled dress.

ZHOU BIAN (*Greets Chunyu Fen*):

Hurry up, Your Highness the Royal Son-in-Law! His Majesty has waited for a long time.

CHUNYU FEN:

Well,

Why is he calling me the Royal Son-in-Law?

(*Whispers*)

I'm glad that Zhou Bian is here with me.

I'd like to ask but cannot get near enough.

DUAN GONG:

Come forward, Your Highness, and kowtow to His Majesty!

> Let's kowtow before the throne.

> (*Chunyu Fen kowtows with Duan Gong*)

DUAN GONG:

> Your humble servant reports
> That Heaven's bliss
> Has brought His Highness to the court.

PALACE ANNOUNCER:

Rise to your feet, Right Prime Minister. Pay tribute to His Majesty, Your Highness the Royal Son-in-Law.

DUAN GONG (*Kowtows*):

Long live the king!

> (*Rises to his feet*)

CHUNYU FEN (*Kneels on the ground and addresses the Ant King*):

The former assistant general in the Huainan troops Chunyu Fen from Dongping kowtows to Your Majesty.

> (*Kowtows three times at the directives of the Palace Announcer*)

PALACE ANNOUNCER:

Your Highness, lie prostrate and listen to the decree of His Majesty!

ANT KING:

My daughter Yaofang, with the title of Princess Golden Branch, is bestowed upon you as your spouse, in obedience to the order of your father.

CHUNYU FEN (*Lies prostrate on the ground*):

Long live the king!

ANT KING:

You may withdraw to the guesthouse.

PALACE ANNOUNCER:

His Majesty is to return to the inner palace.

> (*Exit the Ant King, amid ringing sounds of bells*)

CHUNYU FEN, DUAN GONG (*Kneel on the ground to see the Ant King off*):

> *After an audience with the king,*
> *To the princess will Chunyu cling.*

Scene Twelve
To the Princess Residence

> (Enter the Manager)

MANAGER:

> "*A former assistant in the guesthouse,*

I've been promoted to be the manager.

With the tiny future of an ant,

I have to follow countless manners."

I am manager to the Donghua Guesthouse in the State of Peaceful Locust. His Majesty has just selected his royal son-in-law, who is stopping over at the guesthouse. As this evening bodes good omen, he will go to the Xiuyi Palace to attend the wedding ceremony with Princess Golden Branch. Look, on the way are arrayed twenty pairs of golden lambs and silver wild geese, plus one hundred and twenty pairs of embroidered male and female phoenixes. The music by the female court musicians, the carriages and lanterns are ready for his departure. It is true that the ants have a heavenly marriage as well. His Highness the Royal Son-in-Law is coming in the distance.

(*Enter Chunyu Fen, in full dress*)

CHUNYU FEN (*To the tune of* **Shanglinchun**):

I suddenly find myself in the palace-hall,

Yet feel puzzled as to how that happened.

I am Chunyu Fen. How can it be that a marriage has brought me to this place to meet His Majesty? In talking about the marriage, His Majesty mentioned "in obedience to the order of your father". How queer it is! My father used to be a general serving in the border areas. I do not know whether he is alive or not. Is it possible that the Tartar king in the north has developed friendship with the State of Peaceful Locust while my father served as the go-between? Well, here come three ladies.

(*Enter Sister Shangzhen, with Lady Lingzhi and Princess Qiongying*)

SISTER SHANGZHEN, LADY LINGZHI, PRINCESS QIONGYING (*To the tune of*

Chuduizi):

Our headwear shines bright;

Our headwear shines bright.

Decorated with emerald and gold,

Our embroidered mantles smell sweet at dusk.

Who is it in the Donghua Guesthouse?

Oh, congratulations to you, Mr. Chunyu!

(*Chunyu Fen evades in embarrassment*)

SISTER SHANGZHEN, LADY LINGZHI, PRINCESS QIONGYING:

It is this Mr. Chunyu

That becomes the bridegroom.

Mr. Chunyu!

(*Chunyu Fen bows*)

SISTER SHANGZHEN:

He has grown fatter.

PRINCESS QIONGYING:

He has grown thinner.

LADY LINGZHI:

Get closer to him and feel him to see whether he's fatter or thinner.

(*Chunyu Fen evades in embarrassment*)

SISTER SHANGZHEN:

He is gently rough.

PRINCESS QIONGYING (*Smiles*):

No, he's roughly gentle.

LADY LINGZHI:

He's as innocent as a bull.

(*Chunyu Fen shows signs of impatience*)

LADY LINGZHI:

When we watched the Brahmin dance on the fifteenth day of the seventh month in the Indian Yard of the Chanzhi Temple, you helped Princess Qiongying hang her wet towel on a bamboo. Have you forgotten all about that?

(*Chunyu Fen thinks and sighs*)

PRINCESS QIONGYING:

When we offered the gold hairpins and the rhino-horn case before the altar after we listened to Master Qixuan's preaching on Avalokitesvara Sutra, you enjoyed them very much and lingered a long time before them. Do you still keep this incident in your mind?

CHUNYU FEN (*Thinks*):

> "As it lies deep in my heart,
>
> How can I ever forget it?"

SISTER SHANGZHEN:

Who knows that he has become an in-law with us! Let's go to the Xiuyi Palace and wait for him there!

SISTER SHANGZHEN, LADY LINGZHI, PRINCESS QIONGYING:

> It is this Mr. Chunyu
>
> That becomes the bridegroom.

(*Exeunt*)

(*Enter Tian Zihua in official dress, followed by attendants*)

TIAN ZIHUA (*To the previous tune*):

> The best man,
>
> The best man
>
> Goes to the State of Peaceful Locust.
>
> Princess Golden Branch by the name of Yaofang
>
> Is married to the bachelor Chunyu.
>
> In holiday costume,
>
> He has the lucky star over his head.

(*Greets Chunyu Fen*)

TIAN ZIHUA:

How are you, Your Highness? At the royal edict, I am to serve as your best man.

CHUNYU FEN:

Are you Tian Zihua from Pingyi?

TIAN ZIHUA:

Yes, I am.

CHUNYU FEN:

How is it that you are here?

TIAN ZIHUA:

When I roamed here, I was held in high esteem by Duan Gong, Right Prime Minister and Marquis of Martial Feats. Therefore, I have been staying here.

CHUNYU FEN:

Do you know that Zhou Bian is also here?

TIAN ZIHUA:

Zhou Bian has obtained a high position. As he has great power in his position as the Royal Captain, he has protected me on several occasions.

CHUNYU FEN:

As the three of us are gathered here, I won't feel lonely any more. What a happy coincidence! What a happy coincidence!

    (*Enter the Royal Envoy*)

ROYAL ENVOY:

The time of good omen is approaching for you to enter the palace and attend the wedding ceremony.

TIAN ZIHUA:

It happens that I can watch this grand ceremony today. I wish that he would not desert his old friend. Please ascend the carriage.

    (*The Royal Envoy helps Chunyu Fen onto the carriage*)

    (*Enter the attendants, carrying lanterns in their hands. They walk*)

ALL (*To the previous tune*):

    We march in the capital town,

    We march in the capital town,

    With miles of grand procession,

    With lanterns shining the way.

CHUNYU FEN:

Brother Zihua,

    I feel uneasy sitting in the carriage.

TIAN ZIHUA (*Smiles*):

You deserve this honour, Your Highness.

    Rest at ease

    As there is no need of embarrassment.

    (*Exeunt all*)

    (*Enter Princess Qiongying and her company*)

PRINCESS QIONGYING (*Laughs cheerfully amid music*):

    The embroidered curtains of the princess,

    The embroidered curtains of the princess

    Will be closed at night by the locust-trees.

When we offered incense before the altar,

Our towel and hairpins caused a long dream.

(*Enter Chunyu Fen, followed by his company*)

ALL:

The harmonious bride and bridegroom

Will meet in the bridal room.

(*Exeunt Princess Qiongying and her company while Chunyu Fen and his company make way*)

CHUNYU FEN:

Brother Zihua, these ladies come and go in their own carriages. Their fairy-like music is sweet and bitter, never heard of in the human world.

TIAN ZIHUA:

As the auspicious time is approaching, let's hurry up!

CHUNYU FEN (*To the previous tune*):

The fairy music rings bitter and loud,

The fairy music rings bitter and loud

That comes from the ladies' carriages.

The music sounds like woeful waters and winds,

Making me sad at heart as well.

TIAN ZIHUA:

Since time and tide await no man, why don't you enjoy the music to your heart's content?

Leave the human world aside

And meet in palace your bride!

Here we are at the Xiuyi Palace. Descend the carriage, please. As the fairy ladies are gathering around the gate, I have to be off now. It is true that

While Chunyu goes to his spouse,

I have to head for my own house.

(*Exit*)

Scene Thirteen
Marrying the Royal Princess

(*Enter Princess Qiongying, followed by her company amid music*)

PRINCESS QIONGYING (*To the tune of* **Qingjiangyin**):

The fairy sisters meet the fairy in-law,

Who comes by a fairy carriage.

The fairy music rings to the sky

As the fairy musicians come to the fairy house.

Tell the fairy young man

To descend and bow to the Xiuyi Palace!

LADY LINGZHI:

Royal Princess, please come to the palace hall!

(*Enter Princess Golden Branch, sheltered by fans*)

PRINCESS GOLDEN BRANCH (*To the tune of* **Nüguanzi**):

> No sooner had the clouds dispersed
>
> Than I left my dressing-table and expected.
>
> I have just left my palace
>
> And come to my new residence.
>
> My shadowy secret desire
>
> Makes me shy.

(*Princess Qiongying, Lady Lingzhi and Sister Shangzhen laugh*)

LADY LINGZHI:

May we invite His Highness the Royal Son-in-Law to open the fans please?

(*Enter Chunyu Fen*)

CHUNYU FEN:

> I am about to see the fairy princess,
>
> Who will reveal her flowery face
>
> From behind the sheltering fans.

ALL:

> With a deep root for the marriage,
>
> This princess of distinction
>
> Has selected her royal spouse.

LADY LINGZHI (*Announces*):

The bride and the bridegroom, bow to Heaven and Earth… Bow to His Majesty the King and Her Majesty the Queen… Your Highness, bow to the Princess! Princess, return the bow!

(*Enter the eunuch, bringing the wine*)

EUNUCH:

> "*In the State of Peaceful Locust brews the wine;*
>
> *In the wedding hall a couple is formed at night.*"

The wine is a gift from His Majesty the King and Her Majesty the Queen to celebrate the royal marriage.

(*Chunyu Fen and Princess Golden Branch kowtow to express their gratitude*)

LADY LINGZHI:

The bride and the bridegroom, drink a cup of wine for the wedding!

(*Chunyu Fen and Princess Golden Branch drink the wine*)

CHUNYU FEN (*To the tune of* **Jintangyue**):

> Decorated with a gold cicada on the hat
>
> And a phoenix hairpin on the head,
>
> The warrior marries a beautiful lady.
>
> Embroidered on the robe
>
> Is a thrush darting through the leaves.
>
> After the wedding at the royal decree,

I can see the face of the princess.

ALL:

Light the gold lamp

And you will see the ant princess

In her full beauty in the locust palace.

PRINCESS GOLDEN BRANCH (*To the previous tune*):

I am too ashamed to say

That to face a warrior descendent,

How can I sustain him

In my youthful age?

In the Xiuyi Palace,

I've just learned to make up.

As a princess entitled Golden Branch,

I get married near the locust-tree.

ALL:

Light the gold lamp

And you will see the ant princess

In her full beauty in the locust palace.

LADY LINGZHI, SISTER SHANGZHEN, PRINCESS QIONGYING (*Aside*):

(*To the previous tune*)

Their marriage

Came from the sacred place

Of the Buddhist temple

By sheer chance.

(*Turn back*)

A few remarks

And the hairpins roused his thoughts.

He yearned for the princess,

A born spouse for him.

ALL:

Light the gold lamp

And you will see the ant princess

In her full beauty in the locust palace.

LADY LINGZHI, SISTER SHANGZHEN, PRINCESS QIONGYING:

(*To the previous tune*)

In the natural environment,

The pavilions and gardens

In royal splendour

Form a picture of a visionary world.

In a mystical tune,

Music resounds in the deep cave.

(*Aside*)

The ladies attended the sutra lectures;

The royal princess built a grand palace.

ALL:

Light the gold lamp

And you will see the ant princess

In her full beauty in the locust palace.

LADY LINGZHI, SISTER SHANGZHEN, PRINCESS QIONGYING:

The moon has ascended to the sky.

(*To the tune of* **Zuiwengzi**)

Roll the window curtain

And you see the bright moon shine over the palace.

CHUNYU FEN:

The fairy lady is at the window,

Playing a flute in smile.

Tonight,

In the mist and fog,

I gaze at the mysterious residence.

ALL:

Who has ever seen

A precious flower

Is planted in the locust state?

CHUNYU FEN (*In a low voice*):

(*To the previous tune*)

It is fantastic

That I shall sleep in the palace.

The twenty-four bridges in Yangzhou

Are far away from the pretty maid.

How can I imagine

That I shall go alone

And stay in a magnificent house?

ALL:

Who has ever seen

A precious flower

Is planted in the locust state?

CHUNYU FEN (*Walks*):

(*To the tune of* **Yaoyaoling**)

It is warm in the locust caves,

With flowers in full blossom.

Amid songs in the moonlight,

The ladies are in high spirits,

Outshining the faraway hills.

ALL (*To the previous tune*):

Half drunk at night,

Chunyu will remain in palace,

To join his new bride.

He seems to meet an immortal

In his bed-play.

(*To the tune of* **Coda**)

You'll enjoy the first taste of married life tonight.

Remember to thank His Majesty at dawn!

Paint your eyebrows and make up

If you do not sleep late after your love-making.

(*In the pattern of* **Collected Tang Poems**)

The princess plays the flute and chases her mate,

Under the cloudy sky until late at night.

Remember not to shut the door tight,

So as to catch your carriage to the palace gate!

Scene Fourteen
Potential Enemy

(*Enter the red-faced King of the State of Sandals and Vines, followed by soldiers*)

KING OF THE STATE OF SANDALS AND VINES (*To the tune of* **Heshengchao**):

The earth has undergone great changes,

Forming the State of Sandals and Vines.

Yellow faced, red-footed and slender in figures,

The ant states are fighting all the time.

"A central state is founded in the wilderness,

With the capital encircled by walls of clay.

The field is not large enough for swordplay,

But there is still battle-cry on the way."

I am King of the State of Sandals and Vines to the east of the State of Peaceful Locust. Our state stretches to the east as far as the White Sandals and to the west as far as the Wisterias. Our descendents are scattered in nine streams and eight caves; our houses have a hundred holes and a thousand windows. With two equal lords in the court, who can strive to be the superior? As the locust-tree and the white sandals are both wood for the winter, who can change the order of the seasons? As he is a black ant while I am a red ant, there exists the difference. He thinks that he is a stronger ant and thus looks down upon me. Recently I got a message that he has added the word Great before the State of Peaceful Locust. He is indeed looking down upon me! Across the river is the Nanke County under his reign, which is a land affluent with fish and rice. I intend to gather my tribal troops and loot this area.

(*The soldiers practice martial arts*)

KING OF THE STATE OF SANDALS AND VINES (*To the tune of **Baoziling***):

What difference is there between the ants?

The territories and the armies are on a par.

He bullies us for we are small and lack grains,

But I have a swift army that can march afar.

ALL:

Every one of us is warrior-like.

KING OF THE STATE OF SANDALS AND VINES (*To the previous tune*):

To the west of the river is Nanke County,

Where he amasses meat and grains to threaten us.

To strip the State of Peaceful Locust of its peace,

On our banners are inscribed Great Sandals and Vines.

ALL:

Every one of us is warrior-like.

Bordered on the land of Rakshasa,

We are soldiers of vine shields.

As Nanke County is like a reed,

We'll go and loot on the fields.

Scene Fifteen
Attending the Royal Hunting

(*Enter the Ant King, followed by attendants*)

ANT KING (*To the tune of **Baodingxian***):

Amid gentle breeze in the green locust-trees

I enjoy the leisure on the grand terrace

When the sun shines over the world.

Our tiny state is like the human empire,

Founded in the wilderness at Heaven's decrees.

(*Enter Chunyu Fen with Duan Gong*)

CHUNYU FEN:

His Majesty attends the banquet with his ministers

But battle reports arrive from the frontiers.

CHUNYU FEN, DUAN GONG:

On a tiny land with tiny hills,

The tiny people and tiny steeds

Are hunting in the fields.

(*Kowtow to the Ant King*)

ANT KING (*In the pattern of **Yulouchun***):

"*Our home and hearth lies between Wu and Chu,*

With miniature palaces in the chilly autumn.

CHUNYU FEN:

Chirps resound in the ancient tree,

Announcing the arrival of chilly dew.

DUAN GONG:

The incense smoke goes straight in the still air

While our cave faces the sky that is close by.

ANT KING, CHUNYU FEN, DUAN GONG:

We have no worries from the other ant states,

Except for the State of Sandals and Vines."

ANT KING:

I notice from the memorials yesterday that the State of Sandals and Vines is invading the borders of Nanke County. As our state has been in peace for many years, our people are unacquainted with military actions. The Right Prime Minister advises me to go hunting in the Tortoise Hill to promote military practice. I don't know whether there was ever any warfare in the past during this dynasty.

DUAN GONG:

Yes, there were stories in the past. In the first year of Qianyuan, the Han Dynasty, the people of Henei saw hundreds and thousands of ant troops coming and going from morning till night. In the middle years of Taiyuan, the Jin Dynasty, the family of Huan Qian saw armoured ants holding spears climb the tables and cabinets to grab food. In the first year of Tian'an, the Northern Wei Dynasty, red and black ants were seen fighting in Yanzhou and the red ants died with their heads cut off. In the fourth year of Wuding, the Eastern Wei Dynasty, yellow and black ants were seen fighting in Yedu and the yellow ants returned triumphantly and died. All these are stories about battles in our state.

ANT KING:

Was there any hunting in the past during this dynasty?

DUAN GONG:

In the Southern Qi Dynasty, the family of Xu Xuan saw thousands of ant warriors hunting on the flower-beds and fishing in the Yanshan Lake with hundreds of nets and having a catch of nearly a thousand fish. This is a story of hunting in our dynasty.

ANT KING:

Why should we go hunting on the Tortoise Hill?

DUAN GONG:

Among the constellations in the sky, the Tortoise is a military star. Therefore, we should go to the Tortoise Hill to promote military practice in our state.

ANT KING:

You are right, Right Prime Minister. Have you arranged officers and officials to accompany me?

CHUNYU FEN:

The Royal Captain Zhou Bian will be in charge of military affairs, Consultant Tian Zihua will be in charge of civil affairs, and Right Prime Minister Duan Gong and I will stand on guard for Your Majesty.

ANT KING:

In that case, let's set off!

> (*Walks*)
>
> (*To the tune of* **Haoshijin**)
>
> To travel to the western suburbs,
>
> I set off on an auspicious day.
>
> The flags with emblems of flowers and birds
>
> Disperse the animals and fowls.
>
> The resounding drums
>
> Startle the hills and rills, grass and trees.
>
> I decree at the auspicious hour,
>
> With bugles ringing in the hunting range.
>
> (*Arrives*)

ANT KING:

Is this the Tortoise Hill? It towers to the sky and rises from the earth. The texture at the back of the hill is in the same pattern as the constellations. Therefore, it is only natural that the ancients climbed the Tortoise Hill and slaughtered the turtle in the ninth month. The hill is lush with grass and trees, abundant in animals and fowls. It can equal the Changyang and Shanglin hunting ranges in the human world. Announce my edict that the warriors may start hunting at full scale!

> (*Attendants respond to the edict*)
>
> (*Drumbeats and battle cries*)
>
> (*A tiger is shot and captured*)

ANT KING (*Shoots at a wild goose*):

> (*To the tune of* **Qianqiusui**)
>
> When we use our bows and swords,
>
> The winged animals and fowls cannot escape.
>
> The pellets and guns are shot to the sky
>
> To knit a heavenly net,
>
> To knit a heavenly net,
>
> Directly reaching
>
> The paths to the sea and to the hill.
>
> Kill what is caught
>
> And cudgel what is trodden down!
>
> On foot and on horseback,
>
> Just thrust right and left!

ATTENDANTS (*Shout*):

A pangolin is caught!

ANT KING (*Laughs heartily*):

It is a sworn enemy of our ant state.

ATTENDANTS:

> Although the pangolin can drill a hill,

It cannot escape from the bloody rain

Predestined by Heaven.

TIAN ZIHUA:

On this grand occasion, Tian Zihua, the consultant and a low-rank official, would like to present my *Poetic Essay on the Grand Hunting on the Tortoise Hill, the Great State of Peaceful Locust*.

ANT KING:

Present your essay!

TIAN ZIHUA (*Reads his poetic essay on his knees*):

"How deep and remote is the Great State of Peaceful Locust! It has the Dragon Peak in the front and the Tortoise Hill at the back, which is the essence of the Northern God. To the west is the Tortoise Peak of West Queen Mother; to the east is Mount Tortoise and Mount Meng of the Eastern Prince. The Tortoise Hill, with its vault at the top and its emptiness in the centre, is shaped like the remains of a huge snake in Mount Baqiu, covered with lush grass and trees like the mountains held up by the turtles in the sea. It has grass and trees on its back and animals and fowls in its chest. From the literary point of view, it conforms to the number of Eight Diagrams in the *Picture from the Yellow River* and the *Book from the Luoshui River*; from the military point of view, it bears the appearance of a warrior in armoured coat and helmet. His Highness the Honorary Royal Captain Chunyu Fen, the Right Prime Minister Duan Gong and other ministers raise their heads to the sky and heave a sigh, 'Vast and expansive is the Tortoise Hill! Green and luxuriant is the Tortoise Hill!' If Your Majesty does not go hunting, tigers and rhinoceros will escape from their cages and hurt people; if Your Majesty does not enjoy yourself today, tortoise shell and jade will be damaged in their caskets. Therefore, Your Majesty shares military feats in the fields with the common people. It is now the month when chilly breeze arrives while grass and trees wither and perish. The eagle preys on the fowls and the jackal sacrifices its catch of animals. Your Majesty wears a towering crown and a black robe, carrying the treasure sword and ascending the carriage. The God of Rain sprinkles the way for you while the God of Wind clears the dust for you. The Left Marquis Cheng and the Right Marquis Chunyu lead a multitude of hundreds and thousands of ant-subordinates of various sizes on foot and on horseback. With resounding drumbeats, fluttering flags, roaring guns and glittering swords, the soldiers are marshalled on the tortoise shell when the wind and rain has ceased. When time has arrived for the hunting, the soldiers are on the go. They hang the ape and trample on the snake, break the bear's claw and crush the elephant teeth, eat the leopard and suck the rhinoceros, taste the marrow of wild hens and swallow the brain of wild crows. As to pheasants, hares and the ilk, Your Majesty would not take any notice. A scaled animal is caught at the end of the hunting — it is a pangolin. It has a carapace that can penetrate the hills and a most poisonous mouth that can float above the water. It used to dwell on the slopes of the hill and is now presented before Your Majesty when it is roasted. In great elation, Your Majesty raises your head to the sky and says, 'It is the bliss of the Tortoise Hill that the pangolin meets its doom. I am too insignificant to acclaim the victory!' With soil and rocks as its shell and with grass and trees as its hairs, the Tortoise Hill has been thoroughly combed in this hunting. Afterwards, the hunting comes to an end and the animals of prey are slaughtered; the bells are sounded and toasts are raised; the procession returns triumphantly. After the wining and dining,

I pick up a bamboo slip and write a eulogy to be presented to Your Majesty. The eulogy goes, 'Magnificent is the Tortoise Hill, which is shielded by the Dragon Peak; brilliant is Your Majesty, who goes hunting on the Tortoise Hill. Neither fish nor flesh, rain or shine, the prophecy shows signs of good omen. Your Majesty has displayed militancy without disturbing the people. May the Great State of Peaceful Locust last as long as the Tortoise Hill! May Your Majesty live a long, long life!'"

ANT KING (*Laughs heartily*):

What a nice piece of poetic essay! Emperor Wu of the Han Dynasty did not know Sima Xiangru who wrote such a nice piece of poetic essay as *A Poetic Essay on Sheer Fabrication*. How lucky I am that I know you!

>(*To the tune of **Haoshijin***)
>
>What a striking piece of writing
>
>That depicts the hunting!
>
>How handsome
>
>Is Minister Tian Zihua!
>
>Lofty
>
>Is your spirit that roars to the sky.

Chunyu Fen, this brilliant essay by Tian Zihua must be passed down through the generations. It should be inscribed on a gilded jade slab as a sign to show that our state is rich in talents.

>It adds a tale of distinction to this hill.
>
>What position shall I grant him?
>
>A man who writes about sheer fabrication
>
>Lives during my reign.

Right Prime Minister, how do you enjoy the hunting today?

DUAN GONG:

We are here promoting military practice on this hill, not for pleasure but for the urgent situation in Nanke County. I have inserted a line in the National Chronology.

ANT KING:

What did you write?

DUAN GONG:

In the eighth month, the first year of Yicheng of the Great State of Peaceful Locust, a grand hunting is held on the Tortoise Hill to promote military practice.

ANT KING:

In that case, announce my edict for another military manoeuvre!

>(*Military manoeuvre amid drums and bugles*)

ANT KING (*To the tune of **Qianqiusui***):

>In military manoeuvre,
>
>The beasts of prey are attacked
>
>In rounds and rounds of encirclement.
>
>(*The military manoeuvre goes on*)
>
>Wave the flag,

Wave the flag

And rush forward in battle cries

Lest the enemy should escape!

Wield the rakes

And the spears

In the front

And at the rear —

That is military practice.

The eagle-hunters

Have done merits again.

Announce my edict to finish the hunting and return to the palace!

(*All respond*)

(*Drums and bugles*)

(*To the tune of* **Yuerenhao**)

To return from the hunting,

To return from the hunting,

The drumbeats resound

And the cymbals ring.

Soft and loud

Echoes the music of jade flutes,

Mixed with the blare of bamboo flutes

In perfect harmony.

With spears erect

And in battle array,

On the highway

Stands the procession.

Wearing helmets and waving whips,

They gallop homeward.

While they ride,

They raise a hue and cry.

(*Announces the edict for the procession to go forward*)

(*To the previous tune*)

On the dusty ancient way,

On the dusty ancient way,

The sly animals are carried on the poles,

Which gasped and tried in vain to escape

From the hunting dogs and eagles.

The chilly tree branches

Touch the moist fowl-nests,

Which are deserted now.

The noisy crowd

Whistle a valiant tune

Back and forth.

When they look at the fowls

And carry the animal meat,

They will not say that the land is tiny.

Such a catch

Is by no means small.

DUAN GONG:

Your Majesty, here we are at the capital gate.

(*To the tune of* **Hongxiuxie**)

The soldiers stop their roar,

Stop their roar.

They congratulate His Majesty

On his great catch.

They distribute the meat

And win their rewards,

After they skin the beast

And burn the meat

To share and share alike

And make offerings to the swords.

(*To the tune of* **Coda**)

They go hunting in the autumn day

To serve as camouflage for military manoeuvre.

ATTENDANTS:

May the Tortoise Hill bless His Majesty for years and years!

ANT KING:

Now that the military inspection is over, Chunyu Fen will stay with me and have dinner in the central palace-hall. The Right Prime Minister will entertain the dukes and royal relatives in the Locust Corner Pavilion and discuss the Nanke affairs.

In order to learn and practice military art

Thousands of troops leave the capital town.

How much can His Majesty eat in a meal?

The carts carry the beasts of prey up and down.

Scene Sixteen
Tidings about Chunyu's Father

(*Enter Chunyu Fen and Princess Golden Branch*)

CHUNYU FEN (*To the tune of* **Moshanxi**):

Here in the human world

Live the immortals.

There are vernal sights

In the autumn palace.

PRINCESS GOLDEN BRANCH:

I turn my slender waist

Like a fish in the water.

With coyness between my brows,

I cherish my bridal joys.

CHUNYU FEN (*In the pattern of* **Ruanlanggui**):

"The breeze ruffles the green silken robe,

Spreading fragrant scent over the globe.

PRINCESS GOLDEN BRANCH:

The locust casts shadows o'er the window case

When we rise late and walk out in full grace.

CHUNYU FEN:

I have crossed the dreamland

And waited on the pretty princess —

An experience out of my command.

PRINCESS GOLDEN BRANCH:

Your Highness,

Lest you miss the morning court and drowse,

I have risen early and painted my brows."

Since you came here a month ago, we have cultivated an ever-deepening affection for each other. You have lived a sumptuous life, coming and going in magnificent carriages and attending numerous banquets. Although you are lower in rank than His Majesty, you have tasted enough distinction. However, I have noticed that you often knit your brows and heave deep sighs or remain silent in sorrow. I do not see the reason why.

CHUNYU FEN:

After I fell on wretched days for many years, I have become prosperous all at once. Why should I be discontented with His Majesty and you, my dear wife, let alone all the food and clothing I can now enjoy in the palace? The sorrow you have noticed comes from the sad memory of my late father while I enjoy the heavenly pleasures with His Majesty.

PRINCESS GOLDEN BRANCH:

When did your parents die?

CHUNYU FEN:

Your mother-in-law is buried in our family graveyard near the Chanzhi Bridge. Your father-in-law is a pity indeed.

PRINCESS GOLDEN BRANCH:

Please tell me in detail, Your Highness!

CHUNYU FEN (*To the tune of* **Bailianxu**):

To tell you what is on my mind,

I have to heave a profound sigh.

As a general, my late father

Suffered a defeat where the borders lie.

PRINCESS GOLDEN BRANCH:

After the defeat, did your father return alive?

CHUNYU FEN (*Sighs*):

He died.

PRINCESS GOLDEN BRANCH:

Where did he die?

CHUNYU FEN:

He died in the barbarous area.

PRINCESS GOLDEN BRANCH:

Have you received any message from him in all these years?

CHUNYU FEN:

There is no message for a dozen of years.

But there has been something strange in recent days.

PRINCESS GOLDEN BRANCH:

What has happened?

CHUNYU FEN:

Before our wedding the other day, His Majesty mentioned to me himself that he did all this in obedience to the order of my father. I have been puzzled all the time.

PRINCESS GOLDEN BRANCH:

You have to ask my father.

CHUNYU FEN:

I had not dared to ask until the court banquet after the hunting on the Tortoise Hill. I asked, "Since Your Majesty knows where my father lives, I'd like to ask for leave to pay him a visit." His Majesty replied at once, "Stationed in the north, your father has kept sending me messages. You can write him a letter but cannot go for the time being." Princess,

What is the reason?

Hidden doubts

Have arisen in me.

PRINCESS GOLDEN BRANCH (*To the tune of **Zuitaiping***):

It seems to me

That you were alone in your youth.

Where you meet your wife,

You have found your father.

CHUNYU FEN (*Weeps*):

How is he going in the north?

PRINCESS GOLDEN BRANCH:

As he is stationed in the north,

He must be living happily there.

CHUNYU FEN (*Weeps again*):

Now that I have told you about the story, I shall secretly go north and inquire about my father.

PRINCESS GOLDEN BRANCH:

> How muddle-headed you are!
>
> As the barbarous areas are faraway,
>
> How can you find the way by yourself?

CHUNYU FEN:

Then I shall report to His Majesty and go there in the open.

PRINCESS GOLDEN BRANCH:

> Now that his daughter
>
> Has married for just a few days,
>
> How can he allow you to go?

CHUNYU FEN (*To the tune of* **Bailianxu**):

> It is inconceivable
>
> That he stays in the north
>
> In cold weather and in desolation.
>
> How can it be compared to the cave here?

PRINCESS GOLDEN BRANCH:

Do as my father told you and first send him a letter to express your regard!

CHUNYU FEN:

> I hesitate
>
> To send a letter alone.

PRINCESS GOLDEN BRANCH:

Send him some gifts as well!

CHUNYU FEN (*Weeps*):

> Nothing can express my gratitude.

PRINCESS GOLDEN BRANCH:

In that case, what is to be done?

CHUNYU FEN:

Dear Princess,

> A son like me
>
> Is as good as nothing.

PRINCESS GOLDEN BRANCH (*Aside*):

> (*To the tune of* **Zuitaiping**)
>
> How wretched for him
>
> To be a son-in-law in the royal house!
>
> He has to be pious to his father
>
> And follow the court practice.
>
> (*Turns back*)

How can you stay in my state and send a letter without sending any gifts, Your Highness? I have prepared a pair of longevity stockings and a pair of happiness shoes to go with your letter.

CHUNYU FEN:

Thank you for your kindness!

PRINCESS GOLDEN BRANCH:

> My needlework
>
> Shows the heart of his daughter-in-law.

CHUNYU FEN:

Who will carry the letter for me?

PRINCESS GOLDEN BRANCH:

> When you finish your letter,
>
> I shall report to my father
>
> And the letter will be there in no time.

CHUNYU FEN:

Then, please go to the palace and report to His Majesty as soon as I seal the letter and the gifts!

PRINCESS GOLDEN BRANCH:

No problem.

> Even if I send the letter by a wild goose,
>
> I shall help you
>
> Express your filial piety.

By the way, I have another question to ask you. What kind of official position do you like to take?

CHUNYU FEN:

As a wanderer in the world, I am not well-versed in governmental affairs.

PRINCESS GOLDEN BRANCH:

You just accept the offer and I will give you a helping hand.

> (*To the tune of **Coda***)
>
> I'll enter the palace to send the letter for you
>
> And ask my father to grant you a position.

CHUNYU FEN:

By so doing, I shall become an official through petticoat influence.

PRINCESS GOLDEN BRANCH:

Through petticoat influence or not,

> You will not defame the Chunyu ancestors.
>
> *It's hard to send a letter by the son,*
>
> *Who is just wedded to a pretty wife.*
>
> *The verdant locust is so good*
>
> *That he can live a pleasant life.*

Scene Seventeen
The Position of the Magistrate

(*Enter Duan Gong*)

DUAN GONG (*To the tune of* **Raodiyou**):

> Holding the gold seal and the purple ribbon
>
> As the Prime Minister,
>
> I leave the court when the sun climbs high.
>
> With fewer hair
>
> And narrower waist,
>
> I work for the state heart and soul.
>
> "*I go to the palace at dawn*
>
> *And leave the palace in the morn.*
>
> *Before His Majesty summons me,*
>
> *I close my door in the locust tree.*"

I am Duan Gong, Right Prime Minister and Marquis of Martial Feats. I take charge of the governmental affairs and keep a close watch of the border affairs. As the State of Sandals and Vines is harassing our border regions, His Majesty gave a banquet at the Locust Corner Pavilion to consult with the ministers as to who will be appointed Magistrate of Nanke County. I do not know who is to be appointed yet. Here arrives the Royal Envoy.

(*Enter the Royal Envoy*)

ROYAL ENVOY:

> "*Seldom are the reports to be presented to the king;*
>
> *To inform the intimate ministers is the first thing.*"

(*Greets Duan Gong*)

You must have taken much trouble during the morning audience, Your Excellency.

DUAN GONG:

I was just asking the secretariat about the position of the magistrate of Nanke County. I don't know whether the royal edict has arrived.

ROYAL ENVOY:

You know, no sooner had your memorial been presented than the Royal Princess entered the palace to dispatch His Highness's letter to his father and to ask for an official position for him. I am afraid that this position has fallen into the hands of His Highness.

DUAN GONG:

It's hard to say.

(*To the tune of* **Tiyindeng**)

> Nanke takes a strategic position,
>
> Bordering on the State of Sandals and Vines.
>
> Addicted to drinking,
>
> How can Chunyu shoulder this responsibility?

ALL:

> Shall we agree?
>
> Ill at ease in our hearts,
>
> We can hardly interfere with royal decisions.

ROYAL ENVOY (*To the previous tune*):

> The governmental affairs depend on the ministers,
>
> For there must be somewhere to get suggestions.

However, one thing is clear, that is, the ministers should not get involved in affairs between close relations.

> Now that he lives with the princess,
>
> Rubbing shoulders every day,
>
> Why should he not take this position?

ALL:

> Shall we agree?
>
> Ill at ease in our hearts,
>
> We can hardly interfere with royal decisions.

DUAN GONG:

We have to let it be. I am only afraid that he will do harm to the state when he grows powerful. Well, forget about it.

> *To be appointed the new magistrate*
>
> *Is the yearning of ministers old and great.*
>
> *We have to follow the bent of the King*
>
> *And see who will be the pillar of the state.*

Scene Eighteen
Appointed as the Magistrate

(*Enter Chunyu Fen*)

CHUNYU FEN (*To the tune of* **Xijiangyue**):

> Born in the family of an army officer,
>
> I happen to serve in a royal state.
>
> Since I have won the heart of the princess,
>
> What is there that cannot be revealed?

(*In the pattern of* **Collected Tang Poems**)

> "*A flute girl from the region of Qin*
>
> *Bright and lively in the royal court.*
>
> *I happen to catch sight of her*
>
> *Returning at night by the back door.*"

A few days ago, the princess entered the palace to dispatch my letter and gifts for my father and to ask for an official position for me. I see so many sash lanterns on the street tonight. Here comes the princess.

(*Enter Princess Golden Branch, followed by court ladies carrying lanterns*)

PRINCESS GOLDEN BRANCH (*To the previous tune*):

I attended banquets several nights,

A favour bestowed by my parents.

With lanterns illuminating the street,

I hurry home behind curtains.

(*Greets Chunyu Fen*)

CHUNYU FEN:

I feel so lonely in the several nights when you were in the palace. Have you had my letter dispatched?

PRINCESS GOLDEN BRANCH:

Please listen to me.

(*To the tune of **Yubaodu***)

When I presented your letter,

His Majesty said that it was proper.

He had the letter dispatched at once

And gave advice time and again.

CHUNYU FEN:

I'm afraid that the reply will be delayed.

PRINCESS GOLDEN BRANCH:

Since you have expressed your filial piety,

It does not matter when the reply comes.

(*Enter a young soldier*)

YOUNG SOLDIER:

"*Never become a soldier in your life;*

To be a soldier is full of strife."

I am a young soldier from the north, carrying a letter of peace from the father of His Highness. Here I am to deliver the letter.

(*Kowtows to Chunyu Fen*)

When I delivered your letter in the north, your father was very happy. Here is a letter of reply.

CHUNYU FEN (*With a pleasant surprise*):

Rise to your feet! Rise to your feet! Now I receive the letter of reply at last. Oh, my dear father!

(*Opens the letter and reads*)

"A letter of peace to my son Chunyu Fen." Yes, these eight words do look like my father's handwriting.

PRINCESS GOLDEN BRANCH:

Would you read the letter for me?

CHUNYU FEN (*Reads the letter*):

"At the request of the King of the Great State of Peaceful Locust, I would like you to marry to the Royal Princess. When I receive your letter and the socks, I get to know that the wedding ceremony has been held. How elated I am that Her Highness the Royal Princess is so virtuous!

Since we parted nearly twenty years ago, I have been missing you all the time. Now that you have become an intimate member of the royal house in the locust state, you should be prudent in everything you do. I always keep my old friends in my mind, but I do not know how many kith and kin are still alive. You'd better send me a more detailed letter to relieve me of my cares. I'd like to go and see you, but I am hindered by the hardship of the long distance. I am grieved that I cannot see you in person. Since it is not convenient for you to come to see me for the time being, I hope that I can meet you in the year of the ox."

(*Pats the letter and wails loudly*)

I thought that he was dead since we have not seen each other for nearly twenty years. I did not expect that I should receive his letter and learn that he is safe and sound. What is the use of a son if he cannot see his father?

(*Collapses on the ground for excessive grief*)

PRINCESS GOLDEN BRANCH (*Helps Chunyu Fen to his feet*):

Do not be over-grieved, Your Highness!

CHUNYU FEN (*To the previous tune*):

Safe and sound,

My father gives teachings as of old.

He asks about his kith and kin,

Full of grief for the vicissitude of life.

PRINCESS GOLDEN BRANCH:

It is good that you shall meet him in the year of the ox.

CHUNYU FEN:

Can we meet each other at that time?

How can I sleep with ease of mind?

(*Enter the Royal Envoy, holding the edict in his hands*)

ROYAL ENVOY (*To the tune of **Fendie'er***):

With the edict to appoint the magistrate,

I arrive at the residence of His Highness.

Here arrives the royal edict. Kneel on the ground and listen to the edict, which says, "Ours has been a state with wise people and royal relatives in the court, well-versed in civil and military affairs. As Nanke County is not well administrated, the former magistrate has been dismissed from office. I herewith appoint you as the magistrate and you can go with my daughter. The above is my edict. Give thanks to the Royal Grace!"

(*Chunyu Fen and Princess Golden Branch rise to their feet*)

ROYAL ENVOY (*Kowtows to Chunyu Fen and Princess Golden Branch*):

Congratulations to you on your appointment as the magistrate, Your Highnesses! His Majesty has something else to say.

(*To the tune of **Yubaodu***)

Tell the officials in charge

To prepare the luggage for the magistrate.

Excited at the departure of her dear daughter,

Her Majesty has prepared a sumptuous dowry.

PRINCESS GOLDEN BRANCH:

Is there anything else to say?

ROYAL ENVOY:

> With carriages and servants lining the street,
>
> Her Majesty will see you off in person.

CHUNYU FEN (*Elated*):

> (*To the previous tune*)
>
> How could I expect this in the past?
>
> I used to wander in the world and get drunk.
>
> I have never imagined that I become a son-in-law
>
> Who can drink tasty wine and serve in Nanke.

ALL:

> A predestined marriage brings the couple together
>
> To enjoy all the pleasures of life.

ROYAL ENVOY (*To the tune of* **Coda**):

> To marry the royal princess brings distinction.
>
> Get dressed for the morning court
>
> And thank His Majesty before you leave!
>
> (*Exit*)

776

CHUNYU FEN:

But for your recommendation, I would not have obtained this position.

PRINCESS GOLDEN BRANCH:

The pleasure is mine.

CHUNYU FEN:

I have something else to ask you. It is difficult for me to manage such a large county as Nanke all by myself. Besides, as I have a casual disposition, I intend to have Tian Zihua and Zhou Bian to assist me in managing the county affairs with the consent of His Majesty. What do you think of it?

PRINCESS GOLDEN BRANCH:

It's up to you to decide.

> *Newly appointed as the Nanke magistrate,*
>
> *Chunyu Fen thanks his wife for all the grace.*
>
> *As tomorrow he has friends to nominate,*
>
> *He wakes time and again for that case.*

Scene Nineteen
Recommending the Assistants

(*Enter the Royal Envoy, followed by attendants*)

ROYAL ENVOY (*To the tune of* **Shengchazi**):

> In charge of all the courtly manners,
>
> I stay in the immortal cave at early morn.
>
> Ten thousand tiny creatures are running
>
> When I leave my grand sojourn.

ALL:

The general has arrived at the palace hall. As His Highness the Royal Son-in-Law is to leave the court today, all the ministers please wait on His Majesty here and now!

> (*Enter Chunyu Fen in court dress, holding a memorial in his hands*)

CHUNYU FEN (*To the previous tune*):

> With incense burners in the locust hall,
>
> The forbidden palace favours all.
>
> The magistrate hesitates to go
>
> Along the palace ways that glow.

ROYAL ENVOY:

Please walk along the palace way, Your Highness!

CHUNYU FEN (*On his knees*):

I, Chunyu Fen, the newly-appointed magistrate of Nanke County and the Royal Captain, thank Your Majesty for your grace. As I shall leave for my office today, I have come to take departure.

> (*Kowtows and lies prostrate three times*)

ROYAL ENVOY:

Please read your memorial of gratitude here and now, Your Highness!

CHUNYU FEN:

Besides showing gratitude on my departure, I shall recommend some wise talents to Your Majesty.

> (*To the tune of* **Guizhixiang**)
>
> I come from a general's family,
>
> But lack intelligence.
>
> I am afraid that I might not be qualified
>
> And thus fail to fulfil my job.
>
> I am looking for wise talents,
>
> Wise talents
>
> As my subordinates
>
> To give me assistance.

ROYAL ENVOY:

Whom are you recommending?

CHUNYU FEN:

As far as I know, Royal Captain Zhou Bian from Yingchuan is faithful and upright to be an assistant while Consultant Tian Zihua is prudent and compliant to handle administration. As they have been my friends for a dozen years, they are capable enough to be entrusted. I hope that Zhou Bian will be in charge of law and order and Tian Zihua will be in charge of farming. In that case, I shall distinguish myself in administration and in government by law.

As I am ignorant,

I hope that I shall have assistants

To handle the Nanke affairs.

ROYAL ENVOY:

Please rise to your feet and stand waiting!

CHUNYU FEN (*Rises to his feet*):

I suppose that His Majesty will agree to my proposal. Therefore, Royal Captain Zhou and Scholar Tian will have this opportunity.

ROYAL ENVOY:

This is the royal edict: "I am pleased that His Highness the Royal Son-in-Law recommends talented persons for the state. I give my consent to his proposal."

CHUNYU FEN (*Kowtows*):

Long live the King!

(*Rises to his feet*)

(*Enter Zhou Bian and Tian Zihua*)

ZHOU BIAN, TIAN ZIHUA (*To the tune of **Shenzhang'er***):

His Majesty has approved;

His Majesty has approved.

The magistrate of Nanke County,

Mr. Chunyu Fen recommends us

To be in charge of law and farming.

We are here to thank His Majesty.

(*On their knees*)

Zhou Bian, the newly appointed official in charge law and order in Nanke County and the former Royal Captain, and Tian Zihua, the newly appointed official in charge of farming in Nanke County and the Consultant, kowtow to Your Majesty to express our gratitude.

(*Kowtow*)

Long live the King!

(*Rise to their feet*)

CHUNYU FEN (*Greets Zhou Bian and Tian Zihua*):

Congratulations!

ZHOU BIAN, TIAN ZIHUA:

Thank you for your recommendation!

ROYAL ENVOY:

It's time for Your Highness to set off as His Majesty the King and Her Majesty the Queen are waiting to see you off in the pass to the south of the city.

(*In the pattern of **Selected Tang Poems***)

To be married into a royal house,

He gets promoted because of his spouse.

With two friends to go the same way,

Together they will enjoy the day.

Scene Twenty
The Royal Farewell Banquet

(*Enter two Royal Envoys*)

ROYAL ENVOYS:

> *"Near the palace halls and inscribed boards,*
> *Green canopies and red flags line the street.*
> *When the king and queen arrive,*
> *The princess and her spouse come to greet."*

His Majesty the King and Her Majesty the Queen have prepared a farewell banquet for His Highness the Royal Son-in-Law and Her Highness the Royal Princess to go take up the official position in Nanke County. Here come the royal carriages.

(*Enter the Ant King and the Ant Queen, followed by court ladies*)

ANT KING, ANT QUEEN (*To the tune of **Chuanyanyunü***):

> From the misty palace cave
>
> Arises a beam of sunlight.
>
> When we look back at the palace,
>
> We only see the green tiles.

COURT LADIES:

> The court ladies in service
>
> Accompany the King and the Queen.

ALL:

> We see a pair of phoenixes,
>
> Handsome and pretty.

ROYAL ENVOYS:

Long live the King!

ANT KING:

Is the banquet ready?

ROYAL ENVOYS:

Yes, it is.

ANT KING:

Have the officials concerned prepared the luggage for the magistrate?

ROYAL ENVOYS:

Yes, they have.

COURT LADY:

This is the edict from Her Majesty, "The dowry, jewellery, embroidered satin, carriages, horses and servants are to be displayed on the highway."

ROYAL ENVOYS:

Yes, Your Majesty.

(*Enter Chunyu Fen and Princess Golden Branch*)

CHUNYU FEN, PRINCESS GOLDEN BRANCH (*To the tune of* **Shuying**):

> In elegant dress,
>
> The mirror reflects the image
>
> In full splendour.

PRINCESS GOLDEN BRANCH:

> As if in a dream,
>
> I am always shy,
>
> But ride now in a carriage.

ROYAL ENVOYS (*Urges Chunyu Fen and Princess Golden Branch*):

> As the royal banquet is ready,
>
> You'd better hurry to the green locust.

ALL:

> What a distinguished couple,
>
> A perfect match for each other!

ROYAL ENVOYS (*Reports to the Ant King and the Ant Queen*):

His Highness and Her Highness have arrived.

CHUNYU FEN, PRINCESS GOLDEN BRANCH (*Lie prostrate on the ground*):

We are overjoyed and embarrassed to have the favour of your seeing us off far from the palace.

ANT KING:

780

I would not have parted with you, but I would not worry about Nanke in the south once you are there.

ANT QUEEN (*Weeps*):

You'll suffer from the long journey, my dear daughter!

PRINCESS GOLDEN BRANCH (*Weeps*):

Oh my dear mother!

ANT KING:

When you are at home, you are a princess; when you are married, you are a county lady. What sufferings are you talking about?

CHUNYU FEN, PRINCESS GOLDEN BRANCH (*Kowtow*):

Gratified with all the favours from you, we wish you a long, long life!

ANT KING:

The same to the couple of you.

> (*Chunyu Fen and Princess Golden Branch offer a toast*)

ANT KING (*To the tune of* **Huameixu**):

> When the flowers are bathed in the sun,
>
> I drink toasts in the south of the city.
>
> I rely on you
>
> To keep peace in the south.
>
> Your service in Nanke County
>
> Will ensure the peace of the state.

ALL:

> The grandeur of the Nanke magistrate

Will impress the people of the state.

ANT QUEEN:

From now on, Nanke will be your new home, my dear daughter. All the treasures in the palace will serve as your dowry. Look at the highway!

> (*To the previous tune*)
>
> The towering trees
>
> Cast their shadows on the ground.
>
> I have given you
>
> All you need in your home.
>
> The exotic treasures in the broad day
>
> Will fill cartloads on the way.

ALL:

> The grandeur of the Nanke magistrate
>
> Will impress the people of the state.

CHUNYU FEN (*To the previous tune*):

> To be a county magistrate,
>
> I may not be up to the par.
>
> How dare I bear the honour
>
> Of having you to see us off?
>
> I wish the hills and rills last forever
>
> And the state remain in peace and order.

ALL:

> The grandeur of the Nanke magistrate
>
> Will impress the people of the state.

PRINCESS GOLDEN BRANCH (*To the previous tune*):

> A flower still in the bud,
>
> I bloom in the eastern breeze.
>
> I shall go with my spouse
>
> With cartloads of dowry.
>
> Now that I belong to my man,
>
> I have to leave my parents.

ALL:

> The grandeur of the Nanke magistrate
>
> Will impress the people of the state.
>
> (*Chunyu Fen and Princess Golden Branch kneel on the ground*)

CHUNYU FEN:

What virtue am I endowed to have troubled Your Majesty? May I ask how I am to govern Nanke County?

ANT KING:

As a big county in the country with rich soil and a large population, Nanke is only to be ruled by lenient government. With the assistance of your two friends Zhou and Tian, I hope that you will do your best to relieve my worry.

CHUNYU FEN (*Kowtows*):

I will follow your decree.

ANT QUEEN:

Before you leave, my dear daughter, please listen to my word of advice. Chunyu is robust and vigorous, addicted to drinking. Besides, as he is still young, you'd better be a suppliant lady. If you behave yourself, I shall be free from worries. Nanke is away from here although it is not a long distance. As we are going to part with each other today, how can I refrain from weeping?

> (*Weeps with Princess Golden Branch*)

PRINCESS GOLDEN BRANCH:

I'll follow your instructions.

> (*Kowtows and bids farewell*)

ANT KING (*To the tune of **Diliuzi***):

> Nanke County,
>
> Nanke County
>
> Is by no means inferior.
>
> When you are in office,
>
> When you are in office,
>
> Please forget about your wine.
>
> Go among the farmers
>
> Instead of remaining in office
>
> And taking the leisure all the time.
>
> The people and the affairs
>
> Are rather complicated there.

ANT KING:

Now announce my decree, "Beat the drums, play the flutes and carry the flags to see them off till the Departure Pavilion."

> (*Walks*)

ROYAL ENVOYS, COURT LADIES (*To the tune of **Baolaocui***):

> Amid the hustle and bustle in the street,
>
> Amid the hustle and bustle in the street,
>
> The King and the Queen see the youngsters off
>
> While music accompanies the procession.
>
> The Royal Son-in-Law
>
> Is riding
>
> On a spotted steed.
>
> The King and his son-in-law look so pleased
>
> While the Queen and her daughter look so sad,
>
> Hard to tear themselves away.

ROYAL ENVOYS, COURT LADIES:

We have passed the Departure Pavilion, Your Majesty.

ANT KING:

We shall part sooner or later. Chunyu and Princess, take care!

CHUNYU FEN, PRINCESS GOLDEN BRANCH (*Lie prostrate on the ground*):

We shall always keep your words in our minds. We wish you a long, long life!

(*Exeunt*)

ANT KING:

Announce my decree to return to the palace.

ROYAL ENVOYS (*To the tune of* **Shuangshengzi**):

> Call and cry,
>
> Call and cry
>
> Come from men and steeds.
>
> Do-re-mi,
>
> Do-re-mi,
>
> Rings the music.
>
> With laugh and smile,
>
> With laugh and smile,
>
> They are going,
>
> They are going.
>
> We shall turn around the locust
>
> And return to the palace.
>
> (*To the tune of* **Coda**)
>
> In the prime of their life,
>
> They gallop their way from the capital,
>
> A perfect couple second to none.
>
> (*In the pattern of* **Collected Tang Poems**)
>
> *Two phoenixes fly in the sky,*
>
> *Passing fields and towns on their way.*
>
> *With music ringing happy and gay,*
>
> *It seems to be the prettiest day.*

Scene Twenty-One
The Secretary as the Acting Magistrate

(*Enter the secretary*)

SECRETARY (*To the tune of* **Zizishuang**):

> To serve in office must be strong —
>
> To be a hindrance.
>
> Unable to comment on a document —
>
> Is a fool.
>
> To act as a magistrate —
>
> Is to be in luck.

To grab redemption, money and grains —

Is sheer robbery.

I am the secretary in Nanke County. As the office of the magistrate is in vacancy for the time being, I am temporarily acting in that position. It is already late in the morning, but the clerks and runners have not arrived yet. How detestable! Detestable!

(*Enter a clerk*)

CLERK (*To the previous tune*):

My humble wife calls me a clerk —

A cunning clerk.

I wear a hat with two hard wings —

An official pattern.

To practice deceptions —

I am brazen.

To dine and wine in the countryside —

(*Makes a bow*)

I am back now.

SECRETARY (*Annoyed*):

Oops!

"After days of absence from office,

You come with a mere word of 'I'm back'.

If you try to humbug me,

I'll beat you and give you the sack."

CLERK (*On his knees*):

"Instead of raising a rash alarm,

I should know what to warn.

(*Presents a chicken*)

Look at the chicken I bring from the farm:

It will crow at early dawn."

SECRETARY:

What a fine chicken! What a fine chicken!

CLERK:

Those who came for the lawsuits went home when they heard that you would be late for office because you were fond of sleep. To my mind, you should not waste your brief golden age of taking charge of the office. When I went to the farms, I got hold of two chickens. I ate the hen and have brought the rooster to crow for you at dawn. "A day's work depends on a good start at dawn."

SECRETARY:

Well said, well said. Rise to your feet, please!

(*Kneels on the ground to help the clerk to his feet*)

I do not have a copy of *Book of Laws* in my office. Do you think that I should have one?

CLERK:

You may need one, or you may not need one.

SECRETARY:

Do you think that I should ask for money when I handle a lawsuit?

CLERK:

You may ask for money, or you may not ask for money.

SECRETARY (*Annoyed*):

Why should I take an official position if I do not get money?

CLERK:

If you want money, why don't you buy a copy of *Book of Laws*? There is gold at the back of the book.

(*Enter the messenger*)

MESSENGER (*Bows to the secretary*):

Here is an urgent message.

SECRETARY (*Reads the message*):

"A memorial from the office of the Right Prime Minister mentions the absence of a magistrate in Nanke. According to the royal edict, Chunyu Fen is assigned the position." Alas, the new magistrate is coming. Where are my brief golden days?

MESSENGER:

Here arrives the certificate for the arrival of His Highness the Royal Son-in-Law.

SECRETARY:

Tell the sections concerned to arrange everything and get ready to meet him.

CLERK:

There are set regulations.

SECRETARY:

We'll do something different from the set regulations. We'll build a residence for His Highness and a palace hall for Her Highness. We'll prepare a pearl sedan with gilded umbrellas, shouldered by all females.

CLERK:

Yes, I see. As time is pressing, you'd better write the assignments with both hands.

(*The secretary writes the assignments with both hands*)

CLERK:

One assignment is for the Section of Personnel Affairs to inform the officials. One assignment is for the Section of Revenue to pay the money and grains. One assignment is for the Section of Military Affairs to get ready the musicians, runners, sedans and horses. One assignment is for the Section of Rites to inform the Confucian scholars, senior squires, Buddhist and Taoist monks and a few female singers with slippery tongues.

SECRETARY:

Why do we need the female singers?

CLERK:

They can boast. One assignment is for the Section of Penalty to check the list of prisoners and examine the implements of punishment. One assignment is for the Section of Construction to repair the residence and household utensils. The first thing is to get some toilet joss-sticks.

SECRETARY:

These things can wait.

CLERK:

When the princess gets off the sedan, she will be looking around for the toilet. One assignment is for the archives establishment to sort out the files. One assignment is for the secretariat to write out the positions according to order. One assignment is for the clerk in charge of extra taxes to lay the carpets and put up decorations. One assignment is for the assistant clerk to prepare seal-ink and papers. One assignment is for the courier station to prepare the room and board. One assignment is for the neighbourhood chief to select the gatekeepers, at least two metres tall.

SECRETARY:

Are they too tall?

CLERK:

The new magistrate is three metres tall. That's why we can't make head or tail of him. One assignment is to borrow a pearl sedan canopy from the Temple of Avalokitesvara. One assignment is to borrow the bedding and mattress, rouge and powder from the whorehouse.

SECRETARY:

That won't do. We must have them made to order by night.

(To the tune of **Tingqianliu**)

As this county lies in the south,

His predecessors are ordinary men.

Why is His Highness sent here at this time

To make it a place of prominence?

ALL:

Make a clear list

Of the above-mentioned things.

Tell the secretariat

To make haste and be careful.

SECRETARY (*To the previous tune*):

For the jewellery and gold-thread costumes,

There is neither money nor grains.

CLERK:

If there is neither money nor grains,

Apportion the charges first

And seek the revenues later.

ALL:

Make a clear list

Of the above-mentioned things.

Tell the secretariat

To make haste and be careful.

The acting magistrate has made the loot

Before the new magistrate comes.

They send people with large sums
To meet the new magistrate and salute.

Scene Twenty-Two
Arriving at the County

(*Enter a troop of soldiers*)

SOLDIERS (*In the pattern of* **Collected Tang Poems**):

> *"We change uniforms in times of peace,*
> *While horses gently neigh at pretty sight.*
> *When the fairy moves to a new site,*
> *The music of jade flute floats in the breeze."*

Hi, everyone. At the behest of His Majesty, we are escorting the princess and the royal son-in-law to their new office in Nanke County. By and by we have passed several courier stations. Now the princess and the royal son-in-law have made an early start.

(*Enter Chunyu Fen and Princess Golden Branch, followed by attendants*)

CHUNYU FEN (*To the tune of* **Mantingfang**):

> Dustless on the way from the capital,
> And breezeless near the Painting Bridge,
> The starred flags flutter in the sun.

PRINCESS GOLDEN BRANCH:

> When clouds float in the sky,
> The flower hairpins and the face reflect each other.
> From the farewell banquet,
> I left in the deepest grief.

CHUNYU FEN, PRINCESS GOLDEN BRANCH:

> The road south of the pass
> Is lined with grass on both sides.
> When can I see my parents again?

(*In the pattern of* **Mulanhualing**)

> *"The palace tries to keep the oriole,*
> *Which moves to Nanke instead.*
> *The procession leaves the capital town,*
> *With carriage canopy embroidered.*
> *The man looks with complacency*
> *And asks his wife in a smile.*
> *When they leave the green locust tree,*
> *They look back at the princess garden."*

CHUNYU FEN:

Princess, we have passed several courier stations since we left His Majesty the King and Her Majesty the Queen. We shall soon arrive at Nanke County. Let's be on our way, attendants!

> (*Walks*)
>
> (*To the tune of* **Ganzhouge**)
>
> After the palace banquet,
>
> I ride on a spotted horse
>
> And go on my journey.
>
> The folk in the capital town
>
> Roll up their curtains and gaze.
>
> What official can surpass us
>
> Now that I go with my fairy wife?

ALL:

> In old blue robes
>
> And new hair-do,
>
> A beauty is dressed in the locust palace.
>
> On a magnificent carriage
>
> Driven by robust steeds,
>
> The couple travel in smiles.
>
> (*Enter the messenger*)

MESSENGER:

At the dispatch of the secretary of Nanke County, I am here to present a document and to give you a warm welcome.

CHUNYU FEN (*Takes the document and reads*):

I've signed the document. Go back and do your service there!

> (*The messenger responds*)

CHUNYU FEN (*To the previous tune*):

> Decorated with flowers on my head,
>
> What talent and virtue do I have
>
> To wear a purple ribbon on my waist?
>
> With my tender wife,
>
> I drive through the fields in a carriage.
>
> For love of the beautiful scenery,
>
> I am reluctant to whip the steed.

ALL:

> Bringing his wife,
>
> Riding on a satin saddle,
>
> He goes along the straight highway.
>
> In a spring tour,
>
> The scholar weds a princess wife,
>
> A perfect match in the fairyland.

ATTENDANTS:

Here we are at the border of Nanke County, Your Highness.

(*Enter the secretary*)

SECRETARY:

The secretary of Nanke County is waiting here to greet you.

CHUNYU FEN:

Thank you for your kindness!

SECRETARY:

Not at all. With a new canopy, the guards and sedan-carriers are waiting over there to greet you.

CHUNYU FEN:

Yes, I see. We'll go back at once.

(*Exit the secretary after a response*)

VOICE WITHIN:

All the county officials are here to greet Your Highness.

CHUNYU FEN:

Stand up and wait aside!

VOICE WITHIN:

The Confucian scholars are here to greet Your Highness.

CHUNYU FEN:

Stand up, please! I shall meet you again in the county office.

(*The scholars respond within*)

VOICE WITHIN:

The Buddhist monks, the Taoist priests, and the senior squires are here to greet Your Highness.

CHUNYU FEN:

Stand up and go back!

VOICE WITHIN:

Female singers are here to greet Your Highness.

CHUNYU FEN:

Set off at once!

(*The female singers beat drums and play the flutes to lead the way*)

CHUNYU FEN (*To the previous tune*):

> With jade pendants dangling in my ride,
>
> Ahead I see flags
>
> And officials along the way.
>
> They come to kowtow and greet me,
>
> Gathering on the paths in the fields.

ALL:

> Soldiers and civilians roar,
>
> Men and women call,
>
> While Taoist priests mix with the dancers.

Accompanied by zither music

And drumbeats,

The carriage is hastening its way.

CHUNYU FEN:

What is the place afar that is clouded with mist and luxuriant with trees?

ATTENDANTS:

Ten miles away is the town-seat of Nanke County.

CHUNYU FEN:

What a splendid city, my dear princess!

(*To the previous tune*)

Ten miles ahead,

I can see a dense evaporation,

Which looks like neither fog nor mist.

The birds fly and dance

Above distant terraces and bowers.

A pavilion stands alone in the verdant hills

While fountain waters soak the fields.

ALL:

The sight of pretty hills

And coiling rills

Rouses sighs and deep emotion.

Behind the heavy gates

And walls with flags

Are hidden bowers of the fairyland.

(*Enter men with lanterns to greet the procession*)

ALL:

We have entered the town, Your Highness.

CHUNYU FEN:

I shall take a rest in my residence and go to the office at five tomorrow morning.

(*To the tune of* **Coda**)

Like stars glitter the gauze lanterns,

Which illuminate the streets.

My dear princess,

Let's get off the carriage and enjoy our house!

Endowed with heavenly grace from the king,

We come to a fairyland of a mountain town.

Into the clouds songs and music ring,

To laud the magnificence all around.

Scene Twenty-Three
Missing Her Daughter

(*Enter the Ant Queen, followed by maids of honor*)

ANT QUEEN (*To the tune of* **Yeyouhu**):

> The flowers blossom in the palace
>
> While court garments display splendor.

MAIDS OF HONOR:

> With huge fans on both sides
>
> In the hands of maids of honor,
>
> The Queen misses her daughter in Nanke.

ANT QUEEN (*In the pattern of* **Yiqin'e**):

> "*In the mountains,*
>
> *The fragrance of locust leaves spreads in the breeze.*

MAIDS OF HONOR:

> *Amid green locust leaves*
>
> *In the deep caves*
>
> *Is seen the colorful rainbow.*

ANT QUEEN:

> *My daughter left the palace at fifteen*
>
> *And has to look at the moon from Nanke.*

MAIDS OF HONOUR:

> *The moon sheds shadows*
>
> *Of magpies flying south,*
>
> *Reminding one of departures."*

ANT QUEEN:

I am Queen of the Great State of Peaceful Locust. My daughter has been staying in Nanke for nearly twenty years. A letter came from her yesterday, saying that her children have made her so tired and lean that she cannot bear the heat. She has had the Jade Terrace built in a cool area near the river to shelter from the heat. As she wants to place a thousand volumes of Buddhist sutras in the terrace, I have sent Princess Qiongying to ask Master Qixuan in the Chanzhi Temple for advice. How is it that she has not returned yet?

(*Enter Princess Qiongying, holding the Buddhist sutras*)

PRINCESS QIONGYING (*To the tune of* **Wanxiandeng**):

> Having listened to Zen preaching in the Chanzhi Temple,
>
> I have obtained the Dharma-raja scripture.

(*Kowtows to the Queen*)

> Princess Qiongying kowtows to Your Majesty, the Queen. I wish you a long life.

ANT QUEEN:

Rise to your feet! What is the scripture in your hands?

PRINCESS QIONGYING:

When I went to consult Master Qixuan, he said that all those who have given birth to too many children must have somehow profaned the gods in heaven and on earth. He advised the Princess and her children to obtain *The Nativity Sutra* and eat vegetarian food for three years to show repentance. By so doing, they will evade ill fortune and enjoy good fortune, blessed with health and longevity. Your Majesty,

(*To the tune of* **Yushantui**)

The Nativity Sutra

Is about the infinitely merciful Maudgalyayana.

ANT QUEEN:

What for?

PRINCESS QIONGYING:

Venerable Maudgalyayana went west to rescue his mother. When he passed Zhuiyang County of Yuzhou Prefecture, he saw in the wilderness the Hell of Bloody Basin from which many fettered women in disheveled hair were drinking dirty blood. He asked the yama of the hell why they were suffering in this way. The yama said that these women

Profaned the streams with their blood when they gave birth

And annoyed the virtuous people with the dirty water for tea.

ANT QUEEN:

That's it. As they polluted the tea for the offerings to the Triratna, they had to meet their retribution. And then?

PRINCESS QIONGYING:

On hearing these words Maudgalyayana burst into tears and said, "In that case, my mother has to suffer the same torture for her sin." He went to Buddha for help, prostrating himself devoutly and saying, "Will you the Almighty give me revelations as how to requite my mother by rescuing her from such misery?" Buddha uttered his approval, saying,

If you'd like to requite your mother,

You should eat vegetarian food to show repentance for three years

And chant Namo Amitabha all the time.

ANT QUEEN:

What's the use of chanting Namo Amitabha?

PRINCESS QIONGYING:

It's of great benefit.

The ferryboat turns out to be

The lotus throne over the Hell of Bloody Basin.

ANT QUEEN (*To the previous tune*):

Buddha is so benevolent

That he reveals the truth to the world.

It is women alone that are to suffer, but the sons and daughters belong to both men and women. When women get dazed at childbirth, it is men's fault to pour the dirty water into the streams. In the sutra,

It is overtly stated that dirty waters run outdoors,

Why are women alone to be blamed?

Summon an envoy and tell him to set out at once with a thousand copies of *The Nativity Sutra* and make his way by day and night!

> The royal envoy will bring the sutra to the princess
>
> Lest she should go to the hell in Zhuiyang.

Tell Princess Golden Branch

> To distribute the sutra far and wide
>
> So that I can also ascend to the paradise.
>
> *Where there's mother, there's maternal love;*
>
> *Every mother shares her children's woe.*
>
> *If only she chants the sutra and repents her sin*
>
> *Can she be blessed wherever she is to go.*

Scene Twenty-Four
Street Ballads

(*Enter the Royal Envoy on horseback, carrying the sutra in his hands and the royal edict on his back*)

ROYAL ENVOY (*To the tune of* **Qingjiangyin**):

> On my ride to Nanke County,
>
> I see the mountain scenery like a picture.
>
> While the princess is fine and sweet,
>
> The royal son-in-law fares well in his career.
>
> Here I am,
>
> To dismount the horse and tidy myself up.

Things may vary, but they always follow a course of development. I am the Royal Envoy. Under the royal edict of His Majesty and Her Majesty, I'm here to give the princess the Buddhist sutra for worship and to bring the edict to announce the promotion of the royal son-in-law. No sooner have I entered the Nanke territory than I see the verdant mountains, the blue winding rivers, the flourishing grass and trees, and the thriving birds and beasts. The residential houses are surrounded by tidy gardens and pools, and decorated by orderly eaves. Besides perfect beauty and affluence, they seem to enjoy benevolence and forbearance. On the straight streets, men and women are walking on separate sides. The old and the young bow to each other when they meet in the fields. Much have I traveled but seldom have I seen such a peaceful life. Let me see! I'll ask how the princess is going on so that I can know how the people think of her. Now some villagers are coming this way.

(*Enter some senior villagers, holding joss-sticks in their hands*)

SENIOR VILLAGERS (*To the tune of* **Xiaobaige**):

> With little corvée enforced

And many grains hoarded,

The officials and civilians are in good terms.

The seniors drink to their hearts' content

While the juniors sing in full throat.

What do you think

About our holding

The joss-sticks?

(*Royal Envoy approaches a senior villager and asks*)

ROYAL ENVOY:

Excuse me, sir! How is the princess going?

SENIOR VILLAGER (*With an exclamation*):

(*To the previous tune*)

What do you think

About our holding

The joss-sticks?

(*Exeunt*)

ROYAL ENVOY:

The villagers look so happy, but what is it that they are singing? Some scholars are coming this way, too.

(*Enter some scholars, holding joss-sticks in their hands*)

SCHOLARS (*To the previous tune*):

When village stipulations are followed

And poems set to the music,

Everybody in every family obeys the moral codes.

One learns from all

And all learns from one.

What do you think

About our holding

The joss-sticks?

ROYAL ENVOY:

Excuse me, sir! How is the princess going?

SCHOLAR (*With an exclamation*):

(*To the previous tune*)

What do you think

About our holding

The joss-sticks?

(*Exeunt*)

(*Enter some village women, holding joss-sticks in their hands*)

VILLAGE WOMEN (*To the previous tune*):

With moral codes in sway

And no family violence,

Our marriage life is fit and proper.

> Each family lives in peace;
>
> Each family abounds with children.
>
> What do you think
>
> About our holding
>
> The joss-sticks?

ROYAL ENVOY:

Excuse me, ladies! How is the princess going?

VILLAGE WOMEN (*With an exclamation*):

> (*To the previous tune*)
>
> What do you think
>
> About our holding
>
> The joss-sticks?
>
> (*Exeunt*)
>
> (*Enter a merchant, holding joss-sticks in hand*)

MERCHANT (*To the previous tune*):

> With equal tax
>
> And no extra burdens,
>
> Merchants from afar settle down in this place.
>
> You can pass the checkpoints at any time,
>
> Always safe and sound.
>
> What do you think
>
> About our holding
>
> The joss-sticks?

ROYAL ENVOY:

You look rather familiar to me, brother.

MERCHANT:

I come from the capital and am doing business here.

ROYAL ENVOY:

So that's it. Do you know how the princess is going?

MERCHANT:

We are on our way to pray in the memorial temple of the magistrate. We wish His Highness and the princess a long, long life.

ROYAL ENVOY:

You are not a native here. Why do you wish them a long, long life?

MERCHANT:

Since Magistrate Chunyu came to office twenty years ago, the place has been in such good order that people have no need to lock the door at night and even the dogs are set free. As traveling merchants, we come and go in great ease and comfort. So why shouldn't we acknowledge the duty to requite his kindness?

ROYAL ENVOY:

Before I met you, some senior villagers, scholars and village women had passed, holding joss-sticks in their hands. Where are they going? And what are they singing?

MERCHANT:

There's something you don't know. Since Magistrate Chunyu came to office, Nanke County has always enjoyed timely wind and rain, with contented people living in a country of peace and tranquility. People are enjoying themselves all the year round and singing praise of his benevolent government. A tablet is erected in every village with the name of His Highness inscribed on it. Here is a big temple built in honor of His Highness, with nine rows of walls altogether. The main hall is thirty feet tall, with several fifteen-foot steles to commemorate his virtuous deeds. Within these twenty years, he has done at least 7,200 good deeds, even if he does just one good deed a day. These deeds are really beyond words.

ROYAL ENVOY:

These deeds must have been concocted by some scrupulous scholars or rascal villagers.

MERCHANT (*Annoyed*):

> (*To the previous tune*)
> What do you think
> About our holding
> The joss-sticks?
> (*Exit*)

ROYAL ENVOY:

How ridiculous! How ridiculous! I wonder if there indeed exists such a government as enjoys the ardent support of the people!

> *For his twenty years of virtuous deeds,*
> *They honor him with ballads and incense.*
> *Each stele praises the life he leads,*
> *And each word in the edict makes sense.*

Scene Twenty-Five
Enjoying the Moon

(*Enter the secretary*)

SECRETARY:

> *"As the secretary to the magistrate,*
> *I know something about bookkeeping.*
> *When the magistrate is not in office,*
> *I'll take care of the official seal but have no income at all."*

Something extraordinary has been accomplished recently. The princess, who was brought up in the deep palace, has not got used to the heat in Nanke for all these twenty years. When she got to know that it was cool to the northwest of River Town, she ordered that the Jade Terrace be built for her to shelter from the heat. Zhou Bian and Tian Zihua took charge of the whole project and had it completed in a short time. You may ask why it is called the Jade Terrace, and I can tell you that tall terraces of delicate jade are built outside the four gates. His Highness and the princess will soon arrive to enjoy the moon. Here come Zhou Bian and Tian Zihua.

(*Exit for the moment*)

(*Enter Zhou Bian and Tian Zihua*)

ZHOU BIAN, TIAN ZIHUA (*To the tune of* **Raodiyou**):

> What about human life?
>
> We serve as officials beneath the earth,
>
> But accompany His Highness in leisure times.
>
> Now that the moon has risen
>
> And stars twinkle in the sky,
>
> The perfect couple is coming from the palace.

ZHOU BIAN:

I am Zhou Bian, director of justice and order.

TIAN ZIHUA:

I am Tian Zihua, director of farming affairs.

ZHOU BIAN:

Thanks to the magistrate's favor and trust, we have assisted him in his administrative affairs for many years. The Jade Terrace has just been completed as a summer resort for the princess on the western bank of River Town. His Highness and the princess are coming soon. Today is the fifteenth of the month with the full moon. This is really a joyous occasion.

TIAN ZIHUA:

In my opinion, for all the splendor of the Jade Terrace, it is close to the State of Sandals and Vines. I don't think it convenient for the princess to dwell for long.

ZHOU BIAN:

With the garrison stationed in River Town, safety can surely be ensured.

(*Sounds of clearing the way within*)

TIAN ZIHUA:

Now come His Highness and the princess. We'd better stay away for a while.

(*Exeunt for the moment*)

(*Enter Chunyu Fen and Princess Golden Branch, followed by attendants*)

CHUNYU FEN, PRINCESS GOLDEN BRANCH (*To the tune of* **Poqizhen**):

> Towering above all the surrounding houses,
>
> The Jade Terrace nearly levels the Milky Way.
>
> Under the moonlit sky,
>
> The royal couple
>
> Have dismissed all the officials.
>
> Together we leave the sweet smelling chambers
>
> And ride in the carriage in the evening haze.
>
> Where on earth is better than Nanke County?

(*Enter Zhou Bian and Tian Zihua*)

(*Enter the clerk to report*)

CLERK:

Director of justice and order and director of farming affairs are waiting for an audience.

CHUNYU FEN:

Bring my word that as the princess is here, it is inconvenient for me to see them here. Tell them to go home first.

(*The clerk responds*)

(*Exeunt Zhou Bian and Tian Zihua*)

CHUNYU FEN:

I had this palace built especially for you, my dear princess. Piled with jade, the five gates and the twelve bowers really constitute a fairyland. With the bright moon above us, let's drink to our hearts' content.

(*Enter two maids of honor with wine*)

MAIDS OF HONOR:

"*A perfect couple resides in the gilded bower*
While the moon shines over the Jade Terrace."

Here is the wine.

CHUNYU FEN (*To the tune of **Putianlefan***):

Bathed in the moonlight,

The magnificent palace

Looks like a glaring tower.

Dear princess, you were born in the palace

And are married to me the magistrate.

With incense so fragrant

And flowers so colorful,

Why are you wearing no smiles

But frowning all the time?

In the bright moonlight,

Let me fill your cup with vintage wine.

PRINCESS GOLDEN BRANCH (*Sighs*):

The scenery is beautiful indeed, but I am not in the right mood. I can't help it! I can't help it!

CHUNYU FEN:

Well, as you don't feel like drinking, I'll let our children to urge you. Bring our sons and daughters here!

(*Enter two sons and two daughters*)

SONS AND DAUGHTERS:

"*Under the bright moon, under the bright moon,*
Let's burn incense under the luxuriant tree."

Dad and mom, won't you have a drink?

(*Urge Princess Golden Branch to drink*)

PRINCESS GOLDEN BRANCH (*Smiles*):

I'll drink. I'll drink.

(*To the tune of **Yanguoshafan***)

The Moon Goddess,

I am not as carefree as you.

With so many untrammeled children to raise,

I have to care about each of them.

As twenty years have passed,

My eldest son is studying at school,

My second son is as clever as his brother,

And my little daughters have learned to dress up.

Seeing them in front of me now,

I am brightened up again.

CHUNYU FEN (*To the tune of **Qingbeifan***):

The bright moon

Above the Jade Terrace

Is like a newly polished mirror,

Hanging in the blue sky

For the people to admire.

SONS AND DAUGHTERS:

Come and enjoy

The caresses of the gentle breeze

And the coolness of the limpid dew.

The lingering evening glow

Adds a mystic tint to the moon.

That's why you are called an immortal,

Living in the cool cave,

Inclined to dance off and on.

ALL:

The Great State of Peaceful Locust

Is enshrouded in the moonlight

Of happy reunion in Nanke.

PRINCESS GOLDEN BRANCH:

Together with my man and children, I do enjoy the family reunion. The only thing that worries me is that my two sons have come of age, but neither of them is betrothed yet.

SONS AND DAUGHTERS:

Mom, if you stay up here, won't it be too high and cold?

PRINCESS GOLDEN BRANCH (*To the tune of **Shantaohongfan***):

The thought that occupies me all the time

Is hard to reveal at this time.

The Jade Terrace is no ordinary place,

Rising lonely into the cold sky.

The Moon Goddess seeks shelter in the moon,

But how can I be compared with her?

VOICE WITHIN:

Your Highness, here comes the royal edict.

(*Enter the Royal Envoy to announce the royal edict*)

ROYAL ENVOY:

Here arrives the royal edict. Kneel on the ground and listen to the royal edict, "I am fully aware that the way to run a country well is to respect the virtuous and the able and to love one's kith and kin. This is the basis for bestowing favors and rewards. Princess Yaofang and her husband Chunyu Fen, magistrate of Nanke County, the royal son-in-law and the honorary captain, have taken office in Nanke for twenty years. I am deeply impressed that people sing praise of him for his benevolence. Hence he is to be conferred a fief town of 3,000 households, the title of the Grand General, the post of Grand Secretary of the State Council, and the rank of dukedom. Yet he still holds office in Nanke County. His two sons and two daughters are offered hereditary posts and allowed to be married with members of the royal family and to share the weal and woe with the state. The above is my edict. You are to show your gratitude."

CHUNYU FEN, PRINCESS GOLDEN BRANCH (*Kowtow*):

Long live the king!

ROYAL ENVOY (*Kowtows to Chunyu Fen and Princess Golden Branch*):

Congratulations to you for your promotion!

CHUNYU FEN (*Holds the royal envoy by the arm*):

Thank you very much!

ROYAL ENVOY:

Here is another edict from Her Majesty the Queen: "Here are a thousand copies of *The Nativity Sutra* for the princess to worship and distribute, so that she can evade ill fortune and enjoy good fortune."

CHUNYU FEN:

To run a family and a country well, we need nothing but the Confucian doctrines. Buddhism is entirely out of the way.

PRINCESS GOLDEN BRANCH:

I do not know what the Confucian doctrines are.

CHUNYU FEN:

The Confucian doctrines expound the righteousness between the ruler and the subject, the affection between father and son, the distinction between man and wife, the orderly sequence between old and young, and the fidelity between friends.

PRINCESS GOLDEN BRANCH:

How would you explain the fact that although Confucian doctrines have never been preached in our country, we have righteousness between the ruler and the subject, distinction between you and me, affection between you and your children, and orderly sequence between brothers and sisters?

CHUNYU FEN (*Smiles*):

For all I have said, I'll distribute the sutra for you.

When the princess stays ill in her estate,
The edict brings forth joy to man and wife.

May she live a long and happy life,
As her man will follow the Buddhist fate.

Scene Twenty-Six
Incurring the Covetousness

(*Enter Fourth Prince of the State of Sandals and Vines*)

FOURTH PRINCE (*To the tune of **Lihua'er***):

> Born in this small State of Sandals and Vines,
> As a prince, I am for noise and excitement.
> As a widower, I am clumsy and muddle-headed,
> Well,
> But my late wife used to beat me.

I am the fourth prince of the State of Sandals and Vines. With Sandal Boy as my pet name, I'm of loose and lighthearted personality. My father His Majesty has assigned me three thousand red ants to guard the west region of our state. Yesterday my wife died and I am eager to get a new one. The opportunity to a happy marriage has just fallen upon me. Princess Golden Branch of the Great State of the Peaceful Locust, who married the magistrate of Nanke County and followed him to the post, was so afraid of the heat in their residential place that she got a Jade Terrace built in River Town, which is quite near our country. Heavens! Heavens! How could it be that she fears the heat? She must have got bored with her marital life and want to have fun away from her husband. Obviously this will be a heaven-ordained marriage for me. I will muster one thousand hand-picked soldiers, smash the Jade Terrace and grab the princess. I just wonder whether she falls for me or not. I've already sent a scout to fish for information there disguised as an itinerant peddler of headdress flowers. When will he be back?

(*Enter the scout, beating a rattle-drum*)

SCOUT:

Your Highness, here comes the good news!

FOURTH PRINCE:

Hurry up and tell me all about it!

SCOUT (*To the tune of **Beituobushan***):

> After I set out early from our State of Sandals and Vines,
> I fished for news about Nanke by day and by night.
> A scout can never be too cautious,
> But I have the peddling goods in sight.

What a gorgeous Jade Terrace!

FOURTH PRINCE:

In what sense?

SCOUT (*To the tune of **Zhonglü Xiaoliangzhou***):

> The palace is ornamented with jade and gold,
>
> With maids of honor sauntering around,
>
> Stretching like an emerald Milky Way.
>
> To the acme of perfection,
>
> It is a fairyland in the rosy clouds.

FOURTH PRINCE:

Did you come across the princess?

SCOUT:

I was peddling my flowers when a maid of honor brought me to Her Highness.

> (*To the tune of **Yao***)
>
> When peddling attracted the maids of honor,
>
> I entered the palace as a spy in disguise.

FOURTH PRINCE:

Did Her Highness buy some flowers?

SCOUT:

She asked me what headdress flowers I had. I answered that I had hundreds of flowers, wool flowers, rice-paper flowers, gold-thread flowers and jade-hairpin flowers, to name just a few. She had most of them in the palace, except for two kinds.

FOURTH PRINCE:

What are they?

SCOUT:

> The treasure sandal flower
>
> And the emerald vine flowers —
>
> She put on these two flowers, smiling in the mirror.

FOURTH PRINCE (*Almost faints and topples*):

Fantastic! Fantastic! Sandals and vines are embedded in the name of our state. It is predestined affinity that the princess accepted these two flowers. Scout, her husband won't be able to stop her!

SCOUT:

Her husband has returned to Nanke to handle the official affairs.

FOURTH PRINCE:

How he lacks vigilance!

SCOUT (*To the tune of **Shuahai'er Sansha***):

For her husband,

> What's the point of keeping to his office
>
> While leaving his beautiful wife to herself?
>
> As a scout to fish for information,
>
> I may beat the rattle-drum again in the arcade.
>
> Sun Feihu the bandit will be able to grab the lady;
>
> Wang Zhaojun will be married to the tartar land.
>
> When an affair of the heart has been aroused,

For the covetousness

Of Princess of Golden Branch,

Three thousand ants will fight a sanguinary battle.

(*To the tune of* **Coda**)

Your Highness,

Please feast the soldiers with the betrothal sheep,

And make the military banner with the wedding skirt!

When you seize the princess,

You'll irritate Chunyu Fen to the brink of death

And enjoy yourself to the full.

(*Exit the scout, leaving Fourth Prince on the stage*)

FOURTH PRINCE:

What a stroke of luck! Yes, I'll send an army to pin down River Town while I'll grab the princess in person. As a saying goes,

It's hard for him to cut the sandalwood,

But it's easy for me to grab a wife.

Scene Twenty-Seven
Princess on the Alert

(*Enter maid of honor*)

MAID OF HONOR (*To the tune of* **Haoshijin**, **Part One**):

The lotus leaves float in the autumn breeze;

Coils rise from the incense burner.

The twittering swallows beyond the curtains

Complain about the person lying by the engraved lattice.

I'm one of the maids of honor to attend on the princess. The princess is frail and delicate by nature. Besides, as she is fatigued by the four children, she feels vexed and annoyed for the hot weather. Therefore, she stays in the Jade Terrace to shelter from the heat. She is not up yet now.

(*Enter Princess Golden Branch*)

PRINCESS GOLDEN BRANCH (*To the tune of* **Haoshijin**, **Part Two**):

When the river dims in the cool autumn drizzle,

I feel dizzy in the lingering summer.

A fond dream accompanies the waving fan,

But could I ever become young again?

(*In the pattern of* **Qingpingyue**)

"In the gloomy garden,

Chilly rain comes in my dream.

MAID OF HONOR:

> *The locust twigs dance in the wind*
>
> *When she sleeps till noon within painted walls.*

PRINCESS GOLDEN BRANCH:

> *When I cherish my dream,*
>
> *Incense coils from the golden burner.*

ALL:

> *Married for years to the Honorary Captain,*
>
> *A languid princess does not bother to dress up.*"

PRINCESS GOLDEN BRANCH:

Maid, the Jade Terrace here is cooler than Nanke County.

MAID OF HONOR:

It is already early autumn now.

PRINCESS GOLDEN BRANCH:

Don't you know I am not well?

MAID OF HONOR:

Yes, I know. His Highness is staying in Nanke, and doesn't come back very often.

PRINCESS GOLDEN BRANCH:

He is occupied with a myriad of country affairs. How can he spare any time here? I am so bored.

> (*To the tune of* **Liufangongci**)
>
> With fallen flowers piled in the garden
>
> And evening clouds veiling the pavilion,
>
> I sleep in the autumn days.
>
> Getting up, I feel so weak
>
> That the gold hairpin almost drops from my hair.

MAID OF HONOR:

You've spent a whole summer here.

PRINCESS GOLDEN BRANCH:

> The bamboo mattress is out of use when sweat abates;
>
> The fan is out of use when fireflies no longer fly high.

MAID OF HONOR:

Your Highness, you are too weak and fragile.

PRINCESS GOLDEN BRANCH:

> As I am so fragile
>
> And often fall ill,
>
> I haven't slept well for the past year.

MAID OF HONOR:

This year it has become cold earlier than before.

PRINCESS GOLDEN BRANCH:

> When I feel cold, I'd go behind the gauze curtain;
>
> When I feel hot, I'd take a cold bath.

804

MAID OF HONOR:

It's time for lunch.

PRINCESS GOLDEN BRANCH:

>   As I've lost my sense of time,
>
>   It is well past noon,
>
>   But I lack taste for food.

MAID OF HONOR:

Now that you have such lovely children, why do you still feel melancholy?

PRINCESS GOLDEN BRANCH:

>   Don't mention my children,
>
>   For it is they
>
>   Who have weathered my countenance.

MAID OF HONOR:

I'll prepare a feast to drive away your yearning for the Royal Son-in-Law.

PRINCESS GOLDEN BRANCH (*To the previous tune*):

>   In the morning when I was awakened
>
>   From the dream,
>
>   There is left no trace of my man.
>
>   I had lingered for his caress
>
>   And asked him to paint my brows.

MAID OF HONOR (*Brings wine*):

>   Drink this cup
>
>   And your cheeks will blush.

PRINCESS GOLDEN BRANCH:

No, I don't want to drink.

>   (*Maid of honor kneels down and urges*)
>
>   (*Princess Golden Branch sips a little*)

MAID OF HONOR:

>   I urged three times,
>
>   But you only had a sip.
>
>   How can I get you smile after the drink?

I've got it. I'll ask the young maids to play the flute and zither, sing and dance for you.

>   (*Music from within*)

PRINCESS GOLDEN BRANCH:

How noisy!

MAID OF HONOR:

>   Why are you annoyed at the entertainments?
>
>   Is there a better cure than song and dance?
>
>   (*Sings aside*)
>
>   With her chin cupped
>
>   And her dress trailing on the ground,
>
>   She is woeful although her health has improved.

(Princess Golden Branch looks into the mirror and sighs)

MAID OF HONOR *(Turns back)*:

> In her chronic disease,
>
> She looks depressed in the mirror,
>
> With barely a breath.
>
> *(Enter the eldest son)*

THE ELDEST SON:

> "Beacon-fire lights the Jade Terrace,
>
> For invaders harass the border area."

My dear mother, the State of Sandals and Vines has invaded our territory and is pressing on towards the Jade Terrace. What shall we do?

PRINCESS GOLDEN BRANCH *(Sobs)*:

What shall we do, then? My son, set out for Nanke by night and report to your father! I'll lead the men and women to guard the city.

> *(To the tune of **Fengrusong**)*
>
> I should have stayed in Nanke;
>
> I should not have indulged in the cool weather here.
>
> As I am to blame for all the trouble,
>
> There is imminent danger for war,
>
> But who knows what they are up to?

ALL:

> Men and women will guard the Jade Terrace together!

THE ELDEST SON *(To the previous tune)*:

> To my relief, my mother has somewhat recovered
>
> And will strive to guard the palace while I am gone,
>
> And I'm sure that the palace won't be taken in a short time.
>
> Even if the women soldiers cannot ward off the enemy,
>
> My father and I will come to the rescue.

ALL:

> Men and women will guard the Jade Terrace together!
>
> *(Princess Golden Branch and the eldest son weep and part)*

PRINCESS GOLDEN BRANCH *(To the tune of **Coda**)*:

> There has never been any warfare,
>
> And I feel so scared.

No other generals can help,

> Except for the Royal Son-in-Law, my husband himself.
>
> *(Exeunt Princess Golden Branch and maid of honor)*
>
> *(Enter the eldest son, hurrying on horseback)*

THE ELDEST SON:

Hurry up, soldiers!

> *(To the tune of **Diliuzi**)*
>
> The frontier report is so urgent,

So urgent.

And how can we have a rest?

Take turns,

Take turns

And we change horses all the time.

The more anxiety, the less speed —

Nanke is three hundred miles away,

But I wish to reach it within an instant.

If the palace is taken by the enemy,

What will happen to my mother?

What will happen to my mother?

(*Exit*)

(*Enter the women soldiers, carrying standards and keeping watch on the city*)

WOMEN SOLDIERS (*To the previous tune*):

The frontier report is so urgent,

So urgent.

And how can we have a rest?

Take turns,

Take turns

And we keep watch on the city.

The more anxiety, the less speed —

We'll check the three hundred miles away,

But we wish to check them within an instant.

If the palace is taken by the enemy,

What will happen to the princess?

What will happen to the princess?

SISTER WANG (*Laughs*):

How strange it is! Not a crevasse can be found in the Jade Terrace. Who the hell has reported that there are spies who have sneaked into the city? The princess has just issued the order, "To defend the city, old soldiers and adult men should pass the drawbridge and meet the enemy in battle, while their wives should guard the battlements over the four gates, at each of which a woman chief is to take command." I am Sister Wang. As a woman of some ability, I've been assigned to take charge of the east gate. Oh, Granny Chen and Auntie Zhao, you are here too.

GRANNY CHEN:

I've been assigned to take charge of the west gate.

AUNTIE ZHAO:

I've been assigned to take charge of the north gate. Only the one in charge of the south gate has no turned up yet.

(*Enter a boy carrying a flag on his back*)

BOY:

Allow me to make obeisance to you all, dear aunties!

SISTER WANG:

You're a handsome boy.

THE BOY:

My mother is in charge of the south gate. As she has fallen ill, I've taken the flag for her.

SISTER WANG:

So she is ill. We have to do without her. Here is the order from the princess. The women chief officers carrying the flags should practice the martial arts. Hi, Granny Chen, meet my movement!

> (*She kicks and topples Granny Chen*)

GRANNY CHEN:

Ouch, I'm old now.

SISTER WANG:

Auntie Zhao, let me topple you!

AUNTIE ZHAO (*Topples*):

Ouch, please spare me, Sister Wang!

SISTER WANG:

Come on, boy, taste my kick!

> (*The boy puts Sister Wang down*)

I don't believe I will fall into such disgrace.

> (*Gets up and fights three rounds*)
>
> (*Topples*)

Boy, I can't knock you down with fists. Let's try the spear!

> (*The boy wins with the spear*)
>
> (*Sister Wang shows fear*)

BOY:

Sister Wang, how are you expected to fight against the enemy with such poor skills?

SISTER WANG:

I've got an idea. If the enemy should come up the city wall, we'll pour down the hot stool and urine. I've even brought the chamber pot and the cooking pot here.

GRANNY CHEN, AUNTIE ZHAO:

None of your worthless words! Let's patrol the city and report to the princess!

> (*To the tune of* **Zuiluoge**)
>
> One battlement lines with another;
>
> Posts for the soldiers lie side by side.
>
> The city walls are airtight,
>
> With spears and guns in piles.
>
> The flag-bearers are
>
> These women;
>
> The militiamen are
>
> The youngsters;
>
> They keep watch from dusk to dawn.
>
> (*Sounds of gongs and drums and neighs of horses from within*)

Facing the roaring dust

And looking to the end of the road,

We see the trotting horses by the city wall

And hear the sounds of gongs.

(Report from within, wild beating of gongs)

The enemy soldiers of the State of Sandals and Vines are coming.

BOY:

The situation at the front is critical. Now we shall gather all the families here in combat readiness.

On the four walls of the Jade Terrace,

We have prepared weapons for war.

If the enemy soldiers dare to come,

The women will fight them all.

Scene Twenty-Eight
Army Deployment in the Rain

(Enter Chunyu Fen, followed by attendants)

CHUNYU FEN (*To the tune of* **Xiaoyaole**):

At the spattering of autumn rain on the pond,

I still hold the phoenix fan in my hand.

In the green mansion with the locust shade

I sit alone in the office

And take a nap

Amid the faint fragrance.

"I've been in Nanke for years,

Staying in the mansion with pennants.

Lawsuits are reduced by three thousand a day,

While households reach a million by autumn."

Since I came to Nanke as the magistrate, the produce abounds and people live in peace. The lawsuits are handled with justice and there are fewer thefts. I owe all these achievements to the assistance of Zhou Bian and Tian Zihua. I'd like to drink wine but refrain from it as the princess is absent. As the princess is staying in the Jade Terrace to shelter from the heat, I feel rather lonely. There is a Rain Forecast Hall here, where the moist earth foretells rain. It happens that drizzle indeed comes in early autumn. I have got the wine ready for me to listen to the rain with Zhou and Tian. Wait on us, attendants!

(Enter Zhou Bian and Tian Zihua)

ZHOU BIAN, TIAN ZIHUA:

"The magistrate is easy to approach,

Treating fellow officials as equals."

Attendant, please tell His Highness that we are waiting at the door!

ATTENDANT:

Master Tian and Master Zhou are waiting at the door.

CHUNYU FEN (*Meets Zhou and Tian*):

"The three of us are old acquaintances;

TIAN ZIHUA:

But for your help we won't have assumed office.

ZHOU BIAN:

Thanks for your invitation to listen to the rain,

CHUNYU FEN, ZHOU BIAN, TIAN ZIHUA:

And enjoy the autumn sights in the suburbs!"

CHUNYU FEN (*Serves the wine for Zhou and Tian*):

The feast is set for the rain.

(*To the tune of **Tiying'er***)

The west wind ushers in the autumn

In pattering rains.

The jade pieces jingle on the eaves

In the bright moonlight.

Rainwater drips from the eaves

And goes pitter-patter in foams.

Suddenly I gaze and think

Where I have been carried away;

I am going to meet my wife.

(*To the previous tune*)

The nimbus in the Milky Way may sparkle,

Showering on the lotus leaves.

The raindrops sound like the swimming ducks,

Splashing in the clear pond.

The well railings resound under the parasol trees

While the palm leaves echo the rainfall.

Leaning against the hall

With hanging screens,

I seem to see the fairy lady my wife.

(*To the tune of **Zhuomuli***)

The quiet hall is a good place to drink,

And it is chilly this evening.

I'm afraid the rain might stir the butterflies in pairs

And disturb my dream of coupling mandarin ducks.

When the shorebirds look at the painted boat,

Sweet scent of the wine lingers in the hall.

Amid the melodious music,

Here and now,

I am intoxicated with thoughts.

(*To the previous tune*)

Flurried swallows are busy in the autumn

While sad wild geese file in the sky.

At the sight of the vacant room

And the half-extinguished lamp,

I feel the wretchedness of an official career,

Like a lonely boat on the Dongting Lake.

The memory of days

In the ten long years

Brings tears to my eyes behind the windows.

Mr. Tian, I had a strange dream during the nap. I dreamed of my eldest son reading two lines from *The Book of Poetry*:

"*The storks would hoot o'er the hills;*

My wife would sigh beside the sills."

What omen does this indicate?

TIAN ZIHUA (*Ponders*):

In my humble opinion, the first line means that when the rain approaches, the ants will come out of the hills. Storks like to feed on ants, and that is why they fly and hoot happily. The line "*My wife would sigh beside the sills*" seems to indicate that the princess is in trouble and yearns to meet you. These lines from "The Eastern Hill" describe an expedition by the Duke of Zhou, and they indicate warfare.

CHUNYU FEN:

Thank you for the interpretation! I shall take great care.

(*Drums within*)

What are the urgent drums for?

(*Enter the eldest son on horseback in a hurry*)

THE ELDEST SON:

"*The roving bandits are said to be making trouble,*

So I've come to inform my father posthaste."

Father, the State of Sandals and Vines is making an invasion. Half of their troops are attacking River Town, and the other half are coming towards the Jade Terrace.

CHUNYU FEN (*Alarmed*):

What shall we do? What shall we do? The Jade Terrace is where the princess dwells, and River Town is a frontier fortress. The enemy has come for these two important places; it is hard to guess their real intentions. Mr. Tian and I will lead the troops to the rescue of the princess; Mr. Zhou Bian is to defend the River Town area; you, my son, will guard Nanke. For the time being, you can take a rest.

THE ELDEST SON:

"*To save mother and children,*

Father and son are the best."

(*Exit*)

CHUNYU FEN:

Mr. Tian, so my dream has been confirmed.

ZHOU BIAN AND TIAN ZIHUA:

Yes. The princess is besieged, so we must go to her rescue right away.

(*Enter the soldiers*)

SOLDIERS:

> "*Some will go and rescue the princess in the Jade Terrace,*
>
> *While others will go and defend River Town.*"

CHUNYU FEN:

Listen to my order! Five thousand soldiers shall go to defend the River Town area under Mr. Zhou's command, and a shock brigade of three thousand hand-picked soldiers shall follow me to the princess' rescue by night.

SOLDIERS:

Your Highness, let's display our battle formation!

TIAN ZIHUA:

Your Highness, an ordinary battle array will be all right for the troops to River Town, but the troops to save the princess should follow what *The Book of Poetry* says and form an array of storks.

SOLDIERS (*Respond, form an array and move*):

The battle array of ants is completed.

(*Form an array, dance and respond*)

The battle array of storks is completed.

CHUNYU FEN:

Now Mr. Zhou and I will lead our troops in different directions.

ZHOU BIAN:

Your Highness, to boost the morale of soldiers, only the liquor will do. Throughout my life, the liquor is something I can't do without. Now I beg for your clemency.

CHUNYU FEN:

Give five thousand jars of liquor to the five thousand soldiers. But here is something for Mr. Zhou to keep in mind. I used to be an assistant general in Huaixi, but I bungled matters because of drinking. This is what both of you already know. Since I came to office here as the magistrate, I've given up drinking. Mr. Zhou, you are well-known for your drinking capacity. But now that you are in charge of military affairs, just remember my words, "Drink less and learn more." We'll part and set on expeditions.

CHUNYU FEN, TIAN ZIHUA (*To the tune of* **Guaguling**):

> In high spirits, we set out
>
> To fight in the Jade Terrace.

Princess,

> How can the women defend the Jade Terrace?
>
> The enemy from the State of Sandals and Vines are ferocious.
>
> We'll set up a white altar,
>
> Choose the propitious time and right direction,

To deploy our forces against the invaders.

ALL:

　　When we listen to the autumn rain at sunset,

　　We hear the stirrups clicking in the fields.

　　(*Exeunt Chunyu Fen and Tian Zihua*)

ZHOU BIAN (*To the previous tune*):

　　In the surrounded River Town,

　　We shall bag sands and grains to fight the enemy.

　　We shall keep a close eye on the enemy

　　And reinforce the defenders.

　　As the liquor goes well with the suit of armor,

　　With Chunyu taking command,

　　I'll catch up from the sideways.

ALL:

　　When we listen to the autumn rain at sunset,

　　We hear the stirrups clicking in the fields.

　　The Jade Terrace is far away,

　　But the war has brought man and wife together.

　　They will meet in the battle cries,

　　Crossing the chasm to return in triumph.

Scene Twenty-Nine
The Siege Lifted

(*Enter Fourth Prince of the State of Sandals and Vines, followed by attendants*)

FOURTH PRINCE (*To the tune of* **Jinqianhua**):

　　I am prince of the State of Sandals and Vines,

　　Sandals and Vines,

　　Day and night I am longing for a wife,

　　For a wife.

　　As there is beauty in the Jade Terrace,

　　By building a small bridge,

　　I'll cross the river and take her by force.

　　Will I make it?

　　Chuck, chuck, I chuckle to myself.

It is wonderful that we've hemmed the Jade Terrace around. The palace rises almost to the moon, and shines as brightly as the immortal land. We'll break it at one fell swoop. Won't that be just a piece of cake? Only I'm afraid of startling the princess to miss my purpose. Yesterday we shot our letter of challenge to the city, but how dare she reply? She is only

waiting for her husband to come to her rescue. I've sent another troop to attack River Town, pressing up to Nanke County. I wonder how her husband could get round to coming here. Dear, dear princess, you'll soon be in my hands. Today I've deliberately closed in. When they respond, I'll ask for the princess to speak to me in person on the city wall, so that I can drink in her beauty. Now warriors, close in! Close in!

(*Sounds of beating drums and cheers from within*)

We have closed in.

HEAD OF MAIDS (*Hurries in, weeping*):

My goodness, the enemy troops are pressing on towards us. Soon we'll have no chance of survival. Your Highness, ascend the tent please!

(*Enter Princess Golden Branch, followed by soldiers*)

PRINCESS GOLDEN BRANCH:

Oh heaven! Heaven! What shall I do?

"*Weathering the danger in the Jade Terrace,*

I see the enemy coming below the city wall.

So frightened am I that I grow pale,

And my dear husband will be sad for that.

On the towering parapet wall,

I feel alone to face the approaching war.

Why is Nanke at such a distance

That my flute is not heard there?"

(*Drums from within*)

(*Princess Golden Branch weeps with maids of honor*)

What shall we do?

(*To the tune of **Nanlüyizhihua***)

In my lonely palace

Is heard the tarter flutes.

What man on earth is so vicious

As to scheme against a woman like me?

I am here to seek shelter from the heat

In this quiet palace,

But have incurred covetousness and warfare.

My two months' leisure has been disturbed

By another day in panic.

(*Drums from within*)

PRINCESS GOLDEN BRANCH:

Oh heavens, heavens! What am I to do? Within the Jade Terrace, there is not much wealth or grains. Then what are the enemies up to? Yesterday we received their letter of challenge. At careful thought, I know that women are not to come to grips with men. How can we take them lightly and fight against them? I'll wait for His Highness to come back. Now I'll send someone to ask them. If they are here to grab the goods, I'll give them some and ease the trouble. Tell the interpreter to ask their ringleader what they are up to!

(The interpreter asks within)

FOURTH PRINCE *(Responds)*:

If you want to know the cause of this war, tell your princess to talk with me in person!

INTERPRETER *(Returns and reports)*:

He wants Your Highness to talk with him in person.

PRINCESS GOLDEN BRANCH *(Sighs)*:

I'm the honorable princess of our great state. How dare those bandits talk with me?

INTERPRETER *(Replies the Fourth Prince)*:

Her Highness is the honorable princess of our great state, how is she to talk with you?

FOURTH PRINCE:

I'm not a low-rank general, but the Fourth Prince of our State of Sandals and Vines. Since both of us are from the royal family, your princess is just like my sister. Of course she can talk with me.

INTERPRETER *(Reports to the princess)*:

He says that he is the Fourth Prince of the State of Sandals and Vines and that he regards Your Highness as his sister. Thus you may well talk with him.

PRINCESS GOLDEN BRANCH:

In that case, I'll have to go despite my illness. We might repel the enemy with a few words.

SOLDIERS:

It's hard to know their intentions. Princess, why not put on your martial attire and command a view on the watchtower?

PRINCESS GOLDEN BRANCH:

Right.

> *(Changes to her military attire and carries bow and arrows)*
>
> *(To the tune of **Liangzhoudiqi**)*
>
> How am I to put on the helmet with quivering hands?
>
> I first take off the soft embroidered socks
>
> And shoes that squeeze my tiny feet.
>
> I tidy my helmet ribbon
>
> And fasten my bracers.
>
> My silk dress is tight,
>
> While my embroidered armor is loose.
>
> The shield in front of my chest shines like the crescent moon;
>
> My neat crimson skirt blows up in the wind.
>
> I am a female general, deploying the army
>
> And wearing the armor and wielding the spear.
>
> As an excellent archer I draw the bow
>
> And pick the arrows from the bag.
>
> As a talented strategist I give orders
>
> By writing on the golden plate.
>
> *(The soldiers hail)*

PRINCESS GOLDEN BRANCH:

> Wonderful!
>
> I am worthy of the cheers!
>
> I wear the officer's belt on my slim waist
>
> And wave the signal flags.
>
> A female general is taking command,
>
> Rousing admiring smiles and stares.
>
> (*Drums and shouts from within*)

PRINCESS GOLDEN BRANCH (*Astonished*):

They are terrible! But I'll ask their prince to talk to me.

FOURTH PRINCE (*Laughs*):

Amazing! Amazing! You are really the goddess in the moon, and Avalokitesvara in the clouds. How do you do, Sister Princess!

PRINCESS GOLDEN BRANCH:

How do you do, Your Highness! You live to the north of the river, while I live to the south of the river. We have nothing to do with each other at all. I didn't expect you should invade our state. What for?

FOURTH PRINCE:

Princess, just take a guess at my intentions.

PRINCESS GOLDEN BRANCH (*To the tune of **Muyangguan***):

> In disorderly battle-lines,
>
> You look ferocious,
>
> Intending to break the Jade Terrace like a bowl.
>
> I am full of disdain for your countenance,
>
> And your naked body.
>
> Does great ambition match your small body?
>
> I'll give you some fish and meat,
>
> Plus bits and pieces of firewood.
>
> You have never done anything great.

Prince,

> You are courting death to invade our State!

INTERPRETER:

Your Excellency, Princess Golden Branch says that if you only need bits and pieces of grains and fish bones, we'll give you some and you may leave.

FOURTH PRINCE (*Laughs*):

We're not here for food or drink. You look down upon us! Warriors! Beat the drums and close in!

PRINCESS GOLDEN BRANCH:

Interpreter, tell him

> (*To the tune of **Sikuaiyu***)
>
> Let us know one by one,
>
> What you actually want.

There is no need
To make pretences.
Is livestock what you want?

FOURTH PRINCE:

No.

PRINCESS GOLDEN BRANCH:

You want silver and gold?

FOURTH PRINCE:

No.

PRINCESS GOLDEN BRANCH:

Why don't you want silver, or grains, or livestock?

FOURTH PRINCE:

You don't know that in our State of Sandals and Vines, we suffer from a shortage of women.
This is what we've come here for.

PRINCESS GOLDEN BRANCH:

So the world of women is distant from your state.

FOURTH PRINCE:

We don't lack ordinary women. The only thing is that my wife died recently.

PRINCESS GOLDEN BRANCH:

Oh,
I thought you wanted women with military talents,
But it turns out that you need a second wife!
(*Drums and shouts from within*)

FOURTH PRINCE:

Give me an immediate response! I need a wife badly.

PRINCESS GOLDEN BRANCH:

How a man can be
So lecherous!
Tell him that I'll report to our king to pick a girl for him, and he can leave with his troops now.

FOURTH PRINCE:

I'm prince of our state and I want to be the royal son-in-law.

PRINCESS GOLDEN BRANCH:

There is something he doesn't know.
(*To the tune of **Mayulang**)
Tell him that my father has no more daughters.

FOURTH PRINCE:

Princess, you are his daughter.

PRINCESS GOLDEN BRANCH:

Shut up!
I got married a long time ago,
And have already got several children.

817

FOURTH PRINCE:

You are still tender and lovely.

PRINCESS GOLDEN BRANCH:

>   You may not know it, but I'm well over thirty.

FOURTH PRINCE:

Where is your husband then?

PRINCESS GOLDEN BRANCH:

>   He's gone to Nanke to select military talents.

>   When he comes back,

>   You'll know the serious consequences.

FOURTH PRINCE:

Whether he comes or not, I don't care. Since you've met my man and worn my flowers, why aren't you to be my wife for just one night?

PRINCESS GOLDEN BRANCH (*To the tune of* **Kuhuangtian**):

Ah, ah, ah,

>   This guy is an idiot,

>   A vulgar rascal!

Attendants, ask him where I met his man and wore his flowers!

FOURTH PRINCE:

Both the scented sandals and the green vines were my gifts for you. You accepted them and made an appointment with me.

PRINCESS GOLDEN BRANCH (*Annoyed*):

Ouch, I've been plotted against. Attendants, go and fetch those flowers, tear them into pieces and scatter them down the palace!

>   (*Destroys the flowers*)

Well,

>   A clodhopper fancying to be the royal son-in-law,

>   You're defaming me

>   And belittling my imperial lineage.

>   (*Throws the flowers on the head of Fourth Prince, making him annoyed*)

FOURTH PRINCE:

We are both of the royal descent, but now you've spoiled my flowers. How irritating! I'll shoot an arrow at the bitch and give her a warning.

>   (*Shoots an arrow*)

Princess Golden Branch, this arrow is for you!

>   (*The arrow whizzes*)

PRINCESS GOLDEN BRANCH (*Dodges the arrow with her sleeves and stumbles*):

Ouch,

>   The arrow hit the phoenix hairpin on the jeweled helmet,

>   With its tail feather entangled with my chignon

>   And its hook a near miss of my cheeks.

>   (*Drums from within*)

(Fourth Prince inquires in panic and exits for the moment)

VOICE WITHIN *(Shouts)*:

His Highness the Royal Son-in-Law has arrived with the relief troops.

SOLDIERS *(Report to the princess)*:

The enemy troops have taken to their heels. Amid deafening drums, the Royal Son-in-Law has arrived with the reinforcements.

PRINCESS GOLDEN BRANCH *(Pleased)*:

> *(To the tune of **Quasi-coda**)*
>
> The ant troops have broken through the tight encirclement,
>
> Stirring up dusts on the bloody battlefield.
>
> The Royal Son-in-Law, the Grand Marshall,
>
> Gallops on his steed,
>
> Wearing armors with colored designs.

Now I,

> I shall beat three rounds of drums to cheer his victory.
>
> *(Exit)*
>
> *(Enter Chunyu Fen, followed by his soldiers)*
>
> "A general never invade other states,
>
> But are ready to fight for his dear wife."
>
> *(Enter Fourth Prince, followed by his soldiers)*

CHUNYU FEN:

You little twit from the State of Sandals and Vines, why don't you surrender at once?

FOURTH PRINCE:

I'm the fourth prince of the State of Sandals and Vines. I've just enjoyed a talk with your wife. Are you jealous of me?

> *(They fight)*

CHUNYU FEN *(Asks)*:

He displays the formation of the ants, and so we shall fly above and display the formation of the storks. Only by doing so can we defeat them.

> *(They fight again)*
>
> *(Fourth Prince is defeated and flees)*
>
> *(Enter Princess Golden Branch, followed by attendants)*

PRINCESS GOLDEN BRANCH:

Thank Heavens! The magistrate has returned in triumph. All the troops shall line up at the gate to greet His Highness.

> *(Greets Chunyu Fen)*

CHUNYU FEN:

How scared I was!

PRINCESS GOLDEN BRANCH:

I was nearly frightened to death.

> *(To the tune of **Wuyeti**)*
>
> I was timid and fragile in illness,

Trembling with fear,

Like Xiang Yu's wife besieged in Gaixia,

And like Cui Yingying fighting beyond the bridge.

I was shot on the gold hairpin,

And almost got my rosy cheek spoilt.

On the watchtower I expected you,

Defeating the invaders' chain enclosures on our women garrison.

If you had been late for a short while,

I would have been smashed.

CHUNYU FEN:

We'll feast and offer bounties to the soldiers outside the Jade Terrace. Get the wine for the princess to get over her shock!

PRINCESS GOLDEN BRANCH:

As the siege of the Jade Terrace has just been lifted, we'd better not linger here for long. We should set out immediately and go back to Nanke County.

(*To the tune of* **Coda**)

The sheep are slaughtered at the gate,

And loud drums are heard all the way,

More pleasant than the song and music.

If you had not come to my rescue in person,

And deployed the soldiers,

I would not have been able to see you any more.

Leading soldiers in double formation

And wearing the phoenix helmets,

We gallop on golden stirrups,

Returning in songs of triumph.

Scene Thirty
Zhou Bian Defeated

(*Enter the soldiers dispatched by Fourth Prince*)

ENEMY SOLDIERS (*To the tune of* **Liuyaoling**):

As we are hungry and thirsty in our country,

We've come out to seek food and drink.

With vine armors and wood weapons,

Having crossed the eastern ravine,

We are heading for Nanke County.

Can River Town stop the river and our troops?

Warriors! Now listen! The Fourth Prince of the State of Sandals and Vines is attacking the Jade

Terrace and he has ordered our troops to attack River Town. Let's march on to Nanke County! Here we are at River Town. Let's rush at it!

(*Enter the garrison soldiers*)

GARRISON SOLDIERS (*To the previous tune*):

The beacon fire has been lit in the south,

And is passing on to Nanke.

What is the Magistrate's defense scheme?

Ah!

Those approaching

Are the troops from the State of Sandals and Vines.

Which general will come to defend River Town?

We are garrison soldiers in River Town. Brothers, the enemy troops have come with overwhelming force, yet the general in charge of the defense has not turned up yet. We have to go on patrol on the city wall by ourselves.

(*Enter Zhou Bian, followed by soldiers*)

ZHOU BIAN (*To the previous tune*):

A war has started

With the State of Sandals and Vines.

Five thousand soldiers have left Nanke County,

Hurrying forward in hunger and thirst,

And crossing hills and dales,

Expecting a drinking spree in River Town.

(*The garrison soldiers greet Zhou Bian and his men*)

ZHOU BIAN:

Finally we've reached the destination.

SOLDIERS:

Liquor should be ready in River Town.

ZHOU BIAN:

We are thirsty. We are thirsty.

SOLDIERS:

Yes, we are thirsty, general.

ZHOU BIAN:

Garrison general, has the liquor prepared by the Director of Farming Affairs been brought here?

GARRISON SOLDIERS (*Respond*):

Yes. Every soldier will have one jar of liquor, with five thousand jars for the five thousand soldiers. We have strong liquor, light liquor and the genuine Nanjing white spirit in small bottles. General, which do you prefer, the strong one or the light one?

ZHOU BIAN:

Half light wine and half high strong liquor. The blended liquor can be named "harmony of fire and water". Now bring the liquor and pile up the jars at the city gate of River Town!

(*Enter the soldiers with the liquor*)

SOLDIERS:

Let us count the jars!

> One, two, three hundred,
>
> Two plus three will be five hundred.
>
> Five hundred times five and another two hundred,
>
> Plus five hundred times two and another five hundred.

ZHOU BIAN:

Blend the five thousand jars and drink to your heart's content! Then throw the jars onto the battlefield! You'll take the light liquor and I'll have the strong liquor. There is no limit to how much we drink. We'll drink till our thirst is satiated.

SOLDIERS (*Drink*):

We are still thirsty.

> (*Throw away the jars*)

ZHOU BIAN:

I'm always fond of drinking. Just because of the magistrate's restrictions, I abstain from drinking for fear of breaking the regulations for government officials. Now finally it is time for me to manifest my drinking capacity.

> (*Drinks*)
>
> (*The soldiers get drunk*)
>
> (*Drums within*)

VOICE WITHIN:

Report! The enemy troops are at the town gate.

ZHOU BIAN:

Let them be and go on drinking!

> (*Urgent drums within*)

VOICE WITHIN:

Report! Report! The enemy vanguard is challenging us to a fight.

ZHOU BIAN (*Annoyed*):

How disgusting this guy is! While I'm at the height of my drinking bout, he comes to cause trouble. Soldiers, charge outside the town under the aftereffect of the liquor!

> (*Soldiers respond*)

ZHOU BIAN:

> Flushed with drink, I look like Lord Guan,
>
> Who killed Hua Xiong while the wine was still warm.
>
> (*Exit*)
>
> (*Enter the enemy soldiers, singing*)

ENEMY SOLDIERS:

Warriors! Break into River Town!

> (*Enter Zhou Bian, followed by soldiers*)

ZHOU BIAN:

Aren't you bandits from the State of Sandals and Vines?

> (*They fight*)

(Being drunk, Zhou Bian and his soldiers are defeated)

(Exeunt the enemy soldiers, in a chase)

(Enter Zhou Bian in a hurry)

ZHOU BIAN:

Soldiers, bring me another vessel of strong liquor! I am thirsty after the fight.

(The soldiers bring the liquor)

(Zhou drinks)

(Enter the enemy soldiers)

ENEMY SOLDIERS:

The liquor over there is mellow and delicious. Let's go and grab it!

(They fight again)

(Zhou Bian and his soldiers are defeated again)

(Enter Zhou Bian alone)

ZHOU BIAN:

Ouch, the enemy soldiers are ferocious. So I have to admit defeat for this battle. It's hot and getting late. I'll take off my armor, and go back on horseback by myself in the bright moonlight.

(Exit)

(Enter an enemy soldier)

ENEMY SOLDIER:

Well, well, well, this time we'll race all the way to take Nanke County.

(Stumbles)

Ouch, why have I stumbled? The scent of the liquor fills in the air, and the spilt liquor is dotted all over the ground. So it is the thousands of jars piled at the gate that stand in our way.

(Looks at the sky)

In this weather, it will surely rain. The river will rise and block our way back. We might take the liquor left and return in triumph.

(To the previous tune)

> With the banners and pennants fluttering in the wind,
>
> Drums and gongs are beaten for the victorious army.
>
> We laugh over the hills of meat and ponds of wine,
>
> Oh we gabble!
>
> Oh we jabber!
>
> Our triumphant return from Nanke will be celebrated.
>
> *With thousands of soldiers lost in Nanke,*
>
> *Only the jars still give off a whiff of odor.*
>
> *Drink while you can,*
>
> *And forgive while you may!*

Scene Thirty-One
Zhou Bian Detained

(*Enter Chunyu Fen, followed by attendants*)

CHUNYU FEN (*To the tune of* **Santailing**):

> I've been devising strategies all year round,
>
> But am troubled by worries these days.
>
> It is easy job to annihilate the enemy from Sandals and Vines,
>
> But why aren't there banners and flags of victory on the way?

(*In the pattern of* **Collected Tang Poems**)

> "*On hearing the drumbeats at the city gate,*
>
> *I keep the expedition to the south in mind.*
>
> *Who knows why one night alone in the hall*
>
> *Should have added white hairs to my head?*"

I am Chunyu Fen. I've garrisoned Nanke County for many years, with my fame of military exploits spreading far and wide. The Princess has stayed in the Jade Terrace to shelter from the heat and met trouble; fortunately, the siege by the State of Sandals and Vines has been lifted. Still I'm worried about River Town, where I've sent Zhou Bian to its rescue. I've been looking forward to news of victory, and I've asked the Director of Farming Affairs to arrange a banquet at the Departure Pavilion for Zhou Bian on his return from the expedition. Mr. Zhou should have arrived early.

(*Enter Tian Zihua*)

TIAN ZIHUA (*To the previous tune*):

> The welcome banquet is decorated with flowers,
>
> The wine banners having replaced the battle flags.
>
> While the joyous atmosphere is so overwhelming,
>
> Who knows where the victory goes?

(*Greets Chunyu Fen*)

TIAN ZIHUA:

> "*Your Highness has a wonderful foresight,*

CHUNYU FEN:

> *But your assistance has been indispensable.*

TIAN ZIHUA:

> *Now that wine is ready for celebrations,*

CHUNYU FEN:

> *Let's wait for the frontier news.*"

Mr. Tian, several days have passed since the war started, but there is no report of success yet. I can't help feeling worried and suspicious.

TIAN ZIHUA:

For one thing, His Majesty enjoys boundless blessing; for another, Your Highness is awe-inspiring; for the third thing, Zhou Bian is brave and skillful in battle. Our troops are bound to return in triumph.

(*Enter the scout*)

SCOUT:

> "*The territory is hard to defend,*
>
> *With each bush and tree like an enemy soldier.*"

Report! General Zhou Bian has returned on horseback alone.

CHUNYU FEN:

Mr. Zhou has returned first, which means that most probably he's won. Tell the music players to start!

(*Drums and trumpets from within*)

(*Enter Zhou Bian on horseback, with headscarf on, in a white robe, and carrying a sword*)

ZHOU BIAN (*To the tune of* **Northern Zuihuayin**):

> On horseback alone, I hate the greetings
>
> To none but me and a horse.
>
> Fleeing with soaring dust above my head,
>
> I see the drums beating and flags waving
>
> And hear the welcoming songs in the distance.
>
> (*Looks*)

His Highness the magistrate and the Director of Farming Affairs have prepared a banquet at the Departure Pavilion. Alas,

> They think I am galloping back in triumph,
>
> Ready to congratulate me in due respect.
>
> (*Greets Chunyu Fen*)

Your Highness!

CHUNYU FEN:

Ah, now that you've returned a victor, I've prepared a feast of celebration together with my fellow officials.

ZHOU BIAN:

Thanks! Give me the wine at once!

CHUNYU FEN (*To the tune of* **Southern Huameixu**):

> Seeing stars in the cups,
>
> I'm shocked to see horror in his eyes.

He went to war in gold-threaded armor,

> But why is he baring his back now,
>
> Without armor or helmet?
>
> The whole thing about him rouses my suspicion;
>
> Why is he returning all alone if he has won?

TIAN ZIHUA:

To be frank with you, Your Highness, there is indeed something suspicious about Director Zhou.

ALL:

> Why are there no festival atmospheres?

We have to obtain further news.

ZHOU BIAN (*To the tune* **Northern Xiqianying**):

Why am I baring my back now?

Because I cheered the troops in hot weather.

For ill luck,

With no one to help me,

I was encircled by the bandit troops.

CHUNYU FEN:

Oh, encircled? How did you break through the encirclement?

ZHOU BIAN:

In breaking through the encirclement,

But for my excellent martial skill,

I would have lost my life and all.

CHUNYU FEN:

In that case, you were defeated, but you are still talking about liquor. Let me ask you,

(*To the tune of* **Southern Huameixu**)

When we deploy the troops the other day,

You had five thousand soldiers with you.

They were all able to fend the spears

And evade the arrows.

Why do I see no one come back with you?

You are safe by yourself,

But where are the others?

ALL:

Why are there no festival atmospheres?

We have to obtain further news.

ZHOU BIAN:

I saw them when these five thousand men went with me.

(*To the tune of* **Northern Chuduizi**)

I was assigned five thousand men,

And they were all there at roll-call.

CHUNYU FEN:

Did they show up in the battlefield?

ZHOU BIAN:

They were there during the battle, but I didn't know where they were after the battle.

TIAN ZIHUA:

Were they killed by the soldiers from Sandals and Vines?

ZHOU BIAN:

It's hard to say.

CHUNYU FEN:

Where are their heads?

ZHOU BIAN:

Ending up alone in grief,

Am I to pay for the five thousand heads?

Oh,

I cannot even pay for five thousand clay-heads.

CHUNYU FEN:

I'm talking about human heads, but he's talking about clay-heads. What do you mean? I won't listen to you, but I'll act in accordance with military disciplines. I'll have you executed first and report to His Majesty later.

ZHOU BIAN:

Who dares!

CHUNYU FEN (*Annoyed*):

As a defeated general, dare you to flaunt your abilities?

(*To the tune of **Southern Diliuzi***)

A defeated general,

A defeated general

Saves his life but does harm to the state.

According to the military disciplines,

According to the military disciplines,

You are not to be pardoned;

You should be executed.

Attendants, follow my order

To have him tied up

And beheaded

So as to set an example for others.

(*The attendants with swords try to tie up Zhou Bian*)

ZHOU BIAN (*Refuses to obey*):

(*To the tune of **Northern Guadifeng***)

Alas,

All of a sudden,

He changed face in a rage,

Forgetting the friendship between sworn brothers.

As Royal Son-in-Law in the State of Peaceful Locust,

You abuse your power to bully your subordinates.

You are a member of the royal family,

But I am not from a humble family.

CHUNYU FEN:

Have him beheaded!

ZHOU BIAN (*Sneers*):

I fought my way through the encirclement,

Returning with my head on my neck.

As you are wagging your tongue at will,

Applying the military discipline on me,

How can I obey your order?

"Beheading" is not the word for me.

CHUNYU FEN:

As the commander, don't I have the right to behead you? Executioners! Tie him up!

TIAN ZIHUA:

Your Highness, have a second thought!

(*To the tune of **Southern Didijin***)

A bosom friend from your native land,

He comes to the ant-land for your sake

And is appointed to station in Nanke country.

At your recommendation,

He is promoted to be the commander-in-chief.

Considering his merits in the past,

You should think before you act

And not make a rash decision.

CHUNYU FEN:

In that case, I'll ask him again. Zhou Bian, how did you commit the crime of losing the battle?

ZHOU BIAN:

Neither I nor the five thousand soldiers are to blame. Your five thousand jars of liquor are to blame. When they were thirsty, they drank the liquor and got drunk. At the report of challenge by the soldiers of Sandals and Vines, their limbs were all limp. As the only good drinker, I went to the battle alone. Fighting single-handedly, I had to drop the weapons and flee by night. If you don't believe me, a poem will prove the point.

"*Winter and summer, spring and autumn,*

The sun sets at dusk and the river flows to the east.

Where is the general with his steed?

Woe permeates the flowers and the weed."

It's all the fault of the five thousand jars of liquor.

(*To the tune of **Northern Simenzi***)

You should not have prepared the wine,

The unfiltered wine mixed with narcotics.

The limp legs could hardly move;

The weak arms could hardly lift the swords.

CHUNYU FEN:

In that case, how could they fight?

ZHOU BIAN:

Of course not.

CHUNYU FEN:

Then, the soldiers from Sandals and Vines will march on toward River Town across the river.

ZHOU BIAN:

Don't worry! I left a scheme. When they were about to enter the city, I threw the empty clay jars on the battlefield and stumbled the horses. They failed to enter the city, thanks to the clay jars.

> With jars piled mountain-high
>
> And clay all over the ground,
>
> The bandit troops slipped and retreated.
>
> As my merit is to be registered
>
> To atone for my crime,
>
> I am to be pardoned for I was drunk.

CHUNYU FEN:

Zhou Bian, before you left, I told you to drink less and learn more. You didn't take my words to heart; therefore you will be punished according to the military discipline.

ZHOU BIAN:

Well, who is not fond of drinks since ancient times? If the heaven is not fond of drinks, it will not have the wine star; if the earth is not fond of drinks, it will not have the wine spring. Since both the heaven and the earth are fond of drinks, drinking is the right of a military man. Fan Kuai in the Han Dynasty, Zhou Yu and Guan Yu in the period of the Three Kingdoms are all fond of drinks. I am not the only one who is fond of drinks.

CHUNYU FEN (*To the tune of* **Southern Baolaocui**):

> You are citing the past to allude to the present —
>
> General Fan Kuai got drunk, but he spoiled the Hongmen plot;
>
> Lord Guan had a blushing face not for the sake of drinking;
>
> Compared with Zhou Yu,
>
> You are below par
>
> In drinking the wine.

Well, as you are my fellow countryman and my fellow official, you will not be punished according to the military discipline for the moment. You'll wait for your punishment in the prison. I'll report to His Majesty to make the decision.

> I'll leave your head with you
>
> And put you in the prison,
>
> As I submit a memorial for His Majesty to decide on your fate.

Attendants, put him into prison!

(*The attendants try to tie him up*)

ZHOU BIAN (*Refuses to obey*):

(*To the tune of* **Northern Shuixianzi**)

> Damn! Damn! Damn!
>
> Damn you all!

CHUNYU FEN (*Annoyed*):

Tie him up!

ZHOU BIAN:

> Tie! Tie! Tie!
>
> Tie me and I'll put to the sword!

CHUNYU FEN:

Shut up! Do you think that I can't have you tied? Hang the Royal Command Plate!

(The attendants hang the Royal Command Plate)

TIAN ZIHUA:

Sober up, Captain! Look at the Royal Command Plate!

ZHOU BIAN (*Looks up and gets scared. Aside*):

> He! He! He!
>
> He tells me to open my grim eyes.
>
> *(Wipes his eyes)*
>
> I! I! I!
>
> I'll act the idiot.
>
> *(Looks aslant)*
>
> How! How! How!
>
> How has he hung the Royal Command Plate?
>
> You! You! You!
>
> You must have the secret permission by His Majesty!

ALL:

Captain, why don't you kneel before the Royal Command Plate?

ZHOU BIAN (*With his hands tied behind his back*):

> Why! Why! Why!
>
> Why should a general kneel to a magistrate!
>
> So! So! So!
>
> So I have to kneel in front of the plate.
>
> *(Kneels)*

CHUNYU FEN:

Have you submitted yourself to being tied?

ZHOU BIAN:

I have submitted myself to none other than His Majesty.

> This! This! This!
>
> This is the obligation of a subject.

CHUNYU FEN:

Well, you'll be sent to prison.

> *(To the tune of **Southern Shuangshengzi**)*
>
> The other day,
>
> The other day,
>
> I told you to drink less.
>
> You did not listen,
>
> You did not listen,
>
> But gloss over your promise.
>
> You are lost,
>
> You are lost.
>
> Brag no more!
>
> Brag no more!
>
> You'll wait for His Majesty's decree

In the prison.

(*Enter the jailer*)

JAILER:

I've come to meet you, captain.

CHUNYU FEN:

Defeated captain, you'll stay in the prison for a few days.

ZHOU BIAN (*Annoyed*):

Alas! A hero like me has come to this!

> (*To the tune of* **Northern Coda**)
> I broke through the encirclement,
> But can't break through the prison wall.

My back aches. Please have a look at it!

ATTENDANTS (*Look and laugh*):

It's nothing but a pink ulcer.

ZHOU BIAN:

Let it be! Let it be!

> I'm so angry that ulcer grows on my back.

There is nothing else to blame but the five thousand jars!

> I regret,
> I regret that I didn't sleep on a clay jar
> And die a hero on the battlefield.
> (*Exit*)

CHUNYU FEN:

> *Liquor nearly costs his head;*

TIAN ZIHUA:

> *By now he is kept in the cell.*

CHUNYU FEN, TIAN ZIHUA:

> *When he is sober, he feels the dread,*
> *For he is a loser, but alive and well.*

Scene Thirty-Two
Court Counseling

(*Enter the Ant King, followed by attendants*)

ANT KING (*To the tune of* **Xiaopenglai**):

> Changes take place in the world,
> But the ants remain the same.
> As King of the Peaceful Locust,
> I deploy the troops in Nanke,
> But am worried about the recent events.

(*In the pattern of* **Collected Tang Poems**)

"Poplars and willows are lined on the banks,

While the palace is cold in an autumn day.

As the royal troops are entangled in battles,

When will the garrison be on the homeward way?"

I am King of the State of Peaceful Locust,

At odds with the Sandals and Vines.

When the princess was encircled recently,

The Royal Son-in-Law came to her rescue.

Zhou Bian was sent as enforcement

To assist River Town.

There is no report of victory yet,

And the Right Prime Minister must have some news.

(*Enter Duan Gong, with a memorial*)

DUAN GONG (*To the previous tune*):

I am honored as the Right Prime Minister,

Assisting the king in his handling the state affairs.

Well,

Laws and regulations have been laid down,

But the frontier regions have been neglected.

I shall present the memorial in hot haste.

I am the Right Prime Minister. In the important county of Nanke, His Highness the Royal Son-in-Law has been assigned there for over twenty years and has assumed too much power. To my worry, he is deep-rooted and hard to control. It happened that the princess was encircled and River Town was in trouble. His fame has thus been affected. I would count myself lucky, for things might have been even worse. His Highness sent in a memorial last night, asking about the punishment of Zhou Bian. I'll present the memorial and do as I see fit.

(*Kneels*)

The Right Prime Minister Guan Gong seeks an audience.

ANT KING:

As you have just come in, do you have any news about the war with the Sandals and Vines?

DUAN GONG:

His Highness has sent in a memorial post-haste. Please allow me to read it!

(*To the tune of* **Suochuanglang**)

I am on tenterhooks to report

That we had an encounter with the bandit troops.

ANT KING:

Zhou Bian can lead the army to fight with them.

DUAN GONG:

The troops went on the expedition,

But only one man returned alive.

ANT KING:

So he's badly defeated.

DUAN GONG:

> I am frank
>
> And do not want to cheat you.
>
> I hope that Your Majesty
>
> Will remove me from office.
>
> Zhou Bian is to be punished
>
> For his deadly faults.

ANT KING:

When we are prosperous, we can soar to the sky; when we degenerate, we are restrained like stranded dragons. We are defeated by the tiny State of Sandals and Vines. Oops, the Royal Son-in-Law is imprudent this time.

> (*To the previous tune*)
>
> Nanke is a strategic spot,
>
> Strong enough to resist the Sandals and Vines.
>
> How can an army of ten thousand soldiers
>
> Suffer such casualties!
>
> If the news is leaked,
>
> The enemy will despise us.

Annoying! Annoying!

> In command of the army,
>
> How can the Royal Son-in-Law
>
> Entrust Zhou Bian?

DUAN GONG (*To the previous tune*):

> The error in the frontier is serious,
>
> But His Highness has weathered hardships in twenty years.

ANT KING:

That's it. My son-in-law has been stationed in the border area for years, and the princess has time and again entreated to return to the capital. As no proper person is to succeed him as the magistrate of Nanke, I have dropped the idea.

DUAN GONG:

When His Highness returns, Tian Zihua is still there.

> As he is well-versed in military strategies,
>
> He is able to succeed His Highness.
>
> The princess can return to the capital,
>
> And recuperate her health.

ANT KING:

The minister should take responsibility for the loss of the war. It's Chunyu's fault this time.

DUAN GONG:

> His Highness is to be commended,
>
> But Zhou Bian

Is to be punished.

ANT KING:

Then, Zhou Bian is to be executed for his loss of war.

DUAN GONG:

Zhou Bian is a bosom friend of His Highness. He recommended Zhou Bian twice. I'm afraid that the execution of Zhou Bian will hurt the feelings of His Highness. He'd better be remitted from death and atone for his crimes by meritorious service.

ANT KING:

Your request is consented.

> *Zhou Bian is remitted from death*
> *While Tian Zihua is to succeed the office.*
> *The princess is to follow her man*
> *To return to the capital town.*

Scene Thirty-Three
Summoned to the Capital

834

(Enter Princess Golden Branch, supported by the maid of honor)

PRINCESS GOLDEN BRANCH (*To the tune of* **Yichichi**):

> In fears since I came to the Jade Terrace,
>
> I am deeply worried.
>
> With tears soaking my pillows,
>
> I often wake up from dreams in deep autumn.

MAID OF HONOR:

> She combs at random by the dressing table,
>
> Frowning for her thought of return.

PRINCESS GOLDEN BRANCH (*In the pattern of* **Gutiaoxiao**):

> *"The soul departs,*
> *The soul departs,*
> *With autumn dreams in the Jade Terrace.*
> *I wake up in Nanke again,*
> *Tormented by fragility and illness.*
> *Worsening illness,*
> *Worsening illness*
> *Is the predestined fate for a princess."*

In weak health since my childhood, I feel all the more melancholy as I was frightened by the encirclement, Zhou Bian's loss of war and the anxiety for His Highness. I've asked my parents to bring me to the capital, so as to recover from my poor health, to consolidate the position of His Highness as he might have incurred jealousy for his fame in Nanke for so many years, and to seek titles and offices for my children. I am waiting for the decree by His Majesty.

(Enter Chunyu Fen)

CHUNYU FEN (*To the tune of **Buchangong***):

> Sorrow prevails in the painted hall,
>
> Pearled curtains wavering in the rain.
>
> Picking withered flowers against the rails,
>
> She touches me with her deep affection.

(Greets Princess of Golden Branch)

Are you feeling better?

PRINCESS GOLDEN BRANCH:

I'm afraid that I won't recover. Your Highness, how long have we been here?

CHUNYU FEN:

For twenty years in all.

PRINCESS GOLDEN BRANCH (*Sighs*):

Chunyu, listen to me. Born in the palace, I didn't expect to be married to you. I have assisted you in managing the affairs in Nanke and winning some fame. The loss of war with the Sandals and Vines has diminished your fame. What's more, you have been the magistrate for twenty years. It's time for you to quit the office. I'm afraid I'll die before you.

(Weeps)

(Noise of the locust tree within)

CHUNYU FEN:

What's the noise?

(Enter the eldest son)

ELDEST SON:

Dad and Mom, the locust tree is making the noise.

PRINCESS GOLDEN BRANCH (*Smiles*):

Your Highness, I'm pleased at the clear noise of the tree.

CHUNYU FEN:

You are seldom pleased.

PRINCESS GOLDEN BRANCH:

This locust tree is called the "Sounding Tree". Whenever a Prime Minister is nominated, this tree would make clear noise. By this good omen, you'll be the Prime Minister sooner or later. However, when I'm gone, you'll go through various hardships.

*(To the tune of **Jixianbin**)*

> It's too late for one to repent at the end of his life;
>
> Love is common for the young people,
>
> But dearer for a couple of many years.

I have never treated you shabbily, and so, I hope you will not marry again when I'm gone.

> You'll sleep in the cold quilt in an empty hall.

You won't be the same as before when you return to court.

> You should learn to handle relations
>
> And keep your dignity when I'm gone.

CHUNYU FEN, PRINCESS GOLDEN BRANCH:

>With a painful heart,

>I wish that we shall never die.

CHUNYU FEN (*To the previous tune*):

>(*Weeps*)

Princess,

>Your words will linger in my heart,

>Like cuckoos weeping tears of blood.

>I'll bear the loneliness when you are gone,

>But the children will not feel the same.

Princess,

>With deep affection,

>You have accompanied me all these twenty years.

CHUNYU FEN, PRINCESS GOLDEN BRANCH:

>With a painful heart,

>I wish that we shall never die.

PRINCESS GOLDEN BRANCH (*Weeps*):

>(*To the tune of* **Mao'erzui**)

>Fits of cold and fever

>Have bleached the blush on my cheeks.

Maids,

>Prepare the paper and I'll write a few letters

>To the palace in the capital town.

CHUNYU FEN (*Makes a bow*):

>Oh, heavens!

>At the turn of our lives,

>Please relax your steps!

PRINCESS GOLDEN BRANCH:

At this stage of my illness, I have to give up.

CHUNYU FEN:

How can you speak like this?

>(*To the previous tune*)

>In your fragile health,

>You'd better lower the curtains.

>Keep away from the wind

>And I'll burn the incense under the moon.

PRINCESS GOLDEN BRANCH:

>In dizziness,

>The thread of my life

>Is entrusted to my man.

>(*Enter the eldest son*)

ELDEST SON:

Report! Report! Here comes the royal decree. Dad, as Mom is ill, how is she to receive the decree?

CHUNYU FEN:

My son, support your mom and make a bow here!

ROYAL ENVOY:

Here is the royal decree. Kneel down and listen. The King of the State of Peaceful Locust decrees. Princess Yaofang and the Royal Son-in-Law Chunyu Fen have made meritorious deeds in Nanke for many years. You will be summoned to serve in the court as the Left Prime Minister. The position of Nanke magistrate will be transferred to Tian Zihua, Director for Farming Affairs. The above is the decree. Thank for the royal grace.

(*All shout "Long live the king!" and rise to their feet*)

PRINCESS GOLDEN BRANCH:

Congratulations on your promotion to the position of the Prime Minister! The omen of the clear noise of the locust tree has come true.

CHUNYU FEN:

Thank you for your recommendation!

(*The royal envoy kowtows*)

CHUNYU FEN:

What is to do with Zhou Bian?

ROYAL ENVOY:

By the royal decree, for the sake of Your Highness, he is remitted from death and he is to atone for his crimes by meritorious deeds.

CHUNYU FEN:

It shows the benevolence of His Majesty. Please attend the banquet at the Huanghua Guesthouse!

ROYAL ENVOY:

"*When the kings allots the offices,*

The prime minister will soon return."

(*Exit*)

CHUNYU FEN:

Princess, I've been staying here for years. Now that I am to leave, I shall handle some aftermath of the problems. Our children will go with you in advance, and we shall meet at the palace gate and greet His Majesty together.

PRINCESS GOLDEN BRANCH:

I'll follow your instructions. However, as we have been living in Nanke for twenty years, I can hardly tear myself away from it.

CHUNYU FEN:

Life itself is but a sojourn, let alone the official residence! Take good care of yourself! Get wine, son!

(*Wine is presented*)

(*To the tune of **Zhaoyin'er***)

A cup of wine dispels her sorrow

In the small palace.

Son,

    Take good care of your mom in the long journey!

    Prepare proper food and drink,

    And shun from cold and heat!

    You are old enough to look after her.

ELDEST SON:

    I'll keep your instructions

    And advice in mind.

    I'll take care of Mom

    And tend to her needs.

    Letters of peace

    Will be sent to you.

ALL:

    Blessed by the heaven,

    The family will be in happy reunion,

    Ready for the royal banquet.

    (*Enter the maid of honor*)

MAID OF HONOR (*Reports*):

Your Ladyship and Your Highness, at the news of your return, the officials and civilians are waiting at the door.

PRINCESS GOLDEN BRANCH:

Maid, pass on my words! I am grateful to you for my twenty years of stay in Nanke. As I am returning in illness today, I can only requite you in my next life.

    (*Cries within*)

CHUNYU FEN:

Tell them not to add grief to Her Ladyship.

    The princess is in poor health

    After she stays in Nanke for twenty years.

    When she follows her children to the capital,

    The civilians gaze at her like all the peers.

Scene Thirty-Four
Halting the Way

    (*Enter the old secretary*)

OLD SECRETARY (*To the tune of* **Langtaosha**):

    Worthless as a stray dog,

    I have no hope of promotion.

    I only hope to be safe and sound

In my duty to sign and enact

With plenty of extra income.

I am an old secretary in Nanke County. According to its layout of feng-shui, Nanke County abounds in old officials. Don't you believe my words? His Highness the Royal Son-in-Law has served here for twenty years, so has the Director of Farming Affairs, and so have I as the secretary. I was young and handsome when I came, but I am in grey beard now. By the royal decree, the princess and the magistrate will return to the capital and serve in the court. The princess set out three days ago and His Highness will set out today after he entrusted the county affairs to Tian Zihua, Director of Farming Affairs. To see him off at the Departure Pavilion with a farewell banquet, Director Tian says that His Highness came as the county magistrate and returned as the prime minister. As the highway is not smooth enough, a thirty-*li* sand-bank is built, with arches on both ends inscribed with the words "New Sand-Bank" at the top. Many civilians have come to watch.

(*Enter civilians with a petition*)

CIVILIANS (*To the previous tune*):

The old and young are safe and sound,

Because the officials are clear-handed.

As the virtuous magistrate will return to the court,

The civilians would like to keep him,

But His Majesty is far away and hard to reach.

(*Kneel before the old secretary*)

We want to air our views, Your Honor.

OLD SECRETARY:

What is it?

CIVILIANS:

With His Highness in service here for twenty years, the people have lived in peace and contentment. Our peace is as vast as the ocean, and our contentment is as warm as the springtime. Once he is summoned to serve in the court, how can we tear away from him?

OLD SECRETARY:

It has nothing to do with me.

CIVILIANS:

The civilians in Nanke have signed the petition for His Highness to stay for another ten years. As the capital town is a long way off, we entreat Your Honor get a dozen horses ready to send the petition to the capital by night and day three hundred *li* away. Luck might have it that His Highness will return midway and take his office in Nanke. If we go by ourselves, we might be too late.

OLD SECRETARY (*Surprised*):

So you'd like to retain His Highness. You are afraid that the petition might be too late, so you ask me to get a dozen horses ready to send the petition to the capital by night and day three hundred *li* away. Luck might have it that His Highness will return midway and take his office in Nanke. Well, don't ask me for help!

CIVILIANS (*Weep*):

If you don't want to help, we'll entreat Director Tian.

OLD SECRETARY:

Entreat His Highness? Go if you like!

> (*The civilians rise to their feet*)

OLD SECRETARY:

Wait! Listen to me. Director Tian will take office in Nanke. He will be embarrassed if you ask him.

CIVILIANS:

It turns out that Director Tian will be the new magistrate. It's not convenient for us to ask him. We'll go by ourselves,

OLD SECRETARY:

That's enough for you. Director Tian is coming.

> (*The civilians make way*)
>
> (*Enter Tian Zihua*)

TIAN ZIHUA (*To the tune of* **Yiluosuo**):

> After twenty years as a director in the office,
>
> I am now promoted to be the magistrate.
>
> Seeing off His Highness at the Departure Pavilion,

Well,

> Thousands of people are on the way.

OLD SECRETARY (*Greets Tian Zihua*):

Your Excellency, the banquet is ready.

TIAN ZIHUA:

Look at the crowds of people on the way! Are they seeing off His Highness? Nice people! Nice people!

OLD SECRETARY:

Amid music of drums and flutes, here comes His Highness.

> (*Tian Zihua and the old secretary walk to meet Chunyu Fen*)
>
> (*Enter Chunyu Fen, followed by attendants*)

CHUNYU FEN (*To the tune of* **Lanhuamei**):

> The procession goes in the morning mist,
>
> With people watching all the time.
>
> (*Cries within, "Our lord!"*)
>
> Thousands of people on the way,
>
> What are they doing here?

OLD SECRETARY:

They are trying to retain Your Highness.

CHUNYU FEN:

> With grateful civilians trying to retain me,
>
> What have I done to be worthy of their respect?

Yes, I see. It's the people's kindness.

They are adding a halo over my head.

TIAN ZIHUA (*Kneels down to greet Chunyu Fen*):

Director of Farming Affairs Tian Zihua greets Your Highness.

CHUNYU FEN:

Rise to your feet, Director Tian. I'll get off the carriage and greet you.

(*Gets down the carriage*)

(*Greets Tian Zihua*)

Director Tian, when is this highway completed? Oh, at the top of the colorful arch are the words "New Sand-bank".

TIAN ZIHUA:

Yes, the new sand-bank is built for the prime minister.

CHUNYU FEN (*Smiles*):

I'd like to walk on it with you.

(*Walks with Tian Zihua*)

(*To the previous tune*)

I am promoted to the top at the royal grace;

TIAN ZIHUA:

The new sand-bank is built for the prime minister;

CHUNYU FEN:

The dense trees conceal the horse-bells.

TIAN ZIHUA:

The Departure Pavilion is ahead. I've prepared a cup of wine,

To make a toast at your short stay by the pavilion.

CHUNYU FEN:

The old and new magistrate will meet in haste.

(*Chunyu Fen and Tian Zihua arrive at the pavilion*)

(*Tian Zihua bows to Chunyu Fen*)

CHUNYU FEN:

After I said good-bye to Zhou Bian this morning, I went to your office but did not see you. Let me take this opportunity at the pavilion to thank you, Director Tian!

TIAN ZIHUA:

It's my pleasure.

(*Bows*)

CHUNYU FEN:

"*You are my right hand for twenty years;*

TIAN ZIHUA:

You have showered great favor on me.

CHUNYU FEN:

Please make remedies after I leave;

TIAN ZIHUA:

Please give me a hand in the future."

OLD SECRETARY (*Kowtows to Chunyu Fen*):

841

The Nanke Dream

The old secretary kowtows to Your Highness.

CHUNYU FEN:

Rise to your feet! As a secretary, you have been working hard for twenty years; after I leave, please keep an eye on him, Director Tian!

(*The old secretary kowtows to show his gratitude*)

TIAN ZIHUA:

Bring the wine!

(*Enter the attendant with wine*)

ATTENDANT:

"*The bamboos are reflected in the wine;*

The flowers speed the carriage."

Here is the wine.

TIAN ZIHUA (*Presents the wine*):

(*To the tune of **Shanhuazi***)

With benevolence in Nanke,

You'll return to the Peaceful Locust.

Twenty years of peaceful life

Are ascribed to your merits.

CHUNYU FEN:

I've handed over the seal and all the affairs.

With the golden seal intact

And the documents checked,

I feel the woe in the banquet cups.

CHUNYU FEN, TIAN ZIHUA:

Returning to serve in the court,

The Royal Son-in-Law is further promoted.

CHUNYU FEN (*To the previous tune*):

When the office is transferred to the new magistrate,

Please listen to my advice as a peer!

Don't say that the office is easy matter;

You should know the hardships of the people.

TIAN ZIHUA:

With your instructions kept in mind

And to be followed in the future,

I shall part with my old friend of twenty years.

CHUNYU FEN, TIAN ZIHUA:

Returning to serve in the court,

The Royal Son-in-Law is further promoted.

CHUNYU FEN:

As the princess has set out for a long time, I cannot be delayed any longer. Good-bye!

(*Rises to start on his journey*)

(*Enter the civilians*)

CIVILIANS (*To the tune of **Dahefo***):

    We pray with incense basin on our heads

    For Heaven to retain our gracious magistrate.

    (*Kneel and weep*)

Your Highness,

    Stay a few days for us to send petition to the court!

    Are you willing to tear yourself away from us?

CHUNYU FEN:

Oh, dear fellow countrymen! How can I tear myself away from you?

    But I cannot defy the royal decree,

    Although my stay of twenty years has held my heart here.

CIVILIANS:

    When we think of

    Your favors in twenty years,

    We have always kept them in our hearts.

    (*Weep, clinging to and lying before the carriage*)

Your Highness,

    We have to lie before the carriage,

    Clinging to it in floods of tears.

CHUNYU FEN:

I must be going. Rise to your feet! Rise to your feet!

    (*Walks*)

CIVILIANS (*To the tune of **Wunishang***):

    We stand before the stalwart horses

    And hold the embroidered robe.

CHUNYU FEN (*Weeps*):

    My belt may break but our affection will not break;

    The tie between us will survive for generations.

Director Tian,

    Look after the people for me when I have left!

CIVILIANS (*Weep*):

    As we cannot retain him,

    We'll kneel and pray in his memorial hall at morn and eve.

CHUNYU FEN:

Fellow countrymen, I'm leaving now.

    (*To the tune of **Hongxiuxie***)

    In gratitude they halt the way,

    Halt the way.

    I look back in weeping eyes,

    In weeping eyes.

    Beyond the Departure Pavilion,

    On the painted bridge,

The people kneel,

Facing the benevolent countenance.

The virtuous magistrate

Returns in glory.

Fellow countrymen, please go back!

CIVILIANS:

The Nanke people within territory are seeing you off.

CHUNYU FEN:

Thank you very much!

CIVILIANS (*To the tune of* **Coda**):

The affection makes the departure difficult.

CHUNYU FEN:

As you have fed me for twenty years,

I wish you cherish favorable weather all the time.

(*Exit, followed by attendants*)

CIVILIANS (*Left on the stage*):

Good magistrate, good magistrate! Kowtowing to Magistrate Tian and trying to retain Magistrate Chunyu, we know that His Highness handles affairs better. Let's sit for a while and send a representative to the capital from each region of the county!

(*Allot representatives*)

(*Heralding the way within*)

(*Enter the old secretary*)

OLD SECRETARY:

"*As there are unexpected storms in nature,*

So there are unpredictable vicissitudes in life."

Oh, you are still waiting here?

CIVILIANS:

Your Honor, we're waiting to see off His Highness further.

OLD SECRETARY:

You know, when His Highness was fifty *li* from Nanke, report came that the Princess died.

CIVILIANS:

Pardon?

OLD SECRETARY:

The princess has passed away.

CIVILIANS (*Weep and cry*):

What's to be done? Good Heavens! Is it true?

OLD SECRETARY:

Isn't it true? Director Tian has sent me back to prepare white damask silk, pure satin and sandalwood incense to attend the mourning. Isn't it true?

CIVILIANS:

In that case, His Highness will not be able to return to our county. As the news is true, let's offer joss-sticks for the mourning!

The virtuous magistrate leaves over grace
While the princess is dead and gone.
The grateful civilians in the county
Will weep a thousand years long.

Scene Thirty-Five
Mourning over the Death

(Enter the Ant Queen, followed by maids of honor)

ANT QUEEN (*To the tune of* **Raohonglou**):

The daughter of the royal blood

Has descendants in Nanke County.

As illness may harm her health

And she has been away for a long time,

I feel sad in the inner palace.

(In the pattern of **Qingpingyue**)

"The autumn grass overgrows the jade steps,

Covering the paths with green.

I weep tears of sorrow in my palace,

Growing old without notice.

My dainty daughter in Nanke

Withers for her long illness.

I lean against the door and gaze afar,

Holding a small fan in my hand."

Living in the deep palace, I've heard that my daughter is terrified by the battle at the Jade Terrace and is in woe and worries all day long. I am pleased to know that His Majesty has issued the decree for the couple to return to the court. The report came yesterday that my daughter set out a few days earlier in her illness. I am worried about how she is faring on the way.

(Weeps)

(Enter a court lady)

COURT LADY:

"The messenger bird brings news of happiness,

But there is evil news of the daughter."

Your Majesty the Queen, when I was at the palace gate, I heard from those outside the gate that the princess was seriously ill. I don't know why His Majesty and the attendants are all crying.

ANT QUEEN (*Shocked*):

What's happened?

(*Weeps*)

(*Heralding the way within*)

(*Enter the Ant King, followed by attendants*)

ANT KING (*To the tune of* **Kuxiangsi**):

> It is too late for me to fetch my daughter;
>
> Why should the Heaven grab away her life?

(*Greets the Ant Queen*)

My dear wife, Chunyu's wife has passed away.

ANT QUEEN:

What did you say?

ANT KING:

Yaofang set out a few days earlier from Nanke and died in the Huanghua Guesthouse.

ANT QUEEN (*Cries*):

Oh my dear daughter!

> (*Faints, with the maids of honor supporting her*)

ANT KING:

Don't let her death hurt your health!

ANT QUEEN (*To the tune of* **Hongna'ao**):

> I keep her under my wings with my whole heart;

ANT KING:

> Thinking that she has a bright prospect.

ANT QUEEN:

> I thought that she had an endearing spouse,

ANT KING:

> But her illness confined her to bed.

ANT QUEEN:

> You smiled when she was giving birth,

ANT KING:

> But I choke with sobs for her departure.

ANT QUEEN:

Good Heavens,

> In spite of the Maudgalyayana sutra I copied,
>
> Buddha's power is not felt in face of the ghosts.

ANT KING (*To the previous tune*):

My dear wife,

> I thought there was no worry about her in her palace,

ANT QUEEN:

> But the troubles in the Jade Terrace killed her.

ANT KING:

> There are premature deaths of daughters,

ANT QUEEN:

> But why should my daughter decline like the moon?

ANT KING:

> I remember seeing off the couple off with a drink,

ANT QUEEN:

> Who knows she died on her homeward way.

ANT KING:

> It is predestined in her previous life,
>
> But I loathe mourning before her spirit tablet.

ANT QUEEN:

As His Majesty only has this daughter, the funeral rituals must be elaborate.

ANT KING:

When the funeral hearse arrives, my wife and I will be dressed in mourning and meet her in the suburbs. Her shrine will be set in the Xiuyi Palace, accompanied by half of the royal procession. As to the formalities for entitlement and endowment, the Right Prime Minister and Marquis of Martial Feats will be in full charge.

> *They might have lived in Nanke for a hundred years,*
>
> *But the princess passed away at an earlier date.*
>
> *The state rituals will be duly elaborated,*
>
> *To be bestowed to her in the netherworld.*

Scene Thirty-Six
Returning to the Court

(*Enter Duan Gong*)

DUAN GONG (*To the tune of* **Raodiyou**):

> What is the use of multitude?
>
> One man is the pillar of the state.

Alas,

> Chunyu Fen and the princess
>
> Cherished twenty years of affection
>
> And established power there,
>
> But all ends in a dream.
>
> *"While the bees fall into woe after the Double Ninth,*
>
> *Unawares, the butterflies circle round the boughs.*
>
> *People have changed their minds in different times,*
>
> *As the flowers have not lost their fragrance in one night."*

As far as I know, Chunyu Fen resorted to his relations in staying in Nanke and raising his esteem. For the sake of long-term interest of our state, I sent in a memorial for His Majesty to recall him and give him the position of the Left Prime Minister, so as to curb his power of remote control. Who knows that things are unpredictable! After the princess

passed away, the King and the Queen met the hearse in the suburbs, and the whole state was in mourning for three days. The princess was posthumously titled as Princess Righteousness, with all the ceremonies. At His Majesty's decree, her burial place was discussed. Her burial place could only be selected in Mount Tortoise. I am about to report the choice to His Majesty. I hear that Chunyu Fen will have an audience with His Majesty and will wait here. He may be told to select the place for the burial. Before I finish my words, His Highness has arrived.

(*Enter Chunyu Fen, wearing the court robe and holding a memorial tablet*)

CHUNYU FEN (*To the previous tune*):

Like a broken string hard to repair

And blown away by the autumn wind,

The lovebirds have been separated alive.

(*Stamps his feet and weep*)

While the whole county wails

And the whole state grieves,

I am in deep woe with nowhere to vent my affection.

(*Greets Duan Gong*)

DUAN GONG:

As you are about to have the audience, you'd better stop weeping.

(*Drums within*)

CHUNYU FEN (*Performs the court etiquette and kneels*):

The former Nanke magistrate, the newly-appointed Left Prime Minister, the Royal Son-in-Law and the Royal Captain Chunyu Fen kneels to Your majesty. Long live the King!

VOICE WITHIN:

Here is the royal decree: "I am grieved at the recent loss of his wife by the Royal Son-in-Law. I have decreed that the royal cooks will prepare a banquet in the inner palace. As to the burial place of Princess Righteousness, you may report to me after a discussion with the Right Prime Minister and Marquis of Martial Feats outside the palace gate."

CHUNYU FEN (*Kowtows*):

Long live the King!

(*Rises to his feet*)

How do you do, Right Prime Minister!

DUAN GONG:

How do you do, Royal Son-in-Law!

CHUNYU FEN:

I haven't been to the court gate for a long time. Thank you for your trouble of meeting me a long distance away! As I had not received the audience yet, I did not thank you earlier.

DUAN GONG:

Don't mention it!

CHUNYU FEN:

May I ask where the princess is to be buried?

DUAN GONG:

The cave on Mount Tortoise is propitious.

CHUNYU FEN:

As Mount Tortoise is at the backdoor of our state, what is there to be propitious? I once saw Mount Dragon ten *li* east of the state, with an excellent layout. Why don't we bury her in this place?

DUAN GONG:

Mount Dragon might block the source of the state. We'd better bury her in Mount Tortoise.

CHUNYU FEN:

You know, if Mount Tortoise is selected as her burial site, the tortoise shell might be hurt.

DUAN GONG:

Your Highness, even if Mount Dragon is proper, the one who lies on the dragon nose might hurt its lips.

CHUNYU FEN:

If we choose Mount Tortoise, the tortoise must have a son. Where is the son?

DUAN GONG:

If we choose Mount Dragon, the dragon must have a pearl in its mouth. Where is the pearl?

CHUNYU FEN:

I only want good omens for the children.

DUAN GONG:

Your children all have a good family background. Why should she be buried on Mount Dragon?

CHUNYU FEN:

How can you speak like this? A son must become a general or a prime minister; a daughter must be matched to a king or a marquis. They must share the fate of the state. The burial site is closely related to the fate of the descendants for ten thousand years.

DUAN GONG (*Sneers aside*):

So he is considering for ten thousand years!

(*Turns back and responds*)

If you like. However, as Mount Dragon is positioned too far away from the stars, it might be molested by bees and ants.

CHUNYU FEN:

You do not seem to be an expert in this respect. The dwelling place of a tiger or a dragon has nothing to do with the distance or the size; the swarming of bees or ants only has something to do with the zigzag paths they travel through. Why should we worry about bees and ants?

DUAN GONG (*Laughs*):

If you do not mind being hurt by ants, just present your memorial in the palace hall!

(*Presents his memorial*)

The Right Prime Minister and Marquis of Martial Feats, Duan Gong respectfully presents his memorial.

(*To the tune of* **Matihua**)

To trace the blue blood,

The key lies in the cave on Mount Tortoise.

VOICE WITHIN:

What is the advantage of Mount Tortoise?

DUAN GONG:

It has maids on both sides,

Decrees of entitlement above

And skirt ribbons in the wind.

VOICE WITHIN:

Is Mount Tortoise similar to Mount Dragon?

DUAN GONG:

People only know that peaks grow on Mount Dragon,

But don't know that caves grow in Mount Tortoise.

Will the tortoise alone hang its head,

But will the ants not pile into hills?

CHUNYU FEN (*Presents his memorial*):

The Royal Son-in-Law Chunyu Fen respectfully presents his memorial.

(*To the previous tune*)

Mount Tortoise

Wipes its tears and beats its chest,

But lacks the verdure of Mount Dragon.

Mount Dragon

Has three thousand beauties,

Eight hundred ladies,

And twelve screens.

The jade echoes with each other

While the birds of love make perfect match.

How can we choose the stray tortoise

But discard the genuine dragon?

VOICE WITHIN:

The decree has it that the memorial of the Royal Son-in-Law is accepted. Marquis of Martial Feats will select the propitious date, prepare the ritual procession and bury Princess Righteousness on Mount Dragon. Kowtow to thank the royal grace!

CHUNYU FEN:

Long live the King!

(*Rises to his feet*)

DUAN GONG:

Congratulations! As the genuine dragon is preferred, Mount Dragon is regarded as treasure land. Your Highness, do you happen to know that Zhou Bian died of back ulcer? His son has escorted his body back to his homeland.

CHUNYU FEN (*Wails*):

Alas! Oh my old friend!

DUAN GONG:

Well, the senior noblemen have prepared a banquet in the court lounge.

> (*Enter the senior noblemen, with the banquet ready*)

SENIOR NOBLEMEN (*To the tune of **Busuanzi***):

> Elegantly dressed,
>
> We are most blessed by His Majesty,
>
> Just as the apricots beside the sun
>
> Shining most brightly.
>
> (*Greet Chunyu Fen*)

We bow to you, Your Highness!

CHUNYU FEN:

I bow to you all, dukes and princes!

SENIOR NOBLEMEN:

We bow to you, Right Prime Minister!

DUAN GONG:

Thank you!

SENIOR NOBLEMEN:

As Your Highness had covered a long distance, we welcomed you twenty *li* away. When we burnt incense at the princess residence, we got to know that you had gone to the court. Therefore, we are waiting for you here.

CHUNYU FEN:

Thank you for your trouble, dukes and princes! I do not deserve it.

SENIOR NOBLEMEN:

We'll never forget your gifts we have received in these twenty years. Now that you have returned in the position of Prime Minister, we'll greet you with state-funded wine.

> (*Offer wine*)
>
> (*To the tune of **Bashengganzhou***)
>
> Having no positions, and feeling not yet old,
>
> We congratulate on the promotion of His Highness
>
> As the Prime Minister.

CHUNYU FEN:

> Where is my wife?
>
> I'm sad as dusk clouds and autumn grass.

SENIOR NOBLEMEN:

When Your Highness went to Nanke with the princess, we were all honored to be at the farewell banquet.

CHUNYU FEN:

Yes, I see.

> We went to Nanke as a couple,
>
> And return for ever separated.
>
> (*Weeps*)

ALL:

In the mirror,

You see the tears flooding on your face.

CHUNYU FEN (*To the previous tune*):

(*Sighs*)

Who has ever seen a man in a red robe,

But yearning for his wife in woe

With a waning waist?

SENIOR NOBLEMEN:

The noblemen in the court

Are not on a par with you in talents.

The fragrant wind carries the moon to the sky,

While the moon shines over the fragrant flowers.

ALL:

In the mirror,

You see the tears flooding on your face.

SENIOR NOBLEMEN:

Your Highness, here is a letter of invitation. For the sake of congratulating you on your promotion to the position of Prime Minister, amusing Your Highness, and welcoming you from afar, I, as the eldest of the noblemen, will invite Your Highness to a dinner. All the dukes and princes will prepare dinners in turns. The Right Prime Minister will also be invited on the occasion.

CHUNYU FEN:

There are lots of dukes and princes.

SENIOR NOBLEMEN:

Your Highness, you are a genius. As you are respected, we hope that you will condescend to attend the banquets.

CHUNYU FEN:

I'll accept your invitations.

As Prime Minister with infinite power,

He will show favor to the kith and kin.

All the ministers invite him to dinners,

Making him drunk all day long.

(*Exeunt all*)

DUAN GONG (*Left on the stage alone*):

Look at the overbearing manner His Highness treats the dukes and princes!

(*Sighs*)

Let him be!

"I'll look on the crab,

To see how long he can crawl!"

Scene Thirty-Seven
Sensual Allurement

(*Enter Princess Qiongying, followed by maids of honor*)

PRINCESS QIONGYING (*To the tune of* **Yiqin'e**, **Part One**):

> In court-fashion make-up,
>
> I glance at the emerald green autumn mountains.
>
> I glance,
>
> When I wake up from my sad dream
>
> With flute music flowing in my bed-curtains.

(*In the pattern of* **Tangduoling**)

> "*Of what is sorrow composed?*
>
> *It is the sores of my heart in a row*
>
> *When rain has just stopped in the Locust Palace.*
>
> *In the cool dusk,*
>
> *Who will ascend*
>
> *The tiny bower with me?*"

I am Princess Qiongying. My sister Yaofang was married to Chunyu Fen, who was the magistrate of Nanke and is now the Prime Minister with supreme power. It happened that to the sorrow of the whole country, she suddenly passed away. According to the royal decree, she is buried on Mount Dragon with all the magnificence of the rituals. After his recent return to the court, His Highness is endowed with extraordinary power, for His Majesty esteems his fame in Nanke and Her Majesty favors him and grants him free access to her palace. All the dukes and princes try to seek affiliation with him. He has been attending banquets with songs and dances every day, enjoying all the luxuries and pleasure. The three widows Lady Lingzhi, Sister Shangzhen and I have attended the official ceremonies but have not dined with him in private. As His Highness is handsome and stalwart, how I love him and admire him!

(*To the tune of* **Jinluosuo**)

At the time

> When the three of us went
>
> To listen to the preaching by Master Qixuan,
>
> We met the young man
>
> In front of the Hall of Embroidered Buddha.
>
> At the first glance we made the choice
>
> Of bridegroom for Yaofang,
>
> Who left for Nanke at the age of fifteen.
>
> The bridegroom at the Jade Terrace is above par,
>
> The best match with the princess.
>
> At time appropriate,

I'll allure him into the drunken dreamland,

Dwelling in the bridal chamber

For me to show my love to him.

Yesterday I invited Lady Lingzhi and Sister Shangzhen to burn joss-sticks for Prince Yaofang. I'm sure they'll have a chat with me on their way back.

(*Enter Sister Shangzhen in a Taoist robe, accompanied by Lady Lingzhi*)

SISTER SHANGZHEN (*To the tune of **Yiqin'e, Part Two***):

The colorful clouds may disperse in the wind,

As fine things in the world are frail as glass.

Yaofang is gone,

While Chunyu is alive and well.

(*Greets Princess Qiongying*)

Qiongying, so you are sitting alone in woe. Why don't you burn joss-sticks at the princess mansion to while away some time? There are so many young men!

PRINCESS QIONGYING:

How about the ceremony?

LADY LINGZHI:

We paid tribute by turns. First the princes and their sons, then the marquises and the earls, the civil officials and military officers, scholars and students, Buddhist monks and Taoist priests, civilians old and young, entitled ladies, wives and daughters. Afterwards were people from Nanke, in the same order of the civil, the military, the official and the civilian, to be followed by deputies from various prefectures and counties. The State of Sandals and Vines also sent an envoy to offer one thousand and two hundred *jin* of sandal incense. The piles of silver and rolls of satin presented a magnificent view.

(*To the tune of **Jinluosuo***)

Red silk strings dangle on the green window-frames;

The gauze net is embroidered with lotus-flowers.

In the incense burner,

Sandalwood joss-sticks are offered day and night.

With everybody offering incense,

The deceased princess

Receives unprecedented glory.

The beating of chime-stones resounds to the sky;

Flags and banners cover the ground.

I steal a glance

At His Highness left behind by the princess.

With his strategies and tactics,

With his confident words,

He is worthy of the eternal prime minister.

No matter how he fares in the world, judging from the twenty years of gifts he gave the dukes and princes for greetings, birthdays and festivals, we have to requite him family by family.

(*To the tune of **Liupomao***)

The magistrate knows the ropes,

Sending us gifts on every occasion.

SISTER SHANGZHEN:

Now that he becomes the Prime Minister,

PRINCESS QIONGYING:

We should divert his boredom and relieve his sorrow.

LADY LINGZHI (*Smiles*):

Qiongying, you'd like to divert his boredom, but the three of us are all widows and we need him to divert our boredom.

SISTER SHANGZHEN:

Don't forget that I am a Taoist nun!

(*To the previous tune*)

I've vowed that I'll never look at a man,

Lest he should stir my tranquil heart.

LADY LINGZHI:

I'm afraid you won't hold up to your vow when time arrives.

ALL:

If three cups of wine can let you loose,

You will not refuse the love he shows.

LADY LINGZHI:

So it's settled that when we invite him to our house, we'll make fun by turns and no one is allowed to take advantage.

The son-in-law becomes the prime minister

When his wife has passed away.

Since all of them are of blue blood,

They can make love without delay.

Scene Thirty-Eight
Indulgent Life

(*Enter Chunyu Fen in official dress, walking and followed by attendants*)

CHUNYU FEN (*To the tune of **Lanhuamei***):

As Yaofang and I are now in different worlds,

I feel lonesome in spite of the verdure in the palace.

As I cannot send her letters after her departure,

I shed tears on my court robe before the wind,

But cannot erase my sorrow for her.

ATTENDANTS:

Your Highness, here we are at our mansion.

CHUNYU FEN (*Sighs*):

>(*In the pattern of* **Collected Tang Poems**)
>
>"*With the road lined with old locust trees,*
>
>*The golden hall sees nothing but tear-stains.*
>
>*The son-in-law of the royal court*
>
>*Goes to the west garden in the morn.*"

I am Chunyu Fen. Since the princess passed away, I have been in boredom and sorrow. Fortunately Her Majesty the Queen showed favor on me, for me to go around in the palace at random. She followed my bent on every occasion and the nobles curry favor with me. After the evening court audience, I see maids of honor and entitled ladies dressed neatly and making a noise, but no longer see my wife.

BUTLER:

Report! A court lady is at the gate.

CHUNYU FEN:

Show her into the hall!

>(*Enter a court lady, holding a letter*)

COURT LADY (*To the tune of* **Bushilu**):

>In tiny steps,
>
>I move with emeralds on my bun.
>
>(*Greets Chunyu Fen*)

CHUNYU FEN:

>What is the message?
>
>Is it Her Majesty's decree?

COURT LADY:

No.

>To relieve you from the daily drudgery,
>
>Princess Qiongying and Lady Lingzhi
>
>Will prepare a banquet for you in the evening.

CHUNYU FEN (*Pleased*):

>At their invitation,
>
>I have the rare chance to meet them.
>
>I'll be there in no time;
>
>I'll be there in no time.

COURT LADY:

In that case,

>"*At the message brought by the envoy,*
>
>*His Highness will arrive in haste.*"
>
>(*Exit*)
>
>(*Heralding the way within*)

CHUNYU FEN:

I am languid for I haven't met ladies for a long time. To have the banquet with the princesses, I will drink to my heart's content. It's true indeed,

"Drink while ye may

To enjoy this very day."

(*Enter Princess Qiongying, followed by the court lady*)

PRINCESS QIONGYING (*To the tune of* **Quexianqiao**):

In drowsiness,

I have no one to accompany me,

But a guest will arrive this evening.

(*Enter Lady Lingzhi and Sister Shangzhen*)

LADY LINGZHI, SISTER SHANGZHEN:

For years we have no handsome young men,

To songs and drinks in the jade bower.

(*Greet Princess Qiongying*)

LADY LINGZHI:

"The wind blows at dusk,

Ripping the leaves off the tree.

I have a fervent heart,

But you may not be aware."

SISTER SHANGZHEN:

Qiongying will host Chunyu this evening, with Shangzhen and me to keep company. Before the guest arrives, we'll chat for a while and make some arrangements. I've heard that Chunyu is a heavy drinker. Which of us will be his match?

PRINCESS QIONGYING:

Lingzhi is a heavy drinker.

LADY LINGZHI:

The three of us will get him drunk and make fun.

MAID OF HONOR:

Here arrives His Highness!

(*Enter Chunyu Fen*)

CHUNYU FEN (*To the previous tune*):

I gallop my horse

Toward the warm jade hall

Against the evening glow.

(*Smiles*)

I brighten up in spite of my woe,

For I shall meet the beautiful ladies.

(*Greets the three ladies*)

(*In the pattern of* **Xijiangyue**)

"In the years I am away from you,

You are always lingering in my heart.

PRINCESS QIONGYING:

It's kind of you to keep me in your heart;

We'll have a hearty drink tonight,

LADY LINGZHI:

Regretting that you've recently lost your wife,

SISTER SHANGZHEN:

For the princess has passed away.

CHUNYU FEN:

So Lady Lingzhi and Sister Shangzhen are also here.

ALL:

We are happy to be one family."

CHUNYU FEN:

Since I returned to the court, the nobles have held banquets according to the official etiquettes. Why do you take the trouble to hold this banquet?

PRINCESS QIONGYING:

You know, we hold this banquet for three reasons. Firstly, we'll welcome you from the long journey; secondly, we'll congratulate you on your promotion to the position of Prime Minister; thirdly, we'll soothe your boredom of staying alone. Within the past few days, you have made arrangements with the nobles. We think that Sister Shangzhen is a Taoist nun, Lady Lingzhi and I are widowed. As we are at the end of the host list, we have to wait till now to take turns in preparing the banquet for you. This time I'll serve as the hostess and the other two will keep company.

CHUNYU FEN:

Thank you for your kindness!

PRINCESS QIONGYING:

Serve the wine!

(Enter attendants and a court lady with the wine)

COURT LADY:

"His Highness used to ride with five steeds,

But today he will drink with three ladies."

The wine is ready.

(Princess Qiongying and the other two ladies serve the wine)

PRINCESS QIONGYING, LADY LINGZHI, SISTER SHANGZHEN:

*(To the tune of **Jiesanchengfan**)*

After vicissitude of life in twenty years,

We are happy to see you again.

We'll enjoy ourselves in the Huizhen Bower,

Between Prime Minister and subjects.

Accustomed to make up every day,

Although we do not paint in loud colors,

Please don't hesitate

But watch while holding your golden cup!

CHUNYU FEN *(Serves the wine)*:

(To the previous tune)

I've dreamt of staying in the palace,

With beauties attending on me.

I've dreamt of leaning against the windows,

But being depressed by the raven's caw.

In a swoon I ignore the extinguishing incense,

Idling away the time by the side of beauties.

Unconsciously,

I hold the cup and look them up and down.

PRINCESS QIONGYING, LADY LINGZHI, SISTER SHANGZHEN (*To the previous tune*):

It's said that this is a pleasure palace;

It's said that this is a pleasure palace.

As the gust blows off the flute music,

We are left alone for all our lives.

Here in this world,

Now at the time for leisure,

The ladies will offer you pleasure.

CHUNYU FEN (*Aside*):

Here are the beauties

Under the glimmering lamps.

With song and dance in front of my eyes,

I am entranced by their luring glances.

PRINCE QIONGYING:

At moonrise, Your Highness can drink to your heart's content.

PRINCESS QIONGYING, LADY LINGZHI, SISTER SHANGZHEN:

(*To the tune of **Manerfan***)

The cups of nectar

Are for you to gulp.

PRINCE QIONGYING (*Aside*):

His incessant murmuring reveals his deep affection.

(*Turns back*)

This very affection

Brings the four of us closer

When the moon rises above the railings.

ALL:

In the moonlight the hall is clear and bright.

CHUNYU FEN (*To the previous tune*):

The affection in my heart

Will be bared in their faces,

To lure the three mistresses.

The noble ladies seem to dance in a line,

Flapping sleeves under the moon and lamps.

ALL:

In the moonlight the hall is clear and bright.

PRINCESS QIONGYING, LADY LINGZHI, SISTER SHANGZHEN (*To the previous tune*):

> The breeze stirs the green crepe,
>
> While the moon moves across the corridor
>
> And the dews sizzle on the palace locust-leaves.
>
> Against the mysterious autumn scenes,
>
> We assume graceful poise emitting sweet fragrance.

ALL:

> In the moonlight the hall is clear and bright.

CHUNYU FEN (*To the previous tune*):

> At my visit to the beauties,
>
> The cool jade pillows
>
> Will accompany my long yearnings.
>
> Their make-up has faded in the starlight,
>
> Inviting me to stay overnight.

ALL:

> In the moonlight the hall is clear and bright.

CHUNYU FEN:

I am intoxicated.

PRINCESS QIONGYING:

We've arranged the gauze net for the bed.

CHUNYU FEN:

Won't you stay with me?

SISTER SHANGZHEN:

I'm afraid we won't be so well-behaved.

LADY LINGZHI:

If you don't mind, we'll be with you.

PRINCESS QIONGYING (*Smiles*):

Then we'll wait on you one by one.

PRINCESS QIONGYING, LADY LINGZHI, SISTER SHANGZHEN (*To the tune of **Eya-manduchuan***):

> We vie to take our positions,
>
> Moaning for your favor.
>
> Like butterflies frolicking in the flowers
>
> And fish shuttling in the water,
>
> We flirt and tease with no end.
>
> With our petticoats off,
>
> We take turns on the bed.
>
> We'll enjoy ourselves to the full,
>
> Satiating our needs this evening.

CHUNYU FEN (*To the tune of **Coda***):

> Beauties inside the plum-red gauze net

Are like sister flowers facing the moon.

ALL:

The four of us

Have the same affection in our hearts.

Intoxicated in the ecstasy for a sweet night,

The joy of three beauties is beyond words.

They seem to greet sweet rain after a drought

Or meet bosom friends in a far-off land.

Scene Thirty-Nine
Demotion Predicted

(*Enter Duan Gong*)

DUAN GONG (*To the tune of* **Juhuaxin**):

Dawn comes late for autumn's jade steps

While locust trees with cold dews shelter the palace gate.

I lower my head to tidy my official robe,

Regretting that time flows like the clepsydra.

I am Duan Gong, the Right Prime Minister. I have assisted His Majesty in managing the state and build the Great State of Peaceful Locust into a prosperous country. Out of my expectations, His Majesty invited the Yangzhou drunkard Chunyu Fen to our country and made him the Royal Son-in-Law, who was later assigned as the magistrate of Nanke. I have been worried about him as his fame has soared in recent years. When the princess passed away, he was summoned to the capital and was assigned as the Left Prime Minister, who is above me in status. Her Majesty the Queen is fond of him and calls him into the palace off and on, agreeing to whatever request he raises. I'll say no more about that. As Nanke is rich in resources and produce, the dukes and princes were all bribed by him. Therefore, after he returns to the court, the powerful and distinguished personages have been inviting him to dinners. He has immense power and receives guests all the time. I do not mind the dukes and princes, but even Princess Qiongying, Lady Lingzhi and Sister Shangzhen have been inviting him to dinners by turns. Man and women hang around and enjoy themselves day and night. The heaven is enraged by their debauchery, for the guest star has invaded the constellations according to astrology. I intend to send a memorial to His Majesty about this, but I am afraid that blood is thicker than water. I hear that someone has sent a letter to His Majesty, and if His Majesty should ask me about this, I'll have my say as opportunity comes. Oh Heaven, I shall act like this not out of my jealousy, but out of my concern for the country. Here comes His Majesty; the ministers are to line up to attend the audience.

(*Enter the Ant King, with the eunuchs heralding the way*)

ANT KING (*To the previous tune*):

> In our vast and deep-rooted country,
>
> The ministers head home after the audience is over.
>
> To my great puzzlement,
>
> Why have the constellations been disturbed?

DUAN GONG (*Kowtows to the Ant King*):

Right Prime Minister and Marquis of Martial Feats Duan Gong kowtows to Your Majesty. Long live the king!

ANT KING:

Rise to your feet! Have you heard that someone has sent me a letter?

DUAN GONG:

No, I haven't.

ANT KING:

The letter mentions about an ill omen. It says that the disturbance of the constellations is a foreboding that the country will be in great disorder. The capital town will have to be moved and the ancestral temple of the royal family will collapse. What disturbance have the constellations suffered?

DUAN GONG:

I am about to make the memorial to you that the astrological official has reported that the guest star has invaded the constellations.

ANT KING:

The letter goes on to say that disasters originate outside the house while troubles start from inside the house. I am rather puzzled about the statement.

DUAN GONG:

True, but there are no outsiders in our country. The outsiders will not be able to come inside. Have you got the hint?

ANT KING:

There are no other outsiders but the Royal Son-in-Law Chunyu Fen.

DUAN GONG:

I dare not speak out.

ANT KING:

How can you keep silent when the country will be in trouble?

DUAN GONG:

Please listen to my memorial!

> (*To the tune of **Suochuanglang***)
>
> The guest star invades the constellations
>
> When the visitor returns in a boat.
>
> The constellations symbolize the royal house,
>
> While the guest star is the Royal Son-in-Law.
>
> His Highness is overbearing nowadays,
>
> For he has held office in an important county
>
> And does not take the court to heart.

He and the nobles

Are hanging around day and night.

ANT KING:

Has he degenerated to such a degree?

DUAN GONG:

The unspeakable thing is

That he behaves recklessly with the royal ladies.

ANT KING, DUAN GONG:

The heaven knows

That he is the very trouble-maker.

DUAN GONG (*Sheds tears*):

It is miserable for the country to deteriorate.

ANT KING (*Annoyed*):

Since his departure from Nanke County and return to the capital, Chunyu Fen has been visiting the palace at will and wining and dining with the guests. His insolence with pride has incurred my suspicion, and your words have given evidence to his ruthlessness. How hateful he is! How hateful he is!

（*To the previous tune*）

His extravagance has roused my suspicion,

But I haven't expected that he is so licentious.

He goes about the palace at will,

Coming and going at any time.

My wife favors her son-in-law,

Giving consent to whatever he asks

And permitting him to abuse his power.

That's it. Not a member of our clan, he is not of one mind with us.

（*Sheds tears*）

ANT KING, DUAN GONG:

The heaven knows

That he is the very trouble-maker.

DUAN GONG (*Kneels*):

Please listen to my memorial! As the common saying goes, "Indecision at the critical moment will bring about trouble." As His Highness has come to this, what will Your Majesty decree?

ANT KING:

Listen to my decree:

（*To the tune of* **Yibujin**）

Chunyu Fen is dismissed from his office

And forbidden to leave his residence.

DUAN GONG:

In my opinion, he'd better be sent to his hometown.

ANT KING:

You needn't say anything more.

He will be awakened and sent back to his hometown.

(*Exit*)

DUAN GONG (*Sighs*):

Well, so much so. Chunyu Fen is forbidden to come to the court, but the country is still in danger. As the saying goes,

While the sky is like a dome,

The earth is like a chessboard.

As Chunyu Fen is still in a dream,

He is unaware of shame or esteem.

Scene Forty
Doubts and Fears

(*Enter Chunyu Fen, wearing a white robe and showing signs of melancholy*)

CHUNYU FEN:

"*The paths in the Taihang Mountains are treacherous,*

But straight in comparison with the king's heart.

The waters in the Yellow River are turbulent,

But quiet comparison with the king's heart.

In my service in the State of Peaceful Locust,

Chunyu married the princess in the royal house.

The couple lived like a pair of lovebirds

And like a pair of phoenixes.

The leaves and branches are now torn to pieces,

While the dressing mirror no longer sees my wife.

As the beauty is of no avail now,

I have to leave the court alone."

I am Chunyu Fen, the son-in-law of His Majesty. After my wife died, I left the county and returned to the court to the joy of my colleagues. However, within half a month, His Majesty is angry with me and forbids me to leave my residence. I am rejected from the palace. Not long after my wife passed away, I have no way to go now. If that is all I have to bear, I am worried enough; if I have to bear other misfortunes, what can I do as a foreigner? Oh Heaven! What crime have I committed at all?

(*To the tune of **Shengruhua***)

What can I do for an unwarranted charge?

The result is what I have to face.

As I am forbidden to enter the court

And to attend the parties and banquets,

I have to sit alone at my home.

A multitude of thing have happened these years,

But what has brought me to this situation?

What fault do I have?

A word will reveal the truth

But I am left in the dark.

Is His Majesty suspicious of my doings in Nanke?

I have done no harm to Nanke at all.

In the vicissitude of life, even this old locust tree has lost its vitality. A tree cannot last forever, let alone for a man! I'd like to return to Nanke, but it is impossible now. Well, let it be! I'll doze for a while in front of the memorial tablet of the princess. Oh my dear wife!

(*Enter Chunyu's eldest son, weeping*)

ELDEST SON (*To the tune of* ***Jinjiaoye***):

At the thought of my home and my country,

I shed floods of tears.

(*Collapses when he sees Chunyu Fen*)

My father is whiling away his time

In front of Mom's memorial tablet.

CHUNYU FEN (*Weeps*):

My son, stand up! Stand up!

(*In the pattern of* ***Changxiangsi***)

"*With reason*

Or without reason,

I'm forbidden to attend the court or the parties,

With my hair turning grey.

ELDEST SON:

Whether things end well

Or end ill,

I weep sad tears before my father

And vent my woe before my deceased mother."

CHUNYU FEN:

My son, when we met the other day, His Majesty had mixed feelings of joy and sorrow. Within half a month, I don't know why he is picking fault with me.

ELDEST SON:

This is a matter of right and wrong. Are you not aware of it?

CHUNYU FEN:

As you and your brother stay in the palace while I am forbidden to visit my kith and kin, where am I to find out the truth?

ELDEST SON:

Father, then listen to me!

(*To the tune of* ***Sanhuantou***)

Like a bolt from the blue,

The disaster comes from the sky.

The guest star at night

Invades the constellations.

CHUNYU FEN:

How did His Majesty get to know this?

ELDEST SON:

A countryman sent a letter, saying that the disturbances of the constellations predict great disorder in the country. The capital town will have to be moved and the ancestral temple of the royal family will collapse.

CHUNYU FEN:

What has such ill omen to do with me?

ELDEST SON:

The letter goes on to say that disasters originate outside the house while troubles start from inside the house.

CHUNYU FEN:

Which countryman is so insolent? Even if there are outsiders, how can he know that the outsider is me?

ELDEST SON:

Right Prime Minister Duan Gong viciously slandered that the constellations symbolized the ancestral temple while the guest star invaded the royal family.

CHUNYU FEN:

The princess is your mother.

ELDEST SON (*Weeps*):

He did not mean my mother.

CHUNYU FEN:

Whom did he mean?

ELDEST SON:

The widows Princess Qiongying and Lady Lingzhi

Committed incest with you after cups of wine.

CHUNYU FEN:

Oh, Duan Gong! How viciously he slandered me!

ELDEST SON:

His Majesty flew into a rage, saying that he would not tolerate you for your abuse of power and factional activities.

CHUNYU FEN:

How did Her Majesty the Queen mediate the matter?

ELDEST SON:

When he mentioned that the trouble had started inside the house, how could she say anything more?

CHUNYU FEN:

I do not bear grudges against the countryman or the Right Prime Minister, but against the heaven. Oh Heaven! Why should you bother about the guest star?

ELDEST SON:

    Why should the constellations

    Make trouble with my father?

CHUNYU FEN (*To the previous tune*):

    The slanderous words

    Will not hoodwink His Majesty.

    How can his son-in-law

    Be the guest star?

Your mother was right in saying that I should take precaution at court as the relations are different now. Her words have come true.

    (*Weeps*)

    She warned me of the danger,

    But I am to blame in the end.

    I have had my days of pleasure,

    And now I'll pine away day by day.

ELDEST SON:

Father,

    No more of the word "pleasure"!

CHUNYU FEN, ELDEST SON:

    Forget about the past glory

    But weep before the deceased princess!

    (*Enter the Royal Envoy*)

ROYAL ENVOY (*To the tune of* **Ruzhuan**):

    I gallop out of the East Gate

    And reach Chunyu's residence.

CHUNYU FEN:

    To my astonishment,

    He comes from the palace to my home.

    May I ask what the royal decree is?

ROYAL ENVOY:

    Here comes the royal decree

    To summon you to the court.

CHUNYU FEN (*To his eldest son with a worried look*):

    With a startled heart,

    I wonder about the prospect that awaits me.

ROYAL ENVOY:

    His Majesty wears a smiling face

    And Her Majesty has been missing you

    For your absence from the palace.

CHUNYU FEN:

    There is no time for the fortune-teller,

    But is she really missing me?

ROYAL ENVOY:

> Why are you worried?

> Anyhow you are the Royal Son-in-Law.

CHUNYU FEN:

Envoy, I'm worried about Right Prime Minister.

> With the ulterior motive to usurp the power,

> He has concocted the lie

> That I have disturbed the constellation.

ELDEST SON:

Father,

> You'd better keep silent for the moment;

> Why are you hurting him all the time?

ROYAL ENVOY:

Weigh your words before you respond! I must be going now.

CHUNYU FEN:

My son, what will happen to me this time?

ELDEST SON:

There might be good tidings.

> (*Calls of heralding the way*)
> *The man was standing alone*
> *When his son came across the yard.*
> *As soon as he heard the king's call,*
> *He set out without waiting for the cart.*

Scene Forty-One
Banishment

> (*Enter the Ant King, followed by attendants*)

ANT KING (*To the tune of **Jinjijiao***):

> My auspicious spirit lingers in the sky,

> But a mysterious astrology occurs.

> Who has incurred all the disorder?

> (*Enter the Ant Queen*)

ANT QUEEN:

> Our daughter and her spouse are not to blame,

> (*Sighs*)

> Yet the unexpected accusations

> Are incitements to sow dissention.

> (*Kowtows to the Ant King*)

I wish you a long life, Your Majesty!

ANT KING:

Rise to your feet, my wife!

ANT QUEEN (*In the pattern of* **Zhegutian**):

Your Majesty,

> *"I sit with discomfort in my palace,*
>
> *For I haven't seen the young man for some time.*

ANT KING (*Smiles*):

But you do not know

> *That as he abuses his power to disturb the stars,*
>
> *He has been confined in his residence.*

ANT QUEEN (*Weeps*):

That's it. Oh Heaven, you only know that he

> *Seeks pleasure and wanders about,*
>
> *But he is lonesome in the empty residence.*

ANT KING (*Annoyed*):

> *You only care about trifles at home,*
>
> *But you'll regret when he spoils my state."*

ANT QUEEN:

Your Majesty, how can your son-in-law spoil your state?

ANT KING:

As you stay in the inner palace, you don't know that a countryman sent me a letter saying that astrology predicts disasters. Our capital town might have to move and our ancestral temple might collapse. The disasters originate outside the house while troubles start from inside the house. The outsider is none other than Chunyu Fen!

ANT QUEEN:

Will your son-in-law usurp your state power?

ANT KING:

It's beyond your knowledge. Small as it is, our state is ruled by law, and he has broken the law many times.

ANT QUEEN:

He is but addicted to drinking.

ANT KING:

Addicted to drinking? He is addicted to Princess Qiongying, Lady Lingzhi and Sister Shangzhen as well!

ANT QUEEN:

Who is the witness?

ANT KING:

Are you waiting for the disorder in the palace as the evidence? I'll give him a farewell banquet and send him back to his homeland. Your business is to bring up your grandchildren and keep your mouth shut.

ANT QUEEN (*Weeps*):

Oh Heaven! Won't you pardon him for the sake of our daughter?

(Enter the royal envoy)

ROYAL ENVOY:

His Highness is waiting at the palace gate.

ANT KING:

Bring my decree to summon him in.

    (Drums within)

    (Enter Chunyu Fen in court robe)

CHUNYU FEN (*To the tune of* **Xiaoyaole**):

    Arriving at the court again with mixed feelings

    And with tears in my eyes,

    (Sighs)

    I see His Majesty sitting in the palace hall.

    I am grieved that the princess has passed away,

    Ready to be reprimanded by His Majesty,

    With only Her Majesty to give me a hand.

    "One day from the court

    Creates a vast gap."

Trembling with fear when I enter the palace gate, I have to lie prostrate on the ground in meek submission.

    (Kowtows to the Ant King and the Ant Queen)

The guilty Royal Son-in-Law, Royal Captain, Left Prime Minister Chunyu Fen kowtows to Your Majesty the King and the Queen. I wish you a long, long life!

PALACE ATTENDANT:

Rise to your feet, Your Highness! Come into the palace hall!

    (Chunyu Fen rises to his feet and makes a bow, calling "Long live the king!")

ANT KING:

I mouthed some rash words the other day, and was not polite to you. Please do not take it to heart!

ANT QUEEN:

Oh, Chunyu, how is it that you have waned so much?

CHUNYU FEN (*Bows*):

That's true indeed. I am denounced by His Majesty and confined in my residence. With the help of the princess, I managed the county for quite a number of years without any flaw. Now that I am slandered by the rumors, my heart has really broken.

ANT KING:

I've got wine ready to relieve your sorrow.

    (Enter a palace attendant with wine)

PALACE ATTENDANT:

    "The cold wine in the cup

    Saddens the lonely bird."

Here is the wine.

ANT KING:

I'll offer you a cup of wine today.

> (*To the tune of **Zaoluopao***)
>
> My Son-in-Law, do you remember the day
>
> When I saw you off outside the southern pass
>
> And the two of you rode off in a carriage?
>
> (*Chunyu Fen kneels to drink the wine*)

ANT KING:

Fill in another cup!

> (*Chunyu Fen kneels to drink the wine*)

ANT QUEEN:

Attendant, fill in several cups in succession!

> Since my daughter passed away,
>
> I have not taken good care of you.

CHUNYU FEN (*Kowtows and rises to his feet*):

> After three cups of wine,
>
> A myriad of sad thoughts crowd into my mind.
>
> Where on earth is the guest star?
>
> I hope that you will be lenient to me.

ALL:

> Weal and woe flash by in a moment.

CHUNYU FEN (*Aside*):

Why did he say "Weal and woe flash by in a moment"?

ANT KING:

You seem to be lost in contemplation. Do you know what I mean? The marriage lasted for more than twenty years. Due to her premature death, my daughter could not accompany you to old age. Therefore, I am really sorry for that.

CHUNYU FEN:

After the princess passed away, I am here to give you some comfort.

ANT KING:

There is no need to say these words. The thing is that as you have left your homeland for years, you'd better go back for the time being and meet your relatives.

CHUNYU FEN:

This is my home. Where am I to go?

ANT KING (*Smiles*):

Your own home is not in this land.

> (*Chunyu Fen stands silent in dizziness*)

ANT QUEEN:

He seems to be in a dream.

CHUNYU FEN (*Awakens*):

Oh, yes. My home is in the human world. Why am I in this place?

> (*Wails*)

Oh, thoughts of home suddenly hit me, biting at my heart. I won't be able to wait on you any longer, Your Majesty the Queen.

ANT KING:

Tell the Royal Envoy to show his way home!

CHUNYU FEN:

As my children are staying in the palace, I beg your permission to see them once.

ANT KING:

When my grandchildren stay in the palace, my wife will look after them and bring them up. You don't have to worry about that.

CHUNYU FEN (*Sobs*):

How miserable I am!

ANT QUEEN:

Don't feel miserable! If you keep us in heart, we'll have the opportunity to meet again.

CHUNYU FEN (*Kowtows*):

Farewell to you!

> (*To the previous tune*)
> With my homeland in sight,
> I am suddenly enlightened in my puzzlement,
> Although my eyes are dimmed by tears.

ANT KING:

> I wish you a good journey to the human world
> Now that three cups are drained and songs are over.

ANT QUEEN (*Weeps*):

My son-in-law, you will be gone.

> With your intention to leave,
> You are hard to keep.
> For years of affection,
> There will be nothing left behind.

ALL:

> Weal and woe flash by in a moment.

CHUNYU FEN (*To the tune of* **Yibujin**):

> I shall depart from you and return home,
> In gratitude for your twenty years of grace.

ANT KING, ANT QUEEN:

Chunyu, Chunyu,

> You'll witness the collapse of our state.
> *The guest departs when the wine is drained*
> *As the leaves return to earth when they fall.*
> *Nothing but departing tears remain*
> *When he returns and leaves us all.*

Scene Forty-Two
Waking Up to the Reality

(Enter two Royal Envoys)

TWO ROYAL ENVOYS:

"Without a second thought,

A thing is always done with regret."

The king of the Great State of Peaceful Locust has a daughter, who should have found a spouse in her own country but brought Chunyu Fen from the human world to be her spouse. Chunyu Fen was assigned the magistrate in Nanke and lived there in luxury for over twenty years. After the princess passed away, he was recalled to the court as the prime minister. As he abused his power and disturbed the state affairs, the astrology revealed signs that he would be demoted. As His Majesty was worried and grew suspicious of him, he decreed that we shall send him back with an ox-cart.

(Giggle)

Chunyu Fen, Chunyu Fen, how unlucky you are! It is true to say,

"When the gate is closed on the deep palace,

The ardent spouse becomes a stranger."

(Enter Chunyu Fen in court robe)

CHUNYU FEN:

"The sudden thought to search for home

Has brought tears to my eyes.

Hard to discard the favors done on me,

I am on my way home in heart-breaking sighs."

I am Chunyu Fen. At the sudden thought of home, I am deprived of my glory and have to make my return trip. How can I drop from the yearning for my wife and the service in the court?

(Weeps)

(Greets the two Royal Envoys)

Hi! Are you the Royal Envoys that fetched me twenty years ago?

TWO ROYAL ENVOYS (*Respond sluggishly*):

That's right.

CHUNYU FEN:

Is the carriage and four waiting outside the palace gate?

TWO ROYAL ENVOYS:

Yes.

(They walk)

CHUNYU FEN (*To the tune of **Xiudai'er***):

When I leave the palace in late spring,

Out of the palace gate,

I am caught by a sudden sense of alienation.

Where are my attendants? Is the shabby ox-cart for me to take? Alas!

> Why is there not a single attendant?
>
> Why is there such a shabby ox-cart?
>
> I do not see the reason why.

When I leave the palace, will I be able to come back again?

> I look back with deep affection,

Oh my dear wife,

> With tears dripping on the court robe.

It seems that I'll take this shabby ox-cart today. Let me linger a while! Oh, it's the wall tower with the golden characters. Why do the soldiers and civilians not stand up when they see me? Oops!

> Now I leave this great city to return home,
>
> And set foot on the way by which I came.

It seems that I'll change my coat and set out on my way.

> (*Changes clothes*)
>
> (*In the pattern of* **Changxiangsi**)
>
> "*I put on the court robe*
>
> *And now take it off,*
>
> *The same robe that has lost its distinction.*
>
> *The distant palace looks small.*
>
> *Reluctant to leave*
>
> *And reluctant to move,*
>
> *I shed tears of woeful affection.*
>
> (*Sighs*)
>
> *When on earth can I return to the court?*"

TWO ROYAL ENVOYS:

Get on the cart and hurry up!

> (*Walk sluggishly and sing a limerick in defiance of Chunyu Fen*)
>
> "*A fool is a fool,*
>
> *Who refuses to enter a big hole*
>
> *And to leave a small hole.*
>
> *Isn't he a fool?*"
>
> (*Whip the ox*)

The beast would not go.

CHUNYU FEN:

There is no hurry!

> (*To the previous tune*)
>
> I stop
>
> To watch the scenery that remains the same,
>
> And recall the good old days.
>
> (*The two Royal Envoys whip the ox to make it move faster*)

CHUNYU FEN (*Annoyed*):

Unable to show their usual pomp and glory, these Royal Envoys are indeed vexed.

    (*The two Royal Envoys whip the ox and walk*)

CHUNYU FEN:

Let me ask you when we shall arrive at Guangling County!

    (*The two Royal Envoys make no response, but walk and sing in giggles*)

CHUNYU FEN:

Well, I am asking them in a gentle voice, but they do not respond. Won't I be able to return to the court? Otherwise, I'll mention a few words on my letter of thanks to His Majesty.

    (*The two Royal Envoys sneer*)

CHUNYU FEN:

    They have been keeping silent,

    But I am ill at ease,

    Utterly in a trance.

I have to ask them again in a gentle voice. Envoys, when shall we arrive at Guangling?

TWO ROYAL ENVOYS:

In no time.

    (*Whip the ox and walk*)

CHUNYU FEN (*Looks forward*):

Oh, it looks like Guangling County!

    I can see the dim sight beyond the river,

    And the tunnel is the path I followed when I came.

    (*Walks again*)

Oh, this is the lane where my home is.

    (*Weeps*)

    Fortunately, my hearth and home is still there,

    Which incurs my woeful tears

    In view of the quiet sunset scene.

TWO ROYAL ENVOYS:

Here we are at the entrance. Get off the cart!

    (*Chunyu Fen gets off the cart and steps into the entrance*)

TWO ROYAL ENVOYS:

Climb the steps!

CHUNYU FEN (*Climbs the steps*):

    (*Astonished at the sight of the bed*)

Don't go there! I am in fear.

TWO ROYAL ENVOYS (*Shout aloud*):

Chunyu Fen!

    (*Call three times and Chunyu Fen does not respond*)

    (*Push Chunyu Fen onto the bed*)

    (*Chunyu Fen sleeps in the same manner as before*)

TWO ROYAL ENVOYS:

Where are the locust people? Wake up, Chunyu! We'll be going.

    (*Exeunt in haste*)

CHUNYU FEN (*Frightened*):

    (*Wakes from sleep and calls*)

Envoys! Envoys!

    (*Enter Partridge with wine*)

PARTRIDGE:

What do you mean by "envoys"? I am Partridge.

    (*Enter Liu'er and Sha San*)

LIU'ER, SHA SAN:

Brother Chunyu woke up when we were washing our feet.

CHUNYU FEN:

Where is the sun now?

PARTRIDGE:

It is setting in the west.

CHUNYU FEN:

What's on the window-sill?

LIU'ER:

The half cup of wine is still warm.

CHUNYU FEN:

Oh, the slanting sun has not set behind the west wall and the remaining wine is warm beside the east window. In the twinkle of my dream, I seem to have spent my whole life.

LIU'ER, SHA SAN:

What's in your dream?

CHUNYU FEN (*Thinks for a while*):

Fetch me a cup of hot tea!

    (*Partridge fetches a cup of tea*)

Fetch me another cup of tea! I'm not yet fully awake.

    (*Partridge fetches another cup of tea*)

CHUNYU FEN (*Drinks*):

Well, Brother Liu, Brother Sha, what a distinguished place it is! Princess my wife!

PARTRIDGE:

What princess wife? Have you become a royal son-in-law?

CHUNYU FEN:

Yes, I have.

LIU'ER:

A royal son-in-law in which dynasty?

CHUNYU FEN:

It's a long story. But first help me up!

    (*Liu'er and Sha San help Chunyu Fen up*)

Didn't you see the Royal Envoys?

SHA SAN:

No, we didn't.

CHUNYU FEN:

It's strange. Let me tell you!

>(*To the tune of **Yichunling***)
>
>In the room in the east wing
>
>I was sleeping soundly
>
>When some Royal Envoys came to meet me with a carriage.

Where do you suppose I was going?

>In the cave at the root of a locust tree
>
>Was a pretty princess of Peaceful Locust.

I still remember that her name was Yaofang, who made me her spouse. I went hunting with the King on Mount Tortoise.

PARTRIDGE:

What happened next?

CHUNYU FEN:

To the south of the state is a Nanke County, where I was assigned as the magistrate for twenty years.

LIU'ER, SHA SAN:

You must have enjoyed yourself! What next?

CHUNYU FEN:

The princess gave birth to two boys and two girls. Frightened by the bandits from the State of Sandals and Vines, she died of illness and was buried on Mount Dragon.

PARTRIDGE (*Wails*):

Oh, my poor mistress!

CHUNYU FEN:

>She defended the country on Mount Tortoise
>
>And was buried on Mount Dragon.

SHA SAN:

And then?

CHUNYU FEN:

After the princess passed away, I returned to the court as the prime minister, but things were quite different now.

>As I could hardly stay in that country,
>
>I begged to return from the dreamland.

Seeing that I would like to go home, the King and the Queen had to agree to my request. The Royal Envoys who accompanied me were both of the first rank.

PARTRIDGE:

Oh, I forgot to serve them tea.

CHUNYU FEN:

Brothers, what do you think of my experience?

LIU'ER:

I have no idea.

SHA SAN:

I have no idea, either.

CHUNYU FEN:

What about going to the locust cave?

SHA SAN, LIU'ER:

Maybe the old locust tree has immortalized as a spirit.

> (*To the previous tune*)
>
> Be it the fairy fox or the mountain demon,

Partridge,

> With picks and shovels we'll dig the locust root.
>
> (*Partridge fetches a shovel*)

PARTRIDGE:

Master, master, you used to sleep in drunkenness below the locust tree. Maybe you were bewitched.

CHUNYU FEN:

There is some reason in it. Let's go and have a look!

> (*They walk and look*)

LIU'ER:

There is a big hole below the locust tree.

> (*Digs*)

There are ants! Ants!

> When we explore the cave,
>
> We find ants running along the path.

Let's shovel the earth at the top!

> (*All are surprised*)

Look! The cave is three feet in breadth and three feet in depth, and is bright inside.

SHA SAN:

On the root of the tree, soils are piled up into a city. On each tier of the city is a terrace. Fantastic! Fantastic!

PARTRIDGE (*Surprised*):

Oh! Myriads of ants are gathered in the cave. Terrible! Terrible!

CHUNYU FEN:

Don't disturb them!

> There are tall buildings and city walls,
>
> With a big terrace afar in the centre.

SHA SAN:

The color of the terrace is reddish.

> (*Inspects*)

The two big ants sit side by side, with white wings and red heads, about three inches in length. They are attended by dozens of big ants while all the others dare not come near.

CHUNYU FEN (*Sighs*):

It must be the royal palace of the State of Peaceful Locust.

LIU'ER:

These two big ants are your father-in-law and mother-in-law.

CHUNYU FEN (*Weeps*):

> I have affections for them
>
> As they have treated me with due respect.

LIU'ER:

Let's dig toward the south. Look, on the southern branch, there seems to be an earthen city ten feet in breadth. A small building is inhabited by the ants. Look, at the sight of Brother Chunyu, they either look up, or nod or lie prostrate toward you. Isn't this the Nanke County you mentioned?

SHA SAN:

It's the county you ruled.

> (*To the previous tune*)
>
> On the southern branch
>
> With flat paths and small buildings
>
> Is located Nanke County.

CHUNYU FEN:

This looks like it.

> (*Sighs*)

I was busy here as the magistrate. Did I rule over these ant citizens? The seven thousand and two hundred tablets to commemorate my meritorious management and the memorial temple are all gone, except for the sand dyke leading to the Departure Pavilion.

> What is virtuous management?
>
> It owes to their support in these twenty years.

PARTRIDGE:

Let's dig toward the west!

LIU'ER:

Well, six feet toward the west is a cave high up with a hollow inside. What's this?

> (*Inspects*)

This is a huge tortoise shell, with flourishing wild grass after the rain. As it is situated to the west of the locust tree, isn't it Mount Tortoise?

CHUNYU FEN:

That's it. It is a pity that for Tian Zihua's *Poetic Essay on the Grand Hunting on the Tortoise Hill*,

> A good essay is buried under the pavilion
>
> As a scenic spot for people to visit.

SHA SAN:

Digging eastward for three feet, there is another cave with intertwining ancient roots.

> With the shape of a dragon,
>
> Isn't it where you bury you princess wife?

CHUNYU FEN (*Looks carefully and wails*):

True! The large tomb is where my wife lies. Oh, my dear princess wife!

(*To the previous tune*)

　　With you looming before me,

　　I shed torrents of tears

　　For you cannot lie in the same grave with me!

　　When the King compelled me to leave,

　　Why couldn't you hear my call for help?

Brothers, when I buried my wife, I argued about feng-shui with Right Prime Minister Duan Gong for my children. He said that there might be ants here, but I argued that they do not matter. It looks like as if there are mosquitoes here.

　　What's the use of the dragon according to feng-shui?

The princess once said that

　　She would strive to win distinction for me.

　　(*Wind arises within*)

PARTRIDGE:

A big storm is coming. Let's destroy this nest of ants!

CHUNYU FEN (*Flurried*):

　　Don't try to hurt them!

　　Let's shelter the locust palace for them!

　　(*Covers the cave*)

PARTRIDGE:

The cave is shielded. Let's take shelter from the rain!

ALL:

　　"*Instead of taking shelter from rain,*

　　Who will mind the ant with pain?"

　　(*Exeunt all*)

VOICE WITHIN:

The rain has stopped!

　　(*Enter Partridge, giggling*)

PARTRIDGE:

Funny, funny indeed! Like a child's face, rain and shine in a flash!

　　(*Looks*)

Alas! Master, hurry up!

　　(*Enter Chunyu Fen, Liu'er and Sha San in haste*)

PARTRIDGE:

Look! Where are the ant holes?

ALL (*Astonished*):

How accurate is the prediction!

CHUNYU FEN:

It is predestined! There was the rumor in the ant state that the country would be in great trouble, and that the capital would have to be moved. Isn't the prediction accurate?

　　(*To the tune of* **Dashiyin**)

　　The astrology

Is accurate enough,

For he should not have invited a guest star like me!

SHA SAN:

The great changes in life

Are incurred by your affairs with the ladies.

CHUNYU FEN:

When I walk along the path, everything conforms with the dream, except the State of Sandals and Vines and the River Town.

PARTRIDGE (*Thinks*):

Yes, I see. On the long ditch of the ancient stream to the east of our house, there is a sandalwood tree, intertwined with vines that shelters from the sky. I used to take a day break there and see red ants coming and going. It must be this.

CHUNYU FEN:

That's it. That is the unarmoured army of the State of Sandals and Vines.

These tiny creatures dared to fight,

Defying the valiant General Zhou.

LIU'ER:

Which General Zhou?

CHUNYU FEN:

Zhou Bian is the general. Both he and Tian Zihua were in Nanke with me.

PARTRIDGE:

Really!

CHUNYU FEN:

He got a letter from my father, who promised to meet me in the year of *dingchou*.

LIU'ER:

This year is the year of *dingchou*.

CHUNYU FEN:

How could it be like this! Dubious indeed!

With all things entangled,

Like meeting my dead father,

Am I bewitched to have spirits around me?

SHA SAN:

As to the dead soul, we'd better inquire an enlightened Zen Master.

PARTRIDGE:

Yes, there is one. I happened to meet a monk taking shelter from the rain near the door.

CHUNYU FEN:

Invite him here at once!

(*Exit Partridge to invite the monk*)

(*Enter a monk*)

MONK (*To the previous tune*):

Who is inviting a wandering monk?

(*Greets Chunyu Fen*)

What can I do for you, Master Chunyu?

CHUNYU FEN:

Where are you from, master?

MONK:

I am from Luhe County.

CHUNYU FEN:

May I ask you whether you know the scholar Tian Zihua and the military candidate Zhou Bian in Luhe County?

MONK:

Yes, I know. They are my bosom friends, but they died a natural death on the same day.

CHUNYU FEN:

Then, it's all the more strange.

MONK:

Why is the locust tree dug up?

CHUNYU FEN:

I am just to inquire about this. There are myriads of ants in the cave of this tree. I was taking a nap in the east wing when two envoys invited me to marry the daughter of the king. With the swift passage of twenty years, I woke up to find that it was a dream, with Zhou Bian and Tian Zihua in the dream. Just now I heard from you that they died and became roving spirits. I do not mind that, but I got a letter from my deceased father saying that we are to meet in this year of the ox. I am in great suspicion as to

Whether I shall be in disaster

As it is the year of the ox.

MONK:

It happens that Master Qixuan is at the Gathering of Water and Land to expiate the sins of all the dead souls. Why don't you write a prayer and inquire about the predestined fate at *Moksha-nulha-parishad,* the gathering for almsgiving. The Master will

Reveal to you all the shadows

And explain all the causes and effects.

CHUNYU FEN (*Bows*):

Thank you for your instructions

As if I attended the Ullambana service

And was moved to sing the Bamboo Tune again!

MONK:

This service is much more serious than the Ullambana service. You must fast and confine yourself in a room for forty-nine days. Chant "Amitabha Buddha" thirty-six thousand times within twenty four hours. Then you'll burn your fingertip as incense and write your prayer to be offered before the altar of Buddha. Only in this way will there be some effect.

CHUNYU FEN:

I'll obey your instructions. But I don't know whether the Zen Master will ferry all the citizens in the Great State of Peaceful Locust to the Heaven.

MONK:

Of course he will.

CHUNYU FEN (*To the tune of* **Coda**):

    I'll offer all I have to Buddha,

    To save the ants as the human beings.

    I shall ask Master Qixuan about my haunting illusion.

    The empty existence is not a void,

    But who has the insight to see through?

    I'll go to the sacred Buddhist temple

    To save the citizens of Peaceful Locust.

Scene Forty-Three
Affections Expounded

(*Enter Monk A, holding a banner*)

MONK A:

    (*To the tune of* **Langtaosha**)

    When we lie prostrate before Buddha,

    Beating drums and blow horns,

    The heavens resound with kinnarra, the god of music.

    The everlasting altar lamps with surviving banners

    Shine over the world of suffering.

    (*Enter Monk B, holding a chiming stone*)

MONK B (*To the previous tune*):

    Men inhabit the world of desire,

    In daily apprehension of Yama, the king of hell.

    Is there sorrow in the world of rebirth?

    While all the wheels in the hell are broken,

    What is the world of suffering?

    (*Enter Chunyu Fen, holding an incense burner*)

CHUNYU FEN (*To the previous tune*):

    As the spouse of the king's daughter,

    I once held office in Nanke County.

    What happens in the world of utmost light-purity?

    A man of affections will never be deprived of affections.

    A young man may also be tormented by sufferings.

    (*Places the incense burner on the ground and lies prostrate before Buddha*)

    (*Salutes the monks with his palms crossed*)

My respect to your all.

MONKS:

All the living beings should lie prostrate before Buddha's powerful light, and rely on the

The Nanke Dream

magic power of the Zen Master. There are almsgivers cherishing sincere desires and acolytes obeying the Buddhist disciplines. Thousands of people come to sing praise of Buddha's merits and virtues, with the chanting of sutras like thunders. Those come to worship and pray for forty-nine days are shedding torrents of tears. Those who are unhindered and treat all as equals will impress Buddha with their sincerity. With his wisdom to sever all worries, the Zen Master will bring all the living beings to ascend to the heaven in due order.

CHUNYU FEN:

All the men with affections cherish the common desire of being blessed by Buddha.

(*Enter Master Qixuan in a dignified manner*)

MASTER QIXUAN (*To the tune of* **Northern Xianlu Dianjiangchun**):

> The chanting of sutras
>
> Brings light to the skies
>
> And clarity in the hall.
>
> The karma in the dreams
>
> Will be testified in Buddha's sphere.

CHUNYU FEN (*Bows to Master Qixuan*):

I, Chuyu Fen, bow to the Master.

(*The monks make a bow*)

MASTER QIXUAN:

I have practiced Buddhism to the age of ninety-one before I hold this Gathering of Water and Land to expiate the sins of all the dead souls. Thanks to the piety of the monks, they have fasted forty-nine days and offered the prayer before the altar of Buddha for seven days and seven nights. The floating lamps on the river break the darkness of the night while alms are distributed to all the hungry ghosts. All your pious beseechings will be duly attained. As the gathering will come to an end this evening, do you have any wish that I can help you to fulfill?

CHUNYU FEN:

My first wish is to see my deceased father ascend to the heavens; my second wish is to see my wife Yaofang ascend to the heavens; my third wish is to see all the citizens in the Great State of Peaceful Locust ascend to the heavens.

MASTER QIXUAN:

What great wishes! You may burn your fingertip as the incense and I'll enumerate them for you. They might be fulfilled to reward your piety.

(*The monks beat drums and blow horns*)

(*Chunyu Fen kowtows three times*)

MASTER QIXUAN (*To the tune of* **Hunjianglong**):

> The humble disciple in Huainan,
>
> Chunyu Fen lies prostrate to worship Buddha.

(*Chunyu Fen burns his fingertip*)

MASTER QIXUAN:

> He is willing to skin his fingertip
>
> And burn it as candle or incense
>
> For his deceased father who is buried in the north,

And for the ruined locust palace of his spouse.

His father wrote a letter

And sent it from the underworld

While his ant spouse bares her affection

In the Buddhist Hall.

Oh Buddha, by your immense blessing,

Ferry those affectionate ones into the heavens!

I have prayed for you. And now I shall sprinkle the water with the willow twigs and scatter the sweet flowers.

(*The monks sprinkle water with the willow twigs*)

(*To the tune of **Youhulu***)

I shall twist the willow twigs a thousand times

To sprinkle the cleansing water like nectar.

(*Scatters the flowers*)

The fragrant wind swirls the flowers in the hall

When the fairy comes to scatter them.

The flowers whirl in the sky,

Like the moon in the water

Which reflects the blooming of flowers.

When the insects drink the water-drops,

Their bud-like hearts will burst into lotus flowers.

What time is it now?

MONKS:

The moon has risen to the zenith.

MASTER QIXUAN:

Everyone, please walk around the terrace with joss-sticks in your hands! Chunyu and I shall ascend the terrace and watch the astrology in the sky.

(*The monks respond*)

"*To leave the world of desire,*

We must reach the world of pure saints."

(*Exeunt Master Qixuan and Chunyu Fen*)

(*Chanting with music within*)

MONKS:

"*In the flowery forest*

Where fragrance spreads,

Tathagata Buddha

And Avalokitesvara

Have heavenly eyes

To see through hearts,

With three insights

That disperse darkness."

(*Exeunt the monks*)

(*Enter Master Qixuan with a sword, followed by Chunyu Fen*)

MASTER QIXUAN (*To the tune of* **Tianxiale**):

Ah!

>When I step on the Heavenly Altar,

>The moon is round and the sky fair,

>With three treasures hanging there,

>Clustered by sparkling stars in the cold air.

CHUNYU FEN:

On the Heavenly Altar, why do you bring the sword with you?

MASTER QIXUAN:

This sword will

>Break the cycles of marital affection

>And sever the entangled lust in this life.

>I'll follow the Plough route as the magic.

CHUNYU FEN (*Sighs*):

I am most worried about my father, who won't be able to keep his promise to meet me five years later in the year of the ox unless he ascends to the heavens tonight.

MASTER QIXUAN (*To the tune of* **Nezhaling**):

>If you want to see him,

>Do not fear the springs in the hell,

>As long as you are filial;

>Do not fear the devas or layers of heavens,

>As long as you are pious;

>Do not fear the pratyana or destiny,

>As long as you are determined.

>With determination, he will penetrate through the earth

>And appear on the Heavenly Altar,

>So that you will meet him this very night.

CHUNYU FEN (*Inquires*):

Now I know about my father, but how can the ants turn into human beings?

MASTER QIXUAN:

As they have their nidana, or cause and effect, they have changed their appearances.

CHUNYU FEN:

For what cause have I been brought to the ants' world and made their kin?

MASTER QIXUAN:

It is their affection, nothing but affection, plus a bit of your ignorant nature. Your hindrance of affection has brought about all this.

CHUNYU FEN:

When did my affection with the ants originate?

MASTER QIXUAN:

Do you remember the day when you listened to my preaching in the Xiaogan Temple? I asked you why you brought your kith and kin with you. The two ladies who were offering the phoenix hairpins and the rhino-horn case were the very persons.

*(To the tune of **Jishengcao**)*

In order to meet your love,

You went to live in the ant world.

The human being lived in the ant palace

While the ant became man's spouse

Because fate had brought you to the Buddhist temple.

As the tiny insect have such a good marriage tie,

Why should heaven deny the man his wish?

CHUNYU FEN:

Well, I did not know that she is an ant. Why didn't you reveal the truth to me?

MASTER QIXUAN:

I told the parrot to call "Turn around, ants!" but you mistook the words for "Turn around, lasses!"

CHUNYU FEN:

It was what I heard.

MASTER QIXUAN:

When you asked me three questions about moral afflictions, I hid the truth in half of the couplets in a hymn. The first couplet is "They are like bare locust-trees in the empty palace"; doesn't it refer to the State of Peaceful Locust? The second couplet is "But halting to find a dwelling in the forest"; it refers to your stay in Nanke because of your wife. The third couplet is "When the dream has vanished, the homeward road is barely visible"; it refers to you awakening from the dream to find yourself in your homeland.

CHUNYU FEN:

Yes, I have meditated on these lines.

MASTER QIXUAN *(Aside)*:

I'd like to give him the advice that "All material things are immaterial; all things and phenomena exist in the mind only", but he has not been awakened yet and will not believe it. I shall create another illusion for his kith and kin to show up again when they ascend to the heaven. When he is afflicted by another hindrance of affection, I shall sever them up with the sword and accept him as a Buddhist disciple. That shall be worth my efforts.

(Turns back)

You showed affection for her because you did not know that she was an ant. Now that you know it, will you show affection to her?

CHUNYU FEN:

Since I know the truth now, what affection is there for me?

MASTER QIXUAN:

You say you do not cherish any affection for her, why do you want her to ascend to the heaven? Oh, the heaven's gate is open with a golden flash.

CHUNYU FEN *(Surprised to see it)*:

That's right.

MASTER QIXUAN *(To the tune of **Yao**)*:

When you see a flash of light like lightning,

Do you know which layer of heaven this is?

Has the gate of the heavenly city opened to a palace?

Has the gate of the tower opened to your residence?

Has the heavenly clouds dispersed to reveal a city?

CHUNYU FEN:

Oh, what's the noise from the heaven?

(*The wind rises within*)

I don't know how wide the world is

And why the constellations change at the sound of the wind.

(*Music and a report from within*)

VOICE WITHIN:

The gate to the Indra Heaven is open!

(*Another report from within*)

VOICE WITHIN:

Thirty-four thousand households of ants from the State of Sandals and Vines have ascended to the heavens!

MASTER QIXUAN (*Surprised*):

Reports come from the Indra Heaven that thirty-four thousand households of ants from the State of Sandals and Vines have ascended to the heaven. Look! They have swarmed like rains to the heaven!

CHUNYU FEN:

Alas! I have deep-rooted malignity with the State of Sandals and Vines. All the virtues and merits from this Heavenly Altar have brought them to the heaven. How can it be like this!

MASTER QIXUAN (*Smiles*):

(*To the tune of* **Zhuansha**)

What malignity is there for that one?

What affection is there for this one?

There is no distinction for the senseless heaven.

CHUNYU FEN:

How many ants in Nanke did the State of Sandals and Vines slaughter? What retribution of karma will they receive?

MASTER QIXUAN:

As the slaughtering was committed in their previous lives,

They will ascend to the heaven once they have repented.

CHUNYU FEN (*Wails*):

I want to see my father! I want to see my princess wife!

MASTER QIXUAN:

What about descending with me from the Heavenly Altar and burning another fingertip before the tablet of the thirty-third heaven, or the Indra Heaven?

CHUNYU FEN:

My finger hurts!

MASTER QIXUAN:

Oh!

> If you burn all your fingertips
>
> For the sake of all your family members,
>
> Your flesh-incense will penetrate the heavens.
>
> When the constellation turns,
>
> Step on the Heavenly Altar and watch the sky again!
>
> You may then see your father
>
> And meet your wife.
>
> (*Exit Master Qixuan, dragging Chunyu Fen behind him*)
>
> (*Enter the monks*)

MONKS (*Chanting with music*):

> *"In the flowery forest*
>
> *Where fragrance spreads,*
>
> *Tathagata Buddha*
>
> *And Avalokitesvara*
>
> *Have heavenly eyes*
>
> *To see through hearts,*
>
> *With three insights*
>
> *That disperse darkness."*

Scene Forty-Four
End of Affection

> (*Enter Chunyu Fen, his fingers hurting*)

CHUNYU FEN:

Ouch!

> *"I burn my fingers that hurt to my heart,*
>
> *Hoping for reunion in the past, present and future."*

I am a descendent from a military family, but cannot bear the hurt on my flesh. For the sake of boundless merits and virtues, I burned a fingertip only to ferry the State of Sandals and Vines to the heaven. Now I am led by the Master to the tablet of the thirty-third heaven, burned another fingertip and step on the Heavenly Altar again, waiting for my father and my princess wife.

> (*The wind rises within*)

CHUNYU FEN (*Astonished*):

The heaven's gate is open!

> (*Gazes*)

The voice is coming from the heaven again!

VOICE WITHIN:

Fifty thousand households of ants from the Great State of Peaceful Locust are ascending to the heaven at the same time!

CHUNYU FEN:

Nice! Nice! Fifty thousand households of ants from the Great State of Peaceful Locust are ascending to the heaven. The citizens from Nanke County are all there. But I haven't seen my father and my princess wife yet. This round of my pains has been wasted.

> (To the tune of **Xiangliuniang**)
> Oh heavens! Show mercy on me!
> Oh heavens! Show mercy on me!
> I have neither seen my father
> Nor my pretty wife.
> Move the Heavenly Altar closer to the heaven!
> Move the Heavenly Altar closer to the heaven!
> (Kowtows)
> With piety I am praying
> For the spirits to come up alive!
> I yearn on top of the clouds;
> I yearn on top of the clouds.

Nice! Nice!

> The cloud and mist is coming from the north,
> Accompanied by a miracle.

Oh, the heaven's gate is open again.

> (The wind rises within)
> (Enter Chunyu's father)

CHUNYU'S FATHER:

Chunyu Fen my son, here I am.

CHUNYU FEN (Kneels and weeps):

You are my father!

CHUNYU'S FATHER (To the previous tune):

> My spirit roams for years;
> My spirit roams for years.
> You kind and gentle filial piety
> Has brought us together in the year of the ox.

CHUNYU FEN:

Father, I am guilty since I fail to wait on you when you are alive and fail to bury you when you are dead. Is Mother coming along with you?

CHUNYU'S FATHER:

She's been reborn to this world for quite some time.

> My grave has been intruded by the ants;
> My grave has been intruded by the ants.
> It is a great luck for me

To have the chance to meet you.

I must be going now.

CHUNYU FEN (*Weeps*):

Where are you going, father?

CHUNYU FEN, CHUNYU'S FATHER:

> To ascend to the heaven is a great joy;
>
> To ascend to the heaven is a great joy.
>
> Our practice of Buddhism on both sides
>
> Has brought us together.

CHUNYU FEN:

Father, come down a bit and I'll touch you.

> (*To the previous tune*)
>
> I have been in grief for you for years;
>
> I have been in grief for you for years.
>
> I have often seen you in my dream,
>
> Praying for blessing for you.

CHUNYU'S FATHER:

I've appreciated it all. What will you live on in the future?

CHUNYU FEN:

I shall join the army and become a general.

CHUNYU'S FATHER:

Don't do that! You'll break the moral rule of killing.

> Talk no more of the power of a general!
>
> Serving by the side of Sovereign Shakra,
>
> I am afraid that I'll have to fight the demons.

As time is limited in the heaven, I must be going now.

CHUNYU FEN, CHUNYU'S FATHER:

> To ascend to the heaven is a great joy;
>
> To ascend to the heaven is a great joy.
>
> Our practice of Buddhism on both sides
>
> Has brought us together.
>
> (*Exit Chunyu's Father*)

CHUNYU FEN (*Wails*):

> (*Enter Duan Gong, Zhou Bian and Tian Zihua, dressed as before*)

CHUNYU FEN (*Rises to his feet and looks*):

Oh, so you are Prime Minister Duan, Zhou and Tian!

DUAN GONG, ZHOU BIAN, TIAN ZIHUA:

Yes, we are.

CHUNYU FEN:

Prime Minister, why did you sow discord with slanders all the time?

DUAN GONG (*Smiles*):

Your Highness, where is the good geomantic omen of Mount Dragon?

ZHOU BIAN:

You did enrage me!

CHUNYU FEN:

My twenty years of fame was spoilt by you.

TIAN ZIHUA:

You helped me all those years.

DUAN GONG (*Smiles*):

Let bygones be bygones! Now we must thank His Highness for his prayer to let us ascend to the heaven.

DUAN GONG, ZHOU BIAN, TIAN ZIHUA (*To the previous tune*):

> We served in the court for years;
>
> We served in the court for years.
>
> Our lingering thoughts of gratitude and resentment
>
> Are but merits in Nanke and battles with Sandals and Vines.
>
> We have been haunted by the phantoms;
>
> We have been haunted by the phantoms.
>
> When we see through them,
>
> There is no distinction between good and evil.
>
> (*Drums and bugles within*)

ALL:

The King and the Queen will arrive soon.

DUAN GONG, ZHOU BIAN, TIAN ZIHUA:

> To ascend to the heaven is a great joy;
>
> To ascend to the heaven is a great joy.
>
> Our practice of Buddhism on both sides
>
> Has brought us together.
>
> (*Exeunt Duan Gong, Zhou Bian and Tian Zihua*)

CHUNYU FEN:

They look like His Majesty and Her Majesty.

> (*Kneels to welcome the Ant King and the Ant Queen*)
>
> (*Enter the Ant King and the Ant Queen, surround by court maids holding fans*)

ANT KING (*To the previous tune*):

> The country has been founded for years;
>
> The country has been founded for years.

CHUNYU FEN (*Kowtows*):

Former Left Prime Minister, Royal Son-in-Law and Royal Captain of the Great State of Peaceful Locust, Chunyu Fen kowtows to greet Your Majesties.

ANT KING:

Chunyu, don't stand on ceremony!

ANT QUEEN:

When we parted, I said, "If you keep us in heart, we'll have the opportunity to meet again." My grandchildren have ascended to the heaven. Have you seen them?

CHUNYU FEN:

No, I haven't.

ANT QUEEN:

They have become boys and girls in the heaven.

> All the members of our family
>
> Are heavenly relatives instead of devilish kin.

CHUNYU FEN:

May I ask how ascendance to the heaven is compared to the locust palace?

ANT KING:

> We are going to the boundless universe;
>
> We are going to the boundless universe.
>
> It's different from the small world of ours
>
> With a palace in the size of a tiny grain of sand.

I'm leaving now. The princess and the court ladies will be coming soon.

ANT KING, ANT QUEEN:

> To ascend to the heaven is a great joy;
>
> To ascend to the heaven is a great joy.
>
> Our practice of Buddhism on both sides
>
> Has brought us together.
>
> (*Exeunt the Ant King and the Ant Queen*)

CHUNYU FEN:

As the princess is about to arrive, I'll stand erect waiting for her. We were an affectionate couple for twenty years.

> (*Gazes*)

Why, she is not in sight yet.

> (*Gazes again*)

Several court ladies are riding on the cloud.

> (*Enter Princess Qiongying, Lady Lingzhi and Sister Shangzhen*)

PRINCESS QIONGYING, LADY LINGZHI, SISTER SHANGZHEN (*To the previous tune*):

> We missed affections,
>
> We missed affections
>
> In the lonely palace garden.

CHUNYU FEN:

The princess is not here yet. They are Princess Qiongying, Lady Lingzhi and Sister Shangzhen.

PRINCESS QIONGYING, LADY LINGZHI, SISTER SHANGZHEN (*Laugh*):

His Highness is romantic.

CHUNYU FEN (*Greets them*):

How do you do, fairies!

LADY LINGZHI:

We were having an amazing time together when our intimate affairs were disturbed by the wretched bastard of a countryman.

The Nanke Dream

CHUNYU FEN:

Would you call him countryman? He is that insensible Right Prime Minister!

PRINCESS QIONGYING:

Don't mention this any longer!

CHUNYU FEN:

Come down, as I'd like to talk with you three fairies!

SISTER SHANGZHEN:

We are celestial bodies now. How can we go down?

LADY LINGZHI:

Even if we could go down, your human body is stinking and can no longer attract us now.

> Wretched is the human body;
>
> Wretched is the human body.
>
> As I can find a nice spouse in the heaven,
>
> You are doing a fool's errand!

SISTER SHANGZHEN:

We're leaving now. The princess is coming.

PRINCESS QIONGYING, LADY LINGZHI, SISTER SHANGZHEN:

> To ascend to the heaven is a great joy;
>
> To ascend to the heaven is a great joy.
>
> Our practice of Buddhism on both sides
>
> Has brought us together.
>
> (*Exeunt*)
>
> (*The wind rises within*)

CHUNYU FEN:

How fragrant the wind smells!

> (*Listens*)

Listen! The rings and pendants are tingling on the clouds. Here comes the princess.

> (*Looks up three times, sighing. The wind rises*)
>
> (*Enter Princess Golden Branch*)

PRINCESS GOLDEN BRANCH (*To the tune of* **Northern Xinshuiling**):

> The phoenix flies high above Mount Dragon
>
> On another journey of life.
>
> My tiny feet stepping on the cloud,
>
> My treasure fan moving on the moon,
>
> I fly across the glassy sky,
>
> With my cape flapping in the wind.

CHUNYU FEN:

Is that sky-walker my wife Princess Yaofang?

PRINCESS GOLDEN BRANCH:

Oh Chunyu, my man! It's a long time since we were separated. I bow to you on top of the cloud.

> "*I failed my duty as your wife,*

CHUNYU FEN:

For death cut short our love of twenty years.

PRINCESS GOLDEN BRANCH:

I'd like to vent my woe of life,

CHUNYU FEN, PRINCESS GOLDEN BRANCH:

But clouds have severed us in two spheres."

CHUNYU FEN (*Kneels*):

Princess, I can hardly express my gratitude to you. You may not know how much torment I suffered after you departed.

PRINCESS GOLDEN BRANCH:

I know everything.

CHUNYU FEN (*To the tune of **Southern Bubujiao***):

> I suffered wrongs from Prime Minister Duan,
>
> When sudden death broke us apart
>
> After we had stayed in Nanke for twenty years.
>
> You were buried on Mount Dragon
>
> Until I see you again in the sky.
>
> As soon as you appeared on the clouds,
>
> I took you for the beauty in the Jade Terrace.

My dear, come down! I'd like to chat with you.

PRINCESS GOLDEN BRANCH:

I can't get down.

CHUNYU FEN:

Why not, my dear?

PRINCESS GOLDEN BRANCH (*To the tune of **Southern Zheguiling***):

> Now I ride a cloud carriage,
>
> Walk on the cloud path
>
> And stand on the cloud piles.
>
> In my cloud image,
>
> I speak to you on the top of clouds
>
> And accompany you with cloud emotion.

CHUNYU FEN:

Since you departed, how lonely I have been in the endless night!

PRINCESS GOLDEN BRANCH:

Have you been lonely?

> In the strange adventure of your life,
>
> You had three ladies vying for you,
>
> But did you forget my parting words?

CHUNYU FEN:

I know I was wrong. Princess, at that time I had no choice but take them as sworn sisters.

PRINCESS GOLDEN BRANCH:

> You only knew siblings when you wined and dined,

But discarded your life companion and the children.

CHUNYU FEN:

Now that you have turned into a fairy, I don't think you should take this to heart. Moreover, as my affection for you will never be exhausted, I'd like to have you as my wife once more.

(*To the tune of **Southern Jiangshui'er***)

I am intoxicated in affection day and night,

With everlasting yearning of love.

Princess,

Will you find another spouse in the heaven?

Will you have me again as your man?

Will you come again and meet me here?

Please respond me as to these three things!

(*Weeps*)

Otherwise,

Will you drop something from the sky

As a keepsake in the human world?

PRINCESS GOLDEN BRANCH:

Since you are intent on this, I'll be waiting in the Indra Heaven for you to be my man again, only if you practice the Buddhist conducts with heart and soul.

CHUNYU FEN:

Do man and wife make love in the heaven as in the human world?

PRINCESS GOLDEN BRANCH:

In the Indra Heaven, man and wife make love in the same way as in the human world. The only difference is that they play the game without coming to climax. If you go to the upper heavens, the couple do not have intercourse. When their emotions are roused, they either embrace, smile or smell. My man, the next heaven will be the heaven of separation!

(*Sighs*)

Oh, heavens!

(*To the tune of **Northern Yan'erluo** with **Deshengling***)

If only we sit on the lotus seat for a while,

We'll toss and roll like unstrung pearls.

I'll flirt and tease with you in the world of desires,

But take care not to kick the heaven of separation.

CHUNYU FEN:

When I look at you standing on top of the clouds, you are the very image of Chang'e the moon goddess.

PRINCESS GOLDEN BRANCH:

You know, Chang'e was an ant in the human world, who "changed" into a moth and flew into the sky. She lived under a laurel tree while I lived in the locust palace.

Both palaces were dignified.

When you were selected by the Ant King,

You have won the laurel in the imperial exam

And will rise in the official strata.

(*Sighs*)

You do not have to mind

Meeting a fairy face to face.

To my grievance,

Why is my cloud lowering to the earth?

(*Falls*)

(*Chunyu Fen holds her in his arms*)

PRINCESS GOLDEN BRANCH:

Oh my! How is it that I fell!

CHUNYU FEN:

My wife!

PRINCESS GOLDEN BRANCH:

The human world is different from the heavenly world. Stay away from me, brother!

CHUNYU FEN:

Why did you call me brother?

PRINCESS GOLDEN BRANCH:

You once called me sister in this temple.

CHUNYU FEN (*Thinks*):

Yes, I did.

PRINCESS GOLDEN BRANCH:

You said you want a keepsake. Aren't the phoenix hairpins and the rhino-horn case in front of the statue of Avalokitesvara our first souvenir?

CHUNYU FEN (*Thinks*):

Yes, they are.

PRINCESS GOLDEN BRANCH (*Bows before the statue of Avalokitesvara, fetches the phoenix hairpins and the rhino-horn case and hands them to Chunyu Fen*):

My man, keep the phoenix hairpins and the rhino-horn case! I must be going now.

CHUNYU FEN (*Accepts the hairpins and the case, pulls Princess Golden Branch and kneels, wailing*):

(*To the tune of* **Southern Yaoyaoling**)

As I went under the earth to find you,

How can I let you go when you ascend to the heaven?

Now I pull your skirt ribbon tightly

And beg you not to go alone when you ascend.

PRINCESS GOLDEN BRANCH:

My man, you are not to ascend to the heaven yet.

CHUNYU FEN:

I must go with you!

(*Chunyu Fen and Princess Golden Branch push and pull, in tears*)

(*Enter Master Qixuan with a sword, severing them apart, shouting*)

(*Exit Princess Golden Branch in haste*)

(*Stunned, Chunyu Fen falls to the ground*)

MASTER QIXUAN (*To the tune of* **Northern Wangjiangnan**):

Ah!

> You take the ascending one as your wife,
>
> But raise your head and see where she is!

You say that you know she is an ant, but you are still asking a favor from her. Why are you dwelling on your affections?

> (*Sighs*)
>
> You slept in the locust palace with eyes wide open;
>
> You did not sneeze to burn paper spills before your nose.
>
> Silly as you are, just look and see
>
> What phoenix hairpins are inside the rhino case!

CHUNYU FEN (*Wakes to look*):

Oh! The hairpins are locust twigs and the case is a locust pod. Oops! What do I need them for?

> (*Casts away the hairpins and the case*)

I am awake now. What's the difference between kings and subjects or between man and wife in the human world and the ant world? The weal and woe, the rise and fall are the same in Nanke as in the human world. Everything happens in a dreamland, including the ascension to the heaven! I have been a fool!

> (*To the tune of* **Southern Yuanlinhao**)
>
> I was hoaxed by the ants
>
> With a shadow show of affections.
>
> Everything has its cause and effect,
>
> But where am I to find the cause?

MASTER QIXUAN:

What are you to do next?

CHUNYU FEN:

What am I to do? It is vain to seek the human form; it is vain to seek the heavenly form; it is vain to seek the Buddha form. All is vanity.

MASTER QIXUAN (*Shouts*):

What is vanity?

> (*Chunyu Fen claps his hands and smiles; he puts his palms together and stands silent*)

MASTER QIXUAN:

> (*To the tune of* **Northern Gumeijiu** *with* **Taipingling**)
>
> The living Buddha has no form,
>
> As all forms are unrealistic.
>
> (*Points to Chunyu Fen*)
>
> An ant could have been your best companion.
>
> As you are too late to wake up from your dream,
>
> You have cut short your human experience.
>
> Why did you turn a fool in the twinkling of an eye?
>
> What were the hairpins and the Golden Branch?

Who told you to amass the wealth in a hole?

Who told you to build reputation on a branch?

The parrot revealed the heavenly secret long ago

That you should wake up from the butterfly dream.

I,

I experienced this strange event

To pay off my pagoda debt to the ants

And help them ascend to the heavens.

Oh!

All the living beings have witnessed the cause and effect.

(*Enter the monks with incense, flags and musical instruments*)

MASTER QIXUAN, MONKS (*Shout*):

Chunyu Fen has become a Buddha on the spot!

(*Walk*)

(*To the tune of* **Northern Qingjiangyin**)

It is funny that vain illusions may perturb our eyes

While dreamland scenes may disturb our minds.

Long dreams take but little time;

Short dreams are not inscribed on the steles.

All the men are like ants as in the Nanke Dream.

MONKS (*Kowtow*):

All things are impermanent,

Yet a man has become Buddha.

A fond spring dream is vain like floating clouds,

While Buddhist wisdom cleanses one's yearning heart.

In real life all the audience plays a part

In the busy world of madding crowds.

邯郸记

The Handan Dream

汪榕培 译

Translated by Wang Rongpei

Table of Contents

903

Scene One
Prelude

(Enter Announcer)

ANNOUNCER *(To the tune of **Yujia'ao**):*

> When the sun and the moon shine in the sky,
>
> I hear over the seas the immortal's donkey cry.
>
> Now that peach flowers have burst in full bloom,
>
> Does it mean
>
> That fairy flowers must be applied to the broom?
>
> In dreamland time and tide quietly flow;
>
> Who has made arrangements from below?
>
> It's early when the sun sets in the west;
>
> I look back, smile
>
> And pass Handan without a rest.
>
> *He Xiangu walks alone amid the flowers;*
>
> *Lü Dongbin passes Yueyang city thrice.*
>
> *The pretty Cui waits for wedding in her bowers;*
>
> *The foolish Lu Sheng wakes to see half-cooked rice.*

Scene Two
Riding in the Fields

(Enter Lu Sheng)

LU SHENG *(To the tune of **Poqizhen**):*

> To the distant sky there is a way,
>
> But time drags on day after day.
>
> In three undecorated rooms
>
> With a bed that holds a restless soul,
>
> I toss and turn in glooms.
>
> I open autumn windows
>
> To find no fireflies in the rotten weeds
>
> And gaze at ancient roads
>
> To see the evening crows on poplar trees
>
> While my hair wavers in western breeze.
>
> *(To the tune of **Pusaman** in palindrome)*
>
> *I am upset by autumn scenes east of my house;*
>
> *The autumn scenes east of my house upset me.*

The Lus have been Confucian scholars;
The Confucian scholars have been the Lus.
Why should the unknown be named Lu?
Why should Lu remain unknown?
I've been hurt by profound emotion;
Profound emotion has hurt me.

I am Lu Sheng from the east of Mount Taihang. My ancestors lived in Fanyang Prefecture, deeply rooted there. My late father moved to Handan County and lived a rural life. When I was born, I had an enormous size. Before I reached school age, I had grown to be a handsome lad. With an intent mind, I've read widely; with a deep insight, I'm full of intelligence. Reasoning of whatever insightful depth is at the tip of my pen; writings by whatever top-ranking scholars are stored in my memory. Oops, for all I've said, the lucky star never shines over my head and I've turned twenty-six now. To speak of talented poets, Red Li is White Li's elder brother; to speak of Number One Scholars, Liang the Ninth is Liang the Eighth's younger brother. As for contemporary essays, I'm no worse than these people; as for predestination, I lagged behind them in former days. In ragged clothes, I offend people with my wretched appearance; for all my intelligence, I hold my tongue to pretend ignorance. As the saying goes, "A man of low social standing is never in high spirits; a man of meagre existence is never substantial in words." All I have in my possession is a few acres of arid land, which provides me with crops in autumn. As those who lag behind can never catch up with those who go ahead, what can I do in the name of a gentleman? Now that I'm mixed up with gardeners and farmers, why should I be looked down upon as a lowly man? In late autumn, I have to be dressed in a shabby sheepskin coat; on my way to the inn, I have to ride a colt leaner than a rake. Well, in a plight like this, what am I to do? I'll saddle my lame donkey and take a ride to drive away my cares.

(*Saddles the donkey*)

(*The donkey neighs*)

I've kept company with this donkey for many years. I'll never be able to ride a carriage and four on my way to Handan.

(*Walks on*)

(*To the tune of* **Liuyaojin**)

When I ride on the donkey,

The frosty wind is blowing across the land.

The shabby sheepskin coat

Fails to keep away the dust and sand.

In the arid land the crows caw in the dusk;

Behind ox-back the sun sets in the west.

The ancient roads in autumn breeze

And branching crimson trees,

Branching trees,

Paint the autumn at its best.

Now that the sun is setting, I'd better stop over in the west village and go to the fields tomorrow.

When evening glow enshrouds the country lanes,
To whom shall I bespeak my woe and cares?
With few pedestrians on the ancient road,
The autumn wind bestirs crops unawares.

Scene Three
Converting the Common People

(*Enter Lü Dongbin, carrying a parcel, a gourd and a pillow*)

LÜ DONGBIN (*In the pattern of* **Collected Tang Poems**):

The fairy island of Penglai never sees a single man,
Who slays the monstrous kylin in moonlight.
Immortals leave the earth on wings of wind,
And watch the sunrise from the fairy height.

I am Lü Yan, alias Dongbin, a native of Jingzhao. To my undeserved honour, I succeeded in the imperial examination. By nature I was addicted to drinking and chivalric deeds. After I killed a man on the Xianyang Fair in a drunken state, I had to flee the country. As time went on, I was reduced to poverty. One day I happened to meet Master Zhongli Quan, Man of Midday Sun, who was well-versed in the Taoist charms of ascension. When he saw that I was exhausted from the journey, he alchemised some stones into gold and offered it to me for my use at will. As I was puzzled, I kowtowed to him and asked, "May I ask you, Master, whether the alchemised gold will turn back into stones?" The master said, "The gold will turn back into stones again in five hundred years." I scattered the gold at once, saying that the gold would mitigate my poverty for the moment but would cause trouble to the man who possesses it in five hundred years. The master burst into laughter and said, "Lü Yan, Lü Yan, the purity of your heart will lead you to the Immortal Land." By transmission of heart and by word of mouth, he taught me all the Taoist charms of alchemy and ascension. After more than thirty years of learning, to my undeserved honour, I became one of the Immortals of the Upper Eight Caves. As I was obsessed in Taoist instructions in my previous life, I have been able to do one charm after another in this life. By nature I am entangled in the earthly world and so I am intent on converting the worldly people. A gate to the Penglai Mountain has recently been built at the decree of Emperor Donghua. Outside the gate grows a peach tree of immortality, which begins to blossom in three hundred years. The petals fall at a gust of strong wind and block the heavenly gate. I have converted a certain He Xiangu, who comes to sweep away the fallen petals every day. At the recent decree of Emperor Donghua, He Xiangu has been enlisted in the Immortals. Therefore, Zhang Guolao the Immortal has ordered me to ride the clouds and look for a man to sweep the petals in her stead. Before I can finish my words, I see He Xiangu come in smiles and dances.

(*Enter He Xiangu, carrying a broom*)

HE XIANGU:

What a gale that sends the fallen petals to the wind!

(*To the tune of **Shanghuashi***)

With a broom of phoenix feathers,

I sweep the fallen petals at the heavenly gate.

The wind has swept the fallen petals,

Which fall down in a cloud

And block the way to the heavenly gate.

(*Greets Lü Dongbin*)

Where are you going, Master Lü Dongbin?

LÜ DONGBIN:

Congratulations on your being enlisted in the Immortals at the decree of Emperor Donghua. Zhang Guolao the Immortal has ordered me to go to the earthly world to convert another man lest there be no petal-sweeper since you have been promoted. What a task he has assigned me!

HE XIANGU:

Master Lü Dongbin, it would be a great feat in your path to immortality. By the way, where are you going to convert a man? Will you be in time for the Peach Banquet?

(*To the tune of **Yao***)

Do not miss your target by a hair's breadth,

Nor drink too much in Hermit Donglao's house —

Please look up to the sky.

Master Lü Dongbin,

Let me know when you have found the man.

If you delay,

I'll have to sweep the petals and sigh.

(*Exit*)

LÜ DONGBIN:

Now that He Xiangu is gone, I'd better carry my parcel and porcelain pillow and go on with my trip by riding the cloud.

While the pillow is where the head rests,

The porcelain breeds benevolence at best.

(*Exit*)

(*Enter Attendant*)

ATTENDANT:

At night the clear lake waters lie,

That flow upward into the sky.

I'll sell wine on credit by the Dongting Lake,

To customers from boats nearby.

(*Laughter within*)

VOICE WITHIN:

Brother, you've sworn that you'll never sell wine on credit, but you're going back on your promise again.

ATTENDANT:

The credit is due in a month, but people buy a boatload. I've started a big inn in front of the Yueyang Pavilion. As the Dongting Lake abounds in water, my wine is diluted. These days no one is coming to buy my wine even on credit. Absurd! Absurd!

VOICE WITHIN:

Brother, here come two customers to buy on credit.

ATTENDANT:

Come in, please. Come in, please.

> (*Enter Customers A and B*)

CUSTOMERS A AND B:

> *A wayfarer all my life,*
>
> *Half drunk in autumn days.*

Get us some wine, man.

> (*Attendant responds*)
>
> (*Customers A and B examine the wine-kettle*)

How is it that the characters "Dongting" are inscribed on the kettle?

ATTENDANT:

The kettle is to contain lake water.

CUSTOMER A:

Well, with our holding capacity, we can gulp down several Dongting Lakes.

ATTENDANT:

I'll see which of you two can drink more.

CUSTOMER A:

As I do my business on the Poyang Lake, I can drink eight hundred cups.

CUSTOMER B:

As I come from the Lujiang River, I can drink three hundred cups.

ATTENDANT:

In this way, you can't consume much of my wine. After eight hundred cups for the Poyang guest and three hundred cups for the Lujiang guest, my kettle is still more than half full.

CUSTOMERS A AND B:

What a huge kettle!

> (*Drink and sing to their hearts' content*)

ATTENDANT:

Here comes a Taoist priest.

> (*Enter Lü Dongbin*)

LÜ DONGBIN (*To the tune of **Zhonglü Fendie'er***):

> In the bleak autumn days,
>
> The clouds are floating over towering trees,
>
> Across the world from the Immortal Penglai Island.
>
> On the morning rays,

On the evening glow,

I move on step by step.

With a gourd upon my back,

I'm dressed in appealing pale yellow.

(*To the tune of* ***Zuichunfeng***)

With a warm and carefree heart,

I talk with people who have their minds to bare.

I now descend the mount with my eyes wide open,

And count the places here and there —

Here are the Three Chus and Three Qis,

There are the Three Qins and Three Jins,

But nowhere can one find the Three Wus and Three Shus.

While I am talking to myself, I see the Dongting Lake lying ahead. What a magnificent Yueyang Pavilion!

(*To the tune of* ***Hongxiuxie***)

In the fading glow along the river, a lonely owl flies;

In Xiao-Xiang regions, clouds hang over Cangwu.

Amid drizzling rain at dusk,

The ponds and lakes are muttering.

From sunny peaks I hear people chat in a fair;

By misty waters I see people fishing here and there.

With cool eyes I explore the human hearts.

Here's a big inn. Where's the attendant?

ATTENDANT (*Responds*):

Come in, please. Come in, please.

(*Brings in wine*)

LÜ DONGBIN (*To the tune of* ***Yingxianke***):

As I played the iron flute in Yellow Crane Tower,

So I drink the village wine in the Yueyang Pavilion.

What a beautiful sight! What a beautiful sight! With the Hanyang River in front of me, I can take a look at the Xiao-Xiang Rivers and Mount Cangwu upstream, as well as the area north of Dongting and east of the Yangtze downstream. Will you please come here?

ATTENDANT:

What can I do for you?

LÜ DONGBIN:

Come and make a bow

To the respected Ruler of Dongting Lake now.

ATTENDANT:

Nonsense!

(*Gabbles of wild geese within*)

LÜ DONGBIN:

I hear the wild geese gabble on the strands

And see a lonely sail in the horizon.

Over there the Dongting wanderer sadly stands

As he has missed the boat in the setting sun.

(*In a drunken manner*)

The wine is brewed by the immortals and for the immortals. How can you enjoy the pleasure of drinking!

CUSTOMERS A AND B (*Annoyed*):

Oops! Oops! As the saying goes, "Officials rank first; customers rank second." Aren't we better off than you? Dressed in silk and satin, we eat delicacies and pay in silver. Just look at yourself! Not to mention your food, your dress is simply rags! While we are somber and you are drunk, we won't even care to help you to your feet.

LÜ DONGBIN (*Laughs*):

(*To the tune of* **Shiliuhua**)

I will not argue with you when you say

That you won't even care to help me to my feet;

I am drunk in your sombre eye.

In fact you are much more snobbish than I,

And much more malicious than I.

CUSTOMERS A AND B:

This rustic fox of a Taoist priest is hurting us with his vicious tongue. If you don't get out at once, we'll tear your dress to pieces!

LÜ DONGBIN:

Why should you break my belt

And tear my dress like a beast,

Calling me a rustic fox of a Taoist priest?

CUSTOMERS A AND B:

Ridiculous! Ridiculous! Even his gourd scarcely holds any medicine, but smells of wine.

LÜ DONGBIN (*To the tune of* **Dou'anchun**):

You laugh at my gourd that holds wine

And bits and pieces of souvenirs of mine.

You'd better stand erect

And I'll tell your fortune in the Taoist line.

CUSTOMERS A AND B:

What fortune is there to tell? There is nothing but wine, sex, wealth and temper. They are the inherent traits of human beings.

LÜ DONGBIN:

You regard them as the inherent traits of human beings, but

Wine will corrupt your bowels;

CUSTOMERS A AND B:

What about temper?

LÜ DONGBIN:

Bad temper will burst your breast.

CUSTOMERS A AND B:

What about wealth?

LÜ DONGBIN:

> Greed for wealth keeps man to gold all his life;

CUSTOMERS A AND B:

What about sex?

LÜ DONGBIN:

> Lust for sex keeps man to his wife.
>
> (*To the tune of* **Shangxiaolou**)
>
> Those four evils benefit man the least
>
> And turn man into beast.

CUSTOMERS A AND B:

It's hard to say. To serve the emperor brings wealth and distinction; to have a wife and children brings happiness. Wine, sex, wealth and temper are so essential that no one can tear himself away from them.

LÜ DONGBIN:

> You only care about your emperor,
>
> About your children
>
> And about your dearest wife.
>
> Once you cease to breathe,
>
> Where do you know you have come
>
> And where do you know you will go?
>
> I'm worrying for you
>
> And thinking in your place
>
> That nothing will leave a trace.

CUSTOMERS A AND B:

In a minute, neither will you be able to tell *yang* from *yin* nor will you be able to tell day from night.

LÜ DONGBIN (*Smiles*):

And will you be able to tell?

> (*To the tune of* **Yao**)
>
> Can you tell me what is a crow in the month of Hyades?

CUSTOMERS A AND B:

It comes out when the moon is darkened.

LÜ DONGBIN:

> What is a rabbit in the day of the Scorpius?

CUSTOMERS A AND B (*Think a while*):

That's what you vomit in your room when you've got drunk.

LÜ DONGBIN:

Tell me

> What is the noon of midnight?
>
> What is the leftover of October?

What is the beginning of an hour?

CUSTOMERS A AND B:

Why are we listening to him? He's over-drunk.

LÜ DONGBIN (*Smiles*):

> When I ask,
>
> I ask mediocre people who are tongue-tied.
>
> Is it true
>
> That the priest alone is a man of pride?

CUSTOMERS AND ATTENDANT (*Look at Lü Dongbin's parcel*):

There is a porcelain pillow in his parcel. Let's break it to pieces.

LÜ DONGBIN:

How on earth can you break it?

CUSTOMERS A AND B:

What is it made of that we cannot break it?

LÜ DONGBIN (*To the tune of* **Baihezi**):

> The mould is made of original clay,
>
> Placed in the crescent-moon furnace,
>
> Sealed with seven types of soil
>
> And tempered with water and fire.

CUSTOMERS A AND B:

How do you kindle the fire?

LÜ DONGBIN (*To the tune of* **Yao**):

> I apply the bellows to smelt the mould,
>
> And turn the mercury into pellets of porcelain.
>
> The pink pellets are fired into special tints.
>
> The pillow thus made has no seams at either end.

CUSTOMERS A AND B (*Laugh*):

In that case, the holes at the pillow-ends are for you to relieve your headaches, aren't they?

LÜ DONGBIN (*To the tune of* **Yao**):

> This pillow stops the winds from reaching the earth,
>
> And leans on the sun and the moon to reach the skies.

CUSTOMERS A AND B:

Now you can gaze at the vacant brightness.

LÜ DONGBIN:

> What's vacant for me?
>
> When I lay my head on the pillow,
>
> By and by, the world is at one with my heart and soul.

Will you have a try at the pillow, gentlemen?

CUSTOMERS A AND B:

The pillow is for a bachelor.

LÜ DONGBIN (*Smiles*):

I don't think so.

(*To the tune of* **Yao**)

　　It supports the pretty maid

　　And makes good man and wife.

CUSTOMERS A AND B:

What's the pillow good for?

LÜ DONGBIN:

　　With good news to find,

　　The pillow helps the sleeper change his mind.

CUSTOMERS A AND B:

Is it possible? We don't believe it.

LÜ DONGBIN:

You don't have the luck by fate. I must be off now.

　　(*To the tune of* **Kuaihuosan**)

　　I'm daring not because I have a miraculous sword in my sleeve,

　　But because I sing, travel alone and never grieve.

　　I recite poems and fly across the Dongting Lake

　　To convert those who have the luck.

　　But who will take my advice? Who will take?

　　(*Exit*)

CUSTOMERS AND ATTENDANT (*Laugh*):

We've routed the gentleman out. Let's be on our way.

　　If we meet and do not have a drink,

　　The peach blossoms will laugh at cave's brink.

　　(*Exeunt*)

　　(*Enter Lü Dongbin*)

LÜ DONGBIN:

Ridiculous! Ridiculous! I've found no one to convert on this magnificent Yueyang Pavilion. I have to wander northwestward.

　　(*To the tune of* **Baolao'er**)

　　It's all my fault

　　That I promised my master the other day.

　　Here I have to look for the ferry;

　　There I have to ask the way.

　　I have to read the Taoist rhyme

　　And do some miracles from time to time.

Alas, a deep-blue current of air is floating between the south of Yan and the north of Zhao. Let me turn round the cloud and go with the wind.

　　(*To the tune of* **Mantingfang**)

　　I am not telling fortunes at will,

　　But how is it that neither smoke nor fog hangs overhead,

　　Neither Chu nor Wu is under my feet,

　　And neither black nor red I see?

Is it a current made by the black ox in the Hangu Pass?

Is it a current from a castle in the sky from the East Sea?

As I have no compass to point the direction,

I have to look round and adjust my ride.

Well,

I am approaching the Qing River,

With Handan of Zhao on the other side.

Let me have a closer look. Here I am in Handan. How is it that an immortal seems to be nearby?

(*To the tune of* ***Shuahai'er***)

The Records of the Historian mentions the Handan dancers,

But there are no more heroes like Lin Xiangru for thousands of years.

How is it that auspicious clouds enshroud an extraordinary man?

Who lives in the human world with such good cheers?

Amid the reed catkins and the moonlight, where is the man?

In the hills and by the rills, is the man staying there?

I have a way to find out where he is,

By making his donkey stumble

And by testing whether he is fair and square.

(*To the tune of* ***Coda***)

To look for a petal-sweeper for the Penglai Cave,

I've searched Handan for a man.

If he is predestined in fate,

I'll make him an immortal if I can.

If you meet anyone who is so warm-hearted,

He must have come from Lü's clan.

I ride auspicious clouds from the heavenly palace,

To look for a petal-sweeper in the world.

Whenever the world is brightly lit,

The people will not have groped and erred.

Scene Four
Entering the Dream

(*Enter Innkeeper*)

INNKEEPER:

Cold reigns in late autumn in the north;

My ancestors originated in Handan.

I run an inn to serve millet meals;

Every guest says that life is hard for man.

I've started a small inn to the north of the Zhaozhou Bridge. Half of the land around the inn belongs to the family of Lu from the Fanyang township. Their family members all stop over at my inn when they come and go. Some travelling merchants also take a rest and have meals here. Now that it's time for refreshments, I'll wait and see if there are any guests today.

(Enter Lü Dongbin in laughter, with a parcel and a pillow on his back)

LÜ DONGBIN:

A millet contains the world in it;

A cauldron boils the cosmos in it.

On the Yueyang Pavilion I saw a coil of deep-blue current leading to Handan. I've wandered all the way here, only to find that the current stops at Lu Sheng's house to the west of the Zhaozhou Bridge in Handan County. I have scrutinized Lu Sheng's complexion and found him extraordinary. As Lu Sheng is predestined to be a demi-immortal, I'll go to see him and convert him. However, he is deeply entangled in worldly burdens and has not made up his mind yet. As he is adept at both pen and sword but has not made any success in official career, he keeps aloof and feels depressed all the time. He is not to be moved with mere words.

(In meditation)

I shall act in such and such a way so that he will wake up to reality. I'll go to the inn and wait for him there.

*(To the tune of **Suonanzhi**)*

In a miraculous air

And a green-jade robe,

I lower the clouds and descend from the sky.

I cross the Zhaozhou Bridge

And step on the Handan Road.

(Crowing of roosters and barking of dogs within)

LÜ DONGBIN:

What a relaxing village with its crowing roosters and barking dogs!

INNKEEPER *(Greets Lü Dongbin)*:

Take a seat please, sir.

LÜ DONGBIN:

I put my parcel down

And am well received.

The Yueyang Pavilion

Is farther away than I believed.

INNKEEPER:

May I ask where you are from?

LÜ DONGBIN:

I'm a converting Taoist priest by the name of Hui. I'd like to sit for a while.

(Aside)

Here comes the man on a black donkey.

(Chants incantations)

The donkey, the roosters, the dogs and the people in the human world, all those who have body and soul, do obey my miraculous orders and never violate them. That's my edict!

(*Enter Lu Sheng, dressed in a short fur-coat and riding a donkey*)

LU SHENG (*To the previous tune*):

> While the wind blows at my hat,
>
> In an unbuttoned marten coat,
>
> I whip the black donkey in a sharp note.

INNKEEPER:

Welcome, Master Lu.

LU SHENG:

> With the fields at my heels,
>
> Who's calling me by the waterwheels?

Oh, it's the innkeeper. I'll sit there for a while. Tether the donkey on the stump and let it eat some hay.

INNKEEPER:

Yes, I see.

LU SHENG (*Greets Lü Dongbin*):

> I raise my hand
>
> And make a bow.
>
> When we meet,
>
> I'll say hello now.

Where is the old man from, Innkeeper?

INNKEEPER:

He's from a Muslim country.

LU SHENG:

He doesn't look like a Muslim.

LÜ DONGBIN:

My surname is Hui. I've made my way from the Yueyang Pavilion. May I ask what's your name?

LU SHENG:

I am Lu Sheng. I heard of the Yueyang Pavilion long ago. How does it look like now?

LÜ DONGBIN:

There is an essay entitled *The Yueyang Pavilion*. I'll recite a few lines for you: "The finest sights of Baling are concentrated in the region of Lake Dongting. Dongting, nibbling at the distant hills and gulping down the Yangtze River, strikes beholders as vast and infinite, presenting a scene of boundless variety; and this is the superb view from the Yueyang Pavilion. Since the lake is linked with the Wu Gorge in the north and extends to the Xiao and Xiang rivers in the south, many exiles and wandering poets gather here, and their reactions to these sights vary greatly. During a period of incessant rain, when a spell of bad weather continues for more than a month, chilly winds bellow angrily, tumultuous waves hurl themselves against the sky, the sun and the stars hide their lights, hills and mountains disappear, merchants have to halt in their travels, masts collapse and oars splinter, the day

darkens and the roars of tigers and howls of monkeys are heard. If men come to this pavilion with a longing for home in their hearts or nursing a feeling of bitterness because of taunts and slander, they may find the sight depressing and fall prey to agitation or despair. But during mild and bright spring weather, when the waves are unruffled and the azure translucence above and below stretches before your eyes for myriads of *li*, when the water-birds fly down to congregate on the sands and fish with scales like glimmering silk disport themselves in the water, when the iris and orchids on the banks grow luxuriant and green; or when dusk falls over this vast expanse and the bright moon casts its light over a thousand *li*, when the rolling waves glitter like gold and the silent shadows in the water glimmer like jade, and the fishermen sing to each other for sheer joy, then men coming to this pavilion may feel complete freedom of heart and ease of spirit, forgetting every worldly gain or pain, to hold their wine-cups in the breeze in absolute elation, delighted with life."*

LU SHENG:

What a magnificent sight! You have such a good memory that you can recite the essay so fluently. How many times have you been there?

LÜ DONGBIN:

Not many times, just thrice. As it goes in a poem:

> *I visit Green Void in the morn and Cangwu in the eve;*
>
> *I'm bold since I've a miraculous sword up my sleeve.*
>
> *I'm not known although I've passed Yueyang three times;*
>
> *I fly over Lake Dongting while I recite the rhymes.*

LU SHENG:

What a good poem you've recited! When you mention "I visit Green Void in the morn and Cangwu in the eve", I know that Cangwu is in southern Chu, but where is the Green Void?

LÜ DONGBIN:

The way to Green Void lies ahead of you.

LU SHENG (*Laughs*):

You're hoaxing me.

LÜ DONGBIN:

Then, how are things going with you?

LU SHENG:

Thanks to the gods above, I reaped 7.8 hectolitres last year and 9.9 hectolitres this year.

LÜ DONGBIN:

That's enough for you.

LU SHENG (*Laughs*):

That's true.

> (*Rises to his feet suddenly, looks at his ragged fur-coat and sighs*)

The lucky star is so against me that I'm badly off.

LÜ DONGBIN:

From your appearance, I can see that you are tender-skinned, plump, healthy and talk in a

---

* The translation in quotation marks is by courtesy of *Chinese Literature* (Issue No.10, 1961).

pleasant mood. How can you be badly off?

> (*To the previous tune*)
>
> You enjoy good health
>
> And reap a bumper yield.
>
> We meet here like old friends.
>
> In a good shape, you do not have to pretend;
>
> You have every reason to be overjoyed.
>
> Why are you annoyed
>
> And do not think everything is perfect?
>
> You sigh that you are badly off;
>
> What is it that you expect?

LU SHENG:

You say that I am in a happy mood, but where's the happy mood in my poor life?

LÜ DONGBIN:

How can you be in a happy mood if you are not contented with your present state?

LU SHENG:

A gentleman must do merits to build a fame, be a high-ranking official or general, have sumptuous meals, listen to choice music, have a big family and live a luxurious life. Only in this way can he be in a happy mood.

> (*To the previous tune*)
>
> I am learned
>
> And aim high.
>
> To gain a high position,
>
> I was able to try.
>
> By now, I am score and ten,
>
> But still walk in the fields.
>
> How can I not be annoyed
>
> And think that everything is perfect?
>
> Old man,
>
> You said that I am not badly off,
>
> But what is there for me to expect?
>
> (*In a state of doziness*)

I am feeling dozy.

INNKEEPER:

You must be hungry. I'll prepare a meal of millet for you.

LU SHENG:

I'll take a nap on the bed.

> (*Goes to bed*)

There's no pillow here.

LÜ DONGBIN:

Lu Sheng, Lu Sheng, since you want to be in a happy mood all your life, I'll open the parcel and get a pillow for you.

(*Opens the parcel and gets the pillow for Lu Sheng*)

(*To the tune of* **Coda**)

You feel dizzy and fall asleep.

When you sleep on this pillow,

Everything will be perfect all the time.

Well, Innkeeper, go and

Make the meal of millet while his dream is deep.

(*Exit*)

LU SHENG (*Tosses and turns in bed*):

(*Inspects the pillow*)

(*To the tune of* **Lanhuamei**)

This pillow is not made of silk or rattan,

But seems to be made of some sort of jade.

Oh,

It is of stainless porcelain from Cizhou!

However,

How can there be holes at both ends?

(*Wipes his eyes*)

My sight is blurred, I'm afraid.

(*Looks round*)

The light is penetrating into the room. Maybe it's the sunlight.

(*To the previous tune*)

This room of half a hut is so bright;

Is it the setting sunlight?

Maybe it's because of my blurred eyesight.

Let me get up to take a look.

(*Gets out of bed and is astonished when he looks at the direction of the entrance*)

Why is it growing large and bright?

I'll jump into the gourd and see what is inside,

(*Jumps into the pillow*)

(*The pillow falls off*)

LU SHENG (*Turns to go*):

Alas, how comes this straight highway?

(*Walks on*)

What a huge scarlet wall!

(*To the tune of* **Chaotianzi**)

I walk along a sandy path

And see a residence where the wall turns.

Since the gate is open here, I'll enter the house without invitation.

When the copper ring rolls the curtain,

The flowers in the yard come into view,

Enshrouded in dense mist.

Who owns the residence, a duke or a marquis?

Who owns the residence, a duke or a marquis?

Inside the gate curtain is a big house with a spacious yard. When I look from outside, I can see a Taihu rockery in front of me. Within the hall I can see ancient paintings and lutes, an incense tripod, a bronze crane, green corals and red carpets.

(*To the previous tune*)

In the clean, quiet and well-furnished hall,

People seem to move behind the scarlet gate,

Behind the tiny windows.

VOICE WITHIN:

There's a stranger outside. Stop thief! Stop thief!

LU SHENG (*Flurried*):

I'll hurry down the corridor to avoid trouble.

VOICE WITHIN:

Shut the gate! Stop thief! Stop thief!

LU SHENG (*In a panic*):

What's to be done? The gate is tightly shut now. What luck that there is a hibiscus trellis nearby, where I can hide myself.

I'll keep my mouth shut,

Like fish out of water and a lotus flower on land.

I'll have to linger here;

I'll have to linger here.

(*Enter Maidservant*)

MAIDSERVANT (*Shouts*):

Where's the man? Please come here, mistress.

(*Enter Miss Cui, followed by Meixiang*)

MISS CUI (*To the tune of* **Bushilu**):

Like visionary waves and blooms,

A country girl's soul wanders here and there.

Transformed by an immortal,

I stay in the house and make myself fair.

I am from the family of Cui in Qinghe. This is my maidservant and that is Meixiang. I live in this huge residence and have not got married yet. Someone has entered the yard. Where can he be hiding now?

MAIDSERVANT:

In the thick leaves,

The man

must be hiding behind the hibiscus trellis.

(*Shouts*)

Why don't you come out, man?

We'll have you arrested and your legs broken.

LU SHENG (*Gets scared and comes out of hiding*):

Don't have me arrested. Here I come.

MAIDSERVANT:

None of your fine words! Hang your head!

> (*Grasps Lu Sheng, makes him lower his head and kowtow*)
>
> In this noble residence,
>
> We cannot tolerate your indecency.
>
> How dare you!
>
> How dare you!

MISS CUI:

Ask the man, where is his hometown, what is his first name and what is his last name.

LU SHENG (*To the previous tune*):

> A lover of books,
>
> I'm from the family of Lu to the east of Mount Taihang.
>
> On a leisurely walk,
>
> I've entered your house by mistake.

MISS CUI:

What are your family members?

LU SHENG:

> Alas,
>
> With no wife, no children, no parents.
>
> I'm living alone all by myself.

MAIDSERVANT:

You have no wife, and so you're loafing here?

LU SHENG:

By no means!

> You must know,
>
> A scholar is honest and obeys the law.
>
> How can I behave frivolously?
>
> How can I behave frivolously?

MISS CUI:

Tell the man to raise his head.

LU SHENG:

I dare not.

MAIDSERVANT:

My mistress allows you to raise your head.

LU SHENG (*Looks up*):

Oh, what a pretty lass!

MAIDSERVANT:

How dare you!

MISS CUI (*To the previous tune*):

> I'm from an age-old eminent family,
>
> A family out of the ordinary.

How crafty you are

To peep at a distinguished flower of a lady!

LU SHENG:

I dare not.

MISS CUI:

Meixiang,

Have him arrested at once.

MEIXIANG:

I have no rope with me.

MISS CUI:

The swing ropes are hanging high.

MEIXIANG:

I have no cudgel with me.

MISS CUI:

Give him a hard beating with a drum-stick.

LU SHENG:

How miserable I am! How miserable!

MAIDSERVANT:

Beg for pardon!

LU SHENG:

I know that I'll beg for pardon.

MAIDSERVANT:

The man is kowtowing and begging for pardon.

MISS CUI:

Since he's here either for an illicit affair or for theft, he will not escape punishment by the imperial law. Auntie, ask him whether he wants to settle the problem in private or in court. If he wants to settle it in private, he'll have to remain here and be my husband. If he wants to settle it in court he'll be sent to Qinghe County.

MAIDSERVANT (*To Lu Sheng*):

I've begged pardon for you. The mistress says that if you want to settle the problem in private, you'll have to remain here and be her husband. If you want to settle it in court, you'll be sent to Qinghe County.

LU SHENG:

I'd like to settle it in private.

MAIDSERVANT:

He's ever ready to comply.

(*To Miss Cui*)

Mistress, the scholar is ready to settle the problem in private.

MISS CUI:

In that case, he is pardoned and allowed to rise to his feet.

MAIDSERVANT:

The mistress allows you to rise to your feet.

(*Lu Sheng rises to his feet and laughs*)

MISS CUI (*Looks in an ashamed manner*):

Auntie, lower the curtain at once so that I won't see him.

As he is dressed in indecency,

You'd better

Take him to a bath down the corridor.

Bring word to me by then!

Bring word to me by then!

MAIDSERVANT:

Scholar, the mistress tells you to take a bath in the Fragrant Hall.

LU SHENG (*Smiles*):

She's simply making me embarrassed.

Beneath the eaves of a shed,

I have to bow my head.

(*Exit*)

(*Reenter Lu Sheng, ushered in by Maidservant*)

LU SHENG (*To the previous tune*):

My wife sent me to the Fragrant Hall,

To clean my hands, feet, brows, teeth and all.

MAIDSERVANT:

It's too early to speak of your wife.

Now that you've cleaned and shaved,

Kneel before the steps and cross your hands.

(*Lu Sheng stands respectfully*)

MAIDSERVANT (*To Miss Cui*):

Mistress, the man has taken a bath and changed his clothes.

MISS CUI:

What does he look like?

MAIDSERVANT:

In his intellectual brilliance,

He is now well-dressed and shows elegance.

MISS CUI (*In a low voice*):

What about his inner ability?

MAIDSERVANT (*Giggles lightly*):

Even if he is impotent,

You can play with him.

MISS CUI (*Laughs*):

None of your nonsense!

Roll up the curtain, Meixiang.

(*Meixiang rolls up the curtain*)

MISS CUI:

As I am eager for my first-night love,

Get the bamboo curtain ready at once.

> (*Lu Sheng kneels*)

MISS CUI (*Helps Lu Sheng to his feet*):

> A man has gold under his knees!
>
> A man has gold under his knees!

Lu Sheng, Lu Sheng, I'll keep you company out of pity for your poverty, but there must be a matchmaker. What is to be done?

MAIDSERVANT:

I'll act as your matchmaker so as not to delay your wedding date.

> (*Drumbeats and music within*)
>
> (*Maidservant presides over the wedding ceremony*)

MEIXIANG:

Man and wife drink the wedding wine.

MISS CUI (*Holds the wine in her hands*):

> (*To the tune of **Hexinlang***)
>
> Shy and coy,
>
> With the cup of wine,
>
> My face turns red and bright with joy.
>
> Living an easy and natural Iife,
>
> Why should I walk around like a fairy,
>
> Only to meet my lover?
>
> I grin,
>
> I smile,
>
> For I've become a wife.

ALL:

> The bed scene at night
>
> Is by no means a fright.

LU SHENG (*To the previous tune*):

> A bachelor at thirty years of age,
>
> I happen to stop over in Handan,
>
> In a shabby state.

Out of my expectation,

> I would make love in bed —
>
> A wretched man with a lovely mate.
>
> It will grow;
>
> It will thrust;
>
> It will reach its goal.

ALL:

> The bed scene at night
>
> Is by no means a fright.

MAIDSERVANT:

Man and wife are ready to enter the bridal chamber.

(Leads the way)

ALL *(To the tune of **Jiejiegao**)*:

    From the families of Cui and Lu,

    Two youngsters

    Met by chance and fell in love.

    When she told him to bathe and shave,

    He lost no time

    To make himself clean and tidy.

    His hat is shining bright

    While the lamp sheds tender light.

    Cui is from a house of great renown

    And Lu is a man in his prime.

    (To the previous tune)

    On a raft to cross the Milky Way,

    A man attracts the Weaver Star,

    Who marries him on the same day.

    Do not worry;

    Do not sigh;

    Joy reigns in the sky.

    The man is amazed to see the beauty,

    Who smiles and blows off the candlelight.

    They sleep together tonight

    And fetch the handkerchief when day is bright.

    *(To the tune of **Coda**)*

    Indeed,

    Spring is the best

    When they make love and take a rest.

MISS CUI:

Master Lu,

    By fate we have met and wed.

    I happen to make my wedding plan

    When a scholar comes in sight.

    Leave the porcelain pillow tonight

    As my elbow will support my man.

Scene Five
Recruiting Men of Worth

    (Enter Xiao Song with a manly beard)

XIAO SONG *(To the tune of **Shuangtianxiaojiao**)*:

The clouds and trees down in the south

Ignore the heir of households of renown.

The verdant grass seems to feel for me,

But where is the way to the capital town?

(*In the pattern of* **Collected Tang Poems**)

When vicissitudes of life occur to all,

No one would come to knock my door.

On lavish pleasure-seeking ground,

Who'd please the royal heirs that come around?

I am Xiao Song from Lanling, alias Yizhong. I am a descendent of Xiao Yan, Emperor Wu of Liang, and the grand grandson of Xiao Yu, Duke of Song. With the passage of time, everything in the world has changed. The ancient practice of the pen and the sword has been entirely abandoned, but the ancient interest in music and art has been retained. As I am heavily built with a manly beard, I am predicted to enjoy a long life and high position. Let's drop this subject. I have a sworn brother by the name of Pei Guangting, youngest son of Pei Xingjian, Magistrate of Wenxi County appointed by the capital governor. He is the son-in-law of Wu Sansi, a high-ranking official at the present time. He is well-versed in all the past and present anecdotes. However, he is a little bit jealous, a fault that goes with him all his life. As I haven't seen him for several days, I'm expecting him now.

(*Enter Pei Guangting, with a copy of an imperial edict in his sleeves*)

PEI GUANGTING (*To the previous tune*):

With precious books on my shelves,

I have blue blood in my vessels now.

With the imperial recruiting edict in my sleeves.

I'll go for exams without telling Xiao.

I, Pei Guangting, am well-learned but have not achieved anything yet. It happens that there comes an imperial edict to recruit men of worth. I'm sure that I can become the Number One Scholar, but Brother Xiao is my closest rival. An idea comes across my mind that I'll hide the imperial edict in my sleeves and go for the exam without revealing the truth to him.

(*Greets Xiao Song*)

XIAO SONG:

Brother, please excuse me for having not greeted you properly as I am not in a good mood these days.

PEI GUANGTING:

I've come to say good-bye to you as I'm going to take a sudden leave.

XIAO SONG:

Well, why are you leaving in such a hurry?

PEI GUANGTING:

I can tell you everything except this little privacy. Bye-bye.

XIAO SONG:

Brother, what's rustling in your sleeves?

PEI GUANGTING:

Nothing.

XIAO SONG (*Grabs and inspects*):

It's some yellow paper.

PEI GUANGTING (*Laughs*):

It's a Buddhist donation sheet.

XIAO SONG (*Seizes the paper and reads*):

"The divine emperor issues the following edict: The scholars all over the country may attend the imperial examination in the following middle March. I will decide the final result myself. The above edict must be publicised at once." Well, it's an imperial edict to recruit men of worth. Why are you hiding it in your sleeves?

PEI GUANGTING:

To tell you the truth, when the imperial edict to recruit men of worth arrived at our academy from the Ministry of Supervision, the teacher showed it to me. I thought about none but you because you are talented and will surely go for the examination. Therefore I hid the edict in my sleeves and would go to the capital city without telling you about it. I filled in my name only and sent in the application.

XIAO SONG (*Smiles*):

Is that possible? With so many scholars from all over the country, why do you just worry about me?

PEI GUANGTING (*To the tune of* **Zaoluopao**):

> There are numerous scholars,
>
> Whom I can beat
>
> In a word or two.
>
> All the others in the county are of no worth,
>
> While my only rival is you.

Brother, you will become the Number One Scholar as you are brilliant. If you go for the examination, I will become number two.

XIAO SONG (*Laughs*):

Now I see.

PEI GUANGTING:

> For Chang'e the fairy,
>
> There cannot be two lovers.
>
> When two join in a match,
>
> One will be the loser.
>
> Therefore, I will block your way.

XIAO SONG (*To the previous tune*):

> It's not easy to become a Number One Scholar;
>
> As fate may favour either of us,
>
> Who knows what will happen?
>
> You keep the edict to yourself,
>
> To prevent others from knowing about it.

For one thing, I can at least make way for you in the examination.

> If I bring my talent into full play,
>
> You are none of my rival.
>
> If I do not bring my talent into full play,
>
> You can still be my rival.
>
> I'll even give way on the final contest day.

PEI GUANGTING:

In that case, thank you for your kindness! Let's have a drink of Laurel Red at the inn.

XIAO SONG (*To the tune of* **Coda**):

> Before we finish two kettles of wine,
>
> We'll go to Chang'an the capital town.

Brother,

> The laurel will be either yours or mine.
>
> *Young scholars live a simple way of life*
>
> *To study classics in weathers hot and cold.*
>
> *When they have mastered arts of pen and sword,*
>
> *They serve the emperor with hearts of gold.*

Scene Six
Funding for the Imperial Examination

(Enter Miss Cui)

MISS CUI (*To the tune of* **Raochiyou**):

> To please my sweetheart
>
> I've done my best to give and take
>
> And stay by his side when I wake.
>
> *(Enter Maidservant and Meixiang in smiles)*

MAIDSERVANT, MEIXIANG:

> The man and wife embrace each other
>
> In bed in the dim light.
>
> What an enticing night!

MISS CUI (*In the pattern of* **Chounu'er**):

> *Inside scarlet walls with red blooms and quiet paths,*
>
> *Visitors seldom arrive.*

MAIDSERVANT:

> *With heavenly bliss,*
>
> *A stranger trespassed the yard.*

MEIXIANG:

> *When we found him behind the hibiscus trellis,*
>
> *He'd be punished in private or in court.*

MAIDSERVANT, MEIXIANG:

> *Now that he stays here,*
>
> *He's in ecstasy with his wife.*

MAIDSERVANT:

Sister, a Master Lu dropped from the sky.

MEIXIANG:

Not a Master Lu but a Master Donkey dropped from the sky.

MISS CUI:

You silly maids! You are telling the naked truth. As my family has not accepted a son-in-law without office for seven generations, I'll send him to attend the imperial examinations. What do you think about it?

MAIDSERVANT:

Wonderful! When he comes into office, you will become a distinguished lady.

> (*Enter Lu Sheng*)

LU SHENG (*To the tune of* **Busuanzi**):

> A long chat goes with a long night;
>
> A broad love goes with a broad quilt.
>
> A beauty graceful and coy
>
> Fills me with great joy.
>
> (*Lu Sheng and Miss Cui greet each other*)

MISS CUI:

Master Lu,

> (*In the pattern of* **Collected Tang Poems**)
>
> *You enjoy your life ignoring fame,*

LU SHENG:

> *As I enjoy Utopian life here best.*

MISS CUI:

> *With flower-brewed wine to entertain the guest,*

LU SHENG:

> *I have a fairy beauty to my claim.*

MISS CUI:

Master Lu, since I married you here, we've become man and wife. By enjoying ourselves day and night to the best of our hearts' content, we have tasted all the pleasures of human life. However, as my family has not accepted a son-in-law without office for seven generations, what do you think of your official career?

LU SHENG:

To tell you the truth, I've read all the classics but haven't made much progress in these years. Now that we are living a happy life by heavenly bliss, I won't care about an official career.

MISS CUI:

Alas, how can a scholar talk like this? May I ask how many examinations you have attended?

LU SHENG (*To the tune of* **Zhunu'er**):

> I have forgotten how many exams I attended,

But the examiners never mind what I write.

All those who are at the top of the list

Are from families of wealth and might.

ALL:

When fame and name

Come at the right time,

The prime minister will be yours to claim.

MISS CUI:

Families of wealth and might are not to blame. As you do not have many connections and you have not achieved fame, you have been delayed. Now that most of my relatives are in key positions, you have to pay respects to them when you arrive in Chang'an.

LU SHENG:

Yes, I see.

MISS CUI:

Besides, it's by no means easy to contact these high officials. With the help of my elder brother, you can easily become the Number One Scholar.

LU SHENG:

Will he do that for me?

MISS CUI:

No problem.

>(*To the previous tune*)

>As long as you have the help of my brother,

>I do not care about silver or gold.

But for him,

>You can hardly succeed;

>He will help you beat the others.

ALL:

>When fame and name

>Come at the right time,

>The prime minister will be yours to claim.

LU SHENG:

But I haven't met your brother yet.

MISS CUI:

Who do you think my brother is? He is money. All my money is at your disposal to do the bribery.

LU SHENG (*Smiles*):

Now I see. Thank you for your kindness. To answer for the imperial edict to recruit men of worth, I'll spend all the money you give me to induce the top officials and every word in my essays will become a pearl in their eyes.

MISS CUI:

That's it. Meixiang, fetch some wine to see my man off.

>(*Hands over the wine*)

(*To the tune of* **Yanlaihong**)

Fill the golden cup with wine

And rein the horse to see off my man.

Without a word he looks at the cup and drains it;

Then he refills the cup

And retains his tears at best he can.

ALL:

With straining eyes

We shall expect your success

And hope for good news without surprise.

LU SHENG (*To the previous tune*):

A muddle-headed country scholar

Wins a wife with ambition,

Who gives me gold for my fame.

I hold her hands for a long time,

Before taking a short leave to win a good name.

ALL:

With straining eyes

We shall expect your success

And hope for good news without surprise.

MISS CUI (*Makes a bow*):

(*To the tune of* **Coda**)

You will come back as a renowned spouse;

During this trip,

Be sure not to trespass any place

And I'll be expecting you with knitted brows.

While the emperor values men of worth,

What really values is wealth.

If essays can be done by stealth,

How much is a Number One Scholar worth?

Scene Seven
Rivalling for the Number One Scholar

(*Enter Yuwen Rong*)

YUWEN RONG (*To the tune of* **Yexingchuan**):

Yuwen is a family from Late Wei,

With power and energy in its heyday.

A commanding power

At the royal court,

I stand at the head of ministers.

(*In the pattern of* **Collected Tang Poems**)

With ancestor's power at my back,

I have made another fresh start.

With the best scholars at my heels,

I have followers in every craft and art.

I am Yuwen Rong, Left Prime Minister and Inspector of National Taxation in the Tang Dynasty. I am fond of slanders and good at bribery. When the imperial edict was issued to recruit men of worth, I was entrusted by His Majesty to mark the papers and recommend the best scholars. All my life I have catered to the taste of His Majesty and ingratiated myself to those in power. I've found among the papers one written by a Xiao Song from Lanling County, who is indeed a rare talent, a rare talent. Although he is the descendent of Emperor Wu of Liang, the ruler of the former dynasty, I do not care so much about it. There is also a Pei Guangting from Wenxi County, son of the late prime minister Pei Xingjian and son-in-law of Wu Sansi. He is not so talented as Xiao Song, but I'll rank him as the first and Xiao Song as the second. I've submitted my proposal to His Majesty, but I don't know what His Majesty thinks about it. When the eunuch arrives, I'll try to find out what His Majesty thinks. Attendants, wait outside the door.

(*Enter Eunuch Gao*)

EUNUCH GAO (*To the tune of* **Fendie'er**):

From the palace the green scholar-tree leaves

Reach the examination-room eaves.

ATTENDANT (*Announces*):

Here comes Eunuch Gao, the Ritual Missionary.

YUWEN RONG (*Hurries to greet Eunuch Gao*):

If I had known about your arrival, I would have gone a long way to meet you.

EUNUCH GAO:

It's so kind of you, Your Excellency. I know that you have been busy marking the papers these days.

YUWEN RONG:

I'm just going to submit a secret report to you. May I ask whether His Majesty has decided on the Number One Scholar?

EUNUCH GAO:

Yes.

YUWEN RONG:

Is it Pei Guangting?

EUNUCH GAO:

No.

YUWEN RONG:

Is it Xiao Song?

EUNUCH GAO:

Mention some other name.

YUWEN RONG:

I don't remember the names after them.

EUNUCH GAO:

You know,

> (*To the tune of* **Yifengshu**)
>
> His Majesty has read the papers all along
>
> And decided on Scholar Lu from the east of Mount Taihang.

YUWEN RONG (*Thinks hard*):

Scholar Lu from the east of Mount Taihang?

EUNUCH GAO:

His name is Lu Sheng.

> I don't know how his essay
>
> Has pleased His Majesty.

YUWEN RONG:

Eunuch Gao, has His Majesty indeed decided on Lu Sheng?

EUNUCH GAO:

> I saw His Majesty write on his paper
>
> And Lu Sheng will soon be bestowed the robe of honour.

ALL:

> To attend the royal banquet
>
> As the Number One,
>
> He beat the others and won.

YUWEN RONG:

How strange, how strange! Then, where do Pei and Xiao rank?

EUNUCH GAO:

Xiao ranks second and Pei ranks third.

YUWEN RONG (*To the previous tune*):

> (*Aside*)
>
> I have decided on Xiao and Pei,
>
> But how does it fall on the bastard Lu?
>
> (*To Eunuch Gao*)
>
> It is indeed by fate
>
> That he is held in esteem by the great.

EUNUCH GAO:

You know, it's not His Majesty's views alone. Lu Sheng has got acquainted with all the powerful men in the court and they all say that he is the most talented. I myself have seen his graceful calligraphy.

YUWEN RONG:

I see.

> He knows how to push forward his essay,
>
> But I am blind in the broad day.

ALL:

To attend the royal banquet

As the Number One,

He beat the others and won.

EUNUCH GAO:

I must take leave now. Your Excellency is to attend the royal banquet tomorrow.

(*To the tune of* **Coda**)

In the royal garden you'll help to entertain.

YUWEN RONG:

Of course you'll sit at the front.

EUNUCH GAO (*Smiles*):

I can walk around at the royal court,

Able to assist those who'd like to win fame and name.

(*Exit*)

YUWEN RONG (*To himself*):

How ridiculous, how ridiculous! I've decided on a Number One Scholar, but Lu Sheng has manoeuvred to grab the title and he didn't even curry favour with me!

The royal court can hardly be controlled

And I am getting angry from day to day.

If high positions can be bought with gold,

He who ranks high needn't write an essay.

Scene Eight
Royal Banquet

(*Enter the Royal Chef, wearing a kerchief and a flower on his head*)

ROYAL CHEF:

I am a chef for the Royal Banquet Hall, number one among the 300 chefs. I can cut thin slices and use right seasonings. I can knead glossy steamed bread and make straight noodles. I can also make light pastry and tasty delicacies. So many dishes are served at a banquet that they are more for sight than for taste. The taste of my dishes makes people enticed and the sight of my dishes makes their mouths water. I have cooked not only for the ministers but also for the royal house. Emperor Xuanzong is most fond of my green-onion sausage and Empress Taizhen is most fond of my palace-style dumplings. As a louse was found in a soup for the royal house, I was cudgelled by my superior and dismissed from service. Thanks to the help of my adopted nephew, I was re-employed under a false name.

VOICE WITHIN:

Who is your nephew?

ROYAL CHEF:

He is the most popular ballad-singer in the present day, writing ballads under Eunuch Gao's name. If you ask me why I wear a flower on my head today, I'll tell you that I am here to prepare the royal banquet for the successful scholars in the imperial examinations. First I'll serve light refreshments of all sorts to go with the wine, then I'll serve dishes of various kinds. There are no such things as ritual beef or Xuanzhou chestnuts. In one dish there are half a dozen pieces of shepherd's purse; half a bottle of wine contains some vinegar. A spoonful or two of rice will go with regular tubers of pinellia.

VOICE WITHIN:

Why?

ROYAL CHEF:

You know, as these scholars have suffered from starvation, the tubers of pinellia are good for their stomachs. So much for the random talk. There is a royal banquet today to be held beside the Qujiang Pool for the new Number One Scholar. The imperial edict goes that the examiner Master Yuwen will be the acting host. Here come the guards of honour.

(*Enter Yuwen Rong*)

YUWEN RONG (*To the tune of* **Yejinmen, Part One**):

When the contest is over,

His Majesty offers a royal banquet.

I was once bestowed the royal banquet cake,

But now I can only sigh for old time's sake.

I, Yuwen Rong, am to be the acting host for the royal banquet at the Qujiang Pool. As the new Number One Scholar ranks far behind in the examinations, I am not in a good mood to meet him. Since he is an energetic young man, I shall be flattering him a bit. Ask the chef in the Royal Banquet Hall whether the banquet is ready.

ROYAL CHEF (*On his knees*):

Everything is ready except that the Troupe of Court Music has not arrived yet.

(*Enter the singers*)

SINGERS:

Essays are written in the imperial exam;

Singers are summoned at the royal banquet.

Your Excellency, the singers are kowtowing to you.

YUWEN RONG:

Tell me your names.

SINGER A:

My name is Curtain Show.

SINGER B:

My name is Flower Show.

SINGER C:

My name is Cauldron Show.

YUWEN RONG:

How can you be named like this?

ROYAL CHEF:

I know what her name means. After song and dance, these singers just eat ready food. However, this Cauldron Show serves in the kitchen of the Royal Banquet Hall.

YUWEN RONG:

In that case, she is a cook.

ROYAL CHEF:

That's it. She'll come and soothe Your Excellency.

YUWEN RONG:

Nonsense! Here comes the Number One Scholar. You singers greet him in the distance.

(*Enter Lu Sheng, Xiao Song and Pei Guangting, followed by guards of honour*)

LU SHENG, XIAO SONG, PEI GUANGTING (*To the tune of **Yejinmen, Part Two***):

> We parade the street to show our power
>
> And engrave our names on the city tower.

SINGERS (*Greet the scholars*):

Singers from the Troupe of Court Music are waiting here to greet the Number One Scholar.

LU SHENG, XIAO SONG, PEI GUANGTING (*Laugh*):

Rise to your feet. Rise to your feet.

LU SHENG:

> Thank you for your attendance,
>
> With your song and dance.

YUWEN RONG (*Greets the scholars*):

Come in please, distinguished scholars.

> (*Makes a bow*)
>
> *In search for stalwart steeds,*
>
> *We obtain kylins indeed.*
>
> *When you come to the palace by day,*
>
> *Your brilliance is at full play.*

Congratulations on your great success. I admire you from the bottom of my heart.

LU SHENG:

I owe all my success to the grace of His Majesty.

XIAO SONG, PEI GUANGTING:

We owe all our success to your promotion.

YUWEN RONG:

The royal banquet is indeed a grand fete.

LU SHENG:

As I know there were only some elderly musicians at the banquet in the past, how is it that there are such excellent players this time?

YUWEN RONG:

As His Majesty decided on the Number One Scholar by himself this time, I have paid special attention to the selection.

LU SHENG:

Oh, I see.

YUWEN RONG:

Serve wine!

ROYAL CHEF:

>*Flowers blossom within palace wall*
>*While wine is served in the banquet hall.*

YUWEN RONG (*Presents wine*):

>(*To the tune of* **Xianghuanglong**)
>The Civil Star in the sky
>Shines bright in the royal court
>And rises high.
>The palace wine
>At the royal banquet
>Makes the scholars' faces ashine.

LU SHENG:

>After all the strife
>In my life,
>I've won my fame at heaven's bliss.

XIAO SONG, PEI GUANGTING:

>Enjoy ourselves,
>Drink the wine
>And our demeanour is not fine.

SINGERS (*To the previous tune*):

>Who knows!
>If heaven does not have a feeling heart,
>How can the laurel-holder come
>And Chang'e the fairy queen take part?
>In the elegant world,
>How can the beauties refrain
>From respecting scholars of fame?
>Hush!
>I'll make you happy in bed
>And turn your face red.
>To leave your name,
>Even in a whorehouse
>You can write a poem without shame.

YUWEN RONG:

Sir, as she is inviting you, I shall serve as the matchmaker.

>(*Lu Sheng laughs*)

YUWEN RONG:

Singer, ask for a poem from the Number One Scholar.

LU SHENG:

I'll do that. Where shall I write?

SINGER A:

I have a red handkerchief here.

>   (*Lu Sheng writes*)

YUWEN RONG (*Reads the poem*):

>   *The pretty maiden urges me to write,*
>   *Here I am: His Majesty's student in smiles.*
>   *As His Majesty stands on my side,*
>   *I do not need a matchmaker to find a wife.*

ALL:

What a wonderful poem!

YUWEN RONG:

He seems to have used some phrases to scoff at me.

XIAO SONG:

Master Lu would not have done that.

PEI GUANGTING:

Singer, serve more wine.

>   (*To the tune of* **Huanglonggun**)
>   Together we rank high in the exam;
>   Together we drink nectar here.
>   To be a tiger or to be a dragon,
>   We share the honour alike.
>   Who is to be scoffed?
>   Who is to be lucky?
>   Together we tour the city tower,
>   Inscribe our names
>   And enjoy the grand sight.
>   (*Enter Messenger*)

MESSENGER:

Report, report, report! The imperial edict announces that Master Lu has been appointed Master of the Royal Academy and Edict Drafter; Master Xiao and Master Pei have both been appointed Editors of the Royal Academy. Singers from the Troupe of Court Music are to accompany them to the Royal Academy.

YUWEN RONG:

Congratulations!

>   (*To the previous tune*)
>   He writes the poem in a good hand
>   And rides the horse in good command.
>   Song and music spread in warm spring breeze;
>   Talk and laughter cross the curtain at ease.
>   He has an upright figure,

Behaving in elegant ways.

When he stands

Before the pavilion,

He wins popular praise.

(*Lu Sheng, Xiao Song and Pei Guangting mount horses*)

YUWEN RONG:

Respected scholars,

(*To the tune of* **Coda**)

You shall approach the palace

And rank high in office —

A reward for your persistent efforts.

(*Exeunt all except Yuwen Rong*)

YUWEN RONG (*Sneers*):

Ridiculous, ridiculous! This Lu Sheng becomes the Number One Scholar and behaves arrogantly because he is not my student. I fawned on him by saying, "As she is inviting you, I shall serve as the matchmaker." When he was asked to write a poem, the second line "*Here I am: His Majesty's student in smiles*" was an overt suggestion that he was not my student. Leave this line alone. Well, his fourth line went as far as to say, "*I do not need a matchmaker to find a wife.*" Didn't he want to use such a matchmaker as myself? I'll find some way to do away with him. As he has just been granted a title by the imperial edict, I'll pick bones when he makes mistakes in his function as the Edict Drafter.

> *This young scholar puts on airs*
> *And relies entirely on his essays.*
> *Not until he meets difficult affairs*
> *Will he know someone who betrays.*

Scene Nine
Tribal Invasion

(*Enter Re Longmang and Xi Naluo*)

RE LONGMANG, XI NALUO (*To the tune of* **Nouthern Dianjiangchun**):

The desert is immense

And the Tianshan Mountain rises high —

Thirty thousand feet to the sky.

The dragon and the tiger serve the king alike;

The general and the prime minister stand side by side.

XI NALUO:

I am Xi Naluo, the Tubo Prime Minister.

RE LONGMANG:

I am Re Longmang, the Tubo General.

XI NALUO, RE LONGMANG:

The king is holding a session. Let's wait here.

>   (*Enter the Tubo King, followed by his attendants*)

TUBO KING (*To the previous tune*):

>   White grass and Mongolian gazelles,
>
>   Tens of thousands of huts and tents —
>
>   My possessions have grown.
>
>   I will never submit to Tang,
>
>   When I sit firmly on my throne.
>
>   (*Greets the General and the Prime Minister*)
>
>   *Camels travel to the west of Qinghai Lake*
>
>   *While Mount Bailan abounds in wind and snow.*
>
>   *I have steeds and men at my command,*
>
>   *And the Green Jade River area as my land.*

I am the Tubo King. My ancestor Bald Wugu was the Emperor of Southern Liang. My mother Princess Golden City became the Tubo Queen. With growing population, the tribe is becoming strong and prosperous. We have formed an alliance with the Tang Dynasty by a vow of Golden Goose, but their border generals have often harassed us with armed forces. I am about to summon you to discuss the manoeuvring of our troops.

XI NALUO, RE LONGMANG:

With Song and Liang to the east, He and Shan to the west, Borneo to the south and Turkey to the north, our nation has a hundred thousand troops and a thousand herds of horses.

XI NALUO:

I shall manage the internal affairs.

RE LONGMANG:

I shall go and expand our territory. I shall seize cities and capture officers. The Tang Dynasty will give no cause for anxiety.

TUBO KING:

Which region shall we attack first?

XI NALUO:

We'll grab Hexi first and attack Longyou later.

TUBO KING:

So that's settled. General Longmang is to attack Gua and Sha; Prime Minister Naluo is to provide reinforcements. Warriors, act according to my order!

>   (*All respond*)

TUBO KING (*To the tune of **Qingjiangyin***):

>   From the west
>
>   Comes the Tubo general —
>
>   General Re Longmang.
>
>   The Tubo drums beat;
>
>   The Tubo cymbals sound;

The Tubo horns ring all around.

(*To the previous tune*)

To cross the Tianshan Mountain,

We rely on Prime Minister Xi Naluo,

Who is endowed with wit and powers.

The commanding flags sweep over the nation of Qiang;

The swords point to the nation of Tang;

Their territories will be ours!

A hundred thousand Tubo troops are invincible;

They shoot at gazelles on unsaddled steeds.

Dust and fire arise around the Yinshan Mountain:

Liangzhou regions are the first battlefields.

Scene Ten
Taking a Provincial Office

(*Enter Miss Cui, followed by Meixiang*)

MISS CUI (*To the tune of* **Qiniangzi**):

Number One Scholar for three years,

My man left on horseback —

The sight flashes before my eyes.

Now that another spring is half way through,

With a flower in my hand, I make up with deep sighs.

(*In the pattern of* **Haoshijin**)

To help my man with his career,

I spent all the money I had.

MEIXIANG:

Since the scholar was gone,

She has been living all alone.

MISS CUI:

When I toss and turn in bed,

I regret that I have sent him away.

MEIXIANG:

To worry that beauty fades day by day,

She would sigh and moan.

MISS CUI:

Meixiang, when I lived a secluded life in a remote yard, I met my man at heaven's bliss. We were enjoying ourselves when it suddenly occurred to me that I would send him to the capital to take the imperial examination in the hope of winning an official rank. He became the Number One Scholar and that fulfilled my wishes. Thanks to the grace of His Majesty, he has been assigned to draft the imperial edicts. However, he is not allowed to return home within three years. I am indeed tormented with lovesickness!

(*To the tune of* **Zhenxianxiang**)

We chanced to form the wedlock

And enjoyed wine and music to our hearts' content.

Now that my man has gone far, far away,

I fear to look out of the window.

Amid willow catkins the orioles no longer sing;

Amid blooming flowers the swallows no longer dart.

I gaze and gaze,

Full of worry and woe,

Which are piled on my brows.

(*Enter Messenger*)

MESSENGER:

Report, report, report! The Number One Scholar is about to arrive.

(*Exit*)

MISS CUI (*Pleasantly surprised*):

My man is about to return in honour. Get ready for a banquet.

(*Enter Lu Sheng, followed by his attendants*)

LU SHENG (*To the tune of* **Wangwuxiang**):

Above green lawns and red blooms,

The wind spreads fragrant dusts.

A girl looks pretty by wearing a flower;

A man looks valiant by riding a stalwart horse.

As I am eager to go home,

I wave my whip

And ask the way from time to time —

The house of Cui is in Qinghe County.

(*Greets Miss Cui*)

MISS CUI:

Master Lu, so you have returned in honour.

LU SHENG:

Congratulations to you.

I whipped my way home all the way;

MISS CUI:

That's why the magpies sang early in the day.

LU SHENG:

Now that I have brought an edict from His Majesty,

MISS CUI:

Your renown makes me happy and gay.

I've heard that since you became the Number One Scholar, you have been appointed Edict Drafter for three years in the Central Office. How is it that you are coming home at this time of the year?

LU SHENG:

You are still in the dark. As I am the Edict Drafter, I wrote an edict to grant you a title, submitted it to His Majesty among other edicts and was approved. I've come by night to present you the edict without letting His Majesty know about it.

MISS CUI:

Thank you for your considerations. Master Lu, how did you become the Number One Scholar?

LU SHENG:

Thanks to the money you gave me, I made friends with the elite in the court. They persuaded His Majesty to pick out my paper and nominate me as the Number One Scholar.

MISS CUI:

Alas, you nearly fell to the second place!

LU SHENG (*To the tune of Yufurong*):

> As all the essays are new,
>
> They must be acknowledged by His Majesty.
>
> With palace flowers on my head,
>
> I drank at the royal banquet with honour.
>
> To see me on horseback in high spirits,
>
> Ladies behind pearled curtains would ask, "Whose husband is this?"
>
> You are destined to be a distinguished lady,
>
> With a floral crown on your head.
>
> As of old, Zhuo Wenjun helped her man
>
> To aim high and realise his dream.

MISS CUI (*To the previous tune*):

> You were lucky by birth
>
> To meet a fairy of a wife.
>
> As soon as we met,
>
> We closed the door and started our nuptial life.
>
> I cast my amorous eyes on you,
>
> The amorous eyes of an attractive maiden.
>
> You have succeeded in the imperial exam
>
> And I win the title of County Lady now.
>
> But in all these days,
>
> I have been missing you with knitted brows.

VOICE WITHIN:

Report, report, report! Here comes the official messenger.

(*Enter Official Messenger*)

OFFICIAL MESSENGER:

Running east and going west — that's the official messenger.

(*Bows to Lu Sheng*)

Master Lu, it is odd indeed. When you have obtained the edict and sped home, Master Yuwen found out the trick, and reported to His Majesty, but His Majesty pardoned you. Beyond the

Huayin Mountain there is a Shanzhou city on the way to the east capital. Blocked by rocks, there is no thoroughfare for two hundred and eighty miles. The imperial edict goes that you have been appointed Magistrate of Shanzhou to break the rocks and dig a canal there. You are required to start for your new office without delay.

LU SHENG, MISS CUI:

In that case, get ready for the horse and carriage and we'll go to Shanzhou at once.

> (*To the tune of* **Coda**)
> A scholar with a meagre pay
> Has to manage the Heyang canal.

As man and wife,

> By horse and carriage we'll start on our way.
> *After serving three years in the court,*
> *The scholar returned home with grace.*
> *With imperial edict to dig a canal,*
> *He has to earn his bread in a strange place.*

Scene Eleven
Digging the Canal

> (*Enter the Project Inspector*)

PROJECT INSPECTOR (*To the tune of* **Puxian'ge**):

> Water flows near the Shanzhou Prefecture
> While the road is dry with rocks.
> It has been over a month
> Since the magistrate came to dig the canal.
> It is my turn to check on the project today.

I, a native of Maha, was once enlisted in the capital camp. With some manoeuvring, I became a private adviser to the Shanzhou magistrate. The road from Shanzhou to the capital is two hundred and eighty-eight miles of rocks. It needs a lot of manpower and animal power to transport grain from the east capital to the west capital. There is damage and spoilage on the way and repeated embezzlement of payment. As it is difficult to deal with the complaints lodged by the people, the superiors have decided to dig a canal. Magistrate Lu has agreed to dispense some emergent expenditure. The project has been going on for over a month, but there comes not a single drop of water. The magistrate has told me to check on the project. All the engineers have been doing well, but the Administrative Chief has resorted to various reasons not to report to me. I'll give him a sound beating when he arrives.

> (*Enter the Administrative Chief, holding sacrificial paper money in his hands*)

ADMINISTRATIVE CHIEF (*To the tune of* **Zizishuang**):

> I am the Administrative Chief for ten households,

And ten times of ten households.

The canal diggers try to sneak away

And I have to check the number.

I go from door to door

For trifles.

The Project Inspector tries to extort from me

And I have no way out.

(*Bows to the Project Inspector*)

PROJECT INSPECTOR (*Annoyed*):

Why hasn't that son of a bitch come to wait on me at this late hour?

ADMINISTRATIVE CHIEF (*Kowtows*):

I do not dare to offend you.

PROJECT INSPECTOR:

How come we have not seen a single drop of water now that the project has been going on for over a month?

ADMINISTRATIVE CHIEF:

I don't mean to offend you. Water is the blood of the earth; do you take it as my piss?

PROJECT INSPECTOR:

You bastard! You are in charge of water and you drink water, but do you want to shirk your responsibility?

ADMINISTRATIVE CHIEF:

I am to blame. Here is some paper money for you.

PROJECT INSPECTOR (*Annoyed*):

You son of a bitch! Are you giving me sacrificial paper money?

ADMINISTRATIVE CHIEF:

As the canal has not been completed yet, Magistrate Lu is leading the conscripted labourers and Administrative Chiefs to make a bow at every three steps. They will soon arrive at the Temple of King Yu. This paper money will be offered to King Yu; do you think that it cannot be offered to you?

PROJECT INSPECTOR (*In a panic*):

Alas! The magistrate is going to offer sacrifice in the temple. Why didn't you let me know earlier? Go and burn the joss-sticks and lay the mat at once!

(*Enter Lu Sheng, followed by attendants and labourers*)

LU SHENG (*To the tune of **Lülüjin***):

The mountain is rocky;

The rocks are craggy.

Sweat and blood goes with shovels and spades;

The expenses come from the people.

(*The Project Inspector greets Lu Sheng*)

LU SHENG:

I shall sweep the Divine Temple

And pay tribute to King Yu.

When the water route is cleared for ships and rafts,

I shall come again and requite you.

PROJECT INSPECTOR:

The joss-sticks and sacrificial paper money are ready.

LU SHENG (*Bows*):

(*To the tune of **Jiang'ershui***)

King Yu is here

To accept our consecration.

The rocky road is so slippery

As to hinder the grain carts;

Therefore we are digging a canal to conduct water.

ALL:

When the mountain god opens a way

And the river god arrives,

In a prosperous nation the people will stay.

ALL (*Bow*):

(*To the previous tune*)

To move the rocks for a long way

Is difficult indeed.

It is hard to work with official pay

And it costs a lot to escape from work.

ALL:

When the mountain god opens a way

And the river god arrives,

In a prosperous nation the people will stay.

LU SHENG:

The rites are over. Tell the Heads of Ten Households: one is in charge of ten households and ten are in charge of a hundred households. Beat the drums to inspire work and by no means slack off.

(*All respond*)

(*Drumbeats within*)

LU SHENG (*To the tune of **Guizhixiang***):

You know,

The granaries in Taiyuan are small

And the pass in Lintong is narrow,

Let alone the Dizhu and Sanmen regions

And the regions where we cut the reed-roots.

Look at the mud, sand and rocks,

Look at the mud, sand and rocks!

We have no way to deal with

The mountain that blocks our way.

How miserable it is!

ALL:

We can endure the hardships.

LU SHENG:

> In order to get a single drop of water,
>
> People have to pay with blood and wealth.
>
> (*Drumbeats within*)

ALL (*In surprise*):

That's it, that's it! Master Lu, the water is coming from the east.

LU SHENG (*Pleased*):

I hear the roaring of water.

ALL (*To the previous tune*):

> The passage for the Yellow River
>
> Is allotted by the Mianchi Lake,
>
> From the west of the Princess River
>
> To the Sun Bridge.
>
> Look at the blue water,
>
> Look at the blue water!
>
> We cannot see the water now,
>
> But it is bound to flow here.
>
> How happy we are!

LU SHENG:

We haven't reached the other side of the mountain yet.

ALL:

> We are quenching our thirst by looking at the plums,
>
> But water will come in floods when the time comes.
>
> (*Dig with shovels but to no avail*)

Well, how is it that the shovels won't work?

> (*Look ahead*)

Master Lu, the previous mountains are earthen mountains with a covering of rocks. Now we are facing two rocky mountains: one is called Chicken-Feet Mountain and the other is called Bear-Ear Mountain. The shovels won't work.

LU SHENG (*Thinks aside*):

Chicken-Feet Mountain and Bear-Ear Mountain? When King Yu dug the Gorge of Three Gates in the ancient times, he employed all the five basic elements.

> (*To the labourers*)

Since iron won't work with Chicken Feet and Bear Ear, I'll boil them with salt and vinegar.

ALL (*Laugh*):

Do we have such huge cauldrons?

LU SHENG:

I do not need cauldrons. Just fetch tons of salt and vinegar from the prefecture.

ALL (*Respond and exeunt. Reenter with salt and vinegar*):

Here are salt and vinegar.

LU SHENG:

Get a million bunches of dry wood to burn this mountain. Then sprinkle it with vinegar, hit it with shovel-sticks and the hard rocks will split. Finally spread over the mountain with salt and the rocks will melt into water.

ALL (*Laugh*):

Is it possible?

> (*Set fire to the mountain*)
>
> (*To the tune of* **Dayagu**)
>
> It is a waste of firewood to burn the rocks
>
> And set fire and lightning to the south,
>
> With thunders that crack the cliffs.

Oh, the mountain has turned into charcoal.

LU SHENG:

Get the vinegar at once!

ALL (*Beat drums and sprinkle vinegar*):

> The mountain god used to be a sour scholar,
>
> But will soon suffer from vinegar.
>
> Who would have expected
>
> Such miracles!
>
> (*Laugh*)

Strange, strange! The chicken feet and the bear ears are now well-done!

LU SHENG:

Apply your shovels and axes to the mountain at once to dig a canal.

> (*All beat drums and shovel the mountain*)

LU SHENG (*To the previous tune*):

> The picks peck at the red cliffs,
>
> Which crackle like fish scales and tortoise shells,
>
> Reduced into powder when they split.

Spread salt to make water!

ALL (*Beat drums and spread salt*):

> As spring water flows when snow thaws,
>
> So verdant mountains appear when fire is out.
>
> (*Go on digging*)
>
> (*In astonishment*)

Water is coming from the river source!

> (*Laugh*)
>
> Water-fowl will fly;
>
> Boats and rafts will pass by.

LU SHENG:

My people, the grand feat is accomplished and the canal is completed. We'll cast an iron bull on the riverbank to anchor ships, with its head to the south of the river and its tail to the north of the river. On the one hand, we shall hurry to transport grain to the capital

and attract merchants to bring their merchandise from all over the country; on the other hand, we shall report to His Majesty and invite Him to make an eastern tour to view the beautiful sights and the efforts of the Shanzhou people.

ALL:

Thank you, Master Lu. We shall plant willows along the river to add beauties to the scenes.

LU SHENG (*To the tune of* **Coda**):

> We shall plant willows along the riverbanks
>
> And beg His Majesty to make a tour to the east.

ALL:

> We shall cast an iron bull that will stand forever.
>
> *Having reduced our labour to the least,*
>
> *We are willing to cast an iron beast.*
>
> *When His Majesty hears of this,*
>
> *He will make a tour to the east.*

Scene Twelve
Border Crisis

(*Enter Wang Junchuo, followed by his soldiers*)

WANG JUNCHUO (*To the tune of* **Xidijin**):

> I've braved the ice and waves
>
> And broken the ridges of Mount Jishi.
>
> I've captured rebel kings
>
> And slaughtered their generals;
>
> Stained with frost is my battle robe.
>
> *With warriors standing on my side,*
>
> *The war is looming far and wide.*
>
> *Without the title of a lord,*
>
> *I always carry a bloody sword.*

I am Royal General Wang Junchuo, the Military Commander of Liangzhou. I am a native of Changle County, Guazhou Prefecture. A valiant warrior all my life, I am good at horsemanship and swordsmanship. With the grace of His Majesty, I have been promoted to this position due to my military achievements. I command the troops in Longyou and Hexi to guard the Great Wall against the Tubo tribes. It is said that the Tubo tribes have launched an invasion with strong armed forces, but I don't know who is their commander yet. Now that I shall fight him in the battlefield, how bold and fearless I am!

> (*To the tune of* **Shanhuazi**)
>
> The elderly general brings peace to the nation,
>
> Together with the valiant royal soldiers.
>
> The flags are arranged according to the zodiac,

With the general in the centre of the battle array.

(*Drumbeats within*)

ALL:

There come the drumbeats,

Roaring like thunder.

The soldiers wave their swords and spears,

With their helmets shining like the sun

And their steeds sweeping on the battlefields.

Blessed by His Majesty,

They'll succeed on the border areas.

(*Enter Messenger*)

MESSENGER:

Report, report, report! The Tubo general Re Longmang is galloping towards us.

WANG JUNCHUO:

Get into battle formation and move forward.

(*Marches on*)

(*To the tune of **Qingjiangyin***)

The Tang Dynasty abounds in valiant warriors;

The enemy cannot hinder their movements.

The soldiers hurry on

With the formation stretching long.

To conquer the Tubo troops,

I'll capture the vanguard Re Longmang.

(*Exit*)

(*Enter Re Longmang, followed by his soldiers*)

RE LONGMANG, TUBO SOLDIERS (*To the tune of **Qingjiangyin***):

From the west

Comes the Tubo general —

General Re Longmang.

The Tubo drums beat;

The Tubo cymbals sound;

The Tubo horns ring all around.

(*Enter Wang Junchuo, followed by his soldiers. Wang Junchuo and Re Longmang announce their names respectively*)

RE LONGMANG:

I am the Tubo General Re Longmang. Who are you that dare to fight with me?

WANG JUNCHUO:

I am General Wang Junchuo to fight you here. Take no time to surrender, take no time to surrender!

(*Fighting starts. Re Longmang feigns to be defeated. Exeunt Wang Junchuo and his soldiers, chasing after Re Longmang*)

(*Enter Xi Naluo, followed by his soldiers*)

XI NALUO, TUBO SOLDIERS (*To the tune of* **Qingjiangyin**):

> To cross the Tianshan Mountain,
>
> We rely on Prime Minister Xi Naluo,
>
> Who is endowed with wit and powers.
>
> The commanding flags sweep over the nation of Qiang;
>
> The swords point to the nation of Tang;
>
> Their territories will be ours!

XI NALUO:

I, the Tubo Prime Minister Xi Naluo, am in ambush here to reinforce General Re Longmang. The other day I taught him with a book on the arts of war that if he feigns to be defeated, the Tang soldiers will definitely chase after him, and that if I launch an attack from behind, the Tang soldiers will surely be put to rout. Warriors, rush to the south of the pass and then turn to the west so as to capture the Tang general.

> (*The soldiers respond. Exeunt all*)
>
> (*Enter Re Longmang, chased by Wang Junchuo. They are locked in fight*)
>
> (*Enter Xi Naluo, followed by his soldiers*)

XI NALUO:

Wang Junchuo, Wang Junchuo! Stop for a while to meet the Tubo Prime Minister!

WANG JUNCHUO (*In a panic*):

Alas! I've fallen into their traps! I've fallen into their traps! Soldiers, fight to the last!

> (*Attacked by Re Longmang and Xi Naluo, Wang Junchuo is defeated and killed*)
>
> (*Re Longmang and Xi Naluo greet each other*)

RE LONGMANG:

Thanks to your reinforcement, we have won a complete victory.

XI NALUO:

Now that the Tang soldiers are defeated and their general killed, let's take this opportunity to seize the Yumen Pass without delay!

> *Spur the horses into the dragons' speeds*
>
> *And we shall kill the foes and do heroic deeds.*
>
> *Even if that nation has vast lands,*
>
> *It is controlled all in my very hands.*

Scene Thirteen
Expecting the Imperial Inspection

> (*Enter Station Master*)

STATION MASTER (*To the tune of* **Lihua'er**):

> In the Xinhe Courier Station in Shanzhou,
>
> I am sixty-seven by this year.
>
> I took over office at twenty-one,

Alas,

And need a thousand years to become a minister.

I, master of Xinhe Courier Station in Shanzhou Prefecture, was born with ingenuity. I served as a runner in the county government office, and was later selected to serve in the Ministry of Inspection. As the lucky star was over my head that year, an official in the Ministry of Inspection showed favour on me, indeed showed favour on me. He gave me a sleeveless garment and made me a dispatcher. I was sent to Guangdong and Guangxi, let alone the two capitals in the north and south. A dispatcher was of course awe-inspiring, and when my term of service was over, I took part in the official selection. I was selected as chief of the kitchen for the Six Ministries, but I committed some reprehensible mistakes. Three years later, I played some tricks and was selected as master of Xinhe Courier Station in Shanzhou Prefecture. This courier station is the exit of the Tongguan Pass, sufficient of money, grains and payments. When several sedans, several carriers and several donkeys arrive, there is a strict checking of documents. Then I prepare ten kilos of meat, ten cups of wine, ten eggs to make a dirty lunch or dinner. I can batten on these treatments. When it comes to my share, I can get no more than ten percent. Therefore, I have often been bullied by the official dispatchers. As the saying goes, "Tit for tat and dispatchers beat the station master." For several times I would have run away or simply killed myself, but I still hope to scrape a living. When prisoners on exile come, they come as my subordinates. When they first arrive, they have to pay for the first meeting; when they violate the rules, they have to pay for their offences. If they do not pay their monthly tribute, they will be beaten to death at the cost of a piece of white paper to transcend their souls. Even if the superiors come to check on the roll, there are other prisoners to serve as substitutes. As days go by, there are not enough people to run the ferry. But now an evil star is coming over my head, which really matters.

VOICE WITHIN:

Master, which official is coming by?

STATION MASTER:

Well, who do you think he is? The present Emperor Xuanzong is touring in an extraordinary way. He does not want men to sail the ships, but wants a thousand young women to sing the "Ballad of Picking Water-caltrops". The magistrate has selected nine hundred and ninety-eight singers, and wants two more to line at the head and at the end. I have neither wife nor young daughters. As I cannot find two more young women, I am at my wit's end. It's no small matter to breach the imperial edict. My last resort is to go to the western beams and hang myself there.

(*Puts his neck in the noose*)

(*Enter two female prisoners*)

FEMALE PRISONERS (*Rescue Station Master*):

How is it that you're hanging yourself? If you did not care for your official career, should you not have cared for your life of a dog?

STATION MASTER (*Comes to*):

When I do not care for my life of a dog, how can I care for my official career?

(*Kowtows*)

You are not my sworn sisters, but why are you acting like the Goddess of Mercy?

FEMALE PRISONERS:

Both of us are prisoners in this courier station.

STATION MASTER:

Oh! You are such pretty prisoners. Where have you been hiding, without ever reporting to me? Tell me where your husbands are.

FEMALE PRISONER A:

My husband is called Short Bag. He's gone picking pockets.

STATION MASTER:

What do you mean?

FEMALE PRISONER A:

You allowed him to go so as to pay for the monthly tribute.

STATION MASTER:

It's kind of you.

FEMALE PRISONER B:

My husband is called Wild Talk. He's gone grabbing chickens.

STATION MASTER:

It's a good business.

954

FEMALE PRISONER B:

You told him to go, too.

STATION MASTER:

What do I need chickens for?

FEMALE PRISONER B:

For dinner or for lunch.

STATION MASTER:

Let's talk no more about this. I am fortunate not to have selected you to tow the dragon boat. If you should tell the old emperor about this, he would be afraid to eat my chickens. Now let's talk about something else. Where are you from?

FEMALE PRISONERS:

From the southern bank of the Yangtze River.

STATION MASTER:

Can you sing ballads?

FEMALE PRISONERS:

Yes, we can.

STATION MASTER:

It's all the more wonderful! Since His Majesty is about to come, a thousand female singers are to be selected to tow the dragon boat and to sing the "Ballad of Picking Water-caltrops". As two more singers are needed now, you are lucky enough. Will you take the trouble to sing a ballad, starting from describing the moon, narrating what happens on the ship, containing a word meaning "curved" in each line, containing the word "emperor" in the two middle lines, and making the last line funny?

FEMALE PRISONER A:

Yes, I will.

> (*Sings*)
>
> *The crescent moon is stuck on the skies;*
>
> *In a crooked way the new river lies.*
>
> *I cross my hands round the emperor's neck*
>
> *And bend my feet on the emperor's shoulders.*
>
> *With my feet on his shoulders,*
>
> *The emperor says with a smile on his lips:*
>
> *Your feet are as large as my ships.*

STATION MASTER:

Your song is excellent, excellent! It suits His Majesty's taste exactly.

> (*To Female Prisoner B*)

Your song should contain four words with the meaning of "pointed", contain the word "emperor" in the two middle lines, and have a funny ending.

FEMALE PRISONER B:

Please listen.

> (*Sings*)
>
> *The pointed moon shines over the spears;*
>
> *The piercing nails drive into the oars.*
>
> *My sharp voice enters the emperor's ears;*
>
> *My slender fingers touch the emperor's waist.*
>
> *To touch his waist,*
>
> *What shall I turn round?*
>
> *I'll sail the ship from the skies to the ground.*

STATION MASTER:

Wonderful, wonderful, wonderful! I'll show you to the old emperor, but I'm afraid that you'll offend him because you are inexperienced. You must have some practice.

FEMALE PRISONERS:

There is no one for us to practise on.

STATION MASTER:

What about taking me as the old emperor and practising on me?

FEMALE PRISONER B (*Giggles*):

That'll do.

STATION MASTER:

I'll sing the first two lines and you will go on with the next two lines.

> (*Sings*)
>
> *I the Station Master am as old as a broken boat,*
>
> *Hearing the new river flow while I am afloat.*

FEMALE PRISONERS (*Sing*):

> *You row the oar while you are asleep or awake;*
>
> *We're afraid that you will not row till daybreak.*

(Voice of clearing the way within)

STATION MASTER:

Hurry up, hurry up! The magistrate is coming.

(Enter Lu Sheng, followed by his attendants)

LU SHENG *(To the tune of Xidijin)*:

> Over the stones the waves roar;
>
> On shallow beaches the golden sands glow.
>
> I've decorated the guesthouse into a fairy house,
>
> Waiting day and night for His Majesty to come.

(Station Master bows to Lu Sheng)

LU SHENG *(In the pattern of Xijiangyue)*:

> *His Majesty will come at any time*
>
> *As the canal has been completed.*
>
> *Message comes from the east capital*
>
> *That I must prepare everything.*

STATION MASTER:

> *The first thing is to get gold and grains ready*
>
> *And to get everything well prepared.*
>
> *When the divine emperor makes his tour,*
>
> *Who dares to be not sure?*

Master Lu, if His Majesty leaves the ship and goes on land, where is he going to stay?

LU SHENG:

The Green Peak Palace was built years ago, which can house the empress and the royal concubines. There are also guesthouses for the ministers and generals. The gold and grains for the attachés will be taken care of by the seventy-four prefectures and counties around the east capital. The only trouble is that time is too urgent to get the one thousand female singers. What shall we do about it?

STATION MASTER:

We are short of two female singers only. I've fetched my two sisters by night and taught them to sing. Now we have one thousand female singers ready.

LU SHENG:

Thank you very much.

ATTENDANTS:

The Station Master is lying. They are two female prisoners.

LU SHENG:

You deserve a sound beating!

STATION MASTER *(Kowtows)*:

Although they are prisoners, they have quite pretty looks and are good at singing. It's not easy to find such singers at short notice.

LU SHENG:

You are right. Listen to my orders, Station Master!

> *(To the tune of Yifengshu)*

When the imperial carriage comes to the east,

We need a red crook-handled umbrella.

STATION MASTER:

There is no such thing in the courier station.

LU SHENG:

Borrow it from the warehouse in the Green Peak Palace.

For the imperial banquet,

We need dragon plates decorated with flowers.

STATION MASTER:

I'm afraid that there are not enough delicate dishes and that the old emperor has to do in the rustic areas as the rustics do.

LU SHENG:

I have a thousand ivory plates and dishes in my possession. They are gifts for me and I keep them for gifts too.

STATION MASTER:

I'm also afraid that the accompanying officers and officials are not easy to attend to.

Besides the officers and officials,

The eunuchs are the most difficult to deal with.

LU SHENG:

Never mind. The eunuchs have a chief — Eunuch Gao. I've sent gifts to him and he will not go beyond himself. Still, I'll have to be careful all the same.

Take care

And avoid mistake,

Otherwise my life will be at stake.

I have something else to tell you. Order the grain ships and cargo ships to sail in teams with coloured flags. Each team will carry signs to show the type of grains from a certain region and valued goods from a certain prefecture. Each ship is to burn joss-sticks and play its regional music.

(*Station Master responds*)

(*Enter Messenger*)

MESSENGER (*Reports*):

Master Lu, the eunuch in charge of the advance unit has arrived. His Majesty is 300 miles away.

LU SHENG (*In a hurry*):

Get my horse ready and we'll go and meet His Majesty.

In this area three rivers run forth;

When the emperor arrives, all ships pass with ease.

As all the stars face the north,

So the rivers run to the east.

Scene Fourteen
Imperial Inspection to the East

(*Enter Yuwen Rong and Pei Guangting*)

YUWEN RONG, PEI GUANGTING (*To the tune of* **Taichangyin**):

> Now that His Majesty has travelled a long way,
>
> The roosters crow at the break of a spring day.
>
> When the royal robe glimmers in sunlight,
>
> The towering peaks come into sight.

YUWEN RONG:

I am Yuwen Rong, Supervisory Minister and Right Prime Minister in charge of all state affairs.

PEI GUANGTING:

I am Pei Guangting, Assistant Minister of the Central Office. Minister of the Central Office Xiao Song remains in the capital to take care of state affairs. Right Prime Minister Yuwen Rong and I accompany His Majesty on his inspection to the east. Here we are at the temporary palace outside the Lintong Pass. We shall soon arrive at Shanzhou City, where Lu Sheng serves as the magistrate.

YUWEN RONG (*Smiles*):

It has been three years since Lu Sheng came here. There is no report that the new canal is completed. What a difficult task for him!

PEI GUANGTING:

I am fully aware of his intelligence. The project is bound to complete and he is bound to be commended by His Majesty.

YUWEN RONG:

We'll wait and see whether the canal is completed.

VOICE WITHIN:

His Majesty is having an audience.

(*Enter Emperor Xuanzong, followed by Eunuch Gao and attendants*)

EMPEROR XUANZONG (*To the tune of* **Raochiyou**):

> In a yellow carriage surrounded with flags,
>
> I am on my way from Sanmen.
>
> When night runs out with cockcrows on a spring day,
>
> The sun climbs over the mountain
>
> And starts to shine over the earth.

ALL:

> The nation centres round the throne;
>
> All kowtow to and hail the emperor.

EMPEROR XUANZONG:

> *A road was paved before I arrived at the tents;*
>
> *Upon the palace road is left my trail.*

A thousand flags appear in the shadowy vale;

Ten thousand carriages come amid roaring torrents.

I am Emperor Xuanzong of the Tang Dynasty. On my east inspection by carriage to Luoyang, I stop over outside the Tongguan Pass. Now that breakfast is over, Eunuch Gao, announce my edict to be on the way again.

(*Eunuch Gao announces the edict to set off*)

(*To the tune of* ***Wangwuxiangfan***)

When the stars disappear at the twinkle of an eye,

The flags lead the way into the outskirts of Shanzhou.

Which immortal is preaching on the river?

The fairy princesses are no longer in woe

When ten thousand carriages come by.

LU SHENG (*Kowtows*):

Magistrate of Shanzhou, former Master of the Royal Academy, Edict Drafter Lu Sheng, together with officials and civilians, is here to welcome Your Majesty.

EMPEROR XUANZONG:

Is the magistrate the former Number One Scholar Lu Sheng?

PEI GUANGTING:

Yes, he is.

EMPEROR XUANZONG:

Rise to your feet.

LU SHENG:

A long, long life to Your Majesty!

EMPEROR XUANZONG:

What is it that towers in front of us?

LU SHENG:

As the road outside the pass is precipitous, an overhead passage has been built.

EMPEROR XUANZONG:

Is this an overhead passage? A storm is looming.

LU SHENG:

As the saying goes, "The rain god sprinkles on the way and the wind god sweeps away the dust."

EMPEROR XUANZONG (*Smiles*):

Let's be on our way.

ALL:

Look at the Single Pillar

And the Stone Bridge:

The natural barriers rise above the clouds.

Far away is the temporary palace

And the court set in the tent:

Storms hit the two mausoleums in Mount Xixiao.

EMPEROR XUANZONG:

Pass on my edict to stop awhile to shelter from the rain. Is there a temporary palace in Shanzhou?

LU SHENG:

There is a Green Peak Palace, where Your Majesty once stayed.

EMPEROR XUANZONG:

How do you know it?

LU SHENG:

A poem will serve as evidence.

EMPEROR XUANZONG:

Recite the poem.

LU SHENG:

Now I humbly recite the poem for Your Majesty.

> *When vernal grass turns green in spring,*
> *The wild crab-apple petals have begun to fall.*
> *A white-haired old man is singing a song*
> *Before the Green Peak Palace for Emperor Xuanzong.*

EMPEROR XUANZONG:

When I hear this song, my last inspection seems to revive before my eyes.

LU SHENG:

Your Majesty, as the sky has cleared up, you can be on your way again.

EMPEROR XUANZONG:

Pass on my edict to move slowly.

> (*To the tune of **Jiangduchun***)
> Amid drumbeats resounded in tree branches,
> I gaze at the perilous mountain paths
> And cross the overhead passage.
> The mountains lie between Heyang and Jingzhao
> And now Lintong is far behind me.
> Compared with the dreamlike Mount Taihua,
> The Tongguan Pass looks quite narrow.

LU SHENG:

Your Majesty, we have gone out of the Tongguan Pass and reached the riverside. Please embark on the Dragon Boat.

EMPEROR XUANZONG:

I remember this used to be a rocky road. What's the use of a Dragon Boat?

LU SHENG:

I have dug over three hundred miles of canal for your inspection to the east.

EMPEROR XUANZONG (*Smiles*):

What a miracle! I'll go and have a look.

> (*Gazes afar*)

Oh, what a vast expanse of water and sky!

I look afar

And see a sight of pretty mountains and water.

(*Drumbeats and flute music within*)

(*Emperor Xuanzong and all embark on the Dragon Boat*)

EMPEROR XUANZONG:

Here we are on the Dragon Boat.

LU SHENG:

I have selected a thousand singing girls to tow the boat. They can sing ballads as well.

(*Female singers kowtow and sing boat songs*)

FEMALE SINGERS (*To the tune of **Chuduizi***):

With blessing from Your Majesty,

Thanks to the blessing from Your Majesty,

We have dug a canal between the river and the pass.

With poplars and willows we turn the banks into corridors;

We offer wine and play flutes to the River God.

We sail the boat

From the earth to the Milky Way.

EMPEROR XUANZONG:

How pretty these boat-song singers are!

(*To the tune of **Naofanlou***)

What pretty boat-song singers!

Where songs resound, true beauties appear.

Like the Goddess of Luo River on water surface

And Princess Zhaojun with make-up,

These singers here are pretty indeed.

You ministers should know

That the new canal is best decorated here.

(*Music within*)

LU SHENG:

My wife Cui from Qinghe County has prepared a thousand plates of delicacies for Your Majesty.

EMPEROR XUANZONG (*Smiles*):

I have no objection.

LU SHENG (*Presents wine*):

Your Majesty, I present the wine to wish you a long, long life.

(*To the tune of **Yinghuamei***)

With fairy peach wine in the golden cup,

Like dewdrops containing Your Majesty's grace,

I present the wine to you with submission.

The plates hold delicacies from water and from land;

The ballads sound like heavenly music.

(*Emperor Xuanzong smiles*)

ALL:

> It is our great fortune

> To see Your Majesty smile with pleasure.

EMPEROR XUANZONG:

Distribute the delicacies on the plates among the attendants. Lu Sheng, rise to your feet.

LU SHENG:

Long live the Emperor!

> (*Rises to his feet*)

EMPEROR XUANZONG:

There is music on the teams of thousands of ships in front of us. What ships are these?

LU SHENG:

These are teams of ships transporting grains from the south of the Yangtze River and native products from all over the country. Joss-sticks are burnt team by team and native music is played.

> (*Emperor Xuanzong smiles*)

ALL (*To the tune of* **Didijin**):

> Thousands of ships are sailing in order.

> With army men and civilians on their knees,

> Holding incense burners and playing sweet music.

> The merchant ships are sailing under different colours,

> Followed by grain ships under white flags

> With Muslims dancing on tribal boats.

> All those from the Yangtze and Han

> Gather here to present their treasures.

EMPEROR XUANZONG:

Do you remember the road to Shanzhou in the former days? There were twists and turns on the rocky peaks. It was a hard journey to transport grains from the south of the Yangtze River to this place. Since ancient times, if grains did not arrive in time, we had to move to the east capital for meals. I did not expect that Lu Sheng would have achieved this feat.

> (*To the tune of* **Zhuomu'er**)

> Along the former trails

> Of rocks and stones,

> It was a hard journey to transport grains.

> When everybody drove heavy carts,

> Who had ever thought of using ships?

LU SHENG:

Your Majesty, will you be so kind as to grant the canal a name?

EMPEROR XUANZONG:

I will name it the Eternal Benefit River.

LU SHENG:

Long live the Emperor!

LU SHENG, PEI GUANGTING:

Emperor Xuanzong makes an eastern tour

And names the new river Eternal Benefit.

Grains from the south can arrive every year.

EMPEROR XUANZONG:

What is it that stands erect on the bank in front of us, with its head facing the south of the river and with its tail facing the north of the river?

LU SHENG:

It's an iron bull to control floods.

EMPEROR XUANZONG:

Come forward, Pei Guangting. Since you are good at writing essays, you may write an essay entitled *In Praise of the Iron Bull* to commemorate Lu Sheng's merits.

PEI GUANGTING:

Your Majesty, may I present the essay now?

EMPEROR XUANZONG:

Yes, you may.

PEI GUANGTING:

As Heaven is the originator, it ranks the first; as Earth is subordinate to Heaven, it ranks the second. What originates everything creates the sacrificial bull; what is subordinate to everything is the bull. The bull is the originator of water; iron is a resource of metal. The iron bull is figured with a singular spirit, four firm hoofs, an erect head and two sturdy horns. It was melted in a huge furnace and tempered in the universe. It conforms to the great Tao and displays the power of gods. It reaches the border of Zhou to the east and Guo to the west. It stands on the way to the Hangu Pass, looking as if it were following the immortals; it is near the fortress of Taolin, looking as if it were an animal returning home. When Li Bing was a commander in Shu, he set a stone wild bull in the river; when Zhang Qian opened a road, he watered a bull on the brink of the Hanshui River. The metal stops both water and fire while the bull stays in both mountains and rivers. Therefore, Mount Hua is planted here without feeling heavy and river waters are controlled without leaking because the iron bull is here. Herewith is my eulogy of the iron bull: With distant spirit and chaotic air, the bull is tempered in the furnace and planted in thick earth. The river god splits the mountain with its horns in the west while the Yellow River roars toward the east. The iron bull stands erect with god's blessing and guards the high riverbanks with men's power. When His Majesty names the new river Eternal Benefit, articles of tribute will flow in forever.

EMPEROR XUANZONG (*Smiles*):

What a wonderful eulogy! Lu Sheng's name will be engraved on the tablet. Your magnificent merits will benefit future generations.

LU SHENG:

Long live the Emperor!

EMPEROR XUANZONG (*To the tune of **Sanduanzi***):

High is the river source

That brings currents from the heavenly stream.

Powerful is the intelligent source

That inspires the fluency in your essay.

Lu Sheng,

With your willows you may equal Earl Shao with his pear trees.

Pei Guanting,

Your eulogy of the iron bull is as lucid as the river water.

ALL:

True indeed!

King Yu had a tablet made in commemoration of King Yao alone.

(*Sound of a galloping horse within*)

YUWEN RONG (*Gazes afar*):

A horse is galloping along the riverbank. Is there anything urgent?

(*Enter Messenger*)

MESSENGER:

I gallop from afar to make an urgent report. Master Yuwen, the messenger kowtows to you.

YUWEN RONG:

What's the military situation? Tell me slowly.

MESSENGER (*To the tune of **Zhanshuangji***):

On the border,

On the border,

The Tubo troops come to invade.

YUWEN RONG:

General Wang Junchuo is taking command there.

MESSENGER:

General Junchuo,

General Junchuo,

It's hard to speak of him.

YUWEN RONG:

Do you mean he is killed?

MESSENGER:

For the moment,

The rumour is very much in the air.

YUWEN RONG:

There is the Yumen Pass to stop the Tubo troops.

MESSENGER:

They've broken through the Yumen Pass

And crossed from that side of the pass.

YUWEN RONG:

Do you mean to say that they have crossed from that side and occupied this side?

MESSENGER (*Rises to his feet*):

If they are not on this side,

What am I to report to you?

(Exit)

YUWEN RONG (*To Emperor Xuanzong*):

Your Majesty, there is an urgent report from the border area. Tubo troops have crossed the Great Wall and Wang Junchuo was defeated. We are waiting for your edict.

EMPEROR XUANZONG (*In a panic*):

What shall we do then?

>(*To the tune of **Shangxiaolou***)

>As the border is defenceless,

>I am thrown into a panic.

>How far is it away from Chang'an?

>It is hard to assign a general.

>Among the feeble officials,

>Who has studied the arts of war and will go into battle?

YUWEN RONG (*Giggles aside*):

Lu Sheng has done a deed of merit in digging the canal, and now there's another hard nut for him to crack.

>(*To Emperor Xuanzong*)

I've consulted the officials here. Lu Sheng alone is capable of going into battle.

EMPEROR XUANZONG:

You are right.

LU SHENG:

I am not capable of fierce battles.

EMPEROR XUANZONG:

I know your capability. You should not decline the appointment. You are appointed Supervisory Minister, Administrator and Military Commander of the Four Regions in Hexi and Longyou, and Marshall of Quenching the West. You are to set off by night without delay. I'll give you my war robe for you to wear before my very eyes. That's my edict!

>(*Lu Sheng responds and rises to his feet*)

>(*Sound of drums within*)

LU SHENG (*Changes into the war robe and thanks Emperor Xuanzong*):

Lu Sheng, the newly-appointed Supervisory Minister, Administrator and Military Commander of the Four Regions in Hexi and Longyou, kowtows to Your Majesty.

EMPEROR XUANZONG:

Rise to your feet. With you as the commander, I'll have no worry for the west.

>(*To the tune of **Shuabaolao***)

>As there are troubles in the border area,

>A new general is dressed in the war robe.

>Even if you are a civil official,

>You have to fight on the battlefield.

PEI GUANGTING:

>Fighting on the battlefield

Is more strenuous

Than digging a canal away from the capital.

YUWEN RONG:

I have fought a battle of wits with you

And it's your turn to show how brave you are.

ALL:

By the imperial edict,

You are to leave at once

And hope to become a lord.

(*Sound of drums and flute music within, for the boat to set sail*)

EMPEROR XUANZONG:

Lu Sheng, Lu Sheng,

(*To the tune of* **Coda**)

I'll make a tour to Luoyang

And wait for your news of victory.

By that time,

I'll grant you one title after another.

(*Exit*)

LU SHENG (*Kowtows*):

Long live the Emperor!

(*Rises to his feet*)

Give my order to the officers: as the situation is urgent on the border, we must follow the imperial edict to set off at once without taking leave of our wives. As the saying goes,

I was driven by hunger in the past,

But am pressed by wealth and rank at present.

(*Exit*)

(*Enter Miss Cui with Meixiang*)

MISS CUI:

The Milky Way is the scarlet wall,

That separates the Lu's Jade Hall.

Who is bringing the news to Wang Chang,

The man who knows the lovebirds, thirty-six in all?

I am going with Meixiang to look for my man. Oh, where has he gone?

(*To the tune of* **Saiguanyin**)

Where is my man?

He forgets the inn in Qinghe

And discards his wife Cui from Boling.

MISS CUI, MEIXIANG:

Without a feeling heart,

The river water flows straight to the west.

MEIXIANG (*Makes inquiry*):

Brothers on the riverbanks, do you know where my master is?

VOICE WITHIN:

Emperor Xuanzong has ordered your master to fight the Tubo troops.

MISS CUI (*Weeps*):

I see.

> (*To the previous tune*)
>
> I grow wan and sallow for my man.
>
> The wild geese fly low near the riverbank;
>
> Beyond the willows the sun sets in the mist.

MISS CUI, MEIXIANG:

> The neighing seems to come
>
> From the west of the bridge.

MISS CUI:

Meixiang, let's hurry and try to be in time to see him off.

> (*Walks on*)
>
> (*To the tune of **Renyueyuan***)
>
> I tumble on the ground,
>
> But what am I to do?
>
> Man and wife are about to separate —
>
> At short notice
>
> He is rushing to the battlefield.

MISS CUI, MEIXIANG:

> As the man has gone a long way off,
>
> Where is the wife to pursue,
>
> With tears in her eyes?

MISS CUI:

It's impossible to catch up with him. Let's go back to the prefecture and make other plans.

> (*To the previous tune*)
>
> You may go if you like
>
> And who is going to stop you?
>
> What harm will women do in the army?
>
> When I go home, where will you stay tonight?
>
> Together man and wife should dwell.

MISS CUI, MEIXIANG:

> Sadly, the wife will stay alone,
>
> Except to be with you
>
> In a dream of her own.
>
> *Going to the front when the canal is done,*
>
> *The man is gone and water flows on and on.*
>
> *Where can I look beyond the mountains?*
>
> *Only the moon returns now that he is gone.*

967

The Handan Dream

Scene Fifteen
Sending a Spy to the West

(*Enter two Assistant Generals*)

ASSISTANT GENERALS:

> The terrace frost threatens grass and trees;
>
> The military valour stays with the flags.

We are Assistant Generals in the office of the Hexi Administrator and Military Commander. As Grand Military Commander Lu is going to hold office, we have to wait on him here.

(*Enter Lu Sheng, followed by his attendants*)

LU SHENG (*To the tune of* **Jinlongcong**):

> As Hexi and Longyou are close to the Tubo troops,
>
> Warriors are wounded or killed on the battlefields
>
> And the Yumen Pass is nearly broken.
>
> The emperor is anxious about the west
>
> And makes me commander at the terrace,
>
> For me to fight near Mount Tianshan.

(*In the pattern of* **Collected Tang Poems**)

> I became commander when I was thirty years old
>
> And left my office with the red flags half-rolled.
>
> The vanguards fought on the north of the Jiaohe River
>
> And would conquer the Loulan stronghold.

I am Lu Sheng from Shanzhou. As the Hexi General Wang Junchuo died in fighting the Tubo troops, Hexi and Longyou are in danger. His Majesty is thrown into a panic and orders me to take command and fight in the west. According to the art of war, "When the ruler and the subordinates are in harmony, the nation is unshakable." I intend to send someone to sow discord among the Tubo camp. When Prime Minister Xi Naluo is purged, Re Longmang will be left without assistance and be defeated easily. This is a top secret. I've found out that a scout in the army by the name of Tubo Han can speak thirty-six Tubo dialects. He comes and goes between the Tubo tribes and the Hans as if in a no-man's land. I have summoned him.

(*Enter Scout with a small banner on his back*)

SCOUT (*To the tune of* **Tune One**):

> The vast land on earth
>
> Is severed by mountains and rivers.
>
> As the West Liang region here
>
> Is close to the frontiers,
>
> I am like a wild flower,
>
> With a petal on this side.

(*Kowtows to Lu Sheng*)

LU SHENG:

Are you Tubo Han? Do you speak both the Tubo dialects and the Han language?

SCOUT (*Dances*):

>(*To the tune of* **Tune Two**)
>Tubo Han,
>I am Tubo Han,
>A scout worthy of the name.

LU SHENG:

Are you a Tubo or Han descendent?

SCOUT:

A descendent from southern Tubo, I come to the uninhabited Ganshui and Liangzhou, far away from my native Menmo Mountain. You have enlisted me and I get several portions of salary. I am nimble; I am eloquent. I have been to Yangtong and Dangxiang; I have been to Kunlun and Bailan. I know such Tuluhun words as *gudugulu*; I know such Bieshiba words as *bilibanlan*. I speak Tieli words like *yiliugala*; I speak Shandan words like *tiliutulu*. I can brave dangers to enter enemy camps in the cold desert, wearing a felt hat on my head and a mask on my mouth. I can travel by night and sleep by day, braving wind and storm.

LU SHENG:

"Keep an army for a thousand days and use it once in a while." When I need your service today, are you ready to go?

SCOUT (*To the tune of* **Tune Three**):

>Unless you let me knock an elephant's tusks
>Or break a leopard's tail,
>What else can't I do?

LU SHENG:

The Tubo Prime Minister Xi Naluo is wise and resourceful. He is a sworn enemy of our country. I'd like to ask you to enter the Tubo camps as an agent to tell the Tubo King that Prime Minister Xi Naluo intends to usurp the throne because the Tubo King is old. In this way the Tubo King might kill Xi Naluo. Can you accept this mission?

SCOUT:

>It is a difficult task
>For me to drive a wedge between them,
>As if between the teeth of a tiger.
>Shall I go
>Or shall I refuse?

Your Excellency,

>You tell me to spread the rumour about a rebellion,
>But what shall I do
>And how shall I contact you?

LU SHENG:

Whenever you meet any Tubo soldiers, you just say that Prime Minister Xi Naluo is going to start a rebellion. Suspicion will naturally arise. What contact do you need?

SCOUT:

Heavens!

You tell me to scoff the heaven pillar with my lips

And turn the sea beams with my tongue,

But my words aren't what's to be sung.

LU SHENG:

Since it's difficult to spread the rumour, I have a scheme ready for you. Just write the words "Xi Naluo is to rebel" on a thousand slips of paper and paste them in the Tubo camps. And then the job is done.

SCOUT:

That will do.

(*To the tune of* **Tune Four**)

I look at the slips of paper,

And look at the slips of paper closely.

Well, how can I carry a thousand slips of paper with me?

LU SHENG (*Thinks*):

That's true. I've found out that a stream at the foot of Mount Muye flows into the Tubo King's tent palace. Write the words "Xi Naluo is to rebel" on the tree leaves with a bamboo needle, as if the leaves were bitten by insects. Carry the leaves to the upper stream and let them flow into the tent. The Tubo King will think that the heavenly gods have done the job and will surely be in suspicion. This is the scheme of "Red Leaves in the Royal Ditch".

SCOUT:

Wonderful, wonderful!

You do not use intelligent pretty girls,

But use red maple leaves in cold rills.

I'm going to the shoals

And rouge-coloured hills.

I'll set off at once.

LU SHENG:

I'll give you a red ribbon, ten cups of wine and three thousand coins to buy rations. When the job is done, you will be appointed Chief of a Thousand Households.

SCOUT:

I leave the pass with a wonderful scheme,

Ready to come and go by night.

When I reach the Muye Stream,

I'll take advantage of the flowing water

And deceive the short-witted Tubo King.

LU SHENG:

Repeat to me what is to be written on the leaves.

SCOUT (*To the tune of* **Coda**):

I do not write with a pen but with a bamboo needle,

Mimicking the divine spirit of insects or ants.

I do not write about the woes of palace maids,

But about the rebellion of the Tubo Prime Minister.

(*Exit*)

LU SHENG:

The scout is gone with a firm resolve and he is bound to succeed. I'll get troops ready and advance when opportunity arises.

> *With wise and brave men in the enemy camp,*
> *The best way to defeat them is to sow discord.*
> *I shall soon see victorious flags*
> *And hear good news as my reward.*

Scene Sixteen
Grand Victory

(*Enter Re Longmang*)

RE LONGMANG (*To the tune of* **Northern Yizhihua**):

> Our troops have fought across Mount Helan
> With bloody battles near the border fortresses.
> To expand the Tubo King's territory,
> We have trampled on Han's shields.
> Dressed in felt,
> Embroidered hats and lion bands,
> We rival the Han generals of great power.
> Our swords are wiped with autumn water;
> Our tents are domed in the shape of a lotus-flower.

I am Re Longmang, a Tubo general. I have occupied the Yumen Pass and taken firm command of the troops. I shall be pushing on to Ganshui and Liangzhou and threatening Guanxi and Longyou. As our Prime Minister Xi Naluo is both intelligent and resourceful, planning each move with nine possible consequences in mind, I have sent for his consultations. I know that a good general must rely on the assistance of a good prime minister since ancient times. Nothing can be achieved with single-sided efforts.

(*To the tune of* **Shuanglingjiang'ershui**)

> Prime Minister Xi Naluo,
> Prime Minister Xi Naluo comes to my mind.
> He is a man of men,
> Without equals in the Tubo court.
> He has high inspirations,
> Well-versed in military classics
> And the arts of war.
> He gets along well with me
> And I do better with his help.
> With one in the border area

971

And the other in the court,

The two dragons may disturb the sea.

ALL:

Are you afraid of the vast territory and the wise people of Tang?

RE LONGMANG:

The Hans are said to be wise,

But I do not see how they are wise.

The Tang Dynasty has a vast territory,

And we shall grab from them a vast territory.

I shall turn Mount Tianshan and break Han cliffs.

(*Enter a Tubo soldier with a flag of command on his back*)

TUBO SOLDIER:

Jilishamani, Salihamachi. I report to the general: Prime Minister Xi Naluo has been put to death by the King because he was plotting a rebellion.

RE LONGMANG (*Surprised*):

What did you say?

TUBO SOLDIER:

Prime Minister Xi Naluo has been put to death by the King because he was plotting a rebellion.

RE LONGMANG:

Who has seen it?

TUBO SOLDIER:

The Bodhisattva has seen it.

RE LONGMANG:

How has the Bodhisattva seen it?

TUBO SOLDIER:

You know, a stream at the foot of Mount Muye flows into the King's tent palace, carrying a thousand leaves with the words "Xi Naluo is to rebel" bitten by insects. When the King saw these leaves, he sent men to search the mountain but no one was found. The King said that the heavenly god has sent a message. He told the Prime Minister to drink some horse-milk wine. A copper hammer hit him on the back of his head and his brains dashed out.

RE LONGMANG:

Then, is the Prime Minister dead?

TUBO SOLDIER:

Naturally.

RE LONGMANG (*Weeps*):

Oh my dear Prime Minister Xi Naluo! Gracious heavens! Gracious heavens!

(*Enter Tubo Messenger*)

TUBO MESSENGER:

Report, report, report! Marshal Lu of the Tang Dynasty is leading his army toward us!

RE LONGMANG:

What's to be done? What's to be done?

(*To the tune of* **Coda**)

In haste I mount the steed in front of the camp

And open the camp gate amid drumbeats.

Gracious heavens!

Can I mount the steed

And carry another day?

(*Exit*)

(*Enter Lu Sheng, followed by soldiers*)

LU SHENG (*To the tune of* **Qingjiangyin**):

The Tang Dynasty abounds in valiant warriors;

The enemy cannot hinder their movements.

The soldiers hurry on

With the formation stretching long.

To conquer the Tubo troops,

I'll capture the vanguard Re Longmang.

To conquer the Tubo troops by imperial edict, I have killed Prime Minister Xi Naluo by schemes. It's time to capture the Tubo general now that he is isolated. Soldiers, march on!

(*Exeunt all*)

(*Enter Re Longmang, followed by Tubo soldiers*)

RE LONGMANG (*To the tune of* **Qingjiangyin**):

From the west

Comes the Tubo general —

General Re Longmang.

Tubo drums beat;

Tubo cymbals sound;

Tubo horns ring all around.

(*To Lu Sheng*)

Who are you?

LU SHENG:

I am Marshal Lu of the Tang Dynasty.

RE LONGMANG:

Do you know me, General Re Longmang?

LU SHENG:

It's just because I know you that I can capture you.

RE LONGMANG:

Are you as valiant as Wang Junchuo?

LU SHENG (*Sneers*):

Where is your Xi Naluo?

(*Fights with Re Longmang*)

(*Tubo soldiers are defeated. Exeunt all*)

(*Re-enter all. A fight ensues. Tubo soldiers are defeated. Exeunt all*)

(*Enter Lu Sheng, followed by his soldiers in battle cry*)

Ah, now that Re Longmang has been defeated, our troops will chase the enemy and recapture cities and towns until we push to the west of the Yangguan Pass. It is true indeed,

> *Even if he ran away to Suyama, the top of sky,*
>
> *I'd chase after him and catch him there.*
>
> (*Exeunt all*)
>
> (*Enter Re Longmang, followed by his defeated soldiers*)

RE LONGMANG (*To the tune of* **Tuobushan**):

> I was in high spirits
>
> And looked down upon the Tang troops.
>
> I am now put to the rout,
>
> A case of "tit for tat".

Warriors, what about our men?

> (*Weeps*)
>
> (*To the tune of* **Xiaoliangzhou**)
>
> The warriors die but their spirits remain,
>
> Crying in wild shrieks and howls.
>
> All the soldiers, a hundred thousand in all,
>
> Are now lost,
>
> With arrows remaining on the bows.
>
> (*An uproar within*)

VOICE WITHIN:

The Han soldiers are coming!

RE LONGMANG:

Withdraw, withdraw, withdraw! I'll stop the chasers!

> (*To the tune of* **Yao**)
>
> We expect Tubo reinforcement,
>
> But the Tang soldiers have arrived,
>
> Giving us no escape.
>
> On the bloody battlefield
>
> And amid battle cries,
>
> I can hardly conquer the Hans.

All is lost, all is lost! The Qilian Mountain a thousand miles away is the border between the Tubo and Tang. I have to think a way out.

> (*Wails of wild geese within*)

I have a way out. I'll tear a piece of silk and write a letter to be tied on the foot of a wild goose, begging him to let me go home. There remains the possibility that he'll let me go. Heavens, heavens, heavens, it's a pity that Prime Minister Xi Naluo is dead!

> (*To the tune of* **Shuahai'er**)
>
> The general and the prime minister can never stay apart,
>
> Because it is difficult to fight single-handed.
>
> Like leaves driven by wind or sands floating on waters,
>
> I am in a trance, with no way of escape.

I'm like a defeated jade dragon with shredding scales,

And like a routed beast with wet furs.

I have to beg the wild goose

To wail for me,

Asking for forgiveness.

(*To the tune of* **Coda**)

With attacks from the southern Hans

And roars from the Tubo soldiers,

Home is a long way from here.

My troops are ashamed of my previous victories,

Which come to nought with the last battle.

I look from the Tianshan Mountain

And see battle scenes like boundless seas.

Like a turtledove hit by a pellet,

I have to send letters by wild geese.

Scene Seventeen
Carving the Merits

(*Enter Lu Sheng, followed by his soldiers*)

LU SHENG (*To the tune of* **Yexingchuan**):

We drive along the border fortresses in great speed,

With warriors roaring all the way.

The Yinshan Mountain with its darkened moon,

Yellow clouds and white grass

Is the ancient road toward lordship.

At sunset drums and bugles echo in the camp

When thousands of Tubo soldiers surrender their cities.

Our troops clean their weapons in Fish Sea

And feed their horses on Dragon Hill.

I am Lu Sheng. Taking command of a hundred thousand victorious troops, I have recovered the Yangguan Pass. I have sent speedy report of victory to the court while I push on in the flush of victory for a thousand miles into the Tubo land. However, I must be on guard against tricks and schemes because Re Longmang is known as an expert in the arts of war. I must close the encirclement and guard against any ambush until I capture Re Longmang to crown my victory.

(*The soldiers respond and march on*)

LU SHENG (*To the tune of* **Xinujiaoxu**):

By skilful military strategies,

The Tubo fortresses outside the Great Wall

Fall into our hands one by one.

SOLDIERS:

The commander's orders

Come in stormy power.

On and on,

In cities along the thousand-mile borders,

Tang's flags wave on the city-walls.

One after another,

The passes and fortresses are added

To the Han maps.

(*Enter Messenger*)

MESSENGER:

Report, report, report! As crows are startled in the dale, there might be ambush ahead.

LU SHENG:

That's true. "Where there are black clouds above, there is ambush below." Make a search at

once.

(*Enter a Tubo captain, followed by his soldiers*)

TUBO CAPTAIN:

Shalala, kelele!

(*Starts to fight with the Han soldiers and is defeated. Exit*)

LU SHENG:

What a bandit! I nearly fell into his trap.

SOLDIERS:

This small potato cannot stir up much troubled waters.

(*To the tune of* **Heimaxu**)

What a curse!

For these remaining Tubo troops,

We have made a thorough search.

Like rustles of leaves in the wind,

We have thrown them into utter panic.

LU SHENG:

What destitution!

Blood has stained our swords;

The wind is blowing at our war robes.

(*Wails of wild geese*)

LU SHENG (*Shoots at the wild geese*):

To shoot at the wild geese around,

I stretch my bow

And hit one to the ground.

SOLDIERS (*Hail*):

Here is the wild goose, General. On the foot of the goose, there is a piece of silk with a few lines written on it.

LU SHENG (*Reads*):

> *Here you are in Tianshan,*
> *Which divides Tubo and the Han.*
> *Do not kill all the birds,*
> *Which may requite when they can.*
>
> (*Smiles*)

Stay back, all of you.

> (*Aside*)

This is a letter from Re Longmang, begging me to withdraw my troops. "Do not kill all the birds, which may requite when they can." Yes, when all the birds are killed, the best bow will be shelved. Since Re Longmang is a true warrior, I'll let him go.

> (*To the soldiers*)

What's the name of this mountain?

SOLDIERS:

It's called the Tianshan Mountain.

LU SHENG:

How far is it away from the Yumen Pass?

SOLDIERS:

Nine hundred and ninety-nine miles.

LU SHENG:

Where is the missing mile?

SOLDIERS:

A slab of rock on the Tianshan Mountain occupies one mile.

LU SHENG:

Has anyone else ever marched as far as this mountain?

SOLDIERS:

Never before.

LU SHENG (*Smiles*):

No wonder that an ancient poem reads like this:

> *There remains a slab of stone,*
> *That will for ever stay alone.*

I have started my career as a scholar and crushed the Tubo troops here at the blessing of His Majesty. Therefore, I am fully contented. Brave warriors, let's cut a slab from the Tianshan Mountain and make a victorious return after carving our meritorious deeds on it.

> (*The soldiers respond and begin to cut and carve a slab of rock*)

SOLDIERS (*To the tune of **Yuanlinhaofan***):

> On the towering Tianshan Mountain overhead,
> We apply our hoes and spades
> To cut a slab of rock.
> Taking the mountain as paper and the axe as pen,
> We carve the name of our distinguished commander.

LU SHENG:

I'll make the inscription.

> (*Reads*)

At the imperial edict of Tang to quench the west, the troops went west, marched in the desert for a thousand miles and killed a million Tubo soldiers. The troops have reached the Tianshan Mountain and will return victoriously after carving a slab of rock. This rock will remain forever and ever. The inscription is made by Lu Sheng, Marshall of Quenching the West, on this day, this month, and this year of Emperor Xuanzong's reign.

> (*Lays down his pen and laughs heartily*)

Brave warriors, what will people think of Lu Sheng with the passing of centuries and millenniums?

SOLDIERS (*Respond*):

Naturally.

> (*To the tune of* **Tetelingfan**)
>
> Above is inscribed the year of Tang's Emperor Xuanzong;
>
> Below is inscribed the title "Marshall of Quenching the West".
>
> We went all the way up the Qilian Mountains,
>
> Making twists and turns along the Yellow River.
>
> These lines of inscription
>
> Are carved on a slab of rock
>
> With countless picks and chisels.
>
> With Tang on this side
>
> And Tubo on that side,
>
> The milestone will forever stand on Tianshan.

LU SHENG:

Although we have made the inscription, I am afraid that our merits will be buried in moss after storms or disruptions.

SOLDIERS:

Since the gods will bless His Majesty and you are valiant, the rock will remain unshakable forever and ever.

LU SHENG (*To the tune of* **Shuanghudie**):

> In disregard of the moss and storm,
>
> The lines of inscription
>
> Tower to the sky.
>
> In disregard of the slides and disruptions,
>
> They will shine forever over the mountains and rivers
>
> And scare away the spirits and devils.
>
> Even if the rock becomes a wordless monument,
>
> Once washed, it proves a relic of the past.
>
> (*Enter Messenger*)

MESSENGER:

> *The native country has a vast territory;*

The new grace shines as the sun and the moon.

Master Lu, on seeing your report of victory, His Majesty decreed three days of banqueting for the officials and officers. You have been conferred the title of Marquis of Conquering the West and granted the land tax of three thousand households. When you return to the capital, you will be conferred the titles of Prince Instructor, Defense Minister and Honorary Prime Minister. As His Majesty has sent an envoy to accompany you to the capital, will Your Excellency set off at once?

SOLDIERS:

Congratulations! Congratulations!

LU SHENG:

I should return at once when I hear the favours from His Majesty, but I must make arrangements for everything in the border areas. Within the distance of a thousand miles from the Tianshan Mountain to the Yangguan Pass, you must build three large cities connected with garrison towers. You can cultivate the fields and feed the horses in times of peace; you can reinforce and support each other in times of war. You must follow my instructions.

> (*To the tune of* **Chenzuidongfeng**)
> You must safeguard the Tianshan Mountain
> And never neglect the Lulong region.
> Within the distance of at least a thousand miles,
> The bugles must be heard clearly,
> The troops in garrisons must be on watch
> And always keep high vigilance.

SOLDIERS (*Kneel*):

> We shall follow your instructions
> And obey the imperial rules and regulations
> Laid down by the administrations.

LU SHENG:

In that case, I'm going to change my clothes.

> (*Enter a eunuch with a kerchief and a robe*)

LU SHENG (*Changes his clothes*):

> (*To the tune of* **Jinhuaxiang**)
> Since you will follow my instructions,
> How can I disobey the imperial edict?
> My soul has long crossed the palace bridge.
> (*Sighs*)
> I shall take leave of the warriors
> And take off my battle robe.
> After three years of hardships together,
> I shall leave you behind
> And go to the Yangguan Pass in woe and tears.
> (*Walks on*)

979

The Handan Dream

(*To the tune of **Jinshuizhao***)

The road to the Yangguan Pass

Is the way by which I come and go.

The road to Chang'an

Is not easy to take.

Although I can return before I am too old,

I have been worn with wind and sands.

I have suffered and enjoyed in the army,

Listening to the wild geese in autumn

And the bugles by night.

Amid ringing bells,

Amid ringing bells

And beating drums,

I return on the saddle of a battle steed.

I shall be regarded as Huo Qubing, a famous general,

And return as Ban Chao, an envoy abroad.

(*Sound of drums and bugles within*)

SOLDIERS (*To the tune of **Coda***):

With drums and music echoing in the camp,

The general who has fought on the border will return.

LU SHENG:

Brave warriors,

Do not forget my merits in these years;

Guard well this famous mountain with its monument.

Ministers serve in the palace court,

But I have fought in the battlefield.

I'll be conferred the title of a lord

And have a position firmly sealed.

Scene Eighteen
Good News for the Wife

(*Enter Miss Cui, followed by Maidservant and Meixiang*)

MISS CUI (*To the tune of **Taoyuanyiguren***):

The young Master Lu had a happy marriage —

He married Miss Cui and lived in Qinghe.

Man and wife lived a distinguished life.

But were suddenly separated.

ALL:

May heaven bless us

So that he will return home and live a peaceful life.

MISS CUI (*In the pattern of* ***Changxiangsi***):

> *As there was a Miss Cui in Boling,*
>
> *So there is a Miss Cui in Qinghe.*
>
> *The lovesick Cui Hui is now born again,*
>
> *But who is she in love with?*
>
> *You have gone to Guanxi*
>
> *And crossed the river in Hexi.*
>
> *While you look south and I look north,*
>
> *How the dangling bell tinkles!*

Auntie, I have never heard from Master Lu since he went to fight in the west. I don't know how he is doing with his military affairs.

MAIDSERVANT:

He is bound to win by the blessing of His Majesty. However, you have grown wan these days.

MISS CUI (*To the tune of* ***Tanpojinziling***):

> I have no taste for tea or meals,
>
> Never in a mood to dress and make up.

MAIDSERVANT:

Anyway he is an official.

MISS CUI:

> On business he keeps his mind,
>
> But leaves his wife behind.

MAIDSERVANT:

> When he weathers the wind and sands,
>
> How can we know what he is doing?

MISS CUI:

> He has intelligence
>
> And wisdom to his claim,
>
> But suffers from "fame and name".

ALL:

> Spring is gone
>
> And autumn is near.
>
> The wife shelters her face with her gauze fan
>
> And sheds a flood of tears
>
> For her man's alluring affection.

MISS CUI (*To the tune of* ***Yeyudawutong***):

> I tidy my emerald pins
>
> And face the mirror without a word.

MAIDSERVANT:

What about taking a stroll in the back garden?

MISS CUI (*Walks on*):

> When I leisurely move my feet
>
> And walk slowly,
>
> What if I should trip my steps?
>
> (*Stops*)

MAIDSERVANT:

> If the lotus flowers
>
> Do not blossom for the beloved,
>
> Why should they come into blooms?

ALL:

> With profound affection,
>
> It's easy to pass the long summer day
>
> But is it possible to cut short the winter night?

MAIDSERVANT:

Meixiang, fetch the flute and the lute and play a bit to while away the time.

> (*Meixiang and maidservants play the flute and the lute*)

MISS CUI:

That's enough.

> (*To the tune of* **Tanpojinziling**)
>
> The music of the flute and the lute
>
> Throws me into sorrow.
>
> I'll sit in the room for a while
>
> To idle away my time.
>
> I have nothing to do in this pleasant season.

MEIXIANG:

> You have seduced this man
>
> And made love with him.
>
> And now you'll look for him
>
> And make all the moans.
>
> How is a widow to spend her life?

ALL:

> Spring is gone
>
> And autumn is near.
>
> The wife shelters her face with her gauze fan
>
> And sheds a flood of tears
>
> For her man's alluring affection.

MISS CUI (*To the tune of* **Yeyudawutong**):

> I expect the horse
>
> To bring him back to me.
>
> The hills and rills afar
>
> Are enshrouded in mist.

MAIDSERVANT:

If you don't want to go to the back garden, let's gaze out of the front gate. There might be some message from the border area.

MISS CUI:

That's true. That's true.

> (*Walks*)

VOICE WITHIN (*Sings a ballad*):

> Although young maids worry about their age
>
> With too much regret,
>
> Let's listen to their songs.

MEIXIANG:

> When I lean on the gate and look outside,
>
> I see your knitted brows.
>
> When I look up,
>
> I see your slant phoenix hairpin.

ALL:

> With profound affection,
>
> It's easy to pass the long summer day
>
> But is it possible to cut short the winter night?
>
> (*Enter an officer*)

OFFICER:

> *An urgent message reports victories;*
>
> *Favours come from His Majesty.*

Madam, when His Excellency won victory after victory and sent a quick message to the court, His Majesty was delighted and told the ministers and generals to celebrate for three days. His Excellency has been conferred the title of Marquis of Conquering the West and granted the land tax of three thousand households. His Majesty has sent an envoy to call him back at once, to take up the position of Defense Minister with the titles of Prince Instructor and Honorary Prime Minister. He is to serve at court morning and evening.

MISS CUI:

Thank heavens!

> (*To the tune of* **Coda**)
>
> As the lucky spider hangs on my skirt,
>
> So the sudden good news burns my ears.
>
> Let's arrange song and dance to meet him.
>
> *At the time when he left, I was so sad;*
>
> *When he returns, drums and music ring.*
>
> *May I venture to ask the passing lad*
>
> *How he compares my man with the hero Huo Qubing?*

Scene Nineteen
Slandering

(*Enter Yuwen Rong, followed by his attendants*)

YUWEN RONG (*To the tune of* **Qiuyeyue**):

> The carriage and four
>
> Has just reached the court.
>
> Most of the officials are servile,
>
> But I cannot tolerate those who are thoughtless.
>
> (*Giggles*)
>
> I'll make it today;
>
> I'll make it today.
>
> *To my great joy, His Majesty is biased*
>
> *And listens to me alone on this earth.*
>
> *I would not make trouble this life,*
>
> *But I was wicked by birth.*

I'm Yuwen Rong, the present-day Prime Minister. A few years ago, the Number One Scholar Lu Sheng refused to be a servile student to me. Therefore, I've always borne grudges against him. I tried to get him into the mire by assigning him the job of digging the channels. However, who knows that he achieved the feat of digging a three-hundred-mile canal. When I tried again to get him into trouble by assigning him the job of fighting the Tubo troops, he achieved the feat of expanding one thousand miles of border territory. His Majesty endowed him with the title of Marquis of Conquering the West, Prince Instructor, Defense Minister and Honorary Prime Minister. By now I haven't yet found another way to get him into a trap. After a few days of meditation, I decided to send a reliable agent to probe into his private secrets. It is reported that he bribed the Tubo general into feigning a defeat and thus won an easy victory. When he reached the Tianshan Mountain area, he got a letter from the Tubo general tied at the foot of a wild goose. After he read the letter, he murmured to himself that he would withdraw the troops and stop pursuing the enemy.

(*Giggles*)

Isn't this an evident proof that he had secret communication with the enemy and committed treason? If I let him get away with that, I will never have a better chance. I have drafted an impeachment against him, but I wonder whether the recently promoted Honorary Prime Minister Xiao Song will sign it or not. Now that I've set a trap for him, I don't know when he will come.

(*Enter Xiao Song*)

XIAO SONG (*To the tune of* **Xidijin**):

> Both in the office with topmost claim,
>
> Prime Minister is a worthy name.
>
> (*Smiles*)

With Lu Sheng in charge of military affairs,

He and I become pillars treading on airs.

(Greets Yuwen Rong)

We enter the palace hall at dawn

YUWEN RONG:

And leave the imperial office at dusk.

XIAO SONG:

The fastidious ministers at court

YUWEN RONG:

Spread the gossip in vain.

XIAO SONG:

Your Highness, where comes the gossip?

YUWEN RONG:

Don't you know? It goes around the court that Lu Sheng should be executed for his towering crime of having secret communication with the Tubo troops and committing treason. If we don't report it to the emperor, we'll be held responsible.

XIAO SONG:

What do you mean?

YUWEN RONG:

Why do you think he reached the Tianshan Mountain and suddenly turned back? It happened that he accepted bribery and a private letter from the Tubo general.

XIAO SONG:

As Lu Sheng is a meritorious minister, we'd better refrain ourselves.

YUWEN RONG *(Laughs)*:

*(To the tune of **Bashengganzhou**)*

He cheats and betrays His Majesty;

He keeps illicit relations with foreign nations

And leaks out national secrets.

XIAO SONG:

I don't think that's the true story. As the Tubo general fled out of fear, it's a great success for Lu Sheng.

YUWEN RONG *(Laughs)*:

Re Longmang

May have feigned

To be defeated.

Otherwise,

Lu Sheng should have crushed the Tubo headquarters;

Why should he have read the letter in private?

YUWEN RONG, XIAO SONG:

Don't rush to a conclusion

As it is no small matter.

XIAO SONG (*To the previous tune*):

> To be true or not true —
>
> That is the question.
>
> As the border areas are far away,
>
> We have to make sure.

YUWEN RONG:

The story is absolutely true; otherwise, Lu Sheng should have reported it to His Majesty when he received the letter from the Tubo general.

XIAO SONG:

> The commander in the army
>
> May make decisions according to the circumstances.
>
> What's more, he's recovered the border areas.

YUWEN RONG (*Gets angry*):

You're colluding to deceive His Majesty.

XIAO SONG:

> I'd rather collude to give my advice
>
> Than see a loyal minister to be wronged.

YUWEN RONG, XIAO SONG:

> Don't rush to a conclusion
>
> As it is no small matter.

YUWEN RONG (*Laughs*):

Oh I see. You're defending your colleague instead of your state. I've got everything ready. Here's the manuscript for the impeachment. Just have a look.

XIAO SONG (*Reads*):

Right Prime Minister Yuwen Rong and Left Prime Minister Xiao Song are to present an impeachment against a treacherous general Lu Sheng, the former Administrator and Military Commander in Hexi and the present Marquis of the West, Defense Minister and Honorary Prime Minister, who received letters and bribes from the Tubo general Re Longmang. While Re Longmang feigned a defeat and retreated, Lu Sheng feigned to make advances. On arriving at the Tianshan Region, Lu Sheng received a private letter from Re Longmang and then withdrew his troops. Lu Sheng must be beheaded for high treason. Your obedient ministers Yuwen Rong and Xiao Song bow and report to Your Majesty. Wow! For such critical matters, Your Excellency is going to make a vague impeachment without giving me any previous notice. In such circumstances, you are compelling me to sign it!

YUWEN RONG (*Irritated*):

Do you dare to say three "no's"?

XIAO SONG:

No! No! No!

YUWEN RONG (*Sneers*):

How daring you are! Tell the secretary to fetch a pen and add the lines to accuse you of high treason as well. You will have your time to plead for yourself.

XIAO SONG (*Sighs aside*):

"Misfortune befalls him that contends." It's hard for me to contend with him on these matters. I used to present my memorial to the emperor with the signature of "Faithful", but today I'll have to play some tricks by adding an "un" before my signature so that I may find some excuse in the future.

(*To Yuwen Rong*)

Please calm your anger, Your Excellency. I'm willing to sign it.

(*Signs his name*)

YUWEN RONG (*Laughs*):

I said that you would not be so bold. Let's present our joint-impeachment to His Majesty tomorrow morning.

XIAO SONG:

The heroes are not to be smeared with art and craft;

YUWEN RONG:

The treacherous pretenders must be wiped out.

XIAO SONG:

No gentleman e'er shows regret or doubt;

YUWEN RONG:

No genuine man e'er goes without a vicious heart.

Scene Twenty
Narrow Escape from Death

(*Enter Butler*)

BUTLER:

Medals are conferred from the state
To officials of the topmost rate.

I am the butler to Master Lu, Marquis of Conquering the West. In command of all the troops for several years, Master Lu has been Honorary Prime Minister. All the officers and officials in the court are his disciples. As a special favour to him, His Majesty gives audience to him three times a day. As it's about noontime and Master Lu will soon be back from his second audience in the court, I'll be waiting for him now. Here comes Madame Cui.

(*Enter Miss Cui, followed by Maidservant and Meixiang*)

MISS CUI:

I am Miss Cui. With blessings from His Majesty, my husband has been promoted to the highest civil and military positions. The residence bestowed by His Majesty is equipped with a magnificent gate and decorative buildings. He is highly respected in the court because of his brilliant military exploits in the border areas. Not to speak of my husband, I as his wife am no less influential. I am entitled as the First-Rank Lady and all my grown-up children are promoted to high positions. How extraordinary it is!

(*Noise of tiles being broken within*)

MISS CUI (*Taken aback*):

Old maid, what's the noise?

MAIDSERVANT (*Takes a look*):

A mandarin-duck tile has fallen broken from the eaves.

MISS CUI (*Astonished*):

Alas, how is it that a mandarin-duck tile has fallen broken?

MEIXIANG (*Looks*):

Oh, the tile is broken by a golden pellet shot at a crow.

MISS CUI (*Sighs*):

As is said by a saint: "The crow knows where the wind blows and the ant knows when the rain falls. Misfortunes come when the skin and flesh shivers; good tidings come when the skirt-belt is untied." The mandarin-ducks symbolize the love between man and wife; the crows caw with bad omens; the fallen pellet is a sign of disunion; the broken tile means separation. Gracious heavens, does it mean that shocking news is coming?

> (*To the tune of* **Shanghuashi**)
>
> I sit in my mansion, tall and magnificent,
>
> And see subordinates standing in the hall.
>
> In the shade of trees beside the eaves,
>
> Who can approach the mandarin-duck tiles
>
> And shoot at crows with golden pellets?
>
> (*Noise of an approaching procession*)

MISS CUI:

Now that my man is returning from the court, get the wine ready.

> (*Enter Lu Sheng, followed by his attendants*)

LU SHENG:

I am Lu Sheng. After I consulted on some affairs before His Majesty and ate lunch, I am going home now.

> (*To the tune of* **Yao**)
>
> In a decorative carriage I pass the Donghua Gate
>
> And go home girdled with a jade belt and ushered by gongs.
>
> The new embankment is built on old sands,
>
> But I can hardly enjoy the sights with my wife
>
> Along the palace moat in all its vernal splendour.
>
> (*Lu Sheng and Miss Cui greet each other*)

MISS CUI:

As you are just back from the court, I've opened a jar of royal wine and will make a toast to you.

LU SHENG:

Thank you very much.

> (*Music within*)

LU SHENG:

I'll first drink a few cups with you and have them bottoms up. For each cup you do not drink up, you'll have to drink one more cup of wine.

MISS CUI:

Agreed.

LU SHENG (*Drinks the wine*):

This is a cup for the distinction of man and wife. Bottoms up!

MISS CUI:

You've finished your cup. Now it's my turn. A cup for the distinction of man and wife. Bottoms up!

LU SHENG (*Smiles*):

You haven't drained your cup.

MISS CUI (*Smiles and drinks*):

I've drained this cup. As the poem has it,

> The wine down the narrow orifice is as red as the pearls.

LU SHENG (*Smiles*):

Madam, your orifice is wide enough.

> (*Drumbeats within*)

VOICE WITHIN:

Report, report! It's said that armed soldiers have come out of the Donghua Gate. We don't know why they are coming?

LU SHENG:

Never mind about them. I'll call bottoms up and drain the cup with you.

MISS CUI (*Drinks*):

A cup for the distinction of wife and man. Bottoms up!

LU SHENG:

You've taken the lead and drained this cup. Now it's my turn. A cup for the distinction of wife and man. Bottoms up!

MISS CUI:

You haven't drained your cup.

LU SHENG:

Madam, as the poem has it,

> The wine on the gilded stick flows in drips.

MISS CUI:

Master, your stick is always dripping.

> (*Lu Sheng laughs*)
>
> (*Drumbeats within*)
>
> (*Enter Butler*)

BUTLER:

Report, report! Armed soldiers have come out of the Donghua Gate and filled the streets and lanes. What a roar they're making!

LU SHENG:

Never mind about them. I'll dry the third cup with my wife.

> (*Enter Lu Sheng's sons, weeping*)

SONS:

Dad and Mom, the armed soldiers in battle array are approaching our residence.

LU SHENG (*Startled*):

(*To the tune of* **Northern Zuihuayin**)

In all these days,

I dream a lot while serving the night shift in the court,

Surrounded by pretty ladies in red and green.

My residence should be kept quiet;

In this magnificent mansion,

Who dares to make such a noise?

(*Listens*)

(*Cries of "Arrest him! Arrest him!" within*)

LU SHENG:

They keep shouting

"Arrest him! Arrest him!"

Have the thieves run away or escaped from prison? Otherwise,

Why are there noises of weapons and soldiers?

(*Enter officers with spears and ropes, ordering the soldiers to surround the house*)

(*Exeunt Maidservant and Meixiang in a panic*)

LU SHENG (*Annoyed*):

Who dares!

OFFICERS (*To the tune of* **Southern Huameixu**):

The imperial edict to arrest you

LU SHENG:

Oh, you are imperial envoys. Come in please.

OFFICERS:

Is brought to your house from the Central Office.

LU SHENG (*In a panic*):

Whom are you going to arrest in my house?

OFFICERS:

We've come to arrest you,

To arrest you alone.

LU SHENG (*Frightened*):

So you've come to arrest me. What am I guilty of?

OFFICERS:

The Right Prime Minister has accused you of a serious crime.

It is no ordinary crime,

But a crime that violates the martial law.

LU SHENG:

Why should I come to this when I've done nothing wrong to the country?

OFFICER:

I don't know. Here is the arrest edict. On your knees and listen.

(*Lu Sheng and Miss Cui kneel on the ground*)

OFFICER (*Reads*):

Here is the imperial edict: The former Administrator and Military Commander Lu Sheng exchanged illicit letters with the Tubo general for ulterior motives. He is to be arrested, brought to the Yunyang execution ground and put to death in public without delay. This is the imperial edict.

(*Lu Sheng and Miss Cui kowtow and then rise to their feet crying "Heavens"*)

LU SHENG, MISS CUI:

Gracious heavens!

> Oh, oh!
>
> When misfortune falls from the sky,
>
> How can we air our grievances to His Majesty?

LU SHENG:

Where do all the troubles come from?

> (*To the tune of* **Northern Xiqianying**)
>
> As swift as the wind and the thunder,
>
> Misfortune is a bolt from the blue sky.

I'll air my grievances in front of His Majesty.

OFFICERS:

The imperial court is closed.

LU SHENG:

Will you be so kind as to

> Allow me to see His Majesty in court
>
> By tarrying a bit
>
> So that I can
>
> Wait till the late audience?

OFFICERS:

The imperial edict forbids it.

LU SHENG (*Weeps*):

Madam, madam, I was born to the east of Mount Taihang and had a few acres of land to make both ends meet. Why should I have sought official career and come to this! I shall never be able to go along the way to Handan, wearing a short fur-coat and riding a black donkey again! Fetch a knife!

> I'd better kill myself with a knife.
>
> (*Attempts to kill himself and is stopped by Miss Cui*)

OFFICERS:

According to the imperial edict, you are not to kill yourself but be put to death in public.

LU SHENG:

Yes, that's it. A minister should live a sensible life and die a sensible death. Madam, bring our sons to air grievances in front of the palace gate. I'm going to the execution ground.

> Sooner or later,
>
> I shall be beheaded.

The Handan Dream

Even if I run counter to the imperial edict,

Nothing more comes but death.

(*Exeunt all*)

(*Enter Eunuch Gao*)

EUNUCH GAO:

I am Eunuch Gao. Who will save the Defense Minister? The imperial court is closed today because a meritorious minister is to be put to death. I'll wait and see which minister is going to present a memorial to His Majesty.

(*Enter Miss Cui with her sons*)

MISS CUI:

Now that my man is going to the execution ground, I'm bringing my sons to air grievances in front of the palace gate. I'll make haste and approach the Zhengyang Gate.

(*Shouts*)

Gracious Emperor, Lu Sheng is grievously wronged!

EUNUCH GAO:

The imperial court is closed because a meritorious minister is to be put to death. Who is it that dares to make such a racket?

MISS CUI:

I am Lu Sheng's wife, entitled the First-Rank Lady by His Majesty. I'm bringing his sons to air grievances.

EUNUCH GAO (*Sighs aside*):

No ministers in the court but this woman with her sons are airing grievances. How pitiful she is!

(*Turns back*)

Are you Madam Lu? Just air your grievances here.

MISS CUI (*Kneels on the ground*):

Gracious Emperor, Gracious Emperor! Lu Sheng's wife is airing grievances!

(*To the tune of **Southern Huameixu***)

A longtime enemy

Tries to persecute Lu Sheng.

What wrong has my man done in court

That he is to be put to death?

Illicit relations with the Tubo general

And high treason are concocted crimes.

MISS CUI, EUNUCH GAO:

Oh, oh!

When misfortune falls from the sky,

How can we air our grievances to His Majesty?

EUNUCH GAO (*Weeps*):

How pitiable! How pitiable! Wait here for the imperial edict and I'll present your grievances to His Majesty.

MISS CUI:

I'll take the dust as my incense and pray to Heaven and Earth.

>   (*Kowtows*)

Your obedient servant Cui is airing grievances here. Heavens, heavens! Change the sacred mind of His Majesty and save the life of my man! Such a long time has passed and the imperial edict has not arrived yet.

>   (*Enter Eunuch Gao with Pei Guangting*)

EUNUCH GAO:

Here is the imperial edict: "As there is some injustice in Lu Sheng's case, Pei Guangting is to bring the order of amnesty to the Yunyang execution ground and pardon Lu Sheng from death. Lu Sheng is to go on exile in the Ghost Gate Pass of Yazhou in southern Guangdong. He should set off at once. Pay tribute to the Emperor!"

>   (*Weeps*)

How pitiable! How pitiable!

>   *While no one listens to cranes' weeping words,*
>
>   *An order of amnesty comes with singing birds.*
>
>   (*Exit*)
>
>   (*Drumbeats within*)
>
>   (*Enter Lu Sheng dressed in prison garb and kerchief, escorted by soldiers*)

LU SHENG (*To the tune of **Northern Chuduizi***):

>   The devils with wings stand in line,
>
>   (*Enter the executioner with a sharp knife, who comes forward and kowtows*)

LU SHENG:

Who are you?

EXECUTIONER:

I am the executioner to wait on you.

LU SHENG (*Frightened*):

I'm scared out of my wits.

>   The blade of his knife shows ill omen.

EXECUTIONER:

Please wear the one-word flag on your back, Your Excellency.

LU SHENG:

What's the word?

EXECUTIONER, SOLDIERS:

The word "Beheading".

LU SHENG:

Thanks for the grace of His Majesty. I thought that I would be chopped to pieces, but I shall be beheaded only. I'll wear the flag. I'll wear the flag.

>   (*Amid sound of gongs and drums, the soldiers plant the one-word flag on Lu Sheng's back*)

LU SHENG:

For whom is the banquet prepared on the tent mat?

EXECUTIONER, SOLDIERS:

The Royal Banquet Hall has a dinner ready for the convict awaiting execution. You can wear a flower and enjoy your meal.

LU SHENG:

Yes, this flag

> Serves as the royal flower to guide the dead soul.

The drums and gongs

> Play the music accompanying the late audience.

The dinner

> Provides salted fish for the hungry ghost.

EXECUTIONER, SOLDIERS:

Make haste to dine and wine. It's about time.

LU SHENG:

I've had enough of royal dinners in the court. However,

> *As the underworld has no alehouse sign,*
>
> *From whom can I buy wine?*

I'll kneel on the ground and drink a cup of wine bestowed by His Majesty.

> (*Kneels and drinks*)

How can I gulp it!

> (*To the tune of* **Yao**)

For the moment,

> The wine moistens my throat;

I hope that His Majesty

> Will offer sacrifice to a meritorious minister.

EXECUTIONER, SOLDIERS:

Be on your way now that you've drunk the wine, Your Highness.

LU SHENG (*Kowtows*):

Here's my gratitude to His Majesty for the wine.

EXECUTIONER, SOLDIERS:

Hey, stand aside, onlookers, lest you delay the time.

LU SHENG (*Walks on, tightly bound*):

> With roaring crowds back and forth,

I am squeezed and have to

> Stumble my way to the execution site.

Is it that

> The robbers also enjoy the sight?
>
> (*The executioner and soldiers shout the way amid gong-beats and drumbeats*)

LU SHENG (*Asks*):

What is the place with flag poles?

EXECUTIONER, SOLDIERS:

It is the West Corner.

LU SHENG (*To the tune of* **Southern Diliuzi**):

> Beneath the flagpoles,
>
> Beneath the flagpoles,
>
> A post is set for punishment.
>
> The Yunyang execution ground,
>
> The Yunyang execution ground
>
> Is a refined corner.

EXECUTIONER, SOLDIERS:

You are no exception, Your Highness,

> Many ministers of distinction
>
> Come here alone
>
> And never turn around.

Like caressing the head with glue,

> Your hair will stick to my hands;
>
> There is no alternative.

LU SHENG (*Breaks apart the ropes in anger*):

> (*To the tune of* **Northern Guadifeng**)

Oh,

> My hair stands erect in anger.

EXECUTIONER (*Slips the back of his knife on Lu Sheng's neck*):

Your tender neck can hardly sustain the pain.

LU SHENG:

Alas, for you to test your knife,

> My neck is perfect, without a flaw;
>
> The Yunyang execution ground looks like a grand painting.

EXECUTIONER, SOLDIERS:

Have you killed anyone, Your Highness?

LU SHENG:

Well, by martial law,

> I had countless heads cut at my orders
>
> And now it's my turn to lose my head.

EXECUTIONER, SOLDIERS:

Here we are at the Soul-Leaving Bridge.

LU SHENG:

For several years

> I've been here to look back at the capital
>
> And crossed the Soul-Leaving Bridge.
>
> (*Sound of bugles within*)

EXECUTIONER (*Waves the flag*):

It's time for you to ascend to Heaven, Your Highness.

LU SHENG (*Laughs*):

> *Malicious as you look like a devil,*

You also mouth fine words.

When the knife falls, I shall be born again in Heaven. Alas, please listen to my last words carefully. At that very moment,

>Do not make a miss.

>See to it that you hold my head high

>Lest blood should stain my robe.

EXECUTIONER, SOLDIERS:

On your knees, Your Highness.

>(*Lu Sheng kneels to be bound up*)

>(*The executioner sharpens his knife*)

>(*Sound of wind within*)

EXECUTIONER:

What a gust of wind that blows the sands all over! Oops, where's your neck, Your Highness?

>(*Feels*)

Here it is. Stretch your neck, Your Highness.

>(*Lu Sheng bends his head*)

>(*The executioner raises the knife*)

VOICE OF URGENT SHOUTS WITHIN:

The imperial edict is coming! Stop the execution! Stop the execution!

>(*Enter Pei Guangting in a hurry carrying the imperial edict, followed by Miss Cui*)

PEI GUANGTING (*To the tune of* **Southern Shuangshengzi**):

>The imperial grace is great;

>The imperial grace is great;

>You can beat the drums to air your grievances.

>The imperial edict is coming;

>The imperial edict is coming;

>There will be no execution in Yunyang.

>No punishment today;

>No punishment today.

>Don't be frightened;

>Don't be frightened.

>At a hair's breadth,

>He escapes death from the knife.

Here's the imperial edict: Although Lu Sheng is guilty of a crime that deserves ten thousand deaths, I pardon him from death for heavenly grace. Lu Sheng is to go on exile in the Ghost Gate Pass of Yazhou in southern Guangdong. There should not be a moment's delay. Pay tribute to the Emperor!

>(*Lu Sheng is unbound*)

LU SHENG (*Lies prostrate on the ground and then kowtows*):

Long live the Emperor! I am gratified with the grace of His Majesty. Who is the envoy?

PEI GUANGTING:

This is Pei Guangting.

LU SHENG:

Brother, brother, do I still have my head on me?

PEI GUANGTING:

Let me have a look.

> (*Looks and pats Lu Sheng on the head*)

What a head of longevity you have!

LU SHENG (*To the tune of **Northern Simenzi***):

> My soul lingers at the edge of a knife;

Oh, oh, oh,

> I nearly committed suicide with a knife.

Minister Pei, may I ask why Minister Xiao also signed when the memorial was drafted by Yuwen Rong?

> (*Sighs*)
>
> In a case that involves execution,
>
> How can he sign with the Prime Minister?

PEI GUANGTING:

I'm afraid that Minister Xiao knows nothing about it.

LU SHENG:

> Do you mean to say, do you mean to say that
>
> The old minister could bear a humiliation
>
> By biding his time with inaction?
>
> (*Sighs when wind starts*)
>
> When I look at the sand on the execution ground
>
> And the flowers on the bloody field,
>
> I feel pity for the generals and their steeds.

PEI GUANGTING:

You may say farewell to your wife here. I'll go back and report to His Majesty.

> *Take good care when you are in the swamps*
>
> *As gentle rain will fall when the time arrives.*

Good-bye!

> (*Exit*)

MISS CUI (*Weeps*):

How is it that words get stuck in my throat? I've brought a kettle of wine to calm you down and to see you off.

LU SHENG:

I've wined and dined in prison at the grace of His Majesty. I have had enough.

MISS CUI:

Our sons are kowtowing at the palace gate. Have a look at them before you leave.

LU SHENG:

Forget about it! Forget about it! They will only disturb my mind. Don't let them see me here, Madam.

MISS CUI (*Weeps*):

Oh heavens! I'll give you a toast to show my passions as your wife and on behalf of our sons.

> (*To the tune of* **Southern Baolaocui**)
>
> Oh, oh! Oops, oops!
>
> (*Drops the cup in panic*)

Alas!

> Trembling with fear, I can hardly hold the plate.
>
> I am shivering with cold;
>
> Sobbing and howling,
>
> I moan and cry
>
> In a hoarse voice.
>
> (*Drumbeats within*)

VOICE WITHIN:

Master Lu, hurry up! Hurry up! The imperial edict comes from the capital to urge the departure without delay.

> (*Enter Lu Sheng's sons in tears*)

SONS:

Dear Dad!

MISS CUI:

How can your sons tear themselves away from you!

LU SHENG:

As a woman, you do not know that the imperial court says that I must go on exile outside the Ghost Gate Pass because I have ulterior motives. A criminal on exile has to leave at the fixed time. Oh heavens, as man is not made of soil or wood, who can bear separation from his flesh and blood? I'm afraid that I've involved you and our sons in all the trouble and inconvenience.

> (*Lu Sheng's sons grasp him, eager to go with him*)
>
> You ought not to go with me, my dear sons!
>
> (*Weeps with his sons*)
>
> My sons cannot stay with me;
>
> My wife cannot live with me;
>
> We can only share a bed in death.
>
> (*Miss Cui faints*)

LU SHENG (*Holds Miss Cui*):

> (*To the tune of* **Northern Shuixianzi**)

Oh, oh, oh!

> She's cried her eyes out.

Pull, pull, pull! Pull her up

> Lest she becomes a stone statue.
>
> (*Lu Sheng's sons weep*)

LU SHENG:

Suffer, suffer, suffer!

> They will suffer too much.

Pain, pain, pain!

    The pain stabs at my heart.

I, I, I!

    When I die beside a noxious river,

You, you, you!

    Madam, you will become a widow.

MISS CUI:

Have another look at your sons!

LU SHENG:

Well, well, well!

    My sons cannot take my place.

Now, now, now!

    With these words I've taken leave of His Majesty.

It's time for me to leave. Good-bye!

MISS CUI:

Where are you going?

LU SHENG:

Go, go, go!

    I'm going to the remotest corner of the earth.

    (*Exit*)

MISS CUI (*Weeps*):

Go back home, sons! As his wife, am I not going to accompany him a bit?

    (*To the tune of* **Southern Doushuangji**)

    Although my man is pardoned by His Majesty,

    I feel the sword stabbing at my heart.

    There is no one to help him,

    To help him pack luggage.

    As a minister,

    Why should he have come to this?

    (*Reenter Lu Sheng*)

LU SHENG (*Greets Miss Cui*):

Why are you catching up with me again, Madam?

MISS CUI:

I cannot set my mind at ease because there is no one to accompany you. I've brought a small chunk of silver in my sleeve for you to spend on the way.

LU SHENG:

Who dares to come close to me as a convict? I'll beg my way by myself. Please bring the silver back and buy some rice and firewood. Do not let our sons suffer!

    (*To the tune of* **Northern Coda**)

    Can a convict's family have much hope?

    I fear that other tricks might be done on us.

Madam, madam,

Just keep waiting with patience

Until I come back and win fame again.

A man of worthy deeds is harmed by lies;

On exile to the Ghost Gate Pass he departs.

Weeping eyes look at weeping eyes;

A broken heart sees off a broken heart.

Scene Twenty-One
The Slanderer's Satisfaction

(*Enter Yuwen Rong, in laughter*)

YUWEN RONG (*To the tune of* **Lülüjin**):

I have a honey tongue

And a dagger heart.

Who is so vile as I

And yet serves as a lord?

Those who come must do as I say.

How can a fool like Lu Sheng

Escape from miasma and be on homeward way?

His family is done away with.

I am the slanderous minister Yuwen Rong. In for a chip, in for a chunk. Lu Sheng is a meritorious minister, who has dug 300 miles of canal and expanded 1,000 miles of border territory. When I presented a memorial to His Majesty, saying that he had illicit relations with Tubo, he was to be put to death in public. It is unfortunate that his wife Miss Cui from Qinghe begged His Majesty for pardon from death and Lu Sheng was sent on exile to a place full of miasma in Hainan. How can he escape from death when be crosses the Ghost Gate Pass? He's got into my trap! However, a mere woman as she is, Miss Cui might stir up trouble at the instigation of Xiao and Pei if she is left unrestrained. I presented a secret memorial to His Majesty yesterday, saying, "As the wife of a traitorous minister, Miss Cui should be reduced to the state of a slave maid; as the descendants of a traitorous minister, Lu Sheng's sons should be banished to a distant location." His Majesty decreed, "Lu Sheng's sons are to live outside the capital and Miss Cui is to serve in the Royal Weaving Mill." No sooner had I obtained the imperial edict than I sent a capital envoy to confine Miss Cui in the Weaving Mill and to expel Lu Sheng's sons out of the capital. I'm now waiting for a reply from the envoy.

(*Enter Envoy*)

ENVOY:

An envoy in the capital

Is not an official of the lowest rank.

I've come back to report to you, Your Excellency.

YUWEN RONG:

Have you brought Miss Cui to the Royal Weaving Mill?

ENVOY:

Please listen to me.

> (*To the tune of* **Huangying'er**)
>
> Still pretty in her middle age,
>
> She wept
>
> When she heard of her detention.
>
> She fainted when she heard the edict.
>
> All her properties confiscated,
>
> All her sons on the run,
>
> She is a criminal under custody.

YUWEN RONG, ENVOY:

> It's easily done
>
> That the foe is banished.
>
> How happy we are!

YUWEN RONG:

As you are very capable, you'll be rewarded for your merits. Put in file in the Ministry of Personnel.

ENVOY (*Kowtows to show his gratitude*):

> *Kill one and see him bleed;*
>
> *Do a merit and do it well.*
>
> *As we are of the same breed,*
>
> *You do not have to tell.*

Scene Twenty-Two
Sufferings on Exile

> (*Enter Highwayman A*)

HIGHWAYMAN A:

> *With hairs on my face all my life,*
>
> *I have been nicknamed "Ghost-Head Knife".*

I was born in Lianzhou and have been a highwayman as my life career. As I have nothing to do these days, I'll call on my brother in Gumei Village to resume our business.

> (*Walks on*)

Is my brother in?

> (*Enter Highwayman B*)

HIGHWAYMAN B:

> *A loafer half my life,*
>
> *I'm called "Shave-Up".*

HIGHWAYMAN A:

Why are you called "Shave-Up"?

HIGHWAYMAN B:

If I do not get anything when I say "Money or life", I'll just shave up his chin with a knife.

HIGHWAYMAN A:

Cool, cool! However, what shall we do now that we have got nothing all these days, brother?

(*Tiger roar within*)

HIGHWAYMAN B:

A tiger is coming. Let's wait for the passers-by ahead.

Compared with tigers and wolves,

Men are even more cruel.

(*Exeunt Highwaymen A and B*)

(*Enter Lu Sheng, carrying an umbrella*)

LU SHENG:

Hard is the way;

Hard is the way.

Hard is not the hill;

Hard is not the rill.

Distinction in the morn

And death in the eve.

Hard is the way

That men grieve.

I, Lu Sheng, used to rank high in office for my meritorious deeds, but went on exile after a narrow escape from death without anyone daring to say a word for me. I begged all the way up to Tanzhou, where a former colleague of mine secretly gave me a servant-boy by the name of Trance, who carries the luggage for me. Now that I've passed Lianzhou and approached Guangdong, I have to go on at the risk of my life. Is the servant-boy strong enough to go on?

(*Calls aloud*)

Trance! Trance!

(*Enter Trance, shouldering the luggage with a pole*)

TRANCE:

I'm so tired. Will you carry the luggage for a while?

LU SHENG:

Will you carry the luggage for a little while more?

(*Walks on*)

(*To the tune of **Jiang'ershui***)

I can hardly walk on any more,

In scenes not to be found in the capital,

On my way to Yazhou not conceivable in the Yumen Pass.

TRANCE:

A dark expanse of cloud is pending overhead.

LU SHENG:

Shut up! This is the head of noxious gas, called miasma.

> (*Sighs*)

> The dark clouds of miasma cover the sky.

Let's move on, covering our mouths.

> (*Walks on*)

Well, we've crossed the miasma.

TRANCE:

Another miasma is coming.

LU SHENG:

How can it be? How can it be?

> I cannot rely on Heaven here;

> I have survived in the north,

> But will die in the south.

> (*Tiger roar within*)

TRANCE (*Weeps*):

A tiger is coming. I cannot move a step any more.

LU SHENG:

Are you bewitched? Where's the tiger?

TRANCE:

Don't you see the tiger there?

> (*A tiger jumps onto the stage*)

LU SHENG (*Startled*):

Oh heavens! Heavens!

> (*To the tune of **Teteling**)

> Is it a mountain sprite or a wild cat?

> It does look like a leopard.

As the ancient saying goes,

> *The knife does not kill an innocent man;*

> *The tiger does not eat a fleshless man.*

There's no flesh on me.

TRANCE:

I am even thinner than you.

LU SHENG:

> How can a bony scholar

> Serve as a meal?

> The tiger is more fierce

> Than the hound that bites.

> (*The tiger jumps up*)

LU SHENG:

> It jumps without turning its head,

> A sign of bad omen.

As the tiger usually makes three jumps before attacking, I'll open my umbrella.

(*Opens his umbrella, ready to fight with the tiger*)

VOICE WITHIN:

Behave yourself, you beast!

(*Exit the tiger, holding Trance in its mouth*)

LU SHENG (*Weeps*):

Now that the tiger has carried away Trance, I have to go on all by myself.

(*Walks on*)

It so happens that the silk umbrellas in the imperial court have not sheltered me, but my tattered umbrella has. Those who have received favour from me in the court cannot save my life, but Trance has died in my stead. It seems that everything in the world is predestined.

(*Enter Highwaymen A and B, carrying knives in their hands*)

HIGHWAYMEN A AND B:

Where are you going, man?

LU SHENG (*Frightened*):

I'm going to Hainan.

HIGHWAYMAN B:

Leave your treasures! Leave your treasures!

LU SHENG:

What treasure can I have as a poor scholar?

(*To the tune of **Wugongyang***)

With a raincoat and a wind-cap,

I've been expelled from the court.

HIGHWAYMAN A:

You must have treasures since you are from the court.

LU SHENG:

I used to have treasures,

But tigers and wolves have devoured them.

HIGHWAYMAN B:

Do you mean to say that the tiger has devoured your gold and silver? You're asking for a beating! You're asking for a beating!

(*Beats Lu Sheng with the back of his knife*)

LU SHENG:

Spare me! I'm a man with an intelligent mind.

HIGHWAYMAN B:

What's the use of your intelligent mind?

LU SHENG:

I'm a man with meritorious deeds.

HIGHWAYMAN B:

What's the use of your meritorious deeds? Leave your treasures!

LU SHENG (*Sighs*):

Alas,

You want nothing

But my gold and silver.

Who knows my intelligence?

Where shall I display my feats?

You heartless highwaymen!

HIGHWAYMAN B:

As you do not give me your treasure and calls me names, I'll shave you up with my knife.

(*Kills Lu Sheng*)

(*Lu Sheng feigns to be dead*)

HIGHWAYMAN B:

You are predestined to die this way;

Next year people will commemorate you today.

(*Exeunt the highwaymen*)

LU SHENG (*Comes to life*):

Oh, my neck is slanting aside. How is it that my neck is wet?

(*Looks*)

It's blood! Someone has slipped his knife under my chin. Luck has it that he has not cut my throat. I'll turn my neck to the right position.

(*Turns his neck on tiptoe*)

Oops! Oh, here's the sea!

(*Looks and feels the pain*)

A boat is coming.

(*Enter boatmen*)

BOATMAN A:

Where comes the blood

That pollutes the sea wind?

I'll save your life, man.

(*The other boatmen refuse to let Lu Sheng embark the boat*)

(*Boatman A helps Lu Sheng embark the ship*)

BOATMEN (*To the tune of **Yuzhazi***):

Is it a black boat or a white boat?

The waves are pouring from the sky.

(*Sound of wind within*)

BOATMEN:

A hurricane is coming.

The strong wind breaks the mast,

As if looking for a needle in the sea.

The boat is like a floating leaf,

Carrying little hope with it.

LU SHENG:

Look, the green mountains are looming ahead. We'll soon reach the shore.

BOATMAN A:

Alas, a huge whale is rising out of the water. The boat and the crew will perish.

BOATMEN (*Weep*):

> (*To the tune of **Jiangshenzi***)
>
> The whale looks like a towering mountain;
>
> What shall we do with it?
>
> What shall we do with the whale?
>
> Its eyes are as bright as pearls,
>
> Staring at us all.
>
> Where will its fins fall?
>
> When it wavers its fins,
>
> We can hardly keep alive.
>
> (*Sound of roaring waves within*)

BOATMEN:

It's too bad!

> (*The boat overturns*)
>
> (*Exeunt the boatmen*)
>
> (*Lu Sheng grasps at a plank and floats off stage*)
>
> (*Reenter Lu Sheng, weeping*)

LU SHENG:

Alas, gracious Heavenly Queen Mother! What's the use of a plank?

> (*Sound of wind within*)

Good luck! Gook luck! A gust of hurricane is coming. The shore lies ahead and I'll jump on it.

> (*Jumps*)

Thank heavens!

> (*Sound of roaring wind within*)

LU SHENG (*Holds his neck tightly*):

Well, I'll hold my neck tightly lest it be blown off.

> (*Sound of roaring wind within*)

LU SHENG (*Weeps*):

What shall I do if my neck is blown off? I'll lean against the stone pavilion and collapse.

> (*Falls*)
>
> (*Enter ghosts, dancing in diverse manners*)
>
> (*Enter the Heavenly Minister*)

HEAVENLY MINISTER:

Behave yourselves, ghosts! Well, this man smells of blood.

> (*Looks*)

His neck is hurt by a knife. Pull a lock of my whiskers to fill in his wound.

> (*The ghosts pull a lock of whiskers from the Heavenly Minister and fill in Lu Sheng's wound, joking to each other*)

HEAVENLY MINISTER:

Listen to me now, Lu Sheng:

> *You'll be Prime Minister for twenty years*
>
> *After a thousand days in the Ghost Gate Pass.*

(*Exeunt the Heavenly Minister and the ghosts*)

LU SHENG (*Comes to senses*):

Alas! I've seen so many ghosts! Someone filled in my wound with whiskers and said that I would be Prime Minister for twenty years after a thousand days in the Ghost Gate Pass. Oh, a whisker is indeed growing on my chin.

> (*Enter two woodmen with black faces and dishevelled hair, carrying firewood on their shoulders and singing*)

WOODMEN:

> Gather firewood, gather firewood,
>
> A scholar-tree grows before the Ghost Terrace.

LU SHENG (*Startled*):

Yet two ghosts are coming!

WOODMEN:

Two Black Ghosts are coming.

LU SHENG:

I'll be scared to death!

WOODMAN A:

We are natives here in Yazhou. We are called Black Ghosts because we have black complexions. I am a woodman.

LU SHENG:

Oh I see. Do you have ghosts here in broad daylight?

WOODMAN A:

Haven't you read the gilded characters on the pavilion?

LU SHENG (*Looks and reads*):

Well, I've reached the Ghost Gate Pass. It seems that I can hardly survive.

WOODMAN A:

Who are you that have come here to court death?

LU SHENG:

I'm a meritorious minister of the Tang Dynasty on exile here.

WOODMAN A:

It's said in Yazhou that high officials on exile here are not allowed to live either in government houses or in private houses.

LU SHENG:

How miserable I am!

WOODMAN A:

How pitiful! How pitiful! Come and live in my blockhouse.

LU SHENG:

What is a blockhouse?

WOODMAN A:

You know, there are about forty-eight thousand ghosts in the Ghost Gate Pass. When a hurricane comes, they come jumping around in the broad daylight. These ghosts are as short as three inches and the tallest are no more than a feet. We'll be disturbed if we live

on the plains. That's why we have built wood fences on the cliff and sleep with four-virtue dogs at night.

LU SHENG:

What are four-virtue dogs?

WOODMAN A:

Their first virtue is to bite thieves; their second virtue is to bite beasts; their third virtue is to bite mice; their fourth virtue is to bite ghosts.

LU SHENG:

Well, well, I'll have to sleep with the dogs. The problem is that I am wounded and cannot climb the cliff.

WOODMEN:

We'll carry you up the cliff with ropes.

> (*Carry Lu Sheng with ropes*)
> (*To the tune of* **Qingjiangyin**)
> The dog fence is a wonder,
> Hard for us to build.
> The cliff is steep and tall,
> With thorns sharp and in good shape,
> Climbing their way to the top.
> (*To the previous tune*)
> In a sedan carried by eight men,
> We wind our way up the cliff.
> With straw ropes around our waists,
> We Black Ghosts jump and skip.
> Is this the best a prime minister can enjoy?
> *After a narrow escape from death,*
> *He is like a wren to heave a breath.*
> *Although they are not of his kind,*
> *They are the best he can find.*

Scene Twenty-Three
Sufferings in the Weaving Mill

> (*Enter the Commissioner of the Weaving Mill*)

COMMISSIONER OF THE WEAVING MILL:

> *If a man does nothing wrong,*
> *He will ne'er be hated lifelong.*

I used to be an envoy in the capital. As I did a good job in confiscating Lu's family, I have been promoted to be the Commissioner of the Weaving Mill thanks to the favours of Prime Minister

Yuwen Rong, who would like to further persecute the Lus. Lu's wife is not good at weaving. Whenever her job is not done well, she will get a scolding. However, how can a small potato like the Commissioner of the Weaving Mill insult a First-Rank Lady?

(*Thinks hard*)

Yes, I've conceived a trick: when the eunuch in charge of weaving arrives, I'll instigate him to insult her. For the moment, I'll wait for him here.

(*Enter the eunuch in charge of weaving*)

EUNUCH:

As a ranking eunuch in the palace,

I'm in charge of supplies as well.

I am a eunuch in charge of weaving for the palace. I haven't been to the Weaving Mill for several months. Where's the Commissioner of the Weaving Mill?

COMMISSIONER OF THE WEAVING MILL (*Greets the eunuch*):

Welcome to the mill. I've got tea and dinner ready for you.

EUNUCH:

Have you heard of the good tidings for the imperial court?

COMMISSIONER OF THE WEAVING MILL:

No, I haven't.

EUNUCH:

The Tubo Kingdom has surrendered and has brought ministers from sixteen states to pay tribute to His Majesty. As there are not enough satins to give them as gifts, I've come to speed up the weaving of satins. Are you smart enough?

COMMISSIONER OF THE WEAVING MILL:

Of course I am smart. The pity is that the Weaving Mill is short of money and I've got no cash to present to you.

EUNUCH (*Annoyed*):

You've got no cash to present to me? What a big potato you are!

COMMISSIONER OF THE WEAVING MILL:

May I venture to tell you that there is a handsome sum for you if only you dare to accept it?

EUNUCH:

What do you mean by "a handsome sum"?

COMMISSIONER OF THE WEAVING MILL:

As you haven't been here for half a year, you don't know that a weaving woman has arrived, who is the wife of Minister Lu Sheng. Lu Sheng had illicit relations with Tubo and amassed a lot of gems and pearls, all in the hands of his wife.

EUNUCH:

Do you expect her to offer the treasures at her own free will?

COMMISSIONER OF THE WEAVING MILL:

A horse won't get fat if you do not hang it;

A man will not confess if you do not hang him.

She will offer treasures if you hang her up.

EUNUCH:

I am soft-hearted.

COMMISSIONER OF THE WEAVING MILL:

I'll whisper in your ears as to what to do.

EUNUCH:

So it's settled.

> *As a eunuch all my life,*
>
> *I'll bully Lu's wife.*
>
> (*Exeunt the eunuch and the Commissioner of the Weaving Mill*)
>
> (*Enter Miss Cui and Meixiang, holding satins in their hands*)

MISS CUI (*To the tune of* **Poqizhen**):

> A weaver in the Weaving Mill now
>
> Was First-Rank Lady for ten years.
>
> Reduced to a wretched state
>
> In the Weaving Mill,
>
> I weave with a broken heart.
>
> How can I bear the noise of the mill?
>
> The satin is done,
>
> But tears will soon exhaust.
>
> (*In the pattern of* **Tirenjiao**)
>
> *A Weaving Mill*
>
> *Is enshrouded in the mist.*
>
> *I brighten the lamp*
>
> *And stop my shuttles in a dream.*
>
> *My man on exile*
>
> *Returns at midnight.*
>
> *We are approaching the palace wall*
>
> *When I am awakened by the birdcall.*
>
> *I gaze into the Milky Way*
>
> *And weave with disheveled hair.*
>
> *In the chilly night,*
>
> *I try to embroider the mandarin ducks.*
>
> *At the sight of the river over which birds fly,*
>
> *My tears begin to gush in flood.*

I am Miss Cui of Qinghe, wife of Minister Lu. When my man was sent in exile to the region of miasma, I was sent to the Royal Weaving Mill, with none but Meixiang to accompany me. When my man was serving in the court, the couple of us lived a life of abundance and distinction. For the hundreds of servant boys and servant maids, the boys were decorated with gold and mink while the maids were clothed in embroidery. Who knows the vicissitudes of life? Well, forget about it. How sad I am now that I am separated from my man and my sons!

> (*To the tune of* **Yujia'ao**)
>
> I stop weaving at the thought of my man and sons;

My man has gone south to Hainan,

A place hard to detect on a sea chart.

MEIXIANG:

It's better for her man to stay with her,

Lest she should feel too sad.

Oh, Meixiang!

I used to stay amid silk and blooms,

But now work in the mill in plain dress.

MISS CUI, MEIXIANG:

We'll ask the heavens

Why we should live through two worlds.

MISS CUI:

I have been confined here for three years. No one in the court has ever tried to redress the injustice done on my man.

MEIXIANG:

How miserable we are! How miserable we are!

MISS CUI (*To the tune of* **Tanpodijinhua**):

The grand foe

Has destroyed our career.

A swirl of dust

Has darkened the Heavenly Gate.

I'll learn from the ancient wife,

Who wove a palindrome for her mate.

MISS CUI, MEIXIANG:

If we make a petition to the wise emperor,

There might be a day to get redressed.

MEIXIANG:

Madam, if you weave your petition in a palindrome and have it presented to His Majesty, there might be the possibility of bringing Master Lu home. Here is the ink and the ink-slab. Please write the words to be woven into the satin.

MISS CUI (*Writes*):

Here are two palace poems to the tune of *Pusaman*. I'll get the gold and red silk threads ready and Meixiang will do the weaving with me.

MEIXIANG:

Yes, Madam.

MISS CUI (*Gets the satin ready and starts to weave*):

(*To the tune of* **Tiyindeng**)

I weave the messy silk in a dreary mood,

And try to find the broken thread.

The golden threads go with my endless woe;

My words are hidden in the flowery design.

MISS CUI, MEIXIANG:

The palindrome wears out my tender hands,

While the spindles pass through the stains of tears.

(*Sound of hailing the way within*)

MEIXIANG:

As the satin-collector is coming, you'd better hurry up, Madam.

MISS CUI (*To the tune of* **Mapozi**):

Woven into the royal satin,

My words are worn out.

On hearing crickets chirp in the cold,

I stop the spindles to look afar.

When I weave, tears blur my eyes,

With thoughts flying to the end of the earth.

(*Sound of hailing the way within*)

MISS CUI, MEIXIANG:

While satin-collectors are coming soon,

Woe and worry makes me all the more fragile.

(*Enter the eunuch and the Commissioner of the Weaving Mill, hailing their way*)

EUNUCH (*To the tune of* **Fendie'er**):

Wearing a hat with dumpling-shaped wings,

I walk in haughty strides.

COMMISSIONER OF THE WEAVING MILL:

Here we are at the Weaving Mill.

EUNUCH:

I haven't seen the weavers waiting here to greet us. What a curse! What a curse!

MEIXIANG (*Flustered*):

The eunuch in charge of weaving has arrived. As we are in the mire, we have to greet them, Madam.

MISS CUI:

As I am a First-Rank Lady with dignity, you'll go in my stead, Meixiang.

MEIXIANG (*Responds and kneels to make a greeting*):

The weaver is greeting Your Highness.

EUNUCH (*Giggles*):

Well, stand up, stand up. Are you Madam Lu?

MEIXIANG:

My name is Meixiang.

EUNUCH (*To the Commissioner of the Weaving Mill*):

Why is she called Meixiang?

COMMISSIONER OF THE WEAVING MILL:

Meixiang is a general term for the maids, which means fragrance of the plum-blossom. If you enter the residence in spring, you'll be called Spring Plum-Blossom. If you enter the residence in winter, you'll be called Winter Plum-Blossom. If you have scars on your head, you'll be called Scarred Plum-Blossom. I don't know when she entered Minister Lu's residence that she is called by the general term Meixiang.

EUNUCH (*Giggles*):

Meixiang, Meixiang, what fragrance does she have?

COMMISSIONER OF THE WEAVING MILL:

Meixiang has secret fragrance hidden in the lower half of her clothes.

> (*In a low voice*)

When she is hanged up in the hall, her fragrance will spread all over.

EUNUCH (*Whispers*):

Do you think she knows about the treasures you mentioned?

COMMISSIONER OF THE WEAVING MILL:

As she is a concubine of Minister Lu, how can she know nothing about it?

EUNUCH (*Sighs*):

Even if she is a concubine of Minister Lu, I don't think she knows much about it.

COMMISSIONER OF THE WEAVING MILL:

Never mind. You just burst into anger at my signal.

EUNUCH:

All right.

> (*Makes a greeting*)

Is that Lu Sheng's wife?

MISS CUI:

Thank you, Your Highness.

EUNUCH (*Annoyed*):

Oh, as a weaver under my surveillance, you do not fall on your knees but just say "Thank you" to me. Am I to fall on my knees in front of you? Show me the satin for gifts to the Tubo envoys.

COMMISSIONER OF THE WEAVING MILL:

According to the order of the *Thousand-Word Essay*, there are eight kinds of satin as gifts to the Tubo envoys: "Display Power in Deserts; Subdue the Tubo Tribes." There must be eight bolts for each word, sixty-four bolts in all.

EUNUCH:

Show me the satin samples.

MEIXIANG (*Presents the satin*):

This is the sample for "Display Power in Deserts".

> (*The Commissioner of the Weaving Mill whispers to the eunuch*)

EUNUCH:

Well, the satin is too thin. It won't do. It won't do.

MEIXIANG (*Presents the satin*):

This is the sample for "Subdue the Tubo Tribes".

> (*The Commissioner of the Weaving Mill whispers to the eunuch*)

EUNUCH:

The satin is too soft.

MEIXIANG:

You don't know that the satin with "Display Power in Deserts" should be as thin as gauze and the satin with "Subdue the Tubo Tribes" should be as soft as downs. This is the pattern decreed by His Majesty.

EUNUCH (*To the Commissioner of the Weaving Mill*):

Isn't the pattern decreed by His Majesty? You go and count the bolts!

COMMISSIONER OF THE WEAVING MILL (*Counts*):

There are only forty-nine bolts, lacking sixty-four.

EUNUCH (*Gets angry*):

You are asking for a sound beating.

> (*Beats Meixiang*)
>
> (*Meixiang shelters herself*)

MISS CUI (*Weeps*):

> (*To the tune of* **Putianlefan**)
>
> The Weaving Mill
>
> Urges me;
>
> The weaving office pushes me.
>
> (*The Commissioner of the Weaving Mill whispers to the eunuch*)

EUNUCH:

Yes, the silk in the satin is often broken. For the time being, I'll beat the maid in her madam's stead for her lovesickness and laziness.

MISS CUI:

> How can she be lovesick now that she's in custody?
>
> I'm weaving and thinking of my man all the time.
>
> (*The Commissioner of the Weaving Mill whispers to the eunuch*)

EUNUCH:

Yes, thinking of her man is lovesickness and lovesickness is thinking of her man. Give her a sound beating! A sound beating!

MISS CUI (*Weeps aside*):

> With words woven into the satin,
>
> Can't you see tears mixed with silk?
>
> (*Turns to point at the Commissioner of the Weaving Mill*)
>
> You're spinning yarns for no reason at all.
>
> (*Points at the satin*)
>
> The satin is as fine as the clouds in the sky;
>
> Why on earth
>
> Are you instigating the eunuch?

COMMISSIONER OF THE WEAVING MILL (*To the eunuch*):

She is calling you names. She's calling you son of a bitch, a dog. It's high time for you to burst out.

EUNUCH:

Oops, I am son of a bitch, and aren't you? I am a dog, and aren't you? I'd like to let you go, but you won't allow me to let you go. I'll question you by myself. Come nearer, you woman prisoner! I've heard that your husband had illicit relations with Tubo. How much treasure do you have? Share your treasure with me so that I can decorate my hat and buy a jade belt.

MISS CUI:

Now that everything has been confiscated, what do I have to give you?

(*The Commissioner of the Weaving Mill whispers to the eunuch*)

EUNUCH:

Yes, as the saying goes,

> *A horse won't get fat if you do not hang it;*
>
> *A man will not confess if you do not hang him.*

Hang up Meixiang first.

(*Hangs up Meixiang*)

COMMISSIONER OF THE WEAVING MILL (*Feigns to protect Meixiang*):

Don't beat her, Your Highness. Let her confess by herself.

(*The eunuch beats Meixiang*)

MEIXIANG (*Refuses to comply*):

Alas, while the treasure is all gone, there are some pearls.

EUNUCH:

Where are they?

MEIXIANG:

They are dripping inside my skirts.

(*Pretends to piss*)

EUNUCH:

The fragrance in Meixiang's lower part is rushing out.

(*Sound of hailing the way inside*)

EUNUCH, COMMISSIONER OF THE WEAVING MILL (*In a panic*):

They are hailing the way for the eunuch in charge of gifts.

(*Exeunt*)

(*Enter Eunuch Gao*)

EUNUCH GAO (*To the tune of **Jinjijiao***):

> With my hat decorated in mink,
>
> I wear a dazzling jade belt and a robe with pythons.
>
> A pity that the lady stays alone at home;
>
> When will good tidings come to her?

I am Eunuch Gao.

(*Sighs*)

I have kept a close friendship with Minister Lu for years. Once he was forced to go on exile, his wife was also compelled to work in the Royal Weaving Mill.

(*Sighs*)

As I haven't seen her for quite some time, I don't know how she's getting along.

EUNUCH, COMMISSIONER OF THE WEAVING MILL:

(*Kneel on the ground to greet Eunuch Gao*)

Eunuch in charge of weaving and Commissioner of the Weaving Mill kowtow to greet Your Highness.

EUNUCH GAO:

Step aside.

> (*Enters the Weaving Mill to greet Miss Cui*)

I bow to you, Madam.

MISS CUI:

Excuse me for not greeting you outside as I didn't know you're coming.

EUNUCH GAO:

Have you received the pickled vegetables and fresh vegetables I've sent you off and on?

MISS CUI:

Yes, I have.

> (*Weeps*)

How miserable I am!

> (*To the tune of **Zhunu'erfan***)
>
> The silk is brittle so that I have to take great care;
>
> The silk is moistened when storm comes.
>
> For fear that the lamps will burn out,
>
> I make haste to weave the design.

EUNUCH GAO:

That'll do. That'll do.

MISS CUI:

I have one more word to say. Aside from the royal satin, I've also woven a bolt of pink satin with a palindrome on it to be presented to His Majesty, so that I can lay bare my heart.

EUNUCH GAO:

That's fine. When it is presented to His Majesty, you might be rehabilitated.

EUNUCH GAO, MISS CUI:

> For my miserable fate,
>
> Who would like to care?
>
> Gracious heavens,
>
> Why are you punishing a poor weaver?

MEIXIANG (*Cries aloud*):

Spare my life, Your Highness!

EUNUCH GAO:

Just spare that maid, Madam,

MISS CUI:

It's not I that have persecuted her. I did not dare to tell you that it was the eunuch in charge of weaving.

EUNUCH GAO:

What's the matter?

MISS CUI:

When he came here, he neither urged me on satin nor had a look at the satin. He just made a chaos by extorting treasure or pearls from me. As a convict's wife, what on earth do you think I could give him?

EUNUCH GAO (*Annoyed*):

Oh I see. Untie her at once, man.

> (*The eunuch unties Meixiang in haste*)

EUNUCH GAO:

Military guard, arrest the eunuch and take him to the prison.

> (*Exit the eunuch under arrest*)

MISS CUI:

The Commissioner of the Weaving Mill played a trick on him.

EUNUCH GAO:

Arrest the Commissioner of the Weaving Mill as well.

> (*The Commissioner of the Weaving Mill is arrested*)
>
> (*To the tune of* **Coda**)
>
> Count the cases of satin and bring them with me;

MISS CUI:

> What a depressing song the crickets are singing!

EUNUCH GAO:

Madam, Minister Lu

> Will come back rehabilitated, I'm sure.
>
> *With drops of tears on window-sash like dew,*
>
> *You wove a palindrome as your design.*
>
> *If an edict is bestowed on you,*
>
> *A better future life is sure to ensue.*

Scene Twenty-Four
Revealing the Truth

> (*Enter Yuwen Rong with Xiao Song*)

YUWEN RONG (*To the tune of* **Liuyaoling**):

> As His Majesty is bright with wit,
>
> I fear to wake the dragon when I get the pearl.

XIAO SONG:

> We share the high positions
>
> As prime ministers on earth
>
> And immortals in the sky.

YUWEN RONG:

> The gourd is bound onto the ancient branch;
>
> The gourd is bound onto the ancient branch.

XIAO SONG:

Why do you mention the bound gourd?

YUWEN RONG:

As your feet cannot shrink without being bound, so your position cannot rise without being bound to someone. The Tubo envoys will come to have audience today and His Majesty is going to accept their greetings in the royal palace. It is an honour for all the ministers in the court.

XIAO SONG:

Minister Pei is in charge of foreign affairs in the position of Vice Minister of the Central Office. When he comes to present the memorial, there must be something spectacular.

(*Enter Pei Guangting*)

PEI GUANGTING (*To the previous tune*):

In the guest house of the heavenly empire,

A number of Tubo envoys have arrived.

They follow our etiquettes

And bow in the imperial court,

Calling His Majesty the heavenly khan,

Calling His Majesty the heavenly khan.

How do you do, Your Excellencies. The Tubo envoys have come to the court to greet His Majesty. According to the time-honoured practice, a dinner is to be set in the Royal Banquet Hall and satins made in the Royal Weaving Mill are to be bestowed to them as gifts. Now that everything is ready, we'll wait for His Majesty to come.

YUWEN RONG:

The Tubo envoys should wait on the palace steps.

(*Enter the Tubo envoys*)

TUBO ENVOYS:

While envoys to Han bring a thousand piles of treasure,

Ten thousand bolts of satin are gifts to the kings.

YUWEN RONG:

Tell the Tubo envoys to wait for His Majesty outside the gate.

(*Exeunt the Tubo envoys*)

(*Sound of guards of honour within*)

(*Enter Emperor Xuanzong, followed by Eunuch Gao and all*)

EMPEROR XUANZONG (*To the tune of* **Yexingchuan**):

While the sun shines over the Ever-Bright Palace,

The flags flutter all over the country.

The chiefs of five states

And envoys from three states

Lie prostrate in the palace hall.

(*Yuwen Rong and Xiao Song pay tribute to Emperor Xuanzong*)

PEI GUANGTING (*Pays tribute to Emperor Xuanzong*):

Vice Minister of the Central Office in charge of foreign affairs Pei Guangting presents a memorial to Your Majesty: The Tubo envoy brings envoys from different states to pay tribute to Your Majesty.

EMPEROR XUANZONG:

Transmit my decree: Tell the envoys to listen to my decree outside the palace hall.

PEI GUANGTING:

Long live the Emperor!

YUWEN RONG, XIAO SONG, PEI GUANGTING:

We congratulate Your Majesty on your widespread power. We have prepared a royal banquet for Your Majesty.

> (*Make a toast*)
>
> (*To the tune of* **Haoshijin**)
>
> The flowers dance in the Tang Dynasty
>
> To hail our times of peace.
>
> We're glad to see that the sky is permeated
>
> With mild breeze, sweet rain and benevolent smoke.
>
> Enjoying bliss and longevity,
>
> You hear the chanting greetings
>
> From abroad.
>
> The gentle music is heard in front of the palace hall
>
> And cups of tasty wine are placed on golden plates.

VOICE WITHIN:

The Tubo envoys are to make toasts.

> (*Enter the Tubo envoys*)

TUBO ENVOY A:

Gulu gulu. Lile lile. I am son of the Tubo general Re Longmang. Years ago, my father was defeated and pursued by Marshal Lu. In face of imminent danger, he sent a letter by a wild goose, asking Marshal Lu to withdraw his troops and let him go. The letter says, "Do not kill all the birds; they will requite when they can." When Marshal Lu was held guilty for this, my father could not bear to hear about it and presented a memorial to the Tubo King, ordering me to be the envoy and bring envoys from all the western states to pay tribute to the Tang Dynasty. He told me to appeal for a redress of the injustice done on Marshal Lu when I have an audience with the emperor. It is the time to requite Marshal Lu's kindness. Now that I shall soon meet the Tang emperor, I'll be very prudent.

TUBO ENVOYS:

Gulu, gulu.

> (*Kowtow to Emperor Xuanzong*)

Long live the Emperor!

> (*Kowtow again, rise to their feet and start to dance*)
>
> (*To the tune of* **Qianqiusui**)
>
> Times of prosperity
>
> Reign over the Tang palace alone,
>
> With dragons climbing on the columns.

Amidst drumbeats,

A scroll of longevity

Is presented from the Tubo King.

The envoys dance,

Making twirls and swirls.

On our satin hats,

Twigs with flowers quiver.

Waving long sleeves,

We squat and kneel like lions and elephants,

Lying prostrate before the steps.

We envoys make a toast to the heavenly khan, wishing him a long, long life.

EMPEROR XUANZONG:

Thank you very much for your long journey from your states. What virtue do I have to receive your tribute? Please state your reasons.

TUBO ENVOY A:

The Tubo states used to count on the mountains and rivers to ignore the power of your empire. Since Marshal Lu made the western expedition, the Tubo states have been shocked and have come to understand that the fireflies cannot match the brilliance of the sun. Therefore, we are dispatched as envoys to pay respect to your heavenly dynasty.

EMPEROR XUANZONG:

Yes, I see. Did you mention the former Administrator and Military Commander Lu Sheng? Eunuchs, count and distribute the satin bolts among the Tubo envoys and bring them to the guesthouse to attend the royal banquet.

EUNUCH GAO (*Communicates the imperial edict*):

Envoys, please accept your gifts in front of the palace gate. Down on your knees.

TUBO ENVOYS (*Kowtow*):

Long live the Emperor!

> *When we know the etiquettes of the heavenly empire,*
> *We know how the generals have made their achievements.*
> (*Exeunt*)

EUNUCH GAO (*Counts the bolts of satin*):

Envoys, on your knees to accept the satins: four bolts of fine satin with the design of red flowers, six bolts of satin with the design of pink heavenly horses, eight bolts of satin with the design of purple flying fish, ten bolts of satin with the design of green lakes and lions, twenty bolts of satin with the design of wild geese, thirty bolts of satin with the design of gilded vultures, forty bolts of satin with the design of ball-games on horseback, fifty bolts of satin with the design of universal happiness, and one hundred bolts of red satin for reward. Your Majesty, the royal satins have been distributed among the Tubo envoys. Aside from the royal satins, there is another bolt.

EMPEROR XUANZONG:

Present it for my inspection.

> (*Looks at the satin*)

Oh, there are a few lines of words woven into the satin.

> *(Reads)*
>
> *(To the tune of **Pusaman**):*
>
> *"A far-off scene of plum-blossoms predicts spring;*
>
> *A woeful traveler passes through remote country with miasma.*
>
> *When a lonely wild goose flies homeward,*
>
> *The cold peaks cast their shadows on the green window-sash.*
>
> *When the sun sets behind the weaving room,*
>
> *I weave and weave under pressure.*
>
> *A weaver weeps for her man at dusk,*
>
> *Shedding tears until daybreak."*
>
> *"I look to Heaven for amnesty,*
>
> *A lonely weaver with two bolts of satin.*
>
> *Who will show pity on me,*
>
> *With my man on exile in the swamps?*
>
> *Separated alive,*
>
> *I have my man in the remote land.*
>
> *Heaven far away does not know my heart,*
>
> *That expects the day of pardon."*

PEI GUANGTING (*On his knees*):

As far as I can see, this poem can be read backwards:

> *(Reads)*
>
> *"I weep at dusk when I look at the bright river*
>
> *While I weave and weave under pressure.*
>
> *I leave my satin in the weaving room,*
>
> *With my window-sash permeated with cold.*
>
> *When the wild goose casts its shadow on the hill,*
>
> *A woeful traveler is climbing a peak.*
>
> *He is detained in the land of miasma,*
>
> *The spring scene is dotted with plum-blossoms."*
>
> *"Do you know when my man will be pardoned?*
>
> *He is now on exile in the far-away land.*
>
> *He is dear to me even though we are separated,*
>
> *A man who suffers in the swamps.*
>
> *Who has wept for a man on exile?*
>
> *I stay alone in front of the satin I weave.*
>
> *When I look up at the sky when the satin is done,*
>
> *I weep for the pardon of my man."*

EMPEROR XUANZONG:

How extraordinary! Extraordinary! There must be a signature at the end of the bolt. Yes, here it is. Made by Miss Cui of Qinghe, weaver in the Royal Weaving Mill. Well, Miss Cui, who is Miss Cui?

PEI GUANGTING:

She is the wife of Lu Sheng, the former Administrator and Military Commander of Quenching the West.

EMPEROR XUANZONG:

Oh, she is Lu Sheng's wife, serving as a slave in the Weaving Mill. As she is in such deep remorse, Lu Sheng is to be pardoned.

YUWEN RONG:

Your Majesty, Lu Sheng had illicit relations with Tubo and was guilty of high treason. He is not to be pardoned for his crimes.

EMPEROR XUANZONG:

What's your opinion, Xiao Song?

XIAO SONG:

According to what the Tubo envoy has said, Lu Sheng is a meritorious minister.

YUWEN RONG (*Annoyed*):

Oops, Xiao Song is contradictive in his words and thus shows his disloyalty. Your Majesty, he is to be executed as well.

EMPEROR XUANZONG:

Why do you say that he is contradictive in his words and thus shows his disloyalty?

YUWEN RONG:

The memorial to impeach Lu Sheng has Xiao Song's signature on it.

XIAO SONG:

I have not signed.

YUWEN RONG:

Here is the original copy of the memorial. I'll present the copy to you, Your Majesty.

(*Eunuch Gao accepts the copy*)

EMPEROR XUANZONG (*Reads*):

"Right Prime Minister Yuwen Rong and Left Prime Minister Xiao Song are to present an impeachment..." Yes, Xiao Song's name is on the memorial. I'll have a look at the end of the memorial. Well, here is Xiao Song's signature. How can you say that you haven't signed?

XIAO SONG:

It's not my genuine signature.

EMPEROR XUANZONG:

What is your genuine signature then?

XIAO SONG:

My name is Xiao Song, alias Yizhong, which means "Faithful". I used to present my memorial to Your Majesty with the signature of "Faithful". However, in this case of framing Lu Sheng, Yuwen Rong prefabricated a memorial for me to present with him. I was compelled to make a signature, but added an "un" before "Faithful" to make it "Unfaithful". As Yuwen Rong's memorial revealed his disloyalty, I did not make the signature out of my free will.

YUWEN RONG:

Your Majesty, Xiao Song has cheated the emperor and betrayed his friend. What crime is he guilty of?

EMPEROR XUANZONG (*Irritated*):

Yuwen Rong was a minister of the same rank as Lu Sheng. Who else but Yuwen Rong would like to overshadow Lu Sheng's meritorious deeds by framing a false charge to cheat the emperor and betray his friend? Eunuch Gao, hold him under custody!

(*Eunuch Gao binds Yuwen Rong*)

YUWEN RONG:

Alas, this time misfortune falls on me.

> *Retribution comes in the end,*
> *Whether it's sooner or later.*

(*Exit*)

EMPEROR XUANZONG:

Xiao Song and Pei Guanting, deliver my decree: Lu Sheng is to be fetched back at once and nominated as Prime Minister. His wife Miss Cui is to be released at once, to resume her title as First-Rank Lady and be bestowed a cloak of royal satin. His sons are to be restored to their former positions.

(*Sighs*)

But for the words of the Tubo envoys, I

(*To the tune of **Coda***)

> Have wronged a meritorious minister.
> His whole family is to be rehabilitated.

ALL:

> Your Majesty and your ministers are all virtuous.
> *Unable to see the sun and wronged to the most,*
> *A prisoner is sent on exile in a far-off land.*
> *When he is restored to his former post,*
> *He will serve the emperor and hold command.*

Scene Twenty-Five
Amnesty

(*Enter County Official*)

COUNTY OFFICIAL (*To the tune of **Zhaopixie***):

> A former student in the imperial academy,
> I am eager to pursue my official career.
> Everyday I wine and dine;
> For a remote official, his life is fine.

I am a County Official in Yazhou, A genuine king in a remote land. In dreams of being in a high position, I rise at midnight to piss on the sand. Funny, funny indeed. How can a County Official climb to the position of a minister? It happens that a Minister

Lu has come to settle down here. It is said that he has connections in the court and may be rehabilitated someday. Therefore, I have not pressed him too much. Who knows whether he has connections in the court or not? Yesterday I received a secret letter from Prime Minister Yuwen, saying that he hates Minister Lu the most and asking me to finish off his life. If I do as he tells me, he promises to summon me to the capital and to promote me. Well, if an eighth-rank official can do such an easy job and move to the capital, what is there to be blamed? As my superior is not in office this morning, Lu Sheng will come to pay respects to me.

> (*Enter Lu Sheng*)

LU SHENG (*To the tune of* **Buchangong**):

> I have eaten enough southern olives
>
> With a bitter-sweet taste.
>
> I have become skinny in these three years,
>
> Much skinnier than I can imagine.

I am Lu Sheng, on exile here in Yazhou. As the County Magistrate is not in office and the County Official is in charge, I have to go and see him.

> (*Greets County Official*)

My respects to you, sir.

COUNTY OFFICIAL (*Annoyed*):

Well, who are you?

LU SHENG:

I am Lu Sheng, whom you often meet here.

COUNTY OFFICIAL:

It's all right if you don't mention the name of Lu Sheng. Lu Sheng is a man on exile. As I am in charge of this office to supervise you, shouldn't you kowtow and stand aside to wait on me? As you just greet me with "sir", you're asking for a sound beating! You're asking for a sound beating!

LU SHENG:

Who dares!

COUNTY OFFICIAL:

The attendants will beat you.

> (*The attendants drag Lu Sheng and beat him*)

LU SHENG:

What is my blame?

COUNTY OFFICIAL:

Don't you know?

> (*To the tune of* **Hongna'ao**)
>
> I beat you because you do not greet me properly,
>
> Because you do not stand in the office,
>
> Because you talk all the nonsense,
>
> Because you deserve ten thousand deaths for treason.

LU SHENG:

Yuwen Rong is hateful! Detestable!

COUNTY OFFICIAL:

Are you scolding such a good man as Prime Minister Yuwen?

> I'll beat you because you scold a Prime Minister.

LU SHENG:

Don't worry. I'll return and serve in the court sometime.

COUNTY OFFICIAL:

> I'll beat you because you are so audacious.
>
> (*Lu Sheng laughs*)
>
> I'll beat you till you are bruised and lacerated;
>
> After the sound beating,
>
> I'll burn your head with hot iron.

LU SHENG (*To the previous tune*):

> I'll plead innocence in the higher court,
>
> But not defend myself in your small office.
>
> Now that I live within a dog fence,
>
> How can I expect to suffer tortures across the Ghost Gate Pass?

Well, let it be.

> *Standing under low eaves,*
>
> *I cannot but bow my head.*
>
> I keep silent as to whatever happened in court;
>
> When I resume my position, you will never dare.
>
> As I feel such great pain after the beating,
>
> How can I bear the scorching iron?
>
> (*Lu Sheng is scorched on the head and feet*)
>
> (*Enter Imperial Messenger, followed by attendants carrying a court costume*)

IMPERIAL MESSENGER (*To the tune of **Lülüjin***):

> The gentle rain falls
>
> From the misty sky.
>
> The imperial decree is urgent
>
> To call back the former minister.
>
> The road to high position
>
> Was darkened by the sea wind.
>
> The Imperial Messenger stops here
>
> When he crosses the Ghost Gate Pass.
>
> (*Enter an attendant*)

ATTENDANT:

The Imperial Messenger has arrived to bring the Prime Minister to the capital.

COUNTY OFFICIAL (*Overjoyed*):

Oh Master Yuwen, I haven't done what you've told me yet and you're going to bring me to the capital. I accept your gracious offer. I accept your gracious offer. Take the old man to prison.

> (*Greets Imperial Messenger without kowtowing*)

IMPERIAL MESSENGER (*Asks County Official*):

What rank of official are you that you do not fall on your knees?

COUNTY OFFICIAL:

The Imperial Messenger is to bring me to the capital and to be nominated as the Prime Minister. I am too dignified to kowtow.

IMPERIAL MESSENGER:

Ugh, step aside! Where is Master Lu?

>   (*County Official hurries to bring Lu Sheng*)

IMPERIAL MESSENGER:

Oh, Master Lu, you look so wan and tired! Here's your court costume bestowed by His Majesty.

>   (*Lu Sheng changes into the court costume*)
>   (*County Official is thrown into a panic*)

IMPERIAL MESSENGER (*Reads the imperial edict*):

Here is the imperial edict: The former Administrator and Military Commander of Quenching the West and Defense Minister Lu Sheng, you have got in the mire for three years because I was bemuddled for a moment. Now that Yuwen Rong has been put to death, you will resume your title as Marquis of Conquering the West. When you return to the capital, you will be appointed Prime Minister and take charge of national defense. Wherever you go, you can kill anyone before you report to me. That's my edict.

>   (*Greets Lu Sheng*)

May I venture to ask how long you have stayed here?

LU SHENG (*To the tune of* **Hongshaoyao**):

>   I've been away from the court for three years
>   Since I left my wife and sons on the execution ground.
>   I was fortunate to be pardoned;
>   I've shed floods of tears in the south
>   Amid heat and salt
>   Before the calm climate comes back to me.

ALL:

>   It's good news that Lu Sheng has resumed his position,
>   Thanks to the grace of His Majesty.
>   (*Enter County Official, bound by himself*)

COUNTY OFFICIAL (*Admits his mistake and asks for punishment*):

Who knows that he has indeed been rehabilitated. Yuwen Rong, Yuwen Rong, you have put me in the mire and I have to ask for a death sentence.

>   (*Greets Lu Sheng*)

I am a small man and did not recognize Your Excellency. I've bound myself to ask for a death penalty.

LU SHENG (*Laughs*):

Rise to your feet. You've just followed the way of the world.

>   (*To the tune of* **Hongshan'er**)

Men of the world

Have acted in a blind way.

For people who have done wrong,

I have to let go.

I won't hold any grudge against you.

If you feel ashamed,

You should repent for your vicious tongue.

COUNTY OFFICIAL:

Even if you spare my life now, I won't rest at ease. You'd better finish me off at this very moment.

LU SHENG (*Laughs*):

Are you afraid of my future retaliation?

A great man never goes back on his word;

I swear by the azure sky above.

COUNTY OFFICIAL:

You are indeed broadminded, Your Excellency. I wish you a long life!

LU SHENG:

In answer to the imperial edict, I have to be on my way now.

(*Enter three woodmen*)

WOODMEN:

We Black Ghosts are here to see you off, Your Excellency.

LU SHENG:

Thank you for taking care of me in these three years.

(*To the tune of* **Huiheyang**)

I went all the way through

Qiongzhou, Yazhou, Wanzhou and Zhanzhou.

I thank you for meeting me at the Ghost Gate Pass.

COUNTY OFFICIAL:

A living temple is to be set up in your honour, so that you will be remembered for thousands of years.

LU SHENG:

The living temple is to be set up above their dog fences.

I'll accept homage

In the place where I stayed.

In a dream I've traveled to the South Sea

And embedded my name in the blockhouse.

County Official, take good care of these Black Ghosts when I am gone, so that

These black uncles

Enjoy their life as woodmen,

And men and their wives

Live well in their fishing boats.

I'm leaving now.

(Walks on)

(To the tune of **Hongxiuxie***)*

The imperial edict brings me to the capital,

To the capital.

The horse hooves kick up dust,

Kick up dust.

The vicious minister

Has eaten the bitter fruit.

I owe my gratitude

To the imperial grace.

On my black head is stuck

The former court hairpin,

The former court hairpin.

(To the tune of **Coda***)*

Now that I've cleaned off stains of slander

I'll wash my warrior-coats in the palace lake.

From now on,

The far-away hills and rills

Will serve as scenes on paintings.

On exile I went in plight;

As the Prime Minister I come back.

I look up and see the capital coming into sight

And white clouds hanging over my track.

Scene Twenty-Six
Celebrations

(Enter Chief Commissioner of the Ministry of Works)

CHIEF COMMISSIONER OF THE MINISTRY OF WORKS *(To the tune of* **Dayagu***):*

I serve in the Ministry of Works

To build houses for meritorious ministers

And erect memorial archways.

While Carpenter Lu Ban's rules never change,

High mansions are decorated with gold and jade.

ALL:

We've received numerous rewards from him

And thus wish him high positions and a long life.

CHIEF COMMISSIONER OF THE MINISTRY OF WORKS:

I am Chief Commissioner of the Ministry of Works. By the imperial edict I have erected a memorial archway for the great meritorious Minister Lu, plus about twenty-eight mansions such as Royal Studio, Treasure Mansion, Drinking Hall, Jade Terrace and a garden of rockery and lakes. The Lu family has given me three thousand pieces of silver and plentiful wine. How generous he is!

(*Enter Chief Commissioner of the Horse Stable*)

CHIEF COMMISSIONER OF THE HORSE STABLE (*To the previous tune*):

> I serve in the Horse Stable
>
> To reward meritorious ministers with steeds,
>
> Both white and yellow.
>
> Well-shaped.
>
> The steeds will gallop safe and sound.

ALL:

> We've received numerous rewards from him
>
> And thus wish him high positions and a long life.

CHIEF COMMISSIONER OF THE HORSE STABLE:

I am Chief Commissioner of the Flying Dragon Stable. When His Majesty gave audience to Minister Lu's sons, he saw from the palace that their horses were of different sizes and shapes. He decreed that thirty horses from the Royal Stable be brought to Minister Lu's residence. The Lu's family has given me a piece of gold and given the ninety-odd horse-keepers a hundred strings of coins each. How munificent he is!

(*Enter Chief Commissioner of the Ministry of Revenue*)

CHIEF COMMISSIONER OF THE MINISTRY OF REVENUE (*To the previous tune*):

> I serve in the Ministry of Revenue
>
> To allot fields to meritorious ministers
>
> And establish farms.
>
> How expansive can the farms be?
>
> The well-known farms are better than those in Luoyang.

ALL:

> We've received numerous rewards from him
>
> And thus wish him high positions and a long life.

CHIEF COMMISSIONER OF THE MINISTRY OF REVENUE:

I am in charge of the Registration Office in the Ministry of Revenue. By the imperial edict I allot fields and gardens to meritorious ministers. Thirty thousand hectares of land and twenty-one gardens are allotted to Minister Lu. I have been given ten thousand coins for the contract. How charitable he is!

(*Enter Chief of Musicians, wearing a green coat and a flowery hat*)

CHIEF OF MUSICIANS:

> I serve in the Troupe of Court Music
>
> To entertain meritorious ministers
>
> And provide concubines.

VOICE WITHIN:

Even the bawd went to Minister Lu's residence.

CHIEF OF MUSICIANS:

I've sold a female singer by stealth and my wife went there instead.

> I've prepared music, song and dance;
>
> The only thing is that his wife might interfere.

ALL:

> We've received numerous rewards from him
>
> And thus wish him high positions and a long life.

CHIEF OF MUSICIANS:

I am the newly-appointed Chief of the Troupe of Court Music. His Majesty has bestowed female singers and dancers to the meritorious minister, twenty-four of them from the School of Fairy Music, in accordance with the twenty-four solar periods. At the order of Minister Pei of the Ministry of Rites, they have been brought to Minister Lu's residence. I have been given a flowery hat, a colourful coat, and a thousand strings of coins. How munificent he is!

ALL:

> We've received numerous rewards from him
>
> And thus wish him high positions and a long life.

CHIEF OF MUSICIANS (*Greets the three Chief Commissioners*):

My respects, worthy chiefs.

THREE CHIEF COMMISSIONERS (*Annoyed*):

Ridiculous! Ridiculous! The bawd of a chief musician is greeting us!

CHIEF OF MUSICIANS:

How high is your rank of offices?

THREE CHIEF COMMISSIONERS:

Our rank of offices is not high, but we have all passed imperial examinations, once in three years and thrice in nine years. We are of the sixth rank, serving as magistrates for the common folk. What kind of person are you, just greeting us like this?

> (*Beat Chief of Musicians*)

Well, let him go and watch his girls.

CHIEF OF MUSICIANS:

Your Excellencies, Your Excellencies, not only my girls but also my wife has been brought to Minister Lu's residence.

THREE CHIEF COMMISSIONERS:

In that case, we just take you as a girl and you'll sing us a song. If you sing well, we'll let you go. If not, we'll report to the Ministry of Rites and have your head broken.

CHIEF OF MUSICIANS:

Well, I'll act as a girl and sing a song by the title of *Yinniusi'er*.

> (*Sings*)
>
> *So pretty am I*
>
> *That I bring my sisters to Lu's house,*
>
> *A magnificent house.*
>
> *I return home alone,*
>
> *When the wind blows at my green kerchief,*
>
> *Revealing my nosegay,*

My sleeves and my little shoes.

He puffs up his lips,

Oh devil,

And kisses me on my back,

Leaving me powerless in his hands.

Oh my dear lover,

I'm willing to play with you.

THREE CHIEF COMMISSIONERS:

Wonderful! Encore! Encore!

CHIEF OF MUSICIANS:

That'll do.

> (*The three Chief Commissioners make jokes*)

> (*Sound of hailing the way within*)

ALL:

His Excellency has left the imperial court. Let's go, let's go, let's go! Indeed,

> *A man smiles when he's in a good mood;*

> *He returns with flowers on his hood.*

Scene Twenty-Seven
Extreme Luxuries

> (*Enter Miss Cui, followed by Meixiang*)

MISS CUI (*To the tune of* **Ganhuang'en**):

> As Prime Minister again,

> He returns from a banquet on the bank

> While men vie to have a look at him.

> On his robe sleeves,

> There remains the imperial grace.

> How deep is the imperial grace?

> As deep as the immense sky.

MEIXIANG:

> In the royal garden,

> Beside the royal study,

> The royal music is ready.

MISS CUI:

> Blessed by my man, my sons grew up in luxury.

> And now all serve in the court.

> Time, please stay with us,

> So that we can enjoy.

> (*In the pattern of* **Collected Poems**)

When dust floats into the palace hall,

The scattering flowers bring sweet scents.

Who is not aware of hardships along the borders?

The mansion is what His Majesty presents.

Since his return from the south, my man has been Prime Minister for twenty years. And now he is entitled Duke of Zhao with nine thousand tenant households and is promoted to the position of First-Rank Instructor. All our sons have been promoted as well: Our eldest son Zun becomes Scholar of the Imperial Academy, our second son Ti becomes Assessing Secretary in the Ministry of Personnel, our third son Jian becomes Commander of Royal Guards, our fourth son Wei becomes Palace Announcer. As a concubine to my man, Meixiang also gave birth to a son by the name of Lu Yi. He has been nominated Assistant to the Seals Department because he is still young. Over a dozen of our grandsons are all attending the Imperial Academy. We have enjoyed extreme honour and distinction. A few days ago, when my man and sons attended a royal banquet, His Majesty saw from above that our horses were of different sizes and shapes. He decreed that thirty horses be selected from the Royal Stable and brought to our house. When the banquet was over, His Majesty heard that there were no female singers and dancers in our house, and decreed that twenty-four be brought to our house from the School of Fairy Music, in accordance with the twenty-four solar periods. His Majesty also bestowed us land, gardens, mansions and houses, all of grand size. Now that it's time for my man to leave the palace, I've had a family dinner arranged. I suppose that the dinner is ready by now. My man is coming.

(*Enter Lu Sheng, followed by his attendants*)

LU SHENG:

I entered the palace at dawn

And had dinner at court site.

Soaked with imperial grace,

I return late at night.

I, Lu Sheng, have been Military Commander and Prime Minister at court for over fifty years. Now I have been entitled Duke of Zhao with nine thousand tenant households while my sons are all promoted to high positions. My honour is above all the other ministers and my distinction pervades the whole family. When the royal banquet is over, I now leave the palace and return to my residence. I'm ambling my way home.

(*To the tune of* **Northern Zhonglü Fendie'er**)

How splendid is the Tang Dynasty!

How splendid is the Tang Dynasty!

During the banquet I alone got drunk

Amid toast after toast.

Along the river bank,

On my gentle horse,

I'm intoxicated with the wine.

Turning round the Donghua Gate I see my house,

Ready to drink another cup with my wife.

(*Greets Miss Cui*)

Congratulations, Madam, on your promotion to Lady of Zhao. When the royal banquet is over, the moon is already high in the sky.

MISS CUI:

Since His Majesty has bestowed upon us a few pavilions, I've prepared a family dinner accompanied by the female singers and dancers. I'll drink with you overnight in the Emerald Pavilion.

LU SHENG:

Wait, wait. With guards of honour in front, your four sons wearing jade are coming home on horseback.

(*Enter four sons fully dressed*)

FOUR SONS:

We four brothers are promoted on the same day. Let's go and pay respects to our parents.

(*Bow to Lu Sheng and Miss Cui*)

As descendants of Confucian tradition,

We live in a house of distinction.

The southern mountain is a land of longevity;

The east sea abounds in auspicious clouds.

Please accept our toast of congratulations, Dad and Mom,

(*To the tune of **Southern Qiyanhui***)

Holding cups of sweet wine in our hands,

Your successful sons rise in positions.

We come and go in the palace,

As if visiting a relative's house.

Dear Dad,

Since your place is firm in the court,

The whole family gains distinction.

May Heaven bless you and bring you fame

So that we can also have a good name.

MISS CUI:

Butler, invite them to drink in the hall.

FOUR SONS (*On their knees*):

Dad and Mom, under your auspices, we have received new favours from His Majesty. Therefore, we have formal dinners in our respective offices.

LU SHENG:

Yes, you shouldn't be late for your formal dinners in your offices.

FOUR SONS (*Bow and retire*):

To attend the official dinner,

We'll stride to the jubilant hall.

(*Exeunt*)

(*Music within*)

(*Lu Sheng gasps in admiration*)

MISS CUI:

You don't know, Master, His Majesty decreed that twenty-four female singers and dancers be brought to our house from the School of Fairy Music, in accordance with the twenty-four solar periods. They can play music, sing and dance. They are charming indeed.

LU SHENG:

Alas, I thought that they just played soft music for the family, but they are girls from the School of Court Music. I should not get close to them.

MISS CUI:

Why should you not get close to them?

LU SHENG:

Ordinary girls are pretty but do not have a good voice: this is "dumb beauty". Other girls may have a good voice but are not necessarily pretty; they may dance but cannot sing. Only girls from the School of Court Music not only put on performances like Zither Music, Fairy Dance, Comic Talk, Ballad Singing, Solos and Duets but also are attractive and charming, knowing almost all the ropes. Therefore, a gentleman can watch them but not be indulged in them, can abandon them but not be attached to them. They were fresh and pretty in their earlier years and their teacher taught them to be exquisite. They are beautiful in figure and eloquent in conversation. They will look too pale if they put some white on their faces and they will look too red if they put on some rouge on their faces. They will look too tall if they grow one inch more and they will look too short if they grow one inch less. As *The Book of Poetry* has it:

> How fair the moon shines in the sky!
> How lovely is the lady passing by!
> Complement her dimpled cheeks
> And make her black eyes glow.

Their glowing eyes will trap your heart and their smile with dimpled checks will entice your soul. Therefore it is said, "White teeth and crescent eyebrows are axes that maim your nature; billing and cooing are owls that murder your life; slobber and slaver are poisons that corrode your bowels; bed play is the game that makes you impotent." In Laozi's words, "The five colours can blind one's eyes, and the five tones can deafen one's ears." Therefore, to refrain from sex, an inferior man must refrain his feet; to refrain from sex, a gentleman must refrain his eyes. And so I should not get close to these female singers and dancers.

MISS CUI:

In that case, you are a genuine orthodox scholar. Why don't you present a memorial to His Majesty and send them back?

LU SHENG (*Smiles*):

That won't do. According to *The Book of Rites*, "Never neglect the gifts from the king." That is what we mean by the paradox "To reject is to imply disrespect while to accept is to feel ashamed."

MISS CUI:

Master, as I listen to your preaching, I've missed a few songs. Tell the female singers and dancers to come forward and persuade the master to drink.

(*The female singers and dancers kowtow*)

LU SHENG:

You've come here by imperial edict. Rise to your feet, rise to your feet. You just sing and dance.

SINGERS (*To the tune of* **Northern Shangxiaolou**):

> Like fairies dressed in court fashion,
>
> As if walking on the moon palace in purple dress,
>
> We sing and dance in the best style.
>
> We sound hardwood clappers
>
> And beat exotic drums.
>
> The zither chords ring aloud
>
> And flute music spreads afar.
>
> We sing in full-throated ease
>
> Till yellow millets awake the dreams.

LU SHENG:

Why do you mention yellow millet?

SINGERS:

Oops,

> Till music resounds around the beams.

LU SHENG (*To the tune of* **Southern Qiyanhui**):

> Dignified
>
> And splendid in the magnificent hall,
>
> Stand the court beauties, tinkling with jade.
>
> I thank my wife for her kind heart,
>
> Who tolerates the dozen of beauties.
>
> The flowery girls hold cups at the table,
>
> In coy smile.
>
> I've eaten all kinds of delicacies
>
> And shall taste the beauties as well.

MISS CUI:

May I remind you that we can also wine and dine in the Emerald Pavilion to warm up the new house?

LU SHENG:

What a virtue of a wife! Under moon and cloud, we can enjoy the scenery on the steps. Maidservants, light a hundred sash-lanterns and play some soft music to lead the way. Madam and I shall stroll for a while.

> (*Meixiang and servants walk with lanterns amid light music*)

LU SHENG (*To the tune of* **Northern Huanglonggunfan**):

> Flat and wide are the three step-ways;
>
> Smooth and even is the stretch of plain.
>
> Misty and foggy is the moon-lit sky;
>
> High and bright shine the sash-lanterns,
>
> Which likewise light up the suburb ways.

(Laughs and stumbles)

I'd better stop laughing.

    But for the support of these tender hands,

    I would have stumbled my bowels out.

    (Music, laughter and hailing the way within)

LU SHENG:

Who are they that are hailing the way with dozens of sash-lanterns?

    (Meixiang and servants ask about it)

VOICE WITHIN *(Responds)*:

The four young masters are returning to their private residences from banquets.

LU SHENG:

What a prosperous family! The Emerald Pavilion is right ahead.

    *(To the tune of **Southern Pudeng'efan**)*

    Smoke coils from incense-burners in my sleeves;

    Fallen petals float on the royal moats.

    Gentle music is sounding in the night breeze;

    Zigzag goes the lengthy winding corridor.

    High hangs the jade and golden tablet;

    Supple dangle the willow twigs.

    Densely-lined are the painted eaves;

    Valiant stand the statues of roaring lions,

    Staring at the ball-game field outside the gate.

    (All arrive)

MISS CUI:

Master, look at the thirty-six sights in the Green Lotus Lake in front of the Emerald Pavilion bestowed by His Majesty.

LU SHENG:

They are indeed scenes from a fairyland! Singing girls, help me and Madam upstairs.

    (All climb upstairs)

LU SHENG:

Bring wine in goblets and I'll drink with my wife.

    *(To the tune of **Northern Shangxiaoloufan**)*

    I've climbed the pavilion

    And visited the chambers.

    I lean against the red cloud,

    Step on red lotuses of feet

    And play with the flushing faces.

MISS CUI:

A toast to you, Master.

LU SHENG *(The wine spills and soaks his sleeve)*:

    I laugh and see flowers in the wine

And lamps swirl with the wine.

When wine spills on my sleeves,

The moon seems brighter and the breeze gentler.

MISS CUI:

In the tall pavilion at such a wonderful night, you may enjoy yourself to the full, Master.

(*The female singers and dancers vie to grab at Lu Sheng*)

LU SHENG:

Now listen to me. You will be allotted in separate rooms. A sash-lantern is hung at the door of each of the twenty-four rooms as a signal. Whenever I stay over the night in any of these rooms, the lantern for that room is withdrawn and the others may withdraw the lanterns and go to bed. If I am in a good mood, I may tell two or three of you to wait on me.

(*The female singers and dancers laugh and respond*)

(*To the tune of **Southern Diezifan***)

The girls roar aloud

With passions profound.

The time is running out

In cool breeze and dews.

With a view of birds on the lake,

The red sash-windows are left open.

With fragrance on the pillows,

The girls are eager to please.

As life lasts hundreds of years at the most,

I'd better get drunk and dream a pleasant dream.

MISS CUI:

The night is growing deep. It's time to go to bed, Master.

LU SHENG:

I've enjoyed the best of life today, Madam.

(*To the tune of **Coda***)

For my official career,

I've been Marshal and Premier

In these sixty years of grand feat.

Madam, from now on,

Let's fully enjoy our wealth and distinction.

When heavenly guards open a splendid way,

The senior minister wines and dines every day.

Song and dance goes on night by night;

I visit the pavilion when the lamps are bright.

1037

Scene Twenty-Eight
Friends' Lamentations

(*Enter Xiao Song*)

XIAO SONG (*To the tune of* **Guazhen'er**):

> When the Prime Minister lingers in his life,
>
> I lament over his illness.
>
> The singing girls in the palace
>
> And the dancing girls at court
>
> Are ever in high spirits.
>
> *You survive all my old friends,*
>
> *But now your life is drawing to an end.*
>
> *My face is stained with new tears,*
>
> *Not because of the sad autumn days.*

I am Xiao Song, Honorary Prime Minister at court. Prime Minister Lu is a close colleague of mine. He is over eighty years old now. As he has been ill for three months, he has to do his duties on bed. His Majesty bestows extraordinary grace by requiring all the temples under the Ministry of Rites to pray for him. Minister Pei in the Ministry of Rites has just offered incense in the temples and will surely come over here.

(*Enter Pei Guangting*)

PEI GUANGTING (*To the tune of* **Fanbusuan**):

> As to whether Lu can recover,
>
> His Majesty is anxious.

(*Greets Xiao Song*)

XIAO SONG:

Minister Pei,

> What's the result of this praying?
>
> His illness will certainly take a long time.

Minister Pei, as Prime Minister Lu used to be in good health, how is it that he suddenly fell ill?

PEI GUANGTING (*To the tune of* **Fengrusong**):

> I know something about his illness,
>
> Which is a new story.

XIAO SONG:

Is it because he's too busy in his official duties?

PEI GUANGTING:

> It's not because he's too busy in office
>
> But because he's too busy in his chamber.

XIAO SONG:

Wow, is Prime Minister Lu still potent at his age?

PEI GUANGTING:

> As he thinks that sex will prolong his life,

His Majesty has bestowed on him some girls.

XIAO SONG:

Is that true? Hasn't Madam Lu tried to stop him?

PEI GUANGTING:

It is said that Peng Zu in the ancient times had sex to prolong his life when he was eight hundred years old.

XIAO SONG (*To the previous tune*):

> Old men are like dried paper or remnant of candles;
>
> How can they bear all the troubles?
>
> The Peng Zu of longevity is dead and gone;
>
> Minister Lu took the trouble at a loss.

PEI GUANGTING:

As Prime Minister Lu has enjoyed extreme luxuries, the only thing he thinks is longevity.

XIAO SONG:

That's right.

> Both of us are approaching eighty now;
>
> What's the difference as to age?

Now that he's taken a wrong step, he can hardly survive. Congratulations on you for your coming promotion.

PEI GUANGTING:

I dare not assume that.

> *To cure the minister of his disease,*
>
> *There is no master-hand in court.*
>
> *The tree stands alone in the breeze;*
>
> *To its heirs it can offer support.*

Scene Twenty-Nine
Revelations

(*Enter Miss Cui, with a worried look*)

MISS CUI (*To the tune of **Jinjiaoye***):

> My woe and sorrow is so great
>
> That it won't go away from my gate.
>
> It is difficult for me to talk about it.

Oh heavens, heavens, heavens!

> How can you cure my man for a while?

If you don't think well, sooner or later you'll repent. My man and I have lived to an old age in great wealth and distinction. Now that we are over eighty years old with five sons and ten grandsons, we have enjoyed extreme happiness in the human world. He used to drink with a few maidservants waiting on him and with me taking care of him. Some

time ago, the emperor gave him some female singers and dancers who sang, danced and played music for his entertainment when he drank. However, he followed the advice of an official, who wanted to be promoted, to have sex with the girls. Since there was something wrong with him three months ago, he has been seriously ill all these days. Thanks to the consideration of His Majesty, the officials in the Ministry of Rites are required to pray for him in different temples and relatives of the royal house are required to burn incense for him. We have won extreme favour from His Majesty. I'm afraid that misfortune will follow bliss and that the heavenly gods will not be so merciful. Oh heavens, I won't expect him to live a hundred years, but ninety-nine years will do for him.

(*Enter Lu Sheng, seriously ill, supported by his sons and Meixiang*)

LU SHENG (*To the tune of* **Xiaopenglai**):

> As Prime Minister at the age of eighty,
>
> How much time do I have with me?
>
> I feel so sad in a flash
>
> To think of the swift passage of life
>
> And the hardship of Prime Minister.

(*In the pattern of* **Collected Tang Poems**)

> *With the power of Prime Minister,*
>
> *Who'd like to give up to death?*
>
> *When I drink to lament spring,*
>
> *Wild grass and blooms seem to be so sad.*

Madam, as I'm seriously ill and feel dizzy all the time, I'm afraid I'm at the end of my life. When I first met you, I was all by myself. After I passed the imperial examinations, I became an official at court. I served in large prefectures and consulted in state affairs. When I returned from exile in the south, I resumed my official career. For the past fifty years I've toured at home and abroad, dealing with people of high ranks. The grace of His Majesty has been extended to my sons and grandsons. I have countless mansions and farms, beauties and steeds. There is no equal to my power and distinction. Before I can requite the grace of His Majesty, I've fallen ill. Madam, our sons do not know the hardships we experienced. It is predestined that I have to die at the age of eighty.

(*To the tune of* **Shengruhua**)

> When I studied hard and failed in the examinations,
>
> I rode my lean donkey in the arid farmland.
>
> After I entered your residence by chance,
>
> I passed the examinations and rose high in positions.
>
> It's my fate to experience the vicissitude of life,
>
> Digging canals
>
> And fighting on battlefields.
>
> I had a narrow escape from the execution ground
>
> And went on exile to a land of miasma.
>
> Later I enjoyed fame and wealth until I am over eighty.

ALL:

He used to suffer from toil and terror,

And now he's suffering from illness.

MISS CUI:

Master, predestined as it is, your illness is also your own bitter fruit. How can you hope to gain vital energy by having sex with the girls at the age of eighty?

LU SHENG (*Annoyed*):

Sex, sex, I'm having sex in order to obtain longevity for the benefit of our future generations. Do you think that I have done all this behind your back for my personal joy?

MISS CUI (*To the previous tune*):

You should think for yourself at this age,

Instead of having sex with the girls.

You've done all this for the court,

But you do not care for your health,

Not knowing whether you can ever recover.

Master, I'll say nothing if you are safe and sound. Should there be anything wrong with you, I'll make these twenty-four girls pay for your life.

LU SHENG (*Annoyed*):

None of your nonsense! None of your nonsense!

SONS:

Mom's words are too harsh

While Dad's temper is too hot.

We shall be filial enough

To provide the best food for you.

LU SHENG:

I don't want to eat anything.

SONS:

Here's the liquid medicine.

(*On their knees to present the medicine*)

You'll be able to eat after you've taken the medicine.

LU SHENG (*Annoyed*):

I want none of your medicine.

ALL:

He used to suffer from toil and terror,

And now he's suffering from illness.

VOICE WITHIN (*Announces*):

Report, report, report! Ministers Pei and Xiao have arrived to inquire about Master's health.

MISS CUI:

Who will receive them?

LU SHENG:

Eldest son, you go and receive them in my stead. You just thank Uncle Pei and Uncle Xiao, saying that they are welcome to have a chat here when the court is over.

(Exit the eldest son with a response)

VOICE WITHIN:

A host of dukes, marquises, royal sons-in-law and royal relatives have arrived to inquire about Master's health.

LU SHENG:

Second son, you go and receive them in my stead. These are all our relatives. You just thank them, saying that I'll thank them by myself when I've recovered.

(Exit the second son with a response)

VOICE WITHIN:

Eighty high officials from different ministries have arrived and present their cards to inquire about Master's health.

LU SHENG:

Third son, you go and receive them in my stead. You just thank them all.

(Exit the third son with a response)

VOICE WITHIN:

One hundred and eighty chief officials from different sections have arrived to inquire about Master's health.

LU SHENG:

Fourth son, you go and receive them in my stead. You just say that I know.

(Exit the fourth son with a response)

VOICE WITHIN:

Three thousand and seven hundred minor officials have arrived and presented their letters to inquire about Master's health.

LU SHENG:

Butler, tell them that I know all about it.

(Exit the butler with a response)

VOICE WITHIN:

Report, report, report! At His Majesty's decree, Eunuch Gao has arrived with the court doctor.

(Miss Cui is in a flurry)

LU SHENG:

Madam, get fully dressed and prepare to receive the imperial edict.

(Enter Eunuch Gao, followed by the court doctor)

EUNUCH GAO (*To the tune of* **Diliuzi**):

> The horsemen,
>
> The horsemen
>
> Lead the procession.
>
> By imperial edict,
>
> By imperial edict,
>
> I bring the court doctor along.
>
> I'll meet Minister Lu in his house,
>
> Who is indeed ill,
>
> Without question.

I am cosier than he,

But he's above all other ministers.

(*Arrives at Lu's residence*)

Here comes the imperial edict. On your knees and listen to me. The imperial edict says: You have exerted your virtue to serve as my right hand. You subdued the Tubo troops and managed interior affairs. For the past two decades, I have relied on you. Since you fell ill, I've been expecting that you will soon recover. However, I'm sorry to hear that your illness is becoming more serious. Now I decree that Cavalry General Eunuch Gao visit you in your residence. I hope you will take good care of yourself and do it for me. I hope that you will be all right and I'm expecting good tidings from you. So much for my edict!

(*Miss Cui kowtows and rises to her feet*)

LU SHENG:

Your Highness, I'm greatly indebted to His Majesty's grace and thank you for your coming to my house. I don't know how to requite you.

EUNUCH GAO:

I haven't called on you often enough because I have been occupied with palace management. His Majesty is quite worried about your health. Although he has often sent a minister to inquire about it, he does not feel assured enough. Therefore, he has decreed that I bring a court doctor to make prescriptions for you. He hopes that you will take good care of yourself and live up to his expectations. Court doctor, come forward and see the patient.

COURT DOCTOR (*Feels Lu Sheng's pulse*):

(*To the tune of **Liuhuaqi***)

Raise your hand and I'll look at your fingers;

There is sweat on the back of your hand.

Well,

Like fish and sparrows on the move,

You have a long thread of life.

Minister Lu, I'm good at feeling the pulse. I'm glad to tell you that you and your sons will be promoted again as your pulse goes in a broad way.

LU SHENG (*Smiles*):

Inconceivable! Inconceivable!

COURT DOCTOR (*Aside to Eunuch Gao*):

Prime Minister Lu's pulse is turning for the worse.

His soul will rise to the sky

And he is about to die.

EUNUCH GAO (*Weeps*):

Oh, deplorable Prime Minister Lu, for several dozens of years,

You've thought and acted in the same way,

But now your form and shadow will separate.

COURT DOCTOR:

Prime Minister Lu, here's your prescription.

It is a pity for the court doctor

That he cannot save a life with medicine.

(*Exit*)

LU SHENG:

Your Highness, as I'm seriously ill in my old age, medicine is not of much use. I can hardly requite the grace from His Majesty.

(*To the previous tune*)

What virtue do I have that I receive royal grace

And prescriptions for the immortals?

I'll learn from Jiang Gongwang in ancient days,

Who served the king when he was over eighty.

Your Highness, as I cannot rise from the bed, I have to kowtow on my pillow.

(*Kowtows three times*)

Long live the Emperor!

I'll never forget the heavenly grace

And I'll requite His Majesty in the next life.

Your Highness, Minister Xiao and Minister Pei passed the imperial examinations in the same year as I and we've served His Majesty together for many years. I hope you will give them due help.

EUNUCH GAO:

I've also developed a long-time friendship with them.

LU SHENG:

I have something important to say. You are aware of my grand feats in the past sixty years. I'm afraid that something might be missing when Minister Xiao and Minister Pei compile the national chronology.

EUNUCH GAO:

Since your grand feats are all recorded in the *Book of Meritorious Deeds* and have been checked one item after another, who dares to miss anything?

LU SHENG:

I rely on Your Highness to help my family

And rely on colleagues to keep my record.

May I ask what title I will get when I am dead?

EUNUCH GAO:

His Majesty will take care of it. You don't have to worry about it. I'm off now.

LU SHENG (*Weeps*):

Alas, I have something else to say. My youngest son Lu Yi has not come of age yet. Bring him here and tell him to make a bow to Eunuch Gao.

(*Enter Lu Yi*)

LU YI (*Bows to Eunuch Gao*):

My dear granduncle, please do take care of your grandnephew!

LU SHENG (*Smiles*):

You are smart enough, sonny.

EUNUCH GAO:

He's been assigned Secretary to the Seals Department.

LU SHENG:

I've written about my military feats on the border, but have not written about my feats in digging the canal. I'd like to ask for another position for this youngest son. I hope you will offer some help on this matter.

EUNUCH GAO:

I'll keep it in mind. I must be leaving now.

LU SHENG (*Kowtows in tears*):

Do bring my words to His Majesty, saying that I cannot have another look at his heavenly features.

> (*Weeps*)

EUNUCH GAO:

> *Rather than ask favour from His Majesty,*
>
> *Better requite Him before you die.*
>
> (*Exit*)

LU SHENG:

Alas, alas! I'm sweating now. I feel pain all over. I'm feeling chilly, chilly! Yes, the knife of wind is cutting at my bones. Who can endure the pain in my place? Tell the eldest son to prepare ink and paper for me. Sweep the mat and burn joss-sticks so that I can write my last memorial to His Majesty. When I have expressed my gratitude to His Majesty, I will die at ease.

MISS CUI:

Master, you don't have to write by yourself.

LU SHENG:

You don't know that my calligraphy boasts the Zhong Yao style, of which His Majesty is most fond. The memorial by my own hand will pass down through the generations as a valuable historic relic for the Tang Dynasty.

> (*Enter the eldest son*)

ELDEST SON:

> *With a disease of thirst in old age,*
>
> *He left a Letter on Sacrificial Rites.*

Here's the incense. Dad, will you please draft the memorial?

> (*Lu Sheng kowtows; Miss Cui arranges her hair and dress*)

LU SHENG (*Writes*):

> (*To the tune of* **Jibanling**)
>
> At the end of my life,
>
> I inject my devotion into the incense;
>
> I strive to emit the last ray of my life
>
> Before His Majesty.

Alas, my hand shakes so much that I cannot write any more. Well, I'll make the draft and you will write for me, son.

> I'd like to write the memorial by myself,

I'd like to write the memorial by myself,

But my hands shake so much

That I cannot write a complete line.

You must write in good calligraphy

And remember what I say.

(*Heaves a long sigh and writes*)

ALL:

To make a distinction from the very beginning,

What's the difference between rich and poor?

LU SHENG (*Short of breath*):

Don't make a racket. Eldest son, read the memorial aloud.

ELDEST SON (*Reads*):

I used to be a scholar from the north of Mount Taihang, enjoying my life on the farmland. I was so fortunate to have won favour from Your Majesty that I entered my official career. I have been over-rewarded and received too much grace. I have been Military Commander and Prime Minister. For years I have been working at home and abroad. I'm embarrassed to have received so much grace from Your Majesty but have not done enough for Your Majesty. I've been prudent enough all the time because I may not live up to your expectations and may entice misfortune. I have not been aware that I am growing old day by day. I have risen to the top of positions now that I am over eighty years old. As time goes on, I have become weak in body and in soul. At the last moment of my life, I have to say farewell to Your Majesty. I am extremely grateful to you. The above is a memorial to express my gratitude.

LU SHENG:

That's it. After I draw my last breath, copy this memorial in a clean hand and present it to His Majesty. Madam, please take off my court dress and keep it in my mourning hall for our posterity to pay respects to.

(*Changes into his old clothes*)

I am fully contented with my life. Well, I'm losing my eyesight. I shall be dead and gone.

(*Dies and falls to his former sleeping place*)

ALL (*Weep and sob*):

(*To the previous tune*)

Heaven has ended the husband's life;

The grandfather has passed away.

Set up a mourning hall,

Set up a mourning hall

Where the First-Rank Lady

Weeps and sobs in the centre

And the filial sons

Weep and sob on both sides.

ALL:

To make a distinction from the very beginning,

What's the difference between rich and poor?

(Weep and sob)

MISS CUI *(Removes Lu Sheng's beard covertly, pats Lu Sheng on the back and weeps)*:

Wake up, Master Lu!

    (Exit)

LU SHENG *(Wakes up in surprise)*:

Alas! What a cold sweat! Where are you, Madam?

    (Enter Innkeeper)

INNKEEPER:

What madam?

LU SHENG *(Calls aloud)*:

Where are Lu Zun, Lu Ti, Lu Jian, Lu Wei and my youngest son Lu Yi? Where are they?

INNKEEPER:

Whom are you calling?

LU SHENG:

I'm calling my sons.

INNKEEPER:

How many sons do you have?

LU SHENG:

Five. Well, they are playing around the Royal Studio and the Treasure Mansion in front.

INNKEEPER:

This is a small inn.

    (The donkey neighs within)

LU SHENG:

Have you fed the thirty horses of good breed bestowed by His Majesty?

INNKEEPER:

There is only a lame donkey farting outside.

LU SHENG:

Well, I have taken off my court costume.

INNKEEPER:

You are wearing a worn sheepskin.

LU SHENG:

Oh, how strange, how strange! Where is my white beard?

    (Looks)

Who are you? Are you Miss Cui's butler?

INNKEEPER:

What do you mean by Cui's butler? I am an innkeeper near the Zhaozhou Bridge. I'm cooking yellow millet for you.

LU SHENG *(Thinks hard)*:

Well, is the millet done?

INNKEEPER:

I have to add one more bundle of firewood.

LU SHENG *(Rises to his feet)*:

Can it be true?

(*To the tune of* **Erlangshen**)

It is inconceivable

About the luxuries before my eyes.

I made my way into the pillow some time ago.

(*Takes up the pillow*)

There is a way into the pillow.

The scenes are vivid

As to how I rolled there.

Are these all lies?

I cannot but be puzzled, holding the pillow.

(*Sighs*)

As if in a flash,

In sixty years

The meal of millet is not done yet.

(*Enter Lü Dongbin in laughter*)

LÜ DONGBIN:

The mountain is as silent as in ancient times;

The day is as long as a year.

Have you had a nice sleep, Lu Sheng?

LU SHENG:

Old man, it's fantastic, fantastic! I became the Number One Scholar in the Tang Dynasty, dug three hundred miles of canal and swept across a thousand miles of border regions for the Tang Emperor!

LÜ DONGBIN (*Smiles*):

What grand feats!

LU SHENG:

You don't know and I dare not tell. With such grand feats, I was to be put to death on the execution ground as a result of the slanders of a vicious minister Yuwen Rong. Thanks to the rescue of my wife and sons, I went on exile to the south of Guangdong, as far as the Ghost Gate Pass in Yazhou.

LÜ DONGBIN:

How lucky you are! How lucky you are! And then?

LU SHENG:

With the help of Minister Xiao and Minister Pei, I was rehabilitated and resumed my position of Prime Minister. I obtained countless mansions and gardens, female singers and dancers. My relatives were all of blue blood while my sons and grandsons were promoted. I was in office for over fifty years and I lived till I was over eighty years old.

LÜ DONGBIN:

You said, "A gentleman must do merits to build a fame, be a high-ranking official or general, have sumptuous meals, listen to choice music, have a big family and live a luxurious life. Only in this way can he be in a happy mood." Weren't you in a happy mood when you went through all this? If you reconsider it now, where is your happy mood?

LU SHENG:

There's some truth in it. How sweet is the meal of yellow millet!

LÜ DONGBIN:

Since you have just "had sumptuous meals", would you care for a meal of yellow millet?

> (*To the tune of* **Yuyingti**)
>
> How delicious your court meals are!
>
> The fragrance still remains on the tip of your nose.

LU SHENG:

It's so difficult to cook the yellow millet!

LÜ DONGBIN:

> The millet is cooked with fire and water;
>
> You may ask your wife against the pillow
>
> Whether she'd like to get some millet
>
> To feed your sons.

LU SHENG (*Thinks*):

It indeed takes time.

LÜ DONGBIN (*Smiles*):

> If millet and water do not meet,
>
> The hills and rills are well cooked by now.
>
> Why don't you hope
>
> To enter and visit the pillow again?

LU SHENG (*Smiles*):

Old man, you tell me to visit the pillow again. Is the way by which I went still there?

> (*Looks at the pillow again*)

Well, pillow, pillow, it is because of you that I have a home where I cannot go, and I have a country where I cannot stay. Leave everything else aside, but I feel pity for my sons!

LÜ DONGBIN (*Smiles*):

Did you beget these sons?

LU SHENG:

Who begot them then?

LÜ DONGBIN:

They were transformed from the chickens in the inn.

LU SHENG:

Well, I indeed had a wife, Miss Cui from Qinghe, who married me in her residence.

LÜ DONGBIN:

Your wife Miss Cui was transformed from the donkey you ride. It's a hybrid of you and the horse.

LU SHENG (*Meditates*):

If that is the case, where did the emperor and ministers come from?

LÜ DONGBIN:

They were sheer imaginations of your wandering soul.

LU SHENG (*Sighs*):

Old man, old man, now I come to understand. Human life with all its belongings is like this. Is there anything substantial in human life? All the graces and disgraces, gains and losses, life and death — now I understand everything.

(*To the tune of* **Cuyulin**)

All the romantic encounters

Hardly exist;

Affections of life and death

Are illusions —

Man is simply daydreaming.

When flower shadows go by

And rooster crows die out,

What is the use of lighting the lamps and having supper?

Let it be. As fame and fortune are just external things, I'll forget about them. I'll become your disciple and follow your way.

(*Bows*)

Like the yellow millet,

Worldly life is but a grain,

To be cast away and boiled in a pot.

LÜ DONGBIN (*To the tune of* **Zhuomu'er**):

As to all the horrors

And haste of life,

I have no way to deal with them

When the pillow is broken.

Now that you've become my disciple, you'll follow me in my wanderings.

LU SHENG:

I'll follow you in your wanderings.

LÜ DONGBIN:

A follower of Tao lives on grass and wood, and stays amid dew and wind. How can you enjoy these things as a meritorious minister?

LU SHENG:

You're teasing me again.

LÜ DONGBIN:

I've something else to remind you of. If you as a disciple commit a mistake, the master will hit you on the head with his stick. Even if you are beaten to death, you should not even make a frown.

LU SHENG:

Since I did not make a frown on the execution ground, how can I dread your beating?

LÜ DONGBIN:

Although you're uttering a somniloquy,

I'm afraid your old dream has revived.

LU SHENG:

How can I dream in the broad daylight, Master?

LÜ DONGBIN:

> Even though you can live on pickled vegetables
>
> And won't change your mind in face of torments,
>
> I have to find a witness to talk with you.

LU SHENG:

I'll follow you and look for a witness.

> (*To the tune of **Diliuzi***)
>
> I'll follow my master,
>
> Follow my master
>
> Wandering in hills and rills.
>
> The witness,
>
> The witness,
>
> Where is the witness?
>
> On the road to Handan,
>
> To cook a meal of millet,
>
> The pot is not boiling yet,
>
> While sixty years of life in a dream
>
> Keeps me busy.
>
> (*To the tune of **Coda***)
>
> Awakened, I'll keep busy following Tao.

Where's the witness, Master?

LÜ DONGBIN:

> In a small place called the Penglai Temple.

LU SHENG:

So let's hurry, let's hurry.

LÜ DONGBIN:

As the meal of yellow millet is ready now, we'll go after dinner.

LU SHENG:

Forget about it, forget about it!

> If I wait for the yellow millet,
>
> My immortal dream will be delayed.
>
> (*Exeunt Lu Sheng and Lü Dongbin*)

INNKEEPER:

Funny, funny indeed! A living immortal has converted the scholar Lu Sheng and is gone with him.

> *Life and death upon the road to Chang'an*
>
> *Is the time to cook dinner in Handan.*
>
> *If he knew that lamp was fire,*
>
> *The meal would be done before the dream began.*

Scene Thirty
Gathering with the Immortals

(*Enter Zhongli Quan*)

ZHONGLI QUAN (*To the tune of* **Qingjiangyin**):

　　Zhongli Quan, an immortal for half of his life,

　　Is deformed in features.

　　(*Enter Cao Guojiu*)

CAO GUOJIU:

　　A brother-in-law to the Emperor,

　　I ignore fame and fortune.

ALL:

　　People are fools

　　If they do not follow the immortals!

　　(*Enter Tieguai Li*)

TIEGUAI LI (*To the previous tune*):

　　I use my crutch to stir the cloud

　　And limp my way to the Penglai Island.

　　(*Enter Lan Caihe*)

LAN CAIHE:

　　I sing aloud in my spring tour

　　And play my role in a joking manner.

ALL:

　　People are fools

　　If they do not follow the immortals!

　　(*Enter Han Xiangzi*)

HAN XIANGZI (*To the previous tune*):

　　Han Xiangzi can brew immortal wine

　　And make the buds blossom at once.

　　(*Enter He Xiangu*)

HE XIANGU:

　　My strainer leaks the spring

　　And catches no worries.

ALL:

　　People are fools

　　If they do not follow the immortals!

　　(*The immortals greet each other*)

HE XIANGU (*Smiles*):

Venerable Zhongli, you've ordered your disciple Lü Dongbin to implement Emperor Donghua's decree and convert true immortals in the human world. He has not returned yet. How depressed I am!

TIEGUAI LI (*Strikes at He Xiangu*):

Oops, you are an immortal lady giving way to foolish fancies. I'll break your strainer with my crutch.

ZHONGLI QUAN (*Smiles*):

Let's dance under the peach-blossoms. Zhongli Quan wears his hair in a girl's bun; Cao Guojiu is drunk and waves his court costume. Tieguai Li dozes off on his crutch; He Xiangu mends her strainer with needles. Lan Caihe sings over hills and rills; Han Xiangzi gives up his wife in wind and snow. Zhang Guolao is good at fortune-telling; Lü Dongbin gets drunk thrice on the Yueyang Pavilion.

> (*Exeunt all*)
>
> (*Enter Lü Dongbin, followed by Lu Sheng*)

LÜ DONGBIN (*To the tune of **Northern Xianlü Dianjiangchun***):

> The worldly dusts
>
> Vanish in a hundred years,
>
> Slow and steady.
>
> When he awakes from his dream,
>
> The tea time has long passed.

LU SHENG:

Master, what are the high mountains and flowing rivers in front?

LÜ DONGBIN:

It's the Penglai Island surrounded by the sea, a place to cultivate your virtue.

LU SHENG:

What kind of scenery is there?

LÜ DONGBIN (*To the tune of **Hunjianglong***):

> When you look forward,
>
> The Sea-Immortal Gate stands under peach-blossoms.
>
> There the light always shines
>
> And spring always reigns.

LU SHENG:

Oh, I can see the Penglai Temple over the sea. Are there tigers on the mountains? You know, there are whales and turtles in the sea.

LÜ DONGBIN (*Smiles*):

> Amid the sea waves,
>
> There are numerous whales and turtles;
>
> Upon the mountain island,
>
> There is only one tiger.

LU SHENG:

Where's the ferry boat?

LÜ DONGBIN:

You'll shoulder me across the sea.

> (*Lu Sheng is frightened*)

LÜ DONGBIN:

You just cross the sea with your eyes closed.

LU SHENG (*Carries Lü Dongbin on his shoulders*):

The sea is crossed in a flash.

    (*Looks*)

We are lucky that there is no hurricane. There is neither prefecture nor county here. How desolate it is!

LÜ DONGBIN:

    You say that the immortals' island

    Of thirty thousand feet is desolate

    With neither prefecture nor county,

    But it's much better than the Ghost Gate Pass

    Of eight thousand miles of miasma

    Where you were on exile.

LU SHENG:

Are there highwaymen here?

LÜ DONGBIN:

    The highwaymen only commit misdemeanours,

    While there are more heinous crimes.

LU SHENG:

Are there ghost-hunters?

LÜ DONGBIN:

    As to ghost-hunters,

    There is the righteous immortal

    Who can transform those who go astray.

LU SHENG (*Looks*):

Well, there is a house under the clouds. How is it that there are such people here: in red dress or in green dress, scarred or crippled, old or young? How is it possible that there are people like these?

LÜ DONGBIN:

They are all your witnesses. I'll tell you one by one:

    Zhongli Quan wears his hair in a girl's bun,

    Looking pale and dressed like a Taoist;

    Cao Guojiu has slant eyebrows,

    Like an official with a court tablet;

    Han Xiangzi gives up his positions,

    A Confucian disciple;

    Lan Caihe plays music,

    A musician at court;

    Tieguai Li carries a crutch,

    Somewhat crippled;

    He Xiangu uses a rice-strainer.

Past the prime of her life.

LU SHENG:

What are they doing here day and night?

LÜ DONGBIN:

> Day and night they watch the horoscope
>
> And tell fortunes,
>
> Sitting erect for self-cultivation.
>
> Sometimes they play chess and drink wine,
>
> Facing the universe in smiles.

LU SHENG:

They are born immortals. Can men attain this by cultivation?

LÜ DONGBIN:

> Although they were born human,
>
> They have green eyes and red brains,
>
> With an air of immortals.
>
> They have all undergone cultivation,
>
> Transplanting their backbones and spines,
>
> Changing their pith and tendons.

LU SHENG:

Can I do so as well?

LÜ DONGBIN:

> You were fortunate enough
>
> To marry Miss Cui and live a happy life
>
> And to prosper on the land of Tang,
>
> Giving birth to sons and grandsons.
>
> Yet, when you turn round the road to Handan,
>
> Your fortune ends and your costume is gone;
>
> The millet is boiling and water swirling
>
> In the inn in Qinghe.

LU SHENG (*Smiles*):

I have been hindered by affection all my life.

LÜ DONGBIN:

> Like the burnt wood in the stove,
>
> Your affection is nearing its end;
>
> How is it that the bellows
>
> Awaken the sleeping dumplings in the pot?
>
> As you are fated to be a half immortal,
>
> You meet me to instruct you on the great Tao.

LU SHENG (*Looks*):

How can the coming old man have such long eyebrows?

LÜ DONGBIN:

> I've seen Zhang Guolao

With longer eyebrows.

Although he is not the founder of Taoism,

He ranks high among the immortals.

(*Enter Zhang Guolao*)

ZHANG GUOLAO (*To the tune of* **Qingjiangyin**):

The peach-blossoms have bloomed twice,

But I don't have to ask about the year.

The Penglai Mountain looks beautiful in spring,

If only you are an immortal.

ALL:

People are fools

If they do not follow the immortals!

LÜ DONGBIN (*Nods to Lu Sheng and greets Zhang Guolao, with Lu Sheng kneeling behind him*):

Immortal Zhang, Lü Dongbin bows to greet you.

ZHANG GUOLAO:

Who is kneeling behind you?

LU SHENG:

Lu Sheng, the former Tang Number One Scholar, Prime Minister and Duke of Zhao, kowtows to you.

ZHANG GUOLAO:

Stand up, please. Old Duke, old Prime Minister, you look shabby now.

LU SHENG:

I was dreaming.

ZHANG GUOLAO:

Were you really dreaming? I'm surprised that you were patient enough to endure fifty years of man-to-man disputes. Surprising, surprising!

LU SHENG:

That's true.

ZHANG GUOLAO:

Come forward, Lu Sheng.

(*Lu Sheng kowtows*)

ZHANG GUOLAO:

Although you've reached the desolate mountains, you do not seem to have been severed from your foolish affections. I'll invite the immortals to remind you of your past experience. You'll repent for one item after another.

(*Lu Sheng agrees*)

(*Enter the immortals, singing with drums and clappers*)

IMMORTALS:

Up the magpie bridge,

Down the magpie bridge,

We respond to the stars in the sky

And respond to the tides on earth.

> *We beat the drums to tell tales*
> *And make herb medicine with wine.*
> *The boys smile and the girls are coy;*
> *They make the herb medicine with care.*
> *They enjoy themselves in the open,*
> *Not to miss the thriving spring scene.*
> *(Greet Zhang Guolao)*

We bow to greet you, Zhang Guolao.

HE XIANGU (*Greets Zhang Guolao*):

The obsessed man Lü Dongbin has converted is here.

LÜ DONGBIN:

It's just the time for the Peach Banquet, He Xiangu.

LU SHENG:

Master, you have been called a converting Taoist priest, but in fact you are the living immortal Lü Dongbin. I've found the right master.

ZHANG GUOLAO:

Immortals, please explain the stories in his dream one by one and serve as the witnesses so that I can convert him.

IMMORTALS:

Zhang Guolao gives a good suggestion. On your knees, you obsessed man.

> *(The six immortals raise questions one by one)*
> *(Lu Sheng falls on his knees)*

ZHONGLI QUAN (*To the tune of* **Langtaosha**):

> What is your grand marriage?
> The flower god
> Renovated the house of a female skeleton.
> Where is your Miss Cui?
> You obsessed man!
> *(Lu Sheng kowtows and responds)*

ALL:

> I am an obsessed man.

CAO GUOJIU (*To the previous tune*):

> What is your grand learning?
> You spent money
> To buy your distinction in the palace.
> Where is the Number One Scholar?
> You obsessed man!
> *(Lu Sheng kowtows and responds)*

ALL:

> I am an obsessed man.

TIEGUAI LI (*To the previous tune*):

> What is your grand meritorious minister?

You dug the canal and broadened the territories

But you did harm to the people.

Where is the fame and name inscribed on the rock?

You obsessed man!

(*Lu Sheng kowtows and responds*)

ALL:

I am an obsessed man.

LAN CAIHE (*To the previous tune*):

What is your grand enemy?

You went on exile in a region of miasma

And might be beheaded on the execution ground.

Where are your sufferings?

You obsessed man!

(*Lu Sheng kowtows and responds*)

ALL:

I am an obsessed man.

HAN XIANGZI (*To the previous tune*):

What is your grand rank of office?

Guests flocked into your residence;

Charming girls made you drunk in the pavilion.

Where is the residence you stayed?

You obsessed man!

(*Lu Sheng kowtows and responds*)

ALL:

I am an obsessed man.

HE XIANGU (*To the previous tune*):

What are your grand kith and kin?

You lived to the age of eighty,

Still exerting yourself to protect your heirs.

Where is the noisy mourning hall?

You obsessed man!

(*Lu Sheng kowtows and responds*)

ALL:

I am an obsessed man.

ZHANG GUOLAO:

Wait, Lu Sheng has been reprimanded by the immortals. Has he been awakened and come to understand?

LU SHENG:

Yes, indeed I have.

ZHANG GUOLAO:

Lu Sheng, now listen to my Taoist decree: You were an unsuccessful Confucian scholar on the road to Handan, obsessed with fame and name. You were lucky to stop at the inn where you experienced eighty years of worldly intrigues. When you woke up from your dream, the meal of millet was ready in the human world. Who knows that tides rose near the Zhaozhou Bridge at midnight, but only reached the residence of a prime minister who was daydreaming. You and Miss Cui were obsessed in the daydream when Lü Dongbin revealed the heavenly secret to you. He did not use a single grain of yellow millet, but applied the medicine in his gourd at the right time. He processed mercury with his eyes closed and tempered gold with his very heart. When your heart conforms to nature, you will become aware by yourself and several witnesses will be on your side. You will build a hut and a stove when you are hungry, but we are afraid that you will be perplexed again when you wake up. Tieguai Li, just break the enticing pillow to pieces; He Xiangu, please hand over to Lu Sheng the broom to sweep the petals. He will sweep until the petals are all gone, the earth is gone and even the broom itself is gone and then he will no longer be obsessed. By that time, you will be able to pay respects to the Taoist Emperor by riding on a crane and reap the genuine fruit of your entering a dream by riding on a donkey.

LÜ DONGBIN:

Lu Sheng, accept the broom and thank the immortal!

LU SHENG (*Accepts the broom and bows*):

(*To the tune of* **Chenzuidongfeng**)

I will no longer be my worldly self

And be burdened by wealth and sex.

LÜ DONGBIN:

For three lives,

You're a hybrid with the horse or donkey;

For one life,

You rose high in office,

But the records are vague on the tablet.

ZHONGLI QUAN, CAO GUOJIU:

You went through the vanity fair

And at last became a laughing-stock.

LU SHENG (*To the previous tune*):

I was scared on the execution ground

And had a narrow escape at the Ghost Gate Pass.

LÜ DONGBIN:

You still linger in your dream

And stick to your official stamp;

How many friends and foes did you meet?

TIEGUAI LI, LAN CAIHE:

As the sun has not set in the west yet,

What are you going to consult?

LU SHENG (*To the previous tune*):

To be an immortal is to be blessed;

I've escaped into the mountains in the sea.

1059

LÜ DONGBIN:

When you open the window of flesh

And know the fate of flowers,

The flower-girls will surely awaken you.

HAN XIANGZI, HE XIANGU:

The peach-blossoms bloom another spring

While the human world is still asleep.

LU SHENG (*Sweeps the petals*):

(*To the previous tune*)

As an outsider,

I'm looking at the Handan people with their millet;

As my duty,

I sweep petals on the land of immortals.

Old master, I was so obsessed that I would still be dreaming if I had not met you.

Although I'm awakened from illusions,

I'm afraid it's hard to know the truth.

IMMORTALS:

Why won't you tear yourself away from your soul?

Even if you're too obsessed to part from your dream,

You are now comfortably dreaming an immortal dream.

ZHANG GUOLAO:

Let's pay tribute to the Donghua Emperor.

ALL (*Walk on while beating drums and sounding clappers*):

(*To the tune of **Qingjiangyin***)

To sweep away the fame and fortune of a previous life,

Will perplex an obsessed man.

The peach will be as dry as faggot

And the sea will be as arid as a halo.

When you toss and turn by then,

Will you be waiting for the meal of yellow millet?

(*To the tune of **Northern Coda***)

To convert the single person of Lu Sheng,

We've exhausted the topic of worldly affairs,

So that people will think it over

When they wake from their dreams.

Do not be intoxicated in worldly strife,

Only to awake in the last days of your life.

Make a contract with your heart right now,

Burn incense in your room and make a bow.